D1221232

5th Edition

Labour Market ECONOMICS

Theory, Evidence, and Policy in Canada

Dwayne Benjamin
University of Toronto

Morley Gunderson
University of Toronto

W. Craig Riddell
University of British Columbia

Toronto Montréal Boston Burr Ridge, IL Dubuque, IA Madison, WI New York San Francisco St. Louis
Bangkok Bogotá Caracas Kuala Lumpur Lisbon London Madrid Mexico City Milan New Delhi
Santiago Seoul Singapore Sydney Taipei

McGraw-Hill
Ryerson Limited

LABOUR MARKET ECONOMICS
Fifth Edition

ISBN: 0-07-089154-0

1 2 3 4 5 6 7 8 9 10 TCP 0 9 8 7 6 5 4 3 2

Printed and bound in Canada

Vice President and Editorial Director: Pat Ferrier
Senior Sponsoring Editor: Lynn Fisher
Economics Editor: Ron Doleman
Developmental Editor: Daphne Scriabin
Marketing Manager: Kelly Smyth
Supervising Editor: Carrie Withers
Copy Editor: Rodney Rawlings
Production Coordinator: Madeleine Harrington
Composition: Bill Renaud/Accutype Ltd.
Cover Design: Sharon Lucas
Cover Image: Roy Ooms/Masterfile
Interior Design: Michelle Losier
Art Direction: Dianna Little
Printer: Transcontinental Printing Group

Canadian Cataloguing in Publication Data

Benjamin, Dwayne, 1961–
Labour market economics

5th ed.
Includes bibliographical references and index.
ISBN 0-07-089154-0

1. Labour supply—Canada. 2. Labour economics—Canada.
I. Gunderson, Morley, 1945– II. Riddell, W. Craig (William Craig), 1946– III. Title

HD5728.G85 2001 331.12'0971 C2001-902949-7

To our parents,
Janet Wilson and Harry Benjamin,
Ann and Magnus Gunderson,
and
Ethel and William Riddell

About the Authors

Dwayne Benjamin

Dwayne Benjamin received his Ph.D. from Princeton University in 1989, before joining the University of Toronto, where he is now a Professor of Economics. In 1996–97 he taught at the Woodrow Wilson School, Princeton University, and he has also been a visiting scholar at Australian National University.

Professor Benjamin has published several papers in leading economics journals on a variety of labour market issues, pertaining to Canada, the United States, and especially developing countries. In a Canadian context, he has explored a variety of questions concerning immigration, minimum wages, and retirement. He is currently investigating issues related to aging and retirement, and possible linkages with public pension programs, such as the CPP/QPP. Regarding developing countries, his main interests concern the empirical testing of various models of rural labour markets and investigating the connections between labour market institutions and household welfare. In particular, his recent projects focus on the impact of economic transition and development on household well-being and behaviour in China and Vietnam. These research topics include the role of education in rapidly expanding labour markets; the implications for income inequality and poverty; and the consequences of institutional reform for the health and well-being of the elderly.

Morley Gunderson

Morley Gunderson holds the Canadian Imperial Bank of Commerce Chair in Youth Employment at the University of Toronto, where he is a Professor at the Centre for Industrial Relations (Director 1985–1997) and the Department of Economics. He is also a Research Associate of the Institute of Policy Analysis, the Centre for International Studies, and the Institute for Human Development, Life Course, and Aging, all at the University of Toronto, and an Adjunct Scientist at the Institute for Work and Health. He has a B.A. in Economics from Queen's University (1967) and an M.A. in Industrial Relations (1969) and a Ph.D. in Economics (1971) from the University of Wisconsin–Madison. He has been a Visiting Scholar at the International Institute for Labour Research in Geneva, Switzerland (1977–1978); the National Bureau of Economic Research at Stanford University (1984–1985 and 1991–1993); the North America Forum at the Institute for International Studies at Stanford (Summer 1994–1996); and the Hoover Institution at Stanford (1998–1999).

He has published numerous books and articles on gender discrimination and comparable worth; the aging workforce, pensions, and mandatory retirement; youth employment; public sector wage determination; determinants and impact of immigration; causes and consequences of strikes; child-care arrangements and labour market behaviour; workers' compensation and reasonable accommodation; labour market adjustment and training; volunteer labour supply; and the impact of trade liberalization and globalization on labour markets, policy, and standards, industrial relations, human resource management, and workplace practices.

Professor Gunderson is on the editorial board of the *Journal of Labor Research* and the *International Journal of Manpower*, and is co-editor of the *Labour Arbitration Yearbook*. He is also the recipient of the 2002 Industrial Relations Research Association Excellence in Education Award in Labour Economics.

W. Craig Riddell

W. Craig Riddell is a Professor in the Department of Economics at the University of British Columbia and an Associate of the Canadian Institute for Advanced Research. His research interests are labour economics, labour relations, and public policy. His current research is focused on unemployment and labour market dynamics, the role of human capital in economic growth, experimental and nonexperimental approaches to the evaluation of social programs, unionization, and collective bargaining, gender differences in labour market behaviour and outcomes, unemployment insurance and social assistance, and education and training.

Recent publications include: "Qualifying for unemployment insurance: An empirical analysis," *Economic Journal*, 1997 (with David Green); "Wages, skills and technology in the United States and Canada," in E. Helpman (Ed.), *General Purpose Technologies and Economic Growth*, MIT Press, 1998 (with Kevin Murphy and Paul Romer); "The measurement of unemployment: An empirical approach," *Econometrica*, 1999 (with Stephen Jones); "Canadian labour market performance in international perspective," *Canadian Journal of Economics*, 1999.

Professor Riddell is former Head of the Department of Economics at UBC, former Academic Co-Chair of the Canadian Employment Research Forum, and past President of the Canadian Economics Association. He currently holds a Royal Bank Faculty Research Professorship at UBC.

Brief Contents

Contents

PART FIVE UNIONS

Chapter Fourteen
Union Growth and Incidence 417

Chapter Fifteen
Wage and Employment Determination Under Collective Bargaining 438

Chapter Nineteen
Wage Changes, Price Inflation, and Unemployment 574

Preface

Labour economists study the decisions of everyday life, especially how people earn a living. We even offer the analytic tools to help you decide whether to take labour economics, Shakespearian English, quantum mechanics, or nothing at all (see Chapter 9). In Canada, most people earn a living at their jobs, that is, from the earnings they receive from selling their labour services through the labour market. Not surprisingly, many of the most important issues of public policy hinge on our understanding of how the labour market works. What causes unemployment? Why are some people's earnings so low that they need social assistance? Why are women paid less than men, even in the twenty-first century? Should governments pay subsidies for postsecondary education?

The discipline of labour economics provides a framework for critical thinking about these sorts of questions. At the core of the discipline is the neoclassical supply and demand model. This model allows the construction of logical, internally consistent arguments concerning economic variables, such as employment and earnings. But models have to be used carefully, and evaluated for their applicability in "the real world." Labour economists therefore combine theoretical reasoning with empirical evidence. The interplay between economic theory and evidence is complex. On the one hand, empirical evidence is used as a way to evaluate the theory, and to calibrate the ingredients of theoretical models (e.g., how much taking one year of schooling raises a person's earnings). But, on the other hand, economic theory also serves a vital role in "purely" empirical exercises. Without theory, labour economics would appear as "just one damn fact after another"[1] (which is not to diminish the value of establishing a "fact" in the first place).

In this book we try to provide students with the tools for critical thinking about labour market problems. As the subtitle indicates, we aim to develop student facility at both theoretical and empirical critical thinking. Another important organizing principle is the focus on public policy. The book is meant to provide a consistent theoretical framework that can be applied not only to current policy issues but also to new policy issues as they emerge over time. Policies that are relevant today may not be relevant tomorrow, but a good theoretical foundation will always be relevant. Just as importantly, what constitutes evidence? We are constantly bombarded with claims that a particular viewpoint has "the facts" on its side. How can we recognize specious empirical arguments?

We also believe that economic institutions matter, especially in labour markets. While economic theory and sound empirical methodology is portable to studying labour markets in most countries, we have chosen the balance of topics in this book to reflect Canadian interests. For example, unions are a more important feature of the Canadian landscape than in the United States. Unfortunately, unemployment is also a more prominent feature of the Canadian labour market. Our book reflects these differences. We also provide a corresponding emphasis on the evaluation of Canadian labour market policies, drawing heavily on Canadian evidence. Especially given the explosion of empirical research in Canada during the 1990s, it has been quite easy to maintain an emphasis on Canadian data, examples, institutions, problems, and policies—though harder to keep up with the pace of

[1]Some wags still characterize labour economics this way. The expression is traditionally a cynical description of the discipline of history. Jared Diamond, in Guns, Germs, and Steel: The Fates of Human Societies (New York: W. W. Norton & Company, 1997), provides one of many challenges to this characterization.

research. But that said, given the increased internationalization of the Canadian economy, Canadian issues are discussed within the context of a more general theoretical and empirical framework, applicable to the labour problems of most developed countries.

WHAT'S NEW IN THE FIFTH EDITION

We undertook this revision with two main objectives: first, to improve the readability of the text, making it more student-friendly, and accessible to a broader audience; second, to update the content of the chapters, including clearing out staler material.

Improvements in Pedagogy

- *Figure captions.* The addition of figure captions provides self-contained explanations of the salient features of theoretical graphs and data-based figures. This allows students to review the graphical material without constantly cross-referencing the text.

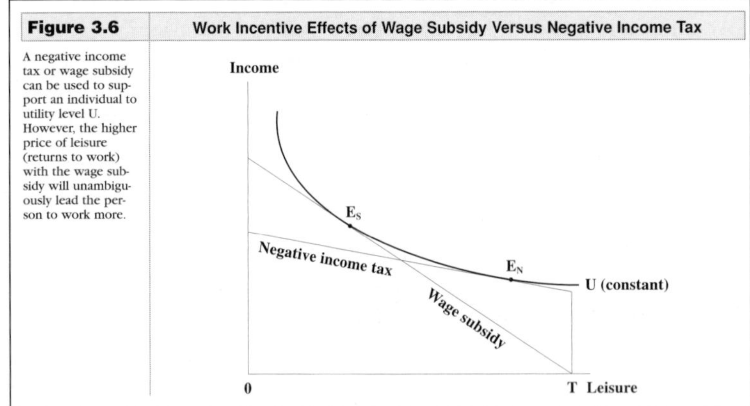

Figure 3.6 Work Incentive Effects of Wage Subsidy Versus Negative Income Tax

A negative income tax or wage subsidy can be used to support an individual to utility level U. However, the higher price of leisure (returns to work) with the wage subsidy will unambiguously lead the person to work more.

- *Chapter summaries.* The objective of the Summary is to provide a concise review of the major themes covered in the chapter. It can be used by students in conjunction with the Keywords as a checklist in evaluating their understanding of the material. More than that, however, the Summaries provide a distinct statement of the main ideas in the chapter.

Summary

- Income maintenance schemes are designed to top up low incomes, which can arise for any of a variety of reasons, permanent or transitory, and may be due either to low wages or hours. By their very nature, means-tested programs can have strong disincentives to earning income.
- The income-leisure (labour supply) framework is a useful way to analyze work incentive effects. While programs vary in details, most will generate income effects (by shifting the opportunity set outward) or substitution effects (by changing the returns to work).
- Demogrants are pure lump-sum transfers, based only on immutable individual characteristics like age or sex. While these transfers are independent of income, they will still have adverse work incentive effects as long as leisure is a normal good.
- Welfare programs are designed to increase the income of individuals with low income. The degree to which they have adverse work incentive effects depends on how strictly benefits are reduced in response to higher earnings. The more severely benefits are reduced with higher earnings, the stronger the disincentives will be for welfare recipi-

- *Questions and problems.* As in other fields of economics, it is impossible to learn labour economics without "doing economics." We have added a significant number of new problems to this edition. They are of two types. Review Questions are slightly easier and designed to direct students to specific parts of the chapter in order to highlight important concepts or issues. The Problems are more analytical and designed to challenge students to apply lessons from the chapter to real-world situations; they vary in difficulty, permitting instructors some flexibility in assigning problems appropriate for their course. Combined with problems in the new *Study Guide*, they should enable students to better develop the skills necessary to "do labour economics."

REVIEW QUESTIONS

1. Use the work-leisure choice diagram to illustrate that, under normal circumstances, if an individual is given a demogrant, take-home pay will not increase by as much as the demogrant. Why is this so?
2. Illustrate the work incentive effects of a demogrant on a disabled person who is unable to work.
3. Use the work-leisure choice diagram to illustrate the following cases where an individual is:
   a. Unwilling to go on welfare because the welfare payment is too low
   b. Indifferent between welfare and work
   c. Induced to move off welfare because of an increase in her wage
   d. Induced to move off welfare because of a change in preferences between income and leisure
   e. Induced to move off welfare by a reduction of the 100 percent implicit tax on earnings
4. In an unemployment insurance diagram like Figure 3.7, depict the case in which the individual must work eight weeks before becoming eligible to collect. Depict the case of a two-third rather than a 60 percent replacement rate.
5. In a diagram like Figure 3.9, depict the worker's compensation system involving a 90 percent replacement of the pre-injury wage earnings.

- *Glossary.* While labour economics is relatively light on jargon (in our opinion), over the course of a textbook we have used plenty of terms that can easily be forgotten from one chapter to the next; we have therefore added a new Glossary, written by David Gray, which should serve as a useful aid to students.

Enhanced Coverage of Topics

Labour economics is a dynamic area of research, especially in Canada. We have tried to ensure that the empirical evidence, for both first-order descriptive statistics and the results of applied research, is up to date. All of the tables and figures were updated with the most recently available data. We gave our reviews of public policy an overhaul, and we have in particular enhanced our discussion of the following topics, which feature prominently in the research agenda of labour economics in the twenty-first century:

- *Supply and demand.* This model is the theoretical workhorse of labour economics, and it is introduced and reviewed more extensively in Chapter 1. The new overview, which includes some of the material from the previous edition's Chapter 7, should offer students a better sense of "the big picture" before moving into the analytic details of Chapters 2 through 7. We include an application of the theory in a slightly expanded appendix on hockey salary determination. On related notes:
  - We have added Exhibit 2.3 on the labour supply of baseball stadium hot-dog vendors; it highlights some of the methodological issues in estimating labour supply elasticities.
  - We have significantly shortened and streamlined Chapter 7, while slightly expanding the treatment of payroll taxes. The new Exhibit 7.1 shows a clever example of how the incidence of payroll taxes can be reliably estimated.
- *Welfare reform and income maintenance.* One of the most significant changes in public policy in the last half of the 1990s was the restructuring of welfare programs in Canada and the United States ("welfare reform"). In order to help the student more carefully evaluate these policy changes, and also understand the rationale for the wide range of income maintenance programs in Canada, we begin Chapter 3 with a general theoretical framework. In that chapter we have also updated the evidence of the impact of welfare reform (see especially Exhibit 3.1 and Figure 3.12) and the discussion of the Self-Sufficiency Project.

- *Economic role of women.* Arguably the most important economic phenomenon of the twentieth century was the increased participation of women in the labour market. Our revision includes increased coverage of related research:
  - In Chapter 4 we discuss some of the broad trends of female employment behaviour. In particular, we have increased our discussion of the linkages between fertility and labour supply (Exhibit 4.2 looks at the role of the birth control pill on women's career paths; Exhibit 4.4 shows how labour economists estimate the impact of children on mothers' labour supply; Exhibits 4.5 and 4.6 discuss the role of public policy in influencing fertility behaviour).
  - Chapter 12 on discrimination has been expanded and updated considerably to include new evidence on the impact of pay equity legislation that requires equal pay for work of equal value, and evidence on the extent of discrimination (see especially Exhibits 12.5, 12.7, and 12.9). There is also a discussion of the recent controversial Federal Pay Equity award that was 15 years in the making (Exhibit 12.13).
- *Globalization and trade.* The Canadian labour market does not exist in isolation from the forces of globalization. We discuss the linkages between international trade and labour market outcomes, including the latest evidence of the impact of NAFTA. In Chapter 11, we have updated the discussion of immigration and its impact on Canada. Also in Chapter 11, we have added new material on the "brain drain," that is, the emigration of Canadians to the United States.
- *Income inequality.* Largely motivated by striking increases of wage inequality in the United States over the 1980s, labour economists devoted considerable energy to documenting and explaining income inequality over this period:
  - We introduce the concept of inequality in Chapter 1, tracing the possible linkages between labour market earnings and overall income inequality (see in particular Figures 1.1 to 1.3). The possible power of supply and demand theory for understanding this question is introduced.
  - Exhibit 8.2 shows how earnings inequality extends to inequality in other job characteristics.
  - Chapter 9 explores the connection between increased returns to education and widening earnings differentials, especially in the United States. The possible linkages between returns to skill, changing technology, and labour market institutions are drawn in Chapter 18. In particular, this entails a comparison of inequality across countries: Canada versus the United States, and Europe versus the United States.
- *Education.* The advent of new data sources and increased exploitation of "natural experiments" led to advances in our understanding of the returns to education.
  - We have rewritten the technical discussion of the methodology of estimating returns to schooling, especially the possible problems posed by ability bias.
  - An example of Canadian evidence exploiting the natural-experiment methodology is provided by Exhibit 9.4, where we summarize how World War II conscription affected the university attainment of Canadian men.
  - We provide a new exhibit on child labour (Exhibit 9.1) that illustrates some of the economics underlying the school attendance decision.
- *Unions.* Unions remain an important institutional feature in the Canadian labour market.
  - In Chapter 16, new material on the impact of unions is added to reflect more recent evidence, when unions are operating under more competitive conditions with respect to factors such as free trade, globalization, deregulation, and privatization. As well, new evidence is added on the extent to which unionization discourages investment in new plant and equipment.
  - In Chapter 14 we provide more international comparative evidence on union growth, and a new Exhibit 14.2 looking at the determinants of recent decline in union density in Canada.
  - While it is only indirectly related to unions, in Chapter 10 we provide a streamlined, updated discussion of the size and nature of public sector employment.

- *Discrimination.* In addition to our traditional discussion concerning earnings differentials between men and women, we have expanded Chapter 12 to cover earnings differences by ethnic groups in Canada.
- *New economics of personnel.* Chapter 13 on optimal compensation has been extensively reoriented to include more material on the "new economics of personnel"—an important new frontier and area of practical importance in labour economics. Topics that are given expanded treatment include:
  - The rise of CEO salaries under globalization
  - Various models of executive compensation: tournament models of compensation; the pros and cons of pay dispersion or compression
  - The free-riding problem in workplace teams; external versus internal promotions; up-or-out rules for promotion (including academic tenure); raiding, offer-matching, and the "winner's curse"
  - Piece-rate systems; alternative payment systems for physicians (i.e., fee-for-service, straight salary, and salary-based on roster of potential patients)
  - Expanded treatment of issues of age discrimination and the legal aspects around mandatory retirement, since they likely will become a more prominent issue given the ageing workforce and possible impending labour shortages
- *Unemployment.* Unemployment is an important feature of the Canadian labour market, with an obvious impact on the well-being of Canadians. There have been significant improvements in our understanding of the nature and causes of unemployment:
  - Many of these improvements concern our interpretation of unemployment statistics, and Chapter 17 has accordingly been streamlined and updated. We have included a new Exhibit 17.2 on supplementary measures of unemployment. We have also highlighted international differences in unemployment, especially comparisons between Canada and the United States.
  - With regard to explaining unemployment, in Chapter 18 we offer an improved presentation of the theory of efficiency wages, and a new section on the role of sectoral shifts. Our discussion of unemployment insurance has been updated to reflect recent changes in policy and more recent econometric evidence of the impact of unemployment insurance on behaviour.
  - Chapter 19 has been revised to reflect more recent Canadian macroeconomic experience. We have included a new section, "Challenges to the Natural Rate Hypothesis," that also includes comparisons of economic performance between Canada, Europe, and the United States. There is also a new section on the role of supply shocks in explaining unemployment.
  - In terms of policy responses to unemployment, in addition to updates of the discussion of unemployment insurance, Exhibit 6.4 presents evidence of the pros and cons of worksharing, based on European experience.

Exhibit 6.4 **Worksharing Isn't for Everyone**

Under what conditions would firms be willing to use worksharing instead of layoffs in responding to depressed market conditions? If a firm needs to reduce labour input by 40 hours per week, it can either lay off one person who usually works 40 hours per week or reduce 40 workers' hours by an hour per week. The choice depends on the relative costs of adjusting workers versus hours of work, which depends on the structure of wages and nonwage costs, as discussed in this chapter. For example, a layoff will allow the firm to avoid all of the recurring fixed costs of employment (such as payroll taxes), whereas small reductions in hours worked may yield no reduction in payroll taxes, especially if there are contribution ceilings. On the other hand, high severance costs may make worksharing cheaper.

In addition to the costs to the firms, the feasibility of worksharing depends on the willingness of other workers to go along with the scheme. Most union seniority rules are biased in favour of layoffs versus worksharing: the youngest workers bear the cost of the downturn, while the others are fully cushioned from the adverse (short-term) shock. Because layoffs are the usual path chosen by firms, governments offer subsidies for firms to adopt worksharing, by topping up the wages paid to non-laid-off workers. Such worksharing, or short time compensation (STC) programs are especially popular in Europe. David Gray (1998) uses

Economics Preparation

The text was written for students who have had an introductory course in economics, and preferably—but not necessarily—a course in microeconomics. Formal mathematical analysis is rarely utilized, though high school algebra and elementary regression analysis are used where appropriate. The text is also suitable as a basis for graduate labour courses in business schools and economics departments.

SUPPLEMENTS FOR INSTRUCTORS

Instructor's Online Learning Centre (www.mcgrawhill.ca/college/benjamin)

The Online Learning Centre includes a password-protected Web site for Instructors. The site offers downloadable supplements and PageOut, the McGraw-Hill Ryerson course Web site development center.

Instructor's Manual (007-089157-5)

Prepared by David Gray, University of Ottawa. Contains answers to questions and comprehensive solutions, and multiple-choice questions. It has been designed with pedagogy in mind.

PowerPoint Presentation (007-090794-3)

Prepared by Erica Morrill, Fanshawe College. This is a balanced presentation with topics presented in the same order as in the chapters. Dynamic builds have been introduced into key graphics in each chapter.

SUPPLEMENTS FOR STUDENTS

Student Online Learning Centre (www.mcgrawhill.ca/college/benjamin)

Prepared by David Wilton, University of Waterloo. This site will include for each chapter: lecture notes, annotated Web links, sample exam questions, chapter summaries, a searchable glossary and access to the CANSIM database.

Study Guide (007-089155-9)

Prepared by David Gray, University of Ottawa. Provides chapter highlights, helpful hints, answers to the end-of-chapter Review Questions and Problems, and multiple-choice questions and answers. In addition to containing step-by-step explanations, it provides a commentary on the point the question is designed to illustrate, making the moral of the story more explicit.

Acknowledgments

Various people have aided in the preparation of this book. Our colleagues and fellow labour economists within Canada are too numerous to mention; however, we are particularly indebted to our colleagues at the University of British Columbia and the University of Toronto, and to a number of anonymous referees who made comments and suggestions for improvements on this and the third edition. Sonia Laszlo provided outstanding assistance in compiling data, and test-driving the new problems. At McGraw-Hill Ryerson, Ron Doleman provided important initial impetus on the direction of the revision, and ongoing support; Carrie Withers provided useful suggestions and prodding; Daphne Scriabin meticulously organized and coordinated the construction of the book—from first drafts to completion—and along with Rodney Rawlings provided valued editorial assistance. We especially wish to thank our wives, Christine, Melanie, and Rosemarie, for their patience, support, and encouragement.

The fifth edition has benefited from a number of perceptive reviews, which were a rich source of suggestions for this revision. Reviewers include:

Ather Akbari	St. Mary's University
David Gray	University of Ottawa
Ibrahim Hayani	Seneca College
Saad Kiryakos	University of Ottawa
Erica Morrill	Fanshawe College
Daniel Parent	McGill University
Isaac Rischall	McMaster University
Brenda Spotton Visano	York University
Glen Stirling	University of Western Ontario
Arthur Sweetman	Queen's University
David Wilton	University of Waterloo

Key to Journal Abbreviations

AER	American Economic Review
BPEA	Brookings Papers on Economic Activity
CJE	Canadian Journal of Economics
CPP	Canadian Public Policy
Ecta	Econometrica
EI	Economic Inquiry
EJ	Economic Journal
IER	International Economic Review
ILRR	Industrial and Labor Relations Review
IR	Industrial Relations
IRRA	Industrial Relations Research Association Proceedings
IER	International Economic Review
JASA	Journal of the American Statistical Association
JEH	Journal of Economic History
JEL	Journal of Economic Literature
JEP	Journal of Economic Perspectives
JLR	Journal of Labor Research
JHR	Journal of Human Resources
JOLE	Journal of Labor Economics
JPE	Journal of Political Economy
JPubEc	Journal of Public Economics
MLR	Monthly Labor Review
PLI	Perspectives on Labour and Income
QJE	Quarterly Journal of Economics
RI/IR	Relations Industrielles/Industrial Relations
R.E. Studies	Review of Economic Studies
R.E. Stats	Review of Economics and Statistics
SEJ	Southern Economic Journal
WEJ	Western Economic Journal

Other journals have been included in the References section without an abbreviation for their title.

The references listed in this text tend to focus on more recent articles, especially those with a Canadian focus; earlier references can be found in previous editions.

Chapter One

Introduction to Labour Market Economics

Main Questions

- *Who are the main actors in the labour market, and what particular roles do they play?*
- *How can features of the labour market be divided into labour supply and labour demand factors?*
- *What types of policy questions does labour economics address?*
- *What characteristics of the labour market make it distinctive from other markets, justifying a special sub-discipline of economics?*
- *What is the neoclassical model of the labour market? Are there alternative approaches?*
- *How does regression analysis contribute to our understanding of labour economics?*

Labour economics studies the outcomes of decisions we can all expect to make over our lifetime. As a subject of inquiry it is both practically relevant to our everyday lives and socially relevant to the broader issues of society. This makes labour economics interesting, practical, and socially relevant, as well as controversial.

DECISIONS BY INDIVIDUALS, FIRMS, AND GOVERNMENTS

Labour market decisions that affect our everyday well-being are made by each of the three main actors or participants in the labour market: individuals, firms, and governments.

For individuals, the decisions include when to enter the labour force; how much education, training, and job search to undertake; what occupation and industry to enter; how many hours to work; whether to move to a different region; when to accept a job; when to quit or look for another job; what wage to demand; whether to join a union or employee association; and when to retire. It may also involve decisions on how to allocate time between market work and household responsibilities.

Many aspects of labour market behaviour are positive experiences, such as obtaining a job, getting a wage increase or promotion, or receiving a generous pension. Other experiences are negative, such as being unemployed or permanently displaced from one's job, or experiencing discrimination or poverty.

Employers also have to make decisions on such aspects as how many workers to hire, what wages and fringe benefits to pay, what hours of work to require, when to lay off workers and perhaps ultimately close a plant, what to subcontract, and how to design an effective pension and retirement policy. These decisions are increasingly being made under pressures from global competition, free trade, industrial restructuring, deregulation, and privatization. As well, the decisions of employers must be made in the context of a dramatically changing work force with respect to such factors as age, gender, and ethnic diversity. The legislative environment within which employers operate also is constantly changing in such areas as human rights and antidiscrimination legislation; employment standards laws with respect to such areas as minimum wages, maternity leave, and hours of work and overtime; legislation on workers' compensation and occupational health and safety; legislation on pensions and on mandatory retirement; and labour relations laws that regulate the process of collective bargaining.

Governments (i.e., through legislators, policymakers, and the courts) also have difficult decisions to make so as to establish the environment in which employees and employers interact. In part this involves a balancing act between providing rights and protection to individuals, while not jeopardizing the competitiveness of employers. It also involves decisions as to what to provide publicly in such areas as training, information, unemployment insurance, workers' compensation, vocational rehabilitation, income maintenance, pensions, and even public sector jobs.

Labour economics deals with these decisions on the part of individuals, employers, and government—decisions that affect our everyday lives and that lead to consequences we can all expect to experience. While this makes labour economics interesting and relevant—and controversial—it also puts a premium on a solid framework from which to analyze these decisions and their consequences. The purpose of this book is to provide and apply such a framework.

Parts of the book are the equivalent of "eating spinach": they may be more challenging and seem less interesting than the sections more obviously related to policy; however, they provide the basic tools and theoretical framework that are crucial to understanding labour market behaviour. In many cases the immediate application of economic theory to labour market issues facilitates understanding the basic tools of economics itself; that is, the application to interesting and important issues in the labour market facilitates a deeper understanding of economic theory.

In labour economics, however, the ultimate usefulness of economic theory is in understanding labour market behaviour. At the risk of carrying the food analogy too far, "the proof of the pudding is in the eating": the usefulness of basic economic theory in the labour area must be demonstrated by its ability to help us understand labour market behaviour. This is one of the objectives of this book.

SUBJECT MATTER OF LABOUR MARKET ECONOMICS

Labour market economics involves analyzing the determinants of the various dimensions of labour supply and demand and their interaction in alternative market structures to determine wages, employment, and unemployment. Behind this simple description, however, lies a complex array of behaviours, decision-making, and dimensions that often interrelate labour economics with other disciplines and areas of study.

Labour supply, for example, involves a variety of dimensions. It includes population growth, which involves decisions pertaining to fertility and family formation, as well as to immigration and emigration, all of which are amenable to economic analysis. Labour supply also involves the dimension of labour force participation to determine what portion of the population will participate in labour market activities as opposed to other activities such as household work, education, retirement, or pure leisure. For those who participate in the labour market, there is the labour supply dimension of hours of work, including trends and cyclical patterns, as well as such phenomena as overtime, moonlighting, part-time work, worksharing, flexible worktime arrangements, and compressed work weeks. This ties labour economics to such areas as demography and personnel and human resource planning.

In addition to these *quantity* dimensions of labour supply, there are also *quality* dimensions that are amenable to economic analysis. Such quality dimensions include education, training, and health. These dimensions, along with labour mobility, are often analyzed as human capital investment decisions, emphasizing that they involve incurring costs today in exchange for benefits in the future. Quality dimensions of labour supply also include work effort and intensity—dimensions that are analyzed in the context of efficiency wage theory and optimal compensation systems. This ties labour economics to issues of personnel and human resource management as well as to the key policy issue of productivity, often involving education and training.

Labour supply analysis also involves determining the work incentive effects of income maintenance and tax-transfer schemes. Such schemes include demogrants (e.g., the Old Age Security Pension), negative income taxes, wage subsidies, income taxes, unemployment insurance, welfare, disability payments, workers' compensation, and private and public pension plans. This ties labour economics to the interesting and controversial areas of poverty and income distribution as well as tax and social welfare policy.

www.hrdc-drhc.gc.ca/isp/common/oastoc_e.shtml

The **labour demand** side of the picture focuses on how firms vary their demand for labour in response to changes in the wage rate and other elements of labour cost, including fringe benefits and legislatively imposed costs. The impact of quasi-fixed costs that may be involved in hiring, in training, and even in terminating workers are also important. Since the demand for labour is a derived demand—derived from the demand for the firm's output—this side of the picture is influenced by such issues as free trade, global competition, industrial restructuring, privatization, public sector retrenchment, mergers and acquisitions, and technological change. It is increasingly important to analyze the demand side in the context of changes that are occurring in the international global environment.

The various dimensions of labour supply and demand are interesting and informative not only in their own right but also because their interaction determines other key **labour market outcomes—wages**, **employment**, and **unemployment**. These outcomes are influenced by the interaction of labour supply and demand in alternative market structures, including the degree of competition in the product market as well as the labour market. They are also influenced by unions and collective bargaining, as well as by legislative interventions including minimum wages and equal pay and equal opportunity laws. This highlights the interrelationship of labour economics with the areas of industrial relations and labour law.

The various wage structures that emerge include wage differentials by occupation (e.g., engineer versus secretary), by industry (e.g., public versus private sector), by region (e.g., Newfoundland versus Ontario), and by personal characteristics (e.g., males versus females). Economic analysis outlines the determinants of these wage structures, how and why they change over time, and how they are influenced by such factors as demand changes, nonwage aspects of employment, and noncompetitive factors including unions, legislation, occupational licensing, and labour market imperfections. For some wage structures, like male-female wage differentials, the economic analysis of discrimination is informative in indicating why wage differentials arise and persist, and how they will be affected by legislation and other policy initiatives.

Wage differentials between union and nonunion workers can be explained by basic economic analysis incorporating bargaining theory. In order to fully understand how unions affect wages, it is also necessary to understand why unions arise in the first place and how they affect the nonwage aspects of employment. Increasingly, labour economics has been applied to understanding why certain institutional arrangements exist in the labour market, including unions, seniority-based wage increases, and personnel practices such as mandatory retirement.

There is increasing recognition that wages can have strong effects on various incentives: to acquire education and training or to move, to stay with a job or quit or retire early, and even to work hard and more productively. These effects are analyzed in various areas of labour market economics: human capital theory, optimal compensation systems, efficiency wages, and private pension plan analysis. This highlights the interrelationship of labour economics with the areas of industrial relations and personnel and human resource management.

The area of unemployment is analyzed at both the microeconomic and the macroeconomic level. At the micro level, the emphasis is on theories of job search, implicit contracts and efficiency wages, and the impact of unemployment insurance. At the macro level, the relationship between wage changes, price inflation, productivity, and unemployment is emphasized.

PRELIMINARY EXPLORATIONS OF LABOUR MARKET OUTCOMES

The fundamental subject matter of labour economics is how individuals earn a living, especially by selling their labour services in the labour market. Labour economists are interested in both the average level of earnings that people get from the market and the distribution: How unequal are labour market outcomes (and why)?

Table 1.1 shows selected descriptive statistics concerning these outcomes. The tabulations are based on a large sample of approximately 20,000 Canadians, referring to their incomes and labour activity in 1994. The sample is drawn from the Survey of Labour and Income Dynamics (SLID), Statistics Canada's primary survey instrument for tracking incomes and labour market activities. In this table we restrict attention to individuals in their prime potential working years, between the ages of 20 and 65. It shows the average levels of various types of income, and the percentage of people with that particular source of income. The averages are also broken down separately for men and women.

www.statcan.ca/
www.statcan.ca/english/sdds/3889.htm

Looking first at the full sample, we see that earnings (from the labour market or self-employment) averaged $21,793 per person. Labour earnings are, by far, the largest source of income for Canadians: they constitute 92.6 percent of non-transfer and 84.5 percent of total income. Eighty percent of Canadians aged 20 to 65 earn income at some point during the year, though they may not work the entire year. Government transfers, such as employment insurance or social assistance, are another important source of income, received by 59.4 percent of the sample. Transfer income is also closely related to labour market outcomes, because it is low labour income that usually qualifies someone to receive the transfer. Finally, note that income taxes reduce earned income by about 20 percent (on average).

Regarding labour market activities, 80 percent of Canadians in the sample worked at least one hour over the year, working an average of 1395 hours. The average wage was almost $16 per hour. Finally, excluding people who worked in self-employment (i.e., worked for themselves), it remains the case that nearly two-thirds (65.3 percent) of individuals had the labour market as their primary source of earned income.

The next four columns compare these outcomes for men and women. Most striking is the gap between men's and women's earnings: the ratio of men's to women's earnings is 1.80. Some of this can be explained by differences in hours worked. Men were significantly more likely to work (87.8 percent versus 73.6 percent), and they worked longer hours, an

Table 1.1 Sources of Income for Individual Canadians, 1994

	Full Sample		Men		Women	
	Mean	**Non-zero**	**Mean**	**Non-zero**	**Mean**	**Non-zero**
Earnings	21,793	79.8	28,028	86.5	15,613	73.2
Investment income	616	29.0	688	28.5	544	29.6
Pension income	541	3.8	805	4.6	278	3.1
Other income	563	14.3	651	15.1	476	13.5
Government transfers	2,289	59.4	2,096	50.2	2,481	68.5
Subtotal	25,801	97.0	32,269	98.7	19,392	95.3
Income taxes	5,131	74.0	7,065	83.7	3,214	64.4
After-tax income	20,670	97.0	25,205	98.7	16,177	95.3
Annual hours worked	1,395	80.6	1,703	87.8	1,098	73.6
Average hourly wage	15.87	64.3	17.51	66.7	14.12	61.8
Worked, but not self-employed	65.3		67.1		63.6	

Notes:
1. Income figures are average values for all individuals aged 20 to 65, in 1994 dollars. The "Non-zero" column reports the percentage of individuals with positive (or negative) income for that source. The income averages are calculated over the whole sample, including individuals with zero income.
2. The "average hourly wage" is the self-reported average hourly wage from the Labour section of the SLID. Note that the product of hours and wages will not equal earnings as they are reported in different parts of the survey. Adapted from Statistics Canada "Survey of labour and income dynamics public use microdata", 1994, Catalogue 75M0001. All computations on these microdata were prepared by the authors. The responsibility for the use and interpretation of these data is entirely that of the authors.

average of 1703 hours per year versus 1098. The male-female ratio of hours worked is thus 1.55, which goes some way toward but falls short of explaining the earnings difference. We can see that the hours explanation is not the whole story, because the ratio of men's to women's wages is \$17.51/\$14.12 = 1.24. Later in this book, we spend considerable time trying to explain the earnings and wage differentials between men and women, in particular assessing the extent to which this differential is driven by discrimination, as opposed to "legitimate" (or "explainable") differences in productivity. Finally, note that some of the earnings differential is offset by the higher taxes paid, and lower government transfers received, by men.

While the averages shown in Table 1.1 are informative, they hide considerable variation, or dispersion, of outcomes across individuals. In Figure 1.1 we plot a histogram of the distribution of labour earnings. In this figure we restrict our sample to those who have positive earnings, and whose earnings come exclusively from wages and salaries (i.e., we exclude the self-employed). Each bar on the histogram shows the fraction of individuals with a particular level of earnings. To aid in interpretation, we also show three reference lines, at the 10th, 50th, and 90th percentiles. While earnings may range from a low of \$500 per year to a high of \$100,000 per year, the majority of people had earnings between \$5000 and \$50,000.[1] The 10th percentile (or first decile) is \$5500. This means that 10 percent of individuals had earnings below \$5500 per year. The median (or 50th percentile) is \$26,000. This means that half of the sample had earnings below, and half above, \$26,000. Finally, the 90th percentile is \$54,000, indicating that 90 percent of people had incomes below this level, or conversely that 10 percent had earnings higher than this. One common measure of income dispersion is the ratio of incomes at the 90th to the 10th percentiles. In this case, a

[1]For clarity of the graphics, we have trimmed the sample of the lowest and highest earners, dropping the top and bottom 1 percent from the sample. However, the percentiles are calculated over the entire sample.

Figure 1.1 **The Distribution of Individual Labour Earnings, 1994**

This is a histogram showing the distribution of labour earnings for a large sample of Canadians in 1994. Each bar shows the proportion of the sample with earnings in the range indicated on the horizontal axis. For reference purposes we also show vertical lines corresponding to the 10th percentile, median, and 90th percentile. Note that the horizontal (earnings) axis has a logarithmic scale.

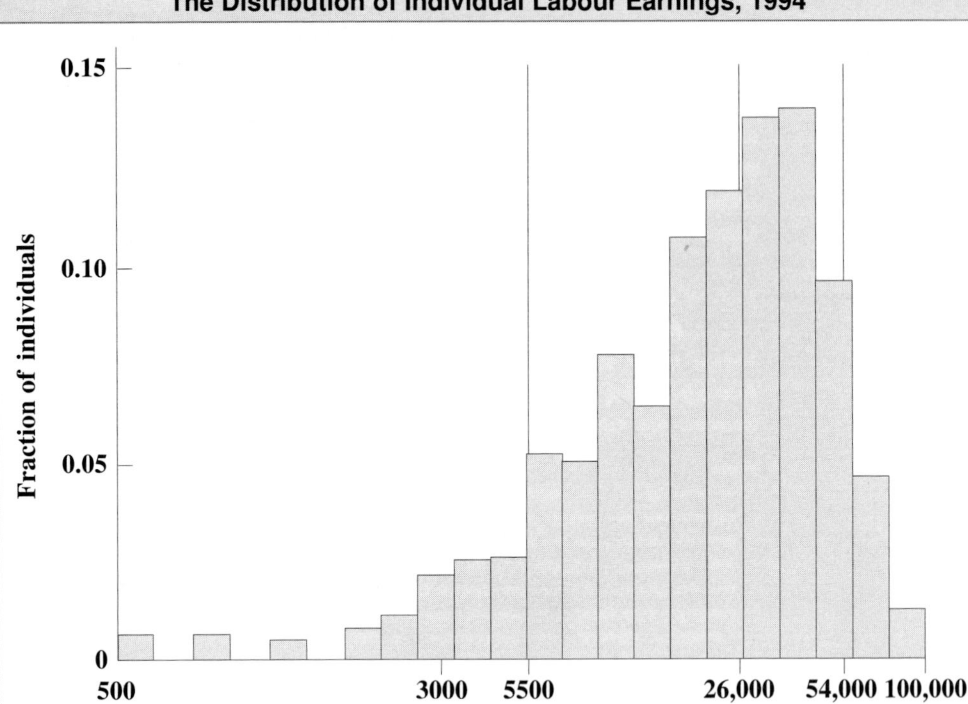

Notes:

1. Adapted from Statistics Canada described in Table 1.1 December 1995. In this figure we show the distribution of average annual wage earnings. For clarity, we only show the middle 98 percent of the distribution, that is, that part of it with labour earnings above the first percentile ($500), and below the 99th percentile ($100,000).
2. Reference lines corresponding to the 10th percentile ($5500), median ($26,000), and 90th percentile ($54,000) are also shown.

"high income" earner (at the 90th percentile) earned about 10 times more ($54000/$5500) than a "low income" person (at the 10th decile).

How much of this difference is due to differences in wage rates, which depend on individual productivity, education, and luck, and how much depends on differences in hours worked, which may depend on a variety of factors, ranging from preferences to the inability to find work (unemployment)? To take a quick look at this, we can break total earnings, WH, into its constituent parts: wages (W) and hours (H). The separate distributions for hours and wages are shown in Figures 1.2 and 1.3.

Looking first at hours, there is considerable variation with hours ranging from as low as 100 hours per year to as high as 3400 hours per year. Recall also that almost 20 percent of individuals do not work at all (i.e., have zero hours), and they are not represented in this figure. Someone may have high earnings because she works a lot (3400 hours corresponds to 65 hours per week, 52 weeks per year, which is even more than a professor works!), or low earnings because she works very little, if at all. Despite the dispersion in hours worked, most people work around 2000 hours per year, which corresponds to the typical 40 hours per week for 50 weeks a year. One of the primary objectives of labour economics is to explain the variation in hours across individuals, in particular explaining why some people work less than 100 hours per year (if at all) while others work more than 2500 hours per year. Are low hours voluntarily chosen, or are they the result of unemployment?

Figure 1.2 **The Distribution of Individual Annual Hours Worked, 1994**

This is a histogram showing the distribution of hours worked for a large sample of Canadians in 1994. Each bar shows the proportion of the sample with hours worked in the range indicated on the horizontal axis.There are 20 bars, so each bar corresponds to (approximately) a range of 150 hours. For reference purposes we also show vertical lines corresponding to the 10th percentile, median, and 90th percentile.

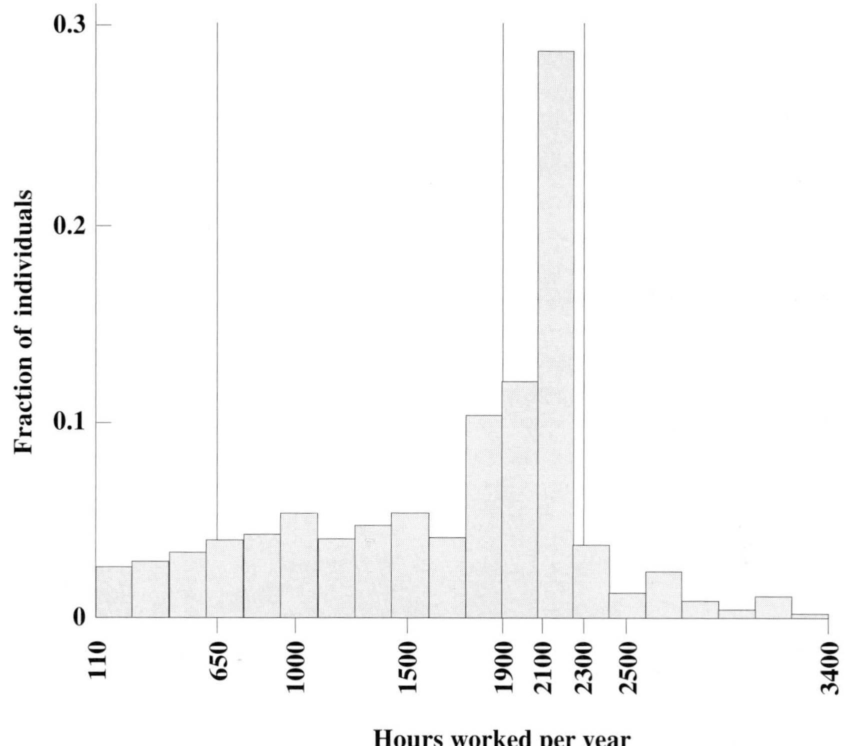

Notes:

1. Adapted from Statistics Canada, '1994 SLID income review: observation and debriefing report' Cat. 75F, Dec. 1995. This figure shows distribution of annual hours worked in 1994. For clarity, we only show the middle 98 percent of the distribution, that is, that part of it with hours above the first percentile (100), and below the 99th percentile (3400).
2. Reference lines corresponding to the 10th percentile (650), median (1900), and 90th percentile (2300) are also shown.

The wage distribution is depicted in Figure 1.3. Wages in this sample ranged from $4.70 per hour to $40. (Again, the graphs have been trimmed of the top and bottom 1 percent.) Most people had wages between $6.70 and $24.70 per hour, corresponding to the 10th and 90th percentiles. Notice that the ratio of wages at the 90th to the 10th percentiles is only 3.69, which is less than the case for earnings: wages are considerably more equally distributed than earnings. The higher inequality of earnings results from the combined inequality of hours and wages. Still, if everyone is created equal, why is there such dispersion in wages? Labour economists attempt to answer this question, exploring the factors discussed in the previous section, and relying heavily on the neoclassical supply and demand model.

THE SUPPLY AND DEMAND MODEL: WORKHORSE OF LABOUR ECONOMICS

The wide-ranging set of topics discussed in the first few pages hint at the breadth of subject matter in labour economics, while the previous empirical explorations show how this broad range of labour market outcomes can be distilled into two variables: employment and wages. Explaining employment and wage outcomes will go a considerable way toward explaining many diverse labour market outcomes. It just so happens that economists have

Figure 1.3

The Distribution of Individual Average Hourly Wages, 1994

This is a histogram showing the distribution of average hourly wages for a large sample of Canadians in 1994. Each bar shows the proportion of the sample with wages in the range indicated on the horizontal axis. For reference purposes we also show vertical lines corresponding to the 10th percentile, median, and 90th percentile. Note that the horizontal (wages) axis has a logarithmic scale.

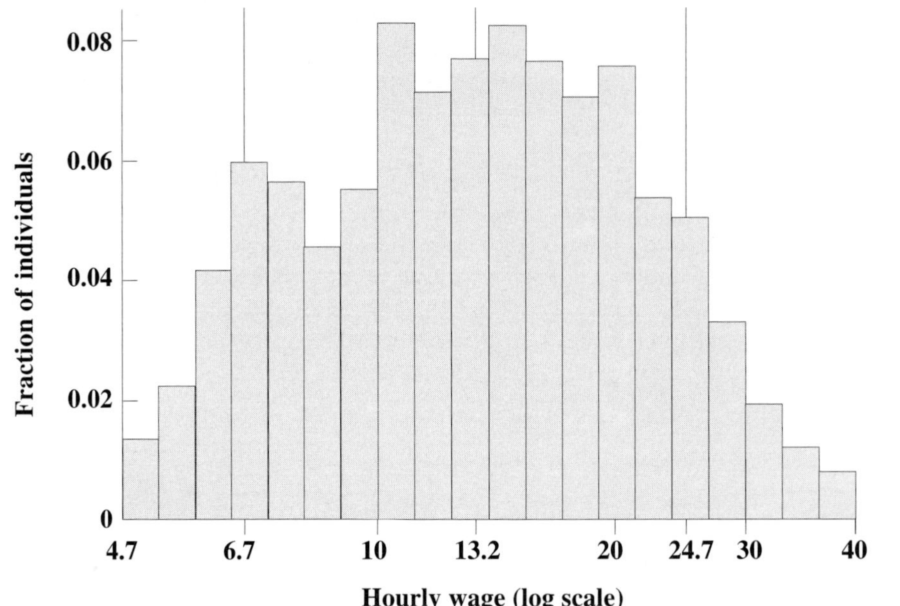

Notes:

1. Adapted from Statistics Canada, described in Figure 1.2. In this particular figure we show the distribution of average hourly wages. For clarity, we only show the middle 98 percent of the distribution, that is, that part of it with wages above the first percentile ($4.75), and below the 99th percentile ($40).
2. Reference lines corresponding to the 10th percentile ($6.70), median ($13.20), and 90th percentile ($24.70) are also shown.

a powerful set of tools with which to explain quantities and prices—in this case, employment and wages. The foundation of that set of tools is the standard supply and demand model, which forms the core of this textbook.

There are two key ingredients in the **neoclassical supply and demand model**:

1. Behavioural assumptions about how buyers and sellers respond to prices and other factors
2. Assumptions about how buyers and sellers interact, and how the market determines the level and terms of exchange

Throughout this textbook we will develop, build upon, and critically evaluate both ingredients. For now we provide a quick overview of the supply and demand framework, with special emphasis on the nature and interpretation of the competitive equilibrium.

The familiar supply and demand model as applied to the labour market is depicted in Figure 1.4. The objective of this model is to yield a prediction concerning the level of employment and wages likely to prevail in a market. With a well-developed behavioural model, we can also conduct "thought experiments," whereby we change assumptions concerning the supply or demand side of the market, and explore the logical consequences for employment and wages.

The supply curve, N^S, represents the behaviour of the sellers' side of the market. We usually imagine that the labour supply decision is made by individuals, and that it depends on many variables. However, in this exercise we hold all factors constant except the wage, and then plot the amount of labour that would be offered for sale at each wage rate. Similarly, the demand function, N^D, shows the amount of labour that firms would be willing to hire at each wage rate. Obviously, labour demand will also depend on many variables besides the wage, but these variables are held constant. The question is then: If individuals and firms simultaneously act in their own best interests, selling and buying labour according to their supply and demand curves, what wage and employment combination will prevail in the market? The assumption of competitive behaviour permits strong predictions concerning the labour market outcomes.

Wages and Employment in a Competitive Labour Market

In the simplest models, buyers and sellers of labour interact competitively in the labour market—that is, they take the market wage as given, and supply or demand the relevant quantity of labour according to their supply or demand functions.

No single agent has the power to affect the market wage by its actions. How is the market wage then determined? We might imagine a mythic auctioneer, using trial and error to establish a market clearing price; however, such an auctioneer does not actually exist. Before discussing how the market wage is determined, economists try to characterize the **equilibrium**, that is, the properties the market wage should satisfy. Of the continuum of possible wages that could prevail in the market, economists focus on that wage that clears the market—the wage that sets supply equal to demand. This equilibrium is depicted in Figure 1.4.

Why is this intersection so appealing to economists? First, at W^*, N^* supply equals demand at W^*, that is, at W^*, N^* is the optimal labour supplied by workers (it lies on N^S), and N^* the optimal labour demanded by firms (it lies on N^D). The easiest way to see why this is at least a reasonable candidate combination of W^* and N^* to prevail in the market, is to consider any other combination. We maintain the assumption that the agents in the labour market are optimizing, that is, they will choose to supply or demand N according to their supply and demand functions. Let us also assume that exchange is voluntary, that is, individuals cannot be forced to buy or sell unless they choose. Consider a wage W' above W^*. At this wage, $N^{D'}$ will be exchanged since firms cannot be forced to hire any more labour. At this wage, supply exceeds demand. There is in principle no reason why this wage will not prevail in the market, but it would be difficult to characterize this as a market equi-

Figure 1.4 **Wages and Employment in a Competitive Labour Market**

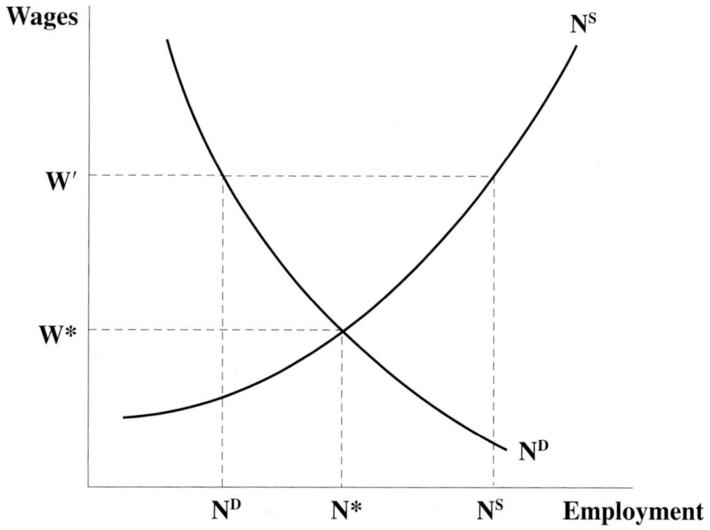

The labour supply curve depicts the desired amount of labour that individuals would like to sell at each wage rate, holding all other factors constant. Similarly, the demand curve shows how much labour firms would like to hire at each wage rate (holding all other factors constant). The equilibrium combination of employment and wages, W^*, N^* is given by the intersection of supply and demand. Only at W^* is it the case that the quantity supplied equals the quantity demanded.

librium. At this wage there would be workers willing to work for slightly less, and firms willing to hire at a slightly lower wage. Thus there would be competitive pressures for the wage to fall. In the absence of rigidities, we might expect wages to fall toward W*. A similar argument (in reverse) would apply to a situation where the market wage was below W*. Thus, if we believe that there are equilibriating mechanisms in the market, the combination W* and N* is a reasonable candidate to prevail in the labour market.

It is worth exploring in more detail some of the features and implications of the competitive equilibrium since this **market-clearing model** underlies most of **neoclassical economics**. One implication is that in markets with homogeneous workers (individuals who are the same in terms of productive characteristics) and homogeneous jobs (jobs which are equally desirable from the workers' point of view) wages will be equalized across workers. Firms would not pay more than the going market wage because they can employ as much labour as desired at the going wage rate. Workers would not accept less than the market wage because there are equally satisfactory jobs available at the going wage rate. We can thus use the supply and demand model to explore the determinants of wages across markets, an important first step in trying to explain wage differentials across different groups of individuals. But our first prediction is that otherwise identical workers should be paid the same. This implication of the basic competitive equilibrium is illustrated in Figure 1.5 for the case of two industries or regions employing the same type of homogeneous labour. Panel (a) shows the situation in which the labour market is not in equilibrium (even though demand equals supply in each individual labour market) because employees in sector A are receiving a lower wage than employees in sector B. In the presence of full information, and in the absence of mobility costs (costs of changing from one sector to another), workers would move from sector A to sector B, thus increasing supply in B and reducing labour supply in sector A. As a consequence, wages would fall in sector B and rise in sector A. This process would continue until wages are equalized across the two sectors, as illustrated in panel (b).

Mobility costs could account for some persistence of earnings differences across sectors, at least in the short run, especially if the sectors are geographically separated. However, these differences are unlikely to persist in the longer run. As older workers retire and young workers enter the labour market, new entrants will tend to choose the higher-paying sector over the lower-paying sector, thus bringing about wage equality across the homogeneous work force.

Another implication of the basic competitive equilibrium is the absence of **involuntary unemployment**. This is also illustrated in panel (b) of Figure 1.5. In labour market equilibrium, there are no individuals who would like to work at the going market wage W_e who are unable to find work at that wage. There are some individuals who are "voluntarily unemployed" in the sense that they would be willing to work at a higher wage (e.g., at wage W_0), but at the wage W_e the value of their time spent in leisure or household production exceeds the value of their time spent in market work. (This aspect is evident from the rising labour supply curves in these two labour markets.) This labour supply decision *may* explain our finding in Figure 1.2 that many individuals choose low hours of work.

The absence of involuntary unemployment implies that there are also no unexploited "gains from trade" that would mutually benefit employers and unemployed workers. For example, if there existed an unemployed worker who would be willing to work at a wage below the existing market wage, both the worker and the hiring firm would benefit from a job match.

A related implication of the basic competitive labour market equilibrium is that there will be no queues for, or rationing of, jobs. The predicted absence of queues follows from the assumed homogeneity of jobs (thus making all jobs equally satisfactory in terms of working conditions, job security, and so on) and the property of wages being equalized

Figure 1.5 **Equilibrium Wages Across Two Sectors**

The supply and demand model can be applied across labour markets. Consider the relative wages of identical (homogeneous) workers in two separate markets (e.g., regions or occupations). In panel (a), the equilibrium wage, W_A, is lower in Sector A than Sector B, W_B. This cannot be a permanent equilibrium, unless there is a barrier preventing workers from sector A from moving to sector B. These barriers could be imperfect information about the higher wage opportunities, or other costs associated with switching regions or occupations. Absent these barriers, we would expect individuals to move to sector B, shifting out the supply curve in sector B, until the wage is equal in the two sectors, and there are no longer incentives for individuals to switch sectors. This cross-sector equilibrium is illustrated in panel (b), where the equilibrium wage is W_e.

(a) Temporary wage differences in markets for homogeneous workers

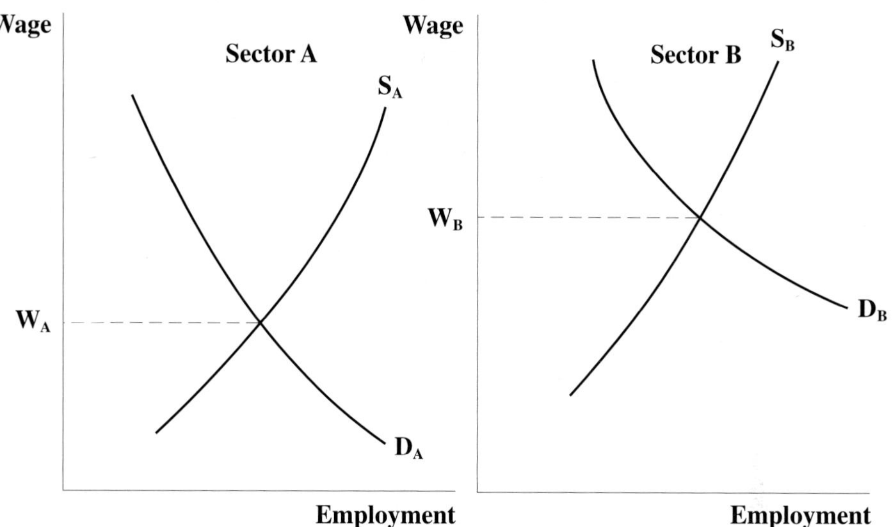

(b) Labour market equilibrium in markets for homogeneous workers

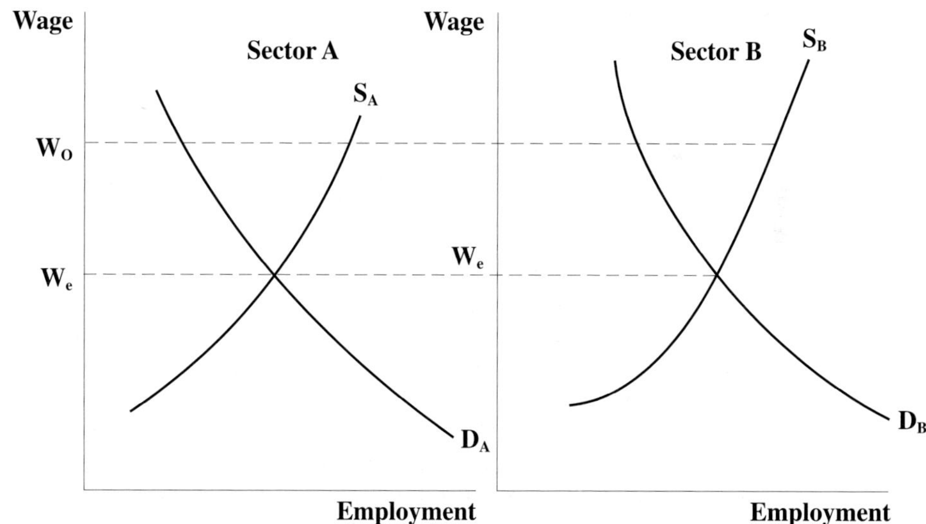

across jobs and sectors. As a consequence, there are no jobs worth waiting for or lining up for. Similarly, in the absence of queues, there is no need for firms to ration jobs.

Whether these predictions of the basic competitive model accord with observed labour market behaviour is another question. Wages may not adjust quickly to "clear" the labour market (i.e., to equate labour demand and supply). Involuntary unemployment of workers appears to be a frequent, if not persistent, feature of many labour markets. Large and persistent differentials in the wages paid to apparently homogeneous workers also appear to prevail. In addition, there is evidence that the jobs that pay the highest wages are also more desirable on other grounds, such as working conditions, job security, career prospects, and nonwage benefits.

These simple observations suggest that this neoclassical model is not strictly true. So why build an entire discipline, let alone a textbook, around such a model? First, it may be there is no better alternative, that other models of the labour market are even worse. More importantly, the model may still serve as a useful approximation, and be useful for looking at policies, especially those that affect prices in the labour market. In essence, the "proof of the pudding is in the eating," so that whether this model is useful will depend in part to what extent it is useful in predicting the consequences of policy changes that affect the labour market.

Nevertheless, it is still unsatisfying that a model, even if useful for some purposes, is at odds with reality. These apparent inconsistencies between the predictions of the basic competitive model and observed behaviour have motivated considerable recent theoretical and empirical research. A central theme of this research is that much of the behaviour we observe in labour markets can be explained in terms of the responses of employers and employees to imperfect information, incentives, and risk and uncertainty, all features of economic life that are ignored in simple supply and demand models. A common feature of these theories, which we will address in this and future chapters, is that the wage performs functions in addition to clearing the labour market—the wage may also act as an incentive device, a risk-sharing mechanism, as part of a matching process, or as a signal of the productivity of the worker on the job. Because the wage rate serves more than one function, it need not—indeed generally will not—perform its market-clearing function fully.

CURRENT POLICY ISSUES

The previous discussion of the subject matter and theoretical methodology of labour market economics highlighted a number of areas of current policy of concern to both public policymakers (e.g., legislators, government policymakers, and the courts) and private policymakers (e.g., employers through their personnel and human resource management decisions and unions through their collective bargaining actions). Labour market economics should be able to shed light on many of these issues, illustrating its social relevance as well as practical relevance in private decision-making.

In the labour supply area, such current policy questions abound. What are the work incentive effects of income maintenance and tax transfer programs such as income taxes, unemployment insurance, welfare, wage subsidies, disability payments, and workers' compensation? How can such programs be designed to achieve their broader social objectives while minimizing any adverse incentive effects that could jeopardize their existence? Why has there been a dramatic increase in the labour force participation of women, especially married women? What accounts for the trend toward early retirement? Can employers use features of their private pension plans to encourage early retirement? What accounts for the long-run decline in the average work week that has occurred? Why do some workers require an overtime premium to work longer hours, while others are willing to moonlight at a second job at a rate that is less than the rate in their primary job? Why has there been an increase in alternative worktime arrangements, including part-time work, flextime, and compressed work weeks? Under what conditions would workers voluntarily accept work-sharing arrangements, for example, a four-day work week in return for no layoffs? What is the impact of increased commuting time and daycare costs on labour force participation and hours-of-work decisions? What factors influence how we allocate time over our life cycle and across different activities? What factors influence our decision to have children, and when to have them?

In the labour demand area, many policy questions have been brought to the fore because of new competitive pressures, many emanating from global competition. What is the impact of wages and other elements of labour cost on the competitiveness of Canadian firms? How is this competitiveness affected by legislated policies with respect to such factors as wages, employment, hours of work, termination, antidiscrimination, human rights, health and safety, workers' compensation, and labour relations legislation dealing with the formation of unions and the conduct of collective bargaining? What is the impact on the labour market of free trade, global competition, industrial restructuring, mergers and acquisitions, privatization, technological change, and the shift from manufacturing to services and high-technology industries? How will employers change their employment decisions in response to legislation on minimum wages, equal pay for work of equal value, severance pay, and advance notice of termination? Can new jobs be created by policies to reduce the use of overtime through higher overtime premiums or regulations on maximum hours of work?

With respect to wage determination and wage structures policy issues also abound. What has been the influence of increased competitive pressures on wages and wage structures and the returns to education? What accounts for the increased wage polarization that has occurred? Do public sector workers receive higher pay than comparable private sector workers? How important are fringe benefits in the total compensation picture, and why do fringe benefits prevail in the first place? How quickly do immigrants assimilate into the Canadian labour market? Does increased immigration lower the wages of native-born Canadians? Are workers in risky occupations compensated for that risk through compensating wage premiums? Do workers "pay" for pension benefits by receiving lower wages than they would receive in the absence of such pensions? Why do male-female wage differentials prevail, and have they been changing over time, especially in response to legislative initiatives? What exactly is meant by the new policies of pay equity (equal pay for work of equal value) and employment equity, and how do they operate? How can employers design optimal compensation systems to induce productivity from their work force, including executives? Why does mandatory retirement exist, and what will happen to wage structures if it is banned? Why do wages seem to rise with seniority even if there is no productivity increase with seniority? Why do some employers seem to pay wages that are excessively high for their recruitment and retention needs?

With respect to unemployment, many old questions prevail and new ones are added. Why has unemployment drifted upwards, even in times of seeming prosperity and inflation? Is unemployment different now than it was in earlier periods? Is permanent job loss more of a problem? What has happened to the unemployment of youths as the baby boomers age through the labour force? Does our aggregate unemployment rate reflect a large number of people experiencing short bouts of unemployment, or a small number of people experiencing long bouts of unemployment? Why do workers and unions not take wage cuts to ameliorate unemployment? Why has the relationship between unemployment and inflation worsened? What impact has unemployment insurance had on our unemployment rate?

These are merely illustrative of the myriad of current policy questions that are relevant for public policy as well as for private personnel and human resource practices and for collective bargaining. They indicate the social and practical relevance of labour economics, and the controversy that surrounds the field. The tools of labour market economics developed in this text will provide answers to many of these questions and shed light on others.[2]

[2]See Riddell (1999) for a more detailed overview of the current state of the Canadian labour market and a discussion of the related policy issues.

SIMILARITIES AND DIFFERENCES BETWEEN THE LABOUR MARKET AND OTHER MARKETS

A key issue in labour market economics is whether the labour market is so different from other markets that the basic tools of economics, especially the supply and demand model described earlier, do not apply. The following discussion illustrates some of these peculiarities and their implications for labour markets.

Various Actors with a Variety of Goals

As discussed previously, the labour market has three main actors or stakeholders—labour, management, and government—each with different subgroups and objectives or agendas. For example, within labour there is union labour and nonunion labour, and within organized labour there are different types of unions (e.g., craft, industrial, professional associations) as well as possible differences between the leadership and the rank-and-file membership. Within management, the goals of stockholders may differ from the goals of chief executive officers, which in turn may differ from the goals of middle management. With increased emphasis on employee participation, the distinction between middle management and workers may be blurred. Within the catchall of government there are federal, provincial, and local levels. As well, there are often differences in the units who make the laws (e.g., legislators and regulators), who enforce the laws (e.g., courts, administrative agencies, and tribunals), and who design the laws and operate particular government programs (e.g., policy units and bureaucrats). As well, the distinction between making, designing, and administering the law and policies often becomes blurred in practice. For example, the jurisprudence and case law of the courts and administrative tribunals can shape the interpretation of the law to such an extent that it can be more important than establishing new laws.

Sociological, Institutional, and Legislative Constraints

More so than most markets, the labour market is riddled with sociological, institutional, legislative, and other constraints. In the sociological area, for example, family and community ties and roles can affect labour mobility, the role of women in the labour market and the household, and their career and educational choices. Social norms may also influence what are considered appropriate wage structures and who should do certain jobs.

Institutions are also important in labour markets. This is most obvious with respect to unions, especially in Canada where almost 40 percent of the work force is unionized. Large corporations may dominate a local labour market and hence set wages, and multinational corporations may follow the wage and workplace practices of their parent company as well as use the threat of plant relocation decisions to influence bargaining. Wage patterns may become institutionalized through pattern bargaining, albeit these may be breaking down under current competitive conditions. Earlier perspectives on labour economics in fact were characterized as "institutional," emphasizing the importance of institutions and institutional arrangements in understanding labour market behaviour.

Legislative constraints are also crucial in labour markets. Employment standards laws set minimal or "community" standards with respect to such things as minimum wages, hours of work and overtime, statutory holidays, parental leave, and severance pay and advance notice requirements. Human rights and antidiscrimination legislation are important, as are laws on health and safety and workers' compensation. Labour relations laws also establish the framework for the formation of unions and the conduct of collective bargaining. Separate statutes often exist for workers in the public sector, sometimes circumscribing the right to strike and providing alternative dispute resolution procedures, including binding wage arbitration. The labour market may also be affected by other laws and regulations, such as those that affect immigration, free trade, unemployment insurance, pensions, training and education, and even environmental protection.

Market Imperfections

The labour market, more so than most other markets, is subject to market imperfections and other constraints. For example, imperfect information may make it difficult to decide which type of education to undertake or whether to make a geographic or occupational move. Asymmetric information (e.g., the employer has information not available to workers) may make it difficult to demand compensating wage premiums for workplace hazards, or to agree to wage concessions in return for employment security. Transactions costs may make it difficult to finance human capital investments in areas like education, training, or mobility. Uncertainty and risk may make it difficult to make occupational choice decisions that are affected by uncertain future demand and supply conditions.

Complex Price, Serving a Variety of Functions

The essential price that gets determined in the labour market—the price of labour services or the wage rate—is a complex price that is called upon to serve a variety of functions. It reflects a variety of factors: the returns to investments in education, training, or mobility; compensation for risk or undesirable working conditions; a "rent" or surplus for being a member of a union or professional association or perhaps being employed in a particular industry; discrimination; and supply and demand decisions on the part of other participants in the labour market. As well, the wage rate is only one component of total compensation, with fringe benefits making up an increasingly larger share.

The **wage rate** is also called upon to perform a variety of functions. It allocates labour to its efficient uses, that is, to particular occupations, industries, and regions. It encourages optimal investments in human capital like education, training, labour market information, job search, and mobility. It is used to enhance performance, work effort, and productivity. It is also called upon to provide an adequate standard of living and family income, and to alleviate poverty and the manifestations of discrimination. In the labour market, issues of efficiency and equity and fairness are intricately related.

In part for these reasons, there are often strong moral overtones to labour market issues and the resultant wage that emerges. This is compounded by the fact that even though the wage is the price of labour services, the fact remains that the labour services and the labourer are inseparable. Dignity, perceptions of self-worth, and social attitudes are tied to the wage. Hence, phrases like a decent wage, a living wage, the social wage, a just wage, and equal pay for work of equal value are common expressions in labour economics.

Clearly, the labour market has a number of characteristics that make it different from many other markets. This raises the issue of whether the basic tools of economics apply in a market with such a complex array of participants and goals; a variety of sociological, legal, and institutional constraints; market imperfections; and a complex price that is called upon to serve a variety of functions.

Our perception is that these are differences in degree and not in kind; other markets have some of these peculiarities as well as others of their own. Moreover, these differences make the basic tools of economics more relevant, not less relevant, to understanding labour market behaviour and the impact of these peculiarities of the labour market. Economic analysis deals with decision-making and tradeoffs under risk, uncertainty, transactions costs, information problems, and market imperfections. It deals with the interplay among various market participants often with conflicting objectives. It deals with the impact of legal, institutional, and even sociological constraints—after all, the methodology of economics is a matter of optimizing the subject to the constraints.

Economics has even proven useful in understanding why many of these constraints and institutional arrangements arise in the first place. As illustrated later in the text, economic efficiency rationales can be given to explain the existence of a variety of phenomena that may appear to be "irrational" or inefficient: pure seniority-based wage increases; the simultaneous existence of moonlighting and overtime; wages that appear "excessive" relative to what is necessary to recruit and retain workers; strikes that appear "irrational"; an unwillingness to accept wage concessions in spite of high unemployment; the provision of job security in the public sector; payment through fringe benefits rather than cash compensation; and the existence of personnel practices like mandatory retirement. In some cases, these phenomena may be the result of mistakes or of bargaining power; but in other cases, they may be the efficient institutional arrangement to deal with other problems in labour markets. Economics can shed light on why these arrangements arise in the first place, as well as indicating their impact on the labour market. This often requires an interdisciplinary understanding that blends labour economics with other areas such as industrial relations, personnel and human resource management, labour law, sociology, psychology, and history.

ALTERNATIVE PERSPECTIVES

Throughout this chapter and the remainder of the book, we emphasize the neoclassical approach to the analysis of labour market equilibrium. One of the central themes of recent research in the neoclassical tradition has been to demonstrate that much of observed labour market behaviour which appears initially to be inconsistent with the basic competitive model is in fact consistent with neoclassical theory, once account is taken of imperfect information, incentives, and uncertainty. There have always been schools of thought, however, that have deemphasized, and at times attacked, the notion of market forces as being the most important factors in wage and employment determination. The severity of the criticism of the neoclassical approach has ranged from saying that economic factors play an important but minor role, to saying that they are distinctly subservient to other political-institutional factors, to the more radical critiques that argue that the economic framework simply masks the forces of power and class conflict that are the real determinants of wages and employment.

While it is always hazardous to try to categorize alternative perspectives and paradigms, they are labelled here as *institutionalism*, *dualism*, and *radicalism*. While there are some basic differences between these perspectives, they have as a common thread a critique of the neoclassical paradigm. In what follows an attempt will be made to briefly summarize each of these schools of thought with respect to their criticism of neoclassical theory, their own contribution, and their own strengths and shortcomings.

Institutionalism

The **institutionalism** tradition in labour economics is one that plays down economic forces and emphasizes the roles of individuals, institutions, custom, and sociopolitical factors. It tends to emphasize descriptive realism as more important than abstract, theoretical reasoning. The case-study and real-world observations are emphasized as important in understanding the behaviour of the labour market.

The institutionalist tradition is evident in the work of Lester (1946), who attacked the assumptions of economics and its emphasis on marginal analysis as being unrealistic. He argued for empirical testing of the assumptions often employed in economics. For example, in responding to interviews and questionnaires, employers said that they did not use marginal analysis in their everyday business decisions and that they seldom responded to wage increases by reducing employment. Lester interpreted this as a rejection of conventional economic analysis.

Dualism

The segmented labour market tradition, or **dualism**, characterizes the labour market as segmented into two main parts, the primary, or core labour market, and the secondary, or peripheral, labour market. The characteristics of the primary and secondary labour markets are given in Doeringer and Piore (1971, p. 165):

> *Jobs in the primary market possess several of the following characteristics: high wages, good working conditions, employment stability, chances of advancement, equity, and due process in the administration of work rules. Jobs in the secondary market, in contrast, tend to have low wages and fringe benefits, poor working conditions, high labour turnover, little chance of advancement, and often arbitrary and capricious supervision. There are distinctions between workers in the two sectors which parallel those between jobs: workers in the secondary sector, relative to those in the primary sector, exhibit greater turnover, higher rates of lateness and absenteeism, more insubordination, and engage more freely in petty theft and pilferage.*

Of crucial importance in the analysis of segmented labour markets is the role of the internal labour market of individual firms in the primary sector. Within each internal labour market, well-developed hierarchies and stable employment relationships develop that are of mutual benefit to both management and workers. The job security and opportunities for career advancement that are so important to workers are also of value to management as ways of retaining a work force that has accumulated enterprise-specific skills and informal on-the-job training. In such circumstances, firms will try to reduce turnover cost by paying high wages, granting job security, and providing career advancement.

Within the internal labour market, the allocation of labour is determined by administrative rules and custom. Competitive forces, according to this perspective, have only a minor influence in determining broad limits within which administered and customary wage and employment policies are carried out.

Radicalism

Following Marx, **radicalism** emphasizes that *economic classes* emerge as a result of the particular way in which productive activity is organized: under capitalism, the working class and capitalists emerge, each group developing a strong subjective identification with its own class. Because of technological change and growth, an *economic surplus* develops over and above the subsistence level necessary to sustain and maintain the economic system. *Class conflict* arises over the division of this economic surplus. Under the current state of capitalism, this surplus tends to be appropriated by the capitalist owners of the means of production and they use the surplus to ensure their continued *power*. In particular, they use the instruments of the *state* (e.g., police, education, granting agencies, tax transfer schemes) to ensure that effective power remains in their hands. These policies could include the granting of concessions to the working class, largely as a way to buy support, co-opt insurgence, and defuse protest.

Over time, however, capitalism develops *internal contradictions*—in essence, it contains the seeds of its self-destruction. In particular, competition, efficiency, and the specialization of labour are necessary for the survival of capitalism, but these very factors dehumanize and alienate the work force, strengthening class consciousness among exploited workers. Eventually, their plight will become intolerable and they will act in a concerted fashion to gain the effective power necessary to improve their position.

An Overall Assessment

Any overall assessment of the various competing paradigms—neoclassical, institutional, dual, and radical—is made difficult by the political overtones that surround any perspective. The matter is further complicated by the fact that the dual and new radical perspectives have not been subjected to the test of time. And when they are judged, it is probably through the perspective of the reigning paradigm—neoclassical economics—with its emphasis on theory that yields implications capable of empirical acceptance or rejection. The extent to which this is a fair test is an open question, especially since the empirical testing itself is geared to the neoclassical paradigm with its emphasis on marginal analysis.

Each of the perspectives certainly does give insights into our understanding of labour market behaviour. Neoclassical economics, with its emphasis on income and relative prices as they affect various facets of labour supply and labour demand in alternative market structures, certainly has provided a systematic and consistent theoretical explanation for various aspects of observed labour market behaviour. This is especially the case when it has been modified to incorporate realistic factors such as uncertainty, transaction costs, incentive structures, and lack of information. While there certainly is no consensus as to which paradigm provides us with the greatest understanding of labour market behaviour, there is certainly more agreement that the insights from all of the paradigms have been useful. As a general proposition it is probably correct to say that the basic neoclassical economic paradigm has not been replaced—at least not yet—by any of the alternatives. Nevertheless, the latter have been useful in pointing out possible weaknesses in the neoclassical paradigm and in pressuring it to analyze institutional phenomena, labour market segmentation, and power relationships—all of which seem to be particularly important in labour markets. The extent to which the neoclassical paradigm is sufficiently adaptable remains an open—and interesting—question.

SUMMARY OBSERVATIONS AND FORMAT OF THIS BOOK

The previous discussion highlighted how labour economics is both practically relevant to our everyday lives and socially relevant to broader social issues. It also indicated how labour economics interrelates with a variety of other disciplines. The discussion also emphasized that the peculiarities of labour economics make economics more relevant, not less relevant, to understanding not only the impact of these peculiarities and institutional features, but also why they arise in the first place. These issues make the study of labour markets relevant, controversial, and interesting.

In covering these issues, the text is divided into 19 chapters, which in turn can be placed into three groups. The first group, Chapters 2 through 7, constitutes the main core of theoretical work in labour economics: the neoclassical supply and demand model. The focus of these chapters is on the determination of employment and wages in a single labour market.

Chapters 2, 3, and 4 examine the supply side of the labour market. The underlying theory of labour supply is first outlined, emphasizing the income-leisure choice framework as a way to analyze the decision of whether and how much to work. While the ostensible objective of this theory is to provide the theoretical underpinnings of the labour supply function in the neoclassical model, it is more fundamentally a theory of individual rationality in the face of economic constraints. This basic theory underlies all of the remaining chapters in the book. While it can be daunting at first, Chapter 2 on labour supply is a "spinach" chapter that forms a foundation even for topics that are not directly related to labour supply. The income-leisure framework is then applied to analyze the work incentive effects of income maintenance programs in Chapter 3. This chapter emphasizes the means by which various features of government policy can be incorporated into the budget constraint, or opportunity set, and ultimately may affect work choices made by individuals. Chapter 4 explores features of labour supply over time, and over an individual life cycle. The retirement decision is also analyzed, emphasizing the role of private and public pensions.

Chapters 5 and 6 address the demand side of the market. Attention turns from the decisions of individual worker-consumers to firms, emphasizing how employers change their demand for labour in response to changes in the wage rate and other determinants of labour demand. The factors affecting the magnitude of the possibly adverse employment effects of wage increases are investigated. Also analyzed are the effects on labour demand and employment of recent trends such as global competition, free trade, industrial restructuring, privatization, and deregulation. Canada's labour cost position in the competitive international environment is outlined, and the usefulness of such information in evaluating the impact of trade on labour markets is discussed. The impact on labour demand and employment of quasi-fixed costs such as hiring and training costs and the cost of certain fringe benefits are also analyzed, especially in the context of the willingness of employers to engage in worksharing or in restrictions on overtime to create new jobs.

Chapter 7 deals with the interaction of labour demand and supply in a single market. Wage and employment determination under a variety of assumptions about the degree of competition is presented. First, the competitive model is exploited, and used to analyze the impact of payroll taxes on employment and wages. Second, we consider the case of imperfect competition, whereby employers have an extreme form of market power, monopsony. The discussion of employment and wage determination under these alternative market structures is then used as background to recent empirical debate regarding the impact of minimum wages.

The second group of chapters (Chapters 8 through 16) extends the neoclassical theory of wage and employment determination in a single market to wage structures *across* markets. Chapter 8 develops the theory of compensating wage differentials that underlies most of the subsequent discussion of earnings structures. Chapter 9 discusses human capital theory and investigates the role of education and training in the labour market. Considerable attention is paid to the empirical analysis of the connection between education and individual earnings. A unifying framework for the study of wage structures, the human capital earnings function, is also developed. This framework is exploited in an analysis of wages by various categories in Chapter 10: occupation, industry, region, firm size. Particular attention is also paid to private-public sector wage differentials.

Chapter 11 looks at the earnings of immigrants, and the degree to which their earnings grow after arrival in Canada. This aspect of the economics of immigration is cast into the wider context of immigration policy, and the impact of immigration on the Canadian labour market. Chapter 12 focuses on earnings differentials by sex and investigates the degree to which these differentials may be attributed to discrimination. The chapter also reviews the various policy initiatives in this area, including pay and employment equity. Optimal compensation systems are analyzed in Chapter 13 and applied to explain, for example, the existence of institutional rules and personnel practices like mandatory retirement.

The last subgroup of chapters, 14 through 16, analyzes the impact of unions on the wage structure. Union growth and the different incidence of unions across industries and regions is discussed, as is a comparison of unionization between Canada and the United States. Union preferences are analyzed and used in the context of contract theory and bargaining theory. Chapter 16 focuses on the impact of unions on wages, employment, non-wage aspects of employment, and productivity.

The third group of chapters (17 through 19) departs from the purely neoclassical model of employment and wage determination to consider the possibility that the labour market does not clear instantly, a fact resulting in unemployment. First, the meaning and measurement of unemployment is analyzed. A great deal can be learned about the nature of unemployment by examining its structure and dynamic properties. Chapter 18 documents many of the suggested leading explanations for the existence of unemployment, ranging from imperfect information and search in a largely neoclassical context to alternative theories that have been offered to explain why wages may not adjust to clear the labour market. Finally, in Chapter 19, the macroeconomic relationship between aggregate wage changes, inflation, and unemployment is examined.

The emphasis in the text is on a balance of theory, evidence, and application to important issues of social policy and private employment practices. By its very nature, however, labour economics has a more empirical tilt than most other fields within economics. While economic theory is a helpful guide when thinking about important policy issues, almost invariably the impact of a policy depends on *how much* a given policy is likely to affect economic outcomes. In the absence of controlled, laboratory experiments, researchers have to infer the impact of economic variables on each other by observing existing or past empirical relationships. Some of these inferences are more plausible than others.

Throughout the book, then, the challenges of conducting empirical research are featured. By its very nature, this research is specific and temporal. While the theory of labour supply and demand is "true" given the assumptions, empirical results that hold at one time may cease to be relevant at another. For this reason, a discussion of evidence is a review of current and past evidence, conducted by specific researchers with specific data. These particular bits of evidence, however, usually contribute to a wider, more consistent mosaic of economic relationships that can serve as a guide to policymakers.

One of the more useful trends in empirical labour economics has been to conduct careful comparative studies of economic outcomes across countries. To some extent, this merely reflects the increased internationalization of our economy, and the need for external benchmarks when assessing magnitudes of variables in Canada. More importantly, however, by comparing economic outcomes between economies as similar as Canada and the United States, differences that exist between these outcomes can be associated with differences in the underlying economic structure or policy environment. While evidence of this nature is only suggestive, it represents some of the more important advances in labour economics over the past few years, and it is highlighted where possible in the text.

APPENDIX: SUMMARY OF REGRESSION ANALYSIS[3]

Throughout this book we emphasize empirical evidence that pertains either to the theoretical model being discussed, or the policy question being analyzed. Empirical labour economists address a variety of such questions, a small sample of which is listed below:

- Do labour supply curves slope upward? (Chapter 2)
- Does unemployment insurance reduce incentives to work, increasing the duration that someone is unemployed? (Chapter 3 and Chapter 18)
- Do minimum wages "kill" jobs? (Chapter 7)
- How much does education increase earnings? (Chapter 9)
- How much of the difference in men's and women's earnings can be attributed to labour market discrimination? (Chapter 12)
- Does increased immigration adversely affect the employment outcomes of the native-born? (Chapter 11)
- Do higher wages adequately compensate individuals for working in unpleasant conditions? (Chapter 8)

[3]More thorough discussions of regression analysis and statistics can be found in Gujarati (1999) and Wooldridge (2000), or any other econometrics textbooks.

- How much do unions affect the wage structure of the economy, that is, what is the premium that workers receive for being organized in unions? (Chapter 16)

Sometimes the evidence is a simple graph, chart, or a table of means. More often in labour economics, because it is relationships between variables that are of direct interest, empirical evidence refers to results from **regression analysis**. Our objective here is not to dwell on the mathematical aspects of regression analysis: several helpful sources that do are listed in the references. Rather, our objective is to review some of the terminology and issues that will allow a more informed reading of the empirical evidence as it is described in the book. With modern computing capabilities, even the most basic of spreadsheets can estimate regressions, so we shall not discuss computational aspects of estimating regressions. Besides, the difficult part of regression analysis or empirical work is not usually the implementation of the estimation procedure, but rather obtaining informative data and choosing a reasonable regression to run in the first place. Our discussion in this brief appendix will therefore focus on how regression results can be interpreted.

The foundation of all empirical work is data, that is, recorded measurements of the variables we are trying to summarize or explain. Increasingly, access to data is becoming quite easy as data libraries and statistics bureaus cooperate in providing computer-readable files. Frequently these data sets can be downloaded over the World Wide Web. Data sets that used to take 20 or more reel-tapes and required large mainframes to process can now be cheaply distributed on CD for use on even the most rudimentary personal computers. Labour economists employ a wide variety of data sets, but there are some sources that we will encounter more frequently in this book. A useful way to catalogue these data sets is by the nature of the unit of observation:

1. **Aggregate or time series data** report economy-wide measures like the unemployment rate, inflation, GDP, or CPI. The variables are usually reported for several years (i.e., over time), and often for several economies (countries or provinces). A common database of such series is Statistics Canada's CANSIM, which has information on literally thousands of variables at the national, provincial, and city level. CITIBASE is a smaller data-base that provides comparable macroeconomic series for the United States.

www.statcan.ca/english/CANSIM

2. **Cross-section microdata** report measures of variables (like earnings, hours of work, and level of education) for individuals at a point in time. Common data sets of this type (of which considerable use is made throughout the text) are the Censuses of Canada, conducted every five years; the (now defunct) annual Survey of Consumer Finances (SCF); the monthly Labour Force Survey (LFS); and in the United States, the monthly Current Population Survey (CPS).

www.bls.census.gov/cps/cpsmain.htm

3. **Panel or longitudinal data** combine the features of cross-section and time series data by following sample individuals for several years. This selection allows economists to study the dynamics of individual behaviour, such as transitions into and out of the labour market. In Canada, the Labour Market Activity Survey (LMAS) and the Survey of Labour and Income Dynamics (SLID) are short panels that follow individuals for a few years. In the United States, the Panel Study of Income Dynamics (PSID) and various National Longitudinal Surveys (NLS) have followed individuals for a longer time, and most panel-data-based studies are based on these sources.

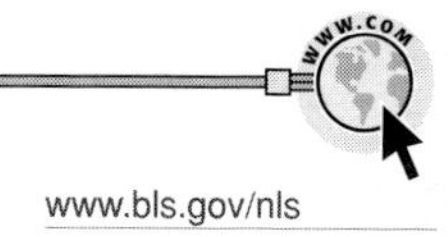

www.bls.gov/nls

In order to illustrate the main ideas of regression analysis, we employ a very simple example that should also provide rudimentary insights into the discussion of earnings determination in later chapters. We explore the relationship between hockey-player performance and player compensation. Specifically, we estimate the relationship between goals scored and player salaries. While the policy relevance of this topic is limited, at least that particular labour market should be familiar to many readers. To keep matters "simple" we also focus only on those players playing forward positions (centre, left wing, and right wing), since salary determination of goal tenders and defencemen will probably be determined by different criteria than those used to evaluate players whose principal function is to score goals.

The underlying theory of player compensation is straightforward. As will be discussed in more detail in the text, individual pay will depend primarily on the economic value of the contribution of one's labour. In this context, we would expect player pay to depend on the amount of additional revenue that he generates (or is expected to generate) for the team. While it involves some additional assumptions, it is not unreasonable to imagine that the main contribution a forward player makes to a team is scoring goals, helping the team win games, and ultimately generating more revenue for the team. What we seek to estimate here is the additional pay a player can expect to make by scoring another goal.

We do this by comparing the salaries of hockey players who score different numbers of goals. We expect the forces of supply and demand to generate higher salaries for the higher scoring players. For example, imagine that there are only two types of players: "stars" who score lots of goals, and "grinders" who serve a primarily defensive or limited offensive role. Presumably, the teams will place a greater value on the higher goal scorers for reasons described above. If we assume that there are two distinct markets for these types of players, then salary determination may be depicted by supply and demand graphs, such as those in Figure 1.A1. Here we can see that the better players earn more because of higher demand and scarcer supply. What we are trying to estimate is the extra earnings a player could expect if he could acquire the skills necessary to move from the "grinder" to the "star" market. Of course, in the real world there is a continuous distribution of hockey talent (goal scoring availability), so we are estimating the returns to marginal improvements in performance.

As suggested earlier, the first step in such an inquiry is to obtain data on the key variables we believe help explain player salaries. In this case, data on player performance statistics and salary are readily available. We use data on player performance in 1999–00, and their salaries in 2000–01. Data on lifetime performance would probably be better, but these more limited data will be sufficient to illustrate the main ideas of regression analysis.

Figure 1.A2 shows a scatter plot of player salaries against the number of goals scored in the previous year. Each point in this scatter plot indicates the combination of goals scored and salary for an individual player. Most of the observations lie below $2,000,000 in annual salary, and 30 goals scored. There are a few observations corresponding to high salaries and higher goal scoring. An "eyeball" summary of this graph suggests that players who score more goals also make more money. Regression analysis is little more than a formalization of this data summary exercise.

In Figure 1.A3 we show a plot of the same data, except that we transform the salaries into "ln(Salary)." Why? It is common practice in labour economics to use logarithms, and some of the reasons are outlined in Exhibit 1A.1, and later in Chapter 9. For our purposes here, the primary reason is that it is easier to summarize the relationship between log salaries and goals with a straight line than the raw levels of salaries. This is especially true given the range of salaries paid to players (from just under $250,000 to $10,000,000).

One simple way to more formally summarize the data in Figure 1.A2 and Figure 1.A3 is to array the average salaries by the number of goals scored. Table 1.A1 illustrates the results of this exercise. Here we can see that player salaries rise from $0.73 million to $1.28 million when "Goals Scored" moves from 0–9 goals per year to 10–19 goals per year, an increase of approximately $550,000 for the extra 10 goals. This implies a return of about $550,000/10 = $55,000 per goal. The return for scoring goals increases as players move to the other categories: average salaries rise by $1 million for moving from the 10–19 to the 20–29 goals per year category; by almost $2 million for moving from the 20–29 to the 30–39 category, and by $2.25 million for moving up to the 40–49 goals per year category. Possibly, these increasing returns reflect the increasing scarcity of higher-goal-scoring players. In terms of logarithms, we see that the log salary rises by about 0.50

Figure 1.A1 **Supply and Demand and the Relative Earnings of "Star" Versus "Grinder" Hockey Players**

Consider the separate markets for two types of players: "grinders" (low skill) and "stars" (high skill). The equilibrium wage for each type of player is determined within each sub-market. Because they generate less revenue, the demand for grinders is lower than for stars. Since it requires less skill to be a grinder, we can also assume that the supply is greater at each wage than for high-skilled players. The combination of lower demand and higher supply results in a lower wage for grinders (W_G) than for stars (W_S).

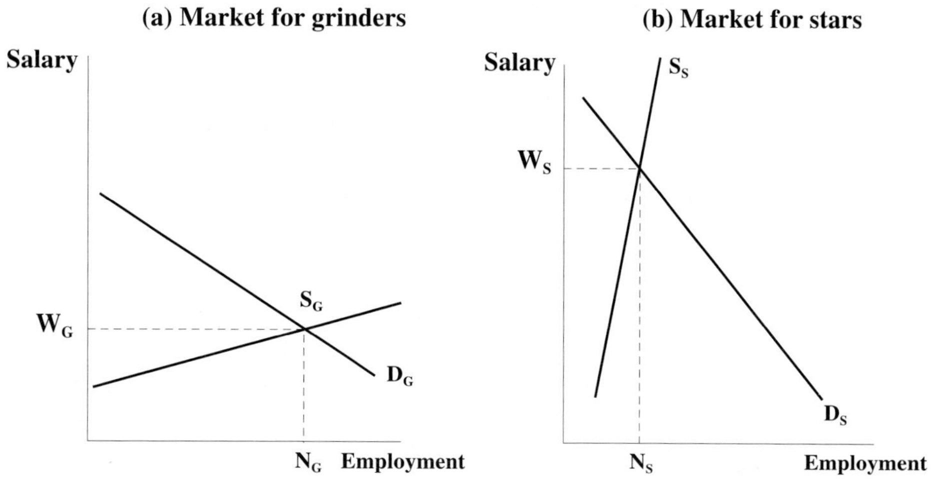

(a) Market for grinders

(b) Market for stars

for 10 goals scored in the below-30-goals range, but increases more as players move to the 50-goals-per-season mark.

All that a regression function accomplishes is to calibrate more formally the relationship that was apparent in the table. Rather than letting our eyes fit a line through the data plotted in Figure 1.A2 and Figure 1.A3, or approximating the relationship between two variables from a table, regressions are calculated to provide an estimate of the function that "best fits" the data. Imagine that we want to estimate the following relationship between salary and goals:

$$\text{Salary} = a + b \times \text{Goals}$$

This is the equation for a straight line. In this example, Salary is the dependent variable, while Goals is the independent, or explanatory variable. If we believed this were an exactly true and complete model of player salaries, all of the data would lie on the line implied by this equation, and estimation would be very simple. Of course, we know that this is only an approximation, and there are many other factors (leadership ability, "marketability," past performance, and luck) that affect player salaries. We can lump all of these factors together into an error term, e, so that our augmented model is:

$$\text{Salary} = a + b \times \text{Goals} + e$$

For any given line that we can draw though the points in the scatter plots, this "model" will fit perfectly. Individual player salaries will equal the "predicted" salary that is on the line, plus the difference between the actual salary and the predicted salary. However, we are interested in explaining as much of the salary as we can with goals, and would like as little as possible left to the residual, e. While there are many ways to formalize this idea, in practice most researchers choose the line that minimizes the sum of the (squared) residuals, or distance between the line and the actual observation. This **ordinary least squares** or **OLS** estimator yields a line that best predicts salary with goals scored, at least according to this criterion. The output of regression analysis will be estimates for the parameters of this line: a, the intercept, and b, the slope.

Exhibit 1A.1 Natural Logging

In labour economics, especially in the presentation of empirical results, it is common to encounter logarithms. Many students find logarithms (or "logs") quite intimidating, but in fact, the use of logs often simplifies economic theory and empirical work. There are at least two (related) contexts in which you will encounter logs in labour economics.

1. First, logs are helpful in expressing elasticities. The elasticity of labour supply with respect to the wage expresses the effect of a change in the wage on hours of labour supply in proportional or percentage terms. This is usually more convenient than expressing the relationship in the original units of measurement. For example, we could state that a $1 an hour rise in the wage increases annual labour supply by 50 hours. In order to facilitate comparison across studies, however, it is usually preferable to report that a 10 percent increase in the wage leads to a 2.5 percent increase in labour supply, that is, that the elasticity is 0.25. The elasticity is unit-free, and gives the proportional (or percentage) change in hours associated with a proportional (or percentage) change in the wage. What does this have to do with logs? The conventional formula for an elasticity is:

$$E = \frac{\Delta Y}{\Delta X} \times \frac{X}{Y} = \frac{\Delta Y}{Y} \div \frac{\Delta X}{X}$$

where "Δ" refers to the change in a variable. As it turns out, changes in the logarithms of variables directly yield the proportional changes, so that the elasticity can be expressed as:

$$E = \Delta \ln Y / \Delta \ln X$$

This is especially convenient in estimating elasticities, because the estimated slope of a regression of ln Y on ln X gives a direct estimate of the elasticity.

2. Second, for many economic phenomena, changes in key variables lead to multiplicative or proportional changes in others. For example, economic growth is usually expressed in percentage terms, rather than in so many billions of dollars. We usually hear that GDP grew by 2 percent, or some comparable figure. An economy with a constant growth rate will grow exponentially, as each year's growth is added to the base of the next year, much as interest is added to the principal in a savings account with compound interest. An approximation of this growth process, or any similar relationship between a variable y and a variable x, is:

$$y = Ae^{rX}$$

This equation is a "simple" representation of a variable y that grows continuously at rate r with X.

In labour economics, many productive characteristics are best described as having a multiplicative effect on wages. For example, an additional year of

Exhibit 1A.1 **Natural Logging *(continued)***

education might raise wages by 10 percent. Each additional year of education would then raise wages by 10 percent as much. In that case, wages can be expressed as a function of years of schooling, as in the equation above. The figure illustrates the relationship between the level of wages and years of schooling for a simple example, where the base wage is $6 per hour, and the return to a year of schooling is 10 percent. Also shown in this graph is a plot of the log wage against the years of schooling. Notice that unlike the relationship in levels, the logarithmic relationship yields an exact straight line. Again, for the purposes of estimating regressions, this is the preferred linear specification of the relationship between wages and education. Transforming such variables into (natural) logs is thus a common exercise.

Useful Properties of Logs

$\ln e = 1$	$\ln (a/b) = \ln a - \ln b$	$\ln (Ae^{rx}) = \ln A + rx$
$\ln ab = \ln a + \ln b$	$\ln a^x = x \ln a$	$\ln (1 + r) \approx r$

A Comparison of W and ln(W) as Functions of Schooling

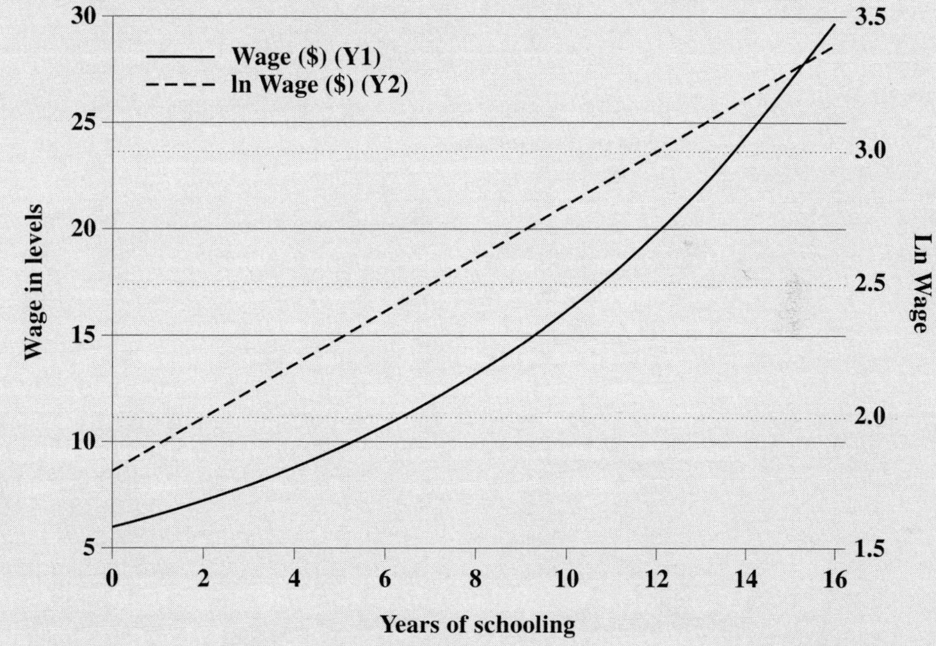

This line shows a hypothetical relationship between wages and the number of years of schooling. In this example, we assume that the logarithm of wages is a linear function of schooling. The dashed line corresponds to the log wage, and the second (right-hand) axis provides the relevant scale. While the log wage is linearly related to the level of schooling, the wage (in levels) is nonlinear, as can be seen by the solid line, and the relevant first (left-hand) vertical axis.

Figure 1.A2 NHL Player Salaries by Goals Scored in the Previous Year, 2000–01

This is a scatter plot of player salaries in 2000-01 against their goals scored the previous year (the 1999-00 season). Each point corresponds to a specific player, relating the number of goals he scored to his salary.

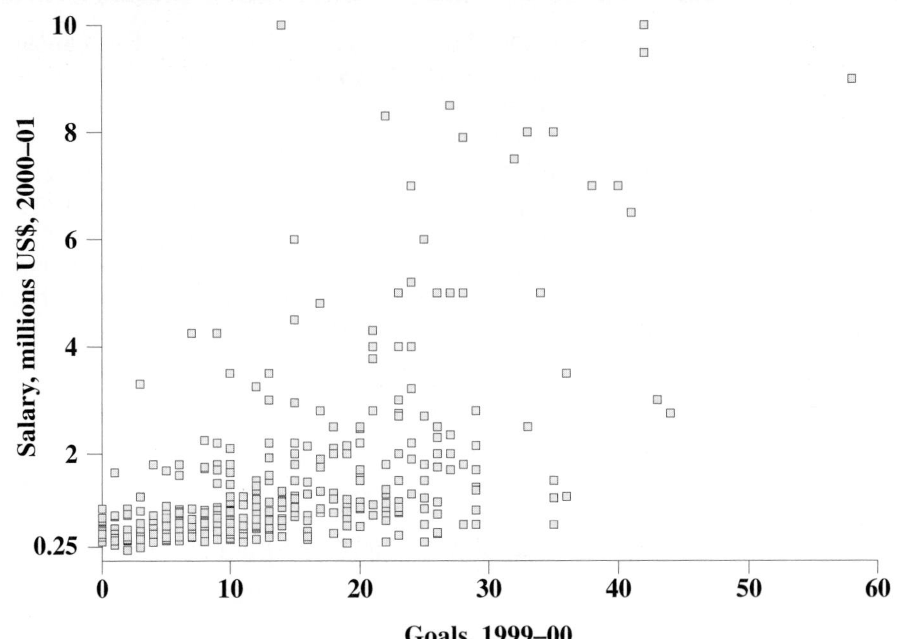

Note: Sample includes only players (forwards) who played at least 20 games in the 1999–00 season. Sample size is 418.

Source: Based on data provided by the NHLPA Web site <www.nhlpa.com>, accessed October 2000.

The estimated regression line for these data is shown in Figure 1.A3. It is upward-sloping, though the precise slope is hard to read directly from the graph. The slope of the line will tell us (on average) how much player salaries rise with goals scored. Specifically, the estimated slope will allow us to conduct the "thought experiment" of how much extra a player would earn if he scored one more goal. The numerical estimates of the regression are reported in Table 1.A2. We show the estimated results for both levels (dollars) and logarithms. In column (1) for levels, we see that each additional goal is associated with $101,325 of additional earnings. In logarithms, column (1) suggests that each goal is

Table 1.A1 Tabulation of NHL Player Salaries by Goals Scored, 2000–01

Goals Scored, 1999–00	Sample Size	Salary ($US million)	ln (Salary)
0–9	184	0.73	13.35
10–19	137	1.28	13.84
20–29	79	2.28	14.36
30–39	11	4.19	14.93
40–49	6	6.46	15.56
50 +	**1**	**9.00**	**16.01**

Notes:
1. Each column indicates the sample size or sample average for the corresponding goal-scoring category.
2. Sample includes only players (forwards) who played at least 20 games in 1999–00. Sample size is 418.

Source: Based on data provided by the NHLPA Web site, <www.nhlpa.com>, accessed October 2000.

Figure 1.A3 **Logarithm of NHL Player Salaries by Goals Scored in the Previous Year, and Fitted Regression Line, 2000–01**

This is a scatter plot of the logarithm of player salaries in 2000-01 against their goals scored the previous year (the 1999-00 season). Each point corresponds to a specific player, relating the logarithm of his 2000-01 salary to his goals scored. In addition, the estimated regression line, based on a regression of log salary on goals scored, is also presented on this graph.

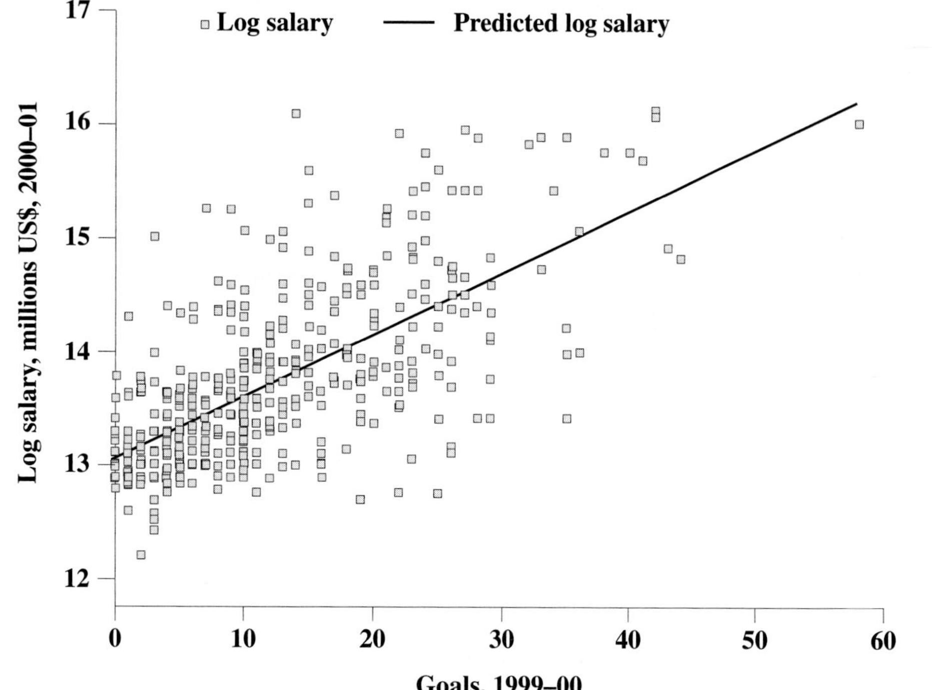

Notes:

1. Sample only includes players (forwards) who played at least 20 games in the 1999–00 season. Sample size is 418.
2. The predicted log salary is based on the regression results reported in Table 1.2A, where Log salary = 13.109 + 0.053 × Goals.

Source: Based on data provided by the NHLPA Web site <www.nhlpa.com>, accessed October 2000.

associated with an additional 0.053 log dollars, which can be interpreted as an additional 5.3 percent in salary.

In addition to the **coefficient**, or **parameter** estimates, regression analysis and the associated statistical theory yield estimates of the stability, or reliability of the estimates, at least within the sample. The **standard errors** of each coefficient provide a measure of the precision with which we are likely to have estimated the true parameter. If the estimation procedure were repeated on other samples of similar hockey players, the coefficients would likely vary across samples even if the underlying salary determination were the same, since no two samples are identical (because of e). The standard error is an estimate of the variability (due to **sampling error**, e) that we would expect for estimates of the coefficient across these samples. Coefficients and standard errors are used together to conduct tests of statistical hypotheses. The most common hypothesis we will encounter is whether a given coefficient is statistically significantly different from zero. Even if one variable has no effect on another, given sampling error it is unlikely that the estimated coefficient would equal zero exactly. For this reason, we generally only pay attention to coefficients that are at least twice as large as their standard errors. This is related to the common "disclaimer" in the reporting of poll results, that the polling procedure yields estimated percentages that are within a given range of the true percentage 19 times out

Table 1.A2 Estimated Effects of Performance on Player Salary (standard errors in parentheses)

	Means	Salary ($US) mean = 1,395,769			ln (Salary) mean = 13.78		
		(1)	(2)	(3)	(4)	(5)	(6)
Intercept		111,033	–37,946	52,841	13.109	13.021	13.046
		(105,182)	(107,941)	(114,739)	(0.048)	(0.048)	(0.051)
Goals	12.68	101,325	63,494	61,771	0.053	0.031	0.030
		(6,626)	(10,573)	(10,549)	(0.003)	(0.005)	(0.005)
Assists	17.77		35,376	31,904		0.021	0.020
			(7,815)	(7,928)		(0.003)	(0.004)
Plus/minus	–0.53			13,712			0.004
				(6,092)			(0.003)
R-squared		0.36	0.39	0.40	0.43	0.47	0.48

Note: Sample includes only players (forwards) who played at least 20 games in 1999–00. Sample size is 418.

Source: Based on data provided by the NHLPA Web site, <www.nhlpa.com>, accessed October 2000.

of 20, so that we should take the specific reported value with a well-defined grain of salt. While this is an approximation of the basic, formal statistics underlying hypothesis testing, it should be sufficient for most empirical research discussed in the book.

The ratio of the coefficient to its standard error is called the **t-ratio**, and the "test" for **statistical significance** is basically a determination of whether this ratio exceeds 2 in absolute value. In the example reported in Table 1.A2, the t-value for goals scored is much greater than 2 (e.g., $101,325/6626 = 15.3), so we can reject the possibility that the estimated relationship between goals and salaries is due to pure chance or sampling error.

Another statistic commonly reported in regression analysis is the **R-squared**. We do not focus much on R-squareds in this text, but the R-squared is a measure of the goodness of fit of the regression. It indicates the proportion of the variance of the dependent variable that is accounted for or explained by the explanatory variables. In column (1) of Table 1.A2, the R-squared is 0.36, which indicates that goals scored in the previous year account for 36 percent of the variation of player salaries. Sadly, this is probably as good a fit of regression as we will encounter in labour economics!

Of course, we do not believe that this simple one-variable regression could possibly explain all of the variation in player salaries. There are other aspects of hockey performance that we also expect to contribute to team victories and revenue. For example, defensive play or setting up goals for other players (assists) may also be rewarded. These other factors can easily be accommodated in **multiple regression** analysis, which is nothing more than adding more variables to the regression equation. At one level, the effect of additional variables, like assists, is of independent interest, and for this reason the expanded set of regressors may be desirable. However, there is a more important reason to add additional variables.

Our objective is to estimate the additional earnings a player can expect to earn by scoring another goal. We accomplish this by comparing earnings across players who have scored different numbers of goals. We thus attribute the additional earnings a 30-goal scorer earns compared to a 10-goal scorer entirely to the extra 20 goals scored. What if the 30- and the 10-goal scorer differ in other ways? What if the 30-goal scorer is also a better player overall (in other dimensions). We may then over-attribute the salary difference to the goal scoring alone. What we really want to do is compare otherwise identical players who only differ in the number of goals scored. We cannot perfectly do this, but by including additional explanatory variables we can control for, or hold constant, these other factors. Of course, we can only hold constant observable, measured factors, and there will always exist the possibility that any estimated relationship between two variables is purely spurious, with one variable merely reflecting the effects of unobserved variables with which it is correlated. We will encounter many such problems as we evaluate empirical research in labour economics. For example, do highly educated individuals earn more because they have the extra schooling, or is schooling merely an indirect indicator of their inherent ability and earnings capacity? Do union members earn higher wages because of the efforts of the union, or because unionized firms are more selective in hiring more productive workers? We must always be careful in noting that regression coefficients indicate correlation between variables. As tempting as it may be, it may be very misleading to apply a causal interpretation to this association.

In columns (2) and (5) we add the variable "Assists" to the regression to see whether goals scored alone was capturing some of the effects of omitted player quality. Apparently this was the case. The estimated return to scoring a goal drops by 40 percent when we control for the number of assists. Players who score more goals also tend to perform well in other dimensions, like assisting other players to score goals. In fact, assists are rewarded almost as much as goals.[4] In column (2), the economic return to scoring a goal, for a player with a given level of assists, is $63,494. In this way, the multiple regression framework holds constant player ability in one dimension to see how variation in another is associated with player salary. Similarly, for players scoring the same number of goals, an extra assist is associated with $35,376 in additional salary.

Finally, in order to see whether forwards are compensated for their defensive abilities, we include a measure of the players' "plus-minus" (the difference between team goals scored for and against while a player is on the ice—a large "minus" for a player indicates that even though he may score goals, the opposing team often scores when he is playing). In columns (3) and (6) we see that the estimated coefficients on "plus-minus" are small, and that including this variable has virtually no effect on the other coefficients. In the levels specification, the plus-minus coefficient is marginally significant, but it is insignificant in the (preferred) logarithmic specification. It appears that forwards are not rewarded for their defensive skills—they are primarily paid to set up or score goals.

Summary

- There are three main groups of actors in the labour market: individuals, firms, and the government. Individuals make decisions concerning how they are going to earn a living: whether and how much to work, what type of work they will do, and what kinds of skills they will acquire in order to work. Firms make decisions about what how much and what type of labour they will hire. Governments set various policies, many of which have direct implications for the decisions of individuals and firms, and also affect the operation of the labour market itself.
- While there are many dimensions to the decisions made by these actors, we can distill the outcomes of the decisions to individual outcomes, especially concerning earnings, employment (or hours), and wages. Preliminary explorations with individual-level data

[4]As it turns out, we cannot reject the hypothesis that the coefficients on goals and assists are the same; that is, given the sampling error, it is possible that the estimated coefficients on goals and assists were generated by a model where goals and assists have the same returns.

show considerable dispersion in these outcomes for Canadians, and systematic differences between men and women. These empirical features, or "labour market facts," merit further investigation in this book.

- The neoclassical supply and demand model is a powerful tool that can be used to analyze these outcomes, especially employment and wages. The model comprises behavioural assumptions concerning buyers and sellers, summarized by the supply and demand curves for labour. In addition, the neoclassical model assumes that the labour market is in equilibrium, that is, that the labour market clears where supply equals demand. This is a very powerful assumption that allows the model to predict a unique employment and wage outcome in a market.
- However, there are other approaches besides the neoclassical model that one can take in studying labour market. These include the institutionalist approach, the dual or segmented labour markets approach, and the radical approach. These other approaches contribute to our understanding of labour markets, but are not covered in this book.
- Most of this book is organized around the supply and demand framework. It begins with a thorough development of the behavioural models underlying labour supply and demand. Next, employment and wage determination in a competitive labour market is summarized, and the assumption of perfect competition is relaxed. The neoclassical framework is then applied to explaining wages across labour markets, especially with respect to the role of education in generating wage differentials. The remainder of the book focuses on markets and outcomes that are not as well characterized by the simple neoclassical model; it includes topics such as discrimination, internal labour markets, unions, and unemployment.
- The appendix to this chapter reviews regression analysis, a statistical tool used to summarize the relationships between variables.

KEYWORDS

labour supply 2
labour demand 3
labour market outcomes 3
wages 3
employment 3
unemployment 3
neoclassical supply and demand model 8
equilibrium 9
market-clearing model 10
neoclassical economics 10
involuntary unemployment 10
wage rate 15
institutionalism 16
dualism 17
radicalism 17
regression analysis 21
aggregate or time series data 21
cross-section microdata 21
panel or longitudinal data 21
ordinary least squares 23
coefficient 27
parameter 27
standard errors 27
sampling error 27
t-ratio 28
statistical significance 28
R-squared 28
multiple regression 28

REFERENCES

Doeringer, P., and M. Piore. 1971. *Internal Labour Markets and Manpower Analysis*. Lexington, Mass.: Health.

Gujarati, D. 1999. *Essentials of Econometrics, Second Edition.* New York: McGraw-Hill.

Lester, R. 1946. Shortcomings of marginal analysis for wage-employment problems. *AER* 36 (March):63–82.

Riddell, W. C. 1999. Canadian labour market performance in international perspective. *CJE* 32 (November): 1097–1134.

Wooldridge, J. M. 2000. *Introductory Econometrics:A Modern Approach*. Cincinnati, Ohio: South-Western College.

Chapter Two

Labour Supply: Individual Attachment to the Labour Market

Main Questions

- *How do we measure labour market attachment? How did labour market attachment evolve over the twentieth century?*
- *What is the labour force participation decision, and how does it fit into the general theory of labour supply?*
- *How can we incorporate the possibly different factors that determine men's and women's labour supply decisions?*
- *Is there any theoretical reason to believe that labour supply increases with the market wage?*
- *What is the evidence regarding the responsiveness of individual labour supply to changes in the wage?*
- *Why are workers paid an overtime premium, rather than just a higher wage, in order to induce them to work overtime?*

At its core, the subject matter of labour supply is how individuals earn a living by selling labour services through the labour market. While there are important quality dimensions to labour supply, such as the levels of skill that someone brings to the market, the focus of the next three chapters is on the quantity of homogeneous labour offered. The guiding theoretical question is whether labour supply is an upward-sloping function of the wage rate.

Why might market labour supply curves increase with the wage rate? In introductory courses, supply curves are commonly drawn as upward-sloping functions of the market price. Why not borrow from this, and merely assert that labour supply, as a special case of "supply," is also upward-sloping in its price? Of course, such reasoning is circular and provides no insight as to why more labour would be offered at a higher wage. The classical economists provide one possible explanation. They argued that labour supply was upward-sloping at least in the long run, because higher wages would spur population growth, increasing the number of labourers. Modern labour economists do not pursue that line of reasoning. Instead, we take the population as fixed at a point in time, and focus on individual decisions of how much to work. These decisions can be broken down into participation (whether to work) and hours (how much to work). Why might both of these dimensions of individual labour supply be increasing in the wage rate? Intuition suggests that people will want to work more if the return for doing so increases. As we shall see, however, intuition alone can be misleading. Nevertheless, incentives to work lie at the heart of the study of labour supply.

In this chapter we develop a model of individual labour supply. The basic theoretical framework is the income- or labour-leisure choice model, and it can be applied to both the participation and the hours dimension. Within this framework, we analyze the effect of changes in wage rates and other economic variables on preferred hours of work, and thus derive the individual's supply curve of labour. An important strength of this model is that it can easily be adapted to explore the impact of more general types of incentives, such as those provided by government tax and transfer programs. Accordingly, we exploit the labour-leisure model in the following chapters. Before turning to the theoretical model, however, we define some important concepts and investigate several labour supply features of the Canadian labour market.

A GUIDE TO THIS CHAPTER

This chapter is a "spinach" one. Much of the material in labour economics, even topics not obviously related to labour supply, such as individual schooling decisions, require an understanding of this theory. This chapter develops the theory of a worker as a rational decision-maker, making choices between various opportunities (good or bad) presented by the labour market. The chapter is divided into two sections:

Section One: The Theory of Labour Supply

The objective of Section One is to begin with a model of individual behaviour, and trace through the implications for the market supply of labour. Ultimately, we derive a labour supply function relating labour supply to the market wage. We begin with an explanation of how economists quantify labour market attachment, dividing this attachment into participation (whether to work) and hours (how much to work) components. After exploring participation and hours patterns in Canada, we develop the basic income-leisure model that underlies both dimensions of labour supply. Using this model, we investigate how participation and hours respond to changes in the economic environment (like the wage). Finally, we summarize the empirical evidence on the effect of wages on labour supply.

Section Two: Extensions and Applications

The objective of Section Two is to use the labour supply model to explore a number of features of the labour market, exclusive of government tax and transfer programs, which we treat separately in the next chapter. In particular, we look at the impact of labour market constraints (like unemployment) on individual labour supply, and the means by which the model can account for multiple jobholding (moonlighting) and the structure of overtime premiums.

Finally, the appendix to this chapter provides a review of the general consumer theory that underlies the income-leisure at the heart of labour supply.

Section One: The Theory of Labour Supply

QUANTIFYING LABOUR MARKET ATTACHMENT

Many students are initially surprised to see the relative attention paid to labour supply by economists. Perhaps based on their own experience, their caricature of a labour supply decision is that virtually everyone wishes a full-time job or career. However, is it really the case that most people participate in the labour market, working the standard work week of around 40 hours? As we shall see, there is actually considerable variation in the degree of attachment of individuals to the labour market.

Labour Force Participation

The **labour force participation decision** is basically a decision to participate in paid labour market activities as opposed to other activities such as unpaid work in the home, volunteer work, education, or retirement. As such, it influences the size and composition of our labour force and it has an impact on household activities, education, and retirement programs.

The policy implications of these changes can be dramatic. Changes in the size and composition of our labour force affect our growth and unemployment rates, as well as the occupational and sex composition of the labour force. The latter, in turn, affect such factors as relative wages, demands for unionization, daycare, and equal pay and equal employment opportunity legislation. Changes in household activities can involve family formation and mobility. Retirement programs can be affected insofar as new labour force participants will add contributions to pension funds, while those who retire (i.e., do not participate in the measured labour force) will be a drain on the funds.

As illustrated in Figure 2.1, the **labour force** consists of those persons in the eligible population who participate in labour market activities, as either employed or unemployed. The eligible population is that portion of the population that is surveyed as potential labour force participants (i.e., civilian noninstitutional population, 15 years and over, excluding the Yukon, Northwest Territories, and those living on Indian reservations). Persons from that potential population of labour force participants (POP) are categorized as either in the labour force (LF) or not in the labour force (NLF). Those in the labour force are either **employed** (E), or **unemployed** (U), with the latter being not employed but seeking work. People are categorized as employed if they are normally employed but they happen not to be at work at the time of the survey because, for example, they are ill or on strike. Individuals on temporary layoff, and those not employed but who have a job to start in the next month, are classified as unemployed. Those not in the labour force are usually students, retired people, persons in the household, those unable to work, or some "discouraged" workers who have simply given up looking for work. According to labour force definitions, the latter are not categorized as unemployed because they are not seeking work.

The **labour force participation rate** (LFPR) is the fraction of the eligible population that participates in the labour force (LFPR = LF/POP). The unemployment rate (UR) is the proportion of the labour force that is unemployed (UR = U/LF).

www.statcan.ca/english/Subjects/Labour/LFS/lfs-en.htm

The Canadian Labour Force Survey (LFS), conducted by Statistics Canada, is currently based on a monthly sample of approximately 62,000 households. The results are published monthly in *The Labour Force* (Statistics Canada, Catalogue No. 71-001), with the survey described in more detail in that publication. The survey began in 1945, first on a quarterly, and by 1952, on a monthly basis. In 1976, and again in 1997, the survey was expanded substantially to collect more detailed information on labour market attachment.

While the LFS provides the most frequently used estimates for our labour force,

Figure 2.1 **Labour Force Concepts (numbers refer to November 2000)**

The labour force is the sum of those individuals either working (employed) or not working, but searching for work (unemployed). The unemployment rate is the percentage of the labour force that is unemployed, while the labour force participation rate is the percentage of the eligible population in the labour force.

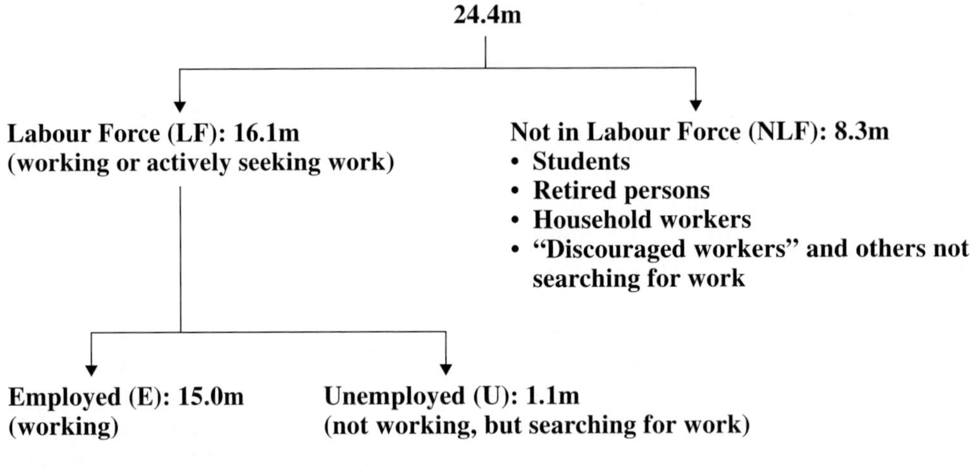

Notes:
"m": million
Labour force participation rate: LFPR = LF/POP = 16.1/24.4 = 66.0%.
Unemployment rate: UR = U/LF = 1.1/16.1 = 6.8%.
Source: Adapted from the Statistics Canada publication "Labour Force", Catalouge 71-001, November 2000.

www.statcan.ca/english/census96/list.htm

employment, and unemployment figures, other sources are available. In particular, the Canadian Census is now conducted every five years, the most recent being in 1996, referring to activity in 1995. The Census is more comprehensive (not being based on a sample from a larger population), and consequently includes richer details on such factors as employment and unemployment by industry and occupation. However, its use is limited because it is conducted only every five years, there is a considerable lag before the results are published, and its reliability on labour force questions may be questioned because, unlike the Labour Force Survey, it does not focus only on labour force activity.

Labour force participation rates have changed significantly over the twentieth century, especially for women. Figure 2.2 shows trends in participation based on census data. As we can see, male participation has declined from just over 90 percent of the eligible population to 76 percent by 1991. Women's rates were below 30 percent as recently as 1961, but they have increased by 10 percentage points per decade to 60 percent in 1991. Results from the 1996 census show that the male participation rate has continued to decline, from 76.4 percent in 1991 to 72.7 percent in 1996. The female rate, on the other hand, has plateaued at 58.6 percent, as against 59.9 percent in 1991. What factors might account for these changes? Was it primarily improvements in contraception or changing attitudes towards women's work that led to increased female participation? Did women's wages rise since 1960, inducing more women to enter the labour force? Did their husbands' wages fall, requiring more women to work to support their families? A well-developed economic model would aid in analyzing these explanations, and also provide alternative testable hypotheses.

Figure 2.2 **Labour Force Participation Rates by Sex, Canada, Census Years 1901–1991**

Labour force participation rates for men an women are plotted by census years, beginning in 1901. The general trends suggest a gradual reduction of labour force attachment for men, in contrast to a sharp increase for women, beginning in the 1950s.

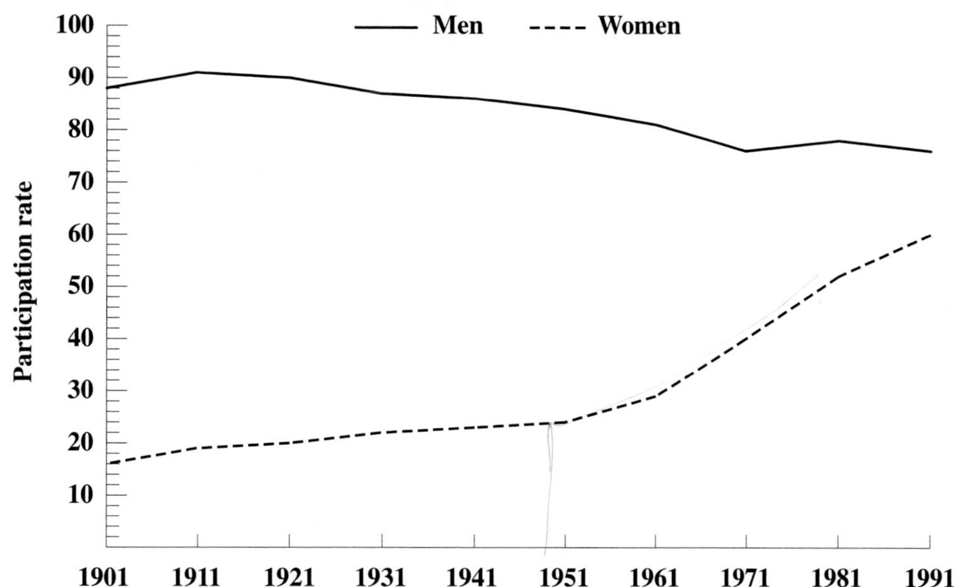

Sources: M. Gunderson, "Work patterns," in *Opportunity for Choice: A Goal for Women in Canada*, ed. G. Cook (Ottawa: Statistics Canada, 1976), p. 97 for 1901–1971, reproduced by permission of the Minister of Supply and Services Canada. Figures for 1981 were computed from the 1981 Census, Catalogue 92-915, Vol. 1, Table 1, p. 1-1. Figures for 1991 were computed from the 1991 Census, Catalogue 93-324, *The Nation: Labour Force Activity*, Table 1.

Figure 2.2 hides as much variation in participation as it shows, as participation also varies significantly by age and marital status. We focus on these demographic and life-cycle elements of labour supply in Chapter 4. However, Table 2.1 highlights another important aspect of cross-sectional variation in participation: variation across countries. The Canadian rates are at the higher end of the range of countries reported, just below that of the United States for both men and women. Generally speaking, the European countries outside Scandinavia have lower participation rates for both sexes (especially men) than North America and Australia, while the less developed countries have higher participation rates for men. Do these participation rates lie along an upward-sloping labour supply curve, with participation rates higher in those countries with higher wages? In fact, this table suggests that the effect of wages may not be uniform: the poorest countries have the highest male participation rates. This table also raises another question: Why do women's participation rates vary so much? Bangladesh and Pakistan have similar levels of development and economic conditions, but quite different patterns of female employment. Is this due to cultural differences, or are other economic variables more important? Clearly, there are several factors at play, and no single theory is likely to explain the intricacies of these numbers. What this table shows, however, is that the relationship between "wages" and participation may not be a simple one.

Hours

The **hours-of-work aspect** of labour supply has a variety of dimensions including hours per day, days per week, and weeks per year. Changes in any or all of these dimensions can alter the hours-of-work aspect of the labour supply decision. Phenomena such as the eight-hour day, the shorter work week, and increased vacation time are institutional embodiments of a reduction in hours of work. Similarly, moonlighting, overtime, flexible

Table 2.1 Labour Force Participation Rates by Sex, Various Countries, 1998

Country	Male	Female	Both Sexes
Denmark	83.1	73.2	78.2
Zimbabwe[a]	79.4	67.5	73.1
Bangladesh[b]	88.8	55.9	72.6
Barbados[a]	73.6	62.1	67.5
USA[c]	74.9	59.8	67.1
Canada[c]	72.4	58.1	65.1
Australia[c]	72.9	53.9	63.3
Hong Kong[c]	75.5	48.5	62.0
Korea[c]	75.2	47.0	60.7
Russia[d]	68.1	50.4	58.5
Argentina[e]	76.2	41.3	58.2
Germany	67.6	47.8	57.3
France	62.2	47.8	54.7
Pakistan[f]	83.1	15.0	50.1
Italy[a, c]	61.3	34.8	47.5

Notes: Participation rates for the population 15 years and older. Ranked in descending order, from highest to lowest labour force participation rate for both sexes. Some figures are preliminary estimates.
a. 1997.
b. 1995–96; excludes armed forces.
c. Excludes armed forces.
d. 1996.
e. 1995.
f. 1996–97; excludes certain regions.

Source: Based on *ILO Yearbook of Labour Statistics*, 1998, 1999.

working time, and compressed work weeks are institutional arrangements that alter the typical pattern of hours of work.

The policy importance of the hours-of-work decision is illustrated in a variety of ways. Changes in hours of work can affect not only the quantity but also the quality of our overall labour supply (and hence national output), as well as absenteeism, turnover, employment opportunities, and the demand for related activities, notably those involving leisure time and flexible working hours. Changes in hours of work, in turn, can be affected by changes in the age and sex structure of the labour force, the prominence of two-earner families, as well as government policies and laws and, of course, the wage rate.

In the short run, hours of work appear to be relatively fixed with little scope for individual variation. The eight-hour day, five-day work week, and fixed vacation period are fairly common for many wage and salary earners. However, the increased importance of flexible working hours is altering these arrangements. In addition, occupational choice provides an element of flexibility as people choose jobs partly on the basis of the hours of work required. Individuals may also be able to combine jobs, perhaps two part-time jobs or a full- and a part-time job, in order to work the desired number of hours for a given wage rate.

Figure 2.3 illustrates the apparent degree of flexibility that Canadian workers have in the number of hours they work per week. The work patterns of women are quite varied. Men are more likely to work the typical 40-hour week. However, even for working men, less than half work 40 to 49 hours per week. Almost a quarter work more than 50 hours, and an equal proportion work fewer than 40 hours. Women, on the other hand, are more likely to work part-time than 40 hours. Might these patterns be explained by labour supply theory? Perhaps relatively higher wages for men lead to higher average hours worked? Alternatively, women may "prefer" to work part-time. As with participation, a good theory of labour supply should be able to accommodate these features of labour market attachment.

Figure 2.3 Distribution of Hours Worked per Week by Sex, May 1996

This histogram shows the distribution of usual hours worked per week for men and women. Less than 50 percent of men or women work 40 to 49 hours per week. Women are more likely to work part-time (under 30 hours per week), while men are more likely to work overtime (more than 50 hours per week).

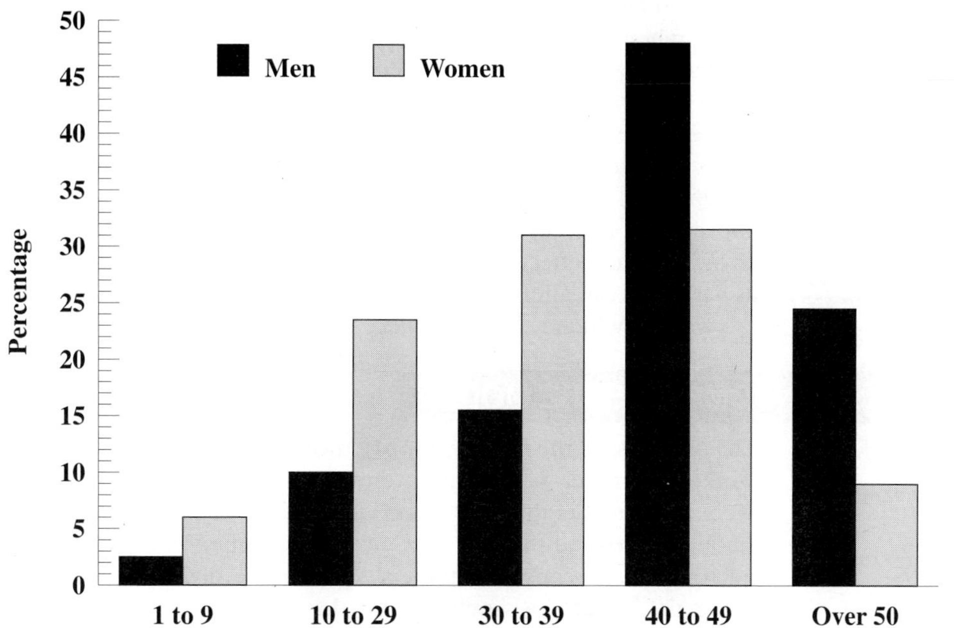

Source: Reproduced by authority of the Minister of Industry, 1996, Statistics Canada, *The Labour Force,* May 1996, Catalogue No. 71-001, Table 20.

Table 2.2 documents further evidence that "typical" hours worked per week are not immutable. This table traces the standard work week in Canadian manu-facturing and shows a pronounced and continuous decline over time in hours of work. Between 1901

Table 2.2 Standard Weekly Hours in Manufacturing, Canada, 1901–1981

Year	Standard Weekly Hours[a]	Hours Net of Vacations & Holidays[b]
1901	58.6	N/A
1911	56.5	N/A
1921	50.3	N/A
1931	49.6	N/A
1941	49.0	N/A
1951	42.6	40.7
1961	40.4	38.1
1971	39.8	36.7
1981	39.2	34.8

Notes:

a. Standard hours are usually determined by collective agreements or company policies, and they are the hours beyond which overtime rates are paid. The data apply to nonoffice workers.

b. Standard hours minus the average hours per week spent on holidays and vacations.

Sources: Figures for 1901–1971 for standard weekly hours are from S. Ostry and M. Zaidi, *Labour Economics in Canada*, 3rd ed. (Toronto: Macmillan, 1979), pp. 80-81. Figures for 1951–1971 for hours net of vacations and holidays are from Labour Canada (1974, p. 6). Both sources used as their primary data the Survey of Working Conditions conducted annually by the Canada Department of Labour and published as *Wage Rates, Salaries, and Hours of Labour*. This survey is also the source for the 1981 figures. Unfortunately, the Survey was discontinued in the early 1980s. Reproduced with the permission of Public Works and Government Services Canada, 2001.

and 1981 the standard work week declined from almost 60 hours to less than 40 hours. The decline slowed down in the depression years of the 1930s, and the war years of the 1940s, and it appears to be slower in the postwar period. However, as the last column illustrates, when vacations and holidays are considered the decline in average working hours is more noticeable. In essence, in recent years the work force has reduced its working hours more in the form of increased vacations and holidays rather than a reduction in hours worked per week. The decline in net weekly hours in the postwar period and in standard hours prior to World War II give a long-run trend reduction of about two hours per decade.

Since real wages have risen over the century, this long-run decline in hours worked appears inconsistent with an upward-sloping labour supply function. Instead, it suggests an independent effect of increased wages: as societies become wealthier, they need not toil as hard, and can afford to take more time off. Hopefully, the theoretical model will clarify the ways in which wages can affect labour supply.

BASIC INCOME-LEISURE MODEL

The objective of the **labour supply model** is to represent an individual's choice of hours worked given her market opportunities and the value she places on her nonmarket time. We wish to model this person as doing the best she can, subject to the constraints of the labour market and the limited availability of time. The model is an extension of standard microeconomic consumer theory. As such, we divide her decision-making problem into two parts: what she would like to do (preferences); and the choices available to her (constraints). The assumption of rationality brings the two parts together, yielding a unique characterization of her choice as a function of her preferences and market constraints.

Preferences

We assume that individual preferences can be distilled into **preferences** over two "goods": consumption of goods and services, and "leisure." **Leisure** embodies all non-labour market activities, including household work and education, as well as pure leisure activities. The phrase "leisure" is somewhat of a misnomer since it includes activities that are not leisure activities. The term is used here, however, because it is the phraseology used by Robbins (1930) in his original work on the subject and it has been retained in the literature as a summary term for "non-labour market activities."

We can graphically represent consumer preferences with **indifference curves**. Indifference curves and budget constraints are used extensively in developing the theory of labour supply. Those unfamiliar with indifference curve analysis should review the appendix to this chapter before proceeding further.

The individual is indifferent (has the same utility, or welfare) between various combinations of consumption and leisure as given by the indifference curve U_0 in Figure 2.4(a). The slope of the indifference curve exhibits a diminishing **marginal rate of substitution** (MRS) between consumption and leisure. For example, at point A, the individual has an abundance of consumption and hence is willing to give up considerable consumption to obtain more leisure; hence the steeply sloped indifference curve at point A. At point B, the individual has an abundance of leisure and hence is willing to give up considerable leisure (i.e., work more) to obtain more labour income and thus consumption; hence the relatively flat indifference curve at point B. At intermediate points such as C, consumption and leisure are more substitutable because the individual is not saturated with either.

While we cannot compare **utility** or welfare levels across individuals, we can compare marginal rates of substitution across consumers. This allows us to represent different preferences, at least partially, by indifference curves with different MRS at various combinations of consumption and leisure. For example, in Figure 2.4(b) we depict two different consumers. For consumer 1, bundle A lies on indifference curve U_0^1, while for person 2,

Figure 2.4 **Consumer Preferences: Consumption–Leisure Indifference Curves**

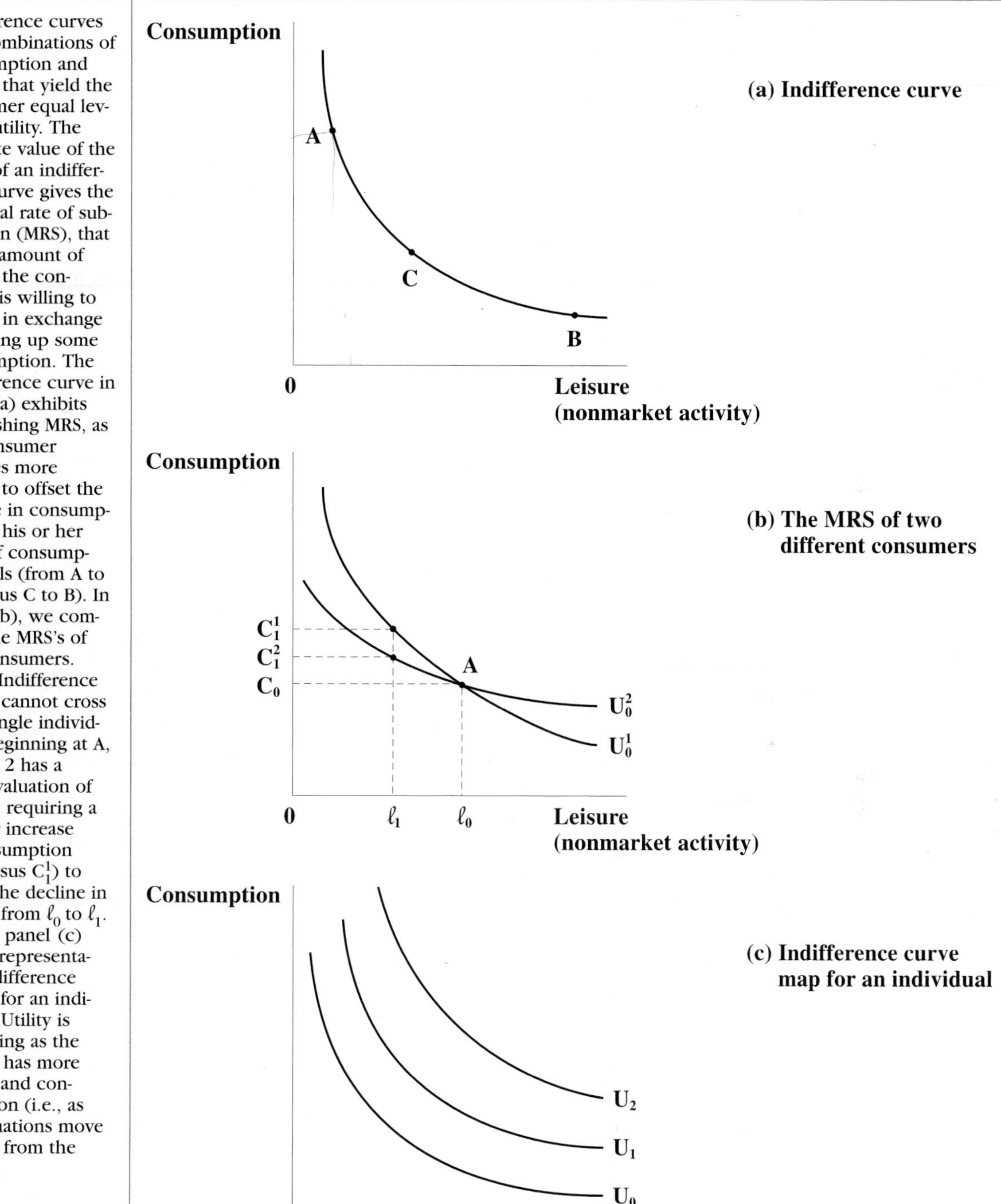

Indifference curves plot combinations of consumption and leisure that yield the consumer equal levels of utility. The absolute value of the slope of an indifference curve gives the marginal rate of substitution (MRS), that is, the amount of leisure the consumer is willing to accept in exchange for giving up some consumption. The indifference curve in panel (a) exhibits diminishing MRS, as the consumer requires more leisure to offset the decline in consumption as his or her level of consumption falls (from A to C, versus C to B). In panel (b), we compare the MRS's of two consumers. (*Note:* Indifference curves cannot cross for a single individual.) Beginning at A, person 2 has a lower valuation of leisure, requiring a smaller increase in consumption (C_1^2 versus C_1^1) to offset the decline in leisure from ℓ_0 to ℓ_1. Finally, panel (c) shows representative indifference curves for an individual. Utility is increasing as the person has more leisure and consumption (i.e., as combinations move further from the origin).

the same bundle lies on indifference curve U_0^2. Person 1 has a higher MRS at A than person 2. This implies that person 1 places a higher value on leisure (at A) than person 2. To induce person 1 to give up leisure from ℓ_0 to ℓ_1 requires compensating him with an increase in consumption from C_0 to C_1^1 to keep him equally happy, whereas it would only require an increase to C_1^2 to compensate person 2. In this way we can incorporate those factors that affect the value of **nonmarket time**, such as the value of work at home, into individual preferences and manifested in the MRS.

We assume that consumers have well-defined preferences over all the conceivable combinations of consumption and leisure. This implies that all combinations lie on some indifference curve. Consumer preferences can then be represented by an indifference curve map, as illustrated in Figure 2.4(c). Higher indifference curves such as U_1 and U_2 represent higher levels of utility since they involve more of both consumption and leisure.

Constraints

The individual will try to reach the highest indifference curve possible, constrained by economic opportunities provided by the labour market. Let the price of consumption be denoted by P, so that the value of consumption is PC. In this simple model we ignore saving, so that we can set PC equal to income. This allows a simple transformation of our model from **consumption-leisure** to **income-leisure**. We now want to summarize the income (or consumption) and leisure combinations from which the consumer can choose. In Figure 2.5 we show a few examples of **potential income constraints**. These are "potential" income constraints because they indicate varying amounts of income that can be obtained by giving up leisure and working. The actual amount of income earned will depend on the chosen amount of work in addition to the amount of income received from other sources, referred to as "nonlabour" income and shown as the amount Y_N. Alternative phrases for the potential income constraint include **budget**, income, and full-income **constraint**.

Consider first a very simple situation where the individual has only three discrete choices, as depicted in Figure 2.5(a). She can do no paid work, spending all of her available time, T, engaged in non-marketed activities, including leisure. In this case, the most that she can consume is given by her nonlabour income, Y_N (which might be 0). This combination is denoted by A. She could work part-time, increasing her income by I_P to $I_P + Y_N$, reducing her leisure by h_P to $\ell_P = T - h_P$ (point B). Alternatively, she could work full-time, earning $I_F + Y_N$ and consuming $\ell_F = T - h_F$ units of leisure (point C). In this case she need only compare the utility of three bundles, choosing the one on the highest indifference curve.

The more conventional potential income constraint is depicted in Figure 2.5(b). This linear budget constraint allows the individual to choose from a continuum of income-leisure bundles, ranging from 0 hours of work to T hours of work. The slope of the constraint depends on the person's wage rate, W. For each hour worked the individual gives up one hour of leisure, but earns W of additional income. The constant slope reflects an assumed constant wage rate for each hour worked. Persons with a higher market wage, such as W_1 where $W_1 > W_0$, will be able to earn more income by giving up leisure and working more; hence, the slope of W_1 is steeper than the slope of W_0.

Perhaps the simplest way to understand how wage changes (as well as other factors such as taxes and transfers, which will be examined later) affect the potential income constraint is to first mark the endpoint on the leisure axis. This endpoint is the maximum amount of leisure available (T); depending on the units in which leisure is measured, it could be 24 hours per day, 7 days per week, 52 weeks per year, or some combination such as 8736 hours per year. The potential income constraint is then derived by plotting the income people receive as they give up leisure and work additional hours; that is, they move leftward from the maximum leisure endpoint. The endpoint on the income axis would be the maximum income the individual could attain by working all of the available time—that

Figure 2.5 **Potential Income Constraints: Summarizing Individual Market Opportunities**

Budget sets, or potential income constraints, show the combinations of income (or consumption) and leisure available to an individual. In panel (a), the individual has only three choices: not working (point A), and obtaining T hours of leisure, no labour earnings, and nonlabour income of Y_N; working part-time for h_P, obtaining ℓ_P hours of leisure, and earnings I_P (plus non-labour income Y_N); or working full-time, obtaining ℓ_F leisure and I_F earnings (plus Y_N). Panel (b) shows the more conventional opportunity set, where the individual is free to choose any number of hours to work at the wage rate, W. Higher wages yield a steeper budget constraint, and higher potential income. Panel (c) illustrates the possibility that the "wage rate" is not constant per hour worked, as would be the case for a self-employed person.

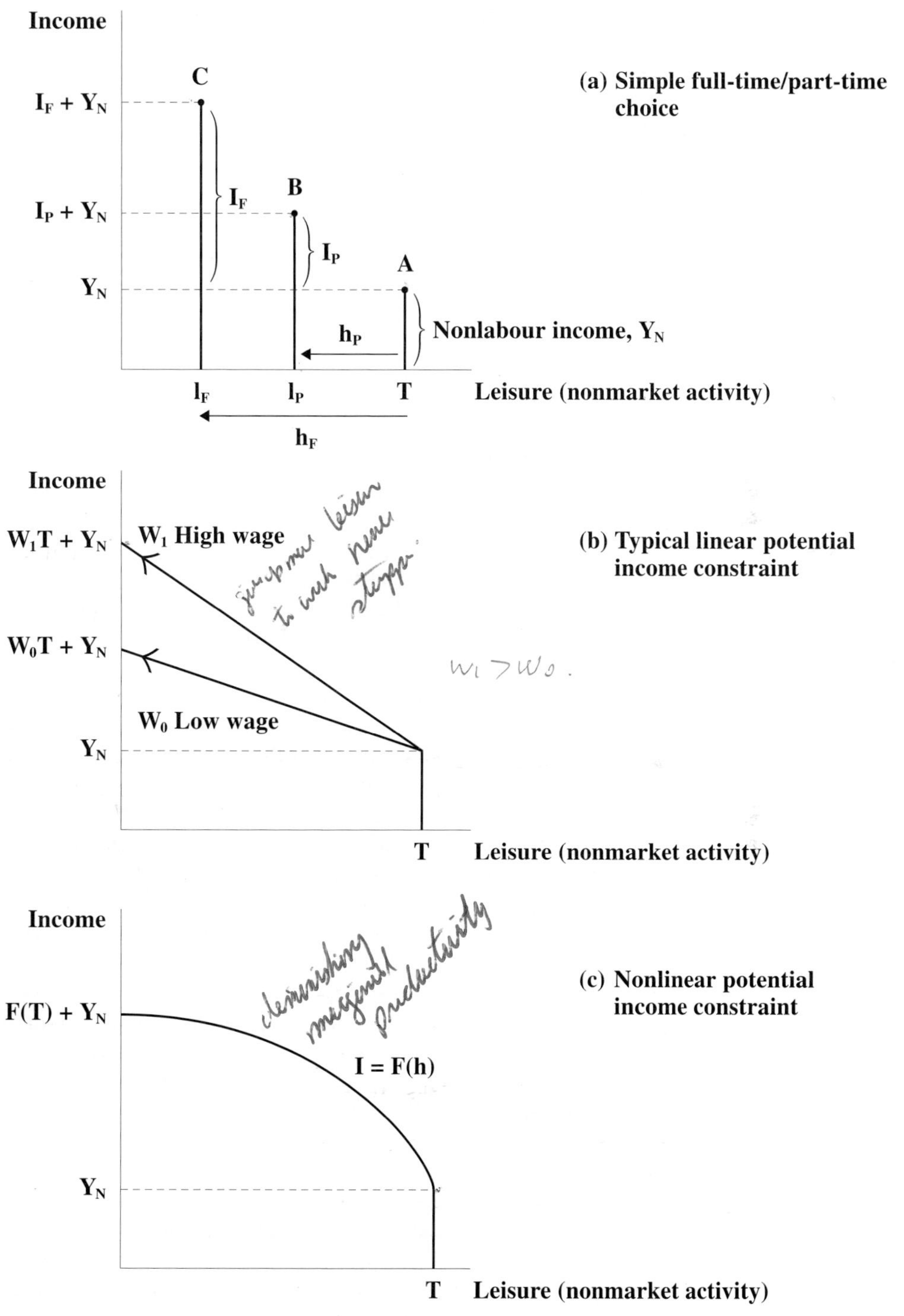

is, by having zero leisure. If individuals choose to work T, the most they can earn is WT + Y_N, commonly called **full income.**

The potential income constraint can be generalized even further, allowing the returns to work to vary with the amount worked. One example would be the case of a self-employed individual (like a doctor or lawyer), who sells output that she produces to the market. Assume that she produces income as a function of hours worked, I = F(h). If she has diminishing marginal productivity for each hour worked beyond a certain point, then her potential income can be depicted by Figure 2.5(c). Here, her income is also a function of the number of hours she works, but the wage rate is the value the market places on an hour's worth of the goods she produces. The treatment of consumer choice in this case would be no different than that in panel (b), though it is analytically more complicated.

The Consumer's Optimum

By putting the individual's potential income constraint and indifference curves together, we can obtain the **consumer's optimum** amount of income and leisure (and hence we can obtain the optimal amount of work, or labour supply). The **utility-maximizing** individual will reach the highest indifference curve possible, constrained by the labour market opportunities as given by the potential income constraint. Figure 2.6 illustrates two types of outcomes to this choice problem.

Panel (a) shows an individual who will not participate in the labour market, given the individual's preferences, nonlabour income Y_N, and market wage rate W_0. The highest possible utility is attained at the point on the budget constraint corresponding to maximum leisure (T), or zero hours of work. This outcome is referred to as a **corner solution** because the individual equilibrium occurs at one of the two extreme points on the potential income constraint.

Panel (b) shows an individual who will participate, given the individual's preferences and constraints. In this case the optimum occurs in between the two extreme points on the potential income constraint, and is referred to as an **interior solution**. With an interior solution, the equilibrium is characterized by a tangency between the budget constraint and the highest attainable indifference curve. At a corner solution, the tangency condition usually does not hold and the slopes of the highest attainable indifference curve and the budget constraint differ. For example, in the situation shown in Figure 2.6(a) the indifference curve is more steeply sloped than the budget constraint. In Figure 2.6(b), the tangency E_0 involves optimal leisure of ℓ_0, and labour supply or work $h_0 = T - \ell_0$, yielding income $W_0 h_0 + Y_N$. One can easily verify that E_0 is the utility-maximizing equilibrium by seeing what would happen if the individual were at any point other than E_0.

A useful way to characterize the consumer's optimum is to compare the individual's marginal rate of substitution (MRS) with the market wage rate. The former measures the individual's preferences or *willingness* to exchange nonmarket time for income, while the market wage measures the individual's *ability* to exchange leisure for income. Consider first the participation decision, and focus on the point of maximum leisure, point A in panels (a) and (b) of Figure 2.6. When the MRS at zero hours of work (slope of indifference curve at A) exceeds the wage rate (slope of budget constraint), as at point A in Figure 2.6(a), the individual's implicit value of nonmarket time is high relative to the explicit market value of that time and the individual will therefore not participate. When the MRS at zero hours of work is less than the wage rate, as at the point A in Figure 2.6(b), the individual's implicit value of leisure time is less than the explicit market value of that time and the individual will participate in the labour market. In this case, the individual increases hours of work until the MRS between income and leisure equals the wage rate, thereby exhausting all "gains from trade" associated with exchanging nonmarket for market time.

In analyzing labour force participation behaviour, economists often use the concept of a **reservation wage**, which is defined as the wage rate at which an individual would be indifferent between participating and not participating in the labour force; that is, the wage at which an individual would be indifferent between work in the labour market as opposed to engaging in nonlabour market activities such as household work, retirement, or leisure activities, all of which require time. If the market wage rate were equal to the

Figure 2.6 **The Consumer's Labour Supply Decision**

The utility-maximizing choice of hours worked is illustrated. In panel (a), the consumer's optimum occurs at A, with leisure equal to T and consumption Y_N yielding the highest utility. This person does not work. The reservation wage is given by the slope of RR', and is the MRS at this point. If the wage were higher than RR', the individual would participate. In panel (b), E_0 is an interior solution, where the indifference curve U_2 is tangent to the budget constraint. This consumer chooses ℓ_0 units of leisure, and consumption (income) of $Y_N + W_0h_0$.

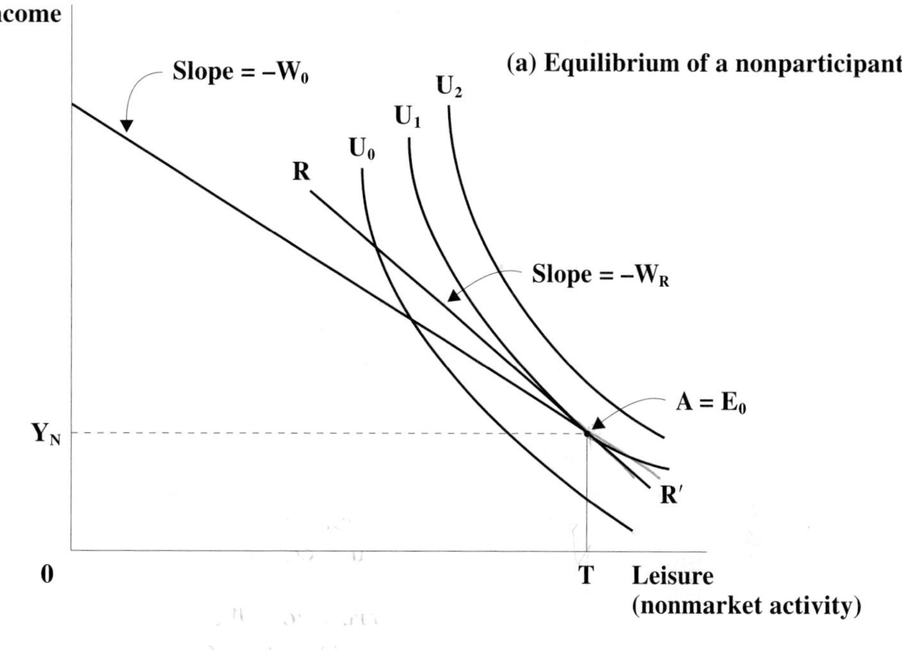

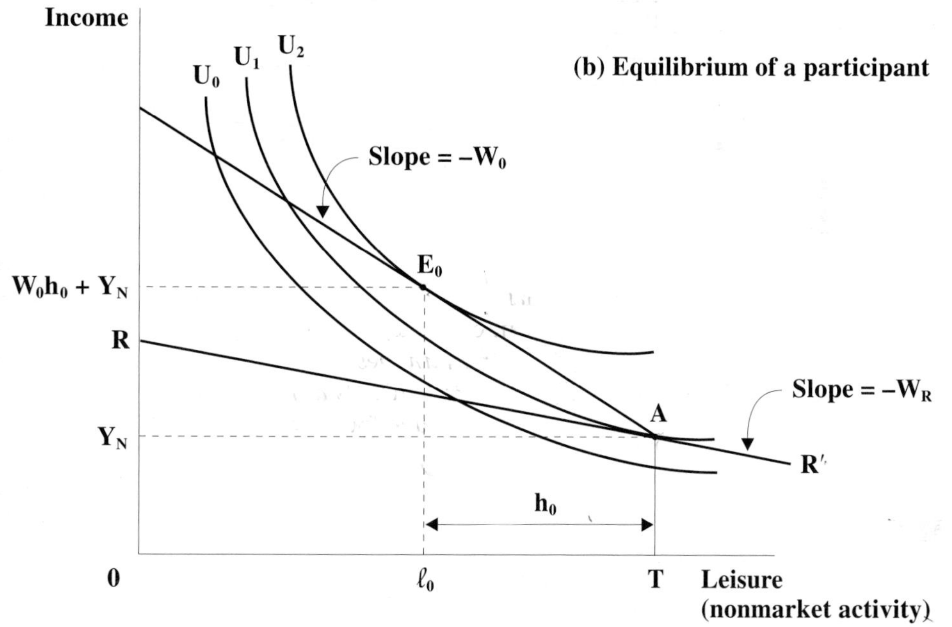

reservation wage W_R, the individual's potential income constraint would be given by the line RR' in Figures 2.6(a) and 2.6(b). That is, the reservation wage is the slope of the individual's indifference curve at zero hours of work. If the market wage is less than the reservation wage, as in Figure 2.6(a), the individual will not participate in the labour force; if the market wage exceeds the reservation wage, as in Figure 2.6(b), the individual will participate in the labour force since the return from engaging in labour market activity exceeds that individual's valuation of time in non-labour market activities.

COMPARATIVE STATICS

We now wish to analyze the effects of changes in key features of the economic environment on an individual's labour supply decision. We focus on the impact on labour supply of changing the wage, holding nonlabour income constant, and similarly, the effect of changing nonlabour income, holding the wage rate constant. The theoretical methodology is quite simple: given our assumption of optimizing behaviour, we need only compare the consumer equilibrium under alternative conditions, comparing the resulting labour supply choice. As we saw above, the decisions on participation and hours are integrated into the same theoretical model. However, given the continuous nature of the hours decision, versus the discrete nature of the participation decision, it is worth treating the two sides of the labour supply problem in sequence.

Hours of Work for Participants

The easiest change to examine in the budget constraint is the effect of changing nonlabour income on desired hours of work. An increase in nonlabour income results in a parallel shift outward of the budget constraint, as depicted in Figure 2.7. This shift outward means that the consumer can purchase more of both goods and leisure. Whether or not she decides to spend more on both depends on her preferences. Goods of which she consumes more in response to an increase in nonlabour income are called normal goods. If leisure is a **normal good**, she will consume more leisure (and work less), such as is depicted in Figure 2.7(a). In this figure, she increases her consumption of leisure (and thus decreases labour supply) from ℓ_0 to ℓ_1 as a result of the increase in nonlabour income. On the other hand, if leisure is an **inferior good**, she will actually consume less leisure, concentrating the additional income (and more) on the purchase of consumption. This possibility is shown in Figure 2.7(b). Economic theory makes no predictions as to whether leisure is normal or inferior. It is an entirely empirical question, depending on individual preferences. However, most available empirical evidence suggests that inferior goods are rare, and in particular, that leisure is not inferior. Through most of our discussion we will thus treat leisure as a normal good—though it must be emphasized this is a matter of pure, albeit reasonable, assumption.

Figure 2.7 **The Effect of an Increase in Nonlabour Income on Labour Supply**

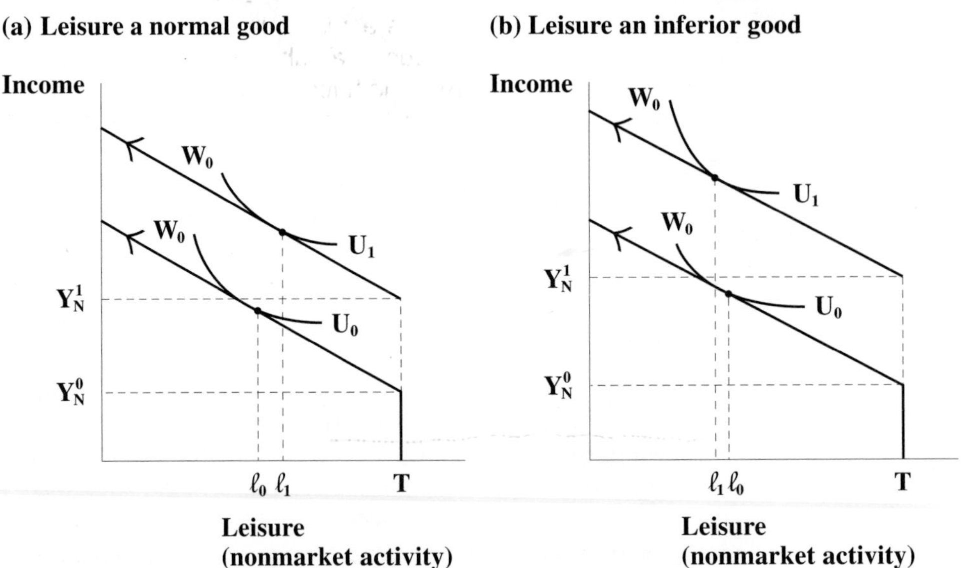

Panels (a) and (b) compare the impact of an increase in non-labour income (from Y_0 to Y_1) on hours worked. In (a), the consumer "buys" more leisure (works less), as leisure is a normal good. In (b), the consumer "buys" more consumption, but less leisure (and works more), as leisure is an inferior good.

What will happen to the equilibrium amount of effort if wages are increased? Among the classical economists, Adam Smith discussed the "short-run" response of labour to an increase in the wage rate:

www.adamsmith.org.uk

> *The wages of labour are the encouragement of industry, which, like every other human quality, improves in proportion to the encouragement it receives. ... Some workmen, indeed, when they can earn in four days what will maintain them through the week, will be idle the other three. This, however, is by no means the case with the greater part. Workmen, on the contrary, when they are liberally paid by the piece, are very apt to over-work themselves, and to ruin their health and constitution in a few years.*[1]

As this quote suggests, a change in the wage rate has two effects. On the one hand, the higher wage rate means that for each quantity of work, the worker now has more income from which to buy more of all goods, including leisure. This is termed the **income effect**, and in the case of a wage increase it leads to reduced work, assuming that leisure is a normal good. On the other hand, the individual may work more because the returns for work are greater; that is, the opportunity cost of leisure or the income forgone by not working is higher and hence the person may substitute away from leisure. This is termed the **substitution effect**, and in the case of a wage increase, it leads to increased work. In the case of a wage change, therefore, the income and substitution effects work in opposite directions; hence it is ultimately an empirical proposition as to whether a wage increase would increase or decrease the supply of work effort.

The income and substitution effects of a wage change are illustrated in Figure 2.8. After the wage increases from W_0 to W_1, the new equilibrium is E_1. This is the net or bottom-line

Exhibit 2.1 Importance of Paying Attention to Both Income and Substitution Effects

The capital of Brazil, Brasilia, was constructed as a planned new city. It was built in the undeveloped heartland of Brazil in the Amazon jungle area. This movement of the capital from the popular coastal area was done, in part, to encourage development in the otherwise isolated area.

Because of that isolation, it was difficult to recruit civil servants to work in the new capital, and wages were raised in order to encourage recruitment. This worked; in essence, it induced a substitution effect whereby the higher wages elicited a voluntary increase in "labour supply" to this region.

Unfortunately, the higher wages also induced an income effect that worked at cross purposes to the objective of encouraging the civil service to permanently move to the new capital and become part of a new, integrated community. That is, with their new, higher income, many of the civil servants could afford to maintain another residence in Rio de Janiero on the coast. They could also afford to fly regularly out of Brasilia, leaving it to spend their greater wealth.

Over time, a more permanent, committed community developed. Nevertheless, it highlights the importance of paying attention to both the income and substitution effects of wage changes. The emphasis on incentive effects in many similar policy discussions often ignores the possibility that an income effect can undo a perfectly reasonable substitution effect.

[1]Adam Smith, *The Wealth of Nations* (ed. E. Cannan), Book I (London: Methuen and Company, Ltd., 1930), p. 83.

Figure 2.8

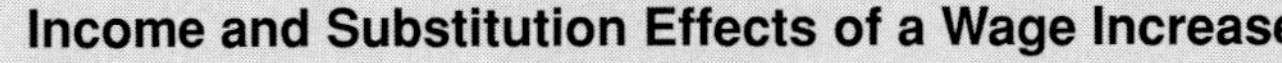

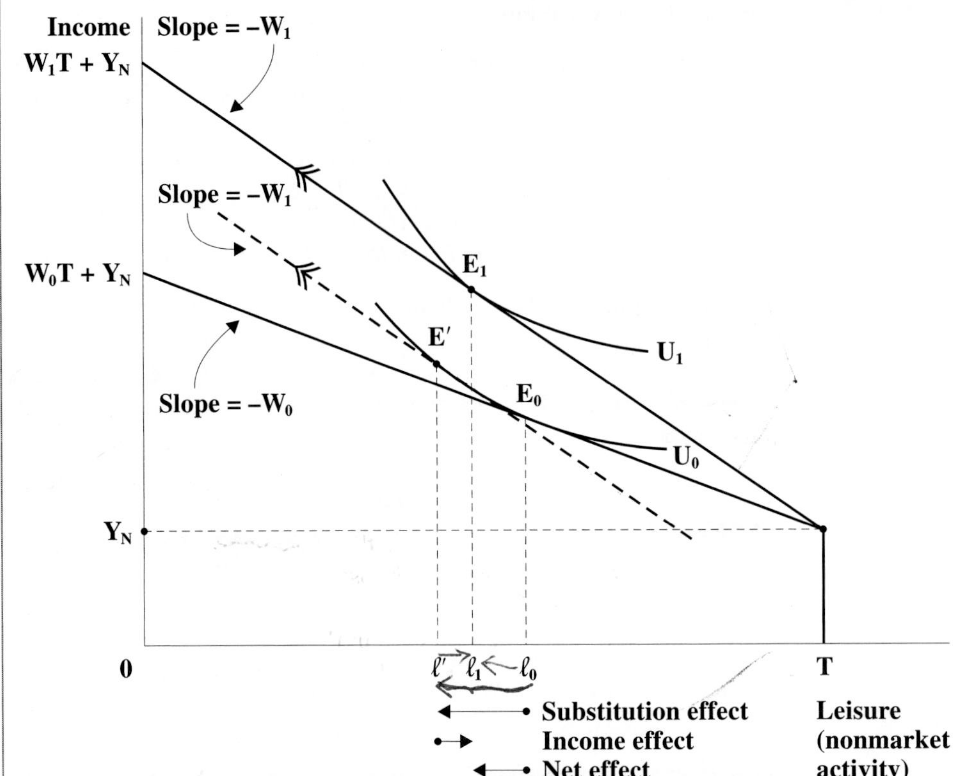

A wage increase from W_0 to W_1 has an ambiguous impact on hours worked. On the one hand, leisure is more expensive, and the substitution effect leads the consumer to switch away from leisure toward consumption (E_0 to E'). On the other, the increase in full income makes the consumer "richer." With leisure a normal good, the income effect leads the consumer to purchase more leisure (E' to E_1). The net result depends on the relative magnitudes of the income and substitution effects. In this example, the substitution effect dominates, and the consumer works more.

effect of the wage change. What we wish to know is: Does economic theory allow us to state whether this new equilibrium entails more or less labour supply? Like all price changes, this increase in the price of leisure can be broken down into an income effect and a substitution effect. This is critical in understanding how wage changes affect labour supply.

The substitution effect represents the effect of a pure increase in the relative price of leisure. That is, the substitution effect is that part of the consumer's adjustment that would occur if she were forced (or allowed) to remain on the original indifference curve U_0, but maintain a tangency with a budget line with slope given by the new wage, W_1. In consumer theory, the substitution effect is sometimes called the compensated price effect, since it refers to the effect of a price change whereby the individual is kept as well-off (i.e., compensated) as she was before the price change. Given our assumption of diminishing MRS, economic theory unambiguously predicts that leisure demand should fall with an increase in its price, holding utility constant. This is depicted in Figure 2.8 with the movement from E_0 to E', and the resulting change in leisure demand, ℓ_0 to ℓ'. In fact, this is the only empirically testable prediction of labour supply theory: the substitution effect for leisure demand is negative, or equivalently, the substitution effect for labour supply is positive. The theory predicts that compensated labour supply curves must slope upward.

The income effect is given by the movement from E' to E_1. The wage rate is held constant at the new wage rate, W_1, but potential income increases to reflect the higher wage rate. The implicit shift in the budget constraint is given by the parallel shift of the constraint from the dashed line to the actual final budget constraint.

If leisure is a normal good, the income effect offsets the substitution effect, since it leads to an increase in the demand for leisure. In Figure 2.8 the substitution effect dominates the income effect; hence in this illustration the wage increase resulted in a net increase in the amount of work. However, the income effect can dominate the substitution effect, in which case a wage increase will result in a decrease in the amount of work supplied.

The overall income effect can itself be broken down into two parts. First, the increase in the price of leisure *decreases* purchasing power, as it would for any other good. With a price increase, all else equal, our command over resources falls. This conventional income effect is offset, however, by the fact that full income also increases with the wage increase. Maximum potential earnings rise by $(W_1 - W_0)T$, the consumer's available time, as valued by the increase in the wage rate. This increase in full income leads to a net increase in income available for the purchase of goods and leisure.

Participation

The effects of changes in the wage rate and nonlabour income on labour force participation are illustrated in Figure 2.9. For a participant an increase in the wage rate has both income and substitution effects; because these are opposite in sign, hours of work may either increase or decrease. However, even if the income effect dominates the substitution effect so that hours of work decline, an increase in the wage rate can never cause a participant to withdraw from the labour force. This prediction of income-leisure choice theory is illustrated in Figure 2.9(a). As the wage increases, the household can achieve higher levels of utility and would never choose to not participate in the labour force which yields the utility level U_0.

For a nonparticipant, an increase in the wage rate may result in the individual entering the labour force or it may leave labour force participation unchanged, depending on whether the now higher market wage exceeds or is less than the individual's reservation wage. As illustrated in Figure 2.9(b), the increase in the wage from W_0 to W_1 leaves the individual's preferred outcome at E_0—that is, out of the labour force. However, the further wage increase to W_2 results in the individual entering the labour force (point E_2). This prediction can be explained in terms of income and substitution effects. An increase in the wage rate raises the opportunity cost of leisure time and tends to cause the individual to substitute market work for nonmarket activities. However, because the individual works zero hours initially, the income effect of an increase in the wage rate is zero. Thus for nonparticipants a wage increase has only a substitution effect which tends to increase hours of work.

These predictions can also be expressed in terms of the reservation wage. An increase in the market wage will not alter the labour-force status of participants because the market wage already exceeds their reservation wage. However, an increase in the market wage may cause some nonparticipants to enter the labour force if the increase in the wage is sufficiently large that the now-higher market wage exceeds the reservation wage.

Together these two predictions of the income-leisure choice model imply that an increase in the wage rate can never reduce and may increase labour force participation.

The effects of an increase in nonlabour income on labour force participation are opposite to those of an increase in the wage rate. If leisure is a normal good, an increase in nonlabour income will never cause a nonparticipant to enter the labour force and may cause some participants to withdraw from the labour force. These predictions follow from the fact that an increase in nonlabour income has a pure income effect. Thus if leisure is a normal good, the amount of time devoted to nonmarket activities must either rise (if the individual was a labour force participant in the initial equilibrium) or not decline (if the individual was already at the maximum leisure point initially).

These predictions of the income-leisure choice model can alternatively be stated using the concept of a reservation wage. If leisure is a normal good, an increase in nonlabour income will increase the individual's reservation wage. (Proof of this statement is left as an

Figure 2.9 The Effect of a Wage Increase on Participation

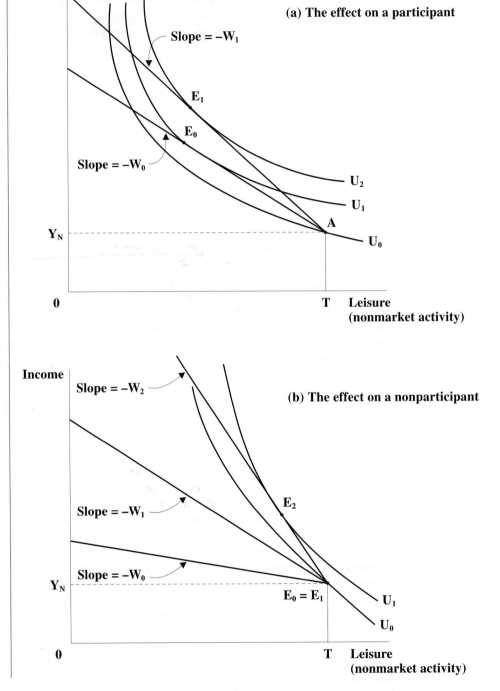

As a wage increase may lead to a reduction in hours worked, it will never induce a participant (in panel (a)) to stop working: the wage is still higher than the reservation wage. A non-participant, however, may be induced to work if the wage rises above the reservation wage. In panel (b), the consumer chooses to work at W_2, but not the lower wages W_0 and W_1.

exercise; see Review Question 5 at the end of this chapter.) Thus some participants will withdraw from the labour force, their reservation wage having risen above the market wage, while nonparticipants will remain out of the labour force, their reservation wage having been above the market wage even prior to the increase in nonlabour income.

The determinants of an individual's labour force participation decision can be conveniently categorized as to whether the variable affects the individual's reservation wage, market wage or both. Other things being equal, a variable that raises the individual's reservation wage would decrease the probability of participation in labour market activities. Such variables could be observable in the sense that data are often available on characteristics such as the presence of children, the availability of nonlabour market income, and the added importance of household work as on a farm. Or the variables could be unobservable in the sense that data are not directly available on the characteristic, such as a preference for household work.

While some such variables may affect primarily an individual's reservation wage and hence have an unambiguous effect on their labour force participation decision, others may affect both their market wage and their reservation wage and hence have an indeterminate effect on their labour force participation decision. An increase in a person's age, for example, may be associated with a higher market wage that makes participation in labour market activities more likely. However, it may also raise their reservation wage if the disutility associated with work increases relative to leisure time, and this may induce them to retire from the labour force.

DERIVING THE INDIVIDUAL SUPPLY CURVE OF LABOUR

We have now met the principal theoretical objectives of this chapter: establishing the avenues through which wage changes affect labour supply, and investigating the slope of the **labour supply schedule**. As the early writings of Robbins (1930) indicate, the income-leisure choice framework can be used to derive the individual's labour supply schedule, which indicates the amount of labour that will be offered at various wage rates. By varying the wage rate, we can obtain a schedule of corresponding desired amounts of work, and hence trace out the individual's labour supply curve.

Derivation of an individual's labour supply schedule is further illustrated by the specific example of Figure 2.10 where leisure and work are measured in units of hours per day and wages in units of wages per hour. Income is the hourly wage rate multiplied by the hours of work. Figure 2.10(a) illustrates the desired hours of work for a wage rate of $6 per hour. In this case, the market wage is below the individual's reservation wage of $7, so the individual does not participate and desired hours of work is zero. The corresponding income is just the value of nonlabour income, $10 per day. This gives us one point on the individual's labour supply schedule of Figure 2.10(c): at $6/h the labour supply would be zero hours. Indeed, this would be the labour supply until the market wage reaches $7/h. In Figure 2.10(b) we see how hours evolve as wages are raised above the reservation wage. At $8/h, the equilibrium hours of work is 8 hours per day, and the corresponding daily income is $64 of earnings, plus nonlabour income, for a total of $74. This gives us the second point on the labour supply schedule: at $8/h labour supply would be 8 hours. As the wage rises to $10/h, hours increase to 12 hours per day. In this particular case, the substitution effect of the wage increase outweighs the income effect so that hours of work increase. This yields a third point on the supply schedule. Finally, in Figure 2.10(b), wages are raised to $14/h and the individual is observed to decrease work effort to 10 hours per day. This yields a fourth point on the supply curve in Figure 2.10(c). At the higher wage rate, the income effect of the wage increase begins to dominate the substitution effect and the labour supply schedule becomes backward-bending. In fact, this may be a reasonable approximation for many individuals: at low wage rates they have an abundance of unmet needs, so that higher wages will induce them to work more in order to fulfill these needs; at higher wages many of their needs are fulfilled, so that additional wage increases will be used to purchase leisure.

Figure 2.10 **Deriving the Individual Supply Curve of Labour**

The individual labour supply curve, relating desired hours of work to the wage rate, can be derived by tracing out the labour supply choices (tangencies) in response to different wages, reflected in the slope of the budget constraint. Labour supply is zero until the wage equals the reservation wage. For higher wages, the slope of the labour supply function depends on the relative magnitudes of the income and substitution effects.

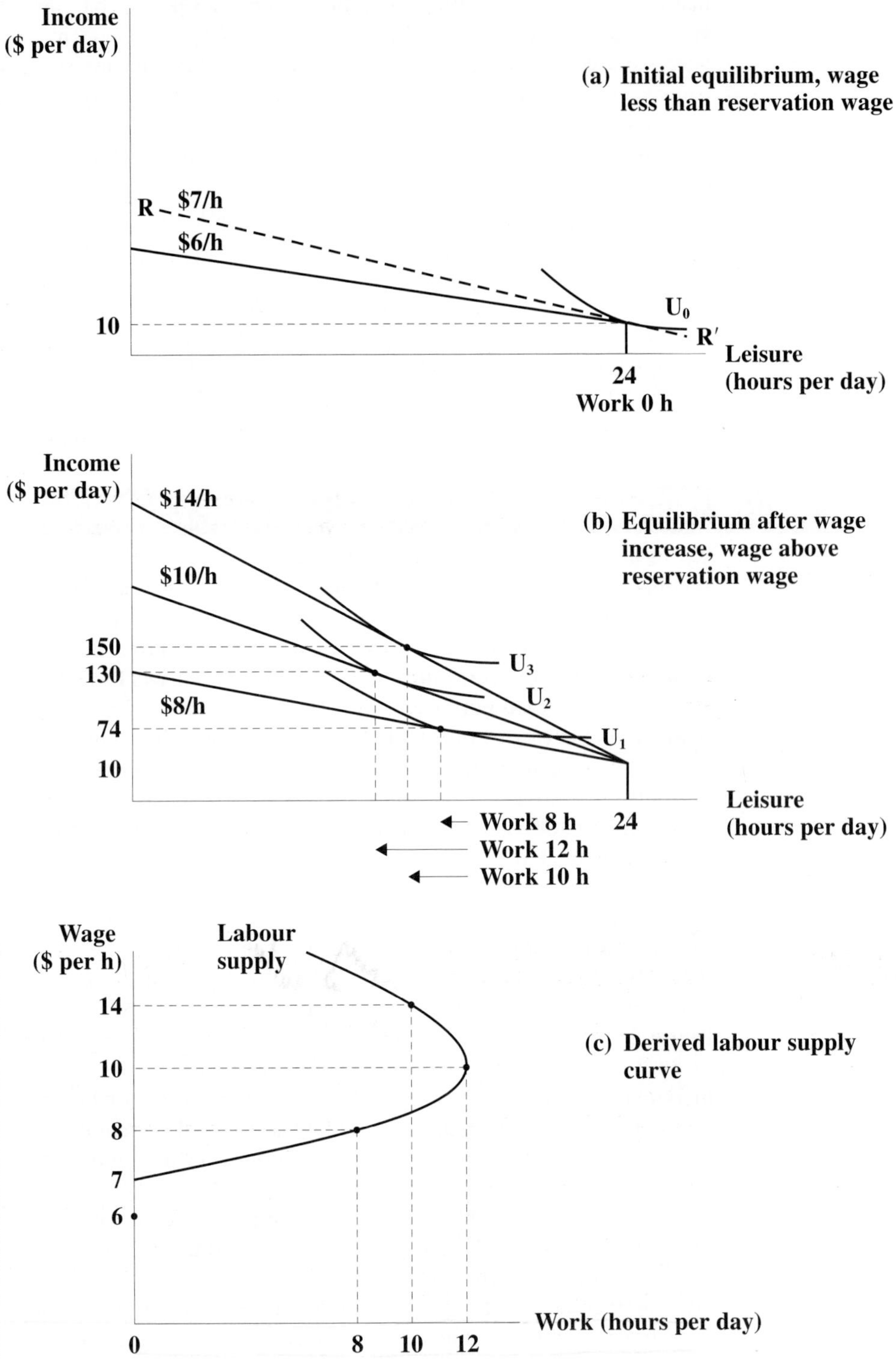

EMPIRICAL EVIDENCE

One of the most active areas of empirical research in labour economics has been the estimation and testing of models of labour supply. The research has focused on two sets of questions: First, does labour supply behaviour conform with the predictions of economic theory, and second, how responsive is labour supply to changes in the wage?

Participation, Married Women

The basic theory of labour force participation is often tested with data on married women since they may have more flexibility to respond to the determinants of labour force participation. In addition, their participation has increased dramatically over the past few decades, and this has policy implications for such things as sex discrimination, family formation, and the demand for child-care facilities.

Empirical evidence in both Canada and the United States tends to confirm the predictions based on the economic theory of participation.[2] For Canada, some illustrative figures are given in Table 2.3. We expect those variables that increase the market wage will be positively associated with participation, while those factors that increase the reservation wage will be negatively related to participation. In the table we show three columns. The first gives the average participation rate by the various categories. The second shows the difference in participation between a given category and the base category. The final column presents estimates of the same differentials as in the second column, but it shows regression-adjusted estimates that control for factors such as age, education, number of children, and husband's income.

Participation for married women appears to peak in the 35–44 age group, with the steepest decline for those over 55 years of age. Whether this can be interpreted as a pure aging or retirement effect will be addressed in more detail in Chapter 4. The effect of children on women's participation is puzzling at first blush: women with no children work less than those with more children. However, this raw correlation confounds the fertility effect with other factors, notably age (married 15-to-24-year-olds may still be in school). In the third column (adjusted differences), we see in fact that labour force participation is strictly declining with the number of children at home.

Exhibit 2.2

The Economics of Sleep

Sleep occupies more of our time than any other activity, with approximately one-third of our adult life devoted to sleeping. Casual observation suggests that many of our students undertake that same time allocation during class!

Presumably, we derive satisfaction from sleeping and it is an important component of leisure, and an input into our production of other activities. Hence, it should be amenable to economic analysis.

Biddle and Hamermesh (1990), in fact, provide empirical evidence from a variety of sources indicating that the demand for sleep is negatively related to the price or cost of sleeping. That is, other things equal, people of higher potential earnings power sleep less because it costs them more (in terms of forgone income) to sleep longer.

[2]Nakamura and Nakamura (1985) and Killingsworth and Heckman (1986) provide a survey of these and related studies.

Table 2.3 Labour Force Participation Rates of Married Women, Canada, 1996

	Participation Rate	Difference from Base Group[a]	Adjusted Difference from Base Group[b]
All Women, Total	**65.0**		
Age			
15–24	72.2	N/A	N/A
25–34	77.0	4.7	5.5
35–44	79.1	6.9	10.2
45–54	73.9	1.7	2.0
55–64	38.1	–34.1	–31.3
65–74	7.5	–64.7	–60.1
Children Under 17 Years Old at Home			
No children	56.5	N/A	N/A
One child	76.8	20.2	–4.6
Two children	75.7	19.2	–8.4
Three children	69.0	12.5	–14.9
Four or more children	57.9	1.4	–24.4
Education			
Less than Grade 9	29.4	N/A	N/A
Grade 9–13 without certificate or diploma	51.5	22.1	8.9
Grade 9–13 with certificate or diploma	66.2	36.8	17.6
Trades (with or without certificate)	74.5	45.1	23.9
Some university (without certificate or diploma)	73.5	44.1	22.2
University with certificate or diploma	77.2	47.8	27.3
University degree	83.4	54.0	30.5
Husband's Income			
Under $10,000	57.8	N/A	N/A
$10,000–$19,999	52.3	–5.4	3.5
$20,000–$29,999	62.9	5.1	5.3
$30,000–$39,999	69.6	11.8	6.0
$40,000–$49,999	71..5	13.8	5.1
$50,000–$59,999	72.0	14.2	3.4
$60,000–$99,999	71.5	13.7	2.0
Over $100,000	66.6	8.9	–1.5

Notes: Sample based on all married women between the ages of 15 and 75 with husband present.
a. Difference in participation rate from the base group (the lowest category).
b. Difference in participation rates from the base group (the lowest category), controlling for the other factors (age, education, fertility, or husband's income), estimated by ordinary least squares.

Source: Statistics Canada, Individual Use Microdata File: 1996 Census of Population.

Education has a pronounced effect on participation. In principle, higher education should be associated with higher market wages, and an increased likelihood of working. Alternatively, education may be correlated with preferences for working, or reduce desired fertility, so that the reservation wages of more educated women may also be lower. The education coefficients alone are not enough to disentangle these competing explanations, though both are consistent with the model of participation. Finally, the results for husband's income illustrate some of the difficulties in identifying "pure" income effects. We would expect that the reservation wages of women with high-income husbands would be higher, at least if the wife's non-market time is a normal good. However, the results in column 3 show that this is the case only for women with very high incomes (over $100,000), at least using women with very-low-income husbands as the omitted category. Using women with husbands earning $30,000–$39,000 as the base category, we would see participation declining with husband's income, at least for incomes $40,000 and higher. Part of the problem in isolating a possibly larger income effect is a consequence of the fact that more-educated, higher-income working women tend to marry more-educated, higher-income husbands. This "assortative mating" confounds the income effect.

Evidence on the Elasticity of Labour Supply

A large number of econometric studies have estimated the "shape" of the labour supply schedule—that is, the responsiveness of labour supply to changes in the wage rate. As discussed previously, there are a number of components to that responsiveness. The total or gross or **uncompensated elasticity** of labour supply is the percentage change in labour supply that results from a 1 percent increase in the wage rate. Its sign is theoretically indeterminate because it reflects both the expected negative income effect of the wage change and the expected positive substitution effect. The **income elasticity** of labour supply is the percentage change in wages that results from a 1 percent increase in non-labour income. It is expected to be negative, reflecting the leisure-inducing effect of the wage increase. The **compensated elasticity** of labour supply is the percentage increase in labour supply that results from a 1 percent increase in the wage rate, after compensating the individual for the increase in income associated with the wage increase (i.e., after subtracting the income effect of the wage increase). The compensated wage elasticity of labour supply is expected to be positive since it reflects the pure substitution effect (movement along an indifference curve) as the wage rate increases the price of "leisure," inducing a substitution away from more expensive leisure and into labour market activities. For this reason, the income-compensated wage elasticity is also often called the pure substitution elasticity.

Knowledge of the separate components of the labour supply elasticity may be important for policy purposes. For example, the uncompensated wage elasticity would be used to predict the labour supply response to a wage subsidy (since it has both income and substitution effects), but the compensated wage elasticity would be used if it was assumed that the higher income would be taxed back. The income elasticity would be relevant to predicting the labour supply response to a lump-sum government transfer.

As indicated, a large number of econometric studies have estimated these various elasticities that constitute the labour supply response to a wage change. The results differ substantially depending upon such factors as the econometric technique and data. Especially for women, the results can differ depending upon whether the labour supply response refers to the participation decision, the hours-of-work decision conditional upon participation, or a combination of both. For women, this can be important because there tends to be more flexibility in their participation decision and hence it is important to take account of potential econometric problems. In particular, the subsample of labour force participants may be a select sample in terms of unobservable characteristics (like attitudes toward career or work) that can influence wages. These characteristics may, in turn, confound the estimated wage elasticity if conventional regression analysis is used. As well, their labour supply decision may be more affected by discontinuities associated, for example, with fixed costs of entering the labour market, such as daycare costs. The differences in female labour supply responses often reflect differences in the extent to which these factors are taken into account in the estimation procedure.

In spite of the substantial variation that exists in the results of the different studies, a number of generalizations can be made. Table 2.4 provides an illustrative representation of those results based on a number of reviews that have been done in the literature (as cited in the source to the table). For example, Hansson and Stuart (1985) review approximately 50 labour supply studies for men and women. They calculate total elasticities for both sexes by weighing the male and female elasticities by their respective share of earnings. They calculate that for both sexes the overall elasticities were: uncompensated 0.10; compensated 0.25; and income elasticity -0.15. However, on the basis of the 13 newer studies, which used more sophisticated econometric techniques to account for many of the previously discussed issues, the elasticities were: uncompensated 0.44; compensated 0.52; and income elasticity -0.08. (These numbers illustrate how the uncompensated or gross elasticity is simply the sum of the compensated and income elasticities.) The numbers used in the first row of Table 2.4 for both sexes are simply based on a "rounded approximation" of those elasticities from the 50 studies and the 13 newer ones. For that reason they are meant to be illustrative and representative rather than strict averages of the results of the different studies. The separate figures for males and females are also meant to be only illustrative.

Exhibit 2.3

Take Me Out to the Ball Game ...

What lessons can economists draw by studying the labour supply of baseball stadium vendors? There is a long history in labour economics of trying to estimate "the" elasticity of labour supply, since it is such an important parameter for public policy. However, the labour supply elasticity almost certainly varies across groups in the population, and also over time. Increasingly, researchers focus their efforts on estimating the impact of specific changes in labour market opportunities on employment decisions, instead of estimating the more general "labour supply elasticity." For example, they may focus on identifying the impact of a tax change or income support scheme on the hours or participation decision. The economic theory of income and substitution effects is still a useful tool in interpreting the results from such exercises.*

But there still remains an important role for trying to estimate "the" elasticity of labour supply, especially in evaluating the one truly testable implication of labour supply theory: that the substitution effect is positive. This is not an easy task for a number of reasons, but especially because of the difficulty of isolating the substitution effect from the income effect. Consider the apparently simple exercise of regressing the number of hours worked on an individual's wage and non-labour income. Ideally, we would like to use the estimated wage coefficient in order to construct the substitution elasticity, under the assumption that we can estimate the income effect from the non-labour income elasticity. A number of statistical problems make this difficult.

First, it is difficult to measure non-labour income. Almost all forms of income are somehow related to labour earnings: government transfer income depends on having low labour earnings (because of either low wages or low hours), and investment income is generally higher for those with higher wages and hours. This could lead to either an over- or an understatement of the true income effect. Second, individual preferences may be correlated with wages. For example, ambitious people may have both higher wages and higher hours. We would thus exaggerate the

The following generalizations are illustrated in Table 2.4:

1. The overall labour supply schedule for both sexes is likely to be slightly upward-sloping; that is, a wage increase does lead to a slight increase in the amount of labour supplied to the labour market. The representative elasticity of 0.25 indicates that a 1 percent increase in real wages would lead to a one-quarter of 1 percent increase in labour supply. This small uncompensated total elasticity is a result of the positive pure compensated (substitution) elasticity slightly outweighing the negative income elasticity.
2. For males, however, the labour supply schedule is likely to be slightly backward-bending; that is, real wage increases are associated with a reduction in the amount of labour supplied to the labour market. This overall effect is very small and could well be zero (i.e., vertical or perfectly inelastic labour supply) or even slightly forward-sloping. The small overall negative elasticity is a result of a weak positive substitution elasticity being outweighed by a weak but slightly larger negative income elasticity.
3. For women, the labour supply schedule is more strongly forward-sloping; that is, an increase in real wages is associated with a more substantial increase in the amount of labour supplied to the labour market. This is the result of a strong positive substitution elasticity outweighing the weak negative income elasticity.

Exhibit 2.3

Take Me Out to the Ball Game ... *(continued)*

impact of wages on their labour supply decision. Third, an increase in someone's wage may have a long-run impact on his lifetime earnings potential, leading to a potentially large income effect. Thus, without a clean estimate of either the wage or the income elasticities, it is difficult to test whether the wage response reflects a positive substitution effect. An ideal "experimental design" would involve comparing an individual's labour supply decisions on a day-by-day basis, when the individual has complete knowledge of his or her "long-run" income, and the patterns of wage rates across different days. In this way, a researcher could attribute higher effort on high-wage days to a pure (positive) substitution effect.

That's where the baseball vendors come in. In a clever study that follows this ideal procedure, Gerald Oettinger (1999) examines the labour supply of vendors in a professional baseball stadium (in Arlington, Texas). He finds that vendors are more likely to work on days where the expected returns (sales, and thus wages) are higher. Apparently, vendors respond to the size of the anticipated crowd, on the basis of the opposing teams, the Texas Rangers' performance, the weather, and promotional events (such as "Free Hat Day"). Even taking into account the fact that the labour supply response also leads more vendors to show up (and thus soak up some of the additional sales), Oettinger estimates that a 1.00 percent increase in the expected daily wage leads to a 0.60 percent increase in the number of vendors working. Because he can identify each vendor's daily choices, he can hold constant individual preferences, non-labour income, and the value of the time-endowment over the entire baseball season, and this response can reliably be interpreted as a pure substitution effect. While the estimated labour supply elasticities may not generalize to other types of workers, Oettinger's paper shows how the careful study of even a very specific group of workers can, more generally, shed light on the possible validity of labour supply theory.

*See Blundell and MaCurdy (1999).

Table 2.4 Compensated and Income Elasticity of Labour Supply

Sex	Uncompensated (Gross, Total) Wage Elasticity of Supply	Compensated (Substitution) Wage Elasticity of Supply	Income Elasticity of Supply
Both sexes	0.25	0.40	–0.15
Men	–0.10	0.10	–0.20
Women	0.80	0.90	–0.10

Sources: As discussed in the text, these are "representative illustrative" numbers based on different reviews of over 50 econometric studies of labour supply. These reviews include Hansson and Stuart (1985), Killingsworth (1983), Killingsworth and Heckman (1986), and Pencavel (1986).

4. The strong positive total elasticity for females is sufficiently strong to outweigh the weak negative total elasticity for males, so that the aggregate supply schedule for both sexes is likely to be forward-sloping, as discussed.
5. The substantial variation in the magnitudes of these effects across studies suggests that these representative numbers be used with caution. As well, there is some evidence[3] that the female labour supply response is closer to the male response than portrayed in many studies—a result that may not be surprising if female labour market behaviour is becoming more like male behaviour over time.

Section Two: Extensions and Applications

One of the most important assumptions of the labour supply model is that individuals can freely choose any package of consumption and leisure along the linear potential income constraint. Unfortunately, this assumption may not be valid for those individuals facing constraints in the labour market. There may be no work available at the going wage rate, resulting in unemployment for the individual. Alternatively, the individual may have only limited choice over the number of hours worked. As we suggested previously, however, the model is quite flexible, and some of these issues can be incorporated into the existing framework.

ADDED AND DISCOURAGED WORKER EFFECTS

Recall that the definition of the labour force includes both the employed (those who wish to work, and have jobs) and the unemployed (those who wish to work, but do not have jobs). One interesting question pertains to how labour force participation responds to changes in the unemployment rate. Specifically, in periods of high unemployment people may become discouraged from looking for work and drop out of the labour force, returning to household activities or to school or perhaps even entering early retirement. This is termed the **discouraged worker** effect. On the other hand, in periods of high unemployment, some may enter the labour force to supplement family income that may have deteriorated with the unemployment of other family members. This is termed the **added worker** effect.

Changes in unemployment are a proxy for transitory changes in expected wages and other income, and thus the discouraged and added worker effects can be interpreted as short-run substitution and income effects respectively. That is, if unemployment is high,

[3]Nakamura, Nakamura, and Cullen (1979) and Robinson and Tomes (1985) for Canadian women. Nakamura and Nakamura (1981) for both Canadian and U.S. women.

then opportunities in the labour market are lowered temporarily: the price of leisure (opportunity cost of forgone income from not working) is reduced temporarily. The wage might fall below an individual's reservation wage, leading him to drop out of the labour force. On the other hand, the high unemployment means that it is more likely that family income is lowered temporarily, lowering other household members' reservation wages and inducing them to participate in labour market activities so as to restore that income.

Since the added and discouraged worker effects operate in opposite directions, one lowering the reservation wage and the other lowering the returns to working, it is necessary to appeal to the empirical evidence to see which dominates. Again, most of the empirical tests have been based on data of married women since they are more likely to respond to changes in unemployment. In the United States, the empirical evidence clearly indicates the dominance of the discouraged worker effect for most married women. That is, in periods of high unemployment, women become discouraged from entering the labour force to look for work, and this dominates any tendency to add themselves to the labour force to maintain their family income. In Canada, however, the empirical evidence is mixed.

HIDDEN UNEMPLOYMENT

The discouraged worker effect also gives rise to the problem of **hidden unemployment**—a topic that we will return to in a later chapter on unemployment. During a recession when the unemployment rate is high, there may also be a large number of discouraged workers who do not look for work because they believe that no work is available. They are considered to be outside the labour force because they are not working or actively looking for work. However, because they would look for work were it not for the high unemployment rate, they are often considered as the hidden unemployed—people whom the unemployment figures tend to miss because they are considered outside the labour force rather than unemployed persons in it.

In this sense, in times of high unemployment our unemployment figures may understate the true unemployment by missing those discouraged workers who constitute the hidden unemployed. The Survey of Job Opportunities (SJO) is an annual supplement to the labour force survey designed to measure the importance of this group. It provides information on the desire for work among nonsearchers, and the reasons for nonsearching for those who desire, but are not looking for work.

www.statcan.ca/english/Dli/ftp.htm

The notion of the discouraged worker is especially important as groups like married women and teenagers become a larger portion of our potential labour force. Such persons often have a loose attachment to the labour force, moving in and out in response to changing economic conditions. They often, but not always, have other family income upon which to rely. For these reasons they are often labelled "secondary" or "marginal workers"—unfortunate misnomers if they are used to belittle their employment problems or the contribution to the family income of such workers. This is especially the case if they are contrasted with "primary workers" or "breadwinners," terms often used to describe the employment position of males.

However, because of their flexibility with respect to labour market activities, married women and teenagers do constitute a large portion of discouraged workers who would enter the labour force and look for work if employment prospects increased. Hence, there is the recent emphasis in labour force surveys (and supplements like the SJO) to find out exactly what these people are doing, and why they are not looking for work.

Clearly the decision to include such persons either in the category of unemployed or as outside of the labour force is a difficult one. Recent work by Jones and Riddell (1999) suggests that while the marginally attached are closer in behaviour to the unemployed than the remainder of the nonemployed, it is not strictly appropriate to pool them with either group.

Exhibit 2.4

Are Women Working to Pay the Mortgage?

In the labour supply model, individuals are assumed free to choose whether to work. As we saw with the added worker effect, someone's labour supply may increase in response to unexpected declines in family income caused by the unemployment of a breadwinner. In such circumstances, increased female participation need not be associated with improvements in family well-being.

Mortgage pre-commitments and borrowing constraints provide another reason why a woman's labour market participation may reflect household constraints, as much as enhanced opportunities for women. Nicole Fortin (1995) examines the labour force attachment of a sample of Canadian women according to the mortgage-holding status of the household. She finds that as a family's mortgage commitments approach the fraction of family income permitted by the bank, the wife's participation rate increases sharply. One (extremely simplified) way to model this is to treat the mortgage payment as a pre-determined financial commitment, outside the household's current choice set. In that case, larger mortgage payments have a similar effect on participation as a reduction in family income. More generally, higher mortgage commitments, especially those close to the maximum that banks will permit, reduce the wife's reservation wage. Of course, this ignores the fact that house purchases are a choice that households make, distinguishing the interpretation from the added worker effect. The joint aspect of the housing and labour supply decision is treated more thoroughly in Fortin's paper. Furthermore, interest rate or housing price swings may lead to genuine changes in the budget constraint that look like typical income effects.

Fortin estimates that the effect of mortgage commitments can be quite large. For example, the effect on a woman's participation of moving into a category where the ratio of mortgage payments to husband's income is close to the maximum of what banks will tolerate has as large an effect as the presence of two preschool children (though in the opposite direction).

MOONLIGHTING, OVERTIME, AND FLEXIBLE WORKING HOURS

Any analysis of the hours-of-work decision must confront the following basic question: Why is it that some people moonlight at a second job at a wage less than their market wage on their first job, while others require an overtime premium to work more? This apparent anomaly occurs because people who moonlight are underemployed at the going wage on their main job while people who require an overtime premium are already overemployed at the going wage on their main job. Underemployment and overemployment, in turn, occur because different workers have different preferences and they tend to be confronted with an institutionally fixed work schedule. The fixed hours of work, in turn, can arise because of such factors as legislation, union pressure, or company personnel policy. The need for interaction among employees (or between employees and the firm's physical capital) may cause the employer to set standardized hours of work, rather than allowing each employee to work his or her preferred number of hours. Again, economic theory will enable us to analyze the labour market impact of these important institutional constraints.

The fixed-hours-of-work phenomenon is illustrated in Figure 2.11(a). In this case, the worker is faced with two constraints. The first is the usual budget constraint TY_1 as

Figure 2.11 **Fixed Hours Constraint, Underemployment, and Moonlighting**

Consumers may be constrained in their choice of hours worked, and confronted with the point C, a fixed hours and income "package." As shown in panel (b), given the wage, the consumer would rather choose D, working $T - L_D$ hours. As this exceeds the available hours of work, the consumer is underemployed. As shown in panel (c), if a second job is available, even one paying a lower wage, the consumer may choose M, working $T - L_C$ on the main job, and moonlighting on the second.

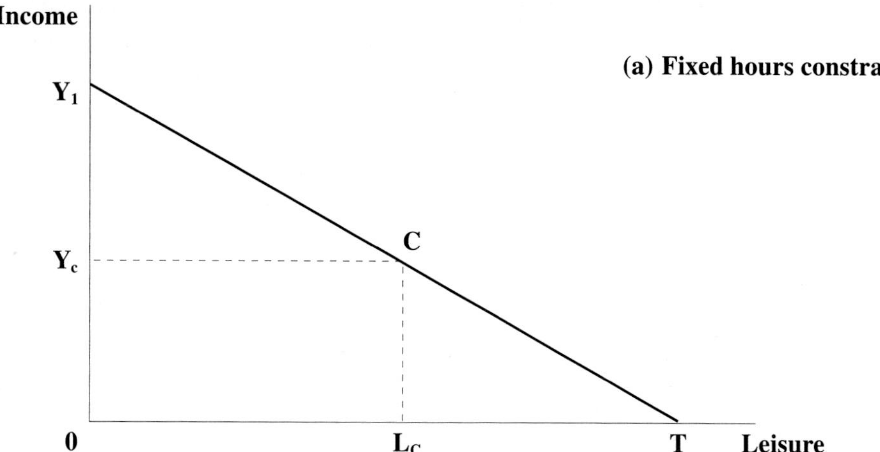

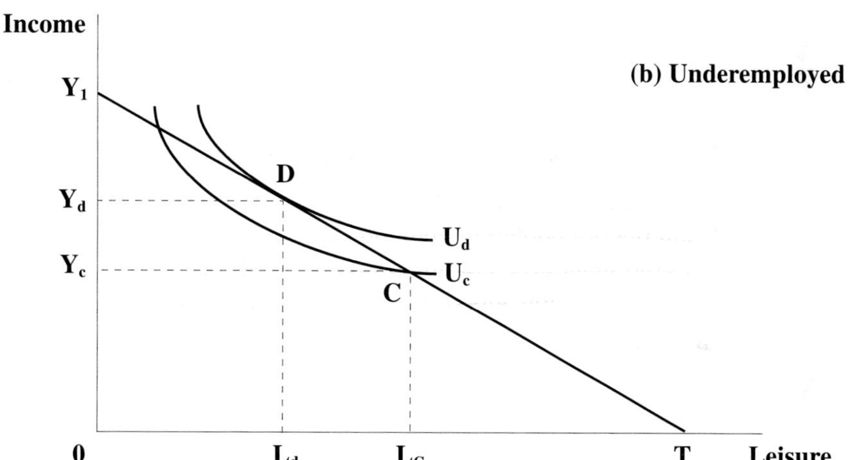

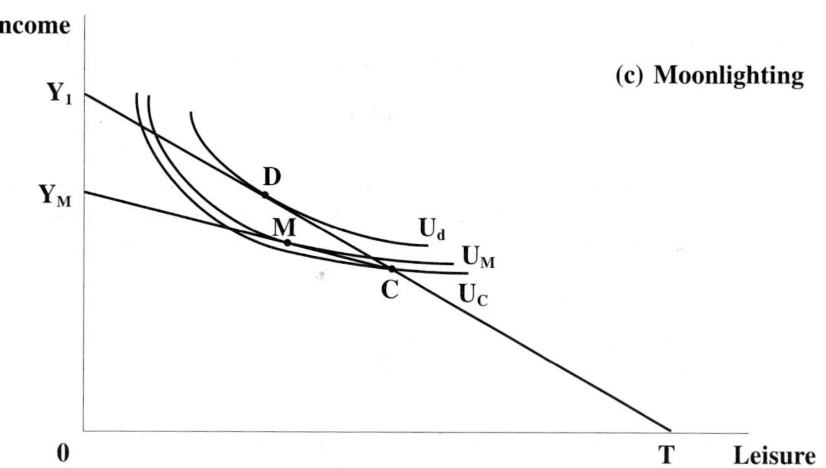

determined by the person's hourly wage. This restricts the worker's maximum choice set to the triangular area TY_1O, where O denotes the origin. The second constraint of the fixed workday of TL_c hours (recall work is measured from right to left) restricts the worker's maximum choice set to the area L_cCY_cO: the worker can take no more leisure than OL_c (work no more than TL_c), and earn no more income than OY_c even if he worked more than TL_c. In effect, this reduces the worker's realistic choice set to the point C since C will always be preferred to other points within L_cCY_cO.

Moonlighting and Underemployment

Some individuals, however, may prefer to work more hours at the going wage rate. Figure 2.11(b) illustrates the case for an individual whose preferences (indifference curve U_d) are such that he would prefer to be at D, working TL_d hours at the going wage and taking home an income of Y_d. However, because of the hours of work constraint, the worker must be at C, obviously being less well off since $U_c < U_d$. In fact, the difference between U_d and U_c is a measure of how much the worker would be willing to give up in order to have the fixed-hours constraint relaxed.

A variety of implications follow from this analysis. The worker is **underemployed** because he would like to work more at the going wage rate. Because of the additional constraint of the fixed working hours, the worker is also less well off ($U_c < U_d$) and may be seeking a different job that would enable him to achieve his desired equilibrium at D. In addition, the worker may be willing to engage in **moonlighting** and do additional work at a wage rate that is lower than the wage rate of the first job.

This moonlighting equilibrium is illustrated in Figure 2.11(c) by the budget constraint CY_m. (To simplify the diagram the details of Figure 2.11(b) have been omitted.) This new budget constraint rotates downward from CY_1 because the moonlighting wage, which is less than the regular wage as given by the slope of CY_1, applies only to hours of work beyond TL_c. In spite of the lower moonlighting wage, the worker is willing to work more hours (move from C to M) because of the greater utility associated with the move ($U_m > U_c$). That is, workers who are underemployed at the going wage rate would be willing to moonlight at a lower wage rate on their secondary job.

Overtime and Overemployment

Other individuals, however, may prefer to work fewer hours at the going wage rate. Figure 2.12(a) illustrates the situation where the worker would prefer (maximize utility) to be at D, working TL_D hours for an income of Y_d. However, because of the institutionally fixed work week, she is compelled to be at C, being less well off ($U_c < U_d$) even though she takes home more income ($Y_c > Y_d$).

Such a worker is **overemployed** at the going wage rate and consequently would support policies to reduce the institutionally fixed work week. In addition, she also may be seeking a different job that would enable her to work fewer hours at the going wage rate, and she may even exhibit absenteeism and tardiness as ways of moving toward her desired work week. Because such a worker is already overemployed at the going wage rate, she would not willingly work more hours at the wage rate; however, she may be induced to do so by an **overtime premium**.

This overtime premium is illustrated in Figure 2.12(b) by the budget constraint CY_o that rotates upward from CY_t because the overtime premium, which is greater than the normal wage that determines the slope of TY_1, applies only to overtime hours of work beyond TL_c. If, for example, the overtime premium is time-and-a-half, then the overtime budget constraint has a 50 percent greater slope than the regular straight-time budget constraint. As long as the worker is willing to give up some leisure for additional income, then there is an overtime premium that will induce her to work more, for example, to move to point O

Figure 2.12 **Overemployment and Overtime**

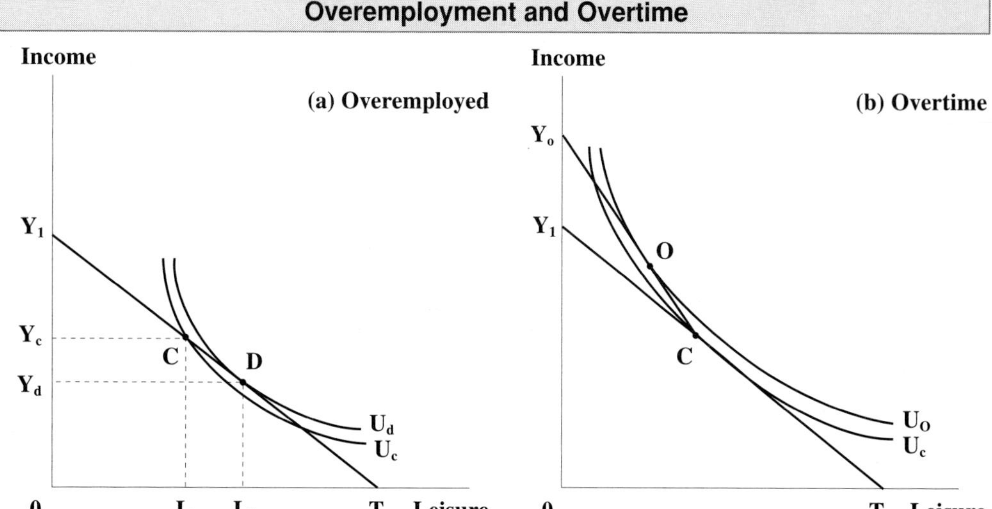

A consumer may be constrained to work more hours than desired. In this case, he or she would prefer to work at D, at fewer hours than C, though C is still preferred to not working at all. However, this consumer could be induced to work more hours, corresponding to point O, if offered a higher wage rate for hours worked after C.

on Figure 2.12(b) (on the indifference curve U_O). Because the worker is overemployed at the going wage rate, the overtime premium is necessary to get her to work more hours.

The person works longer hours even though he is overemployed at the going wage rate because the overtime premium results in a large substitution effect, by making the price (opportunity cost, income forgone) of leisure higher only for the overtime hours. The overtime premium has a small income effect because the budget constraint rotates upward *only* for the overtime hours; consequently, it does not have an income effect for the normal straight-time hours. Recall that the substitution effect was illustrated by a changed *slope* in the budget constraint, while the income effect was illustrated by a *parallel shift* of the constraint. Since the overtime premium changes the slope for the overtime hours, it is primarily a work-inducing substitution effect, with little leisure-inducing income effect.

Overtime Premium Versus Straight-Time Equivalent

The importance of the relative absence of the income effect in the overtime premium can be illustrated by a comparison of the overtime premium with the straight-time equivalent. One might logically ask the question: If workers are constantly working overtime, why not institutionalize that into a longer workday and pay them the straight-time equivalent of their normal wage plus their overtime wage?

This alternative is illustrated in Figure 2.13. The overtime situation is illustrated by the budget constraint TCY_O with TC being the normal wage paid during the regular work period and CY_O being the overtime premium paid for overtime hours. The normal wage is assumed not to change as a result of the overtime premium. The regular work period would be TL_C hours and overtime hours would be L_CL_O. (To simplify the diagram, these points are not shown; however, as in Figure 2.12(a), they are simply the points on the horizontal leisure axis vertically below their corresponding equilibrium points.) The straight-time hourly equivalent for TL_O hours of work is given by the budget constraint TO, the slope of which is a weighted average of the slopes of the regular wage TC and the overtime premium CO. The straight-time hourly equivalent is derived by simply taking the earnings associated with the overtime plus regular time hours of work, TL_O, and determining the straight-time wage, TO, that would yield the same earnings.

A worker who is paid the straight-time equivalent, however, would not voluntarily remain at O, but rather would move to the point S, which involves less work. This is so

Figure 2.13 **Overtime Premium Versus Straight-Time Equivalent**

An overtime premium can be used to induce a worker to choose hours corresponding to the point O, after paying the straight-time wage to point C. Why not simply offer the consumer a straight-time equivalent, equal to the average wage associated with the earnings and hours at O? The income effect associated with the higher wage received from the first hour worked will lead the consumer to choose fewer hours worked (at S) than when the higher (overtime premium) is only paid on hours in excess of those at C.

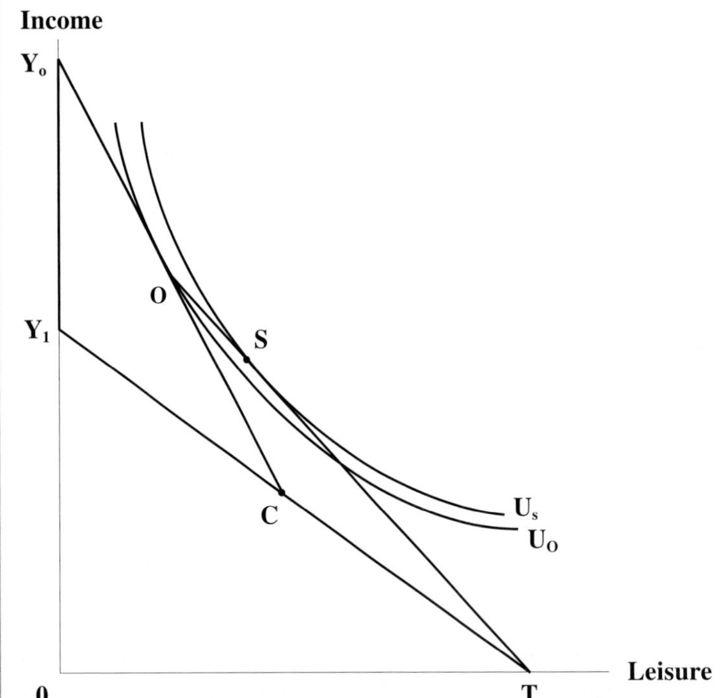

because the wage line TSO has a larger leisure-inducing income effect, whereas the overtime premium COY_0 is dominated by the work-inducing substitution effect (rotation of the budget constraint). In essence, since the overtime premium is paid only for hours *beyond* the regular workday, the person has to work more to get the additional income.

Overtime premiums, therefore, may be a rational way for employers to get their existing work force to voluntarily work more hours, even if they are overemployed at their regular workday. Employers, in turn, may want to work their existing work force longer hours, rather than hiring additional workers, so as to spread their fixed hiring costs over longer hours. The importance of these fixed hiring costs will be analyzed in more detail when labour demand is discussed.

Workers need not be overemployed at their going wage rate for the overtime premium to work. One can easily portray the situation for a worker in equilibrium at the regular wage rate who would unambiguously work more when offered an overtime wage premium, but who may work less if offered a straight-time hourly wage increase. Firms that want to work their existing work force longer hours may prefer a wage package that involves a low regular wage and a high overtime premium to a package that costs them the same but that involves a straight-time wage increase.

Again, what at first glance appear to be costly and irrational actions on the part of firms—in this case the coexistence of overtime and moonlighting rates and a preference for overtime premiums over straight-time equivalent earnings—may well be rational actions when viewed in the larger picture where the parties are optimizing with respect to legal institutional constraints and when the varying preferences of individual workers are considered. Rather than rendering economic theory irrelevant in the force of such constraints, they highlight the usefulness of economics in analyzing the impact of the constraints and in explaining why, in fact, they may arise as an endogenous institutional response to the peculiarities of the labour market.

Allowing Choice in Working Hours

As illustrated previously, the composition of the work force has been changing dramatically in recent years. This is evidenced by such phenomena as the increased labour force participation of women, the dominance of the two-earner family, and the aging of the work force. Given such changes it is not surprising that these different groups would have different tastes and preferences for alternative worktime arrangements in the labour market. As well, they will face different household constraints.

For example, two-earner families may prefer part-time employment for one party, reduced hours of work for the other party, and flexible worktime arrangements, as well as the right to refuse overtime work for both parties. This would enable them to better combine labour market work with their household activities. In contrast, the one-earner family may prefer a long work week (e.g., with regular overtime) for the single earner so as to earn a family income similar to that of the dual-earner family. In essence, the growing diversity of the work force has given rise to a growing diversity of preferences for alternative work-time arrangements. Preferences for such arrangements are no longer dictated by the former stereotypical male "breadwinner" in a single-earner family.

This diversity of preferences is illustrated in the results of the Statistics Canada Survey of Work Reductions, conducted as a supplement to the June 1985 Labour Force Survey (Benimadhu, 1987). According to that survey only about one-third of the work force was content with its worktime arrangements. The two-thirds who were discontented were about evenly divided between wanting more work for more pay and wanting less work for a corresponding reduction in pay. The strongest preference for worktime reductions was from women in the childrearing years (25 to 34) and women with children under the age of five.

The basic income-leisure choice framework can be used to illustrate that there are gains to be had by employers providing alternative worktime arrangements to meet the divergent tastes and preferences of an increasingly heterogeneous work force. These benefits are illustrated in Figure 2.14. Point C illustrates where workers are constrained to operate given the all-or-nothing choice of working TL_c hours (points on the leisure axis are not marked to simplify the diagram) at the going wage (slope of TY_t). However, many workers have different preferences. Some, for example, may prefer to be at point D. Because they are overemployed at the going wage rate, their discontent ($U_c < U_d$) may be exhibited in the form of costly absenteeism, high turnover, and perhaps reduced morale and productivity.

Obviously firms that allowed such workers to work their desired hours of work could save on these costs. Alternatively, such firms could lower their wage rates and still retain their work force. This is illustrated by the wage line TY_f, which could be lowered until the point of tangency, F, with the original utility curve U_c. Workers are equally well off at C and F (same level of utility U_c) even though F implies a lower wage rate, simply because they are at an equilibrium with respect to their hours of work. In essence, they are willing to give up wages in return for a work schedule that meets their preferences.

Competition for such jobs would ensure that firms could offer lower wages in return for more flexible work schedules. In this sense, the gains from flexible work schedules could be recouped by the firm to cover the other costs that may be associated with such schedules. Firms that offer more flexible hours need not lower wages, but may take the benefits in the form of reduced absenteeism, lower turnover, and improved worker morale. Various combinations of reduced wages (downward-rotated wage line) and improved worker morale (higher indifference curve), of course, are possible.

While there are benefits from allowing workers to choose their preferred hours of

Figure 2.14 **Gains from Alternative Work Shedules**

Consumers may be willing to pay for flexibility in choosing their hours worked. A consumer constrained to working at C would be indifferent to any lower wage and hours package lying on the indifference curve U_C. The wage could fall as low as that represented by TY_F, where the consumer would choose hours associated with point F.

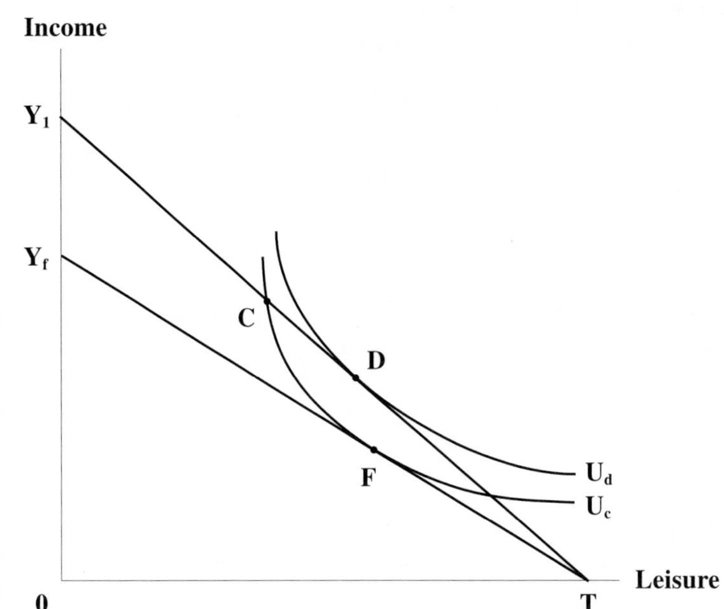

work, there are costs, especially if such flexibility is given to different workers in the same establishment. Individual differences in hours worked can give rise to problems of monitoring, supervision, communication, scheduling, and coordination. One compromise is flextime, whereby the workers are required to work a fixed number of hours (e.g., eight per day), a certain "core" hours (e.g., 10:00 a.m. to 3:00 p.m.), but the beginning and ending times are flexible. This helps meet the divergent preferences of different workers (e.g., late risers versus early risers); it enables some with childraising responsibilities to be home when children return from school; and it facilitates avoiding rush-hour commuting problems.

Compressed work weeks are another alternative worktime arrangement. Common compressed schedules include four 10-hour days or even three 12-hour days. These are often attractive to employees because of the longer "weekends" that are involved. They also enable the amortizing or spreading of fixed daily commute costs over a longer workday. For example, a two-hour commute over three 12-hour days is six hours of commute time per week, as against ten hours based on a five-day week. As well, the 12-hour day may avoid rush-hour commutes. Such compressed work weeks have been used in some areas (e.g., nursing) as a recruiting device to help attract and retain personnel.

Clearly, there may be costs associated with such alternative worktime arrangements and these have to be weighed against the potential benefits. The point made here, and illustrated in the income-leisure framework, is that there are potential benefits to meeting the divergent tastes and preferences of workers. As well, these benefits are likely to be growing as a result of the increasing diversity of the work force.

APPENDIX: CONSUMER CHOICE THEORY

The economic theory of consumer behaviour and labour supply has two main building blocks: preferences and constraints. Preferences summarize what the individual or household wishes to achieve. Constraints summarize what is feasible, that is, what the individual is able to achieve. The key assumption of the theory is that individuals choose from among the feasible outcomes that outcome which yields the highest level of satisfaction or well-being. In this appendix, we review the theory of consumer behaviour, and show how it can be adapted for labour supply.

Constraints

Assume that there are two goods, X and Y, that the consumer can buy in the market. The budget set, or budget constraint, summarizes the set of consumption bundles of X and Y that she can consume. Her expenditure must be less than or equal to her budget M, so that purchases must satisfy

$$P_X X + P_Y Y \leq M$$

where P_X and P_Y are the prices of X and Y purchased in the market. This set of feasible consumption packages is illustrated by the shaded area of Figure 2.A1(a). Because we assume that "more is better" for the consumer, she will exhaust her budget and we can focus on the outer frontier of the budget set, replacing the inequality with equality:

$$P_X X + P_Y Y = M$$

This is simply the equation of a straight line, and we call it the budget constraint.

In labour economics it is important to understand how to manipulate budget constraints, so it is worth reviewing the key features of this very simple budget constraint. It is a simple exercise of high school algebra to see that the slope of the budget constraint is $-P_X/P_Y$ (i.e., rise/run). This slope represents the relative price of X to Y, and it indicates that if the consumer wishes to increase her consumption of X by 1 unit, she would have to give up P_X/P_Y units of Y. The endpoints of the budget line occur where the budget constraint intersects with the X and Y axes. If the consumer spends all her budget on X, she will be able to consume M/P_X units of X, and zero Y. Alternatively, she can buy nothing but Y, consuming a maximum of M/P_Y units of Y.

A simple extension to this framework is illustrated in Figure 2.A1(b). In this case, we assume that the consumer has an initial endowment of $\overline{X}$ units of X. We assume that she can sell all or part of her endowment on the market at the market price for X, P_X. The easiest way to see how this affects her budget set is to assume that she first sells her entire endowment, and then adds the proceeds $P_X\overline{X}$ to her previous budget, M. She can then decide how to spend her budget on X and Y. It is possible to simplify the consumer's problem in this manner because there are no transaction costs associated with buying or selling X. Her new budget constraint is then given by

$$P_X X + P_Y Y = M + P_X \overline{X} = \overline{M}$$

The relative price of X and Y are unaffected, so the slope of this line remains the same. All that has happened to her budget constraint is that it is shifted out by the value of her endowment of X. We can simple relabel her new budget as $\overline{M}$, and treat this budget constraint as if she had no endowment.

Preferences

The individual's preferences can be expressed formally in terms of a **utility function** that shows the level of satisfaction or utility associated with any specific basket of X and Y. The utility function can be written as u = U(X,Y), where X and Y are the quantities of X and Y consumed. In order for the theory to make some testable predictions about behaviour, it is necessary to make some assumptions about the general nature of the preferences of individuals. The following four fundamental assumptions form the basis of the theory of consumer choice:

Figure 2.A1 **Consumer Budget Constraints**

The feasible combinations of X and Y available to the consumer are represented by the shaded area in panel (a). Panel (b) shows how this set is changed when consumers have an initial endowment of $\bar{X}$, which they are free to consume or sell at P_X. The opportunity set is expanded by the market value of the endowment, $P_X\bar{X}$, while the tradeoff between consuming X and Y remains the relative price of X and Y (P_X/P_Y). An endowment of X thus results in a parallel shift of the budget constraint.

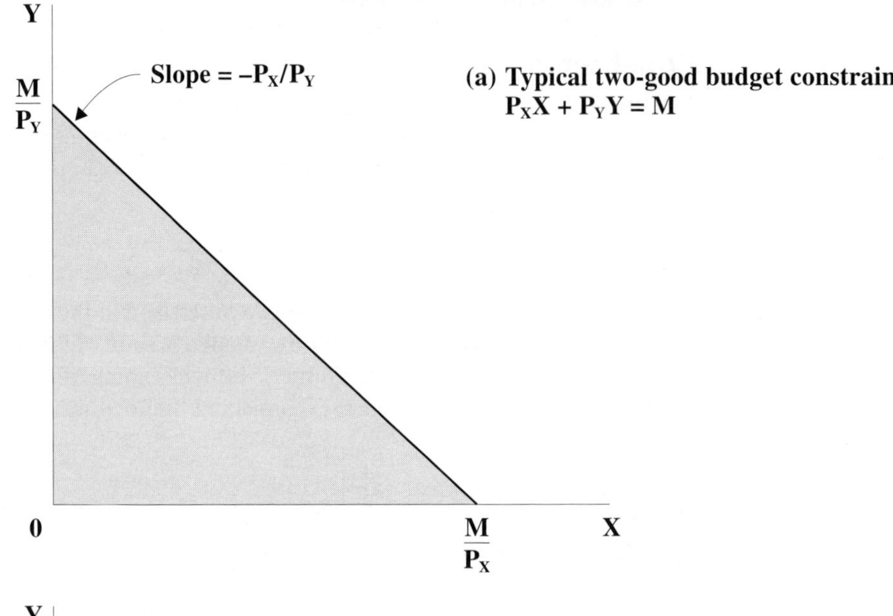

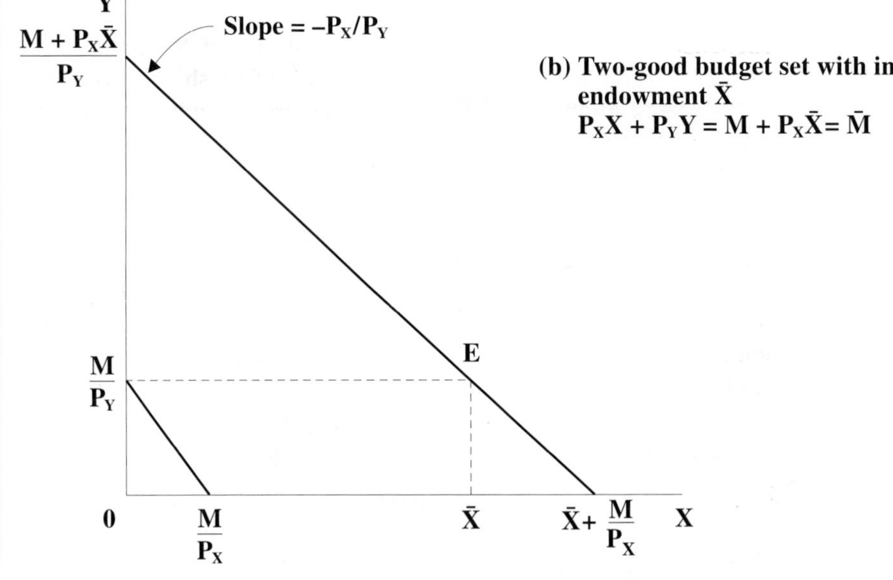

A1. *Complete ordering.* The individual can rank all possible bundles (combinations of X and Y). This assumption means that for any two combinations of X and Y, say bundle A and bundle B, she can state that A is preferred to B, B is preferred to A, or she is indifferent between A and B. In other words, the individual is assumed to know what she derives satisfaction from and, therefore, to be able to say which bundle would yield higher utility or whether both would yield the same utility.

A2. *More of X or Y is preferred.* Both X and Y are assumed to be "goods," not "bads," in the sense that the more of X consumed (holding constant the amount of Y consumed), the higher the level of satisfaction. Similarly, the more Y consumed (holding constant the consumption of X), the higher her level of utility.

A3. *Transitivity.* If bundle A is preferred to bundle B and bundle B is preferred to C, then bundle A must be preferred to bundle C. This assumption implies that preferences have a logical consistency similar to that which holds to objects of different weights: if object A is heavier than B, and B weighs more than C, then A is heavier than C.

A4. *Diminishing marginal rate of substitution.* The individual becomes less willing to substitute X for Y the lower the quantity of X is consumed. More precisely, holding utility constant, the smaller the amount of X consumed, the greater is the amount of Y that would be needed to compensate the individual for one less unit of X.

These four assumptions imply that the individual's utility function has certain properties. Graphically, these assumptions imply that individual preferences can be illustrated in the form of an indifference map as shown in Figure 2.A2(a). Each of the curves labelled U_0, U_1, U_2, and U_3 is called an indifference curve. An indifference curve shows combinations of X and Y that yield the same utility or satisfaction to the consumer. These curves are downward-sloping and have a convex shape. They do not cross or intersect. Indifference curves above and to the right of other indifference curves show combinations of X and Y that are preferred to those on curves lower and to the left (that is, all bundles on U_2 are preferred to any bundle on U_1).

The convex shape of the indifference curves results from the assumption of diminishing marginal rate of substitution. This is illustrated in Figure 2.A2(b). At point A, the individual consumes a large amount of Y (24 units) but has limited X (15 units). Her utility is unchanged if she gives up six units of Y in exchange for one unit of X, thereby moving to point B on the indifference curve. Thus, beginning at the bundle A, she is willing to exchange six units of Y for one additional unit of X. However, beginning at bundle C (which consists of 13 units of Y and 18 units of X), she is only willing to sacrifice one unit of Y for an additional unit of X (i.e., moving from bundle C to bundle D). At point E, which consists of 22 units of X and only eight units of Y, she is only willing to give up a half-unit of Y for one extra unit of X. Thus, the fewer units of Y consumed, the less willing she becomes to give up additional units of Y for extra units of X. As can also be seen in this example, the marginal rate of substitution is equal to the absolute value of the slope of the indifference curve. Thus, the slope of the indifference curve represents the psychic trade-off that the consumer is willing to make between X and Y and remain equally well off.

The Consumer Optimum and Comparative Statics

The consumer's optimal, utility-maximizing choice of X and Y is given by that combination of X and Y on the budget constraint that lies on the highest indifference curve. This is illustrated in Figure 2.A3. Here, at A, the consumer chooses X*, Y*, achieving utility level represented by U*. Notice that the indifference curve U* is tangent to the budget constraint at X*, Y*. This implies that the slopes of these lines are equal at the optimum, that is:

$$MRS = P_X/P_Y$$

This tangency condition has economic content: it indicates that at the optimum, the individual's psychic (or internal) tradeoff between X and Y equals the external, or market, rate of exchange between X and Y. The reader is advised to consider why this would not be an optimum if this condition did not hold.

The objective of the comparative statics exercise is to now examine what happens to the optimal demand for X if the price of X changes, holding M and P_Y constant. Figure 2.A4(a) shows the case of an increase in P_X to P'_X, and the decomposition of the change in optimal X into income and substitution effects. The increase in P_X leads to an inward rotation of the budget constraint. If the consumer wished to buy only Y, her consumption possibility would be unaffected. On the other hand, if she wanted to buy only X, the maximum she could buy is now reduced. The budget constraint is also now steeper, with slope

Figure 2.A2 **Consumer Preferences**

Indifference curves provide a graphical representation of consumer preferences, which rank various bundles (combinations) of X and Y. These indifference curves exhibit diminishing marginal rate of substitution. At higher levels of X, the consumer requires less Y to be compensated for a unit reduction in X. At B, where consumption of X is low, the consumer requires 6 units of Y to compensate for a unit reduction in X, whereas at F, the consumer needs only one-half of a unit of Y to compensate for the same reduction of X.

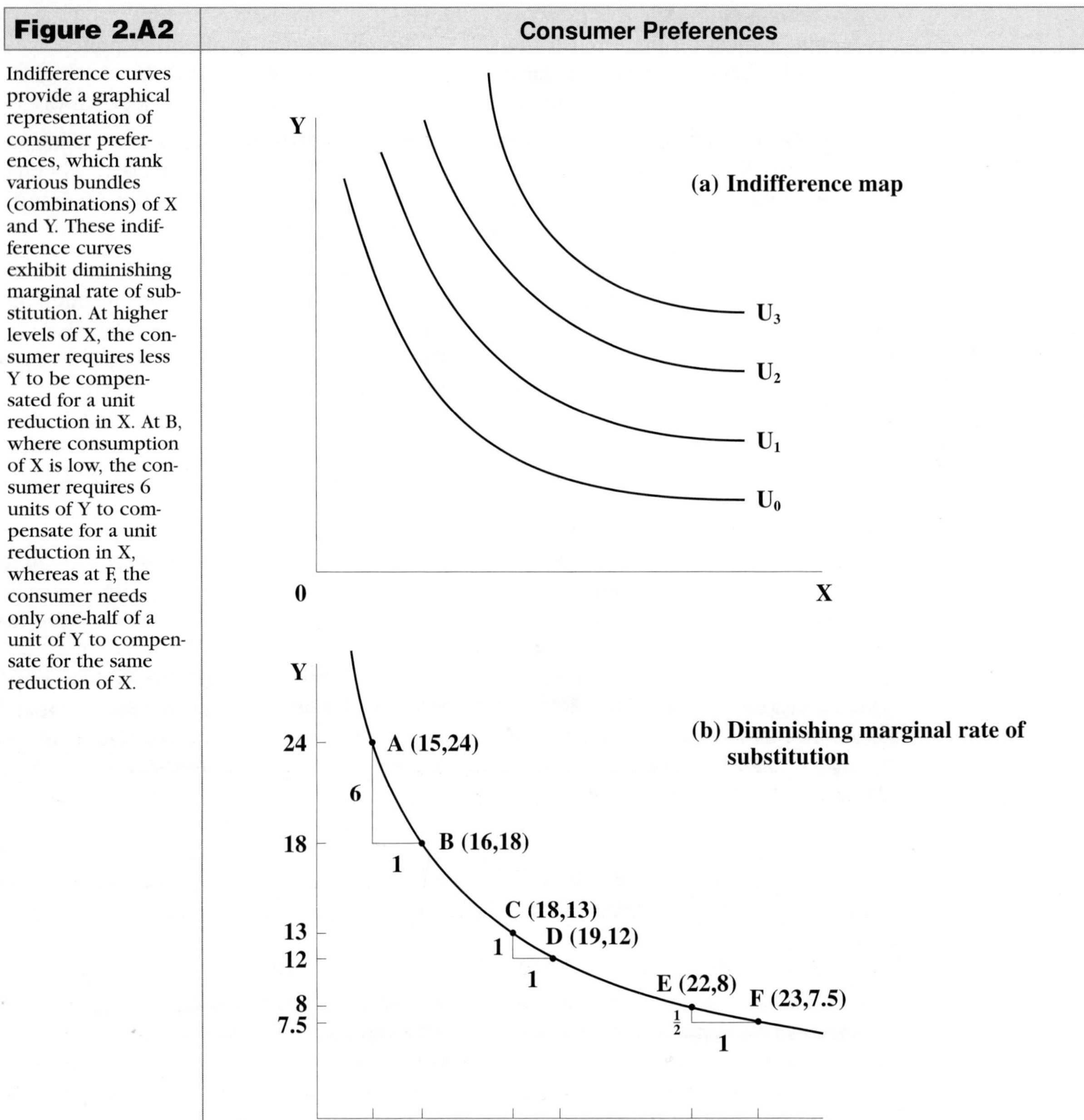

$-P'_X/P_Y$. The optimal consumption bundle moves from A to B. The question we wish to ask is whether this new optimum involves a reduced quantity of X, that is, whether the demand for X is decreasing in P_X.

We can conceptually divide the adjustment into two steps. First, we consider what bundle the consumer would buy if she faced the new relative prices, but had a budget large enough to allow her to attain her original level of utility, U_0. In this case, her consumption of X would decline from X_0 to X'. The shape of the indifference curve insures that a relative price increase results in substitution away from the now more expensive good. This change, called the substitution effect, predicts an unambiguous decline in the demand for

Figure 2.A3 **The Consumer's Optimum**

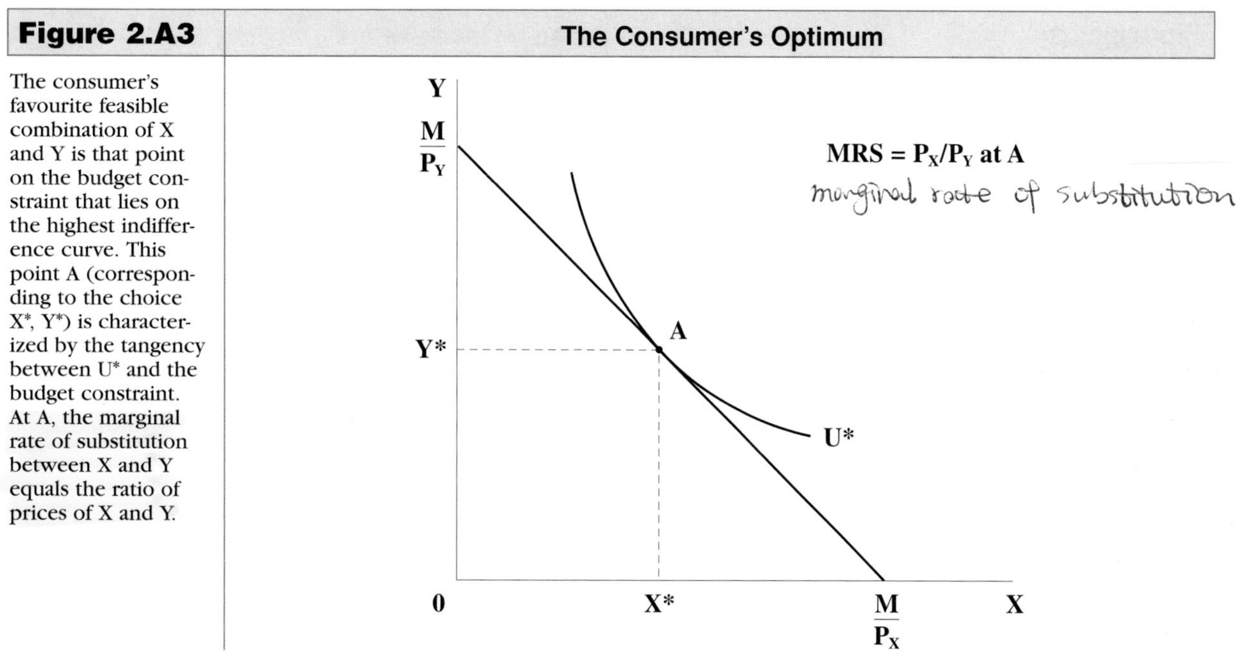

The consumer's favourite feasible combination of X and Y is that point on the budget constraint that lies on the highest indifference curve. This point A (corresponding to the choice X*, Y*) is characterized by the tangency between U* and the budget constraint. At A, the marginal rate of substitution between X and Y equals the ratio of prices of X and Y.

X, at least holding utility constant. Unfortunately for the consumer, in reality she is not compensated for the price increase. In fact, her budget set has been shrunk by the increase in the cost of X. The budget constraint shifts inward, parallel to the original budget constraint, because only income or wealth, and not relative prices have changed. This decline in "purchasing power" leads to another reallocation of her expenditure, denoted the income effect. If X is a normal good, then a decline in purchasing power (or "income") will lead to a further reduction in X consumed, leading her to X_1. Thus, in the case of a normal good, an increase in the price of X leads to an unambiguous decline in the demand of X: the income effect and substitution effect reinforce each other, both leading to a movement away from X.

The exercise is complicated somewhat when we consider the case where the individual has an endowment of X. This case is illustrated in Figure 2.A4(b). Again we can decompose the change into income and substitution effects, but the income effect is more complicated by the fact that the consumer has an endowment of X. The increase in P_X results in a rotation of the budget constraint through the point containing $\bar{X}$ (point E). The slope of the budget constraint has changed exactly as it did in the previous case where the consumer had no endowment. The shift of the budget constraint, and the more complicated income effect is most easily seen by examining the extreme points of the budget constraint. If the consumer wished to consume nothing but Y, the increase in the price of X is a pure windfall: her endowment increases in value, and she devotes all of the proceeds to consumption of Y which has not changed in price. This means that her feasible set has actually increased to the left of point E. On the other hand, if she wants to consume only X, she suffers a net decline in purchasing power because X is more expensive. She can still consume her endowment of $\bar{X}$, but she can purchase fewer units of X from the market.

The substitution effect from the price increase is no different from the previous example, and is given by the movement from A to A'. It unambiguously suggests a decline in the demand for X. We then divide the income effect into two parts. The first is the conventional decline in purchasing power that results from the increase in P_X. We hold constant

Figure 2.A4

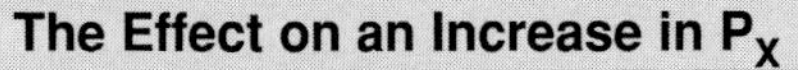

An increase in P_X has income and substitution effects. As X is more expensive, the consumer will substitute away from X toward Y. This is given by the movement from A to A', where the consumer is allowed to remain equally happy as before the price increase. The income effect results from the reduction of purchasing power, which for a normal good leads to a further reduction in X demanded, from A' to B. In panel (b), there is an additional income effect for consumers who have an additional endowment of X. As X is now worth more, the consumer is richer, and the additional income effect may offset both of the "original" income and substitution effects, leading to a net increase in X consumed.

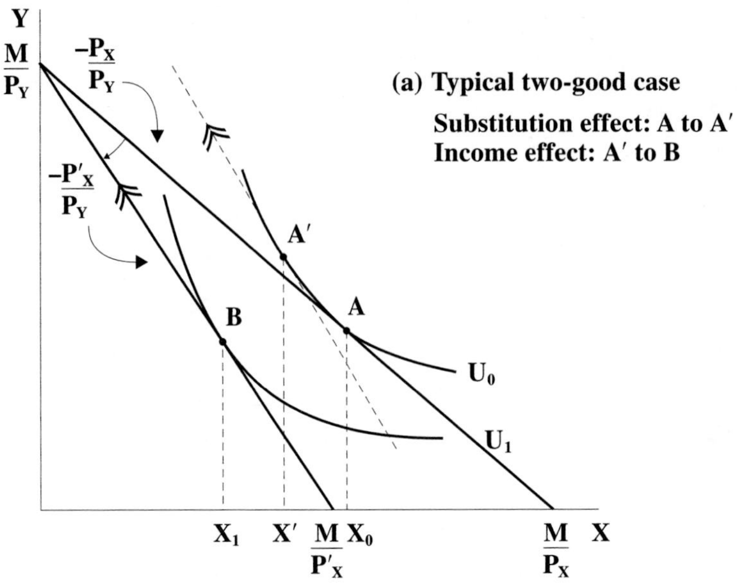

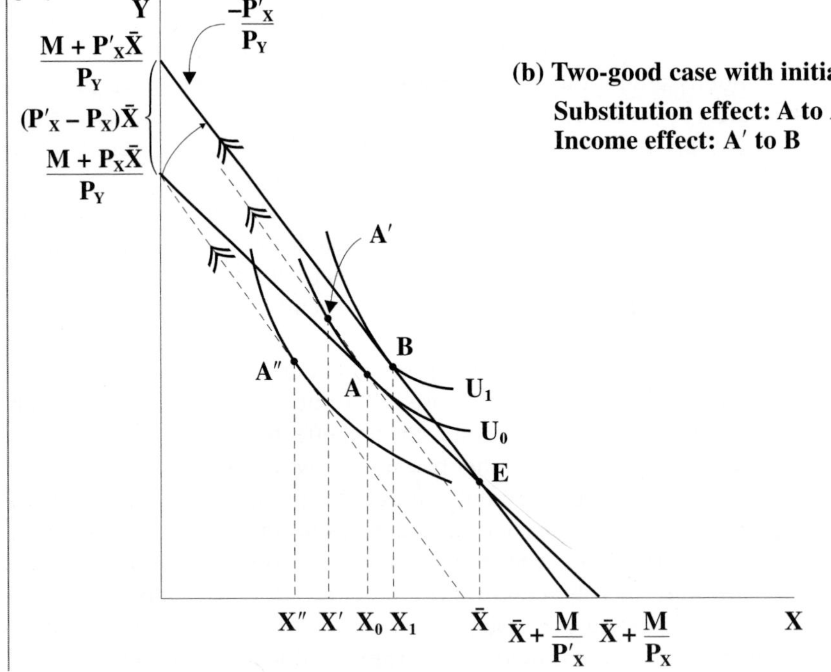

the person's budget, ignoring the fact that he is "richer" because his endowment is worth more. This involves the shift inward of the budget constraint, and the further decline in X as represented by the movement from A' to A'' (assuming that X is a normal good). To this point, we have the conventional result that income and substitution effects reinforce the decline in demand for X. With the increase in the value of the endowment, however, we now consider the consequences for demand for X. This endowment "revaluation" results in the shift of the budget constraint by $P'_X X - P_X X$, and the movement from $A \leq$ to B. If X is a normal good, this will involve an increase in the demand for X. This effect counteracts the previous income and substitution effects. The net effect is ambiguous, though in the case illustrated, the final income effect was large enough to result in a net increase in the demand for X.

Mapping to Labour Supply

The labour supply model can be seen to be a simple relabelling of the standard consumer model with endowments. In the specific notation of the model in this section, Y can be relabelled as consumption of a composite bundle of goods and services. X can be relabelled leisure, where the individual begins with an endowment of T units of leisure that must be allocated between market or nonmarket time. The price of consumption in this case can be normalized to one, while the price of leisure is the wage rate. M becomes non-labour income, while $\overline{M}$ is full income. The one additional wrinkle in the labour supply problem is that there is an additional constraint: total time use cannot exceed the time endowment of T units of time, so that the budget set is truncated at T units of leisure.

Summary

- Individual attachment to the labour market is measured in two ways: first, whether an individual is working, or searching for work (the participation dimension); and second, how many hours he or she works (the hours dimension).
- The microeconomic model of consumer choice can accommodate both dimensions of the labour supply decision. Consumers choose their preferred combination of income (consumption) and leisure (non-market time), as represented by their opportunity set, or budget constraint. If this optimum occurs at zero hours of work, the individual does not participate. If optimal hours are positive, the individual participates, and the marginal rate of substitution between leisure and consumption equals the wage rate.
- The reservation wage is the critical wage to the participation decision: for wage rates above the reservation wage, the consumer will choose to work; for wages below, the consumer will not participate. The reservation wage is given by the marginal rate of substitution between leisure and consumption, at zero hours of work—that is, the person's value of non-market time (in terms of consumption) at zero hours worked.
- The consumer choice model can be used to build an individual's labour supply curve. By varying the wage rate, we can trace out the consumer's optimal choice of hours worked, holding all other factors constant. For wages below the reservation wage rate, labour supply is zero. The consumer moves to positive hours supplied as the wage exceeds the reservation wage. The impact of increased wages on hours worked will then depend on the relative magnitudes of income and substitution effects. If the substitution effect is largest, wage increases lead to increases in labour supply; if the income effect dominates, wage increases lead to decreases in labour supply.
- The labour-leisure choice model can be used to investigate a variety of labour market phenomena, such as the "added worker effect," the structure of overtime wage premiums, and the willingness of individuals to accept flexibility in work hours in exchange for lower wages.

REVIEW QUESTIONS

1. What would happen to an individual's labour supply schedule if leisure were an inferior good? Use an income-leisure diagram to illustrate your argument.
2. A labour force survey yields the following estimates:

Population 15 and older	30m
Employed	22m
Not working, but actively seeking work	1m
Full-time students	2m
Retired	3m
Not working, discouraged because of lack of jobs	0.5m
Not working (household workers)	1.5m

   Calculate the labour force participation rate and the unemployment rate.
3. Use the basic income-leisure choice framework to analyze the possible labour supply response of various groups to changes in their wage rate. The different groups could include the following:
   a. The poor who are at a minimum subsistence, and who aspire to middle-class consumption patterns
   b. The wealthy who have acquired an abundance of material goods and who now aspire to be members of the idle rich
   c. Workers who have a fairly strong attachment to the labour force and who are reluctant to change their hours of work
   d. Workers who have a weak attachment to the labour force and who have viable alternatives to market work
   e. "Workaholics" who have strong preferences for labour market work
4. Illustrate the case where an individual responds differently to a wage increase and a wage decrease of the same magnitude. Specifically, have the person become "locked in" to a certain consumption pattern associated with the higher wage.
5. Use the income-leisure choice model to show that an increase in non-labour income will increase the individual's reservation wage if leisure is a normal good.
6. On the basis of the diagrams of Figure 2.11, illustrate how an underemployed worker would respond to:
   a. An offer to work as many more hours as the worker would like at the going wage
   b. Payment of an overtime premium for hours of work beyond C
   c. An offer to work an additional fixed number of hours, as determined by the employee at the going wage
7. On the basis of the diagrams of Figure 2.12, illustrate how an overemployed worker would respond to:
   a. An offer to work as many hours as the worker would like at the going wage
   b. Payment of the moonlighting rate for hours of work beyond C
8. On the basis of Figure 2.12(b), precisely illustrate the following overtime rates for hours worked beyond TL_C:
   a. Time-and-a-half
   b. Double-time
   c. Time-and-a-half for the first two hours of overtime, and double-time thereafter

PROBLEMS

1. Assume that the following regression equation has been estimated, where P_W is the labour force participation rate of married women (measured as a percentage with

average $\overline{P} = 35.0$), Y_H is husband's wage income (measured in thousands of dollars, with average $\overline{Y}_H = 10$), Y_W is the wife's expected "wage" (expected income from working a fixed number of hours, measured in thousands of dollars, with average $\overline{Y}_W = 6$), and u_H is the male unemployment rate (measured as a percentage, with average $\overline{u}_H$ 6.0):

$$P_W = -7Y_H + 18Y_W - 0.5u_H$$

a. What is the expected effect of an increase of \$1000 in the income of the husbands on the participation rate of their wives?
b. What is the expected effect of an increase of \$1000 in the wage of the wives themselves?
c. Break the latter down into its separate income and substitution effects.
d. Given the magnitude of the latter two effects, what would be the impact on female participation of an equal pay policy that increased the expected wages of females by \$1000 while at the same time decreasing the expected earnings of their husbands by \$1000?
e. Calculate the pure income and the gross or uncompensated wage elasticities of participation, evaluated at the means.
f. Does this equation shed any light on why the labour force participation of married women has increased over time, even though their non-labour wage has also increased?

2. Consider two individuals with endowments of T = 60 hours (per week) of leisure, non-labour income of Y, and facing a wage of \$7.50 per hour. At this wage, assume that workers are constrained by their employers to work 40 hours per week, or not at all.
   a. On a carefully labelled diagram, show the equilibrium for a worker for whom 40 hours is the optimum labour supply; and a worker who would like to work 20 hours, but still prefers the 40-hour week to not working. Compare the marginal rates of substitution for these individuals at 40 hours per week.
   b. The average part-time wage is \$7 per hour, in contrast to \$7.50 wage for full-time workers. Using the above model, provide an explanation for this difference in wage rates.

3. Assume that women's marginal rate of substitution of leisure for consumption is given by the following function:

$$MRS = A(x)\frac{C}{\ell}$$

where C is consumption (with price = 1) and ℓ is leisure. A(x) is a taste-shifting function of the following form:

$$A(x) = \exp(\beta_1 x_1 + \beta_2 x_2 + \ldots + \beta_K x_k + \varepsilon)$$

where the x_j are K different observable factors that affect her preferences, and ε represents unobservable factors that affect the MRS. ε has the property that it can be described as a probability density function, such as the normal or uniform densities.
   a. Show that this functional form for the MRS represents preferences that exhibit a diminishing marginal rate of substitution. Give specific examples of x_j that may affect the MRS, and explain how they will affect the MRS. Give a graphical example.
   b. Assume that an individual woman has non-labour income y (including her husband's income) and a time endowment of T. Derive an expression for this woman's reservation wage, w*. Show that if the market wage is w, this expression implies that a woman will participate if

$$\ln w > \ln y - \ln T + \beta_1 x_1 + \beta_2 x_2 + \ldots + \beta_K x_k + \varepsilon$$

Rewrite this as an expression of the form: Participate if $\varepsilon < Z$, where Z depends on the market wage, non-labour income, and preferences. *Hint*: Remember ln(ab) = ln a + ln b; ln(a/b) = ln a − ln b, etc.

c. Assume that Z has a standard normal distribution. Using your results from part (b), graphically show and explain how non-labour income, the market wage, and the various taste shifters affect the probability of a woman participating in the labour market.

4. Using carefully labelled diagrams, indicate the expected impact on the labour force participation of married women of changes in each of the following factors, other things held constant:
   a. An increase in the education of women
   b. A more equal sharing of household responsibilities between husband and wife
   c. A reduction in the average number of children
   d. An increased tendency to have children spaced more closely together
   e. An increase in the earnings of husbands
   f. Daycare paid out of general tax revenues
   g. Allowing daycare expenses to be tax-deductible
   h. Paying housewives a fixed sum out of general tax revenues for household work
5. Using the income-leisure framework, formally analyze the "added worker" effect, that is, the impact on the wife's labour supply of an adverse shock to her husband's job. For concreteness, assume that the wife has a wage rate of \$10 per hour, and that her husband's employer has forced him to take a pay cut from \$20 per hour to \$15 per hour, but allowed him to continue working at 40 hours per week (if he wishes). Consider two approaches:
   a. In the first, take the husband's hours as given, and analyze the household choice over consumption and wife's leisure.
   b. In the second, focus on the choice of husband versus wife's labour supply, allowing both to adjust their hours, and putting the consumption decision in the background.
   c. Compare the pros and cons of the two approaches. In particular, use the two approaches to compare the impact on the wife's labour supply of unemployment compensation for the husband equal to \$200 per week.
6. Susan claims labour supply theory is nonsense. She determines how much income she needs to support her "addiction" to maintaining and insuring her 1967 Mustang convertible. She then works as many hours as necessary. "No crazy income and substitution effects for me," she asserts. Is she right? Depict her labour supply choice in an income-leisure diagram, and break a wage increase down into its constituent income and substitution effects.
7. Curious George must decide how much to work. He has 60 hours per week available that he can spend either working or engaged in leisure (which for him is creating various kinds of mischief). He can work at a wage rate of \$5 per hour. The Man with the Yellow Hat (who looks after George) also gives him an allowance of \$100 per week, no matter how much George works. George's only source of income that he can use for consumption (mostly bananas) is this allowance plus his wage earnings.
   a. In a carefully labelled diagram, draw George's consumption-leisure budget constraint. Show an equilibrium where George chooses to work 40 hours per week.
   b. In an effort to have George pay for other household expenses, the Man with the Yellow Hat decides to tax George 50 percent of his *wage income*. Using the same diagram you drew in part (a), where George works 40 hours, show what happens to his labour supply. To do this, show one possible outcome, and break the change down into income and substitution effects.

c. Instead of the wage tax, the Man with the Yellow Hat could impose a "poll tax," a lump-sum tax independent of George's wage earnings. This tax must raise the same revenue as the wage tax in part (b), and could be accomplished by reducing George's allowance. Draw the budget constraint with the new tax *and* the wage tax, and compare the work incentive effects of the poll tax to the wage tax in part (b). As in part (b), assume that George was working 40 hours before any taxes were imposed.

KEYWORDS

labour force participation decision 33
labour force 33
employed 33
unemployed 33
labour force participation rate 33
hours-of-work aspect 35
labour supply model 38
preferences 38
leisure 38
indifference curves 38
marginal rate of substitution 38
utility 38
nonmarket time 40
consumption-leisure 40
income-leisure 40
potential income constraint 40
budget constraint 40
full income 41
consumer's optimum 42
utility-maximizing 42
corner solution 42
interior solution 42
reservation wage 42
normal good 44
inferior good 44
income effect 45
substitution effect 45
labour supply schedule 49
uncompensated elasticity 53
income elasticity 53
compensated elasticity 53
discouraged worker 56
added worker 56
hidden unemployment 57
underemployed 60
moonlighting 60
overemployed 60
overtime premium 60
utility function 65

REFERENCES

Benimadhu, P. 1987. *Hours of Work: Trends and Attitudes in Canada.* Ottawa: Conference Board.

Biddle, J., and D. Hamermesh. 1990. Sleep and the allocation of time. *JPE* 98 (October):922–43.

Blundell, R., and T. MaCurdy. 1999. Labor supply: A review of alternative approaches. In *Handbook of Labor Economics*, eds. O. Ashenfelter and D. Card. New York and Oxford: Elsevier Science, North Holland.

Fortin, N. M. 1995. Allocation inflexibilities, female labor supply, and housing assets accumulation: Are women working to pay the mortgage? *JOLE* 13 (July):524–57.

Hansson, I., and C. Stuart. 1985. Tax revenue, and the marginal cost of public funds in Sweden. *JPubEc* 27 (August):333–53.

Jones, S.R.G., and W.C. Riddell. 1999. The measurement of unemployment: An empirical approach. *Ecta* 67 (January):147–61.

Killingsworth, M. 1983. *Labor Supply*. Cambridge: Cambridge University Press.

Killingsworth, M., and J. Heckman. 1986. Female labor supply: a survey. In *Handbook of Labor Economics*. eds. O. Ashenfelter and R. Layard. New York: Elsevier.

Labour Canada. (1974). *Trends in working time.* Ottawa: Wages Research Division, Economics and Research Branch.

Nakamura, A., and M. Nakamura. 1981. A comparison of the labour force behavior of married women in the United States and Canada, with special attention to the impact of income taxes. *Ecta* 49 (March):451–89.

Nakamura, A., and M. Nakamura. 1985. A survey of research on the work behavior of Canadian women. In *Work and Pay: The Canadian Labour Market*, ed. W.C. Riddell. Toronto: University of Toronto Press.

Nakamura, A., M. Nakamura, and D. Cullen. 1979. Job opportunities, the offered wage, and the labour supply of married women. *AER* 69 (December):785–805.

Oettinger, G. S. 1999. An empirical analysis of the daily labor supply of stadium vendors. *JPE* 107 (April):360–92.

Pencavel, J. 1986. Labor supply of men: a survey. In *Handbook of Labor Economics*. Vol. 1, eds. O. Ashenfelter and R. Layard. New York: Elsevier.

Robbins, L. 1930. On the elasticity of demand for income in terms of effort. *Economica* (June):123–29.

Robinson, C., and N. Tomes. 1985. More on the labour supply of Canadian women. *CJE* 18 (February):156–63.

Smith, A. 1776. *The Wealth of Nations*. London: Methuen and Company.

Chapter Three

Labour Supply and Public Policy: Work Incentive Effects of Alternative Income Maintenance Schemes

Main Questions

- *Can the myriad government transfer programs in Canada be analyzed in a common framework? If so, is there a way to determine the "best" type of income transfer program, at least in terms of its effects on work incentives?*
- *Does unemployment insurance unambiguously reduce incentives to work, thereby reducing overall employment?*
- *Can welfare programs be designed in a way that minimizes adverse work incentives, directing benefits to those who most need it?*
- *How can we incorporate disabilities into the labour supply model? Can workers' compensation reduce the incentive of injured workers to return to work?*
- *How do child-care subsidies encourage the labour force participation of women? How can child-care costs be incorporated into the labour supply model?*

As a response to the problem of income loss and poverty, various **income maintenance schemes** have been proposed to raise the income of certain groups and to supplement low wages. Many considerations go into the design of these programs, and no single program can address the multiple reasons why income may be low. However, as we shall see, some programs can have adverse **work incentives**, and these possible incentive problems can be analyzed within the labour supply framework. But before doing so, it is important to understand the motivation for the various types of income maintenance programs. Given that it is desirable that we should transfer income to those with low income, why would governments design a program that discourages work?

In designing a transfer program, consider first the issue of "universality" versus "targeting" of a social program.[1] For simplicity, imagine that there is a well-defined poverty line, z. If a person's income y_i falls below z, we define him or her as poor, and one objective of an income maintenance program may be to eliminate poverty, that is, raise income (at least) to z. An administratively simple program would be to give everyone in the economy the same transfer $t_i = z$, no matter what their income, y_i. Under this universal scheme, poverty would be completely eliminated. However, it is also the most expensive way to eliminate poverty, and many benefits would leak to the non-poor. People who are not poor would receive the same benefits as those who really needed help. An alternative, probably cheaper, program would entail perfect targeting, that is, give everyone exactly enough transfer to reach the poverty line: $t_i = z - y_i$. Only those people with incomes below the poverty line would receive transfers, and they would all attain income level z. As long as individual income is unresponsive to the transfer rule, and ignoring the higher administrative costs associated with means testing, this perfectly targeted program would be cheaper than the universal program. In fact, the perfectly targeted program is the least expensive possible program. However, notice that the perfectly targeted transfer program guarantees that individuals with incomes below z are topped up to z. For every extra dollar of income earned, the transfer is reduced by one dollar. If earning income is a costly activity, individuals may reduce work effort (and thus their income) so that the transfer program becomes more expensive. By their very nature, targeted programs build in disincentives to earn income, because low income is a condition for receiving the benefit. Perhaps surprisingly, those programs whose main selling feature is that they are directed only at the poor, have the worst disincentives for work.

Another issue in program design concerns the permanent or transitory nature of low income. The appropriate response will depend on whether we believe that an individual is having a bad year, or whether she is likely to be poor every year. Imagine that we can describe an individual i's income in year t as the sum of a permanent and a transitory component:

$$y_{it} = y_i^P + (y_{it} - y_i^P) = y_i^P + \Delta y_{it}$$

Some people will have usually low or usually high incomes, y_i^P, but income may fluctuate from one year to the next by Δy_{it}. A person could then be poor in one year, that is, have income such that $y_{it} < z$, for a variety of reasons. If they have usually high permanent earnings, but are having a bad year, then we can design an appropriate social safety net for short-term income loss. Such a safety net is designed for people down on their luck; it is akin to a pioneer community rallying to help a neighbour whose barn has burned down. On the other hand, someone may have permanently low earnings, and need help every year. This requires a quite different type of program.

These considerations can be seen more finely if we decompose earnings into wages and hours. For example, we can write y_{it} as

$$y_{it} = w_{it}h_{it} = w_i^P h_i^P + (w_{it}h_{it} - w_i^P h_i^P)$$

[1]See Besley and Kanbur (1993) for more detailed discussion of these general issues.

so that earnings in year t are the product of the wage and hours worked in year t. This can be written as the sum of "permanent" or usual labour earnings $w_i^P h_i^P$ and the deviation of this year's labour earnings from their usual level. We can further decompose the transitory component as follows:

$$y_{it} = w_i^P h_i^P + (w_{it} h_{it} - w_i^P h_i^P) - w_{it} h_i^P + w_{it} h_i^P$$

$$y_{it} = w_i^P h_i^P + w_{it}(h_{it} - h_i^P) + (w_{it} - w_i^P) h_i^P$$

This simple representation isolates many of the reasons why income may be low in a given year, and the possibly appropriate policy response.

For example, low permanent earnings may result from either low permanent wages, w_i^P, or low permanent hours. Low wages may be the result of a low level of skill or earning power, and no short-run income maintenance program can change that. Such a source of low income may require "active" programs, such as training, in order to raise the productivity of a low-income worker. Alternatively, usual hours h_i^P may be low, perhaps because of a disability to work, or a long-run need to take care of family members. Sometimes, distinctions are made in transfer programs between "employables" and "non-employables." We can imagine non-employables as being those whose usual hours are very low, or that their productivity is permanently low.

Transitory earnings may be low, either because current wages (productivity) are low or because hours worked are low. An obvious example of low transitory hours would be short-term unemployment arising from layoffs. Unemployment insurance, and welfare (for employables) to some extent, are designed to address this problem. Market wages may be temporarily low, either because of a cyclical downturn in low-paying jobs or because of short-run injuries.

In the real world, the distinctions between "permanent" and transitory, are much harder to make. Yet we can see that the various income maintenance programs are designed to address problems arising from different components of the above decomposition. We will also see that hours worked are not immutable to the transfer program, and may depend on work incentives. The income-leisure framework from Chapter 2 is a useful way to analyze these issues, because it can accommodate many of the key elements of our discussion: wages and nonlabour (transfer) income, the choice of hours worked, final income, and consumer welfare (well-being).

We now turn to an analysis of a variety of "programs:" demogrants, welfare, negative income taxes, wage subsidies, unemployment insurance, unemployment-assisted work-sharing, disability payments and workers' compensation, and child-care subsidies. Throughout this chapter, we only discuss "passive" income support, focusing on static work incentives. The possible "dynamic" (or long-run) incentives for investing in human capital (skills) are ignored, as are programs designed to enhance skills. This discussion is deferred until Chapter 9.

STATIC PARTIAL EQUILIBRIUM EFFECTS IN THEORY

The basic income-leisure choice framework provides a convenient starting point to analyze the work incentive effects of alternative income maintenance schemes. The analysis is restricted to the static, **partial equilibrium effects** of alternative income maintenance programs. That is, it does not consider dynamic changes that can occur over time, or **general equilibrium effects** that can occur as the impact of the program works its way through the whole economic system.

Income support programs affect behaviour by altering the individual's opportunities (their potential income constraint). To analyze the effect of specific programs on the income constraint, ask first what is the effect on nonlabour income, and second, what is the effect on the slope of the constraint—that is, what happens as the individual gives up leisure and works more? Throughout this analysis, Y is defined as income after taxes and transfer payments, and E as labour market earnings, equal to wages times hours worked.

Demogrant

Perhaps the simplest income maintenance program to analyze is a lump-sum transfer, or **demogrant**. As the name implies, a demogrant means an income grant to a specific demographic group, such as female-headed families with children, or all persons aged 60 and over, or all family units irrespective of their wealth. There are very few examples of pure demogrants. The best example in Canada is the Old Age Security (OAS) program which provides monthly benefits to individuals over the age of 65. The former Family Allowance program was also a pure demogrant, providing monthly payments to families in respect of each child under 18. Demogrants are characterized by their complete universality: the benefit received does not depend on income or earnings. The Child Tax Credit, which effectively replaced the Family Allowance program, is not a demogrant since the level of benefit depends on family income. Even the OAS is now being "clawed back" for high-income seniors. Nevertheless, demogrants are worth analyzing in their abstract form because many income maintenance programs share the features of demogrants.

www.hrdc-drhc.gc.ca/isp/common/oastoc_e.shtml

As illustrated by the dashed line in Figure 3.1, the demogrant would shift the potential income constraint vertically upwards by the amount of the grant. The slope of the new income constraint would be equal to the slope of the original constraint since the relative price of leisure has not changed. Thus there is no substitution effect involved with the demogrant; the new equilibrium, E_d, would be above and to the right of the original equilibrium; that is, work incentives would unambiguously be reduced. This occurs because the demogrant involves only a leisure-inducing pure income effect. The increase in actual take-home income is less than the amount of the demogrant because some of the demogrant was used to buy leisure, hence reducing earned income. This can readily be seen in Figure 3.1; if the individual did not alter working time, the outcome would be at the point E_1 (yielding income Y_1) vertically above the original equilibrium E_0, whereas income with the demogrant is given by Y_d.

Figure 3.1 Work Incentive Effects of a Lump-Sum Demogrant

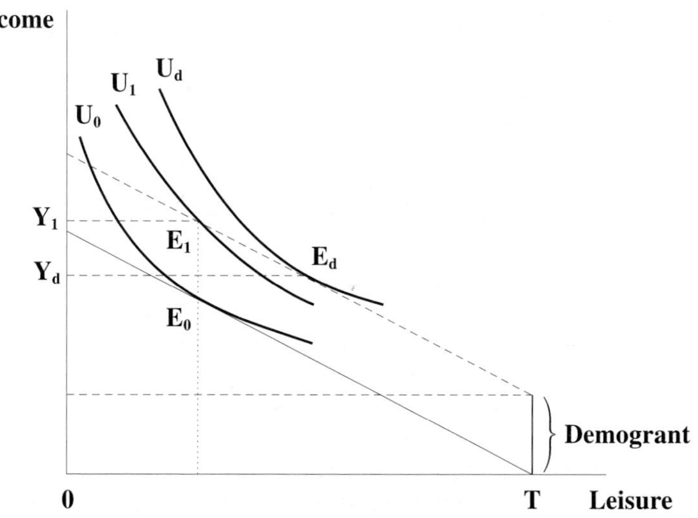

The demogrant generates a parallel shift of the budget constraint. If leisure is a normal good, the new equilibrium will occur at a point like E_d, with lower labour supply than the original E_0. Income will not rise by the full value of the demogrant. This would only occur if E_1 were the optimal choice, with hours of work unchanged. But this cannot happen if leisure is normal.

Welfare

In Canada, **welfare** or **social assistance** programs are administered by the provinces but financed partly (approximately 50 percent) by the federal government under the Canada Health and Social Transfer program. This funding arrangement, implemented in 1995, replaced the Canada Assistance Plan (CAP) that had previously been the avenue for federal-provincial cost-sharing for social assistance. Benefits vary by province and according to other factors such as family type (single parent, couple) and employability. Welfare benefits also depend on the needs of the family and the family's assets and other sources of income. As illustrated in Table 3.1, the total income (including welfare payments) of single parents with one child tends to be about 59 percent of the poverty-line level of income with considerable variation by provinces.

For those who are eligible for welfare their new potential income constraint is given by the dashed line in Figure 3.2. If they do not work, they are given the welfare payment. Hence, at the point of maximum leisure (zero work), their income constraint shifts vertically upward by the amount of the welfare payment. Under some welfare programs, as individuals work and receive labour market earnings they are required to forgo welfare payments by the exact amount of their labour market earnings. In this sense, there is a 100 percent tax on earnings. In fact, the implicit tax may even be greater than 100 percent, if, for example, they also lose medical or housing subsidies. Their potential income constraint is thus horizontal at the amount of the welfare payment: as they work and earn income, they forgo a comparable amount in welfare and hence their income does not increase. Every dollar earned results in a dollar reduction in welfare. Of course, once they reach their original labour market wage constraint, then their take-home pay will be indicated by their original wage constraint: at this point their welfare payments have been reduced to zero so they cannot be "taxed" any further by being required to give up welfare.

Table 3.1 Income[a] of Welfare Recipients by Province, 1999 (single parent, one child)

Province	Annual Income ($)	Income as % of Poverty Line[b]
Newfoundland	13,924	70
Prince Edward Island	11,670	60
Nova Scotia	12,558	63
New Brunswick	12,319	62
Quebec	12,957	57
Ontario	13,704	60
Manitoba	11,328	50
Saskatchewan	11,877	59
Alberta	11,375	50
British Columbia	13,661	60
Average (unweighted)	12,537	59

Notes:

a. Includes basic social assistance (welfare), additional benefits, child tax benefit, provincial tax credits, provincial child benefits, and GST credit.

b. Statistics Canada's low-income cutoffs.

Source: National Council of Welfare. *Revenus de bien-être social 1999* (Ottawa: National Council of Welfare, 2000). Available online, accessed September 17, 2001 <www.ncwcnbes.net/htmdocument/reportwelincome/repwelincome.htm>.

Figure 3.2 **Work Incentive Effects of a Welfare Benefit with 100 Percent "Clawback"**

Without a welfare program, E_0 is the optimal choice, and the person works. With welfare, the person receives a fixed level of income, irrespective of hours worked. From zero hours worked, wage earnings net of reduced welfare benefits are zero, and there are no returns to working (until benefits are exhausted). The optimal choice would thus be E_W, and nonparticipation.

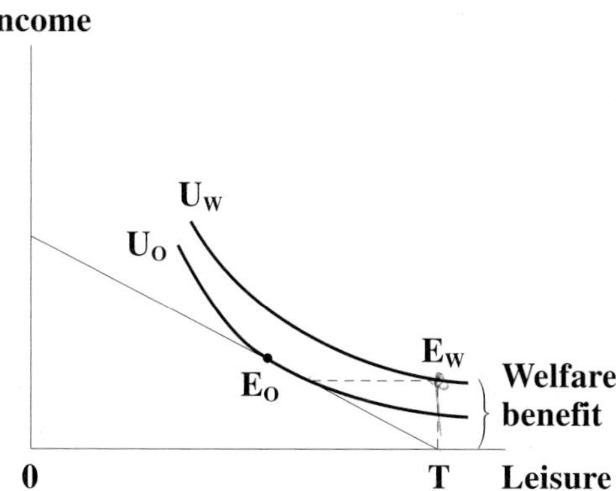

If the welfare payment is sufficiently high, the individual would have a strong incentive to move to the corner solution at E_w where he would not work at all. There is no incentive to work more (move to the left of E_w), because of the 100 percent implicit tax on income from work that arises because the individual has to give up an equivalent amount of welfare for every dollar earned. Even though the person's take-home pay, Y, is lower at E_w than E_0, he chooses E_w because it involves considerably more leisure. Clearly welfare has extreme potential adverse effects on work incentives. Of course, for many people on welfare, work is not a viable alternative if they are perhaps disabled or unemployable. Yet for others, work would be a viable alternative if there would not be this 100 percent implicit tax on earned income.

This analysis suggests a variety of ways of reducing the number of people on welfare. Traditionally we think of making eligibility requirements more stringent or reducing the magnitude of welfare for those who are eligible. These changes would, of course, work. In Figure 3.3(a), for example, if the welfare payment were lowered to an amount lower than the height of U_0 at the point of maximum leisure, there would be no incentive to go on welfare since the individual would be maximizing utility at E_0. Although successful in reducing the number of people on welfare, these changes may have undesirable side effects, not the least of which are denying welfare to those in need and providing inadequate income support to those who are unemployable.

One alternative to these policies would be to increase the market wage rate of those on welfare and thereby encourage them to voluntarily leave welfare and earn income. In Figure 3.3(b), an increase in the market wage rate would pivot the wage constraint upwards from T. At some higher wage rate, the individual clearly would be induced to move to a higher indifference curve that would involve more work effort than under welfare (i.e., a new equilibrium to the left of E_w, E_1). The increased market wage could come about through training, job information, mobility, a government wage subsidy, or institutional pressures such as minimum wages or unionization. Obviously these policies may be costly, or in the case of minimum wages and unionization may involve a loss of jobs. However, they could have the benefit of voluntarily reducing the number of people on welfare and hence increasing work incentives.

Another way of improving work incentives would be to reduce the 100 percent implicit tax on welfare. In most welfare programs, this is accomplished by requiring welfare recipients to give up only a portion of their welfare if they earn income by working. For example, if recipients are required to give up 50 cents in welfare for every dollar earned in the labour market, they would have some incentive to work because the implicit tax rate

Figure 3.3

Other Work Incentive Effects of Welfare Programs

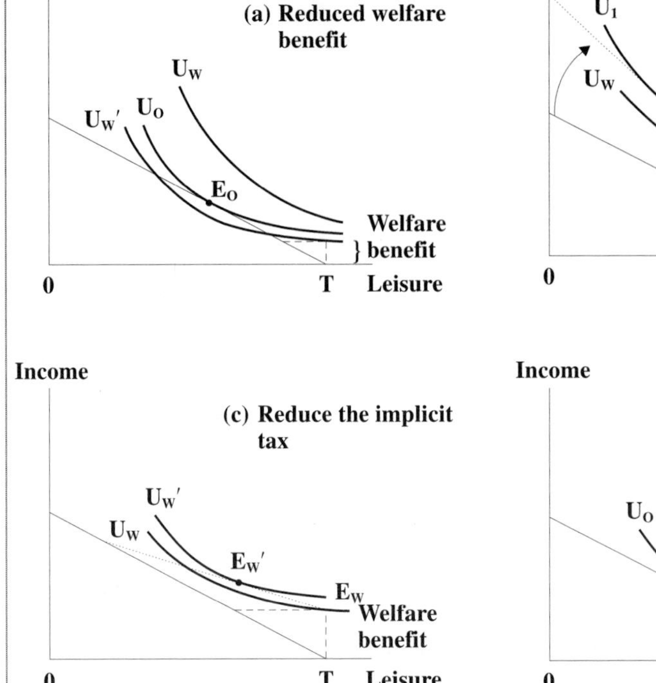

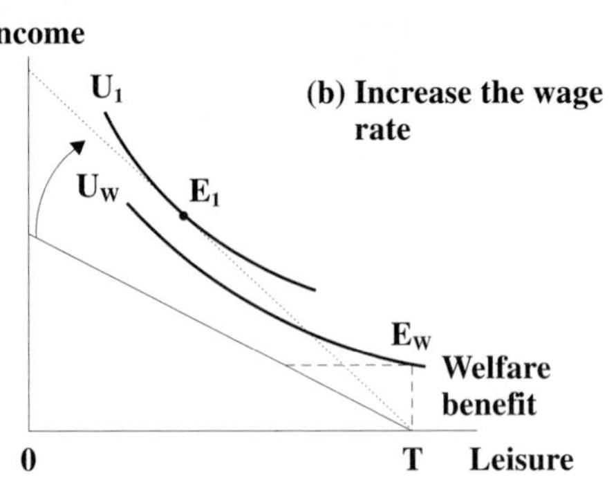

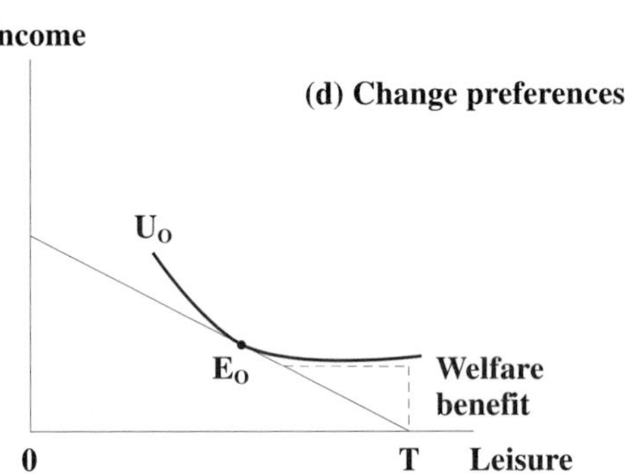

Changes can be made to the welfare program depicted in Figure 3.2 to improve work incentives. In (a), the benefit is reduced so that nonparticipation yields U_w, and the person prefers working E_0. In (b), a higher wage rate can make working more attractive, as E_1 yields utility U_1 versus U_w. In (c), the implicit tax is reduced so that the welfare recipient can keep some of her earnings. This increase in the returns to work can lead to participation at E_w'. In (d), we see the case where sufficient stigma (for example) is attached to being on welfare, so that E_0 is the preferred choice.

would be 50 percent. In Figure 3.3(c), this could be shown by a wage constraint starting at E_w, with a negative slope of 50 percent of the slope of the labour market wage constraint, reflecting the fact that the recipient takes home 50 percent of every dollar earned by working. The negative income tax, discussed below, is a general scheme designed to ensure that individuals receiving income support face an implicit tax on income from work that is significantly less than 100 percent.

An alternative solution to reducing the number of welfare recipients would be to alter the preferences of welfare recipients away from being on welfare and toward labour market activity. In Figure 3.3(d), this would imply changing the shape of the indifference curves. If, for example, at all points to the right of E_0, the indifference curve U_0 were flat, then the individual would not have opted for the welfare equilibrium E_w. The flat indifference curve would indicate a reluctance to accept any cut in income even to get substantial increases in leisure. Traditionally, preferences have been altered by attaching a social stigma to being on welfare. Alternatively, preferences could be altered toward income-earning activities, perhaps by making potential recipients feel more a part of the nonwelfare society or perhaps by attempting to break the intergenerational cycle of welfare.

Recently, welfare reform has also emphasized the distinction between "employables" and "nonemployables" and has often set a requirement that the employables work or be registered in a training program as a condition of eligibility for the receipt of welfare. Such programs—termed *workfare*—have often been directed at single-parent families, given their potential to engage in paid employment. One of the problems, of course, is that this can entail expensive daycare requirements that may be added to the welfare expenses. Nevertheless, it may encourage work incentives as well as the longer-run employability of recipients by providing them with work experience or training.

Negative Income Tax

Negative income tax or guaranteed annual income plans involve an income guarantee, and an implicit tax rate of less than 100 percent applied to labour market earnings. Income after taxes and transfers would be $Y = G + (1 - t)E$, where G is the basic guarantee, t is the implicit tax rate, and Y and E as defined earlier are take-home pay and labour market earnings respectively. Most negative income tax plans differ in so far as they involve different values of the basic guarantee and the tax rate. The term *negative* income tax is used because recipients will receive more from the guarantee than they will pay out in taxes, even though they do face a positive implicit tax rate. Guaranteed annual income schemes have frequently been proposed by policy analysts from a variety of political perspectives.[2]

www.hrdc-drhc.gc.ca/isp/oas/ispb184.shtml

Although a comprehensive guaranteed annual income program has never been implemented in Canada, some programs which apply to particular groups—for example, the Child Tax Credit, which supplements the income of families with children, and the Guaranteed Income Supplement, which supplements the income of individuals over 65—have the negative income tax design. That is, there is a basic guarantee received by those with income below a certain level; those with higher income receive less income supplementation according to the program's implicit tax rate; and those whose income exceeds the program's breakeven point receive no benefits.

A negative income tax plan with a constant rate is illustrated by the dashed line in Figure 3.4. As with the demogrant, at the point of maximum leisure the basic income guarantee shifts the potential income constraint upward by the amount of the guarantee: even if the individual does not work, she has positive income equal to the amount of the guarantee. Unlike welfare, as the individual works, income assistance is not reduced by the full amount of labour market earnings. However, income support does decline as income from work increases; thus labour market earnings are subject to a positive implicit tax rate. Take-home pay does not rise as fast as labour market earnings; hence, the income constraint under the negative income tax plan is less steeply sloped than the original labour market income constraint. At the point B, often referred to as the breakeven point, income received from the negative income tax program has declined to zero. Thus to the left of this point the original income constraint applies.

Assuming leisure is a normal good, the new equilibrium for recipients of the negative income tax plan will unambiguously lie to the right of the original equilibrium: work incentives are unambiguously reduced relative to a situation in which there is no other form of income support. This occurs because the income and substitution effects both work in the same direction to reduce work effort. The tax increase on earned income reduces the relative price of leisure, inducing a substitution into leisure and hence reducing work effort. The tax increase also has an income effect (working in the opposite direction); however, for *recipients* this is outweighed by the guarantee, so that on net their new potential income constraint is always above the original constraint—that is why they are defined as recipients. Because the potential income of recipients is increased, they will buy more of all normal goods including leisure. Thus the income effect works in the same direction as the substitution effect to reduce work effort.

The income-leisure choice framework predicts that work incentives will be unambiguously reduced as a result of a negative income tax plan. But this does not negate the

[2]In one of the most comprehensive studies of its kind, the 1985 Report of the Royal Commission on the Economic Union and Development Prospects for Canada (the Macdonald Commission) recommended fundamental reform of existing income maintenance programs. The centrepiece of its proposal was the Universal Income Security Program (UISP), a negative income tax program that would supplement the income of families with low incomes.

Figure 3.4 **Work Incentive Effects of a Negative Income Tax**

A negative income tax is a welfare program with a less than 100 percent tax-back rate. Such a program will reduce work incentives (compared to no program). The guarantee level, G, shifts out the budget constraint, producing a work-reducing income effect. Leisure is also cheaper, (1 - t)W as against W, so the substitution effect will lead to fewer hours worked. No benefit is received when income is higher than the breakeven level, B.

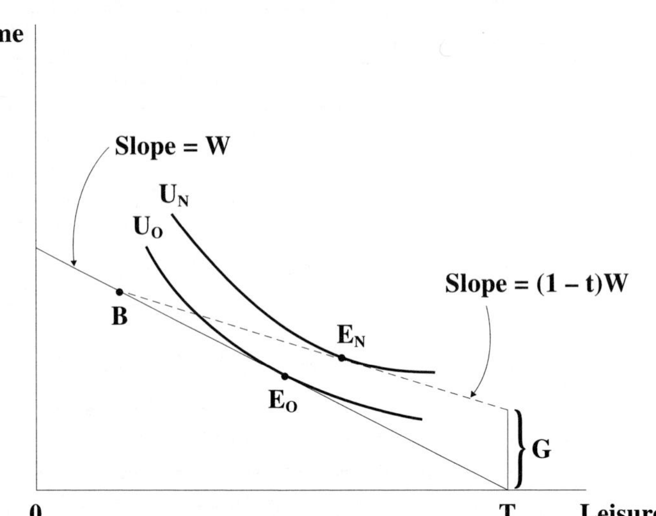

viability of such a program. The adverse work incentive effects may be small, or the increased "leisure" may be used productively as in job search, mobility, education, or increased household activities. In addition, the reduction in labour supply may have other desirable side effects, such as raising the wages of low-wage labour since it is now a relatively scarcer factor of production. Perhaps most importantly, the adverse incentive effects were predicted when a negative income tax was imposed in a world without other taxes and transfers. In most circumstances a negative income tax scheme is intended to replace some welfare programs which have even larger adverse incentive effects. In this sense work incentives may increase relative to incentives under welfare (as will be discussed in more detail in subsequent sections). While the basic conclusions from the work-leisure model should not be ignored, they must be kept in proper perspective. Empirical information is needed on the magnitude of any adverse work incentive effects and on the form in which "leisure" is taken. In addition, the effects on work incentives will depend on the programs that the negative income tax scheme is intended to replace.

Wage Subsidy

Since one of the problems with the negative income tax and welfare is that the tax on earnings may discourage work effort, some have suggested that rather than tax additional earnings, the government should subsidize wages in an attempt to encourage work. Although there are a variety of forms of a **wage subsidy**—most often associated with the proposals of Kesselman (1969, 1971, 1973)—the simplest wage subsidy schemes have the common result that the recipient's per-hour wage rate is supplemented by a government subsidy.

The static, partial equilibrium effect of the wage subsidy is illustrated by the dashed line in Figure 3.5. For the recipients, it is exactly like a wage increase; hence, the potential income constraint rotates upward from the point of maximum leisure T. If the person does not work (i.e., is at T), his income is still zero even though his wage is subsidized. However, as the person works more, his take-home pay rises more under the wage subsidy than if he were only receiving his market wage.

Just as an increase in wages has both an income and a substitution effect working in opposite directions insofar as they affect work incentives, so will the wage subsidy have an ambiguous effect on work incentives. The higher wage means higher potential income from which the individual will buy more of all normal goods, including leisure; hence, work incentives are reduced via the income effect. This income effect will be at work even though the individual has to work to receive the income: the increased leisure could come in the form of reduced hours or longer vacations or periodic withdrawals from the labour force or reduced work from another family member. The higher wage also means that the price (opportunity cost) of leisure has now increased; hence, work incentives are increased via this substitution effect. On net, theory does not indicate which effect dominates; hence the work incentive effects of a wage subsidy are ultimately an empirical proposition.

Although the work incentive effects of a wage subsidy are theoretically indeterminant, other things being equal (the recipients' welfare, their post-transfer income, or the size of the subsidy), the adverse work incentive effects of the wage subsidy are not as great as those of the negative income tax. This is illustrated in Figure 3.6 for the case where the recipients' welfare is held constant at U_0 so that they are indifferent between the two plans. The equilibrium E_S under the wage subsidy *must* lie to the left of the equilibrium E_N under the negative income tax. That is so because the potential income constraint under the wage subsidy is steeper than the negative income tax constraint since it involves a net subsidy to the wage of recipients. Since the wage subsidy constraint must be tangent to U_0 in order for the recipients to be indifferent between the two plans, this tangency must be to the left of E_N because only to the left of E_N is the indifference curve more steeply sloped than at E_N (when we have less leisure, more income is required to give up a unit of leisure and remain indifferent).

Although the work incentive effects are greater under a wage subsidy than a negative income tax, this does not necessarily make the wage subsidy a better plan. One distinct disadvantage of the wage subsidy is that it does nothing to maintain the income of those who are unable to work. Although it may help the working poor, it does nothing to help those who legitimately cannot work. For the latter group, a negative income tax plan would at least provide a guaranteed minimum income. It would also be possible to have both plans and allow individuals to choose between them.

Figure 3.5 **Work Incentive Effects of a Wage Subsidy**

The work incentives of a wage subsidy are the same as for a wage increase: the work-inducing substitution effect may be offset by the income effect (as it is here, in the movement from E_0 to E_S).

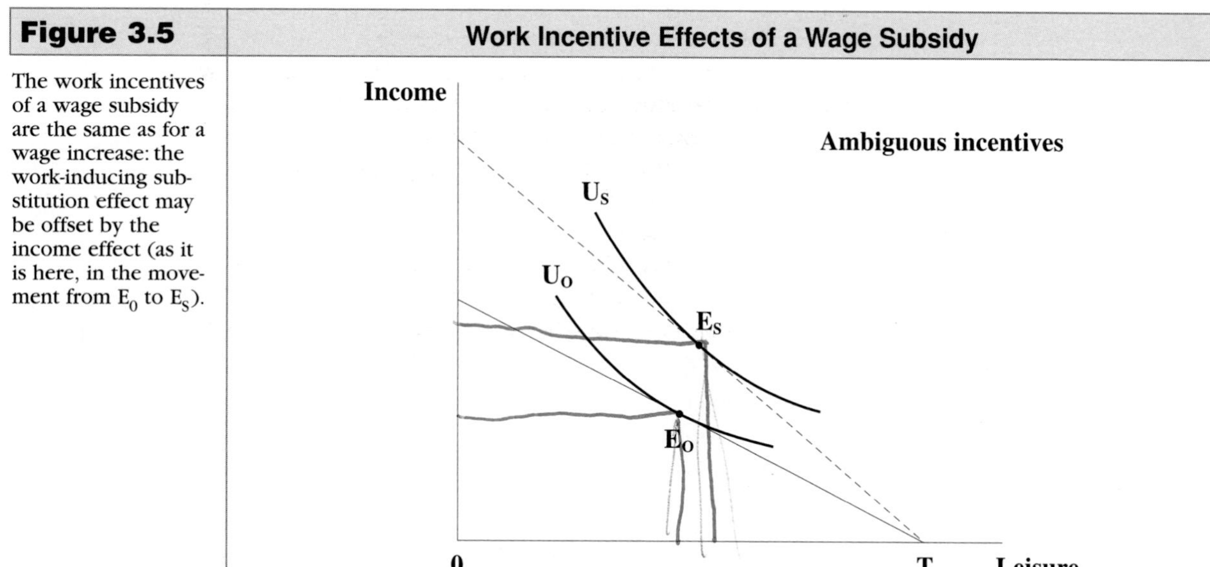

Figure 3.6 **Work Incentive Effects of Wage Subsidy Versus Negative Income Tax**

A negative income tax or wage subsidy can be used to support an individual to utility level U. However, the higher price of leisure (returns to work) with the wage subsidy will unambiguously lead the person to work more.

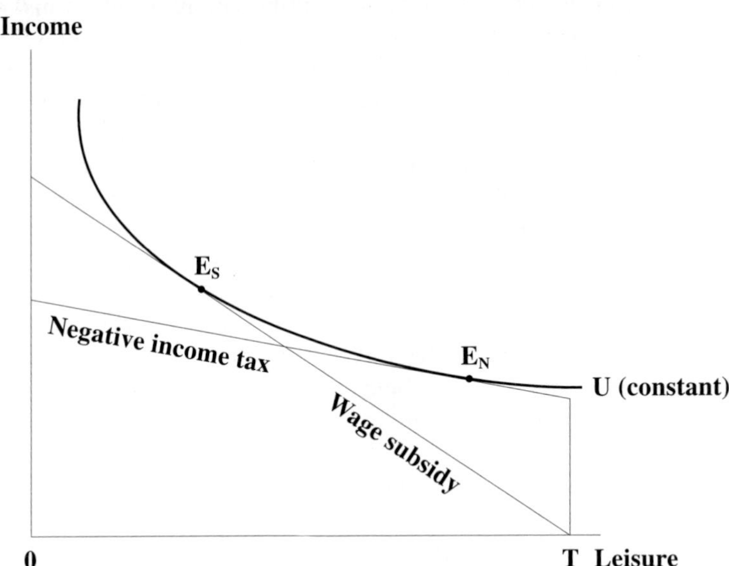

Because funds for income assistance are limited, an important aspect of an income maintenance scheme is the extent to which the program helps those most in need of assistance. Poverty and need are usually defined in terms of family income. For this reason, the negative income tax, which is based upon family income, is more likely to target payments to those in greatest need than a wage subsidy, which is based on individual wage rates. Many low-wage earners—especially youth and spouses of the primary income earner—are members of families with average or above-average income, resulting in a weak association between low individual wages and low family income. Hum and Simpson (1991) compare negative income tax and wage subsidy programs with equal budgets using micro-data on Canadian families in 1981. They conclude that the negative income tax is clearly superior to wage subsidies in terms of its ability to divert payments to those families in greatest need of assistance.

Unemployment Insurance

Unemployment insurance (now called "employment insurance") is the largest single income security program in the country, covering approximately 92 percent of the labour force.[3] UI also accounts for about one-third of non-old-age-related income security expenditure. The replacement rate is 55 percent of lost earnings (subject to a maximum) with the benefit duration ranging from 14 to 45 weeks, depending upon the rate of unemployment in the region. In order to qualify for the benefits, individuals must have worked 420 to 700 hours, the equivalent of 12 to 20 weeks at 35 hours per week, again depending on the unemployment rate of the region.

The income-leisure choice framework can be used to analyze the static, partial equilibrium effect that unemployment insurance will have on work incentives. The theoretical impact of these features of the UI system can be captured by a stylized example of an unemployment insurance scheme that gives recipients 60 percent of their weekly pay for

[3]Throughout this book, we refer to the generic program as "UI," and the specific Canadian program as "EI."

a maximum period of 20 weeks, and that requires a minimum of 14 weeks of employment in order to qualify for benefits.

This hypothetical scheme is illustrated in Figure 3.7, using a one-year time horizon. The solid line AF is the potential income constraint in the absence of a UI program, and the line ABCDF, including the dashed segment ABCD, is the constraint with unemployment insurance. If the individual works less than 14 weeks during the year, he does not qualify for UI benefits and his income constraint is the segment DF. If the individual works 14 weeks, he is eligible for benefits for an additional 20 weeks; thus his income at 14 weeks of work equals his labour market earnings for the 14 weeks plus 20 times 60 percent of his normal weekly wage earnings. His annual income would be Y = 14W + (0.60)20W, where W is weekly wage earnings. This gives the point C in Figure 3.7, the vertical distance equalling (0.60)20W.

As the person works additional weeks (moves from right to left from the point C) he can earn his weekly earnings as well as his unemployment insurance, at least for some period of time. Because he cannot legally work and collect unemployment insurance at the same time, he will reach a point where a week's work "costs" him a week of collecting UI. For example, if he works 50 weeks, he can only collect UI for the two remaining weeks of the year. Any week worked that reduces his 20 weeks of eligible UI collection thus has an additional opportunity cost. So, as long as he does not reduce his entitlement to collect UI benefits, the slope of the income constraint from point C is parallel to the original wage constraint. He can collect his full UI benefits, as well as earn W per week worked. His UI entitlement is reduced as soon as weeks of leisure falls below 20. Thus, this parallel component of the budget constraint is the segment from C to B, at 20 weeks of leisure.

Figure 3.7 **Income Constraint for a Simplified Unemployment Insurance Scheme**

The work incentive effects of unemployment insurance (UI) depend on the original equilibrium. No benefits can be collected until the individual labour supply is at least 14 weeks, so, for some individuals, point C will be preferred to point F (nonparticipation). In the intermediate case, UI benefits provide a pure income effect (once maximum benefits of 20W are earned), so that labour supply will be reduced from c to d. For individuals working more than 32 weeks, each additional week worked reduces potential UI benefits by 0.6W, so the net wage is only 0.4W. This generates a work-reducing substitution effect, so that labour supply may fall from a to b.

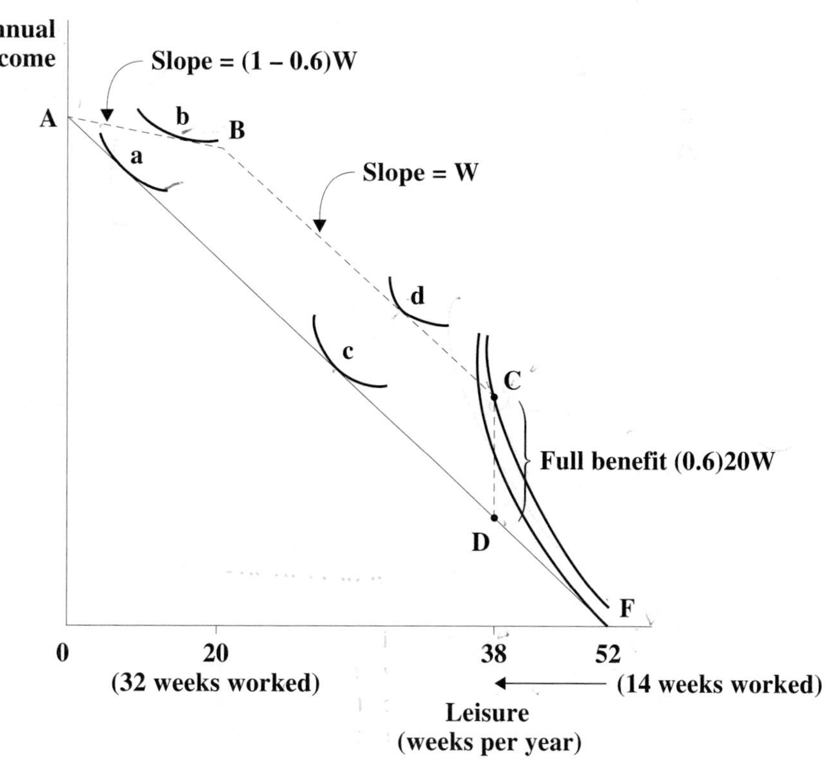

After working 32 weeks, available "leisure," or time for collecting UI is reduced. Thus, the returns to working are less than the wage. Between 32 and 52 weeks worked, the return to working is the labour market earnings minus the forgone UI benefits. Since one week's benefits are equal to 0.6W, the returns to working an additional week over this portion of the budget constraint is W − 0.6W, or 0.4W. This segment is labelled AB in Figure 3.7.

The nature of the work incentive effects of unemployment insurance depend on where the individual would be located in the absence of the UI system. Three different possibilities are shown in Figure 3.7. For individuals working more than 32 weeks (e.g., at the point a on AF), the income and substitution effects work in the same direction to *potentially* decrease weeks worked (moving to the point B on AB). For individuals such as those originally at the point c on AF, the unemployment insurance system constitutes a pure income effect, again *potentially* decreasing work incentives (moving to the point d on BC). These adverse work incentive effects are potential because the vast majority of people will not collect unemployment insurance. Many employees would not leave their job because they may not be able to return once they have exhausted unemployment insurance. However, for those with a guaranteed or reasonably certain job—be it seasonal, or with family friends, or in household activity, or perhaps one of many low-paid dead-end jobs that cannot attract other workers—there may be an incentive to collect employment insurance. In addition, the incentive would certainly be there for those who have lost their job, perhaps because of a recessionary phase in the business cycle, and hence who have no labour market alternatives.

The third possibility illustrated in Figure 3.7 applies to individuals who would be outside the labour force in the absence of a UI program. These individuals are originally located at the point F, reflecting the high value of their time devoted to nonmarket activities. Many such individuals would choose to remain outside the labour force and neither work nor collect unemployment insurance. Others, however, would enter the labour force and work a sufficient number of weeks in order to qualify for unemployment insurance benefits, locating at the point C in Figure 3.7. In this case the UI program has *increased* work incentives by making it attractive for these individuals to devote less time to nonmarket activities and to enter the labour force for relatively brief periods. Similar conclusions apply to those who would work fewer than 14 weeks in the absence of a UI system (i.e., those who would be located in the segment DF).

The previous discussion of the incentive effects of unemployment insurance—as with other income maintenance programs—assumes that if individuals want to increase their labour supply, the jobs are available for them to do so. However, in regions or periods of high unemployment this may be an unrealistic assumption. Individuals may be constrained by the lack of jobs on the demand side. Phipps (1990, 1991) shows that both theoretically and empirically, this can have an important effect in altering the work incentive effects of income maintenance programs like unemployment insurance. Specifically, reforms to UI to increase work incentives may be thwarted, in part at least, by the fact that increasing the *incentive* to work (a supply-side phenomenon) does not guarantee that more people will work, if the jobs are not available (a demand-side phenomenon).

In summary, work incentives may be either increased or decreased by unemployment insurance. Some of those individuals who would, in the absence of a UI system, either be outside the labour force or work fewer weeks than are required to qualify for UI benefits will increase their weeks worked per year in order to receive unemployment insurance. In contrast, some of those individuals who would, in the absence of a UI system, work more than the minimum number of weeks required to qualify for UI will reduce their weeks worked per year and increase the number of weeks during which unemployment insurance benefits are received. Both these consequences of unemployment insurance may increase the unemployment rate, the former because it draws into the labour force individuals with marginal employment attachments who devote much of their time to non-market activities, and the latter because it reduces employment and increases unemployment of those with strong labour force attachment. The impact of the unemployment insurance system on unemployment is discussed further in the chapter on unemployment.

Unemployment-Insurance-Assisted Worksharing

As defined in Meltz, Reid, and Swartz (1981, 3), **worksharing** "is an attempt to combat unemployment by reducing the number of hours each employee works rather than laying employees off when there is a reduction in the demand for labour." In the context of unemployment insurance (UI)-assisted worksharing, the rationale was to encourage the sharing of unemployment among a broader work force rather than having it concentrated in the hands of a few. As pointed out by Reid (1982, 1985) this could be not only more equitable but also more efficient if the larger work force willingly accepted unemployment insurance payments for a small reduction in its work week. Whether UI-assisted worksharing is a socially desirable method of combating unemployment depends on a number of factors such as whether the reduction in demand is temporary or permanent in nature, how the total UI costs associated with the reduction in labour demand are affected, and how the UI program is financed. These issues are discussed further in the chapter on unemployment. Rather than having the unemployment concentrated, for example, in 20 percent of the work force who may be laid off (and receiving unemployment insurance), under UI-assisted worksharing the whole work force of the firm may willingly accept a 20 percent (e.g., one day per week) reduction in their work in return for receiving unemployment insurance for the one day that they are each engaging in worksharing. This, of course, would require modification of the conventional unemployment insurance rules which are based on continuous unemployment, not on being "unemployed" for one day per week.

In 1977 on an experimental basis, and in 1982 on an economy-wide basis, Canada modified its unemployment insurance scheme to allow firms to apply for unemployment insurance for its work force that willing engaged in such worksharing. The scheme, discussed in Reid (1982, 1985) and Gray (2000), basically provides unemployment insurance benefits for giving up an average of one day of work per week so that other workers in the firm would not have to be laid off.

Such an unemployment-insurance-assisted worksharing scheme is illustrated in Figure 3.8, assuming UI benefits (i.e., the replacement rate) to be 60 percent of earnings. The initial equilibrium at E_0 shows a hypothetical situation for a representative worker who works five days per week and takes home a weekly income of Y_0. An unemployment-insurance-assisted worksharing scheme that would allow each worker to choose any amount of work reduction would be illustrated by the dashed-line budget constraint above the original budget constraint. For any work reduction (i.e., movement to the right of E_0) income would not fall by the loss of a day's pay for every day of work reduction, as would be depicted by the original budget constraint. Rather, it would fall by only 40 percent since 60 percent would be supported by the receipt of unemployment insurance. Figure 3.8 depicts the case where the parties agree to a one-day reduction in the work week, and shows that this corresponds to the typical worker's preferred reduction (i.e., E_S is an equilibrium).

In reality, the negotiated reduction need not always correspond to the preferences of the work force, in which case E_S need not be tangent to the new budget constraint; however, it is likely to involve a higher level of utility (i.e., $U_S > U_0$) because the worker gets an extra day of leisure by giving up only 40 percent of a day's pay, the remainder coming from unemployment insurance. Clearly, the unemployment-insurance-assisted worksharing can provide an incentive for workers to voluntarily reduce their working time and enter into

Figure 3.8 **Unemployment-Insurance-Assisted Worksharing**

UI-assisted worksharing can be used to induce someone to voluntarily reduce hours worked. If an individual is originally working five days per week (at E_0), he can be offered UI benefits of 0.6W if he reduces labour supply to four days. The income and substitution effects of this offer will both lead to a reduction in labour supply. In this example, E_S is the optimal days worked under worksharing.

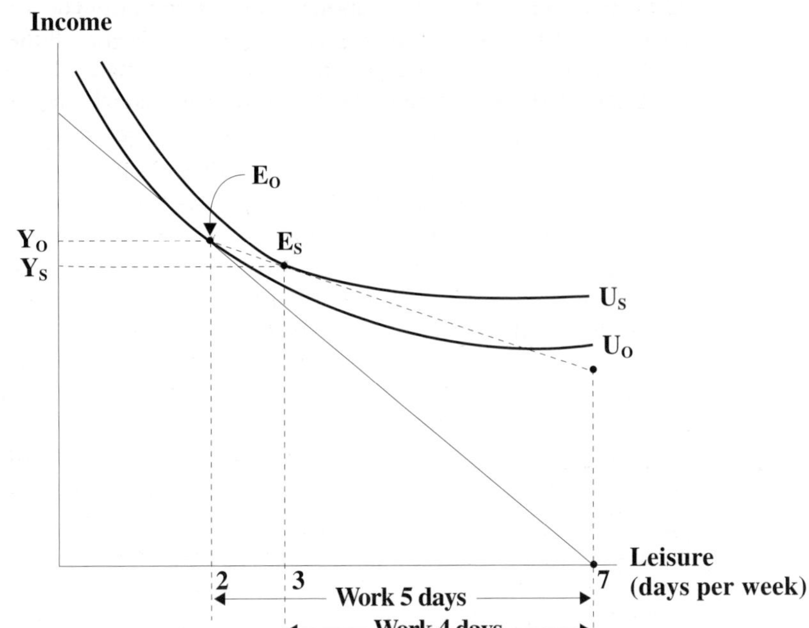

worksharing arrangements. Gray (2000) provides more discussion of worksharing, and we discuss it in more detail in Chapter 6.

Disability Payments and Workers' Compensation

Income maintenance programs for the disabled also exist in a variety of forms such as workers' compensation, disability pension entitlements from public and private pensions, long-term disability insurance (with premiums usually paid from joint contributions from employers and employees), and court awards for personal injury. In most cases, of course, the work incentive effects of such income maintenance programs are not of interest as payment is made precisely because the disability legitimately prevents a person from working and the person may have little discretion over how much to work. In some cases, however, there may be more discretion over whether to work and if so, how much to work or when to return to work. In such cases, the work incentive effects of disability income maintenance programs become a legitimate policy concern.

Prior to examining the impact of disability compensation, it is informative to examine the effect of the disability or injury itself.

Effect of Disability on Budget Constraint Depending upon its nature, the injury may have a number of different effects on the individual's budget constraint (i.e., ability to earn income). A partially disabling injury could reduce the amount of time the individual can spend at the job, but not affect the person's performance and hence wage at the job. This is illustrated in Figure 3.9(a). Without any disabling injury, the worker's choice set is YH_f, given the market wage rate as illustrated by the slope of the budget constraint. In this particular case the worker chooses E_0 with corresponding utility of U_0 and hours of work (measured right to left) of H_0. The partially disabling injury, for example, could reduce the amount of time the worker is able to work from H_0 to H_p. The worker's choice set is now limited to E_pH_f with a corresponding drop in utility to U_p. If the injury were completely disabling so that the person could not work at all, then the person would be constrained to H_f, with no labour market income and utility reduced to U_f. This again highlights the misnomer associated with the phrase "leisure"—it is a catchall for all activities outside of the labour market, ranging from pure leisure to being unable to work because of disability.

In addition to affecting one's ability to earn income, a disabling injury may also require medical expenses. This affects the budget constraint, reducing income by the amount of medical expenses at each level of hours of work, analogous to a reduction in nonlabour income. If the disabling injury led to such medical expenses but did not affect one's wage or ability to work in the labour market, then this would lead to a lower budget constraint like the dashed line Y_mM in Figure 3.9(b). The individual's wage is not affected (i.e., Y_mM is parallel to YH_f), and the individual can work as much as before (i.e., Y_mM is the full-choice set); however, there are some fixed medical costs equal to H_fM which also equals YY_m. If the individual does not work (i.e., the injury is a full disability so that the individual is compelled to move to H_f), then the medical costs are debts, as illustrated by the point M being below the axis (i.e., income is negative).

Because such fixed costs associated with medical expenses shift the budget constraint inward without altering its slope, they will have a pure income effect, unambiguously reducing leisure and increasing hours of work, assuming leisure to be a normal commodity. The reduction in wealth associated with the injury cost means the household will buy less of all normal commodities, including leisure. Alternatively stated, the additional expenses mean that the individual would have to work more to prevent expenditure on goods from falling by the full amount of the medical expenses. This is illustrated in Figure 3.9(b) by the equilibrium E_m with its associated level of utility U_m, where E_m is to the left of E_0 and U_m is less than U_0.

If, in addition to these fixed medical costs, the injury also prevented the person from doing any labour market work, then the segment Y_mM of the budget constraint would not be available. In effect, the individual's "choice" set would be point M, with the corresponding reduced utility level U_f.

A disability that reduced one's ability to earn wages in the labour market would rotate the budget constraint downward as in Figure 3.9(c). This would give rise to conventional income and substitution effects and hence have an indeterminate effect on hours of work. That is, the returns to work are reduced and hence one would work less (substitution effect). But one's wealth is also decreased, hence reducing one's ability to purchase commodities including leisure, thereby inducing more work (income effect).

A disability may also have a differential effect on the disutility associated with work or the ability to enjoy non-labour market activities. For example, if the disability gave rise to more pain and suffering associated with labour market activities than with household work, it would rotate the household utility isoquant as in Figure 3.9(d) so that the indifference curves U_d' and U_d'' are steeper in the disabled state, U_d', than in the nondisabled state, U_0. That is, to remain at the same level of utility, the disabled individual would require more income in return for a given increase in hours of work. For a given market wage rate (as given by the slope of the budget constraint) this would induce a substitution from labour market to non-labour market activities, reducing worktime from H_0 to H_d (work being measured from right to left on the diagram).

Obviously a disability may have a variety of the above effects. They were treated separately here only for expositional purposes. It is a relatively straightforward matter to portray them in various realistic combinations. For example, the disability may reduce the time one is able to work, reduce the wage, impose medical costs, and increase the disutility associated with labour market work as opposed to other activities. In such circumstances, the budget constraint and utility isoquants will change to reflect each of these effects and the incentive to work will be affected accordingly.

Figure 3.9

Effect of Disability

The effect of a disability can be incorporated into the work decision in a variety of ways. In panel (a), the individual's potential working time is reduced to a maximum of H_P or H_F under partial or full disability; in (b), the disability generates fixed medical costs, which have a pure (negative) income effect, leading the person to work more; in (c), the disability reduces productivity, and has the same effect as a reduction in wages; In (d), the worker's opportunity set remains unchanged, but the disutility of work increases. Indifference curves become steeper at H_0 (from U_0 to U_d') and desired work falls to H_d.

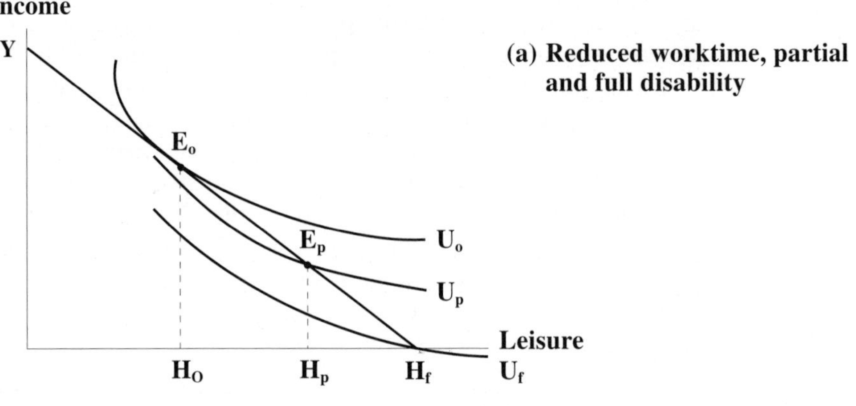

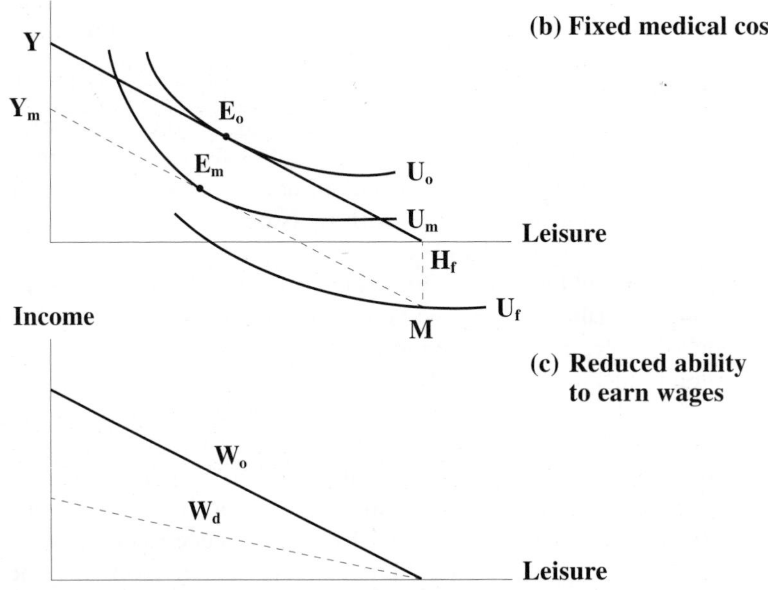

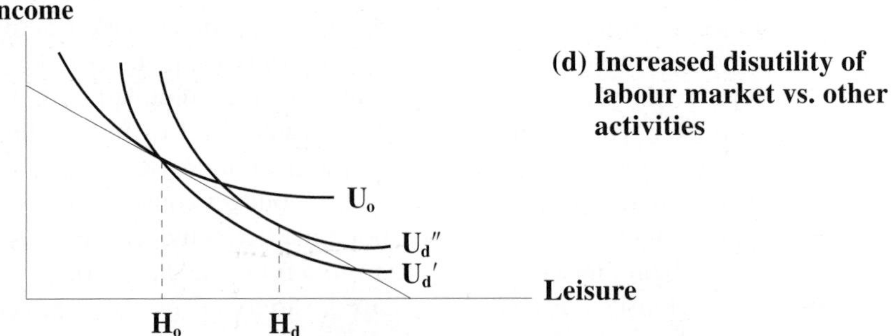

Effect of Compensation To compensate for the previously discussed type of disability, various forms of compensation exist including workers' compensation, disability pension entitlements from public and private pensions, long-term disability insurance, and court awards. The effect of such compensations upon well-being or utility and work incentives depends upon the form of compensation.

Workers' compensation, for instance, is designed to support the recipient's income so it is not reduced by as much as it would be in the absence of the compensation. For example, it may compensate for two-thirds of the loss in one's former potential income, in which case the worker's compensation budget constraint appears as the dashed line $E_0Y_dH_f$ in Figure 3.10(a). That is, as the worker is compelled to reduce work activity (move to the right of E_0), income does not fall by the full drop in take-home pay (as it would along E_0H_f), but rather it falls by the proportion that it is not supported by workers' compensation. If workers' compensation were two-thirds of one's income loss then the fall in income would be one-third.

The policy challenge is to design a compensation scheme that compensates those who are legitimately disabled and hence in need of compensation and yet provides an incentive for them to return to work where feasible. The potential for an adverse work incentive effect for those who could legitimately return to work is exhibited by the fact that the workers' compensation budget constraint is like the previously discussed budget constraint under a negative income tax. That is, the additional income enables one to afford to work less (income effect); further, the reduced opportunity cost of leisure time that comes about because one forgoes disability payments as one increases hours of work (substitution effect) also discourages work activity. Obviously, for those who have no discretion over their ability to engage in more work activity, the incentive effects are not at issue. For some, however, they may discourage a return to work activity that they are capable of doing.

The availability of the full budget constraint $E_0Y_dH_f$ presupposes that such compensation is available for any combination of partial disabilities that would reduce the person's work between H_0 and H_f. That is, depending upon preferences, workers could locate anywhere along the segment E_0Y_d. If the compensation were available only if one could prove full disability, H_f, then the worker's options would be only the points Y_d and E_0. Assuming Y_d were above the indifference curve, U_0, as shown in Figure 3.10(a), then the worker would choose the point Y_d.

Figure 3.10(b) illustrates such a situation where the worker receives workers' compensation for the full disability and has no incentive to return to work, assuming of course that such an option were feasible. The compensation (E_cH_f) is such that the worker is better off by not working, and receiving the compensation (point E_c) than by returning to work (point E_0). That is, utility under compensation (U_c) is greater than utility under work (U_0). Even though income by working would be greater than income under compensation, it is not sufficient to offset the disutility associated with the additional work.

However, not providing any compensation runs the risk that individuals who legitimately cannot return to work have their utility level reduced to U_f. Clearly, lowering the compensation level so that U_c is below U_0 would induce a return to work from those who can legitimately engage in such work; however, it runs the risk of penalizing those who legitimately cannot return to work. Also, when one considers the considerable medical costs and pain and suffering that are often associated with disability, it becomes less likely that compensating someone for a portion of their lost earnings would make them better off.

Different amounts of compensation are also involved depending upon the position to which the recipient is to be returned. Figure 3.10(c) illustrates the situation where a permanently disabling injury prevents the individual from working at all (i.e., forces the individual to locate at H_f) and gives rise to medical costs of H_fM. These events reduce the

Figure 3.10 **Effect of Compensation**

What is the appropriate level of compensation for a worker who has suffered an injury? Workers' compensation conventionally compensates someone (for example) by assuming a full disability (H_F) and providing disability benefits of two-thirds of the pre-injury income, $Y_d = 2/3Y_0$ (in panel (a). Assuming that benefits are reduced by 1/3W for each hour worked, the new budget set is indicated by the dashed line. This may lead the individual to stop working, at E_C (in panel (b), and obtaining utility U_C, which is higher than before the injury (U_0). Panel (c) considers the case of an individual who cannot work, and also has medical expenses M. The "ideal" compensation would be enough to bring him to U_0, which is unobservable. More conventionally, a court may award him Y_0 + M, which yields U_y. Thus, ignoring pain and suffering, he would be overcompensated.

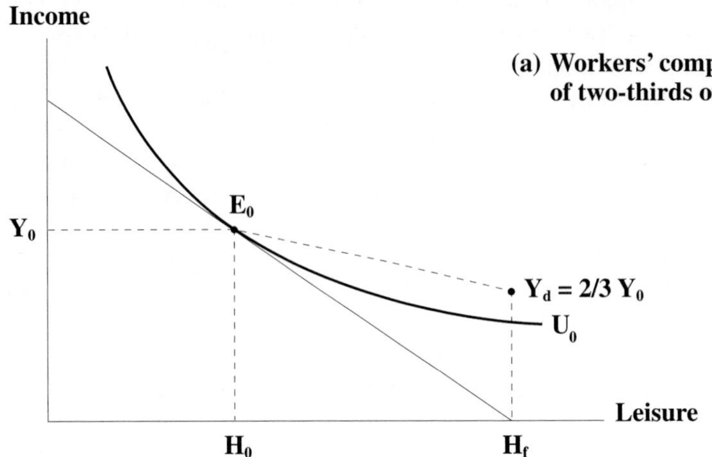

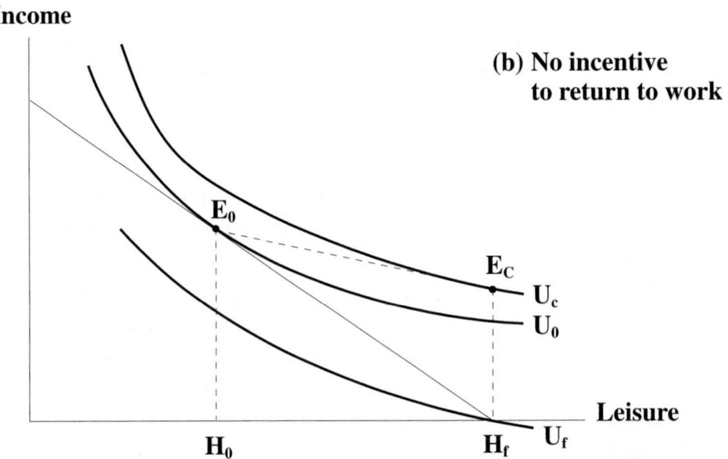

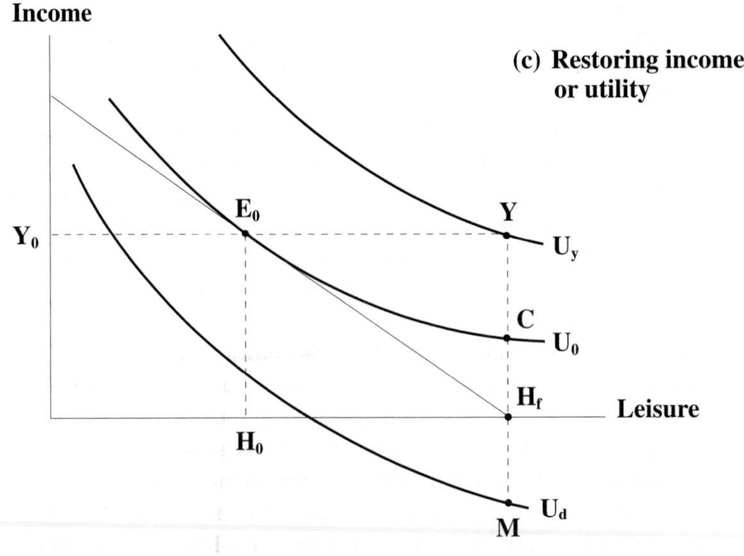

individual's well-being from U_0 to U_d. A court award to compensate for the individual's loss of earnings, YH_f, plus medical costs, H_fM, would lead to a total award of YM. This would clearly leave the individual better off than before ($U_y > U_0$) because the individual is not experiencing the disutility associated with working. If, however, the disability results in pain and suffering then the individual's ability to enjoy goods and leisure consumption may be reduced and the individual could be worse off than before, even with the compensation award of YM (and possibly even with some additional compensation for pain and suffering).

If the court wanted to restore an individual to his former level of well-being or utility, U_0, then an award of CM would be appropriate. The problem is to assess the value the individual may attach to not having to work. This is given in the diagram by YC, which is the income reduction the individual would have willingly accepted to reduce work activity from H_0 to H_f (equal to E_0Y) and to remain indifferent to being at E_0 with utility U_0. The problem is that YC is not observed; all that is observed is the person's income YH_f.

This clearly illustrates the dilemma any court or administrative tribunal would have in arriving at compensation to "restore the person in whole." Different amounts are involved if this is interpreted to be the previous level of income as opposed to welfare or well-being.

Child-Care Subsidy

One of the most hotly debated social programs in recent years has been the provision of daycare or **child-care subsidies** to facilitate the employment of women with children. Analysis of the daycare subsidy requires first investigating how child-care costs might affect a parent's labour supply decision.

Daycare costs can be modelled as a special case of **fixed costs** associated with working. The assumption in this case is that the cost of child care is only incurred if the person works, and that the cost is independent of hours worked. It is a straightforward exercise to extend the analysis to the case where the cost depends on the actual hours worked.

The effect of the daycare cost on the potential income constraint is illustrated in Figure 3.11(a). The fixed cost of daycare is analogous to a vertical drop in the individual's budget constraint immediately upon entering the labour market. That is, immediately upon engaging in labour market activities, the individual incurs the fixed costs m = EM, which are analogous to a drop in income of EM. (The point M is slightly to the left of the vertical line ET to indicate that the costs are only incurred if one engages in labour market activity; that is, moves to the left of T.) These fixed costs are avoided if one does not work in the labour market, but remains at E. In summary, in the absence of child-care costs, the person faces income constraint AE, whereas with fixed child-care costs, the person faces BME.

We can separately examine the effect of these costs on the individual's participation and hours decisions. We first look at participation. In the presence of such fixed costs, the individual's reservation wage is depicted by the slope of the line MM' in Figure 3.11(b). This is the minimum wage above which one would enter the labour market. It is the wage at which one would be indifferent between engaging in labour market activities at E_0, and remaining at home with the children at E. Market wages below the reservation wage would not induce labour market participation because the individual would be better off by engaging in non-labour market activities, like taking care of the children at home, at E, attaining utility level U_0. Market wages above the reservation wage would induce labour force participation and the amount of work would be determined by the tangency of the new higher indifference curve and the higher budget constraint (not shown in this diagram).

Clearly, the individual's reservation wage in the presence of fixed day-care costs is greater than the person's reservation wage in the absence of these costs. This is illustrated in Figure 3.11(b) by the fact that the slope of the line MM' is greater than the slope of the individual's indifference curve at the point E, the latter slope being the person's reservation wage RR' in the absence of fixed costs. (This can be formally proved by the fact that

Figure 3.11 **The Effect of Child-Care Costs on Labour Supply**

Daycare costs can be incorporated into the budget constraint as a fixed cost, m. If a parent does not work, the consumption opportunity is E, but as soon as the parent works, the budget constraint falls to MB. So, effectively, the hours-income budget line is given by EMB. As seen in panel (b), this results in an increase in the reservation wage from RR' to MM'. For a parent who works, the adverse income effect will lead to an increase in labour supply, from H_0 to H_1 (in panel (c)).

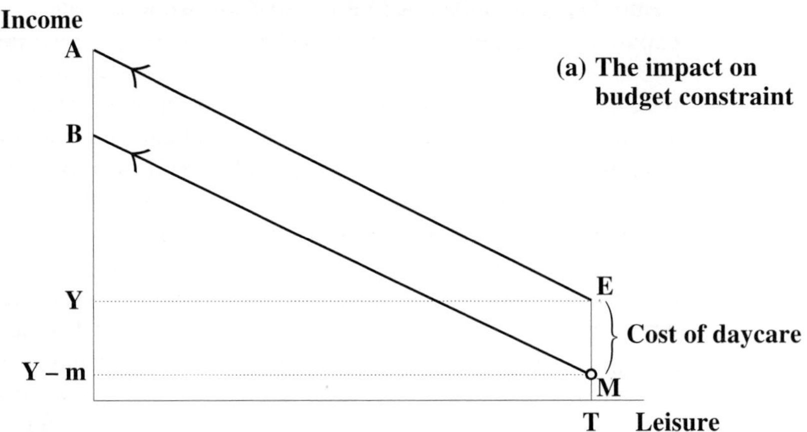

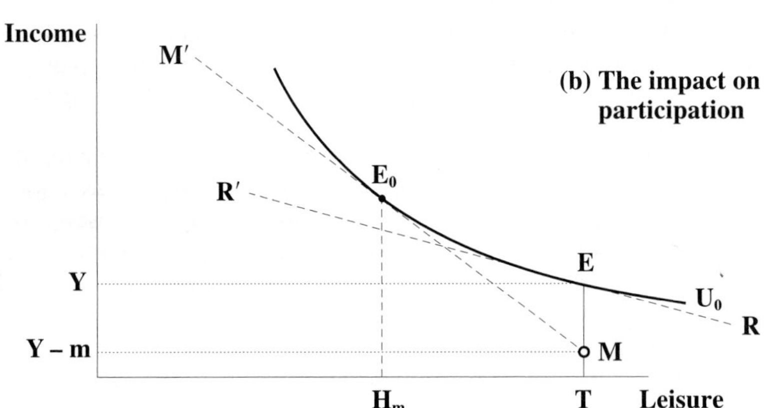

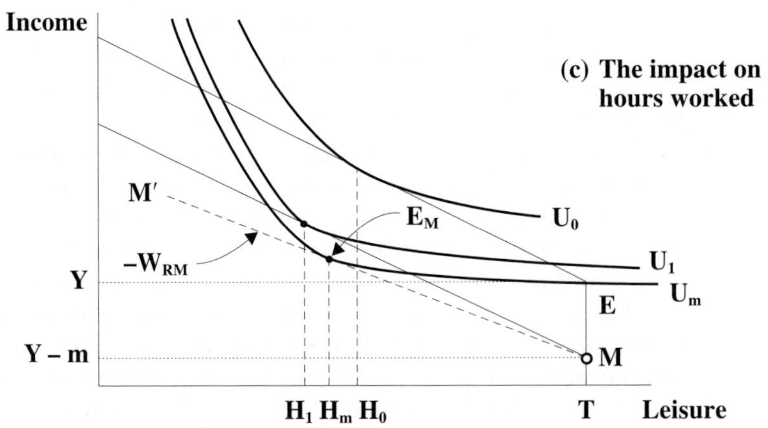

the line MM' is tangent to U_0 at the point E_0 which is to the left of E of the same indifference curve, and the indifference curve becomes steeper as one moves to the left of E because of the hypothesis of diminishing marginal rate of substitution.) Simply stated, child-care costs associated with entering the labour market increase the reservation wage by making labour market work less attractive than caring for the children at home.

Fixed costs can also have an impact on the hours-of-work dimension of labour supply. This impact is more complicated than the labour force participation decision.

First, consider a person for whom the market wage exceeds the reservation wage MM' in the presence of daycare costs. Figure 3.11(c) shows the initial equilibrium at E_0 with hours of work H_0 when there are no child-care costs. The existence of daycare costs m = EM associated with entering the labour market is akin to a reduction in nonlabour income to Y − m. This shifts the budget constraint down in a parallel fashion since market wages have not changed. If leisure is a normal good, this pure income effect from the reduced income increases hours of work from H_0 to H_1. Essentially, when there are fixed costs, one has to work more hours to make up for the income loss associated with the cost of daycare.

In addition to increasing hours of work for those who are participating in labour market activity, fixed child-care costs also create a discontinuity, or "gap," in the implied labour supply schedule. This can be seen in Figure 3.11(c). The distance TH_M indicates the number of hours below which it would not be worthwhile to enter the labour market given the reservation wage W_{RM} created by the daycare costs EM. It is not possible to amortize the fixed costs of entering the labour force over so few hours; hence there is a discrete jump in labour supply from zero to TH_M hours. Geometrically, it is not possible for there to be a tangency between the budget constraint MM' and the indifference curve U_M in the region E_ME. This is so because the slope of MM' is always greater than the slope of the indifference curve to the right of E_M. In this way, daycare costs discourage part-time work.

In summary, fixed child-care costs increase reservation wages and this in turn decreases labour force participation. However, for those who do participate, hours of work will be increased. The fixed child-care costs also create a discontinuity in labour supply, making part-time work less likely. Intuitively, daycare expenses make entering the labour force less attractive, especially for a few hours; however, once in the labour force, the individual will work more hours to compensate for the loss of income associated with the child-care costs. Clearly, fixed costs like daycare have a complicated effect on the various dimensions of labour supply.

To simplify the discussion of the impact of a daycare subsidy, consider a simple program that eliminates the entire cost of child care, for example, the provision of free public daycare. Also, as with the other programs, we ignore the impact of taxes needed to finance the daycare subsidies.

By removing the fixed costs associated with daycare, such subsidies would reduce reservation wages. This, in turn, would induce labour force participation among those who otherwise found the fixed daycare costs to be too inhibiting a barrier to labour force participation. Even part-time work may be attractive since there would no longer be a need to amortize the fixed daycare costs over longer working hours.

For those who are already participating in the labour force the daycare subsidy would not affect their participation decision; that is, it would never cause them to leave the labour force. This is so because if they were already participating, then their reservation wage was already below their market wage, hence, lowering their reservation wage would only strengthen their decision to participate in the labour market.

The daycare subsidy, however, would induce those who already were participating in the labour force to work fewer hours. This is so because the subsidy is like a demogrant, given to those who have children in daycare. This causes them to buy more of all normal commodities including leisure; hence the reduction in hours worked. Alternatively stated, by eliminating the fixed cost of daycare, the subsidy reverses the effect of the fixed cost of working, as illustrated in Figure 3.11(c).

In summary, subsidies to daycare can have a complicated effect on the various dimensions of labour supply, encouraging labour force participation and part-time work, but reducing the hours of work for those already participating (assuming the subsidies are not on a per-hour basis). The net effect on total hours of work is therefore ambiguous. Obviously, making the subsidy available only to those who are not already participating in the labour force would ensure that total hours of work would increase. However, this can create inequities (and some interesting politics!) because similar groups who are already participating in the labour force would not receive the subsidy.

ILLUSTRATIVE EVIDENCE OF INCENTIVE EFFECTS

The theoretical analysis above suggests that income maintenance program parameters can be important determinants of the work incentives of potential recipients; but the model also emphasizes that a person's overall budget constraint matters. Economic opportunities, whether in terms of job availability or of the wage rate, are just-as-important parts of an individual's decision to work in the presence of an income maintenance program. Knowing how large a role is played by the structure of the support program is of obvious importance in the design of policy.

These issues can be illustrated with the example of welfare participation. Consider Figure 3.12, which shows per capita welfare use and a base-case benefit level for Ontario during the past 20 years. While there are differences in the magnitudes and timing, the broad patterns in Ontario are similar to those in other provinces, and also in jurisdictions in the United States. The proportion of per capita welfare beneficiaries increased steadily over the 1980s, with sharp increases in the early 1990s. This was followed by an equally sharp decline over the last half of the 1990s. The real value of the maximum benefit level for single-employables is given by the vertical bars. They track the welfare recipiency rate very closely. There were steady increases in generosity over the 1980s, with significant improvements in benefit levels in the early 1990s. However, the historically high caseloads, combined with fiscal pressures associated with the 1991 recession and the change in federal funding formulas (the replacement of the CAP with the CHST) made the benefit levels politically unsustainable. Welfare benefit levels for employables were significantly cut, and other restrictions on welfare receipt (including workfare provisions) were introduced in 1995.

Looking at these two series alone, there is an obvious correlation between welfare benefits and the number of people collecting benefits. The much harder question is whether the relationship is purely causal, with causality running from benefits to welfare program participation. Moreover, are welfare program parameters the whole story in explaining the pattern of welfare use? It would certainly be premature to draw that conclusion.

First, it is possible that at least some of the correlation is driven by causality running from the level of welfare use to the level of benefits. How are welfare benefits set? This is a political decision, reflecting the preferences and motivations of governments. At least during the late 1980s and early 1990s, Ontario governments viewed themselves as more sensitive to the needs of welfare recipients, who formed an important part of their political constituency. As this became an increasingly sizeable group, benefits were increased to meet their needs. Thus, a larger number of welfare beneficiaries could lead to increased levels of benefits ("responding to need"). The story does not carry easily past 1995, though it is also the case that declining welfare caseloads would remove some of the political pressure to maintain welfare benefit levels. This "story" of how welfare benefits may depend on the number of welfare beneficiaries also extends to using differences in welfare rates to explain differences in welfare use across jurisdictions. A positive correlation may simply reflect the fact that, in some provinces or states, there is a more generous attitude toward

Figure 3.12 Welfare Benefits, Labour Market Conditions, and the Welfare Beneficiaries, Ontario

The average number of welfare beneficiaries per capita (including children) per year is plotted for the years 1980 through 2000. Alongside this series, we show the value of the annual maximum benefits available for a single employable person, expressed in constant year 2000 dollars, and the Ontario unemployment rate.

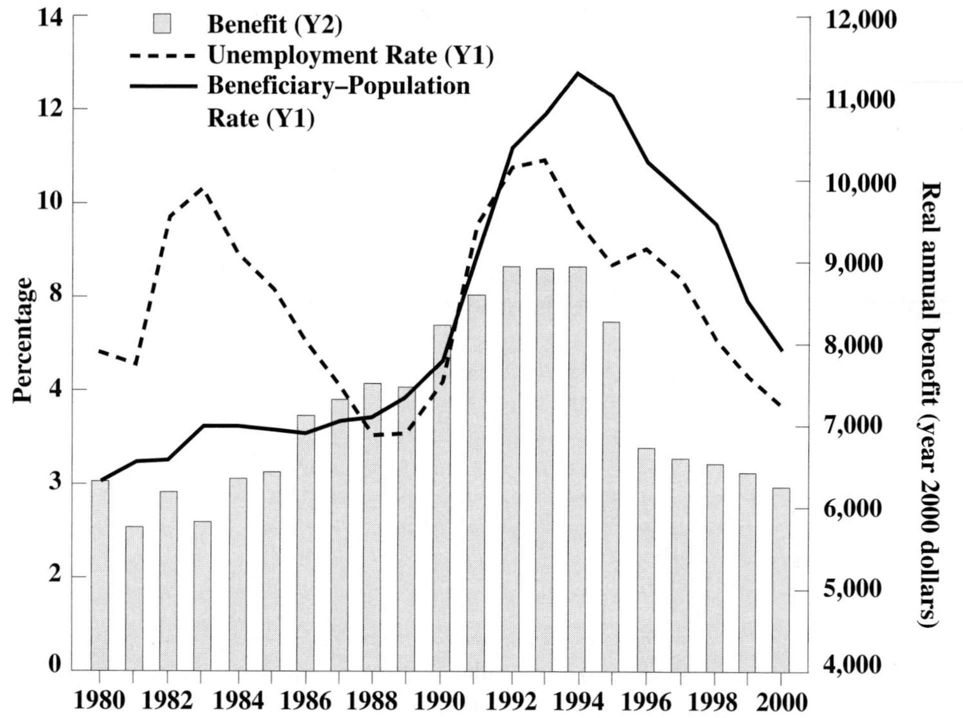

Notes:

1. "Benefit" is the maximum basic welfare benefit for a single employable person, deflated by the Ontario CPI (year 2000 dollars).
2. "Beneficiary-population rate" is the percentage of the population receiving welfare benefits in a given year.
3. "Unemployment rate" is the provincial unemployment rate.

welfare recipients, and this is reflected in both higher levels of benefits and higher numbers of beneficiaries.

But a bigger problem is the possible confounding of welfare benefit changes with other factors. For example, the model of welfare participation underlines the importance of labour market opportunities in the participation decision. Low wages, or high unemployment, will make welfare "more attractive" than work. The unemployment rate is a useful proxy for labour market conditions; it is plotted alongside the other series in Figure 3.12. Especially starting in 1988, there is a strong correlation between the unemployment rate and the number of welfare beneficiaries. At least some of the decline in welfare use in Ontario must be attributed to the strong labour market conditions of the latter 1990s. Note also that in the early 1990s, the high level of unemployment would have had an even larger impact on the welfare rolls, as there were new restrictions on the collection of unemployment insurance benefits, meaning larger numbers would have to turn to welfare instead of UI.

Given these considerations, it is still striking how closely related these series are. How can we formally disentangle the relative impacts? One option would be to extrapolate individual responses to incentives from the nonexperimental literature on general labour supply. But this is a dubious strategy, not only because of their wide variation in results, but also because they generally apply to middle- and high-income families. More reliable evidence on incentive effects of income maintenance programs comes from both nonexperimental and experimental sources directly related to the behaviour of low-income workers in response to changes in specific income support programs. **Nonexperimental**

evidence relates measures of labour supply to various parameters related to the income maintenance scheme, notable wages and nonlabour income. In addition, there have been large-scale "social experiments" in the United States and Canada concerning prototype income support schemes.

Nonexperimental Evidence

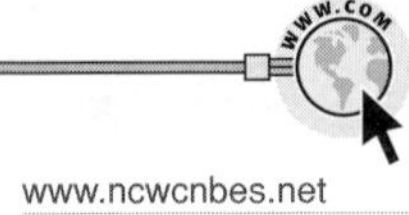

www.ncwcnbes.net

An ideal empirical study of the impact of welfare programs on labour supply and welfare participation would link this joint decision to an individual's wage, nonlabour income, household demographic characteristics, and the welfare program parameters. Using the language of the negative income tax programs, the key parameters would be the guarantee level, G, and the benefit tax-back rate, t. Other real-world parameters would include earned-income exemptions and workfare requirements. A researcher could then evaluate whether individuals facing higher guarantee levels were more likely to be on welfare and work less (if they worked), and whether lower tax rates encouraged welfare recipients to work more hours.

An important caveat must be applied, however, even when interpreting results from an ideal study. As noted by Ashenfelter (1983), welfare participation may be sensitive to program parameters for purely mechanical reasons, having nothing to do with the income and substitution effects described in the labour supply model. Consider first a welfare program with a 100 percent tax rate. Ignoring the value of leisure, an individual can decide whether to collect welfare by comparing income on welfare (G) with earnings off welfare ($Y = Wh$). The individual should participate if $Y < G$. We would thus expect (1) that individuals with lower wages would have lower income, and thus be more likely to participate; and (2) an increase in G would increase the number of people for whom $Y < G$, and therefore the number of beneficiaries. If there is a less than 100 percent tax-back of benefits, the argument easily carries over, only the comparison is between earnings, Y, and the breakeven income, $B = G/t$. In this case, an increase in the tax rate lowers the breakeven income, decreasing the number of people for whom welfare generates more income than working. So even with no marginal "labour supply" decisions, beyond the relatively trivial behavioural assumption that individuals will choose welfare if it yields more income than working, we would expect that increases in G, or decreases in t, would increase the number of welfare beneficiaries. Very few of the studies we discuss make this distinction, and they can thus be viewed more as addressing whether "welfare programs matter" rather than tests of the labour supply models outlined in this chapter.

Setting aside this interpretation issue, data limitations make the "ideal" empirical study virtually impossible, at least in a nonexperimental setting. The primary difficulty is obtaining a data set that contains detailed information on both welfare recipients and non-recipients and their personal characteristics, where individuals face observably different welfare program parameters. Excellent summaries of these, and other challenges facing researchers, as well as evidence for the United States and Canada, are provided by Moffitt (1992) and Lacroix (2000).

One line of research uses administrative data from provincial governments.[4] These data have the benefit of providing detailed income and benefit information for welfare recipients, and especially the ability to track a welfare recipient over a relatively long period of time. Unfortunately, administrative data have limited information on individual socioeconomic characteristics, and, more seriously, there is no information on non-recipients: these data cannot be used to study the welfare participation decision. Also, since the

[4]See Lacroix (2000) for an excellent summary of this research. Important examples of welfare research using administrative data are Duclos, Fortin, Lacroix, and Roberge (1998) for Quebec, Barrett and Cragg (1998) for British Columbia, and Dooley and Stewart (1999) for Ontario.

data are collected at the provincial level, they are not well suited to estimating the impact of program parameters: at any point in time, everyone in the sample faces the same program. While there may be some variation over time, such studies are vulnerable to the problems discussed in connection with Figure 3.12.

That said, these studies yield several important findings, particularly concerning welfare dynamics. First, most beneficiaries use welfare for less than a year before leaving the program. As Lacroix reports, in Quebec, just over one-half of single men who initiate benefits leave welfare during the first year, and slightly fewer single parents. For British Columbia, over 85 percent of single men leave within the first year, indeed three-quarters within the first six months. Similar numbers apply to single parents, with almost 75 percent of welfare spells over in less than a year. This highlights the fact that for most people, welfare serves as temporary income assistance.

However, a less rosy picture emerges when we look at welfare recipients at a single point in time. For any given month, the vast majority of welfare cases are "long-term." Almost 85 percent of single men on welfare in Quebec have been on welfare for longer than one year, and more than 40 percent for over 6 years. For single parents, 95 percent of recipients have been on welfare for more than a year, and almost two-thirds for 6 years or more. The British Columbia numbers are less grim, but the distribution of beneficiaries is still heavily skewed toward long-term, "permanently" low-income users.

One further point is worth highlighting. Most evidence in Canada and the United States suggests that welfare beneficiaries exhibit "negative duration dependence," that is, even controlling for other determinants of being on welfare, the longer one is on welfare, the less likely one is to leave welfare. This may arise because skills deteriorate, employers regard welfare as a negative signal, or those who stay on welfare have conventionally unobserved characteristics (termed unobserved heterogeneity) that are not controlled for in the statistical analysis, and that make them less likely to leave welfare.

www.statcan.ca/english/thesaurus/00004306.htm

Studies of the determinants of welfare participation rely on cross-province differences in the generosity of welfare programs. Allen (1993) uses the 1986 Canadian Census, while Charette and Meng (1994) and Christofides, Stengos, and Swidinsky (1997) use the Labour Market Activity Survey (LMAS) from 1988–89. Each of these studies finds a strong association between labour market earnings potential and welfare use: those with low predicted earnings—a relatively permanent characteristic—are more likely to use welfare. The evidence on the welfare program parameters is more mixed. However, this arises to some extent because of the limited variation in programs, and the difficulty in distinguishing program effects from other, unobserved differences between provinces. Dooley (1999) addresses this limitation by pooling several cross-sectional individual-level data sets (Surveys of Consumer Finances) over a period covering the 1980s to the early 1990s. This allows him to exploit greater within-province variation in program generosity. Dooley's study focuses on single mothers, and he finds very strong evidence linking both the welfare guarantee levels and the individual earnings characteristics to welfare use. He shows that a significant part of the increase in welfare use during the 1980s can be explained by the relative increase in generosity of welfare benefits, combined with stagnant or declining labour market opportunities for low-skilled women.

www.statcan.ca/english/sdds/3502.htm

A third type of study uses aggregate data like that shown in Figure 3.12, pooling data over time periods and across provinces, in order to estimate the impact of provincial welfare programs on welfare caseloads.[5] The consensus from this research is that a variety of factors, including the generosity of welfare benefits, the unemployment rate, and restrictions on the collection of unemployment insurance, all played a role in the increase in welfare caseloads between 1985 and 1994.

[5]See, for example, Fortin (1995), Fortin and Cremieux (1998), Brown (1995), and Dooley and Stewart (1998).

The weight of the nonexperimental evidence thus suggests that welfare participation does indeed depend on the generosity and structure of welfare programs. But it also underlines the other important part of the welfare participation equation: individual labour market and income earning opportunities. While our model is helpful in understanding welfare participation, however, the evidence presented here cannot be taken as evidence that the model is correct in the sense of predicting marginal adjustments in hours in response to welfare program incentives.

Experimental Evidence

The available **experimental evidence** from the experimental negative income tax literature comes from one Canadian and four U.S. negative income tax experiments: New Jersey and Pennsylvania (1968–1972); rural areas of North Carolina and Iowa (1970–1972); Seattle and Denver (1970–1978); and Gary, Indiana (1971–1974). The Canadian experiment was carried out in Manitoba during the period 1975–1979. Different families were given different amounts of basic guaranteed income and their labour market earnings were subjected to various tax rates. Their work behaviour was then compared to that of a control group of similar families that were not under a negative income tax plan.

Moffitt and Kehrer (1981, p. 24) summarize the effect on work incentives of the four U.S. experiments, on the basis of an average tax rate of 0.50 and a guarantee level about equal to the poverty line. The conclusions are: (1) overall hours of work are unequivocally reduced by the presence of the negative income tax; (2) the disincentive effects vary considerably by demographic group with the reduction in hours of work ranging from 1 to 8 percent for husbands, 0 to 55 percent for wives, and 12 to 28 percent for female heads of families; (3) the work reduction for men occurred more in the form of reduced employment to zero hours of work for a small number of men than marginal reductions in the hours of work of those who remained employed; (4) some marginal reductions in hours of work did occur through reduced overtime; (5) the reduced employment often occurred in the form of a lengthening of time spent between jobs for men and increased school attendance for youths, but these responses did not appear to lead to subsequent wage gains; (6) for most groups, disincentive effects generally occurred in response to both the guarantee and the implicit tax rate, although the groups seemed more responsive to changes in the guarantee than the tax rate; (7) the longer the program, the greater the disincentive effects, suggesting that the disincentive effects may be larger for a permanent as opposed to a transitory program. Hum and Simpson (1991) found somewhat smaller impacts of hours worked in the Canadian negative income tax experiment. Hours worked declined between 0.8 and 1.6 percent for men, between 2.4 and 3 percent for married women, and between 3.8 and 5.3 percent among single women.

The Self-Sufficiency Project

While differing substantially in structure from an NIT program, the **Self-Sufficiency Project** provides the most recently available experimental evidence for Canada.[6] This pilot program yielded significant insights into the general question of the role of incentives to the work decision of welfare recipients. The experiments were conducted with a sample of approximately 5600 single parents (mostly women) who had been on welfare for at least a year in New Brunswick and British Columbia over the period 1992–1999. The original sample was randomly divided into treatment and control groups, with the treatment group offered an earnings supplement, and the control group offered nothing.

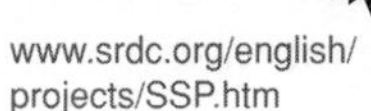

www.srdc.org/english/projects/SSP.htm

The earnings supplement worked as follows. Those in the treatment group were given one year from the beginning of the project to leave welfare for a full-time job, where

[6]See Social Research and Demonstration Corporation (2000) for a complete report on the SSP.

Exhibit 3.1

Welfare Reform in the United States

The early and mid-1990s witnessed several important changes to welfare programs in both Canada and the United States. In general, these changes entailed significant restrictions on welfare eligibility, reduced benefits, and the introduction of work requirements ("workfare") for employable welfare recipients. It is still too early to fully assess the impact of these reforms, but preliminary evidence is available from the United States.

Robert Schoeni and Rebecca Blank (2000) investigate the impact of two rounds of welfare reform in the United States. The first was a series of waivers granted in the early 1990s that permitted states more flexibility in the design and delivery of welfare programs. Usually, when states requested waivers, it was to introduce various forms of workfare. The second, and major, change was the passage of the Personal Responsibility and Work Opportunity and Reconciliation Act, or PRWORA. This act eliminated the traditional welfare program, AFDC (Aid to Families with Dependent Children), and replaced it with TANF (Temporary Assistance to Needy Families). As might be guessed by the name of the act and the new welfare program, the main objective of this act was to make welfare programs stricter, to impose limits on the duration of collection of benefits, and to impose workfare requirements. While this was federal legislation, the timing of its implementation varied across states. Schoeni and Blank use a series of detailed individual-level surveys to construct a time series of state-level data sets for various age-education groups. Their paper explores the impact of the waivers and PRWORA on a variety of indicators, including welfare participation, labour market outcomes, and family income and poverty rates.

Their research highlights the potential difficulties in disentangling the impact of welfare program changes and labour market conditions. For example, states that received waivers (and implemented welfare reforms) saw smaller decreases in their caseloads than non-waiver states, suggesting that welfare reform *increased* welfare use. However, waiver states systematically differed from non-waiver states in other dimensions; notably, they had poorer performing labour markets (which may have generated some of the pressure for welfare reform in the first place). Once proper account is taken of the differences in labour market conditions, Schoeni and Blank find that welfare waivers contributed to the declining welfare caseloads in the United States, as did improving labour market conditions.

Just as importantly, they show that labour force attachment and income levels also improved in the waiver states, over and above the impact of improved labour market conditions. Their results suggest that "welfare matters," in the sense that individual participation depends on welfare program parameters, and moreover (at least so far), that U.S. welfare reforms simultaneously improved the living standards of those who had been on welfare and reduced reliance on welfare.

"full-time" meant at least 30 hours per week. If they took such a job, their welfare benefits would be eliminated, but they would be given an earnings supplement equal to half the difference between their earnings and an earnings benchmark initially set at $30,000 in New Brunswick and $37,000 in British Columbia. Participants could collect this supplement for a maximum of three years. They were also free to return to conventional social assistance at any time. The key idea with this type of program was to make work "pay," contingent on working full-time. So how many took up the offer?

Exhibit 3.2 The Senate Inadvertently Helps Social Science Research

One useful way to determine whether policy parameters affect behaviour is to exploit differences in program parameters across regions. For unemployment insurance, the model described in Figure 3.4 predicts a possible bunching of workers at the minimum weeks worked required to qualify for UI, i.e., 14 weeks. In the Canadian EI system, the qualification period, or entrance requirement (ER) varies across regions according to the local labour market conditions. These Variable Entrance Requirements (VERs) are set higher where the unemployment rate is higher.

To see whether the ER indeed generated a bunching of workers with jobs lasting exactly the minimum number of weeks, Christofides and McKenna (1996) compare the distribution of job durations across regions with different ERs. They find evidence that indeed, there is a correlation between the VERs and the bunching of the job durations at the minimum required weeks.

One potential problem, however, is that the VER is set on basis of the local unemployment rate, so that implicitly the VER may depend on the underlying distribution of job durations. If that is the case, then the causality runs from behaviour to policy, rather than vice versa. To get a clean estimate of whether the ER affects job duration, one would like the VER to be set independently of local economic conditions.

That is precisely what happened in 1990. Unless ratified by the Senate in January 1990, the VERs were to revert to a common ER of 14 weeks in all regions. However, because of a dispute between the House of Commons and the Senate over the introduction of the GST, the necessary legislation was delayed. Thus, for most of 1990, all regions had an ER of 14 weeks, which represented an increase in the ER for those areas with the highest unemployment rates. This "natural experiment" provided an opportunity for economists to study the effect of a change in the ER on the distribution of job durations. Two separate studies—Green and Riddell (1997) and Baker and Rea (1998)—exploit this episode, and find that the job duration distribution was indeed sensitive to the ER. Their results suggest, in part, that individual labour supply reacts to parameters of the UI system.

At the outset of the program, the proportion of welfare recipients working full-time in any given month was 8 percent. By the deadline (after one year), 29 percent of the program group was working full-time. One estimate of the impact of the program would therefore be 21 percent (29 minus 8), that is, that the earnings supplement induced a 21 percentage point increase in the number of mothers leaving welfare for full-time work. But this estimate would be wrong, since some of these women would have left welfare anyway. In order to gauge how many would have left welfare without the offer of the earnings supplement, we can use the control group. The control group also had 8 percent of women working full-time at the outset of the program, but 14 percent after one year. Thus, the true estimate of the "treatment effect" is 15 percent (29 minus 14); that is, the earnings supplement encouraged (caused) an additional 15 percent of welfare recipients to leave social assistance. By the end of the three years, the gap had declined somewhat (to 10 percent), with 28 percent of the treatment group and 18 percent of the controls working in the last month of the program.

The Self-Sufficiency Project generated encouraging results in a number of other dimensions. At the end of three years, only 61 percent of the women were collecting welfare, as against 71 percent in the control group. Of course, some of the program group were collecting the earnings supplement. Taken over the whole sample, the program participants collected an extra $1000 in annual benefits (welfare plus earnings supplement). This combined with the additional average annual earnings of $900 means that their overall living standards improved by almost $2000 per year. So while the earnings supplement was more expensive than welfare, it had the twin benefits of leveraging $1 of transfer income into $2 of total income and getting significantly more women into the labour force, which should have important long-run benefits for the women and their children.

Summary

- Income maintenance schemes are designed to top up low incomes, which can arise for any of a variety of reasons, permanent or transitory, and may be due either to low wages or hours. By their very nature, means-tested programs can have strong disincentives to earning income.
- The income-leisure (labour supply) framework is a useful way to analyze work incentive effects. While programs vary in details, most will generate income effects (by shifting the opportunity set outward) or substitution effects (by changing the returns to work).
- Demogrants are pure lump-sum transfers, based only on immutable individual characteristics like age or sex. While these transfers are independent of income, they will still have adverse work incentive effects as long as leisure is a normal good.
- Welfare programs are designed to increase the income of individuals with low income. The degree to which they have adverse work incentive effects depends on how strictly benefits are reduced in response to higher earnings. The more severely benefits are reduced with higher earnings, the stronger the disincentives will be for welfare recipients to work.
- Negative income taxes, or guaranteed annual income programs, are generalizations of welfare programs. They were proposed as an alternative to welfare programs with steep earnings tax-back rates.
- Unemployment insurance is designed as an insurance scheme, responding to short-run reductions in available hours of work, especially due to cyclical changes in labour market conditions. However, such schemes can also have work incentive effects. For some, the incentives will be to encourage time spent unemployed (voluntary unemployment), but for others, the returns to qualifying for UI will actually encourage them to work.
- Workers' compensation is designed to address income losses arising from workplace injuries. There are a variety of ways to incorporate injuries or disabilities into the labour supply model.
- Child-care expenses can be modelled as fixed costs associated with working. As such, child-care subsidies can be viewed as a reduction of these fixed costs. Generally speaking, these subsidies will encourage labour market participation by parents.
- Estimating the actual (as opposed to the theoretical) impact of income maintenance programs on labour supply is difficult. Many of the empirical issues can be illustrated through the important case of welfare programs. The weight of evidence from research on the impact of these programs shows that both the generosity of welfare benefits and individual labour market opportunities predict participation in welfare programs.

REVIEW QUESTIONS

1. Use the work-leisure choice diagram to illustrate that, under normal circumstances, if an individual is given a demogrant, take-home pay will not increase by as much as the demogrant. Why is this so?
2. Illustrate the work incentive effects of a demogrant on a disabled person who is unable to work.
3. Use the work-leisure choice diagram to illustrate the following cases where an individual is:
   a. Unwilling to go on welfare because the welfare payment is too low
   b. Indifferent between welfare and work
   c. Induced to move off welfare because of an increase in her wage
   d. Induced to move off welfare because of a change in preferences between income and leisure
   e. Induced to move off welfare by a reduction of the 100 percent implicit tax on earnings
4. In an unemployment insurance diagram like Figure 3.7, depict the case in which the individual must work eight weeks before becoming eligible to collect. Depict the case of a two-third rather than a 60 percent replacement rate.
5. In a diagram like Figure 3.9, depict the worker's compensation system involving a 90 percent replacement of the pre-injury wage earnings.
6. Use Figure 3.12 as the basis of a "debate" on the statement, "Welfare reforms in Ontario worked." Construct arguments both for and against this proposition.

PROBLEMS

1. "The negative income tax involves a positive guarantee that has a pure income effect of reducing work effort. It also involves a tax increase on the earned income of recipients, and this has both an income and a substitution effect working in the opposite direction in their effect on work incentives. Consequently, we are unable to predict unambiguously the static, partial-equilibrium effects a negative income tax plan would have on work incentives." Is the last statement true or false?
2. Most jurisdictions allow welfare recipients to earn a small amount of labour market earnings before the tax-back of welfare benefits begins. Using the work-leisure diagram, show how this more realistic welfare program compares to the one described in Figures 3.2 and 3.3. In the late 1990s, the Ontario government increased the amount of labour income disregarded (i.e., allowed before welfare benefits are taxed back), at the same time reducing the overall level of benefits. Analyze the expected impact on labour supply of a prospective welfare recipient of this change in the welfare program.
3. Use the work-leisure framework to illustrate that if we hold the post-subsidy income of the recipients constant, or the size of the subsidy constant, a negative income tax will involve more adverse work incentives than a wage subsidy would.
4. Consider an individual who must drive to his place of work. Assume that there are 16 available hours in the day, that his wage rate is $20 per hour, and that he has nonlabour income of $100 per day. The commute takes one hour each way, and it costs $40 in expenses for the round trip. Using a work-leisure diagram, depict his labour supply choice, including his reservation wage. Analyze the impact of an increase in commuting costs on his participation and hours decision. Analyze the impact, first, of an increase in commuting time from two to four hours per day, and, second, of an increase in driving expenses (from $40 to $60) per round trip (keeping commuting time at two hours).

5. The U.S. Earned Income Tax Credit (EITC) has been described as one of the most successful elements of U.S. antipoverty public policy, especially as it directs benefits toward the working poor. For the 2000 tax year, the EITC works (approximately) as follows. Low-wage workers receive additional income from the federal government, depending on how much they earn and how many children they have. Consider an individual with one child:
   i. There is no credit if nothing is earned.
   ii. The credit equals $0.34 per dollar earned, and peaks at around $2400, when the worker has earned $7000.
   iii. It remains at $2400 until the worker earns around $12,000.
   iv. It is phased out gradually, by $0.16 per dollar earned, until eliminated completely if the worker earns $27,000 or more per year.

   a. Assuming the worker faces no other taxes, graph the budget constraint associated with the EITC for a typical worker earning W per hour.
   b. Analyze how the imposition of the EITC affects hours of labour supplied. Assuming that substitution effects are larger than income effects for the typical low-wage worker, does the credit necessarily increase hours of work for all those who are eligible? Why or why not?

6. Consider the following earnings supplement program, modelled after the Self-Sufficiency Project. An individual can work a maximum of 60 hours per week, at a wage rate of $5 per hour. Welfare benefits are fixed at $200 per week, with a 100 percent tax-back on labour earnings. Finally, the earnings supplement equals half the difference between an individual's labour earnings and the benchmark earnings of $450 per week. This supplement can only be collected if the individual forgoes welfare benefits and works a minimum of 30 hours per week.

   Draw the individual's budget constraint, and analyze the work decision.

KEYWORDS

income maintenance schemes 77
work incentives 77
partial equilibrium effects 78
general equilibrium effects 78
demogrant 79
welfare 80
social assistance 80
negative income tax 83
wage subsidy 84
unemployment insurance 86
worksharing 89
workers' compensation 93
child-care subsidies 95
fixed costs 95
nonexperimental evidence 100
experimental evidence 102
Self-Sufficiency Project 102

REFERENCES

Allen, D. W. 1993. Welfare and the family: The Canadian experience. *JOLE* 11 (Supplement, January):S201–23.

Ashenfelter, O. 1983. Determining participation in income-tested social programs. *JASA* 78 (September):517–25.

Baker, M., and S. Rea. 1998. Employment spells and unemployment insurance eligibility requirements. *R.E. Stats.* 80 (February):80–94.

Barrett, G. F., and M. I. Cragg. 1998. An untold story: The characteristics of welfare use in British Columbia. *CJE* 31 (February):165–88.

Besley, T., and R. Kanbur. 1993. The principles of targeting. In *Including the Poor*, ed. M. Lipton and J. van der Gaag. Washington, D.C.: The World Bank.

Brown, D. M. 1995. Welfare caseload trends in Canada. In *Helping the Poor: A Qualified Case for "Workfare."* Toronto: C. D. Howe Institute.

Charette, M., and R. Meng. 1994. The determinants of welfare participation of female heads of household in Canada. *CJE* 27 (May):290–306.

Christofides, L., T. Stengos, and R. Swidinsky. 1997. Welfare participation and labour market behaviour in Canada. *CJE* 30 (August):595-621.

Christofides, L. N., and C. J. McKenna. 1996. Unemployment insurance and job duration in Canada. *JOLE* 14 (April):286-312.

Dooley, M. 1999. The evolution of welfare participation among Canadian lone mothers, 1973-1991. *CJE* 32 (May):589-612.

Dooley, M., and J. Stewart. 1998. An analysis of changes in welfare participation rates in Ontario from 1983-1994 using social assistance caseload data. Manuscript. McMaster University.

______. 1999. The duration of spells on welfare and off welfare among lone mothers in Ontario. *CPP* 25 (Supplement, November):S47-72.

Duclos, J.-Y., B. Fortin, G. Lacroix, and H. Roberge. 1998. The dynamics of welfare participation in Quebec. Laval University Working Paper, Number 9817.

Fortin, P. 1995. The future of social assistance in Canada. Manuscript. University of Quebec at Montreal.

Fortin, P., and P.-Y. Cremieux. 1998. The determinants of social assistance rates: Evidence from a panel of Canadian provinces, 1987-1996. Manuscript. University of Quebec at Montreal.

Gray, D. M. 2000. *The Work Sharing Program in Canada:A Feasible Alternative to Layoffs?*, C. D. Howe Institute Commentary, Number 146.

Green, D. A., and W. C. Riddell. 1997. Qualifying for unemployment insurance: An empirical analysis. *EJ* 107 (January):67-84.

Hum, D., and W. Simpson. 1991. *Income Maintenance, Work Effort, and the Canadian M-income Experiment.* Ottawa: Economic Council of Canada.

Kesselman, J. 1969. Labour supply effects on income, income-work, and wage subsidies. *JHR* 4 (Summer):275-92.

______. 1971. Conditional subsidies in income maintenance. *WEJ* 9 (March):1-20.

______. 1973. A comprehensive approach to income maintenance: SWIFT. *JPubEc* 2 (February):59-88.

Lacroix, G. 2000. Reforming the welfare system: In search of the optimal policy mix. In *Adopting Public Policy to a Labour Market in Transition*, eds. W. C. Riddell and F. St-Hilaire. Montreal: Institute for Research on Public Policy.

Meltz, N., F. Reid, and G. Swartz. 1981. *Sharing the Work: An Analysis of the Issues in Worksharing and Jobsharing*. Toronto: University of Toronto Press.

Moffitt, R. 1992. Incentive effects of the U.S. welfare system: A review. *JEL* 30 (March):1-61.

Moffitt, R., and K. Kehrer. 1981. The effect of tax and transfer programs on labor supply: The evidence from the income maintenance experiments. In *Research in Labor Economics*, ed. R. Ehrenberg. Greenwich, Conn.: JAI Press.

Phipps, S. 1990. Quantity-constrained household responses to unemployed insurance reform. *EJ* 100 (March):124-40.

______. 1991. Behavioral response to UI reform in constrained and unconstrained models of labour supply. *CJE* 24 (February):34-54.

Reid, F. 1982. UI-assisted worksharing as an alternative to layoffs: The Canadian experience. *ILRR* 35 (April):319-29.

______. 1985. Reductions in worktime: an assessment of employment sharing to reduce unemployment. In *Work and Pay*, ed. W. C. Riddell. Toronto: University of Toronto Press.

Schoeni, R. F., and R. Blank. 2000. What has welfare reform accomplished? Impacts on welfare participation, employment, income, poverty, and family structure. NBER Working Paper, Number 7627.

Social Research and Demonstration Corporation. 2000. *The Self-Sufficiency Project at 36 Months: Effects of a Financial Work Incentive on Employment and Income.*

Chapter Four

Labour Supply Over the Life Cycle

Main Questions

- *Do men's and women's labour supply patterns evolve similarly as they age?*
- *Does the wage elasticity of labour supply change once we account for the fact that individuals may make their labour supply decisions with planning horizons as long as their entire life? What complexities are added to the labour supply framework once we try to model labour supply at each period over a lifetime?*
- *How can economic analysis help in our understanding of fertility behaviour, and the relationship between fertility and women's labour supply?*
- *What factors determine the retirement age? In particular, what roles do public and private pension plans play in this decision?*

The previous two chapters have emphasized the purely "economic" determinants of labour supply—market wages, nonlabour income, and government programs. One of the more interesting other correlates of labour supply is age, and labour economists have spent considerable effort trying to explain why labour supply appears to vary systematically over an individual's life cycle.

As a first step in exploring **life-cycle labour supply**, Figure 4.1 illustrates the labour force participation rates by age groups for men and women. These age-participation profiles are shown for each of three census years: 1971, 1981, and 1991. The men's profiles demonstrate the conventional inverted-U-shaped characteristic of life-cycle labour force patterns in most countries: participation increases sharply as men move into their twenties, peaking for ages 30 to 50, then declining as conventional retirement ages approach. While the profiles are very similar in each census year, notice that the participation rates of older men have declined significantly since 1971, suggesting that men are retiring earlier.

The women's profiles are more complicated and provide an important example of the perils of inferring dynamic behaviour from cross-section data. Focus first on the 1971

Figure 4.1 **Age–Labour Force Participation Profiles**

Each panel shows the participation rates of men or women by age, for three years: 1971, 1981, and 1991. The men's panel shows a strong relationship between age and participation, following the traditional life-cycle pattern. The women's panel is more complicated, because of the shift of the profiles across over time. The cross-section profiles do a poor job of predicting behaviour, because of the confounding of age and cohort effects. The "actual" age effects are indicated by the dashed lines for three selected cohorts.

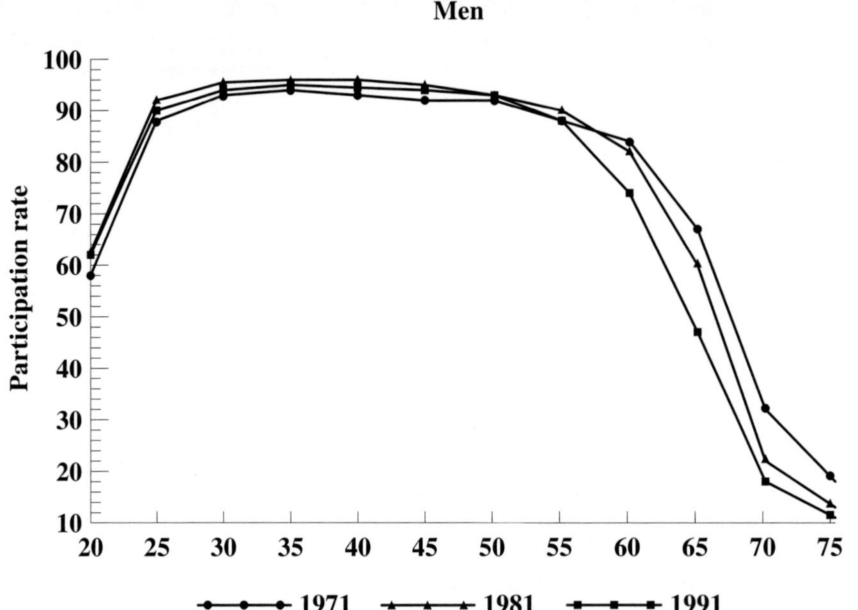

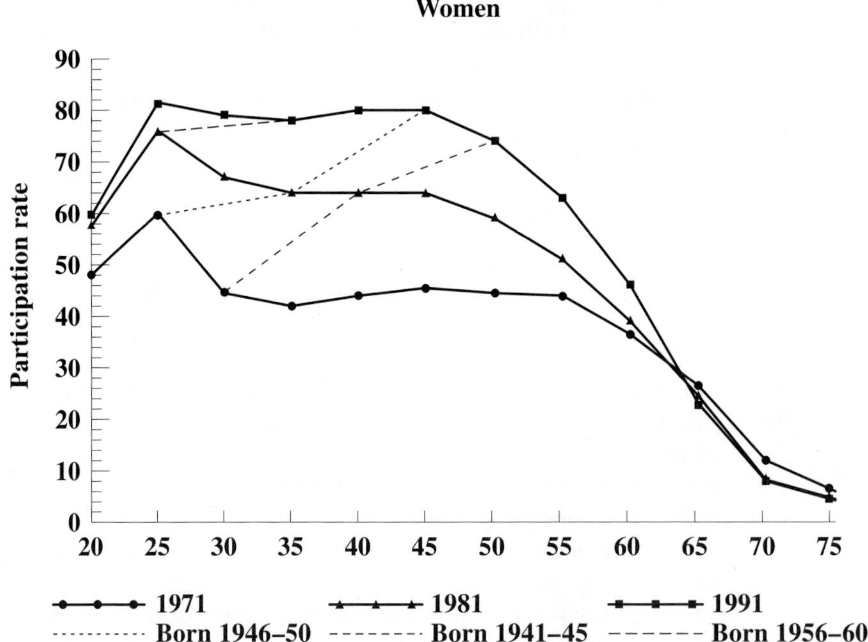

Source: Created from author's tabulations based on Statistics Canada 1971, 1981, 1991 Census of Population.

profile. If interpreted as a stable representation of the pure effects of age on labour force participation, then we can use this profile to predict how many women will work as they age. One can imagine telling the following story: a typical woman increases her labour supply after high school into her mid-twenties, reducing it sharply to raise a family, then gradually returning to work after age 35, until retirement.

However, as can be seen in this figure, predictions based on this story would have been quite wrong. Consider 25-year-old women in 1971. They have a participation rate of around 60 percent, and would be predicted to have a participation rate of around 40 percent when they are 35 years old. By looking at the 1981 profile, we see however that their participation rate was actually higher than in 1971, at around 63 percent. As can plainly be seen from this figure, the age-participation profile has not been stable for women. In 1971 25-year-old women differ from 35-year-old women in more ways than their age: they were born ten years afterward, into a different society with different attitudes toward women working, and possibly different economic conditions surrounding women's work. Thus, it is difficult to disentangle a pure age effect from a birth **cohort effect** in a single cross-section of data. Figure 4.1 shows the actual participation-age path of three different birth cohorts. The labour force participation rate generally increases with age (until retirement). Women's profiles are thus shaped similarly to men's, though with a slower entry into the labour force at younger ages. The figure also clearly shows that the initial participation rate of young women has been rising steadily over the past 30 years.

The focus of this chapter is on reviewing how labour economists explain the pure "age" effects, rather than on why these effects may be changing over time. Nevertheless, there have been a number of important studies that try to document and explain this shift in participation profiles for women. Beaudry and Lemieux (1999) analyze the shifting profiles for Canadian women, and the slowdown in the increase in women's participation in the 1990s. They isolate the pure cohort effects from age and time (business cycle) effects, and their results suggest that most of the changes in participation reflected in Figures 4.1 and 2.2 are driven by (permanent) cohort effects. As for explaining these shifts, most studies, such as Claudia Goldin's 1990 book examining changes in women's participation over the entire century, or Dooley's 1994 paper looking at mothers in Canada, find that the increase in participation rates cannot be explained by changes in economic variables alone, that is, by changing incentives for women to work. These results suggest that changing "preferences" remain an important explanation, and the nature of these changes (e.g., in the attitudes toward married women working), remains an important area of research for both economists and sociologists.

Labour economists seek to assess whether the observed labour force patterns over the life cycle can be explained by changes in the economic environment in a way predicted by theory. For example, does the inverted-U shape of participation derive from a similarly shaped wage profile, mediated by an upward-sloping labour supply function? In this chapter we will examine different approaches to this problem. In addition, there are (at least) three important life-cycle-related phenomena that merit separate attention. The first is the school-work decision: when and whether to acquire education, and the commensurate timing of work. This is a major topic, and is the subject of the chapters on human capital. The second is the fertility decision of women. We have already discussed the theoretical apparatus used to analyze the impact of children on women's labour supply, but in this chapter we explore the economic aspects of the decision to have children in the first place. The third is the decision to retire, or "permanently" withdraw from the labour force. Not only is this an interesting application of labour supply theory, but it is also an increasingly important public policy issue.

Exhibit 4.1

Another U-Shaped Curve: Labour Force Participation and Economic Development

As shown in Table 2.1, women's labour force participation rates vary widely across countries at different stages of economic development. Claudia Goldin (1995) investigates this relationship in detail, both across countries, and over time within the United States. She finds that there is a U-shaped relationship between female participation rates and per capita GDP (a common measure of economic development). Female participation rates are highest in the poorest and richest countries, and lower for those countries in between. Similarly, over the past 150 years in the United States, women's participation rate first declined, and then began its steady ascent early in the twentieth century.

Can this pattern be explained by the labour force participation model of Chapter 2? It is possible that the initial decline in participation is associated with an income effect: as national income rises (reflecting wage growth), women can withdraw from some of the more onerous jobs they were previously performing (especially in agriculture). Eventually, as economic development progresses, and wages rise sufficiently, the substitution effect may dominate, leading more women to work in the market.

Goldin argues that this explanation is incomplete. She argues that an improved version of the labour supply model incorporating social attitudes towards women's working can better explain the U-shaped pattern. As an economy develops, the labour market opportunities actually improve for women, as well as men. However, most of these jobs are in low-status industrial jobs. Social stigmas against *men* whose wives work imposes a psychic cost on families with women working. Men are viewed as poor providers if their wives must work in factories. Thus, the increased income of men allows more women to withdraw from agriculture, but the stigma associated with factory work keeps them at home.

It is only when white-collar, "respectable" jobs emerge that participation becomes acceptable. Less stigma is attached to husbands whose wives are pursuing a career, especially if the job required at least secondary-level education. Thus, an augmented labour force participation model, with due allowance for social attitudes toward women's work, can help explain the U-shaped relationship between national income and women's working.

DYNAMIC LIFE-CYCLE MODELS

There are two distinct approaches we could take in devising a theory of life-cycle labour supply. The objective of the exercise is similar to that in Chapter 2: we would like a model relating labour supply at various points in time to the economic environment over time, specifically wages (and prices) and other income. From such a model we could compare theoretical labour supply for individuals facing different wages, either at a point in time, or over their entire lives.

The first approach would treat an individual's life-cycle labour supply as a sequence of static labour supply problems. Each period, the individual would respond to the economic environment that exists in that period. Such an approach would allow us to use our existing models to make predictions; for example, that as long as the substitution effect dominated, individuals would work most when their wages were highest. If income effects were large, this prediction would be modified accordingly. While this approach is satisfactory for a number of problems, it ignores the possibility that individuals may be forward-looking. If individuals look to the future, they may react today to changes in their anticipated wage path, or to other changes to their future economic environment. Similarly, they may react differently to wage changes that are temporary versus those expected to be permanent.

For these reasons, economists have devised a theoretically more appealing dynamic framework. It turns out that this framework is little more than an extension of the static model we have already described. The basic idea is that individuals plan out their lifetime labour supply, given their expected lifetime economic environment.

For the simplest version of the model we assume that an individual lives and potentially works for N periods, and that there is no uncertainty regarding the values of economic variables in the future. As it turns out, very little is changed by incorporating uncertainty into this framework. The person is assumed to have preferences, not just over "consumption" and "leisure" today, but over consumption and leisure in each of her N periods of life. We can represent these preferences by the utility function

$$u = U(C_1 C_2, \ldots, C_N, \ell_1, \ell_2, \ldots, \ell_N)$$

The individual is then assumed to maximize this utility function, choosing their optimal consumption and leisure in each period, subject to their expected lifetime budget constraint. For simplicity, let us assume that there is no nonlabour income, that the price of consumption is constant, and that the individual knows that she will face wages of W_1, W_2, ... W_N over her lifetime. What does her budget constraint look like?

For ease of exposition, consider the case where there are only two periods (today and tomorrow, or this year and next year). Lifetime labour supply will be summarized by H_1 and H_2, hours worked in each period. It seems reasonable to imagine that lifetime consumption should equal lifetime earnings, or

$$C_1 + C_2 = W_1 H_1 + W_2 H_2$$

This implies that if the consumer chose to do so, she could consume everything in the first period, that is, $C_1 = W_1 H_1 + W_2 H_2$. This assumes that the person can costlessly transfer resources from the future to the present, essentially borrowing her future income to finance current consumption. Try doing this at a bank! A bank will almost certainly charge interest on such loans. Similarly, it is unlikely that our consumer-worker would postpone consumption (or save) unless offered interest on her savings.

Assume that the individual can borrow and lend freely at the interest rate r. The correct relationship between income and consumption is actually given by

$$C_1 + \frac{C_2}{(1+r)} = W_1 H_1 + \frac{W_2 H_2}{(1+r)}$$

so that the **present value** of consumption equals the present value of income. That this is the correct representation can be seen by considering what consumption in period 2 would be if the individual saved or borrowed. First, consider an individual who saved some of her first period earnings to consume in period 2. Her consumption in period 2 would then be her income in period 2, plus the principal and interest from her savings from period 1:

$$C_2 = W_2 H_2 + (1 + r)(W_1 H_1 - C_1)$$

which is a simple rearrangement of the present value representation. If she borrowed on the basis of future income to finance consumption in period 1, her period 2 consumption would be equal to her period 2 income, less the principal and interest on the loan:

$$C_2 + H_2 H_2 - (1 + r)(C_1 - W_1 H_1)$$

which is also a simple rearrangement of the present value formula.

We can rewrite the budget constraint in more conventional terms of consumption and leisure as

$$C_1 + \frac{C_2}{(1+r)} + W_1\ell_1 + \frac{W_2\ell_2}{(1+r)} = W_1T + \frac{W_2T}{(1+r)}$$

In terms of N periods, we merely extend the formula to N periods, so that the discounted present value of consumption and leisure is equal to the discounted present value of the lifetime labour endowment.

The resulting labour supply functions give labour supply in any period as a function of wages in each of the time periods, as well as interest rates and the present value of lifetime resources. The income and substitution effects that form the basis of comparative statics exercises with these **dynamic labour supply** functions are more complicated than the simple static model. MaCurdy (1981) deals with many of these complications, and some of the simpler ones can be illustrated with a diagram based on that source.

Figure 4.2 illustrates two hypothetical age-wage profiles, indicating how wages may at first increase over the life cycle, and then decline later. The higher profile depicts the situation where an individual gets a higher wage at each and every age. The small "blip" in the higher profile illustrates the situation where an individual receives a temporary one-time only, **unanticipated wage increase** at age t. There are three possible sources of wage changes occurring in this diagram and each have different income and substitution effects and hence would lead to different labour supply responses. For illustrative purposes the three wage changes from A to B, B to C, and C to D are assumed to be of the same magnitude as illustrated by the same vertical distance.

The difference between A and B reflects two persons whose wages differ by a permanent amount at each and every age in their life cycle. That difference would be associated with conventional income and substitution effects working in the opposite direction. That is, the high-wage individual at B would have a higher opportunity cost of leisure and hence work more (substitution effect). However, that individual would also have a higher expected lifetime income (a higher present value of the lifetime labour endowment) and hence be able to afford more leisure and work less (income effect). Since the income and

Figure 4.2 **Dynamic Life-Cycle Wage Changes**

The labour supply response depends on how much the income effect of higher lifetime earnings offsets the substitution effect of the higher value of time. A permanent increase in the wage profile (A → B) generates the largest income effect, while a fully anticipated rise in wages (B → C) yields no change in lifetime income, and no income effect. A transitory (temporary) increase in wages (C → D) generates a small (intermediate-level) income effect.

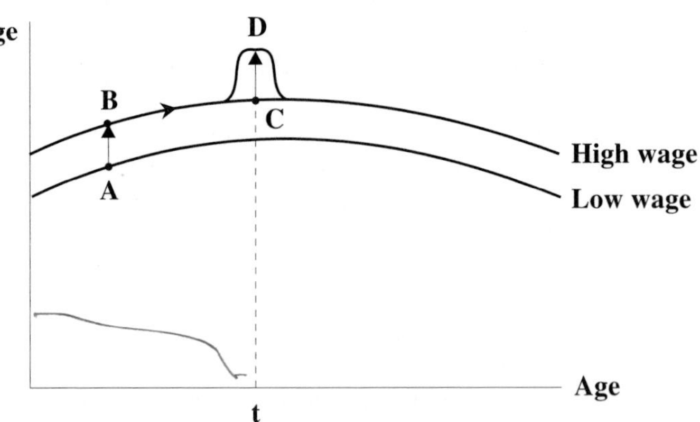

Notes:

A → B Permanent unanticipated wage increase (smallest labour supply response)
B → C Evolutionary anticipated wage increase (largest labour supply response)
C → D Transitory unanticipated wage increase (medium labour supply response)

substitution effects work in the opposite direction, the labour supply of the high-wage individual may be greater or less than the labour supply of the lower-wage individual over their lifetime.

The wage increase from B to C along an individual's given wage profile is an **evolutionary wage change** associated with aging over the life cycle. To the extent that such wage changes are fully anticipated and known with certainty, they will not create a leisure-inducing income effect as they occur. Rather, the income effect is spread over the life cycle, independent of when the wage change occurs. Basically, because it is already accounted for in the consumer's optimization problem (in the present value of the lifetime labour endowment), a fully anticipated wage increase is "no news" to the consumer-worker, so there is no adjustment to a change in resources. The evolutionary wage change, however, does have a substitution effect making leisure more expensive (and hence inducing work) in the years of peak earnings in one's career. The substitution effect essentially reflects that a forward-thinking consumer will buy leisure when it is cheapest, or work more when the returns to doing so are highest. Because there is no leisure-inducing income effect, the labour supply response to anticipated evolutionary, life-cycle wage changes (termed the **intertemporal substitution** response) will be larger than the labour supply response at a given age (i.e., not adding up over the life cycle), to permanent unanticipated differences like the wage profile shift from A to B, the latter labour supply response being muted by the leisure-inducing income effect.

The wage difference between C and D represents a transitory, unanticipated, one-time wage difference between two individuals whose wage profiles are otherwise similar (both high wage profiles) except at age t. It may be associated, for example, with a period of overtime pay that is not expected to be repeated. This wage difference will have the usual work-inducing substitution effect at year t since the income forgone by not working is very high. There will also be a small leisure-inducing income effect spread over the life cycle associated with the fact that the individual with the higher wage at D will have a slightly higher lifetime wealth because of the transitory wage difference. The present value of the lifetime labour endowment is only slightly affected by the one-time-only wage change. Because the wage difference is transitory and not permanent, however, the labour supply response to the transitory wage difference at age t will be larger than the labour supply response to a permanent wage difference as between A and B, at age t, because the latter has a stronger more permanent leisure-inducing income effect. Basically, individuals with the higher **transitory wage** at D will be able to afford to work slightly less over their life cycle; however, they will likely work more at the particular age t to take advantage of the high temporary wage.

Clearly the three sources of wage differences outlined above have different effects associated with whether the wage differences are permanent or temporary and anticipated or unanticipated. The different income effects, in turn, imply different labour supply responses to the wage differences. The anticipated evolutionary change from B to C has a pure substitution effect and is not offset by any leisure-inducing income effect. Hence it will have the largest positive labour supply response to a wage change. The transitory wage difference between C and D mainly has a work-inducing substitution effect; however, there is a mild offsetting leisure-inducing income effect spread over the life cycle. In contrast, the permanent wage difference between A and B, at a given age, has a larger offsetting leisure-inducing income effect and hence will have the smallest labour supply response to a wage increase (in fact, the response may be negative). The labour supply responsiveness to a wage change therefore may be ordered as the largest stemming from an evolutionary change (pure substitution effect), a medium response emanating from a transitory wage change (mainly substitution but slight offsetting income effect), and the smallest (and possibly negative response) emanating from a permanent wage change (reflecting offsetting substitution and income effects).

Clearly, in a dynamic life-cycle context, the substitution and income effects emanating from a wage change can differ depending on whether the wage change is permanent or temporary, and anticipated or unanticipated. This in turn means that the labour supply response will differ, depending upon the source of the wage increase in a dynamic life-cycle setting. While theoretically important, the life-cycle model has been called upon to explain a variety of labour market phenomena, ranging from the pure age related topics that we are about to discuss to year-to-year variations in employment at the macro level. Overall, the empirical performance of the model remains disappointing (see Card, 1994, for a review of the evidence), but the theoretical issues raised, and the insights the model offers over the simple static model, make the life-cycle model hard to set aside.

FERTILITY AND CHILDBEARING

As we saw in Figure 4.1, women's participation is lowest during their childbearing years, suggesting that issues of **fertility** and family formation are important in understanding women's labour supply over the life cycle. In our discussion of labour force participation we addressed the impact of children and child-care costs on the value of women's non-market time and their reservation wages. However, children are not randomly brought to doorsteps by storks, but usually the result of some degree of family planning. It is reasonable to imagine that economic considerations may affect the decision of whether and how many children to have. Certainly, in planning life-cycle labour supply, women must consider the interrelationships between education, work, and having children.

Largely on the basis of the pioneering work of Becker (1960) and Mincer (1963), economists have applied the principles of consumer demand theory to the decision to have children.[1] The more sophisticated analyses of fertility behaviour are cast in a dynamic setting, much like the one outlined in the previous section. A fully dynamic setting allows one to account for the intertemporal nature of the fertility decision, including the possible consequences on future wages of withdrawal from the labour force. A dynamic setting also allows one to look at questions regarding the timing and spacing of births, rather than just the number of children a woman may choose to have. We will restrict ourselves to an overview of the simpler aspects of the economics of fertility, illustrating the potential importance of economic variables in affecting women's labour supply during the childbearing part of their life cycle.

Although many find it obnoxious to think of children, even analogously, as if they are "consumer durables," few would deny that at least some families alter their childbearing decisions because they cannot yet afford to have children (perhaps until they have at least saved for the down payment on a house or have finished paying for their education) or because it is too costly to have a child (perhaps because it would mean an interruption in a wife's career in the labour market). As long as these and other economic factors affect the decision to have children for some families, economic factors will have some predictive power in explaining variations in birth rates.

As suggested by consumer demand theory, the basic variables affecting the fertility decision are income, the price or cost of a child, the price of related goods, and tastes and preferences. Labour supply theory reminds us of the importance of time, the tradeoff between consumption and nonmarket time, and the competing returns to working for pay versus staying at home.

[1]Excellent reviews are found in Hotz, Klerman, and Willis (1997), Montgomery and Trussell (1986), and Schultz (1997).

Exhibit 4.2

The Pill and Women's Careers

While Figure 4.1 shows the shifting age profiles and the associated cohort effects for women's labour force participation, it hides dramatic changes in the nature of women's work: women have moved steadily into professional careers like law, medicine, and dentistry. Several factors are behind these shifts, but what credit can be given to the birth control pill ("The Pill")? *The Economist* (December 1999, p. 102) suggests that oral contraceptives may be considered the technological development "that defines the 20th century," because of their liberating power for women's choices. But why would The Pill make such a difference to women's career paths?

Claudia Goldin and Lawrence Katz (2000) argue that the primary influence was in university dormitories. They explore the role of The Pill in U.S. women's college and marriage decisions from a variety of angles. It was approved for use by the U.S. FDA in 1960, and was quickly adopted by most young, married women. Throughout the 1960s, married women used it, and reduced their fertility. Yet the expectations of reduced fertility did not immediately induce young, single women to enroll in education-intensive occupations. Goldin and Katz argue, instead, that it was not until single women could themselves obtain The Pill that they began making these educational investments. For most of the 1960s it was difficult for single women to get The Pill: there were restrictions on the ability of doctors to prescribe birth control pills to single unmarried women below the age of majority, at the time 21 years old. But in 1971, the age of majority was lowered to 18 by constitutional amendment, with the primary motivation of extending the vote to Vietnam draft-age men. The adoption of this amendment was staggered across states, and there is a striking correlation between when a state lowered its age of majority and when single women in that state started using The Pill. Furthermore, there is a correlation between these dates and increases in the enrollment of women in professional programs, as well as the delay in marriage by young women that facilitates the pursuit of professional careers.

So why would birth control for single women affect their schooling decisions? Goldin and Katz highlight two channels. First, it reduced the possibility of unwanted pregnancies, and allowed women and men to have premarital sex without jeopardizing the woman's educational plans. Second, eliminating the stark choice between sex (and early marriage) versus a career, it allowed women to postpone marriage. This had a ripple effect through the "marriage market." Prior to The Pill, a delay of marriage meant that a woman would face a smaller pool of potential husbands, as many had already matched up with women not pursuing professional careers. But the ability to have sex and delay marriage meant that fewer women were married right out of college, leaving a deeper pool of potential husbands a few years later. Thus, Goldin and Katz argue, the primary liberating effect of The Pill on women's careers was to facilitate the combination of premarital sex with a university education.

Variables Affecting Fertility

Income Economic theory predicts that, *other things being equal*, there will be a positive relationship between income and the desired number of children, assuming children are analogous to "normal goods." The problem is that in the real world other things are not equal. Specifically, factors such as contraceptive knowledge and the cost of having children tend to be related to the income variable, so that it becomes difficult to separate the pure effect of income alone. (See Exhibit 4.3.)

Price or Cost of Children Economic theory also predicts that the demand for children is negatively related to the price or cost of having children. Phipps (1998) calculates the implicit cost of children in Canada by estimating the amount of income it would take to restore a family with one child to the same level of material well-being as a similar childless couple. A typical Canadian couple with a family income of $60,000 would require about $9300 per year to compensate it for the extra costs associated with having their first child. Additional children are slightly cheaper.

Although direct costs such as the additional food, clothing, and housework associated with raising a child are an important aspect of the cost of children, the main element in the cost of having a child is the income forgone by the spouse (in our society this tends to be the wife) who takes time away from labour market activity to bear and raise the child.

An increase in the potential earnings of wives can have both income and substitution effects on the decision to have children. The consumption substitution effect says that wives with high potential earnings will have fewer children because the higher opportunity cost (forgone income) of having a child induces them to substitute away from the expensive alternative of having children and to engage in less expensive activities that do not impinge as much on their earning capacity. The income effect, on the other hand, says that wives with a high earning capacity can contribute more to family income and this will enable the family to spend more on all commodities, implying greater expenditures on children if children are "normal goods." Thus the income and substitution effects of a change in the wife's earning capacity have opposing effects on desired family size.

Price of Related Goods A rise in the price of complementary goods (e.g., medical expenses, daycare, education) would tend to reduce our desired number of children. Conversely, a fall in their price—perhaps from public subsidies—could encourage larger

Exhibit 4.3

Are Children Normal Goods?

In economics, normal goods are ones that we spend more on as our income increases; that is, they have a positive income elasticity of demand. At first glance it appears that children are not like normal goods, in that higher-income families and wealthier countries tend to be associated with small family sizes. Children, like potatoes, seem more like inferior goods which we purchase less of as our income rises!

The problem with the empirical evidence is that the *gross* negative relationship between income and family size is the result of two opposing forces. On the one hand, high-income families and countries have more wealth which should lead to larger family sizes, if children are like normal goods (i.e., a pure income effect). On the other hand, women in high-income families and countries tend to have high potential earnings power and this makes the (opportunity) cost of children higher. That is, women of high earnings power forgo more income if they take time out of the labour market to bear and raise children.

As indicated subsequently, the negative effect of the higher "price" of having a child tends to outweigh the positive income effect whereby higher earnings are used to "buy" more children. When the potential earnings of women is controlled for (e.g., through econometric analysis), a positive relationship between income and family size prevails. Children are like normal goods!

Exhibit 4.4

Fertility and Labour Supply

How much do children reduce the labour supply of women? If parents decide to have an additional child, how much less likely is a woman to work for pay? One way to address this question would be to compare the labour supply decisions of women with different numbers of children. For example, the difference in number of weeks worked of women with one child from that of those with two children could be interpreted as the causal effect of an additional child on labour supply.

However, as this section emphasizes, fertility and labour supply are outcomes of a more complicated, probably joint, decision-making process. It is unlikely that fertility decisions are made independent of labour supply and vice versa. For example, women who choose to have larger families might be less inclined to work in the first place, and this difference in preferences is confounded with the possibly independent effect of fertility on labour supply.

Absent cooperation of a scientifically inspired stork, economists have attempted to identify "natural experiments" whereby the number of children can be treated as exogenous to (or independent of) the labour supply decision. Angrist and Evans (1998) provide a very clever example of this methodology. They point out that among families with two children, parents with "matched sets" (one boy and one girl) are less likely to have a third child than those with two children of the same sex. Presumably, parents like having a mixture of sexes of children. It seems reasonable to treat the sex composition of the first two children as independent of labour supply preferences of parents with two children. It also turns out that women with two children of the same sex (both boys or both girls) are less likely to work than those with one boy and one girl. It is difficult to explain this except by the fact that they are also more likely to have a third child.

Thus, while Angrist and Evans estimate that women with three or more children are 16 percent less likely to work than women with only two children, only 10 percentage points of this is due to the causal effect of children on labour supply, and the remaining 6 percent is due to the underlying preference for women with three children to stay at home anyway.

family sizes. In most cases, the cost of any one of these related commodities is probably not large enough to have any appreciable effect on family size. However, dramatic changes in the private cost of some of these items—such as free university tuition or universally free daycare—could have an impact, as could any trend in the overall extent of government support for medical care, family allowances, maternity leave, education, or daycare.

Tastes and Preferences Economists tend to regard tastes and preferences as exogenously given from outside the economic system. In the area of family formation, our tastes and preferences have dramatically changed, related to our ideas on religion, family planning, and the women's liberation movement in general. These factors have all changed over time in a fashion that would encourage smaller family sizes.

Some would argue that these changes were not really exogenous to the economic system, but rather were a result of some of the more fundamental economic changes. For example, such factors as improved job opportunities for females may have made women's liberation more necessary to ensure more equal employment opportunities. The dramatic increase in the number of women working outside the home may have changed attitudes toward women, their role in society, and the nature of the family. Cause and effect works both ways: tastes and preferences both shape, and are shaped, by the economic system.

Education also has an important bearing on tastes and preferences. Not only does it raise the income forgone from raising children, but increased education may also widen our horizon for other goods (travel, entertainment outside the home), enable family planning, and encourage self-fulfillment through means other than having children.

Technology The term "technology" is often used by economists as a general rubric to describe the general technological and environmental factors that influence our economic decisions. In the area of fertility and family formation, birth control knowledge and contraceptive devices have had an important impact on the number of children, primarily by equilibrating the actual with the desired number of children. Medical advances with vasectomies and tubal ligation can have a similar impact. The reduction in infant mortality that has occurred over time should also reduce the number of births since, in times of high infant mortality, it was often necessary to have large families simply to have a few children survive to adult age.

Most of the technological advances discussed so far are ones that would encourage or enable smaller families. Some, such as reduced danger and discomforts during pregnancy, and advances in fertility drugs and operations, work in the opposite direction to encourage or enable more childbearing. These have been especially important for women who have postponed childbearing to later in their life. Other advances, such as processed food and disposable diapers, have made care for children easier.

Empirical Results

The empirical evidence on fertility behaviour is confusing to interpret because of the difficulty of holding other factors constant when observing actual behaviour. For example, it is difficult to isolate the effect of family income, independent of the effect of the wife's education, because highly educated wives tend to marry husbands with high incomes. If we observe fewer children in high-income families, is this because of their high income, or is it because wives in such families tend to be highly educated and hence their forgone income or cost of having children is high?

Statistical techniques such as multiple regression analysis have been used by econometricians to isolate the effect of a single variable, while holding the impact of all other factors constant. The results of such studies generally confirm the economic predictions. Specifically, there tends to be a negative relationship between the number of children and the cost of having children as measured, for example, by the wife's potential labour market earnings. As well, there tends to be a weak positive relationship between income and family size, after holding constant the impact of other variables, notably the earnings potential of the wife.[2] This positive relationship is especially likely to prevail between income and *expenditures* on children, since higher income is used to "purchase" more

[2]On the basis of Canadian data over the period 1948 to 1975, Hyatt and Milne (1991b) estimate the elasticity of demand for children to be 1.38 with respect to male income, and -1.55 with respect to female wages. These are fairly close to the U.S. estimates obtained by Butz and Ward (1979) for the same period.

This implies that a 1 percent increase in male income gives rise to a 1.38 percent increase in the number of children born, other things held constant. For example, if real average male income increases from $30,000 to $33,000 (a 10 percent increase) then the number of children born would increase by 13.8 percent ($10 \times 1.38\%$). On the basis of the average fertility rate of 1.67 in 1987, this implies an increase in fertility of 0.23 children ($0.138 \times 1.67 = 0.23$) or an increase in average fertility from 1.67 to 1.90.

The negative wage elasticity of -1.55 implies that a 1 percent increase in the wages of women gives rise to 1.55 percent reduction in the fertility rate, other things held constant. For example, if real average female wages increase from $30,000 to $33,000 (as above) this would reduce fertility by 0.26 children (0.155 3 1.67 = 0.26) or a reduction in average fertility from 1.67 to 1.41.

"quality" (as measured by expenditures per child) as well as quantity (number of children).

When the earning potential of the wife is *not* held constant then there tends to be a negative relationship between fertility and income; that is, poor countries and poor families tend to have larger family sizes. This is due, however, to the low earnings potential of women in such situations, with this negative effect of their potential earnings dominating the positive effect of income. This highlights the probability that a viable population control policy, for less-developed countries especially, is to improve the job opportunities for women (see Exhibit 4.5). This will raise the (opportunity) cost of having children, and if the empirical estimates are applicable, this should outweigh any tendency to have more children because of the additional income generated by their employment.

The empirical evidence also indicates that government policies can affect fertility by altering the economic determinants factors that influence family size. On the basis of Canadian data, Hyatt and Milne (1991a) indicate that family allowances, the Child Tax Credit, and maternity benefits under unemployment insurance all had a positive effect on family size. Milligan (2001) investigates the impact of Quebec's tax incentive scheme to increase fertility, and also finds that the policy "succeeded" in encouraging families to have more children (see Exhibit 4.6). On the basis of U.S. data, Whittingham, Alm, and Peters (1990) indicated that the personal exemption for dependents had a positive effect on fertility. Leibowitz (1990) provides evidence indicating that families with free medical care for

Exhibit 4.5

China's "One-Child Policy"

Out of concern for excessive population growth, in 1979 China adopted a "one-child policy" designed to reduce fertility, ideally, to one child per family. The policy was enforced by a variety of mechanisms, including both rewards for complying families and fines for families having too many children. It was applied most strictly in cities, and more unevenly in the countryside. By the early 1990s, the total fertility rate (the number of children ever born to a woman) had declined from three to fewer than two children per woman, and the sex ratio had tilted decidedly in favour of boys.

How much credit or blame should be given to this "central planning" of fertility? As usual, it is difficult to tell. China's pattern of demographic transition, that is, the reduction in births combined with an increase in life expectancy, looks very much like that of other East Asian countries, as they have gone through the process of economic development. As economies develop, and the returns to women's work and education improve, the increase in women's opportunity cost of time naturally leads to a reduction in fertility. Furthermore, as incomes rise parents substitute toward the "quality" of their children's investments (like education) and away from quantity. Several researchers, such as Shultz and Zeng (1999) and Lee (2000), highlight the importance of women's labour market opportunities in their fertility decisions, helping to explain why fertility would have declined for purely economic reasons. However, this does not mean that the policy had no independent effect. Shultz and Zeng (1995) and MacElroy and Yang (2000) show that the economic incentives associated with the "one-child policy" also appear to have influenced the decision of how many children a couple has. Given the dramatic economic and social changes that have occurred in China over the past 20 years, disentangling the impact of fertility policy from economic development will continue to pose a challenge for empirical researchers.

Exhibit 4.6 The Benefits of a Distinct Society (I)

Can governments use cash to encourage Canadian parents to have another child? Given the high costs of raising children, how high would such a subsidy have to be? The government of Quebec offered such a subsidy during the 1990s. The program, Allowance for Newborn Children (ANC), paid non-taxable benefits to families that had children in Quebec, and was in place from 1988 to 1997. When it was first introduced, the program offered $500 for a first child, $500 for a second, and $3000 for a third. By 1997, the subsidy for a third child had risen to $8000! So while the government of China was attempting to reduce fertility, the government of Quebec was trying to increase the number of Quebecers. Were there any takers?

Part of the problem in answering this question stems from the difficulty in knowing what would have happened to fertility in Quebec in the absence of a program. However, given the similarities in fertility behaviour in the rest of Canada, the rest of Canada can serve as a "control group" for the "treatment group" in Quebec. Furthermore, we would expect that the effect of the program would be strongest for parents moving from two three kids, taking advantage of the largest subsidy. Kevin Milligan (2001) exploits this strategy to estimate the impact of the ANC on fertility in Quebec. Some of his results are reproduced in the table below.

Total Fertility Rates by Region

	Quebec	Change (from 1987)	Rest of Canada	Change (from 1987)
1987	1.37		1.66	
1992	1.67	+0.30	1.74	+0.12
1997	1.52	+0.15	1.57	–0.09
DD 1992		+0.18		
DD 1997		+0.23		

Note: DD is the "Difference in Differences" between Quebec and the rest of Canada, comparing the change in TFR from 1987 in the two regions.

Source: Based on numbers reported in Milligan (2001), Table 4.1, in turn based on provincial vital statistics.

In 1987, the TFR (number of children ever born to a woman) was significantly lower in Quebec than the rest of Canada. This reflected a steep decline in fertility in Quebec, in absolute terms and relative to the rest of Canada, beginning in 1960. By 1992, after the program had been in place for five years, the TFR in Quebec had increased by 0.30 children per woman. However, part of this was apparently due to factors unrelated to the ANC, as women in the rest of Canada also had their TFR rise by 0.12. The difference in these changes, the "difference in differences," is 0.18, which may be interpreted as the effect of the "treatment" of the ANC. By 1997, fertility in both regions declined, but the gap between Quebec and the rest of Canada had declined to 0.05, implying an impact of the program of 0.23.

Milligan further shows that the increases in fertility were greatest for those families who had two or more children already, and were thus eligible for the large subsidy. His more detailed econometric analysis employing a variety of data sources also confirms that, for a price, Quebecers could be encouraged to have more children.

three to five years had 29 percent more births than families where medical care was not free. Even in nineteenth-century England, the "family allowance" of the Poor Laws apparently led to increased birth rates (see Exhibit 4.7).

RETIREMENT DECISION AND PENSIONS

The **retirement decision** is essentially a decision by older persons not to participate in the labour force, and it is amenable to analysis utilizing labour force participation theory. The retirement decision is treated separately simply because it is an area of increasing policy concern and, as the references indicate, it has developed its own empirical literature. Here we apply the basic income-leisure framework to the retirement decision. Subsequently, Chapter 13 deals with the reasons for the existence of mandatory retirement rules that lead to a "bunching" of retirement dates, often around age 65.

The notion of retirement has many meanings, ranging from outright leaving of the labour force, to a reduction of hours worked, to simply moving into a less onerous job. The process itself may also be gradual, beginning with a reduction in time worked (perhaps associated with a job change) and ending in full retirement. Throughout this chapter, we will generally talk of retirement as leaving the labour force; however, the importance of various forms of quasi-retirement and the often gradual nature of the retirement process should be kept in mind.

The policy importance of the retirement decision stems from the fact that it can have an impact on so many elements of social policy. For the individuals themselves, and their families, the retirement decision has implications ranging from their financial status to their psychological state. For the economy as a whole, the retirement decision also has macroeconomic implications with respect to such factors as private savings, unemployment, and the size of the labour force, all of which have implications for the level of national income.

In addition, there is concern over the solvency of public pension funds if large numbers retire and few are in the labour force to pay into the fund. This problem may be especially acute around the turn of the century, when the post–World War II baby-boom population reaches potential retirement age and, depending on fertility factors and patterns of female labour force participation, when there may be few other participants in the labour force paying into the funds.[3]

Exhibit 4.7 **Did the "Family Allowance" of the Poor Laws Increase Birth Rates?**

The Poor Laws of early nineteenth-century England essentially provided a system of "child allowances" whereby workers often received additional income from their parish if they had more children. Malthus argued against such laws on the grounds that they simply encouraged larger family sizes which in the long run would simply increase poverty.

There has been, and continues to be, considerable debate on the impact of the Poor Laws. Recent econometric evidence, however, indicates that after controlling for the effect of other variables affecting birth rates (Boyer 1989), the Poor Law system of family allowances did lead to higher birth rates. Malthus appears to have been correct at least in his argument that family allowances leads to higher birth rates.

[3]See Baker and Benjamin (2000) for further discussion of these issues.

The policy importance of the retirement decision is further heightened by the fact that it is an area where policy changes can affect the retirement decision. This is especially the case with respect to such factors as the mandatory retirement age and the nature and availability of pension funds. However, to know the expected impact of changes in these factors, we must know the theoretical determinants of the retirement decision, and the empirical evidence on the retirement response.

Theoretical Determinants of Retirement

Mandatory Retirement Age The term **mandatory retirement provisions** refers to both compulsory retirement provisions and automatic retirement provisions. Under automatic retirement, people *have* to retire at a specific age and cannot be retained by the company. Under compulsory retirement provisions, however, the company can compel the worker to retire at a specific age, but it can also retain the services of a worker, usually on a year-to-year basis.

The term is somewhat of a misnomer, since there is no magic age embodied in *legislation* that says a person *must* retire by a specific age. The mandatory retirement age may be part of an employer's personnel policy, or it may be negotiated in a collective agreement. In addition, there is an age at which public pensions become available, although they do not *prevent* people from continuing to work. As well, aspects of labour legislation may not apply to workers beyond a specific age. Thus the so-called mandatory retirement age—age 65 appears to be the magic number in North America—is really a result of personnel policy and is influenced, but not determined, by government programs. It is neither fixed nor immutable.

This is illustrated by the fact that Europe and the United States appear to be moving in opposite directions with respect to changes in the mandatory retirement age. Presumably to help alleviate problems of youth unemployment, in Europe the tendency is to encourage a lowering of the retirement age. In the United States, on the other hand, the trend seems to be in the opposite direction. Recent legislation has removed any mandatory retirement age in the federal public service and has forbidden a mandatory retirement age below age 70 in most other sectors. Certainly, workers can retire before age 70, and employers may try to induce them to do so. Nevertheless, they cannot be forced to retire.

In Canada, mandatory retirement is banned in Quebec, Manitoba, New Brunswick, and the federal jurisdiction. The Supreme Court of Canada has ruled that mandatory retirement does not constitute age discrimination, which is prohibited under Section 15(1) of the Charter of Rights. Essentially, this decision leaves it up to each individual jurisdiction as to whether it will ban mandatory retirement.

lois.justice.gc.ca/en/charter

Approximately half of the Canadian work force is employed in jobs that are ultimately subject to a mandatory retirement provision (Gunderson and Pesando 1988). Most of these persons have an occupational pension plan in which the mandatory retirement provision is a condition for receiving the pension. Mandatory retirement provisions are most prevalent and pensions most prominent in situations where workers are covered by a collective agreement. These are important observations since they remind us that mandatory retirement provisions tend to exist in situations where workers have a reasonable degree of bargaining power and the income protection of a pension plan. They are not simply imposed by management in a unilateral fashion. This will be an important consideration when the rationale for mandatory retirement is discussed in more detail in the later chapter on optimal compensation systems.

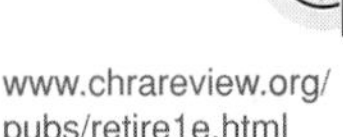

www.chrareview.org/pubs/retire1e.html

The fact that the mandatory retirement age is not immutable suggests that it can change in response to other basic forces that affect the retirement decision and that account for the existence of mandatory retirement itself. These factors are dealt with in Chapter 13, which looks at the rationale for mandatory retirement in the context of an optimal compensation system.

The remainder of this chapter deals with the basic forces that affect the retirement decision, either directly as people are induced to retire or indirectly as pressure is exerted to change the mandatory retirement age or the age at which various retirement benefits become available.

Wealth and Earnings Economic theory, in particular the income-leisure choice theory discussed earlier, indicates that the demand for leisure—as indicated, for example, by the decision to retire early—is positively related to one's wealth, and is related to expected earnings in an indeterminate fashion. The wealth effect is positive, reflecting a pure income effect: with more wealth we buy more of all normal goods, including leisure in the form of retirement. The impact of expected earnings is indeterminate, reflecting the opposing influences of income and substitution effects. An increase in expected earnings increases the income forgone if one retires and therefore raises the (opportunity) cost of retirement: this has a pure substitution effect reducing the demand for retirement leisure. On the other hand, an increase in expected earnings also means an increase in expected wealth and, just like wealth from nonlabour sources, this would increase the demand for retirement leisure. Since the income and substitution effects work in opposite directions, the impact on retirement of an increase in expected earnings is ultimately an empirical proposition. Thus the increase in our earnings that has gone on over time, and that presumably will continue, should have an indeterminate effect on the retirement decision.

Health and the Nature of Work and the Family As people age and approach retirement, their health and the health of their spouses can obviously influence the retirement decision. This can be the case especially if their accumulated wealth or pension income enables them to afford to retire because of health problems.

The changing nature of work may also influence the retirement decision. For example, the trend toward white-collar and professional jobs and away from more physically demanding blue-collar jobs may make it easier and more appealing for people to work longer. Emerging labour shortages may provide an incentive for employers to encourage older workers to return to the labour force. On the other hand, the permanent job loss of older workers due to plant closings and mass layoffs may make earlier retirement more attractive for these workers, especially if their industry-specific skills make it difficult for them to find alternative employment.

The changing nature of the family can also affect the retirement decision, albeit in complicated ways. The decline of the extended family may make retirement less attractive. The dominance of the two-income family may lead to one spouse not retiring from the labour market until the other also retires, given the joint nature of the retirement decision. However, the increased family income associated with both parties working may enable them both to be able to afford to retire early. The "deinstitutionalization" of health care with its emphasis on home care as opposed to institutional care may force the retirement of one spouse in order to care for the other.

In the income-leisure choice framework many of these factors affect the shape of the individual's indifference curve (preferences for labour market work versus preferences for leisure or household work in the form of retirement). Others can affect the budget constraint or wage line, which depicts the market returns to labour market work. For example, health problems that make labour market work more difficult will increase the slope of the indifference curve (requiring more income per unit of work to maintain the same level of utility). This, in turn, will induce a shift toward retirement leisure. Alternatively stated, it increases the individual's reservation wage and therefore makes retirement more likely if the reservation wage exceeds the market wage.

A permanent job loss will lead to a reduction in the market wage if alternative jobs are lower-paid. This downward rotation of the wage line has opposing income and substitution effects, as previously discussed. The returns to work are reduced (substitution effect) and this may induce retirement as the market wage now may fall below the reservation wage. In contrast, income or wealth has fallen (income effect) and this may compel the individual to postpone retirement.

Universal Old Age Security Pension

In addition to being affected by the mandatory retirement age, wealth and earnings, health, and the changing nature of work and the family, retirement decisions can be affected by various features of public and private pension plans. In fact, a growing area of research in labour economics has involved indicating how these various features of pension plans can have intended and unintended effects on retirement decisions. This highlights the fact that pensions are not simply forms of saving for retirement but active policy and human resource management instruments that can be used to influence the retirement decision.

As indicated in Exhibit 4.8, there are a variety of sources of pension income in Canada. The universal "old age" pension is given to all persons over the age of 65. In addition, persons who have worked in the labour market likely will have built up eligibility for the Canada/Quebec Pension Plan (CPP/QPP). As well, many will have an employer-sponsored occupational pension plan. In fact, many receive pension income from all three sources.

www.hrdc-drhc.gc.ca/isp/common/cpptoc_e.shtml

All three tiers of the pension income support system also have features that affect the retirement decision. In fact, increased attention is being paid to utilizing these features of pension plans to influence the retirement decision, for purposes of public policy and human resource management.

www.hrdc-drhc.gc.ca/isp/common/oastoc_e.shtml

For most people, the universal **Old Age Security** (OAS) pension is basically a demogrant, an unconditional grant given to all persons over the age of 65. In the income-leisure choice framework the budget constraint is shifted outward in a parallel fashion, by the amount of the pension. The shift is parallel to the original budget constraint because the pension is given irrespective of the recipient's work behaviour. There is no change in the returns to work—recipients receive their full market wage as well as pension. (This ignores, of course, the income taxes or "clawback" that applies to high earners.)

As a demogrant, the old age pension has the work incentive effects of a demogrant (discussed previously in Chapter 3 and illustrated in Figure 3.1). That is, there is a pure income effect, enabling the recipient to buy more of all normal commodities, including more leisure in the form of earlier retirement. Alternatively stated, the pension enables people to be able to afford to retire earlier.

The **Guaranteed Income Supplement** (GIS) may also be paid to persons over 65 and in need as determined by a means test. There is a 50 percent implicit "tax-back" feature to the GIS in that the payments are reduced by $0.50 for every dollar earned by persons who continue to work and earn income. So the GIS shifts the budget constraint upward by the amount of the supplement, and then reduces its slope by 50 percent (i.e., rotates it downward and to the left) because of the implicit tax-back feature. On net, the budget constraint has both shifted outward and reduced its slope. The outward shift or income effect implies more income or wealth, which in turn implies earlier retirement. The reduction in the slope or substitution effect implies that the returns to labour market work are reduced (i.e., the opportunity cost of retirement is lower) which also increases the likelihood of retirement. That is, both the income and substitution effects of the GIS increase the probability of retiring from the labour force.

Social Insurance Pensions: Canada/Quebec Pension Plan (CPP/QPP)

Social insurance pensions refer to public pension schemes that are financed by compulsory employer and employee contributions through a payroll tax, and that pay pensions based on past earnings to those who qualify by virtue of their age and work experience. Some social insurance pensions (e.g., Social Security in the United States, but not the **Canada/Quebec Pension Plan** in Canada) also have a **retirement test** or work-income test whereby the pension gets reduced if the recipient works and continues to earn income. This is an implicit tax on earnings because it involves forgoing pension payments as one earns additional income. In addition, there is usually an explicit payroll tax on earnings used to finance the social insurance fund.

The retirement test tends to be prevalent in the vast majority of countries with social insurance. Developing economies usually require persons' complete withdrawal from the labour force in order for them to receive the pension (i.e., implicit 100 percent tax on earnings) mainly because such countries cannot afford to pay pensions to people who also work. In contrast, some countries with the longest history of social insurance schemes have no retirement test, allowing the person to retain full earnings and pension. The

Exhibit 4.8

Canada's Three-Tier Public and Private Pension System

1. Universal Old Age Security Pension

- Financed by general tax revenue.
- Demogrant or flat amount paid to all persons over age 65, irrespective of need or past contributions or work history. The maximum monthly benefit for a single person in 2001 was $431.
- May be supplemented by a means-tested Guaranteed Income Supplement (GIS), based on need. The maximum monthly benefit for a single beneficiary in 2001 was $513.

2. Social Insurance Pension: Canada/Quebec Pension Plan

- Financed by compulsory employer and employee contributions through a payroll tax for all workers aged 18–65, whether paid or self-employed.
- Benefits related to contributions based on payroll tax applied to past earnings, but not necessarily self-financing since funds for current pensioners comes from payments from current work force. The maximum monthly benefit in 2001 was $775.
- Canada/Quebec Pension Plan.
- Covered 87 percent of the labour force in 1997, with average CPP contributions of $1237.

3. Employer-Sponsored Occupational Pension Plans

- Financed by employer, sometimes with employee contributions.
- Benefits depend on type of plan: flat-benefit plans pay a flat benefit per year of service; earnings-based plans pay a percentage of earnings per year of service; and defined-contribution plans pay on the basis of returns earned by contributions to the fund.
- Covered 33 percent of the labour force and 41 percent of paid workers in 1998, with average contributions of $3310.
- Coverage differed only slightly by sex, being 33 percent of the male and 32 percent of the female labour force, and 42 percent of the male and 39 percent of the female paid workers.

Also, private savings, privately arranged pensions, and savings through such mechanisms as registered retirement savings plans (RRSPs). In 1998, 29 percent of tax filers contributed to RRSPs, with an average contribution of $4350.

motivation for this may be different: in France it appears to be because pension benefits are low and earnings are needed to supplement income; in Germany it appears to be because of a desire to encourage the work ethic.

In the Canada Pension Plan, the retirement test was eliminated in 1975, while the United States eliminated the retirement test for most Social Security recipients in 2000. In the United States, the retirement test now only applies to individuals who choose to retire before their "Normal Retirement Age."[4] If someone chooses to initiate Social Security benefits between age 62 and the Normal Retirement Age, benefits are reduced by $0.50 for every dollar of earned income above a specific threshold. In 2001, this threshold was $10,080.

These features of the Canadian and American social insurance pension schemes can have a substantial impact on the retirement decision. The pension itself, like all fixed benefit payments, has a pure income effect inducing retirement. In addition, for those who work, the implicit tax of the pension reduction associated with the retirement test, and the explicit payroll tax used to finance the scheme, both lower the returns to work and hence make retirement more financially attractive. That is, both taxes involve a substitution effect toward retirement because the opportunity cost of leisure in the form of retirement is lowered by the amount of tax on forgone earnings. To be sure, the tax on earnings also involves an income effect working in the opposite direction; that is, our reduced after-tax income means we can buy less of everything, including leisure in the form of retirement. However, this income effect is outweighed by the income effect of the pension itself, since for all potential recipients their income is *at least* as high when social insurance is available. Thus, as with the negative income tax plans analyzed in Chapter 3, both the substitution effect and the (net) income effect of the features of social insurance serve to unambiguously induce retirement.

These features of social insurance and their impact on retirement can be modelled somewhat more formally, along the lines of the income-leisure framework developed in Chapter 2. With Y defined as income after taxes and transfers, W the wage rate, T the maximum amount of leisure (ℓ) available, B the pension received upon retiring, p the explicit payroll tax used to finance social insurance, and t the implicit tax involved in the pension reduction through the retirement test, the budget constraint with a social insurance pension is

$$Y_p = B + (1 - p - t)\,W(T - \ell)$$

This can be compared to the constraint without social insurance, which is

$$Y_o = W(T - \ell)$$

The new budget constraint is illustrated in Figure 4.3 for various possible social insurance schemes. Figure 4.3(a) illustrates the case when there is no retirement test (e.g., Canada/Quebec Pension Plans); that is, the recipient is given a pension and is allowed to work without forgoing retirement. (For simplicity, the payroll tax for financing the pension has been ignored. With the payroll tax as a fixed percentage of earnings, the budget constraint would have rotated downward from the point B.) The new budget constraint is $Y = B + W(T - \ell)$ when $p = 0$ and $t = 0$. Such a pension scheme simply has a pure income effect, encouraging potential recipients to retire. Although it is not shown in the diagram, the new indifference curve may be tangent to the new budget constraint, at a point such as E_p above and to the right of the original point E_0. The new equilibrium may also involve a

[4]The "normal retirement age" is defined as the age at which one can retire and receive full pension benefits. Early retirement in the United States can be initiated at age 62 (60 in Canada). The normal retirement age in Canada is 65, while in the United States it is gradually being raised from 65 to 67 (it will be 67 for everyone born after 1960).

Figure 4.3 **Budget Constraints Under Social Insurance Pensions (assuming payroll tax p = 0)**

This figure illustrates the work incentives associated with public pension plans, under varying assumptions regarding retirement tests, or the "clawing back" of benefits. In panel (a), beneficiaries receive benefits Y_B, and there is no penalty for working. In panel (b), the individual faces a 100 percent retirement test, so that earnings are fully clawed back until the benefit is exhausted. In panel (c), the retirement test only applies to earnings over (Y_C - Y_B), when the person works T - L_C, after which benefits are reduced by $0.50 for every dollar earned.

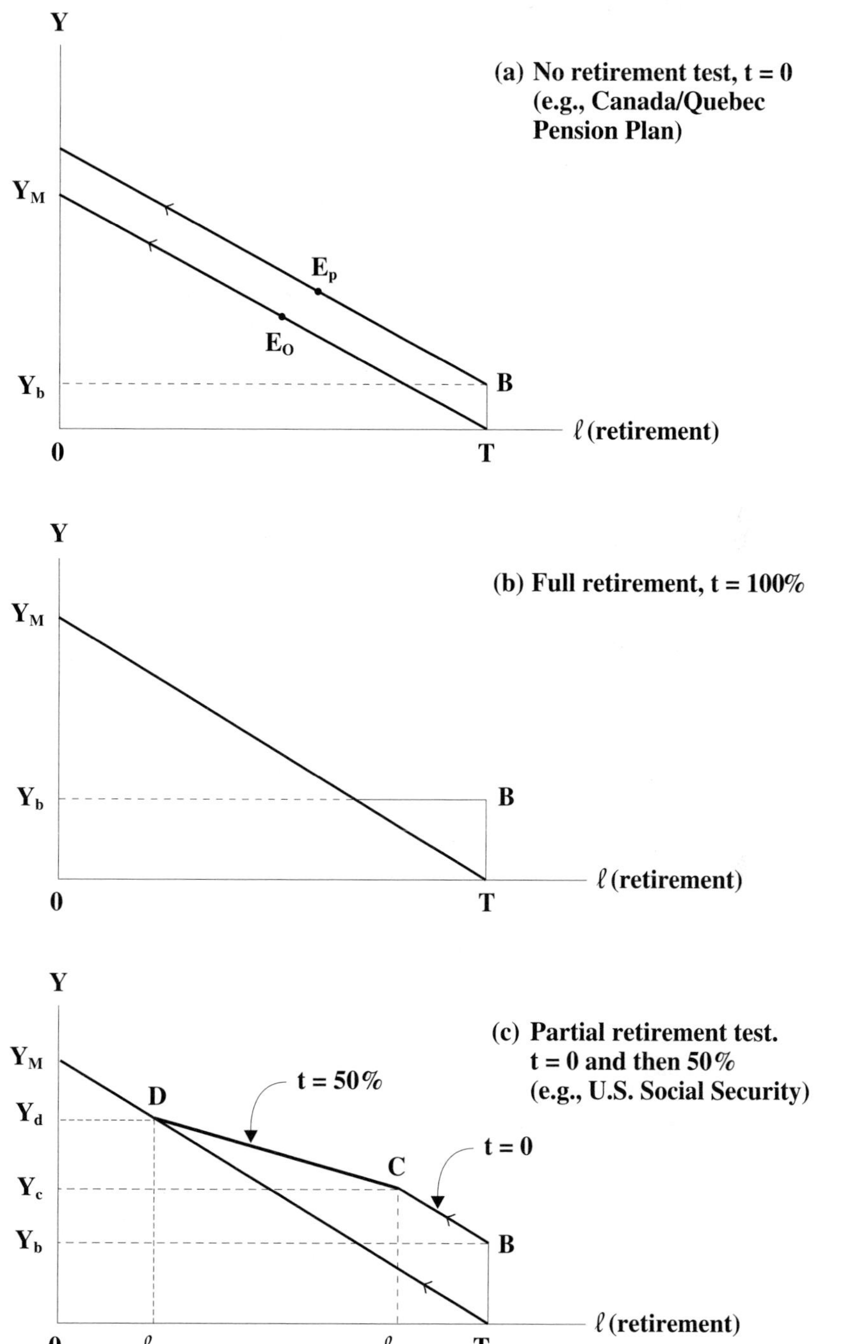

corner solution at B, in which case the recipient retired completely, or it may be at a point like E_p, signifying partial retirement; or, if leisure is not a normal good, it may be at a point vertically above E_0, in which case the recipient continued to work the same as before and received the full pension.

Figure 4.3(b) illustrates the new budget constraint under a full retirement test whereby the pension recipient is required to give up $1 of pension for every $1 earned. This implicit 100 percent tax rate makes the budget constraint similar to the one for welfare discussed in Chapter 3, and the adverse work incentive effects are similar. In particular, there will be a strong incentive to retire completely (move to point B).

The typical case with a partial retirement test is illustrated in Figure 4.3(c). The first arm of the budget constraint, TB, indicates the pension benefits payable upon complete retirement. (Income is Y_b = TB when leisure is OT.) The second arm, BC, illustrates that up to a specific threshold amount of labour market earnings, $Y_c - Y_b$, for working $T - \ell_c$, the recipient may keep the full pension benefits of Y_b (= TB), so that her total income with pension and labour market earnings could be up to Y_c. As indicated previously, this threshold amount of earnings, $Y_c - Y_b$, was $10,080 in the United States in 2001. The new arm of the budget constraint is parallel to the original constraint of TY_m because the implicit tax is zero; that is, recipients who work keep their full labour market earnings.

The third arm, CD, illustrates the implicit tax that is involved when the recipient is required to give back a portion of the pension for the additional labour market earnings of $Y_d - Y_c$ that result from the additional work of $\ell_c - \ell_d$. An implicit tax of 50 percent results in the slope of CD being one half of the slope of the original constraint TY_m; that is, for every dollar earned, the recipient forgoes $0.50 in pension. When the recipient's labour earnings exceed $Y_d - Y_b$, at point D, then the person would no longer receive any pension and any additional work activity of $\ell_d - 0$ would result in additional income as shown by the fourth arm of the budget constraint DY_m.

The work incentive effects of the new budget constraint, $TBCDY_m$, are such as to unambiguously induce retirement. Basically, two things have happened. The budget constraint has shifted outward (upward to the right) from the original constraint of TY_m, and this has a wealth or income effect encouraging the purchase of more leisure in the form of retirement. In addition, the slope of the new budget constraint is always equal to or less than the original constraint; that is, the opportunity cost of leisure is reduced and this would encourage the substitution of leisure for other commodities. Both the income and substitution effect of the partial retirement work in the same direction to encourage early retirement.

Employer-Sponsored Occupational Pension Plans

The third tier of pension income support consists of **employer-sponsored** or **occupational pension plans**, for those who work in establishments with such plans. As indicated in Exhibit 4.9, such plans can be classified on the basis upon which benefits are calculated. Earnings-based plans are most common (especially final-earnings plans), covering about three-quarters of all workers. Flat-benefit plans, which predominate in the union sector, cover about 17 percent of plan members. **Defined contribution plans** cover only about 13 percent of plan members. However, because these tend to exist in small establishments with few employees, about half of all occupational pension plans are defined contribution plans. As well, there is a growing trend toward such plans, in part because of the extensive regulations being put on the defined benefit plans and the uncertainty and conflict over who "owns" the surplus assets that have often been generated in the defined-benefit plans.

The **defined-benefit plans** have a number of features that can influence the retirement decision of workers. In fact, such features can be used to encourage early retirement or to discourage postponed retirement past the normal retirement age established by the plan. This aspect is likely to grow in importance as the aging work force means that more people are in the age groups likely to be affected by early retirement, and as firms view early retirement as a viable way to "downsize" their work force. If the early retirement payments are sufficiently generous, this may also be in the mutual interest of employees, opening

Exhibit 4.9

Employer-Sponsored Occupational Pension Plans, 1998 (% of members in parentheses)

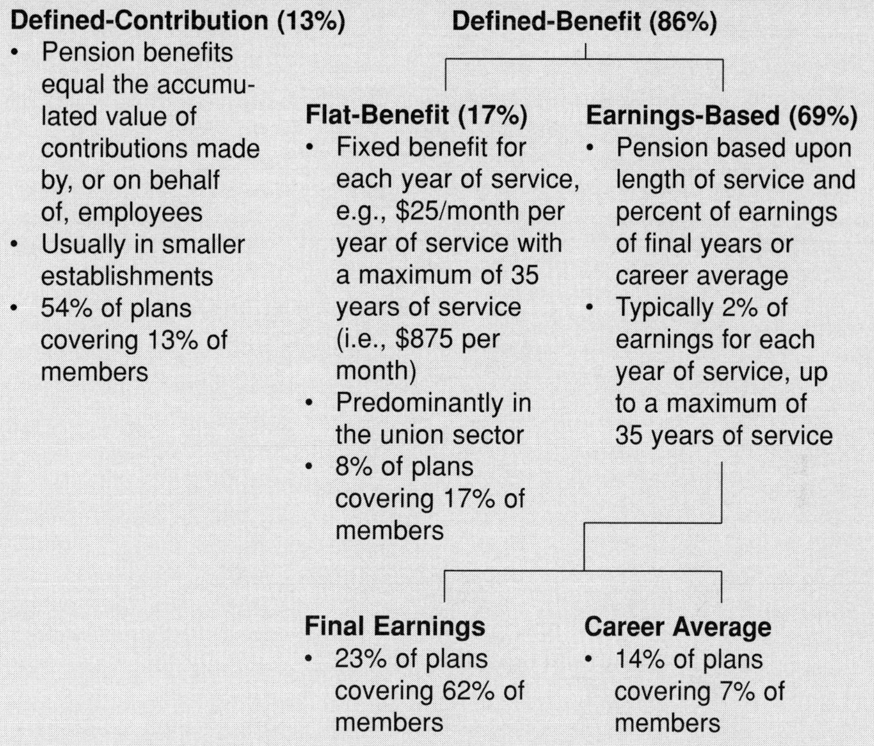

Defined-Contribution (13%)
- Pension benefits equal the accumulated value of contributions made by, or on behalf of, employees
- Usually in smaller establishments
- 54% of plans covering 13% of members

Defined-Benefit (86%)

Flat-Benefit (17%)
- Fixed benefit for each year of service, e.g., $25/month per year of service with a maximum of 35 years of service (i.e., $875 per month)
- Predominantly in the union sector
- 8% of plans covering 17% of members

Earnings-Based (69%)
- Pension based upon length of service and percent of earnings of final years or career average
- Typically 2% of earnings for each year of service, up to a maximum of 35 years of service

Final Earnings
- 23% of plans covering 62% of members

Career Average
- 14% of plans covering 7% of members

Notes: Includes about 1% of composite and other plans. Numbers do not add up to 100 because of rounding.

Sources: Pension Plans in Canada, 1998 (Ottawa: Supply and Services, 1999). In 1998, 33% of the labour force and 41% of employed paid workers were in occupational pension plans. Human Resources Development Canada, reproduced with the permission of the Minister of Public Works and Government Services Canada, 1999.

new promotion opportunities for younger workers, and enabling some of the retired employees to start new careers. As well, if mandatory retirement is banned or becomes less common, voluntary early retirement programs may become more prominent.

The potential work incentive effects of occupational pension plans can be illustrated by various features of a final-earnings plan. Such a plan, for example, could involve the payment of 2 percent of the final 3 years of earnings for each year of service (maximum of 35), which would imply a "replacement rate" of 70 percent (0.02 × 35) of final earnings. For a worker earning $30,000 per year in his final years, this would imply an annual pension of $21,000.

The features that most influence the retirement decision, in addition to the "normal" retirement age for pension eligibility, are: (1) the "backloading" or accumulation of pension benefit accruals, (2) early and special retirement provisions, and (3) postponed retirement provisions.

As indicated in Exhibit 4.10, eligibility for **early retirement** typically occurs at age 55 provided the worker has at least 10 years of service. It usually involves a subsidy in that the pension is actuarially reduced, but by an amount that does not compensate for the fact that it is received earlier and for a longer period.[5] If there is no actuarial reduction in the pension (termed **special retirement**), a larger subsidy is typically involved. Special retirement is less common, usually occurring at ages 60 to 62 and requiring at least 20 years of service. **Postponed retirement** provisions can also exist if workers are allowed to continue working past the normal retirement age, usually 65. Postponed retirement usually involves a penalty because of incomplete actuarial adjustments and/or further benefit accruals are not allowed.

The potential retirement-inducing effect of these features of occupational pension plans can be illustrated through their impact on the expected pension benefits (obligations of employers) that workers accrue as they work additional years with their employer.[6]

These pension benefit accruals, expressed as a percent of the workers' wages, are illustrated in Figure 4.4 for a representative final-earnings plan.

The accruals are substantial, averaging around 18 percent of wages for workers in their 50s and 60s. This means that employers' wage costs for such workers are augmented by about 18 percent to cover the pension obligations that are being accrued by such workers. It also means that for every additional year that such employees work, they are accumulating these substantial pension commitments that they will receive on retirement. The benefits are "backloaded" in the sense that they tend to get larger as the worker ages and accumulates service credits as well as seniority-based wage increases upon which pension benefits are calculated. This makes their total compensation profile (wages plus pension benefit accruals) steeper than otherwise would be the case. This in turn augments any pure seniority effect whereby wages themselves rise with seniority.

In addition to giving rise to substantial benefit accruals that are backloaded, occupational pension plans also can give rise to sharp "spikes" or jumps in benefit accruals at the ages of early retirement (usually 55) and special retirement (usually around age 62 if such a feature exists). As well, negative accruals typically occur after any special retirement spike or after the age of normal retirement when postponed retirement provisions apply.

These features of occupational pension plans can have important incentive effects on the turnover decisions of younger workers and the retirement decisions of older workers. Specifically, the backloading of pension benefit accruals means that younger workers have an incentive to stay with the firm to receive these benefits, and older workers have an incentive not to retire too early and forgo those accruals. This is especially the case just before ages when early or special retirement features would apply. For example, in Figure 4.4, a worker who retired just before age 55 would forgo the wages that would be received at age 55 as well as the pension benefit accrual, which could amount to about 80 percent of wages. The same would be true of a worker who retired just before the special retirement age of 62. Such workers would have an incentive not to retire just before these early or special retirement dates, but to wait at least until these dates. As well, they have an incentive to retire after the special or normal retirement age because of the negative

[5]For example, the reduction formulae could be 5 percent per year for each year that early retirement precedes normal retirement. A worker who retired 10 years early would have an annual pension that is reduced by 50 percent based on a reduction formula of 5 percent for each of the 10 years of early retirement. In the previous example, the worker who received $21,000 per year after the normal retirement age of 65 would have an annual pension of $11,500 commencing at the early retirement age of 55. Even though the annual pension is substantially reduced, a subsidy may be involved because the employee receives the pension earlier (i.e., at age 55) and for a longer period of time (i.e., from age 55 until death). The actual magnitude of the subsidy, and whether it exists, depends upon such factors as inflation and wage growth, as well as actuarial reductions implied by the benefit reduction formula.

[6]These are calculated as the annual present value of the stream of pension income to which a member is legally entitled at the end of the year, less the corresponding value of the previous year, adjusted for the interest factor (Kotlikoff and Wise, 1985; Pesando and Gunderson, 1988).

Exhibit 4.10 **Early and Postponed Retirement Features of Final-Earnings Plans**

Early Retirement Provisions
- Typically at age 55 with at least 10 years' service
- In most earnings-based plans
- May be unsubsidized in that annual pension benefits are reduced by an "actuarially fair" amount to exactly compensate for the fact that it is received early (i.e., at age 55 instead of the normal retirement age of 65) and for a longer period of time
- Or may be subsidized in that the early retirement pension is actuarially reduced by an amount that does not exactly compensate for the fact that it is received early and for a longer period of time

Special Retirement Provisions
- Typically at age 60–62 with at least 20 years' service
- Exists for about 30 percent of workers in earnings-based plans in private sector
- Extensively subsidized in that the special retirement pension is not actuarially reduced to compensate for the fact that it is received earlier and for a larger period of time

Postponed Retirement Provisions
- Typically involve pension "penalties" for postponing retirement past the age of normal retirement (e.g., 65)
- Penalties usually occur because of some combination of not allowing further accrual of pension benefits and/or not actuarially increasing previously accrued pension benefits to offset the fact that they are received later and for a shorter period

accruals that occur after those dates. The negative accruals were around 10 percent in the representative plan of Figure 4.4, but they can easily be in the neighbourhood of 40 percent depending upon other provisions of the plan (Pesando and Gunderson, 1988, p. 257).

In essence, the features of occupational pension plans can have important incentive effects on the retirement decision, discouraging early retirement that would lead to a loss of these backloaded accruals, especially just prior to the substantial accruals that can occur at early and special retirement dates.

Early retirement can be encouraged just after an early retirement date as the benefit accruals have peaked and dropped off thereafter, although, if a subsequent special retirement date also exists then, there may be a reluctance to retire just prior to that date and forgo the option of accruing the special retirement benefits.[7] Retirement is strongly encouraged at the normal retirement date, even if postponed retirement is an option. These incentive effects suggest a bunching of retirement just after the dates of early, special, and normal retirement, with a few retirements just prior to the dates of early and special retirement. As discussed later, these empirical predictions are verified in the data on retirement decisions under occupational pension plans.

[7]This highlights the fact that the turnover and retirement incentives should be formally modelled through "option values" whereby working an additional year yields not only the pension accrual of that year, but also the option to work additional years and consequently to qualify for subsequent retirement provisions. Conversely, retiring means forgoing the income and benefit accruals of that year and subsequent years as well as forgoing the option to work additional years and consequently to qualify for subsequent retirement provisions. See Lazear and Moore (1988).

Figure 4.4 **Pension Benefit Accruals as % of Wages in Representative Final-Earnings Plan**

This figure shows the "spikes" in benefit accrual that characterize many private pension plans (see the source note for details). For example, the provisions of the plan may generate very high returns to delaying retirement from age 54 to 55, or 61 to 62, with the mirror-image disincentives for delaying retirement past these ages.

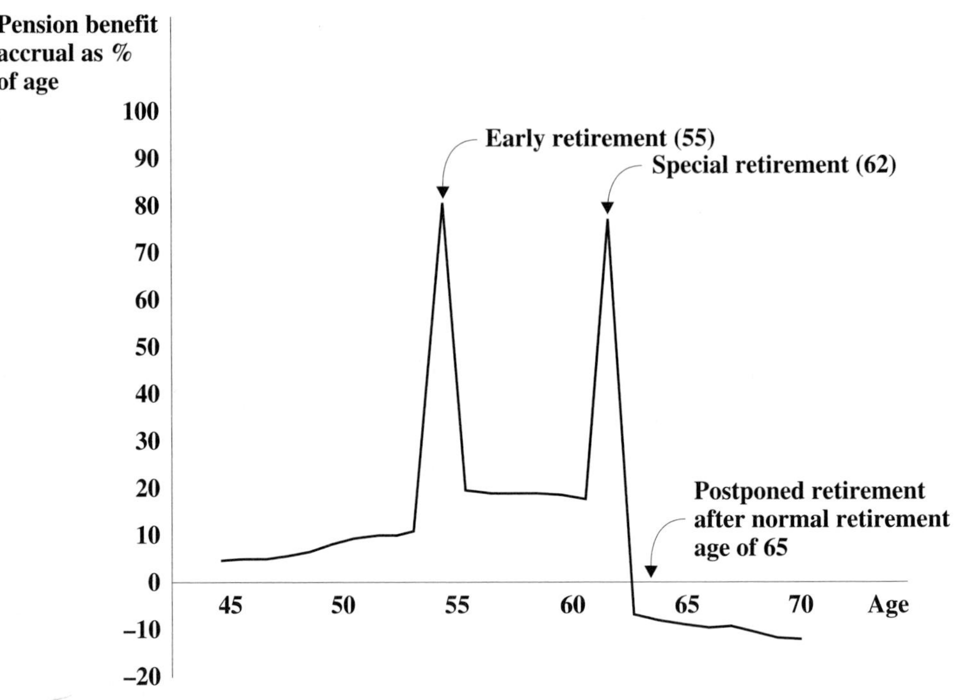

Source: Based on data given in Pesando and Gunderson (1988) for a representative final-earnings plan for an employee who enters the plan at age 30. Early retirement is at age 55 and 10 years of service with benefits being reduced by 5 percent for each year that early retirement precedes normal retirement at 65. Special retirement is at 62 and 20 years of service with (by definition) no reduction in benefits. If retirement is postponed past the normal retirement age of 65, there is a continued accrual of pension benefits but no actuarial increase of previously accrued benefits. Inflation is assumed to be 5 percent, with other assumptions outlined in the original article.

These incentive effects are based on "modelling" only some of the institutional features of occupational pension plans such as early and postponed retirement provisions. Other features such as vesting, bridging supplements, spouse benefits, golden handshakes, and retirement windows are discussed in articles in the references.[8] Clearly, pensions are not only an integral feature of the compensation system but also a key element in the human resource planning strategy of the firm. They can be used both to affect retirement decisions and hence the size and age composition of the firm's work force and to provide income support after retirement. The negative benefit accruals that tend to exist if retirement is postponed after the age of normal retirement may even serve as a substitute for mandatory retirement should mandatory retirement be banned. The sizeable pension obligations also highlight the cost to the firm of an aging work force, where both wages and

[8] *Vesting* refers to employees having the rights to the employer contribution as well as their own contribution. *Surviving spouse benefits* refer to the extent to which benefits are paid to a surviving spouse. *Bridging supplements* refer to additional payments that may be made between the date of early retirement and the date when the member reaches age 65 and thereby qualifies for social insurance pensions like the Canada/Quebec pension plan. *Golden handshakes* refer to special retirement packages given usually to senior executives. *Retirement windows* refer to special periods of time (often a year or less) whereby specific groups of workers can retire early and receive a special retirement bonus.

pension benefits tend to be higher.[9] Pension benefits may also have implications for the magnitude of the male-female wage gap—or, more accurately, the gap in total compensation to include fringe benefits such as pensions.

Empirical Evidence

The general empirical evidence on the determinants of retirement is reviewed in Lazear (1986), Lumsdaine and Mitchell (1999), and Gruber and Wise (1999); while Baker and Benjamin (2000) provide an overview of the Canadian evidence. Researchers use a variety of data sources, including those we have discussed already (labour force surveys and censuses). They also exploit cross-country and cross-jurisdictional data in order to identify the impact of particular features of national public pension schemes (see Exhibit 4.11, for example).

Exhibit 4.11

The Benefits of a Distinct Society (II)

One of the features of Canada's public pension program is that it is split into two separate jurisdictions: Quebec administers the QPP while the federal government (with the provinces) administers the CPP in the rest of Canada. This differentiates Canada from most other countries, which have single, country-wide pension plans. The CPP and the QPP are virtually identical in terms of policy parameters like contribution rates, levels of benefits, and rules governing eligibility. Occasionally, however, the two jurisdictions have been out of step in important ways. This has had real advantages for empirical research on the impact of pension plans on retirement behaviour, since differences across the plans can be exploited to identify possible effects of program parameters on retirement.

In most countries, for example, retirement rates have been trending upward, as more individuals opt for early retirement (retirement before age 65). At the same time, most retirement plans have become increasingly generous, especially with respect to early retirement. It is tempting to causally link these two trends, but one can never be sure whether the correlation is merely spurious and retirement trends are independent of the changes in pension plans. In 1984, Quebec began to allow early retirement for individuals aged 60 to 64, i.e., individuals in this age group could now retire and collect a reduced QPP pension. The CPP did not permit early retirement until 1987. Thus, for three years, early retirement was permitted in Quebec, but not in the rest of Canada. This provided an opportunity to examine the impact of early retirement provisions on retirement behaviour: Did early retirement take off in Quebec relative to the rest of Canada during this interval of different policies? Baker and Benjamin (1999) explore this question, and find that in fact there is little evidence of differential retirement patterns in Quebec over this time period, suggesting that the public pension plans did little to affect behaviour: most of the individuals who opted for early retirement would have done so anyway. Some may have had poor labour market opportunities, while others may have had generous private pensions. Thus, while Canada's constitutional bickering can be quite annoying, it can pay dividends for social science research.

[9] The same general picture also emerges from the flat-benefit plans that tend to predominate in the unionized sector. Periodic enrichments to the flat-benefit formula, usually at the time of the renewal of the collective agreement, lead to a backloading of pension benefit accruals. Spikes in the accruals occur at dates of early and special retirement if they exist. Pesando and Gunderson (1991) simulate these effects for representative flat benefit plans in Canada.

www.umich.edu/~hrswww/

In addition to these more conventional sources, labour economists use two U.S. surveys specifically designed for studying the elderly: the Retirement History Survey (RHS) and the more recent Health and Retirement Survey (HRS). These are longitudinal surveys that follow a sample of older workers for several years. This allows researchers to track the labour force status and relevant economic variables (such as pensions, wealth, and wages) from one year to the next, as the workers age. These sorts of data permit a more detailed investigation of the labour force dynamics associated with retirement. In a similar vein, economists occasionally gain access to company personnel records, which allows a careful analysis of the impact of private pensions on the retirement decision. The most credible studies of this type have been able to exploit "surprises" in the features of private pensions (such as temporary buyouts or offers of early retirement) to explore the sensitivity of the retirement decision to these program parameters.

Most studies find that characteristics of public and private pension plans affect retirement decisions in ways we would expect given the theory outlined above. However, the estimated responses have generally been small—certainly not large enough to "explain" the dramatic changes in retirement behaviour that have occurred over the past 30 years. This is an active area of empirical research, and more recent studies attempt to incorporate information on health, and also recognize that retirement decisions are jointly made by husbands and wives, complicating the simple models outlined here.

Summary

- As individuals age, there are several systematic patterns in their labour supply—withdrawing to have children, and eventually retiring from the labour force—that require modifications of the static labour supply model developed in Chapter 2.
- Interpretation of the cross-section correlation between age and labour force status as representing the "pure" effect of age is problematic, especially for women. This arises because of cohort effects, or the difficulty of separating out "age" from "vintage" (or year of birth) at a single point in time. Specifically for women, the age-participation profiles have been shifting upward over time, as each subsequent cohort of women is more attached to the labour market than previous ones.
- Incorporating individual decisions to work in one time period versus another involves a straightforward extension of the static labour supply model. Principally, this entails allowing for preferences to work at various points in one's life, and more importantly, the specification of the lifetime budget constraint: the present value of lifetime consumption equals the present value of lifetime income.
- The intertemporal labour supply model can be used to conduct a variety of thought experiments concerning the impact of wage changes at different points in the lifecycle on the evolution of work patterns.
- Children can have an important impact on the labour supply of parents, especially mothers; however, children are themselves the outcome of parents' choices. Economic models of fertility explore the connections between economic variables like income and wife's wages on the decision regarding whether and how many children to have, as well as interactions between fertility and labour supply.
- Retirement is another important life-cycle labour supply decision that is affected by a myriad of public and private pension plans. The static labour supply model can easily be augmented along the lines shown in Chapter 3, in order to incorporate some of the main features of public pension plans.

REVIEW QUESTIONS

1. Why has there been a long-run decline in fertility over time, even though income has risen?
2. What does the economics of fertility suggest to us about differences in family size between urban and rural areas of less-developed countries?
3. Discuss the extent to which the mandatory retirement age is both an exogenous determinant of the retirement decision and an endogenous result of the retirement decision.
4. On the basis of Figure 4.3(a) draw the indifference curves, before and after the pension, for persons who:
   (a) Retire completely
   (b) Retire partially
   (c) Work the same as before

   Compare their income in each case.
5. On the basis of Figure 4.3(b), draw the indifference curve for a person who is indifferent between retiring completely and continuing to work. Why would a person ever be indifferent between these two alternatives assuming that retirement is regarded positively? On the basis of the various factors given in the diagram, indicate how people may be induced to stay in the labour force rather than retire.
6. On the basis of Figure 4.3(c), draw the indifference curve for a person who:
   (a) Retires completely
   (b) Works part-time and only earns income up to the maximum amount before it becomes "retirement-tested," that is, benefits are reduced if the individual works "too much"
   (c) Works and earns income up to the maximum amount before it becomes retirement-tested at a 100 percent implicit tax
   (d) Works and earns so much income that no pension is forthcoming

   Compare the pension cost under each alternative.

PROBLEMS

1. The evaluation of the labour supply response to a tax cut can be quite different in a dynamic setting from what it is in a static setting. Discuss the relative impact of a permanent versus a transitory tax cut on labour supply, and compare the analysis to the static model.
2. Use a simple supply and demand diagram to illustrate how either supply- or demand-side factors may underlie the cohort effects implicit in Figure 4.1. What factors could be assigned to the "supply" or the "demand" side in explaining how the curves would shift? How could an empirical researcher disentangle the relative magnitudes of the supply and demand factors in explaining the increase in the number of women working now, as against 1950?
3. Using the economic theory of fertility, analyze the expected impact on the TFR (total fertility rate) and women's labour supply of the following:
   (a) An increase in women's wages
   (b) Elimination of the family allowance for high-income women
   (c) An increase in the deduction for child-care expenses
   (d) Increasing educational levels for women
4. Financial advisors say it's never too early to think about retirement. Analyze the impact on the current labour supply of a 25-year-old of the following news: "The Canada

Pension Plan will be insolvent in 40 years, and in addition to a reduction of pension and old age security benefits, the government will have to increase the CPP payroll tax for all workers."

5. Consider an individual aged 64 who is eligible to collect full Social Security (public pension) benefits of $6000 for a year. She has no other income, but can work at a weekly wage rate of $600 for a maximum of 52 weeks. Receipt of benefits from the Social Security program is retirement-tested. Specifically, the individual can earn up to $9000 in annual wage income without a reduction in benefits; however, after $9000 dollars of earnings, benefits are reduced by 50 percent for every dollar earned, until the benefits are exhausted.
   (a) Carefully draw and label the budget constraint for this individual.
   (b) Consider an individual whose labour supply decision is such that she receives Y_A in social security benefits, so that $0 < Y_A <$ $6000 (i.e., she receives positive but reduced benefits). On the carefully labelled diagram from part (a), show her labour supply decision.
   (c) "Elimination of the retirement test (i.e., allowing the individual to keep all benefits, irrespective of his or her labour earnings) will unambiguously increase the labour supply of the individual described in part (b)." True or false? Explain using a carefully labelled diagram.
6. You have been asked to estimate the impact on retirement of a policy raising the replacement from 40 to 60 percent of final earnings, and of lowering the implicit tax of the retirement test from 50 to 30 percent. You have access to comprehensive microeconomic data where the individual is the unit of observation. Specify an appropriate regression equation for estimating the retirement response, and indicate how you would simulate the impact of the change in the two policy parameters.
7. On the basis of a social insurance pension scheme where income, Y_P, is

$$Y_p = B + (1 - t)E$$

and B is the pension, t is the tax-back rate of the retirement test, and E is earnings, solve for the following:

(a) The breakeven level of earnings, E_b, where the recipient no longer receives any pension income (*Hint:* Income without the pension scheme is $Y_0 = E$, and therefore the breakeven level of earnings, E_b, occurs when $Y_0 = Y_P$ or the pension benefit, $B - tE$, equals zero)

(b) The breakeven level when there is also a threshold level of income, Y_t, before the tax-back rate of the retirement test is applied, so that:

$$Y_P = B + Y_t + (1 - t)E$$

(c) The dollar value of the breakeven level of earnings in parts (a) and (b) when B = $6000, Y_t = $10,000, and t = 0.5.

8. In an income-retirement choice diagram, indicate the effect on an individual's indifference curves and/or budget constraint, and subsequent retirement decision, of each of the following:
   (a) Retirement of one's spouse
   (b) Illness of one's spouse
   (c) Improvements in health of the elderly
   (d) Permanent displacement from a high-wage job in the steel industry to a low-wage job in the restaurant sector
   (e) Improvements in the retirement leisure industry (e.g., condominiums, recreation, travel) such that retirement is now relatively more attractive

KEYWORDS

REFERENCES

Angrist, J., and W. N. Evans. 1998. Children and their parents' labor supply: Evidence from exogenous variation in family size. *AER* 88 (June):450–77.

Baker, M., and D. Benjamin. 1999. How do retirement tests affect the labour supply of older men? *JPubEc* 71 (January):27–51.

Beaudry, P., and T. Lemieux. 1999. Evolution of the female labour force participation rate in Canada, 1976–1994: A cohort analysis. *Canadian Business Economics* 7 (May):57–70.

Becker, G. 1960. An economic analysis of fertility. In *Demographic and Economic Change in Developed Countries*. Princeton: Princeton University Press.

Boyer, G. 1989. Malthus was right after all: Poor relief and birth rates in southeastern England. *JPE* (February):93–114.

Card, D. 1994. Intertemporal labour supply: An assessment. In *Advances in Econometrics: The Sixth World Congress*, ed. C. A. Sims. New York: Cambridge University Press.

Dooley, M. D. 1994. The converging market work patterns of married mothers and lone mothers in Canada. *JHR* 29:600–20.

Goldin, C. 1990. *Understanding the Gender Gap: An Economic History of American Women*. New York: Oxford University Press.

______. 1995. The U-shaped female labor force function in economic development and economic history. In *Investment in Women's Human Capital*, ed. T. P. Schultz. Chicago and London: University of Chicago Press.

Goldin, C., and L. F. Katz. 2000. The power of the pill: Oral contraceptives and women's career and marriage decisions. NBER Working Paper, Number 7527.

Gruber, J., and D. Wise, Eds. 1999. *Social Security and Retirement Around the World*. Chicago and London: NBER Conference Report Series. University of Chicago Press.

Gunderson, M., and J. Pesando. 1988. The case for allowing mandatory retirement. *CPP* 14 (March):32–9.

Hotz, V. J., J. A. Klerman, and R. J. Willis. 1997. The economics of fertility in developed countries. In *Handbook of population and family economics*, eds. M. R. Rosenzweig and O. Stark. Amsterdam, New York, and Oxford: Elsevier Science, North-Holland.

Hyatt, D., and W. Milne. 1991a. Can public policy affect fertility? *CPP* 17:77–85.

______. 1991b. Countercyclical fertility in Canada: Some empirical results. *Canadian Studies in Population* 18:1–16.

Kotlifkoff, L., and D. Wise. 1985. Labor compensation and the structure of private pension plans. In *Pensions, Labor and Individual Choices*, ed. D. Wise. Chicago: University of Chicago Press.

Lazear, E. 1986. Retirement from the labor force. In *Handbook of Labor Economics*, eds. O. Ashenfelter and R. Layard. New York: Elsevier Science.

Lazear, E., and R. Moore. 1988. Pensions and turnover. In *Pensions in the U.S. Economy*, eds. Z. Bodie, J. Shoven, and D. Wise. Chicago: University of Chicago Press.

Lee, D. 2000. China's one child policy: Sex preferences, fertility, and female labour supply. Manuscript, University of Toronto.

Leibowitz, A. 1990. The response of births to changes in health care costs. *JHR* 25 (Fall):697–711.

Lumsdaine, R., and O. S. Mitchell. 1999. New developments in the economic analysis of retirement. In *Handbook of Labor Economics*, eds. O. Ashenfelter and D. Card. New York and Oxford: Elsevier Science, North Holland.

MaCurdy, T. 1981. An empirical model of labor supply in a life-cycle setting. *JPE* 89 (December):1059–85.

McElroy, M., and D. Yang. 2000. Carrots and sticks: Fertility effects of China's population policies. *AER* 90 (May):389–92.

Milligan, K. 2001. Subsidizing the stork: New evidence on tax incentives and fertility. In *Empirical Essays on Behavioural Responses to Taxation*. Ph.D. dissertation, University of Toronto.

Mincer, J. 1963. Market prices, opportunity costs and income effects. In *Measurement in Economics: Studies in Mathematical Economics and Econometrics in Memory of Yehuda Grunfeld*, eds. C. Chris et al. Stanford, Calif.: Stanford University Press.

Montgomery, M. R., and J. Trussell. 1986. Models of marital status and childbearing. In *Handbook of Labor Economics*, eds. O. Ashenfelter and R. Layard. New York: Elsevier Science.

Pesando, J., and M. Gunderson. 1988. Retirement incentives contained in occupational pension plans and their implications for the mandatory retirement debate. *CJE* 21 (May):244–64.

______. 1991. Does pension wealth peak at the age of early retirement? *IR* 30 (Winter):79–95.

Phipps, S. 1998. What is the income "cost of a child"? Exact equivalence scales for Canadian two-parent families. *R.E. Stats.* 80 (February):157–64.

Schultz, T. P. 1997. Demand for children in low income countries. In *Handbook of population and family economics*, eds. M. R. Rosenzweig and O. Stark. Amsterdam, New York, and Oxford: Elsevier Science, North-Holland.

Schultz, T. P., and Y. Zeng. 1995. Fertility of rural China: Effects of local family planning and health programs. *Journal of Population Economics* 8 (November):329–50.

______. 1999. The impact of institutional reform from 1979 through 1987 on fertility in rural China. *China Economic Review* 10 (Fall):141–60.

Whittington, L., J. Alm, and H. Peters. 1990. Fertility and the personal exemption. *AER* 80 (June):545–56.

Chapter Five

Demand for Labour in Competitive Labour Markets

Main Questions

- *Labour demand functions are conventionally drawn as downward-sloping (i.e., decreasing functions of the market wage). Is there any theoretical justification for this convention? Is there corresponding empirical support?*
- *Labour demand decisions are made both simultaneously with other input decisions and after factories and machines have been built. How do labour demand decisions compare in these two circumstances, i.e., how do labour demand decisions differ in the short and long run?*
- *What factors affect the elasticity of demand for labour? For example, does it matter whether a firm operates as monopolist or a perfect competitor in the product market?*
- *How can we characterize the "competitiveness" of Canadian labour? How have the productivities and wages of Canadian workers evolved over time compared to the rest of the world?*
- *How can we trace the impact of "globalization" through labour demand, and its ultimate impact on the wages and employment of Canadian workers?*

The general principles that determine the demand for any **factor of production** apply also to the demand for labour. In contrast to goods and services, factors of production are demanded not for final use or consumption but as inputs into the production of final goods and services. Thus the demand for a factor is necessarily linked to the demand for the goods and services that factor is used to produce. The demand for land suitable for growing wheat is linked to the demand for bread and cereal, just as the demand for construction workers is related to the demand for new buildings, roads, and bridges. For this reason, the demand for factors is called a **derived demand**.

In discussing firms' decisions regarding the employment of factors of production, economists usually distinguish between short-run and long-run decisions. The **short run** is defined as a period during which one or more factors of production—referred to as *fixed factors*—cannot be varied, while the **long run** is defined as a period during which the firm can adjust all of its inputs. During both the short and the long run, the state of technical knowledge is assumed to be fixed; the *very long run* refers to the period during which changes in technical knowledge can occur. The amount of calendar time corresponding to each of these periods will differ from one industry to another and according to other factors. These periods are useful as a conceptual device for analyzing a firm's decision-making rather than for predicting the amount of time taken to adjust to change.

By the demand for labour we mean the quantity of labour services the firm would choose to employ at each wage. This desired quantity will depend on both the firm's objectives and its constraints. Usually we will assume that the firm's objective is to maximize profits. Also examined is the determination of labour demand under the weaker assumption of cost minimization. The firm is constrained by the demand conditions in its product markets, the supply conditions in its factor markets, and its production function which shows the maximum output attainable for various combinations of inputs, given the existing state of technical knowledge. In the short run the firm is further constrained by having one or more factors of production whose quantities are fixed.

The theory of labour demand examines the quantity of labour services the firm desires to employ given the market-determined wage rate, or given the labour supply function that the firm faces. As was the case with labour supply, our guiding objective is in deriving the theoretical relationship between labour demand and the market wage, holding other factors constant. In this chapter we will assume that the firm is a perfect competitor in the labour market. In Chapter 7, we relax this assumption and explore the case where the firm faces the entire market supply curve, and operates as a monopsonist. In that case, it makes no sense to think of the firm as reacting to a given market wage. However, as we shall see, the basic ingredients of the theory of input demand can easily be adjusted to this problem.

In some circumstances, however, it makes no sense to think of either the firm or the labour it hires as operating in a competitive market. The employer and employees may negotiate explicit, or reach implicit, contracts involving both wages and employment. When this is the case, the wage-employment outcomes may not be on the labour demand curve because the contracts will reflect the preferences of both the employer and the employees with respect to both wages and employment. Explicit wage-employment contracts are discussed in Chapter 15 on unions, and implicit wage-employment contracts are discussed in Chapter 18 on unemployment (because of the theoretical links between implicit contracts and unemployment). Even under these circumstances, however, we shall see that the theory of firm behaviour described in this chapter is the foundation for employment determination outside the perfectly competitive framework.

The chapter ends with an extended discussion on the impact of the global economy on the demand for Canadian labour. The relative cost and productivity of Canadian labour is examined, as are the possible channels by which changes in international trade patterns may impact the employment of Canadian workers. In particular, we present evidence on the impact of recent trade agreements (like NAFTA) on the Canadian labour market.

CATEGORIZING THE STRUCTURE OF PRODUCT AND LABOUR MARKETS

Because the demand for labour is derived from the output produced by the firm, the way in which the firm behaves in the product market can have an impact on the demand for labour, and hence ultimately on wage and employment decisions. In general, the firm's product market behaviour depends on the structure of the industry to which the firm belongs. In decreasing order of the degree of competition, the four main market structures are: (1) perfect competition, (2) monopolistic competition, (3) oligopoly, and (4) monopoly.

Whereas the structure of the product market affects the firm's derived demand for labour, the structure of the labour market affects the labour supply curve that the firm faces. The supply curve of labour to an individual firm shows the amount of a specific type of labour (e.g., a particular occupational category) that the firm could employ at various wage rates. Analogous to the four product market structures there are four labour market structures. In decreasing order of the degree of competition the firm faces in hiring labour, these factor market structures are: (1) perfect competition, (2) monopsonistic competition, (3) oligopsony, and (4) monopsony. (The "-opsony" ending is traditionally used to denote departures from perfect competition in factor markets.)

The product and labour market categorizations are independent in that there is no necessary relationship between the structure of the product market in which the firm sells its output and the labour market in which it buys labour services. The extent to which the firm is competitive in the product market (and hence the nature of its derived demand for labour curve) need not be related to the extent to which the firm is a competitive buyer of labour (and hence the nature of the supply curve of labour that it faces). The two *may* be related, for example if it is a large firm and hence dominates both the labour and product markets, but they need not be related. Hence for *each* product market structure, the firm can behave in at least four different ways as a purchaser of labour. Thus there are at least sixteen different combinations of product and labour market structure that can bear on the wage and employment decision at the level of the firm.

In general, however, the essence of the wage and employment decision by the firm can be captured by an examination of the polar cases of perfect competition (in product and/or factor markets), monopoly in the product market, and monopsony in the labour market. We will begin by examining the demand for labour in the short run under conditions of perfect competition in the labour market.

DEMAND FOR LABOUR IN THE SHORT RUN

The general principles determining labour demand can be explained for the case of a firm that produces a single output (Q) using two inputs, capital (K), and labour (N). The technological possibilities relating output to any combination of inputs are represented by the **production function**:

$$Q = F(K,N) \tag{5.1}$$

In the short run the amount of capital is fixed at $K = K_0$, so the production function is simply a function of N (with K fixed). The quantity of labour services can be varied by changing either the number of employees or hours worked by each employee (or both). For the moment we do not distinguish between variations in the number of employees and hours worked; however, this aspect of labour demand is discussed subsequently. Also discussed later is the possibility that labour may be a "quasi-fixed factor" in the short run.

The demand for labour in the short run can be derived by examining the firm's short-run output and employment decisions. Two decision rules follow from the assumption of

profit maximization. First, because the costs associated with the fixed factor must be paid whether or not the firm produces (and whatever amount the firm produces), the firm will operate as long as it can cover its **variable costs** (i.e., if total revenue exceeds total variable costs). **Fixed costs** are sunk costs, and their magnitude should not affect what is the currently most profitable thing to do.

The second decision rule implied by profit maximization is that, if the firm produces at all (i.e., is able to cover its variable costs), it should produce the quantity Q^* at which **marginal revenue** (MR) equals **marginal cost** (MC). That is, the firm should increase output until the additional cost associated with the last unit produced equals the additional revenue associated with that unit.

If the firm is a price-taker, the marginal revenue of another unit sold is the prevailing market price. If the firm is a **monopolist**, or operates in a less than perfectly competitive product market, marginal revenue will be a decreasing function of output (the price must fall in order for additional units to be sold). With capital fixed, the marginal cost of producing another unit of output is the wage times the amount of labour required to produce that output. Expanding output beyond the point at which MR = MC will lower profits because the addition to total revenue will be less than the increase in total cost. Producing a lower output would also reduce profits because, at output levels below Q^*, marginal revenue exceeds marginal cost; thus increasing output would add more to total revenue than to total cost, thereby raising profits.

The profit-maximizing decision rules can be stated in terms of the employment of inputs rather than in terms of the quantity of output to produce. Because concepts such as total revenue and marginal revenue are defined in terms of units of output, the terminology is modified for inputs. The total revenue associated with the amount of an input employed is called the **total revenue product** (TRP) of that input; similarly, the change in total revenue associated with a change in the amount of the input employed is called the **marginal revenue product** (MRP). Both the total and marginal revenue products of labour will depend on the physical productivity of labour as given by the production function, and the marginal revenue received from selling the output of the labour in the product market.

Thus the profit-maximizing decision rules for the employment of the variable input can be stated as follows:

- The firm should produce, providing the total revenue product of the variable input exceeds the total costs associated with that input; otherwise the firm should shut down operations.
- If the firm produces at all, it should expand employment of the variable input to the point at which its marginal revenue product equals its marginal cost.

The short-run employment decision of a firm operating in a perfectly competitive labour market is shown in Figure 5.1. In a competitive factor market the firm is a price-taker; i.e., the firm can hire more or less of the factor without affecting the market price. Thus in a competitive labour market the marginal (and average) cost of labour is the market wage rate. The firm will therefore employ labour until its marginal revenue product equals the wage rate, which implies that the firm's short-run labour demand curve is its marginal revenue product of labour curve. For example, if the wage rate is W_0 the firm would employ N_0^* labour services. However, the firm will shut down operations in the short run if the total variable cost exceeds the total revenue product of labour, which will be the case if the average cost of labour (the wage rate) exceeds the average revenue product of labour. Thus at wage rates higher than W_1 in Figure 5.1 (the point at which the wage rate equals the average product of labour) the firm would choose to shut down operations. It follows that the firm's short-run labour demand curve is its marginal revenue product of labour curve below the point at which the average and marginal product curves intersect (i.e., below the point at which the ARP_N reaches a maximum).

Figure 5.1 The Firm's Short-Run Demand for Labour

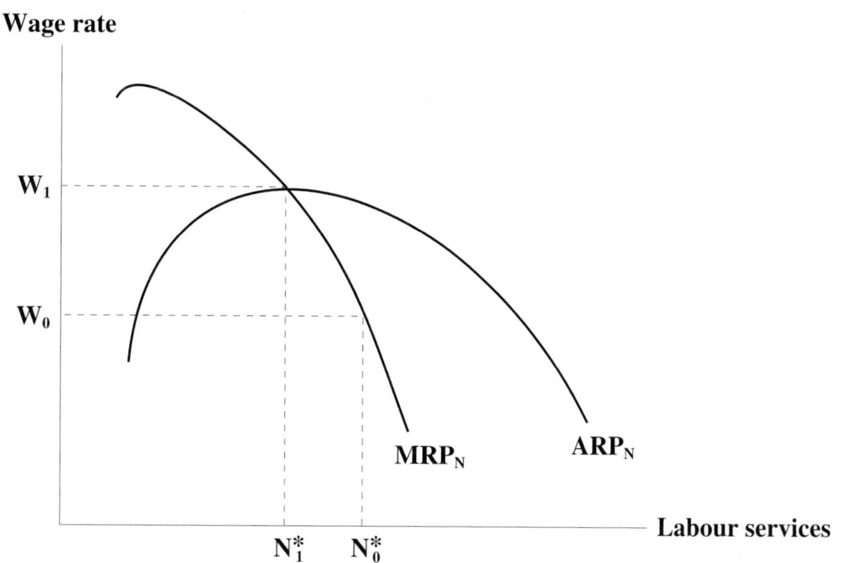

Profit maximization requires labour to be employed until its marginal cost (the wage) equals its marginal benefit (marginal revenue product). For the wage, W_0, the profit-maximizing employment level is N_0^*. At wages higher than W_1, labour costs exceed the value of output, so the firm will hire no labour. The labour demand schedule is thus MRP_N below where ARP_N reaches its maximum.

The short-run labour demand curve is downward-sloping because of **diminishing marginal returns** to labour. Although the average and marginal products may initially rise as more labour is employed, both eventually decline as more units of the variable factor are combined with a given amount of the fixed factor. Because the firm employs labour in the range in which its marginal revenue product is declining, a reduction in the wage rate is needed to entice the firm to employ more labour. Similarly, an increase in the wage rate will cause the firm to employ less labour, thus raising its marginal revenue product and restoring equality between the marginal revenue product and marginal cost.

At this point, it may be worth highlighting a common misconception concerning the reason for the downward-sloping demand for labour. The demand is for a given homogeneous type of labour; consequently, it does *not* slope downward because, as the firm uses more labour, it uses poorer-quality labour and hence pays a lower wage. It may well be true that when firms expand their work force they often have to use poorer-quality labour. Nevertheless, for analytical purposes it is useful to assume a given, homogeneous type of labour so that the impact on labour demand of changes in the wage rate for that type of labour can be analyzed. The change in the productivity of labour that occurs does so because of changes in the amount of the variable factor combined with a given amount of the fixed factor, not because the firm is delving more into the reserve of less-qualified labour.

WAGES, THE MARGINAL PRODUCTIVITY OF LABOUR, AND COMPETITION IN THE PRODUCT MARKET

The demand schedule of a profit-maximizing firm which is a wage-taker in the labour market is the locus of points for which the marginal revenue product of labour equals the wage rate. The marginal revenue product of labour (MRP_N) equals the marginal revenue of output (MR_Q) times the **marginal physical product** of labour (MPP_N). Thus there is a relationship between wages and the marginal productivity of labour.

The marginal revenue of output depends on the market structure in the product market. The two polar cases of perfect competition and monopoly are discussed here. A perfectly competitive firm is a price-taker in the product market. Because the firm can sell additional (or fewer) units of output without affecting the market price, the marginal revenue of output equals the product price; i.e., for a competitive firm

$$MRP_N = MR_Q \times MPP_N = p \times MPP_N \tag{5.2}$$

Because it is the product of the market price and the marginal product of labour, this term is referred to as the **value of the marginal product** of labour; that is, $p \times MPP_N = VMP_N$. A firm that is competitive in both the product and the labour market will thus employ labour services until the value of the marginal product of labour just equals the wage; i.e., the demand for labour obeys the equation 5.3:

$$p \times MPP_N = VMP_N = w \tag{5.3}$$

Equation 5.3 follows from the MR = MC rule for profit maximization; the VMP_N is the increase in total revenue associated with a unit increase in labour input, while the wage w is the accompanying increase in total cost. Alternatively stated, the labour demand curve of a firm that is competitive in both the product and the labour market is the locus of points for which the real wage w/p equals the marginal physical product of labour.

The polar case of noncompetitive behaviour in the product market is that of monopoly. In this situation the firm is so large relative to the size of the product market that it can influence the price at which it sells its product: it is a price-setter, not a price-taker. In the extreme case of monopoly, the monopolist comprises the whole industry: there are no other firms in the industry. Thus, the industry demand for the product is the demand schedule for the product of the monopolist.

As is well known from standard microeconomic theory, the relevant decision-making schedule for the profit-maximizing monopolist is not the demand schedule for its product, but rather its marginal revenue schedule. In order to sell an additional unit of output, the monopolist has to lower the price of its product. Assuming that it cannot differentiate its homogeneous product to consumers, the monopolist will also have to lower the price on all units of its output, not just on the additional units that it wishes to sell. Consequently, its marginal revenue—the additional revenue generated by selling an additional unit of output—will fall faster than its price, reflecting the fact that the price decline applies to intramarginal units of output. The marginal revenue schedule for the monopolist will therefore lie below and to the left of its demand schedule. By equating marginal revenue with marginal cost so as to maximize profits, the monopolist will produce less output and charge a higher price (as given by the demand schedule, since this is the price that consumers will pay) than if it were a competitive firm on the product market.

This aspect of the product market has implications for the derived demand for labour. The monopolist's demand for labour curve is the locus of points for which

$$MR_Q \times MPP_N = MRP_N = w \tag{5.4}$$

The differences between equation 5.3 and 5.4 highlight the fact that when the monopolist hires more labour to produce more output, not only does the marginal physical product of labour fall (as is the case with the competitive firm), but also the marginal revenue from an additional unit of output, MR_Q, falls. This latter effect occurs because the monopolist, unlike the competitor, can sell more output only by lowering the product price and this in turn lowers revenue. Because both MPP_N and MR_Q fall when N increases in equation 5.4, then the monopolist's demand for labour falls faster than it would if it behaved as a competitive firm in the product market, in which case only MPP_N would fall, as given in equation 5.3.

DEMAND FOR LABOUR IN THE LONG RUN

In the long run the firm can vary all of its inputs. For expositional purposes we will continue to assume two inputs, labour (N) and capital (K) and one output (Q); however, the general principles apply to firms which employ many inputs and produce multiple outputs. As in the previous section, the demand for labour is derived by varying the wage rate that the firm faces for a given homogeneous type of labour, and tracing out the profit-maximizing (or cost-minimizing) quantity of labour that will be employed by the firm.

For conceptual purposes, the firm's production and employment decisions are usually examined in two stages. First, the minimum-cost method of producing any level of output is examined. Second, given that each output will be produced at minimum cost, the profit-maximizing level of output is chosen.

Isoquants, Isocosts, and Cost Minimization

As before, output is assumed to be produced according to the technology represented by the firm's production function, Q = F(K,N). Only in this case, capital and labour are chosen together to maximize profits. The first stage of profit maximization (**cost minimization**) is depicted geometrically in Figure 5.2. The top part of the diagram, Figure 5.2(a), gives the firm's **isoquant** Q_0, which shows the various combinations of labour N and capital K that can produce a given level of output Q_0. This isoquant reflects the technological constraints implied by the production function. For any level of desired output, there will be a corresponding isoquant offering the menu of combinations of capital and labour that could be employed to produce the level of output. Higher levels of output will require hgher levels of inputs, and isoquants corresponding to higher output levels (like Q_1) lie to the "northeast" of the Q_0 isoquant.

The slope of the isoquant exhibits a diminishing **marginal rate of technical substitution** (MRTS) between the inputs. The MRTS reflects the ease with which capital and labour can be substituted to produce a given level of output. The diminishing MRTS implies that it becomes harder to substitute away from a factor when there is less of it. For example, in the upper left segment when an abundance of capital is used, a considerable increase in the use of capital is required to offset a small reduction in the use of labour, if output is to be maintained. In the lower right segment when an abundance of labour is used, labour is a poor substitute for capital, and considerable labour savings are possible for small increases in the use of capital. In the middle segment of the isoquant, labour and capital are both good substitutes. Successively higher isoquants or levels of output, such as Q_1, can be produced by successively larger amounts of both inputs.

Clearly, under differing technologies, we expect the difficulty of substitution to vary. If hoeing requires one hoe per worker, purchasing additional hoes without the workers, or hiring extra workers without hoes, will not allow much of an increase in output. In that case, production would be characterized by a low level of substitutability between the inputs. On the other hand, it might be easier to substitute weeding labour for herbicides. One could imagine using a lot of labour, doing all the weeding by hand, or hiring only one worker to apply large quantities of chemicals. Intermediate combinations would also be feasible. In that case, the level of substitutability will be high. The substitutability of one factor for another will clearly have an effect on the responsiveness of producers to small changes in the relative prices of the two factors.

The firm's objective will be to choose the least expensive combination of capital and labour along the isoquant Q_0. The costs of purchasing various combinations of capital and labour will depend on the prices of the inputs. Figure 5.2(b) illustrates the firm's **isocost line** K_MN_M, depicting the various combinations of capital and labour the firm can employ, given their market price and a total cost of C_M. Algebraically, the isocost line is $C_M = rK + wN$,

Figure 5.2 **Isoquants, Isocost, and Cost Minimization**

Cost minimization entails producing a given output, Q_0, using the cheapest possible combination of capital (K) and labour (N), and depends on both technology and the relevant input prices. The technology is represented by isoquants (panel (a)), which show the different ways Q_0 can be produced with K and N. Panel (b) summarizes the costs associated with using any combination of K and N. For example, all points along the line $K_M N_M$ cost the same (C_M). Panel (c) shows the cost-minimizing choice, E_0. Here, Q_0 is produced in the least expensive way: no other point on the isoquant for Q_0 lies closer to the origin (on a lower isocost line). At the point E_0, the firm uses K_0,N_0 to produce Q_0, and, furthermore, the tangency between the isocost line and isoquant implies that the marginal rate of technical substitution equals the ratio of input prices (W_0/r_0).

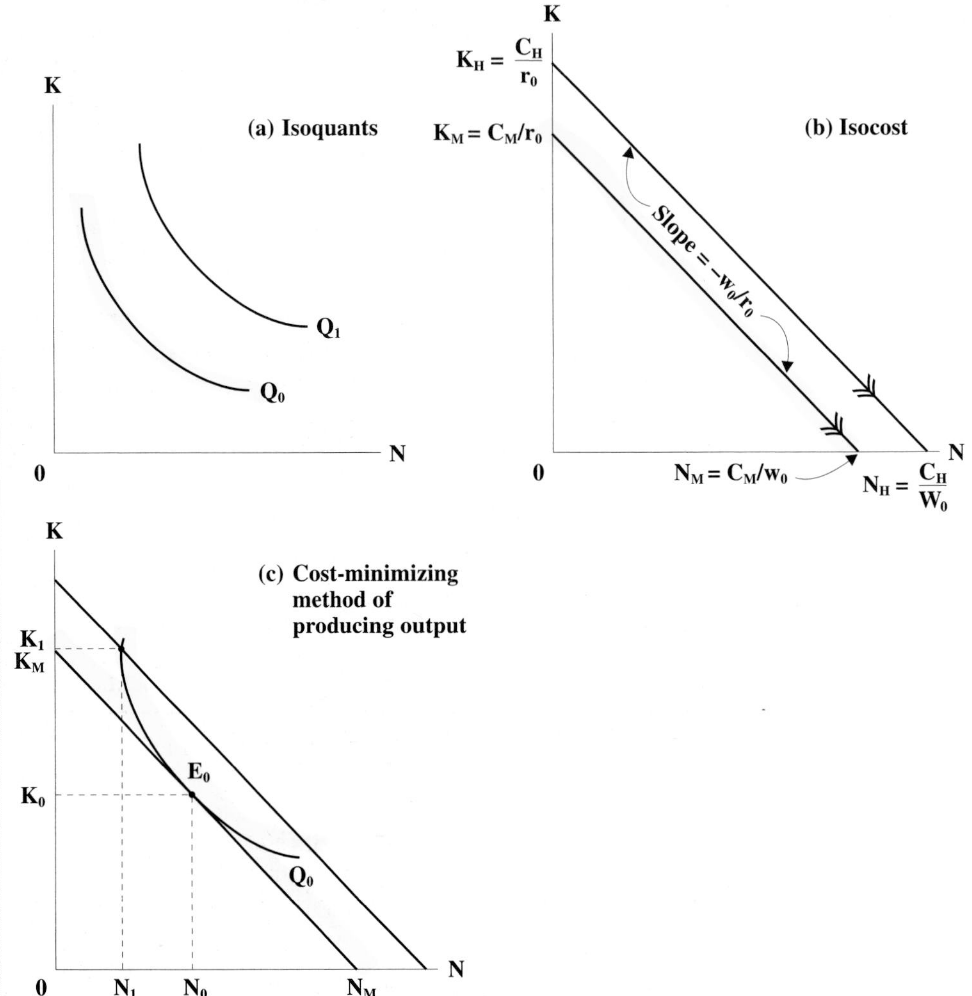

where r is the price of capital and w the price of labour, or wage rate.[1] The position and shape of the isocost line can be determined by solving for the two intercepts or endpoints and the slope of the line between them. From the isocost equation, for fixed prices r_0 and w_0, these endpoints are $N_M = C_M/w_0$ when K = 0, and $K_M = C_M/r_0$ when N = 0. The slope is simply minus the rise divided by the run or $-[C_M/r_0 \div C_M/w_0] = -w_0/r_0$; that is, the price of labour relative to the price of capital. This is a straight line as long as w and r are constant for these given types of labour and capital, which is the case when the firm is a price-taker in both input markets. Isocost lines will pass through each possible combination of capital and labour

[1]If the firm rents its capital equipment. The cost of capital is the rental price. If the firm owns its capital equipment, the implicit or opportunity cost of capital depends on the cost of the machinery and equipment, the interest rate at which funds can be borrowed or lent, and the rate at which the machinery depreciates. In the analysis that follows, we will assume that the firm is a price-taker in the market for capital.

that the firm could hire. For example, a higher isocost line, $K_H N_H$, is also depicted in Figure 5.2(b). Costs are increasing as the isocost lines move to the northeast (away from the origin).

A profit-maximizing firm will choose the cheapest capital-labour combination that yields the output Q_0. In other words, it will choose the combination of K and N on the isoquant Q_0 that lies on the isocost line nearest the origin. Figure 5.2(c) combines the isoquants and isocost lines to illustrate the minimum-cost input choice that can be used to produce Q_0. This is clearly E_0 where the isocost is tangent to the isoquant. That this should be the minimum-cost combination is most easily seen by considering an alternative combination, K_1 and N_1. The isocost line corresponding to this combination is associated with a higher total cost of production. In this case, costs could be reduced by using more labour and less capital, and moving toward the combination at E_0.

As with the consumer optimum described in Chapter 2, the tangency between the isoquant and isocost lines has an economic interpretation. At the optimum for the firm, the internal rate of input substitution, given by the marginal rate of technical substitution (the slope of the isoquant) equals the market rate of substitution, given by the relative price of labour and capital (the slope of the isocost line). This tangency can also be expressed in terms of the relative marginal products of capital and labour:

$$\text{MRTS} = \frac{\text{MPN}}{\text{MPK}} = \frac{w}{r} \tag{5.5}$$

In the short run, we saw that the value of the marginal product of labour was equal to the wage. In the long run, the relative value of the marginal product of labour is equal to the relative price of labour.

The second stage of profit maximization entails the choice of the optimal level of output. The determination of the profit-maximizing level of output (the output at which marginal revenue equals marginal cost) cannot be seen in the isoquant-isocost diagram. What is shown is how to produce any output, including the profit-maximizing output, at minimum cost.

At E_0, the cost-minimizing amounts of labour and capital, respectively used to produce Q_0 units of output, are N_0 and K_0. If Q_0 is the profit-maximizing output, this gives us one point on the demand curve for labour, as depicted later in Figure 5.3; that is, at the wage rate w_0 the firm employs N_0 units of labour.

Deriving the Firm's Labour Demand Schedule

The complete labour demand schedule, for the long run when the firm can vary both capital and labour, can be obtained simply by varying the wage rate and tracing out the new, equilibrium, profit-maximizing amounts of labour that would be employed. This is illustrated in Figure 5.3. An increase in the wage from W_0 to W_1 causes all of the isocost curves to become steeper. For example, at the initial input combination, K_0 and N_0, the isocost line rotates from $K_M N_M$ to $K_P N_P$. Clearly, the total cost of continuing to produce Q_0 using K_0 and N_0 will rise. If the firm chose to rent only capital at the new cost level, C_1, it would be able to rent more capital services than before, up to $K_P = C_1/r_0$. On the other hand, even though costs have risen, if the firm spent C_1 entirely on labour, it could only hire up to $N_P = C_1/W_1$. Finally, panel (a) shows that the cost-minimizing (and profit-maximizing) condition no longer holds at E_0, because the isoquant is not tangent to the new isocost line.

As depicted in Figure 5.3(b), given the higher wage rate W_1, the firm will maximize profits by moving to a lower level of output Q_1, operating at E_1 and employing N_1 units of labour. This yields a second point on the firm's demand curve for labour depicted in Figure 5.3(c); that is, a lower level of employment N_1 corresponds to the higher wage rate W_1, compared to the original employment of N_0 at wage w_0.

To complete the explanation of the firm's response to a wage increase, Figure 5.4 shows

Figure 5.3 **Deriving the Labour Demand Schedule**

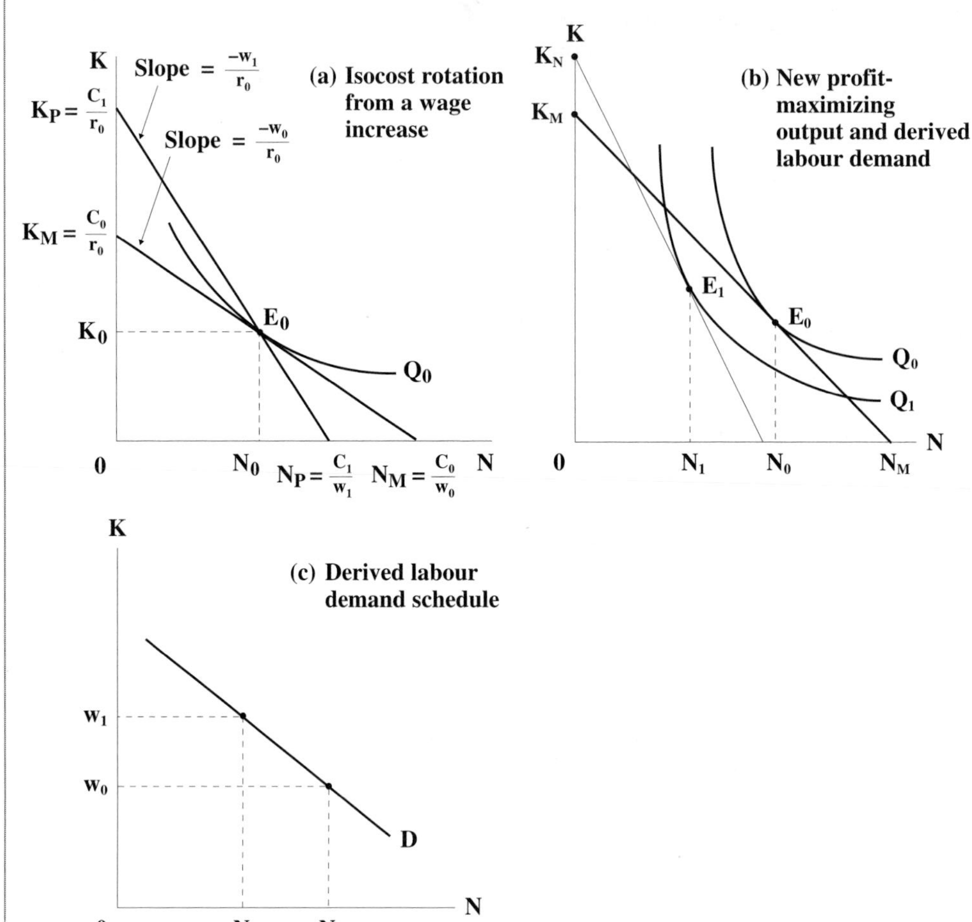

This figure shows how an increase in the wage is associated with a change in the quantity of labour demanded, and ultimately, how a labour demand curve can be traced out. In panel (a), an increase the wage from W_0 to W_1 rotates the isocost curves, and E_0 (the profit-maximizing employment level at W_0) is no longer optimal. The new optimal input combination is depicted in panel (b), where the firm is also producing a lower level of output. The new tangency between the isoquant (for Q_1) and isocost curve yields labour demand of N_1, which is lower than N_0. The relationship between wages (W_0 and W_1) and the optimal quantity of labour demanded (N_0 and N_1) is summarized by the labour demand schedule in panel (c).

how the profit-maximizing output levels (Q_0 and Q_1 in Figure 5.3b) are determined. The wage increase shifts up the firm's marginal and average cost curves. In a perfectly competitive industry, each firm reduces output which raises the market price of the product. In the new equilibrium the output of each firm and total output are lower than in the original equilibrium. The monopolist responds to the increase in costs by raising the product price and reducing output. The analysis of the intermediate market structures (monopolistic competition and oligopoly) is similar; in general an increase in costs, ceteris paribus, leads to an increase in the product price and a reduction in output. Note, however, that although the firm moves to the lower isoquant (Q_0 to Q_1 in Figure 5.3b), its total costs may increase (as shown in Figure 5.3b where $K_N > K_M$) or decrease. Producing a lower output tends to reduce total costs, but the higher wage tends to raise total costs. The net effect therefore depends on the magnitude of these offsetting forces. In this respect the analysis of the response of the firm to an increase in an input price is not exactly analogous to the response of the consumer to a commodity price increase. In consumer theory, income (or total expenditure on goods) is assumed to be exogenously determined. But firms *do not* have predetermined budget constraints. In the theory of the firm, total cost (or total expenditure on inputs) is endogenous rather than exogenous and depends on the profit-

Figure 5.4 **The Effect of a Cost Increase on Output**

The profit-maximizing level of output falls when the wage increases. Profit maximization requires that MC(Q) = MR(Q). A wage increase raises marginal costs, from MC_0 to MC_1, as shown in panel (a). For a competitive firm, marginal revenue equals the price, and at the original output price, P_0, output would decline to Q_0. However, the shift of the MC schedule for all firms leads the industry supply curve to shift from S_0 to S_1, and market price to rise from P_0 to P_1. Each firm produces Q_1 (where $MC_1 = P_1$), while the industry produces q_1. Similar logic applies to a monopolist (panel (b)). The MR function is unchanged by the wage increase, but marginal costs rise from MC_0 to MC_1. This leads to lower output Q_1, where $MR = MC_1$.

(a) Perfect competition

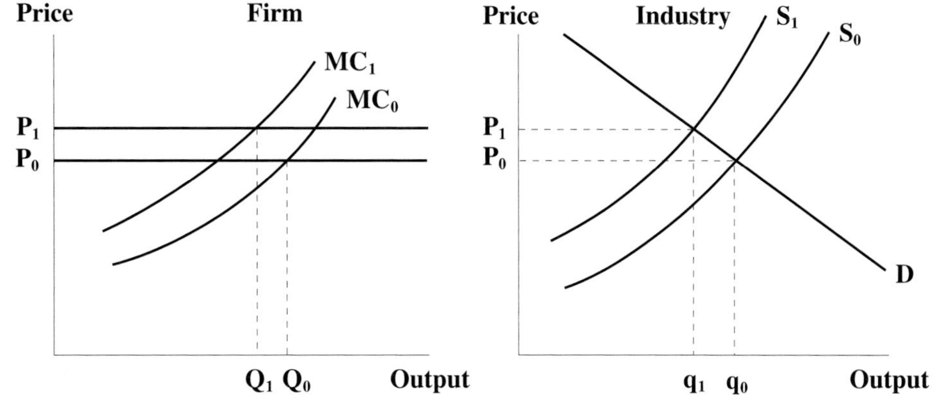

(b) Monopoly

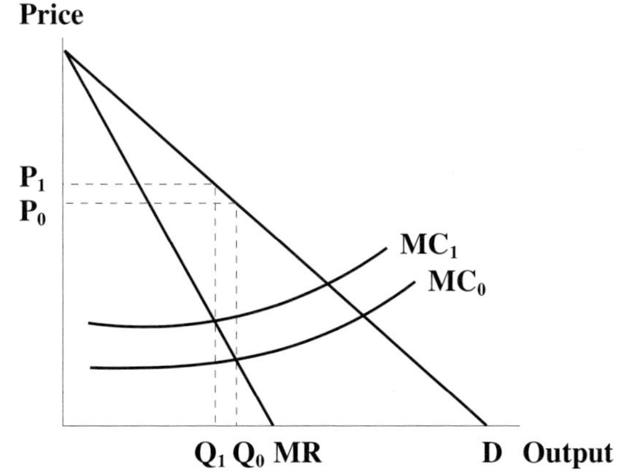

maximizing levels of output and inputs, given the output and input prices. As these change, total costs may change, as depicted previously in Figure 5.3(b).

Clearly one could trace out the full demand schedule by varying the wage rate and observing the profit-maximizing amounts of labour that would be employed. Economic theory predicts that the demand schedule is downward-sloping (i.e., higher wages are associated with a reduced demand for labour) both because the firm would substitute cheaper inputs for the more expensive labour (**substitution effect**) and because it would reduce its scale of operations because of the wage and hence cost increase (**scale effect**). For conceptual purposes it is useful to examine these two effects.

Separating Scale and Substitution Effects of a Wage Change

Figure 5.5 illustrates how the wage increase from w_0 to w_1 can be separated into its component parts—a substitution effect and a scale or output effect. The negative substitution effect occurs as the firm substitutes cheaper capital for the more expensive labour, therefore reducing the quantity of labour demanded. When labour is a normal input, the negative scale effect occurs as a wage increase leads to a higher marginal cost of production which, in turn, reduces the firm's optimal output and hence derived demand for labour. Thus the scale and substitution effects reinforce each other to lead to an unambiguously inverse relationship between wages and the firm's demand for labour.[2]

The scale effect can be isolated by hypothetically forcing the firm to continue producing Q_0. This is illustrated by the hypothetical isocost line that is parallel to the new isocost w_1/r_0, but tangent to the original isoquant Q_0 at E_s. The only difference between E_s and E_1 is the scale of operation of the firm (Q_0 as opposed to Q_1), since the relative price of labour and capital are the same; that is, both are w_1/r_0. Therefore, N_s to N_1 can be thought of as the scale effect—the reduction in employment that comes about to the extent that the firm reduces its output in response to the wage increase. Except in the unusual circumstance in which labour is an inferior input, the scale effect works through the following scenario: wage increases imply cost increases, which lead to a reduced optimal scale of output, which in turn leads to a reduced demand for labour.

The difference between E_0 and E_s, on the other hand, is simply due to the different slopes of the isocost lines. They both represent the same output, Q_0. Consequently, the difference between E_0 and E_s reflects the pure substitution of capital for labour to produce the same output, Q_0. Therefore, N_0 to N_s can be thought of as a pure or output-constant substitution effect, representing the substitution of relatively cheaper inputs for the inputs whose relative price has risen. Both scale and substitution effects work in the same direction to yield an unambiguously downward-sloping demand schedule for labour.

Figure 5.5 **Substitution and Scale Effects of a Wage Change**

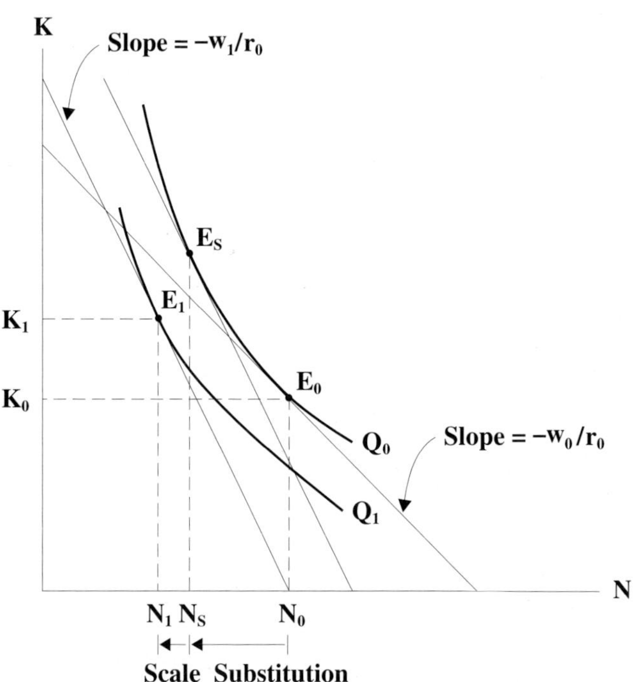

A wage increase from W_0 to W_1 leads to a rotation of the isocost curves. If a firm continued to produce Q_0, the cost-minimizing input combination would move from E_0 to E_S. The associated decline in labour demand from N_0 to N_S is called the *substitution effect*. But the wage increase also leads to a reduction in output, from Q_0 to Q_1. The implied reduction in labour employed from E_S to E_1 is a direct consequence of the output reduction, and the associated reduction in employment from N_S to N_1 is called the *scale effect*.

[2]Nagatani (1978) proves that this is true even when labour is an inferior factor of production.

For capital, the substitution and scale effects of an increase in the wage rate work in opposite directions. The substitution effect (E_0 to E_s) increases the demand for capital as the firm uses more capital and less labour to produce a given level of output. However, the reduction in output from Q_0 to Q_1 causes a reduction in demand for all normal inputs; thus the scale effect (E_s to E_1) reduces the demand for capital. The overall or net effect on capital thus depends on which of the two effects is larger. In general, an increase in the wage may cause the firm to employ more or less capital.

THE RELATIONSHIP BETWEEN THE SHORT- AND THE LONG-RUN LABOUR DEMAND

The division of the firm's response to a wage change into the substitution and scale effects is also useful in understanding the difference between the short- and the long-run labour demand. In the short run the amount of capital is fixed; thus there is no substitution effect. The downward-sloping nature of the short-run labour demand curve is a consequence of a scale effect and diminishing marginal productivity of labour. In the long run the firm has the additional flexibility associated with varying its capital stock. Thus the response to a wage change will be larger in the long run than in the short run, ceteris paribus. This relationship is illustrated in Figure 5.6. The initial long-run equilibrium is at E_0. The short-run response to the wage increase from w_0 to w_1 involves moving to a new equilibrium at E_0^1. Here the firm is employing less labour (N_0^1 versus N_0) but the same amount of capital (K_0). In the long run the firm also adjusts its capital stock from K_0 to K_1, shifting the short-run labour demand curve to the left. The new long-run equilibrium is at E_1. The long-run labour demand curve consists of the locus of points such as E_0 and E_1 at which the firm has optimally adjusted employment of both labour and capital given the wage rate and other exogenous variables.

LABOUR DEMAND UNDER COST MINIMIZATION

Economic analysis generally assumes that firms in the private sector seek to maximize profits. However, organizations in the public and quasi-public sectors—such as federal, provincial, and municipal public administration, Crown corporations, and educational and health institutions—generally have other goals. These goals will determine the quantity of output or services provided and the amount of labour and other productive inputs employed. Although the factors that determine the output of these organizations may vary, such organizations may seek to produce that output efficiently, that is, at minimum cost.

The distinction between the scale and substitution effects is useful in analyzing the demand for labour in these circumstances. An organization whose output of goods and/or services is exogenously determined but which seeks to produce that output at minimum cost will respond to changes in wages by substituting between labour and other inputs. That is, with output fixed (determined by other factors) there will be a pure substitution effect in response to changes in the wage rate. Labour demand will therefore be unambiguously downward-sloping but more inelastic than that of a profit-maximizing firm because of the absence of an output effect.

Although a cost-minimizing organization will respond to a wage increase by substituting capital for labour, its total expenditure on inputs (total costs) will nonetheless rise. This aspect is illustrated in Figure 5.5. The equilibrium E_s involves greater total costs than the original equilibrium E_0. The increase in total costs is, however, less than would be the case if the organization did not substitute capital for labour in response to the wage increase (i.e., if the firm remained at the point E_0 in Figure 5.5).

Figure 5.6 The Demand for Labour in the Short and the Long Run

For a given W_0, consider a firm in long- and short-run equilibrium: it has no desire to change its level of labour or capital. The wage rises to W_1. In the short run, K_0 is fixed, and employment falls to N_0^1. In the long run, the firm adjusts to capital, K_1, and long-run employment of N_1. Long-run labour demand is thus flatter than the "family" of short-run labour demand schedules associated with any fixed level of capital, since the potential for substitution is greater.

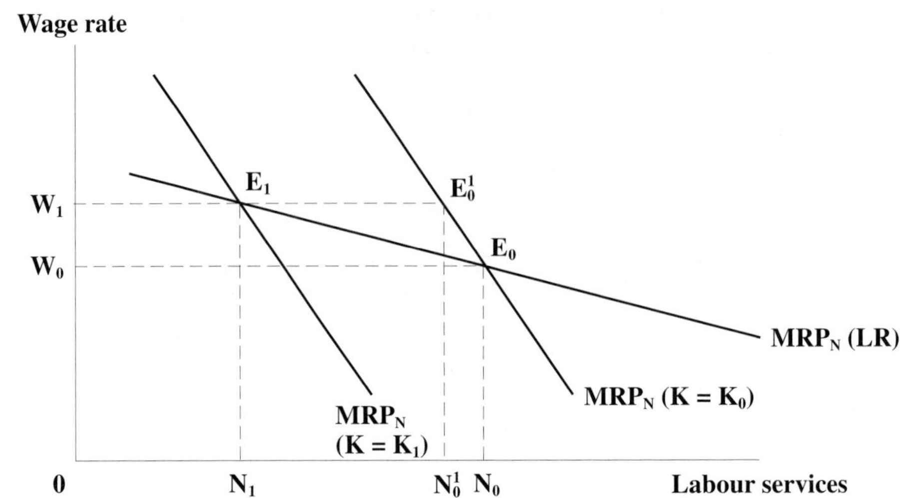

ELASTICITY OF DEMAND FOR LABOUR

The previous analysis indicated that the demand for labour is a negative function of the wage rate. Consequently, in this static, partial-equilibrium framework, an exogenous increase in wages, other things held constant, would lead to a reduction in the quantity of labour demanded. The exogenous increase in wages, for example, could emanate from a union wage demand, a wage parity scheme, or wage-fixing legislation, such as minimum wages, equal pay, fair-wage legislation, or extension legislation. Although there may be offsetting factors (to be discussed later), it is important to realize that economic theory predicts there will be an adverse employment effect from these wage increases. The magnitude of the adverse employment effect depends on the elasticity of the derived demand for labour. As illustrated in Figure 5.7, if the demand for labour is inelastic, as in Figure 5.7(a), then the adverse employment effect is small; if the demand is elastic, as in Figure 5.7(b), then the adverse employment effect is large.

From a policy perspective it is important to know the expected magnitude of these adverse employment effects because they may offset other possible benefits of the exogenous wage increase. Consequently, it is important to know the determinants of the **elasticity of demand for labour.** As originally outlined by Marshall and formalized by Hicks (1963, pp. 241–6 and 374–84), the basic determinants of the elasticity of demand for labour are the availability of substitute inputs, the elasticity of supply of substitute inputs, the elasticity of demand for output, and the ratio of labour cost to total cost. These factors are related to the magnitude of the substitution and scale effects discussed previously. Each of these factors will be discussed in turn, in the context of an inelastic demand for labour in Figure 5.7(a), which implies a wage increase being associated with a small adverse employment effect.

Availability of Substitute Inputs

The derived demand for labour will be inelastic, and hence the adverse employment effect of an exogenous wage increase will be small, if alternative inputs cannot be substituted easily for the higher-price labour. This would be depicted by an isoquant that is more an L-shaped as opposed to a negatively sloped straight line; that is, the marginal rate of technical substitution between other inputs and labour is small. This factor relates to the magnitudes of the substitution effect.

The inability to substitute alternative inputs could be technologically determined, as for example if the particular type of labour is essential to the production process, or it could be institutionally determined, as for example if the union prevents such substitution as contracting-out or the use of nonunion labour or the introduction of new technology. Time also is a factor, since in the long run the possibility of substituting cheaper inputs is more feasible.

Examples of workers for whom substitute inputs may not *readily* be available are construction tradespeople, teachers, and professionals with specialized skills. Even in these cases, however, substitutions are technically possible in the long run, especially when one considers alternative production processes and delivery systems (e.g., prefabricated construction, larger class size with more audiovisual aids, and the use of paraprofessionals).

In declining industries, it may be difficult to substitute new capital for higher-priced labour because of the difficulty of attracting new capital to the industry. As well, if the capital is industry-specific it may have little alternative use, and hence there is little threat of firms moving their capital if complementary labour becomes too expensive. In such circumstances, the demand for labour may not only shift inward (reflecting the declining derived demand for labour), but it may also become more inelastic (reflecting the lack of substitute capital). This can have opposing effects on wages in declining industries, with wages falling because of falling demand, but rising if unions push for higher wage increases, aware that there will not be much of an adverse employment effect given the more inelastic demand for labour. In such circumstances it may be perfectly rational for workers to push for higher wage increases in spite of the declining nature of the industry. Even if profits are declining, unions can still bargain for a larger share of declining rents.

Elasticity of Supply of Substitute Inputs

The substitution of alternative inputs can also be affected by changes in the price of these inputs. If the substitutes are relatively *inelastic* in supply, so that an increase in the demand for the inputs will lead to an increase in their price, then this price increase may choke off some of the increased usage of these substitutes. In general, this is probably not an important factor, however, because it is unlikely that the firm or industry where the wage increase occurs is such a large purchaser of alternative inputs that it affects their price. Certainly in the long run the supply of substitute inputs is likely to be more elastic.

Figure 5.7 **Inelastic and Elastic Demand for Labour**

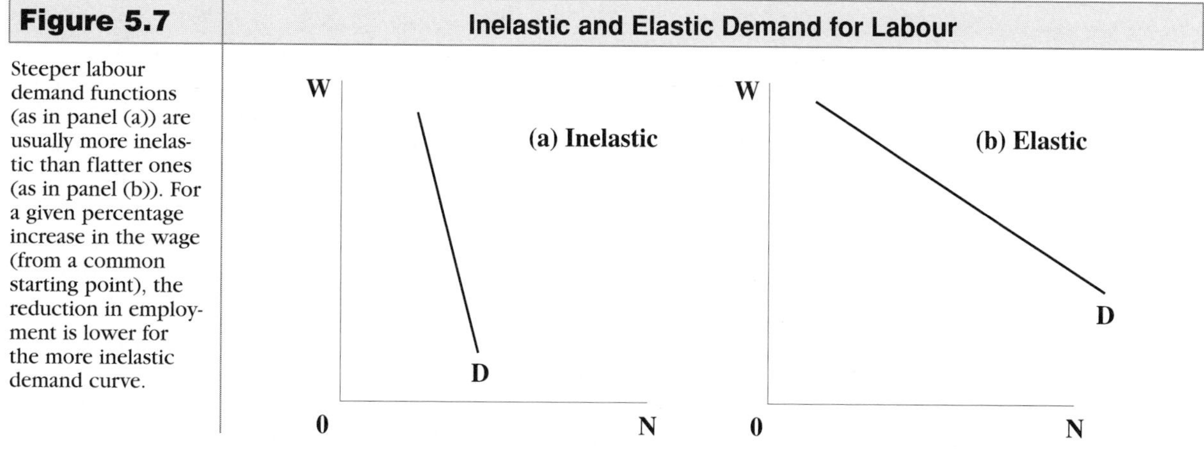

Steeper labour demand functions (as in panel (a)) are usually more inelastic than flatter ones (as in panel (b)). For a given percentage increase in the wage (from a common starting point), the reduction in employment is lower for the more inelastic demand curve.

Elasticity of Demand for Output

Since the demand for labour is derived from the output produced by the firm, then the elasticity of the demand for labour will depend on the price-elasticity of the demand for the output or services produced by the firm. The elasticity of product demand determines the magnitude of the scale effect. If the demand for the output produced by the firm is inelastic, so that a price increase (engendered by a wage increase) will not lead to a large reduction in the quantity demanded, then the derived demand for labour will also be inelastic. In such circumstances, the wage increase can be passed on to consumers in the form of higher product prices without there being much of a reduction in the demand for those products and hence in the derived demand for labour.

This could be the case, for example, in construction, especially nonresidential construction where there are few alternatives to building in a particular location. It could also be the case in tariff-protected industries, or in public services where few alternatives are available, or in most sectors in the short run. On the other hand, in fiercely competitive sectors, such as the garment trades or coal mining, where alternative products are available, then the demand for the product is probably quite price-elastic. In these circumstances, the derived demand for labour would be elastic and a wage increase would lead to a large reduction in the quantity of labour demanded.

Ratio of Labour Cost to Total Cost

The extent to which labour cost is an important component of total cost can also affect the responsiveness of employment to wage changes. Specifically, the demand for labour will be inelastic, and hence the adverse employment effect of a wage increase small, if labour cost is a small portion of total cost.[3] In such circumstances the scale effect would be small; that is, the firm would not have to reduce its output much because the cost increase emanating from the wage increase would be small. In addition, there is the possibility that if wage costs are a small portion of total cost then any wage increase more easily could be absorbed by the firm or passed on to consumers.

For obvious reasons, this factor is often referred to as the "importance of being unimportant." Examples of wage cost for a particular group of workers being a small portion of total cost could include construction craftworkers, airline pilots, and employed professionals (e.g., engineers and architects) on many projects. In such circumstances their wage increases simply may not matter much to the employer, and consequently their wage demands may not be tempered much by the threat of reduced employment. On the other hand, the wages of government workers and miners may constitute a large portion of the total cost in their respective trades. The resultant elastic demand for labour may thereby temper their wage demands.

Empirical Evidence

Clearly, knowledge of the elasticity of demand for particular types of labour is important for policymakers, enabling them to predict the adverse employment effects that may emanate from such factors as minimum wage and equal pay laws, or wage increases associated with unionization, occupational licensing, or arbitrated wage settlements. Estimates of the elasticity of the demand for the particular type of labour being affected would be useful to predict the employment effect of an exogenous wage increase.

[3]Hicks (1963, pp. 245–6) proves formally that this is true as long as the elasticity of demand for the final product is greater than the elasticity of substitution between the inputs—that is, as long as consumers can substitute away from the higher-priced product more easily than producers can substitute away from higher-priced labour. This factor thus depends on the magnitude of both the substitution and the scale effects.

However, even without precise numerical estimates, judicious statements still can be made on the basis of the importance of the various factors that determine the elasticity of the demand for labour.

Hamermesh (1986, 1993) reviews the extensive empirical literature that can be used to calculate estimates of the elasticity of demand for labour. He concludes, largely on the basis of private-sector data from the United States, that the elasticity ranges between −0.15 and −0.75, with −0.30 being a reasonable "best guess."[4] That is, a 1 percent increase in wages would lead to approximately a one-third of 1 percent reduction in employment. This adverse employment effect is roughly equally divided between the substitution and scale effect; that is, the substitution and scale effects are approximately equal. Many of the other propositions regarding labour demand elasticities also seem to be reflected in the empirical evidence. For example, the labour demand elasticity decreases as the skill level of the labour increases.

Canadian studies have obtained broadly similar estimates. For example, Woodland (1975) estimates labour demand functions for ten broadly defined Canadian industries (agriculture, manufacturing, forestry, and mining, and so on) for the 1949–1969 period. One labour input and two capital inputs (structures and equipment) are assumed in the empirical analysis. In each of the ten industries, the estimated labour demand curve is downward-sloping. Estimated elasticities of labour demand are between zero and −0.5 in most industries. Eight of the ten industries exhibited statistically significant substitution among inputs. Woodland concludes that changes in relative input prices appear to play a significant role in determining the demand for factors of production.

There are also a number of more recent Canadian studies based on microeconomic industry or firm level data. These studies also yield elasticity estimates in the middle of the range suggested by Hamermesh. Focusing on employment within Bell Canada, Denny et al. (1981) estimate a labour demand elasticity in the neighbourhood of −0.4. Card (1990) analyzes manufacturing employment in unionized firms, using contract-level data, and finds an implied labour demand elasticity of −0.62. In a study of public sector employment, teachers in school boards in Ontario, Currie (1991) also estimates an elasticity in the neighbourhood of −0.55. Since the technology and market conditions vary across these diverse settings, it is remarkable that the empirical studies paint such a consistent picture of the price elasticity of the demand for labour.[5]

CHANGING DEMAND CONDITIONS AND GLOBAL COMPETITION

Since the demand for labour is derived from the output of firms, then labour demand (and consequently wages and employment) will be affected by changes in the product market conditions that affect employers. Such changes have been substantial in recent years, emanating from such interrelated factors as global competition, free trade, industrial restructuring, technological change, privatization, and subcontracting.

The changing demand conditions emanating from growing international competition have been of special concern to policymakers and the general public alike. Buzzwords like "international competitiveness" proliferate in the media and business sections of bookstores. This focus is likely to continue as world tariffs and nontariff barriers to trade continue to fall under arrangements such as the World Trade Organization (WTO). Trade pressures will also be enhanced by the growing number of trading blocs such as the European Union (EU), the Closer Economic Relations Trade Agreement (CER) between Australia and

www.wto.org
www.sice.oas.org

[4]Hamermesh (1993, p. 135).

[5]See Hamermesh (1993), especially Chapter 3, for a more detailed, comprehensive summary of these and other studies.

New Zealand, the North American Free Trade Agreement (NAFTA) between Canada, the United States, and Mexico, and possible extensions through the FTAA to newly emerging free trade areas in South America such as Mercosur (Argentina, Bolivia, Brazil, Chile, Paraguay, and Uruguay) as well as the Andean Pact (Venezuela, Colombia, Ecuador, Peru, and Bolivia). Competition is constantly felt from the Pacific regions, with the continued success of Japan, the Asian newly industrialized economies (NIEs) of Hong Kong, Korea, Singapore, and Taiwan, and the rapid emergence of China. The transition economies of eastern Europe will also provide increased trade opportunities and pools of relatively untapped labour resources.

While discussions of the merits of trade policies such as NAFTA or the WTO lie ostensibly in the domain of the product market, much of the debate, especially in Canada and the United States, has focused on labour market issues. The labour demand model we have just reviewed provides a useful framework in which to cast some of the key features of the debate. A common question posed by those concerned with the impact of trade on labour markets, is whether "high wage" countries can "compete," i.e., whether increased openness to trade necessitates a reduction of employment, wages, or both.

The Impact of Trade on a Single Labour Market

The simplest way to investigate this question is in the context of a single labour market, for example with a short-run demand for "Canadian" labour. With increased trade liberalization, increased competition from cheaper, foreign-produced goods effectively lowers the price that comparable Canadian-produced goods can sell for. In a competitive market, this leads to a decline in the value of the marginal product of domestic (Canadian) labour, since the $VMP_N = p \times MPN$. This results in a shift inward of the demand curve for Canadian labour. If the wage of Canadian labour remains constant, then this *must* result in a decline in demand for Canadian labour (all else constant). In order to maintain the profit-maximization condition, however, there are two other possible margins of adjustment besides employment. First, the wage rate could decline enough to offset the decrease in the value of Canadian output. Alternatively, the marginal productivity of labour could increase, offsetting the price decrease.

Another approach would be to consider the long-run demand for Canadian labour in global production, where Canadian labour is one of several inputs. A reduction of trade barriers in Canada alone would allow producers to more easily substitute away from Canadian toward foreign labour. They could accomplish this, for example, by moving their factories to the southern United States or some other country. Again, holding the relative price of Canadian and foreign labour constant, this would likely involve a reduction in employment in Canada. Profit maximization requires the maintenance of the condition

$$\frac{MPN_C}{MPN_F} = \frac{W_C}{W_F} \tag{5.6}$$

If the removal of trade barriers effectively reduces the price of foreign labour (W_F), then we would expect to see a substitution toward foreign labour. This simple intuition would seem to suggest that production (and thus jobs) will always move to the lower-wage country. Indeed, all else equal, this would be true if Canadian and foreign labour were perfect substitutes in production.

The important point to note, though, is that the profit-maximization condition involves *both* sides to the equality: while relative labour costs matter, the relative marginal products (marginal rate of technical substitution) matter as much. If Canadian labour is twice as productive with the same level of employment, then a profit-maximizing global employer will choose to hire as much Canadian labour, even at twice the price. This does not diminish the importance of labour costs in assessing the impact of trade on labour markets, but merely emphasizes the need to consider **productivity** at the same time. A focus on labour costs alone ignores the symmetric role that productivity plays. As long as Canadian workers are sufficiently more productive than Mexican workers, firms will not move to Mexico in response to wage differences.

The following tables provide some international comparisons of various aspects of labour costs and productivity. They highlight Canada's changing position in an increasingly integrated world economy. Since it is labour cost relative to productivity that influences competitiveness, the tables provide information on various dimensions: compensation costs (including some fringe benefits); productivity; and unit labour costs which reflect both compensation costs and productivity (i.e., labour cost per unit of output).

Table 5.1 compares compensation costs in Canada to a variety of countries throughout the world. The costs are converted to Canadian dollars on the basis of the exchange rate, and hence they reflect fluctuations in the exchange rate. They are specified on an hourly basis so they are adjusted for differences in hours worked. The costs for each year are indexed to the Canadian costs, which are set equal to 100, so that they are all expressed as percentages of the Canadian costs. For example, in 1999, compensation costs in the highest-cost country, Germany (the part corresponding to the former West Germany), were 173 percent of Canadian costs (i.e., 73 percent above Canadian costs), while the costs in the lowest-cost country of Mexico were 14 percent of those in Canada. The figures of Table 5.1 indicate that Canada is reasonably competitive on an international basis in terms of compensation costs. We are significantly below high-wage countries like Germany, Switzerland, the Netherlands, and the Scandinavian countries, but significantly above low-wage countries like Mexico and the newly industrialized economies of Hong Kong, Korea, Singapore, and Taiwan (though the gap is narrowing). Canadian costs are also lower than those of our major trading partners the United States and Japan. An important point to bear in mind, however, is that one should not be entirely cheered by declining wages. From a welfare perspective, while low wages might make one more competitive, they do not necessarily make one better off. National standards of living depend crucially on high wages derived from high productivity. This further emphasizes the importance of considering productivity along with wage costs.

The continued success of higher wage countries like Germany and Japan shows the viability of being able to compete on the basis of productivity and quality, as opposed to low wages. The extremely low wages of many of the Asian countries and Mexico highlight that it is not possible for Canada to compete on the basis of labour costs alone. Rather, it is important to be able to develop "market niches" on the basis of high productivity and high-value-added production and quality service (i.e., on the basis of a high value of marginal productivity of labour).

Table 5.2 shows how Canadian costs and productivity have evolved over the 1980s and 1990s relative to other countries. Hourly productivity is an estimate of the value of output produced per hour of labour input, and corresponds to the average product of labour. From this table we can see that Canada has the second-lowest productivity growth over this time period of the countries reported in the table. Belgium and Japan had the highest productivity growth, Norway the lowest. However, from a labour allocation perspective, Canadian hourly labour costs grew slowly as well. Canada's compensation cost increase (109 percent from 1979 to 1999), and every other country's, is dwarfed by the increase of the cost of labour in Japan. Most countries had their hourly compensation costs growth exceed their productivity growth. Canada's per-unit labour costs (the average labour cost of producing a unit of output) grew in the low-to-middle range of these countries. A few European countries, like Belgium, Sweden, and the Netherlands, had their productivity and compensation costs increase approximately in tandem over the period, significantly improving their competitive position relative to the other countries. From Canada's perspective, it is important to note that our per-unit labour costs have increased by approximately the same amount as those of our largest trading partner, the United States.

Table 5.1 Compensation Costs,[1] Various Countries,[2] 1980, 1990, 1999 (as % of Canadian compensation costs)

Country	1980	1990	1999
Germany, former West	141	137	173
Norway	133	135	154
Switzerland	127	131	152
Denmark	125	113	148
Belgium	151	121	147
Austria	102	111	141
Sweden	144	131	138
Finland	94	132	136
Japan	64	80	135
Netherlands	139	113	135
United States	114	93	123
Luxembourg[3]	139	105	123
France	103	97	116
Italy	94	109	106
United Kingdom	88	79	106
Australia	98	82	102
Canada	**100**	**100**	**100**
Ireland	68	73	88
Spain	68	71	78
Israel	43	53	77
New Zealand	60	51	59
Greece[3]	43	42	59
Singapore	17	23	46
Korea	11	23	43
Taiwan	11	24	36
Portugal[3]	24	23	36
Hong Kong SAR	17	20	35
Mexico	25	10	14
Sri Lanka[3]	2	2	4
Trade-Weighted Measures[4]			
All 28 foreign economies	76	78	98
OECD[5]	95	97	121
Europe	114	108	131
Asian NIEs[6]	14	23	40

Notes:

1. Defined as (1) all payments made directly to the worker, before payroll deductions of any kind, and (2) employer expenditures for legally required insurance programs and contractual and private benefit plans. In addition, for some countries, compensation is adjusted for other taxes on payrolls or employment (or reduced to reflect subsidies), even if they are not for the direct benefit of workers, because such taxes are regarded as labour costs. All figures are on an hours-worked basis and are exchange-rate-adjusted and therefore reflect exchange rates and wages and fringe benefits.
2. In descending order, from high to low, in terms of 1999 compensation costs.
3. 1999 figures refer to 1998.
4. Averages for groups of countries, weighted by the amount of trade (exports and imports) with the United States as of 1992.
5. Not counting Korea or Mexico.
6. Newly industrialized economies: Hong Kong, Korea, Singapore, and Taiwan.

Source: U.S. Department of Labor, Bureau of Labor Statistics, "International comparisons of hourly compensation costs for production workers in manufacturing." Available online, accessed April 2001 <www.bls.gov/news.release/ichcc.toc.htm>.

Figure 5.8 provides an interesting summary of Canada's competitive position relative to the United States. The graph essentially summarizes the information in Table 5.2, comparing trends in labour costs and productivity in the two countries. There are two important points to note. First, Canada's unit labour costs are slightly higher now than they were in 1980 (relative to those of the United States). This has occurred because hourly compensation has fallen slightly slower than productivity. The second point is that the relative costs fluctuate quite a bit. Most of this fluctuation turns out to be driven by the exchange rate. Notice that Canada's unit labour costs were highest in 1991, corresponding to the first years after the FTA with the United States. These exchange rate–driven high labour costs may have contributed as much as anything else to the changes in employment that coincided with free trade with the United States. They also emphasize the importance of other factors beyond the shoproom floor that can affect Canada's international competitiveness.

Cross-Sectoral Impact of Trade

The above discussion is illuminating on a number of issues related to trade and labour markets. In particular, it emphasizes the important role of the productivity of labour as a determinant, as much as the wage, on where employment is likely to grow in an increasingly global economy. Unfortunately, the single-market framework is too divorced from underlying trade theory to allow us to make more insightful statements about the impact of increased trade on employment and wages.

The following simple trade model illustrates a couple of additional points. It shows the underlying motivation for expanded trade, the possible gains to an economy from increased openness. It also emphasizes the importance of cross-sectoral adjustment in evaluating the

Table 5.2 Change in Productivity,[1] Hourly Compensation,[2] and Unit Labour Costs[3] in Manufacturing, 1979–1999 (various countries)

Country	Hourly Productivity	Hourly Compensation	Unit Labour Cost
Norway	33	142	82
Canada	52	109	38
Germany, former West	62	170	66
Italy	79	139	33
Netherlands	86	96	6
United Kingdom	90	232	75
United States	93	146	28
France	95	133	20
Sweden	96	96	0
Japan	102	303	100
Belgium	110	92	–9

Notes:

All figures represent the percentage increase, relative to 1979 base year.

1. Output per hour.
2. Compensation is defined as (1) all payments made directly to the worker, before payroll deductions of any kind and (2) employer expenditures for legally required insurance programs and contractual and private-benefit plans. In addition, for some countries, compensation is adjusted for other taxes on payrolls or employment (or reduced to reflect subsidies), even if they are not for the direct benefit of workers, because such taxes are regarded as labour costs. All figures are on an hours-worked basis and are exchange-rate-adjusted and therefore reflect exchange rates and wages and fringe benefits.
3. Hourly compensation per unit of output (i.e., adjusted for productivity).

Source: U.S. Department of Labor, Bureau of Labor Statistics, "International comparisons of manufacturing productivity and unit labour cost trends." Available online, accessed April 2001 <www.bls.gov/news.release/prod4.toc.htm>.

labour market effects of trade. While the model is quite simplified, its assumptions provide a useful framework for evaluating the impact of recent trade agreements.[6]

Consider a small economy (relative to the world) that produces and consumes only two products: beer and wine (following Ronald Reagan's analogy at the "Shamrock Summit" with regard to free trade between Canada and the United States). Assume that the economy is completely closed—that is, that it engages in no trade, so that consumers can only consume exactly what they produce. Such an economy is illustrated in Figure 5.9(a). The **production possibility frontier** (PPF) is given by PP'. If labour were allocated entirely in the production of beer, then 100 units (cases) could be produced. Alternatively, if labour were moved entirely into wine production, 15 cases could be produced.

In this economy, consumption possibilities correspond exactly to production possibilities, so a representative or collective consumer must choose from the points on PP' the combination of beer and wine that maximizes utility. This optimal consumption and production

Figure 5.8 **Relative Trends in Labour Costs and Productivity, Canada Relative to the United States (base year 1980)**

This figure shows relative trends in productivity and labour costs in Canada and the United States. Each point shows the ratio of a cost (or productivity) index in Canada to that in the United States, with 1980 as the base year. For example, in 1991 unit labour costs were 30 percent higher in Canada than in 1980, compared to the United States. Note that these figures do not compare the levels of costs between Canada and the United States, only their trends (relative to 1980).

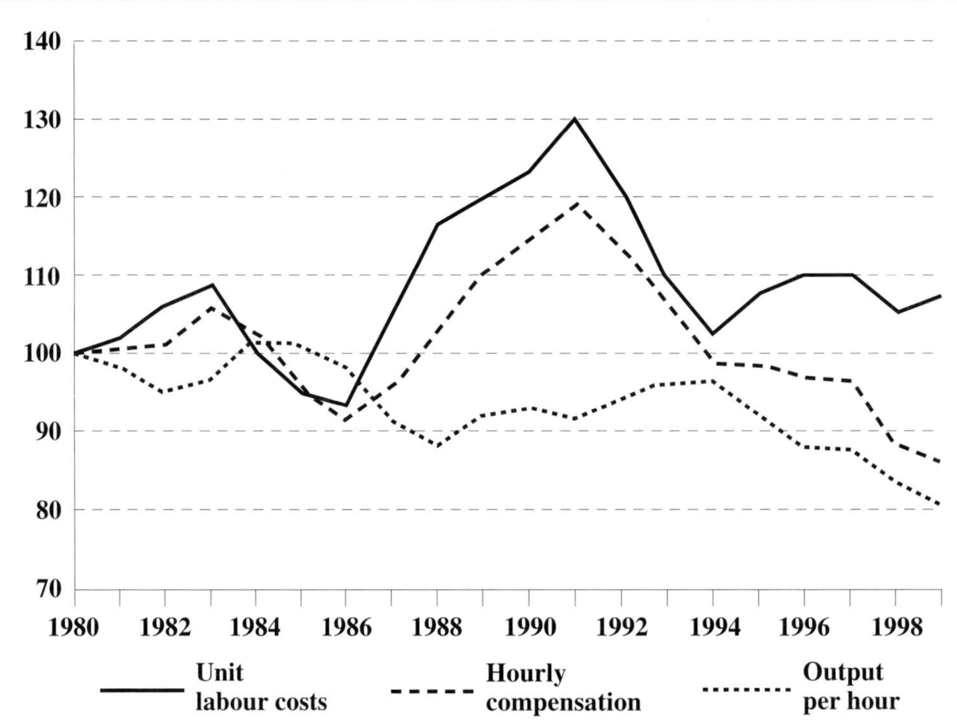

Notes:

Points represent the relative value of indices of Canadian to U.S. labour costs and productivity (as defined in the notes to Table 5.2).

The base year is 1980 (index = 100 for both Canada and the United States).

Source: Author's calculations based on U.S. Department of Labor, Bureau of Labor Statistics, "International comparisons of manufacturing productivity and unit labor cost trends." Available online, accessed April 2001 <www.bls.gov/news.release/prod4.toc.htm>.

[6]See Johnson and Stafford (1999) for a theoretically more rigorous treatment of the links between trade and labour markets, and a summary of evidence pertaining to these links.

package is given by the tangency between the indifference curve U_A and the PP' at point A (for autarky). At this point, the implicit rate of trade (or price) of beer for wine is given by the dashed line, A'A'', and is equal to 5. In other words, 1 case of wine "trades" for 5 cases of beer: the consumer's marginal rate of substitution between beer and wine is 5 (he would be willing to exchange 5 cases of beer for 1 case of wine and remain equally happy); and the marginal rate of transformation is also equal to 5—in order to produce 1 more case of wine, labour would have to be reallocated so that output of beer fell by 5 cases.

Now consider an agent for the world market offering to trade wine and beer with this economy. Note that this agent will only trade wine for beer or vice versa—she will not give either away. Importing (or buying from the agent) necessarily entails exporting (or selling to the agent). Similarly, the small economy will not engage in trade unless it yields an improvement in utility. Suppose that the agent offers to exchange 1 case of wine for 5 cases of beer. This represents no opportunity (on the margin) for the small economy to engage in trade. In order for the international agent to offer something to the small economy, there must be a difference between the world price and the autarkic price. Consider instead a world price of 3 cases of beer for 1 case of wine. On the margin, rather than giving up 5 cases of beer for the case of wine by shifting production on its own, the small economy *could* trade 3 cases of beer for the case of wine, at a savings of 2 cases. This represents an improvement in consumption opportunities, and the set of such opportunities is shown in Figure 5.9(b), under the assumption that production remains exactly as it did before trade. At the extreme, the country could sell its entire production of beer (70 cases) in exchange

Figure 5.9 **Trade, Consumption, and Production in a Simple Economy**

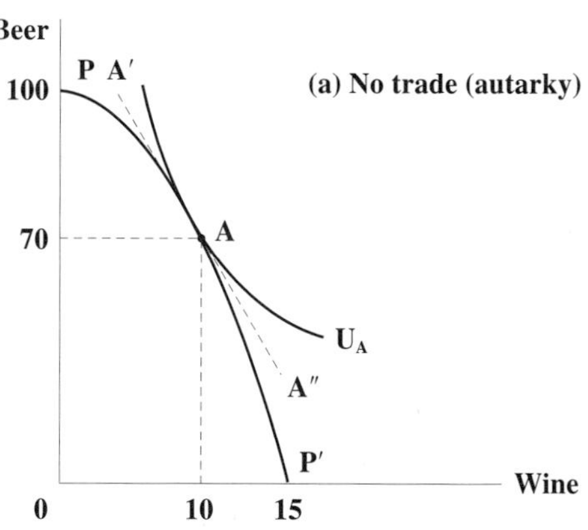

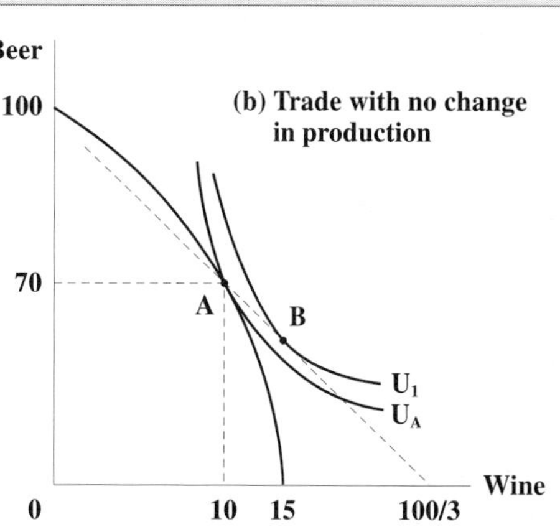

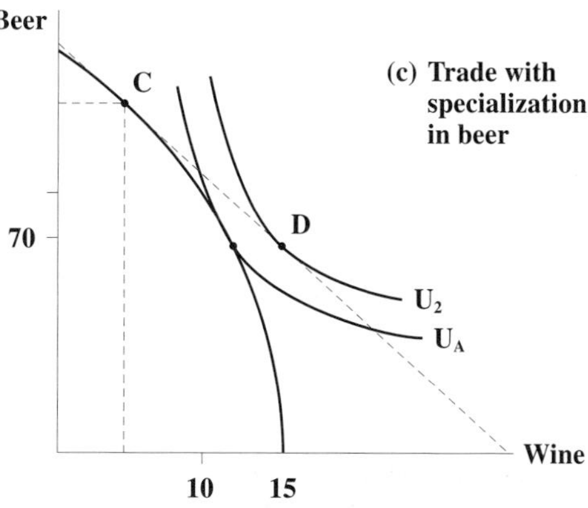

Consumers can be made better off with trade. Panel (a) shows the no-trade outcome, where consumption is based on the domestic production possibility frontier, PP'. At the chosen point A, five cases of beer trade for one case of wine. In panel (b) consumption possibilities expand if wine can be purchased in the world market, at a price of three cases of beer for one case of wine. Even without changing production, consumers can attain utility level $U_1 > U_A$. Consumption expands further (in panel (c)) if the economy specializes in producing beer, moving to the point C. On the basis of this production, consumers can attain U_2, associated with consumption point D.

for 70/3 cases of wine. This would allow it to consume a total of 70/3 cases of imported plus 10 cases of (identical) domestic wine, for a total of 100/3 cases of wine. Consumption need not correspond exactly to production in this case, and the expanded set of consumption opportunities makes the small economy unambiguously better off, allowing it to achieve a level of utility indicated by U_1.

If the economy is willing to reorganize production, by shifting more labour toward the production of beer (and implicitly away from wine), consumption possibilities are expanded further. This possibility is delineated in Figure 5.9(c). Here, production moves to C, while consumption moves to D, corresponding to a higher indifference curve, U_2. Openness to trade can result in increased specialization and enhanced consumption opportunities. Notice that the gains from trade depended only on the divergence of world and internal *relative* prices. It does not matter whether the world beer and wine market is dominated by a "super-mega" producer that can produce beer and wine with less labour than the small economy, or an inefficient producer of both goods. All that matters is the difference in the relative productivity in production of beer and wine. This is the basic notion of comparative advantage, the driving force in the theoretical arguments regarding the gains from trade.

This simple model illustrates why most economists favour free trade as a general principle. Consumers are made unambiguously better off with increased opportunities to trade. The value of the model also lies in its ability to assess the likely impact of increased trade on the labour market. First, it suggests that trade leads to sectoral adjustment— some sectors will expand, while others will shrink. Unless the world economy is "giving away" its output, at least one sector must expand in order for the small economy to be able to purchase the world-produced goods. Looking at aggregate employment statistics may not tell the full story of the effects of trade on the labour market. Second, the argument for the gains from trade assumes that there is a representative consumer, or equivalently, that the consumption pie is shared equally with all members of the small economy. If the labour allocated in the shrinking sector does not share in the increased consumption opportunities, then the argument that trade is necessarily welfare-enhancing is questionable. In more practical terms, unless the "losers" are compensated, or costlessly shifted to the "winning" sector, it is not necessarily the case that freer trade makes the small economy better off. We will be pursuing these issues further in our examination of inequality and wage differentials, later in Chapter 9.

Evidence

With these theoretical insights behind us, let us turn to the more specific question of how freer trade has affected the Canadian labour market, especially since the FTA was implemented in 1989. The effects were expected to be positive: job gains exceeding job losses, increases in real wages, and reductions in unemployment. However, even 12 years after its beginning, controversy remains about its actual effects, with opponents attributing mass layoffs and plant closings to the FTA. It has been difficult to isolate the independent impact of the FTA, in part because it was phased in over a ten-year period, but more importantly because it was only one of many interrelated forces affecting the labour market at the time (Betcherman and Gunderson, 1991). The other forces include those discussed in this section—global competition, industrial structuring, technological change, privatization, and subcontracting. The FTA also coincided with a recession in both Canada and the United States, and a high Canadian dollar (recall Figure 5.8).

An increasing consensus is emerging about the overall impact of the FTA. First, there were definite short-run adjustment costs, especially in heavily protected industries, that is, those that had the largest tariff reductions. Gaston and Trefler (1997) estimate that of the 400,000 jobs lost in Canada between 1989 and 1993, between 9 and 14 percent (around 40,000 jobs) can be attributed to the FTA, netting out the variety of other contributing factors. To some extent, they attribute the adjustment costs to inflexibility (wage rigidity) in the Canadian labour market. Implicit in our discussion of the gains from trade is a costless reallocation of labour from the shrinking sector to the expanding one. If this reallocation is impeded by labour market imperfections, the potentially adverse consequences of trade are magnified. Gaston and Trefler's results emphasize the importance of labour market structure in assessing the benefits of freer trade.

However, Trefler (2001) also shows that while the short-run costs are evident, there have also been significant long-run benefits of the FTA, especially in terms of higher labour productivity. The reallocation of labour out of the less productive into the more productive plants has led to increases in labour productivity of 0.6 percent per year in all of manufacturing, and a "staggering" 2.1-percent-per-year increase in those manufacturing industries most affected by free trade. While painful in the short run, the specialization in more productive activities (or modes of production) generates long-run benefits, largely in line with what we would expect using the simple trade models, such as those discussed in Figure 5.9.

Exhibit 5.1

Free Trade and Jobs

In 1990 and 1991, opponents of free trade linked the Canada-U.S. free trade agreement to the significant job loss experienced in Canada over this time period. Hardly a day went by without the media reporting of one factory or another closing down and moving to the United States. While employment has recovered significantly since that time period, to what extent were FTA opponents correct in laying blame on free trade for these job losses? As it turns out, this is a difficult question to answer. The job losses at the time coincided with four other major adverse economic factors: (1) a severe recession that occurred in both Canada and the United States; (2) a high Canadian dollar, the increased value of which may have offset any favourable effects of U.S. tariff reductions (recall Figure 5.8); (3) high relative Canadian interest rates, which may have contributed to higher relative economic contraction; and (4) ongoing structural adjustment, and other manifestations of technological change and globalization.

Gaston and Trefler (1994, 1997) present a thorough and careful attempt to disentangle these factors. Given lags in data availability, their studies focus on changes up to 1993, corresponding to the depths of the last recession. They point out that any "conviction" of the FTA for job destruction depends on establishing a link between job loss and trade, and furthermore, to the tariff changes that could be associated with changed trade patterns. The aggregate employment conditions at the time cannot be blamed on the FTA, or at least FTA proponents can reasonably argue that other factors might have been responsible. Thus, the Gaston and Trefler studies look at cross-industry variation in employment growth, compared across the two countries.

They show that employment decline, especially in "sunset" or declining industries, was more severe in Canada. This could be associated with changed tariffs. However, some of the more severe employment declines occurred in industries that were less affected by the FTA (automobiles, steel, and lumber for example). In the end, they only attribute about 9 to 14 percent of the overall job loss (around 400,000 jobs) to tariff changes resulting from the FTA. Furthermore, they point out that some of this loss would have been reduced if Canadian wages had adjusted more toward the U.S. level.

Other Demand-Side Factors

As noted previously, there have been a number of other important changes occurring on the demand side of the Canadian labour market. Industrial restructuring has also been prominent, associated mainly with the decline of blue-collar, often unionized, well-paid jobs in heavy manufacturing. As outlined in more detail later in the chapter on wage structures, these middle-wage jobs have been displaced by jobs at polar ends of the occupational distribution. At the high end are professional, managerial, and administrative jobs; at the low end are the low-wage jobs in services and retailing. This phenomenon has been described as the "declining middle" and it has led to increased wage polarization.

The large factories of the heavy-manufacturing, "smokestack" industries have often given way to more flexible, modular factories linked together by advanced communications and "just in time" delivery systems that require little inventory. Flexibility and adaptability are crucial, and the need for these elements has led to increases in subcontracting, permanent part-time work forces, and contingent work forces that are utilized as demand changes. The industrial restructuring has often been accompanied through mergers and acquisitions, often leading to work force reductions ("downsizing") and pressures for concession bargaining.

Technological change has continued its advance, especially in areas of office automation associated with computers. Robotics has been introduced on the factory floor and the assembly line, and computer-assisted technology has been utilized in virtually every aspect of the production cycle.

In the public sector, privatization and subcontracting have been prominent for functions ranging from building maintenance to road maintenance. Crown corporations such as Air Canada have also been privatized.

These various changes emanating from the demand side of the labour market have significant implications both for labour markets and for human resource practices and industrial relations policies in general. They imply greater demands for a flexible and adaptable work force, just like the flexibility that is required from the product market side from which the demand for labour is derived. The work force must be willing and able to do a broader array of job assignments and to integrate quality control as an integral part of the job. The product market changes place greater emphasis on a work force that is trained in the general skills required for continuous upgrading and retraining and is also able to do a variety of tasks ("multiskilling") associated with the broader job assignments and the emphasis on quality control. As part of the individual worker's responsibility for quality control, there is less emphasis on direct supervision and more emphasis on employee involvement in decision-making.

The demand-side changes are also pressuring for compensation that is more flexible and responsive to the changing economic conditions and to the particular economic circumstances of each individual enterprise. This in turn puts pressure toward the breakdown of historical pattern bargaining that often prevailed, whereby establishments frequently followed the wage settlements established by certain key pattern-setting firms. This may no longer be viable given the different demand conditions facing different firms.

The changes emanating from the demand side of the labour market have also led to numerous changes in workplace practices. Jobs have often been redesigned to provide for both *job enlargement* (the horizontal addition of a variety of tasks of similar complexity) and *job enrichment* (the vertical addition of tasks of different levels of complexity).

Whether these changes are part of a fundamental transformation or a continuous evolution of the workplace and the labour market is a debatable issue. What is certain is that the demand-side forces are having a substantial impact. The impact is particularly pronounced because the forces tend to work in the same direction, thereby compounding their individual effects. When coupled with many of the supply-side pressures highlighted previously (aging work force, continued labour force participation of women, dominance of the two-earner family), they emphasize the dynamism that will continue to characterize the Canadian labour market.

Summary

- Labour demand is "derived demand," that is, labour is hired in order to produce goods which are sold in the product market. For this reason, labour demand is always connected to the product market, especially in terms of the degree of competition, whether from foreign or domestic producers.
- Labour is only one of several factors of production. In the short run, we imagine that all of these other factors are fixed, and labour is the only variable input. The profit-maximizing level of labour demand will be chosen so that the marginal benefit equals the marginal cost of hiring an additional unit of labour. The marginal cost is the wage rate, while the marginal benefit is the revenue associated with the extra production by that worker, its marginal revenue product (MRP_N). Therefore, the short-run labour demand function is given by the MRP_N schedule, where employment is determined by $W = MRP_N$.
- In the long run, labour can be substituted with other inputs like capital. An increase in the wage will have two effects on the quantity of labour demanded. First, even if output remains the same, the firm will substitute toward capital and away from labour (the substitution effect). Second, the increase in marginal cost will lead to a reduction in the optimal output, and a further reduction in labour demanded (the scale effect).
- Labour demand curves unambiguously slope downward, in both the long- and short-run. The long-run function is more elastic (at any given wage), because of the greater degree of flexibility in substituting other inputs for labour.
- The impact of globalization on the Canadian labour market can be analyzed in the context of a simple labour demand model, where employment in Canada depends on labour productivity and labour costs in Canada versus the rest of the world. However, a richer model allowing for more than a single sector, provides a better understanding of the cross-sectoral impacts of increased trade on employment, wages, and economic welfare, and also highlights the important role played by comparative advantage in determining trade and employment patterns.

REVIEW QUESTIONS

1. Why is the point E_0 in Figure 5.2(c) a stable equilibrium? Show the firm's expansion path. That is, show how the firm's input mix evolves as output is increased.
2. What is meant by an inferior factor of production? How would the firm's demand for labour be altered if labour were an inferior factor of production?
3. "The firm's demand schedule for labour is a negative function of the wage because, as the firm uses more labour, it has to utilize poorer-quality labour, and hence pays a lower wage." True or false? Explain.
4. Derive the firm's demand schedule for labour if it were a monopolist that could influence the price at which it sells its output. That is, relax the assumption that product prices are fixed, and trace the implications.
5. With reference to Tables 5.1 and 5.2 and Figure 5.8, discuss Canada's changing international competitive position as regards unit labour cost. Discuss the relative importance of the various dimensions of unit labour cost.

6. "Given our wage costs relative to those in the Asian newly industrialized economies, in China, and in Mexico, it does not make sense to try and compete on the basis of restraining labour costs. Rather, we should concentrate on other ways of competing, including the development of market niches that involve a high-wage, high-value-added strategy." Discuss.
7. "Our real concern on an international basis is that our unit labour costs have increased relative to those of the United States, and this has occurred just at the time when we need to be most competitive, given NAFTA. A prudent policy would be to maintain a low exchange rate." Discuss.

PROBLEMS

1. Output of lawn-care services, measured in number of lawns, depends on the hours of lawn-maintenance labour, given a fixed capital stock, according to the production function:

$$Q = 2\sqrt{L}$$

The marginal product of labour is therefore given by $\frac{1}{\sqrt{L}}$.

Assume that the price of lawn services is \$10 per lawn.

(a) Solve for the labour demand function.

(b) Calculate the labour demand, output, and profits for wages equal to the following (i.e., fill in the remainder of the table):

Wage	Labour Demand	Output	Profits
\$1	______	______	______
\$2	______	______	______
\$5	______	______	______
\$10	______	______	______

How do profits vary along the demand curve?

2. Bicycle Helmet Testing Services requires capital (a hammer) and labour to be used in fixed proportions (one labourer per hammer per day of testing). Assume also that it takes one day of steady bashing to fully test one helmet. Show the isoquant for a helmet testing firm corresponding to 100 helmets tested. Show the cost-minimizing input combination if a day's labour costs \$50, a hammer costs \$10 to rent for one day, and the firm wishes to test 100 helmets. Depict the scale and substitution effects if the wage decreases to \$25 per day. What does the short-run labour demand function look like? What does the long-run labour demand function look like?
3. "The provision of health services requires the labour of doctors and nurses. If the wage rate of nurses increases, while doctor's wages are unchanged, the demand for doctors will increase." True or false? Explain.
4. Assume that fruit-picking can be done by children or adults, but that adults are twice as efficient as children (they pick twice as fast). The production function for fruit-picking is thus

$$Q = 10 \times (2L_A + L_C)$$

where output is measured in bushels of apples, labour is measured in days, L_A is the number of days of adult labour, and L_C is the number of days of child labour.

(a) Depict the isoquants for a typical orchard (in terms of fruit-picking).
(b) Assume the wage rate of adults is \$100 per day, and the wage for children is \$60 per day. Show the isocost lines.
(c) Show the profit-maximizing input choice where the profit-maximizing output is 1000 bushels of apples. Depict the scale and substitution effects if the wage of child labour falls to \$25 per day. What does the demand curve for child labour look like?

5. For each of the following examples, choose the case with the lower (more inelastic) wage elasticity, evaluated at a common point where the wage is \$15 per hour:
   (a) A farm's demand for farm labour for weeding, in a jurisdiction where chemical herbicides are banned for environmental reasons, versus a jurisdiction where they are not
   (b) A coal mine's demand for labour, where the mine has a local monopoly in the sale of coal, versus a mine that sells coal in a competitive market
   (c) The demand for workers in a cigarette factory, versus the demand for workers in a fast-food restaurant
   (d) The demand for computer programmers versus secretaries, for factories in Silicon Valley
   (e) The demand for "beer tasters" (quality-control engineers) versus beer production line workers in a brewery

6. Consider a very simple representation of the before-trade Canadian and U.S. economies. Both countries produce only automobiles and food, according to the technology represented in the following production possibility frontiers:

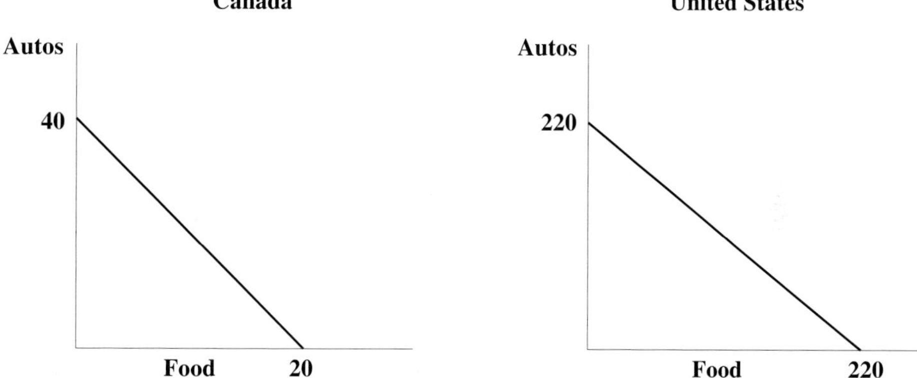

Assume that the working populations of Canada and the United States are 25 and 250 respectively.

(a) Using well-labelled diagrams, show that Canada can gain from trade with the United States. Carefully describe what will happen to Canadian production, employment, and wages after free trade with the United States. Be careful to state your assumptions.
(b) Recognizing that the above model is a simplification of the real world, analyze the likely short- and long-run employment consequences of free trade with the United States on Canadian employment and wages.
(c) "Within four years of the implementation of the Canada-U.S. Free Trade Agreement (FTA) in 1989, employment in Canadian manufacturing dropped by 400,000. This shows that the FTA killed jobs." True or false? Explain.

KEYWORDS

REFERENCES

Betcherman, G., and M. Gunderson. 1990. Canada-U.S. free trade and labour relations. *Labour Law Journal* 41 (August):454–560.

Card, D. 1990. Unexpected inflation, real wages, and employment determination in union contracts. *AER* 80 (September):669–88.

Currie, J. 1991. Employment determination in a unionized public-sector labour market: The case of Ontario's school teachers. *JOLE* 9 (November):45–66.

Denny, M., et al. 1981. Estimating the effects of diffusion of technological innovations in telecommunications: The production structure of Bell Canada. *CJE* 14 (February):24–43.

Gaston, N., and D. Trefler. 1994. The role of international trade and trade policy in the labour markets of Canada and the United States. *World Economy* 17 (January):45–62.

______. 1997. The labour market consequences of the Canada-U.S. free trade agreement. *CJE* 30 (February):18–41.

Hamermesh, D. 1986. The demand for labor in the long run. In *Handbook of Labor Economics*, eds. O. Ashenfelter and R. Layard. New York: Elsevier.

______. 1993. *Labor Demand*. Princeton: Princeton University Press.

Hicks, J. R. 1963. *The Theory of Wages*. New York: Macmillan.

Johnson, G., and F. Stafford. 1999. The labor market implications of international trade. In *Handbook of Labor Economics*, eds. O. Ashenfelter and D. Card. New York and Oxford: Elsevier Science, North Holland.

Nagatani, K. 1978. Substitution and scale effects in factor demands. *CJE* 11 (August):521–526.

Trefler, D. 2001. The long and short of the Canada-U.S. free trade agreement. NBER Working Paper, Number 8293.

Woodland, A. 1975. Substitution of structures, equipment and labor in Canadian production. *IER* 16 (February):171–187.

Chapter Six

Labour Demand, Nonwage Benefits, and Quasi-Fixed Costs

Main Questions

- *How important are nonwage benefits as a share of total compensation? How might these nonwage benefits affect the way that we model labour demand?*
- *In the previous chapter, no distinction was made between workers and hours as components of the labour input. Should this distinction be made, and if so, what potential insights do we gain from doing so?*
- *Many payroll taxes (like employer contributions to employment insurance) have ceilings, or maximum payments per worker. How can this feature of payroll taxes actually reduce employment?*
- *Why might less expensive unskilled labour be more likely to be laid off during a downturn than the more expensive skilled labour?*
- *Can restrictions on the length of the work week, or the amount of overtime permitted, lead to the creation of more jobs for others?*

The previous chapter analyzed the demand for labour when labour is a variable input into the production process. In these circumstances, a change in the amount of labour used in production (the number of employee hours) leads to a proportionate change in labour costs. Furthermore, the change in labour costs depends only on the overall magnitude of the change in the labour input and not on the composition of the change in terms of the number of employees versus hours worked per employee. However, some labour costs may be **quasi-fixed** in the sense that they are independent of the number of hours worked by the firm's work force. These quasi-fixed costs may arise because of the costs of hiring and training new workers, the costs of dismissing employees, and from nonwage benefits such as holiday pay, contributions to pension plans, and unemployment insurance.

Quasi-fixed costs have important implications for a variety of labour market phenomena such as work schedules, part-time work, overtime work, hiring and layoff behavior, and unemployment.[1] This chapter examines firms' employment decisions when labour is a quasi-fixed factor of production.

NONWAGE BENEFITS AND TOTAL COMPENSATION

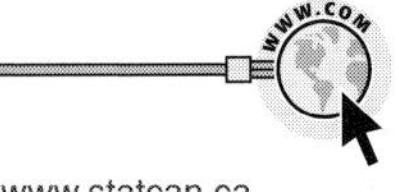

www.statcan.ca

The analysis of labour income and labour demand is complicated by the fact that wages and salaries are only one aspect of total compensation, and therefore only one aspect of the cost of labour to the employer. Figure 6.1 illustrates the main components of total compensation and the most commonly used terminology for these components. Pay for time not worked (holiday and vacation pay, paternal leave) is generally included in wage and salary income as reported by Statistics Canada. However, for some analytical purposes it may be desirable to treat this as a separate compensation category. In particular, for some employees, payment for time not worked is a quasi-fixed cost in the sense that the magnitude of holiday and vacation pay to which the employee is entitled is independent of hours worked.

As is illustrated in Table 6.1, nonwage benefits (indirect labour costs) are a large and increasing component of total compensation. Between 1953 and 1996 nonwage employee benefits as a percentage of direct labour costs (gross payroll) increased from 15.1 to 41.6 percent, though the share declined somewhat in 1998, as wages rose more rapidly than

Figure 6.1 **Components of Total Compensation**

Total compensation comprises wages plus nonwage benefits. The wage and salary component can be further divided into that part directly corresponding to time worked and that part which does not depend on time worked (such as vacation pay).

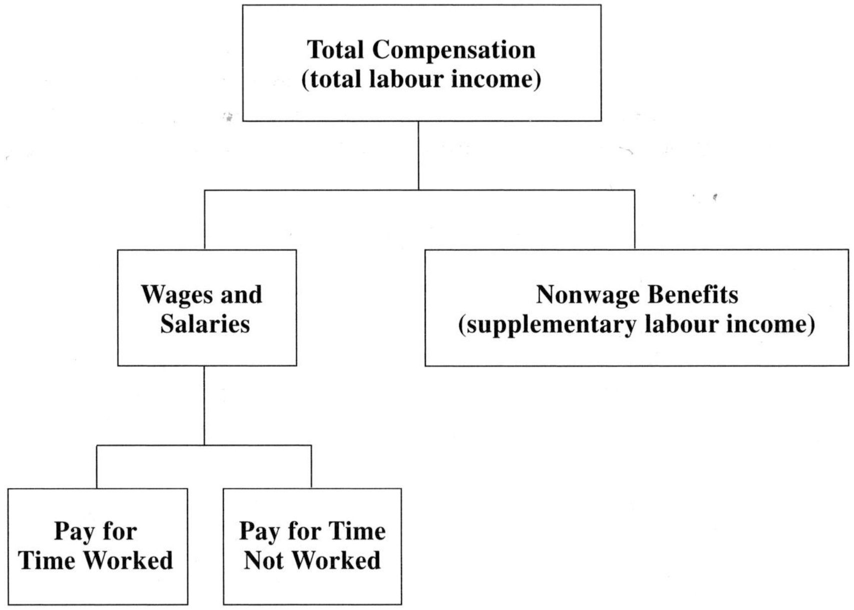

Total Compensation (total labour income)
- Wages and Salaries
  - Pay for Time Worked
  - Pay for Time Not Worked
- Nonwage Benefits (supplementary labour income)

[1]Seminal contributions in this area were made by Oi (1962) and Rosen (1968). Recent contributions include Hart (1984, 1986) and Hamermesh (1989, 1995).

benefits. Pay for time not worked has remained an important category of benefits, and bonuses a small component. The two fastest-growing components have been pension and welfare plans, and legally required payments for workers compensation, unemployment insurance, and CPP/QPP.

The existence and growth of **nonwage benefits** are interesting phenomena to explain, especially given the basic economic proposition that unconditional cash transfers (e.g., wages) are generally more efficient than **transfers-in-kind** (e.g., nonwage benefits). This proposition follows from the fact that recipients who receive cash could always buy the transfers-in-kind if they wanted them, but they are better off because they could buy other things if they wanted them more. Applied to employee benefits, why wouldn't employees and employers prefer wage compensation since it would enable employees to buy whatever benefits they want rather than being given some they may not value?

There are obviously a variety of possible reasons for the existence and growth of nonwage benefits. They are sometimes not taxed and, as taxes have increased over time, this increasingly makes nonwage benefits a preferred form of compensation. There may be economies of scale and administrative economies for group purchases through the employer of such things as pension and insurance plans. However, many of these economies still could be had through completely voluntary group plans. There is the possibility that workers think they are receiving nonwage benefits free in the sense that, if they did not have these benefits, their wages would not rise by a corresponding amount. This possibility, of course, can be true in times of wage controls to the extent that nonwage benefits are exempt or more difficult to control. More likely, workers may simply prefer nonwage benefits because it is an easy way of purchasing benefits that they value. In some cases, like increased vacations and holidays with pay, it is a way of institutionalizing the increased purchase of more leisure that accompanies their growing wealth.

Employers may have accepted the increased role of employee nonwage benefits for reasons that are beneficial to them. Paid vacations and holidays, for example, enable the planning of the production process more than if the workers' desire for increased leisure came in the form of lateness, absenteeism, work slowdowns, or turnover. Similarly, workers' compensation, unemployment insurance, and health insurance can reduce the need for employers to have contingency plans for workers in industrial accidents or subject to layoffs or health problems. In addition, some employee benefits may alter the behaviour of workers in a fashion that is preferred by the employer. Subsidized cafeterias can reduce long lunch hours and keep employees in the plant, the provision of transportation can ensure that

Table 6.1 Nonwage Benefits in Large Firms:[1] Components and Changes Over Time

Nonwage Benefit Categories	Gross Payroll					
	1953	1957	1984	1989	1996	1998
Pay for time not worked	5.9	6.7	14.9	13.9	13.2	12.4
Pension and welfare plans	5.5	6.4	9.4	9.9	14.2	11.5
Payments required by law[2]	1.5	2.0	4.4	5.3	12.1	9.3
Bonuses, profit sharing, other	2.2	1.3	3.7	4.4	2.1	3.5
Total nonwage benefits	15.1	16.4	32.4	33.5	41.6	36.7

Notes:

1. Figures are for all industries. Separate figures for manufacturing and non-manufacturing are not dramatically different.
2. Includes workers' compensation, unemployment insurance, and Canada/Quebec pension plans.

Source: KPMG Peat, Marwick, Stevenson, and Kellogg, *Employee Benefit Costs in Canada* (Toronto), 1989, 1996, and 1998. The last available issue is 1998.

workers get to work on time, company health services can reduce absenteeism and provide a check on a worker's health, and pensions and other seniority-related benefits may reduce unwanted turnover. Employers may also prefer nonwage benefits because they reduce turnover and provide work incentives. Employee benefits such as company pension plans and seniority-based vacation pay represent **deferred compensation** in that these benefits are received later in the employee's career. Workers who leave the firm early in their careers do not receive these benefits. With some of their compensation in the form of deferred benefits, existing employees will be less likely to quit in order to seek or accept employment elsewhere. In addition, deferred compensation raises the cost of being fired for poor work, absenteeism, and so on, thus strengthening work incentives. These effects of deferred compensation on turnover and work incentives are discussed further in Chapter 13.

Deferred compensation can also act as a sorting or screening device, enabling the employer to hire those workers who are most likely to remain with the firm. Employers for whom turnover is very costly—perhaps because of the costs of hiring and training new workers—can screen out those potential employees who do not expect to remain with the firm for an extended period by making deferred compensation a significant proportion of total compensation, a compensation package that is most attractive to potential employees who expect to remain with the firm for a long period of time. Such screening mechanisms are especially valuable when the employer is unable to determine *ex ante* which job applicants are likely to leave the firm after a brief period and which are likely to remain with the firm.

Governments may also prefer nonwage benefits (and hence grant favourable tax treatment) because they may reduce pressures for government expenditures elsewhere.

Exhibit 6.1

Did the Cost of Labour Fall During the 1980s?

Many Canadian workers experienced a decline in real wages during the 1980s. According to the theory of labour demand, this decline in real wages (brought about by nominal wages rising less rapidly than prices) would increase employment, other things being equal. However, as emphasized in this chapter, the cost of labour to the employer depends on both the wage rate and nonwage labour costs. The table below, based on results reported by Pold and Wong (1990), shows that nonwage labour costs have been rising faster than prices. As a consequence, real total compensation per employee declined during the 1977–1988 period, but not to as large an extent as real wages and salaries. This evidence indicates that data on wages and salaries alone would overstate the magnitude of the decline in real labour income and in the real cost of labour. These data also provide further evidence that nonwage labour costs represent an increasingly large fraction of total compensation.

Real Labour Income per Employee in Constant 1988 Dollars

	1977	1988	Percentage Change
Wages and salaries	27,916	26,999	–3.3
Supplementary labour income (nonwage benefits)	2,537	2,970	+17.1
Total compensation (total labour income)	30,453	29,969	–1.6

Source: Pold and Wong, 1990. Reproduced by authority of the Minister of Industry, 1996 Statistics Canada, *Perspectives on Labour and Income*, Catalogue No. 75-001E, Autumn 1990, pp. 42–49.

Employer-sponsored pensions may reduce the need for public pensions; contributions to the Canada (or Quebec) Pension Plan may reduce the need for public care for the aged, at least for the aged who have worked; and increased contributions for unemployment insurance directly reduce the amount the government has to pay to this fund. In addition, many nonwage benefits are part and parcel of the whole package of increased social security, and hence the reasons for their growth are caught up with the reasons for the growth of the whole welfare state.

QUASI-FIXED LABOUR COSTS

General Definition

Employers can change their labour input by changing the number of employees, the hours per employee, or both. The way in which they adjust will depend upon the relative costs of the different options.

Variable costs of labour vary with the *total* hours of labour employed, whether the increase in total hours comes from an increase in the number of employees or from an increase in the hours per employee. For example, if the only cost of labour is the hourly wage rate, then costs will increase by the same percentage whether the labour input is expanded by increasing employment or hours per employee by a given percent. In such circumstances the firm's costs would increase by the same amount whether the labour input was expanded by increased employees or hours per employee.

Wage costs are therefore a variable labour cost, as are nonwage benefits that are proportional to wages. Other labour costs, however, are quasi-fixed costs in the sense that they are incurred per employee and are independent or largely independent of the hours of work per employee. They may be *pure* quasi-fixed costs in the sense that they are fixed per employee and are completely independent of the hours of work of each employee. Or they may be *mixed* variable and quasi-fixed costs in that they increase more rapidly for a given proportionate increase in the number of employees as opposed to hours per employee. In either circumstance, the firm would no longer be indifferent between whether the labour input (employees times hours per employee) expanded by increasing the number of employees or the hours per employee. Increasing the number of employees would be more costly given the quasi-fixed costs.

http://strategis.ic.gc.ca/SSG/ra01275e.html

A distinction should also be made between *recurring* and *nonrecurring* or "one-time" quasi-fixed costs. **Payroll taxes** to finance public pensions and unemployment insurance are examples of recurring nonwage labour costs; these taxes are remitted regularly (e.g., monthly) to the relevant government agencies. Examples of nonrecurring costs include hiring and orienting new employees and dismissing employees whose services are no longer required.

Examples of Quasi-Fixed Costs

At the hiring stage, firms incur quasi-fixed costs associated with the recruiting, hiring, and training of new workers. These costs are independent of the hours the employees subsequently work. Under such circumstances there is an obvious incentive to try to amortize these fixed costs over longer hours and a longer worklife of these employees rather than to hire new employees and incur their additional fixed costs.

Expected termination costs themselves have a fixed-cost component in the sense that at the *hiring stage* the firm may anticipate having to incur such costs should they subsequently lay off or dismiss the worker. Such costs become expected quasi-fixed costs at the hiring stage even though they may not be incurred until a subsequent period. Expectations of such costs are incurred when a new employee is hired but they do not increase, at least by the same proportion as wage costs, when an existing employee works additional hours.

As indicated in Meltz, Reid, and Swartz (1981) and Reid (1985), employers' contributions (payroll taxes) to certain income maintenance programs may also have an element of fixed costs, when such contributions have a ceiling. Employer contributions to workers' compensation and public pensions, for example, have an annual income ceiling, and unemployment insurance a weekly earnings ceiling below which contributions are a certain percent of earnings and beyond which they are zero. Thus, once this ceiling is reached, it pays employers to work these people additional hours since no further payroll taxes are incurred, rather than to hire new employees and incur such payroll taxes. These payroll taxes are variable costs up until the ceiling, and thereafter they become fixed costs, creating the incentive to work existing employees more hours rather than incurring the costs associated with hiring new workers.

Similarly, **employment standards legislation** often requires employees to have been employed for a certain minimum period before they are eligible for such benefits as paid holidays and advance notice of termination. Once the employee reaches this minimum period then these benefits become fixed costs for the employer; they are independent of the additional hours worked by the employee. As with other fixed costs, they encourage the employer to work existing employees longer hours and they discourage the hiring of new employees for whom such costs will be incurred.

Employers' contributions to life insurance and medical and dental plans can also have a quasi-fixed-cost component to the extent that they are fixed per employee. In such circumstances costs are increased by hiring a new employee but not when an existing employee works more hours.

Not all nonwage benefits are ones that have a quasi-fixed component. Some, like employer-sponsored occupational pension plans, may have employer contributions based on a percentage of earnings. In such circumstances the employers' contributions are proportional to earnings and are the same whether the labour input increases through an increase in the number of employees or hours per employee. The same situation prevails for vacation pay that is a percentage of earnings.

General Effect of Quasi-Fixed Costs

As indicated, one general effect of such quasi-fixed costs is to increase the marginal cost of hiring an additional worker (sometimes termed the extensive margin of adjustment) relative to the marginal cost of working an existing worker longer hours (sometimes termed the intensive margin of adjustment). The quasi-fixed costs distort the labour expansion decision of the firm away from employment and toward more hours so as to minimize the quasi-fixed costs. Alternatively stated, the firm will want to amortize its fixed costs over the existing work force as much as possible rather than hire new workers and incur the quasi-fixed costs. This is especially so for skilled workers where such quasi-fixed costs may be especially large, mainly because of training costs.

Just as on the supply side of the market (recall the discussion in Chapter 3), fixed money costs of work reduced the probability that an individual would enter the labour market but would increase the hours of work conditional upon having entered, so too quasi-fixed costs of employment have a differential effect on the demand side. Employers would be reluctant to hire more workers (and incur the fixed costs), but once the workers are hired, the employers would like them to work longer hours so as to amortize the fixed costs.

Nonrecurring fixed costs of employment alter the firm's hiring and layoff decisions, making these longer-term in nature. If the firm must incur some hiring and training costs when a new employee is hired, the firm will not hire the employee unless the addition to revenue is at least as great as the addition to costs, including the hiring and training costs. However, as long as the employee is expected to remain with the firm for several periods, it is not essential that the additional revenue equal or exceed the additional costs *each period*. Rather, the firm will continue hiring additional workers until the present value of additional future revenues equals the present value of additional costs. Thus, rather than hiring until the current wage equals the current value of marginal product (the employment rule discussed previously, summarized in equation 5.1), in the presence of nonrecurring fixed costs of employment the profit-maximizing employment rule becomes

$$H + T + \sum_{t=0}^{N} \frac{W_t}{(1+r)^t} = \sum_{t=0}^{N} \frac{VMP_t}{(1+r)^t} \tag{6.1}$$

where H + T are hiring and training costs (assumed to be incurred in the first period for simplicity),
W_t is the wage rate in period t,
VMP_t is the expected value of the marginal product in period t,
r is the firm's discount or interest rate, and
N is the expected length of employment.

The left-hand side of equation 6.1 is the present value of the costs of hiring an additional worker (i.e., the present value of the marginal costs) and the right-hand side is the present value of the marginal revenue.

Several implications of equation 6.1 are worth noting. The hiring decision depends on the firm's expectations about the future, in particular the expected duration of employment, expected wage rates, and expected product market conditions (which determine the value of the marginal product of labour in future periods). Another implication is that, because of the hiring and training costs on the left-hand side of equation 6.1,

$$\sum_{t=0}^{N} \frac{VMP_t}{(1+r)^t} > \sum_{t=0}^{N} \frac{W_t}{(1+r)^t} \tag{6.2}$$

Thus when hiring an additional worker the firm must anticipate that the value of the marginal product will exceed the wage in most, if not all, future periods. As will be seen below, this prediction of the theory has implications for the firm's layoff behaviour in response to unanticipated changes in demand.

The small but growing empirical literature on dynamic labour demand confirms some of the theoretical discussion on quasi-fixed costs. Hamermesh (1993) reviews the literature in detail, while Hamermesh and Pfann (1996) provide a more recent review of the general literature on **dynamic factor demand**. Most studies find that firms behave as if costs associated with adjusting their level of employment are important. The intuition that the employment level (number of workers) is more costly to adjust than employee hours is also borne out in the data, so that the worker-hours distinction merits further attention. Another important distinction is that between the net and gross costs of adjustment. Hamermesh (1995), for example, uses firm-level microdata and finds that the costs associated with changing the employees (direct hiring and firing costs, or gross costs of adjustment) are as important as costs associated with changing the number of employees (or net costs of adjustment). While there have been fewer direct studies on the relative adjustment speeds of different types of labour, it is generally found that skilled labour is adjusted more slowly than unskilled labour. This has important implications for the incidence of unemployment over the business cycle, a phenomenon we address in the next section.

Some Phenomena Explained by Fixed Costs

The existence and growth of such fixed costs may help to explain, in part at least, the existence and growth of a number of labour market phenomena. The desire of employers to work their existing work force overtime, in spite of overtime premium wage rates and possible fatigue effects, may be explained in part by the fact that fixed costs make it relatively cheaper to work the existing work force longer hours rather than hire new workers. Ehrenberg and Schumann (1982), for example, discuss a number of studies, based on U.S. data, indicating that employers' use of overtime hours are positively related to the ratio of their quasi-fixed employment cost to their overtime premium.

Quasi-fixed costs of employment may also explain, in part, the popularity of temporary help agencies and contracting-out. Employers avoid the quasi-fixed costs of hiring new employees when they contract out or engage the services of temporary help agencies. As with the use of overtime hours, this can be a particularly important way of meeting new demand that may be temporary.

The layoff behaviour of firms will also be affected by quasi-fixed costs of employment. Once an employee has been hired and trained, the associated nonrecurring costs become sunk costs. Because these costs cannot be recovered, they will not influence the firm's decision making with respect to its existing work force (for whom the hiring and training expenses have been incurred), even though they will influence decisions regarding potential employees (for whom the expenses have not been incurred).

At the time an employee is hired, the firm anticipates that the present value of future marginal products will exceed the present value of future wage costs, as shown in Equation 6.2. This excess of the value of the worker's contribution to the firm over the cost of that worker creates a "buffer" which reduces the risk that the worker will be laid off. In particular, even if there is an unanticipated decline in product demand, reducing the value of the marginal product of labour, the firm may nonetheless choose not to lay off any employees because the present value of the revenue associated with an employee, although lower than anticipated, remains higher than the present value of the costs. Because of the unanticipated decline in demand, the firm's return on its investment in hiring and training costs will be lower than expected; however, the return may still be positive, indicating that it is worthwhile retaining the employee. This will be the case especially if the decline in demand is believed to be temporary in nature, or if workers who are temporarily laid off may not be available for recall when demand returns to normal levels. In such circumstances the company may rationally engage in **labour hoarding** of such workers in a cyclical downturn, and they may pay deferred compensation or seniority-related wages or benefits to discourage their experienced workers from leaving.

This implication of nonrecurring fixed employment costs is illustrated in Figure 6.2. Panel (a) shows the case in which there are no fixed costs of employment. At the wage W_0, employment will be N_0^*. A decline in labour demand from VMP to VMP^1 will result in a drop in employment from N_0^* to N_0^1. Panel (b) shows the case in which the employer incurs nonrecurring hiring and training costs H + T. At the wage W_0, employment will be N_0 rather than N_0^* as would occur in the absence of the hiring and training costs. For the N_0 employees hired, the value of their marginal product is VMP_0; because of the fixed costs the employer does not expand employment to the point at which the VMP equals the wage. The "buffer" $VMP_0 - W_0$ implies that employment will not necessarily fall in response to a decline in labour demand. For example, at the wage W_0, employment would remain at N_0 even if the employees' value of the marginal product fell to VMP^1.

Fixed costs of employment can also explain the observation that layoff rates are much higher among low-skilled than high-skilled workers. Considerable evidence exists that hiring and training costs are significantly larger for high-skilled workers. Thus they have a larger "buffer" (excess of value of marginal product over wage rate) protecting them from unanticipated declines in demand compared to unskilled and semiskilled workers. This prediction is illustrated by comparing panels (a) and (b) of Figure 6.2, the former showing the situation facing unskilled workers and the latter that for skilled workers.

Quasi-fixed costs may also foster the segmentation of labour markets into a protected sector (where employment stability is relatively guaranteed so as to amortize the quasi-fixed costs) and a sector that cannot compete for these jobs because firms would have to

Figure 6.2 **Nonrecurring Fixed Employment Costs and Changes in Labour Demand**

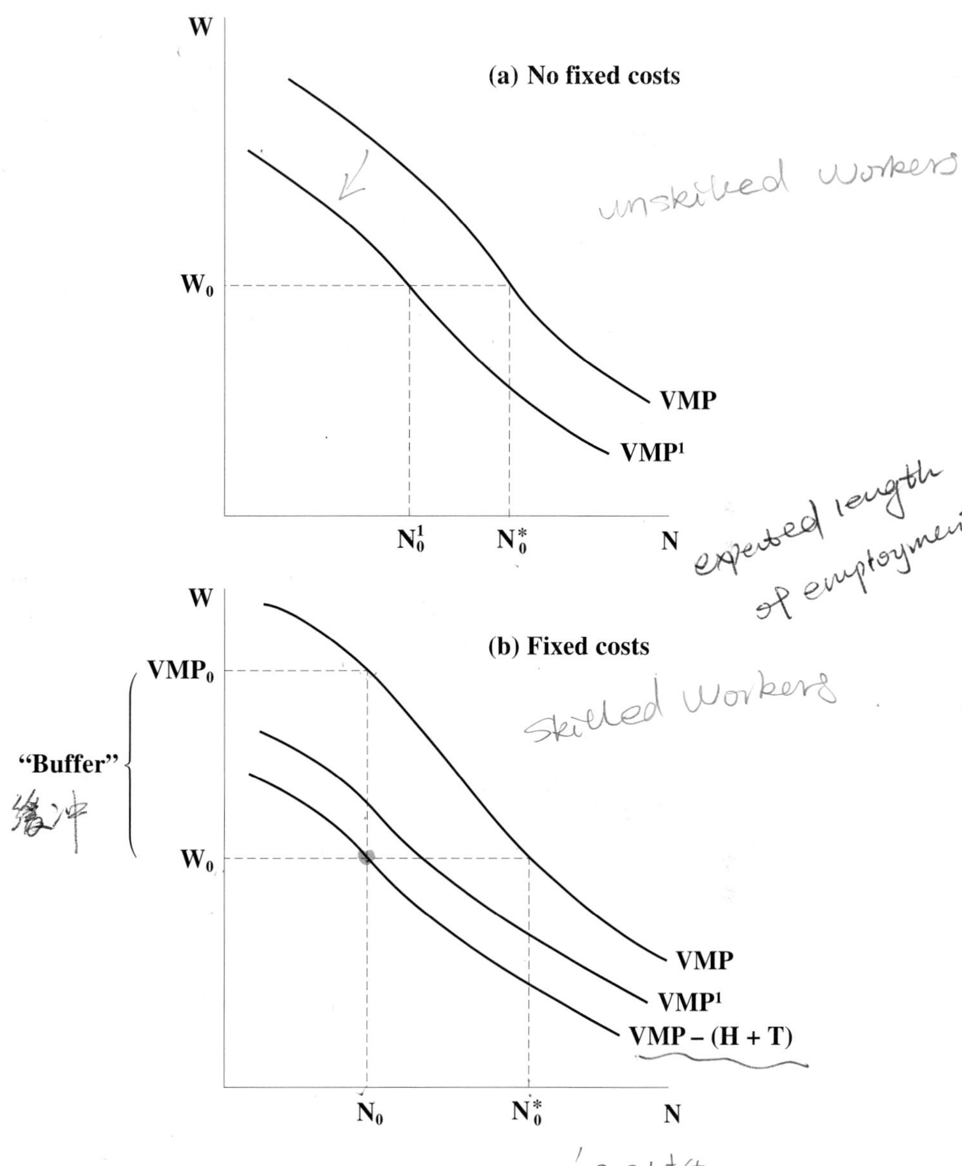

In panel (a), a decline in market conditions leads to an inward shift of the VMP schedule, from VMP to VMP^1. The profit-maximizing level of employment falls from N_0^* to N_0^1 at the prevailing wage of W_0. By contrast, if there are fixed costs of hiring workers, employment may not fall as much. First, the original level of employment will be at N_0, not N_0^*, as employers choose employment so that the wage equals the VMP net of hiring and training costs, VMP – (H + T). At N_0, the VMP (VMP_0) exceeds W_0 by a "buffer" H + T. As long as the new VMP^1 > VMP – (H + T) = W_0, it will not be optimal for the firm to change its employment level from N_0.

incur additional fixed costs upon hiring such workers. In essence, once an employee has been hired and trained, the firm is not indifferent between an existing employee and an otherwise identical potential employee.

To the extent that fixed costs inhibit the hiring of new workers (at the extensive margin), employers may try to meet their labour demand needs by expanding not only at the intensive margin of more hours, but also at the intensive margin of a greater *intensity* of work effort. That is, employers may try to work their existing work force not only longer hours but also harder, rather than hire new workers. Just as labour supply had quality and quantity dimensions, so does labour demand, and these various dimensions may be affected by relative prices including fixed costs.

Quasi-fixed costs may also explain some of the employers' resistance to engage in work-sharing practices. For example, having all of the company's employees work a four-day as

Exhibit 6.2

Labour Hoarding in the Automobile Industry

Most of the evidence suggesting the importance of quasi-fixed costs and labour hoarding is indirect. First, surveys of the labour force confirm that skilled workers are less likely to be unemployed than unskilled workers. This may have nothing to do with labour hoarding, however, since it may simply reflect that skilled workers are employed in firms that are relatively unaffected by business cycle conditions. Second, average labour productivity falls during recessions. This is puzzling because we would expect labour productivity to increase as less labour is employed (by the assumption of diminishing marginal productivity of labour). Labour hoarding would provide one possible explanation: productivity falls during recessions because firms retain workers who have nothing to do, that is, whose productivity is worth less than their wage.

Ana Aizcorbe (1992) provides direct evidence on labour hoarding in the automobile industry. Using plant-level data from car assembly plants in the United States over the period 1978–1985, she shows that firms employed up to 5 percent more workers than necessary given the level of production in each plant. Aizcorbe also investigates another explanation for apparent labour hoarding, besides the quasi-fixed-cost explanation provided in the text. Increasing returns to specialization (or scale) would imply that layoffs, or a reduction in the size of the work force could lower the average productivity of the remaining workers. One possible rationale for these increasing returns arises from the nature of production in assembly plants. The main way that output is reduced is to slow down the assembly line. One cannot, for example, just lay off the part of the line that attaches fenders. The resulting slowdown of line-speed can reduce the intensity and productivity of the remaining workers, especially if they are asked to perform additional tasks. Aizcorbe finds that both of these explanations (increasing returns and conventional labour hoarding) are significant features of employment adjustment in car plants in response to downturns.

opposed to five-day work week, and hiring 20 percent more employees at the same wage, would increase labour costs if there were quasi-fixed costs associated with hiring the new employees. Similarly, having two workers engage in job sharing (e.g., by each working half of the week) would increase the quasi-fixed costs because of the additional employee. Such costs may also make it more expensive to engage part-time employees unless there are compensating offsets in the wage component or in some of the quasi-fixed costs like nonwage benefits.

WORKSHARING AND JOB CREATION

With the high levels of unemployment in the 1980s and 1990s, especially in Europe, increasing attention has been paid to **worksharing** as a way to "create jobs," or at least to share the scarce number of jobs that seem to be available. This emphasis has been buttressed by workers' preferences for flexible worktime arrangements, in part because of the growth of the two-earner family and the changing age and sex composition of the work force.

www.hrdc-drhc.gc.ca/hrib/ws-tp/menu/desc.shtml

Reduced worktime could come in a variety of forms including delayed entry into the labour force, early retirement, a shorter work week, reduced overtime, or increased vacation time. The key question is: Would any of these reductions in the worktime of some individuals lead to new jobs for other individuals?

Exhibit 6.3 Nonwage Benefits and Part-Time Work

Part-time employment, defined as working less than 30 hours per week, has grown rapidly in Canada during the past several decades, both in absolute terms and relative to full-time employment. For example, part-time employment constituted less than 4 percent of total employment in 1953, but has constituted 15 percent of total employment since the early 1980s.

What factors lie behind the growth of part-time and other forms of "flexible" or "nonstandard" employment, such as short-term and contract work, within the temporary-help industry, and certain types of self-employment? The service sector accounts for much part-time employment, and the reasons for the growth of part-time work are interrelated with those accounting for the increase in service sector employment (Economic Council of Canada, 1991). Most part-time employees are women or young workers. Thus, supply-side factors associated with the changing composition of the labour force—particularly the increased participation of women and youths—may also have played a role. However, evidence suggests that demand-side factors also contributed to the rise in part-time employment. In particular, wages of part-time workers are lower than those of comparable full-time workers. The unadjusted earnings differential between part-time and full-time workers is 25 to 30 percent (Simpson, 1986; Economic Council of Canada, 1991, Chapter 5); adjusting for differences in productivity-related characteristics reduces this differential to about 10 percent (Simpson, 1986). Perhaps more importantly, hourly nonwage labour costs are generally substantially lower for part-time workers, due to their lower likelihood of being covered by unemployment insurance, workers' compensation, the Canada and Quebec Pension Plans, their much lower levels of employer-sponsored benefits, and their exclusion from some labour standards legislation (e.g., regulations requiring payment for statutory holidays). Because such nonwage labour costs have been growing rapidly, we would expect an increased tendency for employers to substitute part-time for full-time workers.

Evidence that such substitution has occurred in the United Kingdom is provided in an econometric study by Patricia Rice (1990). Changes in the structure of National Insurance payroll taxes increased significantly the average hourly cost of full-time youth workers, while reducing that of part-time adult workers. In most industries part-time adults and full-time youths were found to be substitutes in production. The consequence of these tax changes was a rise in part-time adult employment and a sharp decline in youth employment.

An important policy issue is whether employers should be required to provide the same benefits (on a prorated basis) to part-time workers as provided to full-time employers, as recommended by the Commission of Inquiry into Part-Time Work (Wallace, 1983). Such a requirement would reduce the substantial gap in total compensation that now exists between those with "standard" full-time jobs and those with "nonstandard" jobs. However, this requirement would also encourage employers to substitute away from part-time employment. Women and youths would be the groups most likely to be affected by this policy. Whether these groups would be better or worse off would depend on whether the positive effects of higher nonwage benefits exceeded the negative consequences associated with reduced employment opportunities.

Overtime Restrictions

In recent years the question has become extremely important with respect to reductions in the work week especially through restricting the use of overtime. The paradox of some workers working overtime, seemingly on a regular basis, while other workers in the same community and often in the same plant are on layoff, has led to increasing pressure to restrict the use of overtime. This restriction could come in a variety of forms: reducing the standard work week beyond which an overtime premium must be paid, increasing the overtime premium, establishing or reducing the statutory maximum hours that are allowed, making it more difficult to get special permission to exceed the statutory limit when exemptions are allowed, or granting workers the right to refuse overtime. Changes in any or all of these features of overtime legislation could be used to restrict the use of overtime.

Unfortunately, we have very little empirical evidence on the extent to which changes in any of these features of overtime legislation would change the demand for overtime hours. Ehrenberg and Schumann (1982) provide empirical evidence based on U.S. data indicating that an increase in the overtime premium from time-and-a-half to double-time would reduce the use of overtime hours. However, the relationship was not overwhelmingly conclusive, being statistically insignificant for the manufacturing sector.

Overtime Restriction and Job Creation

Even if overtime hours can be reduced by policy changes like raising the overtime premium, there remains the question of the extent to which reductions in the use of overtime would translate into new jobs. On this issue there is also considerable controversy. Ehrenberg and Schumann (1982) estimate that the reduction in the use of overtime that would result from a double-time premium could translate into an employment increase in the neighbourhood of 3 to 4 percent, assuming that the overtime hours reduction would be converted directly to new full-time positions. They indicate that this is an upper bound, however, because it ignores a number of the following adjustments that are likely to occur in response to increases in the overtime premium.

For example, firms may not comply fully with the legislation and some workers whose overtime hours were restricted may moonlight. More importantly, although firms may substitute new employees for the more expensive overtime hours, they would also reduce their *overall* demand for labour because it is now more expensive and because the demand for the firm's output will be reduced as it passes some of the cost increase on to consumers in the form of higher product prices. These are, respectively, the familiar substitution and scale effects that occur in response to an increase in the price of a factor of production.

As well, there may be productivity changes that affect the number of new jobs created if hours of work are reduced. If fatigue effects make overtime hours less productive than the hours of work of new workers or rehires, then the number of new jobs created will be diminished because the overtime hours can be replaced by fewer regular hours. Reid (1985), for example, cites European evidence suggesting that the productivity improvements associated with a reduced work week may reduce the employment-creating potential of a reduced work week by one-half. That is, productivity would be sufficiently higher under the shorter work week so that the same output could be maintained with half as many hours in the new jobs to replace the reduced hours of the shorter work week.

Whether this seemingly large productivity offset would be permanent and apply to reductions in overtime hours (as opposed to the standard work week of everyone) remains an open question. Overtime hours may be more susceptible to fatigue effects but workers who work the overtime may already be the most productive of all workers; that is in fact why they are asked to work overtime. If that is the case, then reducing the overtime hours of the most productive workers may have the potential for creating a larger number of jobs for less productive workers, albeit at an obvious cost—a cost that could reduce the job-creating potential because of the substitution and scale effects discussed previously.

The job-creating potential of a reduction of overtime hours also may be offset by the fact that persons who are unemployed or on layoff (who are likely to be less skilled) may not be good substitutes for persons working overtime (who are likely to be more skilled). Unfortunately, the empirical literature that provides evidence on the substitutability between factors of production does not provide information on that point. That literature provides evidence on the substitutability between employment and hours of work of the labour force in general. And it provides some evidence on the substitutability between different groups of labour (e.g., skilled and unskilled, or females and youths). However, it does not do both simultaneously. Formally stated, we do not have estimates of the elasticity of substitution between overtime *hours* of skilled workers and the *employment* of less-skilled workers. In the absence of such information it is difficult to know by how much the job creation potential of reduced overtime hours would be offset by the fact that additional hours of new recruits or even those on layoff may not be good substitutes for reduced hours of those who work overtime.

The job-creating potential of reduced hours of work is further complicated by the fact that in the long run there are not really a fixed number of jobs in the economy. In fact, the notion that there is a fixed number of jobs is known as the "lump-of-labour fallacy." It is a fallacy because it ignores the fact that people who hold jobs have other effects on the economy (known as general equilibrium effects). For example, they may increase aggregate demand through their increased disposable income and they may reduce aggregate wages augmenting the supply of labour. Both of these effects would enhance employment by these groups being in the labour market.

Thus, while an individual who takes a job or works long hours at a particular establishment may be taking a job from someone else who could work at that establishment, this need not be the case for the economy as a whole. What is true for a given establishment may be a fallacy for the economy as a whole. Perhaps this is best illustrated by the example of the increased labour force participation of females. Few analysts today would say that every job taken by a female means one less job for a male. Even though that may be true for a particular job in a particular establishment (just as a job taken by a male means that particular job is not occupied by a female) it is not true for the economy as a whole. Females working in the labour market also create demands for other goods and services, especially those formerly produced in the household. This in turn creates jobs elsewhere.

In essence, a job held by one person does not mean that another person does not have a job. This applies to jobs held by females, by older workers who do not retire, or by persons who work long hours or overtime. Conversely, restricting their work in particular establishments (e.g., by mandatory retirement or by restricting overtime) may open up some new jobs in that establishment but this may not lead to more jobs in the economy as a whole when one considers the general equilibrium effects as previously discussed.

For all of these reasons, the job-creating potential of various forms of worksharing is regarded with some skepticism. This is compounded by the fact that some regard worksharing basically as unemployment sharing, with the fear that any reduced measured unemployment that occurs may take the pressure off governments to follow appropriate policies to reduce unemployment. Nevertheless, as Reid (1985) points out, in times of cyclically high unemployment, worksharing may be a viable temporary method to share scarce jobs until the economy returns to full employment. In addition, it would be important to remove any impediments that may prevent the parties from entering into otherwise mutually beneficial voluntary worksharing arrangements.

Exhibit 6.4

Worksharing Isn't for Everyone

Under what conditions would firms be willing to use worksharing instead of layoffs in responding to depressed market conditions? If a firm needs to reduce labour input by 40 hours per week, it can either lay off one person who usually works 40 hours per week or reduce 40 workers' hours by an hour per week. The choice depends on the relative costs of adjusting workers versus hours of work, which depends on the structure of wages and nonwage costs, as discussed in this chapter. For example, a layoff will allow the firm to avoid all of the recurring fixed costs of employment (such as payroll taxes), whereas small reductions in hours worked may yield no reduction in payroll taxes, especially if there are contribution ceilings. On the other hand, high severance costs may make worksharing cheaper.

In addition to the costs to the firms, the feasibility of worksharing depends on the willingness of other workers to go along with the scheme. Most union seniority rules are biased in favour of layoffs versus worksharing: the youngest workers bear the cost of the downturn, while the others are fully cushioned from the adverse (short-term) shock. Because layoffs are the usual path chosen by firms, governments offer subsidies for firms to adopt worksharing, by topping up the wages paid to non-laid-off workers. Such worksharing, or short time compensation (STC) programs, are especially popular in Europe. David Gray (1998) uses rich industry-level data from France to explore the determinants of the propensity of firms to choose STC over layoffs.

He finds that the determinants of industrial rates of adoption of STC line up with the theoretical discussion above (and in the text). The following summarizes the impact of some of the main variables. (Remember, these are *partial* effects, controlling for the others.)

- *Seniority*. In industries where workers have more seniority, STC is more likely to be chosen by firms. This is arises because of stringent job protection laws that make it relatively expensive to layoff workers with high seniority.
- *Salary*. Industries where workers have higher salaries are less likely to opt for STC. In France, the STC contribution is subject to a maximum, so higher-paid workers must take a bigger pay cut if they workshare. So layoffs are relatively more attractive.
- *Turnover*. Industries already characterized by high rates of turnover and quitting, where adjustment costs are presumably lower, are less likely to use STC.

Gray also finds (not surprisingly) that industries experiencing adverse business conditions are more likely to tap into STC (since they are more likely to need to reduce employment). But what is more troubling is that he finds some evidence that firms in "permanently" declining industries are more likely to use STC, which is inconsistent with the objectives of the STC program.

Reducing Barriers to Employment Sharing

Reid (1985) suggests a number of changes in public policy that could reduce the unintended barriers to employment sharing that are created by these policies. As indicated previously, the ceilings on payroll taxes for workers' compensation, public pensions, or unemployment insurance make it more attractive for employers to work their existing employees longer hours once the ceiling on the payroll tax has been reached, since no further taxes then have to be paid. Having the premiums based on hourly earnings with a ceiling based on hourly earnings would remove the bias against hiring new workers. Similarly, prorating employer contributions to medical, dental, and life insurance plans according to hours worked, rather than having fixed contributions per employee, would reduce their existing bias against employment sharing.

Subsidizing Employment Sharing

One method of encouraging worksharing is to offer financial incentives for firms and workers to choose worksharing instead of layoffs. Chapter 3 showed how EI-assisted worksharing could be used to entice workers to participate. Implicitly, the EI-funded subsidy to shorter work weeks is also a subsidy to firms. Gray (2000) provides a comprehensive review of the Canadian and international experience with "subsidized short time compensation," the more general term for government-subsidized worksharing.

As Gray points out, Canadian experience suggests that the program "works," in the sense that when offered the subsidy, many firms chose to participate. In fact, the program has been oversubscribed, with more firms applying to participate than the budget allows. Program evaluation also suggests that the participating firms reduced layoffs, at least measured by the number of employees enrolled in the program, and the implicit reduction in hours worked. Unfortunately, it is less clear that the subsidy yielded long-run employment protection. Frequently, workers were laid off after the subsidy ran out. Did the firms and workers "take the money and run"? Gray notes, "it would be an exaggeration to characterize the Work Sharing program as prone to widespread misuse by beleaguered, subsidy-hungry firms (and their employees) attempting to avoid restructuring" (Gray, 2000, p. 14). While worksharing subsidies were intended to help firms through short-term downturns, firms and workers may in good faith have believed that demand conditions would soon improve.

Declining firms present problems of their own for policymakers, but long-term employment subsidization of employment is increasingly recognized as the inappropriate response (the Atlantic fishery represents an important example). Gray offers a number of suggestions for fine-tuning worksharing subsidies that try to target the program more effectively to firms genuinely experiencing short-run reductions in demand. For example, subsidies could be restricted to times of aggregate downturn (like recessions) to reduce the possibility that worksharing subsidies are not simply delaying economic restructuring.

Summary

- Nonwage benefits, such as paid vacations, pensions, and other social insurance contributions, account for almost 40 percent of labour compensation. While this is more complicated than the simple "wage" that we use as the price of a unit of labour, the complexity of compensation may not affect the validity of the labour demand model. For example, if nonwage benefits are strictly proportional to the wage, the distinction is not important. However, nonwage benefits are often complex functions of the number of employees and hours worked.
- Many of these compensation costs are "quasi-fixed" in that they are incurred once a worker is hired (possibly recurring annually), but do not change with the number of hours worked. Other labour costs, such as hiring, training, and firing costs, are also "quasi-fixed."
- The fact that some costs do not increase proportionately with hours worked drives a wedge between the marginal cost of hiring an additional worker (the extensive margin) and working an existing worker more hours (the intensive margin). This generates an important distinction between the number of workers and hours worked per worker in yielding a given labour input. Some of these quasi-fixed costs will bias firms toward working their existing employees more intensively instead of hiring additional employees.

- The fixed costs associated with adjusting the number of employees (hiring, training, and firing costs) also generate a wedge between the VMP of labour and the wage rate, since these costs must be paid by the surplus of VMP over wages. This wedge can operate in favour of a worker when demand for a firm's output declines. As long as the lower VMP is still higher than the wage, firms will have an incentive to retain workers instead of laying them off. This, called "labour hoarding," is more likely to apply to skilled workers for whom the quasi-fixed costs are higher.
- Because the labour cost structure may favour layoffs as the way to reduce labour input, governments around the world have introduced various regulations and programs, such as *short time compensation* (worksharing), which are aimed at encouraging firms to reduce hours per worker instead of the number of workers.

REVIEW QUESTIONS

1. Explain the factors that affect the firm's choice between the number of employees and hours per employee.
2. Firms often respond to decreases in demand by laying off some of their work force. However, some groups of workers are more likely to be laid off than others. Provide an explanation for this phenomenon.
3. Would it ever be rational for a firm to retain an employee whose current marginal revenue product is less than their current wage? Explain.
4. "In the absence of hiring, training, and other fixed costs of employment, the firm does not need to forecast the future when making employment decisions. However, in the presence of these fixed costs the firm's employment decision necessarily involves planning for and forecasting the future." Discuss.
5. Discuss how regulations concerning the overtime premium (e.g., mandating it be 2 rather than 1.5 times the wage rate), and subsidies for worksharing, may increase the level of employment. Who benefits from such schemes? Who loses?

PROBLEMS

1. Consider a firm that pays a salary of $10,000 and offers employees a compulsory benefit of 3 units of term life insurance (e.g., term life insurance that pays out 3 times salary if a person dies). Assume that term life insurance can be purchased for $2000 per year per unit in the insurance market.

   Unattached Jane is considering working for this company, and is evaluating her salary and benefits package. She imagines (incorrectly) that she can take the cash equivalent of the life insurance if she chooses.

   (a) Draw her budget constraint, with consumption of non-insurance on the "Y-axis" and units of insurance on the "X-axis," assuming that she can convert the 3 units of life insurance into cash.

   (b) Depict her constrained choice, C, of $10,000 income and 3 units of insurance, and compare this to a situation where she would prefer only 1 unit of life insurance. With these assumptions, is there any way that she is better off with the firm's offer than the cash equivalent?

   (c) What if the implicit price of insurance is cheaper if offered by the firm? Draw the new budget constraint, assuming that she can convert her 3 units of consumption into cash at this cheaper rate. Is it possible that the compulsory 3 units might actually be optimal for Jane? Why might life insurance be cheaper for the firm to offer than Jane could purchase on the open market?
2. Assume that firms have a two-period planning horizon. For any workers hired, the

value of the marginal product of labour in each period is given by VMP_1 and VMP_2, and the wages are W_1, W_2.

(a) Assume that there are no hiring costs. What is the relationship between the VMP and wage rate in each period?

(b) What happens to employment if VMP_2 is lower than expected in the second period?

(c) In order to reduce layoffs in the situation where VMP falls in the second period, the government introduces a "layoff tax." Show how this affects the employment decision in period 2, assuming that the tax was unexpected in period 1.

(d) How would your answer change if the firm was aware of the tax in period 1?

(e) Many European countries have legislation regarding severance pay which makes termination of employees costly to employers. What impact would introducing such legislation have on employer behaviour related to dismissals and new hires? What groups in society are likely to benefit, and what groups are likely to lose, from this type of legislation?

3. Currently, the payroll tax for Employment Insurance and the CPP/QPP are structured (approximately) as follows:

$$\text{Tax} = \begin{cases} tWh \text{ if } Wh \leq \bar{E} \\ t\bar{E} \text{ if } Wh > \bar{E} \end{cases}$$

(a) Why might the government put such a cap on the payroll tax?

(b) Assume that output depends on labour input as the simple sum of the number of hours worked by employees (i.e., an hour worked by an existing or new employee is equally productive). Derive the marginal cost of hiring an additional hour of labour services, depending on the number of hours worked by the employee (incorporating the payroll tax).

(c) Show how the structure of these taxes may affect the firm's choice between workers and hours.

(d) Would it be a good idea to eliminate the cap on the payroll taxes?

4. "The level of benefits offered to part-time workers is often below that offered to full-time workers doing the same job. A priority for labour standards legislation should be to end this discriminatory practice, especially since many part-time workers are women. Part-time workers would be better off if firms were forced to pay them the same benefits." True, false, or uncertain? Explain.

5. Consider a firm that exists for one period. The value of labour's (L) marginal product is given by $VMP_L = P \times MP_L$, where P is the price of output, and

$$MP_L = 10 - 0.5L$$

The wage rate is \$10.

(a) Assume that there are no hiring or training costs. If the firm expects that the price of output to be \$10, what is the optimal level of employment, L_0? If the firm hires these workers, but then finds out that the price of output is \$5, what will the firm do?

(b) Assume now that there are hiring and training costs of \$20 per worker. If the firm expects the price of output to be \$10, what is the optimal level of employment? How does this compare to your answer in part (a)? If the firm hires these workers, but then finds out that the price of output is \$5, what will the firm do? What if the price is \$2? Explain.

(c) Explain (qualitatively) how your answer to part (b) would change if the hiring and training costs were higher or lower. How can these results be used to predict patterns of layoffs across occupations and industries during economic downturns?

KEYWORDS

quasi-fixed costs 172
nonwage benefits 173
transfers-in-kind 173
deferred compensation 174
payroll taxes 175
employment standards legislation 176
dynamic factor demand 177
labour hoarding 178
worksharing 180

REFERENCES

Aizcorbe, A. M. 1992. Procyclical labour productivity, increasing returns to labour and labour hoarding in car assembly plant employment. *EJ* 102 (July):860–73.

Economic Council of Canada. 1991. *Employment in the Service Economy*. Ottawa: Supply and Services.

Ehrenberg, R. G., and P. L. Schumann. 1982. *Longer Hours or More Jobs? An Investigation of Amending Hours Legislation to Create Employment*. Ithaca: New York State School of Industrial and Labor Relations, Cornell University.

Gray, D. M. 1998. When might a distressed firm share work? Evidence from the short-time compensation programme in France. *British Journal of Industrial Relations* 36 (March):43–72.

______. 2000. The work sharing program in Canada: A feasible alternative to layoffs? *C. D. Howe Institute Commentary*, Number 146.

Hamermesh, D. S. 1993. *Labor Demand*. Princeton: Princeton University Press.

______. 1989. Labour demand and the structure of adjustment costs. *AER* 79 (September):674–89.

______. 1995. Labour demand and the source of adjustment costs. *EJ* 105 (May):620–34.

Hamermesh, D. S., and G. A. Pfann. 1996. Adjustment costs in factor demand. *JEL* 34 (September):1264–92.

Hart, R. A. 1984. *The Economics of Non-Wage Labor Costs*. London: Allen and Unwin.

______. 1987. *Working Time and Employment*. Boston: Allen & Unwin.

Meltz, N., F. Reid, and G. Swartz. 1981. *Sharing the Work: An Analysis of the Issues in Worksharing and Jobsharing*. Toronto: University of Toronto Press.

Oi, W. 1962. Labour as a quasi-fixed factor. *JPE* 70 (December):538–55.

Pold, H., and F. Wong. 1990. The price of labour. *PLI* (Autumn):42–9.

Reid, F. 1985. Reductions in worktime: an assessment of employment sharing to reduce unemployment. In *Work and Pay*, ed. W. C. Riddell. Toronto: University of Toronto Press.

Rice, P. G. 1990. Relative labour costs and the growth of part-time employment in British manufacturing industries. *EJ* 100 (December):1138–46.

Rosen, S. 1968. Short-run employment variation in class I railroads in the U.S., 1937–1964. *Ecta* 36 (October):511–29.

Simpson, W. 1986. Analysis of part-time pay in Canada. *CJE* 19 (November):798–807.

Wallace, J. 1983. Part-Time Work in Canada: Report of the Commission of Inquiry into Part-Time Work. Ottawa: Labour Canada.

Chapter Seven

Wages and Employment in a Single Labour Market

Main Questions

- *How is the equilibrium wage and employment level determined in a single labour market?*
- *How does imperfect competition affect the way in which we use the supply and demand model to analyze wages and employment determination?*
- *Are payroll taxes "job killers"?*
- *What is monopsony? How do wage and employment outcomes differ in labour markets where firms have market power in the hiring of labour? How much worse off might workers be if they have few alternative places of employment?*
- *Do minimum wages do more harm than good?*

In this chapter we complete the neoclassical model by analyzing the interaction of labour supply and demand in a single market. The firm may be operating in a **competitive** or **noncompetitive** (monopoly, oligopoly, monopolistic competition) product market. Alternatively, the firm may be competitive or not competitive (i.e., possess some market power, or monopsony) in the labour market. Throughout the analysis we assume that workers are selling their labour on an individual basis; in later chapters we analyze the situation of collective bargaining via unionization.

In dealing with the interaction of supply and demand in various market structures, it is important to be specific about the level of aggregation that is being analyzed. In this section we begin at the level of aggregation of the individual firm, and consequently focus on the firm as the decision-making unit. Subsequently we move to the "market," dealing with higher levels of aggregation such as the occupation, industry, region, and economy as a whole—the levels at which the market wage is determined in competitive labour markets. We then relax the assumption of perfect competition in the product market. As will be seen, this does not substantially alter the supply and demand analysis. We describe the use of the supply and demand framework in policy analysis, with an extended investigation into payroll taxes.

Relaxing the assumption of perfect competition in the labour market has a greater impact on the analysis of wage and employment determination. We move from this discussion of monopsony to an in-depth examination of the impact of minimum wages on the labour market, where the monopsony and perfectly competitive models of the labour market have been brought to bear in the interpretation of recent, potentially anomalous, empirical evidence.

A GUIDE TO CHAPTER 7

Chapter 7 pulls together the components of the supply and demand framework developed in Chapters 1 to 6, exploring how firms and workers interact in the market in determining the level of employment and wages. The key model is the competitive, neoclassical, market-clearing, "supply and demand" model. This model underlies the topics in the remainder of the textbook. The main objective of this chapter, then, is to see how the model works, and to consider some of the ways in which it may be wrong.

One obvious set of ways in which the model may be wrong is in the assumption of perfect competition, that is, the assumption that no one firm or individual can affect the prevailing wage:

- One possible route that imperfect competition may take is via the product market, where employers may have some degree of monopoly power. As we saw in Chapter 5, and will see confirmed here again, is that while the slope of the labour demand function may be affected, the basic labour supply and demand framework is unaffected by imperfect competition in the product market.
- Alternatively, there may be imperfect competition within the labour market itself. For example, there may be only a few (or one) employers, in which case workers have few options of where to work. The case of a single employer is called monopsony, and it significantly affects the way in which employment and wages are determined in a labour market. Imperfect competition could run the other way as well. Labour may be sold to firms on a monopolistic basis by labour unions. Because unions play such an important role in the labour market, we defer their study to separate chapters (Chapters 14–16).

The outline of Chapter 7 is thus:

1. Imperfect competition in the product market, and its impact on the labour demand function.
2. The competitive supply and demand model: solving for and interpreting the equilibrium, and applying the model to an evaluation of payroll taxes.
3. Monopsony in the labour market, or employment determination when firms (but not workers) can affect the wage.
4. Measuring the impact of the minimum wage on employment. Traditionally, this topic would be discussed in a labour demand chapter. However, recent empirical evidence requires an understanding of the impact of minimum wages on monopsonistic markets, before it can be presented.

THE COMPETITIVE FIRM'S INTERACTION WITH THE MARKET

We first examine the case in which the firm is a competitive seller of its output in the product market and a competitive buyer of labour in the labour market. In essence, the firm is so small relative to both markets that it can sell all of the output it wants at the going price of the product, and it can buy all of the labour it wants at the going wage rate. The firm is both a price- and a wage-taker: it cannot influence either the product price or the wage rate.

This situation is depicted in Figure 7.1(a) and (b) for two competitive firms. In both cases, their supply schedules for a given homogeneous type of labour are perfectly elastic (horizontal) at the market wage rate, W_c. The firms are wage-takers, not wage-setters, and consequently can employ all of the labour they want at this market wage rate.

The market wage rate for this specific, homogeneous type of labour is determined by the interaction of supply and demand in the aggregate labour market as depicted in Figure 7.1(c). This aggregate labour market could be a regional labour market for a particular occupational category of labour. For example, it could be the Halifax labour market for junior accounting clerks. By assuming that the firms are in the same region and are hiring the same homogeneous occupational type of labour, we are able to minimize the intervening influence of these factors on the wage determination process, and to thereby focus on the issue of wage and employment determination at the disaggregate or microeconomic level of the firm. In the subsequent chapters on wage structures, these assumptions are relaxed sequentially and the resultant wage structures analyzed.

The demand schedules for labour in the two firms are the schedules of the value of the marginal products of labour, defined as the marginal physical product of labour times the price at which the firms can sell their products. (These were derived formally in Chapter 5.) Since the firms are assumed to be competitive sellers of their products, their product prices are fixed at p_1^* and p_2^*. Only if the firms are selling the same output would their product prices have to be the same; otherwise p_1^* need not equal p_2^*. The magnitude and the elasticity of the demand for labour also are depicted as being different simply to emphasize that the market wage is the same irrespective of these factors. The demand schedules determine the level of employment in each firm: in this case N_1 and N_2 units of labour, respectively in firms 1 and 2.

The **market demand curve**, as depicted in Figure 7.1(c), is the summation of the demand curves of the individual firms, such as those shown in Figures 7.1(a) and (b). Conceptually the market demand curve can be obtained as follows. For any specific wage rate, such as W_0 in Figure 7.1, determine the quantity of labour that each firm in the market would wish to employ. For the two firms depicted in Figures 7.1(a) and (b), these quantities are N_1^0 and N_2^0 respectively. Adding these quantities gives the total market demand at

Figure 7.1 **Competitive Product and Labour Markets**

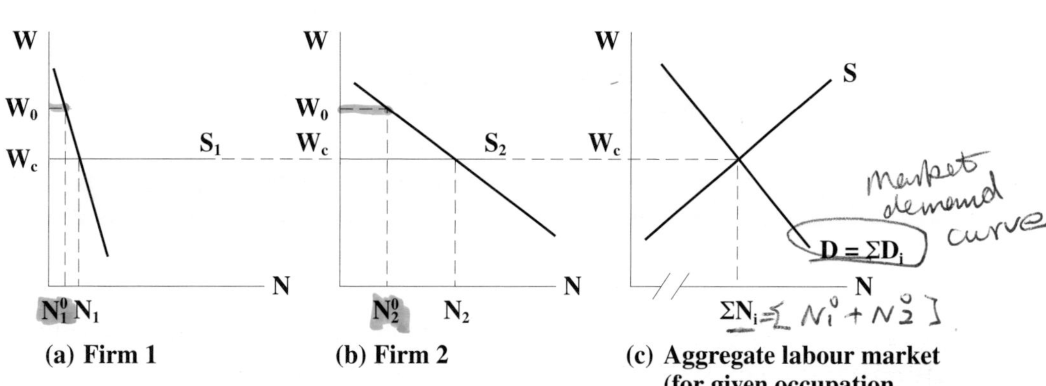

Market demand for labour is the sum of the demand for labour by each firm at each wage. At a wage W_0, market demand is $N_1^0 + N_2^0$, plus remaining firms' demand at W_0. In a competitive market, each firm faces perfectly elastic labour supply at the prevailing wage. For the whole market, the market supply of labour is relevant, and in panel (c), W_C is the equilibrium wage.

that wage rate. Repeating this process for all wage rates traces out the market labour demand curve.

In summary, when the firm is a **competitive buyer of labour**, it faces a perfectly elastic supply of labour at the market wage. When the firm is a competitive seller of its output on the product market, it regards the price at which it sells its output on the product market as fixed, and its derived demand for labour schedule is the value of the marginal product of labour, defined as the marginal physical product of labour times the fixed price at which the firm sells its output. Because the labour supply schedule to the firm is perfectly elastic at the market wage rate, the intersection of the firm's labour supply and demand schedules determines the employment level of the firm for that particular type of labour—wages are determined elsewhere, specifically in the aggregate labour market for that particular type of labour.

The previous analysis was based on the long-run assumption that the firm could get all of the labour it needed at the market-determined wage rate. That is, in order to expand its work force it need only hire additional workers at the going wage rate: there is no need to increase wages to attract additional workers.

In the short run, however, even a firm that is competitive in the labour market may have to raise its wages in order to attract additional workers. This situation is often referred to in the literature as **dynamic monopsony** (Baily 1975). In such circumstances the firm's short-run labour supply schedule could be upward-sloping, as depicted by the schedule S_s in Figure 7.2. In the short run, in order to expand its work force so as to meet an increase in the demand for labour from D to D', the firm may have to pay higher wages, perhaps by paying an overtime premium to its existing work force or by paying higher wages to attract local workers within the community. The resultant expansion of the work force can be depicted as a movement up the short-run supply curve in response to the new higher wage of W_s, occasioned by the increase in the demand for labour from D to D'.

In the longer run, however, a supply influx of other workers will be forthcoming because the firm is paying an above-market wage (i.e., $W_s > W_c$) for that particular type of labour. The supply influx may not be instantaneous, but may occur in the long run because it may come from other firms or perhaps from outside of the labour force, and such adjustments take time.

The new supply influx in response to the higher wage could be depicted by the S_s' supply schedule of labour. The supply influx would depress the temporarily high, short-run wage of W_s back to its long-run level of W_c. Thus the long-run supply of labour schedule to the firm, S_1, can be thought of as a locus of long-run equilibrium points, traced out by various shifting short-run supply schedules of the firm, as the firm tries to expand its work force.

In essence, temporary wage increases above the competitive norm are consistent with the firm being a competitive buyer of labour in the long run. In fact, short-run wage increases can be a market signal for the supply response that ensures that market forces operate in the longer run.

IMPERFECT COMPETITION IN THE PRODUCT MARKET

Monopoly

When an industry is competitive in the product market, the industry demand for labour is obtained by aggregating the labour demand of each of the firms in the industry, as illustrated in Figure 7.1. In the case of monopoly in the product market, the firm *is* the industry, and therefore there is no need to distinguish between the firm's labour demand and that of the industry as a whole.

As discussed in Chapter 5, the structure of the product market has implications for the

Figure 7.2 **Short-Run and Long-Run Labour Supply Schedules to Firm**

Long-run labour supply to the firm, S_1, is perfectly elastic at W_C. In the short run, mobility restrictions may yield upward-sloping labour supply, such as S_S. At higher wages, more workers will want to work at the firm, and at lower wages, the firm will lose some (but not all) of its workers. If demand shifts from D to D', the firm can hire more workers at W_S. In the long run, workers will be attracted to this firm, shifting labour supply to S_S', until the firm is paying W_C.

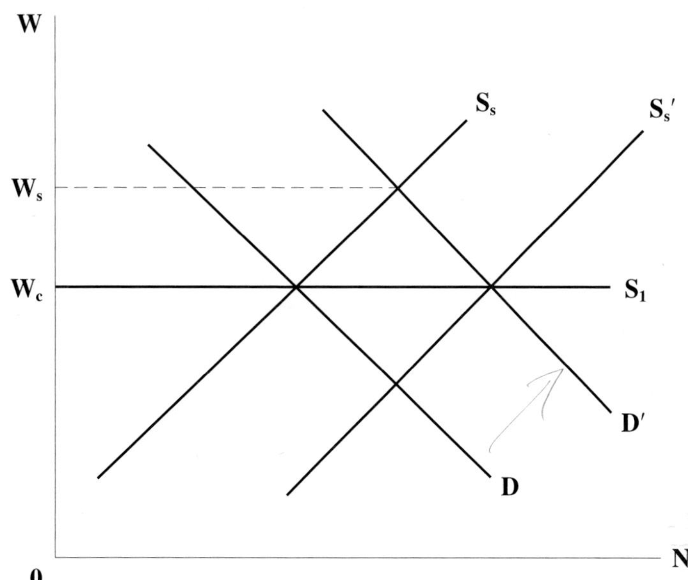

derived demand for labour. As given in Chapter 5, the labour demand schedule for the competitive firm on the product market is given by:

$$w^* = MPP_N \times p_Q^* = VMP_N \text{ [competitor]} \qquad (7.1)$$

This was derived from the more general equation:

$$w^* = MPP_N \times MR_Q = MRP_N \text{ [monopolist]} \qquad (7.2)$$

which applies to the monopolist since its output price is not fixed. Rather, for the monopolist, marginal revenue is the relevant factor.

The difference between equations 7.1 and 7.2 highlights the fact that when the monopolist hires more labour to produce more output, not only does the marginal physical product of labour fall (as is the case with the competitor), but also the marginal revenue from an additional unit of output, MR_Q, falls. This latter effect occurs because the monopolist, unlike the competitive firm, can sell more output only by lowering the product price and this, in turn, lowers marginal revenue. Because both MPP_N and MR_Q fall when N increases in equation 7.1, then the monopolist's demand for labour falls faster than it would if it behaved as a competitive firm in the product market, in which case only MPP_N would fall, as given in equation 7.2.

The difference between the labour demand schedule for a monopolist and the schedule that would prevail if the industry were competitive in the product market is illustrated in Figure 7.3. This comparison is most meaningful if it involves two situations that are identical except for the difference in market structure. To carry out the comparison, begin with a large number of price-taking firms. Aggregating the labour demand of each of the firms in this competitive industry gives the industry demand curve $D_C = \Sigma VMP_N$ in Figure 7.3. Now suppose these firms form a cartel and set the product price to maximize total industry profit, as would a monopolist which owned all of the firms in the industry. The labour demand schedule for the monopolist is $D_M = MPP_N \times MR_Q = MRP_N$. Since $MR_Q < P_Q$ then D_M lies below D_c.

Figure 7.3 **Monopolist Versus Competitive Demand for Labour**

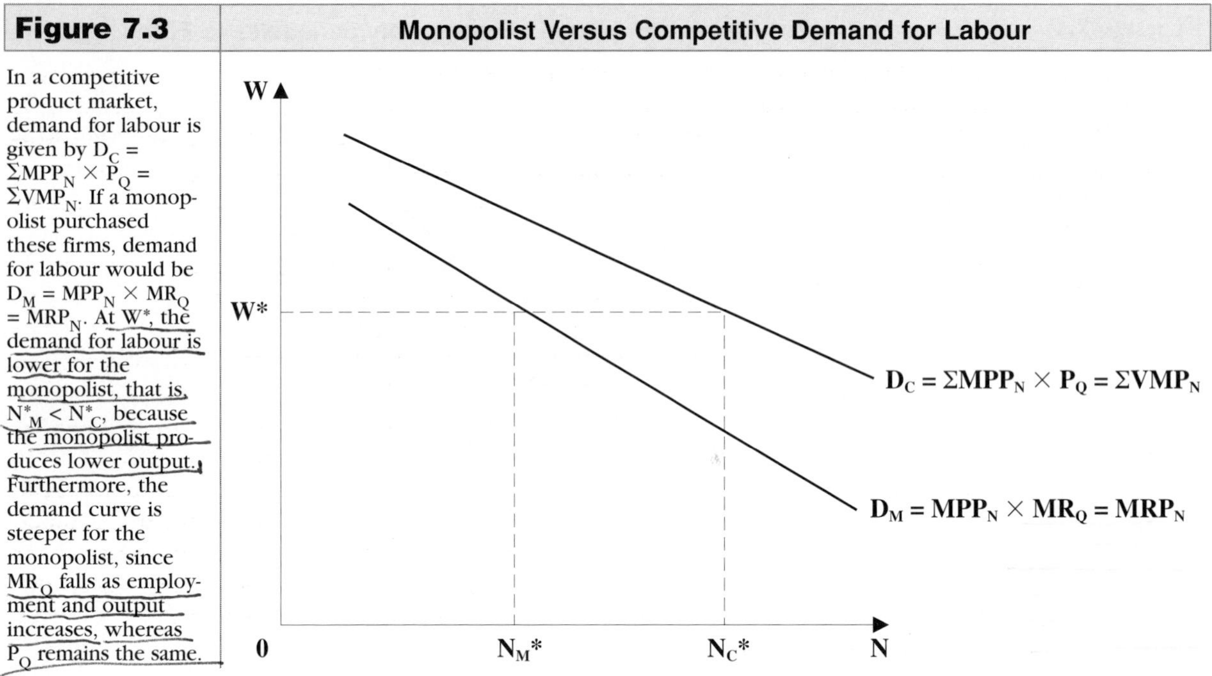

In a competitive product market, demand for labour is given by $D_C = \Sigma MPP_N \times P_Q = \Sigma VMP_N$. If a monopolist purchased these firms, demand for labour would be $D_M = MPP_N \times MR_Q = MRP_N$. At W*, the demand for labour is lower for the monopolist, that is, $N^*_M < N^*_C$, because the monopolist produces lower output. Furthermore, the demand curve is steeper for the monopolist, since MR_Q falls as employment and output increases, whereas P_Q remains the same.

The monopolist (or a cartel of firms acting like a single monopolist) raises the industry price relative to the competitive equilibrium level which reduces output and employment. Thus, at any particular wage (e.g., W* in Figure 7.3), employment will be lower if the industry is monopolized than in an otherwise identical competitive industry.

Product Market Structure and Departures from Market Wages

In theory, the previous analysis has little implication for the wages that monopolists will pay relative to the wages paid by firms that are competitive in the product market. This is so because the firm's behaviour in the product market need not be related to the way the firm behaves in the labour market. Specifically, if the firms are competitive in the labour market then they all face a perfectly elastic supply schedule for labour in the labour market; that is, they are wage-takers, not wage-setters. In such circumstances firms facing different product market structures pay the same market wage, as illustrated in Figure 7.3.

There are reasons to believe, however, that some firms may pay wages somewhat above or below the equilibrium market wage even though the labour market is approximately competitive in nature. Some of these factors are related to product market structure; that is, they serve to imply that monopolists will pay more or less than the market wage. Other factors are unrelated to product market structure; these reasons for departures from market wages are discussed in a subsequent section of this chapter.

In terms of aspects related to the product market, perhaps the main factor suggesting that the monopolist would pay greater-than-market wages is that the monopolist earns monopoly profits, and labour—especially if organized—may be able to appropriate some of these profits. Alternatively stated, the monopolist may be under less pressure to be cost-conscious and hence may more readily yield to wage demands. Being sensitive to their public image, monopolists may also pay higher wages as a way of buying the image of being a good employer. This may especially be the case if the monopolist is regulated and subject to the review of a regulatory agency.

By virtue of simply being a large firm (even though it may be a small employer of certain types of labour), monopolists may also pay high wages. This could be the case, for example, if large firms must use formal methods to evaluate job applicants and hence they pay a high wage so as to have a queue of applicants from which to formally evaluate. In addition, large firms may have to pay a wage premium to compensate for the rigid work schedules and mass-production techniques associated with larger size or to substitute for costly monitoring. Finally, by virtue of their size, large firms may have to follow administratively determined wage policies: unable to pay each worker its marginal product, such firms may pay wages approximating the productivity of the more productive workers within the group. In this way they minimize the risk of losing their more productive workers at a cost of having to pay slightly-higher-than-average wages.

The previously discussed factors suggest why monopolists may pay high wages if they are competitive buyers of labour. Each of these factors, however, could also be associated with lower-than-average wages being paid by monopolists. For example, although monopoly profits could enable the monopolist to pay high wages, they could also enable them to resist wage demands, perhaps by holding out longer against strike activity. In terms of preserving its public image, especially if regulated, monopolists may want to be model employers by paying high wages, but they may also want to appear as cost-conscious to the consuming public and to regulatory agencies. By virtue of their size, monopolists may also be able to pay lower-than-average wages, for example, if their size provided employment security or ample opportunities for advancement, or if turnover was less costly to them because of the availability of standby work forces.

Clearly the various factors that affect the wage determination process do not yield unambiguous predictions on whether a firm will pay above- or below-average wages. Consequently, as is so often the case in economics, we must appeal to the empirical evidence to ascertain the net impact of the variety of factors. This evidence will be examined in a subsequent chapter on wage structures where factors such as the degree of concentration in the product market, the threat of unionization, firm size, and the costs of turnover are viewed as determinants of wages.

Monopolistic Competition and Oligopoly

In between the polar cases of competition and monopoly in the product market are a variety of intermediate cases. Firms can be monopolistically competitive, a situation characterized by many firms which are small relative to the total market, but with products that are differentiated in some way, giving the firm some discretion in its price-setting. In such circumstances the demand for the firm's product is not perfectly elastic, as in the competitive case, but rather has some degree of inelasticity reflecting the fact that if the firm raises its price it will not lose all of its market, and if it lowers its price it will not gain all of the market. Under monopolistic competition, as is the case in perfect competition, there are no barriers to entry by new firms. This "free entry" property implies that firms cannot earn above-normal or monopoly profits in the long run.

Oligopoly industries are characterized by few firms that produce sufficiently similar products that the actions of one firm will affect the other firms. Consequently the firms will react to the actions of the other firms, and will take into account the possible reactions of their rivals in making their own decisions. There are many ways in which the firms can react; consequently, there is a large number of possible ways to categorize oligopoly situations. Oligopoly industries are generally characterized by some barriers to entry by new firms, so that above-normal profits may be earned by oligopolists in the long run.

The general conclusions reached in the previous analysis of perfect competition and monopoly continue to apply to the intermediate cases of monopolistic competition and oligopoly. In particular, market power in the product market is consistent with the firm being competitive in the labour market (or labour markets) in which it operates. Thus firms that exercise some discretion, or even exert considerable control, over the product price may be wage-takers in the labour market. In these circumstances, they would pay the market wage for the types of labour they employ, and could increase or decrease their employment without affecting the prevailing market wage.

However, several of the factors that may cause monopolists to depart from the market wage may also apply to oligopolists. Like monopolists, firms in an oligopoly typically earn above-normal profits that are not competed away by new entrants. Workers may succeed in capturing some of these "economic rents"—especially if the firm's management is satisfied with less than maximum possible profit, perhaps because of a separation of ownership and control. In these circumstances, workers benefit from a less-cost-conscious management and shareholders earn a lower return than they would if the firm paid the market wage, albeit still a greater return than is available in competitive industries. Similarly, oligopolists, like monopolists, are often large firms and they may pay above-market wages for reasons relating to their size.

Under monopolistic competition, free entry implies that firms should not earn above-normal profits in the long run (though they may in the short run, as would occur if there were an unexpected increase in demand for the product). Such firms are also generally small in size, such as retail outlets that are differentiated by location and possibly also by the merchandise carried. Thus, the two characteristics that might cause otherwise wage-taking firms to pay above-market wages—economic rents and large size—are absent in the case of monopolistic competition, as they are in the case of perfect competition. For these reasons we would expect firms that are monopolistically competitive in the product market but perfectly competitive in the labour market to pay the prevailing market wage, over which changes in their employment levels will exert no influence.

Finally, it should be noted that this discussion applies to situations in which the product and labour markets are in equilibrium. Product market structure may also have implications for disequilibrium dynamics—the direction and speed of response to changes in market conditions. For example, because they have some discretion in price-setting, monopolistically competitive firms may respond differently to pressures for wage increases than would perfectly competitive firms, which are not able to pass on wage increases to customers in the form of price increases. Similarly, the response of an oligopolistic firm to a wage increase may depend on how its rivals are expected to react to an increase in the product price.

Concluding Observations on Noncompetitive Product Markets

Clearly the way in which a firm behaves in the product market can affect the way it behaves in the labour market. Since the firm's demand for labour is derived from the demand for the product or service produced by the firm, then whether the firm is a price-setter or a price-taker can influence its employment and *possibly* wage determination.

The term *possibly* is used with respect to the wage determination process because as long as the firm is competitive in the labour market—and it can be competitive in the labour market and not competitive in the product market—then it would have to pay at least the going wage for labour. This fact is important because it suggests that there may be an upward bias toward higher wages in firms that are not competitive in the product market. This upward bias occurs because noncompetitive forces in the product market usually have an indeterminate impact on the wages they would pay to their employees. However, the forces of competition in the labour market would ensure that noncompetitive firms in the product market do not pay below the competitive wage. These same forces, however, may be ignored by noncompetitive firms that pay greater-than-market wages, perhaps out of monopoly or oligopolistic profits.

For example, if a monopolist did not pay the market wage, it might not be able to recruit any work force. Consequently, the forces of competition in the labour market ensure a floor on wages paid by the monopolist. However, if the monopolist paid a greater-than-market wage out of monopoly profits, the same forces of competition need not ensure a ceiling; that is, the excess supplies of applicants could be ignored by the monopolist, who may be under less pressure to be cost-conscious. Because competitive pressures in the labour market ensure a floor, but not necessarily a ceiling on wages paid in noncompetitive sectors of the product market, there may be an upward bias to wages paid in these sectors.

WORKING WITH SUPPLY AND DEMAND

One of the most common types of applied policy analysis is to simulate the effects of a policy change on the equilibrium level of employment and wages. In order to do this, it is necessary to be able to solve explicitly for the market equilibrium. Consider the most general form of the model, with labour supply and demand functions given by

$$N^S = f(W;X)$$

$$N^D = g(W;Z)$$

W, N^S, N^D are **endogenous variables** in this system; while Z, X are **exogenous**. Economic theory guides us in sorting out what are the various shifters Z, X that will affect labour supply and demand.

To solve the system, we invoke market-clearing, and set $N^S = N^D$. Then we solve for W* and N* (two equations with two unknowns). The results, which express N, W as functions of the **parameters** and the exogenous variables, are called the **reduced form**. Once we have solved for the reduced form, we can easily simulate the effect of changing X, Z on the equilibrium.

Linear Supply and Demand Functions

A useful example is to consider the simplest functional form for the supply and demand functions: straight lines. Equations for these functions, depicted in Figure 7.4 are

$$N^D = a + bW; \quad b < 0$$

$$N^S = c + fW; \quad f > 0$$

In order to match the form of the equations with the unconventional economists' reverse representation of functions, it is worth re-expressing these equations in terms of W as

$$W = -\frac{a}{b} + \frac{1}{b}N$$

$$W = -\frac{c}{f} + \frac{1}{f}N$$

These are equations for straight lines. For example, the slope of the demand curve is given by 1/b, while the intercept is −a/b. Many "thought experiments" take the form of changing the "intercept," that is shifting the position of the supply or demand function, keeping the slopes constant. Note that for these linear demand and supply functions, the absolute change or the slope is constant, so the elasticity varies. Since the elasticity is given by: $\frac{\Delta N}{\Delta W} \times \frac{W}{N}$, if the slope is constant, the elasticity will vary with $\frac{W}{N}$.

Setting $N^S = N^D$, we can solve for the equilibrium or reduced form:

$$W^* = \frac{a - c}{f - b}$$

Figure 7.4 **Linear Supply and Demand Functions**

The supply function is given by $N^S = c + fW$, transformed so that the vertical axis is the wage and the horizontal axis is employment, the slope is 1/f, and the intercept is -c/f. The demand function is given by $N^D = a + bW$, but after its axes are switched the slope is 1/b and the intercept is -a/b. The equilibrium N*,W* is given by the intersection of the functions.

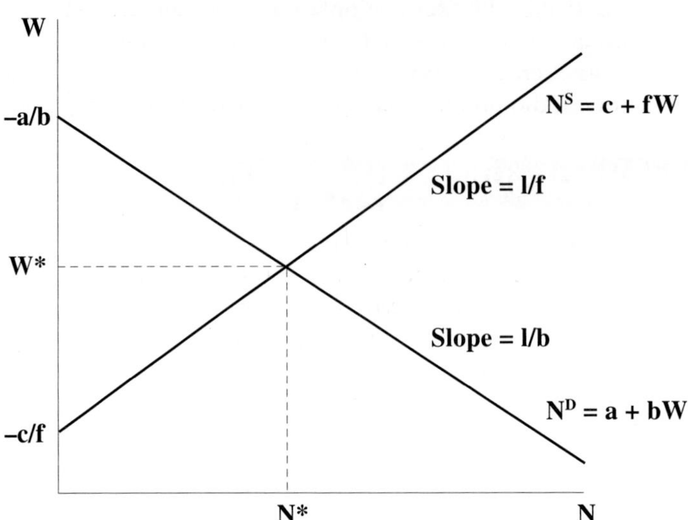

It is easy to add other variables (shifters) like the X or Z, to our models to make them more realistic:

$$a + bW + \delta X = c + fW + \phi Z$$

yielding

$$W^* = \frac{a - c}{f - b} - \frac{\phi Z}{f - b} + \frac{\delta X}{f - b}$$

where Z, X represent other supply and demand factors that shift the position of the supply and demand functions.

We can solve for employment by substituting the equilibrium wage, W*, into either the supply or demand functions:

$$N^* = N^D = a + b\left[\frac{a - c}{f - b}\right]$$

or

$$N^* = N^S = c + f\left[\frac{a - c}{f - b}\right]$$

It is worthwhile confirming that supply equals demand. In either case, N* simplifies to

$$N^* = \frac{af}{f - b} - \frac{bc}{f - b}$$

If we know how policy changes affect the position of the demand or supply function (i.e., how they affect a or c), then given estimates of the other parameters we can simulate the effect of the policy change on the equilibrium.

It is sometimes useful to work with log-linear instead of simple linear functions. In this case, the functional form for the supply and demand functions is given by

$$\log N^D = \alpha + \beta \log W, \quad \beta < 0$$

$$\log N^S = \lambda + \eta \log W, \quad \eta > 0$$

The convenience of the log-linear functional form comes from the fact that the slope parameters β and η are the demand and supply elasticities. The slopes of the log-linear functions are constant, and so too are the elasticities. Because economists often have estimates of these elasticities, the reduced form turns out to be easier to use for simulating the impact of changes in policy.

The solution for the reduced form proceeds identically to the linear case. For simplicity, denote $n^S = \log N^S$, $n^D = \log N^D$ and $w = \log W$. An equilibrium n^*, w^* will occur as before, where $n^S = n^D$, and implicitly $N^S = N^D$.

Application: Incidence of a Unit Payroll Tax

www.hrdc-drhc.gc.ca/isp/common/cpptoc_e.shtml
www.awcbc.org/english

A common use of these equilibrium models is in the evaluation of tax policy. After income taxes, the most contentious tax studied by labour economists is the payroll tax. A payroll tax is a tax levied on employers, based on the level of employment, usually proportional to the firm's payroll. Common examples of payroll taxes in Canada include CPP/QPP premiums, workers' compensation, unemployment insurance, and health insurance levies in some provinces. Table 7.1 illustrates these payroll taxes for 1971 and 1997, drawing on Lin (2000). Generally, payroll tax rates have grown in importance, especially for unemployment insurance and the CPP/QPP. In fact, by 2001 the combined tax rate for employer and employee contributions to the CPP/QPP was 8.6 percent, and is scheduled to rise to 9.9 percent. These taxes are often viewed as taxes on employers, rather than on workers. As such, they are often attacked as taxes on jobs, or "job killers." By investigating the possible impact of such taxes on wages and employment, we can evaluate the truth to these claims. To keep the notation simple, we will consider a simple per-unit tax, T, applied on a per-employee basis to firms. We will use the linear system of equations developed earlier to further simplify the analysis.

Workers are paid the wage W for a unit of work, while firms pay W + T per unit hired, W to the employee, and T to the government. On the face of it, it appears that the common-sense debate has substance: the employers pay the tax to the government (the workers do not), and this is likely to reduce employment because it raises the cost of hiring labour. Unfortunately, this "common sense" ignores the impact of the tax on the labour market and the adjustments that might occur.

The effect of the tax on labour demand is depicted in Figure 7.5. The initial equilibrium is labelled A, with equilibrium employment N_0 and wage W_0. The imposition of the tax shifts the demand schedule N^D down by T units for every employment level. The initial demand curve gives the optimal labour demanded at a cost of W per unit, whereas the shifted curve accounts for the fact that the price of labour is now W (to the workers) plus T (to the government), for a total of W + T. If there were no other changes in the labour market (i.e., the wage stayed the same) demand would fall from N_0 to N'. As we can see, however, as long as the supply curve is not horizontal, the equilibrium wage drops

Table 7.1 Payroll Taxes as a Percentage of Labour Income by Type of Payroll Tax, Canada, 1971 and 1997

Type of Payroll Tax	1971	1997
Workers' compensation	0.73	1.61
Unemployment insurance	1.06	4.98
Canada/Quebec pension	2.12	3.92
Health and/or education	0.21	1.71
Total	4.12	12.23

Source: Authors' calculations based on data provided by Lin (2000).

Figure 7.5 **The Effect of a Payroll Tax on Employment and Wages**

The initial equilibrium is A, at a wage of W_0. The payroll tax, T per worker, raises the price of labour to W + T. This shifts labour demand down by T units at each employment level. The new equilibrium is denoted by B, at the lower wage W_1. Some of the tax is paid by workers through lower wages. The workers' share of the tax is given by the vertical distance BC, while the incidence of the tax on employers is the remainder of T, which is given by CD.

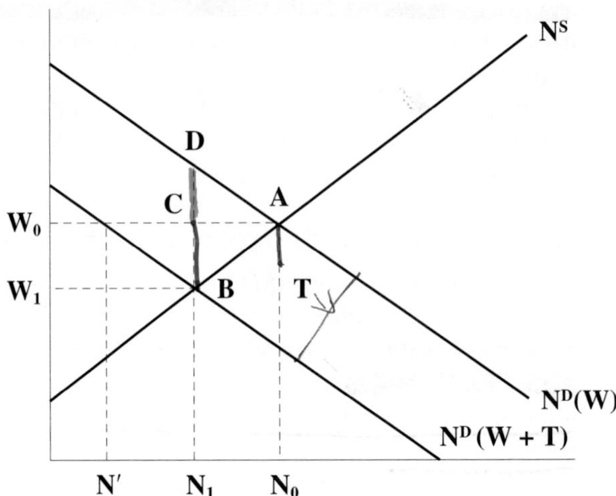

to W_1, and employment only falls to N_1. The lower wage effectively means that the workers pay some portion of the tax. In fact, at the new level of employment, N_1, we can account for who pays the tax. Workers' wages are lowered by $W_0 - W_1$ (given by BC in Figure 7.5), and this represents their share. The remainder of T, CD, is paid by the firm. Therefore, the **incidence of the tax** does not necessarily fall only on the party that physically pays the tax or fills in the forms.

Algebraically, we can see this by substituting the appropriate post-tax prices into the demand and supply equations:

$$N^D = a + b(W + T) = a + bW + bT$$

$$N^S = c + fW$$

So that

$$a + bW + bT = c + fW, \text{ and } W_1 = \left(\frac{a - c}{f - b}\right) + \frac{b}{f - b} \times T < W_0$$

where W_0 is the equilibrium wage in the absence of the tax.

Thus, of the T tax dollars, the worker's wage is reduced from the original level by $\frac{b}{f-b}$ T. This is the worker's share of the taxes. Clearly, the worker's share will depend on the relative slopes of the supply and demand functions. We can use log-linear supply and demand functions to express the incidence in terms of elasticities. Instead of a per-unit tax, T, assume that the payroll tax takes the form tWN, where t is the tax rate, so that the tax is proportional to the payroll, WN. In this case the price of a unit of labour to the firm is W + tW = (1 + t)W. Using the log-linear functional form from earlier, we have:

$$\log N^S = \lambda + \eta \log W$$

$$\begin{aligned}\log N^D &= \alpha + \beta \log[(1 + t)W] \\ &= \alpha + \beta \log W + \beta \log(1 + t) \\ &\approx \alpha + \beta \log W + \beta t\end{aligned}$$

where we use the approximation $\log(1 + t) \approx t$. These equations now resemble the linear case, and the workers' share of the tax t is given by:

$$\frac{\beta}{\eta - \beta}$$

If we choose common estimates of these elasticities, like $\beta = -0.3$ and $\eta = 0.1$, we would calculate the workers' share as 0.75, so that most of the tax is shifted to workers in terms of lower wages.

However, these elasticities may differ in the short and long run. For example, if labour supply is perfectly inelastic in the long run ($\eta = 0$),workers will end up paying the entire tax and the employment level will be unaffected. In the short run, with more elastic labour supply, firms will pay part of the tax, and employment will be lower than before the tax (but again, not as much as would be the case if the market wage did not adjust). It is an empirical question what the ultimate incidence of the payroll tax is.

Kesselman (1996) provides a very useful summary of the state of empirical knowledge on payroll taxes, as well as a critical review of some of the theoretical and practical issues related to the simple model we have just outlined. One of the first important points he raises—and this is very important—is that economists pride themselves on evaluating the unanticipated consequences of a given policy due to unaccounted-for equilibrium effects. Unfortunately, they often fall into the trap of ignoring the greater economic system while concentrating on the specific market they are studying. Given that the government needs to raise a given amount of revenue, it must use some form of tax, and all taxes have distortionary effects on markets. The question is then which tax distorts least. Kesselman reviews a number of reasons why payroll taxes may actually be useful, relatively efficient, tax instruments, especially if the tax is collected for a particular purpose, such as CPP/QPP. For example, compared to income taxes, payroll taxes are generally easier to administer, compliance is easier, and evasion is lower. The growing body of empirical evidence also seems to support the conclusion that in the long run (as suggested by the model above), the incidence of payroll taxes falls largely on workers, and that the disemployment effect is small. There may be some disemployment effects in the short run, but it does not appear that payroll taxes are the "job killers" they are made out to be.[1] The analysis of payroll taxes thus seems to be one area where economists have contributed in a positive way to the evaluation of public policy.

MONOPSONY IN THE LABOUR MARKET

To this point, we have examined the wage and employment decision when the firm is both a competitive seller of its output in the product market and a competitive buyer of labour in the labour market. We also relaxed one of those assumptions—that of a competitive seller of its output—and examined the labour market implications when the firm is a non-competitive seller of its output, but still a competitive buyer of labour in the labour market. In this chapter the assumption of being a competitive buyer of labour is relaxed. So as to trace out the implications of this single change, termed **monopsony**, the firm is still assumed to be a competitive seller of its product. The results of relaxing both assumptions simultaneously—that of competition in the labour market and the product market—follow in a straightforward fashion from the results of each separate case.

[1]See Hamermesh (1993) for an overview of the empirical evidence on payroll taxes. Dahlby (1993), Beach, Lin, and Picot (1996), Beach and Abbott (1997), and Lin (2000) provide up-to-date Canadian evidence. Also see Exhibit 7.1 for interesting evidence from Chile.

Simple Monopsony

The situation in which a firm is sufficiently large relative to the size of the local labour market that it influences the wage at which it hires labour is referred to as monopsony. The monopsonist is a wage-setter, not a wage-taker. In order to attract additional units of labour, the monopsonist has to raise wages; conversely, if it lowers the wage rate it will not lose all of its work force.

Consequently the monopsonist faces an upward-sloping labour supply schedule rather than a perfectly elastic labour supply schedule at the going wage, as was the case when the firm was a competitive buyer of labour. This labour supply schedule shows the average cost of labour for the monopsonist because it indicates the wage that must be paid for each different size of the firm's work force. Since this same wage must be paid for each homogeneous unit of labour, then the wage paid at the margin becomes the actual wage paid to all of the workers, and this same average wage is paid to all.

The firm's labour supply or average-cost-of-labour schedule is not its relevant decision-making schedule. Rather, the relevant schedule is its *marginal* cost of labour which lies above its average cost. This is so because when the firm has to raise wages to attract additional units of labour, in the interest of maintaining internal equity in the wage structure it also has to pay that higher wage to its existing work force (intramarginal workers). Thus, the marginal cost of adding an additional worker equals the new wage plus the addition to wage costs imposed by the fact that this new higher wage must be paid to the existing work force. Consequently, the marginal cost of adding an additional worker is greater than the average cost, which is simply the wage.

This situation can be depicted by a simple hypothetical example. Suppose the monopsonist employed only one worker at a wage of one dollar per hour. Its average cost of labour would be the wage rate of one dollar. This would also be its marginal cost; that is, the extra cost of hiring this worker. If the monopsonist wanted to expand its work force, however, it would have to pay a higher wage of, for example, $1.20 to attract an additional worker. Its average cost of labour is the new wage of $1.20 (i.e., (1.20 + 1.20)/2); however, the marginal cost of adding the new worker is the new wage of $1.20 *plus* the additional $0.20 per hour it has to pay the first worker in order to maintain internal equity in the wage structure. Thus the marginal cost of the second worker is $1.40 per hour, which is greater than the average cost or wage of $1.20. If a third worker costs $1.40, then the average cost or wage of the three workers would be $1.40, while the marginal cost of adding the third worker would be $1.80, composed of $1.40 for the third worker plus the additional $0.20 for each of the other two workers. (This example is further extended in the first three columns of Table 7.1, which is presented later to show the impact of minimum wages on a monopsony situation.)

The monopsony situation is illustrated diagrammatically in Figure 7.6. The essence of monopsony is that the firm faces an upward-sloping supply schedule for labour and hence has a marginal cost-of-labour schedule that lies above the supply or average cost schedule. The firm maximizes profits by hiring labour until the marginal cost of an additional unit of labour just equals the marginal revenue generated by the additional unit of labour. Marginal revenue is given by the VMP schedule in this assumed case of the firm being a competitive seller of its product. This equality of marginal cost and VMP occurs at the employment level N_M.

The VMP curve for the monopsonist is not its demand curve for labour in the sense of showing the various quantities of labour that will be demanded at various wage rates. This is so because the monopsonist does not pay a wage equal to the VMP of labour. For example, in Figure 7.6 at the wage W_M, the quantity of labour demanded is N_M, not W_MV_M, as would be the case if VMP were a demand schedule equating W with VMP. In essence, the demand for labour is determined by the interaction of the MC and VMP schedules and this depends on the shape of the supply schedule (and hence the MC schedule) as well as the

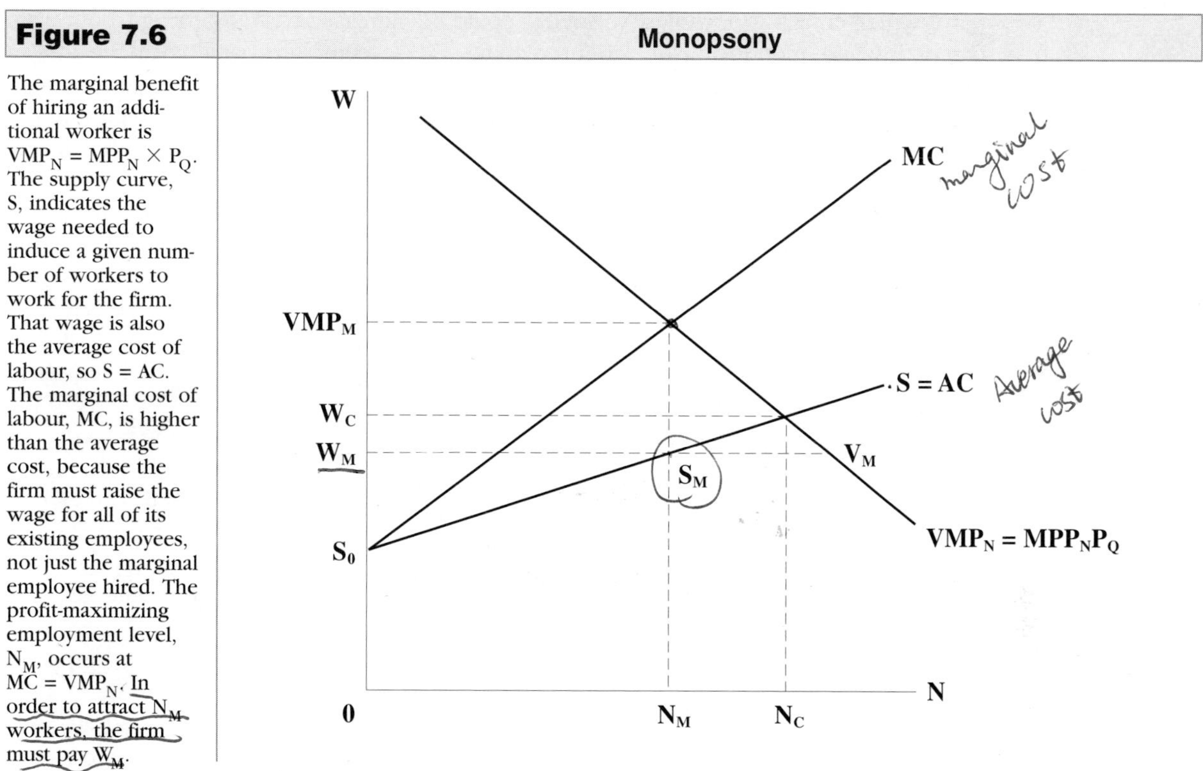

Figure 7.6 **Monopsony**

The marginal benefit of hiring an additional worker is $VMP_N = MPP_N \times P_Q$. The supply curve, S, indicates the wage needed to induce a given number of workers to work for the firm. That wage is also the average cost of labour, so S = AC. The marginal cost of labour, MC, is higher than the average cost, because the firm must raise the wage for all of its existing employees, not just the marginal employee hired. The profit-maximizing employment level, N_M, occurs at $MC = VMP_N$. In order to attract N_M workers, the firm must pay W_M.

VMP schedule. This line of reasoning is analogous to that underlying the fact that a product market monopolist has no supply curve for its product.

Implications of Monopsony

The level of employment, N_M, associated with monopsony is lower than the level, N_c, that would prevail if the monopsonist behaved as a competitive buyer of labour, equating the supply of labour with the demand. The monopsonist restricts its employment somewhat because hiring additional labour is costly since the higher wages have to be paid to the intramarginal units of labour.

For N_M units of labour, the monopsonist pays a wage of W_M as given by the supply schedule of labour. The supply schedule shows the amount of labour that will be forthcoming at each wage and, for a wage of W_M, then N_M units of labour will be forthcoming. This wage is less than the wage, W_c, that the monopsonist would pay if it employed the competitive amount of labour N_c. The monopsonist wage is also less than the value of the marginal product of N_M units of labour. That is, the monopsonist pays a wage rate that is less than the value of the output produced by the additional unit of labour (although the value of that output does equal the marginal cost of producing it). This monopsony profit or difference between wages and the value of marginal product of labour has been termed a measure of the monopsonistic exploitation of labour, equal to $VMP_M - W_M$ per worker or $(VMP_M - W_M) N_M$ for the monopsonist's work force. This monopsony profit accrues to the firm because its wage bill, $W_M N_M$, is less than the market value of the marginal output contributed by the firm's labour force, $VMP_M N_M$.

Because the value of the marginal product of labour for the monopsonist is greater than the value of the marginal product if that firm hired competitively ($VMP_M > VMP_c$, the latter of which equals W_c), welfare to society could be increased by transferring labour from competitive to monopsonistic labour markets. This seemingly paradoxical result—an increase in welfare by expanding noncompetitive markets relative to competitive markets—occurs simply because the value of the marginal product of labour is higher in the monopsonistic market. In effect, transferring labour is akin to breaking down the barriers giving rise to monopsony: it is allocating labour to its most productive use.

Although monopsony leads to a wage less than the value of the marginal product of labour, it is also true that intramarginal workers are receiving a seller's surplus; that is, the wage they are paid, W_M, is greater than their reservation wage as indicated by the supply schedule. The existing work force up until N_M units of labour is willing to work for the monopsonist for a wage that is less than the wage, W_M, they are paid. The wage that they are willing to work for is illustrated by the height of the labour supply schedule, which reflects their preferences for this firm and their opportunities elsewhere. However, to the extent that they are all paid the same wage, W_M, then the existing work force receives a seller's surplus or economic rent equal to the triangle $S_0S_MW_M$.

This is why the term "monopsonist exploitation of labour" should be used with care. It is true that the monopsonist pays a wage less than the value of the marginal product of labour. However, it is also true that the monopsonist pays a wage greater than the reservation wage (opportunity cost, supply price) that intramarginal employees could get elsewhere for their labour.

A final implication of monopsony is that there will be equilibrium vacancies (equal to V_M - S_M in Figure 7.6) at the wage paid by the monopsonist. In other words, the monopsonist would report vacancies at the wage it pays, but it will not raise wages to attract additional labour to fill these vacancies. In this sense the vacancies are an equilibrium, since there are no automatic forces that will reduce the vacancies. The monopsonist would like to hire additional labour *at the going wage* since the value of the marginal product exceeds the wage cost of an additional unit. However, because the higher wage would have to be paid to intramarginal units of labour, the value of the marginal product just equals the marginal cost, and that is why there are no forces to reduce the vacancies. The monopsonist is maximizing profits by having vacancies. It does not reduce the vacancies because it would have to raise wages to do so and the marginal cost of doing so is more than the marginal revenue.

Characteristics of Monopsonists

As long as there is some inelasticity to the supply schedule of labour faced by a firm, then that firm has elements of monopsony power. To a certain extent most firms may have an element of monopsony power in the short run, in the sense that they could lower their wages somewhat without losing all of their work force. However, it is unlikely that they would exercise this power in the long run because it would lead to costly problems of recruitment, turnover, and morale. Facing an irreversible decline in labour demand, however, firms may well allow their wages to deteriorate as a way of reducing their work force.

In the long run, monopsony clearly will be less prevalent. It would occur when the firm is so large relative to the size of the local labour market that it influences wages. This could be the case, for example, in the classic one-industry towns in isolated regions. Such firms need not be large in an absolute sense: they are simply large relative to the size of the small local labour market, and this makes them the dominant employer. Monopsony may also be associated with workers who have particular preferences to remain employed with the monopsonist. In such circumstances, wages could be lowered and they would stay with the monopsonist because their skills or preferences are not transferable.

Thus, a mining company could be a monopsonist, even if it were reasonably small, if it were located in an isolated region with no other firms competing for the types of labour it employed. The same company could even be a monopsonist for one type of labour, for example, miners, while having to compete for other types of labour, for example, clerical workers. Conversely, an even larger mining company might be a competitive employer of miners if it were situated in a less isolated labour market and had to compete with other firms. It is size relative to the local labour market that matters, not absolute size.

Monopsony may also be associated with workers who have specialized skills (specific human capital) that are useful mainly in a specific firm, or with workers who have particular preferences to remain employed with a specific firm. Because their skills or preferences are not completely transferable, such workers are tied to a single employer which therefore possesses a degree of monopsony power. Contractual arrangements in professional sports, for example, often effectively tie the professional athlete to a specific employer (team), giving the employer a degree of monopsony power. At a minimum, the employer need pay a salary only slightly higher than the player's next-best-alternative salary, which would be considerably less than the value of his skills in a competitive market. In practice, a much higher salary is usually paid in order to extract maximum performance. When players are free agents, as for example when different leagues compete, the resultant salary explosions attest to the fact that the competitive salary is much higher than the monopsonist salary.

The professional sports example illustrates the important fact that, although monopsonists pay less than they would if they had to compete for labour, they need not pay low wages. In fact, unique specialized skills are often associated with high salaries, albeit they might even be higher if there were more competition for their rare services. Monopsony does not imply low wages: it only implies wages that are lower than they would be if there were competition for the particular skills.

Perfect Monopsonistic Wage Differentiation

The previous discussion focused on what could be labelled simple monopsony—a situation where the monopsonist did not differentiate its work force but rather paid the same wages to all workers of the same skill, both marginal and intramarginal workers. In terms of Figure 7.6, all workers were paid the wage, W_M, even though intramarginal workers would have been willing to work for a lower wage as depicted by their supply price. The resultant seller's surplus or economic rent (wage greater than the next-best-alternative) is appropriated by the intramarginal workers.

This highlights another implication of monopsony. The monopsonist may try to appropriate this seller's surplus by differentiating its otherwise homogeneous work force so as to pay each worker only their reservation wage. If the monopsonist were able to do this for each and every worker, the result could be labelled **perfect monopsonistic wage differentiation**. In this case the supply schedule would be its average cost of labour *and* its marginal cost, because it would not have to pay the higher wage to the intramarginal workers. In such circumstances the discriminating monopsonist would hire up to the point N_c in Figure 7.6.

In fact there is an incentive for the monopsonist to try to expand its work force by means that would make the cost of expansion peculiar only to the additional workers. In this fashion the monopsonist could avoid the rising marginal cost associated with having to pay higher wages to intramarginal workers. Thus monopsonists may try to conceal the higher wages paid to attract additional labour so as not to have to pay their existing work force the higher wage. Or they may try to use nonwage mechanisms, the costs of which are specific to only the new workers. Moving allowances, advertising, or other more expensive job search procedures, and paying workers for paper qualifications that are largely irrelevant for the job, are all ways in which monopsonists may try to expand their work force without raising wages for all workers.

EVIDENCE OF MONOPSONY

Boal and Ransom (1997) provide an excellent overview of theory and evidence pertaining to monopsony in the labour market. Although the empirical evidence is by no means conclusive, there does appear to be evidence of monopsony in at least some particular labour markets. Scully (1974) finds evidence of monopsony in professional baseball, especially among the "star" players. The dramatic increase in player salaries following the introduction in 1977 of the free agent system (which significantly increased competition among teams for players, who were no longer tied to teams) also indicates that monopsony power was important in this labour market (Hill and Spellman, 1983). However, in their study of salary determination in the National Hockey League, Jones and Walsh (1988) find only modest evidence of monopsony effects on player salaries. Thus, the evidence relating to the importance of monopsony in markets for professional athletes is not entirely conclusive. The professional sports example is also interesting in that it highlights the point that monopsony power need not be associated with low salaries—just salaries that are lower than they would be in the presence of competition in the labour market.

Empirical studies carried out in the United States, the United Kingdom, and Canada have also found evidence of monopsony in the labour markets for teachers (e.g., Landon and Baird, 1971; Dahlby, 1981; Currie, 1991; Merrifield, 1999), professors (e.g., Ransom, 1993), and nurses (see Exhibit 7.1). In Canada, these two labour markets are now highly unionized; thus the employer-union bargaining models developed later in this book may be more appropriate than the simple monopsony model of this chapter. In her study of the labour market for Ontario school teachers, Currie (1991) noted that both a bargaining model and a demand-supply framework are consistent with the data. The estimates associated with the demand-supply framework indicate that labour demand is very inelastic and that labour supply is slightly upward-sloping, that is, that school boards possess a small amount of monopsony power in wage-setting. Further evidence for newspaper printing employees and construction workers is found in Landon (1970) and Landon and Peirce (1971). The extent to which these results can be generalized, even within the occupations where some monopsony was found, remains an open question. In addition, the extent to which it is monopsony power, rather than other factors, that is associated with lower wages could be open to debate.

It is unlikely that monopsony can be an extremely important factor in the long run. Improved communications, labour market information, and labour mobility make the isolated labour market syndrome, necessary for monopsony, unlikely at least for large numbers of workers. As these factors improve over time, monopsony should diminish.

By contrast, monopsony may be quite common in the short run. Most firms can lower their offered wage and still recruit new employees, albeit perhaps at a slower pace than at a higher offered wage. Similarly, firms which offer a higher wage are likely to experience both more applicants and a higher acceptance rate of job offers. In these circumstances, firms face an upward-sloping labour supply curve in the short run, even though they may face a perfectly elastic labour supply curve over a longer horizon. This situation of "dynamic monopsony" is especially likely to occur in an environment of imperfect information in which workers are searching for jobs and employers are searching for employees. These and other implications of imperfect information are examined further in Chapter 18.

MINIMUM-WAGE LEGISLATION

Minimum-wage laws provide a useful illustration of the practical relevance of our theoretical knowledge of neoclassical labour markets. The estimation of the impact of minimum wages has also been an important area of research and considerable disagreement in recent

www.hrdc-drhc.gc.ca/common/workplace.shtml

years. In Canada, labour matters are usually under provincial jurisdiction; hence, each province has its own minimum-wage law. Federal labour laws cover approximately 10 percent of Canadian workers. Industries of an interprovincial or international nature—for example, interprovincial transportation and telephone communication, air transport, broadcasting, shipping, and banks—are under federal jurisdiction. The influence of federal laws may be larger to the extent that they serve as a model for comparable provincial legislation.

Exhibit 7.1

Estimating the Incidence of Payroll Taxes

It is less than ideal to use the theoretical formulae in order to estimate the incidence of a payroll tax: an important distinction must always be made between even well-informed simulation and estimation. In order to estimate the impact of a payroll tax, a researcher would need to provide direct evidence of a link between a change in a payroll tax and a change in employment and wages. This exercise can be difficult for a number of reasons:

- The tax changes may be very small, for example moving from 4 percent to 5 percent. Given the noise and underlying variation in employment and wages, it may be difficult to detect the impact of such a small change.
- Causality may run in both directions. The tax changes may themselves depend on the state of the labour market, being increased when wages and employment are relatively high. In this case, we might find a positive relationship between payroll taxes and employment and wages, yet it would be inappropriate to conclude that the taxes *raised* employment and wages.
- Especially combined with the previous two problems, it may be difficult to hold constant the many other factors that affect employment and wages.

Jonathan Gruber (1997) explores the impact of a dramatic change in payroll taxes in Chile that avoids these problems. In 1981, Chile privatized its social security (public pension) system, moving from a payroll-tax-based, pay-as-you-go system (like the CPP/QPP) to an individual savings-based system. In 1980, the payroll tax to support the old pension system was 30 percent for employers and 12 percent for employees. In May 1981 the new system was implemented, and payroll taxes were slashed, so that they were down to 8.5 percent (for employers) by 1982. The new social security system was financed by contributions from employees.

The obvious question concerning payroll taxes is whether the reduction in payroll taxes led to higher wages, higher employment, or both. To some extent, the tax reduction had to lead to higher wages, because the government legislated firms to increase nominal wages by 18 percent as a consequence of the drop in payroll taxes. However, inflation was running at 25 percent at the time, so it is not obvious that workers enjoyed any real wage increase corresponding to the payroll tax reduction.

Using detailed firm-level data on employment and wages, Gruber explores the impact of the shift in tax regimes. He exploits differences in wages and employment over time (before and after 1981) and in the likely impact of the tax change across firms. His results show that virtually all of the tax reduction led to higher wages, with little effect on employment. His results are thus consistent with the "back of the envelope" calculations that imply that workers bear most of the incidence of payroll taxes and that these taxes have negligible effects on employment.

The recent evolution of minimum wages in Canada and the United States is presented in Figure 7.7. For the Canadian wage we show a population-weighted average of the provincial minima, while for the U.S. we show the federal minimum. The minimum wage is shown relative to the average manufacturing wage, an important benchmark for the relative price of low-skilled labour. The graph shows that the Canadian and U.S. minimum wages track each other quite closely, and that the real value of the minimum wage has declined significantly over the past 25 years, with modest recovery in the 1990s.

The rationale behind minimum-wage laws has not always been clear and explicit. Curbing poverty among the working poor, preventing "exploitation" of the unorganized nonunion sector, preventing "unfair" low-wage competition, and even discouraging the development of low-wage sectors have all been suggested as possible rationales. In the early days of union organizing, it is alleged, minimum-wage laws were also instituted to curb unionization: if the wage of unorganized labour could be raised through government legislation, there would be less need for unions. As is so often the case with legislation, its actual impact may be different from its intended impact, or at least it may have unintended side effects. Economic theory may be of some help in shedding light on this issue.

Expected Impact: Competitive Labour Market

The primary model for evaluating the impact of minimum wages is the neoclassical supply and demand model. Indeed, it is the evaluation of minimum wages that provides one of the most common illustrations of the insights provided by this simple model. Economic theory predicts that a minimum wage in a competitive labour market will have an adverse employment effect; that is, employment will be reduced relative to what it would have been in the absence of the minimum wage. This is illustrated in Figure 7.8 where W_c and N_c are the equilibrium wage and level of employment, respectively, in a particular competitive labour market. After the imposition of the minimum wage, W_m, employers will reduce their demand for labour to N_m. Thus $(N_c - N_m)$ is the adverse employment effect associated with the minimum wage. In addition to the $(N_c - N_m)$ workers who would not be employed because of the minimum wage, an additional $(N_s - N_c)$ workers would be willing to work in this sector because the minimum wage is higher than the previous prevailing wage. Thus the queue of applicants for the reduced number of jobs is $(N_s - N_m)$, with $(N_c - N_m)$ representing workers laid off because of the minimum wage and $(N_s - N_c)$ representing new potential recruits who are attracted to the minimum-wage jobs.

The adverse employment effect $(N_c - N_m)$ occurs as firms substitute other, relatively cheaper inputs for the higher-priced labour, and as they reduce output in response to the higher costs. These are the familiar substitution and scale effects, respectively, that give rise to the downward-sloping demand schedule for labour. (In the short run there would also be a disemployment effect, but the reduction in employment would be less than the long-run effect incorporating the scale and substitution effects.) The adverse employment effect need not mean an increase in measured unemployment: some who lose jobs in the sectors covered by the minimum-wage law may go to the uncovered sectors or drop out of the labour force.

The magnitude of this adverse employment effect depends on the elasticity of the demand for labour. If the demand for labour were relatively inelastic then the adverse employment effect would be small. Unfortunately, in those sectors most affected by minimum-wage legislation—low-wage industries like textiles, sales, service, and tourism—the demand for labour is possibly quite elastic, especially in the long run, reflecting the availability of substitute inputs and products as well as the fact that labour costs are often a substantial proportion of the total cost. In addition, since many of these sectors are often thought of as "fiercely competitive," it is unlikely that the minimum-wage cost increases could be absorbed by the industry through a reduction in monopoly profits.

Figure 7.7 The Ratio of Minimum Wages to Average Wages, Canada and the United States, 1975–2000

This figure shows the relative value of the minimum wage to the average wage, from 1975 to 2000, for both Canada and the United States. For Canada (dashed line), the graph shows the ratio of a weighted average of provincial minimum wages to the average manufacturing wage in each year. For the United States (solid line), the graph shows the ratio of the federal minimum wage to the average manufacturing wage.

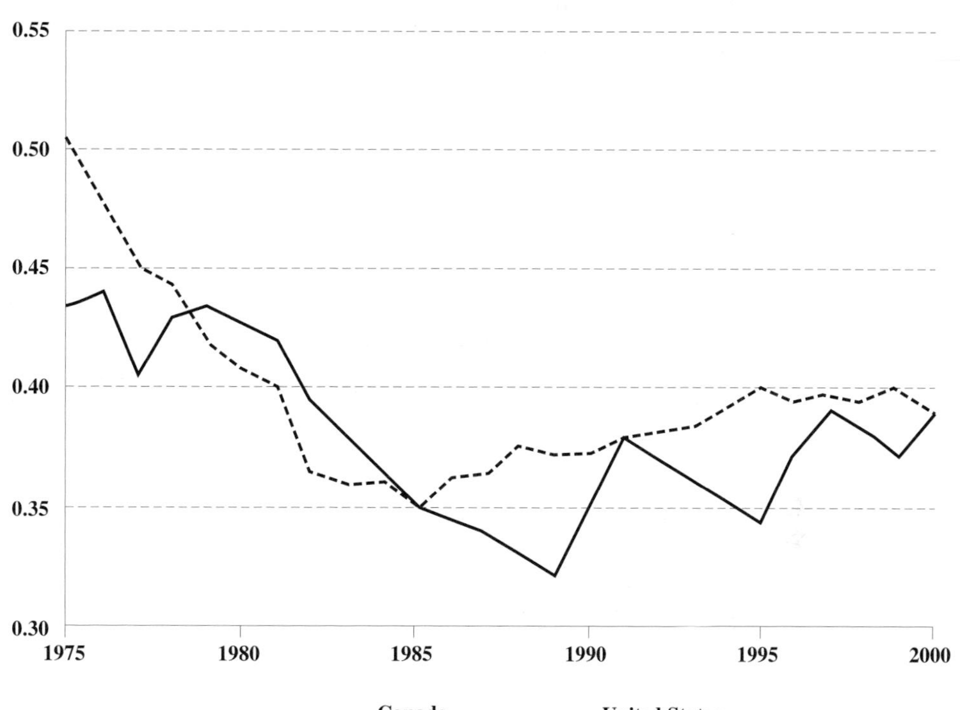

Notes: For Canada, minimum wage is a population-weighted average of provincial minimum wages. The minimum-wage data are reported in Labour Canada, *Labour Standards in Canada*, 1976–1987; and Labour Canada, *Employment Standards Legislation in Canada*, 1989–2000. The average wage is the average manufacturing wage, retrieved from CANSIM. Adapted in part from Statistics Canada CANSIM database, <http://www.cansima.statcan.ca>. For the U.S. minimum wage is the mandated federal amount, while the average manufacturing wage is retrieved from CITIBASE.

Expected Impact: Monopsony in the Labour Market

The existence of monopsony has interesting implications for the employment impact of an increase in the minimum wage. This discussion also applies to other exogenous wage increases, for example, from unionization, equal pay laws, or other forms of wage fixing. Specifically, over a specified range, an exogenous minimum-wage increase may actually *increase* employment in a monopsonistic firm. This seemingly paradoxical proposition first will be demonstrated rigorously, and then explained heuristically and by way of an example.

Formal Exposition Figure 7.9 illustrates a monopsonistic labour market with W_0 being the wage paid by the monopsonist for N_0 units of labour with a value of marginal product of VMP_0. With an exogeneous wage increase, due to the imposition of a minimum wage to W_1, the new labour supply schedule to the firm becomes horizontal at the minimum wage. This is so because the firm cannot hire at wages below the minimum wage. Thus the firm's labour supply schedule becomes W_1S_1S: to the right of S_1 it becomes the old supply schedule because firms can pay higher than the minimum wage.

The relevant marginal cost schedule, therefore, becomes $W_1S_1MC_1MC$. It is the same as the labour supply schedule for the horizontal portion W_1S_1 because both marginal and intramarginal workers receive the minimum wage and consequently marginal cost equals

Figure 7.8 **Minimum Wage**

In this figure, the equilibrium wage and employment level are given by W_C, N_C. If a binding minimum wage, W_m, is set above the equilibrium wage, labour demanded will equal N_m, while labour supply is N_s. Since exchange is voluntary, employment will be determined by the demand side (employers do not have to hire workers if they do not want to). In this case, employment will be N_m, which is below the competitive level, and there will be an excess supply of labour equal to $N_s - N_m$.

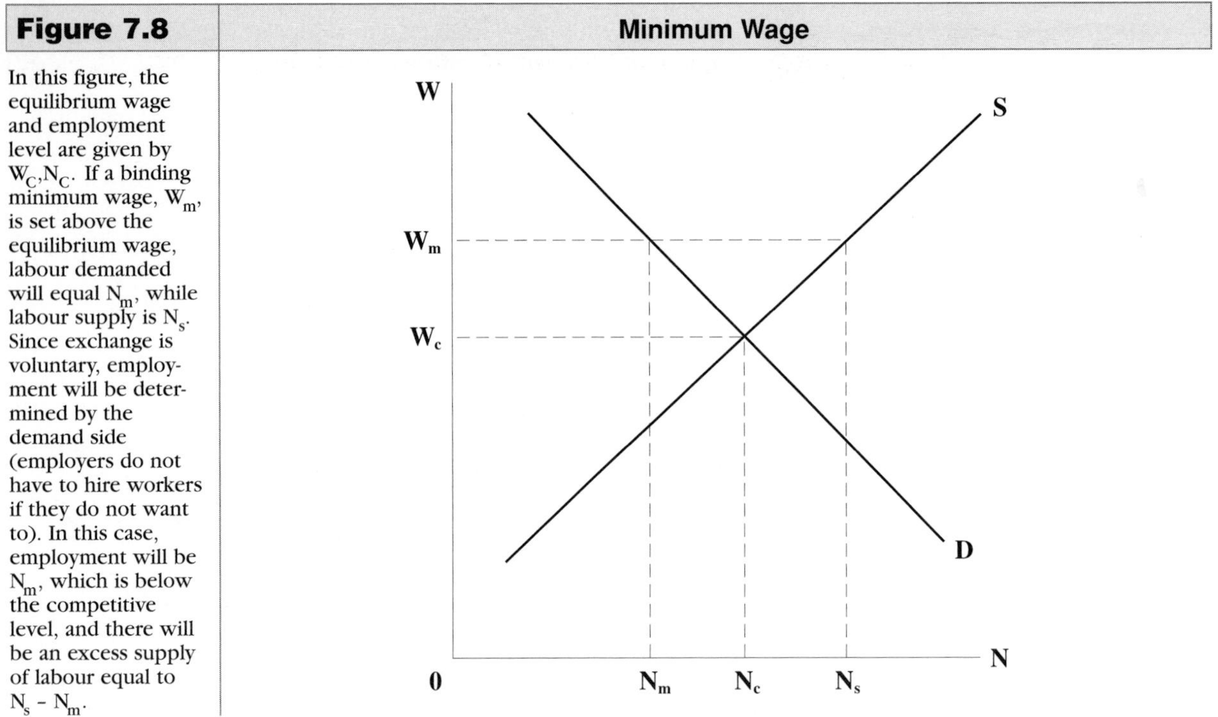

average cost equals the minimum wage. Similarly, to the right of S_1 the marginal cost schedule becomes the old marginal cost schedule MC_1MC reflecting the relevance of the portion of the old supply schedule S_1S. The jump in marginal cost between S_1 and MC_1 occurs because when the firm expands its work force beyond N_1 units of labour it has to raise wages to do so, and the wage increase applies to all intramarginal workers who previously were receiving the minimum wage.

After the imposition of the new minimum wage, the monopsonist would equate MC with MR (i.e., VMP) and hence employ N_1 units of labour at the minimum wage W_1. Wages have increased from W_0 to W_1 and, paradoxically, employment has increased from N_0 to N_1. In fact, for wage increases up to VMP_0, employment would increase, reaching a maximum increase for wages at the intersection of the supply and VMP schedules.

Heuristic Explanation Why would wage increases ever lead to employment increases on the part of the firm? The answer to this seeming paradox lies in the fact that the minimum wage negates or makes redundant a certain portion of the firm's supply and marginal cost of labour schedule. Faced with the new constraint of the minimum wage, the firm no longer need concern itself, at least up to a point, with the fact that if it wants more labour it will have to raise wages and pay these higher wages to all workers. In other words it is no longer inhibited in its employment expansion by the rising marginal cost of such expansion. Consequently it will expand employment because although the wage it pays is higher, the marginal cost of expansion is lower since it already pays the minimum wage to its intramarginal workers.

This does not mean that the monopsonist would welcome a minimum-wage increase because then it would not have to worry about the rising marginal cost of labour. The minimum wage obviously reduces profits to the monopsonist; otherwise it would have self-imposed a minimum wage without the need for legislation. The monopsonist is simply

Exhibit 7.2

Monopsony in the Labour Market for Nurses

The labour market for nurses is often cited as being characterized by monopsony, in part because of a belief that hospitals—the main employer of nurses—possess considerable market power in wage-setting. In addition, the labour market for nurses has frequently displayed persistent shortages, an outcome that is consistent with monopsony. (Recall that a monopsonist will wish to employ more labour at the monopsony wage, and therefore will report unfilled job vacancies. However, the monopsonist will not wish to raise the wage in order to attract more applicants.)

However, skeptics point out that the market for nurses is often national or international in nature, and that nurses are geographically very mobile. Thus, even though a particular hospital may have considerable market power in its own town or city, it must compete in a larger labour market for nurses and may be close to a wage-taker in that larger market.

Thus, on a priori grounds there are arguments both for and against the hypothesis that the labour market for nurses is characterized by monopsony. As is frequently the case in labour economics, the debate can only be resolved by empirical analysis. Indeed, whatever beliefs are held on the basis of a priori reasoning, empirical analysis is needed to determine whether the extent of monopsony is quantitatively significant, or whether the amount of monopsony power is sufficiently small that the market is essentially competitive in nature.

The issue is of considerable practical importance. If monopsony is quantitatively important, unfilled vacancies can be expected to persist and market forces cannot be relied upon to eliminate the "shortage." Furthermore, there may be a role for public policy to alter the allocation of resources, as there is in the case of monopoly in the product market. In addition, proponents of pay equity legislation often claim individuals in female-dominated occupations such as nursing are paid less than those in male-dominated occupations which require similar skills and responsibility. Although lower earnings in the female-dominated occupations is generally attributed to discrimination by employers, monopsony wage-setting would provide an alternative explanation.

A number of empirical studies (e.g., Hurd, 1973; Link and Landon, 1975) tested for evidence of monopsony power by examining the cross-sectional relationship between wages of nurses and employer (hospital) concentration. Most, but not all, such studies find that higher employer concentration is associated with lower wages, evidence which is consistent with monopsony. However, such studies do not provide direct information on the quantitative significance of monopsony. Sullivan (1989) addressed this issue more directly using techniques similar to those used in industrial organization to measure the extent of monopoly power in product markets. His analysis suggests that U.S. hospitals have significant monopsony power in the short run, and that even over a longer time-horizon may exercise considerable market power. In particular, the (inverse) elasticity of labour supply to hospitals is estimated to be 0.79 over a one-year horizon and 0.26 over a three-year horizon. These results indicate that cost-minimizing hospitals will find it in their interest to set wages of nurses below the value of their marginal product.

responding to a different set of constraints: the minimum-wage constraint simply leads to more employment, at least over a limited range of wage rates.

Hypothetical Example The response of a monopsonist to a minimum wage increase is illustrated in the hypothetical example of Table 7.2. The symbols refer to those in Figure 7.9. The firm's labour supply schedule is given in column 2 with hypothetical increments of \$0.20 per hour necessary to attract an additional worker. The resultant marginal cost schedule is given in column 3, rising faster than the average wage cost because of the necessity to pay intramarginal workers the extra wage. In the absence of the minimum wage the monopsonist would equate MC with VMP and hence employ four workers.

With the imposition of a minimum wage equal to \$2 per hour, the firm's labour supply schedule becomes as in column 4. For the seventh worker the minimum wage is redundant, since that worker would not work for less than \$2.20 per hour, as indicated earlier in column 1. With the minimum wage the firm's new marginal-cost-of-labour schedule becomes as in column 5. It is constant at the minimum wage for up until six workers because the firm simply pays the minimum wage to all workers. There is a large jump in MC associated with the seventh worker, however, because to acquire the seventh worker the firm has to pay not only the \$2.20 for that worker but also an additional \$0.20 for each of the previous six workers for a total of \$3.40 (i.e., 2.20 + 6(0.20)).

Given the new marginal cost schedule associated with the minimum wage, the firm will equate MC with VMP by employing five workers. The minimum wage increase results in an increase in employment from four to five workers.

Monopsony profits before the minimum wage were (VMP − w)N = (2.20 − 1.60)4 = 2.40 dollars per hour. After the minimum wage they are reduced to zero in this particular case because the minimum wage was set exactly equal to the VMP of the fifth unit of labour. (In Figure 7.9, for example, there would still be some monopsony profits even after the minimum wage.)

Figure 7.9 **Monopsony and a Minimum Wage**

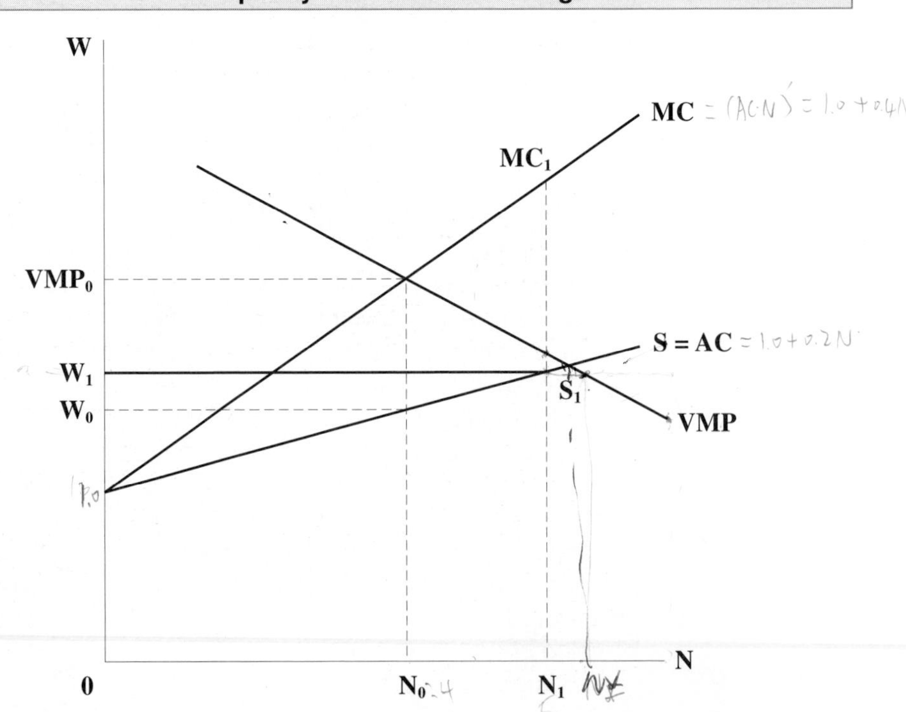

A minimum wage can increase employment under monopsony. The original monopsony wage is W_0, and employment is N_0. If the minimum wage is above W_0, but still below the competitive wage, the resulting marginal cost schedule is given by the minimum wage (W_1) until the firm must pay a higher wage in order to attract workers (at N_1), after which the marginal cost schedule reverts to the original MC schedule (at MC_1). The profit-maximizing level of employment occurs when marginal cost equals marginal benefit of hiring labour, at N_1 in this case. The resulting employment is higher than N_0, but lower than the competitive level.

Table 7.2 Hypothetical Example of Monopsonist Responding to Minimum Wage

Units of Labour	No Minimum Wage		Minimum Wage		Value of Marg. Prod.
	Wages	Marg. Cost	Wages	Marg. Cost	
N	S = AC	MC	W_1S_1S = AC	$W_1S_1MC_1MC$	VMP
(1)	(2)	(3)	(4)	(5)	(6)
1	1.00	1.00	2.00	2.00	3.00
2	1.20	1.40	2.00	2.00	2.50
3	1.40	1.80	2.00	2.00	2.30
4	1.60	2.20	2.00	2.00	2.20
5	1.80	2.60	2.00	2.00	2.00
6	2.00	3.00	2.00	2.00	1.80
7	2.20	3.40	2.20	3.40	1.60

Practical Importance While in theory minimum wage increases can lead to employment increases in situations of monopsony, in practice the importance of this factor depends on the extent to which monopsony is associated with workers who are paid below minimum wages. Examples of low-wage labour markets that would be affected by minimum wages include the garment and textile trades and the service sector, such as hotels, restaurants, and theatres. Employers in these sectors tend to be small and the pool of low-wage labour from which they draw large. On the surface, the conditions giving rise to monopsony do not seem prevalent. Recall, however, our earlier discussion of dynamic monopsony. Even at a fast-food restaurant like McDonald's, it is unlikely that the firm faces a perfectly elastic supply curve, at least in the short run. Perhaps because of imperfect information about job opportunities, small decreases in the wage paid may not lead to a complete abandonment of the firm by its workers. In other words, the firm faces an upward-sloping supply schedule, akin to that of a pure monopsonist.

Expected Impact: Other Possible Offsetting Factors

In a dynamic context, other things are changing at the same time as the minimum wage, and these changes may offset, in part at least, the adverse employment effect. For example, the demand for labour could increase perhaps because of an exogenous increase in the demand for output or because of an increase in the price of substitute inputs. While this may mitigate some, or perhaps even all, of the unemployment associated with the minimum wage, it is still true that employment would be even higher were it not for the minimum wage. Hence, there is still an adverse employment effect relative to the situation with no minimum wage. This can easily be illustrated in Figure 7.9 by shifting the demand schedule upward and to the right and tracing out the new level of employment with and without the minimum wage.

It is possible that some of the adverse employment effect may be offset by what could be labelled a "shock effect." Because of the cost pressure associated with the higher minimum wage, employers may be induced into utilizing other cost-saving devices that they should have introduced even without the minimum wage. The minimum wage simply serves as the catalyst for the introduction of cost-saving efficiencies. Similarly, labour itself may be induced into becoming more productive, perhaps because of the higher wage or perhaps because of the queue of applicants vying for their jobs. The existence of these shock effects, however, requires that there be some slack in the system; that is, that firms were not maximizing profits or minimizing costs in the first place, because otherwise they would have instituted these possibilities even without the minimum wage.

There are possible situations when employers may be able to absorb the wage cost increases without reducing employment. If the firm were an oligopolist and would lose a substantial share of the market by raising its product price, it might try to absorb the wage cost increase. However, it is likely that the low-wage industries that are most affected by the minimum wage are likely to be competitive rather than oligopolistic.

Thus, while there is the theoretical possibility of these factors offsetting, in part at least, the adverse employment effect of minimum-wage laws, their practical relevance is in question. It does not seem likely that they could be of great importance in the long run, especially in those low-wage sectors most affected by minimum wages. Subject to some qualifications, then, economic theory points to the conclusion that, in all probability, minimum-wage laws reduce employment opportunities. In addition, the impact will fall disproportionately on unskilled workers who are often most in need of work experience. This is the case, for example, with respect to younger workers and women who could utilize employment, even at low wages, as a means to acquire the on-the-job training and labour market experience necessary to move on to higher-paying jobs. For this reason, some would argue that minimum-wage laws actually harm the very people they are allegedly designed to help.

This disemployment effect does not necessarily mean that minimum-wage laws are undesirable, although that is likely to be the conclusion of many economists. The benefits of the wage increases to some have to be weighed against the costs of reduced employment opportunities to others. In addition, some would argue that even if minimum wages do reduce employment opportunities, it is in jobs that should not exist in the first place. It may be better to have these jobs eradicated and the unemployed workers trained for higher-wage jobs.

Empirical Evidence on Actual Impact

As may be expected, it is difficult to ascertain the actual impact of minimum-wage legislation, largely because so many other factors are also changing over time, and it may take a long time for all of the adjustments to occur. In addition, the adjustment processes may be subtle and difficult to document empirically. For example, a clothing manufacturer, when faced with a minimum-wage increase, may contract-out to households specific tasks, such as sewing on buttons or collars, or a restaurant may increase its usage of prepackaged foods. How does one accurately compare the employment reduction in the clothing establishment or restaurant with the employment creation in the household or the food processing sector, to arrive at a net employment effect of the minimum wage?

In spite of the obvious difficulties, there have been numerous attempts to measure the employment impact of minimum-wage laws, mainly in the United States. Most of the early research was conducted using aggregate U.S. time series data. A typical study entailed the estimation of a regression of a measure of teen employment as a function of the federal minimum wage, with controls for aggregate labour market conditions. This early research is thoroughly summarized in Brown et al. (1982). Minimum wages were generally found to reduce employment, with the employment elasticity between -0.1 and -0.3. In other words, a 10 percent increase in the minimum wage was associated with a 1 to 3 percent decline in teen employment (all else being equal).

The Canadian evidence to that point reinforced the conclusions from the U.S. research. Both Swidinsky (1980) and Schaafsma and Walsh (1983), for example, found significant disemployment effects. The methodology employed in these studies was somewhat different than those from the United States, in part because the Canadian researchers had the benefit of cross-province in addition to time series variation in the minimum wage. The

Exhibit 7.3

Minimum Wages and Fast-Food Jobs

The best way to measure the effect of a policy change on behaviour is through a controlled experiment. In the context of minimum wages, the ideal experiment might involve imposing a particular minimum wage in one labour market and a different minimum wage in an otherwise identical labour market. The researcher could then compare the different employment outcomes across labour markets. Because the only difference between the two is the level of the minimum wage, any difference in employment could be attributed to the difference in minimum wages. Of course, such experiments cannot be conducted, and labour economists have to seek policy changes in labour markets that as closely as possible approximate the experimental ideal.

Card and Krueger (1994) analyze a change in minimum wages that very closely approximated such an experiment. In April 1992, the minimum wage in New Jersey increased from $4.25 to $5.05 per hour, but remained at $4.25 in neighbouring Pennsylvania. Anticipating an opportunity to measure firm adjustments to the new minimum wages, Card and Krueger surveyed a sample of fast-food restaurants in both states a few months before, and eight months after the increase in the New Jersey minimum wage. *Ex ante*, it is difficult to imagine that an increase of the minimum wage by almost 20 percent would not affect employment. In fact, they found no evidence of a disemployment effect, and if anything, found evidence of relative increases in employment in New Jersey. The employment evidence was thus more in line with the monopsony model, though auxiliary findings on fast-food prices were not consistent with the monopsony story. The Card and Krueger study presented a serious challenge to the conventional view of minimum wages, and not surprisingly, generated an increased interest in minimum-wage research.

Recently, Neumark and Wascher (2000) and Card and Krueger (2000) reevaluated this "experiment" with a variety of corroborating data sets, including new survey data collected by Neumark and Wascher, and administrative records from the federal government, based on payroll data submitted by the firms. As it turns out, there is some sensitivity of the conclusions to the particular data set used to answer the question. However, both of the more recent studies have converged to "agreement" that the impact of the 1992 increase in minimum wages in New Jersey was small, whether it be small and negative (Neumark and Wascher) or small and positive (Card and Krueger). In fact, many of the estimates from both papers are insignificantly different from zero.

Canadian minimum-wage effects also tended to be at the higher end of the range from the United States.

As depicted in Figure 7.7, the minimum wage in real terms declined significantly over the 1980s. The decline was sufficiently large to motivate researchers to investigate whether there was a corresponding increase in teen employment, as would be predicted based on the pre-1980s empirical evidence. However, these studies failed to find an increase in teen employment. In fact, Wellington (1991) and Grenier and Seguin (1991) found the disemployment effect of minimum wages virtually disappeared in the United States and Canadian data respectively. Their results cast doubt on the foundation of the previous consensus among economists.

Exhibit 7.4 Do Higher Minimum Wages Help the Poor?

Most of the discussion surrounding the impact of minimum wages on the poor has focused on the possibly adverse employment effect, whereby the poor may be hurt by a loss of employment, even while some benefit from higher wages. Most of the evidence suggests that this disemployment effect may actually be small. However, a small but convincing body of evidence suggests that higher minimum wages are unlikely to help either. The main reason why the minimum wage may be ineffective in reducing poverty is that the link between poverty (low incomes) and low wages is quite weak. Indeed, this possibility was an important element of George Stigler's (1946) initial criticism of minimum wages. The weak link between low wages and poverty is manifested in two ways:

1. Many of the poor do not work, so raising wages cannot possibly help them.
2. Many low-wage workers live in high-income families.

Recent U.S. studies (Burkhauser and Finegan, 1989; Burkhauser, Couch, and Wittenberg, 1996; and Card and Krueger, 1995) confirm the weak relationship between poverty and minimum wages. Benjamin (2001) and Shannon and Beach (1995) provide comparable Canadian evidence on this point. Shannon and Beach explore the potential distributional effects of an increase in the Ontario minimum wage from $5 to $6.75 (the increase experienced in Ontario over the first half of the 1990s). Using the LMAS, they simulate the effect on individual income of a higher hourly wage rate. For simplicity, Shannon and Beach assume no disemployment effect, or any positive rippling effect through the remainder of the wage distribution.

They find that about 20 percent of Ontario workers would have received a raise from an increase in the minimum wage of this large magnitude. However, this only corresponds to 11 percent of hours worked, since most minimum-wage workers work part-time. The worker-hours distinction is thus one reason why minimum wages might have less an effect on income than on wages. Furthermore, Shannon and Beach show that 60 percent of the affected workers would be young (under 25) and half full-time students. Of course, this still suggests that many minimum-wage workers are older, non-students: the common target of antipoverty policy. Nevertheless, it represents considerable "leakage" of the benefits of higher minimum wages toward a group not usually regarded as disadvantaged. Reinforcing this evidence, they show that only 28 percent of the additional earnings associated with the higher minimum wage went to workers with annual family incomes below $15,000, whereas 31 percent of the extra earnings went to individuals from families with higher than $50,000 income. Clearly, many (but not all) of the beneficiaries are teenagers and college students from higher-income households.

Finally, Shannon and Beach simulate the impact of the higher minimum wage on poverty rates. They show that the Ontario poverty rate would only decline from 16.9 percent to 16.6 percent. The reduction is tiny, primarily because most poor households had no earner. Their findings, coupled with Benjamin (2001) and research from the United States (Burkhauser, Couch, and Glenn, 1996), suggest that redistributive policies of the kind described in Chapter 3, or more creative programs directed at the working poor, may provide "more bang for the buck" than increasing minimum wages.

In part because they had fallen so low, minimum wages were increased in the early 1990s. Several labour economists took advantage of the opportunity to exploit this discrete policy change.[2] Indeed, several states had already increased their minimum wages, providing the opportunity for cross-jurisdictional measurement of the impact of minimum wages. The most influential of these new studies was that of Card and Krueger (1994) (see Exhibit 7.3). In this and a few other associated studies, they did not find evidence of a disemployment effect, and even found evidence suggesting that increases in minimum wages were associated with increases in employment, which is more in line with the monopsony model.[3] Not surprisingly, their results have not gone unchallenged, and a number of studies such as Neumark and Wascher (2000) question the methodology and data employed by Card and Krueger, and provide evidence consistent with the traditional evidence of a disemployment effect.[4]

Baker, Benjamin, and Stanger (1999) incorporate the increases in minimum wages that occurred in most provinces of Canada in the early 1990s. Their research, which benefits from the additional cross-jurisdictional variation in minimum wages across labour markets than is available in the U.S., focuses on the dynamics of minimum-wage responses. To some extent, they provide a reconciliation of the U.S. studies, showing that a zero or positive employment effect is possible in the "short run," but that the "long-run" effect is negative, in line with the earlier studies.

Given the simplicity of the minimum-wage policy lever, it is somewhat distressing that measuring its effect has been so difficult. Nevertheless, the minimum-wage debate provides an interesting example of the difficulty of conducting empirical research in economics. The emerging consensus (subject, obviously, to more evidence) seems to be that minimum wages have small disemployment effects, at least in the long run. Whatever the ultimate resolution, the lessons from the debate extend beyond the effects of minimum wages. Most importantly, they indicate that labour markets are more complicated than the models described in textbooks.

Summary

- In this chapter we bring supply and demand together in order to explore the determinants of employment and wages in a single labour market.
- Irrespective of the competitive structure of the labour market, imperfect competition in the product market will affect the shape of the firm's labour demand function. However, there are no theoretical links between imperfect competition in the product market and imperfect competition in the labour market.
- If the labour market is perfectly competitive, the standard supply and demand model will apply. In this case, by assuming a particular functional form for the supply and demand functions, we can solve explicitly for the equilibrium employment and wage levels. For purposes of policy analysis, it is often useful to solve for the reduced form, expressing the endogenous variables (wages and employment) as functions of the exogenous variables (shifters of supply and demand) and the parameters of the supply

[2]Brown (1999) provides a comprehensive overview of the more recent empirical research on minimum wages.

[3]See Card and Krueger (1995) for a comprehensive review and critique of the empirical research on minimum wages. In this book they also summarize much of the new research that exploits cross-jurisdictional variation in the relative minimum wage, often finding zero or positive employment effects of the minimum wage.

[4]See the collection of book reviews of Card and Krueger's "Myth and measurement" in *Industrial and Labour Relations Review* (1995) for a critical evaluation of their methodology and conclusions. Neumark and Wascher (2000) and Card and Krueger (2000) provide a thorough reconsideration and evaluation of the impact of the 1992 New Jersey minimum-wage change.

and demand functions. Solving for the reduced form is especially straightforward when the supply and demand functions are linear or log-linear.

- Payroll taxes are taxes applied to a firm's payroll or wage bill. These taxes, like unemployment insurance and CPP/QPP premiums, are remitted to the government by employers and employees. However, who actually "pays" the taxes is a separate question, since wages may adjust to the taxes. For example, an increase in payroll taxes to the firm may lead (in a competitive market) to a reduction in wages paid to workers. In this way, the incidence of the tax increase will be shared by firms and workers. The degree to the incidence of the tax falls on firms or workers depends on the supply and demand elasticities. Furthermore, the degree to which the wage adjusts to a payroll tax will determine whether the tax affects employment: unless wages fall by the complete amount of the tax, employment will be lower as a result of the tax. Most evidence suggests that the incidence of payroll taxes is born by workers, and that the disemployment effect is small.
- If a firm is the only buyer of labour in a labour market, it is a monopsonist, and the conventional labour demand model must be modified (analogously to the modification of a monopolist's output decision). Because a monopsonist must pay its workers the same wage, in order to hire an additional worker, the marginal cost exceeds the wage for hiring the marginal worker. This divergence between marginal cost and the wage rate leads the monopsonist to hire less labour than a competitive firm. A monopsonist also pays a lower wage.
- In a competitive labour market, the imposition of a minimum wage above the prevailing (equilibrium) wage will unambiguously reduce employment, as long as the labour demand curve is downward-sloping. On the other hand, a minimum wage set between the monopsony and competitive wage will increase employment in a monopsonistic labour market.
- There is considerable debate about the empirical impact of minimum wages on employment. Recent evidence suggests that the short-run effect is small, though the disemployment effect may be higher in the long run.

REVIEW QUESTIONS

1. Given the demand schedules as shown in Figure 7.1, what would happen to the respective labour demand schedules for firms 1 and 2 if they both became monopolists in their respective product markets? What would happen to the wages they pay? What would happen to the labour demand schedule in the aggregate labour market, and hence the wage and employment level in that market?
2. Combine the results on monopoly in the product market with those of monopsony in the labour market, and illustrate the wage and employment determination process. Is it necessary that monopoly be accompanied by monopsony? Is it possible that the two conditions could go together?
3. The monopsonist's quantity demanded for labour depends on its elasticity of labour supply. Illustrate this proposition in Figure 7.6 by drawing both a more elastic and a more inelastic supply schedule through the point S_M.
4. Is it possible for a multimillion-dollar professional sports player to be subject to monopsonistic exploitation of labour? Is it possible for workers who are subject to monopsony to be receiving an economic rent on the sale of their labour services? Could workers who are receiving an economic rent for their services ever be considered disadvantaged workers?
5. Explain why a minimum-wage increase, over a certain range, would lead to a monopsonist actually increasing employment. Given this possibility, could the monopsony

argument be relied on to negate the critics of minimum-wage legislation who argue that minimum wages will have an adverse employment effect, and hence harm some of the very people they were designed to help? Could minimum wages ever be applied selectively to monopsony situations? Could wage-fixing via unionization be applied more selectively?

6. On the basis of Figure 7.9, discuss the favourable impact on resource allocation of setting a minimum wage at the intersection of the S and VMP schedules. Heuristically, in what sense are resources allocated more efficiently at that point than at the monopsonist's equilibrium? If the monopsonist followed a policy of perfect wage differentiation in the absence of the minimum wage, what would the implications for resource allocation be? Compare the income distribution consequences of the two alternatives of minimum wages and perfect wage differentiation.

PROBLEMS

1. "The imposition of a minimum wage above the prevailing market wage will unambiguously reduce employment." True or false? Explain.
2. There are two types of hockey players: (1) goal-scoring "stars" and (2) "grinders" or "non-stars." Stars are in short supply, so that there are not enough star players to fully stock the teams in the NHL. On the other hand, the supply of non-stars is unlimited. Using carefully labelled diagrams, describe the relative pay of stars and non-stars for each of the following situations:
   (a) Each hockey team in the NHL keeps all of the revenue it generates. Players are drafted by teams and have no ability to change teams on their own accord, that is, they must play for the team that drafted them for their whole career, unless they are traded.
   (b) Players become free agents after a few years. That is, players are free to change teams (going to the highest bidder) after a few years with the team that drafted them.
   (c) There is free-agency for players, but teams agree to share all their gate and TV revenues equally (they put them into a pool and divide it equally among the team owners).
3. Consider a labour market with labour demand and supply functions given by the following equations:

$$L^D = AW^a$$
$$L^S = BW^b$$

   (a) What would you expect the signs of a and b to be? Plot each of these curves, and graphically show the equilibrium wage and employment level.
   (b) Often, it is easier to work with logarithms. Show that the following is an alternative way to represent the above labour supply and demand equations:

$$l^D = A' + aw$$
$$l^S = B' + bw$$

   where lowercase letters represent natural logs, that is, $l^D = \ln L^D$, $l^S = \ln L^S$, $w = \ln W$, and $A' = \ln A$ and $B' = \ln B$.

   Graph these functions with l and w on the axes.

   Algebraically solve for the equilibrium wage and employment levels. Notice that a and b are labour demand and supply elasticities respectively.
   (c) The government is considering a *proportional* payroll tax, so that taxes are col-

lected as a percentage of the wage, where the tax rate is denoted t. With a payroll tax, the effective cost of labour to the firm is thus $(1 + t)W$. Use the approximation that $\ln(1 + t) \approx t$, and solve for the new market wage, the take-home wage of workers, and employment.

Explain how the share of the taxes paid for by the workers depends on the relative supply and demand elasticities. Using reasonable estimates of these elasticities, calculate the probable incidence of this payroll tax. How might your answer differ between the short and the long run?

(d) An alternative tax would have the workers pay an income tax of t percent on their wage income, effectively reducing their wage to $(1 - t)W$. Use the same approximation and logic as in part (c) and show that the level of employment and worker take-home pay will be the same as with a payroll tax with the same tax rate.

4. "Monopsonists are at a disadvantage relative to competitive buyers of labour because, when the monopsonist wants to expand its work force, it has to raise wages, while the competitive buyer can get all the labour it wants at the going wage." True or false? Explain.

5. (a) Consider a firm that sells its output in a perfectly competitive product market, and hires labour in a perfectly competitive labour market. The value of the marginal product of labour (in dollars) is given by:

$$VMP_L = 30 - 2L$$

Assuming that the firm is a profit maximizer and can hire labour at $W per unit, derive its labour demand function.

(b) Given that there are ten identical firms (like the firm described in part (a)) in the industry, show that the market labour demand is given by:

$$L^D = 150 - 5W$$

The supply function of labour to this market is given by:

$$L^S = 10W$$

Solve for the equilibrium wage and level of employment in this market.

(c) In an effort to stimulate employment in this industry, the government offers firms a subsidy of $3 per unit of labour hired. Analyze the effects of the subsidy on the level of employment and the workers' wages.

(d) The government's opposition parties accuse the government of catering to "corporate welfare bums" with the wage subsidy/handout. They suggest that the money would be better spent by putting the money directly into the hands of the workers. They propose that the government should directly give workers an additional $3 for each unit of labour worked.

Evaluate the argument put forward by the opposition parties by comparing workers' employment and incomes (wages plus government bonus) to the scheme in part (c).

6. "Suppose it was found that university professors' salaries depended on the occupation of their spouse. For example, suppose that professors whose husbands were doctors had higher salaries than those who owned businesses. This is clear evidence of monopsony." True or false? Explain.

7. "It is not possible to say on theoretical grounds whether monopolists will pay higher or lower wages than perfectly competitive firms." True or false? Explain.

KEYWORDS

REFERENCES

Baily, M. 1975. Dynamic monopsony and structural change. *AER* 65 (June):338–49.

Baker, M., D. Benjamin, and S. Stanger. 1999. The highs and lows of the minimum wage effect: A time-series cross-section study of the Canadian law. *JOLE* 17 (April):318–50.

Beach, C., and M. G. Abbott. 1997. The impact of employer payroll taxes on employment and wages: Evidence for Canada, 1970–1993. In *Transition and Structural Change in the North American Labour Market*, eds. M. G. Abbott, C. Beach, and R. P. Chaykowski. Kingston: IRC Press.

Beach, C., Z. Lin, and G. Picot. 1996. What has happened to payroll taxes in Canada over the last three decades? *Canadian Tax Journal* 44:1052–77.

Benjamin, D. 2001. Minimum Wages in Canada. In *Labor Market Policies in Canada and Latin America: Challenges of the New Millenium*, ed. A. Berry. Norwell, Massachusetts: Kluwer Academic Publisher.

Boal, W. M., and M. R. Ransom. 1997. Monopsony in the labor market. *JEL* 35 (March):86–112.

Brown, C. 1995. Myth and measurement: The new economics of the minimum wage: Review symposium: Comment. *ILRR* 48 (July):828–30.

______. 1999. Minimum wages, employment, and the distribution of income. In *Handbook of Labor Economics*, eds. O. Ashenfelter and D. Card. New York and Oxford: Elsevier Science, North Holland.

Brown, C., C. Gilroy, and A. Kohen. 1982. The effect of the minimum wage on employment and unemployment. *JEL* 20 (June):487–528.

Burkhauser, R. V., K. Couch, and A. Glenn. 1996. Public policies for the working poor: The earned income tax credit versus minimum wage legislation. In *Research in Labor Economics*, ed. S. Polachek. Forthcoming.

Burkhauser, R. V., K. A. Couch, and D. C. Wittenburg. 1996. "Who gets what" from minimum wage hikes: A re-estimation of Card and Krueger's distributional analysis in myth and measurement: The new economics of the minimum wage. *ILRR* 49 (April):547–52.

Burkhauser, R. V., and T. A. Finegan. 1989. The minimum wage and the poor: The end of a relationship. *Journal of Policy Analysis and Management* 8 (Winter):53–71.

Card, D. E., and A. B. Krueger. 1994. Minimum wages and employment: A case study of the fast-food industry in New Jersey and Pennsylvania. *AER* 84 (September):772–93.

Card, D. E., and A. B. Krueger. 1995. *Myth and Measurement: The New Economics of the Minimum Wage*. Princeton: Princeton University Press.

______. 2000. Minimum wages and employment: A case study of the fast-food industry in New Jersey and Pennsylvania: Reply. *AER* 90 (December):1397–1420.

Currie, J. 1991. Employment determination in a unionized public-sector labour market: The case of Ontario's school teachers. *JOLE* 9 (November):45–66.

Dahlby, B. G. 1981. Monopsony and the shortage of school teachers in England and Wales. *Applied Economics* 13 (September):303–19.

______. 1993. Payroll Taxes. In *Business Taxation in Ontario*, ed. A. Maslove. Toronto: University of Toronto Press.

Ehrenberg, R. G. 1995. Myth and measurement: The new economics of the minimum wage: Review symposium: Editor's introduction. *ILRR* 48 (July):827–28.

Freeman, R. B. 1995. Myth and measurement: The new economics of the minimum wage: Review symposium: Comment. *ILRR* 48 (July):830–34.

Grenier, G., and M. Seguin. 1991. L'incidence du salaire minimum sur le marché du travail des adolescents au Canada: Une reconsidération des resultats empiriques. (The impact of the minimum wage on the labour market of teenagers in Canada: A reconsideration of the empirical results. With English summary.) *L'Actualité Économique* 67 (June):123–43.

Gruber, J. 1997. The incidence of payroll taxation: Evidence from Chile. *JOLE* 15 (Supplement, July):S72–101.

Hamermesh, D. S. 1993. *Labor Demand*. Princeton: Princeton University Press.

______. 1995. Myth and measurement: The new economics of the minimum wage: Review symposium: Comment. *ILRR* 48 (July):835–38.

Hill, J. R., and W. Spellman. 1983. Professional baseball: The reserve clause and salary structure. *IR* 22 (Winter):1–19.

Hurd, R. 1973. Equilibrium vacancies in a labor market dominated by non-profit firms: The shortage of nurses. *R.E. Stats.* 55 (May):234–40.

Jones, J.C.H., and W. D. Walsh. 1988. Salary determination in the National Hockey League: The effects of skills, franchise characteristics, and discrimination. *ILRR* 41 (July):592–604.

Kesselman, J. 1996. Payroll taxes in the finance of Social Security. *CPP* 22 (June):162–79.

Landon, J. 1970. The effect of product market concentration on wage levels. *ILRR* 23 (January):237–47.

Landon, J., and R. Baird. 1971. Monopsony in the market for public school teachers. *AER* 61 (December):966–71. (Comment by R. Thornton and reply, *Industrial and Labor Relations Review* 28 [July 1975]:574–578.)

Landon, J., and W. Peirce. 1971. Discrimination, monopsony, and union power in the building trades: A cross section analysis. *IRRA* 24 (December):254–61.

Lin, Z. 2000. Payroll taxes in Canada revisited: Structure, statutory parameters, and recent trends. *Canadian Tax Journal* 48:577–625.

Link, C., and J. Landon. 1975. Monopsony and union power in the market for nurses. *SEJ* 41 (April):649–59.

Merrifield, J. 1999. Monopsony power in the market for teachers: Why teachers should support market-based education reform. *JLR* 20 (Summer):377–91.

Neumark, D., and W. Wascher. 2000. Minimum wages and employment: A case study of the fast-food industry in New Jersey and Pennsylvania: Comment. *AER* 90 (December):1362–96.

Osterman, P. 1995. Myth and measurement: The new economics of the minimum wage: Review symposium: Comment. *ILRR* 48 (July):839–42.

Ransom, M. R. 1993. Seniority and monopsony in the academic labor market. *AER* 83 (March):221–33.

Schaafsma, J., and W. Walsh. 1983. Employment and labour supply effects of the minimum wage: Some pooled time-series estimates from Canadian provincial data. *CJE* 16 (February):86–97.

Scully, G. 1974. Pay and performance in major league baseball. *AER* 64 (December):915–30.

Shannon, M., and C. M. Beach. 1995. Distributional employment effects of Ontario minimum-wage proposals: A microdata approach. *CPP* 21:284–303.

Stigler, G. 1946. The economics of minimum wage legislation. *AER* 36 (June):358–65.

Sullivan, D. 1989. Monopsony power in the market for nurses. *Journal of Law and Economics* 32 (October): S135–78.

Swidinsky, R. 1980. Minimum wages and teenage unemployment. *Canadian Journal of Economics* 13 (February):158–70.

Welch, F. 1995. Myth and measurement: The new economics of the minimum wage: Review symposium: Comment. *ILRR* 48 (July):842–49.

Wellington, A. 1991. Effects of the minimum wage on the employment status of youths. *JHR* 26 (Winter):27–46.

Chapter Eight

Compensating Wage Differentials

Main Questions

- *What factors determine the relative pay rates across different jobs?*
- *Can workers with identical skills be paid different wages in the neoclassical model?*
- *How might increased safety regulation actually make workers worse off?*
- *Are workers adequately compensated for performing unpleasant tasks or facing the risk of death on the job? Under what conditions might firefighters and police officers be paid the same, assuming their skills were equally valuable to society?*

In previous chapters we discussed labour demand and various aspects of labour supply and how they interact to determine the wages and employment of a homogeneous group of workers. This chapter focuses on the **wage differentials** that arise when workers and jobs are not homogeneous, but differ because of positive characteristics like nonwage benefits and negative characteristics like risk.

PURPOSES OF WAGES AND WAGE STRUCTURES

The discussion of wage determination is complicated by the fact that wages and wage structures are called upon to serve a variety of purposes in our economy. **Wage structures** are the relative prices of labour that are utilized to allocate labour to its most productive and efficient use and to encourage human capital development—education, training, mobility, job search—into areas yielding the highest return. Wages are also the prices that compensate workers for undesirable job characteristics and hence they ensure that the supply of and demand for such characteristics are in balance. In addition wages are an important component of family income and hence may have an important role to play in the achievement of an equitable distribution of income, as we saw in Chapter 1. Our macroeconomic objectives of full employment, price stability, and a viable balance of payments can also be affected by wage developments, just as wage determination is affected by the macroeconomic environment.

There is a complex nexus between wages and productivity. Usually we think of high wages being the result of high productivity that can come about, for example, through various forms of human capital formation, or through technological change. (With respect to the latter factor, wage increases are one way of distributing the gains of general productivity improvements; price reductions are another.) However, there is the possibility of cause and effect working the other way as well; that is, high wages may induce productivity improvements through improved morale, health, and intensity of work effort, as well as by reductions in absenteeism and turnover. In addition wage increases may induce efficient changes elsewhere in the system—changes that should have occurred earlier but that would not occur without the shock induced by a wage change.

The matter is further complicated by the fact that wages and wage structures serve a social role, in that prestige is associated with wages; hence, the importance of *relative* positions in the wage hierarchy and the importance of key comparison groups. The social role of wages is further heightened by the fact that labour services are inseparable from the person who provides the services: hence, the importance of the human element in labour market analysis.

Clearly wages and wage structures are called upon to serve a variety of often conflicting roles in our economic system in particular, and in our social system in general. Perhaps this is why there is so much emotive conflict over various policies—such as minimum wages or wage controls or equal pay legislation—that affect wages.

THEORY OF COMPENSATING WAGES

The idea behind **compensating wage differentials** cannot be stated any more succinctly than originally posed by Adam Smith:

> *The five following are the principal circumstances which, so far as I have been able to observe, make up for a small pecuniary gain in some employments, and counter-balance a great one in others: first, the agreeableness or disagreeableness of the employments themselves; secondly, the easiness and cheapness, or the difficulty and expense of learning them; thirdly the constancy or inconstancy of employment in them; fourthly, the small or great trust which must be reposed in those who exercise them; and fifthly, the probability or improbability of success in them. (Adam Smith,* The Wealth of Nations, *Chapter X, page 100)*

www.adamsmith.org.uk

Wages thus serve the purpose of compensating employees for undesirable working conditions or for negative or costly attributes associated with a particular job. Such conditions include an unsafe or unhealthy work environment, long commute time, undesirable working hours, lengthy training or other human capital requirements, and even the need for workers with discriminatory preferences to work in an integrated work environment. Wages also compensate—by being lower than they would otherwise be—for desirable working conditions such as flexible hours, stimulating tasks, and a pleasant working environment. As illustrated subsequently, many of these characteristics are associated with particular occupations, industries, regions, or firms and hence form part of the rationale for wage structures associated with these factors.

In this chapter, the theory of compensating wages is illustrated with respect to compensating wages associated with the risk of injury or illness that can result from an unsafe or unhealthy work environment—an area where the theory has seen considerable development and empirical application. The analysis would naturally extend to other job amenities or disamenities.

Single Firm's Isoprofit Schedule

Figure 8.1(a) illustrates a single firm's **isoprofit schedule**, I, defined as the various combinations of wages and safety that the firm can provide and maintain the same level of profits. For the firm, both wages and a safe work environment are costly to provide; hence, the negative tradeoff between the two; that is, the firm can provide more safety and maintain profits only if it can pay a lower wage. The isoprofit schedule exhibits a diminishing marginal rate of transformation between wages and safety. That is, in the upper left portion, like at point A, where the firm is providing little safety, it can provide additional safety in a relatively inexpensive fashion with minor basic changes in its safety technology (e.g., better lighting, signs, guard rails). It is in a stage of increasing returns with respect to the provision of safety. In such circumstances, the firm can provide these inexpensive safety features without requiring much of a wage reduction in order to maintain a constant profit level; that is, the isoprofit schedule is relatively flat.

Figure 8.1 **Employer's Isoprofit Schedules and Offer Curve**

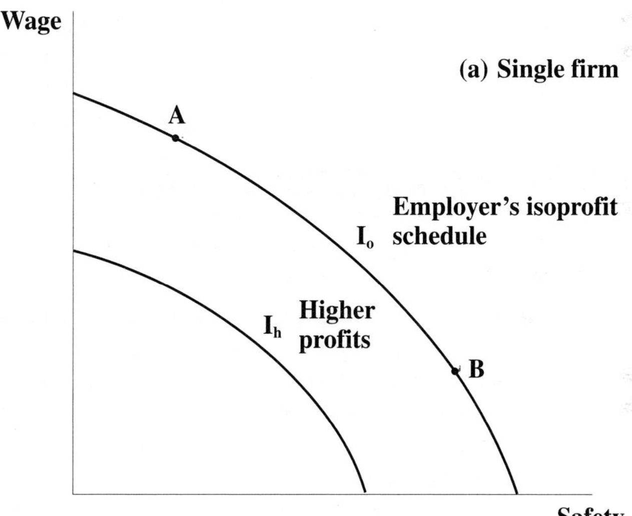

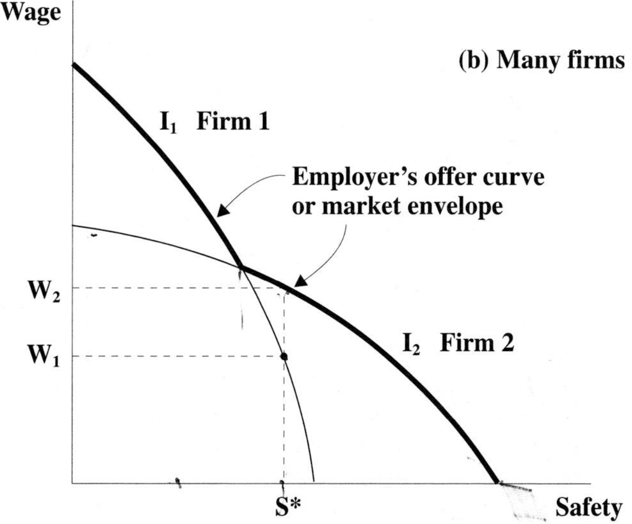

Panel (a) depicts isoprofit schedules, such as I_0, that show combinations of wages and safety yielding the same level of profits. The high-safety/low-wage package at B yields the same profits as the lower-safety/higher-wage package at A. Profits increase as the combinations move closer to the origin, and I_h represents higher profits than I_0. Panel (b) shows the isoprofit schedules of firms with different safety technologies. Firm 2 is inherently safer, and its flatter isoprofit curve (I_2) reflects the fact that it can offer a higher level of safety without reducing wages as much as firm 1 (I_1). The bold line represents the "market envelope" available to workers in equilibrium. At S*, firm 1 can offer W_1, but workers will not accept this, since they could have the same level of safety, but the higher wage W_2, at firm 2. Firm 2 is more attractive at higher levels of safety, but firm 1 will dominate firm 2 at lower levels of safety because it can pay higher wages.

Conversely, in the bottom right segment as at point B, where the firm is providing considerable safety, it can provide additional safety only through the introduction of more sophisticated and costly safety procedures. It is in a stage of diminishing returns in the provision of safety, having already exhausted the cheapest forms of providing safety. That is, as the firm moves from left to right on the horizontal axis and provides additional safety, it will start with the cheapest forms of safety provision and then move to the more expensive. In such circumstances, it will require an even larger wage reduction to compensate for its additional safety costs, in order to maintain the same level of profits; that is, the isoprofit schedule will become steeper as more safety is provided and the firm moves from point A towards B.

Lower isoprofit schedules like I_h in Figure 8.1(a) imply higher levels of profits. That is, profits are the same at all points along I_h just as they are the same at all points along I_0. However, profits are higher along I_h than I_0. This is so because to the firm both wages and safety are costly to provide. Hence, providing both lower wages and lower safety means higher profits.

Different Firms with Different Safety Technologies

Different firms can have different abilities to provide safety at a given cost. Hence different firms may have differently shaped isoprofit schedules even for the same level of profit (e.g., even if they all operate at the competitive level of zero excess profits).

Figure 8.1(b) illustrates the isoprofit schedules for two firms (or industries, or occupations). Firm 1 exhibits rapidly diminishing returns to providing a safe work environment. Additional safety can be provided only if wages drop quite rapidly to compensate for the safety costs, if profits are to be maintained. This could be the case, for example, for firms in sectors that are inherently dangerous, such as mining or logging. In contrast, firm 2 may be in an inherently safer industry and hence be able to provide high levels of safety without having to substantially lower wages to maintain profits. Competitive equilibrium requires that excess profits of firms 1 and 2 are reduced to zero (i.e., $I_1 = I_2 = 0$).

The outer limits of the two isoprofit schedules (bold line), called the employers' *offer* curve or **market envelope curve**, show the maximum compensating wages that will be offered in the market for various levels of safety. Points within the envelope will not prevail in the market because they will always be dominated by points on the envelope. For example, for a given level of safety, S*, firm 2 is able to offer the wage W_2 and maintain its given level of profit, I_2. firm 1, in contrast, can only offer the wage W_1 and continue to meet the zero profit condition. Hence, firm 2's offer will dominate firm 1's offer for levels of safety, like S*, to the right of the intersection of the isoprofit schedules; firm 1's offer will dominate to the left of the intersection. In other words, workers would always go to employers that offer the highest compensating wage for every level of safety; hence, only points on the outer segments of the isoprofit schedules will prevail in a competitive market.

Single Individual's Preferences

As with any other items they value, individuals will have preferences for wages and safety. These preferences can be illustrated by a typical indifference or isoutility curve showing various combinations of wages and safety that yield the same level of utility, as depicted in the top panel, Figure 8.2(a). The curvature of the indifference curve illustrates a diminishing marginal rate of substitution between wages and safety. That is, at points in the upper left segment such as A where the individual does not have a very safe work environment, that individual would likely be willing to give up considerable wages to get a slightly safer work environment. Hence the indifference curve is steep. Conversely, at points such as B where the individual has a safer work environment, the individual may not be willing to give up much in the form of wages to obtain additional safety. Hence, the indifference curve is relatively flat. Higher indifference curves, like U_h, indicate higher levels of utility since the individual has more of both wages and safety, both of which yield utility.

Figure 8.2 **Worker Indifference Curves**

Indifference curves, such as U_0, plot combinations of wages and safety that yield the same utility. Not everyone has the same preferences for safety. At the combination S_0,W_0 (in panel (b)) the indifference curve for person a (U_a) is steeper than for person b (U_b), reflecting a greater willingness to give up wages in return for more safety.

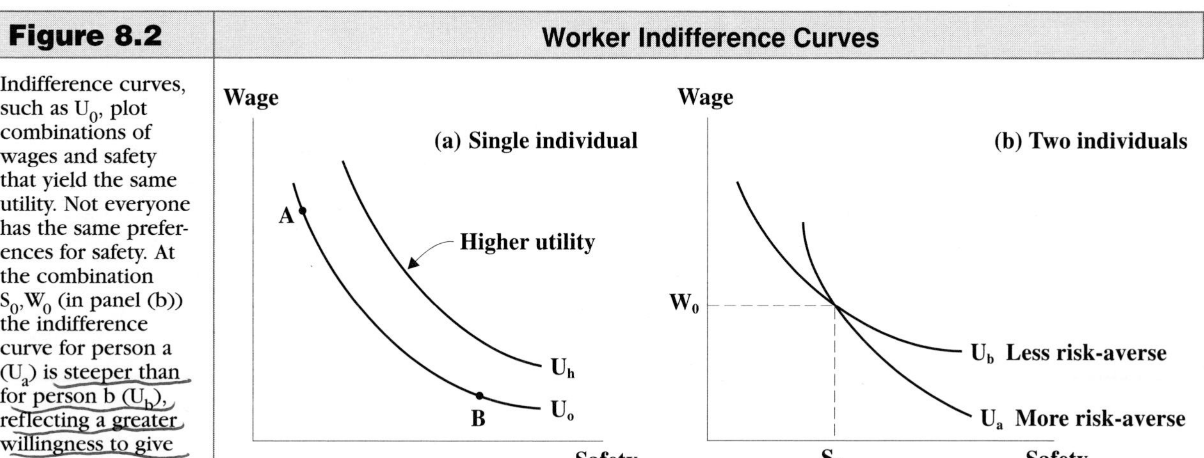

Different Individuals with Different Risk Preferences

Different individuals may have different risk preferences and hence may show a different willingness to give up safety in return for a **compensating risk premium** in the form of higher wages. Figure 8.2(b) illustrates a more risk-averse and a less risk-averse individual. As indicated at the point of intersection of the two schedules, the more risk-averse individual requires a larger compensating wage in return for giving up some safety and accepting a riskier work environment.

Equilibrium with Single Firm, Single Individual

Figure 8.3(a) illustrates the market equilibrium for a single firm and single individual as the point of tangency, E_c, between the firm's isoprofit schedule, I_c, and the individual's indifference curve U_c. This outcome occurs because a perfectly competitive market yields the maximum worker utility subject to the firm's earning zero economic profits. The compensating wage, W_c, given the level of safety, S_c, is the highest the firm is able to offer for that level of safety, given the zero profit constraint. For movements to the left of S_c, the additional wage that the individual requires for accepting more risk (i.e., slope of the indifference curve) is greater than what the firm is willing to give (i.e., slope of the isoprofit schedule) in order to maintain the same competitive profit level. Conversely, for movements to the right, what the worker is willing to give up for additional safety is insufficient to compensate the employer so as to maintain the same competitive profit level. Thus, given the constraint I_c (due to the zero profit condition), worker utility is highest at E_c.

Higher indifference curves are not attainable for the worker, because they would lie outside of the feasible choice set as dictated by the employer's isoprofit schedule, I_c, which gives the competitive level of profits. Higher isoprofit schedules would imply profits that are below the competitive level. Conversely, under competitive conditions, individuals would not have to accept combinations of lower wages and safety that would put them on indifference curves below U_c (and employers on isoprofit schedules that are closer to the origin, implying profits above the competitive norm) because workers could move to firms that would offer higher compensating wages and still maintain competitive profits. Of course, if firms could offer lower combinations of wages and safety (e.g., if worker mobility were restricted or they did not know the risk to which they were exposed), then workers would be on lower indifference curves and firms would have higher profits.

Figure 8.3 **Market Equilibrium**

With a single firm and individual, the equilibrium is given by W_C and S_C. Perfect competition restricts the possible combinations to those on I_C, the firm's zero-profit isoprofit schedule. Workers will choose jobs that yield the highest utility, which is given by the tangency at E_C. Panel (b) shows the case of many firms and individuals. The market envelope is shown in bold, and represents the wage-safety opportunities available to workers (employers' offer curve). Some people will choose to work at less-safe jobs (such as S_L) in exchange for higher wages (such as W_L), while the more risk-averse will opt for greater safety (such as S_H) in exchange for lower wages (such as W_H). The set of equilibrium compensation packages is given by the market wage-safety locus, which shows the rate at which the market compensates individuals for working in less-safe conditions.

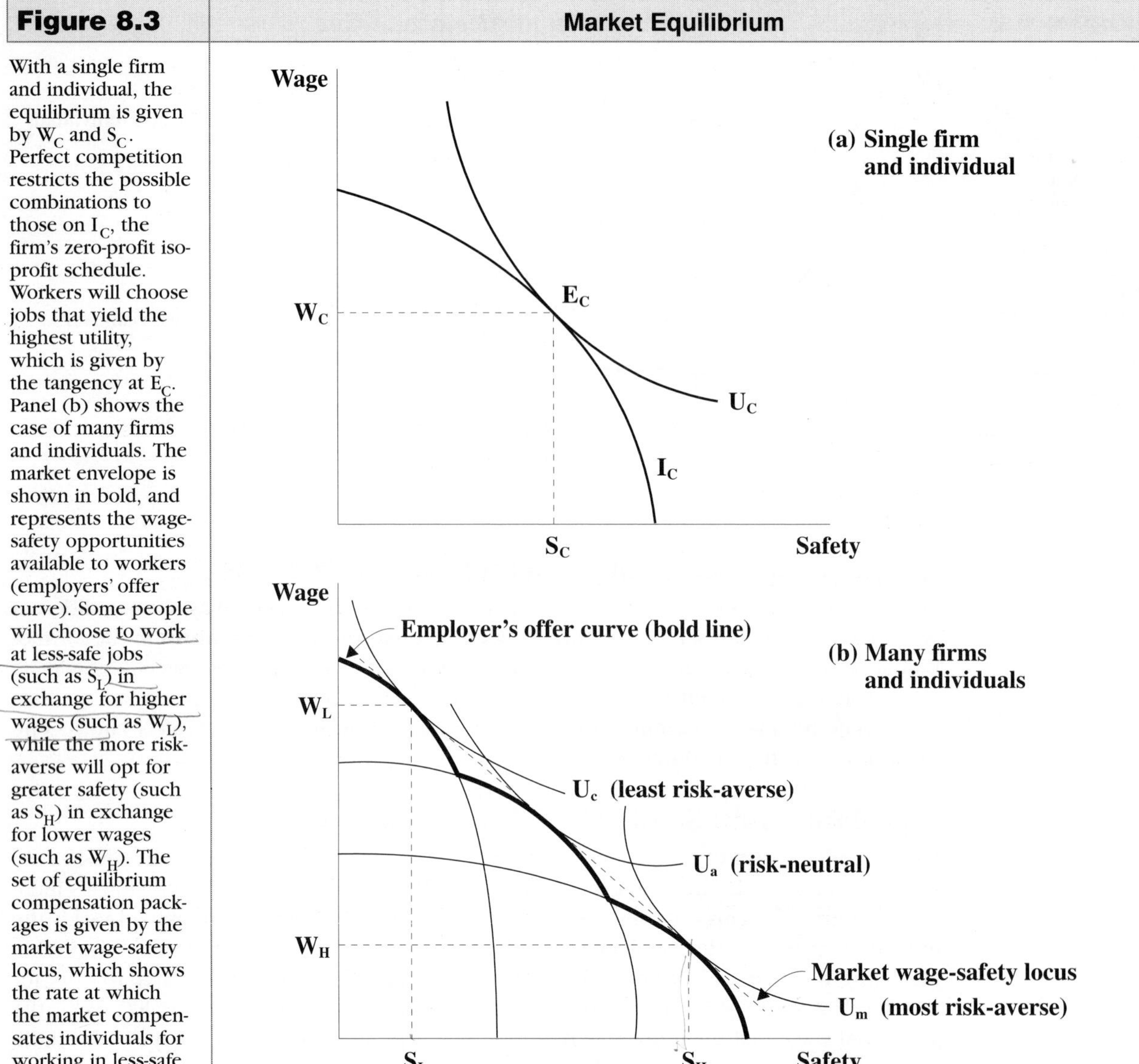

Equilibrium with Many Firms and Individuals

Figure 8.3(b) illustrates the market equilibrium that will prevail when there are many firms and individuals. Assuming perfect competition, individuals will sort themselves into firms (occupations, industries) of different risks (i.e., along the market envelope schedule) and receive differing compensating wages for the different levels of risk. The least risk-averse individual, for example, will enter a high-risk firm in order to get the higher wage, W_L, associated with the low level of safety, S_L. Conversely, the most risk-averse individual will enter the low-risk work environment and accept the lower wage, W_H, in order to have the safe work environment, S_H.

The set of tangencies between the various isoprofit and indifference schedules gives the various equilibrium combinations of wages and safety that will prevail in the market. This is termed the **wage-safety locus** (dashed line in Figure 8.3(b)). The *slope* of that locus of wage-safety combinations gives the change in the wage premium that the market yields for *differences* in the risk of the job. The slope of that line can change for different levels of safety. It is determined by the interaction of workers' preferences and the firms' technology for safety, and these basic underlying determinants may change with the level of safety. The only restriction on the slope of the line is that it be negative, reflecting the fact that compensating wages are required for reductions in safety, given worker aversion to risk and the fact that safety is costly to firms.

The fact that the slope of the wage-safety locus can change magnitude but not direction means, for example, that the compensating wage premium required for *additional* risk may be very high in an already risky environment. Whether that is true, however, is an empirical proposition since it depends upon whether there are sufficient workers willing to take that risk in return for the higher wage, and whether firms could reduce the risk in ways that are less costly than paying a wage premium for workers to accept the risk.

In such circumstances of perfect information and competition (assumptions that will be relaxed later), the market will pay a compensating wage premium for undesirable working conditions, such as risk. This will induce workers to sort themselves into jobs depending upon their aversion to risk. It will also induce employers to adopt the most cost-effective safety standards (not necessarily the safest) since they can save on compensating wages by increasing their safety. In this fashion the need of employers to carry on production in a manner that may involve some risk is required to confront the equally compelling need of workers for desirable working conditions, and vice versa. The price that mediates these competing objectives is the compensating wage paid for the undesirable working conditions. Such prices are often termed **shadow** or **implicit prices** because they are embedded in the market wage rather than being attached explicitly to a job characteristic.

Obviously, the markets for each and every characteristic are likely to be "thin" (i.e., involve few buyers and sellers). For example, a worker who wants (and is willing to pay for) a job that is reasonably safe, close to home, and that allows flexible working hours, may not have a large set of jobs to choose from. Of course, if enough workers want those characteristics, then employers will find it is in their interest to provide them, because of the lower wages they can pay in return for providing the desired work characteristics. Nevertheless, it is easy to see that there may not be a large number of buyers and sellers for each and every characteristic, and hence the shadow price yielded by the market for each characteristic may not be the same as the competitive price that would prevail if there were many buyers and sellers for *each* characteristic.

Alternative Portrayal

The previous analysis was portrayed in terms of conventional indifference curve analysis with wages and safety—both of which are valued by employees—displayed on the axes. Following the insurance literature, the analysis is often portrayed in wage-*risk* space with risk portrayed on the horizontal axis. Since risk is negatively valued by employees, this will obviously alter the portrayal; nevertheless, the same conclusions follow.

In Figure 8.4 the upward-sloping isoprofit schedules illustrate how firms can pay higher wages and maintain profits if risk can be increased because reductions in risk (increases in safety) are costly. The curvature of the isoprofit schedules exhibits diminishing returns; that is, as risk is reduced to very low levels in a firm it becomes extremely costly to reduce risk further and hence a larger wage reduction is necessary to maintain profits. The employers' offer schedule (bold line) indicates the maximum compensating wage that will be offered in the market for each level of risk. Points on employers' isoprofit schedules below that line will be dominated by points on the offer curve. Higher offer schedules yield lower profits, since firms have to pay a higher compensating wage for every level of risk.

Worker indifference curves slope up because workers require a higher compensating

Figure 8.4 **Wage-Risk Space Portrayal**

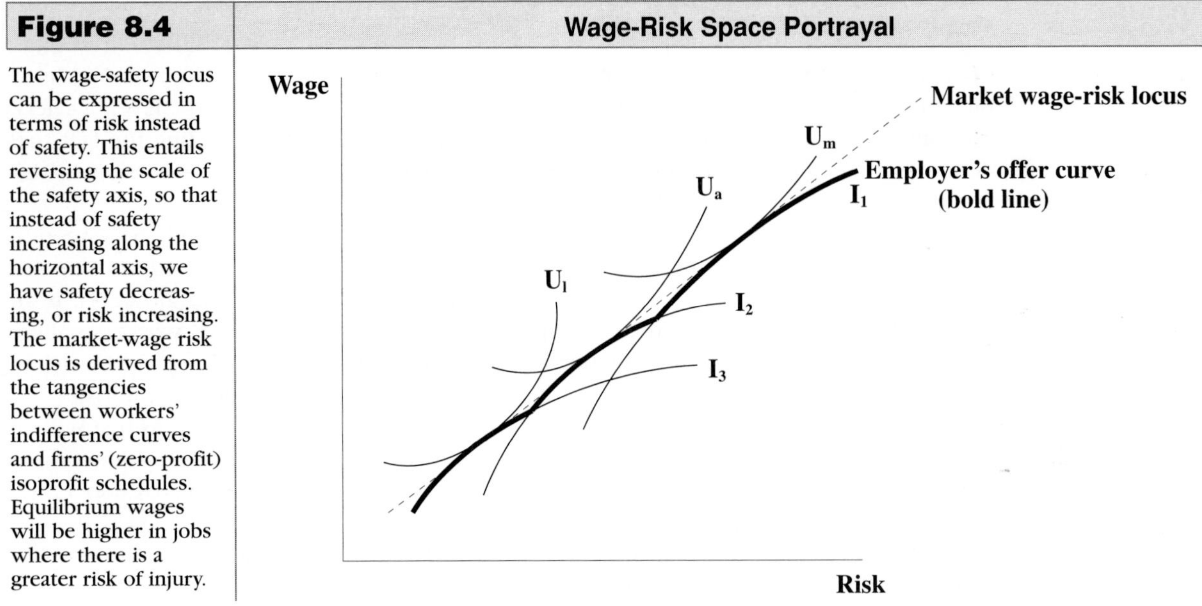

The wage-safety locus can be expressed in terms of risk instead of safety. This entails reversing the scale of the safety axis, so that instead of safety increasing along the horizontal axis, we have safety decreasing, or risk increasing. The market-wage risk locus is derived from the tangencies between workers' indifference curves and firms' (zero-profit) isoprofit schedules. Equilibrium wages will be higher in jobs where there is a greater risk of injury.

wage to remain indifferent to the additional risk. Their curvature illustrates a diminishing marginal rate of substitution between wages and risk; that is, for a given individual to accept more risk and remain indifferent, an ever-increasing compensating wage is required to compensate for the increasing risk. Different individuals have different aversions to risk, as illustrated by the different indifference curves. As depicted at the intersection of the indifference curve for the most risk-averse (U_m) versus the least risk-averse (U_l) individual, the risk-averse individual requires a higher compensating wage to accept additional risk.

Individuals will sort themselves out into different firms (occupations, industries) on the basis of their willingness to accept risk in return for a compensating wage. The locus of tangencies between worker indifference curves and the employers' offer schedule will trace out the market wage-risk locus illustrating the varying wage premium the market will yield for different levels of risk. The market wage-risk locus can be of any configuration, except that it slopes upward, indicating the assumptions that workers require a compensating wage for additional risk and that reductions in risk are costly for employers.

EFFECT OF SAFETY REGULATION

Perfectly Competitive Markets

The effect of safety regulation depends critically upon whether markets are operating properly or not to compensate workers for occupational risk. In markets that are operating perfectly the effect of regulation may be perverse. This is illustrated in Figure 8.5(a). For a single representative firm and individual, the competitive equilibrium is given at E_c, with the wage, W_c, being paid for the level of safety, S_c. In the absence of any external effects on third parties for which the market does not extract appropriate compensation, the level of safety, S_c, can be considered socially optimal in the sense that the price mechanism, through compensating wages, ensures that neither employers nor employees want to move from the level of safety, S_c. By moving from S_c neither party can be made sufficiently better off to compensate the other party so that they are no worse off.

A regulatory agency that required the parties to increase the level of safety to S_r would

Figure 8.5 **Responses to Safety Standard**

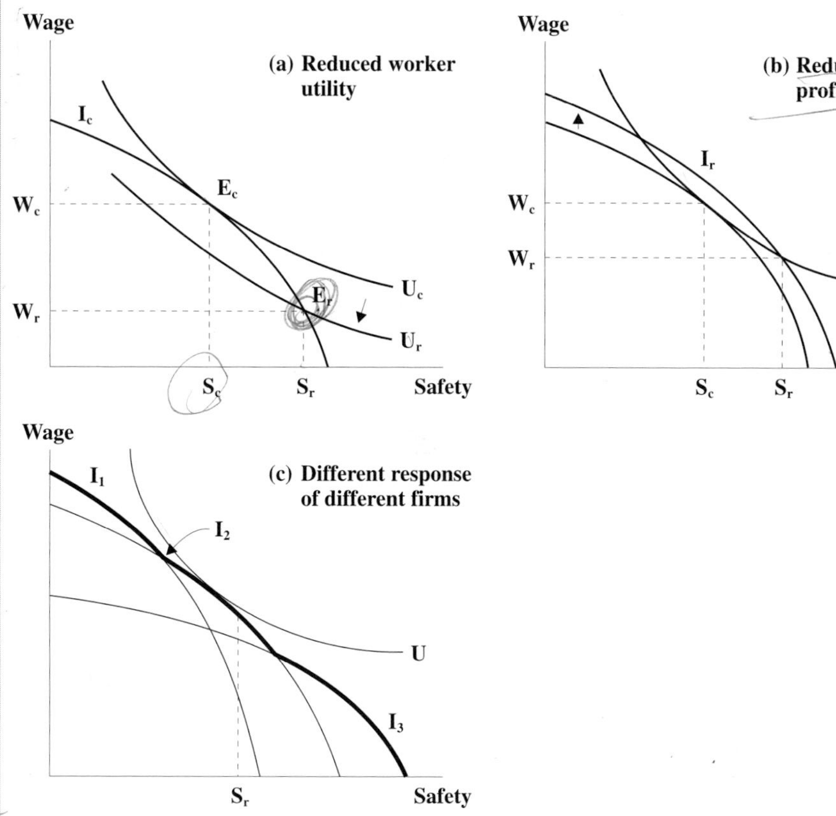

In a competitive market, a legislated increase in safety will make people worse off. In panel (a) the optimal safety level is S_C. At a regulated level of S_r, the zero-profit constraint means that the firm can only provide this at the lower wage W_r. The worker is worse off, as the regulated combination, E_r, lies on a lower indifference curve, U_r. In panel (b), the worker's utility is maintained at U_C, but the firm's profits are reduced to I_r. If profits are negative, the firm will go out of business. Panel (c) extends the argument to several firms. The impact of the regulation will depend on the firm's technology, and some firms (such as firm 1) will go out of business.

actually make one or both parties worse off, in this particular situation of perfectly competitive markets. This is illustrated in Figure 8.5(a), where the firm remains on its isoprofit schedule (it has to if this is the competitive level of zero excess profits) and the individual worker is on a lower level of utility U_r, with compensating wage W_r. The worker's level of utility under regulation is lower (i.e., $U_r < U_c$), because the worker is not voluntarily willing to accept the wage reduction from W_c to W_r in return for the safety increase from S_c to S_r; if given the choice the worker would return to E_c. In this particular example, the firm was no worse off after the regulation (i.e., on the same isoprofit schedule) but the worker was worse off (i.e., on a lower indifference curve). If the firm originally had excess profits it could absorb the cost increase associated with the safety regulation and not go out of business. In such circumstances the worker need not be worse off after the regulation. This is depicted in Figure 8.5(b), where the firm moves to a higher isoprofit schedule, I_r, (with lower profits because it is experiencing both higher wage and safety costs) and the worker stays on the same indifference curve. The worker still receives a reduction in the compensating wage from W_c to W_r, but this is exactly offset by the increase in safety, so that utility remains constant at U_c. In this case, the firm bears the cost of the safety regulation by taking lower profits.

Realistically, the cost of the safety regulation will likely be borne by both workers in the form of compensating wage reductions and firms in the form of lower profits, their respective shares depending upon their relative bargaining powers.

Not all firms will be affected in the same fashion. For some, the safety regulation may be redundant since they are already meeting the standard. Others may be put out of business, unless their work force accepts wage concessions. This is illustrated in Figure 8.5(c) for three firms that are assumed to be operating under a competitive profit constraint so that excess profits are zero (i.e., $I_1 = I_2 = I_3 = 0$). For firm 3, a uniform safety standard of S_r would be redundant since it is already providing a safer work environment than required by the standard; that is, the relevant portion of its isoprofit curve making up part of the market wage envelope always lies to the right of S_r. Firm 2 could meet the standard and stay in business only if its work force were willing to provide wage concessions (and hence receive a lower level of utility) for the firm to stay on its zero profit isoprofit schedule. (For simplicity only the indifference curve for a representative worker of firm 2 is shown.) firm 1 would go out of business because its isoprofit schedule is below that of firm 2 in the relevant region of the safety standard S_r; that is, for the minimal level of safety, S_r, firm 2 could offer a higher compensating wage than firm 1 and still stay in business. Workers in firm 1 would go to firm 2 if the standard were improved, even though they would prefer to be in firm 1 with no standard. This competitive analysis, of course, assumes that firm 2 can absorb the workers, with no adverse general equilibrium effects.

While this analysis suggests that the application of a uniform safety standard has the desirable effect of weeding out firms whose safety technology is such that they cannot meet the standard, it must be remembered that they were able to pay a sufficiently high wage to attract certain workers who were willing to accept the inherent risk. By imposing a uniform standard, the regulators are saying that firms that cannot meet the standard will not be able to operate no matter how much they are able to pay to have workers willingly accept the risk.

Imperfect Information

The previous analysis assumed perfect information about the level of safety involved. Such an assumption, however, may be unrealistic in situations where employers may have a vested interest in not disclosing information about health hazards, and where the latency period before an occupational disease shows up can be very long. In such circumstances, workers may think that they have a higher level of safety, and hence, utility, for the compensating wage they receive.

This situation of **imperfect information** is depicted in Figure 8.6. For a given compensating wage, W_a, associated with an actual level of safety, S_a, workers may perceive their level of safety to be greater at S_p. Their (mis)perceived level of utility would be U_p, while their actual level would be U_a. In such circumstances, any imposed safety standard between S_a and S_r could improve workers' utility without making employers worse off since they would be on the same or a lower isoprofit schedule (lower schedules representing higher profits). The optimal standard would be at the point of tangency, E_o, between the employer's isoprofit schedule and the employee's highest attainable indifference curve.

Providing the parties with the correct information would also lead to the optimal amount of safety because workers would increase their utility by moving to offers in the range of the offer curve between S_a and S_r. Ultimately, they would arrive at E_o, accepting the wage reduction from W_a to W_o in return for the increase in safety from S_a to S_o. With full information, market forces can also lead to the optimal amount of safety.

Rationale for Regulation

www.ccohs.ca

If a perfectly competitive market with proper information can lead to the socially optimal amount of safety at the workplace, why does regulation persist, especially since it runs the risk of making both employers and employees worse off? While no easy answer to this

Figure 8.6 **Effect of Imperfect Information**

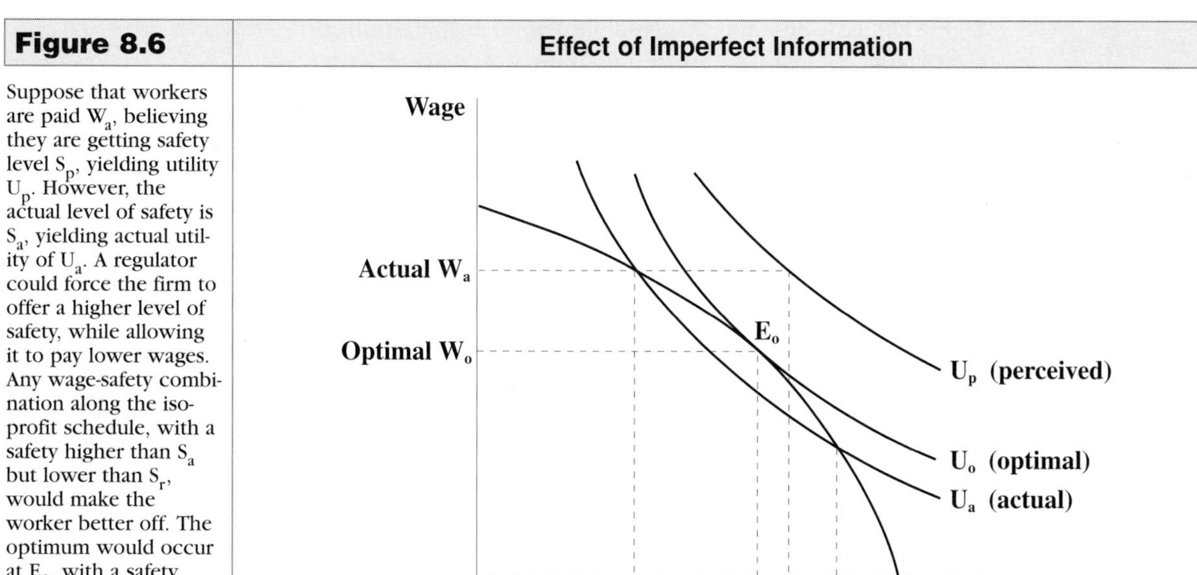

Suppose that workers are paid W_a, believing they are getting safety level S_p, yielding utility U_p. However, the actual level of safety is S_a, yielding actual utility of U_a. A regulator could force the firm to offer a higher level of safety, while allowing it to pay lower wages. Any wage-safety combination along the isoprofit schedule, with a safety higher than S_a but lower than S_r, would make the worker better off. The optimum would occur at E_0, with a safety level S_0 and wage W_0.

question exists, a number of plausible explanations can be given, in addition to the possibility that it may simply be a well-meaning mistake. First, information is not perfect and may be hidden by employers or improperly discounted by workers. Second, competition may not prevail for the buying and selling of each and every job characteristic, including safety in the work environment. Workers simply may not have much choice in the risk of their work. Third, workers who opt for risk in return for a high wage may not pay the full cost of their decisions to the extent that the state bears some of the medical or workers' compensation costs if the risk comes to fruition. Fourth, society may feel that workers ought not to have to sell their health and safety to make a living, even if they are willing to do so. If regulating safety means a lower compensating wage, then it may be best to try to take care of that problem through other income-maintenance schemes. Fifth, the willingness of workers to accept some risk in return for a compensating wage premium may be dictated by the existing amount of risk to which they are currently exposed. If that risk is reduced by law for everyone, they may actually prefer the new level of risk even though earlier they were unwilling to accept the wage reduction to achieve the reduced risk. Although economists tend to regard preferences as given, preferences in fact may be influenced by our existing state. Lastly, there may be the feeling that the market simply may not yield the compensating wages necessary to ensure the socially optimal amount of safety.

EMPIRICAL EVIDENCE ON COMPENSATING WAGES

Obtaining empirical evidence on the existence of compensating wages for undesirable working conditions is difficult because of the problem of controlling the myriad positive and negative job characteristics in order to isolate the separate effect of one characteristic. This is compounded by the fact that situations of strong employee bargaining power often have high wages, good fringe benefits, and good working conditions. While there could still be a tradeoff between wages and a better work environment, there is often insufficient variation in the data to identify the tradeoff with any degree of precision. In some cases it may be direct and explicit. For example, collective agreements or company pay policies may specify a premium for underground as opposed to aboveground mining, or for the night shift as opposed to the day shift. Premiums for an isolation allowance or even hazard pay may be explicitly mentioned with the explicit price stated.

In other circumstances, however, the compensating pay premium is not explicitly given but rather is embedded as part of an individual's wage rate and hence is a shadow price associated with the job characteristic. It can be estimated only by comparing wages in jobs that are similar except for the one characteristic. Given that jobs involve a multiplicity of characteristics, this is not an easy task and usually requires fairly sophisticated statistical procedures.

The most extensive literature in this area pertains to compensating wages for the risk of injury or death on the job. These studies have been plagued by a number of econometric problems that are typical of statistical work in economics, and illustrate the general problems involved with estimating compensating differentials.

For example, in addition to higher wages being paid to compensate for undesirable working conditions, cause and effect may work the other way as undesirable working conditions may result from lower wages—that is, low-wage individuals cannot afford to buy a safe work environment and the forgone income from an accident is less to them. These income and substitution effects, respectively, cause them to buy less occupational health and safety. Failure to account for such reverse causality can lead to a simultaneous equation bias in the estimates of compensating wages for work hazards. Simultaneous equation techniques to account for the two-way causality have been employed in a few studies.

Errors-in-variables problems may also exist, especially in those studies that relate an *individual's* wage to an *aggregate* measure of risk such as the injury rate in the person's industry or occupation. Such aggregate measures of risk are likely to be subject to considerable random error as a proxy for the risk that an individual will face in that occupation. Econometrically, it can be shown that this will lead to an underestimation of the compensating wage paid for risk.

Omitted variable bias may also exist to the extent that crucial variables that affect wages and that are also correlated with risk are not controlled for in the measurement of the wage-risk tradeoff. For example, bargaining power of workers (as represented by unionization) may lead to high wages and low risk. Failure to control for this factor may mean that there appears to be little or no wage premium paid for the risk. In reality, the low wages in risky jobs may reflect the fact that workers with little bargaining power end up in jobs of low wages and high risk. The low wages in risky jobs may reflect the disproportionate absence of bargaining power of workers in those jobs, not the absence of a wage premium for risk. One method to control for such difficult-to-measure variables as preferences or an individual's bargaining power is to use longitudinal or panel data that follows the same individual over time so that such factors can be assumed to be relatively constant or fixed over time. (For example, Brown 1980; see also Hwang, Reed, and Hubbard, 1992 for an alternative approach to this problem.) **Sample selection bias** problems may also prevail to the extent that wage-risk premiums are estimated on a subsample of risky jobs, perhaps because actuarial data is available only on risky occupations (e.g., Thaler and Rosen, 1975). In such circumstances, the risk premiums obtained from the subsample of risk-taking individuals may not give an accurate estimate of the compensating wage paid for a random worker.

More generally, account needs to be taken of the process via which individuals choose jobs, occupations, and careers. Specifically, those individuals who have the least aversion to an undesirable job characteristic (e.g., repetitive work) are, other things equal, the most likely to choose jobs with that characteristic. Thus the compensating wage needed to attract *additional* workers into an occupation may be higher than was needed to attract those already in the occupation. Recent research has tried to take into account this simultaneous determination of job risks and occupational choices (Garen, 1988; Goddeeris, 1988).

Such econometric problems are typical of the applied econometrics literature; hence, the econometric evidence on compensating wages for occupational risk is likely to be neither more nor less reliable than typical econometric estimates. Reviews of such evidence are contained in Digby and Riddell (1986), Rosen (1986), Jones-Lee (1989), Moore and Viscusi (1990), and Viscusi (1993). The general consensus appears to be that compensating wage premiums are paid for work hazards and they increase with the seriousness of the risk; that is, they are larger for risks of death than for risks of injury and, for risks of injury, they are larger for permanent than for temporary injuries. In fact, for less serious injuries, compensating wage premiums are often found not to exist. A limited amount of evidence also suggests that the compensating wage premiums are reduced when the risk is partly covered by workers' compensation systems, and that compensating wage premiums are larger in union than in nonunion environments.

Canadian empirical evidence is relatively recent and tends to confirm the U.S. findings. The traditional obstacle facing researchers is lack of appropriate data (see Digby and Riddell, 1986). Meng (1989) utilizes a unique dataset and finds evidence of significant compensating differentials for job risks in Canada (see Exhibit 8.1). Cousineau, Lacroix, and Girard (1992) examine a large sample of blue-collar and manual workers in Quebec and also find significant evidence of compensating differentials. Controlling for other worker and job characteristics, they find that the wages are higher for jobs with higher probabilities of injury or death. Martinello and Meng (1992) find a compensating wage premium for the risk of fatal and severe injuries, but not for minor injuries. From their estimates they calculate the benefits to society of safety regulations to be \$11,500 for preventing a time-loss injury, \$136,000 for avoiding a severe time-loss injury, and \$5.2 million for saving a life (in 1986 dollars). Meng and Smith (1990) also confirm that, at least for the risk of fatal injuries, market wages appear to reflect compensating wage differentials.

www.wsib.on.ca

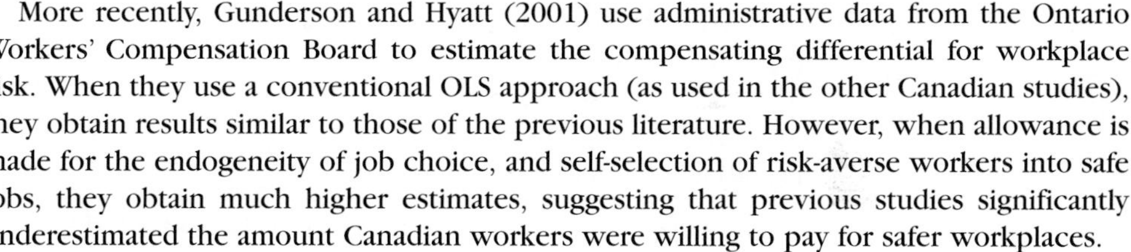

More recently, Gunderson and Hyatt (2001) use administrative data from the Ontario Workers' Compensation Board to estimate the compensating differential for workplace risk. When they use a conventional OLS approach (as used in the other Canadian studies), they obtain results similar to those of the previous literature. However, when allowance is made for the endogeneity of job choice, and self-selection of risk-averse workers into safe jobs, they obtain much higher estimates, suggesting that previous studies significantly underestimated the amount Canadian workers were willing to pay for safer workplaces.

A number of other studies have investigated the presence of compensating differentials associated with other elements of Smith's first factor affecting relative wages ("the agreeableness or disagreeableness of the employments themselves"). Such studies have estimated compensating wages for undesirable job characteristics such as the uncertainty of pension receipts (Smith, 1981; Schiller and Weiss, 1980), the mandatory requirement to work overtime (Ehrenberg and Schumann, 1984), commuting time (Leigh, 1986), shift work (Kostiuk, 1990), retirement characteristics (Ehrenberg, 1980), low pension benefits (Gunderson, Hyatt, and Pesando, 1992), and the willingness of employers to accommodate the return of injured workers (Gunderson and Hyatt,1996). To date, no one has challenged Smith's conjecture that "the most detestable of all employments, that of public executioner, is, in proportion to the quantity of work done, better paid than any common trade whatever" (Smith, p. 100).

Several papers, however, have addressed Smith's conjectured third factor, "the constancy or inconstancy of employment." Smith suggested that individuals would have to be compensated for bearing the risk of unemployment. Describing the seasonal nature of work for a mason or bricklayer, Smith notes that "his employment at all other times depends upon the occasional calls of his customers. He is liable, in consequence to be without any [employment]. What he earns, therefore, while he is employed, must not only maintain him while he is idle, but make him some compensation for those anxious and desponding moments which the thought of so precarious a situation must sometimes occasion" (Smith, p. 103).

Most empirical researchers find evidence of compensating differentials for the risk of

Exhibit 8.1

The Value of Safety in Canadian Industry

What is the value of an increase in safety in the workplace? Because compensating wage differentials associated with workplace risks are implicit prices associated with these negative job characteristics, this question can be addressed by empirical analysis, which estimates these implicit prices. The typical approach is to estimate a regression of individual earnings as a function of the job characteristics, controlling for other influences on earnings (such as education, age, union status, tenure on the current job, and other influences). One bottleneck in the production of such studies is the paucity of data on job characteristics (working conditions), especially detailed enough occupational information to accurately match the riskiness of the job from workplace fatality and injury databases. Meng (1989) uses a unique data source to obtain estimates of compensating differentials associated with several negative job characteristics in Canada. Meng estimated the effect of the following characteristics:

1. Risk of fatal injury on the job (measured as deaths per 1000 workers; sample average 0.19 deaths per thousand workers per year); these risks are computed on an occupational basis and matched to the individual earnings data
2. Non-fatal job characteristics:
   (a) Work under stressful conditions
   (b) Work with machines
   (c) Duties constantly repeated
   (d) Job requires physical exertion
   (e) Ability to control work hours

These negative job characteristics would be expected to be positively associated with wages, compensating workers for the unpleasant conditions. Meng finds that there is a significant positive wage differential associated with the riskiness of the occupation. This estimate is the implicit price associated with the riskiness of the occupation, or the slope of the market wage-risk locus (see Figure 8.4). The estimates indicate that, on average, a typical worker must be paid $2712 (in 1981 dollars, or $5224 in 2000 dollars) more per year to assume an additional 0.001 probability of fatality on the job. In other words, a firm with 1000 workers would save $2,712,000 in annual wage costs ($5,224,000 in 2000 dollars) if it were able to reduce the risk of an occupation-related fatality by a probability of 1 in 1000. Alternatively, a group of 1000 workers would be willing to pay $2,712,000 to reduce the risk of death by one person (among them) per year.

Such estimates are often taken as a way of estimating the value placed on human life, since they use market-based transactions as an indicator of the income people reveal that they are willing to forgo to save a life.

Meng finds no evidence that the other, non-fatal job characteristics had any effect on wages. This result is similar to that found in several studies using U.S. or U.K. data—evidently, only the most adverse working conditions exert effects on earnings which are substantial enough to be measured in the (admittedly imperfect) data available to researchers.

unemployment. This is usually accomplished by investigating the statistical significance of a measure of predicted or anticipated unemployment in a wage regression. Important work in this area is outlined in Ashenfelter and Abowd (1981), Murphy and Topel (1987), Adams (1985), and Li (1986). One complication addressed by these researchers, and Topel (1984), is that we do not observe a pure "market" outcome for the determination of wages and unemployment risk, because of the public provision of unemployment insurance. The existence of alternative forms of insurance reduces the need for wages to accomplish this on their own, and perhaps explains the small differentials found by some researchers. Topel (1984), for example, finds that the compensating differential is much larger once full account is taken of unemployment insurance.

POLICY IMPLICATIONS

A number of policy implications associated with compensating wage differences for undesirable job characteristics have already been discussed. In particular, competitive markets can yield the optimal amount of these characteristics, with compensating wages being the price that equilibrates markets. This ensures that the need of employers to carry on production in a manner that may involve undesirable working conditions is required to confront the need of workers for desirable conditions, and vice versa. This also implies, for

Exhibit 8.2

Inequality of Workplace Amenities

One of the most important—and most studied—features of the U.S labour market is the dramatic increase in wage and earnings inequality beginning in the 1970s, extending into the 1990s. For example, the ratio of the full-time weekly wages of the 90th to the 10th percentile of workers was 3.56 in 1979, rising to 4.66 in 1995 (based on Katz and Autor, 1999, Table 1). As we saw in Chapter 6, wages are only one component of compensation: once due account is taken of nonwage (financial or pecuniary) benefits, total financial compensation inequality increased even more than wage inequality (Farber and Levy, 2000). But what about other aspects of job quality? Was there a potentially offsetting reduction in the inequality of workplace amenities? For example, if there was an across-the-board improvement in workplace safety that workers implicitly value financially, the increase in wage inequality would overstate the increase in total compensation (financial and non-financial) with due allowance for non-pecuniary benefits.

Hamermesh (1999) investigates this question, by exploring changes in the distribution of workplace injuries across industries. Were relative decreases in wages in low-wage industries offset by relative improvements worker safety? Apparently not. If commonly accepted dollar values are attached to workplace safety, overall compensation inequality increased even more than wage inequality! Hamermesh shows that this pattern also happened in the 1960s, when wage inequality was falling. In that time period, relative wage improvements in lower-paying jobs were accompanied by relative improvements in workplace safety. Furthermore, his results extend beyond workplace safety to other amenities. During the 1980s and 1990s, high-wage workers saw relative improvements in their discretion over work hours: evening and shift work was increasingly concentrated among low-wage workers. It appears that when "the rich get richer," they implicitly spend a disproportionate share of their higher wages on improvements in working conditions.

Exhibit 8.3 Who Needs Unemployment Insurance?

Historical data often provide unique opportunities for investigating "pure" market relationships because government intervention was a less important feature of the economy in many historical contexts. In contemporary economies, the existence of government-provided unemployment insurance may reduce or eliminate the need for workers to "purchase" this insurance through lower wages. This is one explanation offered for the weak relationship between wages and the risk of unemployment.

Hatton and Williamson (1991) do not have to contend with UI in their analysis of compensating wage differentials for unskilled labourers from Michigan in the 1890s. In this "purer" market setting, they find very strong evidence that wages were higher for individuals in occupations facing a greater risk of unemployment. Regressions of wages as a function of individual and job characteristics, and the predicted probability or duration of unemployment, were estimated on large samples of contracts for unskilled farm labourers, building trades labourers, and railway workers. For unskilled farm labourers, who faced considerable seasonal and general agricultural risk, the implied compensation for the risk of unemployment was enough to more than offset (on average) the actual lost earnings due to unemployment. Workers in the other trades were not compensated to this degree, though both trades saw significant compensation for workers taking jobs where the risk of unemployment was higher.

Hatton and Williamson further explore the means by which workers coped with unemployment. In addition to having higher average wages, workers relied on their own savings to see them through such periods of potential hardship. Neither other family members, supplementary self-employment, nor generalized poor relief were important sources of relief during unemployment spells. So were market wage premiums and individual thrift enough to fully insure workers against the risk of unemployment? Most workers surveyed at the time indicated that lost earnings due to unemployment significantly reduced their family's ability to purchase necessities.

It would thus appear that while UI may confound economists' attempts to estimate compensating wage differentials, it may yet serve a socially useful role!

example, that the optimal amount of safety is not zero; people are seldom willing to pay the price of attaining that otherwise desirable state.

In such competitive markets, regulations setting a uniform standard, such as a health and safety standard, run the risk of making the parties worse off, largely because compensating wages will adjust in a fashion that workers themselves would not have accepted for the improved working conditions. If there is imperfect information, or markets fail for other reasons, then regulation can make workers better off.

To the extent that wage premiums fully compensate workers for the expected risk of a job, then compensating them if the risk comes to fruition can involve double compensation. Of course, once this is anticipated by the parties, then the compensating wage premium itself will fall, and be paid only for the uncompensated risk. Thus, the compensating wage paid for the risk of injury or of being unemployed will be smaller, respectively, in situations of workers' compensation and unemployment insurance.

Empirical estimates of the compensating wage paid for the risk of death have been used to provide estimates of the **value of life**. This phrase is somewhat of a misnomer since the estimates really reflect what people are willing to pay (as revealed through the market) to reduce the risk of death by a certain percentage. This is then extrapolated to arrive at the total price they would be willing to pay to reduce the risk of death to zero. These values are arrived at through impersonal transactions as people reveal how much in wages they are willing to give up to reduce their risk of death. These are not the values that people would attach to the *certainty* of saving a *specific* life, a value that would likely be incalculable.

For policy purposes such estimates have been used to compensate victims, or their survivors, for the loss of life or limb. They have also been used in decisions on how many resources to devote to lifesaving activities or on the appropriate safety standards to set in industry. Rightly or wrongly, economics with its emphasis on tradeoffs enters into many socially sensitive issues.

The notion that a job involves a set of positive and negative characteristics, each with its own implicit price, also has important implications for the analysis of wage differentials by such factors as occupation, industry, or region. As shown subsequently, the wage that is associated with each of these factors can have a component that reflects the compensating wage premiums paid for certain undesirable characteristics associated with each occupation, industry, or region. This will be important for understanding the existence and persistence of interoccupation, interindustry, and interregional wage structures.

Summary

- While the discussion of Chapters 1 to 7 emphasized that everyone in the "labour market" is paid the same wage, wages clearly vary across individuals. This chapter develops the tools to show why wages can be expected to differ across individuals—even if everyone is equally productive—when the labour market comprises sub-markets that are integrated into a single, more broadly defined, but integrated "labour market."
- Wages will be higher for some individuals in order to compensate them for doing unpleasant jobs (or incurring additional costs of employment), while others will willingly accept lower pay for jobs with more amenities.
- The model of compensating wage differentials can be applied to any job characteristic, but the most common application is workplace safety. Firms can choose their production technology to offer workers greater safety, or they can economize on safety and offer the savings to workers in the form of higher wages. For any firm, there will generally be a tradeoff in offering more safety or higher wages, holding constant the level of profits. In the broader labour market, however, the competition between firms for workers will imply that for any level of safety, the technologically highest possible wage will be offered, while firms earn zero economic profits. The resulting "menu" of wage-safety combinations is called the employers' offer curve.
- Workers have preferences over combinations of wages and workplace safety. Obviously, they would like more of both, but at any level of utility workers are willing to accept some additional risk in exchange for higher wages. Not all workers have the same attitudes toward workplace risk, and will put different values on workplace safety. Workers will sort across firms according to their relative tastes for wages or safety. Those who are least tolerant of risk will choose to work for those firms offering more safety, at the price of lower wages, while those who are less concerned about safety will work at the riskier, but higher-paying jobs.
- In comparing wages across jobs with different levels of safety, the resulting equilibrium choices of workers and firms will yield a "market wage-safety locus." Given that most workers value safety (i.e., on the margin are willing to buy some additional safety in the form of lower wages at *some* price), and that safety is costly for firms to supply, we

expect that the wage-safety locus will show a negative relationship between wages and safety, that is, that wages will be lower for safer jobs *all else equal*.

- Empirical analysis of compensating wage differentials attempts to estimate the extent to which wage differentials across individuals reflect differences in workplace amenities, such as job safety. However, it is difficult to hold everything—such as productivity—constant when doing this analysis, and typically we observe higher-paid individuals also having more job amenities. Nevertheless, most carefully executed studies find that wages are indeed higher (on average) for individuals with more dangerous or unpleasant jobs.
- Primarily as a byproduct of the underlying assumptions of perfect competition and perfect information (workers choose the optimal amount of safety given technological constraints), the theory of compensating differentials can be used to show that government regulation of workplace safety will make workers worse off. However, if the government is more informed about workplace risks than workers, it is possible that government regulation of safety can improve the welfare of workers.

REVIEW QUESTIONS

1. Assume that a firm has predetermined sales revenue of $100, which it produces with one unit of labour. It can produce its output with varying degrees of safety, at a cost of $10 per unit of safety. Its total costs are given by TC = W + 10S, where W is the wage it pays its worker and S is the amount of safety provided.
   (a) Graph the isoprofit schedule for this firm, for level of profits = 0, and profits = 50.
   (b) Assume that there is another firm, with a predetermined level of sales revenue equal to 75. Its total costs are given by TC = W + 5S. Assume that both firms earn zero profits. On a carefully labelled graph, show the "employer's offer curve" for these two firms, analogous to Figure 8.1.
2. A downtown law firm has offered you a summer job sorting and filing papers for 40 hours per week (8:30 a.m. to 5 p.m., with a half-hour hour for lunch), at a wage rate of $15 per hour. Assume that this is your only job. What is the lowest wage rate that you would be willing to accept in order to switch to the following job?
   (a) The same job, but with a "free lunch" at the cafeteria
   (b) The same job, but with extra two paid breaks of a half-hour each per day
   (c) The same job, but with the freedom to work your 40 hours any time of day or night over the course of the week
   (d) A job with the same 8:30–5:00 schedule (with a half-hour for lunch), but working outside for 40 hours a week, picking garbage off the streets
   (e) A job with the same schedule, but as a taste tester at the local brewery
   (f) A job with the same schedule, but as a fashion photographer's assistant for a national men's or women's magazine (take your pick!)
   (g) A job with the same schedule, but working "on the front lines" at a chicken processing plant
3. Referring to Figure 8.3, panel (a), explain why a wage-safety combination with higher safety than S_C, but a lower wage than W_C, will not exist in equilibrium.
4. Is it possible for each individual to have a distaste for working with a particular disamenity (i.e., be willing to accept a lower wage in order to have less of the disamenity), but for there to be no market compensation for working with the disamenity?
5. Explain how improvements in the monitoring of safety in firms will change the benefits or cost of safety regulation in Figure 8.6.
6. Discuss how and why the compensating differential for the risk of death on the job can

be used as the basis for an estimate of the value of human life? Does this seem like a reasonable basis upon which to make such a calculation?

PROBLEMS

1. Suppose there exists a simple economy with two kinds of workers—J (for "jocks") workers who like physical labour, and L (for "lazy") workers who dislike physical labour. Further suppose that in this economy there are two kinds of jobs—O (for "office") jobs which involve little or no physical labour, and F (for "forestry") jobs which involve substantial physical labour. The J workers will work for $6 per hour in the F jobs and $8 per hour or more in the O jobs, while the L workers will work for $6 per hour in the O jobs and $10 per hour or more in the F jobs. Neither group will work for less than $6 per hour. The L workers are indifferent between an F job at $10 per hour and an O job at $6 per hour, while the J workers are indifferent between an F job at $6 per hour and an O job at $8 per hour.
   (a) Draw the supply curve of labour to the two sectors (O and F), assuming that there are 100 of each type of worker.
   (b) Suppose the demand for labour curves (which are derived from the demand for the products of the two sectors) intersect the labour supply curves at L = 150 and L = 50 in the F and O sectors respectively.
      i. What is the equilibrium differential?
      ii. Which workers are earning an economic rent, and what is the amount of the rent earned?
      iii. Which workers are earning no economic rent?
2. A simple economy has two sectors, A and B, both of which use labour as an input in production. A jobs and B jobs are equally desirable from the point of view of workers. Also, all workers have the potential to do either job. However, a training period must precede employment in either job. For simplicity, we will assume that the training is financed by the worker. Each period some workers retire in each sector, and new workers enter the labour force.
   (a) If the training periods for the two jobs are equal in length and cost, what is the equilibrium differential in earnings between the two jobs?
   (b) Assume the conditions given in part (a), and assume further that the labour markets are initially in equilibrium. Then suppose there is an increase in demand for the products of sector A. What will happen in the two labour markets, both immediately and in the long run?
   (c) Suppose job B requires a longer and more expensive training period than job A. Will there be an equilibrium earnings differential between the two jobs?
3. Workers care about only two aspects of their compensation: wages and paid vacations.
   (a) Using carefully labelled diagrams, describe the relationship between wages paid by firms offering longer paid vacations and those offering shorter vacations.
   (b) If you found, in fact, using data from "the real world," that higher-paying jobs also offered longer vacations, would this be evidence against the argument you sketched in part (a)?
   (c) What would happen to the wage structure, if the government forced all firms to offer at least four weeks of paid vacation?
4. After a recent rash of injuries in the Big Choke Coal Mine, members of the Parliamentary Committee in Search of Things to Regulate drafted legislation to increase the level of safety in the mine. Economists hired by the mine countered in the committee hearings that wages at the mine were higher than any other mine, and that by legislating a higher level of safety, the workers would be made worse off.

Outline and evaluate the argument of the economist, describing the conditions under which either the company's economist, or the Parliamentary Committee, have the correct policy recommendation.

5. The current unemployment insurance program, Employment Insurance, offers special benefits to fishers. Because it is seasonal in nature, and fishing regions often have few alternative employment opportunities, fishers usually find themselves unemployed outside of fishing season. They can claim EI benefits for the off-season. Some policymakers have mused openly about eliminating EI benefits for seasonal workers, like fishers.

   "Given the returns to fishing, if EI benefits were eliminated, no one would be able to remain in fishing, and a culturally important way of life would be destroyed." Critically evaluate this statement.

6. A labour economist estimates the following regression relating annual earnings to the risk of on-the-job death in the worker's industry:

$$EARNINGS_i = \alpha + \beta RISK_i + \varepsilon_i$$

   where $RISK_i$ is the annual death rate per 10,000 workers. She obtains a statistically significant estimate of $\hat{\beta} = -30.03$.

(a) Interpret this coefficient. Is this estimate consistent with the economic theory of compensating differentials? If not, does this mean that the theory is wrong?

(b) In a second attempt, the labour economist adds other control variables to the regression, X_i, such as the worker's age, education, union status, and occupation, and estimates:

$$EARNINGS_i = \alpha + \sum_{j=1}^{K} \gamma_j X_{ji} + \beta RISK_i + u_i$$

   and she obtains an estimate of $\hat{\beta} = 43.10$. Why might she obtain a different result than in part (a)? Interpret the new coefficient, and calculate the implied value of a human life. Explain your answer.

7. The William M. Mercer company <www.wmmercer.com> provides annual estimates of rankings of cities based on an index of their "quality of life," an index based on a variety of city characteristics including cultural and recreational amenities, crime, political stability, and traffic congestion. In 2000, Vancouver was the highest-ranked city in the world (tied with Zurich). Montreal and Toronto also scored well, tying for 19th place. If an economist estimated an earnings regression across the 215 cities as follows:

$$W_i = \alpha + \beta QOLI_i + \varepsilon_i$$

   where W_i is the average earnings in city i, and $QOLI_i$ is the "quality of life" index, she would invariably find that $\hat{\beta} > 0$. Does this mean that the theory of compensating differentials, when applied to city amenities, is wrong? Explain how an economist might be able to test the theory with this type of data.

KEYWORDS

wage differentials 223
wage structures 223
compensating wage differentials 224
isoprofit schedule 225
market envelope curve 226
compensating risk premium 227
wage-safety locus 228
shadow or **implicit prices** 229
imperfect information 232
errors-in-variables problems 234
omitted variables bias 234
sample selection bias 234
value of life 238

REFERENCES

Adams, J. 1985. Permanent differences in unemployment and permanent wage differentials. *QJE* 100 (February):29–56.

Ashenfelter, O., and J. Abowd. 1981. Anticipated unemployment, temporary layoffs, and compensating wage differentials. In *Studies in Labour Markets*, ed. S. Rosen. Chicago: University of Chicago Press.

Brown, C. 1980. Equalizing differences in the labour market. *QJE* 94 (February):113–34.

Cousineau, J. M., R. Lacroix, and A. M. Girard. 1992. Occupational hazard and wage compensating differentials. *R.E. Stats.* 74 (February):166–69.

Digby, C., and W. C. Riddell. 1986. Occupational health and safety in Canada. In *Canadian Labour Relations*, ed. W. C. Riddell. Toronto: University of Toronto Press.

Ehrenberg, R. 1980. Retirement system characteristics and the compensating wage differentials in the public sector. *ILRR* 33 (July):470–84.

Ehrenberg, R., and P. Schumann. 1984. Compensating wage differentials for mandatory overtime. *EI* 22 (October):460–78.

Farber, H. S., and H. Levy. 2000. Recent trends in employer-sponsored health insurance coverage: Are bad jobs getting worse? *Journal of Health Economics* 19 (January):93–119.

Garen, J. 1988. Compensating wage differentials and the endogeneity of job riskiness. *R.E. Stats.* 70 (February):9–16.

Goddeeris, J. H. 1988. Compensating differentials and self-selection: an application to lawyers. *JPE* 96 (April):411–28.

Gunderson, M., and D. Hyatt. 1996. Do injured workers pay for reasonable accommodation? *ILRR* 50 (October):92–104.

______. 2001. Workplace risks and wages: Canadian evidence from alternative models. *CJE* 34 (May):377–95.

Gunderson, M., D. Hyatt, and J. Pesando. 1992. Wage-pension trade-offs in collective arguments. *ILRR* 46 (October):146–60.

Hamermesh, D. S. 1999. Changing inequality in markets for workplace amenities. *QJE* 114 (November):1085–123.

Hatton, T., and J. Williamson. 1991. Unemployment, employment contracts, and compensating wage differentials: Michigan in the 1890's. *JEH* 51 (September):605–32.

Hwang, H.-S., W. R. Reed, and C. Hubbard. 1992. Compensating wage differentials and unobserved productivity. *JPE* 100 (August):835–58.

Jones-Lee, M. 1989. *The Economics of Safety and Physical Risk*. Oxford: Basil Blackwell.

Katz, L. F., and D. Autor. 1999. Changes in the wage structure and earnings inequality. In *Handbook of Labor Economics*, eds. O. Ashenfelter and D. Card. New York and Oxford: Elsevier Science, North Holland.

Kostiuk, P. F. 1990. Compensating differentials for shift work. *JPE* 98 (October):1054–75.

Leigh, J. P. 1986. Are compensating wages paid for time spent commuting. *AER* 18 (November):1203–13.

Li, E. H. 1986. Compensating differentials for cyclical and noncyclical unemployment: The interaction between investors' and employees' risk aversion. *JOLE* 4 (April):277–300.

Martinello, F., and R. Meng. 1992. Workplace risks and the value of hazard avoidance. *CJE* 25 (May):333–45.

Meng, R. 1989. Compensating differentials in the Canadian labour market. *CJE* 22 (May):413–24.

Meng, R., and D. Smith. 1990. The valuation of risk of death in public sector decision making. *CPP* 16 (June):137–44.

Moore, M., and W. K. Viscusi. 1990. *Compensation Mechanisms for Job Risks*. Princeton: Princeton University Press.

Murphy, K., and R. Topel. 1987. Unemployment, risk and earnings. In *Unemployment and Its Structure of Labour Markets*, eds. K. Lang and J. Leonard. Oxford: Basil Blackwell.

Rosen, S. 1986. The theory of equalizing differences. In *Handbook of Labour Economics*, eds. O. Ashenfelter and R. Layard. New York: Elsevier.

Schiller, B., and R. Weiss. 1980. Pensions and wages: A test for equalizing differences. *R.E. Stats.* 62 (November):529–38.

Smith, A. 1776. *The Wealth of Nations*. London: Methuen and Company.

Smith, R. S. 1981. Compensating differentials for pensions and underfunding in the public sector. *R.E. Stats.* 63 (August):463–67.

Thaler, R., and S. Rosen. 1975. The value of saving a life: Evidence from the labor market. In *Household Production and Consumption*, ed. N. Terleckyj. New York: National Bureau of Economic Research.

Topel, R. H. 1984. Equilibrium earnings, turnover, and unemployment: New evidence. *JOLE* 2 (October):500–22.

Viscusi, W. K. 1993. The value of risks to life and health. *JEL* 31 (December):1912–46.

Chapter Nine

Human Capital Theory: Applications to Education and Training

Main Questions

- *Why are more-educated workers generally paid more than less-educated workers? What factors determine the market rate of return to education?*
- *If education is such a worthwhile investment, why doesn't everyone have a Ph.D.?*
- *Are more educated people paid more because of the learning they acquired, or do higher education levels merely indicate these individuals' inherently greater productivity?*
- *What is labour market signalling and screening? How might education serve a role as a signal? If education is used primarily as a screening device, why might the private and social rates of return to education diverge?*
- *Are government-funded training programs worth the money?*

In the chapters on labour supply we emphasized the *quantity* aspects of labour supply, ranging from family formation to labour force participation to hours of work. Labour supply also has a *quality* dimension encompassing human capital elements such as education, training, labour market information, mobility, and health. In addition, in the previous chapter on compensating wages, we indicated that compensating wages may have to be paid to compensate workers for the costly process of acquiring human capital like education or training. The hedonic wage approach developed in that chapter can be applied to costly attributes necessary to do a job, just as it can be applied to negative job attributes like risk.

While the economics of education and health are often the subject matter of separate courses and textbooks, they—along with training, job search, and mobility—have a common theoretical thread: that of human capital theory. This chapter presents the basic elements of human capital theory and applies it mainly to the areas of education and training.

HUMAN CAPITAL THEORY

www.epinet.org

The essence of **human capital theory** is that investments are made in human resources so as to improve their productivity and therefore their earnings. Costs are incurred in the expectation of future benefits: hence the term "investment in human resources." Like all investments, the key question becomes: Is it economically worthwhile? The answer to this question depends on whether or not benefits exceed costs by a sufficient amount. Before dealing with the investment criteria whereby this is established, it is worthwhile to expand on the concepts of costs and benefits as utilized in human capital theory. In this chapter, only the basics are touched upon. A wealth of refinements and precise methodological techniques is contained in the extensive literature on human capital theory and its application.

In calculating the costs of human capital, it is important to recognize not only direct costs, such as books or tuition fees in acquiring university education, but also the **opportunity cost** or income forgone while people acquire the human capital. For students in university or workers in lengthy training programs, such costs can be the largest component of the total cost. The evaluation of these opportunity costs can prove difficult because it requires an estimation of what the people would have earned had they not engaged in human capital formation.

In addition, it is important to try to distinguish between the consumption and the investment components of human capital formation, since it is only the investment benefits and costs that are relevant for the investment decision. In reality this separation may be difficult or impossible—how does one separate the consumption from the investment benefits of acquiring a university degree? Nevertheless, the distinction must be made qualitatively, if not quantitatively, especially in comparing programs where the consumption and investment components may differ considerably.

A distinction must also be made between private and social costs and benefits. **Private costs and benefits** are those that accrue to the parties making the investment and as such will be considered in their own calculations. **Social costs and benefits** are all those that are accrued by society, including not only private costs and benefits but also any third-party effects or externalities that accrue to parties who are not directly involved in the investment decision. Training disadvantaged workers, for example, may yield an external benefit in the form of reduced crime, and this benefit should be considered by society at large even though it may not enter the calculations of individuals doing the investment.

A further distinction can be made between real costs and benefits as opposed to pecuniary or distributional or transfer costs and benefits. **Real costs** involve the use of real resources, and should be considered whether those resources have a monetary value or not. Pecuniary or **transfer costs** and benefits do not involve the use of real resources, but rather involve a transfer from one group to another: some gain while others lose. While it may be important to note the existence of such transfers for specific groups, it is inappropriate to include them in the calculation of social costs and benefits since, by definition, gains by one party involve losses by another. For example, the savings in unemployment insurance or social assistance payments that may result from a retraining program are worth noting, and for the unemployment insurance fund they may be a private saving, yet from the point of view of society they represent a reduction in a transfer payment, not a newly created real benefit.[1] Similarly, the installation of a retraining facility in a community may raise local prices for construction facilities, and this may be an additional cost for local residents; yet it is a pecuniary cost since it involves a transfer from local residents to those who raised the prices. While such a transfer may involve a loss to local residents, it is not a real resource cost to society as a whole, since it represents a gain for other parties.

From the point of view of the efficient allocation of resources, only real resource costs and benefits matter. Transfers represent offsetting gains and losses. However, from the point of view of distributive equity or fairness, society may choose to value those gains and losses differently. In addition, costs and benefits to different groups may be valued differently in the economic calculus.

Thus, in the calculation of the benefits from a training program, it is conceivable to weigh the benefits more for a poor disadvantaged worker than an advantaged worker. The appropriate weighting scheme obviously poses a problem, but it could be based on the implicit weights involved in other government programs or perhaps in the progressive income tax structure, or it could simply be based on explicit weights that reflect a pure value judgment.

Care must also be exercised in imputing a macroeconomic impact from investment programs. It is often tempting, for example, to multiply the benefits of some program to capture the multiplier effect as the investment sets up further rounds of spending throughout the economy. Or it is tempting to document the employment expansion that may accompany a particular investment program. The error in this reasoning occurs because it ignores the fact that the opportunities forgone, as resources were devoted to this particular investment rather than to some other one, also have a multiplier and employment creation effect. It is true that the multiplier effects may be different in magnitude (e.g., if they involve different leakages into imports), and they may occur in different regions. While these factors may be worthy of note, they do not justify the imputation of a multiplier effect for all human capital investments.

PRIVATE INVESTMENT IN EDUCATION

The main elements of human capital theory can be outlined by considering decisions relating to investment in education. As noted previously, the basic ideas are more than 200 years old:

www.bibliomania.com/NonFiction/Smith/Wealth

> *When any expensive machine is erected, the extraordinary work to be performed by it before it is worn out, it must be expected, will replace the capital laid out upon it, with at least the ordinary profits. A man educated at the expense of much labour and time to any of those employments which require extraordinary dexterity and skill, may be compared to one of those expensive machines. The work which he learns to perform, it must be expected, over and above the usual wages of common labour, will replace to him the whole expense of his education, with at least the ordinary profits of an equally valuable capital. (Smith,* The Wealth of Nations, *p. 101)*

This passage emphasizes a few key points regarding the investment in and returns to education: (1) the increase in wages associated with the acquired skill is a "pure" compensating

[1]This discussion ignores the possible real resource costs involved in operating and financing unemployment insurance or social assistance programs. If savings in unemployment insurance or social assistance payments reduce the real resources required to operate and finance these programs, then a real externality is involved in addition to the transfer externality.

differential, that is, it is not a payment for innate ability, but merely compensation to the individual for making the investment; (2) the costs of education particularly include the opportunity costs of other pursuits, in terms of both time (the wages of common labour) and other investments; and (3) the analytic framework for the individual decision is analogous to the investment in physical capital.

This decision is illustrated in Figure 9.1 which shows alternative income streams associated with different levels of education: incomplete high school (10 years of education at age 16), high school completion (age 18), and university or college degree (age 22). These three outcomes are used for illustration only; in general we may regard "years of education" as a continuous variable, each year being associated with a lifetime income stream. The earnings in each year are measured in present value terms to make them comparable across different time periods.

The shapes of the earnings streams (or "**age-earnings profiles**") reflect two key factors. First, for each profile, earnings increase with age but at a decreasing rate. This concave shape reflects the fact that individuals generally continue to make human capital investments in the form of on-the-job training and work experience once they have entered the labour force. This job experience adds more to their productivity and earnings early in their careers due to diminishing returns to experience. Second, the earnings of individuals with more years of education generally lie above those with fewer years of education. This feature is based on the assumption that education provides skills which increase the individual's productivity and thus earning power in the labour market. Because of the productivity-enhancing effect of work experience, individuals with more education may not begin at a salary higher than those in their age cohort with less education (and therefore more experience). Nonetheless, to the extent that education increases productivity, individuals with the same amount of work experience but more education will earn more, perhaps substantially more.

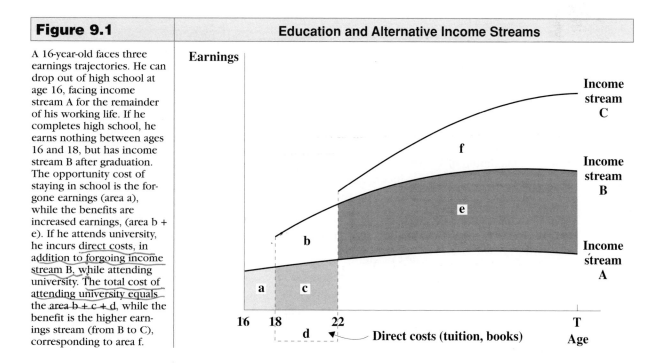

Figure 9.1 **Education and Alternative Income Streams**

A 16-year-old faces three earnings trajectories. He can drop out of high school at age 16, facing income stream A for the remainder of his working life. If he completes high school, he earns nothing between ages 16 and 18, but has income stream B after graduation. The opportunity cost of staying in school is the forgone earnings (area a), while the benefits are increased earnings, (area b + e). If he attends university, he incurs direct costs, in addition to forgoing income stream B, while attending university. The total cost of attending university equals the area b + c + d, while the benefit is the higher earnings stream (from B to C), corresponding to area f.

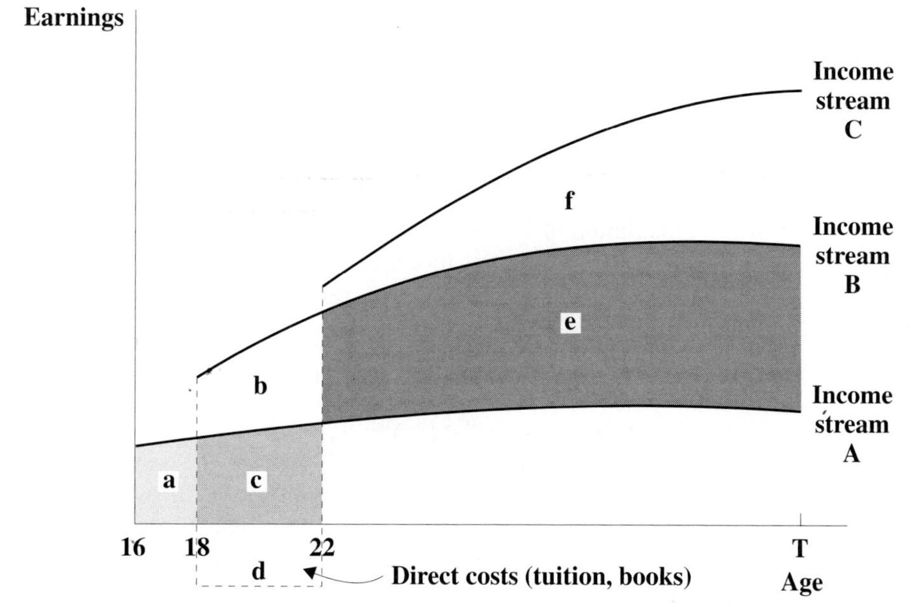

Which lifetime income stream should the individual choose? To address this question we will initially make several simplifying assumptions:

1. The individual does not receive any direct utility or disutility from the educational process.
2. Hours of work (including work in acquiring education) are fixed.
3. The income streams associated with different amounts of education are known with certainty.
4. Individuals can borrow and lend at the real interest rate r.

These assumptions are made to enable us to focus on the salient aspects of the **human capital investment decision**. The first assumption implies that we are examining education purely as an investment, not a consumption, decision. The second assumption implies that the quantity of leisure is the same for each income stream, so that they can be compared in terms of income alone. Assumption three allows us to ignore complications due to risk and uncertainty. The fourth assumption—often referred to as **perfect capital markets**—implies that the individual can base the investment decision on total lifetime income, without being concerned with the timing of income and expenditures. The consequences of relaxing these simplifying assumptions are discussed below.

In these circumstances, the individual will choose the quantity of education that maximizes the net present value of lifetime earnings. Once this choice is made, total net lifetime earnings (or human capital wealth) can be distributed across different periods as desired by borrowing and lending.

As illustrated in Figure 9.1, human capital investment involves both costs and benefits. The costs include both direct expenditures such as tuition and books and opportunity costs in the form of forgone earnings. For example, in completing high school the individual forgoes earnings equal to the area a associated with income stream A between ages 16 and 18. The benefits of completing high school consists of the difference between earnings streams A and B for the remainder of his working life, equal to the areas b + e in Figure 9.1. For a high school graduate contemplating a university education, the additional costs include the direct costs (area d) and forgone earnings equal to area b + c, while additional benefits equal the earnings associated with income stream C rather than B (area f). As Figure 9.1 is drawn, a university education yields the largest net present value of lifetime income. However, for another individual with different opportunities and abilities, and therefore different income streams, one of the other outcomes might be best.

The costs and benefits can be more formally represented in terms of the present value formula introduced in Chapter 4. Consider an 18-year-old high school graduate deciding whether to attend university. She knows that she will work until age T. This means she has a maximum of T - 18 remaining working years. If she forgoes university, she earns income stream B. Denote her income each year, t, along this path from age 18 as Y^H_{18}, Y^H_{19}, Y^H_{20}, ..., Y^H_{T-1}, Y^H_T. The net present value of this sequence of earnings, PV(H), is

$$PV(H) = \frac{Y^H_{18}}{(1+r)^0} + \frac{Y^H_{19}}{(1+r)^1} + \ldots + \frac{Y^H_T}{(1+r)^{T-18}}$$

$$= \sum_{t=0}^{T-18} \frac{Y^H_{t+18}}{(1+r)^t}$$

If she goes to university instead, she will earn nothing for four years, and in fact incur direct costs, D_s, each year she is in university. However, her earnings will be higher when she graduates, corresponding to income stream C. Her sequence of earnings along this path from age 18 is $-D_{18}$, $-D_{19}$, $-D_{20}$, $-D_{21}$, Y^U_{22}, Y^U_{23}, ..., Y^U_T, where we assume that the earnings of someone attending university (Y^U_S) are equal to zero while she attends university (and implicitly, that the direct costs, D_s, are equal to zero after university). The net present value of this stream of earnings, PV(U), is:

$$PV(U) = \frac{-D_{18}}{(1+r)^0} + \frac{-D_{19}}{(1+r)^1} + \ldots + \frac{Y^U_{22}}{(1+r)^4} + \ldots + \frac{Y^U_T}{(1+r)^{T-18}}$$

$$= \sum_{t=0}^{T-18} \frac{Y^U_{t+18} - D_{t+18}}{(1+r)^t}$$

The rational investment decision is to attend university if PV(U) > PV(H).

This decision can be cast in terms of benefits and costs, where costs will include both direct and opportunity costs. The benefit of attending university is the increase in earnings from age 22 (the area f):

$$PV(B) = \sum_{t=4}^{T} \frac{Y^U_{18+t} - Y^C_{18+t}}{(1+r)^t}$$

The cost is the direct cost of university, plus the forgone earnings while attending university (the area b + c + d):

$$PV(C) = \sum_{t=0}^{3} \frac{Y^H_{18+t} + D_{t+18}}{(1+r)^t}$$

So the high school graduate should go to university if PV(B) > PV(C). Careful comparison of the present value formulas PV(B) – PV(C) and PV(U) – PV(H) shows that the decision criteria PV(B) > PV(C) and PV(U) > PV(H) are identical.

The rule for optimal human capital investment can be expressed in a number of alternative, but equivalent, ways. Two common ways of stating this decision rule are illustrated in Figure 9.2. One is in terms of marginal rather than total costs and benefits: the individual should increase years of education until the present value of the benefits of an additional year of education equals the present value of the additional costs. In terms of Figure 9.1, for a high school graduate facing income stream B, the marginal benefits of a university education consist of the area f while the marginal costs consist of the area b + c + d. Marginal benefits generally decline with years of education due to diminishing returns to education and the shorter period over which higher income accrues. Marginal costs rise with years of education because forgone earnings increase with educational attainment. The point at which marginal benefits equal marginal costs yields the maximum net present value of lifetime earnings.

Human capital decisions, like those involving financial and physical capital, are also often expressed in terms of the rate of return on the investment. For any specific amount of education, the **internal rate of return** (i) can be defined as the implicit rate of return earned by an individual acquiring that amount of education. The optimal strategy is to continue investing as long as the internal rate of return exceeds the market rate of interest r, the opportunity cost of financing the investment. That is, if at a specific level of education i > r, the individual can then increase the net present value of lifetime earnings by acquiring more education, which may involve borrowing at the market interest rate r. Similarly, if i < r, the individual would increase lifetime earnings by acquiring less education. Because the present value of marginal benefits and marginal costs are generally declining and increasing functions, respectively, of years of education, the internal rate of return falls as educational attainment rises. The point at which i = r yields the optimal quantity of human capital.

Perhaps the most obvious implication of the theory is that human capital investments should be made early in one's lifetime. Educational investments made at later stages earn a

Exhibit 9.1

Child Labour

To this point, our examples of human capital investment pertain to the decision to attend college or university. In fact, this is the most common education decision that Canadians face, since schooling is compulsory until age 16, and most individuals complete high school. As for those who drop out and never complete high school, it may be difficult to explain their behaviour as the outcome of rational choice. Perhaps these students have high discount rates, so that future income is less important to them. Perhaps the return to completing high school is low.* Or perhaps dropping out of school is just a bad idea.

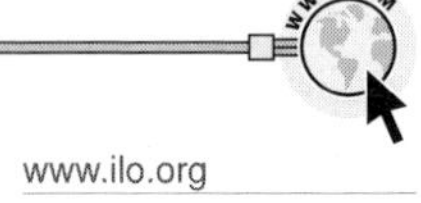

www.ilo.org

But elementary and secondary schooling decisions are still important in many developing countries where attendance is far from universal. Sometimes this reflects poor schooling infrastructure, but frequently it is the "voluntary" choice of families to have children work instead of go to school. The ILO reports that almost 25 percent of the world's children between 5 and 14 years old are economically active (as of 1995).** This number is especially high in Africa, where almost half of children (41.4 percent) work. Many people find child labour offensive, and would like to ban it, or alternatively impose trade restrictions on goods made by child labour. Obviously, this makes sense for the "worst forms of child labour," including slavery, prostitution, and work in the illegal drug trade. Also, it is offensive that children should work in hazardous conditions, though this is more a problem of poor workplace standards than of child labour itself (no one should be compelled to work in unsafe conditions). But the primary argument for more sweeping restrictions on child labour is that it interferes with education, possibly dooming children to a future of poverty.

The puzzle to economists is how these types of restrictions can be reconciled with voluntary, rational human capital (schooling) decisions made by families. According to the human capital model, if education is economically worthwhile, parents would rationally have their children in school rather than working. Conversely, if children are working, it must be the case that parents have decided that the benefits of extra schooling do not outweigh the costs, including the opportunity cost of the child's labour earnings. This may be especially true in rural areas, and for girls. So might it ever make economic sense to ban child labour?

Economists have explored a variety of possible justifications. One possibility is that parents do not act in the interests of their children, so the state should step in on the child's behalf. While it may be true for some parents, this reasoning does

lower financial return because forgone earnings increase with work experience and because of the shorter period over which higher income is earned. A related implication is that individuals who expect to be in and out of the labour force—perhaps in order to raise children—have less financial incentive to invest in education and will (other factors being equal) earn a lower return on any given amount of human capital investment.

This framework can be used not only to explain human capital investment decisions but also to predict the impact of changes in the economic and social environment and in public policy on levels of education. For example, changes in the degree of progressivity of the income tax system are predicted to alter levels of educational attainment. Because optimal human capital investment decisions are based on real after-tax income, an increase in the progressivity of the income tax system would shift down high-income streams (such as C in Figure 9.1) relatively more than low-income streams (such as A), thus reducing the

Exhibit 9.1

Child Labour *(continued)*

not line up with other observations of parental behaviour. For one, child labour (and schooling) is highly sensitive to family income. It is then possible that the inability to borrow on future (children's) earnings may prevent poor households from sending their kids to school. Alternatively, there may be social norms or externalities to human capital, whereby privately rational decisions are not socially optimal. In those cases, everyone could be made better off if the government coordinated the human capital investment decision, forcing all children to school.

Whatever the rationale, many countries have enacted compulsory schooling or child labour laws at some point in their history. Yet it is not obvious that these laws have had any impact, to some extent due to poor compliance. After all, it is difficult to expect a family to send their child to school if it makes no genuine economic sense. Studies of the impact of child labour and compulsory schooling laws implemented in the United States at the end of the 19th century show mixed effectiveness. Margo and Finegan (1996) show that the compulsory schooling laws, combined with child labour laws, had some impact on school attainment. However, Moehling (1999) shows that there is no reliable evidence that these laws had any impact on child labour. To some extent, this reflects the fact that school and work, especially on farms, are not incompatible. More importantly, Moehling argues that it was economic growth, and the accompanying increase in returns to schooling, that led more parents to switch their children from work to school.

The important insight of human capital investment model is that the full cost of schooling includes the opportunity cost of time in school, not just cost of tuition and books. This insight has led to more clever policies aimed at encouraging children to attend school. Some countries have introduced schemes whereby parents are paid subsidies if they send their children to school. This reduces the opportunity cost of attending school, and unlike a ban on child labour, its compliance is easier to measure. Evidence from Ravallion and Wodon (2000) shows that these parental school subsidies do indeed reduce child labour.

*Daniel Parent (1999) shows that this seems to be the case in Canada, unlike the United States.

**See the ILO Web sites below for more information on definitions, regulations, and statistics pertaining to child labour. Basu (1999) provides a useful overview of the economic issues associated with child labour.

<www.ilo.org/public/english/standards/ipec/index.htm>

<www.ilo.org/public/english/standards/ipec/simpoc/stats/child/stats.htm>

demand for education. Similarly, policies such as student loans programs alter the total and marginal costs of education, and thus levels of educational attainment.

Not all individuals have or obtain sufficient information to make the detailed calculations needed to determine the optimal quantity of education. Nonetheless, people do take into account costs and benefits when making decisions, including those with respect to human capital investments. Consequently, as is frequently the case in economic analysis, models that assume rational decision-making may predict the behaviour of individuals quite well, especially the average behaviour of large groups of individuals. Optimization errors that result in a specific individual's choice of education deviating from the optimum level tend to offset each other and thus may have little effect on the average behaviour of large groups of individuals.

Decisions relating to investment in education are also complicated by the fact that the

Figure 9.2 **Two Ways of Stating the Decision Rule for Optimal Human Capital Investment**

Individuals choose the human capital investment that maximizes the net present value of lifetime earnings. One way to show this is illustrated in panel (a). The net benefit of obtaining education level E equals the difference between benefits and costs, and is maximized by setting marginal benefit (MB) equal to marginal cost (MC). The MB of another year of school is the extra earnings generated by the human capital. With diminishing returns, MB will decline with years of education. The MC of another year of school includes direct costs such as tuition fees, plus the opportunity cost of forgone earnings, which generally increase with years of education. The optimal level of education occurs at E*, where MB = MC. Alternatively, the individual could calculate the implicit (or internal) rate of return i for each level of education, corresponding to the discount rate that yields a net present value of zero for the investment. The internal rate of return as a function of years of schooling is given by the schedule I in panel (b). The individual should invest until the internal rate of return equals the opportunity cost of the investment, given by the interest rate, r. This condition yields the same educational choice, E*, as in panel (a).

(a) Marginal benefits equal marginal costs

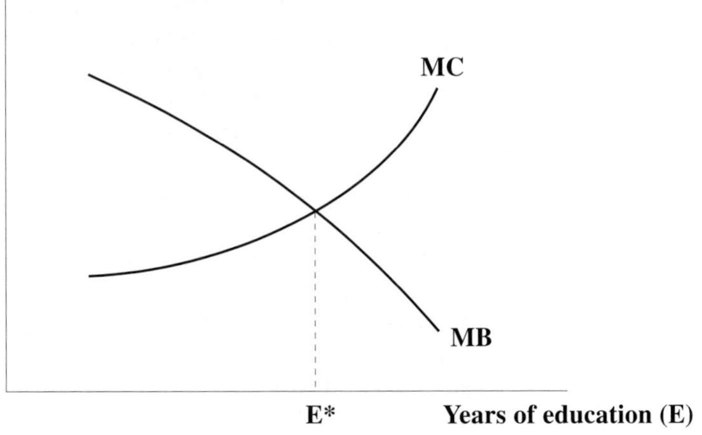

(b) Internal rate of return equals market interest rate

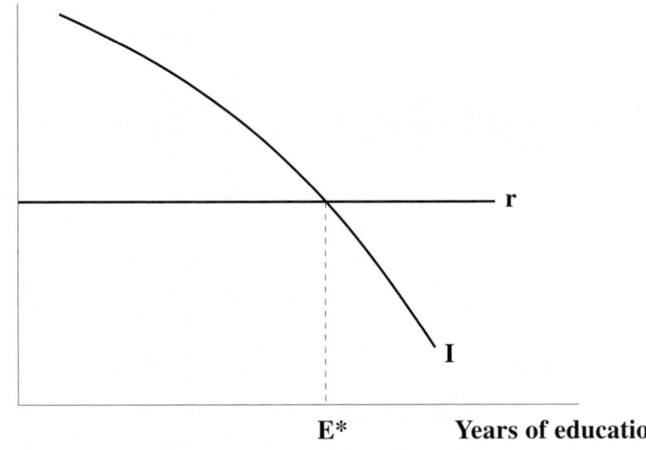

simplifying assumptions used in the above analysis may not hold in practice. The process of acquiring education may directly yield utility or disutility. The existence of this consumption component does not imply that the investment aspect is irrelevant; however, it does indicate that human capital decisions may not be based on investment criteria alone. Individuals who enjoy learning will acquire more education than would be predicted on the basis of financial costs and benefits, and vice versa for those who dislike the process of acquiring knowledge. The decision continues to be based on costs and benefits, but these concepts need to be broadened to include nonfinancial benefits and costs.

In addition to increasing one's future earnings, education may open up a more varied and interesting set of career opportunities, in which case job satisfaction would be higher among those with more education. The consequences may be even more profound; for example, the acquisition of knowledge may alter peoples' preferences and therefore future consumption patterns, possibly enhancing their enjoyment of life for a given level of income. In principle these aspects—to the extent that they exist—can be incorporated in the theory, but they clearly present challenges for measurement and empirical testing. Similarly, the returns to education are unlikely to be known with certainty so that investment decisions must be based on individuals' expectations about the future. Because some alternatives may be less certain than others, attitudes toward risk will also play a role. Risk-neutral individuals will choose the amount of education that maximizes the expected net present value of lifetime earnings, while risk-averse individuals will place more weight on expected benefits and costs that are certain than those that are uncertain.

Financing is generally an important aspect of any investment decision. In the case of human capital investments financing is particularly problematic because one cannot use the value of the human capital (i.e., the anticipated future earnings) as collateral for the loan. In contrast, machinery and equipment, land, and other physical assets can be pledged as loan collateral. There is therefore a fundamental difference between physical and human capital in terms of the degree to which "perfect capital markets" prevail. In the absence of subsidized tuition, student loan programs, and similar policies, the problems associated with financing human capital investments could prevent many individuals from choosing the amount of education that would maximize their net present value of lifetime earnings. Even in the presence of these policies, borrowing constraints may exert a significant influence on decisions regarding education.

This discussion of human capital theory has focused on the private costs and benefits of education because these are the relevant factors affecting choices made by individuals. However, the acquisition of knowledge may also affect third parties, in which case the social costs and benefits may differ from their private counterparts. These issues are discussed further below in the context of public policy toward education.

EDUCATION AND MARKET EQUILIBRIUM

The income streams shown in Figure 9.1 represent hypothetical alternatives available to a given individual. In order to understand the relationship between income and education we need to study the interaction between individuals' preferences regarding different levels of education and employers' preferences with respect to workers with different amounts of human capital. This interaction determines market wage rates associated with different levels of education and employment of workers with various amounts of human capital. The nature of the market equilibrium is very similar to that analyzed in the previous chapter in terms of compensating wages for risk, the difference being that human capital is a positive attribute affecting the productivity of workers while risk is a negative characteristic associated with jobs. Because of the similarity, our treatment in this chapter will be brief.

Figure 9.3 shows indifference curves for two different types of workers (A and B workers) and isoprofit curves for two different types of firms (α and β firms). Two types of each group are assumed purely for illustration. Employees differ in their preferences for education versus income because of such factors as differences in tastes for acquiring knowledge, learning ability, utility or disutility derived directly from the educational process, and need or ability to borrow to finance human capital investments. Because human capital is costly to acquire, both types of employee require a higher wage to induce them to obtain more education. Type A workers have a stronger preference for education, as reflected in the shape of their indifference curves U_A. Holding utility constant, a larger wage increase is required to induce B workers to undertake an additional year of education than is the case for A workers.

Firms' isoprofit curves will be upward-sloping, as depicted in Figure 9.3, if workers with more human capital are more productive. Holding profits constant, a higher wage can be paid to more-educated employees due to their greater productivity. (Otherwise the isoprofit curves would be horizontal straight lines.) However, firms differ in the value of more-

Figure 9.3 **Education and Market Equilibrium**

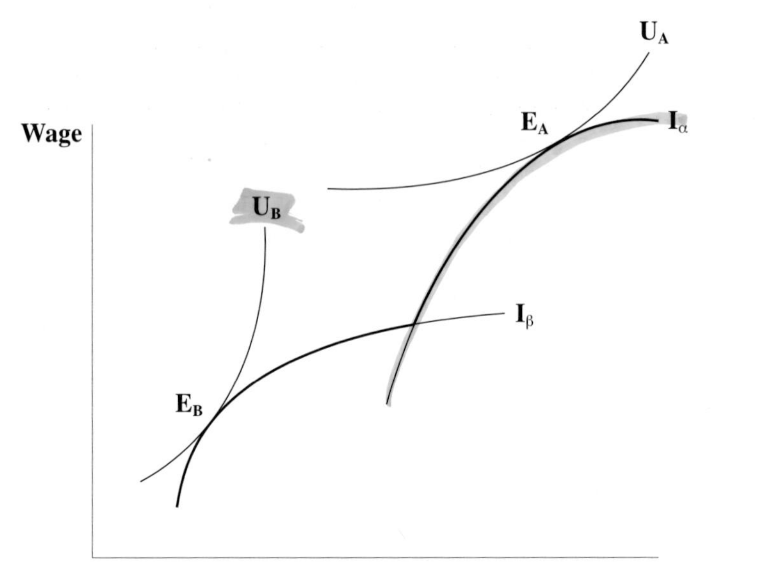

The return to education is determined like other compensating differentials: people need to be compensated for acquiring education, while firms will pay higher wages for more-skilled workers. Worker preferences are given by indifference curves such as U_A, being steeper when education is more costly (such as U_B). If educated workers are more productive, firms can trade off lower-skilled (but cheaper) workers for more-skilled (but more expensive) workers, yielding isoprofit curves, such as I_α. Some firms (such as I_β) are less willing to pay high wages for educated workers. The employers' offer curve is given by the outer envelope of I_β and I_α, and the wage-education locus is given by the tangencies between indifference curves and the offer curve.

educated workers to the production and marketing of their product. More-educated workers are more valuable to the type α firms as reflected by the shape of their isoprofit curves I_α. Holding profits constant, α firms can pay a larger wage increase to workers with an additional year of education than is the case for β firms.

In competitive equilibrium, firms earn zero excess profits (normal rate of return). Thus, if I_α and I_β are the isoprofit curves corresponding to zero profits, the outer limits of these two isoprofit curves (bold lines) constitute the employers' offer curve showing the maximum wage that can be paid for different levels of education consistent with competitive equilibrium. Market equilibrium occurs at points E_A and E_B. This equilibrium has two important properties. First, workers who invest more in human capital receive a compensating differential for doing so. The magnitude of the compensating differential depends on both the preferences of different types of workers regarding income and education and the technology of production and market opportunities of firms. Second, employees with the strongest preferences for education are matched with employers for whom education is most valuable. This sorting equilibrium is Pareto-optimal. Both A and B types of workers are better off employed with the α and β firms respectively than would be the case if they switched to the other firm type.

EDUCATION AS A FILTER

The previous model emphasizes the role of education as enhancing the productive capabilities of individuals. A contrasting view of education, where it has no effect on productivity, is provided by the following simple model, based on the seminal work of Spence (1974).

Imperfect information is a common feature of many labour markets, and gives rise to phenomena that cannot be accounted for by the simple neoclassical model. Some important variables that enter into economic decision-making are not observable (or are observable only at great cost) until after (perhaps a considerable amount of time after) a decision or transaction has taken place. In these circumstances, employers and employees may look for variables believed to be correlated with or related to the variables of interest. Such variables, which are observable prior to a decision or transaction being made, perform the role of being market signals. In this model, worker productivity is unknown when hiring decisions are made, and education plays a role as a signal of the productivity of employees. This model is of importance in its own right because education may act, at least in part, as a **signalling** or sorting device and because it illustrates the more general phenomenon of signalling in labour and product markets.

In the model described here, education acts only as a signal; that is, we assume for simplicity and purposes of illustration that education has no effect on worker productivity. This assumption is made in part to keep the analysis as simple as possible, and in part to illustrate the proposition that job market signalling provides an alternative explanation of the positive correlation between education and earnings.

Employers in the model are assumed to not know the productivity of individual workers prior to hiring those workers. Even after hiring, employers may only be able to observe the productivity of groups of employees rather than that of each individual employee. However, employers do observe certain characteristics of prospective employees. In particular, they observe the amount of education obtained by the job applicant. Because employers are in the job market on a regular basis, they may form beliefs about the relationship between worker attributes such as amount of education and productivity. These beliefs may be based on the employer's past experience. In order for the employer's beliefs to persist, they must be fulfilled by actual subsequent experience. Thus, an important condition for market equilibrium is that employers' beliefs about the relationship between education and productivity are in fact realized.

If employers believe that more-educated workers are more productive, they will (as long as these beliefs continue to be confirmed by actual experience) offer higher wages to workers with more education. Workers thus observe an offered wage schedule that depends on the amount of education obtained. In the model, we assume that workers choose the amount of education that provides the highest rate of return. Any consumption value of education is incorporated in the costs of acquiring education.

To keep the analysis as simple as possible, we assume that there are two types of workers in the economy. Low-ability workers (type L) have a marginal product of 1 (MP = 1), and acquire y units of education at a cost of \$y. High-productivity workers (type H) have a marginal product of 2, and acquire y units of education at a cost of \$y/2. Note, as explained above, that the productivity or ability of workers is given and is independent of the amount of education obtained. Note also that the more-able workers are assumed to be able to acquire education at a lower cost per unit of education obtained. This situation could arise because the more able workers acquire a specific amount of education more quickly, or because they place a higher consumption value on (or have a lower psychic dislike for) the educational process.

The assumption that more-able workers have a lower cost of acquiring education is important. As will be seen, this is a necessary condition for education to act as an informative signal in the job market. If this condition does not hold, low- and high-ability workers will acquire the same amount of education, and education will not be able to act as a signal of worker productivity.

To see what the market equilibrium might look like, suppose that employers' beliefs are as follows:

$$\text{If } y < y^* \text{ then MP} = 1$$

$$\text{If } y \geq y^* \text{ then MP} = 2$$

That is, there is some critical value of education (e.g., high school completion, university degree) and applicants with education less than this critical value are believed to be less productive, while applicants with education equal to or greater than this value are believed to be more productive.

In these circumstances, the offered wage schedule (assuming for the purposes of illustration that the labour market is competitive, so that firms will offer a wage equal to the expected marginal product) will be as shown in Figure 9.4. That is, applicants with education equal to or greater than y^* will be offered the wage $w = \$2$ and applicants with education less than y^* will be offered the wage $w = \$1$. In Figure 9.4 it is assumed that y^* lies between 1 and 2.

Also shown in Figure 9.4 are, for each type of worker, the cost functions $C(y)$ associated with acquiring education. Note that low-ability workers are better off by acquiring 0 units of education. This choice gives a net wage of \$1; because the cost of acquiring zero units of education is zero, the gross wage and net wage are equal in this case. In contrast, low-ability workers would receive a net wage of $w = \$2 - y^* < \$1$ if they were to acquire sufficient education to receive the higher wage offer given to those with education equal to or greater than y^*.

However, the high-ability workers are better off by acquiring education level $y = y^*$. This choice yields a net wage of $w = \$2 - y^*/2 > \$1$, whereas choosing $y = 0$ yields, for these individuals, a net wage of $w = \$1$.

Thus, given the offered wage schedule, if y^* lies in the range $1 < y^* < 2$, the low-ability workers will choose $y = 0$ and the high-ability workers will choose $y = y^*$. Thus employers' beliefs about the relationship between education and worker productivity will be confirmed. Those applicants with low education will in fact be the less productive, and those with higher education will be the more productive. Employers will therefore not have any reason to alter their beliefs, and therefore alter the offered wage schedule. Given the offered wage schedule, workers will continue to choose to acquire the educational "signal" such that the level of education is a good predictor (in this simple model it is a perfect predictor) of productivity. This outcome is a market equilibrium even though by assumption education does not increase the productivity of any individual worker; that is, education acts strictly as a signalling or sorting device in this case. Looked at from the outside, it might appear that education raises productivity because those with more education are

Figure 9.4 **Offered Wage and Signalling Cost Schedules**

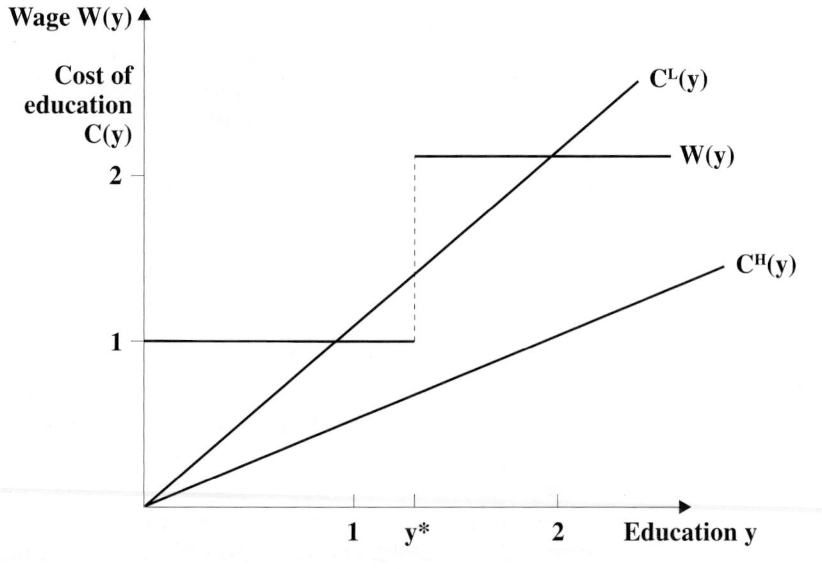

Employers offer the wage schedule $W(y)$ with an educational requirement of y^*, where employees are paid 2 if they have education $y \geq y^*$ and 1 if they have education level $y < y^*$. Low-ability workers' cost of acquiring education is given by $C^L(y)$. Their return acquiring y^* is given by $2 - C^L(y^*) < 1$, so they are better off not going to school, and accepting the lower wage. The net benefit of education to the high-abilitied is given by $2 - C^H(y^*) > 1$, so they are better off acquiring the education level y^* rather than being pooled with the low-abilitied (at wage 1). In this equilibrium, only the high-abilitied acquire education, and all workers are paid their marginal products.

more productive and receive higher earnings. However, this is not the case; education simply sorts the otherwise heterogeneous population into two distinct groups.

This simple model illustrates the central result of the theory of market signalling. This theory has been used to explain numerous other phenomena, such as the use of a high product price to signal the quality of the product, the use of product warranties to signal product quality, and the use by employers of an applicant's employment experience (e.g., number of jobs, amount of time spent unemployed) to signal worker quality.

Of course, we do not expect that education acts strictly as a filtering or signalling mechanism, as is the case in the simple model just outlined. Most educational programs probably provide some skills and knowledge that raise the productivity of workers. However, it is possible that some forms of education or training act primarily as a signal, while other forms involve primarily human capital acquisition which raises productivity and earnings. The extent to which education serves as a signalling device versus a form of human capital acquisition is an interesting and important question. The policy implications of the models, for example, are quite different. For the signalling model, educational subsidies represent a pure transfer to high-ability individuals, and are indefensible on equity grounds.

EMPIRICAL EVIDENCE

Education and Earnings

Because of the importance of the topic, but also an abundance of data sets with information on earnings and education, labour economists have spent considerable effort measuring the **returns to schooling**, and attempting to evaluate the neoclassical human capital model. Figure 9.5 shows age-earnings profiles for four educational categories of Canadian males: (a) eight years or less of elementary schooling, (b) nine to thirteen years of elementary and secondary schooling, (c) some postsecondary education but not a university degree, and (d) a university degree.

As these data indicate, there is a strong relationship between education and lifetime earnings on average. The income streams of those with more education lie above the streams of those with less education. Two additional patterns are evident. First, earnings increase with age and thus (presumably) labour market experience until around age 50 and then decline slightly. As noted previously, this concave relationship between age and earnings is generally attributed to the accumulation of human capital in the form of on-the-job training and experience, a process which displays diminishing returns. Second, earnings increase most rapidly to age 45 or 50 for those individuals with the most education. Thus the salary differential between groups with different amounts of education is much wider at age 50 than at ages 20 or 30.

Data on earnings by age and education can be used together with information on direct costs to calculate the internal rate of return on investments in education, analogously to those described earlier. Such calculations can be useful to individuals wishing to know, for example, whether a university education is a worthwhile investment. They can also be useful input into public policy decisions. In particular, efficient resource allocation requires that investments in physical and human capital be made in those areas with the greatest return.

Table 9.1 shows one such set of estimates of the monetary return to education in Canada as of 1995 (from Vaillancourt and Bourdeau-Primeau, 2001). Like most such estimates, these are obtained by comparing the earnings of individuals with different levels of education at a point in time, rather than following the same individuals over time. Other factors that might also account for earnings differences across individuals are taken into account using multivariate regression analysis. The estimates shown are the private after-tax rates of return to the individual, taking into account such costs as tuition fees and forgone earnings.

Figure 9.5

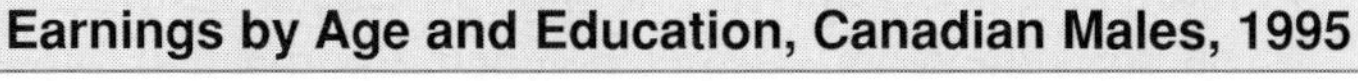

This graph shows the average earnings by age group for different levels of education. For example, the lowest line shows the relationship between age and earnings for those men with no more than elementary school. Their earnings generally increase with age, as they accumulate on-the-job experience. The age-earnings are higher on average for those men with more education, being highest for university graduates.

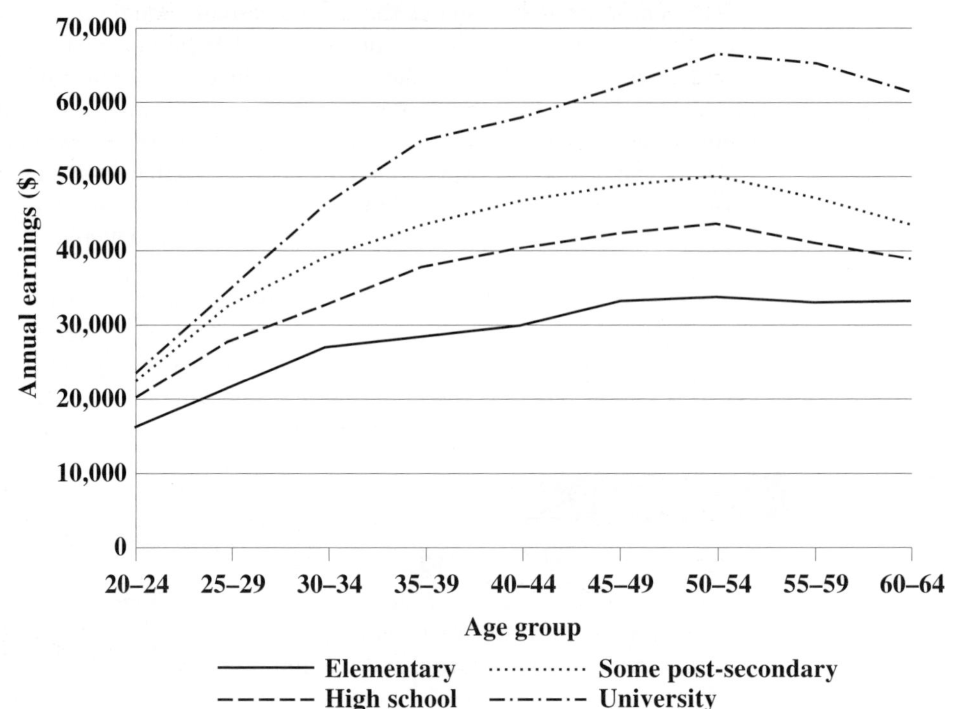

Notes:

1. Earnings are average wage and salary income of full-year (49 plus weeks), mostly full-time (30 hours per week or more) workers.
2. Education categories are defined as: (1) *elementary*: eight years or less of elementary school; (2) *high school*: nine to thirteen years of high school; (3) *some postsecondary*: some postsecondary education, but not a university degree; (4) *university*: at least a bachelor's degree.

Source: Data from Statistics Canada, Individual Public Use Microdata Files: 1996 Census of Population.

Note that the rates of return are highest for the bachelor's level, as would be expected if there is diminishing returns to the level of human capital (e.g., as shown in Figure 9.2). Females benefit more from additional education than males, a result consistent with the general finding that the gap between male and female earnings is largest at low levels of education, and least at high levels of education.

Although rates of return to undergraduate education are generally high, there are also large differences in these rates of return by the type of education obtained. The bottom part of Table 9.1 illustrates these differences for fields of study of a holder of a bachelor's degree. Those obtaining degrees in health sciences (such as medicine, dentistry, and related fields) earn the highest return, while those graduating in humanities and fine arts earn the lowest returns. One need only compare the relative returns to understand the popularity of undergraduate business and commerce programs relative to natural sciences.

The Human Capital Earnings Function

Estimates of the rate of return to education are generally obtained by comparing different individuals at a point in time. After controlling for other observed factors that influence earnings, the differences in individuals' earnings are attributed to differences in educational

Table 9.1 Estimates of the Private Returns[1] to Schooling in Canada, 1995

Level of Schooling	Males	Females
Bachelor's degree[2]	17	20
Master's degree	nc[3]	5
Ph.D.	2	10
Bachelor's Degree by Field of Study	**Males**	**Females**
Education	12	19
Humanities and fine arts	nc	13
Social sciences[4]	13	18
Commerce	18	25
Natural sciences	17	22
Engineering and applied science	22	24
Health sciences	29	30

Notes:
1. Rates of return by level of schooling are calculated relative to the next-lowest level. For example, the return to a bachelor's degree is relative to completed secondary school, and the return to a master's degree is relative to a bachelor's degree.
2. Bachelor's degree includes health (medicine, dentistry, optometry, veterinary) and law degrees.
3. "nc" indicates "not calculated" because that estimated returns were not significantly different from zero statistically.
4. Social sciences includes law degrees.

Source: F. Vaillancourt and S. Bourdeau-Primeau, "The returns to university education in Canada: 1990 and 1995," manuscript, June 2001 (prepared for the C. D. Howe Institute). Reprinted with permission.

attainment. This is primarily accomplished through the estimation of a **human capital earnings function**. In its simplest form, this function is nothing more than a least-squares regression of earnings on education, with controls for other factors believed to affect earnings. Because of its importance to labour economics, however, it is worth reviewing some of the details involved in the specification and estimation of the return to schooling in this regression context.

If an individual i had zero years of schooling, we could think of her receiving the following wage (forever):

$$W_i = W_0(X)$$

where W_0 is her productivity in the absence of education, and depends on X, a set of worker characteristics that affect individual productivity. Now, consider the effect of one year of schooling on her wage. Denote her wage with one year of education as $W_1(X)$, and define

$$r = \frac{W_1(X) - W_0(X)}{W_0(X)}$$

as the rate of return to one year of schooling, that is, $W_1(X) = (1 + r)W_0(X)$. If we assume that the rate of return to schooling, r, is constant for each additional year of schooling, then the second year of schooling will increase wages over one year of schooling by

$$W_2(X) = (1 + r)W_1(X) = (1 + r)(1 + r)W_0(X) = (1 + r)^2W_0(X)$$

In general, for S years of schooling, then, we have

$$W_S(X) = (1 + r)^S W_0(X)$$

Taking logarithms of both sides, the wages of an individual with S years of schooling are given by

$$\ln W = \ln W_0(X) + S \ln(1 + r) \approx \ln W_0(X) + rS$$

since ln (1 + r) is approximately equal to r, at least when r is small (less than 0.2). We could then add more structure to this earnings function by specifying $W_0(X)$. Its simplest specification would be

$$W_0(X) = \alpha + \varepsilon_i$$

In this case, the implication is that earnings in the absence of schooling are equal to a constant, plus a random unobservable component, such as ability or motivation. More generally, based for example on the evidence in Figure 9.5, which showed that earnings rise with age (or experience), we could make the earnings function richer by adding additional variables, like age as a proxy for experience:

$$\ln W_i = \alpha + rS + \beta \text{ AGE} + \varepsilon_i$$

The functional form could be generalized further by permitting the returns to age or schooling to vary with the level of schooling or age, for example, by including quadratic terms in schooling or age.

The human capital earnings function then yields a straightforward regression equation. By regressing log wages on years of schooling, and possibly other factors, we obtain an estimate of the return to schooling. In this particular equation, the return to schooling is simply the coefficient on years of education. The coefficients on the other variables (like age, or potential labour market experience) also have the interpretation as rates of return to the given characteristics.

The easiest way to illustrate the empirical methodology of estimating these earnings functions is to examine some actual earnings-schooling data. We have drawn a random sample of 35-year-old women who held full-time jobs in 1995 from the 1996 census. By comparing the earnings of these women by education level, we can estimate the return to education, holding age constant. This is illustrated in Figure 9.6. The individual observations are plotted, as well as the estimated regression of log earnings on years of schooling from this sample. While the regression function fits quite well, yielding a rate of return to schooling of 8.5% per year, there is still considerable dispersion around this function. On average, earnings rise with education, but there are plenty of examples of low-educated women earning more than the higher-educated ones. These women may be the "anecdotes" used by high school dropouts to justify their decisions, but it is clear that such women are the minority.

In summary, the most conventional approach to estimating the returns to schooling is to estimate the human capital earnings function. The simplest, most common specification replaces age with a quadratic function of **potential experience**:

$$\ln W_i = \alpha + rS + \beta_1 \text{ EXP} + \beta_2 \text{ EXP}^2 + \varepsilon_i$$

This function is linear in schooling, and quadratic in potential labour market experience. Since actual work experience is rarely included in data sets, it is usually approximated by potential experience, equal to

$$\text{Age} - \text{Schooling} - 5$$

Figure 9.6 Log Earnings by Years of Schooling, 35-Year-Old Women

This scatter plot shows the relationship between education and earnings for a sample of 35-year-old women in 1995. Each point represents a particular woman, with her level of education and annual earnings. Also shown is the estimated regression line, which shows the level of predicted earnings for women with a given number of years of schooling. While most observations lie close to the regression line, there are obviously some women whose earnings are higher than predicted, and some whose earnings are lower than predicted.

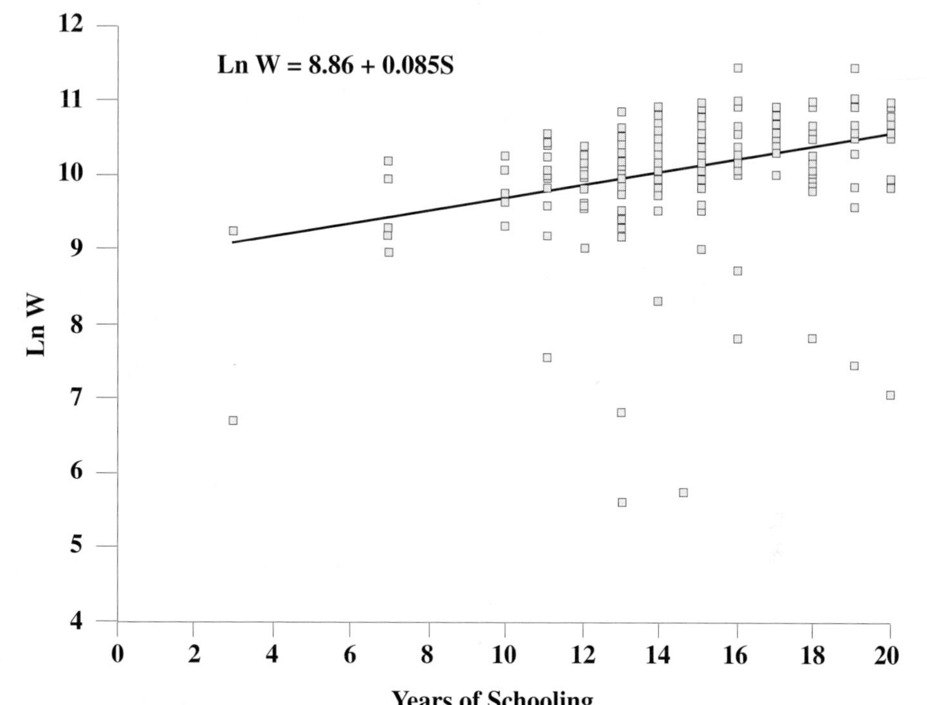

Notes: This figure shows the log annual earnings-schooling pairs and the predicted log earnings from a regression of log earnings on the years of schooling.

Source: Data from Statistics Canada, Individual Public Use Microdata Files: 1996 Census of Population.

www.statcan.ca/english/census96/list.htm

which is an estimate of the number of years an individual was working, but not at school.[2] We have estimated this equation on the full sample of full-year full-time men and women from the 1996 Canadian Census. The results are reported in Table 9.2. The rate of return to schooling for men is estimated as 7.5 percent, while that for women is 9.8 percent. Consistently with Table 9.1, the returns to education are higher for women than men. The returns to experience, however, are significantly lower for women than men. This is perhaps due to the fact that "potential experience" is an especially poor proxy for actual work experience for women, who generally have more intermittent attachment to the work force. We will return to this in our chapter on discrimination.

[2]Age alone might be a poor proxy for labour market experience, since individuals who do not attend school can obtain additional human capital through work experience (as long as they are working). Comparing earnings by education level as in Figure 9.6 (controlling for age alone) would then involve comparing individuals who differed not only by education, but also systematically by work experience. The difference in earnings due to difference in education would be understated, since higher-education individuals also had lower work experience (on average).

Table 9.2 Estimated Returns to Schooling and Experience, 1995 (dependent variable: log annual earnings)

	Men	Women
Intercept	8.473 (519.34)	8.015 (397.30)
Years of schooling	0.075 (98.67)	0.098 (100.05)
Experience	0.056 (63.15)	0.045 (44.38)
Experience squared	–0.0007 (43.27)	–0.0006 (30.64)
R-squared	0.136	0.142
Sample size	98,627	73,386

Notes: The regressions are estimated over the full samples of full-year (49 or more weeks worked in 1995), mostly full-time men and women respectively. Absolute t-values are indicated in parentheses, with t-values greater than 2 generally regarded as indicating that the relationship is statistically significant, and unlikely due to chance.

Source: Data from Statistics Canada, Individual Public Use Microdata Files: 1996 Census of Population.

Signalling, Screening, and Ability

The earnings function provides a convenient framework for summarizing the relationship between education and earnings in the labour market. The estimated rate of return yields the average difference in earnings between groups of individuals with different levels of education. The difficult question, however, is whether this correlation represents a "pure" causal relationship between education and earnings. If the return to education is estimated as 10 percent, then providing an additional year of schooling to a lower-educated group of workers should raise their earnings by 10 percent. If there are systematic differences between the less- and the more- educated that affect both earnings and schooling, then the correlation between earnings and education may reflect these other factors as well. In that case, our estimate of the rate of return to schooling would be biased. One of the advantages of the multiple regression framework is that it allows a researcher to control for these other factors, data permitting.

One potential determinant that is difficult to control for is ability, by which we mean ability in the workplace, not learning ability (though these may be correlated). If more-able individuals are also more likely to invest in education, some of the estimated return to education may in fact be a return to innate ability. In other words, those who are more able would earn more even in the absence of education; we may be incorrectly attributing their higher earnings to education rather than to their innate ability.

One theoretical rationale for the potential importance of "omitted ability bias" is the hypothesis that higher education may act as a filter, screening out the more able workers rather than enhancing productivity directly. According to the extreme form of "signalling/screening hypothesis," discussed above, workers may use education to signal unobserved ability while firms use education to screen. In the equilibrium of this model, workers who obtain more education are more productive and receive higher earnings. Yet, by assumption, education does not affect worker productivity. Thus the signalling/screening hypothesis represents a potentially significant challenge to human capital theory, which attributes the higher earnings of the more-educated entirely to the productivity-enhancing effects of education. In these circumstances, education may yield a private return (more-able individuals can increase their earnings by investing in education) but its social return consists only in its role in sorting the more- from the less-able rather than directly increasing productivity as in human capital theory.

Empirical tests of the signalling/screening hypothesis have not been conclusive (Riley, 1979; Lang and Kropp, 1986). Most would agree that the pure signalling model in which education has no impact on productivity does not appear capable of explaining observed behaviour (Rosen, 1977; Weiss, 1995). Professional educational programs such as those in medicine, law, and engineering clearly are more than elaborate screening devices. However, as Weiss (1995) emphasizes, there is a considerable body of evidence that suggests that education acts as a filter to some degree (see Exhibit 9.2 for example). Furthermore, as discussed by Davies and MacDonald (1984), the informational role of education in terms of matching individuals' interests and abilities may be significant, albeit difficult to measure. As with many controversies in economics, the real world unlikely corresponds to the "either-or" dichotomy in which our discussion is cast.

Even in the absence of education acting as a signal, there may be a correlation between unobserved ability and the level of education. As we emphasized in the human capital model, education is a private investment decision. People acquire additional education if it increases their earnings enough to offset the costs of doing so. For example, two individuals may be comparing the earnings associated with becoming a lawyer versus a plumber. The model outlined earlier assumed that the two individuals were equally able: in terms of

Exhibit 9.2

The Rate of Return to Taking "Serious" High School Courses

Most of the empirical evidence on estimated returns to schooling focuses on the average rate of return to a "year" of education, without any regard for the actual courses taken over that year. Altonji (1995) provides some of the first estimates of the effect of high school course selection on future labour market outcomes. Using the NLS, he observes the wages in 1985 of a large sample of high school graduates from the class of 1972.

Controlling for a variety of family background variables, as well as characteristics of the high schools (or classmates), Altonji finds almost no economic payoff for students who took more academically oriented high school courses. For example, switching from less academically oriented courses (like industrial arts, physical education, or commercial studies) to the same number of science, math, or English courses would increase future earnings by less than 0.3 percent. Thus, the academic "package" of a year's worth of these courses has no higher rate of return than a generic year of high school.

As noted by Altonji, and discussed further in Weiss (1995), this evidence is more consistent with the screening/signalling view of education than the pure human capital model. The premise of human capital theory is that it is the purely productivity-enhancing features of education that employers are paying for. If that is the case, course content should matter more than just the number of years of education. On the other hand, the signalling model suggests that employers infer other characteristics from the level of education, such as individual perseverance and work habits. In that case, employers will care more about whether the person finished high school than whether they took this course or that one. Furthermore, employers may not know about the particular course choices of students, in which case, they will be basing their hiring and compensation decisions on the level of education. It is gaps like the ones detected by Altonji—gaps between measured human capital investments and the labels attached to them—that provide the most convincing evidence of the role of signalling and screening in the labour market.

both their work ability and their ability to complete law school. Assuming that the jobs are otherwise equally desirable, in equilibrium, the return to schooling would be such that these individuals were indifferent between the two career paths: the higher lawyer's salary would be a pure compensating differential for the cost of attending law school. If the one choosing to be a plumber instead went to law school, her earnings would be the same as the person who chose the legal career.

Imagine now that one of the individuals was of higher overall ability. For her, law school would be a relative breeze, so she would choose the legal path. Similarly, because of her higher ability, she would make higher-than-average earnings as a lawyer. Comparing her earnings to the plumber would then overstate the returns to education that the plumber would receive if she had chosen law school. Alternatively stated, the actual difference in earnings would be smaller than predicted if the plumber and lawyer switched career paths. Of course, the bias could work the other way. Ability may be multidimensional. Perhaps the lawyer would make a lousy plumber. In that case, the observed difference in earnings between the plumber and lawyer would understate the difference that would exist if the plumber and lawyer switched occupational paths.

Addressing Ability Bias[3]

The best way to determine how much education improves productivity, and thus increases earnings, would be to conduct an experiment. Separate groups of individuals would be randomly assigned different levels (and possibly types) of education, independently of their ability, family background, and other environmental factors. At a later date, the incomes of these groups would be compared. Because of the random assignment to groups, on average the only differences in earnings between the groups would be due to the different levels (or types) of education. In the absence of such experiments, economists seeking more reliable evidence concerning the relationship between education and earnings have tried to find **natural experiments** that isolate the influence of education from the possible effects of unobserved ability factors.

The basic methodology can be illustrated using a stripped-down earnings function. We specify a simple relationship between earnings and schooling:

$$\ln W_i = \alpha + \beta S_i + \varepsilon_i$$

so that log wages depend only on the level of schooling, S_i, and unobserved talent, ε_i. While it is not exactly the same as the OLS formula, consider the following approximation to our regression estimate of the slope (analogous to an experiment). Imagine dividing the sample into high- and low-educated with levels of schooling S_L and S_H. The slope of the earnings function is given by

$$\beta = \frac{\Delta \ln W}{\Delta S} \equiv \frac{\Delta y}{\Delta S}$$

where we re-label y = lnW. An estimate of the slope is

$$\hat{\beta} = \frac{\bar{y}_H - \bar{y}_L}{S_H - S_L}$$

where $\bar{y}_H - \bar{y}_L$ is the difference in average earnings of high- and low-educated people. $\hat{\beta}$ essentially gives us the average difference in earnings per year of education between

[3]See Card (1999) for a thorough discussion of these issues and an up-to-date review of the empirical literature on the estimation of returns to schooling.

high- and low-educated, a seemingly reasonable estimate of the returns to schooling even if one had never heard of regression analysis. For simplicity, we will refer to this as the *OLS estimator*. We wish to know the conditions under which the OLS estimator gives us the correct estimate of the "true" β on average.

According to the model, "true" earnings are given by

$$y_{Hi} = \alpha + \beta S_H + \varepsilon_{Hi}$$

$$y_{Li} = \alpha + \beta S_L + \varepsilon_{Li}$$

and the average difference in earnings between high- and low-educated people is given by

$$\bar{y}_H - \bar{y}_L = \Delta\bar{y} = \beta(S_H - S_L) + (\bar{\varepsilon}_H - \bar{\varepsilon}_L)$$

The OLS slope estimator can then be expressed as the sum of the true parameter, plus the unobservables:

$$\hat{\beta} = \frac{\Delta\bar{y}}{\Delta S} = \beta + \frac{\bar{\varepsilon}_H - \bar{\varepsilon}_L}{S_H - S_L}$$

On average, if $\bar{\varepsilon}_H = \bar{\varepsilon}_L$, then the OLS estimator $\hat{\beta}$ equals β, and OLS is unbiased. On the other hand, if (on average), $\bar{\varepsilon}_H \neq \bar{\varepsilon}_L$, then OLS is "biased." We term this particular problem **ability bias**. For example, if $\bar{\varepsilon}_H > \bar{\varepsilon}_L$, (high-educated individuals have more talent than low-educated individuals), then $\hat{\beta} > \beta$, and we have an upward-biased estimator. Part of the higher earnings observed for higher-educated individuals is the result of higher average levels of ability, and has nothing to do with their higher levels of schooling. So, the key in evaluating the OLS estimator in this case is whether $\bar{\varepsilon}_H = \bar{\varepsilon}_L$—that is, there is no systematic difference in earnings ability across education groups—in which case we have essentially random assignment.

One of the first approaches taken to "control" for unobserved ability was to exploit data on twins. By comparing identical twins, we have a way of accounting for both genetic "ability" and family background in estimating the return to schooling. The basic idea is quite simple. Label the twins 1 and 2, and their earnings are given by

$$y_1 = \alpha + \beta S_1 + \varepsilon_1$$

$$y_2 = \alpha + \beta S_2 + \varepsilon_2$$

The difference in their earnings is then given by

$$\bar{y}_1 - \bar{y}_2 = \Delta\bar{y} = \beta(S_1 - S_2) + (\bar{\varepsilon}_1 - \bar{\varepsilon}_2)$$

This looks similar to the case above, except that we know we can (possibly) make further assumptions about unobserved ability. Specifically, assume that unobserved ability comprises two components: a common "family" or, genetic effect (λ_F), identical for the twins, and an individual effect (ν_i) that captures all other differences between the twins:

$$\varepsilon_1 = \lambda_F + \nu_1$$

$$\varepsilon_2 = \lambda_F + \nu_2$$

We assume that genetic ability and family background are fully accounted for in the λ_F terms, and that the ν_i are unrelated to these factors. The difference between the twins' unobserved ability is then given by:

$$\varepsilon_1 - \varepsilon_2 = \nu_1 - \nu_2$$

The genetic ability term "drops out," and given our assumptions about the remaining component (ν_1), $\bar{\varepsilon}_1 = \bar{\varepsilon}_2$ on average. This allows us to base an estimate of the returns to schooling on differences between the twins:

$$\ln W_{1i} - \ln W_{2i} = \beta(S_{1i} - S_{2i}) + (\nu_{1i} - \nu_{2i})$$

The difference in earnings between the twins depends only on the difference in education between them, plus random factors. Since ability is genetically the same between the twins, earnings difference cannot be due to differences in ability (by assumption).

Behrman, Hrubec, Taubman, and Wales (1980) provide one of the first examples of this approach. They use a sample of male identical twins who were veterans of World War II. In their data, the simple relationship between education and income indicates that every additional year of schooling adds about 8 percent to annual earnings. However, when attention is focused on twins alone (i.e., the relationship between differences in education and differences in earnings for pairs of twins as described above), the estimated return to an additional year of education falls to 2 to 2.5 percent. These estimates suggest that differences in unobserved ability may account for much of the estimated return to education. However, in this type of analysis, measurement error in the amount of education obtained will bias the estimated returns toward zero. Even small errors in reported education are magnified when looking at differences, instead of levels of education. Thus considerable uncertainty about the true impact of education remained following the Behrman et al. study.

More recently, a team of Princeton University labour economists collected data on a large sample of identical twins attending the annual "Twins Festival" in Twinsburg, Ohio.[4] In addition to the usual measures of earnings and education, they obtained an independent source of information on education level in order to minimize the possible influence of measurement error. They asked each twin about his or her sibling's level of education, giving them a second estimate of the level of schooling for each person. This second estimate could be used to "corroborate" or provide a more accurate estimate of the effects of schooling differences on the earnings differences of the twins.

Using the conventional approach, Ashenfelter and Rouse (1998) estimated an OLS return to education of about 11 percent, slightly higher than most other datasets. Exploiting the twins feature of the data to control for innate ability, the return to education fell to 7 percent, suggesting considerable ability bias. However, once they accounted for the possibility of measurement error, the estimated returns rose to 9 percent, which was still lower than the conventional OLS results. Their results confirm that omitted-variables bias is a problem, but not a large one. A similar result was also found in Miller, Mulvey, and Martin (1995) using an Australian sample of twins. They also found that measurement error in the twins methodology played as great a role in yielding an understatement of the returns to schooling as ability had in inflating it.

Another approach is to try to mimic an experiment by finding a mechanism that affects ("assigns") education levels to groups of individuals in some way independent of the individual's expected returns to schooling. Imagine constructing an estimator based on a grouping of a sample of individuals into two groups (1 and 2). Consider:

$$\hat{\beta}_W = \frac{\bar{y}_1 - \bar{y}_2}{\bar{S}_1 - \bar{S}_2}$$

[4]See Ashenfelter and Krueger (1994) and Ashenfelter and Rouse (1998) for description of the Princeton Twins Survey and a presentation of the empirical evidence.

The model for the groups is given by

$$y_1 = \alpha + \beta S_1 + \varepsilon_1$$

$$y_2 = \alpha + \beta S_2 + \varepsilon_2$$

Similarly to the twins studies, the estimator is based on

$$\bar{y}_1 - \bar{y}_2 = \Delta\bar{y} = \beta(\bar{S}_1 - \bar{S}_2) + (\bar{\varepsilon}_1 - \bar{\varepsilon}_2)$$

The formula for $\hat{\beta}_W$ can be expressed in terms of β as:

$$\beta_W = \frac{\Delta\bar{y}}{\Delta\bar{S}} = \beta\frac{\Delta\bar{S}}{\Delta\bar{S}} + \frac{\bar{\varepsilon}_1 - \bar{\varepsilon}_2}{\Delta\bar{S}}$$

which equals the true parameter (on average) under two conditions:

1. $\Delta\bar{S} \neq 0$, so that the grouping is correlated with the level of schooling (i.e., the two groups have different levels of average education).
2. $\bar{\varepsilon}_1 = \bar{\varepsilon}_2$, so that the groups are otherwise identical in terms of unobservables (on average).

The only potential explanation for differences in earnings between the two groups is their different levels of education. The trick (and main difficulty) is in finding ways to divide a sample of individuals into groups ("treatment" and "control") that satisfy these conditions.

There are a number of studies based on this "natural experiment" methodology, whereby the main innovation is arguing that the division by groups satisfies this condition. One such study uses the natural experiment associated with compulsory school attendance laws (Angrist and Krueger, 1991). Such laws generally require students to remain in school until their 16th or 17th birthday. However, because children born in different months start school at different ages, compulsory attendance laws imply that some children are required to remain in school longer than others. Of course, for those who remain in school longer than the minimum required period, such as those who obtain some postsecondary education, these laws will not influence the amount of education obtained. However, for those who wish to leave school as soon as possible, compulsory attendance laws require students born in certain months to remain in school longer than those born in other months. Because month of birth is unlikely to be correlated with ability or family background, any variation in educational attainment associated with compulsory school attendance laws is likely to be randomly distributed in terms of ability and environmental background. Angrist and Krueger find that season of birth is indeed related to educational attainment in the United States; in particular, those born early in the year (and who therefore attain the legal dropout age earlier in their education careers) have a slightly lower average level of education than those born later in the year. Furthermore, those who attend school longer because of compulsory schooling laws receive higher earnings. They estimate the impact of an additional year of school (due to compulsory attendance requirements) on the earnings of males to be an increase in earnings of 7.5 percent. Because ability is unlikely to be related to month of birth, this estimate should be free of any bias associated with unobserved ability. Of course, this study provides evidence regarding the relationship between schooling and earnings for levels of education around that of high school completion. Other natural experiments would be needed to obtain similar evidence for postsecondary education (see Exhibit 9.4).

Card (1995a) uses proximity to a college as another way to identify the "experimental" effects of acquiring postsecondary education. Individuals born in areas with nearby colleges or universities effectively face a lower cost of schooling. As long as account is taken

Exhibit 9.3

Brothers, Sisters, and the Returns to Schooling

Butcher and Case (1994) provide another example of a study based on a "natural experiment" that can be exploited for estimating the returns to schooling. As is often the case with this genre, their study is interesting not only for its "bottom line" estimate of the returns to schooling, but also for the "first stage" part of the research: explaining educational attainment. Butcher and Case focus on the role of family structure in affecting educational attainment. In particular, they explore the effect of sibling composition (the number of brothers and sisters). They find that at least for women, the number and sex composition of one's siblings has an important effect on educational attainment.

The effect of the number of siblings is relatively straightforward to explain: with more children, parents' financial resources are spread more thinly. If credit markets are imperfect, the average educational attainment of the children may be lowered in families with more children. The effect of sex composition is harder to explain. Butcher and Case found that girls who had only brothers had higher educational attainments than those with only sisters (all else equal). Butcher and Case explore several possible explanations, ranging from the purely economic (parents investing differentially in children on the basis of expected market returns), to more psychological (girls with more brothers have more male role models, and mimic their attitudes toward educational attainment). They find little consistent evidence for any of these explanations.

Whatever the reason for this correlation, the resulting differences in educational attainment among women with different combinations of brothers and sisters provides another possible way to identify the returns to schooling. If sibling size and composition are otherwise independent of future earnings, then differences in earnings across groups of women with different sibling compositions can be attributed to differences in the resulting schooling they received. As in other studies, when they use this technique to estimate the returns to schooling, they find that the estimated returns rise, from OLS estimates of around 7.5 percent, to "natural experimental" estimates on the order of 18 percent.

of other possible differences in family background that may be related to both geographical location and earnings potential, this difference in the cost of education can be used to isolate the returns to education. For example, the sample could be divided into two groups: those who lived near to and far away from colleges. We would expect that the two groups would have different average levels of schooling (the nearby group acquiring more schooling). This difference in schooling between the two groups would have nothing to do with differences in individual ability (though such differences may exist within each group). We could then attribute any differences in average earnings between the two groups to the resulting differences in schooling, since there are no other differences between the groups (having assumed that proximity to a college has no independent effect on earnings). Card found that the standard estimates of the return to schooling were typical, around 7.5 percent. Once college proximity was used to "control" for possible individual ability bias, the estimated returns rose to around 14 percent. Again, there was no evidence of ability bias.

In concluding this discussion of the empirical evidence relating to education and earnings, several observations should be made. First, looking across these recent studies, it

Exhibit 9.4 The Benefits of a Distinct Society (III)

"Conscription if necessary, but not necessarily conscription."

These famous words of Prime Minister William Lyon Mackenzie King spoken during World War II reflected his strong desire to avoid controversy over the issue of conscription (the draft). Canada was deeply divided over whether conscription should be implemented, with the fault line at the Quebec border. In a 1942 referendum on whether the federal government should have the power to draft men into military service, over 70 percent of Quebecers were opposed, while an equally large majority were in favour in the rest of Canada. For many reasons, there were sharp differences between Quebec and the rest of Canada with respect to the war effort in Europe. While there was eventually limited conscription at the end of the war, almost all of Canada's soldiers were volunteers, and regional enlistment patterns reflected the "Quebec–the rest of Canada" attitudes toward the war. Of the male population between the ages of 18 and 45 in 1945, 46 percent of men in Ontario had voluntarily served in the war, as against only 23 percent in Quebec. Basically, men outside Quebec were twice as likely to have served in the Canadian Army, Air Force, or Navy.

What does this have to do estimating the returns to education? In order to ease the return of war veterans into the labour market, the federal government provided strong financial incentives for veterans to attend university or other sorts of training programs. The Veterans Rehabilitation Act (VRA) offered returning soldiers living allowances and covered tuition expenses if they chose to attend university. Because so many more young men from Ontario than Quebec had served as soldiers, they were significantly more likely to be eligible for these benefits. In essence, the combination of the VRA and the differential probability of military service between Ontario and Quebec generates a "natural experiment" for estimating the impact of university attainment.

In terms of the notation in the text, the population can be divided into two groups, for example, 18-to-21-year-olds (in 1945) from Ontario, and the same age group from Quebec. Because they were more likely to be veterans, we would expect that the Ontario men would be more likely to attend university, and thus have higher education than the same-aged men from Quebec. As long as there were no other reasons for differences in labour market outcomes between men in Ontario and Quebec, we could attribute higher lifetime earnings for the Ontario men to their higher education. For example, we would have to assume that the Quebec and Ontario labour markets were otherwise similar, and that veteran status had no independent impact on earnings. David Card and Thomas Lemieux (2001) implement this procedure, including a careful evaluation of the necessary assumptions, to estimate the returns to education. They find that Ontario men born in the mid-1920s (who were 18 to 21 in 1945) were indeed more likely to attend university than comparable men in Quebec, and moreover that they were more likely to attend university than those Ontario men born before or immediately after them (who would not have been eligible for VRA benefits). Card and Lemieux estimate that the VRA increased the education of the veteran cohort of Ontario men by 0.2 to 0.4 years. Furthermore, they estimate an OLS rate of return to schooling of 7 percent, but a much higher (14 to 16 percent) rate of return when they exploit the "natural experiment." As with the growing body of related research, they find that the conventional OLS estimate of the returns to schooling is, if anything, biased downward (possibly by measurement error), as opposed to inflated by ability bias.

seems our initial intuition, that the returns to education were overstated because of ability bias, was exaggerated. Nevertheless, it remains an open question whether these new (higher) estimates of the return to schooling represent the return that a randomly selected individual would receive if given a "dose" of education.[5] More empirical work is needed. Second, the returns to education discussed here are restricted to the private monetary benefits. Additional benefits to the individual—such as any enjoyment derived directly from acquiring knowledge, a more varied and interesting career, or even an enhanced ability to enjoy life—would increase the private returns to education. Third, the social returns to education may differ from the private returns for a variety of reasons. It is also important to note that estimates usually provide the *average* rate of return for all those making a certain educational investment. Policies such as those relating to the allocation of resources should be based on *marginal*, not average, calculations; that is, for social efficiency, funds should be allocated among various physical and human capital investments such that the social rate of return on the last dollar invested in each project is equal.

Finally, note that the calculated returns to education are based on cross-sectional data (different individuals at a point in time). This procedure will only be accurate if the age-earnings profiles for each educational category are approximately constant over time, apart from overall earnings growth affecting all groups. To the extent that earnings differentials by education narrow or widen over time, the actual realized return to educational investments will be smaller or larger than that estimated on the basis of cross-sectional data.

Increased Returns to Education and Inequality

In the previous section, we reviewed the econometric quest for an estimate of "the" return to schooling. Increasingly, researchers have recognized that the return to education is not an immutable parameter, but varies across individuals (Card, 1999) and over time. Labour economists have been particularly interested in the variation of the returns to schooling over time.

Part of the interest derives from a pronounced increase in the returns to schooling during the 1980s and 1990s, especially in the United States. These **increased returns to education** have coincided with more general increases in income inequality in society: the "decline of the middle class," widely discussed in the press. Before examining the evidence, it is worth pausing to clarify the potential linkages between the schooling literature and the wider literature on income inequality. To begin, this entails emphasizing the distinction between wages, earnings, and income.

Most studies of income inequality, such as Blackburn and Bloom's 1993 comparative study of the United States and Canada, focus on the distribution of family income. This measure includes both the income of all family members (i.e., husbands and wives) and labour earnings and non-labour income such as government transfers and investment income. Increases in individual earnings inequality need not translate into increases in inequality of family income, particularly if husbands' and wives' income changes are offsetting, or if government transfers smooth changes in the earnings distribution. Beach and Slotsve (1996), for example, show that overall income inequality did not increase significantly in Canada during the 1980s, even though men's earnings inequality has increased sharply. By contrast, more recent evidence from Picot and Heisz (2000) shows that family income inequality increased sharply over the early 1990s. As Gottschalk (1997) emphasizes, labour economists do not have much understanding to this point how family income (as distinct from individual earnings) evolves in response to changing economic conditions. The determinants of family income are much more complicated. As Picot and Heisz suggest, the increase in Canadian family income inequality is associated with an increase

[5]David Card (1995b) and (1999) provides some preliminary exploration of alternative hypotheses.

in the number of lone-parent families, an increasing tendency for high-earning men and women to marry each other (assortative mating), and a decline in income transfers to low-income households during the early and mid-1990s. Of more interest to us in this section, then, is the distribution of labour market earnings, particularly for men.

The link between earnings inequality and returns to schooling is not quite complete. First, earnings are the product of wages and hours, and changes in hours worked, perhaps due to changes in the incidence of unemployment, may be as important as changes in wages. Some evidence of the importance of this distinction is provided by Beach and Slotsve (1996) and Freeman and Needels (1993). Morissette, Myles, and Picot (1995) and Doiron and Barrett (1996), for example, provide evidence that much of the growing inequality of earnings in Canada over the 1980s can be attributed to a growing inequality in hours of work.

Second, wages themselves may be becoming more unequal in ways that do not correlate with returns to schooling. In fact, most studies of wage inequality focus on the overall distribution, not the relative wages of high- and low-educated. For the United States, the distinction is not important. Katz and Autor (1999), Gottschalk (1997), and Juhn, Murphy, and Pierce (1993) show that the recent trend toward greater wage inequality is the result of both increased returns to schooling and increased inequality within education groups (wage inequality has increased among university graduates, not just between university graduates and high school dropouts). Juhn, Murphy, and Pierce argue, though, that most of the increase in wage inequality is due to increases in returns to "unobserved" skill, as opposed to observable skill (education). In the 1980s, however, the changing returns to observed education were quite pronounced. Given the assumption that wages equal marginal products, many authors blur the distinction between overall wage inequality and returns to schooling, and simply refer to increases in the returns to "skill," rather than restricting the discussion to the returns to formal education.

As it turns out, however, the distinction is much more important in Canada, where there has been a significant rise in wage inequality without an accompanying increase in the returns to schooling. Richardson (1997), Picot (1998), and Picot and Heisz (2000) document the sharp increase in wage and earnings inequality in Canada, and the relatively flat time profile for returns to education. Picot (1998) and Picot and Heisz (2000) emphasize that most of the increase in inequality is associated with age, with older workers faring much better than younger. There appears to be an increase in the returns to age, possibly reflecting increased returns to labour market experience, itself a form of human capital. However, as is carefully illustrated by Beaudry and Green (2000), this is not the case. Instead, the returns to labour market experience have been largely constant, but the entry position of younger workers has been steadily deteriorating, whatever their education level. Thus, earnings differences between young and old reflect possibly permanent "cohort effects" instead of increased returns to aging. Today's young workers have no reason to expect that their earnings will rise to the level of those of current older workers.

In addition to documenting the trends and patterns in the returns to skill (or wage inequality), many studies attempt to provide an explanation. Excellent summaries of these explanations are provided in Bound and Johnson (1992), Johnson (1997), Topel (1997), and Katz and Autor (1999). The explanations can most easily be cast in the context of a two-sector supply and demand framework, with markets for "skilled" and "unskilled" labour. First, increases in the relative supply of unskilled labour might depress the wages of the unskilled. Second, increases in the relative demand for skilled workers would raise their wages. Two hypotheses have been offered for an increase in the demand for skilled workers. Skill-biased technological change, in favour of skilled workers, would increase their relative demand. This would occur if new technologies (such as computers) and educated labour were complements in production. Alternatively, increased globalization and competition from low-skilled labour in developing countries might reduce the demand for less-skilled labour domestically. A third distinct possibility lies outside the supply and demand framework. Labour market institutions, like minimum wages or the influence of trade unions, may have changed in a way that hurt the unskilled more than the skilled. For example, declines in the real minimum wage (documented in Chapter 7) and in the degree of unionization that occurred in the United States (documented in Chapter 14) may have adversely affected the wages of the less-skilled.

Returns to Education During the 1960s and 1970s The first interest in the changing returns to schooling attempted to explain the reverse phenomenon to that studied in the 1990s. Studies of the monetary returns to investments in education during the late 1960s and early 1970s generally concluded that rates of return were substantial, especially for an undergraduate university degree or less (Stager, 1972). Private after-tax returns were usually estimated to be in the 10-to-15-percent range—an excellent investment return, given that these are real (i.e., after taking inflation into account) after-tax returns. During the 1970s the returns to education declined. Dooley (1986) examined changes in the relationship between earnings and education between the years 1971–73 and 1979–81 and found that the largest increases in earnings occurred for those groups with the least education. Using 1981 data, Vaillancourt and Henriques (1986) estimate private after-tax rates of return to university education in Canada ranging from 7 to 14 percent, depending on the region and length of degree program (three or four years). These estimates also indicate that monetary returns to education declined significantly during the 1970s.

In the United States, the financial return to a university or college degree also declined during the 1970s. One explanation of this phenomenon was the substantial increase in the proportion of the population going to university, particularly the entry into the labour force of the "baby boom" generation during the 1970s (Welch, 1979). Freeman (1976, 1980) argued that the demand for educated workers also declined, so that not all of the change in relative earnings could be attributed to temporary developments on the supply side. Dooley (1986) examined these competing explanations in the Canadian setting using data for the period 1971–1981. He concluded that the entry of the large baby-boom cohort during this period did lower earnings growth for this group, but that this demographic effect could not account for the observed narrowing of earnings differentials by level of education. Dooley's results thus suggest that demand-side forces may also have played a role.

Increasing Returns to Education in the 1980s and 1990s The decline in the monetary return to education during the 1970s—which gave rise to the phrase "overeducated American"—was reversed in the 1980s. This reversal was especially sharp in the United States, but it also occurred—albeit to a lesser extent—in Canada (Freeman and Needels, 1993). Careful documentation of the increase in the United States is presented in a number of studies. Katz and Murphy (1992) show the increasing skill premium for both observable and unobservable skill (university education), while Murphy and Welch (1992) focus mostly on increased returns to a university education. Bar-Or et al. (1995) illustrate the changing returns to schooling in Canada. Their study is particularly helpful, since they take full account of the comparability problems present in Canadian microdata. One of the difficulties in conducting such exercises is that changing data definitions can drive some of the apparent empirical patterns. As it turns out, they find that the returns to schooling fell in the 1970s, as noted by the earlier researchers, and increased only modestly (if at all) in the 1980s. Murphy, Riddell, and Romer (1998) also show essentially flat, even declining returns to a university education in Canada through the 1980s to 1994.

Most empirical research has concentrated on explaining the increased returns to education in the United States. Empirical studies generally attempt to sort out the relative contribution of demand and supply factors. On the demand side, the shift in employment out of heavy manufacturing industries and toward financial and business services has brought about a decline in demand for labour in semi-skilled and unskilled blue-collar jobs and an increase in demand for skilled, educated workers in the service sector. The underlying source of this change in demand remains a subject of debate. On the supply side, there were fewer educated baby boomers graduating and entering the United States labour force during the 1980s.

While there is no consensus on the relative contribution of the different supply and demand side factors, there is reasonable agreement that demand-side factors were most important, especially in the 1980s (Katz and Murphy, 1992; Murphy and Welch, 1992; Katz and Autor, 1999). That is, the technological change and industrial restructuring that occurred was biased in favour of more skilled and educated workers. As well, the increased international competition and imports tended to adversely affect low-wage workers, while increased exports positively affect higher-wage workers. On the supply side, there was a slower growth in the influx of educated college graduates so that higher wages were not constrained by that factor in the 1980s. In contrast, in the 1960s and 1970s, supply-side factors, notably the influx of the large cohort of baby boomers, did serve to constrain the wages of persons in those large cohorts (Topel, 1997). Supply and demand changes, as well as legal and institutional factors, also seem to explain the tendency to greater wage equality that occurred in the earlier period of the 1940s and 1950s in the United States. Goldin and Margo (1992) show that the compression of the individual wage structure at that time occurred because of the confluence of a variety of factors: increases in the demand for unskilled workers to work on automated production processes, especially with World War II; increases in the supply of more educated skilled workers; and increases in the minimum wage and union power. These are the flip side of the patterns observed over the 1980s, and they provide some corroboration of the usefulness of examining this question within the context of the supply and demand framework.

While there is some agreement of the overall importance of demand factors (i.e., there is agreement that supply factors cannot explain most of the increase in inequality), there remains disagreement as to which demand factors were most important. Most studies proceed by attempting to relate changes in the skill premium across occupational or industry groups. Because technology is inherently unobservable, it tends to be a "residual" explanation, while trade-based explanations can be more directly evaluated with trade data. Bound and Johnson (1992) and Johnson (1997) emphasize the inability of trade to explain changes in the wage structure, and argue that skill-biased technological change is the most likely explanation. Goldin and Katz (1996) look at the broader patterns of technological change in the twentieth century. They note, first of all, that technological change need not be biased in favour of high-skilled labour. The technological innovations of the industrial revolution tended to hurt skilled artisans in favour of unskilled labour working in factories. However, the twentieth century has seen most technological change complementary with skill, that is, the technological innovations in production have resulted in relative increases in the demand for skilled labour. Krueger (1993) offers a novel study directly linking production technology with wages. He finds that employees who work with computers, all else equal, have higher wages. This provided an indirect suggestion of the association of increased technology in the workplace with increased returns to skill. As it turns out, however, the observed linkage between use of computers and wages may have been spurious, reflecting other unobserved job characteristics. DiNardo and Pischke (1997, using different data from Krueger) show that a similar finding exists for using pencils or telephones on the job, suggesting that Krueger's "computer use" may have been proxying for the type of job, rather than the impact of technology on wages.

Other studies show strong linkages between international trade and the **polarization of wages**. Borjas and Ramey (1994) look at a variety of possible correlates with the skill premium, and find that only the durables trade deficit had a trend that was directly related to the returns to a college education. Borjas and Ramey (1995) extend their results further by showing that the skill premium increased most, not only in industries most open to trade, but also in those that faced the least domestic competition. They suggest that low-skilled foreign competition eroded the monopoly rents that less-skilled workers were sharing. Sachs and Shatz (1996) also find that the cross-industry patterns of changes in the skill premium are consistent with a trade-based explanation. Where import competition increased most, low-skilled workers were hurt most. They also argue that developing countries have seen the flip side of these changes, with improvements in the demand for unskilled labour in these countries. Feenstra and Hanson (1996) explore alternative avenues by which international trade might affect labour demand. They show that U.S. firms have made increasing use of foreign outsourcing, directly shifting the demand for unskilled labour outside the United States. But as Johnson (1997) argues, the trade-based explanation still faces a number of hurdles: the share of U.S. workers in industries affected by international trade is still small, wage inequality has increased in all industries, and the apparent shift in the relative demand for skilled workers goes back almost 40 years, long before the U.S. economy opened up substantially to international trade.

While these demand-side factors were the most important determinants of the growing wage inequality, they were augmented by other, interrelated institutional changes. In particular, DiNardo, Fortin, and Lemieux (1996) and Fortin and Lemieux (1997) show that the decline in unionization in the United States contributed considerably to the relative decline in the fortunes of less-skilled workers. Going even further down the skill distribution, DiNardo, Fortin and Lemieux also show that the real decline in the legislated minimum wage was associated with the widening of the wage distribution.

So why the different experience in Canada? A number of studies have sought to explain differences in both the level and trends in inequality and returns to schooling between Canada and the United States. Some of the answer comes within the supply and demand framework. In their comparative Canada-U.S. study, Freeman and Needels (1993) find that the returns to higher education did not increase as much in Canada as in the United States because of more rapid growth in the supply of university graduates in Canada than in the United States. In other words, the demand for more educated workers increased in both countries, but the greater supply response in Canada kept the relative earnings of the more educated from rising as quickly. In both countries industrial restructuring put downward pressure on the earnings of those with the least skill and education. Murphy, Riddell, and Romer (1998) provide a more formal treatment that confirms Freeman and Needel's main findings. They show that the different trends in returns to schooling between Canada and the United States can be explained by a common shift in the demand curve for skilled labour, combined with a greater offsetting increase in the supply of university-educated workers. As noted in Picot and Heisz (2000), the 1980s and 1990s saw the fraction of the labour force with university degrees almost double, from 10 percent in 1976 to 18 percent in 1998.

But different labour market institutions are also part of the explanation. Freeman and Needels find some evidence that less-educated low-wage workers in the United States were more adversely affected by declining unionism than was the case in Canada, where unions are more important. The greater role of unions is especially highlighted by DiNardo and Lemieux (1997) and Donald, Green, and Paarsch (2000). Both of these studies compare earnings distributions in Canada and the United States, and show that the lower wage inequality in Canada derives from the greater degree in unionization, and indeed DiNardo and Lemieux argue that most of the greater increase in wage inequality (*not* returns to schooling) can be explained by the relative decline in unions in the United States.

Taken together, these findings raise many questions for policymakers. On the one hand, increased returns to schooling make it even more imperative to encourage individuals to acquire education. The penalty for dropping out of high school is becoming increasingly large. These findings suggest that the single easiest way to improve the income distribution may be to reduce inequality in schooling attainment, by encouraging more people to obtain postsecondary education. On the other hand, returns to schooling are increasing, even with dramatic increases in university enrollment. Given that schooling is one of the most important factors leading to income inequality, and that the private returns to schooling have increased significantly, subsidies to education may (if poorly directed) actually contribute to a widening of the income distribution.

TRAINING

Like education, training is a form of investment in human capital in which costs are incurred in the present in the anticipation of benefits in the future. The benefits accrue because training imparts skills which raise the worker's productivity and thus value in the labour market.

In this section, we focus on some *economic* aspects of training rather than on an institutional description of training in Canada: the latter is discussed, for example, in Davies (1986) and Economic Council of Canada (1992). The main focus of our analysis is to shed light on the following questions: Who pays for training? Is a government subsidy warranted? How should training be evaluated?

Who Pays?

In his classic work on the subject, Becker (1964, pp. 11–28) distinguishes between **general training** and **specific training**. General training is training that can be used in various firms, not just in firms that provide the training. Consequently, in a competitive market, firms will bid for this training by offering a higher wage equal to the value of the training. Since competition ensures that the trainee reaps the benefits of general training in the form of higher earnings, then the trainee would be willing to bear the cost of training as long as benefits exceed costs. If a company were to bear the cost of such training they would still have to bid against other companies for the services of the trainee.

This argument is illustrated in Figure 9.7(a). In the absence of training, the individual can earn the alternative wage W_a equal to the value of marginal product without training (VMP_a). During the training period the value of the worker's output is VMP_t (which could be zero). After training, the worker's value to *any* firm in this labour market rises to VMP*. The costs and benefits are as shown. If the investment is worthwhile, the employee can finance the training and earn the benefits by being paid a wage equal to the VMP at each point in time; i.e., the worker receives $W_t = VMP_t$ during training and W* = VMP* after the training period. The firm could incur the costs and hope to reap the benefits by paying the worker W_a before and after training. However, because the employee can earn W* elsewhere, the firm's strategy won't work. Thus, in the absence of bonding arrangements (as are used for limited periods in the armed forces for certain types of general training, such as pilot training), general training will be financed by employees.

With specific training, however, the training is useful only in the company that provides the training. Consequently, other companies have no incentive to pay higher earnings for such training and the trainee would not bear the cost because of an inability to reap the benefits in the form of higher earnings. The sponsoring company, however, would bear the costs providing they exceed the benefits. In addition, the sponsoring company would not have to pay a higher wage for those persons with specific training since other firms are not competing for such trainees.

This case is also illustrated in Figure 9.7(a). The firm pays the alternative wage W_a during and after training, incurring costs of $W_a - VMP_t$ during the training period and receiving benefits of $VMP^* - W_a$ after the completion of training.

Figure 9.7 **Costs, Benefits, and Financing of Training**

Training improves a worker's marginal product, at the expense of lower labour productivity during the training period. Whether the employee or the employer pays for the benefits from training depends on whether the human capital is general (useful to other forms) or specific (only useful to the firm).

Panel (a) illustrates these costs and benefits. In the absence of training, a worker has productivity VMP_a, and can earn W_a elsewhere. After a period of t^* training with reduced productivity, VMP_t, the worker's productivity increases to VMP*. With general training, the worker can finance the training herself, by accepting a lower wage during the training period (equal to VMP_t) in return for a higher wage (VMP*) afterward. The firm has no incentive to pay for this training, since, post-training, she can be poached by other firms for a wage up to VMP*, which would render the firm's investment worthless. On the other hand, if the human capital is firm-specific, the firm can finance the training without concern that the employee will be poached, since her additional training is of no value to other firms. The firm could pay the employee W_a pre- and post-training.

However, even with firm-specific training, given the precarious nature of any employment relationship it may be worthwhile for the employer and employee to share the cost of the investment. Post-training, the employee is paid W*, which is higher than her alternative wage, so she is less likely to quit. In return, the employee helps pay for the training by accepting a lower wage, W_t, during the training period.

In panel (c) earnings rise, and training is offered more gradually. The configuration of wages and marginal product is such that employees accept lower wages early in their career in return for higher productivity and wages later on.

(a) Costs and benefits of training

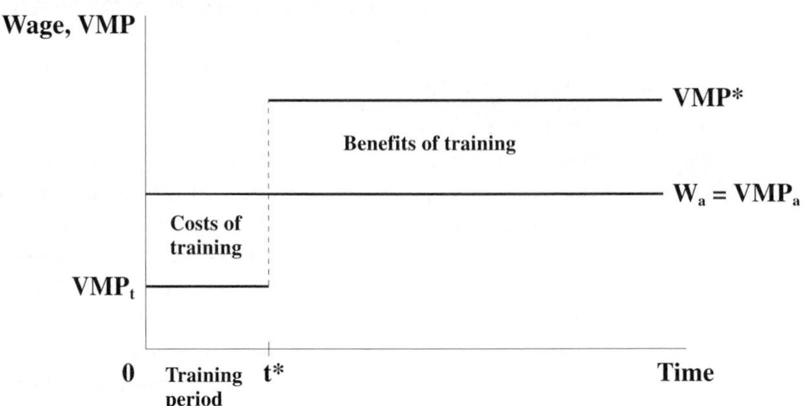

(b) Specific training as a shared investment

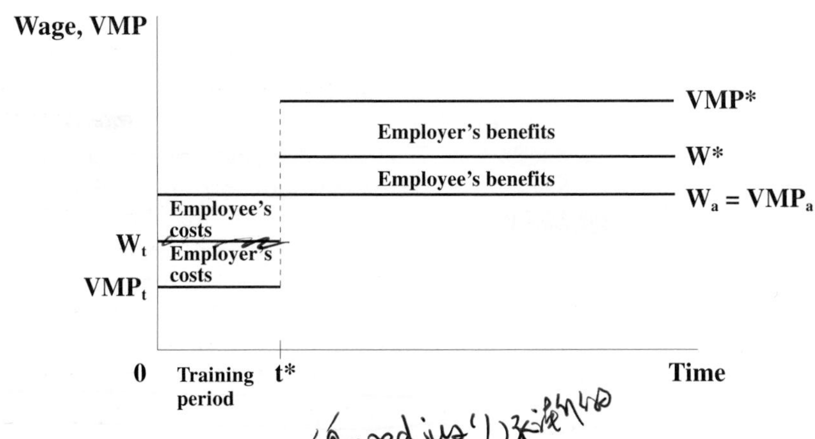

(c) Earnings growth with gradual training

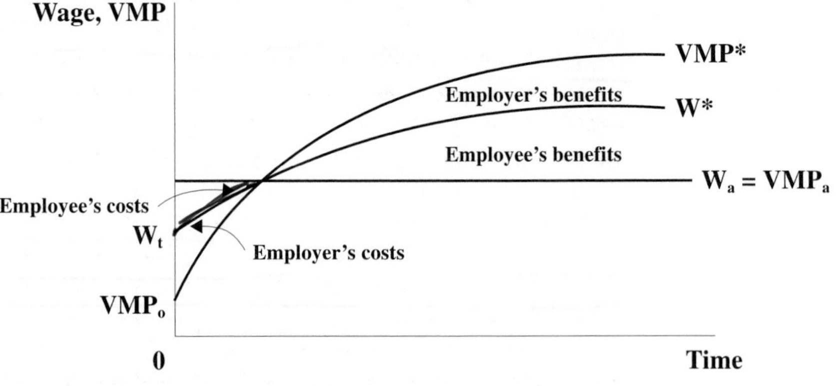

Specific human capital may also be a shared investment. This arrangement is particularly likely when there is some uncertainty about the continuation of the employment relation due to shifts in labour demand affecting the worker's VMP and shifts in supply affecting the alternative wage W_a. If the sponsoring company pays for the specific training, as shown in Figure 9.7(a), it faces the risk that the employee may quit at some point after the training period, thus reducing the employer's anticipated return on the investment. Because the worker is receiving no more than the alternative wage, the cost of quitting is low. Even a small increase in W_a could cause the worker to go elsewhere. However, the cost to the company is high because the trained employee is worth more to the firm than he or she is being paid. In these circumstances, the sponsoring company may pay trainees a wage premium to reduce their turnover and hence to increase the probability that the company will recoup its investment costs. To compensate for the wage premium, the firm may lower the wage paid during the training period, in which case the two parties share the costs and benefits of training.

This situation is shown in Figure 9.7(b). The firm pays $W_t < W_a$ during the training period and $W^* > W_a$ after training. Both parties incur costs and reap benefits as shown. The shared investment minimizes the risk that either party will wish to terminate the employment relation because both the employer and employee are earning rents after the completion of training. The employer's rents of $VMP^* - W^*$ each period reduce the risk that the employee will be laid off due to a decline in demand. Only when the worker's value to the firm falls below W^* will the firm consider layoffs. The employee's rents of $W^* - W_a$ each period reduce the risk that the employee will quit in response to an improvement in labour market opportunities. Only when the alternative wage rises above W^* will the employee consider quitting.

This analysis indicates that specific human capital investments provide an incentive for firms and workers to maintain their employment relationship in the face of external shocks to demand and supply. The return on the shared investment acts like glue keeping the two parties together. These incentives for long-term employment relationships and their consequences are discussed further in Chapter 18 in the context of implicit contracts, in Chapter 13 in the context of deferred compensation, and in Chapter 6 in the context of layoffs.

In competitive markets, then, trainees will pay for general training whereas specific training investments may be paid by the sponsoring company or shared by the two parties. The form of payment may be subtle, as, for example, when trainees in an apprenticeship program forgo earnings by accepting a lower wage rate during the training period, or when companies forgo some output from workers when they provide them with on-the-job training.

The sharp distinction made in panels (a) and (b) of Figure 9.7 between the training and post-training periods may not hold in practice. Much on-the-job training is informal and takes place gradually as employees learn different facets of their job and its place in the overall organization. In these circumstances, earnings can be expected to rise gradually, as shown in Figure 9.7(c), rather than abruptly. The concave shape of the earnings profile reflects the assumption that there are diminishing returns to on-the-job training and work experience. As noted previously, this shape is typical of age-earnings profiles (see Figure 9.5).

In practice the distinction between general and specific training can be difficult to make. Training often contains elements of both. Even training that is geared to the specific production processes of a particular firm often contains elements that are transferable and the completion of such training can serve as a *signal* to firms that the trainee is capable of learning new skills even if the particular skills themselves are not transferable. On the other hand, general training that is provided in a particular firm may be somewhat more useful in the sponsoring company simply because the trainee is more familiar with that company.

Nonetheless, the distinction between general and specific training is useful for conceptual purposes. Furthermore, although training usually contains a mixture of the two forms, occupations and industries will differ in the proportion of training that is general versus specific. Differences across occupations and industries in such factors as earnings growth and layoff and quit rates can therefore be explained in terms of differences in the amount of training and the proportions of general and specific training.

Appropriate Role of Government

If trainees will pay for and benefit from general training and sponsoring companies and employees will share the costs and benefits of specific training, why should governments be involved in the training process? In other words, are there situations when the private unregulated market does not provide a socially optimal amount of training?

This possibility may exist for trainees who cannot afford to purchase training (perhaps by accepting a lower wage during the training period) and who cannot borrow because of an inability to use their human capital (future earnings) as collateral for a loan. Imperfect information, regulatory restrictions, or contract enforceability problems may prevent private institutional arrangements like apprenticeships from fully developing to provide the optimal amount of training (see, however, Gillian Hamilton, 1995, 1996, and 2000 for a discussion of these issues in the context of apprenticeship contracts in early nineteenth-century Montreal). Subsidies to training the disadvantaged may be particularly appealing to taxpayers who prefer to support transfer programs that are associated with work activity. Concern about the working poor who work full-time but at a wage that is too low to yield a level of income above the poverty line also suggests the possibility of supporting training programs for disadvantaged workers.

The private market may also yield a less than socially optimal amount of training to the extent that training generates external (spillover, third-party) benefits that are not paid for in the market. In such circumstances firms and individuals would have no incentive to consider such benefits in their investment calculations and consequently may underinvest in training. Externalities may exist in the form of vacuum effects when trainees move up the occupation ladder and vacate a job that is filled by a member of the unemployed, or they may exist in the form of complementary multiplier effects as trainees reduce structural bottlenecks that previously resulted in the unemployment of related workers.

A sub-optimal amount of general training may also be provided by companies where on-the-job training is a natural byproduct of their production process. Workers simply acquire training in their everyday work tasks. However, because it is difficult to know how much training they are acquiring and at what cost, they may be reluctant to pay for such training. In such circumstances, training may have public-good characteristics in that the training is available to all workers and yet it is difficult to exclude those who don't pay for the training. To be sure, only those who are willing to work for lower wages could be hired (and in this way nonpayers are excluded). However, the indirect nature of the training makes it difficult for the purchasers to know how much training they are acquiring.

At the macroeconomic level, training may also yield benefits to the general public in the sense of helping the economy achieve such goals as growth, full employment, price stability, a viable balance of payments, and a more equitable distribution of income. As an anti-cyclical device to reduce the inflation- unemployment tradeoff, training may be effective in absorbing some of the unemployed during a recession and in providing supplies of skilled workers when structural bottlenecks may otherwise lead to inflation.

Evaluation of Government Training Programs

Our discussion to this point makes clear the importance of education and training in determining individual earnings. It is not surprising that policymakers view training as an important tool, whether or not some of the theoretical arguments in favour of government intervention hold. Given the popularity of proposed training programs, one would imagine that there was evidence that these programs were cost-effective, even if they only displaced the private provision of training. Perhaps surprisingly, the evidence in support of government training programs is quite mixed.

The evaluation of government training programs provides a classic example of the difficulties of performing reliable **program evaluation**. Training is evaluated by the extent to which it improves an individual's earnings, either by increasing his wage rate or by improving his chances of obtaining a job in the first place. The difficulty, which we have encountered before, is that we never observe what the trained individual's earnings would have been in the absence of training. We observe the **treatment** but we may not have a plausible **control group**. Consider first (perhaps cynically) a politician's measure of the effectiveness of training, a comparison of an individual's earnings before and after training:

$$Y_{After} - Y_{Before}$$

There are several reasons why this is a poor measure of the impact of training. Each problem suggests a different solution.

First, the individual's earnings may have been especially low before training. Individuals may be enrolled in programs when they have experienced bad luck in the labour market. On average, even if training had no effect, we would expect these individuals' earnings to revert to their long-run value. Thus, we may attribute an increase in earnings to a "mean reverting" rebound in earnings that would have occurred anyway. The obvious remedy for this problem is to use an appropriate comparison group, where the group comprises individuals who also had extraordinarily low earnings, but did not obtain training. This is a special case of the more general problem plaguing such estimates of the impact of training: the trainees may have experienced wage growth in the absence of training. Whether it is because low earnings are individually transitory, or because there are economy-wide trends upon which trainees can ride, we might observe increases in earnings for individuals that have nothing to do with training. This problem, again, has a straightforward solution: earnings growth of the trainees must be compared to a carefully selected comparison group of individuals who did not receive training. An estimate of the effect of training on earnings would then be

$$(Y_{After} - Y_{Before})_{Trained} - (Y_{After} - Y_{Before})_{Not\ Trained}$$

To address the problems just described, a data set with detailed information on the same types of individuals who received training (but did not) would be sufficient to construct a control group.

Unfortunately, there are difficulties in implementing such a procedure, because one can never obtain data on the "same types" of individuals without an experiment. There are good reasons to believe that individuals who receive and do not receive training will differ in unobservable ways that lead to an overstatement of the impact of training. First, if enrollment in training programs requires initiative on the part of the trainee, then this self-selection will yield a pool of trainees more likely to have these positive unobservable characteristics than the pool of nontrained individuals. Individuals may choose to enroll in training programs if they have private information suggesting they would particularly benefit. The same sort of selection may operate on the part of the training providers. Given resource limitations, administrators of training programs will naturally choose to offer training to those individuals most likely to succeed. It would then be inappropriate to assign the difference in earnings between trained and untrained individuals entirely to training: part of the difference may be the result of innate differences in the earnings capacities of the individuals.

The best solution to this evaluation problem is to conduct an experiment, randomly assigning individuals into training programs or control groups, then following up their labour market outcomes. Such experiments have been conducted in both Canada and the United States. LaLonde (1986) demonstrates some of the advantages of employing these experiments instead of artificially constructing control groups, though Heckman and Smith (1995) point out that these experiments are no panacea, and in fact have their own shortcomings. In fact, as Heckman, Lalonde, and Smith (1999) emphasize, whatever procedure is used, the most important determinant of the reliability of the evaluation is the careful construction of a control or comparison group. If chosen properly, a nonexperimental comparison group can serve almost as well as an experimental one.

Lalonde (1995) and Heckman, Lalonde, and Smith (1999) review the empirical results from evaluating a variety of training programs in the U.S., employing experimental and nonexperimental (econometric) procedures. The results (in terms of cost effectiveness) vary by program. Training is directed to two distinct groups: disadvantaged workers and dislocated or displaced workers. Disadvantaged workers tend to be young, and come from poor backgrounds. They represent a high risk for continued low income (and possible use of welfare). The evidence suggests that there are modest returns to training for disadvantaged women, but little positive evidence for men. Displaced workers tend to be older, blue-collar men, displaced from relatively high-paying jobs. This is the group often discussed when governments propose adjustment programs in response to the impact of globalization or other substantial changes in market structure. There is only limited evidence that training programs help these individuals, and a general consensus that the training programs can never increase earnings to the level before displacement.

As LaLonde points out, however, we may be expecting too much from training. As a crude "back of the envelope" benchmark, consider the returns to a year of full-time university study. This expensive form of training is estimated to raise earnings by about 7 percent (for men). Average earnings for full-year full-time men were about $32,500 in 1990. A 7 percent increase in earnings would be about $2275 per year. The type of training offered in government training programs is much more modest than full-time university, so it is unreasonable to expect that such programs are going to vault large numbers of individuals out of poverty, or restore skilled workers' years of lost industry-specific human capital.

Summary

- The individual decision to acquire education can be treated like any investment. The human capital investment decision is based on a comparison of the present value of the net benefits of obtaining varying levels of education. The optimal choice will maximize the present value of net benefits, accounting for the direct costs of schooling, as well as the opportunity cost of the time spent in school.
- Because it is costly for people to acquire education, workers will need to be compensated in the labour market by higher wages in order to justify the investment in additional human capital. As long as firms are willing to pay these higher wages (because higher-educated workers are more productive), there will be a positive return to education.
- It is also possible for wages to be positively related to education even if education does not improve individual productivity. This can occur when education serves as a signal for underlying ability, and firms cannot otherwise distinguish between high- and low-quality workers. As long as education is correlated with underlying ability, firms will be willing to pay for more highly educated workers.

- The empirical evidence strongly shows that, on average, earnings increase with education. One convenient way to summarize the relationship between earnings and education is through the human capital earnings function. The human capital earnings function relates the log of earnings to the level of education, and other covariates like potential labour market experience. The coefficient on years of schooling in this equation is called the "return to schooling."
- An important interpretation problem arises in determining whether the estimated returns to schooling represent the "causal" effect of schooling on earnings. The estimated coefficient may overstate the true causal effect, if (for example) more highly educated individuals would have earned more than less-educated individuals even with the same amount of schooling as the less-educated. This problem of "ability bias" has been addressed by a number of studies that exploit "natural experiments," where it is believed that differences in schooling are not driven by differences in labour market ability.
- A significant amount of human capital investment occurs through on-the-job training. However, whether the worker or the firm pays for this human capital depends on whether the training yields general or firm-specific human capital. The firm will not pay for general human capital, since workers can be poached away by other firms. The poaching problem does not exist for firm-specific training. However, even with firm-specific human capital, the firm and worker may share the investment, so that the worker will have an incentive to remain with the firm after training.
- Economists and policymakers often want to know whether government training programs improve the incomes of program participants. However, evaluation of these programs requires a carefully constructed "control group," ideally the product of a formal experiment, since a comparison of trainees earnings before and after the training program may overstate the benefits of the training.

REVIEW QUESTIONS

1. Discuss the analogy between physical and human capital.
2. How would you evaluate the extent to which your acquiring a university education is a sound investment economically? Be precise in the information you would require and exactly what you would do with it.
3. You have been asked to evaluate an on-the-job training program in a particular company. Specify exactly what sort of information you require, and what you would do with it.
4. The federal government supports a variety of human resource programs including education, training, mobility, labour market information, and health. Could you suggest any techniques that may be useful to suggest how resources should be allocated to the various functions?
5. Should governments subsidize human resource programs? If so, why? Be precise in your answer by indicating where, if anywhere, the private market may fail to yield a socially optimal amount of human resource development.
6. Give an example of each of the following as errors in a cost-benefit calculation: ignoring opportunity cost, failing to discount benefits, double-counting, considering sunk cost with no alternative value, ignoring a real externality, considering a pecuniary externality, and ignoring consumption benefits.
7. Compare the virtues of on-the-job versus institutional training.

PROBLEMS

1. Assume that you are deciding whether to acquire a four-year university degree. Your only consideration at this moment is the degree as an investment for yourself. Costs per year are tuition fees \$600, and books \$100. The government also pays to the university an equivalent amount to your tuition fees to cover the real cost. If you didn't go to university, you could earn \$6000 per year as an acrobat. With a university degree, however, you know that you can earn \$10,000 per year as an acrobat. Because of the nature of your chosen occupation, your time horizon for the investment decision is exactly ten years after university; that is, if the investment is to be worthwhile, it must be so within a ten-year period after graduation. The market rate of interest is 5 percent. Would you make the investment in a degree?

2. "You can't teach an old dog new tricks—in fact, you shouldn't." Discuss.

3. Madeleine is a high school graduate, deciding whether to go to university. She (like everyone else) lives for two periods after high school. In the first period, she can work (without university) for a salary of Y_H, or she can attend university. If she attends university, she must pay \$5000 in fees (tuition, books), but she will also earn \$5000 from a summer job. In the second period, she will continue to earn Y_H if she did not attend university, or she will earn Y_U if she went to university. The interest rate at which money can be borrowed or invested is r.

   Show that she will attend university if

$$Y_U > (2 + r)Y_H$$

   Explain how an increase in the interest rate would affect her decision to attend university.

4. This question continues the analysis of Madeleine's decision to attend university (from Question 3).

   In order to decide whether to attend university, she needs to know whether the condition (in Question 3) is true, and more generally how much a university education would increase her earnings.

   She has a well-designed labour force survey with information on earnings, education, and other sociodemographic characteristics. If she divides her sample into two groups, 1 and 2, she can estimate the returns to schooling (per year) with the following estimator:

$$\hat{\beta} = \frac{\bar{Y}_1 - \bar{Y}_2}{\bar{S}_1 - \bar{S}_2}$$

   where $\bar{Y}_j$ is average individual earnings from group j, and $\bar{S}_j$ is the average level of schooling for individuals in group j.

   Suppose that the true model of earnings for groups 1 and 2 is given by

$$Y_i = \alpha + \beta S_i + \varepsilon_i$$

   (a) Her first instinct is to divide the sample into two groups: those with a four-year university degree (S_U), and those with only high school (S_H).

   Derive the conditions under which her estimator will yield an unbiased (i.e., correct on average) estimate of β, and interpret.

   (b) Assume that she has information on each individual's parent's income. Assume also that individuals from poorer families face higher borrowing costs than those from richer ones. How might this affect individual university attainment decisions?

Use the condition in Question 3. How might she exploit this information in order to obtain an unbiased estimate of β? Be sure to discuss the necessary assumptions for this strategy to work.

5. Grant has just finished high school. He has three periods of time left in his working life, and is considering three career options:
   - Obtain a job in a hotel, earning $20,000 for each of the remaining three periods of his working life.
   - Attend community college, earning a diploma in human resources. The diploma takes one period to complete, with tuition fees equal to $5000. After graduation, he will earn $50,000 for the remaining two periods of his life.
   - Attend university to obtain his Ph.D. in art history. The degree takes two periods to complete, with tuition fees of $10,000 per period. After graduation, he will earn $90,000 for the one remaining period of his working life.

   Assume that the interest rate is 10 percent per period.

   (a) Which career path should he follow?

   (b) Grant has always wanted to be an art historian. If he chooses to be an art historian, what is the implicit consumption value he places on being an art historian?

   (c) Who among the population is likely to choose this career path—the children of rich or of poor parents? Why?

   (d) Should the government subsidize tuition fees for art history? Why or why not?

6. Assume that there are two types of workers in equal proportion (i.e., 50 percent of each type). High-ability workers have productivity of $50,000, while low-ability workers have productivity of $30,000. Firms will pay workers their marginal product, but they cannot distinguish between the two types of workers. If firms cannot distinguish between workers, they must pay all workers the same wage, equal to the average marginal product. In equilibrium, firms must earn zero profits.

   However, workers can buy S units of education. The cost to high-ability workers to acquire S units of education is $S/2, and for low-ability workers, it is $S. Education has no impact on workers' marginal products.

   (a) What is the equilibrium wage rate for the high- and low-ability workers in the absence of education, that is, assuming that education is unaffordable to either the high- or the low-ability workers?

   (b) Now assume that education is available as described. Assume that firms use the following rules to pay workers:

   If $S < 31{,}000$, then pay the worker $30,000
   If $S \geq 31{,}000$, then pay the worker $50,000

   How much education will the high- and low-ability workers obtain, and what will be their wages? Provide a careful explanation and diagram.

   (c) Returning to the theoretical model, in an effort to encourage low-ability workers to obtain schooling, the government subsidizes and reforms education so that the cost of schooling is reduced. The cost to high-ability workers is now $S/3, and to low-ability $S/2.

   Show that the pay scheme adopted by firms in part (a) does not yield an equilibrium. What is the equilibrium level of schooling and education?

7. A researcher wishes to evaluate the effectiveness of a one-year job skills training program for disadvantaged women. She has surveyed the women as they entered the training program in January 2000, and then one year after the program, in January 2002, obtaining estimates of their average earnings in each year. The women's average earnings in January 2000 were $10,000, and they were $15,000 in January 2002.

(a) "A reasonable estimate of the impact of the training program is that it raised trainee earnings by $5000." Critically evaluate this statement.

(b) The researcher consults her annual reports from Statistics Canada, and reads that the average full-year full-time female worker in Canada had earnings of $35,000 in January 2000, and $38,000 in January 2002. Can she use this information to construct a better estimate of the impact of training? Can you suggest a better comparison group? Explain.

KEYWORDS

REFERENCES

Altonji, J. 1995. The effects of high school curriculum on education and labor market outcomes. *JHR* 30 (Summer):409–38.

Angrist, J. D., and A. B. Krueger. 1991. Does compulsory school attendance affect schooling and earnings? *QJE* 106 (November):979–1014.

Ashenfelter, O., and A. Krueger. 1994. Estimates of the economic return to schooling from a new sample of twins. *AER* 84 (December):1157–73.

Ashenfelter, O., and C. Rouse. 1998. Income, schooling, and ability: Evidence from a new sample of identical twins. *QJE* 113 (February):253–84.

Bar-Or, Y., J. Burbridge, L. Magee, and A. L. Robb. 1995. The wage premium to a university education in Canada, 1971–1991. *JOLE* 13 (October):762–94.

Basu, K. 1999. Child labor: Cause, consequence, and cure, with remarks on international labor standards. *JEL* 37 (September):1083–1119.

Beach, C., and G. Slotsve. 1996. *Are We Becoming Two Societies? Income Polarization and the Myth of the Declining Middle Class in Canada*. Toronto: C. D. Howe Institute.

Beaudry, P., and D. A. Green. 2000. Cohort patterns in Canadian earnings: Assessing the role of skill premia in inequality trends. *CJE* 33 (November):907–36.

Becker, G. 1964. *Human Capital*. New York: National Bureau of Economic Research.

Behrman, J., Z. Hrubec, P. Taubman, and T. Wales. 1980. *Socioeconomic Success: A Study of the Effects of Genetic Endowments, Family Environment, and Schooling*. Amsterdam: North Holland.

Blackburn, M., and D. Bloom. 1993. The distribution of family income: measuring and explaining changes in the 1980s for Canada and the United States. In *Small Differences That Matter*, eds. D. Card and R. Freeman. Chicago: University of Chicago Press.

Borjas, G., and V. Ramey. 1994. Time-series evidence on the sources of trends in wage inequality. *AER* 84 (May):10–16.

______. 1995. Foreign competition, market power, and wage inequality. *QJE* 110 (November):1075–1110.

Bound, J., and G. Johnson. 1992. Changes in the structure of wages in the 1980s: An evaluation of alternative explanations. *AER* 82 (June):371–92.

Card, D. 1995a. Using geographic variation in college proximity to estimate the return to schooling. In *Aspects of Labour Market Behaviour: Essays in Honour of John Vanderkamp*, eds. L. Christofides, E. K. Grant, and R. Swidinsky. Toronto: University of Toronto Press.

______. 1995b. Earnings, schooling, and ability revisited. In *Research in Labor Economics*, ed. S. Polachek. Greenwich, CT: JAI Press.

______. 1999. The causal effect of education on earnings. In *Handbook of Labor Economics*, eds. O. Ashenfelter and D. Card. New York and Oxford: Elsevier Science, North Holland.

Card, D., and T. Lemieux. 2001. Education, earnings, and the 'Canadian G. I. Bill.' *CJE* 34 (May):313-44.

Davies, J. B. 1986. Training and skill development. In *Adapting to Change: Labour market Adjustment in Canada*, ed. W. C. Riddell. Toronto: University of Toronto Press.

Davies, J. B., and G.M.T. MacDonald. 1984. *Information in the Labour Market: Job-Worker Matching and Its Implications for Education in Ontario*. Toronto: Ontario Economic Council.

DiNardo, J., N. Fortin, and T. Lemieux. 1996. Labor market institutions and the distribution of wages, 1973-1992: A semi-parametric approach. *Ecta* 64 (September):1001-44.

DiNardo, J., and T. Lemieux. 1997. Diverging male wage inequality in the United States and Canada, 1981-88: Do institutions explain the difference? *ILRR* 50 (July):629-51.

DiNardo, J., and J.-S. Pischke. 1997. The returns to computer use revisited: Have pencils changed the wage structure too? *QJE* 112 (February):291-303.

Doiron, D., and G. F. Barrett. 1996. Inequality in male and female earnings: The role of hours and wages. *R.E. Stats.* 78 (August):410-20.

Donald, S. G., D. A. Green, and H. Paarsch. 2000. Differences in wage distributions between Canada and the United States: An application of a flexible estimator of distribution functions in the presence of covariates. *R.E. Studies* 67 (October):609-33.

Dooley, M. 1986. The overeducated Canadian? Changes in the relationship among earnings, education, and age for Canadian men: 1971-1981. *CJE* 19 (February):142-59.

Economic Council of Canada. 1992. *A Lot to Learn: Education and Training in Canada*. Ottawa: Minister of Supply and Services Canada.

Feenstra, R., and G. Hanson. 1996. Globalization, outsourcing, and wage inequality. *AER* 86 (May):240-45.

Fortin, N., and T. Lemieux. 1997. Institutional Changes and Rising Wage Inequality: Is There a Linkage? *JEP* 11 (Spring):75-96.

Freeman, R. B. 1976. *The Overeducated American*. New York: Academic Press.

______. 1980. The facts about the declining economic value of college. *JHR* 15:124-42.

Freeman, R. B., and K. Needels. 1993. Skill differentials in Canada in an era of rising labor market inequality. In *Small Differences That Matter*, eds. D. Card and R. Freeman. Chicago: University of Chicago Press.

Goldin, C., and L. Katz. 1996. Technology, skill, and the wage structure: Insights from the past. *AER* 86 (May):252-57.

Goldin, C., and R. Margo. 1992. The great compression: the wage structure in the United States at mid-century. *QJE* 107 (February):1-34.

Gottschalk, P. 1997. Inequality, income growth, and mobility: The basic facts. *JEP* 11 (Spring):21-40.

Hamilton, G. 1995. Enforcement in apprenticeship contracts: Were runaways a serious problem? Evidence from Montreal. *JEH* 55 (September):551-74.

______. 1996. The market for Montreal apprentices: Contract length and information. *Explorations in Economic History* 33 (October):496-523.

______. 2000. The decline of apprenticeship in North America: Evidence from Montreal. *JEH* 60 (September):627-64.

Heckman, J., R. LaLonde, and J. Smith. 1999. The economics and econometrics of active labor market programs. In *Handbook of Labor Economics*, eds. O. Ashenfelter and D. Card. New York and Oxford: Elsevier Science, North Holland.

Heckman, J., and J. Smith. 1995. Assessing the case for social experiments. *JEP* 9 (Spring):85-110.

Johnson, G. 1997. Changes in earnings inequality: The role of demand shifts. *JEP* 11 (Spring):41-54.

Juhn, C., K. M. Murphy, and B. Pierce. 1993. Wage inequality and the rise in returns to skill. *JPE* 101 (June):410-42.

Katz, L. F., and D. Autor. 1999. Changes in the wage structure and earnings inequality. In *Handbook of Labor Economics*, eds. O. Ashenfelter and D. Card. New York and Oxford: Elsevier Science, North Holland.

Katz, L. F., and K. M. Murphy. 1992. Changes in relative wages, 1963-1987: Supply and demand factors. *QJE* 107 (February):35-78.

Krueger, A. 1993. How computers have changed the wage structure: Evidence from microdata. *QJE* 108 (February):33-60.

LaLonde, R. 1986. Evaluating the econometric evaluations of training programs with experimental data. *AER* 76 (September):604-20.

______. 1995. The promise of public sector sponsored training programs. *JEP* 9 (Spring):149-68.

Lang, K., and D. Kropp. 1986. Human capital versus sorting: The effects of compulsory attendance laws. *QJE* 101 (August):609-24.

Margo, R. A., and T. A. Finegan. 1996. Compulsory schooling legislation and school attendance in turn-of-the-century America: A 'natural experiment' approach. *Economics Letters* 53 (October):103-10.

Miller, P. W., C. Mulvey, and N. Martin. 1995. What do twins studies reveal about the economic returns to education? A comparison of Australian and U.S. findings. *AER* 85 (June):586-99.

Moehling, C. M. 1999. State child labor laws and the decline of child labor. *Explorations in Economic History* 36 (January):72-106.

Morissette, R., J. Myles, and G. Picot. 1995. Earnings polarization in Canada, 1969-1991. In *Labour Market Polarization and Social Policy Reform*, eds. K. Banting and C. Beach. Kingston: School of Policy Studies, Queen's University.

Murphy, K. M., W. C. Riddell, and P. M. Romer. 1998. Wages, skills, and technology in the United States and Canada. In *General Purpose Technologies and Economic Growth*, ed. E. Helpman. Cambridge and London: MIT Press.

Murphy, K. M., and F. Welch. 1992. The structure of wages. *QJE* 107 (February):285-326.

Parent, D. 1999. *Labour Market Outcomes and Schooling in Canada: Has the Value of a High School Degree Changed over Time?* Cirano, Scientific Series, Number 99s-42.

Picot, G. 1998. What is happening to earnings inequality and youth wages in the 1990s? Statistics Canada Analytic Studies Branch Research Paper Series, Number 116.

Picot, G., and A. Heisz. 2000. The performance of the 1990s Canadian labour market. *CPP* 26 (Supplement July):S7-25.

Ravallion, M., and Q. Wodon. 2000. Does child labour displace schooling? Evidence on behavioural responses to an enrollment subsidy. *EJ* 110 (March):C158-75.

Richardson, D. H. 1997. Changes in the distribution of wages in Canada, 1981-1992. *CJE* 30 (August):622-43.

Riley, J. G. 1979. Testing the educational screening hypothesis. *JPE* 87:S227-52.

Rosen, S. 1977. Human capital: A survey of empirical research. In *Research in Labor Economics*, ed. R. Ehrenberg. Greenwich, Conn.: JAI Press.

Sachs, J., and H. Shatz. 1996. Trade with developing countries and wage inequality. *AER* 86 (May):234-39.

Smith, A. 1776. *The Wealth of Nations*. London: Methuen and Company.

Spence, A. M. 1974. *Market Signaling: Informational Transfer in Hiring and Related Screening Processes*. Cambridge, Mass.: Harvard University Press.

Stager, D. 1972. Allocation of resources in Canadian education. In *Canadian Higher Education in the Seventies*, ed. S. Ostry. Ottawa: Information Canada.

Topel, R. H. 1997. Factor proportions and relative wages: The supply-side determinants of wage inequality. *JEP* 11 (Spring):55-74.

Vaillancourt, F., and S. Bourdeau-Primeau. 2001. The returns to university education in Canada: 1990 and 1995. Manuscript prepared for the C. D. Howe Institute.

Vaillancourt, F., and I. Henriques. 1986. The returns to university schooling in Canada. *CPP* 12 (September):449-58.

Weiss, A. 1995. Human capital versus signalling explanations of wages. *JEP* 9 (Fall):133-54.

Welch, F. 1979. Effects of cohort size on earnings: The baby boom babies financial bust. *JPE* 87 (October): S65-98.

Chapter Ten

Wage Structures Across Markets

Main Questions

- *Why might wages vary across labour markets, even among apparently identical workers?*
- *Are public sector workers overpaid?*
- *Why are wages lower in Newfoundland than Ontario?*
- *Large firms pay higher wages to workers than small firms: Can this be taken as evidence against the neoclassical, supply and demand model of the labour market?*
- *Which industries and occupations provide the highest wages for their workers? Can these higher wages be accounted for by differences in the skills of the workers?*

There are as many wage structures as there are ways of classifying workers. In Chapter 9, for example, we investigated how wages varied systematically across individuals with different levels of education or skill. Casual observation suggests that there are a number of other interesting dimensions worth exploring:

- Occupation
- Industry
- Region
- Large versus small firms
- Men versus women
- Race or ethnicity
- Immigrant status
- Union status
- Public versus private sector

Some of these categories represent special challenges to the neoclassical model of the labour market we have developed to this point. Others have important policy implications. We cover some of these in separate chapters on immigration, discrimination, and unions. In this chapter we focus on wage variation across occupations, industries, region, firm size, and public versus private sectors.

EXPLORATIONS WITH THE 1996 CENSUS

The easiest way to summarize wage structures across various categories is in the context of the **earnings function** we developed in Chapter 9. Recall that in its simplest form, it is a function relating an individual's earnings to his or her characteristics believed to determine productivity. The most common specification in labour economics is:

$$\ln W_i = \alpha + rS + \beta_1 \text{ EXP} + \beta_2 \text{ EXP}^2 + \varepsilon_i \qquad (10.1)$$

which states that individual (log) wages depend on formal schooling, labour market work experience, plus unobserved ability or luck. When estimated by ordinary least squares, the coefficients on years of schooling (S) and experience (EXP) can approximately be interpreted as rates of return, i.e., the percentage increase in wages associated with a unit change in the productive characteristic.

We can easily augment this equation to allow wages to depend on other characteristics. Consider adding K other measures of individual characteristics X_j:

$$\ln W_i = \alpha + rS + \beta_1 \text{ EXP} + \beta_2 \text{ EXP}^2 + \gamma_1 X_1 + \gamma_2 X_2 + \ldots + \gamma_K X_K + \varepsilon_i \qquad (10.2)$$

In this equation the γ_j also have the interpretation as (approximate) rates of return to the characteristics X_j, controlling for the other factors like human capital.

www.statcan.ca/english/census96/list.htm

To be more concrete, we estimate the earnings function from Chapter 9, augmented with indicators for the individual's occupation, industry, and region. The results are reported in Table 10.1 for men who worked full-year, full-time in 1995, using data from the 1996 census. Consider first the results for region, or province. Table 10.1 shows the percentage difference in annual earnings (wages) across provinces, holding constant the individual's level of schooling, experience, industry, and occupation. Ideally, this represents a "pure" **regional wage differential** that cannot be attributed to the possibility, for example, that wages vary across regions because of differing industrial mixes. We will discuss the challenges of interpreting these differentials later in the chapter. For now, we only wish to summarize the broad patterns.

The reported premiums are the percentage differences in earnings of having a given characteristic different from a base category. The largest category is chosen as the base category. For the provincial indicators, the premium is the percentage difference in wages between that province and Ontario. British Columbia has the highest wages, followed closely by Ontario and Alberta. The Atlantic provinces and Quebec have wages significantly below those in the richest provinces. Note that these differentials account for the fact that the industrial composition is different across provinces. The **occupational premiums** are reported relative to trades. The highest-paid occupational group is "Managerial/business professional." These occupational differentials already account for the fact that education levels vary across these education groups, so the differentials *do not* reflect differences in the level of schooling required for these jobs. For a given level of education, therefore, it appears worth avoiding child-care and other service occupations, if you are interested only in money. If one cannot be a manager, teaching or careers in sciences or health seem like relatively lucrative choices. Finally, the **industry premiums** are reported relative to manufacturing. The largest premium is for "other primary" industries—mostly mining. The lowest paid workers are in accommodation, food, and beverage industries (and note again, this is not because they have less schooling, on average). Having documented the existence of these systematic differences in wages across submarkets, the question then arises as to how these differentials can emerge and be sustained in a competitive, integrated labour market.

Table 10.1 Earnings Differentials by Province, Occupation, and Industry, Canada, 1995

Province

	% Jobs	Premium
Newfoundland	1.4	−13.2
Prince Edward Island	0.3	−23.3
Nova Scotia	2.9	−19.1
New Brunswick	2.3	−14.3
Quebec	24.3	−11.7
Ontario	40.8	—
Manitoba	3.8	−13.2
Saskatchewan	2.7	−9.4
Alberta	9.4	−4.6
British Columbia	12.1	1.7

Occupation

	% Jobs	Premium
Managerial/business professional	15.6	30.3
Clerical/secretarial/ administrative	9.7	−8.4
Natural applied sciences	10.1	15.3
Health	1.6	14.8
Social science/government/ religion	2.4	5.0
Teaching	3.9	15.3
Artistic	1.4	−2.5
Sales	7.2	3.0
Food services	1.7	−10.9
Protective	3.9	6.0
Child care	0.1	−42.9
Other services	5.8	−19.6
Trades	16.4	—
Transport operation	6.1	−9.93
Primary	2.2	−6.4
Supervisors/machine operators/ assemblers	9.7	−8.8
Labourers in processing, manufacturing	2.1	−22.1

Industry

	% Jobs	Premium
Agriculture	1.0	−44.5
Other primary	2.7	23.4
Manufacturing	24.8	—
Construction	4.4	−12.1
Transportation and storage	6.8	−1.0
Communications/utilities	5.5	4.7
Wholesale trade	8.0	−12.0
Retail trade	9.4	−34.9
Finance/insurance	5.0	−5.8
Business services	5.5	−12.5
Government services (federal)	4.6	−2.2
Government services (other)	5.8	−1.7
Educational services	6.1	−13.8
Health and social services	3.4	−23.4
Accommodation/food/ beverages	3.1	−55.4
Other industries	3.9	−31.7

Notes: This table reports the implied earnings differentials in percentage terms, implied by the coefficients on indicator variables for each province, industry, and occupation. The premiums are expressed relative to the base group, the group with the most observations. "% Jobs" indicates the distribution of observations across categories. The earnings function is estimated on a sample of full-year, full-time males with only wage and salary income. The regression includes years of schooling, a quadratic in potential experience, and the indicators for region, industry, and occupation. Observations from the territories are excluded.

Source: Data from Statistics Canada, Individual Public Use Microdata Files, 1996 Census of Population.

THEORETICAL ISSUES

While each type of differential has its own explanation, or raises its own theoretical problems, there are several common conceptual issues. Consider a single labour market comprised of identical workers who can freely choose to work in one of two submarkets. Why might wages vary across these markets? First, there may be different educational requirements for the jobs. In this case, the differences in earnings should simply reflect the returns to schooling. What if the differential remains even after accounting for this difference in human capital? There are a number of possibilities:

- *Compensating differentials.* Earnings may vary because of differences in **nonpecuniary benefits** across sectors. Wages would be higher in the market where jobs were less pleasant.
- **Immobility** *across sectors.* Contrary to our assumption, individuals may not be able to freely choose sectors. This may be because one sector requires a special skill that cannot be acquired through schooling, that is, our assumption that individuals are identical is invalid. Alternatively, there may be barriers to mobility across sectors, caused by government regulation or noncompetitive features in the labour market. In this case, it is not reasonable to treat the two submarkets as parts of a common, integrated labour market. More troubling, the differential may indicate that at least one of the submarkets cannot be characterized by the neoclassical, market-clearing supply and demand model.
- *Short run versus long run.* Perhaps less troubling, the unexplained differentials may only reflect a short-run, transitory, **disequilibrium** across the markets. This may be due to adjustment costs of mobility across markets.
- **Unobserved heterogeneity**. Finally, the differentials may have no theoretical implications, but simply reflect the fact that our data are coarse and imperfectly measured. Differences across the submarkets may be the consequence of differing skills or human capital that are not captured by "years of schooling" or other crude measures of human capital. In this case, we may have a fully integrated labour market, and wage variation across submarkets merely reflects differences in average productivity of the individuals in each market.

While labour economists may find the following wage structures intrinsically interesting, they are more generally interested in whether the earnings differentials indicate that the labour market is not fully integrated, and that there is a significant departure from the neoclassical supply and demand framework.

OCCUPATIONAL WAGE STRUCTURES

www.fedpubs.com/subject/immigration/ccdo.htm

As the *Canadian Classification and Dictionary of Occupations*—hereafter termed the CCDO—indicates, the term **occupation** denotes the "kind of work performed" (p. xiii); that is, "the term 'occupation' is used to refer to a number of jobs that have the same basic work content, even though they may be found in a number of different establishments or industries" (p. xv).

The occupational wage structure refers to the wage structure between various occupations or occupation groups. The occupation groups can be broadly defined, as for example, one of the 23 CCDO two-digit major groups such as managerial, clerical, sales, service, or processing. The 16 occupational classifications in Table 10.1 are aggregates of these groups, the narrowest classification available in Census microdata. Or they can be one of the 496 four-digit codes for which Census data is often available, or a narrowly defined occupation, such as one of the 6700 seven-digit occupations, for example, typist (4113-126) or arc welder (8335-138).

Figure 10.1 illustrates the occupational wage differential (skill differential) that exists between two hypothetical occupations, for example skilled welders and unskilled labourers. The demand schedules for each occupation are simply the aggregation of the demand schedules of the various firms that utilize each type of labour. The schedules could be large or small, elastic or inelastic, depending on the circumstances.

The supply schedules for each of the occupations are upward sloping, reflecting the fact that higher wages are required to attract additional workers into the occupations, away from other occupations, or from nonlabour market activities. The higher wages are often necessary to attract additional workers because of different worker-preferences for the various occupations, or because of increasing costs associated with acquiring the skills necessary to do the work. Those who prefer the occupation or who have a natural talent for doing the work would enter at the lower wages; higher wages would be necessary to attract those who did not have a preference for the occupation or who could do the work only by a more costly acquisition of the skills.

The supply schedule, therefore, can be thought of as reflecting a ranking of actual and potential workers in the occupation, where those who most prefer the occupation or who have an innate talent for it are ranked at the beginning (and hence require a lower wage to enter), and those who least prefer the occupation or for whom the acquisition of the skills would be more costly are ranked at the end (and hence require the higher wage to enter). If all preferences were identical and there were no increasing costs associated with entering the occupation, then the supply schedule would be perfectly elastic at the going wage for the occupation.

The degree of elasticity of the supply schedule to each occupation also depends on the responsiveness of alternative sources of labour supply which, in turn, depends upon such factors as labour market information and mobility, training requirements, immigration, and the general state of the economy. For example, in the short run, the labour supply schedule to an occupation may be inelastic (and hence a demand increase would lead to more of a wage increase than an employment increase) for a variety of reasons: potential recruits to the occupation are not yet aware of the high wages; they have to be trained to enter the occupation; fulfilling some of the occupational demand through immigration takes time; and the labour market is presently tight, so there is no ready surplus of labour from which to draw.

Figure 10.1 **Occupational Wage Differential**

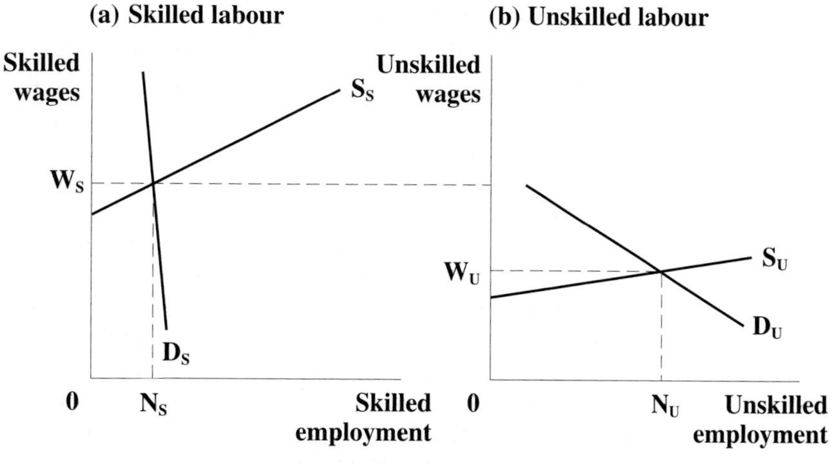

The demand curves for skilled and unskilled labour skilled are given by D_S and D_U. The supply curve represents the number of people willing to work in given occupation at a given wage rate, all else equal. To the extent that skilled labourers incur training costs, we expect the skilled-labour supply curve (S_S) to be higher than the unskilled-labour supply schedule (S_U). We also expect the supply curves to be upward-sloping, as higher wages will attract more workers to that type of job. The equilibrium wages for the skilled and unskilled occupations are given by W_S and W_U.

In the long run, however, most of these factors would adjust to the new demands and the labour supply schedule to the occupation would be more elastic. It may not be perfectly elastic if the new sources of supply are more costly than the original sources. However, in the long run if all of the supply responses had sufficient time to adjust, and if the new sources of supply were not more costly than the original sources, then any inelasticity to the labour supply in an occupation would reflect the different preferences of workers, which would result in a need to raise wages to attract workers who do not have a strong preference for the occupation.

Reasons for Interoccupational Wage Differentials

Given the basic determinants of occupational supply and demand, economic theory predicts that the forces of competition will ensure an equal present value of net advantage at the margin in the long run across all occupations. If this does not prevail, then competition ensures that workers at the margin of decision will move from jobs of low net advantage to ones of high net advantage. This does allow for considerable variation in the occupational wage structure to reflect the main determinants of wage structures: the nonpecuniary aspects of the job (including human capital requirements); short-run adjustments; and noncompetitive forces.

For example, with respect to compensating differences for nonpecuniary aspects, occupations differ in their nonpecuniary characteristics, such as pleasantness, safety, responsibility, fringe benefits, seasonal or cyclical stability, and the certainty of their return (see Exhibit 10.1). As discussed in the previous chapter on compensating wage differentials, **interoccupational wage differentials** may exist, therefore, to compensate for these nonpecuniary differences.

Part of the wage paid in a particular occupation may reflect a compensating wage premium to compensate workers for the costly acquisition of human capital necessary to do a particular job. A competitive wage premium would be one that just yields a competitive rate of return on the investment in human capital.

Individuals may also be *endowed* with skills that are valued in the marketplace, in which case the wage premium that is paid to them reflects their natural embodiment of these skills rather than their costly acquisition of the skills. The individual may be endowed with a skill that is useful in a variety of occupations (e.g., strength, dexterity, or intelligence) or one that is unique to one or a few (e.g., ability to sing or put the puck in the net).

Short-run adjustments factors may also affect the occupational wage structure. For example, an increase in the demand for skilled workers, perhaps because of technological change, would lead to an outward shift in the demand schedule for skilled labour, as in Figure 10.1(a). In the short run, the supply schedule to the skilled occupation may be fairly inelastic because of a long training period required to do the skilled work. Thus wages would rise in this occupation and this would be a short-run signal for workers in other occupations to acquire the skills necessary to work in the skilled occupation.

In response to the short-run wage premium in the skilled occupation, new workers will enter this occupation and this increased supply will reduce the wage premium until it is just large enough to restore an equality of net advantage at the margin; that is, until no further gains in net advantage are possible. The new equality of net advantage may or may not be associated with the old occupational wage differential. This depends on the preferences of workers in the occupations (i.e., on the slopes of the supply schedules to each occupation). If the skilled occupation had an upward-sloping supply schedule, and therefore higher wages were necessary to attract the additional workers, the new skill differential may be greater than before. The skilled workers who were already in the occupation (intramarginal workers) would receive an additional rent because they were willing to work in the occupation at the old wage but now receive the new higher wage that was necessary to expand the number of workers in the occupation.

Exhibit 10.1 **Starving Artist—Myth or Reality?**

Is there any truth to the stereotype of the starving artist—the person who gives up material gain in return for the creative rewards of an artist? In theory, this is a distinct possibility since low monetary rewards are consistent with compensating nonpecuniary aspects of a job, such as fame and creative recognition. As well, artists may bequeath a legacy of art or fame to their heirs. Also, it simply may be an occupation that attracts risk-taking individuals who are willing to gamble for the "big break" that will lead to fame and fortune.

Contrary to the stereotypical view, empirical evidence reported in Filer (1986) indicates that artists tend to have similar earnings than otherwise comparable individuals in other occupations. However, there is more inequality within the artistic profession, confirming the stereotype that some may have very low incomes while others have very high incomes. As well, it tends to be a "younger" profession, suggesting that those who don't make it often leave for other jobs.

The results reported in Table 10.1 also suggest that artists make about as much as everyone else, given their experience and education. Artists in Canada only suffer a 2.5 percent penalty, which may be a very small price to pay, especially for someone who enjoys being an artist.

The evidence therefore suggests that there is more myth than reality to the stereotype of the starving artist. It is true that there are a disproportionate number of artists at the low end of the earnings spectrum within the artistic profession. However, on average, artists earn about as much as otherwise comparable persons who chose more mundane jobs.

Noncompetitive factors can also affect the occupational wage structure. For example, occupational licensing on the part of professional associations, by regulating entry into the profession, can effectively lead to a reduction in the supply of labour to the occupation and hence artificially high salaries. Unions, especially craft unions through the hiring hall and apprenticeship requirements, can also exclude people from some occupations and crowd them into others, raising wages in the former and depressing them in the latter. Other policies may work directly on wages rather than indirectly through the supply of labour. Minimum wage legislation would affect low-wage occupations and equal pay for equal work laws would affect wages in female-dominated occupations.

REGIONAL WAGE STRUCTURES AND GEOGRAPHIC MOBILITY

The existence of pronounced regional wage differentials is a well-documented fact in Canada as in most economies (see Table 10.1, for example). As with most wage structures, however, what is less well known are the reasons for the differentials and the extent to which a pure geographic wage differential would persist in the very long run.

Reasons for Regional Wage Differentials

Economic theory predicts that the forces of competition would ensure an equality of net advantage at the margin associated with identical jobs in each region. That is, if the nonwage aspects of employment (including the probability of obtaining employment) were the same, competition would ensure that wages for the same job would be the same across all regions. Competitive forces could operate in the form of workers moving from the low-wage regions to the high-wage regions, or in the form of firms moving from high-wage regions to low-wage regions to minimize labour cost. As workers leave the low-wage region, the reduced supply would raise wages, and as firms enter the low-wage region, the increased demand would also increase wages. The converse would happen in the high-wage region and the process of the mobility of labour and/or capital would continue until an equality of net advantage were restored in the long run.

To the extent that different people have different geographic preferences, the supply of labour for a given occupation in a particular region may not be perfectly elastic. That is, for a region to expand its work force, higher wages may have to be paid to attract workers from other regions. This could obviously be the case in the short run, but it may also be the case in the long run to the extent that geographic preferences exist. In such circumstances, some workers may be receiving location rents in the sense that they would prefer to remain in a particular region even if wages were lower.

The equality of net advantage at the margin predicted by economic theory does allow for considerable variation in the interregional wage structure; however, as with interoccupational wage differentials that variation would have to reflect compensating differences, short-run adjustments, or noncompetitive factors.

The compensating differences are most obvious and they include wage compensation for such factors as cost of living, remoteness, and climate. They may even include compensation for nonprice externalities such as pollution and congestion. Short-run interregional wage differentials could also be present and, in fact, serve as the signals that are necessary to induce the mobility that will lead to a long-run equilibrium.

Noncompetitive factors may also affect the regional wage structure. Not only is geographic mobility hindered by the barriers that arise because of the high direct and psychic costs of moving, but also it can be hindered by artificial barriers and by public policies that have an indirect, and perhaps unintentional, impact on mobility.

Occupational licensing, for example, can hinder geographic mobility. Some provinces may not recognize training done in other jurisdictions, others may have residency requirements, and others may even require citizenship. In addition, trade unions that control hiring (i.e., have the "hiring hall") can require that people who have worked in the zone be hired first, hence discouraging others from entering the zone. While these policies do achieve other objectives, they also reduce the effectiveness of interregional mobility as a force to reduce interregional wage differentials.

Social transfer programs that try to reduce income disparities will obviously have different regional impacts and this could reduce regional mobility. In such circumstances governments are faced with a basic dilemma: as they use transfer programs to reduce income inequality, they reduce part of the incentive for people to engage in regional mobility, unless the transfer programs are conditional upon geographic mobility. Regional expansion policies can encourage capital to move into low-income areas, but this also reduces the mobility of labour from that region and hence reduces some of the market forces that would reduce inequalities. Obviously these policies can achieve other important objectives—noticeably, perhaps, a more equitable distribution of regional income—but they do have the effect of reducing the effectiveness of geographic mobility as a force to reduce geographic wage differences.

Migration Decision

As the previous section indicates, economic theory predicts that the forces of competition would serve to reduce pure regional wage differentials so that they reflect compensating differences, short-run adjustments, or noncompetitive factors. Those forces of competition were the movement of capital from high- to low-wage areas, and the movement of labour from low- to high-wage areas.

This latter movement—geographic mobility or **migration**—can be treated as a human capital decision, the determinants of which are discussed in Chapter 9. That is, geographic mobility will occur as long as the marginal benefits exceed the marginal costs to the individuals making the decision. Benefits can include such factors as expected income (which in turn can be a function of earnings and job opportunities as well as transfer payments), climate, and the availability of social services. Costs can include the usual costs of information-seeking and moving, as well as the psychic costs associated with geographic moves. In addition the migration decision may depend on one's ability to finance the move—a problem that is particularly acute in human capital theory because one cannot legally use human capital (e.g., the larger expected earnings) as collateral to finance any necessary loan.

The human capital framework provides a variety of empirically testable propositions concerning the mobility decision. Other things being equal, relative to older workers, younger workers would tend to engage in more job mobility because they have a longer benefit period from which to recoup the costs, their opportunity cost (forgone income) of moving is lower as are their direct costs if they do not have a home to sell or family to move, and their psychic costs are probably lower because they have not established long ties in their community. In addition, they may not be locked in by seniority provisions or pensions that are not portable. Mobility should be from areas of high unemployment toward areas of low unemployment. It should also increase at the peak of a business cycle when job opportunities are more abundant, and decrease in a recession when jobs are scarce. Mobility in and out of Quebec is likely to be lower than in other regions of Canada because of language and cultural differences. In addition distance is an inhibiting factor because it increases moving costs and uncertainty as well as the psychic costs associated with being uprooted from one's familiar environment.

Empirical evidence tends to verify the implications of migration as a human capital decision.[1] Osberg, Gordon, and Lin (1994) explore the determinants of interregional and interindustry mobility of individuals in the Maritimes. Using the 1986–87 LMAS, they find that younger individuals and those with higher expected wage gains are more likely to migrate. Finnie (2000) uses a database of longitudinal tax records that allow him to accurately follow individuals over a 13-year period (1982–1995). His analysis of the determinants of interprovincial migration is in accordance with what we would expect from the human capital model. Younger workers are more likely to move, as they have a longer period over which to reap the benefits of moving. It is more costly for people who are married with children to move, and, not surprisingly, they have lower mobility. Francophones are also less likely to leave Quebec, as their language skills do not transfer easily to other provinces. Finally, Finnie finds that individuals who are down on their economic luck are more likely to move, especially if they live in a high-unemployment province. Similar results concerning migration decisions and the human capital model are found by Cousineau and Vaillancourt (2000), using the 1991 Canadian Census. The economic incentives of government programs can also affect the migration decision. Day (1992) shows that interprovincial migration flows reflect the fact that people tend to move to provinces with more generous social programs, lower taxes, and higher expenditures on health and education.

But why do regional wage disparities persist? Migration should tend to reduce wage differentials, at least to the point where there is no incentive (on the margin) for people to move. Low-wage regions would simply be nicer places to live, as workers accept lower wages in return for local amenities. Similarly, investment flows should reduce earnings differentials, as firms build factories in low-wage areas. In fact, evidence from the United States and Canada suggests that regional earnings differences are eroding over time. For example, empirical evidence from the United States indicates that the wage differential between North and South had disappeared by the 1970s, after controlling for the

[1]Early evidence on interprovincial migration in Canada can be found in Courchene (1970, 1974), in Grant and Vanderkamp (1980), and in the extensive work of John Vanderkamp (1968, 1971, 1972, 1976, and 1986).

differences in cost of living and the human capital endowments of the work force (Bellante, 1979; Bishop, Formby, and Thistle, 1992; Leolho and Gahli, 1971; Farber and Newman, 1987). This wage convergence occurred as firms located to the low-wage South (thereby reducing the demand for labour in the North and increasing it in the South) and as workers left the South for jobs in the high-wage North (thereby increasing the supply of labour in the North and reducing it in the South). Economic convergence of incomes also appears to be happening in Canada. Coulombe and Day (1999) and Cousineau and Vaillancourt (2000) show that interprovincial differences in per capita income levels are diminishing. However, both studies also highlight correlations between the labour market and provincial income differentials. Coulombe and Day point to the labour market as a "smoking gun" impediment to further reductions of income differentials, since it appears that some of the low-income, and slow-growing, provinces also have lower levels of employment and higher levels of unemployment. Presumably, if more people would move, income differentials would fall. Coulombe and Day speculate that government policy, in particular unemployment insurance and regional income transfers, may be contributing to the discouragement of migration. But as noted by Cousineau and Vaillancourt, some of the reduction in mobility in Canada may be the result of narrowing income differentials across provinces. Sorting out these explanations remains an important priority for future research.

INTERINDUSTRY WAGE DIFFERENTIALS

www.statcan.ca/english/Subjects/Standard/sic-c/sic-c.htm

As the Canadian *Standard Industrial Classification* manual indicates, industrial designations refer to the principal kind or branch of economic activity of establishments in which individuals work. The industries may be broadly defined sectors, as, for example, agriculture, mining, manufacturing, construction, transportation, trade, and public administration. Or they may be more narrowly defined. For example, within the nondurable manufacturing sector there are food and beverage, tobacco, rubber, textile, and paper industries. The interindustry wage structure indicates the wage differential between industries, however broadly or narrowly defined.

Theoretical Determinants of Interindustry Wage Differentials

The average wage in an industry will reflect a variety of factors, including the occupational composition and personal characteristics of the work force, and the regional domination of some industries. Consequently, pure **interindustry wage differentials** are difficult to calculate because they reflect other wage structures, notably those by occupation, region, and the personal characteristics of the work force.

If we could net out the effect of these other wage structures, however, so that we were comparing wages across industries for the same occupation, the same type of worker, and the same region, then the pure interindustry wage differential would reflect only the different characteristics of the industry. This is what we attempt to do with the exercise reported in Table 10.1. Many of these different wage-determining characteristics are similar to the ones analyzed as determinants of the interoccupational wage structure—nonpecuniary aspects of the jobs in each industry, short-run adjustments, and noncompetitive forces. If there are no differences in any of these aspects, competitive forces should ensure that all industries pay the same wage for the same type of labour. The basic determinants of interindustry wage differentials, therefore, can be categorized according to the basic determinants of any wage structure: nonpecuniary characteristics of the industry, short-run demand changes, and noncompetitive factors.

Interindustry wage differences, for example, may exist to compensate for differences in the nonpecuniary aspects of the work in different industries. Such factors could include unpleasant or unsafe work conditions, or seasonal or cyclical employment. Workers in the construction industry, for example, may receive a wage premium in part to compensate for risk as well as the seasonal and cyclical nature of much of the work.

Interindustry wage differences may also reflect short-run demand changes. The wage differences are the price signal necessary to encourage reallocation from declining sectors to expanding ones. Different industries are affected in different fashions by various demand changes emanating from such factors as technological change or free trade and global competition. For example, freer trade will lead to an expansion of export-oriented industries and to a contraction of industries most affected by imports. This should lead to a wage premium in the expanding export sector, which in turn is the price signal to encourage the reallocation of labour from the declining import sector to the expanding export sector.

There may also be a variety of noncompetitive factors that could affect the interindustry wage structure. Monopoly rents may differ by industry and these may be captured, in part, by workers, especially if they are unionized. Even in declining industries, or industries subject to severe import competition, the rents going to workers could increase if they were able to appropriate a larger *share* of the declining rents. This could occur, for example, if the declining nature of the industry meant that there was no threat of entry, and the firm had no alternative use for its plant and equipment, and therefore no viable threat to relocate if labour appropriate a larger share of the rents. In essence, labour is still able to "milk a dead cow," at least for a time.

Other noncompetitive factors can also affect the interindustry wage differential. Minimum wage laws obviously affect low-wage industries such as personal services (laundries, hotels, restaurants, and taverns), retail trade, and parts of nondurable manufacturing, especially clothing. Equal pay laws will affect industries with a high proportion of females (and which also often are low-wage industries), for example nondurable manufacturing retail trade, services and finance, insurance, and real estate. Fair wage laws and wage extension laws tend to be most important in the construction sector. Occupational licensing and unionization tend to be most prominent in high-wage industries—in part, of course, because they may have raised wages in those industries. In summary, basic economic theory suggests that, in the long run, competitive forces should eliminate pure interindustry wage differences. To the extent that they exist, interindustry wage differences should reflect only such factors as compensating wages for the nonpecuniary characteristics of the industry, short-run demand changes, or noncompetitive factors.

Efficiency Wages and Interindustry Wage Differences

As will be discussed in more detail in Chapter 18 (Unemployment: Causes and Consequences), firms may rationally pay wages above the market-clearing level so as to improve morale, reduce turnover and absenteeism, elicit effort, reduce shirking, reduce the threat of unionization, and to have a queue of applicants so as to reduce recruiting and hiring costs. It may be efficient for the firm to pay wages above the market-clearing wage because of its positive effects on labour productivity or on reducing costs in these other areas. These productivity-enhancing wages are called **efficiency wages**. Such higher wages are rents to the workers who receive them in the sense of being payments in excess of the market-clearing wage and in excess of their next-best-alternative job, assuming it is at the market-clearing wage. In fact it is the receipt of this rent or excessive wage payment that elicits the desirable behaviour on the part of workers. Although they are payments above the market-clearing wage, these are competitive wage differentials in the sense that they are consistent with the profit-maximizing behaviour of firms and will not be eliminated by the forces of competition.

The desirability of paying efficiency wages may well differ by industry, thereby giving rise to persistent interindustry wage differentials.[2] For example, industries that utilize expensive capital equipment or for which the training costs make turnover costly, may find it profitable to pay such efficiency wages to have a trustworthy work force and low turnover. Such interindustry wage differentials may also persist over time if the efficiency rationales for paying a pure wage premium also persist over time.

Such high-wage jobs also correspond to the notion of "good jobs" as opposed to "bad jobs." The good jobs are those in industries that pay wages in excess of the market-clearing wage. Workers in those jobs are fortunate in the sense that the efficiency wage premium is a pure rent, not a compensating wage premium paid for undesirable working conditions or costly human capital. It is a rent or wage premium designed explicitly to make it a good job so that workers will not want to lose the job. As such, they are likely to exhibit good work characteristics with respect to such factors as absenteeism, turnover, and honesty. Obviously, to the extent that there is disutility associated with having to deliver such good work characteristics, then the higher wage would simply be a compensating wage premium associated with such characteristics. The essence of efficiency wages, however, is that they are rents or pure wage premiums and not compensating wages.

Efficiency wage premiums are different from conventional rents in that they are not extracted from the firm through, for example, the monopoly power of a union. Rather, they are voluntarily paid by the firm to serve a positive human resource management function such as eliciting loyalty or honesty or reducing turnover. Workers are paid the marginal product of their labour; that marginal product is simply enhanced by the productivity-inducing aspects of the higher wage. For workers, however, it is like a conventional rent in that the wage premium is greater than any disutility they experience from the actions (increased loyalty and honesty, reduced turnover, absenteeism, or shirking) that they undertake as a result of the efficiency wage premium.

Workers who are displaced from those "good" jobs (perhaps because of industrial restructuring or import competition) would lose those rents if they are displaced to jobs that may simply pay the market-clearing wage. The loss of such efficiency wages may be one of the reasons for the large wage losses that are often experienced by workers who are displaced because of a plant closing or permanent job loss.

The existence of efficiency wages may also provide a theoretical rationale for industrial policies designed to protect the so-called "good wage" jobs (Dickens and Lang, 1988; Katz and Summers, 1989a). Such policies could include subsidies to "high-tech" or other industries where such jobs may prevail, or even minimum wage laws that reduce employment in low-wage jobs that are unlikely to embody any efficiency wage. Tariffs could also protect good jobs in industries that pay efficiency wages; however, in developed countries, high-wage industries tend to be export-oriented ones and low-wage industries tend to be subject to import competition. Therefore, freer trade to enhance both exports and imports should increase the number of "good jobs" related to low-wage jobs; that is, free trade and not protectionism would be the best policy to enhance the number of jobs that pay efficiency wage premiums, especially if workers can be reallocated from the lower-wage import-competing jobs to the higher-wage export-oriented jobs.

In summary, countries may want to protect or encourage jobs that pay efficiency wages because they are good jobs in the sense that firms want to pay the high wages (i.e., it is in their profit-maximizing interest to do so) and workers obviously want to receive such high

[2]In theory, efficiency wages could vary by any of the factors that give rise to wage structures, such as occupation or region as well as industry. In practice, however, the theoretical rationales for efficiency wages suggest that they will differ by industry and by firm size and not so much by occupation and region. Hence, the efficiency wage literature tends to be associated with the literature on wage differences by industry and firm size, and not by the other factors that give rise to wage structures.

wages because they are rents in excess of their next-best-alternative wage. Countries that happen to have such jobs are fortunate, just like countries that happen to have endowments of natural resources.

While efficiency wages can provide a *theoretical* rationale for industrial policy to protect certain good jobs, this should not be taken as a justification for all such policies. Most are likely instituted to protect monopoly rents or to provide subsidies or protection that is politically motivated and likely comes at the expense of consumers having to pay higher product prices. At a practical level, it may be extremely difficult to distinguish efficiency wages from pure rents so as to target the protection and encouragement only of the jobs that pay efficiency wages. Issues of equity and fairness may also be involved since the jobs that pay efficiency wages are likely to be high-wage jobs for reasons other than efficiency wages.

Furthermore, there is legitimate debate over the existence and magnitude of pure efficiency wages. It is difficult to statistically control for all of the other factors that influence wages, and yet this is crucial in this area since one would expect firms to be able to hire the best workers in terms of both observable characteristics (the influence of which can be controlled for through statistical techniques) and unobservable factors (the influence of which is difficult to control for). As such, the efficiency wages may simply reflect a return to an unmeasured characteristic. As well, competition on the part of workers for such good jobs should put a cap on the magnitude of the efficiency wage that is necessary to ensure that these are regarded as good jobs. There are also likely to be other compensation mechanisms besides paying efficiency wages to elicit the desired behaviour on the part of workers. One such mechanism, discussed subsequently in the chapter on optimal compensation systems, is deferred compensation whereby workers are "underpaid" when young and "overpaid" when older as a way to encourage them to want to stay with the firm.

In spite of these theoretical and empirical problems in using industrial policies to encourage the "good" jobs that pay efficiency wages, the potential policy importance of the area merits that more consideration and research be given to the topic. This is especially the case because the encouragement and protection of efficiency wages is subject to a degree of policy control. Sensible policy application, however, requires answers to a number of questions: Can efficiency wage premiums be precisely identified so as to target policies to encourage such jobs? What will be the ultimate outcome if all jurisdictions (countries, provinces, states, regions, etc.) compete for such jobs? Are there ways of dealing with the distributional consequences if the already high-wage jobs effectively become protected or subsidized? If industrial policies are used to protect or encourage efficiency wages, what will happen when employers and employees try to have other jobs protected and encouraged in the same fashion? Answers to these and other questions would be useful to shed light on this important policy issue.

Empirical Evidence on Interindustry Wage Differences, Efficiency Wages, and the Impact of Deregulation

Systematic evidence on the existence of pure interindustry wage differences is difficult to compile because of the problem of controlling for other factors that affect the wage difference across industries. Different industries, for example, utilize different skill mixes, and they are concentrated in different regions and are composed of firms of different sizes. Hence, interindustry wage differences often confound wage differences by other factors such as occupation, region, or plant size.

With the advent of microeconomic data sets using the individual worker as the unit of observation, however, it has been possible to use econometric techniques to control for the influences of some of these different factors, and to thereby isolate a pure interindustry wage differential. The econometric results indicate that interindustry wage differences do reflect the conventional determinants of wage structures: nonpecuniary differences in the jobs, short-run demand changes, and noncompetitive factors. However, the studies also indicate that even after controlling for these factors a pure interindustry wage differential or efficiency wage seems to prevail.[3] Some industries simply pay higher wages than appear necessary to compensate for the nonpecuniary aspects of the job, or to meet short-run demand changes, or because of noncompetitive factors. As well, this interindustry wage pattern appears quite stable over time; high-wage industries tend to remain high-wage industries.

That these are rents or payments above the market-clearing wage is supported by other indirect evidence. Workers who change industries are likely to gain or lose the full amount of the rent premium associated with that industry, suggesting it is the industry and not their own individual characteristics that gave rise to the wage premium. As well, the wage premium goes to workers throughout the occupational spectrum in an industry (e.g., secretaries, blue-collar workers, and managers) suggesting that it is something in the industry itself that generates the premium. The higher wages also tend to be associated with lower quit rates and large queues of applicants, and this would not prevail if the premium were simply a compensating premium for skills or nonpecuniary aspects of the job. While these observations suggest that the wage premiums are rents, it is more difficult to determine whether they reflect efficiency wages or the results of noncompetitive factors associated with each industry.

The interindustry wage structure tends to be quite stable over time and across different countries (Katz and Summers, 1989b; Krueger and Summers, 1988). That is, high-wage industries tend to be high-wage industries for considerable periods of time, and they tend to be high-wage industries in countries with very different labour market structures and institutional features. Industries that pay efficiency wages tend to be capital-intensive, and typically are composed of large firms with considerable market power and ability to pay. These industries are also usually highly unionized and have a work force of above-average education and with low quit rates.

Table 10.2, based on Canadian data, illustrates the magnitude of the pure interindustry wage differential that prevails after controlling for the effect of a wide range of other factors that can influence wages across industries. Clearly the differences are substantial. High-wage industries like tobacco products and mineral fuels respectively pay wage premiums of 33.4 percent and 2.5 percent above the competitive norm (i.e., above the average wage paid to workers of comparable wage-determining characteristics in other industries). Conversely, the service industries tend to pay wages considerably below the competitive norm—31.8 percent below in religious organizations, and 20.3 percent below in accommodation and food services.

These extreme examples of the largest differences above and below the competitive norm also highlight the potential difficulty of fully controlling for the other factors that could affect interindustry wage differences. For example, some of the wage premium in tobacco products could reflect a compensating premium for the uncertainties associated with the restructuring of that industry. Some of the wage disadvantage in accommodation and food services may reflect the fact that some of the compensation may occur in the form of "tips." Some of the wage disadvantage in religious organizations may reflect perceived compensation in nonmonetary forms.

[3]Dickens and Katz (1987), Katz and Summers (1989b), Krueger and Summers (1987, 1988), and Murphy and Topel (1987) for U.S. data, and Gera and Grenier (1994) for Canadian data. These studies also review the earlier studies that documented a substantial interindustry wage differential based on aggregate industry data.

Whether these interindustry wage premiums reflect noncompetitive factors or efficiency wages, there is empirical evidence to suggest that industry wage premiums will be dissipated by international competition. This has been documented in studies that tend to find a negative correlation between average industry wage levels and the extent of import

Table 10.2 Pure Interindustry Wage Differentials, Canada, 1986*

Industry	Wage Premium	Industry	Wage Premium
Primary Industries		Construction	
Mineral fuels	25.5	Special trade	17.0
Mining services	22.7	General contractors	11.4
Forestry	18.9	Related services	–2.4
Metal mines	18.9	Transportation, Communication, Utilities	
Nonmetal mines	13.7	Utilities	14.4
Quarries and pits	0.1	Communications	10.5
Fishing and trapping	–9.5	Transportation	8.7
Manufacturing		Storage	6.3
Tobacco products	33.4	Trade	
Petroleum and coal	20.8	Wholesale trade	3.8
Chemicals	14.4	Retail trade	–11.1
Paper	12.0	Finance, Insurance, Real Estate	
Primary metals	11.5	Insurance carriers	13.7
Wood products	8.7	Finance	9.3
Transport equipment	7.2	Insurance and real estate agencies	–4.1
Rubber and plastics	7.1	Other Services	
Printing and publishing	6.4	Business management	4.8
Nonmetallic minerals	4.8	Education	–1.0
Metal fabricating	3.7	Miscellaneous	–2.8
Electrical products	2.6	Health and welfare	–3.1
Machinery	0.8	Amusement/recreation	–11.4
Miscellaneous manufacturing	–3.4	Personal services	–16.7
Food and beverages	–3.5	Accommodation/food	–20.3
Clothing	–8.1	Religious organizations	–31.8
Leather	–10.0		
Furniture and fixtures	–14.4		
Textiles	–19.0		

*Percentage wage differential between the wage in each particular industry and the average two-digit industry wage, after controlling for the effect of other wage-determining factors. Data is from Statistics Canada's 1986 Labour Market Activity Survey. The industries are listed in descending order of the magnitude of the industry wage premium within each major industry group.

Source: Gera and Grenier, 1994, pp. 86–8.

penetration into the industry.[4] It has also been documented in a number of recent studies that relate individual wages to measures of import penetration into the industry in which the individuals work.[5]

There is also empirical evidence indicating that industries that are concentrated in the sense that they are dominated by a small number of firms in the product market tend to pay higher wages, presumably because of their monopoly profits. In his study of Canadian interindustry wage differentials, Grey (1993) finds that more concentrated industries, as well as those with more export orientation, have higher unexplained wage differentials. Industries that are regulated also pay higher wages, presumably because the higher wage costs can be passed to consumers in the form of rate increases without there being much of a reduction in the demand for the regulated service and hence in the derived demand for labour. Ehrenberg (1979), for example, found that workers in the regulated telephone industry in New York were paid about 10 percent more than comparable workers in other industries. Shackett and Trapani (1987) found regulatory wage premiums of around 10 percent for males and 15 to 20 percent for females in regulated industries like trucking, airlines, banks, utilities, and insurance in the mid-1970s in the United States.

Conversely, the deregulation that has occurred in recent years has led to substantial reductions in wages in those industries. Rose (1987), for example, found that the union wage premium was cut almost in half after deregulation of the trucking industry in the United States. The wages of unionized truck drivers fell by almost $4000 or 14 percent as a result of deregulation. Prior to deregulation, she indicates that unions had captured two-thirds of the regulatory rents or excess profits generated by the regulatory protection. In such circumstances, it is not surprising that unions tend to strongly oppose deregulation. This is especially the case because the new firms that enter the industry after deregulation tend to be nonunion, and the ones that fail after deregulation tend to be union operations.

In the case of the airline industry, Card (1986) also found that wage reductions occurred after deregulation, albeit the magnitudes were smaller than in trucking. This was attributed in part to the fact that the large airline carriers were still able to maintain a monopoly position because of their control over key airline terminals as a result of the "hub and spoke" system.

In summary, the empirical evidence strongly suggests that industries that are subject to greater competitive pressures on the product market (e.g., import competition, deregulation, more competing firms) tend to pay lower wages. The evidence also suggests the existence and persistence of pure interindustry wage differentials or rents that are consistent with the payment of efficiency wages. More empirical work is necessary, however, to document the precise magnitude of these wage differences and their basic determinants.

INTERFIRM WAGE DIFFERENCES AND FIRM SIZE

Wage differences may also exist across firms within the same industry and region and for the same occupational group. As with other wage structures, economic theory suggests that such wage differences should reflect the basic determinants of wage structures: nonpecuniary differences in the nature of the jobs, short-run demand changes, and noncompetitive factors. Firms that pay high wages, for example, may have poor working conditions, or short-run demand increases, or noncompetitive conditions such as a monopoly position in the product market or a union in the labour market, or they may find it in their interest to pay efficiency wages above the competitive norm.

[4]See, for example, Grossman (1986, 1987), Lawrence and Lawrence (1985), Revenga (1992), and Grey (1993).

[5]See, for example, Dickens and Lang (1988), Freeman and Katz (1991), Katz and Summers (1989a), and Gaston and Trefler (1994, 1995).

One of the puzzling empirical regularities that seems to prevail is the positive relationship between wages and firm size, with larger firms tending to pay higher wages (see Brown and Medoff, 1989, for a comprehensive review of the evidence). This relationship has been somewhat of a puzzle to economists because there is little theoretical reason to expect such a relationship once one has controlled for the effect of other factors that influence wages.

Certainly other factors that influence wages may be correlated with firm size, giving the appearance that it is the size of the firm that affects wages. For example, large firms tend to be unionized and hence may pay a union wage premium. Even if they are not unionized, they may pay that premium to minimize the threat of being organized. Large firms may be more likely to have monopoly profits that may be shared with labour. They may also be more likely to be capital-intensive and hence employ more skilled workers, thereby confounding the occupational wage differential with a firm-size wage differential. Some of the wage advantage in large firms may be a compensating wage premium for their more structured and formalized work requirements.

In such circumstances, the wage premium in large firms arises because large firms are more likely to have these wage-enhancing characteristics: unionization, skilled workers, rents, and undesirable working conditions. It is not firm size per se that matters, but rather the correlation of firm size with these other wage- determining factors.

These characteristics may be conventionally observable factors, as were the previously mentioned ones, or they could be conventionally unobservable factors that are difficult to control for in statistical procedures that isolate the pure effect of firm size on wages. Such unobservable factors could include motivation or skills that are not measured by years of education or training. Large firms may attach a premium to these characteristics because of their importance in the capital intensity and interrelated production of such firms. It may also be harder for large firms to get rid of their "mistakes" given their (usually) more formal personnel systems and discipline procedures. Having the best workers (even if more expensive) may also be more important to large firms since monitoring and supervision may be more difficult. Having the best workers may be an important way of conserving on scarce managerial time, and this may be especially important for large firms if they employ the most talented managers so as to amortize that talent over the large firm size. To the extent that large firms tend to employ workers with conventionally unobserved characteristics that attract a wage premium, then some of the firm size wage effect may simply be the wage premium for these conventionally unobserved factors.

Large firms may also be more likely to pay efficiency wages. As discussed previously, these are wage premiums above the market-clearing wage. They are voluntarily paid by firms in order to encourage loyalty and reduce costs associated with turnover, shirking, monitoring, and supervision. These may be more important for large firms, given their capital-intensity and their possibly higher costs of monitoring and supervision. In essence, a high-wage policy may pay more for large firms than smaller firms. In such circumstances, the wage premium need not be a premium for workers who have better observable or even unobservable characteristics. It can be a pure rent or "prize" that elicits the positive behaviour on the part of workers so as not to risk losing the prize. Large firms may find it more cost-effective to pay such prizes rather than devote resources to continuous monitoring and supervision. This is analogous to the cost effectiveness of setting a large penalty (i.e., the loss of the efficiency wage) when it is costly to detect or prosecute malfeasant behaviour.

Morissette (1993) uses 1986 LMAS data from Canada to try to disentangle the relative importance of each of these factors contributing to the positive relationship between firm size and wages. He controls for a number of worker and firm characteristics, but still finds a large firm-size premium. A worker moving from a firm with less than 20 employees to one with over 500 employees would expect a wage increase of almost 19 percent. Morissette also eliminates the simple compensating wage differential explanation, by showing that large firms tend to have better working conditions, for example, reflected in the provision of pension plans. This evidence seems to suggest that efficiency wage or noncompetitive explanations underlie the firm-size effect. Reilly (1995) uses a sample of workers from the Maritimes (the General Segmentation Survey) and arrives at the opposite conclusion. He shows that controls for most firm and worker characteristics, indeed, have no effect on the firm-size premium. However, once he adds controls for whether the firm owned or had access to a computer, the firm-size effect vanishes. These data were collected in 1979, when less than half of the firms had access to this technology, and firm size was significantly positively correlated with computer use. Reilly's results suggest that the firm-size premium reflects unobserved worker productivity associated with high technology production, and may have nothing to do with noncompetitive features of the labour market. Certainly, Reilly's evidence highlights the difficulty of using unexplained wage differences as evidence in favour of a particular model of the labour market.

PUBLIC-PRIVATE SECTOR WAGE DIFFERENTIALS

The issue of **public-private sector wage differentials** is a topic of interindustry wage determination since the public sector is simply one of many industries. However, the public sector is singled out for special attention for various reasons: it is a large sector; it is the subject of policy concern mainly because of strikes and wage settlements; its impact may spill over into the private sector; and it has peculiarities that make wage determination somewhat unusual.

As our earlier discussion indicated, the theoretical determinants of interindustry wage differentials include compensating adjustments for nonpecuniary differences, short-run adjustments, and noncompetitive factors. Just as these broad categories provided a convenient framework for analyzing the determinants of interindustry wage differentials, they also are convenient for categorizing the theoretical determinants of the particular interindustry wage differential examined in this chapter—the public-private sector wage differential.

The public sector can be broadly defined to include education, health, and government enterprises, and the more narrowly defined government employment at the federal, provincial, and municipal levels. This definition is based on whether the employer is either funded or owned by the government. Figure 10.2 shows the breakdown of public sector employment in Canada from 1981 to 2000. Total public sector employment grew through the 1980s, peaking in 1992 when there were over three million employees—approximately one-quarter of the employed labour force—working for the government, or government-funded employers. Public sector employment dropped sharply in the mid-1990s, but has since levelled off, and actually grew (slightly) in 2000, so that public sector workers now account for 19 percent of the employed labour force.

The total employment figures hide different trends in the sub-components. The main declines occurred through downsizing of all three levels of public administration (government), and the privatization of government enterprises, such as Air Canada, Canadian National, and Petro-Canada. The health and education sectors also shrunk slightly over the 1990s, but are now a larger share of the public sector than in 1981, so that the education sector now accounts for 29 percent of public sector workers (as against 24 percent in 1981) and the health sector accounts for 26 percent (as against 22 percent in 1981). Clearly, even with the downsizing of the 1990s, the public sector is a large and important employer.

Theoretical Determinants of Public-Private Wage Differentials

Compensating Adjustments for Nonpecuniary Differences Interindustry wage differentials may reflect compensating adjustments for differences in the nonpecuniary aspects of employment across industries. With respect to the private and public sectors, nonpecuniary advantages may exist with respect to such factors as job security, fringe benefits, and political visibility. To the extent that these advantages prevail in the public sector, we would expect a correspondingly lower wage to compensate for the advantages. However, to the extent that these advantages are dissipating over time, we may also expect public sector wages to rise relative to those in the private sector to compensate for the loss of these nonpecuniary advantages.

Job security often is discussed as being more prevalent in the public than in the private sector. Theoretically this may be the case because job security could be necessary to prevent the abuses of political patronage. That is, without a modicum of job security, civil servants could be replaced each time a new political party came into power, or whenever a politician wanted to gain favour by granting patronage in the form of civil service jobs. To avoid this potential abuse, and to ensure a degree of continuity in the public sector work force, a degree of job security may be granted. Larger elements of the public sector also may be able to easily provide such job security because their size gives them a portfolio of jobs within which to reallocate their work force.

Figure 10.2 **Public Sector Employment, Canada, 1981–2000**

This graph shows the level of employment in the broadly defined public sector in Canada from 1981 to 2000. Each bar is divided into four sections, the height of each segment corresponding to the level of employment in each subcategory: (1) government (public administration), (2) health and social services, (3) education (schools, colleges, and universities), and (4) government-owned businesses. The total height of each bar equals average total public sector employment in that year.

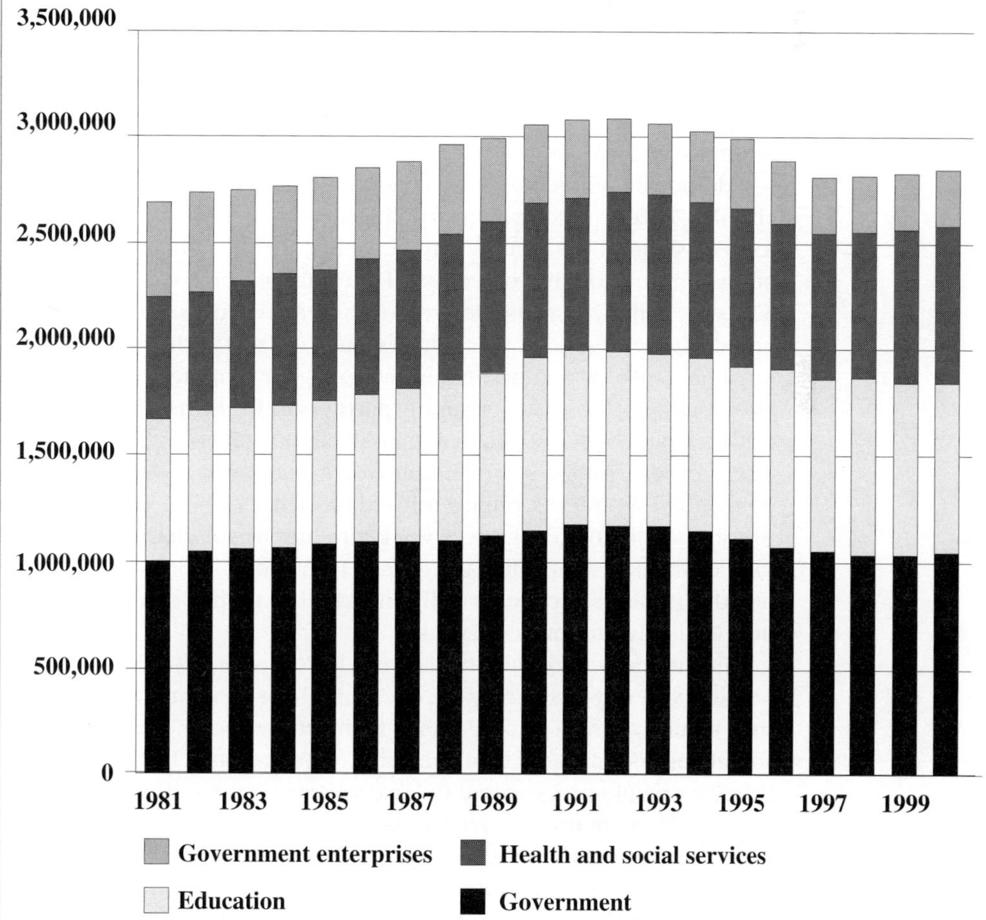

Notes: Each bar represents annual average employment in four public employment sectors: government (federal, provincial, and municipal governments), education (local school boards, colleges, and universities), health and social services, and government-owned businesses.

Source: Authors' calculations based on Statistics Canada, CANSIM series D466212, D466028, D466358, D466371, D466384, D466240, D466266, and D466490. <http://cansima.statcan.ca>

As with job security, there are theoretical reasons to suggest that the public sector may provide more liberal fringe benefits. This occurs because in the public sector there are not adequate checks to prevent employers from saving on *current* wage costs by granting liberal retirement benefits and pension schemes, the cost of which may be borne by *future* generations of taxpayers. Fringe benefits that are payable in the future, such as early retirement plans and employer-sponsored pensions, can be viewed as deferred wages in the sense that workers would willingly give up some current wages for these future benefits. Such deferred compensation systems may be a way for the public sector to shift costs to future generations of taxpayers; however (as discussed in the later chapter on optimal compensation systems) deferred compensation also may exist as part of an optimal compensation system to ensure honesty and work effort. Such a system may be especially important in the public sector, to the extent that other mechanisms, such as the threat of dismissal or the monitoring of output, are not available.

In the private sector there is a built-in check to ensure that employers are constrained in their granting of such deferred benefits: eventually they have to meet the obligation of paying for them. However, in the public sector, unless such benefits are fully funded, their costs will be borne by future taxpayers. To the extent that they have little or no say in the current political process, there is no automatic mechanism to prevent public sector employers from saving on current wage costs by granting liberal deferred cost items, such as early retirement or substantial pensions or pensions indexed for future inflation. The only check is the possibility that future generations may not honour such commitments made by their predecessors, or the possibility that local property values may fall to the extent that they reflect the future tax obligations associated with such future cost commitments.

Additional nonpecuniary advantages offered by the public sector could include political visibility, access to control over political rules, and the opportunity to provide public service. For some, these factors may be valued for their own end; for others they may be valued as a means to other objectives. For example, some workers may regard a period of public sector employment as a low-wage apprenticeship period that provides them with inside knowledge, access to power sources, and contacts in the political arena. These factors may be of immense value (and hence lead to higher remuneration) in future private sector jobs as consultants, lobbyists, or simply partners in firms that do business with the government or that would benefit from inside political information.

For others, public sector employment may provide "the nonpecuniary satisfaction of doing good"—to use a phrase utilized by Reder (1955). This could be a reason, for example, for people to do volunteer work for churches or charities, or for some to accept lower salaries in such nonprofit institutions. It may be a more prevalent phenomenon throughout the public sector, especially in teaching or health care. The term "public service" means just that to many persons.

The nonpecuniary factors that we have discussed—job security, fringe benefits, and political visibility—generally are ones for which there are theoretical reasons to believe that they would be greater in the public than private sector. Certainly conventional wisdom and casual empiricism seem to suggest this to be the case. To the extent that it is true, the public sector would be expected to have lower wages to compensate for these factors.

While these nonpecuniary factors may be greater in the public than private sector, there are reasons to believe that the gap may be dissipating over time. Certainly this seems to be the case with job security and it may be the case with fringe benefits to the extent that the public sector may have reached diminishing returns with respect to the fringe benefits it can provide, and the private sector is now catching up. Even with respect to the opportunity to do public service, attitudes seem to be changing so that public sector jobs are done in return for pay, like most other jobs. To the extent that these nonpecuniary factors have diminished in the public sector, one would expect the wages of public sector workers to rise relative to those of their private sector counterparts.

Short-Run Adjustments Interindustry wage differentials may reflect a short-run disequilibrium situation. In fact the disequilibrium wage serves as the signal for new entrants, and this supply response should restore the interindustry wage structure to its long-run equilibrium level. This scenario could be relevant to the public sector. In essence, the expansion of the public sector that occurred from the 1950s through the 1980s would lead to increases in the demand for public sector labour, and hence to increases in their wages. The higher wages would enable public employers to recruit the necessary work force associated with the expansion of the public sector. Conversely, recent contractions in the public sector would lead to downward pressure on wages and reductions in the number of workers seeking employment in the public sector, to the point where it becomes difficult for the government to recruit and retain employees.

Noncompetitive Factors Interindustry wage differentials may also reflect noncompetitive factors and it is in this area that the differences between public and private sector labour markets become most pronounced. Specific features that have important implications for public-private wage differentials and their changes over time revolve around the fact that the public sector can be characterized as subject to various peculiarities including a political constraint rather than a profit constraint, possible monopsony, an inelastic demand for labour, and a high degree of new unionization. Each of these factors will be discussed in turn, with an emphasis on their implications for public-private wage differentials and their changes over time.

Political Rather Than Profit Constraint The public sector usually is not subject to a profit constraint as traditionally exists in the private sector. Rather, the profit constraint is replaced by an ultimate political constraint and there is the belief that the political constraint is less binding. This occurs because taxpayers are diffuse, often ill-informed, and can exert pressure only infrequently and with respect to a package of issues. Public sector managers also are diffuse in the sense that lines of responsibility are not always well defined and "buck-passing" can prevail. Workers in the public sector, on the other hand, are often portrayed as a unified, distinct interest group providing direct pressure for wage increases. A more serious imperfection of the political process arises from the fact, discussed earlier, that *future* taxpayers have little or no representation in *today's* political process.

While these features of the political constraint suggest the possibility that it is less binding than the profit constraint, there still are constraining influences on wage settlements in the public sector. Taxpayer scrutiny is now extremely strong and in fact politicians may gain by appearing to be cost-conscious guardians of the public purse by reducing wage costs. Public sector workers may also be called upon to set an example of moderate wages to curb inflation as was evident in recent wage controls applied to the public sector. Even the alleged diffuse nature of management in the public sector may work against employees; it can be difficult to win wage gains if one doesn't know with whom one is bargaining.

Perhaps the most important feature of the political constraint that works against public sector workers is that, during a strike, tax revenues keep coming in to the public sector even though wage expenditures are reduced and public services are not provided. This is in contrast to the private sector, where employers are under considerable pressure to settle because they are losing customers and sales revenues during a strike. To be sure, there can be pressure from taxpayers to have the wage savings go into general tax revenues or into tax reductions because services are not provided. Nevertheless, the fact remains that this political pressure is less stringent than the profit constraint when firms lose customers and revenues during a strike.

Monopsony To the extent that the government sector is often the dominant employer in particular labour markets, governments may utilize their monopsony power to pay lower wage rates than if they behaved competitively. Political forces may pressure them to act as model employers and not utilize their monopsony power; nevertheless, there is also pressure to be cost-conscious and this may lead them to exercise their monopsony power.

In fact, the empirical evidence cited earlier in the chapter on monopsony suggested that for at least two elements of the public sector—teaching and nursing—there was some evidence of monopsony. The extent to which these results can be generalized for other elements of the public sector, or for the teaching and nursing professions as a whole, remains an unanswered empirical question.

To the extent that monopsony power exists and is exercised in the public sector, public sector wages would be lower than they would be in the absence of monopsony. However, the pressure of monopsony also means that, for a range of wage increases, unions would not have to be concerned about employment reductions. In fact, as illustrated in the chapter on monopsony, wage increases may actually lead to employment increases, suggesting the possibility of a substantial union wage impact in monopsonistic labour markets.

Inelastic Demand for Public Sector Labour The possibility of a substantial union impact on wages in the public sector is furthered by the possibility that the demand for labour in the public sector may be wage-inelastic. In such circumstances unions could bargain for substantial wage increases without worrying about large reductions in the employment of their members. The inelasticity of the demand for labour may occur because noncompetitive forces restrict the utilization of substitute inputs as well as substitute services.

Many of the services produced in the public sector are so-called essential services that are not provided in the private sector, and when they are so provided, they are often under governmental regulation. Since consumers (taxpayers) are unable to substitute other services for those provided by the public sector, their demand for these services may be relatively price(tax)-inelastic. In essence, wage increases can be passed on to taxpayers in the form of tax increases for the essential services without taxpayers reducing their demand for these services and, hence, the derived demand for labour.

This is strengthened by the fact that there are often few good inputs to substitute for public sector labour as it becomes expensive. This may reflect the nature of the public sector production function, but it may also reflect the fact that the public sector is heavily professionalized, and professional labour tends to have a degree of control over the utilization of other inputs, including nonprofessional labour.

While these factors suggest that the demand for public sector labour would be wage-inelastic, other factors are at work in the opposite direction. Specifically, the high ratio of labour cost to total cost in many public services suggests that the demand would be elastic. In addition, substitute inputs and services certainly could be utilized, especially in the long run. Even the essentiality of the service may work against public sector employees by restricting their right to strike and reducing public sympathy during a strike. In addition, the employers may stall in the bargaining process, knowing that the essential elements of the service will be maintained and, as indicated earlier, tax revenues are still forthcoming.

Since theory does not indicate unambiguously whether the demand for public sector labour would be elastic or inelastic, we must appeal to the empirical evidence. The evidence from various U.S. studies indicates that the demand for labour in the public sector is inelastic, and that the more essential the service, the greater the inelasticity (Gunderson and Riddell 1991, p. 167).

Unionization A final noncompetitive factor—unionization—may also affect the wages of public sector workers relative to their private sector counterparts. This is especially the case when the unionization is coupled with the other factors discussed in this chapter—the inelastic demand for public sector labour, the possible monopsony in some public sector markets, and the absence of a profit constraint.

In Canada, the growth and high degree of unionization in the public sector is documented, for example, in Ponak and Thompson (1992). Some sectors, like the federal civil service, are organized almost to their full potential. Others, like teaching and health, are now predominantly unionized.

Competitive Floor But Not Ceiling The previously discussed factors—absence of a profit constraint, monopsony, inelastic demand, and the high degree of recent unionization—all suggested that wage determination may be different between the public and private sectors, and that noncompetitive factors may give rise to an interindustry wage differential between the public and private sectors. Most of the factors, with the exception of monopsony, would appear to favour a noncompetitive wage advantage in the public sector, although a variety of subtle constraining influences are present.

However, there is a stronger reason to expect the wage advantage to be in favour of public sector workers. This is so because the forces of competition would ensure that wages in the public sector would not fall much below wages in the private sector for comparable workers. If they did, the public sector would not be in a competitive position to recruit labour, and would experience problems of recruitment, turnover, and morale. That is, competition would ensure a competitive *floor* on wages in the public sector.

These same competitive forces, however, need not provide an effective *ceiling* on wages in the public sector. To be sure, if public sector wages exceeded wages of comparable workers in the private sector, there would be queues of applicants and excessive competition for public sector jobs. Nevertheless, employers in the public sector are not under a profit constraint to respond to these disequilibrium signals; they need not lower their relative wage. They *may* not pay an excessive wage if the political constraint is a binding cost constraint; nevertheless, there is no guarantee that this will be the case. In essence, the forces of competition ensure a floor, but they need not provide an effective ceiling on wages in the public sector. Hence the potential bias, in theory, for wages in the public sector to be in excess of wages in the private sector for comparable workers.

Empirical Evidence

Empirical studies of wage differentials between the public and private sector try to isolate the "pure" public sector premium, that is, the impact of working in the public sector, controlling for human capital, age, sex, industry (type of service), occupation, and possibly

Exhibit 10.2 Are There Queues for Government Jobs?

One of the best measures of whether a job is "overpaid" and whether incumbent workers therefore receive economic rents, is whether there are queues of qualified applicants for such jobs. This is so because queues provide a good "bottom-line" measure of the total compensation of the job (wages and fringe benefits) relative to the requirements and working conditions of the job. That is, as an alternative to trying to estimate, for example, pure public-private wage differentials after controlling for the effect of other legitimate wage-determining characteristics, it may be desirable to estimate queues of qualified applicants.

Krueger (1988a, 1988b) does so on the basis of a number of different U.S. data sets. He finds that there are substantial queues for federal government jobs. As well, as the ratio of federal earnings to private sector earnings increases, the application rate for federal government jobs increases, as does the quality of such applicants.

union status. The simplest way to do this is within a regression framework, such as that in equation 10.2. The researcher includes an indicator variable (or "dummy variable") of whether a worker works in the public sector, along with the other control variables (X). The coefficient on the public sector indicator is interpreted as the public sector pay premium. An alternative approach generalizes the regression approach, and takes into account the possibility that the pay structure may differ in the two sectors. For example, the impact of gender may be different in the public sector because of more stringent pay equity provisions, or the experience profiles may be flatter. This decomposition procedure, which is more fully developed in Chapter 12 on discrimination, divides the public-private differential into two parts: (1) that part due to differences in skills or endowments of the worker and (2) surplus returns or economic rent (the "pure" public sector premium).

www.statcan.ca/english/Subjects/Labour/LFS/lfs-en.htm

The two approaches yield similar conclusions. Recent Canadian evidence is provided in Gunderson, Hyatt, and Riddell (2000).[6] Using Labour Force Survey data from 1997, they estimate that public sector workers earn a premium of about 9 percent. Generally, the premium is higher for women, reflecting the impact of pay equity policies, and lower for

Exhibit 10.3 What Do Public Sector Wages and Environmental Issues Have in Common?

The empirical evidence discussed in this section suggests that severe policies to curb public sector settlements are not necessary, at least at this stage. There is one area, however, where constant vigilance is required.

Neither market nor political forces are likely to provide a sufficient check to ensure that current taxpayers do not shift some of the costs of public sector settlements to future generations of taxpayers through deferred compensation arrangements. Such deferred compensation could include pensions, job security, and seniority-based wage increases, all of which tend to be more prominent in the public sector as opposed to the private sector.

While checks on "shifting the bill" to future generations of taxpayers are necessary, the problem is that the current taxpayers have little incentive to put such checks in place. Reducing the deferred compensation package would mean that they would likely have to incur higher current costs, which falls on their tax bill. In contrast, deferred compensation falls on the tax bill of future generations of taxpayers.

It is in that sense that public sector compensation and environmental issues have something in common. Current generations may have insufficient economic incentives to preserve the environment for future generations, since preserving the environment can be costly for the existing populace. What is needed are mechanisms whereby the current generations are required to pay for the full costs of their decisions. This applies to public sector compensation decisions as well as to environmental decisions. The irony is that the current population has little incentive to put such mechanisms in place.

[6] Gunderson, Hyatt, and Riddell (2000) employ the simpler, "dummy variable" approach. For evidence employing the alternative (decomposition) approach, see Gunderson and Riddell (1995). For other surveys of evidence on the public sector premium in Canada, see Gunderson (1998).

higher-skilled employees, reflecting wage compression in the public sector. One of their more striking findings, using census data from 1971, 1991, and 1991, is that the public sector pay premium has actually been rising over the past 30 years, from about 5 percent in 1971 to 9 percent in the 1990s. The Canadian evidence agrees with results from the United States, where the estimated public sector premium is also in the 5-to-10-percent range.[7]

These empirical results, which suggest only modest premiums, suggest that severe policies are not necessary, at least at this stage, to restrain public sector wage settlements. Nevertheless, constant vigilance is required especially to prevent current taxpayers from passing public sector costs on to future taxpayers in the form of deferred compensation (Exhibit 10.3).

Summary

- The wage (or earnings) structure can be cut along many dimensions besides workplace amenities and education that we explored in the previous chapters. In particular, we are often interested in how earnings vary by occupation, region, industry, and public versus private sector. The human capital earnings function is especially helpful in summarizing how earnings vary in these dimensions, because it allows us to isolate the "pure" impact of working in a specific region or job, controlling for all of the other factors, especially age and education (skill).
- Simple supply and demand diagrams can be used to explain why wages differ across sectors. In equilibrium, we expect wage differentials to exist because of differing demand conditions, combined with differences in the supply of workers. That said, wage differentials may be exacerbated by impediments to mobility of workers between sectors, and non-equilibrium wage differences may persist, even in the long run, if workers cannot move from the low- to the high-wage sector.
- While barriers to mobility can often explain persistent wage gaps across sectors (like regions in Canada), these gaps may be generated by more complicated economic behaviour. For example, interindustry wage differentials may be generated by "efficiency wages," whereby firms pay higher wages because worker productivity depends on the wage rate. In this case, some industries will be "high-wage industries," even in the long run, despite queues of workers who would like to switch from lower-wage industries. Because it would reduce worker productivity, firms in high-wage industries are unwilling to cut wages to increase employment, and thus clear the cross-industry labour market.
- The public sector accounts for about one-fifth of the employed labour force in Canada, including workers in government (public administration), as well as government-owned or funded firms and agencies (hospitals, schools, colleges, universities, and Crown corporations). An important policy question is how much public employees should be paid, and in particular whether through their unions and political pressure they are able to extract excessive wages. Most evidence suggests that there is a small premium (5 to 10 percent) for working in the public sector, controlling for observable human capital determinants of earnings.

[7]Borland and Gregory (1999) provide a detailed summary of the methodological issues entailed in estimating the public sector wage premium, as well as extensive international evidence.

REVIEW QUESTIONS

1. Discuss the various factors that determine the shape of the labour supply schedule for an occupation. Give an example of an occupation that may have an elastic supply schedule and one that may have an inelastic one, and indicate why this is so. If the two occupations received an equal increase in the demand for their labour, what would happen to the skill differential between them?
2. Discuss the expected impact on the occupational wage structure of each of the following policies:
   a. An increase in unionization
   b. An increase in public subsidies to education, training, job search, and mobility
   c. Wage-price controls
   d. Child labour laws
   e. Laws governing the minimum age one can leave school
   f. A reduction in rural-urban migration
   g. An increase in immigration
   h. An exogenous influx into the labour force of younger workers and married women
   i. Stricter control of entry into the medical profession
3. It could be argued that market forces will not prevent cities from growing beyond a socially optimal size, because pollution or congestion externalities associated with city growth are not accounted for through the market mechanism. Discuss the extent to which wage adjustments may reflect these externalities. Will the wage adjustments ensure a socially optimal city size?
4. Discuss the ways in which government social transfer programs may decrease or increase geographic mobility. To the extent that they decrease mobility, should they be removed? Are there ways of mitigating their adverse effects on geographic mobility?
5. Why might large firms pay higher wages than small firms? Why might this relationship prevail even after controlling for the effect of other wage-determining factors such as the differences in the skill distribution and in working conditions?
6. On the basis of your knowledge of the determinants of the elasticity of demand for labour (for a review, see Chapter 5), would you expect the demand for public sector labour to be inelastic or elastic? Why? Why might one expect the elasticity to differ across different elements of the public sector?
7. Criticisms of public sector wages as being too high often implicitly assume that private sector wages are the correct norm. What is so virtuous about private sector wages, given that they can reflect market imperfections, unequal bargaining power, and a variety of non-economic constraints? Discuss.

PROBLEMS

1. "In a competitive economy, there can be no such thing as a pure interindustry wage differential in the long run." True or false? Explain.
2. "Efficiency wages cannot prevail in the long run, because there would always be a queue of qualified applicants for the jobs that paid the efficiency wage premiums. In such circumstances, the employer could increase the hiring standards or the job requirements and the wage premium would therefore reflect a compensating wage for the greater skill requirements or more difficult requirements of the job." True or false? Explain.
3. Consider an economy of only two industries, one high-wage and the other low-wage. Each employs the same number of workers, equally divided between two groups,

skilled and unskilled. Skilled workers are identical with each other in the two industries, and so are the unskilled. The low-wage industry pays its skilled labour \$10 an hour, and its unskilled labour \$5 during both a recession and an expansion; that is, it has a rigid wage structure. The high-wage industry pays its skilled labour \$20 per hour in both a recession and an expansion, but it pays its unskilled workers \$5 during recession and \$15 during expansion; that is, only its skilled wages are rigid over the business cycle.

For the whole economy, calculate the interoccupational wage differential (ratio of skilled to unskilled wages) in both the recession and the expansion. Calculate the interindustry wage differential (ratio of high- to low-wage industries) for both skilled and unskilled workers in both the recession and the expansion. Why does the interoccupational wage differential contract in the expansion and widen in the interindustry?

4. A researcher has access to the 2000 Labour Force Survey, and estimates the following regression:

$$\ln W_i = 10.46 + 0.336 PUBLIC_i$$

where W_i is individual annual earnings, and $PUBLIC_i$ is an indicator of whether the individual works in the public sector. Calculate the implied ratio of public to private sector earnings. The researcher concludes that this is evidence that public sector workers earn economic rents, that is, that they are overpaid. Critically evaluate the researcher's conclusions, and explain how the researcher could refine her estimate.

5. Differences in the elasticity of demand for labour between the public and private sectors, by themselves, are not sufficient conditions for a wage differential between the two sectors. True or false? Explain.

6. Grant, a young Newfoundlander, has just graduated from high school and is deciding what to do with the rest of his life, which lasts two periods (like everyone else's). His main decision is whether to stay in Newfoundland or migrate to Toronto.

   If he stays in Newfoundland, he will earn Y_0 in period one and Y_1 in period 2. If he moves to Toronto, he will incur a moving cost of M (in the first period), and he will be unemployed (with zero earnings) for the first period. In his second period in Toronto, he will earn Y_T. The interest rate at which money can be borrowed or invested is r.

   a. On a carefully labelled diagram, illustrate Grant's migration decision, that is, show his earnings paths as a function of time, depending on whether he lives in Newfoundland or Toronto.
   b. Show that he will move to Toronto if

   $$(Y_T - Y_1) > (1 + r)(Y_0 + M)$$

   What is the economic intuition underlying this result? How does an increase in the interest rate affect the migration decision? Why?
   c. As a potential labour economist, Grant realizes that he needs to have estimates of Y_T and Y_1 in order to make a wise migration decision. He reads in the newspaper that average earnings of Newfoundlanders in Toronto are $\overline{Y}_T$, while Newfoundlanders earn an average of $\overline{Y}_1$, if they stay in Newfoundland. (Both magnitudes refer to second-period earnings) With specific reference to the result in part (b), discuss the potential error that Grant may make by using $\overline{Y}_T$ and $\overline{Y}_1$ as the basis of his estimate of the return to migration.

7. Debbie is deciding which career to pursue. She cannot decide between becoming a veterinarian or a pharmacist. Assume that both careers require the equivalent of six

years of postsecondary education. A recent increase in the demand for pharmacists has led to shortage, and incomes of pharmacists are about $20,000 higher than those of veterinarians. All else equal, Debbie would rather be a veterinarian, but for a $20,000 higher salary, she is tempted to study pharmacy. As a rare, economically literate guidance counsellor, use a figure like Figure 10.1 to advise Debbie on her career choice. Be sure to distinguish between the short- and the long-run supply of labour to an occupation.

8. Assume that, on average, an applicant waits 12 months before being hired into a government job (as a mail clerk). George could work as a mail clerk in the private sector immediately for a salary of $2500 per month, but he chooses instead to remain unemployed and wait for the government job. In the meantime, he collects $500 per month in unemployment insurance benefits (for 12 months). Assume that the government job lasts two years, that his private sector job will last just as long (plus the year he can wait for the government job), that salaries are constant, that the interest rate is 10 percent per year, and that leisure has no value to George. Determine the minimum public sector premium that must exist for George's decision to be rational.

   What are the pros and cons of using queues as a measure of rents or excess payments paid to workers in the public sector?

KEYWORDS

earnings function 288
regional wage differential 288
occupational premiums 288
industry premiums 288
nonpecuniary benefits 290
immobility 290
disequilibrium 290
unobserved heterogeneity 290
occupation 290
interoccupational wage differentials 292
migration 294
interindustry wage differentials 296
efficiency wages 297
public-private sector wage differentials 304

REFERENCES

Bellante, D. 1979. The North South differential and the migration of heterogeneous labor. *AER* 69 (March):166–75.

Bishop, J., J. Formby, and P. Thistle. 1992. Convergence of the South and Non-South income distributions, 1969–1979. *AER* 82 (March):262–72.

Borland, J., and R. G. Gregory. 1999. Recent developments in public sector labor markets. In *Handbook of Labor Economics*, eds. O. Ashenfelter and D. Card. New York and Oxford: Elsevier Science, North Holland.

Brown, C., and J. L. Medoff. 1989. The employer size wage effect. *JPE* (October):1027–59.

Card, D. 1986. The impact of deregulation on the employment and wages of airline mechanics. *ILRR* 39 (July):527–38.

Coulombe, S., and K. Day. 1999. Economic growth and regional income disparities in Canada and the northern United States. *CPP* 25 (June):155–78.

Courchene, T. 1970. Interprovincial migration and economic adjustment. *CJE* 3 (November):550–76.

______. 1974. *Migration, Income and Employment: Canada 1965–1968*. Montreal: Howe Research Institute.

Cousineau, J.-M., and F. Vaillancourt. 2000. Regional disparities, mobility and labour markets in Canada. In *Adopting Public Policy to a Labour Market in Transition*, eds. W. C. Riddell and F. St-Hilaire. Montreal: Institute for Research on Public Policy.

Day, K. 1992. Interprovincial migration and local public goods. *CJE* 25 (February):123–44.

Dickens, W., and L. Katz. 1987. Industry wage differences and industry characteristics. In *Unemployment and the Structure of Labor Markets*, eds. K. Lang and J. Leonard. Oxford: Basil Blackwell.

Dickens, W., and K. Lang. 1988. Why it matters what we trade: A case for active policy. In *The Dynamics of Trade and Employment*, eds. L. Tyson, W. Dickens, and J. Zysman. Cambridge: Ballinger.

Ehrenberg, R. 1979. *The Regulatory Process and Labor Earnings*. New York: Academic Press.

Farber, S., and R. Newman. 1987. Accounting for South/Non-South real wage differentials and for changes in those differentials over time. *R.E. Stats.* 59 (May):215–23.

Filer, R. 1986. The "starving artist"—myth or reality. *JPE* 94 (February):56–75.

Finnie, R. 2000. The who moves? A panel logit model analysis of inter-provincial migration in Canada. Statistics Canada Analytic Studies Branch Research Paper Series, Number 142.

Freeman, R. B., and L. F. Katz. 1991. Industrial wage and employment determination in an open economy. In *Immigration, Trade, and the Labor Market*, eds. J. Abowd and R. Freeman. Chicago: University of Chicago Press.

Gaston, N., and D. Trefler. 1994. Protection, trade, and wages: Evidence from U.S. manufacturing. *ILRR* 47 (July):574–93.

______. 1995. Union wage sensitivity to trade and protection: Theory and evidence. *Journal of International Economics* 39 (August):1–25.

Gera, S., and G. Grenier. 1994. Interindustry wage differentials and efficiency wages: Some Canadian evidence. *CJE* 27 (February):81–100.

Grant, E. K., and J. Vanderkamp. 1980. The effects of migration on income: A micro study with Canadian data, 1965–71. *CJE* 13 (August):381–406.

Grey, A. 1993. Interindustry wage differentials in manufacturing: rents and industrial structure. *CJE* 26 (August):525–35.

Grossman, G. 1986. Imports as a cause of injury: The case of the U.S. steel industry. *Journal of International Economics* 20 (May):201–23.

______. 1987. The employment and wage effects of import competition. *Journal of International Economic Integration* 2 (Spring):1–23.

Gunderson, M. 1998. Government compensation: Issues and options, CPRN Discussion Paper, Number W03.

Gunderson, M., D. Hyatt, and W. C. Riddell. 2000. Pay differences between the government and private sectors: Labour force Survey and census estimates, CPRN Discussion Paper, Number W10.

Gunderson, M., and C. Riddell. 1991. Provincial public sector payrolls. In *Provincial Public Finances*, ed. M. McMillan. Toronto: Canadian Tax Foundation.

______. 1995. Public and private sector wages: A comparison. Government and Competitiveness Series, School of Policy Studies, Queen's University.

Katz, L. F., and L. H. Summers. 1989a. Can inter-industry wage differentials justify strategic trade policy. In *Trade Policies for International Competitiveness*, ed. R. C. Feenstra. Chicago: University of Chicago Press.

______. 1989b. Industry rents: Evidence and implications. *Brookings Papers: Microeconomics*:209–90.

Krueger, A. 1988a. Are public sector workers paid more than their alternative wage? Evidence from longitudinal data and job queues. In *When Public Sector Workers Unionize*, eds. R. Freeman and C. Ichniowski. Chicago: University of Chicago Press.

______. 1988b. The determinants of queues for federal jobs. *ILRR* 41 (July):567–81.

Krueger, A., and L. H. Summers. 1987. Reflections on the inter-industry wage structure. In *Unemployment and the Structure of Labor Markets*, eds. K. Lang and J. Leonard. Oxford: Basil Blackwell.

Krueger, A. B., and L. H. Summers. 1988. Efficiency wages and the inter-industry wage structure. *Ecta* 56 (March):259–93.

Lawrence, C., and R. Lawrence. 1985. Manufacturing wage dispersion: An end game interpretation. *BPEA* 1:47–106.

Leolho, P., and M. Ghali. 1971. The end of the North-South wage differential. *AER* 61 (December):932–37; comment and reply, 63 (September 1973):757–62.

Morissette, R. 1993. Canadian jobs and firm size: Do smaller firms pay less? *CJE* 26:159–74.

Murphy, K., and R. Topel. 1987. Unemployment, risk and earnings. In *Unemployment and the Structure of Labour Markets*, eds. K. Lang and J. Leonard. Oxford: Basil Blackwell.

Osberg, L., D. Gordon, and Z. Lin. 1994. Interregional migration and interindustry labour mobility in Canada: A simultaneous approach. *CJE* 27:58–80.

Reder, M. 1955. The theory of occupational wage differentials. *AER* 45 (December):833–52.

Reilly, K. T. 1995. Human capital and information: The employer size-wage effect. *JHR* 30 (Winter):1–18.

Revenga, A. 1992. Exporting jobs: The impact of import competition on employment and wages in U.S. manufacturing. *QJE* 107 (February):255–84.

Rose, N. 1987. Labor rent sharing and regulation: Evidence from the trucking industry. *JPE* 6 (December):1146–78.

Shackett, J., and J. Trapani. 1987. Earnings differentials and market structure. *JHR* (Fall):518–31.

Vanderkamp, J. 1968. Interregional mobility in Canada: A study of the time pattern of migration. *CJE* 1 (August):595–608.

______. 1971. Migration flows, their determinants and the effects of return migration. *JPE* 79 (September/October):1012–31.

______. 1972. Return migration: Its significance and behaviour. *WEJ* 10 (December):460–66.

______. 1976. The role of population size in migration studies. *CJE* 9 (August):508–16.

______. 1986. The efficiency of the interregional adjustment process. In *Disparities and Interregional Adjustment*, ed. K. Norrie. Toronto: University of Toronto Press.

Chapter Eleven

The Economics of Immigration

Main Questions

- *How have patterns of immigration to Canada changed over the past 45 years? From which countries do immigrants come, and where do they settle upon arrival in Canada?*
- *What is the "points system," and what impact does it have on immigration to Canada?*
- *Overall, does immigration have a positive or negative impact on the labour market outcomes of the native-born? In particular, are higher levels of immigration associated with downward pressure on wages, or increases in unemployment?*
- *In what respects do immigrants assimilate? How long does it take for an immigrant's earnings to catch up to those of a native-born Canadian?*
- *Are immigrants a net drain on the public treasury, especially through higher dependence on social assistance?*

From the narrow perspective of the human capital earnings function, immigrant status may be viewed as just another determinant of individual wages. In fact, documenting and interpreting the correlation between immigrant status and earnings is currently the subject of intense research in labour economics. However, this focus arises from a much wider interest in the economics of immigration.

While immigration has always been an important feature of Canadian labour market policy, several factors have conspired to move it to the forefront of economic policy discussion. First, there is some concern that immigration may be contributing to a deterioration in labour market conditions, especially in the form of higher unemployment and wage polarization. Second, government fiscal pressures have led to cutbacks in social programs and there is some perception (perhaps unwarranted) that immigrants pose a special burden to these programs. Third, immigrants come from an increasing diversity of countries, substantially changing the ethnic composition of the Canadian population. Some view these changes as a challenge to Canadian multiculturalism policy. Others note that immigrants from non-European countries may face greater difficulties in assimilation than was the case with earlier immigrants. To the extent that the new immigrants come from developing countries, their skills (vocational or language) may indeed be less of a match for the Canadian labour market. Finally, whatever the particular policy motivation, immigrants are a numerically important group in the labour market. This is true, not just in the traditional immigrant-receiving countries like Canada, the United States, and Australia, but also the United Kingdom, France, Germany, and other parts of Europe. Immigration, as much as trade, is an important manifestation of globalization in the Canadian labour market.

Even confined to its economic aspects, immigration is too large a topic to cover in one chapter. There are a number of potential subtopics that would be worth describing. Among them are:

1. *Economic models of migration.* How might we model the individual decision to migrate to a particular country? To what extent can we explain immigrant flows across countries by the economic variables implied by these models?
2. *Economic performance of immigrants.* Once they arrive in Canada, how quickly do immigrants adjust to their new labour market? What factors seem to explain success (or failure) in the Canadian labour market?
3. *The impact of immigrants on native outcomes.* Do immigrants adversely affect the labour market outcomes of the native-born population? Are some groups hurt more than others? Are immigrants net contributors to the public treasury?
4. *Policy evaluation.* What policy mechanisms are at the government's disposal to minimize the adverse effects of immigration (or maximize the benefits)? Should immigration levels be increased or decreased? Should family reunification be the dominant criteria for admission to Canada? Does it really matter who is admitted to Canada?

Our discussion is confined to the last three topics. The economic model of migration is a straightforward extension of human capital theory, briefly outlined in Chapter 10.

A PROFILE OF IMMIGRATION TO CANADA

Any description of the main features of immigration to Canada is principally a confirmation of the prominence of immigrants in the Canadian labour market. As such, the following provides a backdrop for the discussion of public policy toward immigration, and the potential impact of immigration on the labour market.

Figure 11.1 shows the level and patterns of immigration by source region since 1955. Green (1976, 1995) provides more detailed documentation of these patterns, including an important historical perspective on immigration over the twentieth century. This figure illustrates a number of important points. First, until the mid-1980s, overall immigration levels fluctuated considerably. Subsequently, Canada steadily admitted over 200,000 immigrants per year, with the exceptions of 1998 and 1999. However, these numbers are not unprecedented. The annual flow is not much higher than was experienced in the late 1950s, mid-1960s, and mid-1970s. On a per capita basis, immigration levels are actually slightly lower. In the past, however, immigration levels were more cyclical, with levels significantly curtailed during recessions. The recessionary years of the early 1990s did not see such a decline in immigration. Second, the source regions have changed dramatically. In the mid-1960s, the main source countries were the United Kindgom, the United States, and western Europe. By 1995, the largest region was "Asia" (a decidedly coarse grouping). Other countries, principally in South and Central America, have also gained in relative importance. Table 11.1 provides a more detailed breakdown of the source countries for 1998–2000. The top ten countries, seven of which are in Asia, accounted for over half of all immigrants to Canada. China alone, including Hong Kong, represented 16 percent of immigrants. Combined, the United States and the United Kingdom accounted for less than 5 percent.

Figure 11.1

Immigration to Canada by Source Region, 1955–2000

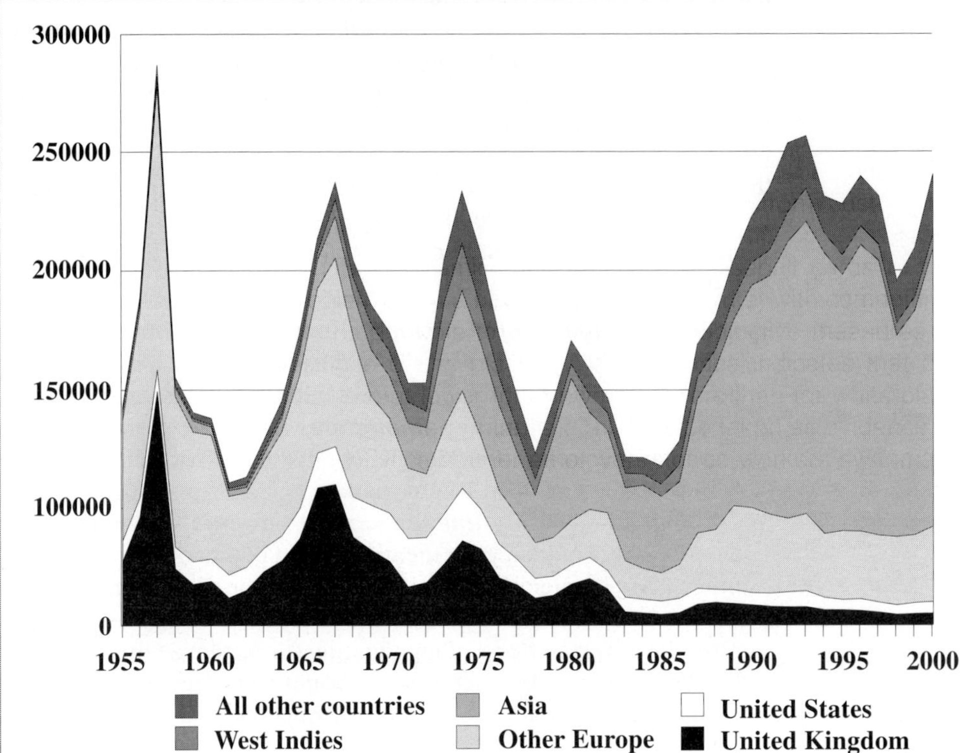

This figure plots the number of immigrants to Canada from six major immigrant source regions, for each year from 1955 to 2000. The distance between each line and the one below it represents the number of immigrants from that region, so that the areas (the bands) between lines shows the relative size of immigration from the region. Total immigration is given by the sum of immigration from the six regions. The figure thus illustrates patterns in the total flow of immigration, fluctuating with peaks around 200–250 thousand, as well as a declining share of immigrants from the United Kingdom and the United States, and an increasing share from Asia.

Notes: United Kingdom figures include Australasia. "Other Europe" is total Europe minus the United Kingdom.

Source: Reproduced with permission of the Minister of Public Works and Government Services Canada, 2001.

While this changing mix of source countries may not have any bearing on the economic consequences of immigration, it certainly affects public perceptions of immigration, and more objectively, has a clear impact on the ethnic composition of the population.

Figure 11.2 demonstrates another important feature of immigration to Canada. Based on the 1996 census, this figure shows the regional variation of immigrant concentrations across major metropolitan areas. Immigrants are defined to be those individuals born outside of Canada. In 1996, 17.4 percent of all Canadian residents were born outside Canada, as against approximately 9 percent of residents in the United States. However, such an aggregate, national figure masks the potential impact of immigration. Immigrant concentrations vary considerably, from over 40 percent in Toronto and 35 percent in Vancouver, to under 5 percent in the Quebec cities outside Montreal. Figure 11.2 also shows that this concentration varies slightly differently for recent arrivals compared to older immigrants. Around 20 percent of the populations of Toronto and Vancouver are made up of immigrants who arrived in the past 15 years. While economists often speak of the impact of immigration on the national labour market, it is likely that the impact varies across cities. This variation also represents a possible source, unexploited in Canada, of identifying the impact of immigration on the labour market.

While Figure 11.2 shows the concentration of immigrants in each city, it does not show the allocation of immigrants across cities. In separate tabulations, the census further shows the urban nature of immigration. Of all immigrants, 85.0 percent reside in the

Figure 11.2

Immigrant Concentration by Census Metropolitan Area, 1996

This bar chart shows the fraction of the population of Canada's largest cities (Census Metropolitan Areas, or CMAs) who are immigrants (i.e., born outside Canada). Each bar is divided into two parts, corresponding to recent immigrants, who arrived between 1980 and 1995, and older immigrants, who arrived prior to 1980. The cities are sorted in descending order of the fraction of the population that consists of immigrants.

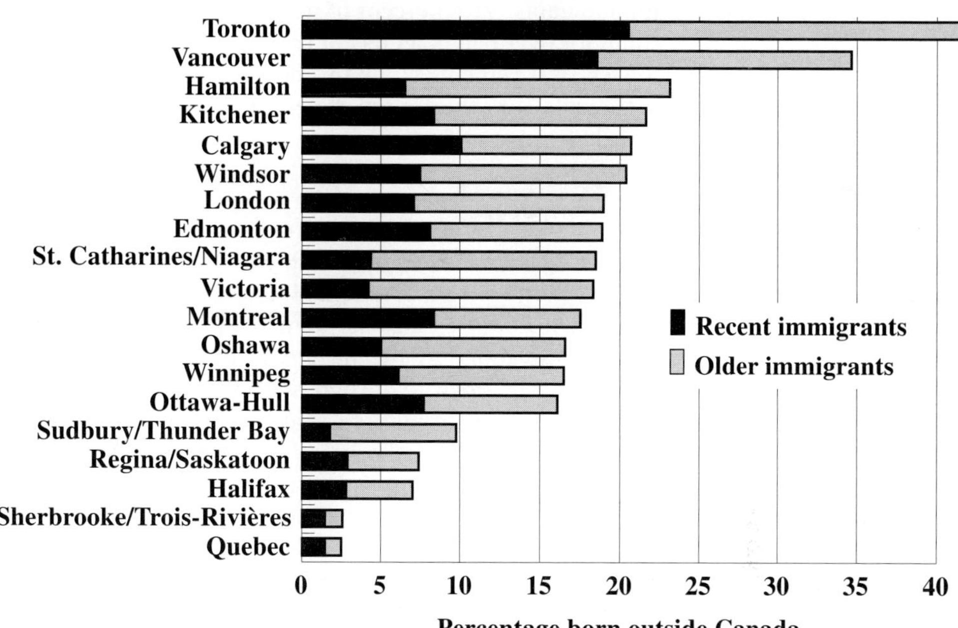

Notes: Recent immigrants are those who arrived between 1980 and 1996. Older immigrants are those who arrived prior to 1980. Reported figures are the percentage of each CMA that was born outside Canada.

Source: Adapted from Statistics Canada, Individual Public Use Microdata File: 1996 Census of Population.

Table 11.1 Immigrant Landings (All Classes), Top Ten Source Countries, 1998–2000

Country	1998	Rank	1999	Rank	2000	Rank
China (including Hong Kong)	19,766	1	29,116	1	36,664	1
India	15,350	2	17,431	2	26,004	2
Pakistan	8,086	4	9,299	3	14,163	3
Philippines	8,183	3	9,163	4	10,063	4
South Korea	4,913	8	7,213	5	7,602	5
Sri Lanka	N/A	N/A	4,720	9	5,832	6
USA	4,786	9	5,539	7	5,806	7
Iran	6,768	7	5,905	6	5,598	8
Yugoslavia	N/A	N/A	N/A	N/A	4,699	9
Great Britain	N/A	N/A	4,480	10	4,644	10
Taiwan	7,178	6	5,478	8	N/A	N/A
Russia	4,285	10	N/A	N/A	N/A	N/A
Hong Kong	8,079	5	N/A	N/A	N/A	N/A
Top Ten Total	**87,394**		**98,344**		**121,075**	
Percentage	50		52		53	
Other countries	86,686		91,570		105,762	
Percentage	50		48		47	
Total	**174,080**		**189,914**		**226,837**	

Note: "N/A" indicates that immigration numbers from a particular country did not place it in the top ten for that year.

Source: "Planning now for Canada's future: Introducing a multi-year planning process and the immigration plan for 2001 and 2002," Citizenship and Immigration Canada Web site, accessed October 10, 2001 <www.cic.gc.ca/english/pub/anrep01e.html>.

CMAs listed here, compared to only 55.2 percent of the native-born, who are relatively more likely to live in smaller communities. This concentration is even more pronounced for recent immigrants, 91.5 percent of whom live in these cities. Toronto and Vancouver alone account for over half of all recent immigrants, with Toronto receiving 40.8 percent, and Vancouver 16.0 percent. While this detail will be glossed over when we look at evidence for "Canada," or "the United States," it remains an important qualification of the empirical evidence that follows.

THE POLICY ENVIRONMENT

Immigration policymakers essentially have two "levers" that they can manipulate: (1) the number of immigrants to be admitted and (2) who among the set of potential immigrants is admitted. The history of Canadian immigration policy illustrates the extremes in the application of these tools. At the beginning of the twentieth century, immigration to Canada was essentially open to anyone, with the notable exception of immigrants from China. While there was a strong preference to recruit immigrants from northern Europe, only the very sick, destitute, and criminals were actively screened (Green, 1995). By the mid-1960s, both the quantity and type of immigrants were significantly restricted, though there ceased to be active discrimination on the basis of country of origin. Before outlining how these immigrant admission tools are used, it is worth discussing the fundamental, though largely unresearched, question regarding the objectives of immigration policy. It is difficult to assess the failure or success of immigration policy without some idea of what policymakers are trying to achieve.[1]

We begin by ignoring the important political dimension of immigration policy, and assume that policymakers are attempting to maximize "national welfare." The question is then whose welfare enters into this objective function. What are the relative weights attached to the existing stock of Canadian residents versus potential immigrants? Most likely, the greater weight is placed on maximizing the benefit of immigration to the existing population. Immigrants, for example, may be admitted for the skills they bring to the Canadian labour market, alleviating specific skills shortages or more generally contributing to economic growth. The problem with the delineation between current residents and immigrants, however, is that the "existing population" evolves as new immigrants join the club. The welfare of the existing population and potential immigrants cannot be neatly separated, because today's immigrants are tomorrow's residents. For example, today's immigrants will ultimately wish to be reunited with family members. Family reunification then becomes another motivation for immigration that is addressed to maximizing the welfare of the "ultimately" current residents of Canada.

http://lois.justice.gc.ca/en/I-2

Humanitarian concerns for potential immigrants will provide another motivation for admitting individuals to Canada. Such concerns may be purely for political reasons (to provide individuals sanctuary from political persecution) or they may be economic (to provide individuals with sanctuary from poverty). In practice, it is difficult to disentangle these factors, and it may be easier to summarize them as merely providing immigrants with an opportunity to better their lives.

Canadian immigration policy has been driven by both the self-interested and the altruistic (humanitarian) concerns described above. This is reflected in the historical development of the immigration policy levers. Green (1977, 1995) and Green and Green (1995, 1999) provide a comprehensive summary of the history and details of Canadian immigration policy.

[1]Borjas (1996) provides a non-technical discussion of these issues, while Borjas (1995) offers a slightly more technical presentation of the economic benefits of immigration. Green and Green (1995) document the variety of goals—economic and non-economic—that have played important roles in the evolution of Canadian immigration policy.

As will become apparent, the two policy dimensions, the number and nature of immigrants, are not independent. Nevertheless, it is worth discussing them separately. Every year, the federal government announces the planned number of immigrants to be admitted the following year. These levels are chosen in consultation with the provinces, with an eye to minimizing any adverse impact of immigration. Accordingly, planned admissions would be reduced in recessionary times. Of course, fewer immigrants would find Canada an attractive destination during a recession. The ultimate level of immigration would then be the result of a mixture of immigrant supply and demand factors.

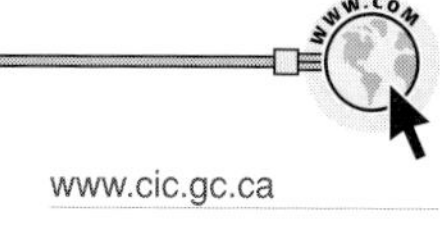

www.cic.gc.ca

Immigrants enter Canada by a number of different avenues, each reflecting the competing motivations for immigration described above. Broadly speaking, immigrants can be divided into **assessed and nonassessed classes**. The assessed classes are those immigrants who are evaluated on the basis of their likely contribution and success in the Canadian labour market. These include the traditional **independent immigrants**, most commonly described in economic models of migration. These are individuals who apply for admission to Canada on the basis of their skills, and are evaluated on a relatively objective **point system**. This system, introduced in 1967, currently applies to the majority of immigrants. Points are awarded for the specific skills that the immigrant has, with extra points awarded for skills perceived to be in shortage in Canada. The details of the point allocation are described in Exhibit 11.1. The point system provides the government with the most direct method of controlling the types of immigrants admitted to Canada. In principal, with enough information, the point system could be used to limit immigration only to those individuals virtually certain to succeed in Canada, with no possible displacement of Canadian workers. There are other, smaller economically assessed classes. The business classes, which include investors, entrepreneurs, and self-employed are not evaluated under the same point system as skilled workers, but must meet certain economic objectives. Assisted relatives are basically skilled workers, admitted under the point system, but who obtain extra points for having relatives in Canada. Finally, immigrants are admitted as retired workers, or under special occupational programs, such as those for domestic workers and nannies.

The nonassessed classes (**family class** and **refugee class**) currently comprise 40 percent of all immigrants, a lower proportion than in the early 1990s. Reunification of family members with Canadian residents is a high priority of government policy. The definition of "family" has varied over the years, with the closeness of relative admissible under these criteria changing. Unlike assisted relatives, who undergo skills evaluation, family class immigrants are not selected with any consideration of the likelihood of their success in Canada. The same is true of refugees. In fact, likelihood of economic success is of no consideration for refugees, since they are admitted on the basis of humanitarian grounds, usually to facilitate escape from political persecution or violence.

Figure 11.3 plots the time series of immigration to Canada by broad class of immigrant, since 1966. A few patterns are worth noting. First, the economically assessed classes are the largest group, comprising over half of immigrants (58 percent) in 1999. However, the relative importance of this group has fluctuated over time with changes in immigration policy. When the point system was first introduced in 1967, most immigrants were assessed. Over the mid-1970s the family class grew steadily in importance, and until the mid-1990s formed the "base" of the immigration numbers in any given year. The size of the family class was not very sensitive to economic conditions, or the total number of immigrants admitted to Canada. In fact, it was the assessed classes in this time period that essentially formed the margin of adjustment, being substantially reduced when immigration totals were cut. This changed in the mid-1990s when concerns of the economic performance of immigrants led to an increased emphasis on skills, and the assessed classes became more prominent. The refugee class fluctuates with global political conditions, peaking, for example, in the late 1970s with Vietnamese refugees, and more recently with refugees from eastern

Figure 11.3 **Immigration to Canada by Class of Immigrant, 1966–1999**

This figure plots the number of immigrants to Canada each year from 1966 to 1999 by class of entry. "Economically assessed" immigrants are primarily "independent," assessed under the point system, and the (small) business (or investor) class. The class "Family" are those immigrants sponsored by Canadian residents (as family members).

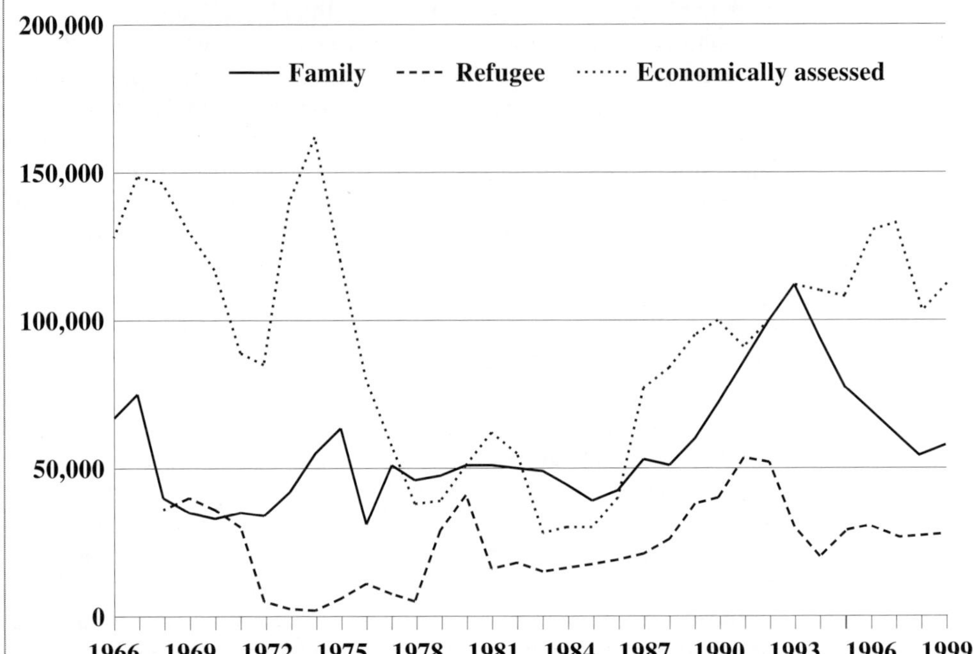

Note: Reported figures are the annual totals of immigration to Canada by class of entry. The economically assessed class is an aggregate of business, retired, assisted relatives, and other skilled worker classes.

Source: Data reported in Employment and Immigration Canada, *Immigration Statistics,* various issues, Supply and Services Canada; and Citizenship and Immigration Canada. The 1996 data is from Citizenship and Immigration Canada, "Facts and figures 1998: Immigration overview," Minister of Public Works and Government Services, 1999. The 1997–1999 data is from Citizenship and Immigration Canada, "Facts and figures 1999: Immigration overview," Minister of Public Works and Government Services, 2000.

Europe. Smoothing out the peaks, there has also been a slight upward trend in the number of immigrants admitted as refugees.

A number of policy questions immediately arise. How much of a problem for the Canadian economy is created by the fact that the family class is unassessed? Do family class immigrants perform more poorly than independent immigrants? Even within the assessed classes, how well does the point system pick those most likely to succeed? How sensitive is immigrant performance to the overall level of immigration?

To address these particular, as well as more general issues, policymakers need to know the answers to a few important empirical questions:

1. *What is the impact of immigrants on the Canadian market?* If immigrants have no adverse effects (or possibly even positive ones), then this permits humanitarian concerns to dominate. It reduces the need for governments to intensively assess potential immigrants. On the other hand, if there are adverse consequences, then it will matter more how many and who is let in.
2. *How do immigrants fare in Canada?* Answering this informs the policy maker of what factors are important for success in Canada, and yields possible evidence on the failure or success of previous admissions policy. It also provides indirect evidence regarding the first question. If immigrants have difficulty in adjusting to the Canadian labour

Exhibit 11.1 **Canada's Immigration Point System, 2001**

Independent class immigrants are admitted under a point system. Applicants are assigned points for a variety of characteristics believed to be useful predictors of success in the Canadian labour market. Applicants must obtain a minimum of 70 points to be considered for admission to Canada. Interested individuals can assess their likelihood of admission with a self-assessment guide available, for example, on the Internet, at the Citizenship and Immigration Web site: <www.cic.gc.ca>.

Factor	Maximum Points
1. *Age.* Maximum points are given for individuals ages 21–44, with declining points given for older individuals (zero for age 49 and older).	10
2. *Education.* Increasing points for level of education, for example with 0 for incomplete high school, 15 for a bachelor's degree, and 16 for advanced degrees.	16
3. *Specific vocational training.* Since occupation is a primary determinant of admission, occupational qualifications make up a large part of the assessment.	18
4. *Occupation.* Points are assessed according to the perceived demand for an individual's skills in the Canadian labour market. An applicant is automatically disqualified if he/she obtains zero points in this category.	10
5. *Arranged employment/designated occupation.* If an individual has a prearranged job, he/she gets ten points. Points are also awarded for being in a "designated" occupation.	10
6. *Work experience.* Points are awarded for years of experience, with the most points being awarded for experience in occupations in high demand.	8
7. *Language ability.* Points are awarded for fluency in English or French. Fluency in one language yields 9 points, while fluency in both official languages yields 15 points.	15
8. *Demographic factor.* This is essentially an "intercept" factor, and is currently set to 8 points for everyone.	10
9. *Personal suitability.* Points are assigned on the basis of an interview, providing a more subjective evaluation of the probability of success in Canada.	10
10. *Relative in Canada.* 5 points are awarded if the applicant has a relative who is a permanent resident of Canada.	5

market, it seriously questions the ability of the labour market to absorb the level and type of immigrants being admitted. Furthermore, if immigrants perform poorly, they may have more direct adverse effects on the Canadian economy, potentially becoming a burden on transfer programs. Of course, the evidence could just as easily show that immigrants are on average quite successful, and net contributors to the public treasury.

THE IMPACT OF IMMIGRANTS ON THE LABOUR MARKET

Of most direct interest to policymakers in setting immigration levels is the **impact of immigrants** on the labour market. A simple supply and demand model can be used to outline the principal theoretical issues.[2] Most directly, the addition of new immigrants to a labour market increases the population of potential workers, and increases the supply of labour. This first-order effect on the labour market is illustrated in panel (a) of Figure 11.4. One can easily see why the native-born might oppose immigration. Wages are unambiguously depressed, unless the demand curve is perfectly elastic (horizontal). While employment increases, if for some reason the wage does not fully adjust to clear the market, unemployment might also ensue.

This simple-minded representation ignores many other effects of immigration on the labour market that could offset these adverse consequences. First, as described above, immigrants are often selected on the basis of their occupational skills. If these skills are in shortage, so that the market is in temporary disequilibrium, then immigrants may relieve the shortage without any adverse effect on wages or unemployment. Of course, only a small minority of immigrants are likely to fill this role, so skills shortages alone are unlikely to offset the negative impact of immigration on wages, assuming Figure 11.4 (a) is the otherwise correct representation of the labour market.

More likely, immigrants may cause the demand curve to shift outward, as illustrated in Figure 11.4(b). Immigrants purchase goods and services in Canada, and this will increase the derived demand for labour. Immigrants may also alter trade patterns in ways that could affect the demand for labour (Kuhn and Wooton, 1991; Globerman, 1995; Baker and Benjamin, 1997a; and Head and Ries, 1998). This could arise because of improved information flows between new immigrants and their source countries. Alternatively, "importing" labour may be a substitute for importing the goods produced by that labour in the originating country. Immigrants may also disproportionately invest into Canadian firms, creating additional employment. Clearly, this is the motivation for the admission of business class immigrants. Even if immigrants themselves do not invest, others may invest in productive facilities that take advantage of the new immigrant labour. In Figure 11.4 (b) the increase in demand is drawn in such a way that there is no adverse effect on wages. Whether this is the relevant outcome depends on the relative shifts of the supply and demand curves, as well as the slopes (elasticities) of the functions. Economic theory can only take us so far in this policy exercise.

Another important consideration is to ask what the relevant labour market is, upon which we expect immigration to have an impact. Is it the national labour market? Is it the Vancouver, Toronto, Montreal, or Regina labour markets? Is it the high-skill or low-skill labour markets? Can we view these markets in isolation, or are there important linkages across the markets? For example, the admission of high-skilled immigrants might lower the price of high-skilled labour, but if this labour is complementary with low-skilled labour, then demand for low-skilled labour would be positively affected. A similar argument would hold if immigrants were low-skilled, but the beneficiaries of immigration would be the high-skilled. The overall impact on the market would then depend on the skill composition of immigrants, as well as the complementarity of high- and low-skilled labour.

As it turns out, estimating the impact of immigration on the labour market is quite difficult. Part of the problem arises because of the factors outlined above: the impact may be complicated, vary across markets, and be diffuse at the national level. This makes it more

[2]For a detailed discussion of the impact of immigrants on the labour market, Borjas (1994, 1995) and Friedberg and Hunt (1995) provide quite readable and comprehensive surveys. Borjas (1999) provides a more technical, and also a more general, overview of the immmigration literature.

Figure 11.4 The Impact of Immigration on Employment and Wages

An increase in the number of immigrants will shift out the supply curve of labour, from S_0 to S_1. If this is the only change in market conditions, the new equilibrium will have lower wages, W_1 as against W_2, and higher employment, N_1 as against N_0. Panel (b) allows for the possibility that immigration also shifts out the demand curve. In this example, the increase in demand is exactly enough to offset the change in supply, so that the new wage W_1 equals the original wage, W_0, and all the new immigrants are employed.

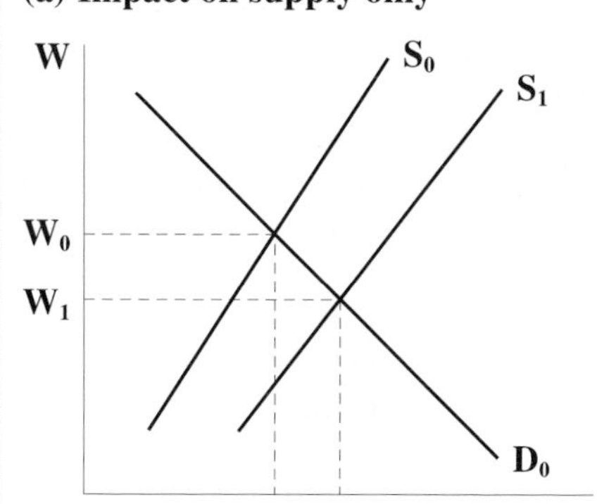

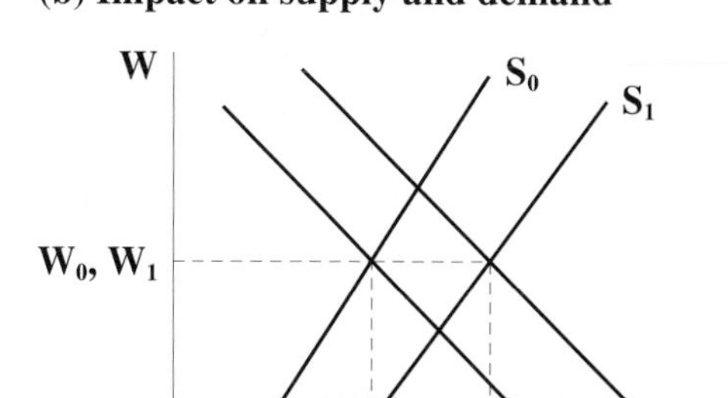

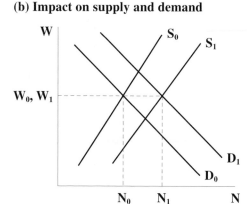

difficult to know where to begin to look for the effect of immigration. Unfortunately, even where there is some confidence that one can isolate a market in which immigration should have an effect (positive or negative), economists encounter the same problem as in most other empirical exercises. We never observe what labour market conditions would prevail in the absence of immigration, that is, we do not observe the **counterfactual** case. The absence of a reasonable comparison market is compounded by the fact that, with few exceptions, immigrants do not arrive randomly in a particular market. Immigrants are generally attracted by good economic prospects, whether in terms of higher wages or employment probabilities. This simultaneous determination of immigration and labour market outcomes confounds the evaluation of the impact of immigration. The most credible empirical investigations of the impact of immigration focus on this issue, and have adopted different strategies for constructing counterfactual evidence.

For reasons that will soon become clear, there have been very few cross-market studies of the impact of immigration in Canada. Two broad approaches have been taken instead. The first is quite indirect. Rather than estimate the impact of immigration on the labour market, the objective is to measure the substitutability of immigrant and native-born labour. As noted above, if immigrant labour is complementary to native labour, then the impact of immigration is likely to be more positive than if immigrants and natives are substitutes. These studies estimate aggregate production functions using cross-industry or cross-occupation mixes of immigrants to identify the substitutability of the labour. Akbari and DeVoretz (1992) are representative of this approach. They find that the implied displacement effect of immigrants is quite small, and concentrated in lower-skilled labour markets. Another, more direct approach is adopted by Marr and Syklos (1995). They explore the impact of immigration on unemployment at the national level, using standard time series econometric techniques. They find that there are only very small adverse effects on the unemployment rate. To some extent, the higher unemployment may only reflect the short-run adjustment of the immigrants themselves in Canada, since the aggregate numbers cannot be separated by immigrant status. On the other hand, the impact of immigration may be more diffuse in aggregate data, and their findings would understate the impact on more localized labour markets. Nevertheless, their results are similar to most of the micro-based studies described below which are able to focus more directly on submarkets where the effect of immigration would be more pronounced.

One promising approach is to exploit cross-city variation in immigration. Consider again Figure 11.2. If the economies were otherwise identical, one could imagine comparing labour market outcomes in Toronto, with an immigrant concentration of over 40 percent, with Montreal, with an immigrant concentration of just over 15 percent. With a 25 percent higher concentration of immigrants, if immigrants had a depressing effect on the labour market, one would expect that Toronto would have lower wages and higher unemployment than Montreal. The problems with this procedure are manifest in this prediction. There may be other features of the cities that differ and have nothing to do with the fraction of immigrants. One way to address this problem is to relate *changes* in labour market outcomes to *changes* in immigrant shares within cities. Looking at changes across cities will net out other, potentially unobservable permanent differences in the labour markets across cities. From Figure 11.2, we would then base our inference on the differences in changes in wages and unemployment between Montreal and Toronto, compared with the difference in the share of recent immigrants (approximately 21 versus 8 percentage points). Again, we can see the limitations of this approach. Presumably, immigrants move to the city where economic conditions are most promising, that is, where labour market outcomes are likely to be improving. We never really see what the economy of Toronto would have looked like without immigration, and looking at changes in the Montreal economy may not be informative. Nevertheless, by finding variables that help predict immigration but are relatively independent of economic factors (e.g., the preexisting ethnic composition of a city), progress can be made in addressing this problem.

No studies have exploited this approach in Canada, primarily because of data limitations. Because of the larger sample sizes and larger number of cities (markets), this approach has been used in the United States, where Altonji and Card (1991) use cross-city variation in immigration patterns between 1970 and 1980 to identify the impact of immigration on a variety of labour market outcomes. Because most immigrants to the United States are low-skilled, they also focus their attention on the labour market outcomes of comparably low-skilled native-born. As mentioned, the positive correlation between immigration and positive labour market outcomes is likely to lead to an understatement of adverse labour market consequences, if such consequences exist. For this reason, Altonji and Card also try to account for this simultaneity by using previous immigration patterns to help predict cross-city flows of immigration. They find virtually no evidence of a link between immigration and labour market outcomes. In a more recent paper, Card (2001) extends the cross-city approach, using the 1990 U.S. census, and more importantly, exploiting within-city differences in the skill mix of immigrants, and potential impacts on the local occupational wage structure. His results are consistent with previous studies (small overall effects), except he finds that where increases in immigration led to disproportionate increases in the share of unskilled workers, the wages of low-skilled workers were slightly adversely affected. He estimates that high levels of low-skilled immigration, like those experienced over the 1980s, adversely affected the wages of low-skilled workers in the most affected cities (such as Miami and Los Angeles) by 1 to 3 percent.

Borjas, Freeman, and Katz (1996) criticize the cross-city approach by showing that the results can be sensitive to the choice of geographic unit. If the geographic area is broadened, they show that the estimated impact (using the 1980 and 1990 censuses) is more negative. One possibility is that native out-migration reduces the immediate impact of immigration on the narrowly defined CMA (city), dampening the outward shift of the supply curve. However, this is addressed (and discounted) in Card's (2001) study. Another possibility is that trade or investment patterns adjust to the changed immigrant concentrations in particular cities, so that the adverse consequences of immigration are shifted elsewhere. Borjas, Freeman, and Katz (1992, 1996) prefer to use the more indirect approach described earlier. They estimate the impact of immigration on the supply of various skill groups, then simulate the effect on wages and employment, analogously to the discussion surrounding

Exhibit 11.2 Fidel Castro and Immigration Research

Because immigrants are likely to settle in labour markets that provide the best economic opportunities, comparing the economic outcomes of high- and low-immigrant cities may not provide a clean estimate of the impact of immigration. Even if immigrants depressed wages in the high-immigration city, this effect might be masked by the otherwise better economic performance of that city. One way around this problem is to find examples where political, rather than economic motivations, were the principal determinants of immigrant settlement.

David Card (1990) exploits one such episode. Emigration from Cuba is tightly restricted, but between May and September 1980, Fidel Castro permitted approximately 125,000 Cubans to leave Mariel for the United States. About half of these immigrants settled permanently in Miami, leading to a 7 percent increase in the labour force, especially of low-skilled workers. Associated with this immigration was an immediate downturn in the Miami economy. The unemployment rate rose from 5 percent in April 1980 to 7.1 percent in July. The homicide rate rose by 50 percent, and there were serious riots in the poorer sections of Miami, with 13 deaths.

So, does this suggest that the Mariel boatlift hurt the Miami labour market? The answer is no: even cities that did not receive these immigrants suffered similar deteriorations in their labour markets. We can think of Miami as the "treatment" group in a "natural experiment," and the measured impact on Miami cannot be interpreted without a reference or "control" group. Card constructs a control group with a composite of comparable cities with similar characteristics to Miami (Atlanta, Houston, Los Angeles, and Tampa). The "difference in differences" methodology then estimates changes in the Miami labour market before and after the arrival of the Mariel immigrants, compared to the comparison group. For example, to estimate the effect on the labour market (Y) two years after the Mariel boatlift, one only needs to estimate:

$$(Y_{1982} - Y_{1979})_{\text{Miami}} - (Y_{1982} - Y_{1979})_{\text{comparison}}$$

Statistically significant differences could be interpreted as evidence of the effect of immigration on the Miami labour market.

Card finds no detectable effect of the Mariel boatlift on the Miami labour market. There is no evidence that the unemployment rates or wages of even the low-skilled workers were adversely affected by this major labour market shock. This finding has spawned a research agenda that explores (1) whether the Miami experience is unique and (2) what features of the Miami labour market made it able to absorb this significant increase in immigrant labour.

Figure 11.4. Using this approach, they argue that while the overall impact of immigration on wages and employment is limited, United States immigration patterns have had a negative impact on the employment and wages of low-skilled natives, which is qualitatively similar to Card's (2001) conclusions. In fact, they point to immigration as one of the more important factors leading to increased wage polarization.

While the cross-market approach has much appeal, it will always be limited by the possibility that immigration and labour market outcomes are jointly determined. While econometric technique and simulated "experiments" can go a long way toward addressing this problem, the evidence is potentially more convincing where a clear case can be made that immigration was "exogenous" or independent of the economic conditions in the labour market. There have been a few such studies that exploit historical episodes where immigration was determined by political factors, and a relatively convincing case can be made for the exogeneity of the immigration. The empirical method is otherwise similar to the cross-city approach. Comparisons are made between the economic outcomes in the market receiving the "immigration shock" to markets that did not receive the shock. Not surprisingly, the method may suffer from the same flaws, and the results can be sensitive to the choice of comparison market. Even if we believe that the immigration shock is exogenous, we only observe the "treatment" market, and may not have a perfect counterfactual, or "control" market (see Borjas, 1999).

The first paper to use this approach is Card (1990) (see Exhibit 11.2). He examines the impact of the Mariel boatlift on the Miami labour market, and finds very little evidence of an adverse effect of this historically large influx of immigrants. Several more recent papers look at similar episodes of major, politically motivated migration on labour markets. Two papers look at the impact of the repatriation of European "colonials" on their home country labour markets. Hunt (1992) examines the impact of the return of Europeans to France after Algerian independence in the 1960s, while Carrington and deLima (1996) explore the impact of the return of Portuguese citizens following Marxist revolutions in former Portuguese colonies in Africa. While the evidence is mixed, neither of these studies conclude that these significant shocks to the labour markets were associated with adverse outcomes for natives. Friedberg (1996) looks at the effect of large-scale Russian immigration to Israel from 1989 to 1994. Over this period, the arrival of 450,000 Russian immigrants increased the Israeli labour force by 13 percent. By exploiting the uneven occupation distribution of the Russian Jews (both before and after their arrival in Israel), and the subsequent changes in the Israeli occupational wage structure, she shows that this increase in immigration had no adverse effect on the wages of native-born Israelis.

Taken together, and despite looking very hard, economists have found virtually no evidence that immigrants have an adverse impact on the labour market outcomes of natives. Borjas, Freeman, and Katz (1996), and more recently Card (2001), provide some qualification of this finding, noting that the adverse impact may be concentrated among the less skilled. Nevertheless, the research in this area provides very little guidance for policymakers attempting to choose the optimal level of immigration, beyond the important possibility that at least at historical levels, it doesn't really matter, and if given the option, one should select more skilled immigrants.

ECONOMIC ASSIMILATION

Primarily because of the relative abundance of data, most research on immigration has focused on the immigrants themselves. By charting immigrant economic performance, especially over time, economists obtain at least indirect evidence on the absorptive capacity of the labour market. By correlating economic success with observable characteristics, results from this exercise can, in principle, aid in the design of admission criteria. Finally, since one of the general public's concerns is that immigrants do not succeed and subsequently become burdens of the state, evidence on immigrant performance can directly support or allay these concerns.

Economic assimilation can occur in a number of possible dimensions. Immediately after arriving in Canada, immigrants may face a period of unemployment as they search for a job. Thus, we might expect immigrants to assimilate in terms of their hours worked: perhaps starting out at a lower level than similar native-born individuals, but catching up after spending time in Canada. We may expect their wages to follow a similar pattern. Upon arrival in Canada, immigrants may lack some of the less observable skills that the native-born have—language, knowledge of the local labour market, more specific (but unobservable) skills particular to firms in Canada. Their educational credentials may not be fully recognized. With time, however, we would expect their wages to grow to the level of native-born. In fact, if immigrants are **positively selected**, that is, that immigrants are among the most motivated and able (in terms of unobservables), their wages may eventually exceed that of natives. Earnings growth may also reflect the dissipation of discrimination, at least to the extent that immigrants who have been in the country for a longer period are likely to be less discriminated against than recent arrivals.

Most studies of assimilation focus on earnings as a summary of economic performance. Earnings will summarize both hours worked and wages, though by focusing on full-year full-time workers, these studies effectively concentrate on wages. The objective of most of this research is the immigrant assimilation profile. Figure 11.5 shows the key features of this profile. Consider two otherwise identical individuals: one native-born entering the labour market at age 20, and the other a 20-year-old immigrant entering the labour market immediately upon arrival in Canada. The native-born Canadian will experience wage growth as he ages (the returns to experience). Initially, the immigrant may suffer an earnings penalty, called the **entry effect**. As the immigrant ages, his earnings should also rise. Assimilation will refer to the difference in the returns to age experienced by the immigrant and the comparable native, and is usually measured as a function of **years since migration** (YSM). If immigrants experience assimilation (i.e., enjoy additional returns to age), it is possible that their earnings will catch up to the native-born. This catch-up or time to equality is marked by T in Figure 11.5. After T years of YSM, immigrant earnings exceed that of natives. If assimilation is slow, or the entry effect is sufficiently large, then the implied time to catch-up may exceed the individual's working life. In that case, immigrants effectively never catch up to the native-born.

Early studies of immigrant assimilation, such as Chiswick's 1978 investigation for the United States, found large entry disadvantages offset by rapid earnings growth. The methodology employed in these studies was quite straightforward. Most census data include information on individual human capital characteristics, earnings, and immigration

Figure 11.5 **Hypothetical Assimilation Profile, 20-Year-Old Immigrant**

We typically measure assimilation by the extent to which immigrant earnings catch up to those of the native-born. Consider two otherwise identical people at age 20, one native-born and the other a new immigrant. At age 20, the immigrant's years since migration (YSM) equals zero, and his earnings are initially below those of the native-born, due to what is called the *entry effect*. Over time, the native-born wages will rise with age for conventional reasons, as would the immigrant's. However, with years in Canada, the immigrant's earnings may grow even faster, as he accumulates Canada-specific human capital. These excess returns to age, or returns to YSM, are due to what is called *assimilation*. If the rate of assimilation is high enough, immigrant earnings may catch up, for example, by age T.

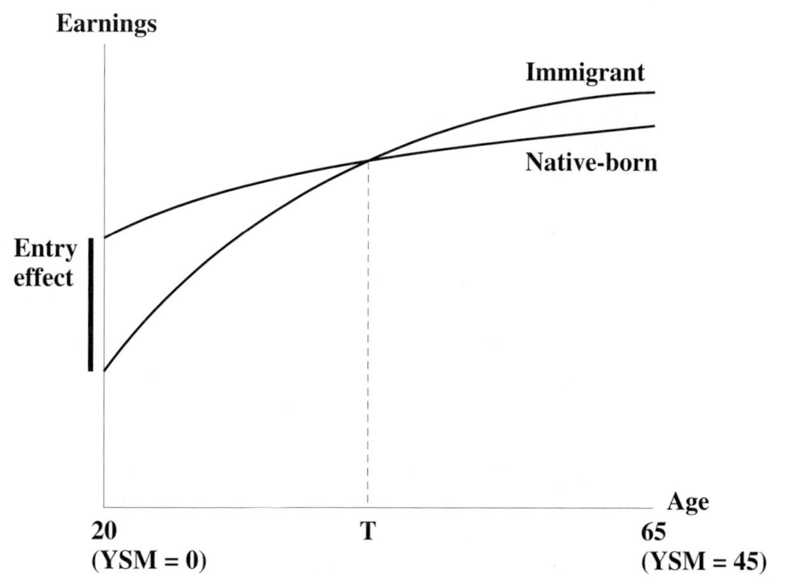

status. One can then estimate a conventional earnings function, augmented by the indicators of immigrant status. By comparing recently arrived immigrants to comparable natives, one can readily estimate the entry effect. By then comparing earnings of recent immigrants to those who have been in the host country longer, one can impute the rate of earnings assimilation. As pointed out by George Borjas (1985), however, such a procedure can lead to misleading results regarding assimilation, and also miss important changes in the entry effects of immigrants. This would be the case if immigrant performance is deteriorating (or improving) over time. Because it illustrates some of the general empirical problems involved in estimating assimilation, as well as outlining some of the important areas of debate in the recent literature, we describe this problem in some detail.

The problems of using a single cross-section of data to estimate assimilation profiles are illustrated in Figure 11.6. Panel (a) illustrates the ideal scenario, for which the single-cross

Figure 11.6 **Measuring Earnings Assimilation: Disentangling Cohort and Assimilation Effects**

This figure shows the potential pitfalls of using cross-sectional data to rates of assimilation. Panel (a) shows the ideal case. Each cohort of immigrants has the same starting point (entry effect) and same rate of assimilation. A cross-section estimate of assimilation is based on comparing the earnings of IM7680 to IM8185 in 1985, where the immigrants who arrived between 1976 and 1980 (IM7680) have been in Canada five years longer than the newer immigrants (IM8185). This difference is given by BD, which corresponds to the actual earnings growth of IM7680 who started out at A, the same level as IM8185 (at D). Panel (b) shows what happens if the entry position of immigrant cohorts is shifting. Here, genuine earnings growth of IM7680 is given by BF, but the difference in earnings between IM7680 and IM8185 is BD. Part of the difference is due to the lower starting point, or cohort entry effect of IM8185 (D versus A). The cross-section estimate of earnings growth for IM8185 (BD) would overstate assimilation, confounding actual growth and the change in initial earnings. Only with data from 1980, and following IM7680 from A to B, would the genuine assimilation of BF be identified.

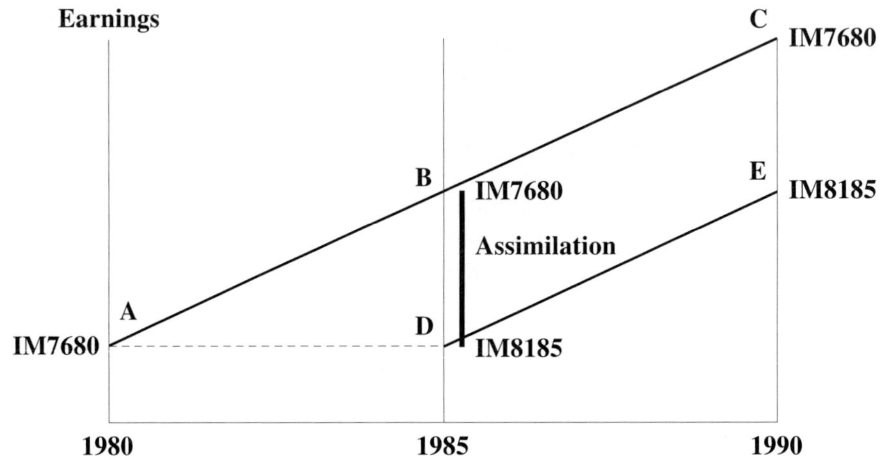

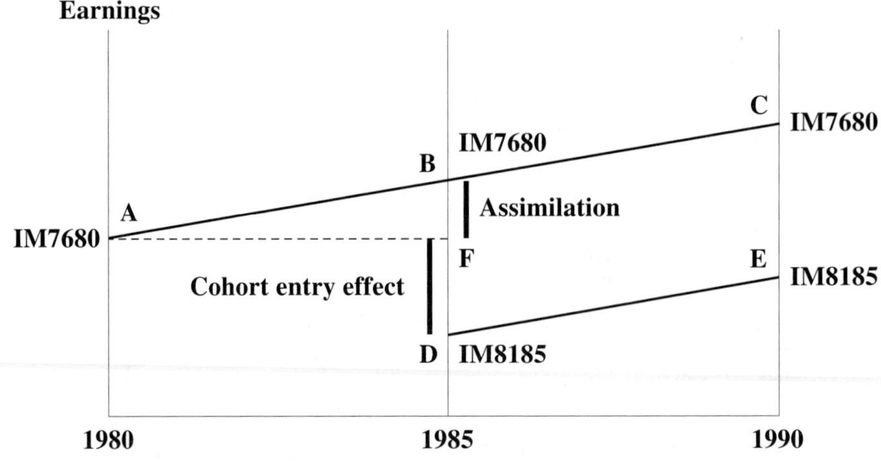

section would be appropriate. Consider the earnings of the cohort of immigrants who arrived between 1976 and 1980, labelled IM7680. Their initial earnings are at the level labelled A, and they grow by the indicated amount to point B in 1985. Now, assume that we have data in 1985 that allows us to compare the earnings of the most recent cohort, IM8185, to IM7680. Because IM7680 immigrants have been in Canada on average for five years longer, we might attribute the difference in earnings between the two groups (point B versus point D) to assimilation (ignoring, for the moment any other sources of earnings growth in the economy). If entry and assimilation rates are the same across cohorts, this will be an accurate estimate.

Now consider the situation in panel (b), where the assimilation rate is constant across cohorts, but their entry positions differ. IM7680 begins at point A, and has their earnings rise to point B in 1985. However, we would seriously overstate immigrant assimilation by attributing the entire difference in earnings between IM8185 and IM7680 in 1985 (point B minus point D) to the latter's five years in Canada. Their earnings are also higher because they started out at a better position: IM8185 starts off at point D rather than the earnings associated with point A. By looking at 1985 data alone, there is no way to disentangle the changing entry, or cohort, effect (the distance from D to F) from genuine assimilation (the distance from F to B). For this reason, the only credible way to obtain estimates of assimilation is to follow cohorts of immigrants over time, for example by combining data from 1985 and 1990. For IM8185 this would entail a comparison of point E with point D. Even with this method, there may be pitfalls. One possibility is that out-migration of immigrants leads to systematic changes in the composition of the underlying immigrant cohorts (see Lam, 1994). The immigrants comprising IM8185 in 1990 may have a different composition than they did when they first arrived in 1981. On one hand, some of the unsuccessful immigrants may have returned home; on the other, some of the more successful may have migrated to the United States. Average incomes of the IM8185 cohort might then be different in 1990 than 1985 for reasons that have nothing to do with earnings growth of the average immigrant arriving in 1981.

Cohort effects represent more than just a nuisance for labour economists measuring assimilation. The changing entry position of immigrants is of considerable interest in its own right. If immigrant performance is deteriorating, it becomes important to document and explain. Is it because the immigrants themselves are not as capable as previous cohorts? If so, can this be linked to changes in immigration policy? Alternatively, is it the economy that is changing, whereby the labour market is less able to provide employment for immigrants with particular skills?

Figure 11.7 illustrates the issues described above by arraying immigrant earnings by cohort for the 1991 and 1996 censuses. Here average annual earnings (expressed in 1995 dollars) are shown for a sample of full-year, full-time men so that the patterns primarily reflect differences in wages. Focus first on the 1990 means (the black bars). By looking from right to left, we can see that average earnings rise as we compare immigrants who have been in Canada longer. To some extent, these differences reflect the fact that those immigrants are older, but they may also reflect genuine assimilation. The entry effect can be estimated by comparing the most recent immigrants (1986–1990) with the native-born. In this case, the entry effect is approximately \$10,604 (25 percent less than for natives). Now consider the exercise of predicting the assimilation of the IM8185 cohort for the next five years (to 1995), on the basis of the observed cross-sectional profile in 1990. A cross-section prediction of assimilation can be obtained for the 1981–1985 cohort (IM8185), by comparing their earnings to the 1976–1980 (IM7680) cohort, who had been in Canada five years longer. In 1990, IM8185 earned \$37,592 while IM7680 earned an average of \$40,462. The difference is \$2870 (7.6 percent of IM8185 earnings) and this can be interpreted as the effect of being in Canada five years longer. If assimilation profiles are the same for all groups, we would expect IM8185 to experience the same earnings growth to 1995.

Figure 11.7 **Annual Earnings by Immigrant Cohort, 1990 and 1995**

A cross-section estimate of assimilation compares the earnings of immigrant cohorts within a given year: looking right to left, immigrants who have lived in Canada longer have higher earnings. A "quasi-panel" estimate of assimilation follows actual cohorts' earnings over time (between 1990 and 1995). This entails a comparison of the height of the black and the gray bars for each cohort. Between 1990 and 1995, all cohorts' earnings declined, suggesting negative assimilation. However, a better estimate of assimilation nets out changes to aggregate economic conditions, using native-born earnings as a benchmark. In this case, those cohorts that experienced smaller declines in earnings than the native-born have positive earnings assimilation.

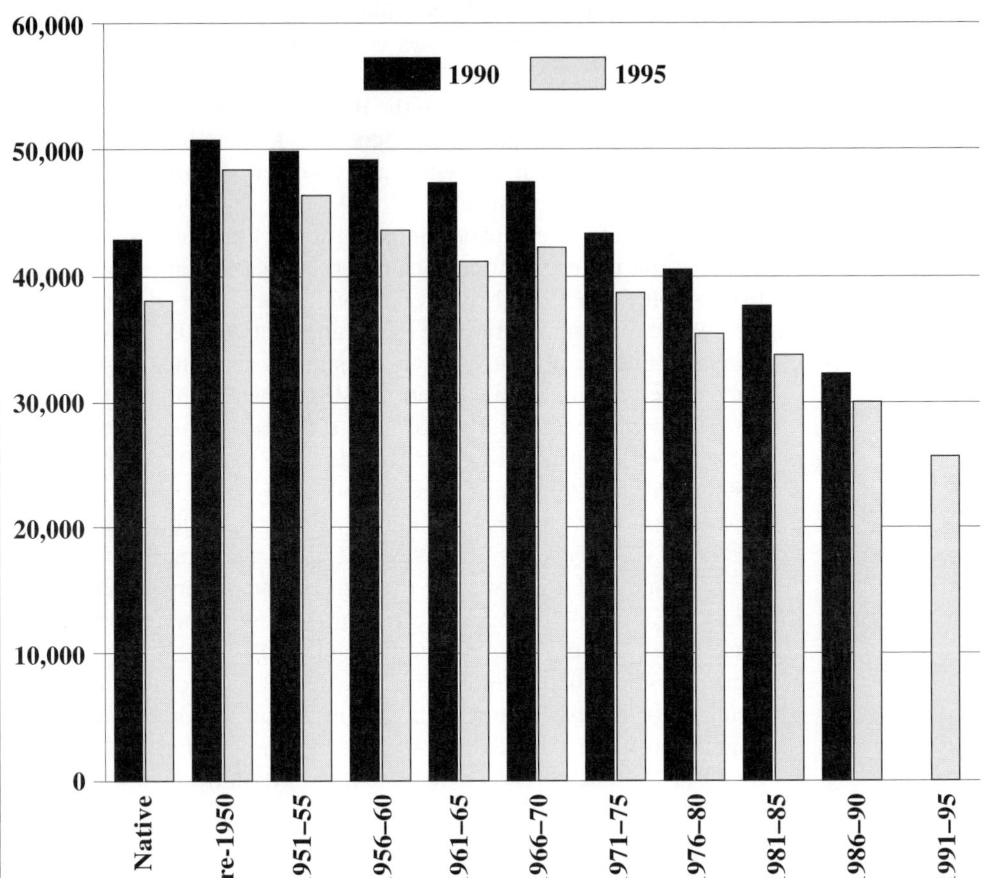

Note: Reported figures are average annual earnings of men by immigrant cohort. "Native" refers to Canadian-born, while each immigrant cohort is grouped by year of entry. Averages are computed for full-year, full-time men between 20 and 64 years of age who had only wage and salary income. Because of coding in the 1996 Census, individuals from the Atlantic provinces are excluded. 1990 incomes are adjusted by the CPI to 1995 dollars.

Source: Adapted from the Statistics Canada Individual Use Microdata File: 1996 Census of Population.

The **quasi-panel**, genuine cohort assimilation rate would be estimated by comparing the earnings of each cohort across censuses, that is, comparing the heights of the black and gray bars for each cohort. Every immigrant cohort saw earnings *fall* between 1990 and 1995. IM8185, for example, experienced an earnings decline to $33,711, a drop of $3,881, certainly not what we would have predicted on the basis of IM7680's earnings in 1990. However, the decline in earnings of this cohort does not provide an estimate of assimilation, since some of this decline was due to earnings declines for everyone in the economy, associated with the general deterioration of the labour market between 1990 and 1995. For this reason, we want to net out aggregate wage "growth," using the native-born as a benchmark. Native-born earnings fell by (a staggering) $4,835, so the estimated earnings assimilation for IM8185 is the net difference, -$3881 - (-$4835) = $954, or about 2.5 percent their initial earnings. In this case, the quasi-panel estimate of assimilation is significantly lower than cross-section. The IM8185 cohort did not reach the same level of earnings as IM7680 when they had been in Canada the same length of time, even factoring in the poorer economic conditions of 1995. The gap in earnings between the cross-section and the quasi-panel provides an estimate of the deterioration in immigrant fortunes. This can also be obtained by comparing the position of IM8185 after ten years in Canada (in 1995) with IM7680 at the same point along its assimilation profile (in 1990). In fact, this can be done for any set of cohorts. What is of concern to policymakers is that recent immigrants in 1995 (IM9195) had real earnings considerably below those of recent immigrants (IM8690) in 1990. Even accounting for lower general earnings in 1995, this suggests a significantly worsening entry effect for new immigrants.

www.statcan.ca/english/Dli/ftp.htm

For now, we review empirical findings of assimilation in Canada, most of which are from studies conducted before the release of the 1996 census. We begin with immigrant men. The first evidence is based on cross-sectional evidence from the Job Mobility Survey (JMS), conducted in 1973 covering earnings in 1972. While restricted in their ability to control for immigrant cohort effects, Meng (1987) and Abbot and Beach (1993) exploit other advantages of the JMS, especially the detailed measures of work experience. The survey also covered immigrant earnings in a time period when cohort effects were smaller. These papers report immigrant entry effects on the order of 15 percent, with immigrants catching up to natives between 9 and 14 years, depending on the specification. Abbot and Beach also confirm the higher return for immigrants than natives for actual Canadian work experience.

Baker and Benjamin (1994) and Bloom, Grenier, and Gunderson (1995) use different empirical strategies exploiting the 1971 through 1986 censuses. Baker and Benjamin estimate cohort-specific assimilation rates and confirm a steep decline in the entry position of immigrants in the Canadian labour market. They also find only negligible evidence of assimilation: for most cohorts, one cannot reject the hypothesis that there was zero assimilation. Baker and Benjamin also find that up to one-half of the declining initial position of immigrants is correlated with the changing source country composition of immigrants that occurred in the 1970s.

Bloom, Grenier, and Gunderson also paint a pessimistic picture of immigrant assimilation. They find that more recent cohorts began at increasingly worse positions in the labour market. For example, the 1981–85 cohort is estimated to have an entry effect of -34 percent, as against -19 percent for the 1976–80 cohort, who themselves were in a worse position than their predecessors. The assimilation rate is also estimated to be very small, at 0.25 percent per year. If one is prepared to extrapolate the assimilation rate to recent cohorts, this would imply a 137-year catch-up time! The empirical evidence up to 1986 suggests that immigrant men in Canada face increasing difficulties, and that economic assimilation is negligible, especially in comparison with the United States. Borjas (1995) estimates assimilation rates for immigrants to the United States that are approximately double those in Canada, though he also charts a significant decline in immigrant fortunes over time, similar to that which happened in Canada.

But as is often the case in economics, extrapolations can be misleading. More recent evidence suggests that the pessimism based on data from the early 1980s did not carry over to the more buoyant late-1980s. Mary Grant (1999) applied the methodology of Baker and Benjamin (1994) to the 1991 and 1986 censuses, and found significant evidence of immigrant assimilation, as high as 17 percent for the IM7680 cohort. She also found an arrest to the decline in immigrant entry effects. As Grant showed, there is nothing in the observable characteristics of the immigrants that would have predicted the reversal of fortune. Instead, the explanation for the improved immigrant fortunes probably lies in the stronger Canadian labour market of the late 1980s. This serves as a cautionary tale on using any two survey years to estimate assimilation profiles, since immigrant performance may be sensitive to the business cycle. Indeed, this is the conclusion reached by McDonald and Worswick (1998). They show that the identification of cohort effects and assimilation rates is sensitive to the choice of survey year, and this is driven primarily by the fact that immigrants fare especially poorly in recessions. Immigrants are more likely to be unemployed in downturns, and this can have lasting effects on their ability to accumulate work experience in Canada, let alone the adverse direct impact on immigrant earnings (McDonald and Worswick, 1997).[3] The work of Grant and of McDonald and Worswick thus not only serve a methodological caution but also dampen the pessimism of the earlier studies.

As a postscript to this research, the results reported in Figure 11.7, based on the 1996 census, confirm the methodological point raised by McDonald and Worswick, but not their optimism. Labour market conditions were especially poor in the early 1990s (recall the aggregate decline in real wages), and the entry effect for the 1991–1995 cohort is significantly below that of the arrivals in the late 1980s, suggesting a further deterioration in immigrant performance. Clearly, the immigrant "assimilation" rate, while an important parameter to policymakers, is not immutable and depends on domestic economic conditions.

Immigrant women have been studied less than immigrant men. To some extent, this reflects the reluctance of researchers to compare earnings for women across groups and across time where the labour supply differences, and possible selectivity problems, are potentially important. The few studies that exist suggest that assimilation patterns for immigrant women are quite different than for men. Beach and Worswick (1993) use the Job Mobility Survey to chart immigrant women's earnings compared to native-born women. They find that immigrant women actually have (on average) an earnings premium over the native-born. Highly educated immigrant women, though, suffer an earnings penalty. Immigrant women's earnings, however, do not grow faster than native-born women, that is, they do not assimilate. This basic pattern is confirmed with more recent data in Bloom, Grenier, and Gunderson (1995). While they do not find an entry premium, they do find much smaller entry penalties across cohorts than for men, but zero assimilation.

One explanation, described in Beach and Worswick (1993), and Duleep and Sanders (1993), for example, is the **family investment hypothesis**. The basic idea in this hypothesis is that facing borrowing constraints, immigrant families specialize their labour market activities across husbands and wives. Immigrant wives enter the labour market into jobs with little promise of earnings growth in order to subsidize the acquisition of human capital by their husbands. This strategy would explain the differential earnings assimilation patterns. Baker and Benjamin (1997b) provide a detailed evaluation of this model, comparing its predictions to a more conventional family labour supply model. Primarily by eliminating other explanations, and as well comparing the earnings and labour supply behaviour of immigrant women married to immigrant men (who need to invest) versus native men (who do not need to invest), they find empirical support for the family investment hypothesis.

Worswick (1996, 1999) also explores immigrant family labour supply. Like Baker and Benjamin, he finds no direct evidence of the family investment hypothesis, but does find that women's labour supply plays a particularly important role in immigrant families. He also finds that some of the immigrant wife's labour supply—at least for recent immigrants—can be explained by credit constraints (i.e., the inability of these households to borrow.). It remains an important agenda for future research whether this family labour supply behaviour represents "investment" in the husband's economic assimilation.

Taken together, the evidence on economic assimilation suggests that assimilation rates are low, unless immigrants arrive when the economy is booming. Immigrants will likely take a long time to catch up to the native-born, especially if large numbers arrive during a recession, as happened in the 1990s. This need not imply that immigration has an adverse

[3]McDonald and Worswick (1998) also directly highlight the importance of the acquisition of human capital in the assimilation process, by noting that some of the entry effect and low immigrant earnings can be explained by their shorter job tenure and thus lower level of firm-specific human capital.

impact on the labour market, or on the economy more generally. One possibility, however, is that immigrants who cannot obtain employment or who have low earnings capacity may turn to social welfare programs, and this may have adverse effects on the public treasury. Baker and Benjamin (1995a, 1995b) and Crossley, McDonald, and Worswick (2001) directly examine this question (see Exhibit 11.3) and show that despite poor economic outcomes, immigrants make significantly less use of unemployment insurance and social assistance. Lui-Gurr (1995) confirms this basic finding for immigrants to British Columbia: even recent immigrants are no more likely to collect social assistance. At least using the native-born as a benchmark, there is no evidence that immigrants represent an extra burden to taxpayers. In fact, Akbari (1995) uses the 1991 census to estimate a balance sheet of immigrant net contributions to the Canadian treasury, and finds that taxes paid by immigrants far exceed the value of transfers received from the government.

IMMIGRANT OUTCOMES AND PUBLIC POLICY

One of the more important questions regards possible linkages between immigration policy and the patterns of immigrant assimilation just described. For example, how effective have the policy levers described at the beginning of the chapter been in selecting immigrants most likely to succeed in Canada? Unfortunately, answering such questions has been difficult because, until recently, there were no publicly available data linking immigration selection criteria (class of immigrant, points, etc.) with economic outcomes. Researchers have had to explore alternative avenues for drawing out the possible relationships between policy and outcomes.

One of the most fruitful approaches has been to compare immigrant performance in Canada and the United States. Since Canada introduced the point system in 1967, immigration policy has differed significantly, at least in principle, between the two countries. In the 1960s, both countries adopted policies designed to eliminate the pro-European orientation that dominated immigration policy to that point. Canada instituted the point system to more objectively evaluate the suitability of immigrants to Canada, while the United States instead moved to a family-reunification-based immigration system.[4]

Despite the different systems, however, the two countries have seen similar patterns in immigrant assimilation over the past 25 years, namely, a marked decline in the entry position of recent immigrants. While assimilation rates are higher in the United States, the entry position of immigrants is generally lower. George Borjas (1993) examines observable skills (like schooling) as well as the earnings of immigrants to the two countries, in order to assess the possible effects of Canada's point system. He argues that the main effect of the point system has been to tilt immigration to Canada away from source countries that provide, on average, low-skill workers. For example, he suggests that immigrants to Canada have a higher education level than those to the United States, not because the point system favours the most skilled from a given country, but because it reduces admissions from less-developed countries, where workers are less skilled on average.[5] He shows that the resulting differences in immigrant source countries account for most of the difference in immigrant performance (in terms of entry position) between the two countries. In another interesting exercise, he compares the performance of U.S. immigrants in Canada to Canadian immigrants in the United States. If the point system was effective in picking winners, especially compared to the more open U.S. policy, we might expect American

[4]See Alan Green (1995) for a detailed comparison of immigration policy between the two countries.

[5]Educational differences between immigrants and natives are also documented in Duleep and Regets (1992) and Baker and Benjamin (1994). Green (1999) explores skill differences along occupational dimensions, and shows that immigrants are more highly represented in skilled occupations.

Exhibit 11.3

Immigrants and Government Transfers

A common concern expressed about the impact of immigration is that immigrants are prone to using Canada's social transfer system, be it the collection of welfare, unemployment insurance, or residence in public housing. Baker and Benjamin (1995a, 1995b) directly examine this question, asking whether immigrants make more use of social insurance than the native-born. Using the Survey of Consumer Finances (SCF) for 1985 and 1990, they compare use of social services by various immigrant cohorts, and track their use over time. The following table illustrates some of the patterns of program use in 1990:

	Men Collecting EI	Families Receiving Social Assistance	Households Receiving a Rent Subsidy
Native-born	16.8%	9.4%	3.9%
Immigrants 1966–70	13.4	5.1	2.5
Immigrants 1976–80	16.7	8.8	3.7
Immigrants 1986–90	13.4	10.4	5.9

Source: SCF, 1991, reported in Baker and Benjamin (1995a).

As a group, immigrants are less likely to use each of these programs than the native-born. The differences are even more pronounced once one controls for differences in economic characteristics, including the fact that recent immigrants have poor labour market economic outcomes. A much harder question concerns trends in welfare and transfer program use. Are new immigrants becoming more reliant on these programs over time? Do immigrants tend to use transfer programs the longer they are in Canada? Baker and Benjamin find evidence of an increasing trend toward welfare use, mirroring the deteriorating labour market outcomes. To some extent, this can be explained by the disproportionately high fraction of refugees (who were not allowed to work) in the late 1980s. They also find evidence that immigrants assimilated *into* (not out of) transfer programs. However, Crossley, McDonald and Worswick (2001) show that identifying the dynamics of transfer program use is problematic when using only two surveys. In fact, they find no evidence of deteriorating immigrant outcomes, and certainly not of assimilation into transfer programs. Instead, they emphasize the importance of business cycle conditions in determining the propensity for immigrants to use transfer programs, like UI or welfare. Despite these difficulties, the two sets of researchers agree that immigrants are less likely than the native-born to rely on government transfers.

immigrants to do better in Canada than Canadian immigrants in the United States. He shows that the opposite holds, that is, that Canadians do better in the United States than vice versa.

Other studies have challenged the sharpness of the Borjas conclusion, arguing that the point system indeed had some impact on "picking winners" from particular source countries, though these studies also reinforce his conclusion that the changing source country mix is correlated with changing immigrant fortunes. Green and Green (1995) provide a detailed investigation on the linkages between immigration policy changes (like the point system) and the occupational mix of immigrants.[6] They show that overall, it is difficult to find an impact of the point system on the occupational mix of immigrants, especially accounting for source country characteristics. This, and their finding of the importance of source country composition, is in accordance with Borjas' interpretation. However, they further show that the absence of a "post-1967" effect on immigrant skills is not due to ineffectiveness of the point system, but rather that the point system is dominated by immigration nonassessed classes (family and refugee). Thus, they argue that the point system actually has a significant impact on tilting immigrant selection toward more skilled groups, once full account is taken of the limited nature in which it is applied.

Their findings are reinforced by Wright and Maxim (1993). They relate estimated immigrant entry earnings by country and cohort to administrative records on the class composition of those immigrant groups. They find that the class-of-entry information has the predicted effect—independent immigrants fare better than family class and refugee immigrants. They also find (as did Borjas) that immigrants from developing countries suffered the largest earnings deficit. Research on the importance of class of admission has been significantly advanced by the assembly of the Longitudinal Immigration Database (IMDB). This database links immigrant characteristics from landing (admission) records—notably immigrant class, education, and other skills—to income-related information from income tax records. The database is longitudinal, so that it permits following an (anonymous!) individual immigrant's earnings over time. A recent series of reports (Citizenship and Immigration Canada, 1998; Citizenship and Immigration Canada, 1999) shows unambiguous evidence that economically assessed immigrants have more skills (language and education) than other immigrants, and that, in turn, they fare much better in Canada: they earn more, their earnings grow faster, and they are less likely to require unemployment insurance or social assistance. Untangling the reasons behind these differences across classes—that is, whether they are due to differences in source country, education and other skills, or unobservable talent—remains an important topic for future research. What certainly appears to be the case, however, is that immigration policy affects the types of immigrants who are admitted to Canada, and this in turn is related to their economic performance.

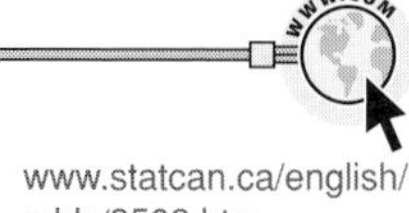

www.statcan.ca/english/sdds/3502.htm

THE IMPACT OF IMMIGRATION ON SOURCE COUNTRIES

While it does not enter significantly in Canadian immigration policy determination, one of the most interesting and controversial aspects of international migration is the issue of the so-called **brain drain**. The problem arises because countries, especially less-developed ones, may lose their most-skilled labour to the more-developed countries. It is the skilled workers that tend to leave because they can afford to do so, they have the knowledge of foreign opportunities (perhaps acquired while studying abroad), and they can usually amass sufficient points to enter the host country.

www.canadasbraindrain.ca

The problem is especially acute with countries that heavily subsidize the education and training of their workers. In such circumstances, the home countries bear the cost of the education, and the skilled emigrant reaps all of the benefits in the form of higher earnings in the host country. In many circumstances these skilled workers are the very persons that the developing economy can least afford to lose.

[6]David Green (1995) evaluates the correlation between the intended and actual occupation of immigrants. Intended occupation is the basis of admission through the point system. He finds that the correlation is quite high, though primarily because of observable skills on the part of immigrants, rather than any additional predictive power of their stated intended occupation.

The brain drain often occurs when students from less-developed economies go to more-developed economies for advanced education and training. The psychic costs associated with the cultural and environmental change have already been incurred, and the direct cost of education or training is often borne by the home country. By definition, the income opportunities are greater in the more-developed host country and hence the temptation to stay.

For countries that are net losers of highly skilled labour, there are some possible remedies, but they all involve other problems. Having the individuals themselves pay for their own education and training would at least ensure that they were paying the costs for the benefits they could receive if they emigrate. However, especially in developing economies, this may hinder large numbers of otherwise poor people from acquiring the education or training. Placing an "exit tax" equal to the amount of the human capital cost borne by the state is theoretically possible, but practically difficult to enforce, and it may be politically unpopular as it becomes compounded with issues of human rights. Recruiting your own students abroad and encouraging their return is a policy that is utilized, but it does have costs and it may be vacuous if viable job opportunities cannot be provided. Providing job opportunities at high wages, of course, is easier said than done, especially in countries that have followed a conscious policy of minimizing wage differentials, possibly for equity reasons. Clearly, as in so many elements of public policy, a variety of delicate tradeoffs are involved.

The Brain Drain and Canada

While the immigration to Canada by skilled individuals from developing countries does not cause loss of sleep for most Canadians—we're happy to poach the best and brightest from anywhere in the world—the brain drain is relevant to Canada to the extent that it, too, is a source country, especially of immigrants to the United States. Indeed, the emigration of highly skilled Canadians to the United States has received considerable media attention, and is often used as one argument in favour of income tax cuts. Despite the hyperbole, and for a variety of reasons (especially data limitations) research on the brain drain remains thin. However, economists have recently addressed a number of relevant questions in this area.

http://strategis.ic.gc.ca/sc_ecnmy/mera/engdoc/07.html

The first pertains to the size of the brain drain, and whether it is in fact getting worse. It turns out that answering this question is difficult (see Zhao, Drew, and Murray, 2000). To start with, the Canadian government does not collect data on people leaving Canada. This leaves only indirect Canadian sources. One is the "Reverse Record Check," a double-check performed by Statistics Canada to evaluate the coverage of the census. This survey is helpful for establishing the residence of those sampled, and whether they have moved to the United States. It is therefore helpful in counting exits in census years, but it yields no other information on the migrants. A second source is tax records. By tracking tax filers, it is possible to identify the year they switch from Canadian to U.S. addresses. Again, this is useful for counting people who leave Canada, with the added bonus of revealing the taxpayer's income before leaving Canada. On the negative side, tax data contain very little in the way of demographic information, and there are no observations for people who do not file income taxes. The other sources are from the U.S. perspective. The decennial U.S. censuses collect information on country of birth, so Canadian-born residents of the United States can be identified, along with information on their income and demographic characteristics. Unfortunately, since the census is conducted only every ten years, it is less useful for identifying trends in emigration. A second U.S. source is the Current Population Survey (CPS), the U.S. equivalent of the Labour Force Survey. The CPS collects information on country of birth, so this can be used to estimate the number of Canadians living in the United States on a regular basis, though the sample sizes are small. Finally, administrative data from the Immigration and Naturalization Service (INS) can be used to tally the number

www.ins.gov

of Canadians obtaining visas to the United States. However, it can be difficult to sort out permanent from temporary migration using these data.

Once the pros and cons of the various data sources are taken into account, it is possible to get reasonable estimates of the flow of Canadians into the United States. As Zhao, Drew, and Murray (2000) report, approximately 22,000 to 35,000 Canadians move to the United States every year, about half of whom are taxpayers (income earners). There has also been a steeply rising trend of emigration over the 1990s, facilitated to some extent by labour mobility provisions in NAFTA. However, as noted by Helliwell (1999) and others, the current level of migration to the United States is low by historical standards. More alarming is the composition of the migrants; they are disproportionately highly educated and high earners. There is an especially high flow of doctors, nurses, natural scientists, and university professors. While the annual flow represents less than 1 percent of the current stock of these occupations in Canada, it can be a large fraction of new graduates. For example, one-quarter of the new classes of nurses and doctors in the mid-1990s moved to the United States. Similarly, movers were disproportionately drawn from Canadians who earned over $100,000 before they left.

The second question concerns the impact of the brain drain. To some extent the analysis could proceed along the lines of Figure 11.4, only in reverse. However, at least in aggregate, it is unlikely that an annual outflow of 25,000 people would have much impact on the Canadian labour market, given that it is difficult to detect the impact of adding 200,000 immigrants. But in more narrowly defined markets, emigration may matter: It could be the case that doctors and nursing shortages are exacerbated by the brain drain, which increases the wages of those who remain. In this sense, the brain drain may increase health care costs by increasing the price of health care professionals. Another way to measure the impact of the brain drain is to calculate the loss of goods and services produced by Canadians in the United States. For example, one estimate of the current stock of highly skilled Canadians living in the United States on TN-1 (NAFTA) visas is 60,000.[7] If they earn the equivalent of C$150,000 in the United States, this represents a loss of $9 billion worth of GDP, and about $3 billion of tax revenue every year. And this number does not include permanent migrants to the United States! If we take 20,000 as an estimate of the number of earners leaving Canada every year, and assume that they earn an average of C$50,000, this corresponds to the further loss of $1 billion per year (which gets added to the stock living in the United States). To the extent that the migrants are disproportionately high-income earners, and these individuals pay a disproportionate share of income taxes, the brain drain has an undeniable effect on the Canadian treasury. However, as our "back of the envelope" calculations show, it is not hard to "cook up" estimates of the cost of the brain drain, including some outrageously high ones. More problematic is the task of constructing the "counterfactual," that is, in estimating how much income these emigrants would have made had they stayed in Canada. Presumably, they moved to the United States because they could make more money, that is, they were more productive there than in Canada. As the income differential for an individual in the two countries reflects his or her higher productivity in the United States, it is unreasonable to assume that their incomes could be replicated in Canada.

The final question concerns what, if anything, to do about the brain drain. The policy implications have received increasing attention.[8] A common proposal is to cut income taxes, making it more attractive to remain in Canada. There are a number of potential problems with this suggestion (at least in this context). First, potential emigrants remain a small fraction of the population, and it does not make sense to let the "tail wag the dog," in

[7]See Hoefer, Norris, and Ruddick (2000).

[8]See Finnie (2001), Kesselman (2001), and a recent IRPP symposium (1999) for discussions of the policy issues.

setting tax policy. Obviously, the responsiveness of Canadians to taxes is an important ingredient in setting tax rates, but it would be an overstatement to assume that most high-income Canadians are on the verge of moving to the United States. Second, an important key input in evaluating the benefits of a tax cut to stem the brain drain is knowledge of the sensitivity of migration to the tax rate. Yet when asked about the importance of various factors in their decisions to move, a sample of recent (1995) graduates living in the United States ranked higher Canadian taxes low on their list of reasons for leaving Canada (Frank and Belair, 1999). The most important reason was a better job, and the corresponding higher income. Using the survey of 1995 *Graduates Who Moved to the United States*, Frank and Belair estimate that comparable science graduates earn starting salaries of \$47,400 in the United States, as against \$38,400 in Canada. These salaries, both expressed in Canadian dollars and adjusted for differences in the cost of living (but not taxes), yield a significant difference not only in short-term but also in life-time earnings. If we take the estimated age-experience profile from Table 9.2, and simulate a person's earnings growth over a 40-year career, assuming a 5 percent discount rate yields a present value of \$292,439 for taking the U.S. job instead of the Canadian. The most striking mystery (to economists) is why anyone faced with this decision would stay in Canada at all![9] It is also clear that small changes in the income tax rate will do little to change this calculation.

A second policy prescription is to ensure that emigrants are replaced by immigrants from outside Canada. In fact, Zhao, Drew, and Murray report that for every university-educated emigrant, Canada receives four university-educated immigrants, including one at the Masters or Ph.D. level. Clearly, immigration can at least partially offset the loss of human capital to the United States. However, no matter how many qualified immigrants come to Canada, it would presumably be better to have both the new immigrants and those people who moved. In the long run, there will continue to be a brain drain as long as the United States provides better opportunities than Canada. Defining the set of policies that would create this happy situation certainly lies outside the scope of this textbook, and is an obvious topic for future research.

Summary

- Canada currently receives over 200,000 immigrants per year. This number has fluctuated over time, for example, sometimes being lower during economic downturns. Compared to 30 years ago, immigrants are significantly more likely to come from Asia than western Europe. Most immigrants settle in large cities, especially Toronto and Vancouver.
- The Canadian government has two main policy instruments for controlling immigration. First, it can set a target number of total immigrants. Whether the target binds will depend to some extent on the supply side by the number of people who want to immigrate to Canada. Second, the government can affect the mix by determining how many immigrants will be admitted in the assessed and nonassessed classes. Over the 1990s the government tilted the mix toward more-skilled immigrants, by increasing the number of immigrants assessed by the points system and decreasing the size of the family-reunification class.
- Policymakers and economists can use the simple supply and demand framework in order to simulate the potential impact of immigration on the labour market (i.e., on the employment and wages of the native-born). If the only effect of immigration is to shift

[9]DeVoretz and Iturralde (2001) address this very question, and explore a broad variety of determinants of mobility from Canada to the United States.

out the supply curve, we would predict that immigration would depress wages. However, the impact of immigration may be offset by shifts of the labour demand curve, in which case the impact of immigration is indeterminate.

- Empirically evaluating the impact of immigration on the labour market is difficult, because it is impossible to know what would have happened in the absence of immigration. A common approach, for example, is to compare native-born wages across cities with different levels of immigration. This can be a difficult empirical strategy if immigrants choose to go to cities with more prosperous labour markets; if native-born workers move in response to immigration; or if firms invest in factories to take advantage of the pool of immigrant labour. All of these factors will make it difficult to detect an adverse effect, even if one exists. Researchers have employed a variety of strategies to circumvent these problems, including exploiting "natural experiments," whereby there were large sudden inflows of immigrants to particular labour markets. The "consensus" estimates of the impact of immigration suggest that the impact is modest, though possibly that increases in unskilled immigrants lower low-skilled wages.
- Another important empirical question is how immigrants perform in their new labour markets. Economists are particularly interested in how much lower are earnings of immigrants than those of the native-born when they first arrive (the entry effect), how quickly immigrant earnings grow after arrival (assimilation), and ultimately, whether they catch up to those of the native-born. It can be difficult to estimate these assimilation profiles, unless one uses data sets that permit following cohorts (or samples of cohorts) of immigrants over time. The assimilation rate in Canada has generally been low over the past 30 years, with the exception of the economic expansion in the late 1980s.
- Emigration is the opposite of immigration, and the flow of emigrants from Canada to the United States has received considerable attention in the context of the "brain drain." The data suggest that the number of migrants to the United States is small on an annual basis, but many of these migrants come from high-skilled occupations in short supply in Canada.

REVIEW QUESTIONS

1. Visit the Citizen and Immigration Web site <www.cic.gc.ca>, and review the information for applicants to Canada. In this section there is a detailed discussion of the point system described in Exhibit 11.1. Evaluate yourself, and determine whether you qualify as an immigrant to Canada.
2. Describe the point system and its role in Canadian immigration policy. Discuss the policy objectives it is designed to meet, and review the empirical evidence that reflects upon its effectiveness.
3. Carefully define economic assimilation in the context of a human capital earnings function. Outline some of the empirical difficulties encountered in estimating earnings assimilation. How can evidence on assimilation patterns of immigrants in Canada and the United States be used to evaluate the impact of Canadian immigration policy?
4. "An increase in the immigration of low-skilled workers has an unambiguously adverse impact on the wages of low-skilled native-born workers." Discuss the theoretical and empirical validity of this statement using a framework similar to Figure 11.4.
5. Explain how the data summarized in Figure 11.2, on cross-city variation in the concentration of immigrants, could form the basis of an empirical investigation of the impact of immigration on the Canadian labour market. Critically review the evidence from the United States that employs such a procedure.

6. Most studies of earnings assimilation find quite different patterns for women and men. Carefully describe two models that may account for this difference.
7. Discuss what is meant by the brain drain, why it arises, and possible solutions to the problem.

PROBLEMS

1. Consider the following tabulation of (fictitious) average earnings for natives and two cohorts of immigrants.

	Year of Observation	
Group	**1990**	**1995**
Native-born	40,000	41,000
Immigrants, 1986–1990	32,000	36,000
Immigrants, 1981–1985	38,000	39,000

Use these data to provide a description of the immigrant assimilation profile (entry effect and assimilation rates).

2. A researcher wishes to investigate the impact of immigration on the Canadian labour market. She uses time series data on the number of immigrants and the national unemployment rate from 1961 to 2000 to estimate the following relationship:

$$dur_t = \alpha + \gamma d \ln imm_t + \varepsilon_t$$

where dur_t is the change (from one year to the next) in the unemployment rate, and $d \ln imm_t$ is the change in the logarithm of the number of immigrants arriving in Canada.

(a) Explain what economic theory suggests should be the sign of γ.

(b) She obtains the following regression estimates (with standard errors in parentheses):

Intercept	0.015 (0.147)
$d \ln imm_t$	-1.56 (0.75)

She interprets her results as showing that, far from adversely affecting the Canadian labour market (and increasing the unemployment rate), increases in immigration actually reduce unemployment. Critically evaluate her interpretation. In your answer, you should discuss:

i. Under what conditions her interpretation may be correct
ii. The reasons why her interpretation may be flawed
iii. Any evidence that you know sheds light on these issues

3. The following table shows the average earnings of various immigrant cohorts and the native-born for 1990 and 1995 (all values expressed in 1995 dollars), corresponding to Figure 11.7.

a. Calculate the cross-sectional entry effect (in levels) for the 1991-1995 (IM9195) cohort. Interpret.

b. Use the 1990 cross-section to estimate the effect on earnings of being in Canada an additional five years for the IM8690 cohort, that is, the effect of being in Canada 7.5 instead of 2.5 years. Use this to predict IM8690's earnings in 1995.

c. Compare your estimate from part (b) to IM8690 earnings in 1995. Provide a better estimate of the earnings assimilation of the IM8690 cohort. Explain and interpret. Compare this to the cross-sectional estimate from part (b) and suggest an explanation of why they are different.

Average Earnings by Immigrant Cohort

Cohort	Label	1990 YSM	1990 Earnings ($)	1995 YSM	1995 Earnings ($)
Native-born	Native	N/A	42,838	N/A	38,002
Pre-1950	IM50P	42.5	50,748	47.5	48,387
1951–1955	IM5155	37.5	49,855	42.5	46,362
1956–1960	IM5660	32.5	49,166	37.5	43,601
1961–1965	IM6165	27.5	47,352	32.5	41,113
1966–1970	IM6670	22.5	47,412	27.5	42,229
1971–1975	IM7175	17.5	43,332	22.5	38,633
1976–1980	IM7680	12.5	40,462	17.5	35,382
1981–1985	IM8185	7.5	37,593	12.5	33,711
1986–1990	IM8690	2.5	32,233	7.5	29,960
1991–1995	IM9195			2.5	25,653

Note: "YSM" refers to the average years since migration.

4. Assume that the labour market can be described by the following supply and demand equations:

$$S : e = a + bP + cW$$
$$D : e = \alpha + \beta P + \eta W$$

where e is the log of employment, W is the log wage, and P is a log of the "population."

(a) Interpret b and β. Explain how immigration may shift the population. Define γ as the elasticity of population, P, with respect to immigration, I. Why might γ vary across markets?

(b) Solve for the equilibrium wage and employment level as a function of the population.

(c) Assume the following parameters: $c = 0.1$, $\eta = -0.3$, which are in accordance with the empirical literature. Using the answer to part (b), evaluate the impact of an increase in immigration on equilibrium employment and wages under two scenarios:

i. $\beta = 0; b = 1$

ii. $\beta = 1; b = 1$

Assume that the elasticity of population with respect to immigration is 1. Interpret your results, using a figure like Figure 11.4.

5. Assume that the starting salary for a computer programmer in the United States is C$75,000 as against C$50,000 in Canada; that the starting age is 25; and that the person expects to be continuously employed until age 65. Assume further that earnings can be expected to grow at 6 percent per year in both jobs.

Calculate the present value of earnings under the two alternatives, assuming a discount rate of 5 percent. How much would a potential migrant have to value living in Canada in order to stay? What factors can you identify (and possibly value) that might offset the benefits of moving? Calculate the present value of moving at each age. When would you expect a person to move, if he or she were going to move?

It is recommended that you use a spreadsheet in order to make these calculations. (In Excel, the relevant function for calculating present values is "NPV.")

KEYWORDS

assessed and nonassessed classes **321**
independent immigrants **321**
point system **321**
family class **321**
refugee class **321**
impact of immigrants **324**
counterfactual **325**
economic assimilation **328**
positively selected **329**
entry effect **329**
years since migration **329**
cohort effects **331**
quasi-panel **332**
family investment hypothesis **334**
brain drain **337**

REFERENCES

Abbott, M. G., and C. M. Beach. 1993. Immigrant earnings differentials and birth-year effects for men in Canada: Post-war 1972. *CJE* 26 (August):505–24.

Akbari, A. 1995. The impact of immigrants on Canada's treasury, circa 1990. In *Diminishing Returns*, ed. D. DeVoretz. Toronto: C. D. Howe Institute and Laurier Institution.

Akbari, A. H., and D. J. Devoretz. 1992. The substitutability of foreign-born labour in Canadian production: Circa 1980. *CJE* 25:604–14.

Altonji, J., and D. Card. 1991. The effects of immigration on the labor market outcomes of less-skilled natives. In *Immigration, Trade, and the Labor Market*, eds. J. Abowd and R. Freeman. Chicago: University of Chicago Press.

Baker, M., and D. Benjamin. 1994. The performance of immigrants in the Canadian labor market. *JOLE* 12 (July):369–405.

______. 1995a. Labour market outcomes and the participation of immigrant women in Canadian transfer programs. In *Diminishing Returns*, ed. D. DeVoretz. Toronto: C. D. Howe Institute and Laurier Institution.

______. 1995b. The receipt of transfer payments by immigrants to Canada. *JHR* 30 (Fall):650–76.

______. 1997a. Asia-Pacific immigration and the Canadian economy. In *The Asia Pacific Region in the Global Economy: A Canadian Perspective*, ed. R. G. Harris. Calgary: University of Calgary Press.

______. 1997b. The role of the family in immigrants' labor market activity: An evaluation of alternative explanations. *AER* 87 (September):705–27.

Beach, C. M., and C. Worswick. 1993. Is there a double-negative effect on the earnings of immigrant women? *CPP* 19 (March):36–53.

Bloom, D. E., G. Grenier, and M. Gunderson. 1995. The changing labour market position of Canadian immigrants. *CJE* 28 (November):987–1005.

Borjas, G. J. 1985. Assimilation, changes in cohort quality, and the earnings of immigrants. *JOLE* 3 (October):463–89.

______. 1993. Immigration policy, national origin, and immigrant skills: A comparison of Canada and the United States. In *Small differences that matter: Labor markets and income maintenance in Canada and the United States. National Bureau of Economics Research Comparative Labor Markets Series*, eds. D. Card and R.-B. e. Freeman. Chicago and London: University of Chicago Press.

______. 1994. The economics of immigration. *JEL* 32 (December):1667–1717.

______. 1995. Assimilation and changes in cohort quality revisited: What happened to immigrant earnings in the 1980s? *JOLE* 13 (April):201–45.

______. 1995. The economic benefits from immigration. *JEP* 9 (Spring):3–22.

______. 1996. The new economics of immigration. *Atlantic Monthly* 278 (November):72-80.

______. 1999. The economic analysis of immigration. In *Handbook of Labor Economics*, eds. O. Ashenfelter and D. Card. New York and Oxford: Elsevier Science, North Holland.

Borjas, G. J., R. Freeman, and L. Katz. 1992. On the labor market effects of immigration and trade. In *Immigration and the Workforce: Economic Consequences for the United States and Source Areas*, eds. G. Borjas and R. Freeman. Chicago: University of Chicago Press.

______. 1996. Searching or the effect of immigration on the labour market. *AER* 86 (May):246–51.

Card, D. 1990. The impact of the Mariel boatlift on the Miami labor market. *ILRR* 43 (January):245–57.

______. 2001. Immigrant inflows, native outflows, and the local labor market impacts of higher immigration. *JOLE* 19 (January):22–64.

Carrington, W. J., and P.J.F. de Lima. 1996. The impact of 1970s repatriates from Africa on the Portuguese labor market. *ILRR* 49 (January):330–47.

Chiswick, B. 1978. The effect of Americanization on the earnings of foreign-born men. *JPE* 86 (October):897–921.

Citizenship and Immigration Canada. 1998. *The Economic Performance of Immigrants: Immigration Category Perspective*. Ottawa: IMDB Profile Series, Citizenship and Immigration Canada.

______. 1999. *The Economic Performance of Immigrants: Education Perspective*. Ottawa: IMDB Profile Series, Citizenship and Immigration Canada.

Crossley, T. F., J. T. McDonald, and C. Worswick. 2001. Immigrant benefit receipt revisited: Sensitivity to the choice of survey years and model specification: Comment. *JHR* 36 (Spring):379-97.

DeVoretz, D. J. 1999. The brain drain is real and it costs us. *Policy Options* (September):18-24.

DeVoretz, D. J., and C. Iturralde. 2001. Why do highly-skilled Canadians stay in Canada? *Policy Options* (March):59-63.

Duleep, H. O., and M. C. Regets. 1992. Some evidence of the effects of admissions criteria on immigrant assimilation. In *Immigration, Language, and Ethnicity: Canada and the United States*, eds. B.-R. e. Chiswick. Washington, D.C.: AEI Press; distributed by University Press of America.

Duleep, H. O., and S. Sanders. 1993. The decision to work by married immigrant women. *ILRR* 46 (July):677-90.

Emery, H. 1999. The evidence vs. the tax-cutters. *Policy Options* (September):25-29.

Finnie, R. 2001. The brain drain: Myth and reality—what it is and what should be done. School of Policy Studies, Queen's University, Number 13.

Frank, J., and E. Belair. 1999. *South of the Border: Graduates from the Class of 1995 Who Moved to the United States*. Human Resources Development Canada and Statistics Canada.

Friedberg, R. 1996. The impact of mass migration on the Israeli labor market. Brown University Working Paper, Number 96-28.

Friedberg, R., and J. Hunt. 1995. The impact of immigrants on host country wages, employment and growth. *JEP* 9 (Spring):23-44.

Globerman, S. 1995. Immigration and trade. In *Diminishing Returns*, ed. D. DeVoretz. Toronto: C. D. Howe Institute and Laurier Institution.

Grant, M. 1999. Evidence of new immigrant assimilation in Canada. *CJE* 32 (August):930-55.

Green, A. G. 1976. *Immigration and the Postwar Canadian Economy*. Toronto: Macmillan.

______. 1995. A comparison of Canadian and U.S. immigration policy in the twentieth century. In *Diminishing Returns*, ed. D. DeVoretz. Toronto: C. D. Howe Institute and Laurier Institution.

Green, A. G., and D. A. Green. 1995. Canadian immigration policy: The effectiveness of the point system and other instruments. *CJE* 28 (November):1006-41.

______. 1999. The economic goals of Canada's immigration policy: Past and present. *CPP* 25 (December):425-51.

Green, D. A. 1995. Intended and actual occupations of immigrants. In *Diminishing Returns*, ed. D. DeVoretz. Toronto: C. D. Howe Institute and Laurier Institution.

______. 1999. Immigrant occupational attainment: Assimilation and mobility over time. *JOLE* 17 (January):49-79.

Head, K., and J. Ries. 1998. Immigration and trade creation: Econometric evidence from Canada. *CJE* 31 (February):47-62.

Helliwell, J. F. 1999. Checking the brain drain: Evidence and implications. *Policy Options* (September):6-17.

Hoefer, M., D. Norris, and E. Ruddick. 2000. Canadians authorised to work in the United States under NAFTA provisions. Presentation at 5th International Metropolis Conference, Vancouver, November.

Hunt, J. 1992. The impact of the 1962 repatriates from Algeria on the French labor market. *ILRR* 45 (April):556-72.

Iqbal, M. 1999. Are we losing our minds. *Policy Options* (September):34-38.

Kesselman, J. 2001. Policies to stem the brain drain—without Americanizing Canada. *CPP* 27 (March):77-93.

Kuhn, P. J., and I. Wooton. 1991. Immigration, international trade, and the wages of Native workers. In *Immigration, Trade, and the Labor Market*, eds. J.-M. Abowd and R.-B. e. Freeman. A National Bureau of Economic Research Project Report, Chicago and London: University of Chicago Press.

Lam, K.-C. 1994. Outmigration of foreign-born members in Canada. *CJE* 27 (May):352-70.

Lui-Gurr, S. 1995. The British Columbia experience with immigrants and welfare dependency, 1989. In *Diminishing Returns*, ed. D. DeVoretz. Toronto: C. D. Howe Institute and Laurier Institution.

Marr, W., and P. Syklos. 1995. Immigration and unemployment: A Canadian macroeconomic perspective. In *Diminishing Returns*, ed. D. DeVoretz. Toronto: C. D. Howe Institute and Laurier Institution.

McDonald, J. T., and C. Worswick. 1997. Unemployment incidence of immigrant men in Canada. *CPP* 23 (December):353-73.

______. 1998. The earnings of immigrant men in Canada: Job tenure, cohort, and macroeconomic conditions. *ILRR* 51 (April):465-82.

Meng, R. 1987. The earnings of Canadian immigrant and native-born males. *Applied Economics* 19:1107-19.

Stewart-Patterson, D. 1999. The drain will be a torrent if we don't staunch it now. *Policy Options* (September):30-33.

Watson, W. 1999. If we're number one, why would anyone leave? *Policy Options* (September):39-43.

Worswick, C. 1996. Immigrant families in the Canadian labour market. *CPP* 22 (December):378-96.

______. 1999. Credit constraints and the labour supply of immigrant families in Canada. *CJE* 32 (February):152–70.

Wright, R. E., and P. S. Maxim. 1993. Immigration policy and immigrant quality: Empirical evidence from Canada. *Journal of Population Economics* 6 (November):337–52.

Zhao, J., D. Drew, and T. S. Murray. 2000. Brain drain and brain gain: The migration of knowledge workers from and to Canada. *Education Quarterly Review* 6 (May):8–35.

Chapter Twelve

Discrimination and Male-Female Earnings Differentials

Main Questions

- *How can otherwise equally productive men and women be paid different wages in a competitive labour market? Will competitive market forces dissipate discrimination?*
- *What methods are used to measure the extent of discrimination in the labour market?*
- *How much discrimination against women exists in the Canadian labour market? Is there evidence of discrimination against other groups?*
- *What policies have been adopted to address the effects of discrimination? Which policies have been effective?*

The economic analysis of discrimination provides a good application for many of the basic principles of labour market economics. In addition, it indicates the limitations of some of these tools in an area where noneconomic factors may play a crucial role. In fact, many would argue that discrimination is not really an economic phenomenon, but rather is sociological or psychological in nature. While recognizing the importance of these factors in any analysis of discrimination, the basic position taken here is that economics does have a great deal to say about discrimination. Specifically, it can indicate the labour market impact of the sociological or psychological constraints and preferences. More importantly, economics may shed light on the expected impact of alternative policies designed to combat discrimination in the labour market.

Although the focus of this analysis is on gender discrimination[1] in the labour market, it is important to realize that discrimination can occur against various groups and in different

[1]The terms *sex discrimination* and *gender discrimination* are used interchangeably in this chapter, although the former is often used to denote biological differences and the latter to denote cultural and socially determined differences.

markets. Discrimination can occur in the housing market, product market, capital market, and human capital market (e.g., education and training), as well as in the labour market. It can be based on a variety of factors including race, age, language, national origin, sexual preference, or political affiliation, as well as on sex. Sex discrimination appears to have existed for a long time, at least as evidenced by the fact that the Bible recommended paying females 60 percent of the pay of males—a ratio that is fairly close to that which prevails today (see Exhibit 12.1).

The focus of the chapter is on labour market discrimination that occurs when groups who have the same productivity, or productivity-related characteristics such as education, experience, and training, are treated differently purely because of their demographic group or personal characteristics such as sex, race, age, national origin, or sexual preference. The different treatment could occur in such forms as wages or the occupation into which they are placed, and it can occur at various phases of the employment relationship, for example, recruiting, hiring, promoting, training, and terminating. The discrimination can be overt or intentional, or it can be subtle, inadvertent, and unintentional, perhaps as a byproduct of other employment practices or requirements such as when unnecessary height requirements effectively preclude some women from obtaining the job, even through they can do the work. The later is often termed "systemic" discrimination (not to be confused with "systematic") to indicate that it is a result of a system of practices.

In order to better understand the economics of gender discrimination, the reasons, sources, and forms of sex discrimination are first discussed. Various theories of discrimination are then presented and empirical evidence is given to document the existence of sex discrimination in the labour market. The chapter concludes with a discussion of alternative policies to combat discrimination in the labour market.

DISCRIMINATION: REASONS AND SOURCES

Reasons for Discrimination

Labour market discrimination against females may result because males have a preference for working with or buying from fellow males. This prejudice would be especially strong against females in supervisory positions or in jobs of responsibility.

Discrimination may also occur because of erroneous information on the labour market worth of females. Such erroneous information could come from females who consistently underestimate their own capacity in the labour market or it could come from employers who consistently underestimate the productivity of females. Erroneous information on the part of employers may come from the subjective reports of co-workers or supervisors, or it may be based on sex-biased test scores.

Because information on individual workers is extremely costly to acquire, employers may judge individual females on the basis of the average performance of all females. **Statistical**

Exhibit 12.1 **It's Been 0.60 Since Biblical Times**

"The Lord spoke to Moses and said, 'Speak to the Israelites in these words. When a man makes a special vow to the Lord which requires your valuation of living persons, a male between twenty and fifty years old shall be valued at fifty silver shekels, that is shekels by the sacred standard. If it is a female, she shall be valued at thirty shekels'" (Leviticus 27:1–4).

Clearly, a female/male earnings ratio of 30/50 = 0.6 is not a new phenomenon. It has existed—or at least been endorsed—at least since biblical times.

and signalling theories of discrimination are discussed in Coate and Loury (1993a, 1993b), Lundberg (1991), Lundberg and Startz (1983), Oettinger (1996), and Phelps (1972). If efficiency wage premiums are paid to reduce costly turnover, individual females who expect to stay in the labour market may find it difficult to credibly signal their intent. In such circumstances, employers may judge them as having the average turnover of all women (which employers perceive to be higher than that of males) and hence may not place them in the jobs that pay the efficiency wage premiums. Although, from the employers' viewpoint, such statistical judgment may be efficient, it could be inequitable for many individual females.

Males may also discriminate for reasons of job security. To protect their high-wage jobs from low-wage female competition, males would use the forces of governments, unions, and business cartels to ensure that power remains in their hands and is used to further their own ends.

Obviously, discrimination can occur for any, or all, of the previously mentioned reasons of preference, erroneous information, statistical judgment, or job security. As we shall see later, the effectiveness of policies designed to combat discrimination often depends on the reasons for the discrimination.

Sources of Discrimination

Labour market discrimination can come from a variety of sources. *Employers* may discriminate in their hiring and promotion policies as well as their wage policies. To a certain extent the forces of competition would deter employers from discriminating since they would forgo profits by not hiring and promoting females who are as productive as their male counterparts. However, profit-maximizing firms do have to respond to pressure from their customers and male employees. For this reason they may be reluctant to hire and promote females, or they may pay females a lower wage than equally productive males. In addition, firms in the large not-for-profit sector (e.g., government, education, hospitals) may be able to discriminate without having to worry about losing profits by not hiring and promoting females.

In addition to discrimination on the part of employers, *male co-workers* may also discriminate for reasons of prejudice, misinformation, or job security. Akerlof and Kranton (forthcoming), for example, provide examples of how males in typical "male" jobs may find their masculinity threatened, and thereby refuse to cooperate with or informally train female co-workers. Representing the wishes of a male majority, craft unions may discriminate through the hiring hall or apprenticeship system, and industrial unions may discriminate by bargaining for male wages that exceed female wages for the same work. Another potential source of discrimination is *customers* who may be reluctant to purchase the services of females or who may not patronize establishments that employ females, especially in positions of responsibility (see Exhibit 12.2).

THEORIES OF LABOUR MARKET DISCRIMINATION

Alternative theories of sex discrimination in the labour market can be classified according to whether they focus on the demand or supply side of the labour market, or on noncompetitive aspects of labour markets.

Demand Theories of Discrimination

Demand theories of discrimination have the common result that the demand for female labour is reduced relative to the demand for equally productive male labour. The decreased demand for female labour would reduce the employment of females and, unless the supply of female labour is perfectly elastic, the decreased demand would reduce the wages of females relative to the wages of equally productive males. How does discrimination lead to a reduction in the demand for female labour?

Exhibit 12.2 **Discrimination or Productivity Differences? Evidence from Baseball Cards**

Conventionally, the extent of discrimination is measured by estimating the earnings differential between, for example, males and females or blacks and whites, after controlling for productivity differentials that could be regarded as legitimate determinants of wages. It is extremely difficult, however, to control for productivity differentials. Even if the extent of discrimination can be estimated, it is difficult to determine the extent to which it emanates from customers, co-workers, or employers.

Nardinelli and Simon (1990) examine the market for baseball cards to get around many of these problems. It is a highly competitive market with competitive prices for the cards and it is possible to link the price to objective measures of productivity (i.e., performance of the players). The evidence indicates that the price of cards is 10 to 13 percent lower for nonwhite players than for white players of the same productivity (i.e., performance). This can be taken as evidence of pure *customer* discrimination since neither employers nor co-workers systematically influence the price.

According to Becker (1971, p. 14), employers act as if $W_f(1 + d_f)$ were the net wage paid to females, male co-workers act as if $W_M(1 - d_m)$ were the net wage they receive when working with females, and consumers act as if $P_c(1 + d_c)$ were the price paid for a product sold by a female. In all cases, the discrimination coefficient, d, represents the cost, in percentage, associated with hiring, working with, or buying from females. For example, a firm that has a discrimination coefficient of 0.10 and that can hire all the female labour it wants at \$6 per hour, would act as if it paid \$6 (1 + 0.10) = \$6.60 each time it hired a female. Clearly such discrimination reduces the demand for females relative to equally productive males.

Arrow (1973) gives a neoclassical theory of discrimination based on the firm's desired demand for labour when the firm maximizes utility (rather than simply profits) and the firm's utility is increased by employing fewer workers from minority groups. Again, this results in a reduced demand for female labour and lower female wages.

The demand for female labour relative to male labour also depends on information concerning their relative productivity. To the extent that employers consistently underestimate the productivity of females, they would correspondingly reduce their demand for female labour. This misinformation on the part of employers may be due to their own ingrained prejudices as well as to erroneous information fostered by male customers and co-workers.

Supply Theories of Discrimination

Supply theories of discrimination have the common result that the supply of female labour is increased by discrimination or, conversely, that the female asking wage is reduced by discrimination.

The **crowding hypothesis**, as formalized by Bergmann (1971) and analyzed by Sorensen (1990), implies that females tend to be segregated into "female-type" jobs. The resulting abundance of supply lowers their marginal productivity and hence their wage. Thus, even if females are paid a wage equal to their marginal productivity, their wage will be less than male wages that are not depressed by an excess supply.

In a similar vein, dual labour market theory posits two separate and distinct labour markets. The primary or core labour market (unionized, monopolistic, expanding) provides secure employment at high wages. The secondary or peripheral labour market (nonunionized, highly competitive, declining) is characterized by unstable employment at low wages. Men tend to be employed in the primary labour market, women in the secondary labour market. Prejudice on the part of the dominant group and its desire to exclude female competition will prevent the entry of women into the primary labour market. Unions, occupational licensing, discriminatory employment tests, and barriers to education and training can all work against the entry of females into the core labour market. Female immobility may also result because of women's stronger ties to the household and their tendency to move to the places of their husbands' employment. For these various reasons, females tend to be crowded into jobs in the secondary labour market with its concomitant unstable employment and low wages. Their low wages and undesirable working conditions in turn create high absenteeism and turnover which further depress wages in the secondary labour market.

Females' attitudes of their own labour market worth also may induce them to lower their asking wage when seeking employment. Because of conditioning in a male-dominated labour market, females may erroneously underestimate their own labour market worth. This would tend to lower female asking (reservation) wages; that is, the female labour supply schedule would be shifted vertically downward. Employers would naturally foster these attitudes because they lead to lower labour costs. Supply theories of discrimination also emphasize the importance of preferences in determining various decisions with respect to education, training, hours of work, working conditions, and occupational choice—all of which can influence the jobs that women take and the pay they receive. The importance of these preferences are emphasized, for example, in Butler (1982), Daymont and Andrisani (1984), and Filer (1983, 1986). Of course, the extent to which these "choices" reflect preferences or discriminatory constraints, perhaps arising from outside of the labour market, is an interesting and important question.

Noncompetitive Theories of Discrimination

In theory, male-female wage differentials for equally productive workers are inconsistent with competitive equilibrium. As long as females could be paid a wage lower than that of equally productive males, firms that do not have an aversion to hiring females would increase their profits by hiring females. The resultant increased demand for females would bid up their wages, and the process would continue until the male-female wage differential is eliminated. Firms that do not have an aversion to hiring females would be maximizing profits by employing large numbers of females; firms that have an aversion to hiring females would be forgoing profits by employing only males. According to competitive theory, discrimination leads to a segregation of males and females, not wage differentials. It also implies that discrimination should be reduced over time since firms that discriminate will go out of business as they forgo profits to discriminate.

Some would argue that these predictions of competitive economic theory are at variance with the facts. Male-female wage differentials seem to persist, and discrimination does not appear to be declining over time. What then are some of the factors that may explain this persistence in the face of competitive forces? Thus, there arise **noncompetitive theories of discrimination**.

Arrow (1973) attributes the persistence of male-female wage differentials to costs of adjustment and **imperfect information**.[2] Even if they do acquire the information that profits can be increased by hiring low-wage females to do certain jobs performed by

[2]The importance of imperfect information and search costs in sustaining discrimination in otherwise competitive markets is also emphasized in more recent papers by Black (1995) Borjas and Bronars (1989). Evidence on the extent to which competitive pressures dissipate discrimination is provided in Ashenfelter and Hannan (1986).

higher-wage males, firms cannot immediately replace their male workers by an all-female work force. There are fixed costs associated with recruiting and hiring; consequently, firms want to spread these fixed costs as much as possible by retaining their existing work force. Firms may replace male turnover by new female recruits, but they would be reluctant to immediately replace their male work force. In essence, Arrow implies that the long run may be a very long time.

Queuing theories based on efficiency wages may also explain the persistence of male-female wage differentials for equally productive workers. Arrow argues that some firms pay efficiency wages that are wages greater than competitive market wages in order to reduce turnover, improve morale, or secure the advantages of always having a queue from which to hire workers. Other firms pay greater than competitive wages because of union or minimum wage pressure, or because of a necessity to share monopoly or oligopoly profits with their workers. The resultant higher-than-competitive wage enables these high-wage firms to hire from a queue of available workers. Rationing of the scarce jobs may be carried out on the basis of discrimination or nepotism where nepotism is a form of discrimination in that it involves favouring a particular group, which disadvantages the group not receiving the favouritism. Thus, discriminatory wage differentials may exist in a long-run competitive equilibrium when profit-maximizing firms minimize labour costs by paying high wages in order to reduce turnover or improve morale, or because they face institutional constraints such as unions or minimum wage legislation.

The persistence of discrimination can also be fostered by non-competitive pressures, when political pressures can replace market pressures. Reflecting majority wishes, governments can discriminate both in their own hiring practices and in the provision of education and training. In the case of sex discrimination, this would reduce the skill endowment of minorities and reduce the number of professional-managerial females who would hire fellow females. Also reflecting the wishes of a male majority, unions could discriminate against females, especially in apprenticeship and training programs. Social pressure can foster discrimination, especially when profits can be made through discrimination. Majority groups may use the power inherent in governments, unions, and business monopolies to further their own ends through discrimination and segregation.

A more radical perspective regards discrimination as deliberately fostered by employers as part of a conscious policy of divide-and-conquer (Reich, 1978; Roemer, 1979). Employers will consciously pit workers against each other and utilize a reserve of unemployed workers as ways of disciplining the work force and reducing working class solidarity and power. In this perspective, group power is more important than the economic forces of supply and demand in determining wages.

Monopsony is another noncompetitive factor that can affect female wages relative to male wages, mainly in two ways. First, if females tend to be employed by monopsonists, their wages will be reduced correspondingly. Because of their immobility (tied to household and to husbands' places of employment), females may not have the effective threat of mobility necessary to receive a competitive wage. Second, monopsonists may try to differentiate their work force so as to pay the higher wage rate only to some employees. One obvious way of differentiating workers is by sex. Thus, the company may pay higher wages to male employees and yet not have to pay these higher wages to its female employees who do the same work, simply because the female employees do not consider themselves direct competitors with male employees doing the same job. Employers find it in their interest to foster this attitude, since it enables them to maintain the wage differentials based on sex. The formal monopsony model of sex discrimination with separate male-female labour supply schedules was discussed earlier in Chapter 7.

The concept of **systemic discrimination** (not to be confused with *systematic discrimination*) has been advanced to explain discrimination that may be the unintended byproduct of historically determined practices. It may result, for example, from informal word-of-mouth recruiting networks (the "old-boy system") that perpetuate the existing sex composition of the workforce. Or it may result from certain job requirements pertaining to height or strength that may no longer serve a legitimate purpose. In situations where wages are institutionally set above the competitive norm, such job requirements may simply serve to ration the scarce jobs and serve little or no function related to productivity.

Productivity Differences: Choice or Discrimination?

Female wages may differ from male wages because of productivity differences that arise from differences in the human capital endowments and differences in the absenteeism and turnover of males and females. The human capital endowments could include *acquired* attributes such as education, training, labour market information, mobility and labour market experience, as well as more *innate* characteristics such as intelligence, strength, perseverance, or dexterity. In general there is little reason to believe the endowment of these *innate* characteristics to differ in an important manner between the sexes, and in an increasingly mechanized society the innate characteristic for which there may be the greatest difference—physical strength—takes on reduced importance. It is in the area of acquired human capital endowments that productivity differences may arise.

Human capital formation will occur until the present value of the marginal benefits (usually in the form of increased earnings) equals the present value of the marginal cost (both direct cost and the opportunity cost of the earnings forgone while acquiring human capital). Because of their dual role in the household and in the labour market, women traditionally have a shorter expected length of stay in the labour market. Consequently, they have a reduced benefit period from which to recoup the costs of human capital formation. In addition, their time in the labour market can be intermittent and subject to a considerable degree of uncertainty. Depending upon the nature of the household tasks they perform, this can lead to a depreciation of their human capital that is valued in the labour market and inhibit them from acquiring continuous labour market experience. For this reason it may be economically rational for females (or firms) to be reluctant to invest in female human capital that is labour-market-oriented. Of course, if the skills they develop in household activities are valuable in the labour market (e.g., time management and multitasking, or doing a wide range of different tasks) their human capital need not deteriorate from spells of household work.

The human capital decision therefore may reflect rational choice, but it may also reflect discrimination as well as rational choice subject to discriminatory constraints. Females may be discriminated against in the returns they receive for acquiring human capital as well as in borrowing to finance the cost of human capital formation. In addition, family and peer group pressures may close off certain avenues of human capital formation. Young girls, for example, may be conditioned to become nurses and not doctors, or secretaries and not lawyers.

Most important, female responsibility for household tasks (see Exhibit 12.3) may reflect discrimination more than choice. Whatever the reason, females tend to acquire less labour-market-oriented human capital than males, and consequently their wages and employment opportunities are reduced in the labour market. This occurs even if in the labour market there is no discrimination on the part of firms, co-workers, or customers. Differences in wage and employment opportunities may reflect productivity differences, which in turn may come about because of rational economic choice as well as discrimination prior to entering the labour market.

Productivity and hence wage differences may also occur because of differences in the absenteeism and turnover of females. This is especially the case if female turnover occurs primarily as a result of leaving the labour force (which would reduce earnings as explained

Exhibit 12.3

Do Differences in Family Commitments Affect the Pay Gap Between Male and Female Managers?

On the basis of survey data of middle-managers in a large Canadian organization, Cannings (1991) determined that female managers spend about four times as much time on household work than male managers. Only 15 percent of the females, but 69 percent of the males, thought that their own careers were more important to their families than the careers of their spouses. Ten percent of the females had professional or managerial husbands who would be willing to move for the sake of the career of their wife; in contrast, 28 percent of the males had professional or managerial wives who would be willing to move for the sake of the career of their husband.

Clearly, family commitments and constraints are more important to female managers than they are to male managers. Statistical analysis of the determinants of the earnings of male and female managers indicates that these differences in family commitment accounted for about 20 percent ($900) of the earnings gap that prevailed between otherwise similar male and female managers.

earlier), and male turnover occurs primarily as a result of moving to a higher-paying job. The empirical evidence on differences in quit rates and turnover rates by sex tends to be mixed. Some studies find quit and turnover rates to be higher for women than men so that women accumulate less tenure, seniority, and training at a particular job (Becker and Lindsay, 1994; Donohue, 1988; Hall, 1982; Sicherman, 1996; Ureta, 1992). However, other studies find that after controlling for the effect of other variables that affect turnover (e.g., wages, education, occupation, age) there is no significant difference in the turnover rates of men and women (Blau and Kahn, 1981; Viscusi, 1980; Meitzen, 1986). In other words, to the extent that women have higher turnover rates then men, it tends to be because women are employed in occupations and low-wage jobs that have high turnover. As well, most studies find that any differences in turnover rates tend to be declining over time, and that the wage gap is smaller when comparisons are made between males and females with the same continuity in the labour forces (Light and Ureta, 1990, 1992).

The absenteeism of women tends to be much higher than that of men, but this difference also becomes negligible after controlling for the effect of other determinants of absenteeism, notably the presence of small children in the household. Boulet and Lavallée (1984, p. 67), for example, cite Canadian evidence indicating that while total absenteeism was only slightly higher for females than males without children or with school-age children only, it was about seven times higher for females than males with preschool-age children. In addition to causing lower wages, higher absenteeism and turnover may be the result of low wages: cause and effect work in both directions to reinforce each other.

Differences in household responsibilities and in the division of labour within the household can be quite pronounced. Gunderson and Muszynski (1990, p. 26) for example, cite Canadian evidence indicating that when both the husband and wife work full-time in the labour market, the wife tends to work an average of 16 hours per week on household tasks while the husband averages about seven hours.

Differences in household responsibilities can lead to a situation where women develop a comparative advantage in household tasks and men develop a comparative advantage in labour market tasks, leading to each specializing in their area of comparative advantage. This is reinforced by discriminatory behaviour against women in labour market tasks. The specialization, in turn, leads to cumulative effects whereby women become less prone to accumulate the continuous labour market experience that leads to higher earnings. This leads them to be especially vulnerable in case of divorce or if they return to the labour market after a prolonged absence due to childraising.

The fact that the household responsibility of females is so important in these aspects of productivity makes it more understandable that there will be increased pressure for a more equitable division of labour in the household as well as more daycare facilities for children. In addition, in empirical work that attempts to control for productivity differences between males and females, we should be careful in interpreting the productivity-adjusted wage and employment patterns as ones that are free of discrimination. The discrimination may simply be occurring outside of the labour market.[3]

Feminist Perspectives

Feminist perspectives on economics in general may also shed light on alternative theories of discrimination. Examples include Bergman (1986, 1989), Cohen (1985), Ferber and Nelson (1993), and Woring (1988), plus references cited in those studies. While such perspectives are continuously being articulated, they tend to have a number of common elements. Many of these are similar to the segmented labour market and radical perspective discussed earlier.

Exhibit 12.4 provides an admittedly stark contrast of the elements of differences between conventional economics and feminist perspectives on economics. Certainly not all feminists would share the feminist perspective, just as not all economists would share this stylized

Exhibit 12.4 **Feminist Versus Traditional Economic Perspectives**

Traditional	Feminist
• Rational choice and optimization	• Power, tradition, dependence, coercion
• Market exchange	• Human interactions and processes
• Self-interest, individualism	• Human relations
• Budget constraints and endowments	• Constraints from broader society and family
• Often emphasis on material needs and objectives	• Broader social and nonmaterial needs and goals
• Objectivity, reasoning, and analytical inquiry	• Additional emphasis on subjectivity and holistic approach
• Mathematical statistical approach	• Alternative methodologies
• Dominated by males	• Male dominance in field of economics determines the issues and methodologies

[3]Lundberg and Startz (1996) analyze the cumulative effect of post- and pre-labour-market discrimination, and review the earlier literature on that topic.

www.ruf.rice.edu/~femec

view of traditional economics. As well, many economists would argue that the conventional tools of economics can be applied to most of the approaches advocated by the feminist perspective. In fact, the journal *Feminist Economics* started in 1995 is a manifestation of the significant methodological common ground between the two perspectives.

Nevertheless, the feminist perspective highlights a set of critical issues that are important for understanding discrimination. The issues are sufficiently important and complex that our understanding of them could be enhanced by a variety of alternative approaches—feminist perspectives, conventional economics suitably modified, and other approaches.

EVIDENCE ON MALE-FEMALE EARNINGS DIFFERENTIALS

Empirical studies have employed a variety of techniques to estimate the male-female earnings differential and to see how much of the differential reflects discrimination. The results are quite varied, in part because of different data sources and methodology, but also in part because of an emphasis on different aspects of discrimination. Some studies focus on wage discrimination within the same establishment and occupation; others involve measures of sex discrimination that also reflect the crowding of females into low-wage establishments, occupations, and industries; and other studies utilize measures of earnings differentials that could reflect discrimination outside of the labour market, perhaps in educational institutions or in households.

Figure 12.1 indicates the ratio of the average earnings of females relative to males in Canada, *before* controlling for the effect of other factors also believed to influence earnings. On average, females tend to earn about 60 to 65 percent of what males earn, with the ratio being more like 70 percent or slightly higher for full-year, full-time earners. The ratio has been increasing steadily but very slowly since the 1960s.

Gunderson and Riddell (1991) discuss how the ratio of female to male earnings in Canada varies by other factors. The ratio is much larger (i.e., the gap is much smaller) after controlling fully for differences in hours worked. Specifically, it is more in the neighbourhood of 75 to 80 percent when comparisons are made between the hourly wages of men and women (see Exhibit 12.5). The ratio is also much higher for younger workers under the age of 24 (above 80 percent), for single persons (almost 90 percent), and for university graduates (above 70 percent). Baker, Benjamin, Desaulniers, and Grant (1995) refine these observations by exploring the interactions between age, education, and the raw differential. They show the ratio is highest for young university graduates (over 90 percent), and lowest for older high school dropouts (59 percent). Baker et al. also point out that the differential is higher (i.e., the ratio is lower) for the highest-paid women within these age-education groups. This reflects the greater compression of the women's wage distribution compared to men. One interpretation of this compression is that higher-paid women face **glass ceilings**, invisible barriers due to discrimination that keep them from the highest-paid jobs within organizations.

These raw or unadjusted earnings ratios do not simultaneously control for the variety of other factors besides gender that can influence wages. Such factors include age, education, race, training, labour market experience, seniority, marital status, health, hours of work, city size, region, quality of schooling, absenteeism, and number of children. The individual's industry and occupation can also affect earnings, but these are more likely to be channels through which discrimination can occur, rather than exogenous wage-determining variables.

Econometric studies, however, have estimated the separate impact of many of these other determinants of wages, with the intent of isolating a pure male-female wage differential that remains after controlling for the effect of productivity-related factors that are regarded as "legitimate" or nondiscriminatory determinants of the wage gap. The net or adjusted wage gap that remains is then taken as a measure of discrimination. The most

Figure 12.1 **Female-Male Earnings Ratio, Canada, 1967–1994**

The ratio of female/male earnings has slowly but steadily increased over most of that time period for both full-year, full-time earners (top line) and all earners (bottom line). The ratio is also higher for full-year, full-time earners than for all earners compared, since the latter group also includes part-year and part-time workers and females are disproportionately in those groups. That is, a substantial portion of the male-female earnings gap reflects that fact that females disproportionately work part-year and part-time and this lowers their annual earnings relative to those of males. The drop in the ratio for both full-year, full-time workers and all workers beginning around 1993 likely reflects the effect of the recession of the early 1990s—a recession that disproportionately affected the earnings of females relative to males.

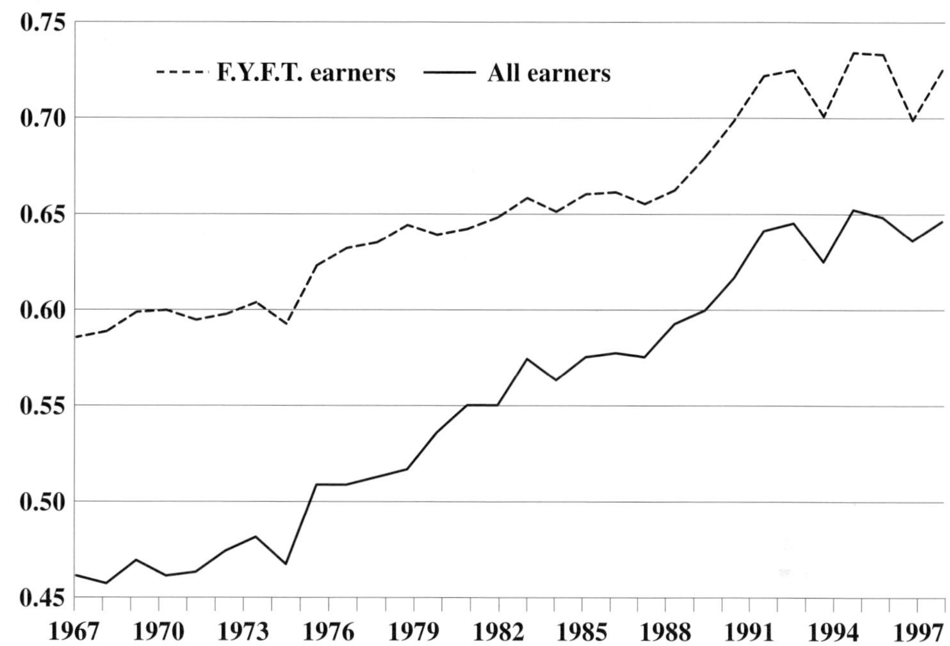

Note: "F.Y.F.T." refers to full-year, full-time workers.

Source: Statistics Canada, *Earnings of Men and Women,* 1988, and subsequent updates, No. 13-217 and 13-577 (Ottawa: Supply and Services, 1989, for years 1967–1994. Reproduced with the permission of the Minister of Public Works and Government Services Canada, 1977. For years since 1994, Statistics Canada Web site <www.statcan.ca/english/Pgdb/People/Labour/Labor01a.htm>. Statistics Canada computes these ratios using data from the Survey of Consumer Finance until 1996, thereafter from the Survey of Labour and Income Dynamics.

common procedure is to estimate equations of the determinants of earnings, separately for males and females. The overall average earnings gap is then decomposed into a component attributable to differences in the endowments of wage-determining characteristics and another attributable to discrimination, defined as differences in the economic returns to the same wage-determining characteristics (outlined in next section).

Measuring Discrimination

Defining discrimination is much easier than measuring it. It is rare, though not unheard of, to find cases of discriminating firms engaging in overtly and directly observable discriminatory practices. Instead, economists and others look for indirect evidence of discrimination as reflected in unequal outcomes between groups. Of course, for any two groups there may be legitimate differences in earnings that have nothing to do with discrimination. Economists therefore look for evidence of unequal outcomes (like pay or promotion rates) *net* of differences in productivity. Unfortunately, productivity is rarely measured.

Where equally qualified men and women perform the same job in the same firm, but are paid differently, this is generally taken as prima facie evidence of discrimination (economically and legally). But such situations represent only a tiny fraction of the potential discrimination in the economy, and publicly available, firm level data sets are very rare (though see Exhibits 12.3 and 12.11).

Exhibit 12.5 Female/Male Hourly Wages

www.statcan.ca/english/sdds/3889.htm

Maria Drolet (1999) uses data from the Survey of Labour and Income Dynamics (SLID) to illustrate how hourly wages (and annual earnings) differ between males and females and how that difference varies by the characteristics of males and females. In addition to doing an econometric analysis to control for the effect of various wage-determining factors, she also tabulates the ratio of female/male hourly wages (times 100 to convert to percentages) by various characteristics (her Table 6). Some highlights of that tabulation include:

- 80.3% overall ratio
- 86.1% age 25–34
- 96.4% single, never married
- 85.0% no children
- 95.5% 0–2 years of work experience
- 86.6% covered by a collective agreement

Clearly, there is substantial variation in the ratio of female/male wages. Econometric analysis from this study, and also others reviewed in this study and discussed later in this chapter, indicate how the male-female pay gap varies by these different characteristics after controlling for the effect of the other wage-determining factors.

Most economic research focuses on the economy-wide earnings ratio depicted in Figure 12.1. It is in this wider arena where the unobservability of productivity becomes an empirical problem. Viewed differently, it is another manifestation of the more general empirical problem in economics. Because we cannot perform controlled experiments to address every empirical question, we have to artificially construct counterfactual evidence. In this case, we have to construct counterfactual evidence for women's earnings: What would women earn if they were men? We wish to hold all productive characteristics constant, and imagine changing the workers' sex to see how their pay would be adjusted. (In this case, the difficulty of conducting the experiment is evident, though individual cases exist.) Any difference in pay that cannot be accounted for by productive characteristics might be deemed discrimination.

The framework most commonly employed by economists is a straightforward application of the human capital earnings function previously developed. The procedure is due to Blinder (1973) and Oaxaca (1973), though it is usually referred to as a **Oaxaca decomposition**. The objective is to decompose the difference in earnings between men and women (or any two groups) into that part due to productivity and that due to discrimination.

To begin, we wish to explain

$$\frac{Y^M}{Y^F} \text{ or } \frac{Y^F}{Y^M}$$

that is, the ratio of women's to men's wages. Our earnings functions provide models for the levels of pay for men and women. Suppose that we have our standard human capital models of earnings:

$$\ln Y^M = \beta_M X_M$$

and

$$\ln Y^F = \beta_F X_F$$

where X_M and X_F are men's and women's productive characteristics, and β_M and β_F are the market rewards (rates of return) or pay schedules for these characteristics. Then, taking logs of the male-female wage ratio, we have the simple expression

$$\ln\left(\frac{Y^M}{Y^F}\right) = \ln Y^M - \ln Y^F = \beta_M X_M - \beta_F X_F$$

By adding and subtracting the term $\beta_M X_F$ we obtain

$$\ln Y^M - \ln Y^F = \beta_M X_M - \beta_F X_F - \beta_M X_F + \beta_M X_F$$

Rearranging, we get

$$\ln Y^M - \ln Y^F = \beta_M (X_M - X_F) + (\beta_M - \beta_F) X_F$$

which yields the decomposition.

In the absence of discrimination, pay differences should only arise from differences in the X's (productive characteristics), not differences in the β's (the pay scales). The first part of this expression, $\beta_M(X_M - X_F)$, gives the predicted difference in earnings that would arise if men and women were paid on the same basis, but had different characteristics. The second component, $(\beta_M - \beta_F)X_F$, yields the part of the differential due to differences in pay structure. The first component is often referred to as a measure of the differential due to **pre-market characteristics**, while the second, unexplained component, is often labelled as that due to labour market discrimination.

The basic framework is illustrated in Figure 12.2. This figure shows two pay scales, one for men and one for women, as well as the wage corresponding to two individuals, a woman with productive characteristic X_F, and a man with X_M. The woman is paid $\ln Y^F$ according to her pay schedule (measured by the vertical distance to point A), while the man is paid $\ln Y^M$ according to his pay schedule (measured by the vertical distance to point D). The overall differential is thus the vertical distance between points A and D. The point B represents what the woman would have been paid if she had been paid according to the man's pay schedule. In this way, the "counterfactual" is constructed. The difference between A and B is thus labour market discrimination, or the difference in earnings due entirely to differences in pay schedules. The vertical distance CD is the additional pay that the man earns because of his higher level of X (according to the male pay schedule), and is thus that part of the earnings difference that can be explained by pre-market characteristics.

With data on the X's and Y's, the earnings functions or pay scales can be estimated. The decomposition can then be based on the regression coefficients and average measured male and female characteristics.

$$\ln Y^M = \hat{\beta}_{0M} + \hat{\beta}_{1M}\overline{X}_{1M} + \ldots + \hat{\beta}_{KM}\overline{X}_{KM}$$
$$\ln Y^F = \hat{\beta}_{0F} + \hat{\beta}_{1F}\overline{X}_{1F} + \ldots + \hat{\beta}_{KF}\overline{X}_{KF}$$

Thus, we can decompose the differences in mean log earnings (and thus the raw earnings ratio) into that part due to differences in observable X's and that part due to differences in β's: **explained and unexplained differentials**, respectively. A simple, fictitious example is provided in Exhibit 12.6.

While the procedure is relatively simple to employ, there are a number of important caveats for interpretation, and difficulties in implementation. First, there is the question of what are the admissible X's (productive, "pre-market" characteristics). Most researchers would agree that the standard human capital variables, like experience and education, are legitimate predictors of productivity and earnings. However, schooling decisions of women and men may be affected by discrimination in the labour market. A neat separation of pay differences due to "pre-" and "post-" labour market discrimination may therefore be

Exhibit 12.6

Hypothetical Oaxaca Decomposition

Consider the case where Y^M = 40,135 and Y^F = 28,001. This implies that the female-male wage ratio is approximately 0.70.

In terms of logarithms, $\ln(Y^F/Y^M) = \ln Y^F - \ln Y^M = 10.60 - 10.24 = \ln(0.70) = -0.36$.

Consider the very parsimonious human capital earnings function:

$$\ln Y^M = \alpha_M + \beta_M S_M$$

and

$$\ln Y^F = \alpha_F + \beta_F S_F$$

In this case, the Oaxaca differential for ($\ln Y^M - \ln Y^F$) is equal to:

$$\alpha_M(1 - 1) + \beta_M(S_M - S_F) + (\alpha_M - \alpha_F)1 + (\beta_M - \beta_F)S_F$$

Attaching numerical values to these parameters, assume we have:

$$\ln Y^M = 9.2 + 0.10S_M \qquad S_M = 14$$

and

$$\ln Y^F = 9.4 + 0.07S_F \qquad S_F = 12$$

Thus, we have

$$[9.2 \times (1 - 1) + 0.10 \times (14 - 12)] + [(9.2 - 9.4) \times 1 + (0.10 - 0.07) \times 12] = 0.20 + 0.16$$

In this case, the "unexplained" differential is 0.16, which is 44 percent of the overall gap of 0.36. The "explained" differential (due to differences in schooling in this case) is the remainder, or 0.20, which is 56 percent of the overall gap.

This implies an unexplained, or "adjusted" female-male earnings ratio of $\exp(-0.16) = 0.85$.

difficult. Empirically, demographic variables like marital status and number of children also affect earnings, though their relationship to productivity is less clear cut. Are these legitimate variables that can be used to "explain" earnings? More problematic are variables like industry and occupation. These variables might be more legitimately viewed as outcome variables themselves, and may embody the effects of discrimination. They are certainly difficult to label "pre-market." Nevertheless, they will capture some of the skill differences between men and women that may be legitimate earnings determinants. It might also be interesting to see to what extent these variables "explain" earnings differences, even if we are not prepared to dismiss the possibility that these variables are contaminated by discrimination. For this reason, it is usually worthwhile to estimate the decomposition for a number of specifications, including ones that do not control for the differences in the occupational and industrial distributions of men and women.

A second problem arises with the opposite specification problem: What variables are omitted from the regressions that may lead to a systematic bias in the estimation of discrimination? At one extreme, a diehard believer that there is no discrimination could attribute the entire unexplained difference in earnings to legitimate, unobserved productivity differences between men and women. More reasonably, there are specific variables that we

Figure 12.2 **Graphical Illustration of the Oaxaca Decomposition**

The lines indicate the relationship between pay (vertical axis) and productive characteristics (horizontal axis) separately for males (top line) and females (bottom line). The positive slope of both lines indicates that both males and females receive higher pay for more productive characteristics. The fact that the male line is steeper than the female line indicates that males also receive a higher return (i.e., greater pay) for additional productive characteristics. The fact that the intercept is higher for males than for females indicates that males also receive greater "base" pay than females. Since the base pay (i.e., intercept) of males and the monetary returns to productive characteristics (i.e., slopes) are greater for males than for females, the male line is always above the female line—that is, male pay is always higher than female pay for any given level of productive characteristics.

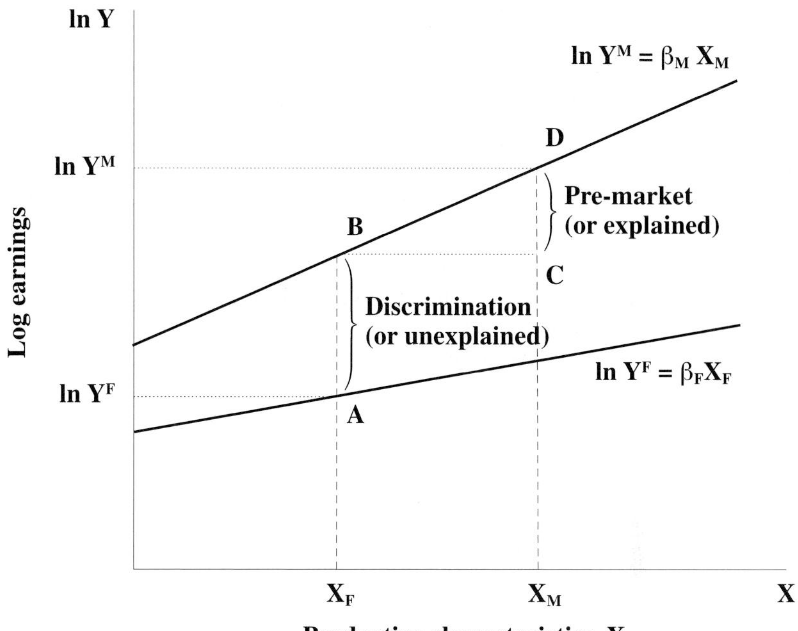

might imagine are systematically poorly measured for women. One such variable is experience. As discussed in Chapter 9, labour market experience is proxied by "potential experience," which is essentially a function of age. Women's labour market attachment has been historically lower than men's, especially as women withdraw from the labour force for child-care purposes. Potential experience may then be a poor proxy for women's actual experience compared to men. We might then expect men to have higher estimated returns to experience, not because of discrimination, but because of measurement error. The data rarely provide a clear-cut way to assess these possibilities.[4] At the very least, we must be careful in interpreting the results of this exercise, and be prepared to examine the numbers underlying the "bottom line" reported differentials. There is also a high return to finding data sets that permit one to address some of these econometric problems.[5]

Empirical Results on Male-Female Differentials

A number of studies review the evidence based on the econometric studies of gender discrimination.[6] While there are exceptions to almost every statement, a number of generalizations do emerge from the evidence on gender differences in earnings.

[4]Studies that do have measures of actual experience find that differences in labour market experience do account for a substantial portion of the male-female earnings gap, and, importantly, the increased experiences of women accounts for a substantial portion of the reduction of the gap in recent years (Blau and Kahn, 1993; Light and Ureta, 1995; and Wellington, 1993).

[5]Data sets that provide information on choice of college major, for example, suggest that a substantial portion of the male-female earnings gap for college graduates reflects differences in such choices (Brown and Corcoran, 1997; Paglin and Rufolo, 1990; and references cited therein). The extent to which such "choices" reflect discrimination, of course, remains an unanswered question.

[6]Reviews of earlier Canadian and U.S. studies are contained in Gunderson (1989a) and of U.S. studies in Altonji and Blank (1999), Willborn (1986), Cain (1986), and Blau and Ferber (1987).

www.chass.utoronto.ca/datalib/major/scf.htm

Even after controlling for a wide range of wage-determining variables using the Oaxaca procedure, a pure wage gap appears to remain that is attributable to discrimination. The gap is narrowed considerably after controlling for the effect of these other determinants of wages; nevertheless, a residual wage gap appears to remain. Based on the 1991 *Survey of Consumer Finances*, Baker et al. estimate a raw earnings differential of 0.402. Depending on the specification, they find that 0.374 to 0.338 of this gap remains unexplained (i.e., only 0.028 to 0.064 of the gap is explained). Using LMAS data for 1989, and looking at wages instead of earnings, Kidd and Shannon (1994) estimate a raw differential of 0.295. Using traditional measures of labour market experience, they find that 0.22 of this differential is unexplained. However, as noted above, it is not clear that it is appropriate to control for the effect of many of these other factors, since differences in these factors themselves may reflect discrimination and, in fact, may be a channel through which discrimination operates. This is the case, for example, with respect to such factors as hours worked, training, labour market experience, seniority, and type of education.

Discrimination and inequality of responsibilities and opportunities originating from outside of the labour market may be as important a source of male-female wage inequality as discrimination from within the labour market itself. This is especially the case with respect to the unequal division of labour with respect to household responsibilities (especially childraising) which can manifest itself in different labour market behaviour pertaining to such factors as hours worked, absenteeism, turnover, mobility, career interruption, training, and occupational choice. In fact when Kidd and Shannon (1994) use predicted labour force attachment, which is primarily a function of household responsibilities, to correct the measure of labour market experience, they find that the unexplained component of the earnings differential drops in half. Hersch and Stratton (1997) find that hours devoted to household work has a negative effect on women's wages. This evidence highlights the limited scope of policies that focus only on labour market discrimination.

Wage differences arising from differences in the occupational distribution between males and females are also an important contributor to the overall wage gap. A number of Canadian studies, however, find that the occupational segregation of women into lower-paying jobs does not explain a large portion of the male-female wage gap in Canada (Baker et al., 1995; Baker and Fortin, 1999, 2000, 2001; Kidd and Shannon, 1994; with similar evidence for the U.S. given in Macpherson and Hirsch, 1995). This reflects the fact that a large part of the gap reflects the segregation of females in low-wage establishments and industries. Also, there is not a strong negative relationship between female pay and the proportion of females in the occupation. Baker and Fortin (2000, 2001) attribute this to the high degree of unionization in Canada, especially in public sector jobs such as education and health and welfare, where women are relatively well paid. However, as pointed out by Kidd and Shannon (1996b), to some extent this reflects the poor measures of occupation. Occupation has greater explanatory power with more narrowly defined occupations (e.g., separating out doctors and nurses from "health occupations"). Again, beyond an accounting exercise, it is doubtful that we want to treat occupation as a pre-market characteristic. Nevertheless, these findings highlight the potential importance of policies to reduce occupational segregation and to encourage the occupational advance of women. Such initiatives include equal employment opportunity policies, as well as the provision of education and training that is labour-market-oriented. They also highlight the limitations of conventional equal pay legislation involving comparisons between men and women within the same job in the same establishment, since pay differences are likely to be small in those circumstances.

In addition to being disproportionately employed in low-wage occupations, women tend to be employed in low-wage establishments and industries. This further emphasizes the limitations of equal pay policies, since comparisons are allowed only within the same establishment and therefore also the same industry. Kidd and Shannon (1996a) emphasize this point in their comparison of earnings differentials in Australia and Canada. In Australia, these cross-firm and cross-industry wage comparisons can be made within centralized (and administered) wage setting and guidelines.[7] As a result, the gap in Australia is only 0.14 (most of which is still unexplained), half the level in Canada where such wage-setting procedures will likely never occur.

The productivity-adjusted wage gap tends to be smaller in the union sector as opposed to the nonunion sector, and in the public sector as opposed to the private sector. Within the private sector, it tends to be smallest when product markets are competitive, highlighting that competitive market forces can dissipate discrimination. The gap seems to be declining slightly over time, with most of the decline coming from improvements in the productivity-related characteristics of women including their increased labour market experience (see Exhibit 12.7).[8] Interestingly, women who are more likely to be discriminated against are less likely to report discrimination (see Exhibit 12.8).

Most of the empirical studies from which the empirical evidence on discrimination was derived use variants of the Oaxaca decomposition or similar procedures to indirectly estimate the extent of discrimination. More direct procedures (see Exhibit 12.9) also provide evidence of discrimination.

Empirical Results for Other Groups

Most empirical research on discrimination in Canada has focused on male-female earnings disparities. Very little attention has been paid to other potentially disadvantaged groups (but see Exhibit 12.10). This has not been the case in the United States, where a high percentage, including most of the pioneering theoretical and applied work, of discrimination research has focused on racial discrimination, especially black-white differentials (for a recent review see Altonji and Blank, 1999). Partially due to data limitations, evidence and research on earnings differentials by ethnic groups in Canada is somewhat scanty, but what little there is has raised a number of important questions for future research.

George and Kuhn (1994) examine white-**Aboriginal earnings differentials** using the 1986 census. Focusing on natives (Aboriginals) living off reserves, they find a raw gap of 0.14 for men with any Aboriginal origins, and 0.087 for women with any Aboriginal origins. Depending on the breadth of controls included in the earnings function, they find that anywhere from one-quarter to one-half of this differential can be explained by observable characteristics. Promisingly, they find that education plays an important role in diminishing the earnings difference between whites and native people. Less promisingly, they find that Aboriginal outcomes look much worse once those living on reserves are included in the sample.

Exploration of **ethnic-white earnings differentials** for other groups inevitably confronts the problem that most nonwhites in Canada are also immigrants. This makes research difficult for two reasons. First, it requires a separation of earnings differences that are to be attributed to immigrant status as distinct from ethnicity. This is best accomplished by comparing immigrants of different ethnicity separately from native-born of different ethnicity (e.g., comparing immigrant whites to immigrant blacks, and native-born whites and native-born blacks as separate exercises.) This is where data constraints become a problem,

[7]Wages in Australia are not entirely market determined. Wages for approximately 80 percent of employees are determined by centrally administered tribunals at the state and federal level (see Kidd and Shannon, 1996 for more details).

[8]See, for example, Ashraf (1966), Blau and Kahn (1997), and O'Neill and Polachek (1993). Blau and Kahn emphasize that the gap would have narrowed even further were it not for the fact that wage differentials between skilled and unskilled workers widened, and this disproportionately depressed women's wages.

Exhibit 12.7 Good News, Bad News on the Male-Female Earnings Gap

The following table, from Gunderson (1998, p. 114), is based on a decomposition of the overall male-female wage gap in Canada into its component parts: a portion attributable to differences in their wage-determining characteristics and a portion attributable to differences in the pay they receive for the same characteristics (i.e., discrimination). The analysis is based on census data for the years 1970, 1980, and 1990—the year 2000 data not being available at that time. Because of the necessity of having a common specification of the earnings equations across the three years, fairly simple earnings equations were estimated, on the basis of annual earnings.

		Portion Attributed to Differences In:	
	Overall Differential	Characteristics	Discrimination
Year	(1)	(2)	(3)
1970 annual earnings	0.469 (100%)	0.166 (35.5%)	0.302 (64.5%)
1980 annual earnings	0.403 (100%)	0.135 (33.5%)	0.268 (66.5%)
1990 annual earnings	0.326 (100%)	0.096 (29.5%)	0.230 (70.5%)

The good news is that the overall male-female earnings gap declined consistently over that time period (column 1). Although this is not shown, female earnings as a percentage of male earnings increased consistently from 61.6 percent in 1970, to 66.6 percent in 1980, to 71.4 percent by 1990. Further good news is portrayed in column 2: the portion of the gap attributed to differences between males and females in their wage-determining characteristics declined from 35.5 percent of the gap in 1970 to 29.5 percent by 1990—females were becoming more like males in terms of their wage-determining characteristics. The bad news is that the portion of the overall gap attributed to differences in pay for the same characteristics (i.e., discrimination) increased from 64.5 percent in 1970 to 70.5 percent by 1990.

Fairly similar results are found in Baker, Benjamin, Desaulniers, and Grant (1995) based on slightly different specifications and combining different data sets. However, they highlight the fact that the results are extremely sensitive to possible selection bias associated with the possibility that women who enter the labour market have unobserved characteristics that enable them to earn higher wages. The difficulty of identifying the effect of these characteristics, however, leads them to suggest that this is a topic in need of further research.

since there are often very few native-born members of ethnic minorities in publicly available data sets. For example, Baker and Benjamin (1994) report that there are only 60 native-born blacks in the public use samples of the 1981 census who had the earnings characteristics usually required for estimation of wage regressions.

Nevertheless, there have been a few studies that provide preliminary evidence on ethnic wage differentials in Canada. Stelcner and Kyriazis (1995) catalogue Oaxaca decompositions for several ethnic groups (mostly European) from the 1981 census. They find that most ethnic groups have similar earnings to Canadians of "British" ethnicity. For visible minorities, they find that African-Canadian men earned 18 percent less than British

Exhibit 12.8 Are Women Who Are Discriminated Against Most Likely to Report Discrimination?

Conventionally, one would expect persons who are most subject to discrimination to also be most likely to report themselves as being subjected to discrimination. However, based on both Canadian and U.S. evidence, Peter Kuhn (1987) finds that women who are most subject to objective measures of wage discrimination are the least likely to subjectively self-report that they are subject to discrimination. The objective measure of discrimination is the statistical evidence of discrimination based on the decomposition analysis from male and female earning equations as discussed in the text. The subjective measure of perceived discrimination is whether the woman self-reports on a confidential survey that she is subject to discrimination. Kuhn's analysis indicates that younger, well-educated women, for example, are more likely to report discrimination, even though they appear to be less subject to wage discrimination.

Kuhn attributes this difference in reporting behaviour to possible differences in nonstatistical aspects of discrimination. For example, younger, more-educated women may work in mixed occupations where male comparator jobs are more readily observed, or they may be more perceptive of the subtle forms of discrimination, or they may have not yet sorted themselves into jobs where they perceive less discrimination, or they have greater expectations of nondiscriminatory norms.

Barbezat and Hughes (1990) also indicate that employees may be less likely to engage in discrimination in ways that can be measured and used against them, if they feel that such information is more likely to be reported by particular groups such as younger and more-educated women. Consequently, the degree of statistically measured discrimination is likely to be smallest against such groups precisely because they are more likely to report discrimination.

Exhibit 12.9 Direct Evidence of Discrimination from Interviews and Blind Auditions

The vast majority of empirical evidence on discrimination is indirect, based on estimating wage equations and conducting Oaxaca-type decompositions of the male-female wage gap. More direct evidence—sometimes termed audit studies—also confirms the existence of such discrimination.

Neumark (1996), for example, had two otherwise equally qualified male and female college students apply for jobs in a variety of restaurants. He found that the males were more likely to get interviews and ultimately job offers (at a higher wage) in the higher-priced restaurants, while females got them in the lower-priced restaurants, and at a lower wage. He interpreted this as reflecting customer discrimination: apparently customers, for whatever reason, were prepared to pay more to be waited on by a male waiter in the more expensive restaurants.

Goldin and Rouse (1996) analyze the effect of "blind" auditions adapted by a number of orchestras in the United States in the 1970s and 1980s. In such auditions, the performer was separated from the judging panel by a screen so that the panel would not know the personal characteristics of the performer. They found that the blind auditions had a large and positive effect on the hiring of female musicians after controlling for other characteristics that could influence such hiring. They argue that this accounted for a large amount of the increased proportion of female musicians that were hired in recent years.

Exhibit 12.10

Discrimination Against the Homely

Are better-looking people paid more? If so, does this represent employer discrimination against the less attractive? Hamermesh and Biddle (1994) explore the role of physical beauty in the labour market. They use survey data from Canada and the United States that contain subjective measures of looks. Interviewers were asked to rate photographs of the respondents on 1 to 5 scale (strikingly handsome through homely). Most people were judged average-looking. Very few were rated at the extremes, and Hamermesh and Biddle focus on the average, the above average, and the below average.

Controlling for human capital characteristics, they find that the penalty for being unattractive (rather than average) is around 5 to 10 percent. The penalty is slightly higher for men than women. The premium for beauty was estimated to be slightly smaller, at about 4 to 5 percent, again similar for men and women. An obvious question is whether this reflects employer discrimination. Because of consumer discrimination, better-looking employees may actually be more productive, in the sense that they increase profits for their employers. This is obviously true for modelling agencies and movie studios, and may also be important in occupations where interpersonal contact is important. Hamermesh and Biddle use the fraction of an occupation that hires better-looking workers as a proxy for occupational productivity of good looks. They find that there is some evidence that this measure of occupational productivity affects earnings, but that individual looks still matter, even for those employed in occupations where beauty is less likely to be important. Their results suggest that the attitudes of employers toward nonproductivity-related characteristics of their employees may affect individual pay.

Canadians, with most of this differential unexplained. On the other hand, Chinese Canadians also earned 18 percent less than British Canadians, but this was actually more than would be predicted on the basis of their observable characteristics. Christofides and Swidinsky (1994) use the 1989 LMAS to compute decompositions based on a coarse "visible-minority" indicator. They find that men from visible minorities earned about 15 percent less than whites, and that most of this differential could not be explained by observable characteristics. The differential was much smaller for women, at about 3 percent.

Reitz et al. (1999, p. 421) also find that the earnings disadvantage for immigrants varies considerably according to the country of origin of the migrant. For example, relative to other male European immigrants, earnings were lower by 6 percent for Italians, 15 percent for West and South Asians and Chinese, and up to 25 percent for Greek, black, and other Asian groups. Reitz and Breton (1994) also provide survey evidence for Canada indicating that negative attitudes toward immigrants vary substantially by ethnicity.

Baker and Benjamin (1997) provide decompositions by ethnic group and immigrant status based on the 1991 census. Following the lead of Reitz and Breton (1994), they also provide a comparison of the Canadian findings with those from the U.S., in order to assess the question of whether Canadian multicultural policy provides a more hospitable environment for minorities in Canada than the "melting-pot" of the United States. Their results are summarized in Table 12.1, with the results for Canada in the top panel and for the United States in the bottom panel. In Canada there is generally a substantial overall gap between the unadjusted or gross earnings of whites and the various ethnic groups who are born in Canada. The gap is largest for South Asians (e.g., Bangladesh, India, Pakistan) and smallest

Table 12.1 Ethnic Wage Differentials, Various Groups Born in Canada or United States

	Black	South Asian[a]	Southeast Asian[b]	Chinese	Aboriginal
Canada					
Total gap	0.293	0.536	−0.022	0.193	0.179
"Discrimination"	0.171	0.222	0.023	0.058	0.091
United States					
Total gap	0.328	0.176	−0.079	−0.205	0.304
"Discrimination"	0.123	0.055	−0.007	−0.047	0.136

Notes: The total gap is the percentage by which the earnings of whites exceed those of the ethnic group, reflecting both the differences in their wage-determining characteristics and the differences in pay for the same characteristics. The latter is the differences in the regression coefficients from a Oaxaca-type decomposition as discussed in the text, and is labelled here as "Discrimination."

[a]E.g., Bangladesh, India, Pakistan.

[b]E.g., Philippines, Korea, Vietnam.

Source: Baker and Benjamin (1997, Tables 5 and 11, specification 3 including industry and occupation controls).

(actually negative) for Southeast Asians (e.g., Philippines, Korea, Vietnam). After controlling for differences in various wage-determining characteristics, the "unexplained gap" or "discrimination" appears to account for roughly half of the overall gap. The pure ethnic earnings disadvantage relative to whites is 22 percent for South Asians, 17 percent for blacks, 9 percent for Aboriginals, 6 percent for Chinese, and 2 percent for Southeast Asians. It is labelled a pure ethnic earnings gap or "ethnic discrimination" because it reflects ethnic status after controlling for the effect of various observable wage-determining characteristics including immigrant status.

Reasons for the variation in this pure ethic earnings gap across the different ethnic groups are not obvious, and in fact the variation highlights the fact that it likely does not all reflect discrimination since there is no obvious reason why pure discrimination should vary so much across the different groups. Some of the variation likely reflects differences in such factors as the quality of schooling or in credential recognition, or perhaps in ethnic social capital and networks of the different groups. More research is necessary to uncover these underlying factors.

Interestingly, the pure ethnic earnings gap attributable to "discrimination" is smaller in the United States compared to Canada for every ethnic group except Aboriginal persons. In fact, two of the five ethnic groups (Southeast Asians and Chinese) receive higher returns (i.e., the gap is negative) for their wage-determining characteristics than white Americans with the same observable characteristics. Furthermore, the ranking of the different ethnic groups with respect to the magnitude of the gap is not the same in the Unites States as in Canada, raising further questions about why this should be.

Clearly this analysis raises numerous interesting questions in need of further research. Why do the pure ethnic earnings differentials vary across the different ethnic groups in both countries? Why do they differ between Canada and the United States? And why does the ranking of the different groups in terms of the magnitude of the gap differ across the two countries?

Pendakur and Pendakur (1998, p. 530) do a similar analysis for persons who designate themselves as visible minorities—another way of designating ethnic status. They also find that after controlling for various wage-determining characteristics, visible minorities have an earnings disadvantage relative to otherwise comparable "whites" in Canada. For males, the earnings disadvantage was 8.2 percent for visible minorities who were born in Canada, and it doubled to 16.2 percent for visible minorities who were new immigrants. The 8.2 percent estimate is taken as a pure estimate of the effect of visible minority status independently of immigrant status since it exists for visible minorities who were born in Canada and hence who are not immigrants. Interestingly, for females, they found no earnings disadvantage for visible minorities who were born in Canada, and a smaller disadvantage of 7.8 percent for visible minority women who were new immigrants.

Hum and Simpson (1999) do a similar analysis to isolate the pure wage effect associated with visible minority status, after controlling for the impact of various wage-determining characteristics. They also attempt to control for the possible selection bias that could occur because persons in the labour market may have different wage offers than persons who do not enter the labour market, although such effects are extremely difficult to identify. They find that most visible minority groups experience a significant wage disadvantage relative to otherwise comparable Canadian-born persons. However, when they do the analysis separately for foreign-born and Canadian-born visible minorities, they find that the earnings disadvantage of being a visible minority arises mainly among the foreign-born immigrants. Visible minorities who are born in Canada do not generally experience any significant wage disadvantage, except for black males. This leads them to conclude (p. 392) that "there is no significant wage gap between visible minority and non-visible minority group membership for native-born workers. It is only amongst immigrants that the question of wage differentials for visible minorities arises." Clearly, this points up the fact that more research would be desirable to reconcile these results with those of Baker and Benjamin (1997) and Pendakur and Pendakur (1998).

POLICIES TO COMBAT SEX DISCRIMINATION

Because of the variety of sources and forms of discrimination, policies to combat discrimination have also tended to take a variety of forms. The main thrusts of public policy have been in three areas: equal pay legislation (including pay equity or equal pay for work of equal value); equal employment opportunity legislation (including employment equity or affirmative action); and policies designed to facilitate female employment and to alter attitudes and preferences. Each of these will be discussed in turn.

Conventional Equal Pay Legislation

All Canadian jurisdictions have **conventional equal pay legislation** which requires equal pay for equal work within the same job and within the same establishment. The courts and

Exhibit 12.11 **Are Female Managers as Likely to Be Promoted as Male Managers?**

Discrimination can occur in the form of differential promotion opportunities as well as unequal wages for the same work. In a survey of large Canadian corporations, Kathy Cannings (1988a) found that female managers earned on average 87 percent of the pay of male managers. However, they were only 80 percent as likely to be promoted in any given year of their career with the organization.

Some of this difference in promotion opportunities can be explained by differences in such factors as formal education and productivity-related characteristics. However, even after controlling for differences in these factors, female managers were significantly less likely to be promoted than male managers.

enforcement agencies have generally interpreted equal work as work that is *substantially similar*, with minor differences being allowed, especially if offset by differences in other aspects of the work performed. For example, the work could be considered the same even if males do occasional heavy lifting, especially if females do other occasional tasks not done by males.

The scope of conventional equal pay legislation is limited by the fact that it deals with only one aspect of discrimination—wage discrimination within the same job within an establishment—and as our earlier discussion of the empirical evidence indicated, this is probably a quantitatively small aspect of discrimination. In addition, the enforcement of the law can be difficult because it usually relies upon individuals to complain and because there are problems of interpreting what is meant by equal work, although the courts have interpreted this rather broadly.

Equal Value, Pay Equity, or Comparable Worth Legislation

In part because of the limited potential for conventional equal pay policies to narrow the overall male-female earnings gap, further legislative initiatives have been advocated on the pay side in the form of equal pay for work of equal value. The phrases equal value, **pay equity**, and **comparable worth** are usually used interchangeably, although "equal value" is often used internationally, "pay equity" is usually used in Canada, and "comparable worth" is used most often in the United States.

Existence of Equal Value Legislation

Table 12.2 catalogues the relevant pay equity legislation for each province in Canada, effective as of the beginning of 2000. Legislation, and its interpretation and enforcement in this area, are in a constant state of flux. Nevertheless, this table provides an overview of the differences to which different jurisdictions have chosen pay equity legislation as a key part of their antidiscrimination policy.

http://canada.justice.gc.ca/en/news/nr/2001/doc_26466.html

In Canada, pay equity or equal value legislation or regulation exists in all jurisdictions except Alberta. It has been in place in Quebec since 1976, although most cases in that province tended to be conventional equal work cases with comparisons being made between males and females in the same job. In 1996 the law was revised (to be implemented in 1997 with the first adjustments to begin in 2001) to be a so-called proactive system, whereby employers are required to initiate gender-neutral job evaluation plans and to make the appropriate wage adjustments whether or not a complaint has been filed, or there is prima facie evidence of discrimination. This is in contrast to a complaint-based system, whereby a complaint is required before the process will be instigated.

In most Canadian jurisdictions, pay equity legislation is restricted to the public sector either by law or by practical application. In a number of jurisdictions (Newfoundland, British Columbia, and Saskatchewan) governments have voluntarily agreed to apply it to other public sector employees, rather than have it legislated. Only Ontario (since 1987) and Quebec (since 1996) have both a proactive system and a requirement to be applied also to the private sector. In fact, these two characteristics make Canada's equal value legislation the most extensive in the world (Gunderson, 1994).

In the United States, by the mid-1960s over a dozen states had passed comparable worth legislation covering state employees; however, these laws were rarely enforced (Ehrenberg and Smith, 1987). More recently, however, Gardiner and Daniel (1998) indicated that eight states have implemented comparable worth for their state employees, Washington State, Minnesota, and Iowa receiving the most attention. At the local level a larger number of cities, counties, or school districts (mainly in California, Washington, and Minnesota) were experimenting with or studying the concept; however, it has yet to be adopted on a widescale basis in the United States.

Table 12.2 Existence of Pay Equity in Various Canadian Jurisdictions, 2000

Jurisdiction	Year	Private Sector[a]	Enforcement
Pay Equity			
Federal	1977	Yes[d]	Complaints-based
Manitoba	1985	No	Proactive[e] plans
Yukon	1986	No	Complaints-based
Ontario	1987[b]	Yes	Proactive[e] and complaints
Newfoundland	1988	No	Collective bargaining[f]
Nova Scotia	1988	No	Proactive[e]
Prince Edward Island	1988	No	Proactive[e] and complaints
New Brunswick	1989	No	Proactive[e]
Northwest Territories	1990	No	Complaints-based
British Columbia	1990	No	Collective bargaining[f]
Quebec	1996[c]	Yes	Proactive[e] and complaints
Saskatchewan	1997	No	Collective bargaining[f]
Conventional Equal Pay			
Alberta	1957	Yes	Complaints-based

Notes:

a. Also the public sector.

b. The legislation was passed in 1987 to commence on January 1, 1988. Wage adjustments were to commence no later than January 1, 1990 in the public sector, and no later than January 1, 1991 in the private sector. Smaller private sector employers must begin adjustments in subsequent years.

c. The law, passed in November 1996, to be implemented November 1997, was revised to be proactive (see note e) and to apply to the private sector, but the first adjustments do not have to be made until 2001.

d. Almost all cases have been in the public sector.

e. Employers are required to initiate gender-neutral job evaluation plans and to adjust wages in female-dominated jobs to ensure equal pay for work of equal value, whether or not a complaint has been made or there is prima facie evidence of discrimination. When applied in the private sector, small employers are not required to establish a plan, but they are required to implement the policy.

f. Legislation has not been passed, but the government has committed itself to pay equity for its civil service, through the collective bargaining process.

Source: Updated from Gunderson and Robb (1991). More detailed analysis is given in Weiner and Gunderson (1990).

In Europe, the principle of equal pay for work of equal value is incorporated into the European Community law (Gunderson, 1994, p. 59). Its practical application, however, is severly limited by the fact that it is largely complaints-based, enforcement tends not to be prominent, and job evaluation procedures that are used to determine the "value" of a job are not common in Europe.

In Australia, a form of comparable worth was adopted in 1972 when their national wage awards made by their wage tribunals (which set wages for the majority of workers) eliminated wage differentials across occupations that were designated as predominantly male and predominantly female. However, this decision, which substantially raised the wages of females, was based on legislative fiat, not on the results of job evaluation procedures, and hence is not a comparable worth procedure in the conventional sense. The centralized process where wages tend to be set by arbitration through tribunals is particularly conducive to making equal value awards (Borland, 1999), although they tend not to be based on formal job evaluation procedures as in North America (Gunderson, 1994, p. 66).

Equal Value Procedures

Equal value policies generally require an equality of pay between jobs of equal value where value is determined by a job evaluation scheme that is free of gender bias. Such schemes generally involve comparisons between jobs that are designated as predominantly male and predominantly female, where gender predominance is designated, for example, as involving 70 percent or more of either sex. The next step involves the determination of the *factors* such as skill, effort, responsibility, and working conditions that are believed to be the important determinants of the value or worth of a job. For the various jobs, job evaluators then usually assign point scores for each of these factors. The points are then summed to get a total point score for each job (which implies equal weights for a point score for each of the factors) or different weights or ranges of scores could be assigned to the scores of each factor on an a priori basis. Predominantly female jobs are then compared to predominantly male jobs of the same total point score, and the wages adjusted to those of the predominantly male jobs. In situations where this equal value approach has been applied, wages in female-dominated jobs typically have been only 80 to 90 percent of wages in male-dominated jobs of the same job evaluation point scores. The jobs can be in different occupations as long as they have the same job evaluation point scores. One case in the federal jurisdiction, for example, involved a comparison of predominantly female librarians with predominantly male historical researchers.

Economic Versus Administrative Concepts of Value

This procedure highlights the fact that equal pay for work of equal value involves an **administrative concept of value**, where value is determined by the *average* value of the *inputs*, such as skill, effort, responsibility, and working conditions, that are involved in a job. This is in contrast to the *economic* concept of the value of the marginal product of labour whereby value is determined by the value of the *output* produced by an *additional* unit of labour. The administrative concept of value is akin to the notion of value-in-use (i.e., the average value of inputs) while the economic concept involves value-in-exchange (i.e., marginal contribution to the value of output). According to the economic concept, inputs that are in abundance in supply may have little value-in-exchange (and hence command a low market wage) even though they may have a high value-in-use because they involve substantial average inputs of skill, effort, responsibility, and working conditions. This is analogous to the diamond-water paradox whereby diamonds have a high value-in-exchange (because of their scarcity) but water has a low value-in-exchange (because of its abundance) in spite of its high value-in-use.

The equal value concept in fact explicitly rejects the notion that market forces should be the prime determinant of the value and hence pay for jobs. This rejection is based on the belief that market forces reflect discrimination. Even if market forces enable employers to hire workers in predominantly female jobs at rates of pay that are lower than those paid to workers in predominantly male jobs, proponents of comparable worth would argue that such an outcome is socially unacceptable because it reflects discriminatory segregation and the systematic undervaluation of female-dominated jobs. The belief is that females should not have to leave female-dominated jobs to get the same pay as in male-dominated jobs that require the same inputs of skill, effort, responsibility, and working conditions (Robb, 1987).

In essence, the primacy of market forces of supply and demand is rejected in that the value and hence remuneration of a job is not deemed to be low simply because there is an abundance of labour willing to do the work, or because there is little demand for that type of labour. This is in contrast to the economic emphasis on the market forces of supply and demand to determine the value and hence remuneration of a job.

While there is a sharp contrast between the economic and comparable worth concepts of value, the two concepts do not have to be diametrically opposed to each other. Skill, effort, and responsibility are scarce resources and hence will receive a market premium, just as they are assigned point scores by job evaluators. Similarly, compensating wage premiums are paid in the market for undesirable working conditions, just as they can be assigned point scores by job evaluators. In fact, it is possible to use the premiums that the market yields for the various factors of skill, effort, responsibility, and working conditions, based only on the male-dominated jobs, and then to apply those premiums to weigh the scores of the female-dominated jobs to arrive at the value of those jobs had they been paid the same market premium as the male-dominated jobs. This procedure is termed a **policy capturing approach** in that it is a policy that simply captures the pricing mechanism that is used for the male-dominated jobs and extends it to the female-dominated jobs. Comparable worth approaches can also pay attention to market forces by allowing exceptions for occupations that are in scarce supply.

Clearly market forces do not have to be ignored by the principle of comparable worth, but it is equally clear that the comparable worth concept of value is different from the economic concept of value. The former is an administrative concept of value based upon job evaluation procedures; the latter is based upon market forces of supply and demand.

Rationale for Equal Value Initiatives

Equal value initiatives have been rationalized on the grounds of being able to deal with *both* wage discrimination and occupational segregation—the latter on the grounds that comparisons can be made across different occupations as long as they are of the same value as determined by job evaluation procedures. This is important because occupational segregation generally is believed to be a more important contributor to the overall earnings gap than wage discrimination, and conventional equal pay can only deal with the latter. Equal value policies have also been rationalized on the grounds of securing redress for those women who do not want to leave predominantly female jobs to get the same pay as predominantly male jobs of the same value, as determined by job evaluation procedures.

Scope of Equal Value Initiatives

The scope of equal value policies is potentially large because it enables comparisons across occupations, unlike conventional equal pay policies, which enable comparisons only within the same occupations. However, the scope of equal value policies will be limited in a complaints-based system by the fact that it is difficult for individuals or even groups to lodge a complaint under such a complicated procedure. For individuals, the fear of reprisals may also deter complaints. For this reason, supporters of comparable worth have advocated a **proactive system-wide** procedure whereby employers would be required to have a bona fide job evaluation system in place to help achieve pay equity. Even if such a system were in place, the scope of comparable worth would be limited by the fact that comparisons can be made only within the same establishment and hence also industry. This means that comparable worth could not reduce that portion of the overall earnings gap that reflects the segregation of females into low-wage establishments or industries (Carrington and Troske, 1995). Using U.S. data, for example, Johnson and Solon (1986) indicate that these restrictions mean that even if comparable worth completely eliminated the relationship between wages and the sex composition of an occupation, it would reduce the average male-female earnings gap by only a small amount. In Canada, the scope is limited even further by the evidence, discussed previously, suggesting that there is not a strong negative relationship between female pay and the proportion of females in an occupation.

Design Features of Comparable Worth

If comparable worth becomes more prominent as a policy initiative, a large number of program design features will have to be worked out to facilitate the practical implementation of the policy.[9] Such design features include: the definition of gender predominance for comparing male-dominated with female-dominated jobs; the job evaluation procedure for establishing the value of a job; the procedure for relating the job evaluation point scores to the pay of jobs; the procedure for adjusting pay in undervalued jobs and in overvalued jobs; the definition of establishment and of pay itself; the appropriate exemptions if any; and the optimal enforcement procedure including whether a complaints-based or more proactive, system-wide procedure should be followed. These and other design features can have a substantial impact on the scope of equal value initiatives and hence on their positive and negative consequences, illustrating the maxim "The devil is in the details."

Pay Equity Example

A hypothetical example can illustrate many of the issues associated with the application of pay equity. In Figure 12.3 the job evaluation points for each job are plotted on the horizontal axis, and the pay for each job is plotted on the vertical axis. The upper line is the **payline** for the male-dominated jobs (e.g., 70 percent or more males) and the bottom line is the payline for the female-dominated jobs (e.g., 70 percent or more females). The points around each line are the particular male or female jobs in the establishment. The points illustrate the combination of pay and points associated with each job. The paylines could

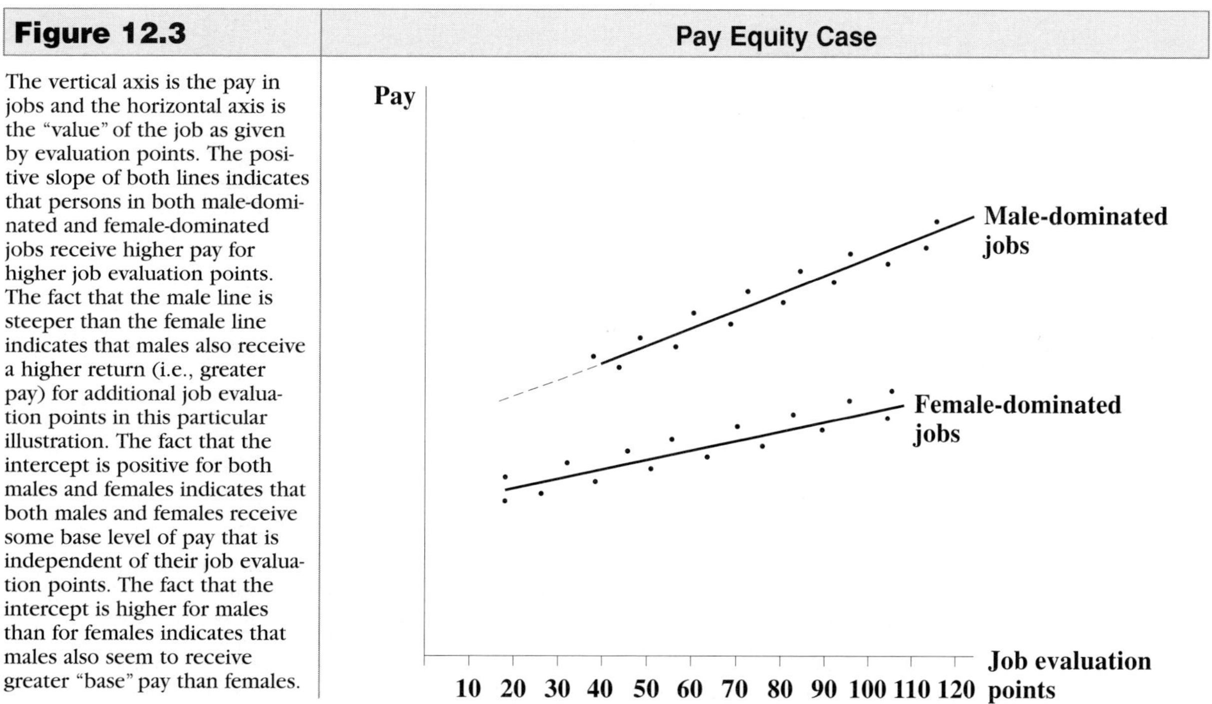

Figure 12.3 Pay Equity Case

The vertical axis is the pay in jobs and the horizontal axis is the "value" of the job as given by evaluation points. The positive slope of both lines indicates that persons in both male-dominated and female-dominated jobs receive higher pay for higher job evaluation points. The fact that the male line is steeper than the female line indicates that males also receive a higher return (i.e., greater pay) for additional job evaluation points in this particular illustration. The fact that the intercept is positive for both males and females indicates that both males and females receive some base level of pay that is independent of their job evaluation points. The fact that the intercept is higher for males than for females indicates that males also seem to receive greater "base" pay than females.

[9]These design and implementation features are discussed in more detail in Gunderson (1989, 1994) and Gunderson and Robb (1991).

have been simply drawn or "eyeballed" to fit the scatter of points, or they could be estimated by statistical techniques such as regression analysis. They could be straight lines, as in this example, or nonlinear if the relationship between pay and points is nonlinear. The slopes could be the same, in which case the same absolute pay difference would be associated with different job values, and therefore the percentage difference would be smaller in the jobs of high pay and points. Or the slopes could be different, as in this example where the higher-paying jobs are associated with higher absolute wage differences, albeit a possible constant percentage differential.

A number of observations are worth noting. The male payline is above the female payline indicating that male-dominated jobs tend to receive higher pay than female-dominated jobs of the same value, where value is measured by job evaluation points. Typically, the female payline is 80 to 90 percent of the height of the male payline, indicating that female-dominated jobs tend to be paid 80 to 90 percent of the pay in male-dominated jobs of the same job evaluation score. (They are drawn further apart here simply to avoid clutter in the diagram.)

Some of the female-dominated jobs at the lower end of the job evaluation scores do not have direct male **comparator jobs** of the same value. This raises the issue of whether projection of the male payline would be allowed (the dashed line segment) to provide hypothetical male comparators (sometimes termed **phantom jobs**) that indicate what such male jobs would have been paid, on the basis of the relationship between pay and points in the other male jobs. In fact, there may even be an issue of whether extrapolation of the male payline is allowed within the sample points of the male-dominated jobs, or whether a male comparator job of comparable job evaluation points is required before a comparison can be made.

Although not shown in this particular diagram, it is possible that some female "dots" (pay for points) could lie above the male payline, or above a male "dot" of the same value. This would simply indicate that some female jobs could pay more than male jobs (hypothetical or actual) of the same job evaluation score. Similarly, a male "dot" could lie below the female line. Such outlying dots are not likely to occur, but they are possible. It is also possible to have multiple male or female "dots" at the same point score. This would simply indicate that unequal pay for work of the same value can exist within female-dominated jobs or within male-dominated jobs.

The diagram also illustrates alternative wage adjustment procedures that are possible. The **line-to-line** procedure would raise the female payline to the male payline, thereby eliminating the systematic differences in pay between male-dominated and female-dominated jobs. The random deviations in pay that previously prevailed around the female payline would remain, just as they remain for male-dominated jobs around the male payline. Some female jobs would be "overvalued" (i.e., above the male payline), and others would be "undervalued" (i.e., below the male payline) just as they were overvalued and undervalued relative to the previous female payline, and just as some male-dominated jobs are overvalued and others undervalued relative to the male payline.

The **point-to-line** procedure, in contrast, would raise all the points around the female payline to the male payline. This would remove both the systematic differences as evidenced by differences in the heights of the paylines, as well as the random deviations that previously prevailed around the female payline. Random deviations for male jobs around the male payline would still prevail, unless it became a company policy to try to remove such random deviations. This would be hampered, however, by the fact that pay equity legislation invariably prohibits the wages in any job to be reduced as a result of pay equity, in which case male points above the male payline could not be brought down to the male payline.

Other adjustment procedures are also possible. A **point-to-point** procedure would raise the female point to the closest male comparator point (as is specified in the Ontario legislation). This would not require the estimation of paylines, but it would require decision rules for the choice of particular male comparators jobs. An average payline could be used that is an amalgam of the male and female lines, or a corridor approach could be used whereby the female payline is raised only to a lower boundary of the male payline. A single average adjustment could be calculated, with the same amount then allocated to each female-dominated job.

These are meant to be simply illustrative of the technical and administrative issues that can be associated with the implementation and design of pay equity. They can have a substantial impact on the magnitude of the awards that are made, and hence are likely to be subject to considerable debate if the policy becomes more extensively applied.

Equal Employment Opportunity Legislation

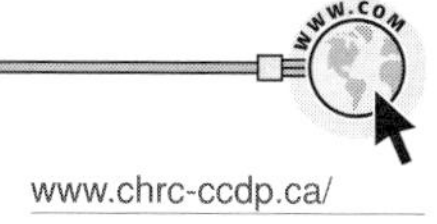

www.chrc-ccdp.ca/

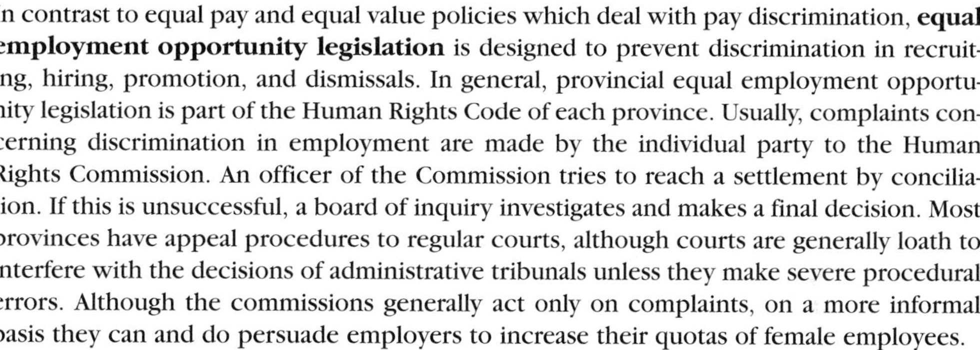

In contrast to equal pay and equal value policies which deal with pay discrimination, **equal employment opportunity legislation** is designed to prevent discrimination in recruiting, hiring, promotion, and dismissals. In general, provincial equal employment opportunity legislation is part of the Human Rights Code of each province. Usually, complaints concerning discrimination in employment are made by the individual party to the Human Rights Commission. An officer of the Commission tries to reach a settlement by conciliation. If this is unsuccessful, a board of inquiry investigates and makes a final decision. Most provinces have appeal procedures to regular courts, although courts are generally loath to interfere with the decisions of administrative tribunals unless they make severe procedural errors. Although the commissions generally act only on complaints, on a more informal basis they can and do persuade employers to increase their quotas of female employees.

In spite of the fact that this procedure is time-consuming and cumbersome, equal employment opportunity legislation does have the virtue of increasing the demand for female labour at the recruiting, hiring, and promotion stages. This, in turn, should increase female wages *and* employment. Unlike equal pay laws which increase female wages at the expense of their employment, equal employment opportunity legislation would work through the market to increase both the wages and employment of females. However, equal employment opportunity legislation is likely to be more beneficial to new recruits or women seeking to change their jobs; it may do little to help incumbent females in their existing jobs.

Some have argued that equal pay and equal employment legislation are complementary, in that one is useless without the other. The argument is that without equal employment opportunity legislation, equal pay would result in employers refusing to recruit, hire, and promote females. Similarly, without equal pay, equal employment opportunity legislation would result in employers hiring females but paying them lower wages than equally productive males. However, this ignores the economic argument that the increased demand for females resulting from equal employment opportunity legislation would work through the market to increase female wages. Equal pay may be a natural byproduct of equal employment opportunities.

Affirmative Action or Employment Equity

While equal employment opportunity legislation is designed to remove discriminatory barriers so as to ensure an equality of *opportunity*, affirmative action is a more intrusive form of intervention, focusing on *results* and not just opportunities. The rationale is that an equality of opportunity is insufficient to compensate for the legacy of a cumulative history of discrimination as well as systemic discrimination that may be the unintended byproduct of certain personnel policies. True equality may require some preferential treatment for women, at least on a temporary basis, to ensure an equality of starting points. The hope is that temporary affirmative action programs may break the circle of entrapment whereby women are relegated to low-wage dead-end jobs, which in turn foster labour market behaviour that keeps them in such jobs.

Affirmative action legislation tends to be called **employment equity** legislation in Canada—a phrase coined by the 1984 Abella Commission—in part to differentiate it from the earlier U.S. initiatives which tended to be criticized on the grounds of requiring rigid quantitative quotas for the hiring of the target groups. In Canada, legislated employment equity currently exists only in the federal jurisdiction, which covers about 10 percent of the Canadian work force. It is embodied in the Employment Equity Act of 1986, amended in 1995 to also include the federal civil service. A separate employment equity program was also adopted in 1986 for federal contractors as part of a federal contract compliance program. Employment equity programs have also been adopted in particular cities or municipalities and can be utilized on a voluntary basis without being considered a form of reverse discrimination by the courts.

The federal programs were to apply to four designated groups which were identified by the Abella Commission as particularly susceptible to systemic discrimination. The four designated groups are: women, visible minorities, disabled persons, and Aboriginal people.

Employment equity essentially involves four steps.

- First, an internal audit is conducted within the firm, usually based on a survey, to determine the internal representation of the designated groups and their position within the firm.
- Second, this internal representation is compared to the external availability of these groups in the relevant external labour market, as given for example by census data.
- Third, targets or goals are established to achieve an internal representation of the designated groups that is similar to their availability in the relevant external labour market.
- Fourth, a plan and timetable for achieving these targets is established.

In the United States, affirmative action has a longer history. It is part of the federal contract compliance program under Executive Order 11246 of 1965, and subsequent orders. It can also be imposed by the courts as a form of redress under the general antidiscrimination legislation: Title VII, the Equal Employment Opportunity Provision, of the Civil Rights Act of 1964. When first instituted, affirmative action was targeted toward blacks, but in the 1970s it was also targeted toward women.

Policies to Facilitate Female Employment

In addition to the various direct policies such as equal pay and equal employment opportunities legislation, and affirmative action, there are a variety of policies that can indirectly affect the employment opportunities and wages of women. These could be labelled **facilitating policies**, in that they are generally designed to expand the range of choices open to women and hence to facilitate their participation in labour market activities in a nondiscriminatory fashion.

Currently, women tend to have the primary responsibility for household tasks, especially the raising of children. This may reflect historical tradition, comparative advantage (which itself may be historically determined), or discrimination within the household. Whatever the origin, this responsibility can create tensions over the equitable division of labour within the household when both parties engage in labour market work.

To minimize some of this tension, and to expand the employment opportunities available to women, facilitating policies have been suggested. Improved availability of daycare, flexible working hours, part-time jobs, and childbirth leaves are examples of such facilitating policies. In the interests of equality they would apply to males as well as females, so as to maximize the opportunities of households to allocate their labour among various market and nonmarket alternatives.

Certainly such policies are not without their costs, which could be substantial in some areas such as subsidized daycare. Consequently there is legitimate debate over the efficiency of such policies. What is less contentious, from the perspective of economics at least, is that at a minimum such facilitating policies be allowed to emerge in response to market demands. This may require, for example, that daycare expenses be tax-deductible or that quality regulations do not restrict excessively the availability of daycare. Or it may require that government policies not discourage flexible working arrangements by increasing quasi-fixed costs of employment which may encourage employers to utilize only a core of male workers.

To a large extent these institutional features—flexible hours, part-time jobs, child-care leaves and daycare arrangements—are emerging as endogenous responses to the increased labour market role of women. Their emergence, however, may be subject to impediments reflecting discrimination, government policies designed to achieve other objectives, or simply the slow operation of market forces subject to inertia and fixed costs.

Considerable debate emerges over the appropriate role of public policy in this area. Some would argue that such facilitating policies should be discouraged in order to preserve the traditional sex division of labour. Others argue that public policies should be neutral by simply removing impediments to the emergence of these facilitating policies. Others argue for a more active role—subsidized daycare, extended child-care leave—to compensate for discrimination elsewhere in the system, including past discrimination.

The role of **protectionist labour standards** policies takes on an interesting light in the context of policies designed to facilitate the labour market work of women. Such protectionist policies could include special provisions requiring employers to provide free transportation for women on night shifts, or prohibiting the employment of women in some specific occupations, or restrictions on the hours of work for females.[10] Some may argue that such protective devices would enable women to take on some jobs they would otherwise be reluctant to do. Most would argue that such protective devices simply protect male jobs by reducing the employment opportunities of females and by perpetuating the stereotype of women as in need of outside protection. If such protection is desirable, it should be provided to all workers, male and female, through labour standards laws or collective agreements.

This suggests another institutional arrangement for facilitating the labour market work of females—unionization. The rationale for increasing the role of women in unions is really twofold. The first is to have women share in the wage and job security gains that unions obtain for their members. In order to obtain these gains, it is not only necessary for women to unionize;[11] they must aspire to powerful positions within the union or at least ensure that their minority rights are guaranteed. The second rationale for increasing the role of women in unions is to ensure effective monitoring of equal pay, equal employment opportunities, and affirmative action.

Females may be more willing and able to press for equal pay and employment opportunities through the union both because the apparatus is available (shop steward, grievance procedure) and because reprisal by the company is less likely when the worker is protected by a union.

Alter Preferences and Attitudes

Economics traditionally regards tastes and preferences as exogenously given, and then inquires into what happens to the demand for something when such factors as relative prices and income change. In the area of sex discrimination, this is a legitimate inquiry. Equal pay and equal employment opportunity legislation can be viewed as policies designed to raise the "price" of discrimination to those who discriminate. The price in this

[10]The earliest labour standards laws in Canada had their origins in the Factory Acts of the 1890s, designed to "protect" women and children.

[11]Doiron and Riddell (1994), for example, provide evidence for Canada indicating that unions narrow the male-female wage gap because the union impact is greater for females than for males, but this is almost exactly offset by the fact that women tend to be less unionized.

case is the legal costs which include court costs and the expected fine. The contention is that raising the price of discrimination will reduce the quantity demanded.

In the area of discrimination, however, some have suggested the utilization of public policies designed to alter the basic tastes and preferences that give rise to discrimination, since tastes and preferences of employers, co-workers, and customers are an important source of discrimination. The dominant group, for example, may find it important to foster uniform preferences for discrimination and to punish nondiscriminators. Preferences are also shaped by the media, the education system, and the socioeconomic system in general. Preferences are not immutable over time, nor are they likely to be the same for all firms, employees, or customers. For this reason, many antidiscrimination policies are designed to alter basic tastes, preferences, and attitudes. Recent work in economics, for example, has emphasized **endogenous preferences** (i.e., understanding why and how preferences are formed) rather than simply taken them as exogenously given.

In practice, of course changing basic tastes and attitudes is a difficult task. Specific policies have been instituted and include: removal of sex stereotyping in schoolbooks, guidance programs, and television; provision of information on the labour market performance and attachment of females; and politicization of women to raise their own group awareness. The process will be slow, but many argue that the results at least will be long-lasting.

IMPACT OF POLICY INITIATIVES[12]

While there is considerable empirical evidence on the magnitude of the male-female wage differential and its determinants, there is much less evidence on the impact of various policy initiatives.

Conventional Equal Pay Policies

The Canadian evidence on the impact of equal pay policies is so far restricted to conventional equal pay policies which require equal pay for *equal work*, rather than the broader concept of work of equal value. Econometric studies in the area of equal pay for equal work have found those policies not to have had any impact on closing the male-female earnings gap (Gunderson, 1985). This lack of impact likely reflected the limited scope for such policies, since they could only deal with male-female wage differences within the same occupation and establishment, and such differences are unlikely to be very large compared to differences across occupations and establishments. As well, reliance on a complaints procedure may deter enforcement since individuals may be reluctant to complain.

In the United States, conventional equal pay policies are combined with equal employment opportunity initiatives under Title VII of the Civil Rights Act; therefore, the separate impact of equal pay is difficult to disentangle, especially because both should serve to raise the wages of women. The econometric studies of that legislation (reviewed in Gunderson, 1989) tends to find somewhat inconclusive results. Some studies find positive effects on the earnings of women, some find no effect, and when the effects are positive they tend to be small.

In contrast, more positive effects of equal pay policies are found in Britain (Zablaza and Tzannatos, 1985a, 1985b) where it was incorporated into the process of centralized collective bargaining that occurs in that country. This suggests that conventional equal pay policies may be more effective in reducing the earnings gap when it is incorporated by the private parties into more formal systems of centralized collective bargaining, rather than legislative systems relying on complaints in the more market-oriented decentralized systems of wage determination and collective bargaining that prevails in North America.

[12]Much of the evidence from this section is summarized in more detail in Gunderson (1989, 1995).

Exhibit 12.12 **Ignorance Is Bliss**

One of the ironies of pay equity settlements is that recipients of the awards often do not know why they received the pay adjustment. This occurs because employers prefer the employees to feel that they received a large wage increase that was voluntarily given by the employer rather than mandated by legislation. In unionized environments, the union also has an incentive to make it appear they bargained for the wage increase. In part for these reasons, Evans and Nelson (1989) found that in the substantial pay equity award that was made in Minnesota, fewer than half of the employees knew that their wage increase came from a pay equity settlement.

Affirmative Action

A number of econometric studies (reviewed in Altonji and Blank, 1999; Gunderson, 1989) have evaluated the impact of affirmative action under the federal contract compliance of Executive Order 11246 in the United States. That legislation did benefit the minority groups to which it was targeted—mainly black males in the earlier years of the program. Much of that benefit, however, came at the expense of losses to other minority groups—mainly white females—to which the program was not targeted in the earlier years. However, when the affirmative action programs began to be more targeted toward females, they too benefited from them. The legislative initiatives also tended to be more effective in an expanding growing economy than in a recession (Beller, 1982) and when it was aggressively enforced (Beller, 1982; Leonard, 1984, 1985; Osterman, 1982).

Comparable Worth and Pay Equity

The impact of comparable worth (pay equity) programs has also been analyzed in a number of studies, usually based on the application of the policy in a number of public sector jurisdictions in Canada and the United States.[13] Average wage adjustments of $3000 to $4000 per recipient are common, although there is considerable variability in the adjustments. However, such adjustments only occur in particular organizations and go to the portion of the work force that is in female-dominated jobs that are undervalued. (See Exhibit 12.13 for a discussion of the now famous federal pay equity case in Canada.) When the costs are amortized over the whole work force of the particular public sector, they are in the neighbourhood of 4 to 8 percent of payroll costs. Typically, in those public sector work forces, the ratio of female earnings to male earnings (in all public sector jobs, not just those that receive the adjustment) is around 0.78 before the comparable worth adjustment and 0.84 after the adjustment (but see Exhibit 12.14). This increase of 0.06 in the earnings ratio implies that comparable worth closes about one-third (i.e., 0.06/0.22) of the earnings gap of 0.22 (i.e., 1.00–0.78).

These estimates of the impact of comparable worth are based on particular public sector cases where the policy has been applied. They are also based on estimates of the gap

[13]The studies are reviewed in Gunderson and Riddell (1991) and Gunderson (1995), and some are discussed in Altonji and Blank (1999). The jurisdictions where the policy has been applied in the public sector include Manitoba, Ontario, Minnesota, Iowa, Michigan, Minnesota, Washington State, and the City of San Jose in California. For a discussion of the lack of knowledge of employees of the source of their pay equity adjustment see Exhibit 12.12.

Exhibit 12.13

www.psac.com

So It Took a Little While: The Federal Pay Equity Award

On December 19, 1984, the Public Service Alliance of Canada (the largest union of federal government employees) filed a pay equity complaint to the Canadian Human Rights Commission (responsible for handling federal human rights issues) against the Treasury Board of Canada (the employer of federal government employees). PSAC alleged that the predominantly female clerical and regulatory group was paid lower wages than the predominantly male program administration group even though their work was of equal value. This subsequently mushroomed into complaints filed on behalf of other female-dominated occupation groups. On July 29, 1998, the federal Human Rights Tribunal, in a 203-page decision based on 262 days of hearings, ruled in favour of PSAC, giving the parties one year to voluntarily agree to the specifics of the implementation procedure or it would be imposed by the Tribunal. The Treasury Board appealed to the Federal Court of Canada, but the appeal was rejected. The parties then came to an agreement on October 29, 1999—almost 15 years after the original complaint. Clearly, the mills of the gods grind slowly.

The settlement was for approximately $3.6 billion (most of which was back pay) affecting approximately 230,000 current and former federal employees, of which only about 54,000 were still working for the government at that time—many of the others were deceased. The awards occurred in such female-dominated jobs as clerks, secretaries, librarians, data processors, hospital workers, and education support staff. The settlement averaged over $15,000 per employee, by far the largest and most significant pay equity award in history.

The process involved 15 job evaluation committees evaluating 1700 jobs from nine female-dominated groups and 1407 jobs from 53 male-dominated groups. There was endless wrangling over issues such as gender bias in job evaluation as well as the appropriate wage adjustment procedure with phrases like "level to segment" comparisons and "female points to the weighted quadratic male composite line" being part of the debate.

For details of what has been appropriately named "A Pay Equity Saga" see Sulzner (2000).

within a particular public sector employer, and this gap of around 0.22 is only a little over half of the earnings gap that prevails in the economy as a whole. Simulations of the potential economy-wide impact of comparable worth in the United States have estimated that the policy would close at most 8 to 20 percent of the overall gap of 0.41 (Johnson and Solon, 1986) or 15 to 20 percent of the gap (Aldrich and Buchelle, 1986). The policy can only close a portion of the overall gap because much of the gap reflects the segregation of females into low-wage firms and industries, and comparable worth does not involve comparisons across different firms or industries.

The potentially limited impact of comparable worth in the wider labour market is confirmed with preliminary evidence from Ontario. Gunderson (1995) examines early evidence from surveys of firms, and finds that the pay adjustments were smaller on average in the private sector. These smaller settlements were reflected in much smaller changes in wage costs for private firms: 0.6 percent of payroll for large firms, versus 2.2 percent in the public sector. McDonald and Thornton (1998) also report that few females received pay equity adjustments in the private sector firms they surveyed in Ontario.

Exhibit 12.14

It Pays to Lobby

In 1985 the state of Iowa announced a pay equity award to its state employees that would have raised the ratio of female-to-male wages from 0.78 to 0.88, closing 44 percent of the male-female pay gap (Orazem and Mattilla, 1990). However, male-dominated union and professional groups lobbied for modifications to the award to enhance their own pay. Because of their pressure, the award was subsequently amended so that the ratio of female-to-male wages was only 0.83, with the award thereby closing only 22 percent as opposed to 44 percent of the pay gap. Clearly, in a public sector environment, where political factors can be important in setting pay in the first place, those same factors can influence any changes in pay. What the state gives, the state can take away.

These studies suggest that comparable worth would likely close about one-third of the pay gap within particular elements of the public sector. For the economy as a whole, it would likely close a smaller portion, perhaps 8 to 20 percent of the gap. This highlights the fact that the policy can close a substantial portion of the earnings gap, but most would remain even after a comprehensive application of the program.

An even more pessimistic view of the potential for pay equity legislation emerges from Baker and Fortin (2000) in their comprehensive analysis of Ontario pay equity legislation (Exhibit 12.15).

Employment Effects of Comparable Worth

As indicated in Exhibit 12.15, Baker and Fortin (2000) found only small employment effects of pay equity in Ontario, likely reflecting the fact that they found small or no wage effects.

Ehrenberg and Smith (1987) simulate the potential adverse employment that would result from the widespread application of comparable worth to the public sector in the United States. On the basis of the magnitude of the wage adjustments that occurred in a number of comparable worth cases in the United States, they assume that comparable worth would lead to a 20 percent increase in the wages of females in the state and local public sector. On the basis of existing estimates of the elasticity of demand for public sector labour, this in turn would yield an employment reduction of only 2 to 3 percent. These adverse employment effects are small because of the existing lack of substitutability between males and females in the public sector. Whether this would be true in the long run when there is sufficient time to substitute away from female-intensive activities remains an unanswered question. Aldrich and Buchelle (1986) also estimate that comparable-worth wage increases of 10 to 15 percent in the *private* sector would lead to employment reductions of about 3 percent. Kahn (1992) finds no adverse employment effects of comparable worth in the city of San Jose, California.

Orazem and Matilla (1998) indicate that paradoxically pay equity could increase the proportion of women in both female-dominated and male-dominated jobs. This occurs because the elasticity of labour supply is greater for females than for males in female-dominated jobs, and the opposite in male-dominated jobs. So when real wages increase in female-dominated jobs, females enter those jobs in proportionately larger numbers than males, making them even more female-dominated. When real wages decrease in male-dominated jobs, males disproportionately leave, making them less male-dominated.

Gregory and Duncan (1981) also estimate the employment effect that resulted from the Australian pay awards emanating from their wage tribunals, which set wages for the

Exhibit 12.15

A Comprehensive Evaluation of Ontario's Pay Equity

Baker and Fortin (2000) provide a comprehensive and systematic econometric analysis of the effect of Ontario's pay equity legislation as it applies to the private sector. Their study is particularly important because it is the first to comprehensively examine the impact of proactive (as opposed to complaints-based) pay equity in a decentralized, private-sector labour market. Their results are quite startling and will likely generate considerable controversy. Their findings indicate that the legislation had the following effects on wages and employment (actually wage and employment growth) and the wage gap:

- No substantial impact on women's wages in female-dominated jobs, in part because such jobs tend to be in the smaller firms where implementation and compliance is difficult
- A reduction in male wages in the female-dominated jobs
- A slight reduction in the male-female wage gap in female-dominated jobs, mainly because of the fall in male wages
- A reduction of female wages in the male-dominated jobs which tended to be in the larger firms where compliance was more prominent
- An increase in male wages in the male-dominated jobs
- An increase in the male-female wage gap in those male-dominated jobs as a result of the decreased female wages and increased male wages
- Overall, across all occupations, no substantial change in the male-female wage gap because the reduction in the gap in the female-dominated jobs was largely offset by the increase in the gap in the male-dominated jobs
- A small decrease in female employment in the larger firms where compliance is more likely
- A small increase in female employment in the smaller firms where compliance is less likely
- No substantial change in female employment as a result of these offsetting forces

The lack of any substantial impact of the legislation is attributed largely to the fact that compliance and enforcement is extremely difficult in the small firms that employ the majority of women. This in turn reflects a variety of factors:

- The high cost of implementing the legislation in small firms given the difficulty of amortizing the costs of job evaluation and consultants over a small number of employees
- The difficulty of finding male comparator jobs (or estimating male paylines) when there are few male employees
- The fact that female pay tends not to be substantially lower in female-dominated jobs

majority of the work force. Between 1972 and 1978 those awards led to an increase in the ratio of female to male wages from 0.774 to 0.933. This in turn led to a statistically significant but quantitatively small reduction in the growth of female employment relative to male employment. That is, female employment growth averaged 3.0 percent per year as opposed to the 4.5 percent that would have occurred without the substantial wage increase. Most of the reduced growth occurred in the manufacturing and service sector, not in the public sector where employment growth was relatively insensitive to the wage increases. While these various studies suggest either a small or nonexistent adverse employment effect from fairly substantial comparable worth wage increases, Killingsworth's (1990) results, based on data from Minnesota, California, and Australia, suggest otherwise. He tends to find that the long-run adverse employment effects are small (certainly relative to the normal growth of female employment), but this occurred because the long-run wage increases from comparable worth were small. If they had been larger, then the adverse employment effect would have been substantial because he estimates a very elastic demand for female labour. In essence, Killingsworth tends to find a small adverse employment effect because of a small wage effect combined with a large elasticity of demand for female labour. The other studies tended to find a small adverse employment effect because of a substantial wage effect but a small elasticity of demand for female labour. Clearly, more work is necessary to resolve the important differences in this area.

Summary

Although it is hazardous to draw a conclusion about the impact of the various policy initiatives from such a limited number of studies, some tentative generalizations can be made. The effect of equal pay and equal employment opportunity policies tends to be inconclusive, although there is some evidence that affirmative action policies in the United States have been effective for the target groups to which they have been applied. Comparable worth policies have reduced the earnings gap and resulted in considerable awards in the few situations where they have been applied, albeit on a comprehensive basis their scope will be limited by an inability to deal with the considerable portion of the wage gap that reflects the segregation of females into low-wage establishments and industries. The evidence on the adverse employment effects from comparable-worth adjustments tends to be inconclusive.

It should be kept in mind, however, that estimating the impact of such policy initiatives is extremely difficult, especially given the other dramatic changes that are occurring simultaneously in the female labour market. This is especially the case since the policy initiatives themselves may be a function of the policy problem they are designed to eliminate, and the initiatives may be related to other unobservable factors that are the true cause of the changes in labour market behaviour. Such problems are not unique to these policy initiatives; they apply to estimating the impact of almost any social program.

REVIEW QUESTIONS

1. "If females are paid a wage equal to their marginal productivity, then sex discrimination in the labour market does not exist." Discuss.
2. "Male-female wage differentials for equally productive workers will not persist in the long run because the forces of competition would remove these differentials." Discuss.
3. If we adjusted the gross male-female wage differential for all of the productivity-related factors that influence wages (e.g., education, experience, absenteeism, turnover, etc.) and found that the wage gap would be zero if males and females had the same productivity-related characteristics, would this indicate the absence of gender discrimination?
4. What impact would equal pay laws have on the wages and employment of female workers? What impact would equal employment opportunity laws (fair employment laws) have on the wages and employment of female workers?
5. For policy purposes does it matter if the reason for discrimination is prejudice,

erroneous information, or job security? Does it matter if the main source of discrimination is employers, co-workers, or customers?

6. Why might the wage gap be negligible for single never-married males and females? If it is negligible would this reflect the absence of discrimination?
7. Discuss reasons for the limited potential scope of pay equity legislation.
8. Would you expect the overall, unadjusted male-female pay gap to be increasing or decreasing over time, and why?
9. "Comparable worth" is akin to the elusive notion of a "just price," where the price is determined independent of the basic forces of demand (reflecting what people are will to pay for a service) and supply (reflecting what people are willing to accept to provide the service). Discuss.
10. Discuss the pros and cons of the following design or implementation features of comparable worth: (a) defining gender dominance as 60 percent as opposed to 70 percent of either sex; (b) constraining the male and female paylines to have the same slope as opposed to different slopes; (c) allowing projection of the male payline outside of the sample range of the data in cases where the female-dominated jobs otherwise have no male comparator groups; (d) following a point-to-line versus a line-to-line versus a point-to-point wage adjustment procedure.
11. Would you expect discrimination to be greater in the public sector or in the private sector, and why? Would you expect it to be greater in union or nonunion sectors, and why?
12. From your knowledge of the various components of the overall male-female wage, discuss the potential scope of the various possible policy initiatives.
13. In designing a viable equal value policy, what steps might you take to minimize any inherent conflict between administrative concepts of value (as implied by job evaluation procedures) and economic concepts of value (as implied by market-determined wages)?
14. Assume that you have used a job evaluation procedure to establish the point scores for a number of male-dominated jobs and a number of female-dominated jobs in your organization. Indicate how you would estimate a payline between point scores and pay for each of the predominantly male and predominantly female jobs. What is the appropriate functional form for such paylines? Should they each have an intercept? If the pay in the undervalued female-dominated jobs is to be adjusted, should the female payline be raised to the male payline (line-to-line adjustment) or should the pay in each female job be raised to the male payline (point-to-line adjustment), or to some other value such as an average line or the pay of the closest male job? Should interpolation of the paylines be allowed, within the sample range of the data? Should extrapolation of the paylines be allowed outside of the sample range of the data?

PROBLEMS

1. Suppose that a pay equity plan has just been put in place in your organization. The pay equity consulting firm did a job evaluation and assigned points to each of the male-dominated and female-dominated jobs. They then estimated the following male and female pay lines by ordinary least squares regression, where Y denotes annual earnings, P denotes job evaluation points, and the subscripts m and f denote male and female respectively:

$$Y_m = 5000 + 100P_m$$

$$Y_f = 4000 + 80P_f$$

______. 1998. Male-female supply to state government jobs and comparable worth. *JOLE* 16(1):95–121.

Paglin, M., and A. Rufolo. 1990. Heterogeneous human capital, occupational choice, and male-female earnings differentials. *JOLE* (January):123–44.

Pendakur, K., and R. Pendakur. 1998. The colour of money: Earnings differentials among ethnic groups in Canada. *CJE* 31(August):518–48

Phelps, E. 1972. The statistical theory of racism and sexism. *AER* 62 (September):659-61.

Reich, M. 1978. Who benefits from racism. *JHR* 13 (Fall):524-44.

Reitz, J., and R. Breton. 1994. *The Illusion of Difference: Realities of Ethnicity in Canada and the United States*. Toronto: C.D. Howe Institute.

Reitz, J. G., J. R. Frick, R. Calabrese, and G. C. Wagner. 1999. The institutional framework of ethnic employment disadvantage: A comparison of Germany and Canada. *Journal of Ethnic and Migration Studies* 25(3):397–443.

Robb, R. 1985. Equal pay policy. In *Towards Equity*. Ottawa: Supply and Services.

______. 1987. Equal pay for work of equal value. *CPP* 13 (December):445-61.

Roemer, J. 1979. Divide and conquer: micro-foundations of a Marxian theory of wage discrimination. *Bell Journal of Economics* 10 (Autumn):695-706.

Royalty, A. 1996. The effects of job turnover on the training of men and women. *ILRR* 49:506–21.

Sicherman, N. 1996. Gender differences in departures from a large firm. *ILRR* 49:484–505.

Simpson, W. 1990. Starting even? Job mobility and the wage gap between young single males and females. *Applied Economics* 22 (June):723-37.

Sorensen, E. 1986. Implementing comparable worth: a survey of recent job evaluation studies. *AER* 76 (May): 364-7.

______. 1987. Effect of comparable worth policies on earnings. *IR* 26 (Fall):227-39.

______. 1989. Measuring the pay disparity between typically female occupations and other jobs. *ILRR* 42 (July):624-39.

______. 1990. The crowding hypothesis and comparable worth. *JHR* 25 (Winter):55-89.

Stelcner, M., and N. Kyriazis. 1995. An empirical analysis of earnings among ethnic groups in Canada. *International Journal of Contemporary Sociology* 32 (April):41-79.

Sulzner, G. 2000. A pay equity saga: The Public Service Alliance of Canada vs. the Treasury Board of Canada Secretariat. *Journal of Collective Negotiations in the Public Sector* 29(2):89–122.

Ureta, M. 1992. The importance of lifetime jobs in the U.S. economy, revisited. *AER* 82 (March):322-35.

Viscusi, K. 1980. Sex differences in worker quitting. *R.E. Stats.* 62 (August):388-98.

Weiner, N., and M. Gunderson. 1990. *Pay Equity: Issues, Options and Experiences*. Toronto: Butterworth.

Wellington, A. 1993. Changes in the male/female wage gap (1976–85). *JHR* 28:383–411.

Willborn, S. 1986. *A Comparable Worth Primer*. Lexington: D.C. Heath.

Woring, M. 1988. *If Women Counted: A New Feminist Economics*. San Francisco: Harper and Row.

Zabalza, A., and Z. Tzannatos. 1985a. The effect of Britain's anti-discrimination legislation on relative pay and employment. *EJ* 95 (September, comments and reply *Economic Journal* 98 [September 1988] 812-43):79-99.

______. 1985b. *The Effects of Legislation in Female Employment and Wages*. Cambridge: Cambridge University Press.

Chapter Thirteen

Optimal Compensation Systems, Deferred Compensation, and Mandatory Retirement

Main Questions

- *In what ways might internal labour markets within firms differ from external labour markets outside firms? What are the implications for neoclassical supply and demand models?*
- *Why do wages rise with seniority? Does worker productivity rise continually over the life cycle?*
- *Why are superstars paid so much more than "average" performers, when the difference in their performance level may be relatively small?*
- *What is "mandatory retirement"? Does it represent age discrimination, or might it be an important feature of a well-functioning labour market?*
- *Why are the salaries of some CEOs and executives so very high and why has their pay relative to the pay of an average worker increased in recent years?*
- *Why does academic tenure exist?*
- *Under what circumstances would organizations match the offers of raiding firms?*

Many features of our compensation system in particular (and personnel policies in general) seem peculiar and inefficient. For example, promotion and pay are often based on seniority and not necessarily merit. Workers are often required to retire from specific jobs even though they could carry on many of the necessary functions. Certain individuals receive astronomical pay, certainly relative to what they would receive in their next-best alternative activity, even though they appear to be only slightly better performers than others. In many circumstances, pay seems to resemble a tournament prize rather than payment equal to the marginal revenue product of the employee to the firm. Retroactive cost of living adjustments are often made to the pensions of retired workers, even though neither the firm nor the incumbent employees have a formal obligation to the retired workers. In many circumstances wages appear to be in excess of the amount necessary to recruit and retain a viable work force to the firm.

To some, these examples are simply taken as illustrations of the fact that **internal labour markets** within the firm do not operate in the textbook fashion predicted by neoclassical supply and demand theory. They are regarded as inefficient pay practices or the results of constraints imposed by unions. In recent years, however, basic economic principles have been applied to help explain, in part at least, the existence of various institutional features of labour markets, including compensation systems. An efficiency rationale was sought to explain their survival value. This is part of the trend away from simply regarding these institutional features as exogenously given and analyzing their impact, and toward explaining these institutional features (i.e., to regard them as endogenous) using basic principles of economics.

Explaining the variation in the use of such workplace and human resource management practices over time and across different work environments is an important new area of research in labour economics. "The new economics of personnel" is the phrase often used to describe this area. Lazear (1995, 1998, and 1999) is generally considered the modern founder, placing that literature in the mainstream of neoclassical labour economics.[1] That literature also highlights the interrelationship of labour economics with practical issues of human resource management including compensation practices.

As will be illustrated in many of the subsequent examples and in the materials cited in the footnote to the previous paragraph, it is a literature that often relies on game theory dealing with "mechanism design issues" (in this case personnel practices) in a world of uncertainty, monitoring cost, and information asymmetries. This provides a significant "barrier to entry" for specialists in the field of personnel and human resource management, and hence there has been minimal interaction between such specialists and economists who work in this area. Hopefully such interaction will expand in the future—and in fact, students who read this chapter may be motivated to "arbitrage that gap." As stated by Gibbons (1998, p. 30): "Much of the best economics on this subject [economics of personnel] is still to come, and it will exhibit stronger connections both to broader literature on organizational economics and to other disciplines that study organizations." Examples of such efforts include Barron and Gjerde (1997), Drago and Garvey (1998), Kandel and Lazear (1992), Lazear (1991), Lindbeck (1997), and Main, O'Reilly, and Wade (1993), many of which deal with group norms and teamwork.

The new economics of personnel also suffers from a lack of data. This reflects in part the fact that conventional data sets focus understandably on easy-to-quantify measures such as labour force participation, hours of work, and wages. The measures that are more the

[1]Discussions, summaries, and reviews of some of that rapidly emerging literature are also given in Baker and Holmstrom (1995), Blakemore (1987), Gibbons (1998), Gibbons and Waldman (1998), Gunderson (2001), Holmstrom and Milgrom (1994), Malcomson (1998), Mitchell and Zaidi (1990), Parsons (1986), and Prendergast (1999).

focus of personnel economics, such as effort, motivation, bonuses, and individual performance, are often more difficult to quantify and hence not collected in conventional data sets. They are occasionally obtained from confidential, proprietary personnel records of firms, but this makes them more difficult to verify and replicate, and it focuses attention on large firms. Consequently, the literature in this area has often been theoretical—too many theories and too few facts (see Exhibit 13.1).

AGENCY THEORY AND EFFICIENCY WAGE THEORY

In many instances the theoretical framework that has been applied is part of what is termed **principal-agent theory.** That perspective deals with the problem of designing an **efficient contract** between the principal (employer) and the agent (employee) when there are incentives to cheat. The problems are particularly acute when **monitoring costs** are an issue or there is **asymmetric information** (i.e., one party has better information than the other and there is no incentive to reveal that information). In such circumstances the parties may try to design contracts that elicit "truth-telling" and that ensure incentive compatibility so that no party has an incentive to cheat on the contract.

In such circumstances the pay of workers need not equal their marginal revenue product to the firm at each and every point in time (a condition economists label the "spot" or "auction market"). Rather their *expected* pay would equal their expected productivity over their expected lifetime with the firm. Such circumstances are often characterized by explicit contracts like collective agreements that provide a degree of guarantee of the receipt of payment. Or they are often characterized by **implicit contracts** that rely largely upon reputation. Where reputation is weak, a compensating wage may be paid for the risk that the contract may be broken. Economists term such markets "contract" markets to highlight the long-term contract nature of the arrangements (Carmichael, 1989; Lazear, 1991).

The growing literature on efficient compensation systems is also related to the literature on **efficiency wages** (discussed previously, and in Chapter 18) which argues that wages may affect productivity as well as wages being paid according to the value of the marginal product of labour in the firm; that is, causality can run both ways. This efficiency wage literature has had a number of applications. The economic development literature has often emphasized the subsistence wage necessary for basic levels of nutrition. The Marxist literature has emphasized the subsistence wage necessary for the reproduction of the labour force. As will be discussed in the chapter on the impact of unions, much of the new literature on the impact of unions has emphasized that unions may arise in response to high wages (in addition to the conventional view that unions *cause* higher wages) and that such unions can have a positive influence on productivity. As discussed previously, one possible response to minimum wage legislation (or any other form of wage fixing) is for employers to be "shocked" into more efficient practices; again higher wages induce higher productivity. High pay also enables employers to hire from a queue of applicants and this may serve as a worker discipline device, making the cost of layoff high to the worker, especially if there is a pool of unemployed. The personnel literature, and many private personnel practices, has long recognized the potential efficiency gains of paying high wages (see Exhibit 13.2). Pay (and especially perceptions about the fairness of pay) has long been recognized in the personnel literature as potentially being able to affect productivity. In all of these examples the causality runs in the direction of pay affecting productivity. This supplements the conventional economic emphasis that pay is given in return for the value of the marginal product of labour to the firm. This two-way causality must be recognized in the design of any **optimal compensation system**.

Exhibit 13.1

Too Many Theories, Too Few Facts

The problem of lack of data to test the theoretical predictions of personnel economics has been recognized by many who work in the field. Here are some examples:

- "Most of the early work in personnel was theoretical. Primarily because of data shortcomings, research focussed on dreaming up theories that might explain the empirical regularities of human resource management" (Lazear, 1999, p. 200).
- "There are simply no easily accessible data bases with personnel data" (Prendergast, 1999, p. 56).
- And as indicated by the title of one review article: "Internal Labor Markets: Too Many Theories, Too Few Facts" (Baker and Holmstrum, 1995).

While they are rare, there are a growing number of studies that have utilized firm-level data sets linking individual measures of performance to the personnel practices of firms. These include:

- Ichniowski, Shaw, and Prennushi (1997), linking clusters of human resource practices in steel mills to productivity performance
- Kahn and Sherer (1990), linking contingent performance-based pay to managerial performance
- Baker, Gibbs, and Holmstrom (1994a, 1994b), linking compensation practices to performance

ECONOMICS OF SUPERSTARS

Optimal compensation systems must also consider the fact that the value of the marginal product of labour may reflect the size of the market as well as the contribution of an employee to the productivity of others. As emphasized by Rosen (1981) small differences in the skill input of certain individuals may get magnified incredibly in the value of the marginal product of the service consumed by the public or co-workers in certain circumstances. This could be the case, for example, in a collectively consumed consumption good like a concert or TV performance, where the size of the audience does not usually detract from the ability of others to watch. In such circumstances of a common demand, people are willing to pay to hear the best person because the additional price they have to pay to hear the best is shared among a large group of collective recipients. The additional *per person* cost of hearing the best person is small because it is shared among the large audience. Hence, "the best" person may command a **superstar** salary that is astronomical relative to the next-best person even though the superstar's ability or skill may only be marginally better than that of the next-best person. Small differences in skill get magnified into large differences in the value of the marginal product of the service when that service can be consumed by a large audience that can share the cost.

Similarly, if an individual can have a positive effect on the productivity of other workers in the job hierarchy then the value of the marginal product of that person's labour to the organization may be high, even if that positive effect is small for each person. A small

Exhibit 13.2

Do High Wages Pay for Themselves?

Ratt and Summers (1987) ask whether Henry Ford paid efficiency wages. On January 14, 1914, Henry Ford overnight doubled the going wage rate to $5 per day. As a result there were hugh queues of applicants, so much so that rioting developed and the lines of job applicants had to be controlled with fire hoses.

Worker performance and productivity improved dramatically. Within a year, turnover fell to one-eighth, absenteeism to one-quarter, and dismissals to one-tenth of their previous level.

Henry Ford touted the high-wage policy—it was termed profit sharing—as good business, rather than altruism. It certainly did have the effect of improving work effort and productivity, and it reduced the need for costly supervision. This raises the possibility that high wages may "pay for themselves," at least to a degree.

It is interesting to note that women and "girls" were excluded from eligibility for the $5 a day, largely on the grounds that they were not supporting a family. As well, a Sociological Department with 150 inspectors was established, with the power to exclude workers from eligibility if they engaged in excessive drinking, gambling, untidiness, and consumption of unwholesome food!

www.time.com/time/time100/builder/profile/ford3.html

positive effect on each person can cumulate to a large total effect when the number of affected persons in the organization is large. Hence, we may expect certain executives or talented individuals to receive a much larger salary than the next most talented individual, even though there may not be much difference in the skills of the two individuals. Small differences in skill get magnified into large differences in the value of an individual to an organization when those skills can improve the productivity of a large number of persons. The expansion of world markets through globalization and trade liberalization that has occurred in recent years may account for some of the astronomical increase in the pay of CEOs of large multinationals; their talent may now be spread over a world market of customers, employees, and suppliers. Even if the CEOs are only slightly more talented than the next-best person, that small additional talent is worth a huge amount to an organization if it affects thousands of employees, millions of customers, and thousands of suppliers. We would also expect such talented individuals to be drawn to large organizations where the benefits of their talents could be spread over larger numbers.

As pointed out by Rosen (1982), superstar salaries may also be necessary to ensure that the best persons get sorted into their best match or highest-valued use, especially if they have unique talents peculiar to an organization and other persons are not good substitutes. A huge salary may not be necessary to motivate such persons to work hard, but it may be necessary to ensure that their specific talents are matched with the right organization. This is especially the case when the effect of their talent gets spread over a large base of customers, employees and suppliers, as discussed previously.

SALARIES AS TOURNAMENT PRIZES

As pointed out in Lazear and Rosen (1981) and Rosen (1986), executive salaries often seem to resemble prizes for the winners of contests rather than compensation in return for the value of the marginal product of one's services. **Salaries as tournament prizes** are starkly illustrated in the situation of a company that has a number of vice-presidents, all of whom are of roughly comparable ability. However, the one who gets promoted, presumably on the basis of being the best, gets a huge increase in salary. The salary difference between the president and the vice-president seems to reflect a prize for winning a contest more than differences in ability or the value of the person to the organization. That is, the president is probably slightly more capable than the vice-president and yet the salary difference seems much more than the ability difference.

Such a compensation system may be efficient, however, if the organization is only able to *rank* its executives according to the relative value of their contribution to the organization. That is, the organization may be able to say that individual A is better than B who is better than C, and so forth. However, the organization is not able to assess the precise contribution of each individual or by how much the contribution of one individual exceeds that of another. If the organization is able to assess the productivity of the group, then it could pay individual wages equal to the *average* productivity of each person. However, this compensation system may not create much incentive to perform since the individual's pay would be based on the productivity of the group, not the individual. In fact, it may create perverse incentives for individuals, who themselves know that they have below-average productivity, to enter the group and get the average pay. This adverse selection procedure (a common problem in markets with asymmetric information) could lead to a situation where the bad workers drive out the good workers.

In order to create performance incentives in such markets, organizations may pay a top salary that resembles a prize to the winner in the group. Even if most are paid a wage equal to the average productivity of the group, there will be an incentive to perform in order to be promoted to win the prize. The organization can judge the winner in order to award the prize because, by assumption, the organization can rank individuals on the basis of their performance, even though it cannot gauge their individual productivity.

Such compensation in the form of prizes may be particularly important for senior persons who otherwise have few promotional opportunities left in their career. There may still be an incentive to perform if one of those promotions means the prize of a large salary increase.

Such compensation systems in the form of prizes can also create perverse incentive structures. For example, they may discourage cooperative behaviour since that could lead to one's competitor receiving the prize, unless of course the organization is able to identify and reward such "team players." Such compensation systems may even encourage individuals to disrupt the performance of their competitors for the prize so as to enhance their own probability of winning the prize. One can win a tournament by performing well, or by making one's opponents play poorly! Drago and Garvey (1998), for example, found that compensation schemes based on relative performance can discourage workers from sharing their tools with fellow workers. The firm is also limited in the extent to which it can use prizes since risk-averse individuals would not enter a contest for which the runner-ups (e.g., vice-presidents) would receive nothing. Hence, it must balance the needs to provide an incentive to win a large prize against the needs to guarantee some payment to get people to enter the contest.[2]

EFFICIENT PAY EQUALITY, TEAMS, AND EMPLOYEE COOPERATION

In establishing the pay structure within an organization, trade-offs are involved in determining the **optimal degree of inequality** of pay, as well as competitive and cooperative behaviour amongst employers.[3] Some dispersion of inequality of pay is necessary to

[2]Empirical evidence generally confirming predictions of tournament theory include Bognanno (2001), Drago and Garvey (1998), Ehrenberg and Bognanno (1990), Eriksson (1999), Hutchens (1987, 1989), Leonard (1990), and Main, O'Reilly, and Wade (1993).

[3]Much of the material in this section is based on Lazear (1989).

provide an incentive to perform well in order to advance up the hierarchy and perhaps ultimately reach the top. However, too much inequality or dispersion may be inefficient in that it can discourage cooperative behaviour and **teamwork** if only a few can rise to the top. It may even encourage sabotage to prevent your fellow employees, if they are competitors, from being promoted if that reduces your own chance of promotion. As well, a large degree of salary inequity may not be attractive to persons with a degree of risk-aversion, or who are motivated by concepts of fairness.

The challenge for compensation specialists and human resource managers is to establish the optimal degree of pay equality or salary compression to provide performance incentives and yet to encourage teamwork and cooperative behaviour if that is important. The optimal degree of pay equality likely differs across different situations. A greater degree of pay equality or salary compression will be efficient if workers affect each other's output; it is difficult to measure each individual's contribution to the team, and cooperative effort is important for team production. In such circumstances, cooperative behaviour and teamwork have a greater potential to enhance group productivity, while sabotage has a greater potential to do the opposite. In the extreme, a completely egalitarian pay structure may prevail, although this suffers from the **1/N problem** (see Exhibit 13.3).

Exhibit 13.3

The 1/N Problem: What Do Team-Based Compensation, Joint Publishing, and Restaurant Bills Have in Common?

In workplace teams (a growing phenomenon in the workplace), paying people on the basis of the average performance of team members is often advocated. This can make sense if it is difficult to measure individual performance, if team production is highly interrelated, and if cooperative team effort is to be encouraged. However, such an egalitarian compensation structure suffers from the "1/N problem. "Individuals only receive 1/N (i.e., the same share as everyone else) of the total results of the team effort. This can be a very small amount if the workplace team is large, providing little incentive to work hard and contribute to the team since hard workers would get the same as shirkers (Holmstrom, 1982). In small teams and partnerships, on the other hand, peer pressure can be brought to bear to deter shirking (Barron and Gjerde, 1997; Kandel and Lazear, 1992).

As an aside, the same issues apply to academics writing joint articles for publication. To the extent that they share equally in the credit, there may be a tendency to free-ride on the efforts of the others. This is mitigated somewhat by the fact that such free-riders will seldom be asked to continue as co-authors. If they do not do their share on one article, they can still make it up by doing more than their share on other articles, as long as this "inter-temporal substitution" averages out. When it does, the coalitions will be stable and continue over time. Of course, there can also be other reasons for coalitions changing (e.g., interests and comparative advantages may change).

At a more pragmatic level, the 1/N problem applies to the sharing of restaurant bills as well. If the bill is shared, each individual has an incentive to eat or drink too much and order the more expensive food and drinks, since they only pay 1/N of the cost of what they all eat and drink. (Of course, they may be constrained by the fact that they pay the individual cost of indigestion and a hangover!) As the group size increases, this problem becomes more severe since the individual actions are not as transparent. In contrast, in a small group that repeatedly eats together such transgressors may not be asked out too often.

Different pay incentive schemes also may be appropriate for different levels within an organization, as well as for different organizational structures. For example, at higher levels within an organization the potential for cooperative or sabotaging behaviour may be greater than at lower levels. As well, the types of persons who achieve those higher levels may be disproportionately "hawkish" and willing to engage in aggressive competitive behaviour. In such circumstances, it may be sensible to pay higher-level managers bonuses on the basis of individual or group output, rather than paying them on the basis of their relative performance. The latter could encourage noncooperative behaviour and even sabotage, on their own part as well as on the part of their peer with whom they compete.

Firms may also try to discourage noncooperative behaviour or sabotage by keeping such opposing contestants at arm's length, for example, by having them each head relatively autonomous separate business units. Selecting a president from "within" a company (i.e., **internal promotion**) also may be more feasible if that person is chosen from a group of vice-presidents who head autonomous units whose relative performance can be evaluated easily, and who cannot affect the relative performance of the other competing vice-presidents through noncooperative behaviour or sabotage. If such opportunistic behaviour is possible, then it may be necessary to choose a president from the "outside" (i.e., **external promotion**), though this may dilute the incentive of inside vice-presidents because of the reduced probability for internal promotion.

External promotion may also be necessary to prevent the internal contestants from colluding. That is, if the internal contestants know that one of them will be promoted and that this will be based on their relative performance, they may have an incentive to collude and not work hard (i.e., to avoid the "rat race"), since one of them will still be promoted. The individual incentive to "defect" or cheat is obvious, so the group will have to be able to discipline such "rate busters" who work hard! In such circumstances, the firm may promote (occasionally at least) from the outside so that they have a credible threat of promoting from the outside to discipline the internal contestants.[4]

The optimal degree of competition and cooperation amongst employees is also likely to differ across firms and individuals. Some firms may get higher output, more innovation, and better quality by fostering competition; others may do better by fostering cooperation amongst employees. Some workers may thrive on competition; others may be devoured by it and do their best work in a cooperative environment. In such circumstances it is incumbent upon human resource managers to appropriately "mix and match" such workers. Workers themselves cannot always be relied upon to sort themselves into their appropriate environment, since there may be an incentive for the more "hawkish" competitive employees to disguise that trait, enter the more "dovish" cooperative work environment, and then dominate that environment by their noncooperative behaviour. In such circumstances, it may be rational for human resource managers to use personality traits as a hiring criterion so as to appropriately mix and match employees on the basis of the importance of competitive versus cooperative behaviour.

These examples highlight the fact that human resource policies which at first glance may appear to be inefficient (e.g., an egalitarian wage policy, paying attention to personality in the hiring decision) may be efficient practices to encourage cooperative behaviour among employees. In essence, basic economic principles may be able to explain the existence of a variety of human resource practices and compensation policies, including egalitarian wage structures within a firm, personality as a criterion in hiring, the establishment of semi-autonomous business units, and promotion from within the firm as opposed to

[4]The pros and cons of external promotion versus internal promotion from within, are discussed, for example, in Baker, Gibbs, and Holmstrom (1994a, 1994b), Bognanno (2001), and Chan (1996) as well as references cited therein.

from the outside. Explaining the variation in the use of such practices across time and across different work environments is an important new area of research in labour economics. It also highlights the interrelationship of labour economics with practical issues of human resource management and compensation practices.

Up-or-Out Rules

Up-or-out rules are an example of a set of personnel practices that at first glance seem inefficient but that very well may have an efficiency rationale given imperfect and especially asymmetric information.[5] Under such rules employees are evaluated usually at a specified point in their career, and are either promoted (i.e., "up") or terminated (i.e., "out"). These rules are common in universities (where assistant professors come up for promotion and if they do not make the cut they are effectively terminated) and such rules are common in law firms where junior personnel either become a partner or leave. This appears to be an inefficient practice since it would seem more efficient to simply pay a lower wage to those with lower performance rather than losing them altogether. In other words, the rule seems to preclude normal market transactions or trades—lower wages for lower performance.

In a world of asymmetric information, however, when employers have better information on the value of the employee to them and on their true ability to pay, they have an incentive to not reveal that information and not promote the person to the higher-paying position. Up-or-out rules can encourage such information revelation, since employers are not given the low-cost option of not promoting good employees to the higher-paying job. If they bluff and argue that the employee is not a good performer or they cannot "afford" the employee they are compelled to terminate that person, and this imposes a cost on them if the employee in fact is a good performer. As is common in models of asymmetric information, the institutional rules are an information revelation mechanism designed to get the parties with the private information to reveal that information, by making the bluffing strategy costly to them.

Up-or-out rules can also serve a purpose when there are a relatively fixed number of junior, non-promoted slots in an organization. In such circumstances, the organization may want to use some of these slots to evaluate a potential new candidate. If a non-promoted employee continues to occupy a slot, they preclude that opportunity to bring in a new potential candidate. As stated by O'Flaherty and Siow (1992, p. 347): "If screening can be done only on the job, then the junior position has two roles. First, it is a direct factor of current production. Secondly, it allows the firm to observe the suitability of the junior employee for promotion to senior rank, thereby increasing future production. Even if a junior is capable in his current position, the firm may fire him in order to use his slot to observe another candidate with more promise for the senior rank."

Up-or-out rules can also exist in tournament-type compensation systems to deal with one of the disadvantages of tournament systems: they create losers as well as winners, and losers may be disgruntled employees if they remain. They may in fact try to sabotage the winner to indicate that a mistake was made. In contrast, if they leave they may have a strong incentive to perform well in their new job to indicate that a mistake was made. Revenge can be a strong motivator! In such circumstances where the employee may be a counterproductive performer if they remain but a very productive employee if they leave, up-or-out rules may well be efficient contracts.

Up-or-out rules can also compel managers to make hard decisions and not to simply "coast" and take the easy way out by retaining mediocre performers rather than termin-

[5]Up-or-out rules are discussed in Kahn and Huberman (1988), O'Flaherty and Siow (1992, 1995), and Waldman (1990).

ating that person.[6] Up-or-out rules compel the manager to make a more extreme decision—retain the person and promote him or her to a higher position, or terminate the person. The middle option of retaining them without a promotion is not possible.

While **tenure** at universities is an up-or-out rule that may exist for the reasons discussed above, it may also exist to provide job security so that senior employees have an incentive to hire new persons who are better than themselves (see Exhibit 13.4).

Raiding, Offer-Matching, and the Winner's Curse

Asymmetric information issues can also give rise to the problem of the **winner's curse** when organizations engage in **raiding** other organizations for top talent (Lazear, 1986). Because the person being raided has already been employed at the organization that is being raided, that organization presumably has better information on the person than the raiding organization does. In such circumstances, the organization being raided presumably would engage in **offer-matching** of the outside offer *if* the person were truly worth that amount, and they would not match the offer if the person were not worth that amount. The raiding organization then would only be successful for persons who were *not* worth their offer—hence, they would be subject to the "winner's curse."

There are, of course, mitigating circumstances that would alter that scenario, otherwise we would not expect to observe such raiding. Some individuals may be a better fit or match in the organization doing the raiding; hence, it would not make sense for the insti-

Exhibit 13.4

Why Is There Academic Tenure?

Historically, academic tenure was perceived to be necessary to ensure freedom of expression in the university environment. Other rationales have been offered, including the possibility that it encourages researchers to undertake potentially risky but innovative research projects, since unsuccessful projects will not lead to job loss.

Carmichael (1988) offers an alternative explanation in that such job security is necessary to provide an incentive for more senior professors to hire junior professors who are better than themselves. Without such job security, professors would be reluctant to hire their potential replacement.

Tenure is prominent in the academic field because the recruiting method is unusual in that the search and hiring decisions are done usually by the employees themselves (i.e., by professors). In a sense, the university can be thought of as a workers' cooperative, run by the workers themselves! In order to provide an incentive to hire the best young people, academics are granted the job security of tenure after meeting certain competency requirements, usually after about six years as an assistant professor.

Again, what appears to be an inefficient work rule may well be an efficient practice, given the policy of recruiting and hiring being done by professors themselves. On the other hand, it may also be a convenient rationale for those of us with tenure!

[6]Prendergast (1999, p. 30) cites evidence from the personnel literature of the tendency to compress evaluation ratings because of a reluctance to give poor "grades" to poor performers. This is also one of the reasons for compelling relative evaluations.

tution being raided to try to pay that "match-specific" offer. In such circumstances, raiding would ensure that individuals are allocated to their most valued use.

The raided institution may also not want to match the outside offer because that may engender disgruntlement among their existing personnel if they do not get a similar pay increase. In such circumstances, the disgruntled employees may devote their time and energy into obtaining outside offers (some of which may be productive activity, but some of which may be a diversion from their normal activity). Or they may alter their effort margin or work intensity if they have no intention of leaving.

It is also the case that in many situations the information on a person's productivity is generally well known; it is "public" and not private information possessed only by the institution being raided. Most university departments, for example, know their superstars as do other universities. Universities that raid other universities also generally know who are "good citizens" because they generate positive externalities within their departments. Most even know who are disruptive citizens because they generate negative externalities, though that information may not be so publicly known. In such circumstances, the raiding institution is not likely to be subject to the winner's curse.

Piece Rates

Under piece rates,[7] workers are paid on the basis of the output (number of "pieces") they produce. They have positive work incentive effects, because workers are rewarded directly for working harder and smarter, and hence producing more output. They also have positive sorting effects for firms, because piece-rate systems would attract good workers willing to work hard. Firms would not have to worry about supervising and monitoring worker inputs and hence would save on the costs of such monitoring.

Piece-rate systems, however, require that the output of the individual can be readily monitored so that payment can be based on that output. This can be costly and it can lead to disputes if the parties do not agree on the accuracy of the monitoring. As well, such systems are harder to sustain if the individual does not have a large degree of control over the output, perhaps because it is affected by the work of others, or by actions of the firm or by technological or other changes. A technological or other change that enables workers to produce twice as much output as before with no additional effort, will lead to a renegotiation of the piece rate (or price per unit of output), and this may be difficult to establish depending upon whether the change emanated from actions of the firm or it was truly an exogenous change. Individuals on piece-rate systems may also be reluctant to do other tasks that could benefit the organization but for which a piece rate is not paid (e.g., assist other employees, unless reciprocal favours are possible). As well, under piece-rate systems workers may not care about the quality of the product or service unless it is tied to other rewards or penalties.

Overall, piece-rate systems will be more effective when it is simple to measure and monitor the quantity and quality of the *output* produced, while the more conventional time rate systems will be more effective when it is easy to measure and monitor the quantity and quality of the *input* that is provided. In such circumstances, it is not surprising that the use of piece-rate systems vary considerably by the characteristics of the product or service market and by the nature of the workplace and production process.

Paarsch and Shearer (1997) provide empirical evidence on the incentive effects of piece-rate systems for tree planters in British Columbia—an industry suited for utilizing and evaluating piece rates because "planter output is easily observable on a daily basis" (p. 654). Specifically, other things equal, paying 1 cent more per seedling planted (on the basis of the average payment of 25 cents per seedling) increased average daily output by 67

[7]Piece rates are analyzed, for example, in Gibbons (1987) and Kraft (1991).

trees. They emphasize the importance of controlling for the endogeneity of the piece rate in that higher piece rates have to be paid in situations of difficult planting conditions; otherwise, workers will not work under piece rates. Without controlling for these planting conditions, higher piece rates led to lower output (where the lower output resulted from the difficult planting conditions) which would give the appearance of negative incentive effects—the opposite of what is predicted by theory. After controlling for the fact that higher piece rates have to be paid to compensate for the lower output associated with the more difficult planting conditions, the positive relationship between piece rates and productivity held, as predicted by the theory.

Lazear (2000) also provides evidence on the effect of shifting from hourly wages to piece rates in a large U.S. company that installed car windshields. The shift to piece rates increased productivity (output per worker) by about 44 percent. About half of this was due to the incentive effect of employees working harder because their effort was directly rewarded. The other half was due to "sorting": the least productive workers left the company, and more productive workers stayed or joined the company.

Perhaps somewhat surprisingly, piece rates also exist in the medical profession. Medical doctors are typically paid in one of three main ways, each creating a different incentive structure. *Fee for service* is essentially a piece-rate system in which the doctor is paid for each service unit performed. This can occur in market-based systems where patients or insurance carriers essentially pay for the services performed during a visit (e.g., in the United States). Or it can occur in regulated systems such as in Canada where the government sets the fee for the different services, but the number of services performed depends largely on the decisions of the patient and the doctor (though it is usually subject to some government monitoring with respect to the need for the services, and sometimes subject to regulations with respect to the maximum amount that can be earned from fees). This system encourages doctors to "work hard" since they are paid by the "piece" (i.e., the service they produce). But it runs the risk that they may cut quality since they are not paid directly for better-quality service, although patients may not return if they feel they are not getting quality service (to the extent that they can judge quality in this area). It also runs the risk that doctors may have an incentive to "churn" patients through the system, having them come back for repeat visits, follow-ups or—in the extreme—visits that are not necessary. If there are maximum limits on the amount doctors can earn from fees (or reductions on the fee paid after a certain limit is earned), it can create the incentive to rapidly move patients through the system until the maximum is earned, and then to do other activities. It is for these reason that the public provider often has to monitor the output—in this case the need for the service—and often has an incentive to introduce co-payments (shared by the patient) so that the patient has some monetary incentive not to abuse the system. Queues or waiting lists are often used to ration scarce services when prices are not used. Governments are also not able to know their costs in advance, although that is mitigated somewhat if there are caps on payments.

An alternative payment system for doctors is on the basis of *capitation* or the number of potential patients in the doctor's service area or roster (e.g., in Britain). In effect, the doctor is on a form of salary, although that salary is contingent on the number of patients they can be expected to serve based on their roster. In such circumstances, the doctor does not have a monetary incentive to see more patients or to provide quality service (or any service) since their pay is based on potential patients and not actual patients or actual services performed. They do have an incentive to try to get a roster of healthy patients or at least patients who will not come in for services. In this system, governments are able to know their costs in advance since it is essentially a form of salary.

A third payment system for doctors is on the basis of straight *salary* where their pay is independent of the number of potential or actual patients they see. Such systems exist in the health maintenance organizations (HMOs) in the United States and they can exist for doctors employed by companies or other organizations. While such doctors do not have a direct monetary incentive to "work hard," neither do they have an incentive to rush patients through the system or cut quality. As with the capitation system, governments are able to determine their costs in advance since it is essentially the salary.

Clearly difficult tradeoffs exist in trying to design an optimal compensation system that provides the best incentives in this important and costly area. As is typically the case in designing optimal compensation systems, those tradeoffs depend upon such things as difficulties of monitoring the output or the input, and on information asymmetries and the extent to which doctors and patients respond to monetary incentives in the system.

EXECUTIVE COMPENSATION

The issue of **executive compensation** has received increased attention and public scrutiny in recent years. Executive pay has increased relative to the average pay of workers, and it is much higher in the United States (where the attention has focused) in relation to other countries like Japan. Stories abound in the popular press of skyrocketing executive pay that has occurred in spite of the poor performance of their companies, suggesting that executive pay is not tied to performance.

The previous discussion of tournaments and superstars suggests that high executive salaries may be motivated in part by the need to pay "prizes" to the top persons, as a way to induce incentives amongst other executives so as to win the "tournament prize." Making sure that the top person gets the job is especially important for a top executive who is responsible for an extremely large organization. Correct decisions in these circumstances, for example, can have huge ramifications for the performance of large numbers of workers. In that vein, the incentive that is important is not the incentive for the executive to work hard or to acquire managerial skills, but rather it is to make sure that the executive with the right talent gets *matched* with the organization that needs and values that talent the most (Rosen, 1982). Paying a person a million dollars as opposed to half a million dollars a year is not likely to make her work any harder or be more productive. It may not even be necessary to have such a large "prize" to improve the incentives of potential candidates to be promoted and "win" the prize. However, it may be necessary to ensure that the appropriate person goes to the organization where her talent is valued most. Such organizations are likely to bid for that talent if they can identify it as being of particular use to their organization. This need to pay high salaries as prizes may be tempered by the negative ramifications of excessive inequality if, for example, it induces noncooperative behaviour or feelings of resentment if such high salaries violate norms of fairness.

Popular impressions to the contrary, the empirical evidence tends to suggest that the compensation of top executives *is* positively related to the performance of their firm but the pay-performance linkage is generally weak (Antle and Smith, 1986; Murphy, 1985; Jensen and Murphy, 1990; Zhou, 2000; and references in those studies). Whether this link is sufficiently strong to induce appropriate incentives, or is in fact unnecessarily and excessively strong, is subject to considerable controversy. It is also not clear that the underlying determinants of executive compensation have *changed* sufficiently in recent years to explain the rapid *increase* in their relative compensation that appears to have occurred.

The link between executive compensation and firm performance is complicated by the institutional arrangements whereby executive compensation is set. Executive compensation usually consists of a base salary and **stock options**—the latter of which provide an incentive for the CEO to improve the stock market value of their firm. Typically, the compensation process involves the board of directors approving the executive pay recommendation made by a compensation committee. The boards of directors may have an incentive to award high executive salaries because they themselves are usually executives, and they are often appointed by the CEO whose salary they are determining. Shareholders may not be able to provide an effective check because of the complexities of evaluating the magnitude of the compensation package. As a result of these institutional arrangements for setting executive pay, some reforms have focused on making the process more open to the scrutiny of shareholders to serve as an effective check.

DEFERRED WAGES

Evidence

Compensation often appears to be deferred in the sense that wages are above an individual's productivity for the more senior employees (Figure 13.1(a)). Alternatively stated, wages rise with seniority or experience, independently of the individual's productivity. Evidence on **deferred compensation** is reviewed in Lazear (1999) and Prendergast (1999).

The deferred wage aspect would be even larger when one considers the fact that pension accruals become important in the years just prior to retirement. That is, for every additional year an individual works, that individual experiences not only a wage increase but also pension increments that are a cost to the employer but a compensation benefit to employees. Pension benefits themselves also can be considered part of the deferred compensation package (Lazear, 1990; Pesando and Gunderson, 1988; Pesando, Gunderson, and Shum, 1992).

Associated Characteristics

Obviously such deferred compensation systems will exist only in situations where there is some long-term commitment on the part of the firm to continue the contracted arrangements. Otherwise the firm has an incentive to dismiss employees at the time when the workers' pay begins to exceed their productivity (at the point of intersection, S_B, of the pay and productivity schedules of Figure 13.1(a)). Firms that engaged in such opportunistic behaviour, however, would develop a bad reputation and have to pay a higher regular compensating wage in return for the risk that employees may not receive their deferred wage.

Of course, firms that find themselves with an aging work force with accumulated seniority and few younger workers (perhaps because of a decline in their hiring due to a decline in their product demand), may find it "profitable" to declare bankruptcy and hence sever their deferred wage obligations, especially if they can relocate elsewhere and hire younger workers at a wage less than their productivity. Obviously, if this were known by the new recruits, then a compensating wage would be required for accepting employment in a firm that deliberately restructured to avoid its deferred compensation obligations. However, the true rationale for such bankruptcy can be difficult to detect, especially in situations of asymmetric information where the firm has more information than employees on the true profitability of the firm. As well, with "footloose capital" and the ability to relocate plants throughout the world, firms may have less need to worry about their reputation if they close plants in one country and reopen in another.

Given the fact that firms have a short-run incentive to renege on the deferred wage obligation when that obligation becomes due, such a compensation system will prevail only when there are certain checks and balances to ensure that the deferred compensation is paid. Such checks and balances include the reputation of the firm, the payment of wages related to seniority, legal protection against unjust dismissal, and the fact that unions can provide a degree of "due process" to ensure that their members are not arbitrarily dismissed. These checks and balances are characteristic of the longer-term "contract market," where a longer-term employment relationship is expected, rather than the "spot" or "auction" market, where wages would equal the workers' productivity at each and every point in time (Figure 13.1(b)).

Figure 13.1 **Wage Productivity Profiles**

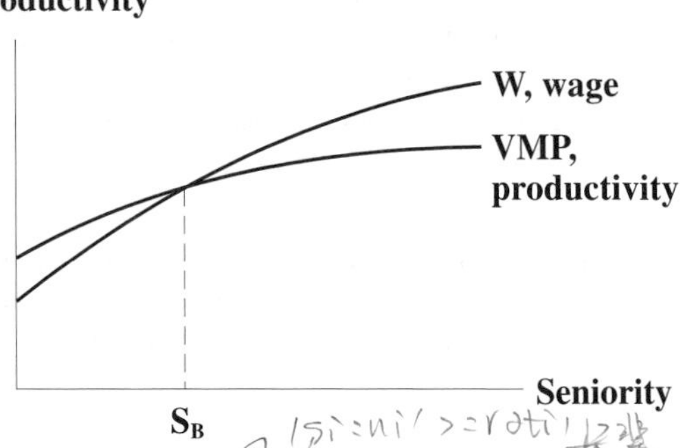

(a) Deferred wages contract market

Productivity or the value of marginal productivity is assumed to rise with seniority, though tapering off at higher level of seniority. Wages start off below the individual's productivity profile (indicating underpayment relative to productivity) but they rise more rapidly than productivity, eventually reaching a breakeven point, and then being above productivity at the higher levels of seniority (indicating overpayment relative to productivity).

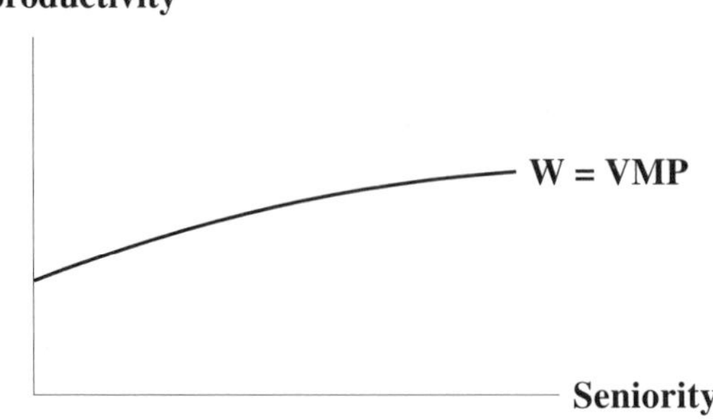

(b) Spot market

Wages are equal to productivity at each and every level of seniority; that is, workers are always paid the value of their marginal product.

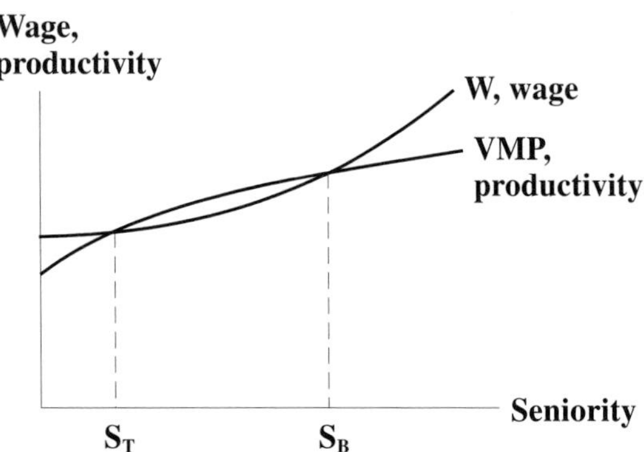

(c) Deferred wages with company-specific training

Wages are above the individual's productivity during the initial period up to S_t while they receive company-specific training. The sponsoring company benefits by that training (since it is usable only in that company) and hence it "pays" for the training, by accepting the fact that the worker will have lower productivity during that training period. Thereafter a deferred wage profile prevails.

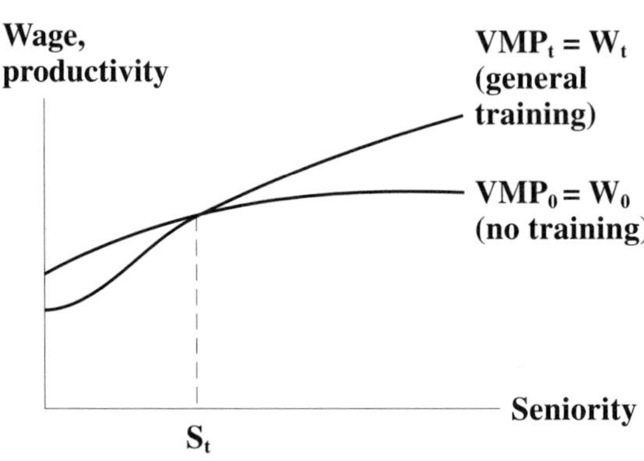

(d) General training

Wages are considerably below productivity in the initial period up to S_t, not only because of the deferred wage but also because the trainee is "paying" for the general training by accepting a lower wage during the training period. Trainees pay for the general training because they benefit by it; other firms will bid for their services since the training is generally usable in a wide range of organizations.

Rationales for Deferred Compensation

Such deferred compensation systems may serve a number of important functions and hence have an efficiency rationale. As emphasized by Lazear (1979, 1981), they may ensure honesty and work effort because the worker wants to stay with the company to get the deferred wage. It is like the worker posting a bond (equal to the excess of the worker's productivity over wages when young) that will be returned (in the form of wages in excess of productivity) when the worker has accumulated seniority with the firm. The returning of the bond (deferred compensation) will be done conditional upon the worker having performed satisfactorily after a period over which past performance can be observed. Workers whose performance has not been satisfactory can be dismissed, subject to the checks and balances discussed previously. The greater honesty and work effort that results from such a system enhances productivity and hence provides the means for such workers to receive greater compensation over their expected work life.

Such a compensation system also reduces the need for constant everyday monitoring of the productivity of workers. With deferred wages monitoring can be made on a periodic, retrospective basis (i.e., examining past performance) with the worker being promoted and hence receiving the deferred wage conditional upon satisfactory performance (again subject to the previously discussed checks and balances). In contrast, under the spot market system (Figure 13.1(b)), where wages are equal to productivity at each and every point in time, productivity and performance must be assessed or known on a regular basis in order to compensate accordingly. The paradigm of the spot market is the piece-rate system, where payment is made directly according to output—a system that can exist only where output is easily measured (e.g., sales, logs cut, buttons sewn).

Deferred wages may also reduce unwanted turnover and hence enable firms to recoup their quasi-fixed hiring and training costs that are usually incurred early in the employee's career with the company. Such costs to the firm are illustrated in Figure 13.1(c), by the area above the value-of-marginal product, VMP, line and below the wage line. In order to recoup these costs and amortize them over a longer work life of their employees, firms may want to defer compensation in order to provide employees with an incentive to stay with the firm.

The training here is *company-specific* in the sense that it is usable mainly in the company providing the training. As discussed in the previous chapter on human capital theory, if the training were *generally usable* in other firms then the employee would have the incentive to pay for the training, often in the form of accepting a lower wage during the training program. In this case the trainee's productivity and wage during training ($VMP_t = W_t$ in Figure 13.1(d)) would fall below what their productivity and wage would have been in the absence of training ($VMP_0 = W_0$). After the training period, the employee's productivity would increase and, since general training is usable anywhere, so would the trainee's wage (i.e., $VMP_t = W_t$ and both lie above $VMP_0 = W_0$ in the post-training period). In the case of general training, where the employee bore the cost of accepting a lower wage during the training period, the company would not have incurred any quasi-fixed costs, and hence would have no incentive to pay a deferred wage, at least for that reason. In such circumstances the wage profile would equal the productivity profile (i.e., $W_t = VMP_t$) as in a spot market. If deferred wages were desirable for other reasons, then they could be superimposed upon the general-training wage profile.

Deferred wages may also exist so as to provide workers with a financial interest in the solvency of the firm. Under the pure spot market of Figure 13.1(b), except for the transactions costs of finding a new job, the employee would be indifferent as to whether the firm went bankrupt since employees would get a wage equal to their productivity elsewhere. With deferred wages, as in Figure 13.1(a), however, the employee stands to lose the deferred wage portion if the firm goes bankrupt. Thus deferred wages, including pension obligations, provide employees with an interest in the financial solvency of the firm. The loss of deferred wages, for example, may be one reason for the larger income losses that are incurred by older workers when they lose their jobs and are displaced to their next-best-alternative employment.

Deferred wages may discourage "bad" workers ("lemons") from applying for such jobs since information on their productivity will be revealed over time. This gets around the asymmetric information problem emanating from the fact that potential employees have better information than firms about such factors as their motivation, commitment, and willingness to work hard.

Public sector employers may prefer deferred wages because this arrangement passes costs to future generations of taxpayers, the only check being the willingness of the future generations to honour these commitments. Such deferred compensation may come in the form of more liberal pension benefits or greater job security so that one's *expected* wage (i.e., wage times the probability of receiving the wage) is higher. Deferred wages may also be legitimately needed more in the public than private sector to the extent that honesty is more important in the public sector and to the extent that monitoring and the measurement of current output is more difficult.

Deferred wages may also be preferred by employees since they facilitate the synchronization of income and expenditures over the life cycle. That is, the shortfall of wages below productivity for junior people can be regarded as a form of forced savings, paid out later in the form of wages in excess of productivity in later years (Exhibit 13.5). Whether this corresponds to their years of greatest expenditure needs and whether saving in the form of deferred wages is better than private saving through capital markets is an open question. Deferred wages may also correspond to a sense of equity and fairness to employees so that they receive wage increases commensurate with seniority, even if their productivity does not increase or even declines. As well, if deferred wages have positive efficiency effects, employees may share in those gains by having higher wages over their life cycle.

Clearly there are a variety of possible rationales for deferred wages that can confer mutual benefits on both employers and employees. Even when the initial benefits would go mainly to employers (e.g., increased work incentives, reduced monitoring costs, reduced unwanted turnover) such benefits would provide the means for them to compensate employees for any adverse effects of deferred wages. Employees could be compensated in

Exhibit 13.5

Do Workers Also Prefer Deferred Wages?

While there are good reasons why *employers* prefer deferred wages (i.e., rising wage profiles), it is less obvious why *workers* should also prefer them. This is especially the case since having a positive discount rate, given the uncertainties of the future, implies that people should discount the future and hence not prefer to give up current wages in return for future wages.

Loewenstein and Sicherman (1991) surveyed individuals and found that they actually *preferred* the rising wage profiles. They maintained this preference even when they were told that they could have higher lifetime income by having the money sooner and investing it.

This "irrational" preference may occur as people regard deferred wages as a form of forced saving or because they get satisfaction from anticipating future consumption. Whatever the reason, individuals seem to prefer to give up current wages in return for future wages. For that reason they would willingly accept deferred wage profiles, which are also preferred by employers.

the form of a higher lifetime wage profile and more job security. As mentioned previously, employees may also benefit from the lifetime employment aspects of the contract market, from the periodic rather than everyday monitoring, from the due process and seniority rules that provide security to ensure that deferred wages are paid, and from the possible synchronizing of income and expenditures and the sense of equity and fairness that may be associated with wages based on seniority.

RATIONALE FOR MANDATORY RETIREMENT

To Enable Deferred Wages

While there clearly can be efficiency and equity reasons for deferred wages to exist, such a contractual arrangement requires a termination date for it to exist. Otherwise, employers run the risk of paying wages in excess of productivity for an indefinite period (as illustrated in Figure 13.1(a)). In such circumstances a contractual arrangement involving deferred wages could not persist.

Lazear (1979) argues that **mandatory retirement** provides the termination date for such contractual arrangements with deferred wages, and he provides empirical evidence indicating that mandatory retirement provisions are more prevalent in situations of deferred wages. The mandatory retirement date, MR in Figure 13.2, provides an equilibrium condition, enabling the expected present value of the wage stream to be equal to the expected present value of the productivity stream to the firm. Without that termination date to the existing contractual arrangement it would be difficult or impossible for the deferred wage contract to exist, since the firm would be paying a wage in excess of productivity for an indefinite period. Mandatory retirement is the institutional rule that gives finality to the existing contractual arrangement. Viewed in this light, it is an endogenous institutional feature of labour markets that arises for efficiency reasons to allow deferred compensation systems to exist; it is not an exogenously imposed constraint, as is often perceived.

As discussed in the earlier chapter on retirement, the phrase "mandatory retirement" is somewhat of a misnomer since it does not mean that the person is required to retire from the *labour force*. It means that the existing contractual arrangement is now terminated, and the employee must renegotiate an alternative arrangement with another employer or with the same employer (the latter being possible under compulsory but not automatic retirement). Presumably any new arrangement would be for a wage commensurate with the worker's productivity and this may involve a substantial wage drop since deferred

Figure 13.2 Mandatory Retirement Age

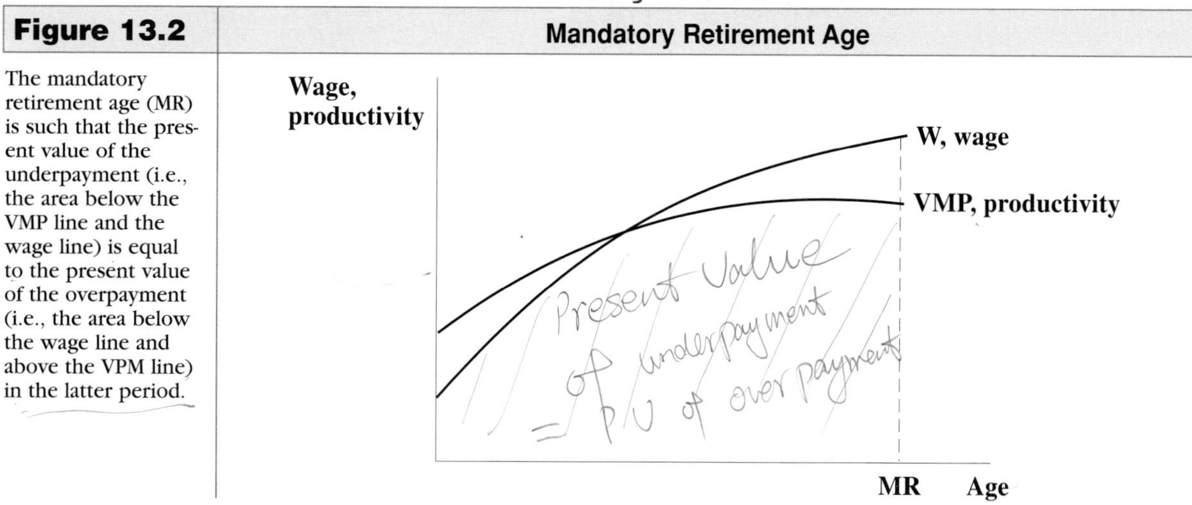

The mandatory retirement age (MR) is such that the present value of the underpayment (i.e., the area below the VMP line and the wage line) is equal to the present value of the overpayment (i.e., the area below the wage line and above the VPM line) in the latter period.

wages no longer would be paid. The wage drop need not reflect a decline of productivity with age; rather it occurs because deferred wages are in excess of productivity for senior employees (in return for wages being below productivity in their early years with the company). In fact, this emphasizes that mandatory retirement need not exist because productivity (correctly or incorrectly) is perceived to decline with age. The appropriate response to such a phenomenon, if it existed, would be wage reductions, rather than requiring that the person must leave the job. Mandatory retirement could be an efficient compensation rule even if productivity continues to increase throughout a worker's working life (as it in fact does in the diagram).

Other Possible Rationales for Mandatory Retirement

In addition to enabling a deferred wage compensation system, other possible rationales may exist for mandatory retirement. It may facilitate worksharing by opening up promotion and employment opportunities for younger workers. While this may be true in particular firms and industries, as indicated in our previous discussion of worksharing, caution should be used in applying this argument to the economy as a whole so as to avoid the "lump-of-labour fallacy." That is, there need not be a fixed number of jobs in the economy so that the job held by an older worker would mean that a younger worker would not have a job. The younger worker may not have that *particular job*, but by working longer the older worker may be generating other jobs through increased consumption expenditures and through affecting wage levels.

Mandatory retirement may also create a greater degree of certainty about when an employee will retire from a particular job. For employers, this may facilitate planning for new staffing requirements, pension obligations, and medical and health expenditures, the last of which can be quite high for older workers. For workers, the advent of mandatory retirement may encourage pre-retirement planning and preparation of eventual retirement, preparation they may otherwise postpone indefinitely if the retirement date were not fixed. Retirement may also be facilitated by the fact that pensions, as a form of deferred compensation, are prominent in situations of mandatory retirement.

Mandatory retirement also reduces the need for the monitoring and evaluation of older workers and it enables them to "retire with dignity" since they are retiring because of a common retirement rule, not because they are singled out for incompetence. Less productive workers can be "carried" to the retirement age by employers or co-workers because that may be a short period and it is known with certainty. In contrast, without mandatory retirement, the performance of older workers will have to be monitored and evaluated, and dismissals may occur more frequently.

Arguments Against Mandatory Retirement

The arguments against mandatory retirement tend to rest on human rights issues, with mandatory retirement being regarded as a form of age discrimination (see Exhibit 13.6). The appearance of age discrimination is further enhanced by the fact that employment standards or human rights legislation often has an age limit, not covering workers who are 65 years of age and older. The rationale for this age limit beyond which protection does not apply is to accommodate mandatory retirement, but by doing so it effectively precludes protection from age discrimination for persons beyond age 65. This apparent sanctioning of mandatory retirement provisions certainly makes the provisions look like a form of age discrimination. Stereotypes that give rise to discrimination are likely to be as prominent against older workers as against women, racial groups, or any other visible minorities.

Even if certain rules may be efficient, they may not be socially justifiable if they discriminate against individuals. Thus even if mandatory retirement creates certainty for employers and employees, and it facilitates retirement with dignity, if this occurs at the

Exhibit 13.6

Do Age Discrimination Laws Facilitate Deferred Compensation Even Though They Ban Mandatory Retirement?

When mandatory retirement is banned, it is done through age discrimination legislation that prohibits mandatory retirement. If mandatory retirement exists in part to facilitate deferred compensation schemes (by providing a termination date to such arrangements as those discussed in the text) this would suggest that age discrimination laws, by prohibiting mandatory retirement, would reduce the extent of deferred compensation schemes. This can be termed a "banning of mandatory retirement" effect whereby banning mandatory retirement reduces the likelihood of deferred compensation.

Neumark and Stock (1999), however, indicate that age discrimination laws may provide a degree of employment security and protection to older workers who may be receiving deferred wages. They may protect older workers from employers who may behave opportunistically and lay off or fire workers when they begin to receive their deferred wage (whereby their wage begins to exceed their productivity). By providing this "protection effect" age discrimination laws may facilitate deferred wages even though they ban mandatory retirement. Neumark and Stock suggest that the age discrimination "protection" effect that would facilitate deferred wages is likely to dominate the "banning of mandatory retirement" effect that would discourage deferred wages because firms could use subsidy and penalty features of their pension plans to substitute for mandatory retirement. That is, they could reduce pension benefits for those who carried on working if mandatory retirement were banned and this would discourage continued employment with the firm.

Neumark and Stock exploit the cross-section variation in the extent of age discrimination legislation across different states in the United States to estimate the impact of age discrimination legislation on deferred compensation. They find that age discrimination legislation facilitated deferred compensation even though it banned mandatory retirement. In essence, the positive effect of age discrimination legislation in "protecting" deferred wages for older employees dominated the negative "banning of mandatory retirement" effect on deferred wages.

It is possible, however, to have age discrimination legislation and to still allow mandatory retirement (e.g., to exempt it as not constituting age discrimination if, for example, there is the protection of a collective agreement and/or an employer pension plan). In such circumstances, deferred wages should be facilitated both by the protection of age discrimination and by the existence of mandatory retirement that terminates the deferred compensation arrangement.

expense of some who want to continue working, and are capable of working, it still may be regarded as discriminatory against those individuals.

The abolition of mandatory retirement has also been supported on the grounds of improving the viability of public and private pensions, a growing concern as the aging population puts increasing pressure on pension obligations at the same time as a declining work force provides fewer persons paying into pension funds. If workers continue to work beyond what was the former retirement age they will be less of a drain on pensions. Of course, this argument assumes that those who continue to work will not draw full pension income, an assumption that is seldom explicitly stated. In fact, many unions tend to be concerned that banning mandatory retirement is simply a veiled excuse to reduce private and public pension obligations.

A Middle Ground

Given the pros and cons of mandatory retirement it is not surprising that the debate over banning mandatory retirement is conducted at an emotive level. The real question, however, is: To what extent should legislation ban parties from entering into contractual arrangements (like mandatory retirement) that inhibit their freedom at some time in the future, presumably in return for other benefits such as job and promotion opportunities when they are younger, pensions when they retire, and the benefits of a deferred compensation scheme? Clearly legislation sanctions some contracts like marriage contracts and loan contracts that can inhibit freedom at certain points in time, presumably because of the other benefits they bring. Yet the state does forbid other contracts like indentured service or separate pay or promotion lines for females or racial groups, even if the individuals themselves are willing to enter into such contractual arrangements. Not all contractual arrangements are sanctioned by the state, especially if people can be misinformed or if they can be exploited because of a weak bargaining position.

One possible solution to prevent the worst abuses of mandatory retirement and yet to preserve its benefits would be to remove the age ceiling on antidiscrimination legislation but to exempt bona fide collective agreements or employees covered by a bona fide pension plan. This would enable people to enter into arrangements involving mandatory retirement if they had the protection of a union. Presumably the union would be informed of the tradeoffs involved and it would represent the interests of its older workers, because all of its members could expect to become older and subject to any constraints like mandatory retirement. Exempting employees covered by a bona fide pension plan would ensure that when workers become subject to the mandatory retirement constraint, they would retire with an adequate pension.

Such exemptions, however, would allow mandatory retirement to continue much in its present form since most workers who are currently subject to mandatory retirement are also protected by a collective agreement and/or a pension plan. However, it would prevent potential abuse by the employer who engages in age discrimination or who requires mandatory retirement but does not provide a pension.

Impact of Banning Mandatory Retirement

www.eeoc.gov/laws/adea.html

In the United States, mandatory retirement was effectively banned through the 1986 amendments to the Age Discrimination in Employment Act, although there were some exemptions including one for university professors (an exemption which expired in 1994). In Canada, the legal status of mandatory retirement is more complicated. It is allowed in provinces that have an age limit of 65 in their human rights code (with that limit existing to allow mandatory retirement) or if being under a certain age is considered a *bona fide occupational qualification* (BFOQ) necessary to perform the job. Supreme Court decisions in Canada have also generally upheld mandatory retirement provisions (Gunderson, 2001).

In the United States, earlier studies had suggested that the banning of mandatory retirement would not have a large effect on the continued employment of older workers, since most wanted to retire at or around the mandatory retirement age in large part because penalties in the public and private pension system would discourage older workers from continuing on in employment (Burkhauser and Quinn, 1983). More recent evidence from Neumark and Stock (1999, p. 1109) also indicate that banning mandatory retirement had little effect on postponing retirement, although they suggest that this may reflect limitations of their data. On the basis of better data (albeit data limited to only university professors) Ashenfelter and Card (2000) provide evidence that suggests that banning mandatory retirement has had a substantial effect on delaying the retirement of university faculty in the United States, the effect being largest at private research institutions where teaching loads are lowest.

While research on the effect that banning mandatory retirement will have on the continued employment of older workers is scant (and not in agreement), there is virtually a complete absence of research on the impact that banning retirement will have on other aspects of the employment relationship. On the basis of the theoretical reasons for the existence of mandatory retirement in the first place, Gunderson (1983) outlined the *expected* impact a legislative ban on mandatory retirement would have on various aspects of the employment relationship.

To the extent that deferred compensation is no longer as feasible, then the wages of younger workers will rise and the wages of older workers with more seniority will fall, as wage profiles will now have to more closely approximate productivity profiles (i.e., the profiles will be more like Figure 13.1(b) than 13.1(a)). The wages of older workers may drop quite substantially to compensate for any increase in age-related fringe benefit costs like medical and disability insurance. Those adjustments, in turn, may bring charges of age discrimination in pay practices. Until such wage adjustments occur, however, older workers may receive substantial "windfall gains" from the abolition of mandatory retirement, as their wages could now exceed their productivity for an indefinite period of time (i.e., beyond MR in Figure 13.2).

Not only will the wage profile "tilt" downward toward the productivity profile but the whole productivity profile and wage profile will drop to the extent that productivity was enhanced by the deferred wage system, for example, because of enhanced work incentives and reduced monitoring. New efforts will also be made to restore the deferred wage system in a fashion that does not rely upon mandatory retirement for its existence. For example, periodic bonuses may be more prominent. If deferred wages are continued, employee voluntary buyouts or "golden handshakes" may become more prominent to encourage voluntary retirement. Actuarial reductions in pension benefits may also be used to encourage people to voluntarily retire. Pensions themselves may become less prominent to the extent that they were a part of the deferred compensation scheme.

Monitoring and evaluation of workers will likely increase to the extent that it is less feasible to use periodic evaluations based upon past performance. In addition, it will be more necessary to detect early signals of performance in younger workers and to provide documentation in the case of dismissals or wage reduction of older workers so as to avoid age discrimination charges.

The employment and promotion opportunities of younger workers may be reduced in particular jobs when older workers continue past the usual retirement age. The extent to which other job opportunities may open up because of the spending activities of those who remain in the work force, or because of their effect on wage levels, is an empirical unknown. To the extent that deferred wages are not as prominent, promotion will take on a different meaning, since it will not mean promotion to receive the deferred wage. If wages are now equal to the worker's value of marginal product at each and every stage of the life cycle, then promotion by itself will be less important.

Training will decrease to the extent that deferred wages can no longer exist to discourage the unwanted turnover of those who receive company-specific training. However, training may increase to the extent that the expected benefit period, without mandatory retirement, is longer. Forecasting and planning will be more difficult given the greater uncertainty about retirement ages.

Jobs may be redesigned to accommodate the older workers who stay, but they may also be designed to encourage them to leave. Some dismissals of older workers who otherwise may have been "carried" to the mandatory retirement age will be inevitable, and this will likely increase the amount of litigation over unjust dismissal cases. Layoffs of older workers may also be more prominent to the extent that seniority declines as a work rule that was coexistent with deferred compensation.

These are meant to be simply illustrative of the sorts of adjustments that may occur if one aspect of the intricate employment relationship is changed, in this case if mandatory retirement is abolished. The adjustments may be minor if they are going on already in anticipation of mandatory retirement being banned, or if alternative procedures can arise to enable deferred wages, or if workers continue their trend toward earlier retirement. Nevertheless, we do not know if that trend will continue especially as the proportion of the white-collar work force grows, as retirement plans have more lead time to change, as larger numbers of co-workers postpone retirement, and if pensions dissipate. In addition, as discussed in the chapter on retirement, Canadian public pension plans do not have a tax-back feature as exists in the United States, so that Canadian workers may be more prone to postpone retirement than their American counterparts.

Clearly, the current debate over the pros and cons of banning mandatory retirement is not one that is likely to be resolved easily, and if it is resolved in favour of banning mandatory retirement, a number of repercussions are likely to follow. Hopefully, the application of some basic principles of economics can narrow the focus of the debate, though it may also make the issues more complicated than they appear at first glance. At the very least, these principles should provide us with information on the repercussions of a policy change and the alternative and complementary policies that may be desirable.

Summary

- Considerable new work is occurring in labour economics (often under the rubric of the "new economics of personnel") trying to explain the economic rationale that may lie behind the existence of various human resource and workplace practices within the internal labour markets of firms. Such practices at first glance often appear inefficient, but they may have a more complex efficiency rationale given uncertainty, monitoring costs, and information asymmetries.
- Examples of such practices discussed in the chapter include:
  - Efficiency wages or wage premiums that "pay for themselves"
  - Superstar salaries that are exorbitant
  - Egalitarian or compressed internal wage structures designed to encourage cooperation especially among work teams
  - External compared to internal promotions from within the organization
  - The free-riding or "1/N" problem that exists in partnerships, workgroups, and workplace teams
  - "Up-or-out" rules (including academic tenure at universities) under which employees are evaluated and then either promoted or terminated
  - Raiding and offer-matching
  - Piece rates (with an application to fee-for-service compensation schemes in medical practices)
  - Executive compensation systems that seem to resemble tournament prizes with large rewards for the winner
  - Deferred compensation systems where employees tend to be underpaid when younger and overpaid relative to their productivity when older
  - Mandatory retirement
- The theoretical framework underlying much of this work is agency theory, dealing with how to design efficient explicit or implicit contracts between the principal (employer) and the agent (employee or their representatives) when there are incentives to cheat,

largely arising from uncertainty, monitoring costs, and information asymmetries. The contractual arrangements are often self-enforcing, in the sense that they are designed to elicit the private information of the parties, providing them an incentive to engage in "truth-telling" that improves market efficiency.

- Unfortunately, much of the work in this area has remained at the theoretical level, since there are few data sets linking individual employees to such practices, and when they exist they are often not publicly available (and hence capable of being replicated) or they are from a single large organization, which raises the issue of generalizability. However, this is changing and empirical research in this area is a new frontier in labour economics.

REVIEW QUESTIONS

1. Discuss the pros and cons of efficiency wages as opposed to deferred compensation as compensation systems to deter shirking and encourage work effort.
2. What should happen to the pay of superstars if there is technological change or increased globalization that enables the very best to reach a wider audience?
3. Under what circumstances would it be optimal for a firm to have a compressed versus a dispersed wage structure?
4. What is the "1/N problem," and how can it be dealt with?
5. What are "up-or-out rules," and what are their pros and cons?
6. What is the "winner's curse" when organizations engage in offer-matching of raiding organizations?
7. "If deferred compensation prevails and firms face an exogenous, unanticipated permanent reduction in their demand conditions, then they may have a strong incentive to engage in permanent layoffs or even bankruptcy." Discuss.
8. "While there may be advantages to deferred compensation, there are other ways besides mandatory retirement to enable deferred compensation." Discuss.
9. If mandatory retirement exists in part to enable deferred compensation, discuss the implication of banning mandatory retirement for different elements of the personnel function, including compensation policies.
10. "The relevant question is not: Are you for or against mandatory retirement? Rather, it is: Under what conditions should governments prohibit private parties from entering into arrangements like mandatory retirement?" Discuss.
11. "Any theory of executive compensation must be able to consistently explain two stylized facts—the increase in executive compensation that has occurred relative to average pay, and the higher executive compensation in the United States relative to that in other countries." Discuss.

PROBLEMS

1. On the basis of the deferred wage profile of Figure 13.1, how would the analysis change if productivity began to decline after a certain age? Draw the new figures.
2. On the basis of the mandatory retirement portrayal of Figure 13.2, what would happen to the wage and productivity profiles if mandatory retirement were banned? Draw the new figures.
3. You are the human resource manager at a large organization. Each worker in your organization produces output valued at $10 per hour (i.e., VMP = $10). You want to deter shirking and turnover by paying a deferred wage profile where the hourly wage

$W = 2/3T$, where T is the tenure or length of time that the person remains with the firm (i.e., after 10 years the person would earn $W = 2/3(10)$ or \$6.67 per hour).

(a) Draw the diagram of the deferred wage profile.
(b) Could this profile persist?
(c) Solve for the breakeven point or length of time the person would have to stay with the firm so that their wage would just equal their productivity.
(d) Determine the length of time they would have to stay with the firm for their expected wage over that period to just equal their expected productivity (assume no discounting so that a dollar today is the same as a dollar in the future).
(e) If the vast majority of the people start working with the firm at age 35, what mandatory retirement age would you pick to provide a termination date to that contractual arrangement?
(f) If a positive discount rate were assumed, what would that do to the mandatory retirement age?
(g) If you behaved in a short-run, opportunistic fashion and terminated all of your employees at the breakeven point, what would happen to that profile?
(h) If you had to downsize but wanted to maintain your reputation, you might want to offer an early retirement buyout package equal to the magnitude of the deferred compensation. What would that magnitude be for someone who has been at the firm for 15 years (assume 2000 working hours in a year or 50 weeks at 40 hours per week).
(i) Assume that you had unjustly dismissed an employee two years prior to his mandatory retirement age. An arbitrator deemed that you must compensate that employee for wage loss from the fact that if he had to obtain a job elsewhere it would be only at a wage equal to his value of marginal product at another firm (assumed equal to his VMP with your firm). Calculate the amount of that arbitration award.
(j) Assume that you have ten workers, all of whom started at the same age of 35 and are now at the breakeven point in terms of how long they have been employed in your organization. You are a real hard-hearted person and you are trying to determine whether you should declare bankruptcy given your aging (and more expensive) workforce. You know that you can open up a new organization elsewhere and pay people the value of their marginal product. However, there are costs associated with going bankrupt and opening elsewhere. What is the magnitude of those costs that would make you indifferent between going bankrupt and continuing with your existing operation?

4. Outline the pros and cons of the different payment systems that exist for medical doctors, being sure to discuss the incentive effects they create. Who should like which scheme and why (among doctors, patients, and governments)? In your discussion, analyze the following schemes:
   - Fee-for-service with no annual maximum
   - Fee-for-service with an annual maximum
   - Capitation or fixed salary based on the number of patients in the doctors' roster
   - Fixed salary independent of the services rendered
5. One of the difficulties of a fee-for-service system is determining the (piece) rates that are to be paid for doctors for the different services performed. In Canada, these fee schedules are set by negotiations between the provincial governments and medical associations. One of the complications is that technological change can alter the amount of time or skill that it takes to perform a particular service. Discuss how this is a typical problem in piece-rate systems.

6. Ferrall, Gregory, and Tholl (1998) do an econometric analysis of the determinants of the working time of Canadian physicians. They obtain the following results after controlling for the various other factors that determine working time:
   - Physicians who are in solo practice work many more hours than those who work in group practices where they share the returns.
   - Physicians in Quebec (which tend to have the most stringent caps on earnings) work significantly fewer hours than physicians in other provinces.
   - Physicians who work under fee-for-service see more patients but work fewer hours than physicians on salary.

   Are these facts consistent with the predictions of the theory of piece rates and of the 1/N problem presented in this chapter?

KEYWORDS

REFERENCES

Antle, R., and A. Smith. 1986. An empirical investigation into the relative performance of corporate executives. *Journal of Accounting Research* 24 (Spring).

Ashenflelter, O., and D. Card. 2000. How did the elimination of mandatory retirement affect faculty retirement? University of California Centre for Labor Economics Working Paper 25.

Baker, G., and B. Holmstrom. 1995. Internal labor markets: Too many theories, too few facts. *AER* 85:255–59.

Baker, G., M. Gibbs, and B. Holmstrom. 1994a. The internal economics of a firm: Evidence from personnel data. *QJE* 109:881–919.

______. 1994b. The wage policy of a firm. *QJE* 109:921–55.

Barron, J., and K. Gjerde. 1997. Peer pressure in an agency relationship. *JOLE* 15:234–54.

Blakemore, A. (Ed.). 1987. The new economics of personnel. *JOLE: Supplement,* 5(Part 2).

Bognanno, M. 2001. Corporate tournaments. *JOLE* 19:290–315.

Burkhauser, R., and J. Quinn. 1983. Is mandatory retirement overrated? Evidence from the 1970s. *JHR* 18:337–58.

Carmichael, L., 1988. Incentives in academics: Why is there tenure? *JPE* 96 (June):453-72.

______. 1989. Self-enforcing contracts, shirking and life-cycle incentives. *JEP* 365–83.

Chan, W. 1996. External recruitment versus internal promotion. *JOLE* 14:555–70.

Drago, R., and G. Garvey. 1998. Incentives for helping on the job. *JOLE* 16:1–25.

Ehrenberg, R., and M. Bognanno. 1990. Do tournaments have incentive effects? *JPE* 98 (December):1307-24.

Eriksson, T. 1999. Executive compensation and tournament theory: Empirical tests on Danish data. *JOLE* 17:262–80.

Gibbons, R. 1987. Piece-rate incentive schemes. *JOLE* 5 (October):413-29.

______. 1998. Incentives in organizations. *JEP* 12:115–32.

Gibbons, R., and M. Waldman. 1998. Careers in organisations: Theory and evidence. In *Handbook of Labor Economics*, eds. O. Ashenfelter and D. Card, Vol. 3B (pp. 2373–92). New York: North Holland.

Gunderson, M. 1983. Mandatory retirement and personnel policies. *Columbia Journal of World Business* (Summer):8-15.

______. 2001. Economics of personnel and human resource management. *Human Resource Management Review* 11:1–22.

Hamlen, W. 1991. Superstardom in popular music. *R.E. Stats.* 73 (November):729-32.

Heisz, A. 1996. Changes in job tenure. *PLI* 8 (Winter):31-5.

Holmstrom, B. 1982. Moral hazard in teams. *Bell Journal of Economics* 13:324–40.

Holmstrom, B., and P. Milgrom. 1994. The firm as an incentive system. *AER* 84:972–91.

Hutchens, R. 1987. A test of Lazear's theory of delayed payment contracts. *JOLE* 5, Part 2 (October):S153-70.

______. 1989. Seniority, wages and productivity. *JEP* 3 (Fall):49-64.

Ichniowski, C., K. Shaw, and G. Prennushi. 1997. The effects of human resource management practices on productivity: A study of steel finishing lines. *AER* 87:291–313.

Jensen, M., and K. Murphy. 1990. Performance pay and top management incentives. *JPE* 98 (April):225-64.

Kahn, C., and G. Huberman. 1988. Two-sided uncertainty and "up-or-out" contracts. *JOLE* 6:423–44.

Kahn, L., and P. Sherer. 1990. Contingent pay and managerial performance. *ILRR* 43(3)(Special Issue): S107–S121.

Kandel, E., and E. Lazear. 1992. Peer pressure and partnerships. *JPE* 100 (August):801-17.

Kraft, K. 1991. The incentive effect of dismissals, efficiency wages, piece rates and profit sharing. *R.E. Stats.* 73 (August):451-9.

Lazear, E. 1979. Why is there mandatory retirement? *JPE* 87 (December):1261-84.

______. 1981. Agency, earnings profiles, productivity and hours restrictions. *AER* 71:606–20.

______. 1986. Raids and offer-matching. *Research in Labor Economics* 8:141–65.

______. 1989. Pay equality and industrial politics. *JPE* 97:561–80.

______. 1990. Pensions and deferred benefits as strategic compensation. *IR* 29:263–80.

______. 1991. Labor economics and the psychology of organisations. *JEL* 5:89–110.

______. 1995. *Personnel Economics*. Cambridge, Mass. and London: MIT Press.

______. 1998. *Personnel Economics for Managers*. New York: Wiley.

______. 1999. Personnel economics: Past lessons and future directions. *JOLE* 17:199–236.

______. 2000. Performance pay and productivity. *AER* 90:1346–61.

Lazear, E., and S. Rosen. 1981. Rank-order tournaments as optimum labor contracts. *JPE* 89 (October):841-64.

Leonard, J. 1990. Executive pay and firm performance. *ILLR* 43(Supplement):13–29.

Lindbeck, A. 1997. Incentives and social norms in household behavior. *AER* 87:369–77.

Loewenstein, G., and N. Sicherman. 1991. Do workers prefer increasing wage profiles? *JOLE* 9 (January):67-84.

Main, B., C. O'Reilly, and J. Wade. 1993. Top executive pay: Tournament or teamwork? *JOLE* 11:608–28.

Malcolmson, J. 1998. Individual employment contracts in labor markets. In *Handbook of Labor Economics*, eds. O. Ashenfelter and D. Card, Vol. 3B (pp. 2291–372). New York: North Holland.

Mitchell, D., and M. Zaidi. (Eds.) 1990. The economics of human resource management. *IR* (Special Issue) 29(2).

Murphy, K. 1985. Corporate performance and managerial remuneration. *Journal of Accounting and Economics* 7:11-42.

Neumark, D., and W. Stock. 1999. Age discrimination laws and labor market efficiency. *JPE* 107:1081–1125.

O'Flaherty, B., and A. Siow. 1992. On-the-job screening, up-or-out rules, and firm growth. *CJE* 25 (May):346-68.

______. 1995. Up-or-out rules in the market for lawyers. *JOLE* 13 (October):709-35.

Paarsch, H., and B. Shearer. 1997. Fixed wages, piece rates and incentive effects: Statistical evidence from payroll records. Society of Labor Economists Conference Paper, May 2–3.

Parsons, D. 1986. The employment relationship: Job attachment, work effort, and the nature of contracts. In *Handbook of Labour Economics*, eds. O. Ashenfelter and R. Layard. New York: Elsevier.

Pesando, J., and M. Gunderson. 1988. Retirement incentives contained in occupational pension plans and their implications for the mandatory retirement debate. *CJE* 21:244–64.

Pesando, J., M. Gunderson, and P. Shum. 1992. Incentive and redistributive effects of private sector union pension plans in Canada. *IR* 30:179–94.

Prendergast, C. 1999. The provision of incentives in firms. *JEL* 37:7–63.

Raff, D., and L. Summers. 1987. Did Henry Ford pay efficiency wages? *JOLE* 5 (October): 57-86.

Rosen, S. 1981. The economics of superstars. *AER* 71 (December):845-58.

______. 1982. Authority, control and the distribution of earnings. *Bell Journal of Economics* 13:311–23.

______. 1986. Prizes and incentives in elimination tournaments. *AER* 76:921–39.

Waldman, M. 1990. Up-or-out contracts: A signalling perspective. *JOLE* 8:230–50.

Zhou, X. 2000. CEO pay, firm size, and corporate performance: Evidence from Canada. *CJE* 33(1):213–51.

Chapter Fourteen

Union Growth and Incidence

Main Questions

- *What fraction of Canadian workers are members of unions? How has this evolved over time? How does this differ from other countries?*
- *Which types of workers are most likely to be covered by union contracts?*
- *What factors determine the level of unionization in the labour market?*
- *Union density in the United States has fallen dramatically since 1970, while unionization rates have been relatively stable in Canada. Given the similarities between the two countries, how can we explain this divergence in unionization rates?*

Unions are collective organizations whose primary objective is to improve the well-being of their members. In Canada, this objective is met primarily through **collective bargaining** with the employer. The outcome of this process is a collective agreement specifying wages, nonwage benefits such as those relating to pensions, vacation time, and health and medical expenses, and aspects of the employment relation such as procedures relating to hiring, promotion, dismissal, layoffs, overtime work, and the handling of grievances.

There are two basic types of unions. **Craft unions** represent workers in a particular trade or occupation; examples are found in the construction, printing, and longshoring trades. **Industrial unions** represent all the workers in a particular industry regardless of occupation or skill; examples are found in the automobile, steel, and forest industries. Some unions combine elements of both types.

In addition to their collective bargaining activities, unions play a role in social and political affairs. Close ties between unions and social democratic political parties are common, especially in western Europe. In Canada the union movement provides financial and other support for the New Democratic Party. Unions also seek to influence the government in power, and accordingly have been involved in various forms of consultation and collaboration with governments and, in some cases, representatives of the business community. Although these and other political and social aspects of unions are important and deserve study, the major function of Canadian unions is to represent their members' interests in collective bargaining with employers, and it is this aspect of unions which is studied here.

This chapter begins with a brief discussion of the nature and significance of unions and collective bargaining in Canada. The extent of unionization in the labour force, how this has changed over time, how it compares with other countries, and the legal framework governing unionization and collective bargaining are described. We then examine the determinants of the extent and incidence of unionization in the economy: what factors result in some groups of workers being represented by a union while other groups of workers remain unorganized? The following chapters are devoted to understanding the economic consequences of unions and collective bargaining.

UNIONS AND COLLECTIVE BARGAINING IN CANADA

http://labour.hrdc-drhc.gc.ca/doc/wid-dimt/eng

For a significant fraction of the Canadian labour force, wages and other conditions of employment are determined by collective bargaining. Table 14.1 provides several measures of the quantitative significance of unions in the labour market. Over time, an upward trend is evident until the 1980s, with a modest decline since that time. **Union membership** as a proportion of the civilian labour force increased from about 9 percent in 1920 to about 26 percent in 1998. Union membership as a proportion of (civilian) nonagricultural paid workers—a measure which excludes from consideration the self-employed and those employed in agriculture—increased from 16 to 33 percent over the same period.

The influence of unions may extend further than is suggested by these measures of the extent of union organization or **union density**. For example, the extent of unionization is much higher among nonoffice than office employees. The wages and benefits negotiated for production workers may set a standard for nonunion office employees in the same establishment. More generally, union agreements may influence the wages and working conditions of unorganized workers in the same industry, urban area, or region. As discussed below, in some countries the wages and working conditions in union agreements are extended to nonunion workers in the same industry or sector.

THE LEGAL FRAMEWORK

Union representation and collective bargaining in Canada are regulated by an elaborate legal framework. The evolution of this framework reflects the changing social attitudes toward the role of unions and collective bargaining in Canadian society, and has played a role in the increase in union organization evident in Table 14.1. In general terms, the law with respect to collective bargaining in Canada has passed through three main phases. (For a more detailed description of the evolution of Canadian labour legislation, see Weiler, 1986.) In the first phase, the period mostly prior to Confederation, the law discouraged collective bargaining. Judges interpreted the common law to hold that collective action by employees constituted a criminal conspiracy. There were also other criminal and civil constraints on both individual and group action by workers. In the second phase, which began in the 1870s, the law was "neutral" with respect to collective bargaining. In particular, the Trade Unions Act of 1872, amendments to criminal law, and other legislative actions removed many of the restrictions on union formation and the collective withdrawal of labour. However, the law did not encourage or facilitate unionization. This neutral stance lasted in Canada until the enactment in 1944 of the National War Labour Order, Order-in-Council P.C. 1003, after which labour law facilitated union formation and, in turn, encouraged the spread of collective bargaining. P.C. 1003, which was partly modelled on the National Labor Relations Act (the Wagner Act) of 1935 in the United States, provided most private sector employees with the right to union representation and collective bargaining, established certification procedures, provided a code of unfair labour practices primarily

Table 14.1 Union Membership and Union Density in Canada, 1920–1998

Year	Union Membership (000s)	Union Membership as a Percentage of Civilian Labour Force	Union Membership as a Percentage of Nonagricultural Paid Workers
1920	374	9.4	16.0
1925	271	7.6	14.4
1930	322	7.9	13.9
1935	281	6.4	14.5
1940	362	7.9	16.3
1945	711	15.7	24.2
1951*	1,029	19.7	28.4
1955	1,268	23.6	33.7
1960	1,459	23.5	32.3
1965	1,589	23.2	29.7
1970	2,173	27.2	33.6
1975	2,884	29.9	35.6
1980	3,397	29.2	35.7
1985	3,666	28.3	36.4
1990	4,031	28.5	34.5
1995	4,003	27.0	34.3
1998	3,938	25.6	32.5

*The survey was not conducted in 1950.

Sources: Human Resources Development Canada, *Directory of Labour Organizations in Canada*, various issues. Reproduced with the permission of the Minister of Public Works and Government Services Canada, 1997, 2001.

intended to prevent employers from interfering with employees' right to union representation, and established a labour relations board to administer the law. Thus, in the post-World War II period, legislation encouraged collective bargaining.

http://lois.justice.gc.ca/en/P-35

These three phases in the history of collective bargaining applied primarily to the private sector. With the passage of the Public Service Staff Relations Act (PSSRA) in 1967 at the federal level and similar acts at provincial levels, governments encouraged collective bargaining and union formation in the public sector, which was also at that time an area of rapid growth in employment.

The Canadian labour relations policy which emerged in the 1940s had the following central features (Weiler, 1986):

1. Workers who met the statutory definition of employee had the right to join and form unions.
2. Collective bargaining rights were protected under unfair labour practices legislation, which prohibited acts by both employers and unions to discourage or interfere with the employees' prerogative to bargain collectively.
3. A system of defining appropriate bargaining units and certifying bargaining representatives was established.
4. Once certified, the union became the exclusive bargaining representative of all employees in the bargaining unit.
5. Unions and employers were required to bargain in good faith.

6. These rights and obligations were administered and enforced usually by a labour relations board, but in some cases in court.

This Wagner Act framework was combined with the traditional Canadian labour policy, expressed in the Industrial Disputes Investigation Act of 1907 and subsequent legislation, of regulating the use of work stoppages. These features included:

1. Compulsory "cooling-off" periods/postponement of strikes and lockouts, coupled with compulsory mediation and/or conciliation procedures.
2. Prohibition of strikes or lockouts during the term of the collective agreement coupled with a requirement that each collective agreement provide some alternative means for the resolution of grievances concerning the interpretation and application of the agreement.
3. While the content of the collective agreement was left largely to the parties, Ottawa and the provinces increasingly began to require certain items to be included in collective agreements, such as a recognition clause, a no-strike/no-lockout clause, a clause providing for a peaceful mechanism to resolve grievances arising during the term of the agreement, and provision for a date of termination of the agreement.

Another important aspect of the legal framework is the division of powers between the federal and provincial governments over labour legislation. The Constitution Act, 1867, has been interpreted by the courts as implying that jurisdiction over labour relations matters rests primarily with the provinces. Federal jurisdiction is limited to about 10 percent of the labour force—federal public servants, employees of federal Crown corporations and those employed in rail, air, shipping and truck transportation, banks, broadcasting, uranium mines, and grain elevators.

FACTORS INFLUENCING UNION GROWTH AND INCIDENCE

Inspection of Table 14.1 reveals that during the past six decades union growth in Canada has been substantial but erratic. In some periods union membership declined in absolute terms (1920–1935; 1990–1998), in others it increased absolutely but declined relative to the labour force (1955–1965; 1975–1990), while in others union membership grew substantially more rapidly than the labour force (1965–1975; 1940–1950). The causes of union growth—both the upward trend and the variations around the trend—have long been a subject of scholarly research and debate. There are also significant cross-sectional differences in the extent of unionization—across countries, industries, regions, and occupations—which call for an explanation.

Table 14.2 shows two measures of the extent of union organization in the economy for the years 1980 and 1994 in several OECD countries. Union density—defined in this table as union membership as a percentage of paid (wage and salary) workers—in Canada is higher than in France, Japan, or the United States, but much lower than in the Scandinavian countries (Denmark, Norway, Sweden, and Finland). Also evident is the general tendency for union density to decline over the period 1980–1994 in most advanced economies. The principal exceptions are the Scandinavian countries, where unionization, already high by international standards, increased further. Canadian behaviour falls into a middle category, in terms of both the level of union density and the relative stability over the period 1980–1994. The divergent patterns displayed by Canada and the United States are particularly striking and are discussed in Exhibit 14.1.

The second measure of unionization is **collective agreement coverage**—the percentage of paid workers whose wages and working conditions are covered by a collective agreement. In countries such as Canada, Japan, and the United States, most bargaining takes place between an individual employer and union, and the collective agreements reached do not generally cover other workers. In contrast, centralized bargaining at the

Table 14.2 Union Density and Collective Agreement Coverage in Selected OECD Countries, 1980 and 1994

	Union Membership as a Percentage of Paid Workers		Collective Agreement Coverage as a Percentage of Paid Workers	
	1980	1994	1980	1994
Australia	48	35	88	80
Austria	56	42	98	98
Belgium	56	54	90	90
Canada	36	34	37	36
Denmark	76	76	69	69
Finland	70	81	95	95
France	18	9	85	95
Germany	36	29	91	92
Italy	49	39	85	82
Japan	31	24	28	21
Netherlands	35	26	76	81
New Zealand	56	30	67	31
Norway	57	58	75	74
Portugal	61	32	70	71
Spain	9	19	76	78
Sweden	80	91	86	89
Switzerland	31	27	53	50
United Kingdom	50	34	70	47
United States	22	16	26	18

Source: Organization for Economic Co-operation and Development, *Employment Outlook* (Paris: OECD, July 1997).

level of the industry, sector, or entire economy is common in many European countries and Australia. In addition, agreements reached between unions and employers are often extended to cover nonunion workers in related firms and sectors. In these circumstances there may be a substantial difference between union membership and collective agreement coverage. The extreme case in is that of France, where union membership had fallen to less than 10 percent in 1994, yet 95 percent of wage and salary workers were covered by collective agreements! On the basis of a comparison of union density, one might have concluded that unions play a much smaller role in the French economy than in Canada (union density of 9 percent in France as against 34 percent in Canada) but the data on collective agreement coverage indicates that this is unlikely to be the case. More generally, collective agreement coverage in Canada is much lower than in most of these OECD countries, and exceeds only that of New Zealand, Japan, and the United States.

www.oecd.org

Canadian labour legislation provides that, once certified, the union is the exclusive bargaining representative for all employees in the bargaining unit, whether or not they are union members. Because some members of the bargaining unit choose not to join the union (although they are generally required to pay union dues), collective agreement coverage exceeds union membership. However, the gap between membership and coverage is small in Canada, Japan, and the United States, compared to that in Australia and many European countries.

The extent of union organization in Canada varies considerably by industry, occupation, region, and various individual employee or employer characteristics. Table 14.3 shows

Exhibit 14.1

The Divergence of Unionization Between Canada and the United States

As illustrated in Figure 14.1, Canada and the United States displayed similar patterns of union growth from the early 1900s until the mid-1950s. Since that time, trends in unionization have diverged sharply, with union density declining steadily in the United States, but growing in Canada until the mid-1980s and subsequently declining modestly. As a consequence, a huge intercountry differential has emerged in the extent of union coverage—so that since the mid-1980s the fraction of the Canadian labour force represented by unions has been approximately double that of the United States.

A number of explanations have been advanced for the dramatic decline in union strength in the United States. Perhaps the most common explanation has to do with the changing structure of the economy and labour force. Specifically, most of the employment changes that have occurred in the past three decades—away from manufacturing and toward services; away from blue-collar and toward white-collar; away from male and full-time and toward female and part-time; away from large firms and toward small firms—represent declines in the relative importance of sectors which traditionally have been highly unionized and increases in the relative importance of sectors which traditionally had low union density. Thus if union density remained constant in each sector, or for each type of worker, the economy-wide extent of unionization would decline due to these structural shifts.

Another explanation involves changes in the U.S. legal regime (the laws, their interpretation, and their administration and enforcement) relating to unions and collective bargaining during the post–World War II period. A related view is that the decline in U.S. unionization can largely be attributed to the rise in management opposition, both legal and illegal, to unions. Increased management opposition to unions may be due to changes in the legal regime, a more competitive economic environment, and a substantial union-nonunion wage differential.

Another hypothesis is that there has been a reduction in the desire for collective representation because of the growth of substitute services. Governments have gradually provided more of the employment protection and nonwage benefits that were originally important factors underlying workers' desire for union coverage. In addition, employers have become increasingly sophisticated in their human resource practices and now provide services (e.g., grievance procedures) that workers previously only received in unionized firms.

A final hypothesis, which is perhaps the simplest and most profound, is that there has been in the United States a reduction in public sympathy toward unions and a reduction in workers' desire for collective representation.

Some evidence supporting each of these explanations has been put forward.

some of these variations. Unionization is highest in nursing, teaching, and blue-collar occupations such as construction, trades, and machine operators, and lower in many sales and service occupations. Industry differences are also substantial. Public sector employees are much more likely to be unionized than workers in the private sector. Public administration (federal, provincial, and municipal public employees), health care, education, and utilities are extensively unionized, while trade, finance, and business and professional services have little unionization. Full-time workers are more likely to be unionized than part-time workers, and males are slightly more unionized than females. (See also Exhibit 14.2 on the

Exhibit 14.1 **The Divergence of Unionization Between Canada and the United States *(continued)***

However, beginning with Weiler (1983, 1984), the value of adopting a comparative Canada-U.S. perspective has increasingly been recognized. In particular, the many similarities between the economies of the two countries and their industrial relations systems results in a situation with elements of a controlled experiment, thus perhaps enabling some explanations of the decline in U.S. union strength to be rejected because they cannot account for the observed behaviour in Canada.

Many of the structural changes described above (rise in service sector, in female and part-time, and in white-collar employment) also occurred in Canada. Thus it appears unlikely that the "structuralist" hypothesis can account for the behaviour of union density in both countries. Using comparable micro-data on union incidence in the two countries, Riddell (1993) concludes that structural differences account for about 15 percent of the intercountry differential in union coverage; 85 percent is attributed to the fact that a Canadian worker with given characteristics is much more likely to be covered by a collective agreement than a U.S. worker with the same characteristics. The most important structural difference is the greater extent of public sector employment in Canada, which accounts for about 7 percent of the unionization gap. (Public-sector workers are much more likely to be unionized in both countries.)

Riddell (1993) also shows that underlying social attitudes toward unions, as measured by public opinion polls, are very similar in the two countries. Public attitudes toward unions have become less favourable during the last three decades on both sides of the 49th parallel, and to a similar degree. In addition, the impact of unions on wages in the private sector is very similar in the two countries. Thus, these hypotheses do not seem capable of explaining the observed behaviour in both societies. Equally unlikely is the "growth of union substitutes" view; Canadian governments have gone further than their U.S. counterparts in providing social and employment security.

These findings suggest that differences between Canada and the United States in the legal regime governing unions and collective bargaining may be able to explain the decline in the U.S. union movement and the divergent patterns of union growth in the two countries. Differences in such areas as certification and decertification procedures, bankruptcy and succession rights, first-contract negotiation, and union security arrangements have been argued to be factors contributing to the intercountry differential in union coverage (Weiler, 1983, 1984). Institutional differences in the two countries' labour movements and industrial relations outcomes, detailed in Kumar (1993), also appear to be consistent with this perspective.

male-female unionization gap.) There are also important differences by age; the likelihood of being unionized increases sharply with age to 45–54 years of age, and then declines. One of the strongest relationships is between unionization and workplace size, with workers in large establishments being much more likely to be represented by a union than those in small establishments.

Explaining these differences in unionization—over time and across industries, regions, and occupations—is of considerable interest for its own sake. As discussed subsequently, this understanding is also important in interpreting research findings on the consequences

Table 14.3 Union Membership and Collective Agreement Coverage as a Percentage of Paid Workers in Canada, 1999

	Percentage of Paid Workers Who Are:	
	Union Members	Covered by a Collective Agreement
By Gender		
Both sexes	29.8	32.2
Females	28.9	31.1
Males	30.6	33.2
By Age		
15 to 24	11.7	13.4
25 to 44	30.3	32.8
45 to 54	41.4	44.1
55 and over	34.4	36.5
By Education		
Less than Grade 9	27.4	28.7
Some high school	23.2	24.8
High school graduate	27.2	29.0
Some postsecondary	23.1	25.3
Postsecondary diploma	33.4	36.0
University degree	34.9	38.3
By Province		
Newfoundland	38.6	40.0
Prince Edward Island	27.4	29.5
Nova Scotia	28.7	30.0
New Brunswick	26.2	27.9
Quebec	35.4	39.5
Ontario	26.4	28.1
Manitoba	34.8	36.9
Saskatchewan	32.7	35.2
Alberta	22.5	25.3
British Columbia	33.9	35.4
By Work Status		
Full-time	31.6	34.2
Part-time	21.5	23.0
By Sector		
Public sector	70.5	74.7
Private sector	18.1	20.0
By Industry		
Agriculture	3.5	3.8
Natural resources	26.8	28.6
Utilities	67.6	72.0
Construction	29.9	31.9
Manufacturing	31.0	33.7
Trade	12.5	13.9
Transportation, warehousing	42.1	44.4
Finance, insurance, real estate	7.8	9.7
Professional, scientific, technical	4.1	5.7
Management, administrative	10.5	11.9
Education	68.8	73.6
Health care, social assistance	52.1	54.7

Table 14.3 Union Membership and Collective Agreement Coverage as a Percentage of Paid Workers in Canada, 1999 *(continued)*

	Percentage of Paid Workers Who Are:	
	Union Members	**Covered by a Collective Agreement**
Information, culture, recreation	26.5	28.7
Accommodation and food	6.3	7.0
Other services	8.6	10.2
Public administration	64.7	70.0
By Occupation		
Management	8.6	11.7
Business professional	16.6	18.6
Financial and administrative	21.8	24.4
Clerical	27.8	30.1
Natural and applied sciences	24.6	27.4
Health professional	35.8	41.8
Nursing	80.2	82.5
Health technical	59.1	61.2
Health support staff	53.8	56.3
Legal, social, religious	38.4	41.2
Teachers, professors	76.8	80.8
Culture and recreation	25.4	27.9
Wholesale sales	5.9	7.6
Retail sales	12.5	13.5
Food and beverage	8.8	9.5
Protective services	52.7	60.0
Child care and home support	32.9	35.7
Travel and accommodation	25.3	26.8
Contractors and supervisors	27.5	33.3
Construction trades	39.4	40.4
Other trades	41.3	43.6
Transportation equipment operators	34.6	36.8
Helpers and labourers	33.7	35.4
Unique to primary industries	15.8	16.9
Machine operators and assemblers	38.0	40.9
Production labourers	37.7	39.7
By Workplace Size		
Under 20 employees	12.0	13.5
20 to 99 employees	30.0	32.7
100 to 500 employees	44.1	47.2
Over 500 employees	55.4	58.3
By Job Tenure		
1 to 12 months	13.8	16.0
Over 1 year to 5 years	19.9	22.1
Over 5 years to 9 years	32.2	34.6
Over 9 years to 14 years	41.6	44.3
Over 14 years	55.8	58.6
By Job Status		
Permanent job	30.9	33.2
Non-permanent job	22.0	24.7

Source: Adapted from Statistics Canada, *Perspectives on Labour and Income*, Catalogue 75-D01, Autumn 2000.

Figure 14.1 Union Density in Canada and the United States, 1920–1998

Union density is defined here as union membership as a percentage of non-agricultural paid workers. Union density rates for Canada and the United States are plotted at five-year intervals over the period since 1920. Union growth followed a similar pattern in the two countries from 1920 to the mid-1960s, after which time there has been a substantial divergence.

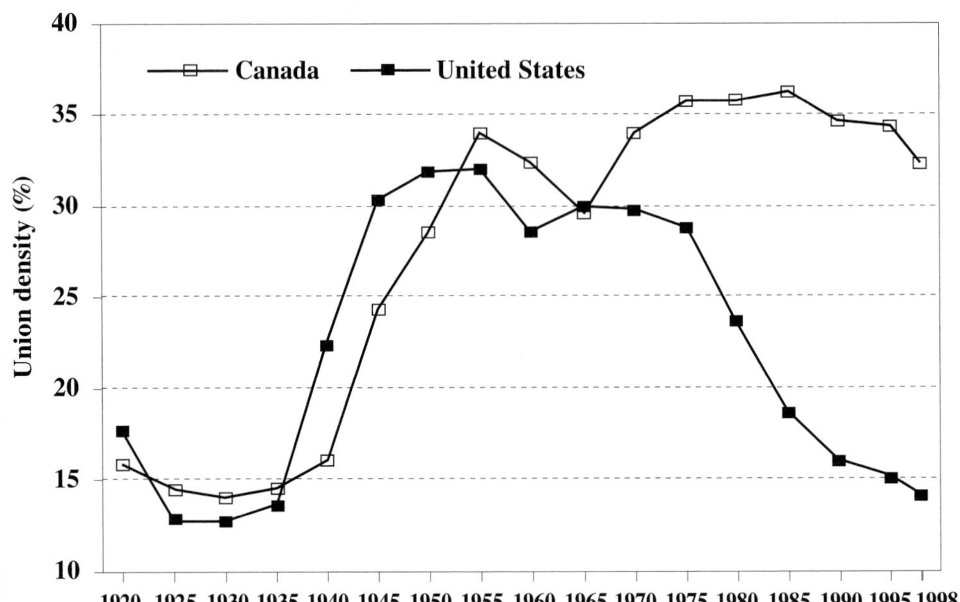

of unions. Indeed, a central theme of recent research has been that union/nonunion status and the wage and nonwage effects of unions are jointly determined. That is, unionization may result in higher wages and improved working conditions, but also higher wages as well as other factors related to higher wages may make unionization more likely to occur.

The growth and incidence of union organization can be analyzed using a demand and supply framework.[1] The **demand for union representation** emanates from employees and depends on the expected benefits and costs of union representation. The **supply of union representation** emanates from the organizing and contract administration activities of union leaders and their staff. These demand and supply forces are discussed in turn.

On the demand side the potential benefits of union representation may include higher wages and nonwage benefits, greater employment security (through protection from dismissal other than for cause) and protection from arbitrary treatment by management. Potential costs include direct costs such as union dues and time devoted to union activities, potential loss of income in the event of a work stoppage, and costs associated with the employer's actions, should the employer be willing and/or able to attempt to discourage unionization. Several factors may be net benefits or costs depending on the individual employee's circumstances. Higher wages will benefit those who retain union jobs but may reduce employment opportunities of others. Unions typically alter procedures for determining promotions and layoffs—usually placing more emphasis on seniority—which will enhance some workers' opportunities and reduce those of others.

On the supply side, administering the contracts covering existing union members and organizing new (or previously nonunion) workplaces are costly activities. Unions need

[1]This approach can be traced to Berkowitz (1954) and Ashenfelter and Pencavel (1969). There is also a substantial institutional and historical literature on the causes of union growth.

to allocate their scarce resources to the activities that are expected to yield the greatest return, measured in terms of the union's objectives. Success in organizing new workplaces and in maintaining membership and union representation in existing organizations will depend on a variety of factors including the resources devoted to contract administration and organizing drives, the activities of employers, and the economic and policy environment.

This demand and supply framework provides a useful conceptual model for analyzing the extent of union organization at a point in time and changes in unionization over time. The central concept is that the extent of unionization depends on the choices made by employees, the organizational and contract administration activities of union leaders, and the actions of employers. Those enterprises in which a majority of the employees perceive substantial net benefits from being represented by a union and in which the actions of the employer will not significantly reduce these benefits will have a high demand for unionization, and vice versa. The supply of union organizational and contract administration effort will be high to those enterprises in which the per-worker cost of organization and representation is low. The interaction of these demand and supply forces determines an equilibrium extent of union organization at a point of time. Some enterprises will be organized while others—because of either low demand or high organizational costs—will remain unorganized. Changes over time in the factors influencing demand and supply will result in changes in union density.

Under the Canadian legislative framework there are several dimensions to the way the demand and supply factors interact and determine the **union status** of individual workers. First, a group of workers must become represented by a labour union, a process known as **certification**. Second, once certified, the union remains the exclusive bargaining representative of that group of employees (known as a **bargaining unit**) unless the union becomes decertified. Although the details of the mechanisms vary somewhat across provincial and federal jurisdictions and over time, certification and **decertification** are essentially majority decisions by the workers in the bargaining unit.

At any point in time the stock of unionized and nonunion enterprises and firms is thus a reflection of past certification and decertification decisions. The third influence on union status consists of the decisions of individual workers about whether to seek employment in unionized or nonunion organizations. Fourth, the decisions of employers about which applicants to hire (and, in the case of workforce reductions, which workers to lay off) will also influence which individuals obtain (or retain) union jobs. Finally, because the economy and labour force are continually changing, the growth and decline of union and nonunion firms over time will also impact on the union status of individual workers.

For these reasons, the determination of the union status of individual workers is the outcome of a complex set of forces, reflecting both past decisions and current developments. Because the stock of union and nonunion employers at any point in time is, to an important extent, the outcome of past decisions, union density (or other measures of the extent of union organization in the economy) displays considerable inertia. Changes over time tend to be gradual, reflecting the extent to which growth in employment in unionized firms exceeds or falls short of growth in nonunion employment, certifications of new or previously nonunion organizations, and decertifications of previously union enterprises.

EMPIRICAL EVIDENCE

This demand and supply framework was used as the basis for econometric analyses of union growth in the United States by Ashenfelter and Pencavel (1969) and the United Kingdom by Pencavel (1971). Subsequently, Bain and Elsheikh (1976) carried out an extensive econometric study of union growth in Australia, Sweden, Great Britain, and the United

States. Empirical studies by Swidinsky (1974), Bain and Elsheikh (1976), Abbott (1982), and Kumar and Dow (1986) have applied and extended this approach in the Canadian setting. These studies employed aggregate data.

More recently, the demand and supply framework has been used to analyze microdata in which the union status of each individual is observed. The supply and demand for unionization themselves are inherently unobservable. In a conventional market, we can appeal to an equilibrium assumption that supply equals demand, given by the observed quantity exchanged. With this assumption, the observed level of unionization would correspond to actual supply and demand. However, given the high degree of government regulation, and the imperfectly competitive nature of the "market" for unionization, this would be an untenable assumption. With mobility into the nonunion sector, at least relative to the union sector, the most common characterization of the disequilibrium is one of excess (or unsatisfied) demand for unionization. That is, there are generally queues for union jobs, and those unable to obtain a job in a unionized organization either remain unemployed (waiting for a union job to open up) or take employment in the nonunion sector.

The data requirements in this situation make precise measurement very difficult. Nevertheless, there exist a few data sets that ask individuals whether they desire to be unionized, and this permits estimation of demand, which combined with actual union status, permits the estimation of unfulfilled demand. The probability of union coverage, given that an individual wishes to be covered, is taken as a measure of supply. Analogously, the proportion of uncovered individuals desiring coverage is taken as a measure of unfulfilled demand. Riddell (1993) uses this methodology, developed by Farber (1983), to explore whether the current difference in Canada and U.S. unionization rates is due primarily to demand or supply factors. If supply factors dominate, this would suggest that legislative or other cost of unionization factors are most important. Riddell finds that about two-thirds of the difference in rates (a gap of 26.5 percent) can be attributed to differences in supply.

Farber and Krueger (1993) also use this methodology to examine the decline in union coverage in the United States over the 1980s. They attribute most of the decline to a drop in demand for union representation. They also re-estimate the Canada-U.S. decomposition with more recent data than Riddell, and additional information that allows a more precise comparison of the data from the two countries. Farber and Krueger attribute a slightly higher fraction of the gap to demand factors (only one-third to supply differences). The results from the two studies are thus quite similar, though both highlight the limitations of the approach, and a preference for data on more directly observable economic variables associated with unionization (see Exhibit 14.1).

There have been a number of studies of the cross-sectional incidence of unionization according to more observable factors such as industry, enterprise and personal characteristics, region, and legislative jurisdiction. Although this literature will not be reviewed in detail here, the main findings and their consistency with the demand and supply framework will be discussed. Several factors suggested by the demand and supply framework have been investigated in empirical studies.

Social Attitudes Toward Unions and Collective Bargaining

Both the receptiveness of employees to union representation and the resistance of employers may be affected by the prevailing attitudes regarding the role of unions and collective bargaining in society, a factor which is, however, difficult to measure. In their U.S. study, Ashenfelter and Pencavel (1969) find that the percentage of Democrats in the House, a measure of pro-union sentiment, has a significant effect on U.S. union growth. Because society's attitudes toward unions tend to be reflected in labour legislation and its administration, measures of the legal regime (discussed below) capture social attitudes to some degree.

In the United States, attitudes toward unions have become less and less favourable since the 1950s, leading some observers to explain the decline in unionization in that country in terms of less supportive social attitudes (e.g., Lipset, 1986). However, a very similar decline in favourable attitudes toward unions also occurred in Canada, casting doubt on this explanation (see Exhibit 14.1).

The Legislative Framework Governing Unionization and Collective Bargaining

Legislation governing the right of workers to act collectively and the machinery for administering and enforcing these rights are likely to exert an important influence on the demand for and supply of union representation. However, it must be recognized that labour relations legislation and its administration itself reflects certain underlying factors such as society's attitudes toward unions; in the absence of good measures of social attitudes, it will be difficult to determine the independent impact of the legislation. Further, union growth and a legislative environment that is conducive to union growth may be joint manifestations of underlying societal attitudes. Without favourable attitudes, legislation may not have an independent influence.

The changes in the Canadian legislative framework described earlier have lowered the cost to employees of collective action and have increasingly restricted the employer's ability to attempt to discourage unionization. The former increases the demand for unions by raising the net benefits to workers of union representation; the latter increases the supply by lowering the costs of organizing and representing workers. The legislative changes are therefore predicted to have encouraged union growth. Although this trend in labour legislation and its administration has occurred gradually over time, particularly important changes took place in the 1870s (e.g., the Trade Unions Act of 1872), the early 1900s (the Industrial Disputes Investigation Act of 1907 contained an implicit form of union recognition by banning strikes or lockouts over recognition issues), the 1940s (the enactment of P.C. 1003 gave workers the right to form and join unions and made illegal a number of practices by employers previously used to discourage collective bargaining; similar legislation was enacted in most provinces following World War II and the end of federal emergency powers), and in the 1960s (the extension to public sector employees of the right to collective bargaining).

Examination of Table 14.1 suggests that the changes in the legislative framework around 1944 and 1967 may have had a positive impact on union growth in Canada. Econometric studies by Abbott (1982) and Kumar and Dow (1986) support the view that labour legislation has had a significant effect on the union growth process. In addition, the divergent patterns of union growth in Canada and the United States since the 1960s has been argued to be associated to a considerable extent with differences between the two countries in labour relations legislation and its enforcement (Exhibit 14.1).

Legislative changes introduced in several provinces during the 1980s and 1990s appear to have made new union organizing more difficult. Perhaps most significant has been the trend toward requiring secret-ballot elections for union certification (and decertification) decisions in Canadian jurisdictions. Exhibit 14.2 discusses the evidence on the impacts of these developments.

Other Economic and Social Legislation

The extent of union organization may also be affected by other economic and social legislation, although the direction of the effect is ambiguous. The setting (and raising) of employment standards such as those with respect to minimum wages, overtime premiums,

Exhibit 14.2

Round Up the Usual Suspects: What Caused the Recent Decline in Unionization in Canada?

Although union density rates in Canada and the United States have diverged substantially since the mid-1960s (see Exhibit 14.1), the recent trend in the two countries has been similar—downward (see Figure 14.1 and Table 14.1). For example, between 1984 and 1998 collective agreement coverage fell by 7 percentage points in Canada—from 40.3 percent to 33.5 percent, a decline of 17 percent—versus 8 percentage points in the United States—from 23.1 percent to 15.2 percent, a decline of 34 percent (Riddell and Riddell, 2001). What are the principal causes of this recent decline in Canadian union strength?

Many of the "usual suspects" are summarized in Exhibit 14.1. Recent research provides some evidence about the relative importance of these various explanations.

Riddell and Riddell (2001) use data on individual workers in 1984 and 1998 to investigate the contributions of structural changes in the economy and labour force—such as the relative shift from manufacturing to services, the more rapid growth in part-time than full-time work, the rise in female labour force participation, and shifts in the industrial and occupational composition of employment. They find that very little of the recent decline (less than 10 percent of the total change) in union coverage in Canada can be attributed to such structural changes. Instead, almost all the decline in union coverage can be attributed to a fall in the *likelihood that a worker with a given set of characteristics will be unionized.* This evidence indicates that we need to look at other explanations for the recent drop in union strength.

One hypothesis involves the recent trend toward legislation believed to deter unionization. In particular, an increasing number of provincial governments have instituted mandatory voting as the union certification procedure. As has traditionally been the case in the United States, many unions in Canada must now win a secret ballot election to be certified as the exclusive bargaining agent of the proposed bargaining unit. This contrasts dramatically with the traditional "automatic certification" or "card-signing" procedure in Canada—in which unions simply had to obtain signatures of a sufficient proportion of the proposed bargaining unit to achieve certification. Before the 1980s only one province—Nova Scotia—had mandatory voting for union certification. By the year 2000, however, there were five provinces with such laws, including Newfoundland, Manitoba, Nova Scotia,

statutory holidays, workplace health and safety, notice of layoff, and severance pay may narrow the gap in wages and working conditions between organized and unorganized workers, thus reducing the demand for unionization. On the other hand, such policies may have aided union growth by reducing competition from the lower labour costs that otherwise would have prevailed in the nonunion sector in the absence of extending such benefits to unorganized workers through employment standards. Social programs such as those respecting public pensions, medical and health care, and unemployment insurance may also have offsetting effects. Neumann and Rissman (1984) have suggested that the provision of certain welfare benefits by governments in the United States accounts for some of the decline in union strength there. In Canada, however, union density rose during the postwar period, an era of rapid expansion of the welfare state and significant increases in employment standards.

Exhibit 14.2 **Round Up the Usual Suspects: What Caused the Recent Decline in Unionization in Canada? *(continued)***

Ontario, and Alberta. From 1984 to 1993 British Columbia also had mandatory voting laws.

What is the evidence on the impact of this legislation on unionization? Martinello (2000) conducts a study using data from Ontario over the period 1987–1998 and finds that overall union-organizing activity and union-organizing success rates were higher under the legislation introduced by the NDP regime of Bob Rae than under the legislation introduced by Mike Harris' Progressive Conservative regime. Johnson (2001) uses data from every province except Prince Edward Island to estimate the impact of various types of legislation on certification success over the period 1987–1996. She uses the variation over time and across provinces to identify the effect of mandatory voting and finds that a mandatory voting regime reduces union organizing success rates by 9 percentage points.

Why should mandatory voting deter unionization? One reason could be the absence of peer pressure from union organizers and pro-union co-workers. Under a card-signing system such pressure is likely to be considerably greater relative to a secret ballot election, in which no one can observe the vote cast by any one individual. A second factor revolves around management opposition to the organizing drive. Specifically, it has been argued—first by Weiler (1983)—that because of the inherent nature of a secret ballot vote coupled with the reduction in union peer pressure power and lengthier organizing drives, management opposition is likely more effective in a mandatory voting regime.

What does the evidence suggest? Thomason (1994) examined the impact of management opposition on union organizing success in Ontario over the period 1980–1988 and found that while management opposition did reduce support within the proposed bargaining unit, it was not sufficiently effective to reduce overall success rates. Ontario, however, did not introduce mandatory voting until December 1995. In a study based on data from British Columbia over the period 1987–1988, Riddell (2001) finds that management opposition was highly effective in defeating union organizing drives. British Columbia did have a mandatory voting law in effect at that time. Hence, there is some evidence that legislative changes (in particular the introduction of "U.S.-style" mandatory voting in union certification procedures) and management opposition may have contributed to the recent decline of unions in Canada.

Aggregate Economic Conditions

Early institutional economists such as Commons (1918) emphasized the role of the business cycle in the growth of unions. Subsequent econometric studies have investigated the influence of such variables as the unemployment rate, the rate of growth of employment that is eligible for unionization, and the rate of price inflation. The general finding that the rate of union growth varies directly with the rate of growth of employment that is eligible for unionization is consistent with several hypotheses, including: (1) employer resistance to union formation is lowest when product demand is high and the labour market is tight and (2) the ability of unions to secure wage and benefit increases (and thus the perceived net benefit of being represented by a union) is highest when there is excess labour demand. However, even in the absence of these cyclical effects, a positive relationship between union growth and growth in employment eligible for unionization is expected. Employment growth in existing organized enterprises will result in an increase in the unionized labour force unless the employees decide to decertify the union. In addition, some new enterprises and their employees will have characteristics (discussed below) which make them likely to become organized.

Although the above reasons suggest that union growth will be pro-cyclical in nature, the experience of the Great Depression—during and subsequent to which the union movement displayed strong growth, especially in the United States—led Ashenfelter and Pencavel (1969) to hypothesize that severe business contractions will raise worker discontent, which in turn will be a spur to unionization, perhaps with a lag. Although U.S. studies generally find that union growth is positively related to the severity of past recessions, Canadian evidence on this issue is mixed (Abbott, 1982; Kumar and Dow, 1986).

Time series studies also generally find that union growth varies directly with the rate of price inflation. This finding is consistent with the hypothesis that unions are viewed by workers as an effective vehicle for maintaining real wages.

Industry and Enterprise Characteristics

As Table 14.3 shows, there are substantial differences across industries in the extent of union organization. Cross-sectional studies have found that union density tends to be higher in industries with larger firms or establishments, in more concentrated industries, in industries with more capital-intensive production processes and in industries with more hazardous jobs. Martinello and Meng (1992) is a good example of this type of study with Canadian data.

These results can be interpreted using the demand-supply framework. The demand for union representation is likely to be higher in larger establishments because individual action becomes less effective the larger the group; and the need for formal work rules, communications, and grievance procedures is greater in larger organizations. In addition, the per-worker cost of union organizing is lower in larger establishments. Industries with hazardous jobs are also likely to be characterized by greater demand for a collective "voice" to represent workers' interests in the internal regulation of workplace health and safety.

Capital-intensity may be associated with several effects. As with job hazards, capital-intensive production processes may entail greater need for a collective voice relating to the organization and flow of work—aspects such as the speed of assembly lines, scheduling of shifts, and overtime regulations. In addition, high capital-intensity implies that labour costs are a small fraction of total costs. This tends to make labour demand more inelastic and thus increases the potential wage gains from unionization.

The finding that more concentrated industries tend to be more heavily unionized may reflect several factors. Concentrated industries typically have significant barriers to entry; there is thus less threat of nonunion competition in the form of new entrants. In addition, unions may enable workers to share in the excess profits or rents earned by the established firms. Organizing costs may also be lower in more concentrated industries.

Because of these differences across industries in the extent of union organization, changes over time in the economy's industrial structure will be accompanied by changes in union density, other things equal. In Canada and most other industrialized countries, significant changes in industrial structure have occurred in the postwar period: employment has grown rapidly in services-producing industries and the share of service-sector employment increased substantially; goods-producing industries (manufacturing and construction) have experienced slower employment growth and a decline in the share of total employment; employment in agriculture both declined absolutely and relative to the share of total employment; and other primary industries (mining, forestry, fishing, and trapping) have experienced positive employment growth but declining shares of total employment.

These trends in the industrial composition of employment have had offsetting effects on union growth. Several factors tend to increase union density: the decline in employment in agriculture, an industry with little unionization; and the rapid growth in employment in public administration (employees of the federal, provincial, and municipal governments), a sector which has become extensively unionized since the mid-1960s. Robinson (1995) examines the incidence of unions in the public sector, in an attempt to isolate some of the underlying sources of this growth. Netting out differences in industry and personal characteristics, which turn out to have only a limited effect on unionization, he attributes most of the relative increase in public sector unionization to the lower per-member cost of organizing the large "plants" that characterize the public sector.

However, other changes in industrial structure have tended to reduce the extent of union organization in the economy: declining employment shares in manufacturing, mining, and forestry (sectors with above-average unionization); and increases in the share of employment in trade, finance, insurance, real estate, and other private sector services (industries with low degrees of unionization).

Personal Characteristics

A number of personal characteristics affect the propensity to be a union member or to be represented by a union. Part-time workers and workers with intermittent labour force attachment are less likely to be organized. For these individuals, the net benefits of union representation—especially in the form of seniority provisions, pension benefits, and other forms of deferred compensation—are lower than is the case with full-time workers and employees with a permanent labour force attachment. The costs of organizing part-time workers and workers with intermittent labour force attachments may also be high. Largely because they are more likely to work part-time and have tended to have less permanent attachment to the labour force, women are less likely to be represented by a union than men. (See Exhibit 14.3.)

As noted earlier, the extent of union organization is much higher among blue-collar than white-collar workers. Blue-collar workers are more likely to demand union representation because of less identification with management and possibly greater need for a collective voice in the determination of working conditions.

Age and experience have also been found in a number of studies to be related to the propensity to be organized (see, for example, Farber and Saks, 1980; Duncan and Stafford, 1980). Although there are some conflicting results, this relationship appears to be concave; that is, the propensity to choose union representation at first increases, reaches a maximum, and subsequently decreases with age and/or experience. This result, which is also suggested by the tabulations in Table 14.3, is consistent with the view that, when members' preferences differ according to some characteristic like age, unions tend to represent most closely the preferences of members in the middle of the distribution of preferences (i.e., the median member).

An individual's position in the earnings distribution may also affect the net benefits of being represented by a union. As explained subsequently, unions tend to increase the wages of those at the lower end of the wage distribution by a relatively large amount and those in the upper tail of the wage distribution by a relatively small amount. Thus individuals whose earnings would be above average in the absence of a union are less likely to favour union representation.

Exhibit 14.3 Gender Differences in Unionization

www.statcan.ca/english/sdds/3830.htm

During the past three decades, significant changes have occurred in the extent of union organization of Canadian males and females. In the 1960s, males were more than twice as likely to be unionized as females. For example, in 1966 union density of males was over 38 percent, whereas that of females was about 16 percent (Mainville and Olineck, 1999). However, the male-female unionization gap has subsequently narrowed considerably—reflecting the fact that female unionization has grown substantially whereas that of males has fallen moderately. The data shown below, based on a series of special surveys by Statistics Canada, show that the gender gap in unionization narrowed by almost half during the 1980s—from about 12 to 6 percentage points.

	Extent of Collective Agreement Coverage		Gender
	Male	Female	Unionization Gap
1981*	38.6	26.8	11.8
1984	46.0	36.6	9.4
1986	43.7	35.2	8.5
1988	37.6	28.7	8.9
1990	40.5	34.3	6.2
1999	33.2	31.1	2.1

*Union membership.

In an empirical study analyzing the 1981, 1984, and 1988 surveys, Doiron and Riddell (1994) find that the gender unionization gap is mainly due to differences between males and females in labour force characteristics; in particular, females possess fewer of each of the characteristics which make unionization likely. The occupation and industry distributions of females are the most important such characteristics, followed by job tenure and full-time work. Differences between males and females in the impacts of labour force characteristics on the probability of unionization contribute relatively little to the gap in union coverage.

Over time, males and females have become more similar in their labour force characteristics (experience, education, part-time employment, etc.). Thus the gender gap in union coverage has narrowed.

From a longer-term perspective, the rapid expansion of female employment in the public and quasi-public (health, education, and social services) sectors, together with increased unionization of public and quasi-public sector employees since the mid-1960s, has also contributed significantly to the increased unionization of Canadian women (Akyeampong, 1998).

Because unionized workers typically earn more than their nonunion counterparts, this narrowing of the male-female unionization gap may have raised the earnings of women relative to those of men. Doiron and Riddell find that the male-female earnings differential would have widened by about 7 percentage points in the absence of the increase in female unionization relative to that of males.

Gender differences in unionization have also declined substantially in the United States; however, in the U.S. this was brought about by a steep decline in male unionization while that of females remained approximately constant. Even and Macpherson (1993) find that the greater decline in male unionism is responsible for about one-fifth of the 13-percentage-point decline in the gender wage gap which occurred between 1973 and 1987.

Summary

In summary, the growth of unions over time and the extent of union organization across industries, regions, occupations, and establishment and employee characteristics are systematically related to a number of economic, social, and legal variables. These observed relationships are generally consistent with the demand-supply framework, which appears to provide a valuable conceptual device for understanding the growth and incidence of unions.

- Unions are collective organizations whose primary objective is to improve the well-being of their members. In Canada this objective is met primarily through collective bargaining with the employer.
- There are two basic types of unions. Craft unions represent workers in a particular trade or occupation while industrial unions represent the workers in a specific industry. Some unions combine elements of both types.
- A significant fraction of the Canadian labour force—about 26 percent in 1998—are union members. The importance of unions in Canada has increased over time. Union membership as a percentage of non-agricultural paid workers—a commonly used measure of union density—rose from 16 percent in 1920 to 33 percent in 1998.
- Union representation and collective bargaining in Canada are regulated by an elaborate legal framework that has changed substantially over time. The law provides workers with the right to form and join unions, and establishes procedures for administering and enforcing these rights. Canadian labour legislation has also traditionally regulated the use of work stoppages.
- Jurisdiction over labour legislation rests mainly with the provinces, with federal jurisdiction limited to about 10 percent of the labour force.
- The extent of union organization differs substantially across countries. On the basis of union density, Canada is in the middle of the pack among the OECD countries. However, collective agreement coverage in Canada is lower than in most OECD countries, and substantially below levels that prevail in many European countries.
- In Australia and many European countries there is a large difference between union membership and collective agreement coverage. These differences arise because of centralized bargaining at the level of the industry, sector, or entire economy, and because union agreements are frequently extended to cover unorganized workers in the same industry or sector. In these circumstances, union membership may substantially understate the influence of unions in the economy. In Canada, the gap between union membership and collective agreement coverage is relatively small.
- The extent of union organization varies considerably by industry, occupation, region, and various individual employee and employer characteristics. Workers in the public and quasi-public sectors (public administration, education, and health care) are the most heavily unionized, as are workers employed in large establishments.
- Economists use a demand-supply model to explain variations in unionization over time and across industries, regions, and types of workers at a point in time. The demand for union representation emanates from employees and depends on the expected benefits and costs of union representation. The supply of union representation emanates from the organizing and contract administration activities of union leaders and their staff. Employers' actions may influence either the demand or supply of union representation by altering the costs and benefits to employees and union leaders and organizers.
- The growth of unions over time, and the extent of union organization across industries, regions, occupations, and establishment and employee characteristics, are systematically related to a number of economic, social, and legal/institutional variables. Both

social attitudes toward unions and the legislative framework governing collective bargaining (which in turn may reflect society's views of unions) appear to influence union growth and decline. Aggregate economic conditions—in particular, employment growth, unemployment, and inflation—also affect union growth over time. Industry and enterprise characteristics such as establishment size, industry concentration, capital-intensity of production, and the extent of job hazards contribute to explaining the large variations in union incidence across industries and establishments. Finally, worker characteristics such as part-time employment, blue collar employment, age, experience, and position in the wage distribution also contribute to the determination of union status. These observed relationships are generally consistent with the demand-supply framework for understanding the growth and incidence of unions.

REVIEW QUESTIONS

1. Account for the differential growth of unionization between Canada and the United States in recent years.
2. "Differential legislative structures may account for some of the differential union growth between Canada and the United States; however, that raises the question of why the legislative structures are different. That is, legislation should be regarded as an endogenous variable and its existence explained." Discuss.
3. Discuss differences in the concepts of union density based on union membership and the proportion of the work force that is covered by a collective agreement. What accounts for the differences in the magnitude in Canada? Which of the two best measures the significance of unions in the determination of wages and working conditions?
4. Outline the main legislative initiatives in Canada that have facilitated the development of unionization and collective bargaining.
5. The extent of unionization in Canada varies from one province to another. Discuss factors which could account for these differences.
6. Discuss the general factors that would explain the differences in union density across industries, occupations, and employee characteristics shown in Table 14.3.

PROBLEMS

1. "Any theory of union growth must be able to explain not only its long-run trend and short-run cyclical variation, but also why unionization varies across countries and across industries, regions, and occupations within a country." Discuss.
2. Given the determinants of unionization, discuss the future prospects for union growth in Canada.
3. Ashenfelter and Pencavel (1969) carry out an econometric analysis of the determinants of union growth in the United States between 1900 and 1960. Would their estimated equation over-predict, accurately predict, or under-predict the subsequent union growth in the United States? If you believe their equation would under- or over-predict the subsequent growth, what variable or variables may have been omitted?

KEYWORDS

unions 417
collective bargaining 417
craft unions 417
industrial unions 417
union membership 418
union density 418
collective agreement coverage 420
demand for union representation 426
supply of union representation 426
union status 427
certification 427
bargaining unit 427
decertification 427

REFERENCES

Abbott, M. 1982. An econometric model of trade union membership growth in Canada, 1925-1966. Princeton University, Industrial Relations Section Working Paper, #154.

Akyeampong, E. 1998. The rise of unionization among women. *PLI* 10(4)(Winter):30-43.

Ashenfelter, O., and J. Pencavel. 1969. American trade union growth: 1900-1960. *QJE* 83 (August):434-48.

Bain, G., and F. Elsheikh. 1976. *Union Growth and the Business Cycle.* Oxford: Blackwell.

______. 1976. Trade union growth in Canada: A comment. *RI/IR* 31 (No. 3):482-90.

Berkowitz, M. 1954. The economics of trade union organization and administration. *ILRR* 7 (July):575-592.

Commons, J., et al. 1918. *History of Labor in the United States, I.* New York: Macmillan.

Doiron, D., and W. Riddell. 1994. The impact of unionization on male-female earnings differences in Canada. *JHR* 29:504-34.

Duncan, G., and F. Stafford. 1980. Do union members receive compensating wage differentials. *AER* 70 (June):335-71.

Even, W., and D. MacPherson. 1993. The decline of private sector unionism and the gender wage gap. *JHR* 28 (Spring):279-96.

Farber, H. 1983. The determinants of the union status of workers. *Ecta.* 51 (September):1417-37.

Farber, H., and A. Krueger. 1993. Union membership in the United States: The decline continues. In *Employee Representation: Alternatives and Future Directions*, eds. B. Kaufman and M. Kleiner. Industrial Relations Research Association.

Farber, H., and D. Saks. 1980. Why workers want unions: The role of relative wages and job characteristics. *JPE* 88 (April):349-69.

Freeman, R. 1986. Unionism comes to the public sector. *JEL* 25 (March):41-86.

______. 1988. Contraction and expansion: the divergence of private sector and public sector unionism in the United States. *JEP* 2 (Spring):63-88.

Johnson, S. 2001. Card check or mandatory representation vote? How the type of union recognition procedure affects union certification success. *EJ* (Forthcoming).

Kumar, P. 1993. *From Uniformity to Divergence: Industrial Relations in Canada and the United States.* Kingston: IRC Press.

Kumar, P., and B. Dow. 1986. Econometric analysis of union membership growth in Canada, 1935-1981. *RI/IR* 41 (No. 2):236-53.

Lipset, S., ed. 1986. *Unions in Transition: Entering the Second Century*. San Francisco: ICS Press.

Mainville, D., and C. Olineck. 1999. Unionization in Canada: A retrospective. *PLI* II (Summer, Supplement: 3-35).

Martinello, F. 2000. Mr. Harris, Mr. Rae, and union activity in Ontario. *CPP* 26 (March):17-34.

Martinello, F., and R. Meng. 1992. Effects of labor legislation and industry characteristics on union coverage in Canada. *ILRR* 46 (October):176-90.

Neumann, G., and E. R. Rissman. 1984. Where have all the union members gone? *JOLE* 2 (April):175-92.

Pencavel, J. 1971. The demand for union services: An exercise. *ILRR* 24 (January):180-90.

Riddell, C. 2001. Union suppression and certification success. *CJE* 34 (May): 396-410.

Riddell, C., and W. C. Riddell. 2001. Changing patterns of unionization: The North American experience, 1984-1998. University of British Columbia, Department of Economics, Discussion Paper 01 C.23, June.

Riddell, W. 1993. Unionization in Canada and the United States: A tale of two countries. In *Small Differences that Matter: Labor Markets and Income Maintenance in Canada and the United States*, eds. D. Card and R. Freeman. Chicago: University of Chicago Press.

Robinson, C. 1995. Union incidence in the public and private sectors. *CJE* 28 (November):1056-76.

Swidinsky, R. 1974. Trade union growth in Canada: 1911-1970. *RI/IR* 29 (No. 3):435-50.

Thomason, T. 1994. The effect of accelerated union certification procedures on union organizing success in Ontario. *ILLR* 47 (January):207-26.

Weiler, J. 1986. The role of law in labor relations. In *Labour Law and Urban Law in Canada*, eds. I. Bernier and A. Lajoie. Toronto: Royal Commission on the Economic Union and Development Prospects for Canada and University of Toronto Press.

Weiler, P. 1983. Promises to keep: Securing workers' rights to self-organization under the NLRA. *Harvard Law Review* 96 (June):1769-829.

______. 1984. Striking a new balance: Freedom of contract and the prospect for union representation. *Harvard Law Review* 98 (December):351-420.

Chapter Fifteen

Wage and Employment Determination Under Collective Bargaining

Main Questions

- *What motives underlie union behaviour? How, for example, do unions evaluate the tradeoff between higher wages and improved job security?*
- *Can union behaviour be reasonably represented by a purely economic model?*
- *How do firms and unions interact in the setting of employment and wages?*
- *In what sense might unions lead to inefficient production decisions?*
- *Can economic theory account for apparently inefficient union practices like "featherbedding" and other restrictions placed on firm employment decisions?*
- *How can we incorporate "bargaining power" into a model of firm-union interaction?*

The previous chapter was concerned with explaining which organizations are unionized and which are nonunion. We now turn to the behavioural implications of unionization and collective bargaining. In order to understand and predict the consequences of collective bargaining we begin by examining union objectives and the constraints unions face in attempting to achieve those objectives. Then we examine the firm's objectives and constraints and how the two parties interact to determine collective bargaining outcomes. Much of this chapter focuses on the determination of wages and employment. Various nonwage aspects of employment—such as grievance procedures, seniority provisions, workplace health and safety, and fringe benefits—are discussed in the next chapter.

THEORY OF UNION BEHAVIOUR

The economic analysis of firms and households begins from the assumption that the decision-maker maximizes an objective function subject to the constraints imposed on the agent by the economic environment. Private sector firms are usually assumed to maximize profits subject to the production function (which summarizes the technical possibilities available to the firm), the demand conditions in the product markets, and the supply conditions in the markets for inputs. This is the theory that underlies the demand for labour discussed in Chapter 5 of this book. It is a theory rich in testable implications, and one which has generally been found to accord with the available evidence. Similarly, the household is assumed to maximize utility (which depends on the quantities consumed of various goods, including leisure) subject to the budget constraint (which depends on the prices of goods and the wage rate). This is the theory that underlies the demand for goods and services in product markets and the theory of labour supply discussed in Chapter 2 of this book. This theory is also rich in testable implications, and has generally been found to be consistent with the evidence on household behaviour.

Economists have generally agreed that an understanding of union behaviour and its consequences must likewise begin with a theory of union objectives. The union can then be assumed to maximize its objective or utility function subject to the constraints imposed on the union and its members by the economic environment. However, our ability to characterize union preferences has long been and remains controversial. The major aspects of this controversy were debated several decades ago by Dunlop (1944) and Ross (1948). Dunlop advocated an "economic" approach in which the union is modelled as attempting to maximize a well-defined objective function subject to labour market constraints. (The specific objective function suggested by Dunlop is discussed below.) Ross criticized this approach and argued that union decision-making can only be understood by treating the union as a political institution. Although this debate has not been fully resolved, the modern approach to union behaviour recognizes some merit in both positions in that the union is modelled as attempting to maximize a well-defined objective function but attention is paid to the political nature of union decision-making.

UNION OBJECTIVES

Unions are collective organizations whose leaders represent members of the bargaining unit—the rank-and-file—in collective bargaining with the firm. **Union objectives** refer to the goals of the organization. These need not be identical to the objectives of the individual members or to those of the union leaders. Three factors influence the relationship among the preferences of the members, the union leaders, and those of the union as a whole: (1) the information available to the rank-and-file about the available options, (2) the nature of the union's political decision-making process, and (3) the degree of homogeneity of the individual members' preferences. If the rank-and-file are well informed and the union's decision-making processes are highly democratic, the union leaders will make choices that have the support of a majority of the members. (Otherwise they will be quickly replaced.) In these circumstances, the union's objectives are those which a majority of the rank-and-file would favour. However, asymmetric information (the members being less informed than the leaders) or imperfectly democratic decision-making processes may allow the union leaders to pursue their own objectives to some degree. In these circumstances the objectives of the members and those pursued by the union may differ.

The degree of homogeneity of individual members' preferences is another important factor. If the rank-and-file have very similar preferences it will be easy for the union leaders to determine the group's preferred choices. However, if preferences differ significantly across individuals or groups of individuals the task of the union leaders is more difficult and selecting an option that will be supported by a majority may require considerable skill and judgment.

Although various union objectives have been postulated, most involve two key aspects—the wages and employment of union members (abstracting from the various non-wage aspects of working conditions for the moment). This suggests a union objective or utility function whereby utility is a positive function of both the wage rate and the employment of union members (and which may also depend on other variables as discussed below). Combinations of the wage rate and employment which are equally satisfactory to the union—the union's indifference or iso-utility curves—must be downward-sloping because a higher wage is needed to compensate for lower employment, and vice versa. Furthermore, it is plausible to hypothesize that union preferences display a diminishing marginal rate of substitution between wages and employment; that is, holding utility constant, the union will be less willing to accept a wage reduction in return for a given increase in employment the higher the level of employment, and vice versa. This implies that the indifference curves have the convex shape displayed in Figure 15.1. (See the appendix to Chapter 2 for a review of indifference curves.)

Union objectives are likely to depend on several additional variables. One is the overall price level, or the cost of living. Clearly what matters to the workers (and thus to the union leaders) is the real wage rate. A 10 percent increase (or decrease) in the nominal wage rate accompanied by a 10 percent increase (or decrease) in the price level leaves the workers' real income and, therefore, consumption and leisure possibilities unchanged. Union utility is also likely to depend on the **alternative wage** (i.e., the wage rate that union members could earn if employed elsewhere). Few workers will be willing to bear the costs of union representation (union dues and other costs discussed earlier) unless their compensation is equal to or greater than that available elsewhere for comparable work. For this reason the alternative (real) wage is shown as a lower bound to the union's indifference curves in Figure 15.1.

Figure 15.1 **Union Objectives and Constraints**

Union indifference curves plot combinations of wages and employment that yield equal utility. The indifference curves display diminishing marginal rate of substitution as the union requires more employment to compensate for a one-unit reduction in the wage, the lower the wage. The indifference curves do not fall below the alternative wage because no level of employment would be sufficient to compensate for a wage below what union members could earn elsewhere. If the firm chooses employment, the union's constraint is the labour demand curve. The combination of wages and employment that yields maximum union utility is point a_0, where the indifference curve is tangent to the labour demand curve.

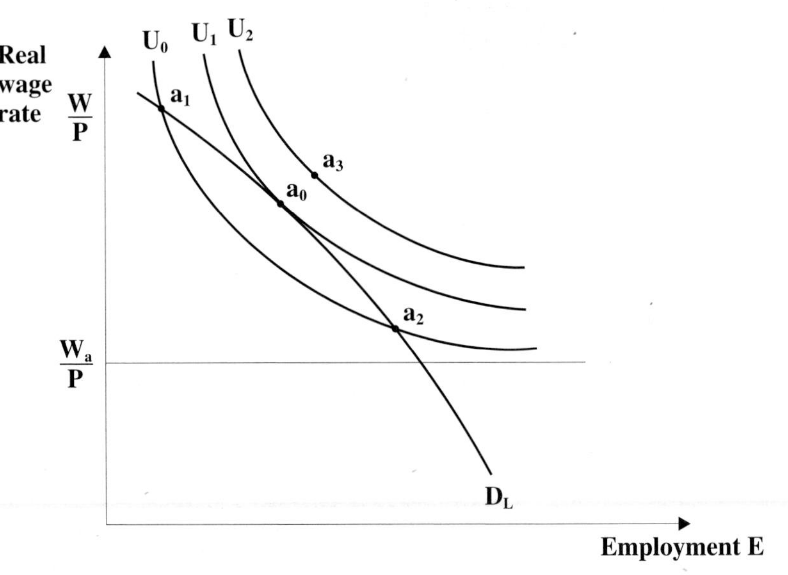

In using the term "employment" we have not distinguished between hours worked and number of employees. Implicitly hours worked are held constant, so that employment refers to the number of workers. This assumption is innocuous at this stage, but needs to be relaxed when examining issues such as worksharing versus layoffs in response to temporary reductions in demand. Also, we have not discussed how the size of the union membership is determined. Membership size will matter to both the union leadership and the existing union members—the former because a larger membership implies more revenue from dues and possibly more power and prestige, and the latter because a larger membership may imply reduced employment opportunities, depending on how scarce jobs are rationed when employment demand is insufficient.

SOME SPECIAL CASES

As noted earlier, various union objective functions have been suggested in the literature on union behaviour. Several of these are special cases of the utility function illustrated in Figure 15.1, and examining these may increase our understanding of union objectives.

Maximize the Wage Rate W

This would imply that the union places no weight on employment, that is, that the indifference curves are horizontal straight lines, as shown in Figure 15.2(a). Although this may seem implausible, the notion that, in negotiating wages, unions do not take into account the employment consequences of higher wages has a long tradition including the influential work of Ross (1948), and is often stated by union leaders today.

Maximize Employment E

This is the opposite extreme of the previous objective, and implies indifference curves which are vertical straight lines, as shown in Figure 15.2(b).

Maximize the (Real) Wage Bill wE

This objective, proposed by Dunlop (1944), implies that the indifference curves are rectangular hyperbolas as shown in Figure 15.2(c). (wE = a constant is the equation of a rectangular hyperbola.) It has the advantage that the union attaches weight to both wages and employment. The wage bill is, of course, total labour income. It may appear plausible that union members would attempt to maximize their total income, especially if there is some mechanism for sharing the income between employed and unemployed members. The main defect of this objective function is that it disregards the alternative wage; indeed it implies that the union may be willing to allow the wage to fall below W_a in exchange for higher employment.[1]

Maximize (Real) Economic Rent $(w - w_a)E$

This objective is analogous to profit-maximization for a monopolist; the alternative wage is the opportunity cost to each union member, so **economic rent** is analogous to total revenue (wE) minus total cost (w_aE). In this case the indifference curves are rectangular hyperbolas with respect to the new origin (W_a,0), as shown in Figure 15.2(d).

This objective is probably the most plausible of the group, in that it hypothesizes that the union members seek to maximize their "total return," given what they could earn elsewhere. Again, the objective is most plausible when there is some mechanism for sharing the income between employed and unemployed union members.

[1]To avoid this difficulty, Dunlop (1944) suggested that the union maximize the wage bill subject to a "membership function" which shows the wage rate needed to attract a given number of union members. The membership function is analogous to a labour supply function.

Figure 15.2 **Union Objectives: Some Special Cases**

The panels illustrate four special cases of the union utility function. In panel (a) the union maximizes the wage, placing no weight on employment. The indifference curves are horizontal straight lines in wage-employment space. In panel (b) the union maximizes employment, placing no weight on the wage. The indifference curves are vertical straight lines. In panel (c) the union maximizes the wage bill, wages times employment. The indifference curves are rectangular hyperbolas, and display diminishing marginal rate of substitution between wages and employment. In panel (d) the union maximizes economic rent, the product of employment times the difference between the union wage and the alternative wage. The indifference curves are rectangular hyperbolas in wage-employment space above the alternative wage, and display diminishing marginal rate of substitution between wages and employment.

(a) Maximize wage rate

(b) Maximize employment

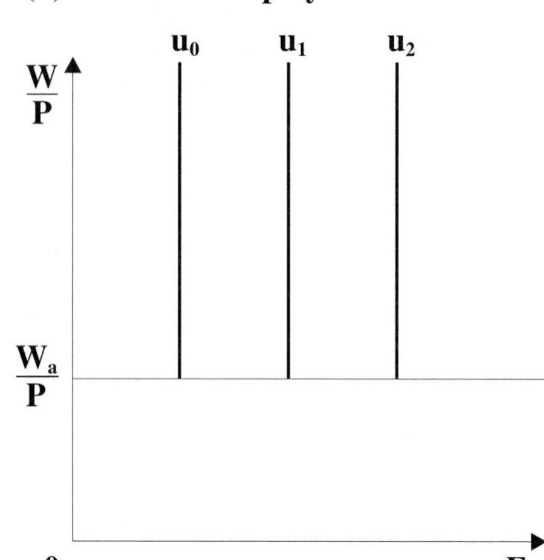

(c) Maximize wage bill

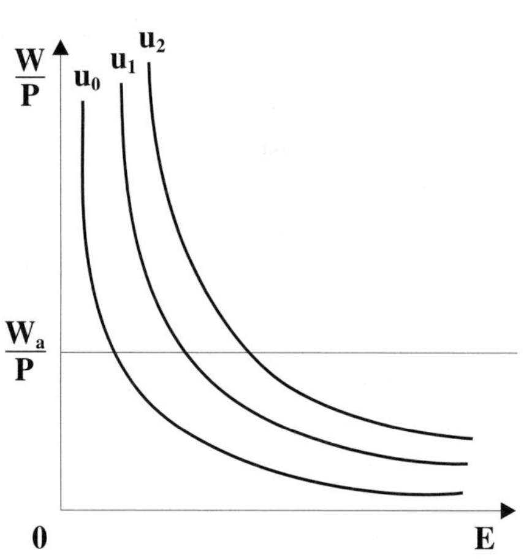

(d) Maximize economic rent

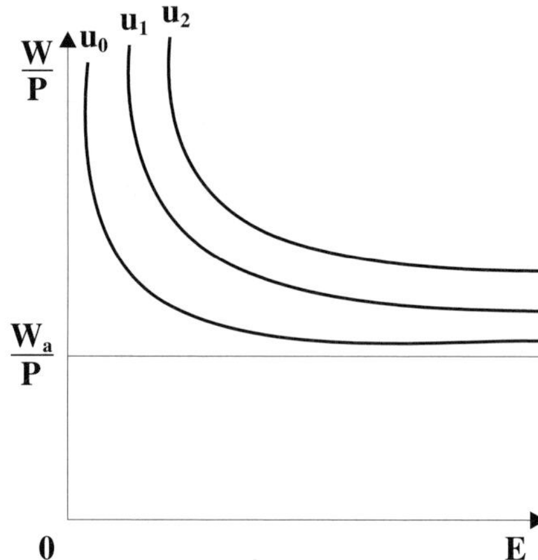

UNION PREFERENCES: SOME ADDITIONAL CONSIDERATIONS

The task of deriving union objectives from the preferences of the constituent members is simplest (though not necessarily simple) when: (1) members' preferences are homogeneous, (2) union leaders are constrained by democratic decision-making processes and the availability of information from pursuing their own objectives, and (3) union membership is exogenously determined. When these conditions do not hold, the economics of union behaviour is more complex.

Heterogeneous Preferences

The preferences of individual union members may differ for a variety of reasons. The union may represent several groups of employees with different occupations or skills. Industrial unions often contain highly skilled employees (usually a minority) in addition to semiskilled and unskilled workers. Alternatively, workers performing similar jobs may differ according to a number of personal characteristics such as age, seniority, marital status, and alternative employment opportunities. Individual preferences may depend in a systematic way on these characteristics. For example, older workers may desire a greater emphasis on pensions and other forms of deferred compensation and less emphasis on current earnings in the total compensation package. Those with good alternative employment opportunities (high W_a's) may prefer a higher union wage than those with limited opportunities, for given levels of employment security. If layoffs take place in accordance with seniority, more senior workers may wish to place more emphasis on wages and less emphasis on employment in union objectives. Clearly these sources of heterogeneity may be important in particular settings and the economic analysis of union behaviour should be able to account for their implications.

The conditions under which heterogeneous individual preferences can be aggregated into a group or social objective function is a central issue in the theory of public choice. One well-known result is the **median voter model** which states that when choices over a single variable are made in a democratic fashion (i.e., by voting among alternatives) then under certain conditions the group's preferences will be identical to those of the median voter. The reason is that the outcome preferred by the median voter will defeat all others in a sequence of pairwise elections. In the union context this result implies that if, for example, the members' preferences with respect to the wage rate depend on the worker's seniority, the union's objective function will be that of the member with the median seniority (i.e., that individual for whom half the members are more senior and half the members are less senior).

The conditions under which the median voter model holds are fairly stringent. One key requirement is that the choice or voting set must be defined over a single variable (e.g., the wage in the union setting). Thus, with heterogeneous members, union preferences over multiple objectives (wages, employment, nonwage benefits, working conditions) cannot be derived from the assumption of pairwise voting among alternatives except under special conditions.

When the required conditions do not hold, a voting equilibrium will generally not exist; that is, no single set of outcomes will defeat all others in a sequence of pairwise elections. In these circumstances, the organization's choice will depend on factors such as the order in which alternatives are presented for voting.

Clearly the assumptions of the median voter model do not apply precisely in the union setting. Unions typically do not choose among alternatives by conducting a sequence of pairwise votes. Most choices are made by union leaders who are elected periodically by the membership. In addition, the union leaders often face tradeoffs among several alternatives such as wages, nonwage benefits, and employment. Nonetheless when union members' preferences are heterogeneous the median voter model may predict union behaviour reasonably well. Union leaders wishing to remain in office will adopt positions that a majority of the membership support. When the members can be ordered by a preference-related factor such as age or seniority the choices of the median member, because of their central position in the distribution of preferences, may be more likely to receive majority support than any other set of choices.

Union Leaders Versus Union Members

Unions, like societies, generally do not make choices in a fully democratic fashion in the sense of conducting a referendum each time a decision must be made. Rather, union leaders are elected to implement policy and their position of authority may allow them to pursue their own interests to some extent. Furthermore, because they specialize in contract administration and collective bargaining with the employer, union leaders generally have greater access than members do to information regarding the feasible options.

In addition, the information that is received by the rank-and-file can be filtered to some degree by the leadership.

These observations suggest that union leaders may be able to pursue their own interests—such as maximizing dues revenue, expanding the union's membership and influence, and raising their own personal income. Nonetheless, the desire to remain in office (and perhaps other considerations) does constrain the leaders from deviating too far from the wishes of the membership. How binding these constraints are may well vary according to individual circumstances. A theory of union preferences based solely on the wishes of the members may not be able to account for all aspects of union behaviour in all settings. Nonetheless, it may provide a good approximation to observed behaviour.

Union Membership and Union Objectives

Changes in union membership may alter union preferences. For example, if employment in the industry or firm is expanding rapidly, not only will membership size increase but the age and seniority of the median member will probably fall. The union's objectives, if the union represents members' preferences, will adjust to reflect the wishes of the younger, less senior worker. The opposite is likely to occur in declining sectors.

In formulating wage policy, the current union membership also influences the size of future membership and thus future union preferences. If the union pursues a high-wage policy, future membership will be reduced as employers substitute capital for labour and consumers substitute less expensive products. Thus union preferences may not be stable over time, but may depend on the wage policies adopted.

UNION CONSTRAINTS

The union cannot choose whatever wage and employment outcomes it desires, but must negotiate with the firm and must also take into account the consequences for its members of the outcomes of these negotiations. Initially we will assume that the two parties negotiate over the wage rate, leaving the firm free to choose the level of employment at whatever wage rate is agreed upon by collective bargaining. (The possibility of negotiating over both wages and employment is discussed subsequently.) In these circumstances, the firm will choose the level of employment that maximizes profits given the negotiated wage; i.e., will choose employment according to the labour demand curve.[2] It follows that when the firm can unilaterally determine employment the union is constrained by the firm's labour demand curve. That is, the firm's labour demand curve is analogous to a budget constraint for the utility-maximizing union.

In this situation, the union's preferred wage-employment outcome is the point a_o in previous Figure 15.1, where the iso-utility curve u_1 is tangent to the labour demand curve. Wage-employment combinations such as a_1 and a_2 are attainable but the union prefers a_o to a_1 and a_2. Outcomes such as a_3 are not attainable if the firm can choose employment.

The firm will prefer wage-employment outcomes at which profits (π) are higher to those at which profits are lower. The firm's **isoprofit curves**—combinations of wage rates and employment which yield equal profits—are shown in Figure 15.3. Note that lower curves imply higher profits; that is, $\pi_3 > \pi_2 > \pi_1 > \pi_o$. This is so, because for any given level of employment, say E*, profits are higher when wages are lower, other things equal.

Each curve attains a maximum at the point at which the isoprofit curve and the demand for labour curve intersect. This is so because if we fix the wage at, say, W*, then profits

[2]In the public and nonprofit sectors the labour demand curve is derived under different assumptions about the organization's objective, for example cost minimization. In these circumstances the demand curve shows the cost-minimizing level of employment for each wage rate.

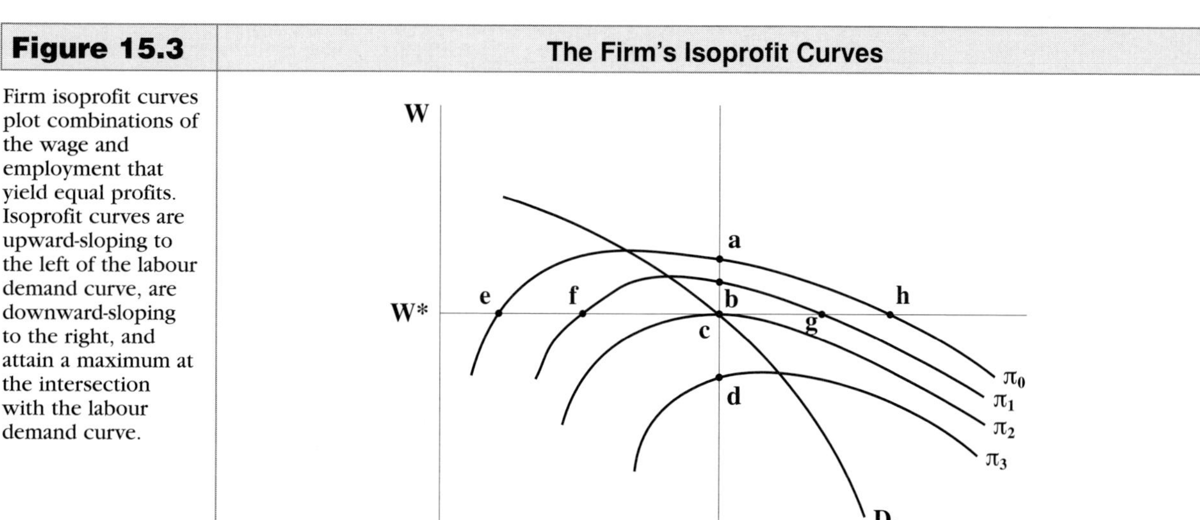

Figure 15.3 **The Firm's Isoprofit Curves**

Firm isoprofit curves plot combinations of the wage and employment that yield equal profits. Isoprofit curves are upward-sloping to the left of the labour demand curve, are downward-sloping to the right, and attain a maximum at the intersection with the labour demand curve.

must be highest at c because D^L shows the profit-maximizing quantity of E at each wage. Thus, as the firm increases employment from e to f to c, π must increase (i.e., the firm must be moving to isoprofit curves with higher profit levels), reflecting the fact that each additional worker hired adds more to total revenue than to total cost (i.e., MRP > W where MRP is the "marginal revenue product," the change in total revenue that results when one additional employee is hired). Similarly, as the firm increases employment from c to g to h, π must fall, reflecting the fact that for E > E*, MRP > W (i.e., each additional employee adds less to total revenue than to total costs).

It is important to recognize that although the firm is maximizing profits at each point on the labour demand curve, the firm is not indifferent among these points because each corresponds to a different level of profits. The higher the wage rate, the lower the maximum attainable level of profits.

Because profits rise as the firm moves down and to the right along D_L, the firm will prefer lower points on D_L to higher points. However, the firm is constrained by the fact that it cannot pay wages below the alternative wage that employees could get elsewhere. Thus in Figure 15.4, I_f (I for "ideal") is the firm's preferred (W,E) combination while I_u is the union's preferred (W,E) combination. The **bargaining range** is the interval [W_a,W_u]. The firm would not want the wage rate to fall below W_a, and the union would not want a wage higher than W_u because a higher wage would not be worth the reduction in employment. Within the bargaining range, however, higher wages make the union better off and the firm worse off (and vice versa).

The bargaining range may be further limited by the need for the firm to earn a normal rate of return (zero economic profits) in order to remain in business, a constraint analogous to the requirement that employees receive a wage at least equal to that available elsewhere. The isoprofit curve corresponding to zero economic profits is shown as π_o in Figure 15.4; thus if the wage were higher than W_0 the firm would go out of business. The wage at which profits are zero (W_0) may be above or below the union's preferred wage, W_u. (In a competitive equilibrium W_0 and W_a coincide, and there is no scope for raising wages without forcing some firms to shut down operations.) When W_0 is below W_u, the upper limit to the bargaining range is W_0.

Figure 15.4 **The Firm's and Union's Preferred Wage-Employment Outcomes and the Bargaining Range**

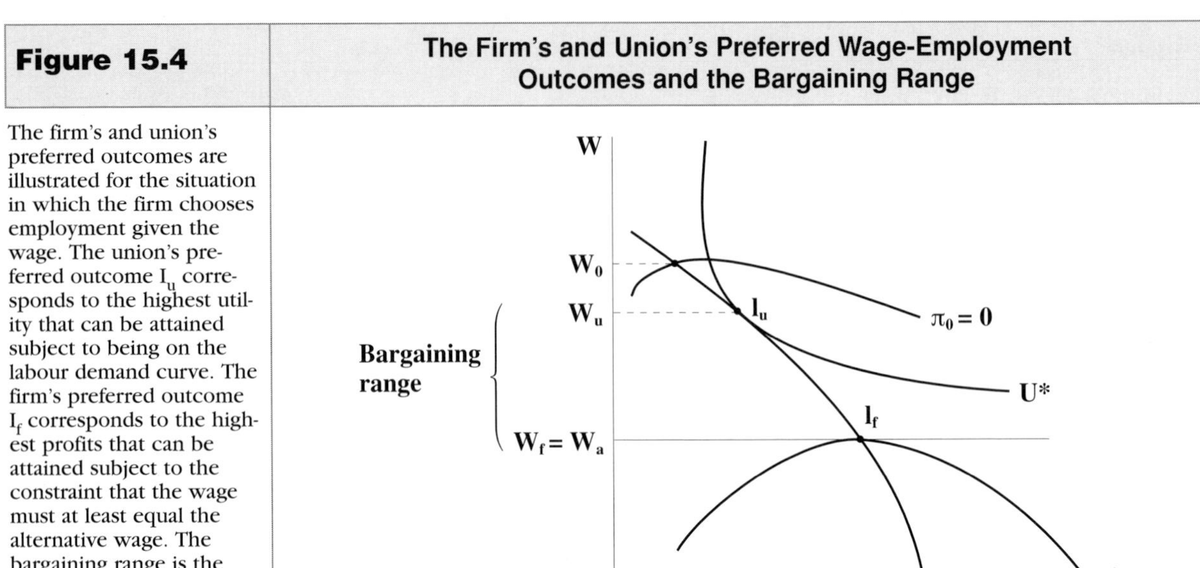

The firm's and union's preferred outcomes are illustrated for the situation in which the firm chooses employment given the wage. The union's preferred outcome I_u corresponds to the highest utility that can be attained subject to being on the labour demand curve. The firm's preferred outcome I_f corresponds to the highest profits that can be attained subject to the constraint that the wage must at least equal the alternative wage. The bargaining range is the set of wages between W_f and W_u.

The theory outlined thus far does not predict a unique wage and employment outcome, but rather predicts that the wage rate will lie somewhere in the bargaining range (W_a, W_u) with the corresponding level of employment being determined according to the labour demand function. To complete the theory we require an explanation of the determination of the bargaining outcome arrived at by the two parties. This requires a theory of bargaining, a subject taken up later. First we examine two closely related possibilities: (1) that the union may attempt to alter the constraint and (2) that the firm and union may bargain over both wages and employment, rather than leaving the latter to be unilaterally determined by the firm. In addition, the way unions can achieve their objectives by restricting supply is also discussed.

RELAXING THE DEMAND CONSTRAINT

Through collective bargaining with the employer, the union will attempt to reach a wage-employment outcome as close as possible to its preferred outcome I_u. However, unions can also enhance the set of available options by altering the constraint—either increasing labour demand or making the demand for labour more inelastic, so that increases in wages will have less severe consequences for employment. Various union practices attempt to achieve these results. With respect to the goal of making labour demand more inelastic, recall from Chapter 5 that the elasticity of labour demand depends on (1) the elasticity of product demand, (2) the elasticity of substitution between labour and other inputs, (3) the share of labour in total costs, and (4) the elasticity of labour supply of other inputs. Union activity is thus often directed at restricting substitution possibilities by consumers in product markets and by employers in labour markets, the latter including the substitution of nonunion for union labour in addition to the substitution of capital and other inputs for labour. Some restrictions come about through collective bargaining with the employer, while others are achieved by influencing public policy.

Because of the derived nature of labour demand, some attempts to alter the constraint focus on the product market. These include: support for quotas, tariffs, and other restrictions on foreign competition in order to reduce the number of substitutes for union-produced goods and services (observed, for example, in the Canadian auto, textile, and shoe industries); opposition to deregulation, which generally enhances product market competition and may facilitate entry by nonunion competitors (observed, for example, in the communications and transportation industries); advertising of the product (e.g., union label on beer); and union attempts to organize all the firms in an industry in order to minimize substitution of nonunion-produced for union-produced goods and services.

Other union policies focus on the labour market. Unions are generally strong supporters of various forms of wage-fixing for nonunion labour such as minimum wage laws and "fair wage" provisions in government contracts. Raising the wage of nonunion workers reduces the potential for substitution of nonunion for union labour—both directly through arrangements such as contracting-out of work by unionized employers and indirectly by the growth of nonunion firms at the expense of union firms. Advocating "fair wages" for unorganized employees and higher minimum wages for both organized and unorganized workers may also be viewed by the union movement as an effective method of raising the living standards of the labour force and increasing labour's share of national income. Union support for full employment policies may reflect similar desires; such support can also be viewed as an attempt to increase labour demand generally, including the demand for union labour, as well as reducing the size of the pool of unemployed workers competing for jobs and thus weakening the position of employed union members.

Attempts to alter the constraint can have offsetting effects; in these circumstances the union's optimal strategy will depend on the magnitude of the opposing effects. For example, raising the wages of unorganized workers limits the potential for substitution of nonunion for union labour, but may also reduce the incentive for these workers to organize. The growth paths adopted by early craft unions also illustrate opposing effects. Some craft unions remained narrowly focused, representing a small group of highly skilled workers. An advantage of this arrangement is that the earnings of these workers often account for a small fraction of total cost. Other craft unions expanded to cover semiskilled and unskilled workers in the same enterprise and industry in order to minimize the substitution among different types of labour that would occur in response to an increase in the wage of the highly skilled group.

The potential for labour market substitution can also be reduced by restrictions on labour supply—such as limited immigration and control of entry through occupational licensing and apprenticeship arrangements. Restrictions on labour supply into the occupation or trade are most frequently employed by craft unions and professional associations such as those representing doctors and lawyers. Unions also attempt to limit the employer's substitution possibilities by negotiating contract provisions such as those relating to technological change, contracting-out of work, and work practices. This feature of collective bargaining involves the two parties in the negotiation of contracts relating to both wages and employment, a topic examined next.

EFFICIENT WAGE AND EMPLOYMENT CONTRACTS

Because unions generally care about the employment prospects of their members, we would expect the union to use its bargaining power to negotiate over employment as well as wages. Of course, the employer may resist this attempt because agreeing to certain levels of employment will have implications for the firm's profits. Nonetheless, if the union and its members care enough about employment, they may be willing to accept a lower wage in exchange for higher levels (or greater security of) employment. In these circumstances, the union and the firm may discover that an agreement with respect to both wages and employment is to their mutual advantage. Such **efficient wage and employment contracts** may be explicit (i.e., contained in the collective agreement) or implicit (i.e., an understanding that both parties respect).

In general, the firm and union can each benefit from negotiating a contract covering *both* wages and employment rather than having the firm choose employment subject to a fixed wage. That is, wage-employment outcomes on the labour demand curve imply unexploited "gains from trade" and thus are inefficient in the Pareto sense. (Recall that an outcome is said to be *Pareto-efficient* or *Pareto-optimal* if no individual or group of individuals can be made better off without making some individual or group of individuals worse off.)

This is illustrated in Figure 15.5. Starting at points on the labour demand curve such as A and B, it is possible to make one or both parties better off by moving to outcomes in the respective shaded areas. At A' both the union and firm are better off than at A, while at A'' the union is better off than, and the firm as well off as, at A. Note that at A'' it is not possible to move in any direction that does not make at least one party worse off. Thus A'' is a **Pareto-efficient wage-employment outcome.**[3] It is characterized by the union's indifference curve being tangent to the firm's isoprofit curve. This is a necessary condition for an efficient wage-employment arrangement.

The reasoning underlying this condition is as follows. The slope of the indifference curve measures the union's willingness to trade off wages against employment, holding utility constant. That is, it shows the largest wage reduction the union would accept in exchange for an increase in employment of one unit. Similarly, the slope of the isoprofit

Figure 15.5 **Efficient and Inefficient Wage-Employment Contracts**

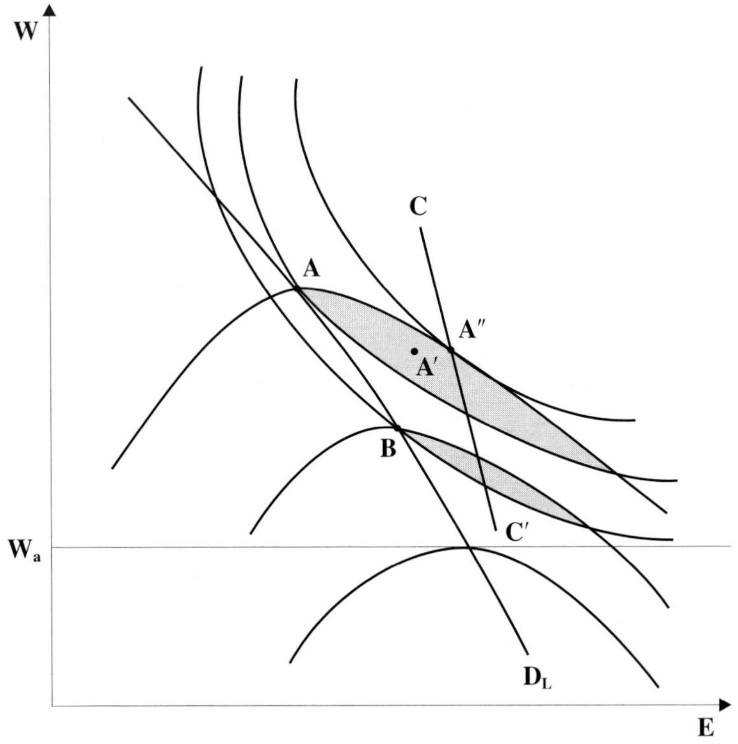

Wage-employment contracts on the labour demand curve are inefficient. For example, compared to the point A on the labour demand curve, both parties are better off at point A' which yields higher union utility and higher firm profits. The set of Pareto-efficient wage-employment contracts, called the contract curve and shown as CC', is the locus of points at which a union indifference curve is tangent to a firm isoprofit curve. Because the union indifference curves are downward-sloping, this set of tangencies must occur to the right of the labour demand curve, where the firm isoprofit curves are also downward-sloping.

[3]Pareto-efficiency is defined here in terms of the interests of the two parties. Whether such wage-employment outcomes are socially efficient (Pareto-efficient in terms of the interests of society as a whole) is unclear and will depend on a variety of other factors.

curve measures the firm's ability to substitute between wages and employment while holding profits constant. That is, it shows the minimum wage reduction the firm would require in exchange for an agreement to increase employment by one unit. When these slopes are not equal, unexploited gains from trade must exist. That is, by increasing employment by one unit and reducing the wage by more than the minimum the firm would require to maintain constant profits but less than the union would accept to maintain constant utility, both parties are made better off.

The locus of the Pareto-efficient wage-employment outcomes is called the **contract curve** and is shown as CC' in Figure 15.5. When the union cares about wages and employment (i.e., if the indifference curves are downward-sloping), the contract curve must lie to the right of the labour demand curve. This follows from the fact that the isoprofit curves are upward sloping to the left of the labour demand curve, have a slope of zero where the two intersect, and are downward sloping to the right of the labour demand curve. Thus the tangency conditions can only be met to the right of the labour demand function, where both the isoprofit and iso-utility curves slope downward.

In summary, both the firm and the union can benefit from negotiating a wage-employment outcome on the contract curve. Of course, the two parties will have differing views about which *particular outcome* on the contract curve should be chosen. Moving up CC', the union becomes better off and the firm worse off, and vice versa. As before, there is a bargaining range and where the parties end up within that range depends on their relative bargaining strengths. The lower limit of the bargaining range is determined as before; the firm would not want the wage rate to be lower than would be required to attract workers. The upper limit is determined by a zero economic profit condition; in general the union would not want wages and employment set at a level which caused the firm to cease operations.

Several implications follow from this analysis. Perhaps the most important implication is that the two parties have an incentive to negotiate wage-employment arrangements which may appear to be wasteful. Outcomes on the contract curve must involve the firm employing more labour than the firm would choose on its own, given the wage rate; i.e., hiring redundant personnel or spreading a given number of tasks among more workers. Such outcomes can be enforced by work rules of various kinds—arrangements which are often referred to as restrictive work practices or featherbedding. The above analysis shows why such practices may be to the mutual advantage of the employer and the union.

A second important implication is that, in the context of efficient contracts, the anticipated negative relationship (other influences being held constant) between wages and employment may not hold. The contract curve may be vertical or upward- or downward-sloping. Thus it need not be the case in this setting that higher wages imply reduced employment, and vice versa. A more powerful union will generally be able to achieve higher wages *and* employment than a less powerful union, other things equal. (The meaning of the term *union power* is discussed further later in this chapter.) Nonetheless, any particular union ultimately faces a tradeoff between wages and employment, even when the contract curve is upward-sloping, because the union is ultimately constrained by the need for the employer to earn a satisfactory level of profits in order to continue producing. Thus the union is constrained by the locus of wage-employment combinations that yield this satisfactory level of profits, illustrated by the isoprofit curve π_0 in Figure 15.4, a locus which is downward-sloping to the right of the demand curve.

Obstacles to Reaching Efficient Contracts

While there is an incentive for firms and unions to bargain over both wages and employment and reach an outcome on the contract curve, there are also reasons for believing that outcomes on the labour demand curve may be more likely. One reason is that the information needed to recognize that there are unexploited gains from trade may not be available to both parties. For example, suppose the two parties are currently located at point A in Figure 15.5. As long as each has some information about the other side's preferences, then both will recognize that they are both better off at A' than at A. What this requires is the firm knowing something about the union's willingness to trade off wages against employment, and similarly for the union. However, if neither party trusts the other, then each may be unwilling to reveal information about their preferences to the other, perhaps because of a fear that the other will later use this information to their own advantage. Indeed, there may even be an incentive to misrepresent one's preferences in bargaining situations—that is, not to "tell the truth, the whole truth, and nothing but the truth." In these circumstances it may be difficult for the two bargainers to recognize a Pareto-improving change.

Also, while an agreement over wages is easily enforced, an agreement about employment may be difficult (i.e., costly) to enforce. Some enforcement mechanism is needed to prevent the firm from "cheating" on the agreement; this follows from the fact that at each wage rate the firm's profits are highest at the level of employment given by the labour demand curve. Thus even though both sides are better off on the contract curve, given the negotiated wage rate the firm always has an incentive to cut employment.

If the demand for labour is expected to remain constant during the contract period (the period during which the collective bargaining agreement is in effect), then an agreement about employment should not be difficult to enforce. Presumably the union can keep track of its employed members, and if the firm is caught cheating (e.g., not replacing a worker who quits, retires, or is fired) the union will attempt to punish the firm (e.g., a strike, slowdown, etc.). However, many collective agreements cover a period of two or more years (almost all provide for a duration of at least one year) so that it is unlikely that labour demand will remain constant over the contract period. Thus an agreement concerning employment would have to specify the level of employment for each of the many sets of circumstances that may prevail in the future.[4] This is the case for such factors as the future state of the product market and the costs of other inputs for the firm. From the workers' point of view, important variables would be the cost of living and wages in other firms and industries. Clearly it may be very difficult and expensive to negotiate and enforce such a "contingent" agreement, depending on the different states of nature that may prevail.

The obstacles to negotiating efficient wage-employment contracts are often evident in concession bargaining. Unions have generally been reluctant to engage in concession bargaining unless job guarantees are part of the package, recognizing that without such guarantees the concessions may save few union jobs and may simply lead to higher firm profits. Firms are often reluctant to make explicit employment guarantees because of potential changes in product and labour market conditions.

Since an agreement covering all possible contingencies is unlikely to be workable, the two sides may try to approximate such an arrangement. This can be accomplished by tying employment to the output of the firm or to the use of other inputs. The most common such arrangement is to specify the minimum number of employees to be used for a given task; examples of such provisions are observed in railroads (size of freight train crews), airlines (number of pilots per aircraft), teaching (class size provisions), and musical performances (minimum size of orchestra). (Some of these provisions may also reflect other objectives, such as safety.) Such rules may not be difficult to enforce; further, they have the advantage that they allow the firm to adjust employment in response to fluctuations in the

[4]If D_L shifts, so does the set of Pareto-efficient (W,E) combinations. Even if an agreement for a specific level of employment could be enforced, there is no incentive for the two parties to reach such an agreement if the demand or supply of labour is expected to shift.

demand for the firm's product, yet oblige the firm to hire more employees in each state of demand than the firm would choose on its own.

The practice of negotiating work rules that restrict the firm's ability to control employment can thus be interpreted as a mechanism for approximating an efficient contract. In effect the unconstrained demand curve D_L is replaced by a constrained demand curve D_L^C which shows the firm's profit-maximizing level of employment, given the work rules implicitly or explicitly agreed to by the two parties (see Figure 15.6). Although this constrained demand curve (or "approximately efficient" contract curve) is unlikely to coincide exactly with the contract curve, for each outcome on D_L there is a Pareto-superior outcome on D_L^C (i.e., a wage-employment outcome that makes both parties better off than on D_L).

Previously we noted that if the union is constrained by the labour demand curve, it is in the union's interest to shift the demand curve to the right or make it more inelastic. What wasn't clear was why the firm would accede to such requests. A primary insight of the analysis in this section is that featherbedding rules or restrictive work practices which force the firm to operate to the right of the unconstrained labour demand curve can be to the mutual advantage of both parties.

Efficient Versus Inefficient Contracts: Summary

Two alternative models of the determination of wages and employment in unionized settings have been outlined. The first—which can be termed the **labour demand curve model**—involves the two parties negotiating the wage rate and the firm unilaterally setting employment. Because the firm retains discretion over employment, this is also referred to as the "right to manage" model. The alternative model—the contract curve or "efficient contracts" model—involves the two parties negotiating over both wages and employment. Which of these two models applies in any particular setting is an empirical question. The observation that both parties can improve their welfare by negotiating both wages and employment suggests strong incentives to reach an outcome on the contract curve and provides an explanation of negotiated work rules as a rational response to these incentives. However, in many settings, employment is unilaterally determined by the firm and work rules appear to play a minimal role. This suggests that in many settings the costs of monitoring and enforcing an efficient contract are too high, given the variability in demand, to make this type of arrangement worthwhile.

Figure 15.6 **Inefficient, Approximately Efficient, and Efficient Contracts**

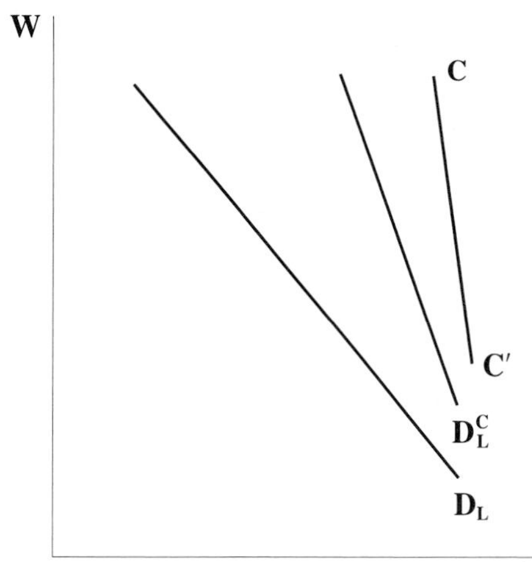

The contract curve or set of efficient wage-employment contracts lies to the right of the labour demand curve D_L. However, the costs of writing, monitoring, and enforcing contingent contracts may prevent the two parties from reaching the contract curve in all situations. Rather, the firm and union may agree to the set of approximately efficient contracts, denoted by D_L^C, by negotiating work rules that restrict the firm's ability to control employment. For each point on the labour demand curve there is a wage-employment outcome on D_L^C that both the firm and the union prefer.

EMPIRICAL APPLICATIONS

Compared to the large number of empirical studies of the product demand and labour supply behaviour of households and of the production and cost behaviour of firms, the number of studies of wage and employment determination in unionized labour markets is limited. Nonetheless, following pioneering research by Farber (1978) and Dertouzos and Pencavel (1981), a number of studies have been carried out.

Empirical applications of the theory of union wage and employment determination face several obstacles:

1. Choosing an appropriate specification of union preferences
2. The presence of two alternative models of wage and employment determination which are plausible on a-priori grounds
3. The need for a theory of firm-union bargaining to predict the specific wage-employment outcome chosen by the parties

These are clearly major challenges. As noted previously, the issue of whether it is appropriate to characterize unions as attempting to maximize an objective function has long been a matter of scholarly debate. With respect to obstacles (2) and (3), the studies by Farber (1978), Dertouzos and Pencavel (1981), Pencavel (1984) and Carruth and Oswald (1985) assume that observed wage-employment outcomes lie on the labour demand curve and that the union is sufficiently powerful that it can achieve its preferred outcome, I_u in Figure 15.4.

In contrast, studies such as those by Abowd (1989) are based on the assumption of efficient contracts, that is, that wage-employment outcomes are on the contract curve. Another group of studies—including Brown and Ashenfelter (1986), MaCurdy and Pencavel (1986), Eberts and Stone (1986), and Martinello (1989)—have addressed the question of whether observed wage and employment outcomes are more consistent with the labour demand or contract curve models. The studies by Svenjar (1986) and Doiron (1992) have begun the difficult task of incorporating bargaining into empirical models of wage and employment determination in unionized industries.

www.bgsu.edu/colleges/library/cac/ms0038.html

The Dertouzos and Pencavel study focuses on the International Typographical Union (ITU), a once-powerful closed-shop union representing printers. The employers are mostly newspaper firms. Recently there have been important technological changes in the industry (computer typesetting, etc.) and employment has fallen drastically. The period studied, 1946–1965, is before these drastic changes to the collective bargaining setting.

Dertouzos and Pencavel argue that the union has a dominant power position, and that this justifies the assumption that the union can determine the wage. The union's power derives mainly from the vulnerability of local newspaper firms to a prolonged period of nonproduction. This vulnerability results from several factors: (1) the product cannot be stored, (2) both advertisers and subscribers have various alternative media they can turn to in the event of a strike, and (3) it is often costly and difficult to regain former subscribers and advertisers after a strike.

For the union local examined in the most detail, the *Cincinnati Post*, Dertouzos' and Pencavel's estimates imply that the union cares about both wages and employment, but that relatively more weight is put on employment than would be the case if the union's objectives were maximization of economic rents. Pencavel (1984) finds that larger union locals have preferences which are approximately those of rent maximization, while smaller locals place more weight on employment.

www.umwa.org

Farber (1978) analyzes the wage and employment behaviour of the United Mine Workers in the U.S. bituminous coal industry over the period 1946–1973. The union was a dominant force in the industry due to the fragmented market structure (large number of essentially competitive firms), and is thus assumed to be able to dictate the wage. However, the union is constrained by the position and shape of the labour demand curve, which depend on substitution: (1) between coal and other fuels in the product market, (2) between labour and other inputs in coal production, and (3) between union-produced and nonunion-produced coal.

Farber's estimates imply that the union places a relatively high weight on employment relative to wages and benefits, higher than would be implied by wage bill or economic rent maximization. Other studies based on the labour demand model also find that unions place a relatively high weight on employment. Carruth and Oswald (1985) analyze the National Union of Mineworkers in the United Kingdom over the period 1950–1980. Their estimates imply that the union places less weight on employment than its U.S. counterpart, the United Mine Workers, but nonetheless a high weight relative to that on wages. Martinello (1989) analyzes the behaviour of the International Woodworkers of America (IWA) in the British Columbia forest products industry. Although his primary objective is to compare the performance of the labour demand and contract curve models, his estimates for the labour demand model (assuming the union can set the wage) also imply that the union places a relatively high weight on employment.

On the basis of these studies based on the labour demand curve model, there appears to be agreement on several issues: (1) both employment and wages are important to unions, (2) union preferences display a diminishing marginal rate of substitution between wages and employment, (3) union preferences are sensitive to the alternative wage, (4) unions generally place relatively more weight on employment than wages, (5) wage bill maximization is rejected as a union objective function, and (6) economic rent maximization is rejected in the majority of cases. In assessing these conclusions, it is important to keep in mind that only a small number of unions have been analyzed using modern econometric methods and that the conclusions are conditional on some key assumptions, in particular that the union can dictate the wage and the firm unilaterally sets employment.

The task of testing between the contract curve and labour demand models has been addressed in a number of papers. The basic methodology is to test whether, controlling for the contract wage, w, the alternative wage, w_a, helps predict employment. The alternative wage is taken as an indirect indicator that union preferences help predict employment, off the demand curve but on the contract curve. This would be the case, for example, if union preferences resembled those depicted in Figure 15.2(d) (maximize economic rent). In this case the contract curve is vertical (see Problem 4 at the end of this chapter), so the level of employment is independent of the contract wage and varies only with changes in the alternative wage. In contrast, under the labour demand curve model, the contract wage should be the only wage relevant for employment determination.

Most studies employ contract-level data for specific unions and industries. For example, Brown and Ashenfelter (1986) and MaCurdy and Pencavel (1986) explore wage and employment outcomes in a sample of ITU contracts in the U.S. Eberts and Stone (1986) examine New York State public school teachers, and Card (1986) focuses on airline mechanics in the U.S. There are also a few studies that employ Canadian contract data. Martinello (1989) tests the contracting and labour demand models for a sample of British Columbia forestry workers in the IWA. Christofides (1990) and Christofides and Oswald (1991) use an extensive contract-level data set covering 420 Canadian firms and 68 unions to try and distinguish between the models.

At this point there is not a consensus on the question of which model performs best. Most studies find that the contract curve model is more consistent with their data: alternative wages help predict employment levels, and contract wages are often only weakly related to employment (e.g., see Christofides and Oswald, 1991). However, the evidence is far from conclusive. In particular, whether the efficient bargaining model is better than alternative frameworks that allow the outcome to be to the right of the demand curve remains to be seen. Furthermore, Manning (1994) questions whether the aformentioned empirical approaches can actually distinguish between the two models. As Card (1990)

Exhibit 15.1 **Are Ontario Teachers' Contracts Efficient?**

Janet Currie (1991) attempts to distinguish between the monopoly union and efficient contracts models of union employment and wage determination for a sample of Ontario public school teachers over the period 1975 to 1983. She finds that controlling for the contract wage, the alternative wage (the average wage in adjoining school districts) is negatively related to the level of employment, while the contract wage is insignificant. These findings are consistent with a vertical contract curve—that is, efficient employment determination in which employment is independent of the union wage.

However, as she notes, these results are also consistent with an entirely different model of the market for teachers: a simple supply and demand model. In that model, alternative wages shift the supply curve for teachers to a given school board. The supply of teachers would be lower to those boards paying wages below the neighbouring boards. Currie shows that, indeed, employment and wage determination in school boards is statistically consistent with a supply and demand model. Her results suggest that despite the obvious violations of the assumptions governing firm-worker interaction in a unionized market, a competitive model may yet capture the essential features of employment and wage determination.

shows with Canadian contract data, the alternative wage may affect current employment because it helps predict future contract wages, and need not have an efficient bargaining interpretation. As Currie (1991) notes, correlation of employment with alternative wages may actually be consistent with a perfectly competitive model of a unionized labour market (see Exhibit 15.1). The conditions under which outcomes are on the labour demand curve or the contract curve (or perhaps in between) is an important research topic.

Perhaps the most important aspect of union wage and employment determination that is not addressed by the above studies is the incorporation of firm-union bargaining in the empirical analysis. In general, the labour demand and contract curve models predict a range of possible wage-employment outcomes rather than a unique outcome. In order to determine the particular settlement the parties will reach we require a theory of bargaining, a subject to which we now turn.

THEORY OF BARGAINING*

Bargaining theory is concerned with predicting the outcome in any particular bargaining situation, and explaining what factors this outcome depends on. Because of the importance of bargaining in many aspects of life, bargaining theory has received considerable attention from social scientists. There is not yet, however, any single widely accepted theory of bargaining. In this section we examine some important contributions, with particular emphasis on their implications in the collective bargaining setting.

Although each bargaining situation may be unique, all share some common features: there is a set of possible outcomes, with minimum acceptable outcomes for each party; because agreement is voluntary, neither party will agree to an outcome worse than their minimum acceptable outcome. Whether the parties bargain over wages alone or over wages and employment, there is a set of feasible outcomes, with upper and lower limits

*More difficult material.

representing the minimum outcomes acceptable to the union and the firm. This type of situation is illustrated in Figure 15.7(a). The point d = (d_1,d_2) shows the utility of each party if no agreement is reached; this is referred to as the "disagreement" or **threat point**. Neither party will agree to an outcome worse than d and each can threaten to impose this outcome on the other by failing to agree. The bargaining set S consists of feasible outcomes in which one or both parties is better off than they would be without an agreement. This diagram illustrates the bargaining situation in terms of the parties' utilities because what ultimately matters to each party is the satisfaction obtained from an agreement. However, the parties do not bargain over utilities but rather over outcomes such as wages and employment, and in some cases the analysis is best carried out in terms of these outcomes.

In bargaining there are incentives for both cooperation and conflict. The incentives for cooperation are evident from the fact that there are various feasible outcomes that make both parties better off than if no agreement is reached. As long as the employees' utility is at least as great as they can obtain elsewhere and the employer's profits at least as great as can be earned elsewhere, both sides are better off continuing the employment relationship. Indeed, the two parties have an incentive to cooperate at any Pareto-inferior outcome, such as the point C in Figure 15.7(a), because both can gain from this process. The incentives for conflict arise because, once all Pareto improvements have been realized, such as at the point A in Figure 15.7(a), actions which make one party better off result in the other becoming worse off. Further, the recognition by each party that the other benefits from reaching an agreement may create an incentive to threaten the other with nonagreement. For example, recognizing that the firm is better off with outcome f_1 than d_2 the union may threaten the firm with nonagreement unless the firm agrees to the outcome A. Alternatively the firm may threaten nonagreement unless the union agrees to B. Because of these incentives for both cooperation and conflict, most bargaining situations contain an uneasy mixture; on the one hand, recognition of the importance of reaching agreement

Figure 15.7 The Bargaining Problem and the Nash Solution

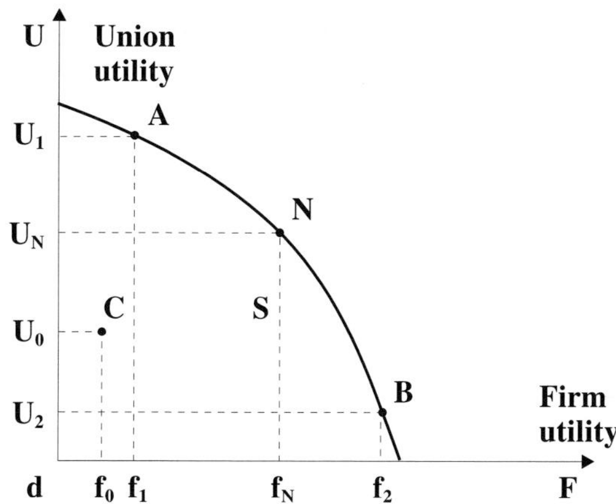

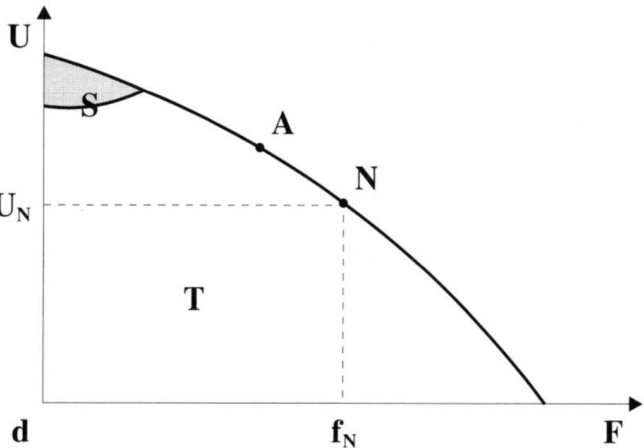

Panel (a) illustrates common features of bargaining situations. Union utility is plotted on the vertical axis and firm utility on the horizontal axis. The point d shows the utility of each party if no agreement is reached. The bargaining set S consists of the set of feasible outcomes in which one or both parties are better off than without an agreement.

Panel (b) illustrates the Nash solution (point N) and the "independence of irrelevant alternatives" axiom. An example of an irrelevant alternative is the shaded area in the upper corner of S.

and, on the other, attempts to mislead, outmanoeuvre or otherwise gain advantage over the other party.

SOLUTIONS TO THE BARGAINING PROBLEM*

A number of solutions to the bargaining problem have been proposed. These can be classified into two groups: theories of the bargaining process and theories of the bargaining outcome. The former not only predict the outcome but also model the process by which that outcome is reached. The latter model the bargaining outcome, by specifying a number of properties or axioms which the outcome should obey. Leading examples of each type are outlined below. The theories described here assume full information; each party knows the set of feasible payoffs or outcomes, the preferences of the other side, and therefore the set of feasible utility outcomes, S in Figure 15.7. However, this does not imply that there is no uncertainty; although each party is aware of the outcomes available to itself and the other party, it may well be uncertain about what the other will do. As is common in uncertain situations, the parties are assumed to maximize expected utility.

Nash's Bargaining Theory

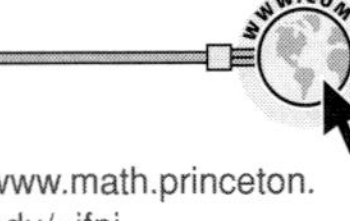

www.math.princeton.edu/~jfnj

Following the publication by Von Neuman and Morgenstern in 1944 of the *Theory of Games and Economic Behaviour*, the Princeton mathematician John Nash proposed a solution to the bargaining problem which is still widely used today. Nash (1950) specified four axioms that the solution should obey:

A1. *Pareto-efficiency*. Only Pareto-efficient bargains will be agreed to.

A2. *Symmetry*. If the feasible bargaining set S is symmetric (i.e., if it doesn't matter which party's utility is measured on which axis), the solution will give equal utility increments (relative to the disagreement outcome) to each party.

A3. *Transformation invariance*. The solution is not altered by linear transformations of the utility function of either party.

A4. *Independence of irrelevant alternatives.* Suppose that the solution to the bargaining problem has been reached for a particular bargaining set S; for example, the point A in Figure 15.7(b). Then the solution will not be altered if some outcomes other than A are unavailable (such as the shaded area in Figure 15.7(b)). That is, if A is the solution with the bargaining set S then A will also be the solution if the same two players face the bargaining set T (S less the shaded area).

The first axiom can be regarded as a natural consequence of the rationality of the two bargainers and the full information assumption. Why would they agree to an outcome such as C when both can be made better off at outcomes such as A and N? The second axiom can be viewed as stating that the bargaining power of each side is reflected in the nature of the set of feasible bargaining outcomes and the disagreement outcome. If the set of bargaining outcomes is symmetric, the two parties must be equally powerful because they both stand to gain or lose equally from agreement or nonagreement. Thus the solution should reflect this equality of bargaining power, and give each an equal gain from agreement.

The third axiom states that the units in which utility is measured should not matter. Utility functions simply represent an individual's preference-ordering of outcomes, and any pair of functions that order outcomes in the same way are equally valid for this purpose. In expected utility theory, cardinal utility functions are needed; any linear transformation of a cardinal utility function will preserve the ordering and therefore be a valid utility

*More difficult material.

function. The measurement of temperature is analogous; the Fahrenheit and Celsius scales are equally valid measures of temperature, one being a linear transformation of the other. Because this axiom states that the actual numerical scale used to measure utility is arbitrary, its main consequence is to rule out interpersonal comparisons of utility.

The fourth axiom has probably been the most controversial. According to this axiom, if the parties chose the outcome A from all the alternatives in the set S, then the same outcome should be chosen from the set T because the only difference between the two situations is the absence of the outcomes in the shaded area, outcomes which have already been rejected in favour of A by the two bargainers. An analogy in the case of individual decision-making is the following. You go out to a restaurant for dinner, and are told by the waiter that there are three choices: chicken in mustard sauce, veal with a chanterelles sauce, and salmon with a cucumber sauce. You decide to order the veal. The waiter subsequently informs you that they are out of salmon. Would you want to change your order? Obviously not—you chose veal over salmon and chicken, so should choose veal over chicken alone. Whether this reasoning applies in a two-person bargaining situation is a more complex question—which is why the axiom has generated controversy.

Nash's (1950) remarkable result was that assumptions A1 to A4 imply a unique solution to any bargaining situation: the outcome that maximizes the product of the two parties' utility increments from the disagreement point—that is, maximizes $(U - d_1)(F - d_2)$. The **Nash solution** is shown as the point N in Figure 15.7. Geometrically, the Nash outcome maximizes the area within the set S; that is, the area dU_NNf_N in Figures 15.7(a) and (b) exceeds the area of any other rectangle contained in the bargaining set.

A number of other axiomatic theories of the bargaining outcome have been proposed; Roth (1979) provides a survey of these theories and Roth and Malouf (1979) and others have tested these competing theories in experimental settings. The Nash solution predicts the outcomes of some bargaining experiments well; however, in other situations the outcomes appear to contradict axiom A3, and a theory that assumes the parties make interpersonal utility comparisons predicts outcomes better than the Nash solution.

It can be debated whether the axiomatic approach constitutes a positive or normative theory of bargaining. The approach proceeds by stating properties that the solution ought to obey, and therefore may be more appropriate for the analysis of arbitration decisions (i.e., decisions about what the outcome ought to be) than collective bargaining outcomes. For the latter purpose, theories that explicitly model the bargaining process may be more appropriate. It should be noted, however, that although the axiomatic theories do not specify the process by which the outcome is reached, they may be consistent with one or several such processes. For example, in an early contribution to the theory of bargaining, Zeuthen (1930) proposed a model of the concession behaviour of each party. The assumed concession process results in the outcome that maximizes the product of the two utility increments, an outcome identical to the Nash solution. Recent contributions have provided more general theories of the bargaining process, and these are examined next.

Rubinstein's Bargaining Theory

In an important contribution, Rubinstein (1982) obtains a solution to the bargaining problem using some concepts of non-cooperative game theory. The type of bargaining situation analyzed in **Rubinstein's bargaining theory** has the following characteristics. The two bargainers take turns making offers. If an offer is accepted, the process ends; if the offer is not accepted the other party makes a counteroffer in the next period. However, delay is costly to both sides. Each period the total "pie" to be shared by the two parties gets smaller. This situation is illustrated in Figure 15.8. As before, there is a bargaining set which shows the outcomes available to each party. In the first period this is the set bounded by du_1f_1. However, if an agreement is not reached in the first period, the set of utility outcomes avail-

Figure 15.8 The Rubinstein Solution to the Bargaining Problem

(a) Rubinstein's solution to the bargaining problem

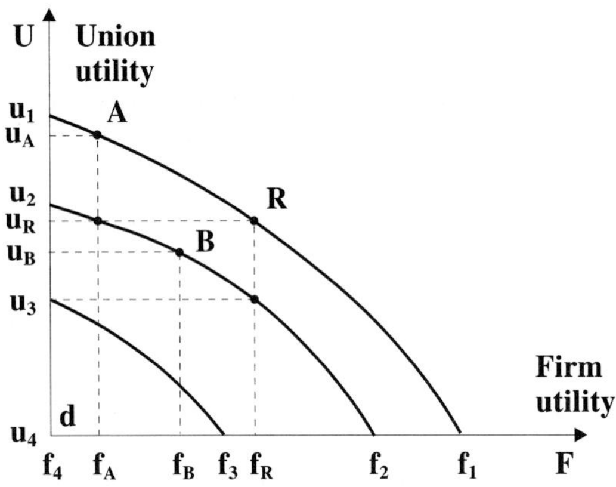

Panel (a) illustrates a non-cooperative bargaining game in which the parties make alternating offers that the receiving party may either accept or reject and both parties incur delay costs. In round 1 the set of feasible outcomes is du_1f_1 but if no agreement is reached the parties face the reduced set du_2f_2 in round 2, du_3f_3 in period 3, and du_4f_4 in period 4. If the union makes the first offer, the Rubinstein solution is point R.

(b) The effect of delay costs on the Rubinstein outcome

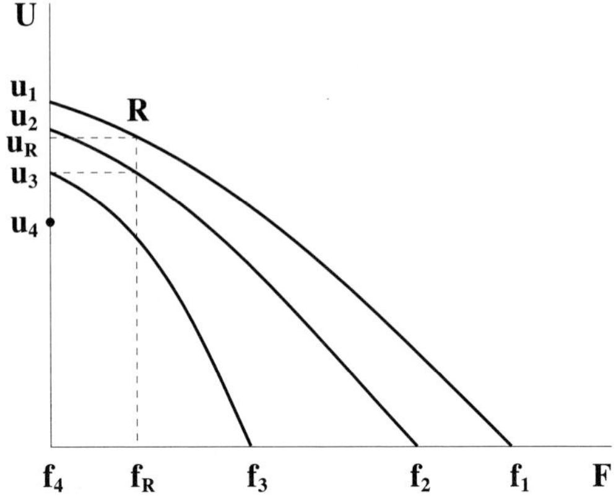

Panel (b) illustrates the effects of an increase in the delay costs to the firm, holding constant the costs to the union. This change leads to an outcome R with higher union utility and lower firm utility.

(c) The effect of a proportional change in disagreement costs on the Rubinstein solution

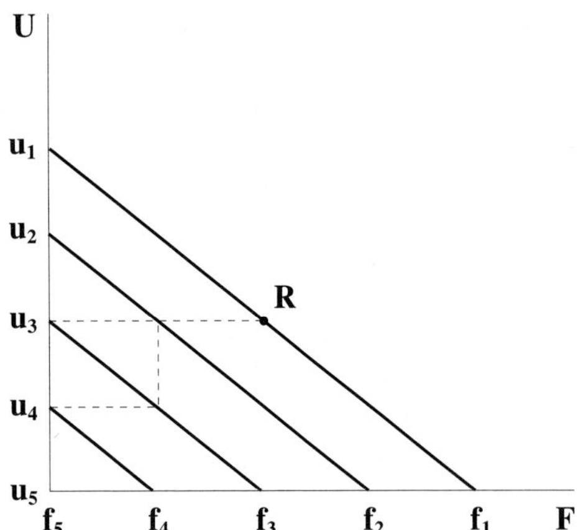

Panel (c) illustrates the effect of a change in delay costs that affects both parties by the same proportion. In bargaining situation 1, the parties face bargaining set du_1f_1 in period 1, du_2f_2 in round 2, du_3f_3 in round 3, du_4f_4 in period 4, and du_5f_5 in the final round. The solution is the outcome R. In situation 2, delay costs are proportionally larger for both parties: they face du_1f_1 in round 1, du_3f_3 in period 2, and du_5f_5 in period 3. The solution is again outcome R, which illustrates the prediction that a change in delay costs that affects both parties by the same proportion will not alter the outcome.

able in period two shrinks to that bounded by du_2f_2. Similarly in period three the bargaining set becomes du_3f_3, and in period four the only feasible outcome is the disagreement point $d = (u_4,f_4)$. Thus in this example the "pie" which the parties can share has shrunk to zero by period four. In general it may require delay of more than four periods in order to reach the situation where both parties gain nothing from an agreement (if, indeed, this situation is ever reached); the assumption that this outcome is reached quickly is made simply for ease of illustration.

As before, both parties are assumed to possess full information about the bargaining situation. That is, each knows the size of the "pie" available to be shared in the first period, the other party's preferences and the costs of delay (or disagreement) to both sides. Thus each can infer the nature of the bargaining set they will face in subsequent periods.

Each party is assumed to be concerned only with its own self-interest; that is, it wants to obtain the highest possible utility from the bargain, and cares only about the outcome, not how it was reached. Also, each behaves rationally (and expects the other to do likewise) in the sense that neither will believe threats that would not be in the interest of the threatening party to carry out. For example, suppose it is the union's turn to make an offer in period one. The union could offer $A = (u_A,f_A)$ and threaten to refuse to accept or make any future offers unless the outcome A is accepted. If the firm believed the threat, it would accept because f_A is better than f_4, which is what the firm would receive if the offer A is rejected and the union carries out the threat. However, the threat is not credible. Suppose the firm rejects the offer. In period two the bargaining set becomes du_2f_2 and if the firm offers the outcome B, the union will accept because u_B is better than u_3, the best outcome the union could obtain in the next period. For this reason, the firm knows that the union's threat in period one is not credible and it will therefore not believe it.

We can now turn to the solution. Suppose that in the initial period it is the union's turn to make an offer. Rubinstein's analysis predicts that the union will offer and the firm will accept the outcome $R = (u_R,f_R)$; that is, the Rubinstein outcome is the point R in Figure 15.8. To see why this solution is predicted to occur, we proceed by backward induction. In the second period it will be the firm's turn to make an offer and in the third period the union's turn. In the fourth period there is nothing left to be shared. Now look at the situation facing the union in period three. Both parties recognize that the best the firm can attain next period is the outcome f_4. Thus in period three the firm will accept any offer equal to or better than f_4. The union would therefore offer (u_3,f_4) and the firm would accept. Now go back to the situation facing the firm in period two. The firm knows that the best the union can expect next period is u_3. Thus the firm won't offer more than u_3; i.e., will make an offer in the interval between (u_3,f_R) and (u_4,f_2). However, the firm also knows that next period the union will offer and the firm will accept (u_3,f_4). Thus in period two the firm will offer and the union will accept (u_3,f_R). Now go back to period one and the union's choice of offers. The same analysis leads to the conclusion that the union will offer and the firm will accept (u_R,f_R). Thus the point $R = (u_R,f_R)$ is the bargaining outcome; the costs of delay and the rational behaviour of the two parties result in an agreement that avoids incurring any disagreement costs.

Clearly **delay costs** play an important role in generating agreement in the Rubinstein model. The existence of these costs—and the fact that both parties are aware of them—gives each some power over the other. For this reason the relative magnitude of delay costs exerts an important influence on the negotiated outcome. This result is illustrated in Figure 15.8(b). The bargaining set du_1f_1 is identical to that in Figure 15.8(a), as are the delay costs to the firm (measured by the outcomes f_1, f_2, f_3, and f_4). However, the union's disagreement costs are less than in Figure 15.8(a), as indicated by the outcomes u_1, u_2, u_3, and u_4. As a consequence, the outcome predicted by Rubinstein's theory is more favourable to the union and less favourable to the firm.

It is important to recognize that *relative* disagreement costs determine the extent to which the negotiated outcome favours one party or the other. By holding constant the firm's disagreement costs and lowering the union's in the comparison between the situation in Figure 15.8(a) and (b), the union's relative delay costs declined. The consequence is a more favourable outcome for the union and a less favourable outcome for the firm. However, suppose the disagreement costs fall by the same proportion for both parties, leaving relative costs unchanged. This situation is shown in Figure 15.8(c). Two bargaining situations are depicted in the same diagram. In the first case the outer boundary of the bargaining set is u_1f_1 in the first period, u_2f_2 in the second period, and so on, reaching the disagreement point (u_5,f_5) in the fifth period. In the second bargaining situation, disagreement costs are proportionally higher for both parties; the boundary of the bargaining set is u_1f_1 in the first period, u_3f_3 in the second, and the disagreement point in the third period. In both cases the firm makes the first offer. The solution is unchanged by the proportionate increase in delay costs, illustrating the reason for emphasizing the role of relative disagreement costs in bargaining outcomes.

As a description of the collective bargaining process, the Rubinstein model is highly simplified. For example, in most bargaining situations either party can make an offer in any period. Nonetheless, this theory captures important aspects of collective bargaining, in particular the role played by the costs of delay or disagreement in bringing about a negotiated settlement. The negotiations process itself consumes scarce resources; thus the sooner an agreement is reached the lower the direct negotiations costs to each party. But the major disagreement costs are those associated with attempts of one side to bring pressure to bear on the other to make concessions. Although there are a variety of relatively inexpensive (and possibly also ineffective) methods for exerting pressure on the other party (e.g., work-to-rule actions, refusal to work overtime), the primary mechanism is the strike or lockout.

The strike involves the collective withdrawal of union labour in an attempt to halt or sharply curtail production. The lockout denies union members access to their normal job and source of income. Both types of work stoppage impose costs on the employer and the employees represented by the union (and also possibly on third parties). The firm loses profits and the workers lose income. In addition to the costs incurred during the strike or lockout, there may be costs of a more permanent nature. Clearly rational bargainers (and perhaps even irrational bargainers) will, in the negotiations process, take into account the magnitude of the costs that they and the other party will bear in the event of a strike or lockout. Rubinstein's theory confirms our intuition that the relative size of the costs of a work stoppage will be an important determinant of the negotiated settlement. Further, it is not necessary for a strike or lockout to occur in order for the costs associated with a work stoppage to influence the outcome.

UNION BARGAINING POWER

The term **bargaining power** arises frequently in discussions of firm-union bargaining. Like many terms that are widely used, the precise meaning is not always clear. In this section we contrast two possible meanings of union bargaining power. For simplicity we assume that the two parties negotiate over wages alone, leaving the firm to set employment. The extension of these ideas to the case of bargaining over wages and employment is straightforward.

One meaning of bargaining power is related to the elasticity of labour demand. A union facing an inelastic demand for labour can raise wages substantially with only minor adverse employment consequences. This notion of bargaining power is associated with the *willingness* to increase wages; other things equal, the more inelastic the demand for labour, the more willing is the union to raise the wage rate.

Figure 15.9 Alternative Aspects of Union Power

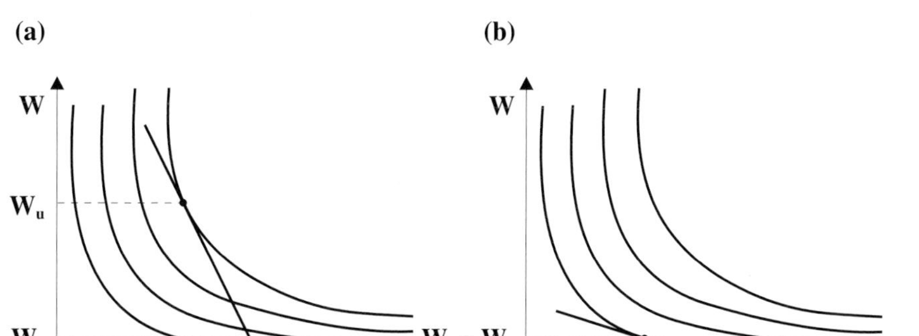

Two alternative aspects of union power—the "willingness" and "ability" to raise wages—are illustrated. Panel (a) shows a situation in which the union is willing to raise wages substantially because the demand for labour is relatively inelastic. Nonetheless, the union is limited in its ability to increase wages—it is only able to achieve the outcome W_c, which is substantially below its preferred wage. Panel (b) illustrates a union that is able to negotiate a contract wage W_c equal to its preferred wage W_u, but is not willing to raise the wage substantially due to the highly elastic demand for labour.

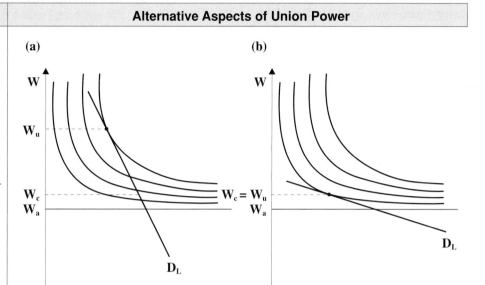

An alternative notion of bargaining power is associated with the *ability* to raise wages. According to this meaning of the term, a powerful union is one that can obtain a negotiated outcome close to its most preferred outcome. This aspect of union power depends not on the elasticity of labour demand but primarily on the relative costs of disagreement to each party.

Because these two aspects of bargaining power depend on different variables, it is possible for a union to be powerful according to one definition but weak according to another. This possibility is illustrated in Figure 15.9. Panel (a) shows a union that is willing to raise wages substantially but is unable to do so; the negotiated wage W_c is considerably below the union's preferred wage W_u. Panel (b) shows a union that can obtain its preferred outcome but is not willing to raise wages substantially because of the employment consequences. Of course, in some circumstances a union may be powerful (or weak) according to both meanings. However, neither aspect of bargaining power alone ensures that the negotiated union wage will be substantially higher than the alternative wage.

UNION POWER AND LABOUR SUPPLY

Most unions attempt to improve the wages and working conditions of their members directly by bargaining with the employer, and the strike threat is their primary source of bargaining power. However, craft unions and professional associations can raise the wages and working conditions of their members indirectly by controlling labour supply. For these organizations, restrictions on the supply of labour can constitute an important source of union power.

Restricting Supply: Craft Unions

By restricting the supply of labour, unions can raise wages artificially relative to the situation where competition prevailed in the supply of labour. Craft unions generally have sought to raise the wage of their members by controlling entry into their craft through the apprenticeship system, discrimination, nepotism, high union dues, and such devices as the closed shop (the worker has to be a member of the union *before* being hired, i.e., the union controls the hiring hall). Because the supply of labour to the craft is reduced, wages will rise above the wage that would prevail in the absence of the craft restrictions.

Needless to say the craft union will try to control the whole trade; otherwise the benefits of the supply restriction would also go to nonunion craft workers. Hence the importance to the union of apprenticeship licensing, the closed shop, the union shop (the worker has to join the union after a probationary period of employment), or the agency shop (the worker must pay union dues but need not be a member of the union).

At the artificially high union wage rate, the quantity of labour supplied will exceed the quantity demanded. To the extent that the union controls entry, the scarce jobs can be rationed to the large number of workers who would like the jobs by such devices as discrimination, nepotism, or high union dues. To the extent that employers have a say in who is hired, they may ration jobs on the basis of discrimination or nepotism, but they may also ration on the basis of productivity-related factors such as education or training or experience. While these productivity-related factors obviously are useful requirements for employers, they may be set *artificially* high because the employer has an excess supply of applicants, given the higher unionized wage.

Restricting Supply: Professional Associations

Professional associations can also behave much like craft unions in their control over labour supply, largely through the processes of occupational licensing and certification. This setting of standards is deemed necessary, ostensibly to protect the public interest in circumstances where it is important but difficult for the consuming public to judge the quality of the professional service. The job of governing the profession has usually gone to the profession itself—hence the term *self-governing professions*—because only members of the profession are deemed qualified to set standards. Traditionally, this has occurred in the stereotypic professions such as medicine and law, where an uninformed clientele purchases complex services from a self-employed professional. Increasingly, however, professionals are becoming employed on a salaried basis, and the rationale for self-governing powers for salaried professionals can be questioned when the employer can provide an effective mediator between the consuming public and the salaried professional.

The techniques of occupational control utilized by professional associations usually involve occupational licensing or certification. Under certification only those with the professional certificate have the right to use the professional designation or title; that is, they have a *reserve-of-title certification*. However, other practitioners are allowed to practise in the profession, albeit they cannot use the certified title. Under licensing, only those with the professional licence can practise; that is, they have the *exclusive right-to-practise licence*. Clearly the exclusive right-to-practise licence involves more control over the occupation than the reserve-of-title certification; hence, it is sought after by most professional and quasi-professional groups.

Under licensing the supply of labour to the occupation is restricted only to those with the licence. Under certification the supply restrictions are less severe in the sense that others can practise in the profession, although competition is restricted because others cannot use the professionally designated certification. Whatever the impact on the quality of the service performed, the supply of labour to the occupation is restricted and wages rise accordingly. In this sense, professional associations like craft unions raise the wages of their members.

Although they receive higher wages, members of the profession may bear costs associated with the occupational licensing requirements. Such costs could include lengthy education periods as well as practical training periods, such as internship for doctors or articling for lawyers. There is a danger, however, in that the *incumbent* professionals may try to have the brunt of the licensing costs borne by *new* entrants into the profession. This could be accomplished by having increasingly stringent education or training requirements as a qualification for entry into the profession, with so-called "grandfather" clauses exempting those who are already practising. In this fashion, the new entrants bear more of the licensing costs (they will do so as long as the wage premium outweighs these costs), the existing practitioners who control the profession benefit from the restricted competition, and the consuming public gets increasingly qualified practitioners, albeit at a higher cost. Restricting grandfather clauses, or having licensing requirements set by persons other than existing practitioners, could go a long way to correcting this potential abuse of occupational licensing.

Summary

- The theory of union behaviour has long been a subject of debate. Some advocate an "economic" approach that assumes the union seeks to maximize an objective function subject to constraints. Others criticize this approach as not paying enough attention to the union as a political institution in which union leaders are elected to represent the wishes of the members and may perhaps also pursue their own objectives. The modern approach to union behaviour recognizes some merit in both positions in that the union is modelled as attempting to maximize a well-defined utility function, but attention is paid to the political nature of union decision-making, especially the relationship between the preferences of individual members and those pursued by union leaders.
- Union objectives refer to the goals of the organization. The relationship between the preferences of the members, those of the union leaders, and the objectives of the organization as a whole depend on several factors, including: (1) the information available to the rank-and-file about the available options, (2) the nature of the union's political decision-making process, and (3) the degree of homogeneity of the individual members' preferences.
- Union utility is postulated to be a function of the union wage and the employment of union members. Union indifference curves are downward-sloping in wage-employment space, because a higher wage is needed to compensate for a reduction in employment, holding utility constant. Further, it is plausible to hypothesize that union preferences display a diminishing marginal rate of substitution between wages and employment, so that the indifference curves are convex in shape.
- Union objectives also depend on the price level and the alternative wage available to union members in their best alternative job. What matters to union members is their real wage, that is the wage rate relative to the cost of living. The benefits to union members of belonging to the union also depend on the union or contract wage relative to their best alternative wage.
- The general union utility function depends on the real union wage, total employment of union members, and the real alternative wage. Some special cases of this utility function that have been proposed include: (1) maximize the (real) wage rate, which places no weight on employment in union preferences, (2) maximize employment, which places no weight on the union wage, (3) maximize the wage bill—the product of employment and the wage rate—which ignores the alternative wage, and (4) maximize economic rent, the product of employment and the difference between the union wage and the alternative wage. The latter is the most plausible of these special cases, and is analogous to the union acting as a monopoly seller of labour to the firm and maximizing the "total return" or profit.
- The task of deriving union objectives from the underlying preferences of individual members is easiest when individual members' preferences are relatively homogeneous. When this is not the case (e.g., older members wanting to place more weight in union

decision-making on pensions and less on current wages than younger members), the median voter model may be a good way to represent union preferences. According to this model, the preferences of the organization as a whole will be those of the median member (e.g., the member of median age in the case of preferences that differ according to the age of the member). The median voter model can be derived under certain conditions from a political model of union decision-making.

- Union leaders may pursue their own objectives to some extent, but they are constrained by the desire to remain in office. A theory of union objectives that is based solely on the wishes of the members may not be able to account for all aspects of union behaviour, but may provide a good approximation to observed behaviour in most circumstances.
- Because union utility depends on the preferences of individual members, changes over time in union membership may lead to changes in union objectives. For example, an increase in product demand will lead to an influx of new and possibly younger members, reducing the age and seniority of the median member.
- When the firm chooses employment subject to the negotiated wage rate, the union is constrained by the firm's labour demand curve. In this situation the union's preferred wage-employment outcome occurs where the union indifference curve is tangent to the labour demand curve. The firm would prefer to pay the alternative wage, the minimum wage rate needed to attract labour to this sector. This leads to the "labour demand curve" or "right to manage" model in which the two parties negotiate the wage rate and the firm chooses employment. The negotiated wage will lie somewhere in the bargaining range, between the alternative wage and the union's preferred wage rate.
- Unions may be able to enhance their available wage-employment outcomes by relaxing the demand constraint—either by increasing labour demand (shifting the demand curve to the right) or making labour demand more inelastic (making employment less responsive to increases in the wage). Such policies may include support for restrictions on competition in the product market, opposition to deregulation, and support for wage-fixing legislation such as minimum wage laws and "fair wage" provisions.
- In general the firm and union can each benefit from negotiating a contract covering both wages and employment. Outcomes on the labour demand curve imply unexploited "gains from trade" that can be attained by exchanging a lower wage rate for increased employment such that both firm profits and union utility rise. The set of Pareto-efficient wage-employment contracts occurs where the union indifference curves are tangent to the firm's isoprofit curves, so that the rate at which the two parties are willing to exchange wages for employment is equalized at the margin. This set of Pareto-efficient contracts, called the *contract curve*, lies to the right of the labour demand curve, thus implying that the higher wages that generally accompany unionization may not be associated with reduced employment.
- Although in principle both the employer and union can benefit from negotiating over wages and employment, in practice there are several obstacles to reaching efficient contracts. First, the parties must reveal to each other sufficient information to realize that there are unexploited gains from trade. Second, because demand may shift several times during the term of the agreement, thus altering the contract curve and the efficient levels of wages and employment, the contract must stipulate the employment level under a variety of contingencies. Third, there is a need for costly monitoring because, for any given contract wage, the firm has an incentive to reduce employment to the labour demand curve, where profits are maximized at that wage rate. The costs of negotiating, monitoring, and enforcing such "contingent contracts" may be too high to make the effort worthwhile.

- Approximately efficient contracts may allow the firm and union to achieve most of the gains from trade associated with moving toward the contract curve without negotiating a fully contingent contract. These can be accomplished by tying employment to the output of the firm or to the use of other inputs. These arrangements allow employment to change in response to shifts in demand, but also constrain the firm to employ more workers than the profit-maximizing level at the contract wage. Examples of such contractual arrangements are observed in many sectors, including railroads (size of freight train crews), airlines (number of pilots per aircraft), and teaching (class size provisions). The theory of efficient wage-employment contracts helps explain the existence and persistence of such "restrictive work practices"—practices that may appear to be socially wasteful.
- Empirical studies of union wage and employment determination face several challenges: (1) choosing an appropriate specification of union preferences, (2) the presence of two alternative models of wage and employment determination that are plausible on a priori grounds, and (3) the need for a theory of firm-union bargaining to predict the specific wage-employment outcome chosen by the parties.
- The earliest empirical studies assume that observed wage-employment outcomes lie on the labour demand curve and that the union is sufficiently powerful to achieve its preferred outcome. Another set of studies assumes that observed outcomes are efficient (i.e., on the contract curve). Recently scholars have begun the difficult task of incorporating bargaining theory into the empirical analysis of union wage and employment determination.
- Studies of several unions and industries based on the labour demand curve model generally agree on a number of findings: (1) both employment and wages are important to unions, (2) union preferences display a diminishing marginal rate of substitution between wages and employment, (3) union preferences are sensitive to the alternative wage, (4) unions generally place more weight on employment than wages.
- Several studies have attempted to test between the "labour demand curve" and "efficient contracts" models using contract-level data for specific unions and groups of firms. At this point there is not a consensus on which model performs best.
- Bargaining theory seeks to predict the outcome in any given bargaining situation, and to explain what factors this outcome depends on. In any bargaining situation there are incentives for both cooperation and conflict. The incentives for cooperation arise because of "gains from trade"—there is a set of feasible outcomes that make both parties better off than if no agreement is reached. The incentives for conflict arise because once all the mutually advantageous trades have been made, actions that make one party better off make the other worse off.
- Two principal types of solutions to the bargaining problem have been proposed. Theories of the bargaining process not only predict the outcome but also model the process by which that outcome is reached. Theories of the bargaining outcome specify a number of properties or axioms that the solution should obey.
- Nash's bargaining theory specified four axioms the bargaining solution should obey. Together these four properties imply a unique solution to any bargaining situation: the outcome that maximizes the product of the two parties' utility increments from the disagreement point (the utility of each party if no agreement is reached). Nash's solution to the bargaining problem is widely used in theoretical and empirical work, and has been tested in laboratory experiments.
- Rubinstein's solution to the bargaining problem uses non-cooperative bargaining theory, and assumes a process of alternating offers that the receiving party can either accept or

reject. There are costs of delay, so the size of the "pie" to be shared by the two parties shrinks the longer it takes to reach agreement. Even though under full information the two parties would never delay reaching an agreement, the relative magnitudes of the delay costs facing each negotiator influence the Rubinstein outcome. In collective bargaining this implies that the relative costs of a work stoppage (strike or lockout) influence the negotiated outcome even though a strike or lockout may not occur.

- Two possible meanings of the term "union bargaining power" are implied by the analysis in this chapter. One is related to the elasticity of labour demand. A union facing an inelastic demand for labour can raise wages substantially with only minor adverse employment consequences. This notion of bargaining power is associated with the *willingness* to raise wages. The second notion is associated with the *ability* to raise wages. According to this meaning of the term, a powerful union is one that can obtain a negotiated outcome close to its most preferred outcome. This aspect of union power depends not on the elasticity of labour demand but principally on the relative costs of disagreement to each party.
- Most unions attempt to improve the wages and working conditions of their members directly by bargaining with the employer. However, craft unions and professional associations can raise wages and improve working conditions indirectly by controlling labour supply. Mechanisms for restricting labour supply include limiting entry through the apprenticeship system, occupational licensing, and certification.

REVIEW QUESTIONS

1. Discuss the reasons why the objectives of union leadership may differ from the objectives of the rank-and-file. Discuss the implications of such differences.
2. Draw the union indifference curves (iso-utility curves) for the following situations:
   (a) Wages and employment are perfect substitutes.
   (b) There is a minimum wage below which union members will not reduce their wages in order to increase employment.
   (c) At the current level of employment within the union, unions attach more disutility to a given employment reduction than the utility they attach to a corresponding employment increase.
   (d) As their wealth increases, union members attach more weight to job security than to real income gains.
   (e) The union objective is to maximize the wage bill.
   (f) The union objective is to maximize total economic rent.
3. Discuss the effect of an increase in the alternative wage rate on the utility of the union.
4. Discuss the error in the following statement: "Because the firm is maximizing profits at each point on its demand curve, it is indifferent among these points."
5. Discuss the constraints that limit the "bargaining range" between unions and employers.
6. Discuss various ways in which unions may try to make the demand for labour more inelastic so as to minimize any adverse effect emanating from any wage increase.
7. Discuss why efficient wage and employment contracts are not on the firm's labour demand curve. That is, show how both labour and management potentially could be better off by agreeing to wage and employment combinations that are not on the firm's labour demand curve.
8. Discuss the obstacles that unions and management may face in arriving at efficient wage-employment contracts.
9. "Craft unions and professional associations will affect the wages of their members in

a different manner than industrial unions." Discuss, and indicate why this may be the case.

10. "Self-government is an anachronism for salaried as opposed to self-employed professionals." Discuss.
11. Distinguish between occupational licensing and certification. Give examples of each.

PROBLEMS

1. Discuss why union members may differentiate in their preferences between hours of work and employment. What are the implications for union preferences?
2. Discuss the implications of unions being a democratic institution, reflecting the preferences of the median union voter. Why would the preferences of the median voter dominate in such a situation? What are the implications for minority rights within the union?
3. "If unions engage in concession bargaining to maintain job security they should specifically bargain for a specific level of security to be associated with their wage concessions rather than simply agreeing to the concessions and allowing the firm to choose the level of employment." Discuss.
4. Show that if the union's objective function is to maximize economic rent, the contract curve is vertical and employment corresponds to the level of employment that would prevail if the firm set employment subject to the constraint of paying the alternative wage.
5. What determines where the parties will settle on the contract curve? Could the indeterminacy of where the parties will be on the contract curve ever prevent them from arriving at an efficient contract?
6. Discuss how certain featherbedding rules may be efficient and sustain themselves in a competitive market environment. Does this mean that firms will never try to "buy out" such seemingly inefficient practices?
7. Some trade unionists have argued that wage concessions have not preserved jobs. Use the material developed in this chapter to illustrate the circumstances under which this concern may be legitimate, and the conditions under which the concern is not correct.
8. Show that if the union's objective is to maximize the wage paid, and if the firm and the union negotiate an efficient contract, then the contract curve will correspond to the labour demand schedule.
9. "The main foe of any union is various forms of substitution, not the firm."
   (a) Explain the various forms of substitution that unions need to be aware of in formulating their bargaining objectives, and elaborate on the relationship between these forms of substitution and union bargaining power.
   (b) The United Mine Workers studied by Farber (1978) had two instruments for affecting the monetary returns to and employment of their members—the hourly wage rate and the output tax (tax per ton of coal produced), the proceeds from which were distributed to members. Under what circumstances would the use of these two instruments allow the union to achieve outcomes that could not be achieved by affecting the wage rate alone?
10. Indicate conditions under which one may expect unions to have a substantial impact on the wages of their members.
11. If craft unions or professional associations are able to raise the wages in their trades above the competitive norm, excess supplies of applicants would result. Discuss how the scarce jobs may be rationed.

12. "If occupational licensing is necessary, the only group that could be entrusted not to abuse the powers of licensing would be the alumni of the profession, or at least members who were about to retire. Only they have knowledge about the profession, without having a self-interest in abusing the power of licensing. Existing practitioners, while knowledgeable about the profession, have a self-interest to restrict entry by putting unnecessarily costly entry requirements on new entrants into the profession. New entrants may not find it in their self-interest to put unnecessary restrictions on their entry into the profession, but they do not yet have sufficient knowledge about the profession and what is required for proper qualifications. The general public, while having an interest in ensuring quality performance without unnecessary restrictions, may not be able to judge what requirements are necessary for professional competence. Only alumni have knowledge of the profession without having a self-interest in excessive quality restrictions; consequently, they are the persons who should be entrusted with the powers of occupational licensing, if it is necessary." Discuss.
13. "Restrictions on the use of grandfather clauses would go a long way in reducing the abuses of occupational self-licensing." Discuss.
14. Indicate why incumbent practitioners in a profession may want to put excessive restrictions on entry into the profession.

KEYWORDS

union objectives 439
alternative wage 440
economic rent 441
median voter model 443
isoprofit curves 444
bargaining range 445
efficient wage and employment contracts 447
Pareto-efficient wage-employment outcome 448
contract curve 449
labour demand curve model 451
bargaining theory 454
threat point 455
Nash solution 457
Rubinstein's bargaining theory 457
delay costs 459
bargaining power 460

REFERENCES

Abowd, J. M. 1989. The effect of wage bargains on the stock market value of the firm. *AER* 79 (September):774–809.

Brown, J., and O. Ashenfelter. 1986. Testing the efficiency of employment contracts. *JPE* 94 (July):S40–87.

Card, D. 1986. Efficient contracts with costly adjustment: Short-run employment determination for airline mechanics. *AER* 76 (December):1045–71.

______. 1990. Unexpected inflation, real wages, and employment determination in union contracts. *AER* 80 (September):669–88.

Carruth, A, and A. Oswald. 1985. Miners' wages in post-war Britain: An application of a model of trade union behavior. *EJ* 95 (December):1003–20.

Christofides, L. 1990. Non-nested tests of efficient bargain and labour demand models. *Economics Letters* 32 (January):91–6.

Christofides, L., and A. Oswald. 1991. Efficient and inefficient employment outcomes: A study based on Canadian contract data. In *Research in Labor Economics, Volume 12*, ed. R. G. Ehrenberg. Greenwich, Conn.: JAI Press.

Currie, J. 1991. Employment determination in a unionized public-sector labour market: The case of Ontario's school teachers. *JOLE* 9 (November):45–66.

Dertouzos, J., and J. Pencavel. 1981. Wage and employment determination under trade unionism: The international typographical union. *JPE* 89 (December):1162–81.

Doiron, D. 1992. Bargaining power and wage-employment contracts in a unionized industry. *IER* 33 (August):583–606.

Dunlop, J. T. 1944. *Wage Determination Under Trade Unions*. New York: Macmillan.

Eberts, R., and J. Stone. 1986. On the contract curve: A test of alternative models of collective bargaining. *JOLE* (January):66–81.

Farber, H. 1978. Individual preferences and union wage determination: The case of the United Mine Workers. *JPE* 86 (October):923–42.

Macurdy, T., and J. Pencavel. 1986. Testing between competing models of wage and employment determination in unionized markets. *JPE* 94 (July):S3–39.

Manning, A. 1994. How robust is the microeconomic theory of the trade union? *JOLE* 12 (July):430–59.

Martinello, F. 1989. Wage and employment determination in a unionized industry: The IWA and the B.C. wood products industry. *JOLE* 7 (July):303–30.

Nash, J. 1950. The bargaining problem. *Ecta.* 18 (April):155–62.

Pencavel, J. 1984. The tradeoff between wages and employment in trade union objectives. *QJE* 99 (May):215–32.

Ross, A. 1948. *Trade Union Wage Policy*. Berkeley: University of California Press.

______. 1979. *Axiomatic Models of Bargaining*. New York: Springer-Verlag.

Roth, A., and M. Malouf. 1979. Game theoretic models and the role of information in bargaining. *Psychological Review* 86 (6) (November):574–94.

Rubinstein, A. 1982. Perfect equilibrium in a bargaining model. *Ecta.* 50 (1) (January):97–110.

Svenjar, J. 1986. Bargaining power, fear of disagreement and wage settlements: Theory and empirical evidence from U.S. industry. *Ecta.* 54 (September):1055–78.

Von Neumann, J., and O. Morgenstern. 1944. *Theory of Games and Economic Behaviour*. Princeton, N.J.: Princeton University Press.

Zeuthen, F. 1930. *Problems of Monopoly and Economic Warfare*. London: G. Routledge and Sons.

Chapter Sixteen

Union Impact on Wage and Nonwage Outcomes

Main Questions

- *By how much are unions able to raise the wages of their members? Which types of workers benefit most?*
- *What effects do unions have on the wages of nonunion workers?*
- *Do unions increase or decrease the overall level of income inequality?*
- *How much economic inefficiency can be blamed on the consequences of unionization?*
- *Are there positive effects of unionization on labour productivity?*
- *On balance, do unions reduce the profits of firms?*

This chapter focuses on the impact of unions on various labour market outcomes. We begin by examining the impact of unions on the wages of their members and on the wages of other employees. The final part of the chapter discusses various nonwage consequences of unions—including their impact on fringe benefits, productivity, firm profitability, turnover (quits and layoffs), income distribution, and the allocation of resources.

UNION WAGE IMPACT

The impact of unions on wages has received more attention from economists than any other aspect of union behaviour. Most of the empirical research has been directed at measuring the **union-nonunion wage differential**, the (percentage) difference in wages between union and otherwise comparable nonunion workers. Our discussion of this research begins by outlining the relevant theoretical background and explaining some of the conceptual and measurement issues involved; we then proceed to a summary of the main empirical findings and a discussion of how these empirical results should best be interpreted.

The basic issues can be illustrated by imagining what evidence could be brought to bear on the question, "What is the (average) effect of unionization on an individual worker's wage?" The simplest way to tackle the question would be to compare the average wages of union (W_U) and nonunion (W_N) workers. The percentage difference in wages would be given by:

$$\hat{d} = \frac{\overline{W}_U - \overline{W}_N}{\overline{W}_N} \approx \ln \overline{W}_U - \ln \overline{W}_N$$

The first problem that one confronts is that the wages of nonunion members may not be the same as the wages that would prevail in the complete absence of unions from the labour market (say, W_0). There are a number of theoretical reasons to believe that unions affect the wages of those employed in the nonunion sector. We never really observe the counterfactual case to a union member's wages that would prevail if unions were removed entirely from the economy, and the wages of nonunion employees may be a poor proxy.

The second problem is more practical, and concerns the more limited objective of measuring the impact of changing an individual's union status, given the level of unionization in the economy. The above measure, $\hat{d}$, only measures the "pure" effect of union status if union status is the sole difference between the union and nonunion workers. For reasons discussed below, this may not be the case, and more complicated statistical procedures have had to be employed in order for the estimator $\hat{d}$ to approximate a "pure" union effect.

Theoretical Background and Conceptual Problems

In many respects, the basic theory of the union wage impact is similar to that underlying the impact of other wage-fixing arrangements such as minimum wages. However, there are some unique aspects of union wage determination and these will emerge in what follows. We first examine the union wage impact in the simplest setting, and subsequently introduce additional complications.

In the analysis of union wage and employment determination in the previous chapter, the union workers' alternative wage—which in many situations may be taken to be the nonunion wage—was taken as exogeneously given. At this stage, however, it is important to recognize the impact of unions not only on the wages of union members but also on the wages of others. This requires a general equilibrium model. Most of the basic principles can be illustrated with a two-sector model, as shown in Figure 16.1(a). The two sectors A and B can be thought of as two different industries or regions employing the same type of labour, which is assumed to be homogeneous. There is a sufficiently large number of firms and workers that, in the absence of unions, the labour market is competitive. The equilibrium wage in the absence of collective bargaining is therefore W_0. (If there are differences in the desirability of jobs in the two sectors, a compensating wage differential would exist in equilibrium, as discussed in Chapter 8 of this book; allowing for this possibility would not affect the analysis other than to make it more complex.) Now suppose a union organizes the workers in sector A and is able to raise the wage to W_u. Employment in sector A will therefore decline to E_1^A. (We are assuming here that the firm can unilaterally set employment; the possibility of wage-employment outcomes to the right of the labour demand curve is discussed below.) The workers who are unable to obtain (or retain) employment in sector A will search for jobs in sector B, increasing labour supply to that sector by $a = E_0^A - E_1^A$. The additional labour supply depresses the wage in sector B, resulting in a new equilibrium wage of W_N. Employment expands to E_1^B, an increase (the amount b in Figure 16.1(a)) which is smaller than the reduction in employment in sector A. The difference (a - b) in Figure 16.1(a) is due to the upward-sloping supply of labour to

Figure 16.1 Two-Sector Model of General Equilibrium

(a) Union wage impact in a two-sector model

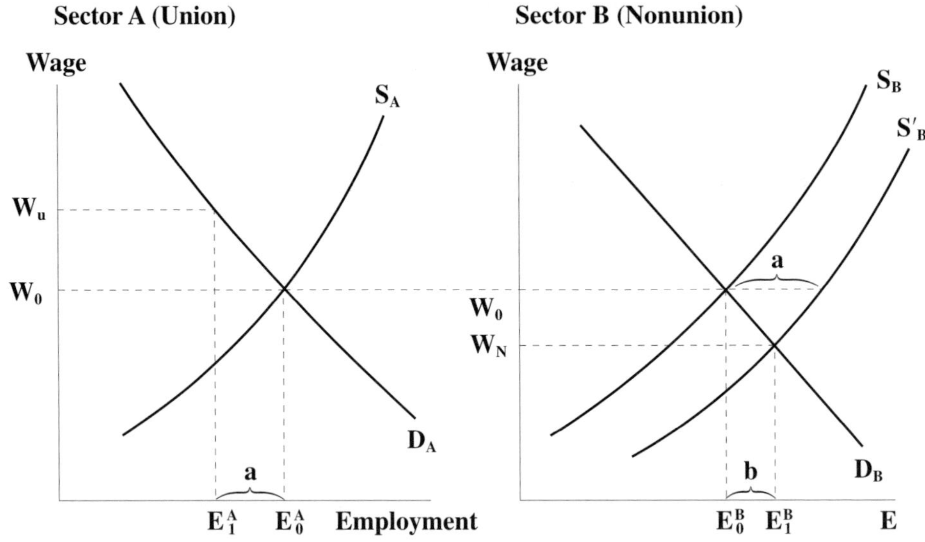

Both sectors start off with the competitive wage W_0. Unions raise wages from W_0 to W_u in the union sector, creating a reduction in employment of a. These displaced workers go to the nonunion sector shifting out the nonunion supply schedule by a and reducing wages from W_0 to W_N. This induces some persons in the nonunion sector to leave that sector (i.e., there is a movement down the supply curve given the lower wage), presumably to leave the labour force altogether.

(b) Union wage impact with a threat effect

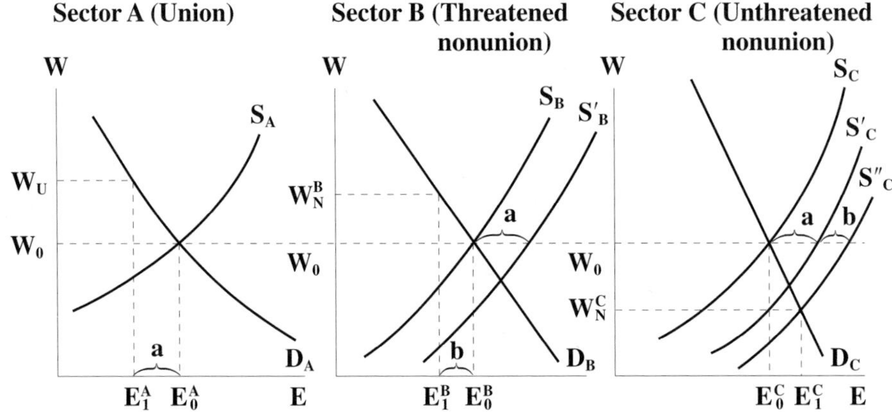

The nonunion sector is broken into two subsectors. In sector B, the nonunion firm raises its wage to W_n^b to reduce the threat of being unionized. The displaced workers b go to the nonunion sector C that does not respond with a threat effect, further augmenting the increased labour supply of a that already came from the union sector.

Figure 16.1 **Two-Sector Model of General Equilibrium *(continued)***

(c) Union wage impact with a vertical contract curve

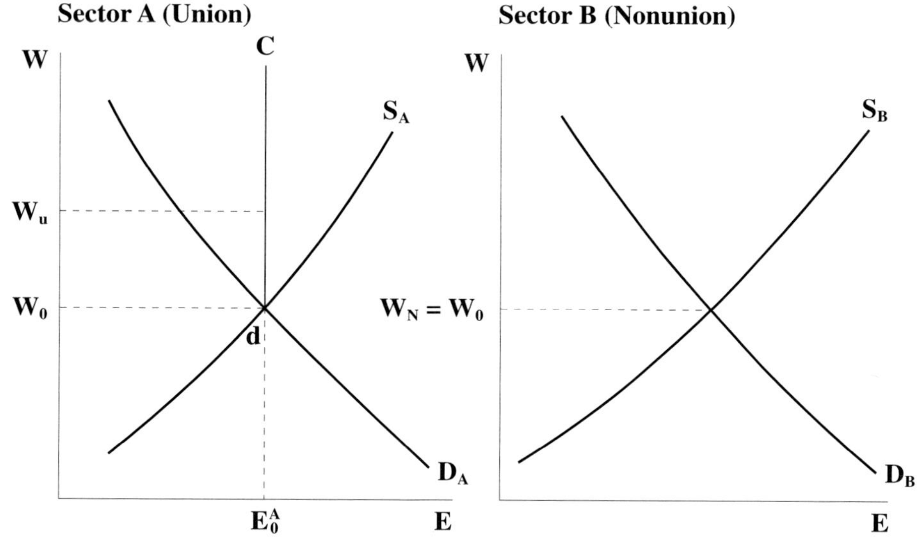

With a vertical contract curve Cd the union bargains for retaining the same level of employment, in spite of the higher wage. There is no adverse employment effect and hence no augmentation of labour supply in the nonunion sector.

(d) Union wage impact with wait unemployment

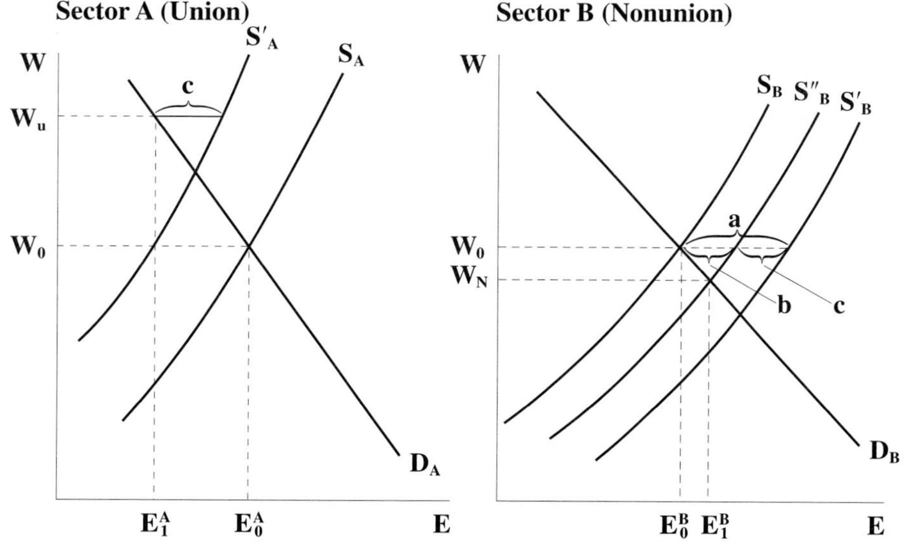

This is the same as panel (a) except that some of the displaced workers (the horizontal distance c) prefer to engage in "wait" unemployment, looking for jobs in the union sector. The net increase in employment in the nonunion sector B thereby is only b = a – c.

the economy; as the market wage falls in sector B, some individuals drop out of the labour force, the market wage falling below their reservation wage.

In this economy the union-nonunion wage differential would be $d = \frac{W_u - W_N}{W_N}$. Note that this is greater than the difference between the union wage W_u and the wage union members would receive in the absence of unionization (W_0). The difference arises because the higher wages associated with unionization force more workers to seek employment in the unorganized sector, depressing wages there. In this respect, the impact of unions on wages in the two sectors is similar to that of firms in sector A paying efficiency wages, as discussed in Chapter 10.

According to this basic **two-sector model**, the magnitude of the union-nonunion differential depends on: (1) the elasticity of labour demand in each sector, (2) the ability of the union to raise wages in the organized sector, and (3) the elasticity of labour supply.

This basic model is consistent with the notion of a dual labour market. The primary sector (A) consists of firms or industries that have characteristics—such as establishment size, concentration in the product market, stability of employment, and the nature of production—that make unionization likely. The secondary sector (B) consists of firms or industries with the opposite characteristics. The reduction in employment in the primary sector (relative to what employment would be in the absence of wage increases associated with unionization) creates a widening of the wage gap between the two sectors as those who cannot obtain employment in the unionized sector crowd into the nonunion labour market, depressing wages even further in the secondary sector. These low wages may in turn be a source of many of the phenomena—such as high absenteeism and frequent turnover—that are characteristic of the secondary sector.

Contrary to the belief that union wage increases tend to depress the wage of unorganized workers is the perspective that nonunion firms may raise the wages of nonunion labour in order to compete with unionized firms for the work force. In addition, firms with both union and nonunion workers may raise the wages of nonunion labour in order to preserve traditional wage differentials. While this belief has intuitive appeal, especially because comparability appears to be so important in wage determination, it ignores the market factors—in particular the supply influx from workers who cannot get jobs in the unionized sector—that would enable employers to pay lower wages to nonunion labour. In essence, there may not be a need to compete with the unionized sector because there is a large pool of labour to hire that cannot get jobs in the high-wage unionized sector. It is true that the unionized sector may get the top applicants because of the high wages, and it is the case that the reserve of labour may dry up in periods of prosperity (hence compelling the nonunion sector to pay higher wages), but it is also true that those who cannot get jobs in the union sector are a supply influx into the nonunion sector, and this lowers wages in that sector.

Nonetheless it is the case that *some* nonunion employers may raise wages in order to reduce the threat of their employees choosing to become unionized. This **threat effect** will be greater if the union wage premium is high, the nonunion sector is easy to organize, the potential union is aggressive, or the employers have a strong aversion to unionization. In such circumstances, nonunion employees may be paid close to the union wage (perhaps even higher if the firm has a strong aversion to unionization) and provided with working conditions similar to those of union workers. Such employees could receive the benefits of unionization without bearing such costs as union dues or possible strike costs. However, such benefits may be precarious in that they hinge on the willingness of employers to provide them.

To illustrate the operation of the threat effect, we need to distinguish between those firms that choose to pay higher wages to avoid unionization—perhaps because of a strong aversion to unionization or because they are easy to organize—and those that will choose to pay the lowest wage needed to attract labour. This situation is shown in Figure 16.1(b). As before, the equilibrium in the absence of collective bargaining is the wage W_o in each sector. The establishment of a higher union wage W_u causes some employers (sector B) to raise wages to W_N^B, despite the supply of individuals willing to work at lower wages. (W_N^B may be above or below the union wage, depending on the employer's aversion to unionization.) Employment declines in sectors A and B; thus wages fall further in sector C than in the absence of the threat effect. In dual labour market analysis, sector C would be identified as the secondary labour market.

The impact of the threat effect on the union-nonunion wage differential is ambiguous. The nonunion wage is a weighted average of W_N^B and W_N^C with weights being the employment in each sector. This average nonunion wage may be higher or lower than the nonunion wage that would prevail in the absence of a threat effect, W_N in Figure 16.1(a).

Two additional theoretical points should be noted; these can also be explained using the basic two-sector model. One is the possibility that the firm and union will negotiate wage-employment outcomes to the right of the labour demand curve, for reasons discussed previously in Chapter 15. Figure 16.1(c) illustrates the case in which the parties negotiate outcomes on a vertical contract curve. (Recall from Chapter 15 that the contract curve may be upward-sloping, downward-sloping, or vertical.) In these circumstances, the higher union wage is not associated with reduced employment in the union sector and therefore with depressed wages in the nonunion sector. The union-nonunion differential in this case is identical to the difference between the union wage and the wage union members would earn in the absence of collective bargaining. If the contract curve is downward-sloping, the higher union wage will result in some displacement of labour to the nonunion sector and therefore lower wages in that sector; however, these impacts will be smaller than will be the case if employment is on the demand curve.

The final complication to be discussed is that of **wait** or **queue unemployment**. The rationale behind this phenomenon can be understood by returning to the two-sector model illustrated in Figure 16.1(a). In that case it was assumed that all of the workers unable to obtain jobs in the union sector would seek employment in the nonunion sector. However, because union jobs pay relatively well, it may be rational to wait for a union job to turn up rather than seek employment elsewhere. This strategy is most likely to be sensible when there is rapid turnover in the union sector (so that union jobs become available fairly frequently) and when it is difficult to queue for a union job while employed. When these conditions apply, some individuals may choose to remain attached to the union sector, albeit unemployed. As a consequence, the increase in supply to the nonunion sector will be less than the reduction in employment in the union sector; compare Figures 16.1(a) and (d). The union-nonunion wage differential will be smaller than in the case of no queuing unemployment, though higher union wages nonetheless have some depressing effect on the wages of nonunion workers.

Higher union wages may also affect the demand for labour in the two sectors. This outcome is most likely to occur when the sectors constitute two groups of firms—possibly one group easy to organize and the other difficult to organize—in the same industry. Unless offset by higher labour productivity (a possibility discussed later) the union-nonunion wage differential may enable nonunion firms to expand their market share at the expense of union firms, thus shifting the demand for nonunion (union) labour to the right (left). The final equilibrium in this case will generally involve a smaller union-nonunion wage differential than that shown in Figure 16.1(a).

The above analysis of the union wage impact was based on several simplifying assumptions, including a homogeneous labour force and competitive labour markets (in the absence of collective bargaining). Several implications follow from relaxing these assumptions. With several different types of workers, changes in the wages of any one group will generally alter the wages of other groups. If union and nonunion workers are employed in the same firm or industry, an increase in union wages will increase (reduce) the demand for nonunion labour if the two groups are substitutes (complements) in production, and therefore increase (reduce) the wages of nonunion workers in that firm or industry. In addition, the wages of nonunion workers may be affected by various forms of wage-fixing such as minimum wage rates and fair wage provisions, many of which are supported by unions to reduce competition based on lower nonunion wages. In these circumstances the wage in the unorganized sector may not decline sufficiently to absorb the workers displaced by higher wages in the union sector. Jobs will be rationed in both sectors and there will be a number of individuals willing to work at existing wage rates but unable to find employment.

In summary, collective action (in particular the strike threat) will generally enable unions to raise wages relative to a hypothetical labour market equilibrium without unions, thus creating a wage differential between union and comparable nonunion workers. The magnitude of this differential depends not only on the ability and willingness of unions to raise wages but also on the impact on the wages of nonunion workers. Clearly the various factors discussed above can be at work simultaneously affecting the wages of nonunion workers, and since they do not all work in the same direction, economic theory does not provide unambiguous predictions of the effect of unions on the wages of nonunion workers. The wages of some nonunion workers may increase because of the increased demand for substitute nonunion labour, as a result of the threat effect, in response to legislative wage-fixing, or as part of the nonunion sector adjusts to restore old wage relativities. In contrast, some nonunion wages may decrease because of a decrease in the demand for complementary inputs, or because of the supply influx into the nonunion sector created by the reduced employment opportunities in the unionized sector. Ultimately, the impact of unions on the wages of nonunion workers is an empirical proposition.

Some Problems in Measuring the Union Wage Impact

Attempts to measure the union-nonunion wage differential face a number of interrelated problems, the most important being those of controlling for other wage-determining factors, accounting for the joint determination of union status and the union wage impact, and separating cause and effect.

In estimating a *pure* union-nonunion wage differential, it is important to control for other wage-determining factors so as to be able to attribute the differential purely to unionization. If, for example, unionized establishments tend to utilize more skilled labour than nonunionized establishments, it is crucial to control for these skill differences. Otherwise, the union-nonunion wage differential may simply reflect the skill differential, not a pure union impact on wages. Controlling for differences in labour quality between the union and nonunion sectors is especially important because, as indicated earlier, if unionized establishments pay a wage that is greater than the competitive wage, they may have a queue of applicants and may be able to hire the "cream of the crop" of applicants. Union firms faced with higher labour costs may also try to increase the job assignment, for example by increasing the pace of work; however, such adjustments are likely to be resisted by the union.

In these circumstances it is extremely important to control for differences in the characteristics of workers and job assignments. Otherwise these omitted variables are likely to impart an upward bias because the union-nonunion wage differential would reflect better-quality workers and perhaps more onerous job assignments in the union sector in addition to the pure wage impact of unions.

Most contemporary studies use individual micro-level data to estimate the impact of union status on earnings. This permits the researcher to try to control for labour quality differences by including variables such as education, training, and experience in a multiple regression framework. In fact, the most common procedure is to embed union status in the human capital earnings function described in previous chapters. In this way, the inclusion of the other regressors allows the investigator to control for all of the observable factors believed to affect earnings in the absence of unions. The implicit model is then

$$\ln W_i = \beta_0 + \beta_1 X_1 + \dots \beta_K X_K + \beta_U \text{IUNION} + \varepsilon_i$$

where the X's are the standard human capital variables and ε captures all the other, unobserved worker characteristics. An estimate of β_U, would then be an estimate of the impact of union status (IUNION) on individual earnings, controlling for observed earnings characteristics.

Unfortunately, some of the factors believed to affect labour quality and earnings (e.g., motivation, work effort, and reliability) may not be observed by the economist. If these characteristics are correlated with union status, then some of the estimated effect that is attributed to union status may, in fact, merely reflect these unobserved differences between union and nonunion workers. For example, information relating to the pace of work and job assignments is also often unavailable, although some studies (e.g., Duncan and Stafford, 1980) have been able to control for these factors. Many studies are able to include only crude controls (such as occupation, industry, and region) for the characteristics of the job. Thus it is not clear that the available data enables researchers to *fully* control for differences in productivity-related factors, although as will be explained below the quality of the available data has steadily improved.

These issues illustrate the problem of **selection bias** or the nonexperimental nature of union status, in the context of the union wage impact. As discussed in Chapter 14, union status is the outcome of decisions made by individual workers, employers, and union organizers. The omission from the estimated earnings equations of unobserved variables which are related to wages (such as motivation, work ethic, reliability) will not bias the estimates of the union wage impact if these unobserved factors do not also influence the decisions relating to union status; that is, if the unobserved factors affecting wages do not also influence selection into the union sector. However, if factors unobserved by the researcher influence wages and selection decisions—for example, if ability is not observed by the researcher but is known by employers, perhaps because of screening procedures, and used to decide which applicants to hire—then the estimated union wage impact will be subject to "selection bias." Addressing the selection bias problem is quite difficult, as it entails simultaneously explaining individual union status as well as the effect of unionization on wages.

The issue of the selection process determining which workers enter the union sector illustrates the more general problem of sorting out cause and effect in studies of the union impact. Usually the argument is advanced that unions cause higher wages. However, there is the possibility that cause and effect also works in the opposite direction. That is, some firms may simply be high-wage firms, perhaps because of efficiency wage considerations relating to productivity and morale, perhaps because they are trying to reduce the turnover of workers with firm-specific human capital, or because they want to be known as a model employer, or because they want a queue of applicants from which to hire. Unionization may be more likely to emerge in high-wage sectors because they are easier to organize or because the workers may be more likely to demand union representation. Workers in these firms will be reluctant to leave because wages are so high. Knowing that they want to stay in the high-wage establishment, and knowing that they will probably stay there for a considerable period of time because of the high wages, they may turn to devices to try to improve the everyday work conditions of the job. One such device may be unionization with its emphasis on due process, regulating the work environment, and administered rulings that provide a degree of certainty and security for the unionized workers.

In Hirschman's (1970) terminology, the restriction of **exit** increases the use of **voice**. In this case, voluntary quitting (exit) is reduced because of the high wages, and hence workers seek to have more of a say (voice) in their job by collective bargaining.

This possibility of cause and effect working in both directions suggests that some of the wage advantage of union establishments may not be due to unions, but may be attributed to other factors; in fact, unionism itself emerges because of the wage advantage. This suggests that econometric studies of the impact of unions should be based on simultaneous equation models, which allow wages to be a function of unionism as well as unionism to be a function of wages.

EMPIRICAL EVIDENCE ON UNION WAGE IMPACT

In varying degrees the numerous empirical studies of the wage impact of unions have attempted to deal with the measurement and modelling problems just discussed. Research has passed through several phases. Early studies based on aggregate data (e.g., industry or region) have given way to those using data based upon the individual worker as the unit of observation. Recent studies have attempted to account for the joint determination of union-nonunion status and the union wage impact and for unobserved quality differences between union and nonunion workers. Much of the research has been carried out in the United States and our summary reflects this fact. However, during the 1980s a number of data sets with information on the union status of individual employees became available in Canada. Accordingly, there is now a growing body of empirical literature on this important aspect of the Canadian labour market.

Early Studies

The classic work of H. Gregg Lewis (1963) both reviewed and reanalyzed the existing literature in the United States and provided new estimates up to 1958. While there was considerable variation in the estimated impact of the studies reviewed by Lewis, he attributed much of the variation to methodological differences. Lewis's estimate of the union-nonunion differential, based on his own work and a reanalysis of earlier studies, was approximately 10–15 percent for the U.S. economy as a whole, being larger in recessions and smaller in the boom phase of the business cycle. This estimate of a 10–15 percent differential was associated with an increase in the average union wage of 7 to 11 percent and a decrease in the average nonunion wage of approximately 3 or 4 percent.

Data availability imposed important limitations on these early studies. Because separate union and nonunion wage series were not available, the union-nonunion differential often had to be inferred from the average wage and the extent of unionization. This inference can be made only under certain restrictive assumptions; thus the estimates should be treated with caution.

Since Lewis's work there have been numerous additional studies, most utilizing new data sets where the unit of observation is the individual establishment or worker. Estimates of the union-nonunion wage differential based on individual cross-sectional data have tended to be higher than the 10–15 percent recorded by Lewis. These studies thus suggested that the union wage impact is higher than was previously believed. However, this conclusion is subject to the qualification that some of the difference between union and nonunion wages (after controlling for other wage-determining factors such as education, age, and experience) may be a reflection of reverse causality and/or unmeasured quality differences between union and nonunion workers. Recent research has focused on these issues.

Modelling Union Incidence and Impact

A number of recent studies have attempted to account for the joint determination of union status and the union wage impact. Ashenfelter and Johnson (1972), who were the first to formally deal with the **simultaneity** issue, used aggregate U.S. time series data. They found that higher wages make unionization more likely, and that the estimated union wage impact is considerably smaller when the two-way causality is taken into account. Most subsequent studies have applied simultaneous equation methods with individual data. Generally these studies model the wage determination process in the union and nonunion sectors and the selection process determining which workers are employed in each sector. Thus the researchers account for the possibility that the sample is not randomly generated with respect to union status; that is, some individuals have unobserved characteristics that make them more likely to be represented by a union than others.

Longitudinal Studies

Another recent development has been the availability of **longitudinal or panel data** which provide observations on the same individuals over time. With longitudinal data, person-specific characteristics which are conventionally unobservable to the researcher (e.g., reliability, work effort, and motivation) can be taken into account if these characteristics are constant for each individual over time. In these circumstances taking first differences (differences from one period to the next) in the data provides a natural way of removing the effects of such characteristics. This cannot be done with conventional cross-section estimates, which compare different individuals at the same point in time.

The procedure can be illustrated with the earnings regression introduced above. We assume that the unobservable component of individual i's earnings in year t, ε_{it}, has two components as follows:

$$\varepsilon_{it} = \lambda_i + \nu_{it}$$

In this case, λ_i captures all of the fixed characteristics of the individual that we believe may be correlated with his union status, while ν_{it} represents a purely random error term that is uncorrelated with union status (or any other regressor). If we have two observations on each individual (e.g., in two different years), then we can take first differences:

$$\ln W_{it} - \ln W_{it-1} = \beta_1(X_{1t} - X_{1t-1}) + \ldots \beta_K(X_{Kt} - X_{Kt-1}) + \beta_U(\text{IUNION}_t - \text{IUNION}_{t-1}) + \varepsilon_{it} - \varepsilon_{it-1}$$

By assumption,

$$\varepsilon_{it} - \varepsilon_{it-1} = \lambda_i + \nu_{it} - \lambda_i - \nu_{it-1} = \nu_{it} - \nu_{it-1}$$

that is, the λ_i term falls out, so that the error term in this regression is independent of these unobserved, fixed individual characteristics. If the unobserved variables are indeed constant over time, the use of longitudinal data allows the researcher to identify the union impact from the wage change for those individuals who *change* union status (IUNION_t - IUNION_{t-1}). Essentially the estimated differential is an average of the earnings gain of those who moved from nonunion to union jobs and the earnings loss of those who moved from union to nonunion jobs, after controlling for other observable factors.

Longitudinal analyses in the United States (e.g., Mellow, 1981; Mincer, 1983; Moore and Raisian, 1983; Jakubson, 1991) generally find that the estimated union-nonunion wage differential is about 10 percent, substantially smaller than suggested by cross-sectional estimates. Indeed, when cross-sectional analyses are carried out on the same data sets, the estimated differentials are approximately double those obtained using data on those who change union status. This finding could be due to unobserved (by the researcher) differences in worker quality between union and nonunion workers which are quantitatively significant; if true, this conclusion has important implications for the interpretation of not only observed earnings differences between organized and unorganized workers but also observed differences in labour productivity between the two sectors. However, the assumptions underlying the longitudinal estimates could also be invalid.

In addition, longitudinal data have some deficiencies. There is evidence of error in the measurement of union status which may bias downward the estimated union-nonunion wage impact (Freeman, 1984). Thus the estimated average wage impact of 10 percent may be too low. Card (1996) presents direct evidence in this regard. Using 1987 and 1988 matched (longitudinal) CPS data, he estimates cross-section union wage effects on the order of 16 percent (typical of the literature). Estimation of a conventional **fixed-effects** (first difference) **model** yields a much smaller union wage effect of about 6 percent. This suggests a significant amount of selectivity bias. However, external validation of the CPS union indicator suggests that approximately half of the individuals who appear to change union status are miscoded. The longitudinal approach depends on a reliable estimate of the earnings that individuals actually earn in their unionized and nonunion state. If half of the individuals we believe we observe in the different states are actually miscoded, then the genuine wage differences associated with changing union status will be offset by the "noise" of the mismeasured observations. In the extreme case where union status is randomly reported, there should not be any systematic relationship between wages and "unknown" union status. This will generally lead to an understatement of the union effect. Card takes account of the misclassification problem, and finds that the resulting fixed-effect estimator leads to an estimated union effect of 16 percent, similar to the cross-section estimate.

A further problem is that the number of individuals changing status is typically only 3–5 percent of the total sample, resulting in small and possibly unrepresentative samples. Furthermore, the facts that those individuals who change status may not be typical individuals and that changes in union status may themselves be associated with other unobservable factors suggest that it would be hazardous to rely exclusively on the estimates from longitudinal studies.

Summary of Average Impact in United States

Clearly important advances have taken place in the measurement of the union wage impact, a reflection of improved data sources and more sophisticated econometric methods. The accumulated U.S. evidence indicates that there is a statistically significant difference between the wages of union and otherwise comparable (to the researcher) nonunion workers—probably on the order of 10 to 20 percent for the economy as a whole after controlling for observed worker characteristics other than union status. In a major extension of his earlier work, Lewis (1985) reviews almost 200 empirical studies of the impact of unions on wages in the United States. He concludes that the average union-nonunion wage differential over the period 1967–79 was 15 percent.

However, there remains uncertainty about the magnitude of the union-nonunion wage differential when the joint determination of unionization and its impact is taken into account. Unfortunately the availability of better data and the application of more sophisticated techniques have not yet resulted in greater consensus about the magnitude of the average union wage impact. Indeed, the range of estimates produced by these studies is sometimes wide, a reflection both of differences in data sets and differences in model specification. Accordingly, recent research has attempted to determine which specification is most appropriate (Robinson, 1989b; Jakubson, 1991; Green, 1991; Card, 1996).

Canadian Evidence

Canadian studies of the average union wage impact are summarized in Table 16.1. Studies using aggregate industry data, plant-level data, and individual data have been

Table 16.1 Estimates of the Union-Nonunion Wage Differential in Canada

Author	Time Period	Estimated Differential (%)	Characteristics of Sample; Other Comments
1. Kumar (1972)	1966	17–23	Unskilled workers in manufacturing; aggregate data
2. Starr (1973)	1966	10–15	Unskilled male workers in Ontario manufacturing; disaggregate data (base wage at plant level)
3. Grant and Vanderkamp (1980)	1971	15	Individual data; annual earnings; "union member" includes membership in professional associations
4. Maki and Christensen (1980)	1974	51	Aggregate data, manufacturing
5. Christensen and Maki (1981)	1971–75	32	Aggregate data, manufacturing
6. MacDonald and Evans (1983)	1971–76	16	Aggregate industry data; 30 manufacturing industries
7. MacDonald (1983)	1971–79	20	Aggregate industry data; 30 manufacturing industries
8. Grant, Swidinsky, and Vanderkamp (1987)	1969–71	12–14 (1969) 13–16 (1970)	Individual longitudinal data, annual earnings; "union membership" includes professional associations
9. Robinson and Tomes (1984)	1979	24	Individual data on hourly paid workers
10. Simpson (1985)	1974	11	Microdata on wage rates for narrowly defined occupations
11. Kumar and Stengos (1985)	1978	10	Union and nonunion earnings data by industry
12. Kumar and Stengos (1986)	1981	12	Individual data; hourly earnings, representative sample
13. Robinson (1989)	1979–81	19–22	Individual data on hourly-paid workers
14. Green (1991)	1986	15	Individual data on males; hourly earnings
15. Swidinsky and Kupfeschmidt (1991)	1986	15	Individual data on job changers
16. Lemieux (1993)	1986–87	20 (males, cross-section) 29 (females, cross-section) 16 (males, longitudinal) 17 (females, longitudinal)	Individual cross-section and longitudinal data on males and females
17. Doiron and Riddell (1994)	1984	15 (males) 24 (females)	Individual data on males and females
18. White (1994)	1989	18–20 (all workers) 9–10 (professionals)	Individual data; samples of all workers, and professionals and managers
19. Christofides and Swidinsky (1994)	1989	7 (white males 11 (white females) –14 (minority males) 21 (minority females)	Individual data
20. Kuhn and Sweetman (1998)	1983	9–14	Panel data of displaced workers who lost union job
21. Renaud (1998)	1989	10	Individual data
22. Gunderson, Hyatt, and Riddell (2000)	1997	8	Individual data

carried out. The estimated union impact generally differs substantially across individual workers; the estimates reported in Table 16.1 are for the average individual in the sample. The estimates are broadly similar to those obtained in comparable U.S. studies. Average differentials (for the samples used) generally lie in the 10–25 percent range, with 15 percent being the estimate provided by Kuhn (1998) in his review. The estimated union wage impact is also sensitive to the econometric specification employed and to the nature of the sample (e.g., manufacturing, hourly-paid).

VARIATION IN THE UNION WAGE IMPACT

As would be expected on theoretical grounds, the estimated union-nonunion wage differential varies considerably across firms, industries, and workers. The average differential also varies over time. A number of generalizations about these variations emerge from the empirical literature, although for most generalizations there are exceptions in particular studies.

The union-nonunion wage differential tends to be larger when a high proportion of the relevant jurisdiction (industry, occupation, region) is organized. The relationship, however, is nonlinear; once a certain proportion of the jurisdiction is unionized, further increases have little additional effect on the differential. These findings can be interpreted in terms of two aspects of union power discussed previously: the elasticity of demand for union labour and the threat effect. As the fraction of the industry (or occupation or region) unionized increases, the possibilities for the substitution of nonunion for union labour decline, reducing the elasticity of demand for union labour. However, as more of the industry is organized, the remaining nonunion firms may face a higher possibility that their work force will organize and thus will tend to raise their wages. The gap between union and comparable nonunion workers in the same jurisdiction will thus not continue to widen, and may even narrow.

Firm or establishment size has also been found to be positively related to both union and nonunion wages in the majority of studies. The relationship is considerably stronger for nonunion workers; thus the wage differential between union and comparable nonunion workers declines with firm or establishment size. This outcome may reflect several forces. Unions usually attempt to standardize wage rates across firms and occupations—to "take wages out of competition"—which implies raising wages more in smaller firms, given the positive relationship between wages and firm size in the absence of unionization. Further, the threat of union organization is generally higher (due to reduced organizational costs per prospective member) in larger firms. Thus larger nonunion firms are more likely to match union wage scales than their smaller counterparts.

Large differences in the estimated union-nonunion differential are usually found to exist across occupations and industries. The impact is higher for blue-collar workers than for white-collar workers; higher in nonmanufacturing than manufacturing industries; and it can be exceptionally high in certain specific sectors such as construction. Skilled workers typically gain less from unionization than their semiskilled and unskilled counterparts (MacDonald, 1983; Simpson, 1985; Robinson and Tomes, 1984; and Renaud, 1998 for Canadian evidence), although there are specific examples of skilled trades—usually organized in craft unions—that exhibit large earnings differentials. As indicated in Table 16.2, the estimated union-nonunion differentials decline almost monotonically with skill level; indeed, in the most skilled categories, nonunion wages exceed union wages. This outcome may largely reflect the fact that in many unions—especially industrial unions—skilled workers constitute a minority with little influence on the union's wage policy.

An alternative perspective on the relationship between union and nonunion wages and skill level is shown in Figure 16.2. (It should be understood that all other wage-determining factors are held constant.) Wages increase with skill level in both sectors; however, the increase is more gradual under collective bargaining, and at high skill levels the union may

Figure 16.2 The Relationship Between Union and Nonunion Wages and Personal Characteristics

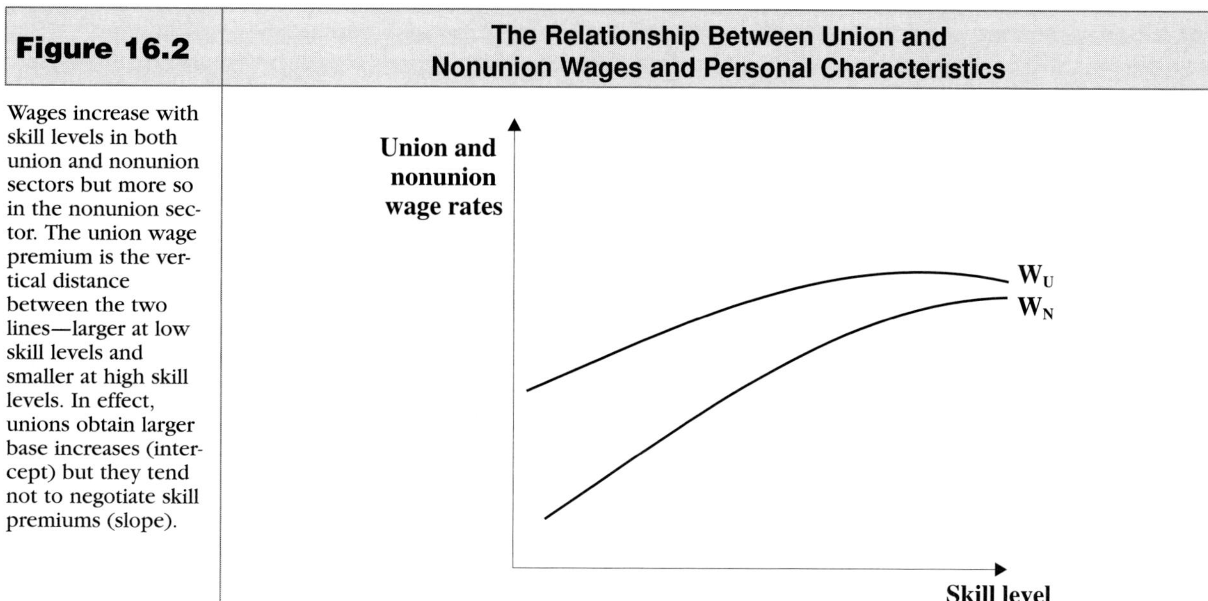

Wages increase with skill levels in both union and nonunion sectors but more so in the nonunion sector. The union wage premium is the vertical distance between the two lines—larger at low skill levels and smaller at high skill levels. In effect, unions obtain larger base increases (intercept) but they tend not to negotiate skill premiums (slope).

even fall below the nonunion wage. This type of relationship applies to a number of productivity-related characteristics (e.g., experience, education) in addition to skill. Simply stated, union wages are typically found to be less responsive to the personal characteristics of workers. The relationship between earnings and such factors as age, experience, education, and even marital status is weaker (i.e., age-earnings profiles are flatter, albeit higher) in the organized sector. When fringe benefits—which are typically of greater benefit to older, more experienced workers—are included together with wages this outcome is weaker, at least with respect to age and experience, but nonetheless remains.

Direct evidence on the possible shapes of the earnings-skills relationships depicted in Figure 16.2 is provided in Lemieux (1993) for Canada and Card (1996) for the United States. They provide longitudinal estimates of the union wage gap for workers with different skill levels, and find strong evidence that the wage gap is highest for low-skill workers,

Table 16.2 Estimates of the Union-Nonunion Percentage Wage Differential by Skill Level, Canada, 1974

Skill Level	All Industries	Manufacturing	Non-manufacturing	Public Sector[a]	Private Sector
1 (Low)	33.2	26.5	33.7	12.0	32.9
2	28.9	17.1	29.6	2.9	28.7
3	18.1	11.0	22.6	2.3	19.1
4	17.9	3.3	23.4	–1.0	19.0
5	12.4	–1.9	14.9	4.8	10.2
6	13.1	14.1	9.5	–24.3	15.0
7 (High)	–10.7	–11.1	–14.2	–33.4	–9.4
All Levels	18.6	11.5	20.9	–10.6	18.9

Note: [a]Includes workers in health and education as well as public administration.

Source: Simpson (1985, pp. 164–81).

and is possibly zero for high-skill workers. For example, Lemieux estimates a wage gap of 21 percent for the lowest-skill group, and less than 1 percent for the top-skill group. Card estimates a wage gap of 28 percent for the bottom fifth of the skill distribution; but 0 and 11 percent for the top 2 quintiles of the skill distribution.

U.S. studies generally find that union and nonunion wages are approximately equally responsive to gender. Lewis (1986) surveys 48 U.S. studies dealing with the impact of unions on male and female wages; the union-nonunion wage differential for females is generally estimated to be similar to that for males. However, in Canada there is evidence of a larger union-nonunion differential for females (Christofides and Swidinksy, 1994; Doiron and Riddell, 1994; Kumar and Stengos, 1986; Lemieux, 1993; and Renaud, 1998). Unionization thus has two offsetting effects on the average earnings of Canadian males and females. Females benefit less from unionization because they are less likely to be covered by a collective agreement (see Exhibit 14.2 in Chapter 14). However, unions raise the wages of females more than those of males. Doiron and Riddell (1994) find that these two effects tend to offset each other.

In the United States the union wage impact tends to be smaller in the public than in the private sector (Mitchell, 1983; Ehrenberg and Schwartz, 1986; Freeman, 1986). This finding may appear somewhat surprising, given that the elasticity of labour demand is generally estimated to be lower in the public sector. However, there are other important differences between the two sectors, and these may account for the observed behaviour. Unlike their private sector counterparts, many U.S. public sector employees do not have the right to strike. Thus the *willingness* of public sector workers to raise wages may be higher than in the private sector, but their *ability* to do so may be lower. In addition, union-nonunion wage differentials for the private sector workers who are most similar to those in the public sector—those in white-collar, service-sector employment—are significantly lower than for employees in blue-collar, goods-producing jobs. Thus, once one controls for the nature of employment, the public-private sector differences in union impacts narrow considerably.

Canadian evidence generally supports the conclusion that the union wage impact is smaller in the public sector (Renaud, 1998; Robinson and Tomes, 1984; Simpson, 1985). Robinson and Tomes (1984) find modestly lower differentials for hourly-paid workers in the public sector (27 percent versus 34 percent in the private sector); however, only a minority of public sector workers are paid on that basis. As shown in Table 16.2, Simpson (1985) concludes that union-nonunion wage differentials are significantly lower in the public than private sector for each skill group. Indeed, the differentials for higher-skill groups in the public sector are sufficiently negative that unionized public-sector workers are estimated to earn *less* than comparable nonunion public sector workers, while unionized private sector employees earn substantially more than their nonunion counterparts. Lemieux (1993) confirms the higher union wage gap in the private sector in the cross-section specification, but finds the returns to union status are virtually identical in the first differenced (longitudinal) specification.

In his earlier work, Lewis (1963) concluded that unionism has probably lowered the wages of nonunion workers, this effect accounting for about 3 to 4 percentage points of the total estimated differential of 15 percent. Subsequent studies utilizing better data (Kahn, 1978, 1980) also reach this conclusion; however, some more recent studies find small positive effects of unions on the wages of nonunion workers (Corneo and Lucifora, 1997; Ichniowski, Freeman, and Lauer, 1989; and Neumark and Wachter, 1995) at the city level, but negative effects at the industry level. As well, the overall average effect masks considerable variability, with some groups such as nonunion white males receiving a large wage increase from unionism. This outcome suggests the operation of both the threat and labour supply effects of union wage increases, as analyzed previously.

Lewis also concluded that the union-nonunion wage differential varies cyclically, widening in recessions and narrowing in booms; that is, union wages are less responsive to variations in economic and labour market conditions than nonunion wages. This behaviour may partly result from the fact that collective agreements typically provide for fixed nominal wage rates—often for durations of two to three years—and these agreements overlap each other. At any point in time, only the fraction of union contracts being renegotiated are able to respond to changes in economic conditions. In the nonunion sector, agreements are implicit rather than explicit and wages can be adjusted in response to variations in economic conditions. However, even if union wage contracts were renegotiated frequently and did not provide for fixed durations (as is the case, for example, in the United Kingdom), union wages may well exhibit less cyclical variation than nonunion wages. For reasons discussed subsequently, unions are likely to prefer employment reductions to wage reductions as a method of responding to temporary reductions in labour demand.

Recent U.S. research has generally supported Lewis' conclusion that the union-nonunion wage differential varies countercyclically, although some conflicting results have been reported. Changes in the extent of cost of living allowance clauses in collective agreements is one of several factors that may alter the cyclical behaviour of union wage rates. Because the price level varies procyclically (in the absence of supply shocks), indexing union wages to the cost of living tends to increase their responsiveness to variations in aggregate economic conditions.

Canadian evidence on the time series behaviour of the union-nonunion wage differential is extremely limited. As can be seen from Table 16.1, nine years (1971–1979) is the longest period for which estimates are available. MacDonald (1983) finds the differential rose almost continuously during this period from 16.4 percent in 1971 to 22.8 percent in 1979. Because this was a period of generally rising unemployment and increasingly slack economic conditions, these results are broadly consistent with the hypothesis that the union wage impact varies countercyclically. Renaud (1997) finds that the union impact was approximately 15 percent at the beginning of the 1970s, rising to a peak of around 25 percent by the end of the 1970s and falling to around 10 percent by the end of the 1980s. Gunderson, Hyatt, and Riddell (2000) also found that the union impact was approximately 8 percent by 1997.

UNION WAGE IMPACT: CONCLUDING COMMENTS

Although exceptions can be found in particular studies, a number of generalizations emerge from the substantial body of empirical research on the wage impact of unions:

1. There is substantial evidence of a significant wage differential between union and nonunion workers who are otherwise comparable in terms of observable characteristics. In Canadian studies, the average differential appears to be approximately 15 percent (in the range of 10 to 25 percent), similar in magnitude to estimates based on U.S. data. The earnings gap between union and comparable nonunion workers varies across industries, firms, regions, occupations, and over time with aggregate economic conditions.
2. The overall impact of higher wages in the union sector on the average wage in the nonunion sector is both theoretically and empirically inconclusive, with early studies tending to find small negative effects on nonunion wages, but some more recent studies finding the opposite.
3. In unionized enterprises, wage differences among workers who differ according to various productivity-related personal characteristics—such as education, age, experience, skill, and marital status—are smaller than in nonunion enterprises, and evidently smaller than they would be in the absence of unionization. Thus the financial "return" to

additional amounts of these attributes—for example, years of education or experience—is generally lower with collective than individual bargaining.

4. The union-nonunion wage differential is generally higher in the private than the public sector, higher in small firms and enterprises, higher for blue-collar than white-collar workers, higher when a large proportion of the relevant jurisdiction is organized, and higher in recessions than booms.

Canadian empirical evidence is consistent with these conclusions; however, only a limited number of studies have been carried out with Canadian data and there is considerable scope for further research.

Clearly a great deal has been learned about the effects of unions on wages. Nonetheless, several unresolved issues remain:

1. On theoretical grounds there is reason to believe that unionized firms will respond to higher wages and the concomitant larger queue of applicants by hiring "higher-quality" workers. The extent to which estimated union–nonunion differentials reflect this difference in labour quality rather than a pure differential remains largely unknown. U.S. evidence from longitudinal studies suggests that unobserved personal characteristics may account for a substantial proportion—perhaps as much as one-half—of the estimated wage differential. However, the differences between longitudinal and cross-sectional analyses could be due to other factors.
2. Unionized firms may also respond to higher wages by attempting to increase the job assignment. Although empirical studies have generally been able to control for a variety of measured worker characteristics, few have been able to control for attributes of the job. Some studies have concluded that estimated union-nonunion differentials partly reflect compensating differentials for more hazardous jobs, faster work pace, more structured work settings, and less flexible working hours (Duncan and Stafford, 1980; Leigh, 1982).
3. Uncertainty exists regarding the extent to which earnings differences between union and comparable nonunion workers are caused by unions raising their members' wages as opposed to unions being more likely to exist in firms that would choose to pay relatively high wages even in the absence of unions.

UNIONS, WAGE DISPERSION, AND THE DISTRIBUTION OF INCOME

As documented by Belman and Heywood (1990), Freeman (1980a, 1982, 1993), Hirsch (1982), and Quan (1984), for the United States and DiNardo and Lemieux (1997), Meng (1990), and Lemieux (1993, 1998) for Canada, there is significantly less **wage dispersion** among union workers than among comparable nonunion workers. This smaller variance is related to several aspects of union wage policy noted above. Unions tend to reduce wage differentials among workers that differ according to factors such as skill, age, experience, and seniority. Unions also attempt to standardize the wages of similar workers across establishments, especially those in the same industry or region. Further, unions have a larger impact on the wages of blue-collar than on white-collar workers. These policies imply that unions typically raise the wages of those at the lower end of the pay scale proportionally more than those at the upper end. As a result, the union wage distribution is both to the right and less dispersed than the nonunion distribution, as shown in Figure 16.3.

Although wage dispersion is substantially lower in the union than in the nonunion sector, it does not necessarily follow that unionism is associated with reduced wage dispersion in the economy as a whole. By creating a wage differential between union and comparable nonunion workers, unions also increase the variability of earnings relative to a hypothetical economy without collective bargaining. Because of these offsetting

Figure 16.3 **Wage Dispersion in the Union and Nonunion Sectors**

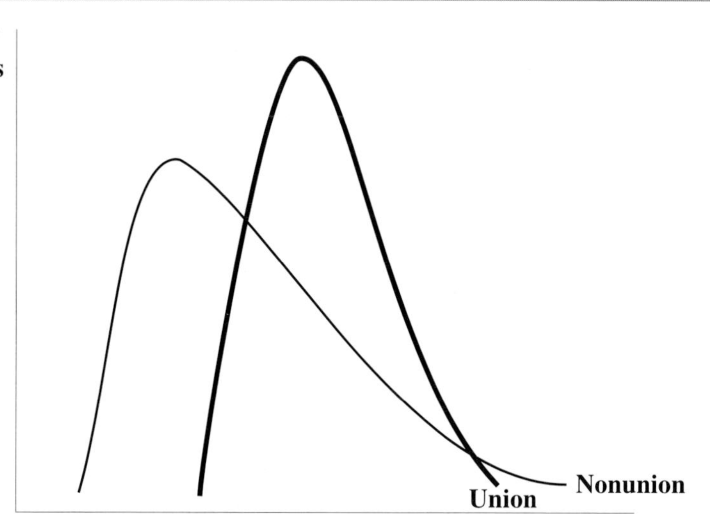

In the union sector the wage distribution is more compressed (less dispersed) with fewer workers receiving low wages and few receiving very high wages. In effect, the tails of the distribution are compressed into the higher spike at the middle of the wage distribution in the union sector. The union distribution also tends to be to the right of the nonunion distribution reflecting the higher wages generally received in the union sector.

factors—lower wage dispersion within the union sector but greater inequality between union and nonunion workers—the direction of the overall impact of unionism on the wage distribution is indeterminate.

Studies by Hyclak (1979, 1980), Freeman (1980a), and Quan (1984) indicate that in the United States the net effect of unionism is to reduce wage dispersion. In a detailed analysis of the impact of labour market institutions on the distribution of wages, DiNardo, Lemieux, and Fortin (1996) confirm the significant equalizing effect of unions. In fact, they attribute an important role to the decline in unions for contributing to the increasing wage inequality in the United States (see Chapter 14). They note that the decline in unions is associated especially with a drop in middle-level-paying jobs—better-paying blue-collar jobs traditionally associated with the union sector. Lemieux (1993) uses a Canada-U.S. comparison to gauge the extent to which differences in unionization rates contribute to the different levels of wage inequality in the two countries. He estimates that the greater extent of unions in Canada explains 40 percent of the difference in wage inequality, suggesting that unions play an important role in reducing income inequality. DiNardo and Lemieux (1997) also find that the much greater decline in unionization that occurred in Canada compared to the United States over the period 1981 to 1988 accounted for two-thirds of the greater growth in wage inequality that occurred in the United States compared to Canada.

UNION IMPACT ON RESOURCE ALLOCATION AND ECONOMIC WELFARE

Because they alter wages and employment, unions affect the allocation of labour and other resources in the economy. The nature and magnitude of this effect depends on several factors discussed previously in the context of the union wage impact. As was done earlier in this chapter, the consequences of unions are studied by comparing the situation with unions to a hypothetical economy without unions.

Figure 16.4 shows the allocative consequences of the union wage impact in a simple two-sector general equilibrium model in which outcomes are on the labour demand curve and the supply of labour to the economy is completely inelastic. With homoge-

Figure 16.4

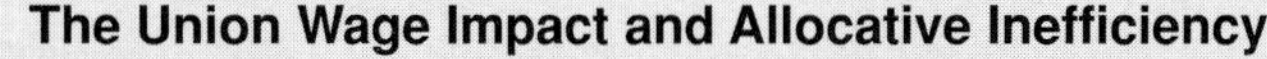

The Union Wage Impact and Allocative Inefficiency

With no unions both sectors start with the competitive wage W_0 and employment E_0. Unions raise wages in the union sector to W_u, reducing employment by $(E_1 - E_0)$ all of whom go to the nonunion sector. This creates deadweight losses—the triangles of acb in the union sector and dgf = dfe in the nonunion sector. These losses are greater the larger the union-nonunion wage differential (i.e., the height of the triangles), and the greater the elasticity of demand for labour and hence the resulting employment reallocation (i.e., the base of the triangles).

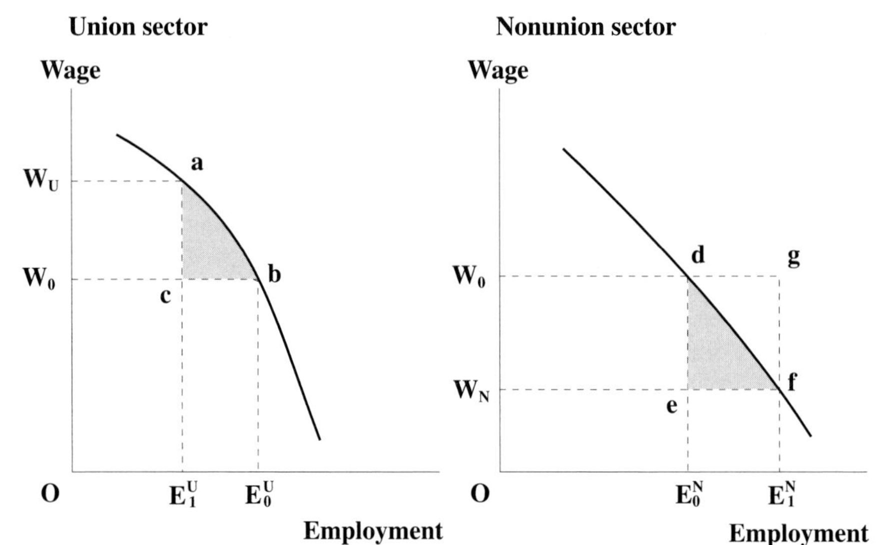

neous workers and competitive labour markets, the equilibrium in the absence of unions implies a common wage (W_0) in both sectors. Because of the higher union wage W_u, employment declines to E_1^u in the union sector and increases to E_1^N in the nonunion sector, reducing the wage there to W_N. With inelastic labour supply the increase in employment in the nonunion sector $(E_0^N E_1^N)$ equals the reduction in employment in the union sector $(E_1^u E_0^u)$.

These changes in wages and employment result in an **inefficient allocation** of society's resources and a reduction in the total output and income generated by the economy. The magnitude of this allocative inefficiency can be illustrated using the fact that, because the labour demand curve is the marginal revenue product curve, the area under the labour demand curve equals the total value of the output produced. Thus the value of the output produced by the union sector declines by E_1^u a b E_0^u as a result of the union wage impact, while the value of output produced by the nonunion sector increases by E_0^N d f E_1^N. Total income declines by E_1^u a b E_0^u minus E_0^N d f E_1^N, an amount equal to the sum of the two shaded areas cab and edf. (This follows from the fact that the area E_1^u c b E_0^u equals the area E_0^N d g E_1^N and the area def equals the area dgf, assuming a linear demand curve.)

An alternative way of viewing the losses is to distinguish between deadweight or real resource losses and transfer losses, the latter representing a redistribution, not a loss, of output or income. For example, the loss of output E_1^u a b E_0^u in the union sector consists of two components: the loss of income E_1^u c b E_0^u to the displaced workers (which is a transfer loss since employers and ultimately customers are not paying that amount), and a real resource or deadweight loss abc, which represents what consumers are willing to pay for the output over and above what the workers were willing to accept to produce the output. When the displaced workers move to the union sector $(E_1^u E_0^u = E_0^N E_1^N)$, their income is reduced from E_1^u c b E_0^u in the union sector to E_0^N e f E_1^N in the nonunion sector. They therefore lose income of edgf. However, edf of that is a gain to the rest of society, reflecting their value of the output E_0^N d f E_1^N over and above what they have to pay for the additional output E_0^N e f E_1^N. Therefore, the only real resource loss is dgf, which equals edf given a linear demand curve. Thus the total real output loss is abc plus def: the former represents what consumers are willing to pay for the loss of output in the unionized sector over and above what workers required to produce that output; the latter represents the loss associated with the fact that the output increase is valued less in the nonunion sector than the output loss in the union sector. The sum of these two components constitutes the welfare loss from union wage-fixing in an otherwise competitive market.

This reduction in the value of total output is referred to as a **deadweight loss** because it is not offset by a benefit elsewhere. The misallocation of labour resources occurs because higher wages and reduced employment in the union sector push other workers into less-productive and more poorly paying jobs in the nonunion sector. As a result there are too few workers employed in the union sector and too many in the nonunion sector. The use of other resources is also affected. Relative to an efficient allocation of resources, firms will respond to the wage differential by utilizing excessively capital-intensive production techniques in the union sector and excessively labour-intensive techniques in the nonunion sector.

The existence and magnitude of a deadweight loss associated with the union wage impact depend on several factors discussed earlier: the elasticity of labour supply, the amount of queuing unemployment, and the extent to which firms and unions negotiate wage-employment outcomes to the right of the demand curve. Depending on these various factors, the magnitude of the reduction in total output may be lower or higher than that shown in Figure 16.4. For example, in the situation depicted in Figure 16.1(c), in which union wages and employment lie on a vertical contract curve, employment in the two sectors is identical to that which would occur in a competitive labour market equilibrium, and no misallocation of labour resources results. In these circumstances, the higher union wage alters the distribution of income (increasing labour's share) but not total income. On the other hand, an additional output loss will occur if some individuals leave the labour force because the nonunion wage falls below their reservation wage and/or some individuals choose to remain unemployed, hoping to receive a union job.

The potential allocative inefficiency associated with the union wage impact was illustrated using as a reference point an economy in a competitive equilibrium. From this starting point, any distortion such as monopoly in the product market or wage-fixing in the labour market will result in a misallocation of resources and a reduction in total income. However, if the starting point is an economy with existing distortions, then it is not necessarily the case that adding another distortion (e.g., union wage impact) will cause a reduction in society's economic welfare. (This is the central proposition of the "Theory of Second Best" associated with Lipsey and Lancaster, 1956.) The Canadian economy contains numerous distortions which would cause it to deviate from a first-best (Pareto-optimal) allocation of resources in the absence of unions; therefore it is an empirical question as to whether the union wage impact improves or worsens allocative efficiency.

http://internationalecon.com/v1.0/ch100/100c030.html

Early estimates of the deadweight loss were based on fairly crude methods and did not take into account other distortions in the economy. These studies estimated the loss for the United States to be about 0.15 percent of GNP (Rees, 1963) and 0.33 percent of GNP (Johnson and Mieszkowski, 1970) when the union-nonunion wage differential was 15 percent. More recently, De Fina (1983) reports estimates based on a computable general equilibrium model of the U.S. economy incorporating several existing distortions. De Fina estimates the deadweight loss to be considerably less than that of earlier studies; when the union-nonunion wage differential is 15 percent, the loss is less than 0.1 percent of GNP, while a differential of 25 percent produces an estimated loss of 0.2 percent of GNP. More recent work by Fisher and Waschik (2000) for Canada, based on a general equilibrium model that incorporates other distortions and trade, finds considerably smaller estimates of the deadweight loss of 0.04 percent (i.e., 0.0004) of GNP. They attribute these smaller effects in part to the fact that they did not simply impose an exogenous union wage increase, but also allowed unions to bargain for more efficient contracts over both wages and employment (discussed previously in Chapter 15).

UNION IMPACT ON NONWAGE OUTCOMES

Unions bargain for a wide range of factors in addition to wages, and a more complete understanding of the economic and social consequences of unions will emerge from examining these other outcomes of collective bargaining. We begin by discussing the impact of unions on fringe benefits and proceed to working conditions, quit and layoff behaviour, and productivity and profitability.

Unions and Fringe Benefits

Nonwage or fringe benefits refer to employer payments such as those for pensions, medical and life insurance, vacations, holidays, and sick leave. Omitting these benefits understates both the cost of labour to the employer and the benefit received by the employee; thus total compensation is the relevant measure for both labour demand and supply decisions. (See Chapter 5 for a discussion of nonwage benefits and their effects on labour demand.) The omission of fringe benefits would not bias estimates of the impact of unions on the total compensation of union and nonunion workers if nonwage benefits were the same proportion of total compensation in both sectors. However, evidence indicates that nonwage benefits account for a greater proportion of total compensation among union than nonunion enterprises; that is, unions tend to have a greater impact on fringe benefits than on wages (Freeman, 1981; Freeman and Medoff, 1984; Renaud, 1998). This implies that estimated union-nonunion differentials understate the total compensation gap between organized and unorganized workers.

There are numerous reasons why all parties—employees, employers, and governments—may prefer fringe benefits over wages as a form of compensation. (These are discussed in more detail in Chapter 5.) Workers may prefer fringe benefits because they are often not taxable or taxes are deferred; in addition there may be economies of scale and administrative simplicity associated with group purchases. Employers may benefit from the fringe benefits provided to employees to the extent that they facilitate the planning and operation of the production process, provide appropriate work incentives, and reduce turnover. In periods of wage control both parties may favour compensation via nonwage benefits. Governments may prefer fringe benefits (and hence grant favourable tax treatment) because private sector expenditures on items like pensions, workers' compensation, and unemployment insurance may reduce pressure for government expenditures in these areas.

While there are these reasons for the existence and growth of fringe benefits, the question remains as to why their magnitude is greater in the union than the nonunion sector. There are several theoretical reasons why this is so.

To the extent that union workers are made better off by unionization, they can afford to buy more of everything, including fringe benefits. Thus, if the income elasticity of demand for nonwage benefits exceeds unity, union workers will devote a larger share of total income to fringe benefits than comparable nonunion workers. Compounding this effect is the fact that the effective price or cost of non-taxable fringe benefits falls as income (and therefore the marginal tax rate) rises.

The union's role in articulating its members' preferences regarding nonwage benefits may also affect the share of total compensation devoted to fringe benefits. As discussed previously, because of their political nature unions can be expected to represent the wishes of the median union voter. In contrast, nonunion employers will design their compensation packages to appeal to the marginal worker—the employee on the verge of joining or leaving the firm—who is likely to be younger and more mobile than the member of median age or seniority. Because the demand for such fringe benefits as pensions and life, accident, and health insurance increases with age, seniority, and family responsibilities, compensation packages in unionized enterprises are thus expected to devote a greater share to these nonwage benefits.

Fringe benefits in the form of deferred compensation are also expected to be more prevalent in unionized establishments. As discussed in Chapter 13, employers may prefer deferred compensation because of favourable work incentive effects (employees will work diligently in order to retain their jobs and thus receive the deferred payment later in their careers) and because it reduces turnover (employees who quit lose some or all of their deferred compensation—for example, pensions and vacation rights). Deferred compensation will be attractive to employees if they are given a sufficiently high wage to compensate for some of it being deferred (and hence its receipt being uncertain), and/or if they are provided with sufficient guarantees that employers will ultimately pay the deferred wages. Such guarantees are more binding when they are provided in a collective agreement which, for example, protects against arbitrary dismissal. Thus deferred compensation arrangements are expected to be more acceptable to union than nonunion employees, other things equal.

Freeman's (1981) empirical analysis indicates that unionism increases fringe benefits both directly and indirectly (through higher levels of compensation for union workers). This suggests that the tendency of unions to represent the preferences of the median or inframarginal worker and the increased acceptability of deferred compensation to workers protected by a collective agreement help account for the increased significance of nonwage benefits in the union sector.

Union Impact on Working Conditions

In addition to their impact on wages and fringe benefits, unions affect a variety of working conditions. These changes may reflect both the collective bargaining objectives pursued by the union and the firm's response to the higher labour costs associated with unionism.

Union workplaces tend to be governed much more by various rules than comparable nonunion settings. Collective agreements typically stipulate such factors as the way grievances are to be handled, the role of company service, and the scheduling of worker hours. Nonunion enterprises, although not without their own bureaucratic procedures such as personnel policies, tend to be less rules-oriented, and to exhibit more worker and management flexibility.

In addition to a more structured work setting and less flexible hours, there is also evidence that unionized environments are characterized by a faster work pace. This may reflect the fact that unionism is more likely to occur in response to such working conditions or that employers are able to respond to the union wage effect by changing the conditions of work. Without being able to disentangle the true cause and effect, Duncan and Stafford (1980) estimate that about two-fifths of the union-nonunion wage differential reflects a compensating wage for these more onerous working conditions. This conclusion is relevant to interpreting empirical evidence not only on union-nonunion wage differences, but also on productivity differences between union and nonunion workers, discussed subsequently.

In response to the economic realities of the new economic environment, unions may also be changing their bargaining strategy in order to survive. In particular, they may be deemphasizing wage gains and emphasizing issues related to working conditions and work rules (see Exhibit 16.1).

Union Impact on Turnover and Mobility

Unions also affect various aspects of **labour market turnover** and mobility—quits, layoffs, rehires, promotions, and terminations. Numerous U.S. studies (e.g., Freeman, 1980b, 1980c; Blau and Kahn, 1983; Rees, 1994) and a Canadian study (Swindinksy, 1992) have found that the quit rate is significantly lower among union workers than comparable nonunion workers. In part this reflects the reluctance of workers to leave the higher-wage union environment. However, even after controlling for differences in wages, union workers quit less frequently than their nonunion counterparts.

There may be several explanations for this phenomenon. As discussed previously, deferred compensation is more prevalent in union enterprises; such benefits provide an extra inducement to remain with the employer. Causality may also operate in the other direction. Deferred compensation such as pensions and vacations tied to length of service is more attractive to individuals who expect to remain with the firm for a long time. Thus this type of compensation tends to act as a sorting or screening mechanism, attracting to union firms workers who are less likely to quit (and vice versa in nonunion firms).

The lower quit propensity among union workers can also be interpreted as reflecting their substitution of a "voice" mechanism for an "exit" mechanism (Freeman, 1980b; Freeman and Medoff, 1984). Union employees dissatisfied with their working conditions can attempt to bring about improvements through collective bargaining, while the main mechanism available to dissatisfied workers in nonunion enterprises is the threat of seeking employment elsewhere.

Unions also affect the use of temporary layoffs, hours reductions, and wage reductions as mechanisms for responding to short-term fluctuations in demand. Collective agreements typically provide for a fixed nominal wage rate, possibly indexed to the cost of living but rarely indexed to other variables such as the state of the firm's product demand. With

Exhibit 16.1

Are New Unions Changing Their Stripes to Survive?

Freeman and Kleiner (1990) argue that newly formed unions in the United States in the 1980s may be changing their bargaining strategy in order to survive. Specifically, they argue that newly formed unions at that time may be moving away from their "monopoly" phase of trying to win large wage increases, and toward their "collective voice" phase of emphasizing practices that are important to unions such as grievance procedures, seniority protection for layoffs and recalls, and posting and bidding for internal promotions. They argue that the collective-voice aspects may be emphasized more in the 1980s for a variety of reasons:

- Unions may have been under more pressure to be cost-conscious because of deunionization, deregulation, global competition, and high unemployment.
- New unions in the 1980s may have wanted to solidify their position by bargaining for items that give them a greater degree of security.
- New unions in the 1980s tended to disproportionately organize minorities and females, and since organizing was less frequent at that time (unions were declining) the plants they organized may have had particularly bad labour-management relations—hence the emphasis on collective-voice aspects more than money.

Freeman and Kleiner provide empirical evidence indicating that union wage gains in those newly formed unions in the 1980s were low (i.e., less than 5 percent) by historical standards, but that they did win improvements in grievance procedures, seniority protection for layoffs and recalls, and posting and bidding for internal promotions. They conclude that this represents a shift in union strategy in response to the realities of the new environment, with unions emphasizing their collective voice rather than their more costly monopoly union function.

wages fixed, union firms rely more heavily on layoffs and recalls to respond to temporary fluctuations in demand than otherwise comparable nonunion firms, who make greater use of adjustments in wages and hours of work (Medoff, 1979; Blau and Kahn, 1983). In addition, seniority receives more weight in determining the order of layoffs and recalls in union firms. These differences in adjustment behaviour are consistent with the view that unions tend to represent the preferences of the median member. Having substantial seniority, such workers are unaffected by layoffs except in the case of extremely large reductions in the work force. In contrast, nonunion employers respond to the preferences of the marginal worker. Being younger and less senior, such workers would prefer that all workers take a reduction in wages and/or hours rather than some workers being laid off in reverse order of seniority.

Internal mobility also differs between union and nonunion employees and organizations. Promotion decisions depend much more on seniority in union than in nonunion organizations, as do decisions about employee terminations (Blau and Kahn, 1983). As with layoffs, the greater weight given to seniority in these organizational decisions can be seen as reflecting the preferences of the median union member.

Union Impact on Productivity, Profitability, and Investment

Although the impact of unions on various aspects of **productivity** has been debated for a long time, the subject received little quantitative analysis until recently. This recent literature has confirmed that unions can have both positive and negative effects on productivity, so that the overall impact depends on the magnitude of various offsetting factors.

In discussing the impact on productivity it is important to distinguish between the effects that occur directly as the outcome of collective bargaining and those that occur indirectly in the form of a behavioural response to higher wages. It is also important to recognize that unions may affect productivity not only in unionized firms but also elsewhere in the economy.

Economic theory predicts that firms will respond in several ways to the increase in labour costs associated with unionization. Relative to their nonunion counterparts, union firms will utilize more capital and other inputs and less labour per unit of output. Union employers will also attempt to hire more productive workers, and may try to increase job assignments and the pace of work.

Each of these responses to the union wage impact tends to raise labour productivity (output per worker) in the union sector and lower labour productivity in the nonunion sector. Thus a union-nonunion productivity comparison that does not control for differences in the amount of capital per worker, productivity-related worker characteristics, and the nature of the job assignment may well conclude that union workers are more productive than their nonunion counterparts. Although this conclusion would be correct, it would not necessarily follow that unions benefit society as a whole by raising worker productivity. For example, as discussed previously, the union wage impact and its consequences for the allocation of labour and other resources results in a reduction in society's total output and income, even though output per worker in the union sector rises. Similarly, society as a whole will, in general, not benefit from distributing the labour force such that unionized firms employ the more productive workers and nonunion firms the less productive. For these reasons, empirical analyses have attempted to determine whether unions and collective bargaining have direct effects on productivity in addition to those which arise as a consequence of the union wage impact. Such direct impacts, if positive, do imply a social benefit; if negative, they imply a social loss.

A common belief is that unions reduce productivity directly by inducing work stoppages and by negotiating restrictive work rules which compel the employer to use excessive amounts of union labour and/or prevent the employer from introducing technological innovations. However, as emphasized by Freeman and Medoff (1979, 1984), unions may also have positive effects on productivity by reducing turnover, improving morale and cooperation among workers, improving communications between labour and management, and by "shocking" management into more efficient practices.

Turnover is generally costly to firms because of expenses associated with hiring and training new workers to replace experienced personnel. While some turnover costs—for example, expenditures on job advertising—may not affect measured productivity, others—for example, existing personnel devoting less time to their own tasks and more to training new workers—do have this effect. In addition, lower turnover implies greater incentives for firms to engage in on-the-job training which enhances productivity. For these reasons, the lower quit rate in union enterprises is expected to result in higher productivity than in otherwise comparable nonunion enterprises. As discussed earlier, the differential in turnover can in turn be partly attributed to the union-nonunion wage differential and partly to the direct impact of collective bargaining.

Unions may affect employee morale, the amount of cooperation among workers, and communications between labour and management in several, possibly offsetting, ways. Employee morale may be enhanced through better wages, benefits and working conditions, by providing workers with a mechanism for expressing their collective preferences, and by negotiating grievance, dismissal, and other procedures which protect workers from arbitrary treatment by management. Better morale may in turn raise productivity, although it is also possible that grievance procedures can be abused by workers—resulting in management and employee time being devoted to trivial matters—and that making dismissal more difficult may reduce work effort and protect the incompetent. By making promotions much more dependent on seniority, unions may increase the amount of cooperation among workers because there will be less competition among employees for advancement. On the other hand, competition among workers for promotion may also enhance work effort and thus raise productivity. Unions also provide a formal mechanism for communication between workers and management, and these communications channels can be used to provide the firm with information about potential improvements in production techniques, product design, and the organization of the workplace. However, the union-management relationship can also become adversarial, with the consequence that there is less communication between the firm and its employees about potential improvements than in nonunion organizations.

Some analysts have also suggested that unionization—and the accompanying increase in labour costs—may shock the firm into adopting more efficient production and management techniques. This **shock effect** hypothesis assumes the existence of organizational slackness or inefficiency prior to unionization and is therefore consistent with "satisficing" behaviour on the firm's part, but not with optimizing behaviour (profit maximization and/or cost minimization). Although logically separate, the shock effect is difficult to distinguish empirically from the response of an optimizing firm to a change in relative factor prices—in this case, implementing a variety of changes in production techniques, hiring practices, and job assignments which result in the more efficient utilization of union labour.

In summary, economic theory suggests a variety of mechanisms through which unions may affect productivity. Because these mechanisms tend to both raise and lower productivity, the net impact is ambiguous. Empirical studies have found evidence of both positive and negative net impacts, suggesting that in some circumstances the productivity-enhancing mechanisms dominate while in others the opposite occurs. To the extent possible, the studies have attempted to control for such factors as differences in capital per worker and in productivity-related worker characteristics such as education and experience. The purpose, then, is to estimate the direct impact of unions on productivity, that is, to exclude those effects which are a consequence of the union-nonunion wage differential.

Broadly based studies using aggregate data have generally produced inconclusive results. Using cross-sectional data for U.S. manufacturing industries, Brown and Medoff (1978) found a large positive union impact on productivity when certain strong assumptions were made regarding the technology of production in union and nonunion firms, but found no statistically significant impact under more general assumptions. With data for Canadian manufacturing industries, Maki (1983) obtains results which are even more sensitive to econometric specification, being positive when the Brown-Medoff assumptions are imposed but significantly negative under more general conditions. Canadian evidence presented in Mitchell and Stone (1992) is also sensitive to the econometric specification. Adding to the conflicting results, Warren (1985) finds evidence of a negative union impact on productivity using aggregate U.S. time series data.

Empirical studies based on more disaggregated data generally appear to be much less sensitive to changes in specification. Using a large sample of individual U.S. firms, Clark (1984) estimates a small negative union impact on productivity. The growing number of econometric studies of individual industries provides evidence of both positive and negative impacts. In detailed studies of the U.S. cement industry, Clark (1980a, 1980b) finds that union labour was 6 to 8 percent more productive than nonunion labour, an amount which approximately offsets the higher labour costs associated with the union wage impact. Large productivity effects have been estimated in residential and office construction (Mandelstamm, 1965; Allen, 1984), a sector in which the union-nonunion wage differential is also substantial. However, union and nonunion labour are estimated to be equally productive in the construction of schools (Allen, 1984). The difference may be due to the high degree of competition in residential and office construction relative to that for schools. Consistent with the hypothesis that product market competition plays an important role in the impact of unions on productivity is the general finding that there is no union-nonunion productivity differential in the provision of public sector services such as municipal libraries (Ehrenberg, Sherman, and Schwarz, 1983), hospital services (Sloan and Adamache, 1984), and building department services (Noam, 1983), although Hoxby (1996) finds unions to have had a negative effect on the productivity of public school teachers.

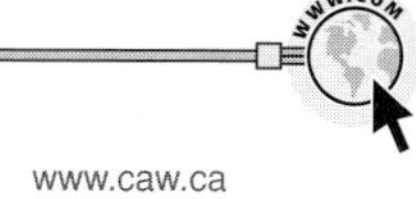

www.caw.ca

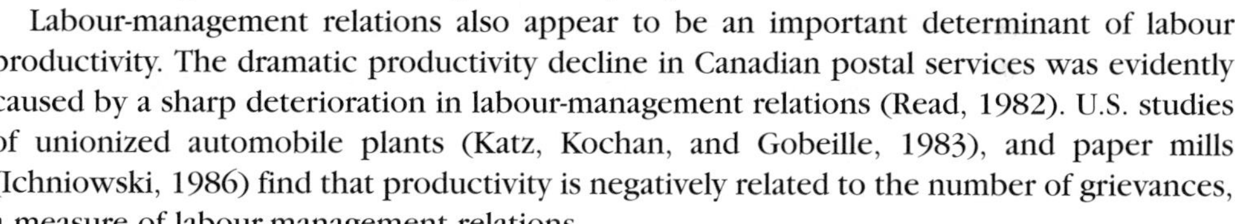
Labour-management relations also appear to be an important determinant of labour productivity. The dramatic productivity decline in Canadian postal services was evidently caused by a sharp deterioration in labour-management relations (Read, 1982). U.S. studies of unionized automobile plants (Katz, Kochan, and Gobeille, 1983), and paper mills (Ichniowski, 1986) find that productivity is negatively related to the number of grievances, a measure of labour-management relations.

Management response to unionization may also play a significant role. In his study of cement plants that became unionized, Clark (1980a) found that existing managers were replaced with new managers who were less paternalistic or authoritarian, and who placed more emphasis on controlling costs, setting production standards, and improving communication and monitoring. This adjustment can be interpreted either as a "shock effect" or as an optimizing firm's substitution of higher-quality managerial input in response to an increase in the relative price of production labour.

In summary, the impact of unions on productivity, long a controversial issue, has received considerable attention recently. Evidence on the average economy-wide impact is inconclusive. However, in specific industries union labour has been found to be more productive, in some cases substantially so, than comparable nonunion labour. This productivity differential persists after controlling for differences in capital per worker and observed productivity-related worker characteristics, differences which can be attributed to the union-nonunion wage differential. However, the existence of a positive union impact on productivity is by no means assured. The direction and magnitude of the effect appears to depend on the management response to unionization, the quality of labour-management relations, and perhaps the degree of product market competition.

The conclusion that in some industries union labour is significantly more productive than comparable nonunion labour will no doubt surprise those who believe that, by restricting management flexibility and negotiating various work rules, unions reduce production efficiency. Sceptics are correct in claiming that several interpretations can be given to such evidence. Unions may organize the most productive firms in the industry, perhaps because these are the most profitable and have the greatest potential for wage gains. Alternatively, as discussed previously in the context of the union wage impact, there may be unobserved differences in worker characteristics and/or job assignments which account for observed productivity differences. However, it also may be the case that, for the various reasons discussed above, union representation makes otherwise comparable workers more productive.

One interesting consequence of a positive union productivity effect is that it may explain the coexistence of both union and nonunion firms in the same industry. In a perfectly competitive industry unions must either organize all the firms in the industry (and credibly threaten to organize potential entrants) or the cost-increasing consequences of the higher union wages must be offset by higher productivity. When barriers to entry or other factors enable firms to earn above-normal profits, it is not essential that union wage gains be offset by the higher productivity of union labour. In these circumstances unions may be able to capture some of the economic rents that would otherwise accrue to the firm's managers and/or owners. Empirical evidence indicates that this in fact occurs. Despite differences in data sources, measurement of **profitability**, and methodology, numerous U.S. studies are unanimous in concluding that union firms are less profitable than comparable nonunion firms.[1] However, unions do not appear to reduce profits by so much as to drive firms into bankruptcy and thereby "kill the goose that lays the golden egg" (see Exhibit 16.2).

The Canadian evidence is more equivocal. To some extent, this may reflect the differences in data sources (especially measures of profitability) and empirical methodology.

Exhibit 16.2 **Do Unions Commit the Worst Crime Against Working People?**

www.dol.gov/dol/oasam/public/programs/laborhall/sg.htm

Freeman and Kleiner (1999) cite Samuel Gompers, the first president of the American Federation of Labour in the late 1900s, when he said "the worst crime against working people is the company which fails to operate at a profit." Gompers clearly recognized the mutual interest that workers and employers had in the survival of the organization. As an aside, Gompers' facility with one-liners is also exhibited by his famous response to the question "What does labour want?" His response was simple—"more"—but, he obviously recognized, not so much "more" as to jeopardize the financial viability of the organization.

Recognizing that unions generally reduce profitability, Freeman and Kleiner (1999) analyze whether they do so by so much as to induce some firms into bankruptcy—to commit the "worst crime against labour." They find that unionized firms are no more likely to declare bankruptcy than nonunion firms. They therefore conclude that while unions reduce profits they do not "kill the goose that lays the golden egg."

[1]Abowd (1989), Becker and Olson (1989, 1992), Belman (1992), Bronars and Deere (1990, 1994), Hirsch (1991a, 1991b), Ruback and Zimmerman (1984), and Voos and Mishel (1986).

Maki and Meredith (1986) investigate the relationship between unionization rates and industry-level profitability for a cross-section of Canadian industries over the period 1971–1981. They find that most measures of profits are negatively associated with unionization, consistent with the U.S. findings. Laporta and Jenkins (1996) find that unions reduced profits in monopolistic industries but increased them in competitive ones. Martinello et al. (1995) focus more narrowly on the impact of unionization on a sample of Ontario firms. Using share prices as an indicator of profitability, they estimate the effect of different types of union certification (including first-time certification) on the value of firms. They find very little relationship between changes in union status and firm share prices, suggesting that unions do not adversely affect profits (see Exhibit 16.3).

Their results also contrast with those of a comparable U.S. study, Ruback and Zimmerman (1984), who find that the effect of unionization on firm profits is anticipated by stock market participants. Equity values fell significantly when an application for a union representation election was announced. The decline was substantially higher in those cases in which the union subsequently achieved certification, suggesting that investors were also able to anticipate the outcome of the representation vote.

Pearce, Groff, and Wingender (1995), however, found that shareholder wealth did not increase when unions were decertified, perhaps reflecting the costs and uncertainty associated with implementing the new managerial strategies.

If unions reduce profitability one would expect to see less investment in unionized plants. This is especially the case if there is a risk of a **hold-up problem** whereby unions are able to appropriate the benefits of successful investments given that capital is fairly fixed and difficult to move once it is in place. Multinationals especially may allocate more of their investment in nonunion organizations if their unionized ones are less profitable.

Exhibit 16.3

Do Unions Hurt Shareholders?

Martinello, Hanrhan, Kushner, and Masse (1995) estimate the effect of union certification on the share prices of firms. If financial markets are efficient, then the share price should capture all relevant information regarding shareholders' expectations about future profits. A "surprise" certification application should then have an adverse effect on stock prices if shareholders believe that unionization will harm firm profits.

Martinello et al. use a conventional **event study** methodology to isolate the certification effect. This procedure is similar to the "difference in differences" approach described earlier in the text, except that there is no "control" group. Basically, one looks for unexplained changes in the share price around the timing of the "event" being analyzed (similar to a "before" and "after" study). Martinello et al. examine a sample of 66 firms that experienced unionization drives (official applications for certification to the Ontario Labour Relations Board) over the period 1975–1991. Not all of these were for new unions (some were "raids" by other unions), and not all applications were ultimately successful. Nevertheless, even across these different types of certification application, most firms seemed to experience increases in share prices within 6 months (before and after) of the application. This suggests that the unions were not expected to have an adverse effect on firm profits. Another explanation, however, would be that union certification drives were correlated with periods of relatively good firm performance. Acknowledging this potential problem, these results still contrast with findings from the United States employing a similar methodology.

www.gov.on.ca/lab/olrb/eng/homeeng.htm

This negative overall investment effect may be offset somewhat, however, by the possibility of substituting capital for labour if labour becomes more expensive because of a union wage premium or rigid work rules. As well, unions may actually bargain for additional investment to sustain employment.

The empirical evidence generally finds a negative effect of unions on investment (e.g., Odgers and Betts, 1997 for Canada).[2] An interesting exception is Menezes et al. (1998), who find that in Britain the negative effect disappears if one excludes the high-tech industries that tend to invest considerably in research and development, and that tend to be nonunion. In the other industries, unions do not appear to deter investment. They suggest that much of this may reflect the fact that British unions tend to emphasize jobs over wages and hence are reluctant to bargain in a way that may deter investment. In the United States, Karier (1995) is another exception, finding that firms in heavily unionized industries in the United States are no more likely to transfer their investments out of the country than less unionized industries.

Overall, the evidence on the impact of unions on productivity, profitability, and investment suggests the following:

- Unions generally reduce quits and increase productivity, although there is conflicting evidence in the latter area.
- These positive effects tend not to offset the higher cost associated with unions, especially because of their higher wages and fringe benefits.
- As such, profitability is generally lower in unionized firms.
- However, unions are careful not to push firms into bankruptcy.
- In part because of this lower profitability, there tends to be less new investment put into unionized plants.
- For almost all of these results, however, there are exceptions—as is usually the case with empirical work.

Summary

- Unions affect the wages not only of their members but also of nonunion workers, though in an indeterminate fashion. Some workers who are displaced from the union sector because of the adverse employment effect of the union wage premium go to the nonunion sector with that supply spillover depressing nonunion wages. As well, the demand for nonunion labour may change, but in opposing ways. On the one hand, the demand for nonunion labour may decrease (and hence nonunion wages fall) to the extent that it is a complement to union labour. On the other hand, the demand for nonunion labour may increase (and hence nonunion wages rise) to the extent to which it is a substitute for the now higher-priced union labour. The wages of nonunion labour may also increase directly if employers raise their wages to reduce the threat of becoming unionized. Wages of nonunion labour can also be affected by legislative initiatives that are often supported by unions (e.g., minimum wages) or if employers try to restore old wage relativities.
- Methodological problems associated with measure the union impact include: difficulties of controlling for other factors that influence wages, especially because employers have

[2]For the United States, see Allen (1988), Becker and Olson (1992), Bronars, Deere, and Tracy (1994), Cooke (1997), Fallick and Hassett (1999), and Hirsch (1991a, 1991b, 1992).

an incentive to alter items such as qualifications and job requirements in response to the higher union wage; the selection bias that may occur if workers sort themselves (or are sorted by employers) into the union or nonunion sector on the bases of unobserved factors; and reverse causality if high wages induce unionization.

- Although there are always exceptions, empirical studies on the impact of unions tend to find:
  - The union-nonunion wage differential is likely around 15 percent, and within the range of 10–25 percent.
  - The union wage impact is falling in more recent years and now may be more in the neighbourhood of 10 percent.
  - The impact on nonunion wages is likely small, although there is not a consensus as to whether it is positive or negative.
  - The union impact is larger at low skill levels and smaller at high skill levels, as unions tend to garner flat wage increases but reduce the returns to factors related to skill levels such as education or training.
  - The union impact tends to be higher: in the private sector compared to the public sector; in small firms compared to large firms; for blue-collar compared to white-collar workers; when a larger portion of the relevant jurisdiction is organized; in recessions compared to booms.
- In the United States the union wage impact is similar for females and males, but in Canada it is larger for females compared to males. However, because women tend to be less unionized, fewer women obtain the union wage premiums with these opposing effects cancelling out such that unions tend not to affect the overall male-female wage differential.
- Unions tend to compress wage structures within the union sector, but they also create a union-nonunion wage differential that widens wage inequality, with most studies finding on net that unions reduce wage inequality in the economy.
- Because of the distortions created by their wage and employment effects, unions create welfare losses to society as a whole but those losses are small.
- The union impact on fringe benefits tends to be greater than the impact on wages.
- Unions reduce turnover and quits, and many studies (but by no means all) find that they have a positive impact on productivity. These positive effects tend not to offset the higher cost associated with unions, especially because of their higher wages and fringe benefits.
- As such, profitability is generally lower in unionized firms, although unions are careful not to push firms into bankruptcy and "kill the goose that lays the golden egg."
- In part because of this lower profitability, there tends to be less new investment put into unionized plants.

REVIEW QUESTIONS

1. Discuss the various wage structures and wage levels that unions can affect.
2. Discuss the various ways in which unions can affect the wages of nonunion labour.
3. Why may one expect the skill level of union workers to be different from the skill level of nonunion workers? What does this imply about union-nonunion wage differentials? Why may one expect high wages to cause unionism, as well as vice versa, and what does this imply about union-nonunion wage differentials?

4. If you expect the wage impact of unions to differ systematically with respect to certain conditions (e.g., extent of unionization in the industry or extent of concentration in the product market), how would you capture the interaction effect in a regression equation designed to measure the impact of unions?
5. Discuss why the union wage impact may vary according to such factors as industry, occupation, the stage of the business cycle, and the size of the firm.
6. Discuss the pros and cons of using longitudinal data to estimate the impact of unions.
7. Discuss the various ways in which unions can affect wage inequality in the economy.
8. Discuss the effect of unionization on the efficient allocation of resources. How would you measure these "welfare" effects?
9. Discuss the effect of unions on fringe benefits and working conditions.
10. Discuss the various ways in which unions may affect productivity.
11. In their article "The two faces of unionism," R. Freeman and J. Medoff state:

    According to our recent research on the subject, treatment of unions as organizations without solidaristic or purposive values, whose sole function is to raise wages, is seriously misleading. While unions appear to raise wages above competitive levels, they also have significant nonwage effects which influence diverse aspects of modern industrial life. By providing workers with a voice both at the work place and in the political arena, unions can and do positively affect the functioning of the economic and social systems.

    Elaborate and assess this claim.
12. For each part, classify the statement as either true, partly true but incomplete, or false, and explain your reasoning:
    (a) "Unions tend to raise wages for unionized workers and lower wages for most nonunion workers. Thus unions tend to increase the amount of income inequality in the economy."
    (b) "A powerful union is one for which the costs of a strike to the firm are very high, while a weak union is one for which costs of a strike are low."
    (c) "Empirical research has found that unionized labour is more productive than comparable nonunion labour. This proves that unions increase the total value of output in the economy."
    (d) "Unions can't raise wages in competitive industries because firms earn zero economic profits in equilibrium in these industries."

PROBLEMS

1. Assume the following union impact equation:

$$W = 0.5CA + 0.004CA \times U + 0.003CA \times CR$$
$$- 0.01CA \times RLC + \text{Other control variables}$$

where W is the wage rate in the establishment; CA represents the existence of a collective agreement in the establishment; U represents the percentage of the industry that is unionized; CR represents industry concentration; and RLC is the ratio of wage labour cost to value added.

(a) Theoretically justify the use of each of these explanatory variables.
(b) What sign would you expect for each regression coefficient?

(c) Why are the explanatory variables entered in the equation in that particular fashion—that is, multiplied by CA?

(d) What is the effect on wages of being covered by a collective agreement as opposed to not covered?

(e) Evaluate this effect at the following mean values of the explanatory variables: $\overline{U} = 40$, $\overline{CR} = 7$, $\overline{RLC} = 36$.

(f) Compare this union impact in an establishment with the impact that would occur if the industry in which the firm operated was completely unionized, other things being equal.

(g) Compare the union impact of part (e) with the impact that would occur if the ratio of wage labour cost to value added were only 20 percent as opposed to 36 percent.

(h) What does such an equation imply about the impact of the control variables on union and nonunion workers?

(i) How would you relax that implied assumption?

2. Assume you have estimated the following wage equations where W is the mean wage (or benefit), X is a vector of the mean values of the wage-determining characteristics, β is a vector of the estimated coefficients or returns to the characteristics, and the subscripts denote union and nonunion status.

$$W_u = X_u\beta_u \text{ for union workers}$$

$$W_n = X_n\beta_n \text{ for nonunion workers}$$

(a) Illustrate the hypothetical wage, W_u^*, that union workers would receive if they had their own characteristics (i.e., X_u) but were paid according to the nonunion pay structure for those characteristics.

(b) Show that the difference between this hypothetical wage and the actual wage of union workers is attributable to differences in the endowments of wage-determining characteristics between union and nonunion workers, since both are paid according to the same pay structure, in this case the nonunion returns which are taken as the competitive norm.

(c) Show that the difference between the actual wage of union workers and the hypothetical wage they would earn if they were paid according to the nonunion pay structure is attributable to differences in their returns for the same wage-determining characteristics, in this case the union characteristics.

(d) Add the differences calculated in (a) and (b) above to show that the average wage differential between union and nonunion workers can be decomposed into two components: differences in the average value of the wage-determining characteristics, $(X_u - X_n)$, evaluated according to the nonunion returns, β_n; and differences in the pay structure between union and nonunion workers, $(\beta_u - \beta_n)$, evaluated with the union characteristics, X_u.

(e) Give an interpretation to each of these two components in terms of union rents or wage premiums and endowments of wage-determining characteristics such as education or experience.

3. Assume you are head of the newly formed Airlines Pilots' Association and your brother is head of the newly formed Garment Workers' Association. Your union faces an elasticity of demand for labour of -0.2 and your brothers' union faces an elasticity of demand for labour of -0.6. You both can only bargain over wages.

(a) If you both negotiated the average union wage premium of 10 percent that exists in the economy, what employment effects would result?

(b) If you both were willing to accept a 2 percent reduction in the employment of your membership, what wage increase would you each bargain for?
(c) If the airline that you bargained against just bought out another airline so there was very little competition, and this cut the elasticity of demand for labour that you faced by half, what wage would you now bargain for if you were willing to accept a 2 percent reduction in the employment of your membership?
(d) If your brother's union now was bargaining with employers who were just exposed to increased international competition from countries with low-wage labour and this increased the elasticity of demand for labour that he faced from -0.6 to -1.0, what wage increase would he now bargain for if he were willing to accept a 2 percent reduction in employment?
(e) Under these circumstances would you support or oppose the merger and your brother support or oppose free trade?

4. From Figure 16.4, the efficiency losses from the wage distortion imposed by unions is the triangle abc in the union sector plus the triangle dgf in the nonunion sector. Assuming linear demand curves, this is equal to

$$\tfrac{1}{2}(W_u - W_0)(E_1 - E_0) + \tfrac{1}{2}(W_0 - W_n)(E_0 - E_1), \text{ or}$$

$$\tfrac{1}{2}(W_u - W_n)(E_1 - E_0), \text{ since } (E_1 - E_0) = (E_1 - E_0)$$

It can be shown that this efficiency loss can be expressed as a percentage of national income in the economy (Rees, 1963) as:

$$\tfrac{1}{2}\Delta W_u \times \Delta E_u \times D_u \times L/Y, \text{ where}$$

ΔW_u = percentage union wage impact

ΔE_u = percentage reduction of employment in the union sector

D_u = union density or percent of labour force that is unionized

L/Y = labour's share of national income

Assuming that elasticity of demand for labour is -0.5 (so as to calculate the employment reduction), that 0.30 of the labour force is unionized (as is the case in Canada), and that labour's share of national income is 0.75, calculate this efficiency loss as a percentage of GNP on the basis of the following scenarios:
(a) A union wage impact of 0.15, which is an approximate "best guess" for Canada
(b) A union wage impact of 0.10, which may be the case in more recent years given international competitive pressures and other forces
(c) A union wage impact of 0.15, but only 0.15 of the labour force being unionized as is approximately the case in the United States
(d) A union wage impact of 0.15 and a unionization rate of 0.30, but an increase in the elasticity of demand for labour from 0.5 to 1.0 given increased foreign competition
(e) A union wage impact of 0.10, but in return for the concession of such smaller wage gains unions getting guarantees of smaller employment adjustments that effectively reduce the elasticity of demand for labour from 0.5 to 0.25

KEYWORDS

union-nonunion wage differential 470
two-sector model 474
threat effect 474
wait or queue unemployment 475
selection bias 477
exit 478

voice 478
simultaneity 479
longitudinal or panel data 479
fixed-effects model 480
wage dispersion 486
inefficient allocation 488
deadweight loss 489
labour market turnover 491
productivity 493
shock effect 494
profitability 496
hold-up problem 497
event study 497

REFERENCES

Abowd, J. 1989. The effect of wage bargains on the stock market value of the firm. *AER* 79:774-809.

Allen, S. 1988. Productivity levels and productivity change under unionism. *IR* 27:94-113.

______. 1984. Trade unionized construction workers are more productive. *QJE* 99 (May):251-74.

______. 1986. Unionization and productivity in office building and school construction. *ILRR* 39 (January):187-201.

Ashenfelter, O., and G. Johnson. 1972. Trade unions and the rate of change of money wages in United States manufacturing industry. *R.E. Studies* 39 (January):27-54.

Becker, B., and C. Olson. 1989. Unionization and shareholder interests. *ILRR* 42 (January):246-62.

______. 1992. Unions and firm profits. *IR* 31:395-415.

Belman, D. 1992. Unions and firm profits. *IR* 31:395-415.

Belman, D., and J. Heywood. 1990. Union membership, union organization and the dispersion of wages. *R.E. Stats.* 72 (February):148-53.

Blau, F., and L. Kahn. 1983. Unionism, seniority, and turnover. *IR* 22 (Fall):362-73.

Bronars, S., and D. Deere. 1990. Union representation elections and firm profitability. *IR* 29:15-37.

______. 1991. The threat of unionization, the use of debt, and the preservation of shareholder wealth. *QJE* 106 (February):231-54.

______. 1994. Unionization and profitability: Evidence of spillover effects. *JPE* 102:1281-88.

Bronars, S., G. Deere, and J. Tracy. 1994. The effects of unions on firm behaviour. *IR* 33:426-51.

Brown, C., and J. Medoff. 1978. Trade unions in the production process. *JPE* 86:355-78.

Card, D. 1996. The effect of unions on the structure of wages: A longitudinal analysis. *Ecta.* 64 (July):957-79.

Chaykowski, R. 1995. Union influence on labour market outcomes and earnings inequality. In *Labour Market Polarization and Social Policy Reform*, eds. K. Banting and C. Beach. Kingston: Queen's University School of Policy Studies.

Christofides, L., and R. Swidinsky. 1994. Wage determination by gender and visible minority status: Evidence from the 1989 LMAS. *CPP* 20:34-51.

Christensen, S., and D. Maki. 1981. The union wage effects in Canadian manufacturing. *JLR* 2:355-367.

Clark, K. 1980a. The impact of unionization on productivity: A case study. *ILRR* 33 (July):451-69.

______. 1980b. Unionization and productivity. *QJE* 95 (December):613-40.

______. 1984. Unionization and firm performances: The impact on profits, growth, and productivity. *AER* 74 (December):893-919.

Cooke, W. 1997. The influence of industrial relations factors on U.S. foreign investment. *ILRR* 51:3-17.

Corneo, G., and C. Lucifora. 1997. Wage formation under union threat effects. *Labour Economics* 4:265-92.

De Fina, R. 1983. Unions, relative wages, and economic efficiency. *JOLE* 1 (October):408-29.

DiNardo, J., N. Fortin, and T. Lemieux. 1996. Labor market institutions and the distribution of wages, 1973-1992: a semi-parametric approach. *Ecta.* 64 (September):1001-44.

DiNardo, J., and T. Lemieux. 1997. Diverging male wage inequality in the United States and Canada, 1981-88: Do institutions explain the difference? *ILRR* 50 (July):629-51.

Doiron, D., and W. Riddell. 1994. The impact of unionization on male-female earnings differences in Canada. *JHR* 29:504-34.

Duncan, G., and F. Stafford. 1980. Do union members receive compensating wage differentials. *AER* 70 (June):335-71.

Ehrenberg, R., D. Sherman, and J. Schwarz. 1983. Unions and productivity in the public sector: A study of municipal libraries. *ILRR* 36 (January):199-213.

Fallick, B., and K. Hassett. 1999. Investment and union certification. *JOL* 17:570-82.

Fisher, T., and R. Waschik. 2000. Union bargaining power, relative wages, and efficiency in Canada. *CJE* 33:742-765.

Freeman, R. 1980a. Unionism and the dispersion of wages. *ILRR* 34 (October):3-23.

______. 1980b. The exit-voice trade-off in the labour market: Unionism, job tenure, quits and separations. *QJE* 94 (June):643-73.

______. 1980c. The effect of unionism on worker attachment to firms. *JLR* 1 (Spring): 29–62.

______. 1981. The effect of unionism on fringe benefits. *ILRR* 34 (July):489–509.

______. 1982. Union wage practices and wage dispersion within establishments. *ILRR* 36 (October):3–21.

______. 1984. Longitudinal analyses of the effects of trade unions. *JOLE* 2 (January):1–26.

______. 1986. Unionism comes to the public sector. *JEL* 25 (March):41–86.

______. 1993. How much has de-unionization contributed to the rise of male earnings inequality? In *Uneven Tides: Rising Inequality in America*, eds. S. Danziger and P. Gottschalk. New York: Russell Sage Foundation.

Freeman, R., and M. Kleiner. 1990. The impact of new unionization on wages and working conditions. *JOLE* 8 (January):8–25.

______. 1999. Do unions make enterprises insolvent? *ILRR* 52:510–27.

Freeman, R., and J. Medoff. 1979. The two faces of unionism. *The Public Interest* (Fall):69–93.

______. 1984. *What Do Unions Do*. New York, NY: Basic Books.

Grant, E., R. Swidinsky, and J. Vanderkamp. 1987. Canadian union-non-union wage differentials. *ILRR* 41 (October):93–107.

Grant, E., and J. Vanderkamp. 1980. The effects of migration on income: A micro study with Canadian data 1965–1971. *CJE* 13 (August):381–406.

Green, D. 1991. A comparison of estimation approaches for the union-nonunion wage differential. UBC Department of Economics Working Paper 91-13.

Gunderson, M., D. Hyatt, and W. C. Riddell. 2000. *Pay Differences Between the Government and Private Sectors: Labour Force Survey and Census Estimates.* Ottawa: Canadian Policy Research Networks. Available online <www.cprn.org>.

Hirsch, B. 1982. The interindustry structure of unions, earnings, and earnings dispersion. *ILLR* 36:22–39.

______. 1991a. Union coverage and profitability among U.S. firms. *R.E. Stats.* 73 (February):69–77.

______. 1991b. *Labor Unions and the Economic Performance of Firms.* Kalamazoo, MI: Upjohn Institute for Employment Research.

______. 1992. Firm investment behavior and collective bargaining strategy. *IR* 31:95–121.

Hirschman, A. 1970. *Exit, Voice and Loyalty*. Cambridge, Mass.: Harvard University Press.

Hoxby, C. 1996. How teachers' unions affect production. *QJE* 111:671–718.

Hyclak, T. 1979. The effect of unions on earnings inequality in local labour markets. *ILRR* 33 (October):77–84.

______. 1980. Unions and income inequality: Some cross-state evidence. *IR* 19 (Spring):212–5.

Ichniowski, C. 1986. The effects of grievance activity on productivity. *ILRR* 40 (October):75–89.

Ichniowski, C., R. Freeman, and H. Lauer. 1989. Collective bargaining laws, threat effects, and the determination of police compensation. *JOLE* 7:191–209.

Jakubson, G. 1991. Estimation and testing of the union wage effect using panel data. *R.E. Studies* 58 (October):971–91.

Johnson, H., and P. Mieszkowski. 1970. The effects of unionization on the distribution of income: A general equilibrium approach. *QJE* 84:539–61.

Kahn, L. 1978. The effects of unions on the earnings of non-union workers. *ILRR* 31 (January):205–16.

______. 1980. Union spillover effects on unorganized labour markets. *JHR* 15 (Winter):87–98.

Karier, T. 1995. U.S. foreign production and unions. *IR* 34:107–18.

Katz, H., T. Kochan, and K. Gobeille. 1983. Industrial relations performance, economic performance, and QWL programs: an interplant analysis. *ILRR* 37 (October):3–17.

Kuhn, P. 1998. Unions and the economy: What we know and what we should know. *CJE* 31:1033–56.

Kuhn, P., and A. Sweetman. 1998. Wage loss following displacement: The role of union coverage. *ILLR* 51:384–400.

Kumar, P. 1972. Differentials in wage rates of unskilled labour in Canadian manufacturing industries. *ILRR* 26 (October):631–45.

Kumar, P., and T. Stengos. 1985. Measuring the union relative wage impact: A methodological note. *CJE* 18 (February):182–9.

______. 1986. Interpreting the wage gap estimate from selectivity correction techniques using micro data. *Economic Letters* 20:191–5.

Laporta, P., and A. Jenkins. 1996. Unionization and profitability in the Canadian manufacturing sector. *IR/RI* 51:756–76.

Leigh, J. 1982. Are unionized blue collar jobs more hazardous than non-unionized blue collar jobs? *JLR* 3 (Summer):349–57.

Lemieux, T. 1993. Unions and wage inequality in Canada and the United States. In *Small Differences that Matter*, eds. D. Card and R. Freeman. Chicago: University of Chicago Press.

Lewis, H. 1963. *Unionism and Relative Wages in the United States: An Empirical Inquiry*. Chicago: University of Chicago Press.

______. 1985. *Union Relative Wage Effects:A Survey*. Chicago: University of Chicago Press.

______. 1986. Union relative wage effects. In *Handbook of Labor Economics*, eds. O. Ashenfelter and R. Layard. New York: Elsevier Science.

Lipsey, R., and J. Lancaster. 1956. The general theory of second best. *R.E. Studies* 24 (December):11-32.

MacDonald, G. 1983. The size and structure of union-nonunion wage differentials in Canadian industry: Corroboration, refinement and extension. *CJE* 16 (August):480-5.

MacDonald, G., and J. Evans. 1981. The size and structure of union-nonunion wage differentials in Canadian industry. *CJE* 14 (May):216-31.

Maki, D., and S. Christensen. 1980. The union wage effect re-examined. *IR/RI* 35, 210-30.

Maki, D. 1983. Trade unions and productivity: conventional estimates. *RI/IR* 35 (No. 2):211-25.

Maki, D., and L. Meredith. 1986. The effect of unions on profitability: Canadian evidence. *RI/IR* 41 (No. 1):54-68.

Mandelstamm, A. B. 1965. The effects of unions on efficiency in the residential construction industry: A case study. *ILLR* 18 (July):503-21.

Martinello, F., R. Hanrahan, J. Kushner, and I. Masse. 1995. Union certification in Ontario: Its effect on the value of the firm. *CJE* 28 (November):1077-95.

Medoff, J. 1979. Layoffs and alternatives under trade unions in U.S. manufacturing. *AER* 69 (June):380-95.

Mellow, W. 1981. Unionism and wages: A longitudinal analysis. *R.E. Stats.* 63 (February):43-52.

Menezes-Filho, N., D. Ulph, and J. Van Reenen. 1998. R & D and unionism: Comparative evidence from British companies and establishments. *ILRR* 52:45-63.

Meng, R. 1990. Union effects on wage dispersion in Canadian industry. *Economic Letters* 32 (April):399-403.

Mincer, J. 1983. Union effects: wages, turnover, and job training. In *New Approaches to Labor Unions*, ed. J.J.D. Reid. Greenwich, Conn.: JAI Press.

Mitchell, D. 1983. Unions and wages in the public sector: A review of recent evidence. *Journal of Collective Negotiations* 12 (4):337-53.

Mitchell, M., and J. Stone. 1992. Union effects on productivity: Evidence from western US sawmills. *ILRR* 46:135-45.

Moore, W., and J. Raisian. 1983. The level and growth of union/non-union relative wage effects, 1967-1977. *JLR* 4 (Winter):65-80.

Neumark, D., and M. Wachter. 1995. Union effects on nonunion wages: Evidence from panel data on industries and cities. *ILRR* 49:20-38.

Noam, E. 1983. The effect of unionization and civil service on the salaries and productivity of regulators. In *New Approaches to Labor Unions*, ed. J.J.D. Reid. Greenwich, Conn.: JAI Press.

Odgers, C., and J. Betts. 1997. Do unions reduce investment? Evidence from Canada. *ILRR* 51:518-36.

Quan, N. 1984. Unionism and the size distribution of earnings. *IR* 23 (Spring):270-7.

Pearce, T., J. Groff, and J. Wingender. 1995. Union decertification's impact on shareholder wealth. *IR* 34:58-72.

Read, L. 1982. Canada Post, a case study in the correlation of collective will and productivity. In *Research on Productivity of Relevance to Canada*, ed. D. J. Daly. Ottawa: Social Science Federation of Canada.

Rees, A. 1963. The effects of unions on resource allocation. *Journal of Law and Economics* 6 (October):69-78.

Rees, D. 1994. Does unionization increase faculty retention? *IR* 33:297-321.

Renaud, S. 1997. Unions and wages in Canada. *Selected Papers from the 33rd Annual CIRA Conference*. Quebec: Canadian Industrial Relations Association, pp. 211-26.

______. 1998. Unions, wages and total compensation in Canada. *IR/RI* 53:710-27.

Robinson, C. 1989. The joint determination of union status and union wage effects: Some tests of alternate models. *JPE* 97 (June):639-67.

Robinson, C., and N. Tomes. 1984. Union wage differentials in the public and private sectors: A simultaneous equations specification. *JOLE* 2 (January):106-27.

Ruback, R., and M. Zimmerman. 1984. Unionization and profitability: Evidence from the capital market. *JPE* 92 (December):1134-57.

Simpson, W. 1985. The impact of unions on the structure of Canadian wages: An empirical analysis with micro data. *CJE* 18 (February):164-81.

Sloan, F., and K. Adamache. 1984. The role of unions in hospital cost inflation. *ILRR* 37 (January):252-62.

Starr, G. 1973. *Union-Non-union Wage Differentials: A Cross-Sectional Analysis*. Toronto: Research Branch, Ontario Ministry of Labour.

Swidinsky, R. 1992. Unionism and the job attachment of Canadian workers. *IR/RI* 47:729-751.

Swidinsky, R., and M. Kupferschmidt. 1991. Longitudinal estimates of the union effects on wages, wage dispersion, and pension fringe benefits. *RI/IR* 46:819-38.

Voos, P., and L. Mishel. 1986. The union impact on profits: Evidence from industry price-cost margin data. *JOLE* 4 (January):105-33.

Warren, R., Jr. 1985. The effect of unionization on labor productivity: Some time series evidence. *JLR* 6 (Spring):199-207.

White, F. 1994. The union/non-union earnings differential for professionals. *Proceedings of the 30th Canadian Industrial Relations Association*:269-280.

Chapter Seventeen

Unemployment: Meaning and Measurement

Main Questions

- *How is the unemployment rate measured? Who is considered to be unemployed?*
- *How do the incidence and duration of unemployment separately contribute to the overall unemployment rate?*
- *How long is a typical Canadian unemployed? Does this vary across groups in the population?*
- *Why is Canada's unemployment rate so much higher than in the United States?*
- *Does the unemployment rate accurately reflect the amount of hardship felt by the jobless?*

With the possible exception of the Consumer Price Index, no single aggregate statistic receives as much attention as the unemployment rate. To a considerable extent this attention reflects concern about the hardship which unemployment may impose on affected individuals and their families and the waste of human resources that may be associated with unemployment. In addition, the unemployment rate is used as a measure of the overall state of the economy and of the degree of tightness (excess demand) or slack (excess supply) in the labour market. However, in spite of this evident interest, there is often confusion about what is meant by our unemployment statistics. This chapter examines the meaning and measurement of unemployment. The causes and consequences of unemployment and the role of public policy in this area are discussed in the following chapter.

MEASURING UNEMPLOYMENT

The unemployed are generally defined as those who are not currently employed and who indicate by their behaviour that they want to work at prevailing wages and working conditions. In Canada, measurement of the unemployed can be obtained from the Labour Force Survey, the Census, or from the number of claimants of the Employment Insurance program. While there are these alternative measures, and different ones can be useful for different purposes, the unemployment measure according to the Labour Force Survey is the one that receives the most attention: it is the one that is so often quoted by the press and utilized for general policy purposes.

Labour Force Survey

www.statcan.ca/english/Subjects/Labour/LFS/lfs-en.htm

The **Labour Force Survey** (LFS) is conducted monthly by Statistics Canada. According to the LFS, people are categorized as **unemployed** if they did not have work in the reference period but were available for and searching for work. There are two exceptions to this general principle. The unemployed also includes persons who were available for work but who were not seeking work because they were on temporary layoff from a job to which they expect to be recalled, or they had a new job to start within four weeks.

Apart from these exceptions, the general principle is that to be counted as unemployed, one has to be available for and searching for work. That is, it is necessary to engage in some form of job search—such as contacting employers or checking job ads—to be classified as unemployed. Job search is defined in the LFS as having looked for work sometime during the previous four weeks. Individuals who are not employed and who are not seeking work (such as students, persons engaged in household work, those permanently unable to work, and retirees) are classified as being out of the labour force.

Persons are categorized as employed if they did any work for pay or profit, including unpaid work on a family farm or business, or if they normally had a job but were not at work because of such factors as bad weather, illness, industrial dispute, or vacation. The employed plus the unemployed make up the labour force, and the unemployment rate is defined as the number of unemployed divided by the labour force.

Census

www.statcan.ca/english/census96/list.htm

The Canadian Census, conducted every ten years since 1871, also provides information on the unemployed, at least since 1921. (A smaller census containing more limited information is also conducted in between the ten-year census.) Rather than being based on a sample of the population, the Census is based on the whole relevant population, with detailed information coming from approximately one-fifth of this population. Consequently, Census data is more comprehensive and provides detailed information on such factors as unemployment by industry and occupation, as well as a wealth of demographic and economic information on the respondents. For this reason the Census data has proven useful in detailed statistical and econometric analysis of labour market behaviour. However, the usefulness of the Census data is limited by the fact that it is conducted infrequently and its reliability on labour force issues may be questioned because of the fact that it covers so many issues in addition to labour force activity. In addition, there is a time lag of about two years before the Census data are available, whereas the Labour Force Survey results are available within a few weeks of the survey.

Unemployment Insurance Claimants

A third data source—unemployment insurance claimants—can be used to obtain estimates of the unemployed. Comparisons of the number of unemployed according to unemployment insurance figures versus Labour Force Survey figures are given in Levesque (1989).

While the number of unemployed according to the Labour Force Survey may be similar to the number claiming unemployment insurance or registered in an unemployment insurance office, the two series generally differ. The number of unemployment insurance claimants may exceed the Labour Force Survey number because some people may be collecting unemployment insurance but are not actively seeking work. These people could range from persons on maternity or sick leave who are legally entitled to collect unemployment insurance, to persons who traditionally do seasonal work and collect unemployment insurance for part of the year, to outright cheaters who simply don't bother looking or who may even be working illegally. Such persons may be collecting unemployment insurance, but they need not indicate, in the confidential Labour Force Survey questionnaire, that they are actively seeking work.

On the other hand, the number of unemployed according to the Labour Force Survey could exceed the number of unemployment insurance claimants. New job seekers, for example, may not be eligible for unemployment insurance, or the long-term unemployed may have exhausted their benefit period. Some, such as the self-employed, may not be covered by unemployment insurance; others may not register because then they would have to accept a job. They (or their parents who may be the respondents) may still indicate on a Labour Force Survey questionnaire that they are actively seeking work.

Clearly the two series need not be identical since they indicate somewhat different things. Because, from a policy perspective, what is usually wanted is an indicator of the number of persons who are available for work and actively seeking work, then the Labour Force Survey figures are the ones that are commonly used.

Canadian Experience

As Figure 17.1 illustrates, Canada's unemployment rate fluctuated widely during the period 1921–1996, to a considerable extent because of cyclical fluctuations in business activity. With the onset of the Great Depression in 1929, the unemployment rate soared from about 3 percent to almost 20 percent. A lengthy period of declining unemployment

Figure 17.1 **Unemployment in Canada, 1921–2000**

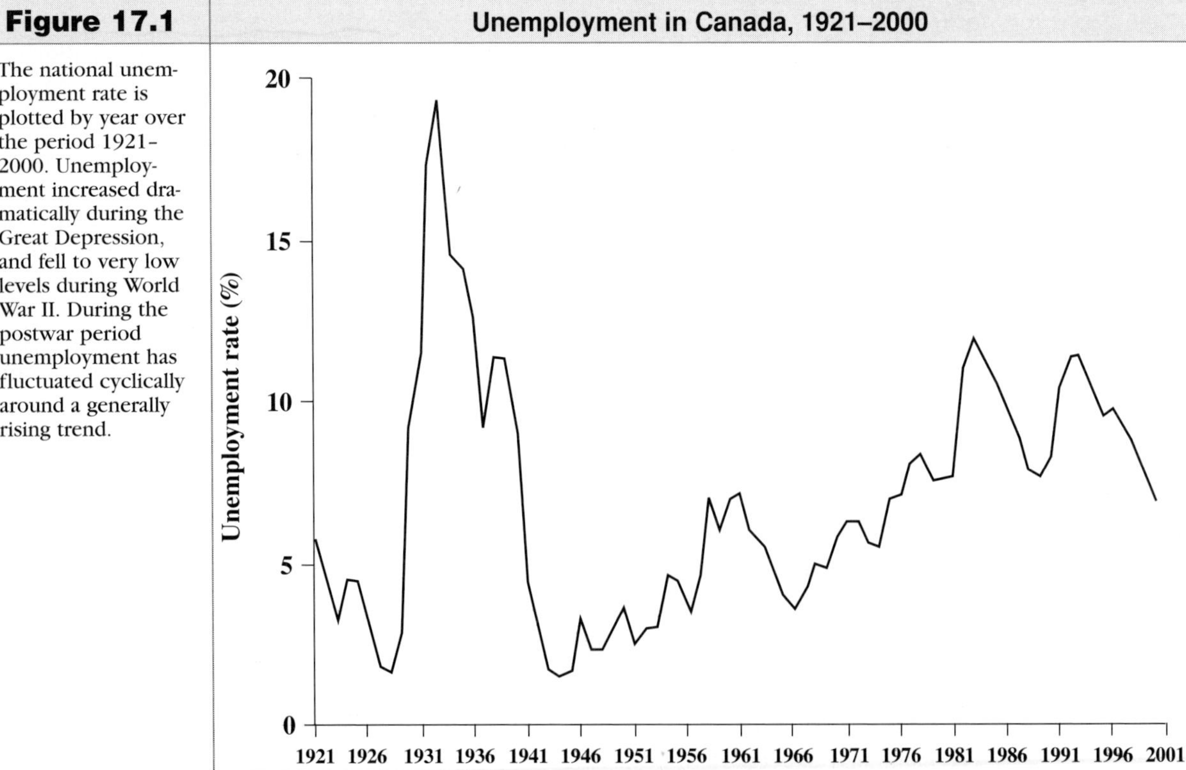

The national unemployment rate is plotted by year over the period 1921–2000. Unemployment increased dramatically during the Great Depression, and fell to very low levels during World War II. During the postwar period unemployment has fluctuated cyclically around a generally rising trend.

Source: *Historical Statistics of Canada (1921–1926)*, Catalogue 11-516 from Statistics Canada CANSIM database, Matrix 600 <cansima.statcan.ca>.

followed, and during World War II unemployment fell to very low levels. Following the war, unemployment remained low until the recession of 1957–58. As the economy recovered from this recession, the unemployment rate gradually declined, reaching 3.4 percent in 1966. Since that time the overall trend in unemployment has been upward, although fluctuations around the trend have continued to occur. The most significant increases occurred in the recession of 1974–75, in the severe recession of 1981–82 which resulted in the unemployment rate reaching 11.8 percent, the highest level since the Great Depression, and in the recession of 1990–92. During the economic expansion which followed the 1981–82 recession, the unemployment rate gradually declined to a low of 7.5 percent in 1989. By 1992 the unemployment rate was back above 11 percent. However, as a consequence of the recovery and expansion in the latter part of the 1990s, the unemployment rate declined to 6.8 percent in 2000—its lowest level since the early 1970s. The behaviour of unemployment in the 1990s suggests that the upward trend evident throughout most of the post–World War II period may have levelled off.

The **unemployment rate** is the most commonly used measure of aggregate labour market activity and the degree of labour force utilization. Two alternative measures are the labour force participation rate (the ratio of the labour force to the population of working age, or source population) and the **employment rate** (the ratio of employment to the source population). These statistics are shown for selected years in Table 17.1. (The years 1956, 1966, 1973, 1981, 1989, and 2000 correspond to the peak years of the business cycle in the postwar period. Because they focus on somewhat different aspects of labour market activity, these three measures need not always move together. For example, since 1966 the unemployment rate has risen sharply, yet at the same time both the employment rate and the fraction in the labour force have risen rather than fallen. Additional perspective on these divergent patterns is provided by the fourth column of Table 17.1; the rate of growth of employment between 1966 and 1981 was the most rapid of the postwar period. The combination of rapid employment growth and rising unemployment rates reflected several

Table 17.1 Labour Force Participation, Employment, and Unemployment, Canada, 1946–2000[a]

Year	Labour Force Participation Rate	Employment Rate	Unemployment Rate	Rate of Growth of Employment[b]
1946	55.0	53.1	3.4	
				1.8
1956	53.5	51.7	3.4	
				2.5
1966	55.1	53.1	3.6	
				3.0
1973	59.7	56.4	5.6	
				3.2
1981	65.0	60.0	7.6	
				1.8
1989	67.2	62.1	7.5	
				1.3
2000	65.9	61.4	6.8	

Notes:

[a]All statistics are based on authors' calculations from data on the civilian labour force (annual averages) derived from the CANSIM database.

[b]Civilian employment; growth rates are averages of compound annual increases from the level in the year in the row one line above to the level in the year one line below.

Source: Created from author's calculations based on data from the Statistics Canada CANSIM database, Matrices 600 and 3450 <cansima.statcan.ca>.

Exhibit 17.1 International Differences in Unemployment

Canada and the United States measure employment, unemployment, and labour force participation in very similar ways, using monthly surveys (the Labour Force Survey and Current Population Survey respectively) that share many features. Measures used in other countries differ in a variety of ways; however, the unemployment rate statistics shown below have been adjusted so that they are comparable to the U.S. concepts.

As these data indicate, the unemployment rate has varied substantially over time within most countries, and also varies considerably across countries. During the 1950s and 1960s, unemployment rates in North America were substantially higher than those in Australia, Japan, and most European countries. However, after the first OPEC oil price shock in 1973, unemployment rose sharply in several European countries (e.g., France, Germany, the Netherlands, and the United Kingdom) and then escalated further during the 1980s. The 1990s saw further increases in unemployment in France, Germany, and Italy but lower unemployment in the Netherlands and the United Kingdom. Australia followed a pattern similar to the United Kingdom's. Japan, as well as a few European countries (e.g., Sweden), did not experience this dramatic rise in unemployment during the 1970s and 1980s, but both Japan and Sweden have had much higher unemployment in the 1990s.

Thus Canadian and American unemployment rates, which were unusually high by international standards during the first two decades of the postwar period, were no longer so during the 1980s and 1990s. Indeed, unemployment rates in North America declined substantially during the long periods of economic expansion following the recessions of the early 1980s and early 1990s, whereas those in many European countries remained stubbornly high. Japan and Sweden stand out as countries that were somehow able to adjust to the economic shocks of the 1970s and 1980s without experiencing dramatic increases in unemployment. However, both experienced large increases in unemployment during the 1990s, and by 2000 the unemployment rate in the United States was lower than that in Japan and Sweden, two countries with a tradition of low unemployment. Explaining these large differences in international experience is an important challenge for social scientists.

Civilian Unemployment Rates, 1959–2000 (approximating U.S. concepts)

Year	U.S.	Canada	Australia	Japan	France	Germany	Italy	Netherlands	Sweden	U.K.
1959	5.5	5.6	(A)2.1	2.3	1.6	2.0	4.8	N/A	(S)1.7	2.8
1960	5.5	6.5	(A)1.6	1.7	1.5	1.1	3.7	N/A	(S)1.7	2.2
1961	6.7	6.7	(A)3.0	1.5	1.2	0.6	3.2	N/A	1.5	2.0
1962	5.5	5.5	(A)2.9	1.3	1.4	0.6	2.8	N/A	1.5	2.7
1963	5.7	5.2	(A)2.3	1.3	1.6	0.5	2.4	N/A	1.7	3.3
1964	5.2	4.4	1.4	1.2	1.2	0.4	2.7	N/A	1.6	2.5
1965	4.5	3.6	1.3	1.2	1.6	0.3	3.5	N/A	1.2	2.1
1966	3.8	3.4	1.6	1.4	1.6	0.3	3.7	N/A	1.6	2.3
1967	3.8	3.8	1.9	1.3	2.1	1.3	3.4	N/A	2.1	3.3
1968	3.6	4.5	1.8	1.2	2.7	1.1	3.5	N/A	2.2	3.2

phenomena, including the substantial number of youths and women who entered the labour force, particularly after the mid-1960s. Although employment grew rapidly between 1966 and 1981, the growth in labour supply was even more substantial; thus the unemployment rate rose. During the 1980s and 1990s the rate of growth in employment has fallen substantially. The growth rate of 1.3 percent per year in the 1990s represents the slowest rate of employment growth in the postwar period.

Exhibit 17.1 **International Differences in Unemployment *(continued)***

1969	3.5	4.4	1.8	1.1	2.3	0.6	3.5	N/A	1.9	3.1
1970	4.9	5.7	1.6	1.2	2.5	0.5	3.2	N/A	1.5	3.1
1971	5.9	6.2	1.9	1.3	2.8	0.6	3.3	N/A	2.6	3.9
1972	5.6	6.2	2.6	1.4	2.9	0.7	3.8	N/A	2.7	4.2
1973	4.9	5.5	2.3	1.3	2.8	0.7	3.7	3.1	2.5	3.2
1974	5.6	5.3	2.7	1.4	2.9	1.6	3.1	3.6	2.0	3.1
1975	8.5	6.9	4.9	1.9	4.2	3.4	3.4	5.1	1.6	4.6
1976	7.7	6.8	4.8	2.0	4.6	3.4	3.9	5.4	1.6	5.9
1977	7.1	7.8	5.6	2.0	5.2	3.4	4.1	4.9	1.8	6.4
1978	6.1	8.1	6.3	2.3	5.4	3.3	4.1	5.1	2.2	6.3
1979	5.8	7.2	6.3	2.1	6.1	2.9	4.4	5.1	2.1	5.4
1980	7.1	7.2	6.1	2.0	6.5	2.8	4.4	6.0	2.0	7.0
1981	7.6	7.3	5.8	2.2	7.6	4.0	4.9	8.9	2.5	10.5
1982	9.7	10.6	7.2	2.4	8.3	5.6	5.4	10.2	3.1	11.3
1983	9.6	11.5	10.0	2.7	8.6	6.9	5.9	11.4	3.5	11.8
1984	7.5	10.9	9.0	2.8	10.0	7.1	5.9	11.5	3.1	11.7
1985	7.2	10.2	8.3	2.6	10.5	7.2	6.0	9.6	2.8	11.2
1986	7.0	9.2	8.1	2.8	10.6	6.6	7.5	10.0	2.6	11.2
1987	6.2	8.4	8.1	2.9	10.8	6.3	7.9	10.0	2.2	10.3
1988	5.5	7.3	7.2	2.5	10.3	6.3	7.9	7.7	1.9	8.6
1989	5.3	7.0	6.2	2.3	9.6	5.7	7.8	7.0	1.6	7.2
1990	5.6	7.7	6.9	2.1	9.1	5.0	7.0	6.2	1.8	6.9
1991	6.8	9.8	9.6	2.1	9.6	5.6	6.9	5.9	3.1	8.8
1992	7.5	10.6	10.8	2.2	10.4	6.7	7.3	5.6	5.6	10.1
1993	6.9	10.7	10.9	2.5	11.8	7.9	10.2	6.5	9.3	10.5
1994	6.1	9.4	9.7	2.9	12.3	8.5	11.2	7.2	9.6	9.7
1995	5.6	8.5	8.5	3.2	11.8	8.2	11.8	7.1	9.1	8.7
1996	5.4	8.7	8.6	3.4	12.5	8.9	11.7	6.3	9.9	8.2
1997	4.9	8.2	8.6	3.4	12.4	9.9	11.9	5.3	10.1	7.0
1998	4.5	7.5	8.0	4.1	11.8	9.3	12.0	4.0	8.4	6.3
1999	4.2	6.8	7.2	4.7	11.2	8.7	11.5	3.4	7.1	p6.1
2000	4.0	5.8	6.6	p4.8	p9.7	p8.3	p10.7	N/A	p5.9	N/A

Notes: N/A = not available. p = preliminary. A = The Australian labour force survey was initiated in 1964. Unemployment rates for 1959–1964 are estimates made by an Australian researcher. S = The Swedish labour force survey was initiated in 1961. The published data for 1959–1961 are estimates made by the OECD.

Source: Comparative Civilian Labor Force Statistics, Bureau of Labor Statistics, August 2001.

Which of these three measures is used for analyzing aggregate labour market activity will depend on the purpose of the analysis. The employment and labour force participation rates focus on the fraction of the source population which is employed and in the labour force respectively, while the unemployment rate measures the fraction of the labour force which is out of work and searching for work. Because this chapter deals with unemployment, the main aggregate statistic referred to is the unemployment rate. However, in many circumstances the employment and labour force participation rates may provide useful additional information on labour market developments.

Hidden Unemployment/Marginal Labour Force Attachment

The measurement of unemployment raises some difficult and controversial issues. Hidden unemployment or **marginal labour force attachment** refers to situations in which individuals may be without work, yet they desire work but are not classified as unemployed according to the official statistics. Such individuals are attached to the labour force to some degree, but are not sufficiently strongly attached that they are seeking work. One important example—especially during recessions and in regions where few jobs are available—is the phenomenon of the **discouraged worker**. This refers to individuals who are not employed, who may wish to work at prevailing wages, but who are not seeking work because they believe that no work is available. Other examples include: individuals still awaiting recall after more than six months on layoff; forms of underemployment, such as individuals working fewer hours than they desire to work or normally work; and those

Exhibit 17.2

Supplementary Measures of Unemployment

The question of how best to measure unemployment has long been controversial. We frequently hear claims that the "true" amount of unemployment is much greater than the official measure because of underemployment or "disguised" unemployment such as discouraged workers who have stopped searching but still desire work. On the other hand, others claim that the official measure may overstate the amount of underutilization of labour because much unemployment is very short-term in nature, representing mainly normal turnover in the labour market, and some searchers may not be serious about finding work.

www.statcan.ca/english/indepth/71-005/feature/lfhi1999003003s2a.htm

Recognizing that there is no single best measure of unemployment suitable for all purposes, Statistics Canada produces a number of "supplementary measures of unemployment" (Statistics Canada, 1999). As shown below, in 1998 these ranged in magnitude from R1 = 1.1 percent to R8 = 11.5 percent when the official rate (R4) equalled 8.3 percent.

R1	Counting only those unemployed one year or more	1.1%
R2	Counting only those unemployed three months or more	3.3%
R3	Made comparable to the U.S. official rate	7.6%
R4	Official rate	8.3%
R5	Official rate plus discouraged workers	8.8%
R6	Official rate plus those waiting for recall, waiting for replies, and long-term future starts	9.0%
R7	A measure of both unemployment and underemployment (involuntary part-time employment) expressed in full-time equivalents	10.6%
R8	Official rate plus discouraged workers, those waiting for recall, those waiting for replies, and long-term future starts, and the underutilized portion of involuntary part-time workers	11.5%

Measures R1 and R2 focus on groups for whom unemployment may represent temporarily employed in jobs that do not utilize their skills or training. Each of these examples illustrates the difficulties involved in making a satisfactory distinction between "employment," "unemployment," and "out of the labour force."

As discussed in Exhibit 17.2 and by Statistics Canada (1999), some evidence on the quantitative significance of hidden unemployment in Canada is available. Since 1979 an annual supplement to the Labour Force Survey (the Survey of Job Opportunities) has identified those who want work, are available for work, but are not seeking work for "personal" or "economic" reasons.[1] These "persons on the margin of the labour force" typically number between one-quarter and one-third of the officially unemployed. Exhibit 17.2 shows the consequences of including two types of "marginally attached" workers. In 1998, including discouraged workers increases the unemployment rate by 0.5 percentage points, and including a "waiting" group—those who state that they desire work but are not searching because they are waiting for recall, for replies from employers, or for a new job to start—adds 0.7 percentage points. Including these two groups with the officially unemployed raises the unemployment rate from 8.3 to 9.5 percent, an increase of 1.2 percentage points or about 15 percent.

Exhibit 17.2 **Supplementary Measures of Unemployment *(continued)***

particular economic hardship. Measures based on duration of unemployment may also be informative about the extent of mismatch between the skills and/or location of unemployed workers and available jobs, as discussed under the topic of "structural unemployment" in the next chapter.

R3 measures the Canadian unemployment rate on a comparable basis to the methods used in the United States. Differences in the Canadian and American definitions of unemployment are discussed later in this chapter. During the 1990s these differences resulted in the U.S. unemployment rate being 0.7 to 0.8 percentage points lower than its Canadian counterpart for purely measurement reasons.

R5 adds to the officially unemployed those individuals who state that they desire work but are not searching because they believe no work is available in their area or suitable to their skills.

R6 includes the officially unemployed and three "waiting" groups who are conventionally classified as "out of the labour force": (1) waiting for recall to a former job, (2) waiting for replies from employers, (3) have a job to start more than four weeks from the reference week of the survey. Note that the "waiting for recall" group does not include "temporary layoffs" who are included among the officially unemployed even if not searching. Similarly, "long-term future starts" does not include "future starts" who are included among the officially unemployed if they report that they have a job to start within four weeks.

R7 adds to the officially unemployed a measure of underemployment—those working part-time who state that they desire full-time work. Because this notion of underemployment is based on the gap between actual and desired hours of work, it is converted to full-time equivalents to make it comparable to measures of unemployment based on number of individuals rather than hours.

R8 adds to the officially unemployed all of the groups in R5, R6, and R7.

[1]Since 1997 this information is collected in the monthly LFS.

Whether individuals who desire work but are not seeking work should be classified as unemployed is a controversial issue. The observation that they are without work and want work (assuming the response to the survey is accurate) may argue for including them among the unemployed. According to this view, the fact that they are not searching for work may simply be a rational way to spend their time, for example if they believe that no jobs are available. Similarly, waiting more than six months for recall may be sensible behaviour rather than wishful thinking, especially if the chances of recall are good and the job to which the individual expects to return is attractive relative to potential alternatives. In contrast, the absence of job search may indicate a low degree of labour force attachment, justifying the classification "out of the labour force."

These phenomena respond to changes in aggregate economic conditions. The number of discouraged workers increased substantially during the 1981–82 recession and subsequently declined as the economy gradually recovered. An increase, albeit smaller, was also observed during the 1990–92 recession (Akyeampong, 1992). The number of individuals awaiting recall after more than six months displayed a similar pattern. As a consequence, the increase in the unemployment rate in recessions is smaller than would be the case if those desiring but not seeking work were classified as unemployed. Similarly, the decline in the unemployment rate during the recovery is smaller than would be the case if these individuals were included in the unemployed.

Some evidence on the significance of underemployment is also available from the Labour Force Survey. For example, in 1998 about 5 percent of those working part-time would have preferred full-time work (Statistics Canada, 1999). Once again, the measured unemployment rate may understate the extent of unutilized labour services, especially in recessionary periods.

Jones and Riddell (1999) provide more evidence on how "persons on the margin of the labour force" may distort measures of unemployment. They formally test whether these individuals behave more like the unemployed, or those out of the labour force (where they are currently classified). Jones and Riddell show that the marginally attached behave as a distinct group, different from both the unemployed and the remainder of the "not in the labour force" category. Interestingly, "discouraged workers" are not the subgroup that most resembles the unemployed (rather than out of the labour force, where they are currently classified), but instead it is the group of individuals waiting for promised or potential jobs who most behave like the unemployed.[2]

The major lesson to be learned from this discussion is *not* that the official unemployment rate is a poor measure of unemployment, but rather that the concept of unemployment is not sufficiently well defined that any single measure will suit all purposes. For many purposes the official unemployment measure will be appropriate; however, in other situations this should be supplemented by measures of hidden unemployment and underemployment. Because no single measure is likely to be suitable for all purposes, Statistics Canada publishes several "Supplementary measures of unemployment," described in Exhibit 17.2.

LABOUR FORCE DYNAMICS

Since the early 1970s, research by economists has emphasized the dynamic nature of the labour force. The Labour Force Survey provides a snapshot at a point in time, an estimate of the stock of persons in each labour force state. However, even if the magnitudes of these stocks remain approximately constant from one period to another, it would be a mistake to conclude that little change had taken place in the labour force. In fact, as Figure 17.2

[2]The group waiting for promised or potential jobs is included in Statistics Canada's measure "R6" (see Exhibit 17.2).

Figure 17.2 **Labour Market Stocks and Flows, 1976–1991**

This figure illustrates the large flows that occur each month between the labour force states of "employment" (E), "unemployment" (U), and "not in the labour force" (O). On average, every month 235,000 unemployed workers obtained jobs (i.e., moved from U to E), and 190,000 workers lost or left jobs and joined the pool of job searchers (i.e., moved from E to U). The average net monthly flow was thus 235,000 - 190,000 = 45,000 from U to E. The probability of an unemployed worker becoming employed the following month equals 0.22 and the probability that an employed worker becomes unemployed equals 0.02.

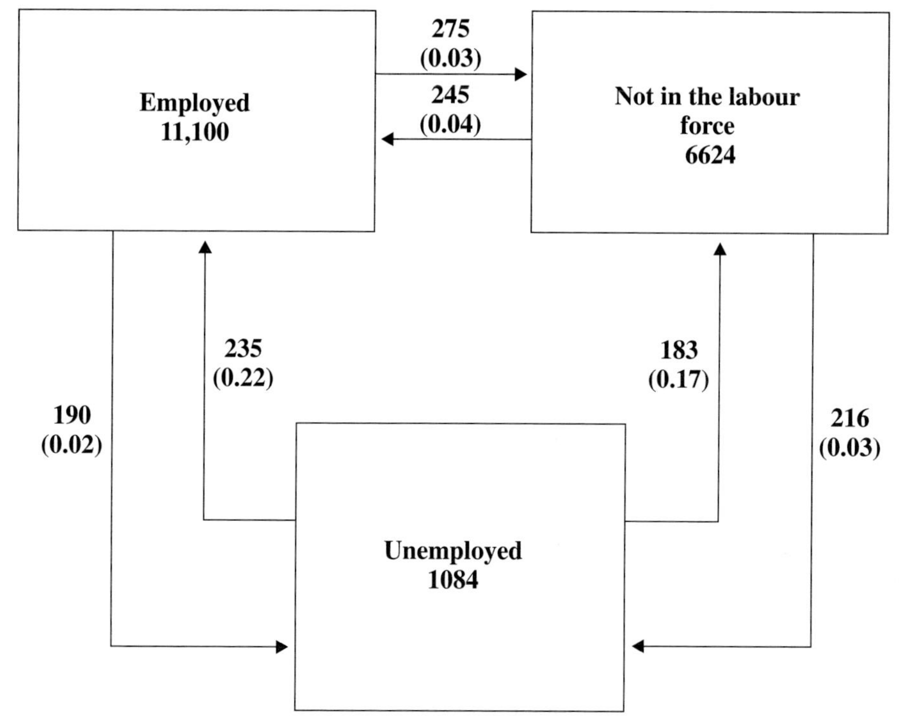

Notes:
1. All numbers are in thousands.
2. All flows and stocks are averages of monthly values from 1976 to 1991.

Source: Stephen R.G. Jones, "Cyclical and seasonal properties of canadian gross flows of labour." This article first appeared in Vol. XIX:I March 1993 of *Canadian Public Policy—Analyse de Politiques*. By permission.

illustrates, the flows between the three labour force states (employment, unemployment, out of the labour force) are large in comparison to the stocks and the **gross flows** are huge in comparison to **net flows**. For example, on average over the period 1976–1991 between any pair of months the number of unemployed declined only slightly (by 12,000). However, 235,000 individuals, 22 percent of those unemployed in an average month, became employed by the following month. This large gross flow from unemployment to employment was offset by a movement of 190,000 individuals in the opposite direction; the average net flow from unemployment to employment was thus 45,000 (235,000 minus 190,000). Similarly, 183,000 individuals, 17 percent of those unemployed, left the labour force between the average pair of months. However, this change was more than offset by the 216,000 individuals who entered the labour force and sought work. The net addition to unemployment of 33,000 due to the movements between unemployment and not in the labour force thus partially offset the net decline of 45,000 associated with the flows between unemployment and employment.

Below each flow (in parentheses) is the average probability of moving from the origin state to the destination state. For example, on average over the period 1976–1991, the probability of an unemployed individual being employed in the following month was 0.22; the probability of moving from employment to unemployment was 0.02.

In summary, even though the number of unemployed changes only marginally from one month to the next, many of the individuals unemployed in one month are no longer unemployed in the next month, with about 22 percent having obtained work and about 17 percent no longer seeking work. The picture that emerges from these data is that of a highly dynamic labour force in which there is a great deal of movement among employment, unemployment, and outside of the labour force each month.[3]

Table 17.2 provides data on the significance of the various flows into unemployment. The picture of unemployment consisting almost entirely of individuals who lost their job (either temporarily or permanently) is clearly misleading; such job losers account for 40 to 60 percent of all unemployment. In recessions (such as during 1982-1983 and 1990-1992) the absolute and relative importance of job losers increases, and the relative importance of job leavers declines. New entrants and re-entrants (those moving from out of the labour force to unemployed *and* who previously were in the labour force) constitute a substantial proportion (one-quarter to one-third) of the unemployed.

Incidence and Duration of Unemployment

Because of the dynamic nature of labour force movements, the understanding of unemployment requires information on the flows between various labour force states in addition to the stocks in each state at any point in time. Useful measures for this purpose are the **incidence of unemployment**—the proportion of individuals who become unemployed in any period—and the **duration of unemployment**—the length of time spent in the unemployed state before obtaining employment or leaving the labour force.[4] For any particular group of workers, incidence measures the probability of a member of the group becoming unemployed, while duration measures the length of time the individual can be expected to remain unemployed. Using the data in Figure 17.2, the incidence of

Table 17.2 Decomposition of Unemployment by Reason, 1975–2000

	National Unemployment Rate (%)	Reason for Separation		
		Job Losers (%)	Job Leavers (%)	New Entrants and Re-entrants (%)
1976–1979	7.7	3.4	1.3	2.2
1980–1981	7.5	3.4	1.2	2.3
1982–1983	11.5	5.9	1.3	2.9
1984–1987	10.1	4.8	1.4	2.6
1988–1989	7.7	3.5	1.3	2.0
1990–1992	9.9	5.0	1.3	2.4
1993–1996	10.2	4.5	1.0	2.9
1997–2000	7.9	3.0	0.8	2.8

Notes:
1. All statistics are based on authors' calculations from data on the civilian labour force (annual averages).
2. Components do not sum to the total because reasons for separation "Reason unknown" and "Future starts" are omitted.

Source: Statistics Canada, *Labour Force Historical Review*, Catalogue 71F0004, 2001.

[3]Gross flows data are subject to some limitations; see Jones (1993).

[4]This is sometimes referred to as the duration of a "completed spell of unemployment" to distinguish it from the duration of an "interrupted spell" (i.e., a spell in progress). For further discussion of these duration concepts see Corak and Heisz (1995).

unemployment for those employed in the average month was 1.7 percent (190,000 out of 11,100,000) while the incidence of unemployment among those out of the labour force in the average month was 3.3 percent (216,000 out of 6,624,000). The overall incidence among those either employed or not in the labour force was 2.3 percent. More commonly, incidence of unemployment is measured as a fraction of the labour force, so that it measures the percentage of the labour force that is newly unemployed. With this measure, the incidence of unemployment would be 3.3 percent.

The amount of unemployment at any point in time is affected by both the incidence and duration. Indeed, the unemployment rate (UR) can be expressed as the product of the incidence (I) and duration (D).[5]

$$UR = I \times D \tag{17.1}$$

Table 17.3 shows the breakdown of the unemployment rate into its incidence and duration components. As it turns out, there are a number of statistical problems associated with estimating the average duration of unemployment, so the table also illustrates three approaches that can be taken in addressing these problems. To keep the discussion focused, we shall only discuss the decomposition for 1993, the bolded row. In that year, the average monthly unemployment rate was 11.4 percent. Incidence is measured as that portion of the labour force who have been searching for work for less than one month, that is, new entrants into the pool of the unemployed. In 1993, incidence was 2.6 percent, which implies that the probability of someone attached to the labour force becoming unemployed in a given month was 2.6 percent.

Three measures of duration are shown. The first (D1) is reported monthly by Statistics Canada, and is the average duration of unemployment (in months) of the currently unemployed. This statistic answers the question, "How long has the average unemployed worker been searching and without work in the survey month?" Because the search spells are still incomplete and economic conditions may be changing, this measure may actually be a poor measure of how long the newly unemployed can expect to be without work. For this reason, more sophisticated measures have been proposed. One such measure, the expected duration of completed spells, which takes account of the incomplete nature of the observed spell is provided by Picot and Heisz (2000) and reported as D2. Finally, we show the estimate of duration that is implied by the **steady-state condition** (equation 17.1), by backing out duration from the unemployment and incidence rates (D3).

It is only for these sets of numbers (D3) that equation 17.1 holds with identity. In this case (by construction), the unemployment rate (11.4 percent) is exactly the product of incidence (2.6 percent) and duration (4.3 months). The unemployment rates implied by D1 and D2 (through equation 17.1) are reported as U1 and U2. Neither lines up perfectly, but the Picot and Heisz measure comes close. These discrepancies suggest that the assumption of "steady state" may be a poor approximation of labour market dynamics. Finally, in the last column we provide another indicator of unemployment duration: the fraction of the unemployed who have been unemployed for more than three months. In 1993, it appears that about half of the unemployed could be expected to find work in the first three months of search.

Table 17.4 shows the unemployment rate and the incidence and duration of unemployment for various age-sex groups in Canada in 1995. The most striking feature of the data in Table 17.4 is that the groups with the highest unemployment rates (males and females

[5]When the labour force is in a steady-state equilibrium (i.e., the fraction of the labour force in each state and the proportions flowing between states are constant) this relationship is exact. Otherwise the relationship is only approximately correct. Equation 17.1 is an example of the steady-state identity that the stock at any point in time equals the flow times average duration.

Table 17.3 Incidence and Duration of Unemployment, Canada, 1976–2000

	Unemployment Rate			Incidence	Duration (Months)			% Long
Year	Actual	U1	U2	Actual	D1	D2	D3	Spells
1976	7.0	7.1	6.1	2.2	3.2	2.8	3.2	37.4
1977	8.0	8.2	9.3	2.5	3.3	3.7	3.2	38.4
1978	8.3	8.8	9.2	2.5	3.6	3.7	3.4	40.5
1979	7.5	8.2	8.1	2.4	3.4	3.4	3.1	38.2
1980	7.5	8.3	8.3	2.4	3.4	3.5	3.1	37.3
1981	7.6	8.7	8.7	2.5	3.5	3.5	3.0	37.3
1982	11.0	12.0	13.9	3.0	4.0	4.6	3.7	43.4
1983	11.9	13.9	12.8	2.7	5.1	4.7	4.4	51.2
1984	11.3	14.6	12.6	2.9	5.0	4.4	3.9	48.2
1985	10.7	14.0	11.5	2.8	5.0	4.1	3.8	47.8
1986	9.6	12.7	10.5	2.7	4.7	3.9	3.6	45.2
1987	8.8	11.7	9.5	2.5	4.7	3.8	3.6	45.2
1988	7.8	10.0	8.7	2.4	4.2	3.6	3.3	42.2
1989	7.5	9.6	8.5	2.3	4.2	3.7	3.3	41.8
1990	8.1	9.8	9.7	2.5	3.9	3.9	3.2	40.6
1991	10.3	12.1	12.4	2.7	4.5	4.6	3.8	46.1
1992	11.2	14.3	13.6	2.8	5.2	4.9	4.0	49.8
1993	**11.4**	**15.3**	**12.0**	**2.6**	**5.8**	**4.6**	**4.3**	**52.2**
1994	10.4	14.8	10.9	2.5	5.9	4.4	4.2	51.4
1995	9.4	13.8	10.4	2.5	5.6	4.2	3.8	48.2
1996	9.6	14.8	11.2	2.7	5.5	4.1	3.6	47.2
1997	9.1	14.8		2.9	5.1		3.2	43.8
1998	8.3	12.4		2.7	4.7		3.1	41.8
1999	7.6	10.6		2.5	4.3		3.1	40.4
2000	6.8	9.3		2.3	4.0		2.9	37.7

Notes: The actual unemployment rate is the official unemployment rate reported by Statistics Canada (all ages), and is the average monthly unemployment rate. Actual incidence is estimated as the fraction of the labour force unemployed 1–4 weeks in a given month. Duration is measured three ways. The first (D1) is the reported average weeks of unemployment and corresponds to interrupted spells. The second (D2), from Picot and Heisz (2000), is expected completed duration of unemployment in months (unavailable after 1996 due to a break in the series). The third (D3) is calculated from the actual unemployment rate and incidence rate from the formula UR = I × D. The resulting implied unemployment rates from these different measures of duration are U1, based on the interrupted spell duration, and D2, based on the Picot and Heisz measure of duration. "Long Spells" is the fraction of unemployed who have been unemployed 14 weeks or longer (more than three months).

Sources: Garnett Picot and Andrew Heisz, "The performance of the 1990s Canadian labour market," *Canadian Public Policy* 26(July 2000, Supplement):S7–S26, and calculations by the authors from data in Statistics Canada, *Labour Force Historical Review,* Catalogue 71F0004, 2000.

15–24 years of age) have the lowest duration (2.2 and 2.0 months respectively). The very high youth unemployment rate is associated with a high probability of becoming unemployed rather than an unusually long time being required to find a job or to exit from the labour force. Older workers, on the other hand, have the lowest unemployment rates within each sex group. This reflects the fact that older workers are less likely to become unemployed; those that do become unemployed require a longer than average period to find employment or leave the labour force. The incidence and duration of male and female unemployment is very similar, as is their overall unemployment rate.

Table 17.4 Incidence and Duration of Unemployment by Age and Sex, Canada, 2000

Sex or Age Group		Unemployment Rate	Incidence Rate	Duration (Months)	Unemployed > 6 Months
Men	15–24	13.9	6.3	2.2	8.6
	25–44	6.0	1.7	3.5	21.6
	45+	5.0	1.2	4.0	28.0
	All	6.9	2.3	3.0	19.1
Women	15–24	11.3	5.6	2.0	6.4
	25–44	6.0	1.9	3.1	16.8
	45+	5.2	1.4	3.6	24.9
	All	6.7	2.4	2.8	15.7

Notes: The incidence rate is calculated as the percentage of the labour force that has been unemployed between 1 and 4 weeks. The average duration is calculated from the formula UR = I × D, given the incidence and unemployment rates in the first two columns.

Source: Statistics Canada, *Labour Force Historical Review*, Catalogue 71F0004, 2001.

Changing Perspectives on Unemployment

Public policy toward unemployment has occupied a central role in Canada, certainly since the Great Depression. Economists have often been charged with the task of discovering "a cure" for unemployment. As with any economic problem, the first step in designing an effective policy is to understand the "pathology" of unemployment. A common portrayal (or caricature) of unemployment in the media is that a 10 percent unemployment rate corresponds to 10 percent of the population engaged in a long-term and futile search for nonexistent jobs. The data summarized to this point goes a long way in dispelling this simple image. Several conclusions can be drawn:

1. The labour force is highly dynamic, with large flows into and out of unemployment each period.
2. About half the flow into unemployment in an average year is due to individuals losing their job; the remainder is associated with job leavers, new entrants, and re-entrants.
3. The average duration of unemployment in an average year is approximately $4\frac{1}{2}$ months, with less than half of all unemployment spells lasting more than 3 months.
4. The age groups with the highest unemployment rates have the shortest average unemployment durations, but the highest incidence of unemployment.

These general findings have important implications for the role of policies to deal with unemployment. The large amount of turnover in the labour force, the fact that job losers account for only about half the flow into unemployment, and the relatively short average duration of unemployment (especially among the groups with the highest unemployment rates) suggest that much unemployment may be caused not by a general shortage of jobs but by employment instability—brief spells of employment followed by periods of job search and/or exit from the labour force. In particular, the short observed duration of unemployment was regarded as evidence that most people could find an acceptable job fairly quickly. Feldstein (1973) used the term "the new unemployment" to describe this view of unemployment being primarily associated with rapid turnover and employment instability; this contrasted with the "old view" in which the unemployed were regarded as a stock of individuals without work for a lengthy period while waiting for a business upturn (the caricature painted in the previous paragraph). The new view suggested that policies aimed at reducing turnover and employment instability may be more successful in achieving lower levels of unemployment than policies aimed at increasing the number of jobs.

Subsequent research, such as that of Clark and Summers (1979) and Akerlof and Main (1980) for the United States and Hasan and de Broucker (1982) and Beach and Kaliski (1983) for Canada, indicated that the "new view" of unemployment contained important elements of truth but was an overly simplistic picture of unemployment. Three conclusions emerged from this research; taking these into account resulted in a "modified new view." First, although the average duration of completed spells of unemployment is fairly short, much unemployment is accounted for by those suffering lengthy spells of unemployment. An example may help to illustrate this point. Suppose that five individuals become unemployed, four for spells of one month each and the fifth for eight months. The average duration of unemployment for this group is 2.4 months, but two-thirds of all the unemployment (8 out of 12 months) is associated with the one long spell.

A second important consideration is that not all periods of unemployment end in employment. As Figure 17.2 suggests, a significant number of individuals end their search for work by withdrawing from the labour force. Some may leave the labour force to return to school, raise children, or work in the home; however, as discussed previously, some may want paid work but have stopped searching for work because they believe no work is available or for other "economic reasons." By not classifying as "unemployment" the period during which these individuals wanted work but were not searching for work, the duration of unemployment may be considered to be understated. For example, consider an individual who becomes unemployed, searches for work for two months, gives up and stops searching for three months, and then resumes the job search, finding work after a further two months. According to the official statistics, this person would have experienced two spells of unemployment, each lasting a brief two months. However, it could be argued that the individual experienced a single bout of unemployment lasting seven months. Even if this argument is rejected (i.e., the job search requirement for being considered unemployed is retained), it is clear that, when many spells of unemployment end in withdrawal from the labour force, the fact that the average duration of unemployment is fairly short does not imply that most of the unemployed can find an acceptable job fairly quickly. A related observation is that spells of unemployment which end in employment are, on average, longer than those ending in withdrawal from the labour force. Thus the average length of time required to successfully find a job is understated by the duration statistics such as those reported in Table 17.3.

The third modification is related to the distribution of unemployment across the population. The implications of a specific unemployment rate differ according to how widely the unemployment is distributed. For example, an unemployment rate of 8 percent could mean that 8 percent of the labour force is unemployed all year (i.e., the distribution of unemployment is highly concentrated) or that all of the labour force is unemployed for 8 percent of the year (i.e., the distribution of unemployment is widely dispersed). The high rate of labour force turnover and the short average duration of unemployment led some analysts to believe that unemployment must be widely distributed among the labour force. In fact, this conclusion turns out not to be correct: unemployment is highly concentrated among a minority of the labour force. The reason for these apparently contradictory findings is that even though the average duration of unemployment is short, a minority of individuals suffer repeated spells of unemployment, sometimes interrupted by periods out of the labour force. For these individuals—the "chronically unemployed"—obtaining employment, especially durable employment, appears to be a difficult task.

Recent behaviour of Canadian unemployment has been dominated by cyclical changes: the recession of 1981–82, recovery and expansion from 1983 to 1989, recession of 1990–92, and recovery and expansion from 1993 to 2000. During 1983 the unemployment rate reached 11.9 percent, its highest level of the postwar period (Figure 17.1 and Table 17.3). Only by 1989, following a long period of economic growth, did the unemployment rate return to its prerecession level (however briefly). During the recession of 1990–92, unemployment again climbed above 11 percent, and did not fall below 8 percent until 1999. The 1980s and 1990s were thus characterized by higher unemployment rates at each point in the business cycle than was experienced in the 1960s and 1970s.

Subsequent recent research and policy attention has focused on international differences in unemployment experience, especially the dramatic increases in European unemployment since the 1970s and the persistence of high unemployment in those countries. As noted in Exhibit 17.1, during the 1950s and 1960s European countries typically had much lower unemployment than their North American counterparts. However, beginning with the OPEC oil price shocks of the 1970s and continuing during the 1980s and 1990s, unemployment rates shot up during economic downturns and have shown much less of a tendency than in North America to decline during the subsequent expansion. In contrast to Europe, unemployment rates in the United States during the 1990s were very similar to those experienced in the 1960s and 1970s (see Exhibit 17.1). Relative to the United States, Europe has gone from being a "low unemployment region" to being a "high unemployment region," with the Canadian experience lying in between these two extremes.

Accompanying the rise in European unemployment has been a substantial increase in the extent of long-term unemployment. Table 17.5 summarizes recent experience for the same ten countries whose unemployment rates are reported in Exhibit 17.1. In France, Germany, and Italy, between 40 and 60 percent of the unemployed have been unemployed for a year or more. These proportions are lower in the Netherlands, Sweden and the United Kingdom, but they are nonetheless much higher than in North America, where the fraction of long-term unemployment is about 10 percent in Canada and 5 to 6 percent in the United States.

For these reasons, the 1980s and 1990s saw a shift in emphasis away from concern about employment instability and high turnover in the labour force toward unemployment that remains persistently high and is longer-term in nature. This shift was especially evident in Europe where the problem of long-term unemployment was particularly severe. It thus appears that the "new" view of unemployment put forward in the 1970s needs to be

Table 17.5 International Differences in Long-Term Unemployment

	Long-Term Unemployment as a Percentage of Total Unemployment			
	1990		2000	
	6 Months and Over	12 Months and Over	6 Months and Over	12 Months and Over
Australia	41.0	21.6	43.6	27.9
Canada	20.2	7.2	19.5	11.2
France	55.5	38.0	61.9	42.5
Germany	64.7	46.8	67.6	51.5
Italy	85.2	69.8	75.3	60.8
Japan	39.0	19.1	46.9	25.5
Netherlands	63.6	49.3	46.5	32.7
Sweden	22.2	12.1	41.5	26.4
United Kingdom	50.3	34.4	43.2	28.0
United States	10.0	5.5	11.4	6.0

Source: OECD, *Employment Outlook 2001* (Paris: OECD, 2001).

replaced, or at least significantly modified. The changing nature of unemployment over time and across countries makes it difficult to design single, universally applicable policies to address unemployment.

The Divergence of the Canada and U.S. Unemployment Rates

Throughout most of the postwar period, unemployment rates in Canada and the United States tracked each other very closely, as illustrated in Figure 17.3. Average unemployment rates were nearly equal in the two countries during the 1950s and 1960s, and only slightly higher in Canada during the 1970s. However, since 1982 the Canadian unemployment rate has been two to five percentage points higher than in the United States, with the gap being larger in the 1990s than in the 1980s.

The emergence of a large Canada-U.S. unemployment gap has sparked much speculation about and research into its causes. Initially many observers argued that the gap reflected the more severe economic downturn in Canada in 1981–82. However, the persistence of the differential throughout the subsequent expansion and the decade of the 1990s suggests the emergence of a permanent or structural difference between the two countries rather than a short-run cyclical phenomenon. Given other similarities between the economies, it is hoped that an understanding of the sources of this divergence can help explain the underlying factors responsible for the increased level of unemployment over the 1980s.

Figure 17.3 Unemployment Rates, United States and Canada, 1953–2000

The national unemployment rates for the United States and Canada are plotted annually over the period 1953–2000. Unemployment rates in the two countries followed each other closely throughout most of the postwar period, but diverged substantially in the 1980s and 1990s.

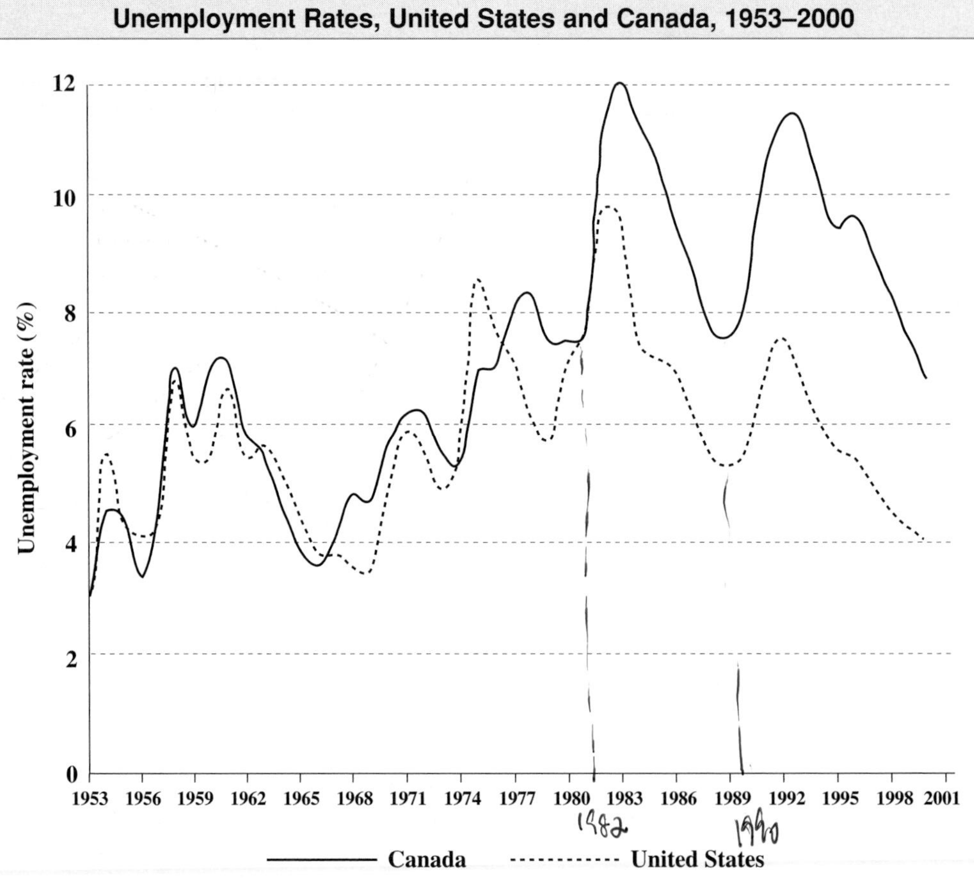

Source: Created in part from author's calculations on the basis of data from the Statistics Canada CANSIM database <cansima.statcan.ca>.

As it turns out, a number of key insights on the nature of Canadian unemployment emerge from an investigation of differences in the structure of unemployment in the two countries.

Some of the gap is simply due to differences in the way unemployment is measured in the two countries. One of the most important such differences is the treatment of "passive" job searchers—such as those whose sole search method was "looked at job ads." The United States requires "active" job search—that is, taking an action that could result in a job offer—to be classified as unemployed, whereas in Canada any form of job search is sufficient. During the 1990s, this and other measurement-related differences between the two countries account for about 0.8 to 0.9 percentage points of the Canada-U.S. unemployment rate differential (Statistics Canada, 1998; Riddell, 1999). The bulk of the gap therefore remains to be explained by behavioural factors.

In their analysis of the **Canada-U.S. unemployment differential**, Card and Riddell (1993 and 1997) point out that intercountry differences in other measures of aggregate labour force activity actually converged during the 1970s and 1980s, in contrast to the divergence observed in the unemployment rate. Traditionally, labour force participation in Canada was lower than that in the United States; however, by the late 1970s Canada's participation rate had caught up to the U.S. rate, and during the 1980s consistently exceeded the U.S. rate. Perhaps indicative of the mutable nature of economic knowledge, this convergence in labour force participation was reversed after 1990. Similarly, although intercountry differences in the unemployment rate and nonemployment rate (1 minus the employment rate) followed the same cyclical pattern, the gap in the nonemployment rate actually closed in the 1980s, at the same time the unemployment gap widened. Thus, a comparison of relative employment rates and participation rates paints a much brighter picture of the Canadian labour markets during the 1980s than a comparison of the unemployment rates. Since 1990, however, the participation, nonemployment, and unemployment rates have painted a similarly grim picture of the Canadian labour market.

These aggregate data suggest that the Canadian and U.S. labour forces became more alike during the 1980s in terms of the amount of time spent in the labour force and the amount of time spent employed. Yet they became less alike in terms of the amount of time spent unemployed. How can these apparently contradictory trends be explained? The answer lies in the way nonworking time is spent. In their analysis of Canadian and U.S. microdata, Card and Riddell find that much of the intercountry unemployment differential up to 1989 can be attributed to a rise in the fraction of nonemployment time spent unemployed (i.e., searching for work) rather than out of the labour force. This finding illustrates the fact that alternative measures of labour market activity can sometimes appear to indicate contradictory trends. It also suggests that an understanding of the emergence of a substantial Canada-U.S. unemployment gap must account for the rise in the likelihood of a nonemployed Canadian being engaged in job search (rather than being out of the labour force) compared to a nonemployed American. The widening gap in both unemployment and nonemployment since 1990, however, presents itself as an additional challenge to our understanding of these labour markets.

Further results on the Canada-U.S. unemployment gap are presented in Baker, Corak, and Heisz (1998). They investigate relative changes in incidence and duration of unemployment in the two countries over the 1980s. They note that before the gap emerged, while unemployment rates were similar, incidence and duration followed different patterns. Unemployment spells lasted about 25 percent longer in Canada, but incidence was about 25 percent lower. Since 1981, however, the incidence of unemployment has dropped significantly in the United States, but has remained approximately constant in Canada, so that incidence is now about the same in the two countries. In the United States, duration has followed the same cyclical and trend patterns as in Canada. Thus, while the higher duration of unemployment in Canada is most associated with the level of the difference in unemployment rates between the two countries, it has been the relative decline in incidence in the United States that is most responsible for the emergence of the unemployment rate gap over the 1980s. Baker, Corak, and Heisz estimate that almost 70 percent of the widening gap can be explained by the relative decline in the incidence of unemployment in the United States. Their findings indicate that explanations of the gap that rely on increased duration of unemployment (perhaps due to differences in UI) will be able to account for less than one-third of the gap.

Gray and Grenier (1998) focus attention on differences in the level of unemployment duration between the two countries. Using comparable surveys of laid-off (displaced) workers, they estimate the determinants of unemployment duration. They find that local labour market conditions (like the local unemployment rate) explain a significant fraction of the difference in durations experienced by Canadian and U.S. job seekers. This suggests that a lack of jobs is a contributing factor to the longer unemployment spells in Canada. On the other hand, they also find that Canadian job seekers are less responsive to changes in labour market conditions, possibly because of incentives provided by unemployment insurance.

Taken together, the evidence on the Canada-U.S. unemployment rate differential should provide no comfort to policymakers. The widening gap is a complicated product of changes in the number of jobs, as well as differences on the labour supply side. If nothing else, however, this research should deflate those commentators who point to a single explanation for Canada's disappointingly high unemployment rate. It also illustrates the amount of insight that can be gained on this question simply by understanding how unemployment is measured.

UNEMPLOYMENT RATE AS A SUMMARY STATISTIC

The unemployment rate is widely used as an economic and labour market indicator about such things as the aggregate state of the economy, the tightness or looseness of the labour market, or the extent of hardship in the population. However, much of the previous discussion suggests that is unwise to rely on the unemployment rate alone for these purposes. It is not that the unemployment rate is wrong; rather, it may be asking too much of a single measure to indicate all these things, especially when dramatic demographic changes have occurred in the labour force, and institutional changes have occurred in programs such as unemployment insurance, pensions, and social assistance.

The unemployment rate is arguably most suited as a measure of the amount of unutilized labour supply. This purpose accounts for the emphasis placed by statistical agencies on being "available for work" and currently "searching for work" in the official unemployment statistics. The concept of unutilized labour supply is necessarily somewhat ambiguous, because, as discussed in Chapter 2, both theory and evidence on labour supply behaviour indicates that the amount people want to work depends on how well they will be remunerated for their time and effort. The fact that those classified as unemployed are currently searching for employment is taken as evidence that they are willing to work at prevailing wages and working conditions.

Nonetheless, even as a measure of unutilized labour supply, the unemployment rate is imperfect and should be supplemented with additional measures such as those described in Exhibit 17.1. Groups on the margin of the labour force may desire employment at prevailing wages but may not be currently searching because of discouragement or various forms of "waiting" for jobs to become available. These groups may display a weaker attachment to the labour force than those officially classified as unemployed, but also a stronger attachment than the remainder of those not in the labour force for reasons such as schooling, household production, and retirement.

The need to supplement the unemployment rate with other indicators increases when we consider some other uses to which this widely cited statistic is applied. As we have seen in this chapter, the unemployment rate provides a useful measure of the state of the economy and aggregate labour market—increasing in periods of slow or negative economic growth and falling in expansionary times. However, as illustrated in Figure 17.1, the time series behaviour of unemployment displays not only these cyclical ups and downs but also a clear upward trend since the 1960s. Thus an unemployment rate of 6 percent is not likely to indicate the same degree of labour market tightness or looseness today as it did in earlier decades. At the present time, we would regard an unemployment rate of 6 percent as "low" and probably associated with an economy at or near a cyclical peak. In contrast, this level would have been regarded in the 1960s as very high and likely an indicator of a weak labour market and a slumping economy.

The labour force participation rate and the employment rate are measures of aggregate labour market activity that can be used to provide a more complete picture of the state of the labour market. Often the three measures will move together—for example, a downturn in the economy is usually accompanied by rising unemployment and declining participation and employment rates. But, as we have seen, Canada and other countries have also experienced periods such as 1966-1973 and 1973-1981 in which the employment rate, the participation rate, and the unemployment rate were increasing (recall Table 17.1). In these circumstances focusing on movements in the unemployment rate alone is likely to be misleading.

The unemployment rate is also often used as an indicator of the extent of hardship in an economy, region, or time period. Here the need for considering additional measures is especially strong. Today, many of the unemployed are in families in which one or more other members are working. The rise of multi-earner families with two working parents and one or more working teenagers or young adults has resulted in a weaker link between unemployment and low family income than was the case in the past when there was more likely to be a single "breadwinner" in the family. At the same time, the unemployment rate is uninformative about the earnings levels of the employed, and the degree to which they may have fallen below a poverty level. Increases in earnings inequality may be associated with greater hardship without accompanying movements in unemployment.

Summary

- The unemployed are generally defined as those who are not currently employed and who indicate by their behaviour that they want to work at prevailing wages and working conditions. The primary source of data on unemployment in Canada is the Labour Force Survey, carried out monthly by Statistics Canada.
- According to the Labour Force Survey, individuals are categorized as unemployed if they did not have work in the reference period but were available for and searching for work. Two exceptions to this principle are those on temporary layoff from a job to which they expect to be recalled and those with a job to start within the next four weeks.
- Canada's unemployment experience has varied widely. The onset of the Great Depression saw the unemployment rate soar from about 3 percent to almost 20 percent. During World War II unemployment fell to very low levels. The post-World War II period has been characterized by cyclical variations around a general upward trend. The behaviour of unemployment during the 1990s suggests that the upward trend may have ended.
- The unemployment rate is the most commonly used measure of labour market activity. Two additional measures are the employment rate and the labour force participation rate, defined respectively as the fractions of the adult population employed and in the labour force. Because they focus on somewhat different aspects of labour market activity these three measures need not always move together. For example, since the mid-

1960s the unemployment rate has risen substantially but the labour force participation rate and employment rate have risen, not fallen.

- The measurement of unemployment raises difficult and controversial issues. Hidden unemployment or "marginal labour force attachment" refers to situations in which individuals may be without work, desire work, yet they are not officially classified as unemployed because they are not searching for work. Examples include discouraged workers and those who are waiting for potential or promised jobs to become available. The major lesson is not that the official unemployment rate is a poor measure, but rather that no single measure of unemployment is likely to be suitable for all purposes. Accordingly, Statistics Canada publishes several "supplementary measures of unemployment."
- Canada's labour market is highly dynamic. Gross flows between the three labour force states (employment, unemployment, and out-of-the-labour force) are large in comparison to the stocks in each state at any point in time, and huge in comparison to the net flows.
- Unemployment does not consist almost exclusively of individuals who lost their job, either temporarily or permanently. Job losers account for 40 to 50 percent of flows into unemployment, with the proportion being highest in recessions. The remainder is accounted for by job leavers (10 to 20 percent) and new entrants and re-entrants (25 to 35 percent).
- Useful concepts for understanding unemployment dynamics are the incidence and duration of unemployment. For any group of workers, incidence refers to the probability of a member of the group becoming unemployed, while duration measures the length of time the individual can expect to remain unemployed. In a steady state the unemployment rate can be expressed as the product of incidence and duration.
- Young workers have much higher unemployment rates than adults, but lower average duration of unemployment. The high youth unemployment rates are due to the high probability of becoming unemployed in any period. The incidence and duration of unemployment are very similar for men and women, as are their unemployment rates.
- Perspectives on unemployment have evolved substantially. During the 1970s the traditional view—in which the unemployed were regarded as a mainly unchanging stock of individuals without work for a lengthy period—was challenged by a "new view" that emphasized the importance of employment instability and turnover in the labour market. Subsequent research modified this "turnover" view by noting that although the average duration of unemployment is fairly short, much of total unemployment is nonetheless accounted for by those experiencing long spells of joblessness. Furthermore, many unemployment spells end in labour force withdrawal rather than in employment, suggesting that unavailability of suitable employment is a reality for some workers. In Canada, the 1980s and 1990s have been dominated by cyclical developments: the deep recessions of 1981–1982 and 1990–1992 and recovery from these downturns. These two recessions—the worst of the postwar period—saw sharp increases in both the incidence and the duration of unemployment, but both declined substantially during the subsequent expansions. In contrast, in many European countries increases in unemployment persisted and the incidence of long-term unemployment grew dramatically.
- Unemployment rates in Canada and the United States behaved very similarly during most of the postwar period, but diverged in the 1980s and 1990s. Differences in the way unemployment is measured account for 0.8 to 0.9 percentage points of the unemployment rate gap in the 1990s. Most of the differential is due to a relative increase among Canadians in the fraction of non-working time spent searching for work compared to that of Americans. The emergence of the unemployment gap was also associated with a decline in the incidence of unemployment in the United States relative to Canada.

- The unemployment rate is widely used as an indicator of the amount of unutilized labour supply, the state of the labour market and economy, and the degree of hardship in the population. For each of these purposes, it is unwise to rely on the unemployment rate alone.

REVIEW QUESTIONS

1. (a) Discuss the various ways in which the number of unemployed typically are measured in Canada.
   (b) Which is the measure that receives the most publicity?
   (c) Discuss the strengths and weaknesses of the various measures.
2. Explain the difference between the following measures of the duration of unemployment:
   (i) The average duration of all spells ongoing at a point in time
   (ii) The expected completed duration of all spells beginning during a certain period
   Which of these measures is most useful, and why? Which of these measures corresponds to the "average duration of unemployment" reported by Statistics Canada?
3. (a) Explain the meaning of the following measures of labour force utilization: (i) labour force participation rate, (ii) employment rate, and (iii) unemployment rate.
   (b) For each of these measures, describe circumstances under which that measure would be preferred to the other two.
   (c) Under what conditions will these three measures all move in the same direction? Under what conditions would they move in opposite directions?
4. Explain the concept of hidden unemployment. Discuss the pros and cons of including the hidden unemployed in our unemployment statistics.
5. Explain the distinction between gross flows and net flows among various labour force states.
6. In discussing the nature of unemployment, some analysts stress a shortage of jobs while others emphasize labour force turnover and employment instability.
   (a) Elaborate these competing perspectives on unemployment.
   (b) Describe research findings which attempt to distinguish between these competing perspectives. Which view is correct?
7. Why might we expect younger workers to have higher unemployment rates than older workers, and what does this imply about the changes in our aggregate unemployment rate over time?
8. Why is it that the groups with the highest unemployment rates also have the shortest average duration of unemployment?
9. (a) Indicate some of the uses for which our aggregate unemployment rates are often used.
   (b) Why might this single measure increasingly be inadequate for these purposes?
   (c) What are some of the alternatives and what are their strengths and weaknesses?

PROBLEMS

1. Canada includes "passive" job searchers among the unemployed, whereas the United States classifies those who use only "passive" search methods as not in the labour force.
   (a) Which country's measurement procedures are preferable, and why?
   (b) What empirical evidence could be used to help answer part (a)?
2. Explain what is currently known about the causes of the Canada-U.S. unemployment rate gap. What questions remain unanswered?

3. Examine the time series plot of the number of discouraged workers in Canada over the period 1979-1999 (see Chart 18 in Statistics Canada, 1999).
   (a) During which years were there relatively more discouraged workers? Why?
   (b) The number of discouraged workers did not increase as much during the recession of 1990-1992 as it did during the recession of 1981-1982. What factors might account for this difference?

KEYWORDS

Labour Force Survey 507
unemployed 507
unemployment rate 509
employment rate 509
marginal labour force attachment 512
discouraged workers 512
gross flows 515
net flows 515
incidence of unemployment 516
duration of unemployment 516
steady-state condition 517
Canada-U.S. unemployment differential 523

REFERENCES

Akerlof, G., and B. Main. 1980. Unemployment spells and unemployment experience. *AER* 70 (December): 885-93.

Akyeampong, E. 1992. Discouraged workers—where have they gone? *PLI* (Autumn):38-44.

Baker, M., M. Corak, and A. Heisz. 1998. The labour market dynamics of unemployment rates in Canada and the United States. *CPP* 24 (Supplement: February):S72-S89.

Beach, C., and S. Kaliski. 1983. Measuring the duration of unemployment from gross flow data. *CJE* 16 (May):258-63.

Card, D., and W. Riddell. 1997. Unemployment in Canada and the United States: A further analysis. In *Trade, Technology and Economics: Essays in Honour of Richard G. Lipsey*, eds. B. Eaton and R. Harris. Cheltanham: Edward Elgar.

______. 1993. A comparative analysis of unemployment in Canada and the United States. In *Small Differences That Matter: Labor Markets and Income Maintenance in Canada and the United States*, eds D. Card and R. B. Freeman. Chicago: University of Chicago Press.

Clark, K., and L. Summers. 1979. Labor market dynamics and unemployment: A reconsideration. *BPEA*:13-60.

Corak, M., and A. Heisz. 1995. The duration of unemployment: A user's guide. Statistics Canada Research Report #84.

Feldstein, M. 1973. The economics of the new unemployment. *Public Interest* 33 (Fall):3-42.

Gray, D., and G. Grenier. 1998. Jobless durations of displaced workers: A comparison of Canada and the United States. *CPP* 24 (Supplement: February):S152-S169.

Hasan, A., and P. de Broucker. 1982. Duration and concentration of unemployment. *CJE* 15 (November):706-34.

Jones, S. 1993. The cyclical and seasonal properties of Canadian gross flows of labour. *CPP* 19:(March).

Jones, S., and W. Riddell. 1999. The measurement of unemployment: An empirical approach. *Ecta* 67 (January):147-61.

Levesque, J. 1989. Unemployment and unemployment insurance: A tale of two sources. *PLI* 1 (Winter):49-53.

Picot, G., and A. Heisz. 2000. The performance of the 1990s Canadian labour market. *CPP* 26 (Supplement, July):S7-S26.

Riddell, W. 1999. Canadian labour market performance in international perspective. *CJE* 32 (November):1097-1134.

Statistics Canada. 1998. *Labour Force Update: Canada-US Labour Market Comparison.* Ottawa: Statistics Canada.

______. 1999. *Labour Force Update: Supplementary Measures of Unemployment.* Ottawa: Statistics Canada.

Chapter Eighteen

Unemployment: Causes and Consequences

Main Questions

- *What are the different types of unemployment? Do they have a common cause, and if not, what different sets of policies might be appropriate in addressing them?*
- *What role does wage rigidity play in explaining unemployment? What alternative theories to the conventional neoclassical model can help explain why wages may not adjust, even in the face of considerable unemployment?*
- *In what sense can unemployment be "voluntary"? Is voluntary unemployment a positive, necessary feature of the labour market?*
- *How does imperfect information manifest itself in the labour market? In what ways might imperfect information be an important cause of unemployment? What are the appropriate (or inappropriate) government responses to this malfunctioning of the labour market?*
- *What role does unemployment insurance play in affecting the structure of unemployment in Canada? Does it do more harm than good?*

The previous chapter discussed the meaning and measurement of unemployment and described the salient aspects of the Canadian experience. In this chapter we examine the causes and consequences of unemployment and the role of public policy in this area. Given the diverse nature of unemployment, both across different groups in the population, as well as over time, it should hardly come as a surprise that there is no single explanation of why the unemployment rate should be at a particular level.

In this chapter we focus on the microeconomic sources of unemployment. As we shall see, most of the theoretical work addresses the question of why the market wage rate fails to adjust downwards to clear the labour market. Most of the models in this area explore the ways in which the labour market diverges from the neoclassical model that forms the core of the book. From a policy perspective, the most contentious aspect of government policy toward unemployment is the provision of unemployment insurance. From being viewed as an important, progressive part of the social safety net in the early 1970s, by 1990 unemployment insurance (UI)[1] was painted as a major villain in the increases in unemployment witnessed during the 1980s. We trace the debate on the role of unemployment insurance, and examine the still accumulating evidence on its role in affecting the unemployment rate.

Section One: Types of Unemployment

Economists usually distinguish among several types of unemployment. These differ according to their causes, their consequences, and the policies that are likely to be effective in dealing with them. The most common categories are frictional, structural, deficient demand, and seasonal unemployment. Each of these will be discussed in turn. As will become evident in the ensuing discussion, the distinctions are often not clear-cut, either conceptually or practically.

FRICTIONAL UNEMPLOYMENT

Frictional unemployment is associated with normal turnover in the labour force; it can thus be thought of as unemployment that would prevail even in a well-functioning labour market. Change is a pervasive feature of modern economies. As discussed previously, in each period some individuals enter the labour force to search for work while others leave to return to school, retire, or work in the home. Similarly, new jobs open up in some firms and disappear in others. As a consequence, unemployed workers and unfilled job vacancies will coexist at any point in time. This unemployment exists even if jobs and workers are potentially matched in the sense that the unemployed workers are qualified for the available jobs and are willing to fill these jobs; they simply have to be brought together and this process takes time. For this reason, frictional unemployment is often associated with job search activity within a given labour market. Because suitable unfilled vacancies exist for the frictionally unemployed, this type of unemployment will typically be of short duration; however, the optimal duration will depend on the benefits and costs of continued search, as discussed below.

Unfilled job vacancies and unemployed job seekers coexist because of imperfect information. Time and money are required for the unemployed to discover the available jobs, their rates of pay, and their working conditions. Such is also the case for employers to identify applicants and determine their suitability. The process of matching job seekers with job vacancies yields benefits—both to the individual employers and employees involved and to society—but it also involves costs. By improving the flow of information, it may be possible to reduce the amount of frictional unemployment. However, it is unlikely that such unemployment could be eliminated, nor is it necessarily the case that reducing frictional unemployment would be desirable. In many circumstances the benefits of search and the acquisition of information by employers and job seekers will exceed the costs. In such cases it is both privately and socially optimal for the parties to engage in such activity. Furthermore, the additional benefits of reducing frictional unemployment—perhaps by reducing the time needed to locate job vacancies—may not exceed the additional costs associated with bringing about this change. In these circumstances it would not be desirable to implement policies intended to reduce frictional unemployment.

Frictional unemployment may also take the form of **temporary layoffs**. Even in the

[1]"UI" is used for convenience to refer to unemployment insurance in general, not a specific program.

absence of fluctuations in aggregate economic activity, individual firms and industries are affected by changes in product demand due to changes in international economic conditions, consumer demand, weather, work stoppages, and so on. Employers may respond to reductions in demand in a variety of ways: inventory accumulation, wage and/or hours reduction affecting most or all of the work force, or temporary layoffs affecting a portion of the work force. The combination chosen will depend on a variety of factors discussed below. For some firms and industries temporary layoffs are a common form of adjustment to changing circumstances. As explained previously, individuals who have been laid off and are expecting to be recalled to their former employer are classified as unemployed even though they may not be searching for work. Temporary layoffs typically account for 7 to 12 percent of unemployment in Canada (Kaliski, 1985). About 20 percent of workers on temporary layoff search for work, perhaps because they are uncertain about being recalled or perhaps because they are using the opportunity to try to find a better job. Workers on temporary layoff are considered to be frictionally unemployed in the sense that the fluctuations in individual markets which give rise to layoffs are part of the normal "frictions" of a decentralized market economy. However, temporary layoffs are conceptually different from other forms of frictional unemployment in that job vacancies for these workers do not necessarily exist at the time of the survey; rather, the unemployed are waiting for their previous jobs to reappear.

Temporary layoffs in response to fluctuations in demand can be an efficient arrangement from the perspective of both employers and employees if other forms of adjustment (inventory accumulation, wage and/or hours reductions) are costly, and if the costs to workers of brief periods of temporary unemployment (and reduced income) are not too high.

STRUCTURAL UNEMPLOYMENT

Structural unemployment results when the skills or location of the unemployed are not matched with the characteristics of the job vacancies. Unemployed workers and job vacancies are considered to be in different labour markets, either by virtue of geography or because they do not coincide in terms of qualifications and characteristics. The analogy that is often used is that of matching square pegs to round holes. As is the case with frictional unemployment, structural unemployment is characterized by the coexistence of unemployed workers and job vacancies. However, in this case, successful matching of workers and jobs requires more than acquisition of information. In particular, employees or employers will either have to relocate—when there are job vacancies in one region and unemployed workers in another—or alter their characteristics or requirements (in the case of mismatching along occupational and skill lines). Proposed solutions to structural unemployment usually involve improving the human capital characteristics of the workers by education or training programs or encouraging labour mobility and job search in other regions. They could also include adapting the characteristics of the jobs themselves by altering entrance requirements, rearranging the basic job components to adapt to available skills, and even job enrichment and job enlargement. Regional development policies which attempt to expand employment opportunities in areas with high levels of structural unemployment have also been used in Canada.

One of the most difficult issues relating to structural unemployment involves determining whether a particular situation is temporary or permanent. For example, suppose that there is an increase in demand in one industry, occupation, or region, giving rise to job vacancies in that sector and a decrease in demand in another industry, occupation, or region, giving rise to unemployed workers in that sector. If these changes in demand are permanent in nature, the resulting unemployment is clearly structural and the best course of action will usually be to adjust to the structural change, perhaps via retraining or relocation. However, if the changes in demand are temporary in nature, the resulting unemployment is more frictional than structural and the best course of action may well be to simply wait for demand to return to normal levels in each sector. In these circumstances, costly activities such as relocation or retraining are inappropriate because they yield negligible (perhaps zero) benefits. Unfortunately, it is not always evident in advance which situations are temporary and which are permanent. From the perspective of individuals adversely affected by economic change, this uncertainty implies that it may not be clear whether investments such as retraining or relocation are worthwhile. In these circumstances, some individuals may wait for the uncertainty to be resolved before taking action. Providing it is based on a careful assessment of the likelihood of demand returning to previous levels, and not on "wishful thinking," waiting for the resolution of uncertainty can be viewed as a productive activity analogous to the acquisition of information associated with job search. Waiting can result in the acquisition of information about future developments while job search can result in acquiring information about current job opportunities.

When the changes giving rise to structural unemployment are clearly permanent in nature, the best course of action—both from the perspective of the individuals involved and from that of society—usually will be to adjust to the altered circumstances. An exception occurs for people near the end of their working lives. For these individuals, the benefits of retraining or relocation may not justify the costs, and alternatives such as early retirement may be best, given the available options.

The distinction between frictional and structural unemployment can be blurred conceptually, and in practice it can be difficult to clearly delineate the two. Nevertheless, these are differences in degree if not in kind. Frictional unemployment is a result of the matching process; structural unemployment occurs when there is mismatching. Frictional unemployment is associated with job search in an individual labour market; structural unemployment involves more costly solutions, ranging from retraining for a job within the individual labour market to job search and relocation in other labour markets. Frictional unemployment is associated with a productive activity—the acquisition of information regarding job opportunities and applicants—and thus policies designed to reduce frictional unemployment are not necessarily desirable. Structural unemployment that is clearly permanent in nature is not associated with a productive activity and actions to reduce this type of unemployment should be taken, providing the benefits from doing so exceed the costs. What the two have in common is that they are related to the characteristics of the workers and the job, not to the general state of aggregate demand in the economy. Even here, though, the distinction between demand-deficient unemployment and non-demand-deficient unemployment (frictional, structural) may become blurred as the characteristics of the work force and of jobs themselves may be related to the aggregate state of the economy.

DEMAND-DEFICIENT UNEMPLOYMENT

Demand-deficient unemployment exists when there is insufficient aggregate demand in the economy to provide jobs. It is not a matter of workers engaging in normal job search or lacking the correct skills or being in the wrong labour market; rather it is a matter of insufficient aggregate demand to generate sufficient job vacancies. Therefore, job vacancies would fall short of the number of unemployed job seekers. That is, defining labour supply as employed plus unemployed, and labour demand as employed plus vacancies, then insufficient demand, defined as being less than supply, would imply vacancies being less than the number unemployed.

Demand-deficient unemployment is usually associated with adverse business cycle conditions; hence, the term **cyclical unemployment** is often used. However, it may also be associated with a chronic (as opposed to short-term cyclical) insufficiency of aggregate demand as occurred, for example, in the Great Depression of the 1930s. Since the cause of such unemployment is a deficiency of aggregate demand, its cures usually involve macroeconomic policies to increase consumption, investment, exports, or government spending, or to decrease imports and taxes. Monetary, fiscal, and exchange rate policies are the traditional macroeconomic instruments.

SEASONAL UNEMPLOYMENT

Seasonal unemployment is often associated with insufficient demand in a particular season. In this sense it can be considered demand-deficient unemployment; nevertheless, it is different in the sense that it is not a shortage of aggregate demand for the economy as a whole, but rather a shortage of demand in a particular season. The patterns are usually predictable over the year and specific to particular industries. For example, seasonal unemployment is usually prevalent in the winter months in construction, agriculture, and the tourist trade. Seasonal fluctuations in labour supply may also occur, the most significant example being the large number of college and university students who enter the labour force during the summer.

Seasonal unemployment is analogous in several respects to temporary layoffs, and is therefore often included under the rubric of frictional unemployment. Both seasonal unemployment and temporary layoffs involve workers returning to their previous job or employer. To the extent that layoffs or seasonal unemployment are anticipated, employees generally will receive some compensation ex ante in the form of a wage premium to compensate them for the probability of being unemployed.

To a certain extent seasonal jobs could be adapted to employ more people over the slow season. Some construction jobs could be modified so as to be more continuous throughout the year. Tourist facilities can likewise adapt; for example, winter ski areas can become summer schools in other sports or crafts. In some industries, like agriculture, migrant labour often moves to other labour markets, following the seasonal patterns of demand.

Clearly the fact that such adaptation of jobs and workers can and does go on illustrates that seasonal unemployment is not immutable. It is related to the costs and benefits of reducing such unemployment, and the private market will respond to changes in these costs and benefits. For example, to the extent that the cost to employers and employees of seasonal unemployment is reduced by the availability of unemployment insurance benefits, then one may expect more seasonal unemployment.

Aggregate unemployment rates are often referred to as seasonally adjusted or unadjusted. The seasonally unadjusted figures simply show the unemployment rate as it is in a particular month, unadjusted for seasonal fluctuations. The seasonally adjusted figures show the unemployment rate that would have prevailed had the particular month not been associated with unusually high or low seasonal demand conditions. Those who are seasonally unemployed are not removed from the figures; they are simply averaged in over the year.

INVOLUNTARY UNEMPLOYMENT AND WAGE RIGIDITY

Another distinction often made is that between **voluntary and involuntary unemployment**. According to the most common definition of these terms, individuals are involuntarily unemployed if they are willing to work at the going wage rate for their skills or occupation but they are unable to find a job. Voluntary unemployment exists when a job is available but the worker is not willing to accept it at the existing wage rate. These definitions are based on the willingness to work at the prevailing wage, rather than on the reason for becoming unemployed, such as job loser or job leaver. Nonetheless, many job losers may be involuntarily unemployed and many job leavers voluntarily unemployed.

Cyclical unemployment is often viewed as being largely involuntary in nature because evidence suggests that many of those unemployed in economic downturns would accept work, even at wages below the prevailing wage. This phenomenon could be associated with a failure of the wage to adjust to a decline in aggregate demand, creating excess supply of labour at the existing wage rate. For this reason, involuntary unemployment and **wage rigidity** are often regarded as being closely linked. Explaining why wages may not adjust to "clear" the labour market is a puzzle that has challenged economists for many years. Leading responses to that challenge are examined in the next section.

Section Two: Explanations of Unemployment

The economic theory of frictional, structural, and demand-deficient unemployment has received considerable attention, especially in the past three decades. To a considerable extent this interest has been motivated by the increase in unemployment that occurred in many countries during the 1970s and 1980s, remaining stubbornly high during the 1990s. In addition, many economists believed that the theory of unemployment suffered from a lack of clear microeconomic foundations similar to those which provide the basis for the theory of household or firm behaviour. Traditional macroeconomic theories of unemployment merely assumed that unemployment was characterized by wages being set too high, above the market clearing level. What could keep wages rigid, even in the face of the competitive force of the "reserve army of the unemployed"? Significant recent developments that tackle this question include search theory, implicit contracts, efficiency wages, and insider-outsider theories.

SEARCH UNEMPLOYMENT

The **job search** and **matching** process is associated with imperfect information on both sides of the labour market. Unemployed workers are not aware of all available jobs, their rates of pay, location, and working conditions. Employers with job vacancies are not aware of all individual workers and their characteristics. If both sides were fully informed, the process of matching workers and jobs could take place in a few days, if not hours. However, because the acquisition of information about job opportunities and job applicants takes time, unemployment and unfilled vacancies coexist.

Following the important early contributions of Stigler (1962) and Phelps et al. (1970), the economics of job search has received considerable attention in the past three decades. To illustrate the main ideas we focus primarily on the job search process of employees. Original work on employer search is discussed in Lippman and McCall (1976) and in the Canadian context in Maki (1971, Chap. 3).

Job search is an economic decision in that it involves both costs and benefits. There are two main aspects to the decision: (1) determining whether it is worthwhile *initiating* the job search process and (2) once begun, determining when to *discontinue* the process. For employees, initiating a job search or continuing to search rather than accepting the first job offer that comes along may yield benefits in the form of a superior job offer involving higher wages or better working conditions. Similarly, by continuing to search rather than filling the job with the first "warm body" that becomes available, the firm may obtain benefits in the form of more suitable or more qualified applicants. In both cases the magnitude of these benefits is uncertain; their size depends on the employee's expectations regarding the probability of receiving a superior job offer or on the firm's expectations regarding the quality of future applicants. Those engaged in search must make their decisions on the basis of expectations—that is, the information available ex ante. The realized or ex post benefits may turn out to be larger or smaller than the expected benefits.

The expected benefits have to be weighed against the costs of search. These include both the direct costs—such as the firm's costs of advertising positions and interviewing applicants and the employee's costs of sending applications and travelling to interviews—and the indirect or opportunity costs. For employees the opportunity costs are measured by the best alternative use of their time devoted to job search. For those who quit their previous job to search for a better one their opportunity cost would be their previous wage. For others the opportunity cost would be measured by the best job offer received so far or the wage that could be earned in some job that is known to be available. It could also be an individual's implicit home wage or the value of their time doing household work. For employers the opportunity cost of continuing to search is the difference between the value of the output that would be produced by the best known applicant and the wages that would be paid to that applicant.

Not all job seekers are unemployed; some individuals will search for a better job while employed. Employed search has the advantage of being less costly. However, it may also be less effective because of the difficulties associated with contacting potential employers and following up promising opportunities while working, especially if employed on a full-time basis. In some circumstances individuals may choose to quit their current job in order to search for a better one, while in other circumstances employed search will be the preferred method.

The central assumption in the economic analysis of job search is that individuals will search in an optimal fashion—that is, will choose their search activities in order to maximize their expected utility. Note, however, that the assumption of optimal search behaviour does not imply that all unemployed job seekers have *chosen* to be unemployed or that all search unemployment is voluntary in nature. Individuals who quit their previous job in order to search for a new job—the "job leavers" in Table 17.2—may have chosen unemployment. Rational employees would not do so unless the expected utility of searching for a new job exceeds the expected utility of remaining in the existing job. However, as Table 17.2 indicates, about half the unemployed are "job losers"; many of these individuals may have preferred to remain in their previous job. Nonetheless, given that they have lost their previous job, rational individuals will carry out their job search in an optimal fashion. In the case of a person who is risk-neutral, this assumption implies that the individual will choose the amount of search activity that maximizes the net expected benefit (expected benefits minus expected costs). Risk-averse employees will also take into account the costs and benefits of search, but will attach a greater weight to benefits and costs which are certain compared to those which are uncertain. The basic principles of optimal job search are most easily explained in the context of risk-neutral searchers. However, very similar principles and conclusions follow when individuals are risk-averse.

In order to maximize the net expected benefits of job search, employees should continue searching until the marginal expected benefit of search equals the marginal expected cost. This condition is simply another example of the rule that the net benefit of any activity is maximized by expanding the activity to the point at which its marginal benefit equals its marginal cost. Figure 18.1 shows the way in which the benefits and costs of search are likely to be related to the amount of time devoted to job search. The case in which search is worthwhile is illustrated (i.e., total expected benefits exceed total costs). For low levels of search, the marginal costs of search are fairly low because low-cost, usually informal, search processes can be used. For example, friends and relatives can be contacted, want ads examined, and perhaps a few telephone calls made. As the search continues, however, more costly processes are often necessary to acquire additional labour market information. For example, it may be necessary to apply directly to a company or to sign up with an employment service. In some cases it may even be necessary to change locations or to quit working if one already has a job. For these reasons the marginal cost of search probably rises with the amount of job search undertaken, as depicted in Figure 18.1.

The marginal benefits of search, on the other hand, probably are a declining function of the amount of search undertaken. One starts out the search process with an examination of the most promising alternatives and then continues examining further activities in the

Figure 18.1 **Optimal Job Search**

The expected optimal time spent searching for a job will maximize the present value of the difference between the expected benefits and costs of search. The expected benefits, B, are increasing with time spent searching, and the expected costs of search, C, also increase with search duration. The optimal amount of search will maximize the difference between B and C. This difference is maximized when the expected marginal benefit of search equals the expected marginal cost, at expected search duration S_e. As shown in the bottom panel, shorter expected searches than S_e yield a situation where an extra "day" of search has a higher expected benefit than cost, and is thus worth conducting. Similarly, longer searches reduce net benefits.

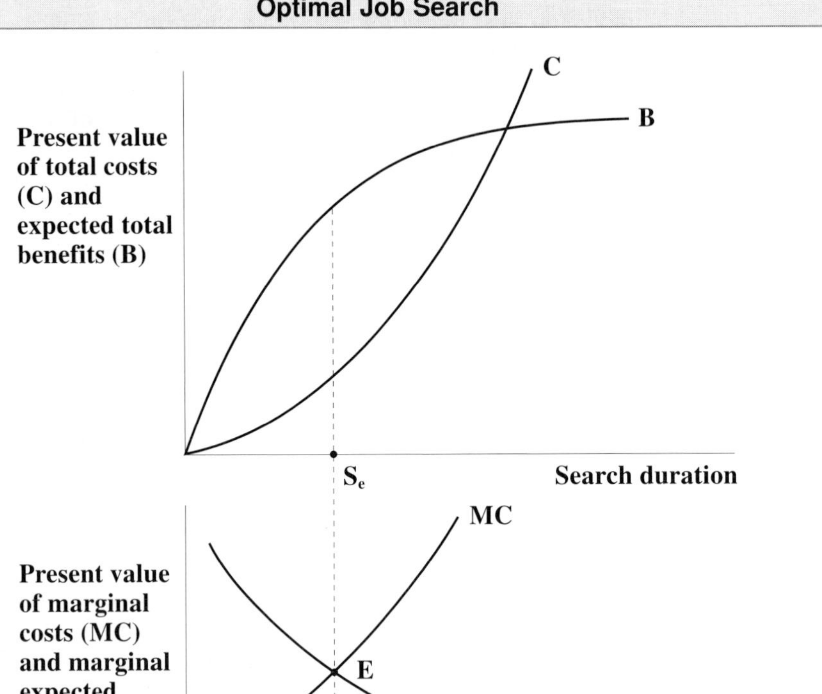

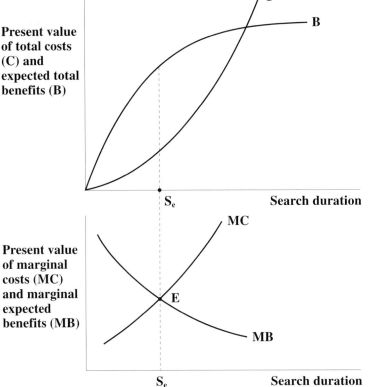

hope of finding an even better one. Obviously, a better alternative may occur; however, one may encounter diminishing returns with respect to the additional information. As search continues it becomes less likely—but still possible—that a better offer will be received simply because there are fewer options left to examine.

Given the costs and benefits of additional search, the rational individual will acquire labour market information and engage in search until the point E, where the marginal expected benefits equal the marginal cost. To the left of E, the benefits of additional search exceed the cost and hence additional search is worthwhile; to the right of E, the benefits of additional search are not worth the costs. In this sense E will be an equilibrium with S_e being the optimal amount of expected search activity. Note, however, that S_e is the *expected* amount of search required to maximize net benefits. The actual amount of search undertaken in any particular situation may turn out to differ from S_e. For example, a lucky individual who receives an extremely good job offer during the first week will experience an actual search duration less than S_e because the best course of action will be to accept the job and discontinue the search. Similarly, an unlucky individual may have to search longer than anticipated, or accept a lower-paying job than expected.

The conditions for optimal search can alternatively be stated in terms of a **stopping rule**: the individual should choose a minimum acceptable wage and search until a job paying this wage or better is found. The minimum acceptable wage is often referred to as a **reservation wage**, although this concept is not identical to the reservation wage discussed in Chapter 2 on labour force participation. Choosing a minimum acceptable wage is equivalent to choosing an expected search duration. On average, given the distribution of wage offers in the market and the rate at which firms can be contacted, the individual will require the expected search duration to find an acceptable job. The minimum acceptable wage is therefore chosen to equate the marginal benefits and marginal costs of search.

Note that these decision rules imply that workers and firms will, in general, discontinue their search activities before they are fully informed. That is, optimal decision making implies that it is typically worthwhile to acquire some information prior to making a decision (information for which the marginal benefits exceed marginal costs) but to not acquire all the available information. Because of diminishing returns to information acquisition, and possibly also rising marginal costs of information acquisition, workers and firms will discontinue their search activities prior to being fully informed.

Several implications follow from these optimal search decision rules. First, a labour market characterized by imperfect information will not "clear" instantaneously. While the process of *matching* workers and jobs proceeds, demand will not equal supply at each moment. Indeed, because search, information acquisition, and matching take time, unsatisfied demand (unfilled job vacancies) and unutilized supply (unemployed job seekers) will coexist at any point in time.

A related implication of imperfect information is that there generally will be a distribution of wage rates even in a labour market with homogeneous workers and jobs. This situation is illustrated in panel (a) of Figure 18.2, in contrast to the full-information case shown in panel (b). Some employers will pay wages above the market average, both because they are not fully informed about wages offered by other firms and they may wish to expand their work force at a rapid rate, an aspect which is discussed further below. Similarly, other firms may offer wages below the market average. In fact, this dispersion of wages is necessary for search to exist in the first place. Because workers are not fully informed about the wages offered by all firms, some unemployed job seekers may accept employment at firms offering below average wages, an outcome that would not occur under full information.

A further, and closely related, implication is that under imperfect information employers possess some short-run monopsony power, even though the market is otherwise

Figure 18.2 Wage Distributions Under Imperfect and Perfect Information

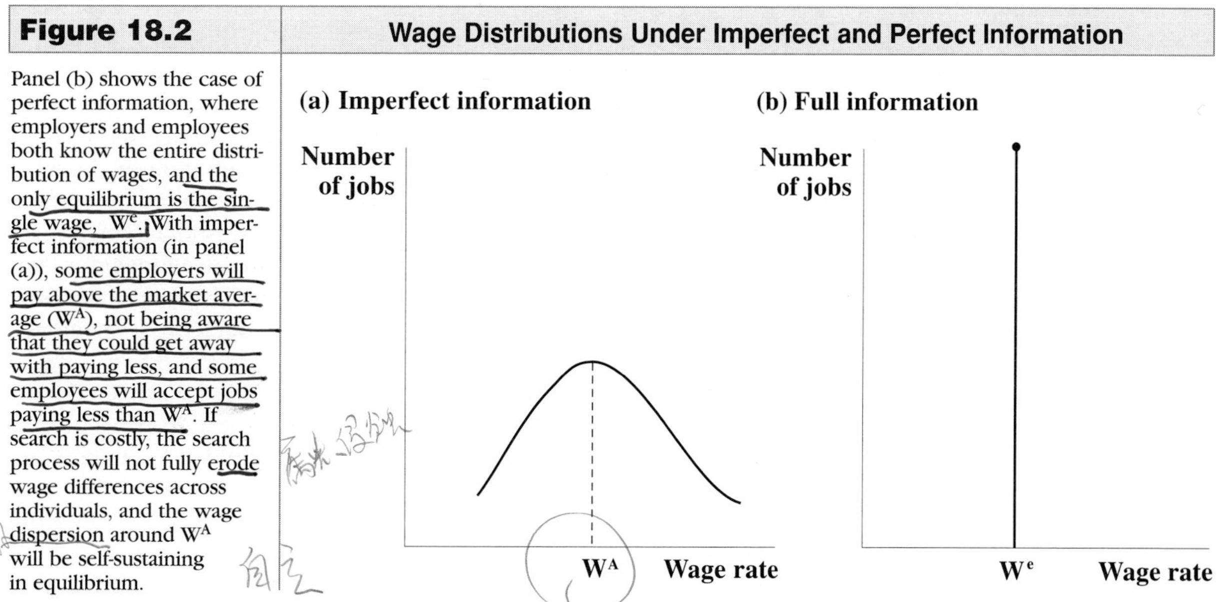

Panel (b) shows the case of perfect information, where employers and employees both know the entire distribution of wages, and the only equilibrium is the single wage, W^e. With imperfect information (in panel (a)), some employers will pay above the market average (W^A), not being aware that they could get away with paying less, and some employees will accept jobs paying less than W^A. If search is costly, the search process will not fully erode wage differences across individuals, and the wage dispersion around W^A will be self-sustaining in equilibrium.

perfectly competitive, and employers are wage-takers in the long run. This situation—referred to as **dynamic monopsony**—is most readily understood by assuming that workers have some information about the distribution of wage rates available in the market, that is, the distribution illustrated in Figure 18.2(a), but do not, in the absence of search, know the wage rates offered by individual employers. In these circumstances, when an unemployed job seeker receives a job offer, she must decide whether to accept the offer or continue searching. She will be more likely to accept an offer that appears to be above average (based on her beliefs about the distribution of wage rates available in the market) than one that appears to be below average. Thus, from the perspective of the employer with unfilled job vacancies, paying a high wage (relative to what other firms are believed to be paying) increases the probability that an offer will be accepted and vice versa for offering a low wage. In other words, the employer faces an upward-sloping labour supply curve in that the higher the offered wage the greater is the acceptance rate of job offers, or hiring rate.

This discussion also indicates that in markets characterized by imperfect information the wage rate does not adjust instantaneously to equate labour demand and supply. Employers who find that their acceptance rate of job offers is low will, over time, adjust upward their offered wages, especially if it is very costly to leave jobs unfilled. Similarly, employers who discover that their offers are immediately accepted may lower their offered wages. These adjustments can be expected to occur gradually because it takes time for employers to become aware of how their offered wages compare to those available elsewhere, as well as to observe the rate at which their offers are accepted.

Factors Determining Optimal Search

This framework is useful to illustrate how the optimal amount of search depends on the various factors underlying the cost and benefit schedules and how search activity will respond to shifts in these schedules. For example, factors affecting the expected benefits of job search are the dispersion of wage offers (for otherwise comparable jobs) and the expected duration of the job. If there is little variation in the attractiveness of different jobs in terms of wages and working conditions, there is little point in continuing to search once an offer has been received. In contrast, if some jobs are much more desirable than others, the optimal strategy may be to continue searching even after receiving an average job offer. Similarly, if some potential jobs are more desirable than others, it will be rational to devote more time to search if it is anticipated that the duration of employment will be long, because of the longer period over which the benefits of a superior job can be enjoyed.

These two factors may help explain the observed differences in the average duration of unemployment across age and sex groups, as summarized in Table 17.4. Because of their limited work experience, youths typically face a less dispersed distribution of potential wages than older workers. In addition, many youths try out a variety of jobs before settling on a career; thus, on average, their expected duration of employment is much lower than is the case for adult workers. For both these reasons, there is less incentive for youths than for adult workers to continue searching in the expectation of obtaining a better job. These considerations are consistent with the observation that the average duration of unemployment of youths is significantly lower than that of adults.

Shifts in the schedules may affect the number of searchers as well as the expected duration of search. For example, an increase in expected total benefits or a decrease in total costs will imply a larger number of people for whom search is worthwhile. As a consequence the following may be observed: more entry and reentry into the labour force, an increase in the number of quits as more employed workers seek a new job, and more search by the employed.

Given the central role played by imperfect information in the job search model, impor-

Exhibit 18.1

Mandatory Notice and Unemployment

Employment protection laws take a variety of forms, including severance or redundancy pay, mandatory notice, and requirements to establish adjustment programs to assist displaced workers. In Canada, mandatory notice is the primary legal obligation on employers who wish to reduce their work force for "economic" reasons. All jurisdictions (federal, provincial, and the territories) have some form of advance notice requirement for individual layoffs or dismissals. Several provinces have additional requirements for mass layoffs. In addition, under Canadian common law, "reasonable" notice must be provided to employees dismissed for economic reasons.

Does mandatory notice reduce unemployment? By giving employees time to search prior to the termination of their existing job, some may be able to move from one job to another, without an intervening period of nonemployment, thus reducing the incidence of unemployment. Others may be able to begin the search process during the notice period, and to thereby reduce the duration of unemployment.

The impact of mandatory notice on unemployment has been examined by Jones and Kuhn (1995) using a sample of workers laid off due to plant closures in Ontario. They find that even small amounts of notice are quite helpful in reducing the number of workers who experience some unemployment following displacement (the incidence of unemployment). For example, giving notice of less than one month reduces the proportion of workers in a shutdown who experience unemployment from 92 percent to 76 percent. However, Jones and Kuhn also find that there are few, if any, additional gains from providing notice of more than one month, and they even find some evidence that notice of more than six months can be harmful to workers.

Unfortunately, there appears to be little scope for using advance notice to reduce the long-term unemployment that results from many mass layoffs. In particular, Jones and Kuhn find that, no matter how much notice is given, about 30 percent of workers remain unemployed one year after shutdown. The reason appears to be that, except in small amounts, pre-displacement search is significantly less effective than post-displacement search in obtaining re-employment, a conclusion also reached in several U.S. studies of displaced workers (e.g., Swaim and Podgursky, 1990; Ruhm, 1992).

tant factors determining the value of job search are the institutional mechanisms for disseminating labour market information. These mechanisms are currently undergoing dramatic change, and there are literally hundreds of "jobs.com" sites in existence. These Web sites range from the very general to the very specialized (e.g., "Meat and Poultry Online"), significantly facilitating information exchange between employers and employees (see Kuhn, 2000a). Other factors affecting the benefits and costs of search include the number of employers with job vacancies, the rate at which employers make job offers, the value of "leisure" time (time spent not searching or working), the number of other searchers competing for the available jobs, and the occupational and regional segmentation of labour markets. Social and labour market policies can also alter the costs and benefits of search and hence its amount and duration. Unemployment insurance and portable pensions would reduce the total and marginal costs of search and hence increase the number of searchers and the optimal duration of search. Improving the arrangements for

www.jobs.com
www.workopolis.com

disseminating labour market information would increase the total benefits and, in most cases, the marginal benefits as well. Thus the number of job seekers would increase but the expected duration would fall. The total amount of search unemployment may either increase or decrease, depending on which effect is larger.

Aggregate economic conditions can also affect the schedules and hence the amount and duration of job search. In recessions the expected benefits of search decline because there are fewer unfilled vacancies and more job losers competing for the available jobs. The downward shift in the benefit schedule can be expected to result in fewer employed workers quitting their jobs to search for a new job, which explains why the quit rate varies pro-cyclically. The tendency for quits to decline in recessions is partially evident in Table 17.2, which shows that the proportion of job leavers as a share of separations falls as the unemployment rate rises, and rises as the economy recovers. The decline in the benefits of search will also result in less entry into and more withdrawal from the labour force, as fewer of the unemployed find search worthwhile. This "discouraged worker" phenomenon was discussed previously in the context of hidden unemployment. Because of this phenomenon the labour force participation rate also varies pro-cyclically. As a further consequence, in a recession the rise in unemployment will be less than the decline in employment; the opposite occurs as the economy recovers from the recession.

The job search paradigm may also help explain why wages adjust slowly to excess supply or demand in the labour market. As noted above, the optimal search strategy involves choosing an acceptance wage and searching until a job offering this wage or better is found. Thus wages are not adjusted downward even if an acceptable job is not found quickly. Over time, unemployed searchers will revise downward their acceptance wages if they discover that their initial beliefs regarding the distribution of wage offers and the rate at which job offers are made were too optimistic, as would be the case if there were more labour supply or less demand than originally anticipated. However, because this learning process takes time, the adjustment of wages to excess demand or supply will occur less quickly than in the presence of complete information.

Empirical Evidence

www.statcan.ca/english/Subjects/Labour/LFS/lfs-en.htm

A significant amount of job searching takes place. Table 18.1 provides information on job search activity for 1995, based on the Labour Force Survey. First, note that more than 5 percent of all employed workers are looking for another job. Part-time workers are disproportionately represented in this group, as they are presumably looking for better jobs. Most of the unemployed are also looking for full-time work. Among those individuals who are searching, Table 18.1 indicates that the most common search activities are directly contacting employers and looking at job advertisements.

Grenon (1998, 1999) provides further detail on search methods and their relative success. His tabulations confirm that directly contacting employers is the most common search activity because it is the best: almost half of all jobs were ultimately found this way. Informal discussions with friends and relatives was the next most popular and effective means of search, accounting for a quarter of successes. Perhaps most surprising is the small and diminishing role played by government employment agencies. But as mentioned earlier, the mechanisms of search are not stable, and are subject to technological change. The Internet, most importantly, facilitates information exchange between job seekers and potential employers. Employees also have much better information about the wage distribution. Peter Kuhn (2000a) reports U.S. evidence showing that 15 percent of unemployed, and 7 percent of employed, workers use the Internet to scout for jobs. This number can be expected to grow as Internet use becomes more widespread and the Web sites more sophisticated.

Table 18.1 Search Activity of the Employed and Unemployed, 1995

Group and Search Activity		Number Using Activity (thousands)	% Using Activity[a]
Employed:[b]	Full-time	426	3.9
	Part-time	311	12.4
Unemployed:	Did not search	306	20.8
	Searched for full-time work	983	66.9
	Searched for part-time work	180	12.3
Search activity:	Contacted employers directly	730	49.7
	Used public employment agency	380	25.9
	Looked at advertisements	583	39.7
	Used other methods	420	28.6

Notes:
[a]For search activities, the sum of the methods does not equal the total because many of the individuals use more than one method.
[b]Data on employed search comes from the *Labour Force Annual Averages*, 1995.

Source: Adapted from Statistics Canada, "Labour force annual averages," Catalogue 71-220, 1999 (See note b for Employed data).

There is an extensive empirical literature estimating formal models of search behaviour, testing some of the propositions outlined here.[2] For example, in a series of papers exploiting administrative data, Belzil (1993, 1996) explores the relative efficiency of unemployed and employed job search. Belzil (1993) finds that if job quality is measured by the duration of the accepted job, then those who use employed job search ultimately obtain better jobs. In Belzil (1996), this finding is confirmed and refined. For younger workers, unemployed job search may actually be more effective. His findings may provide a partial explanation for the patterns reported in Table 17.4, where the incidence of unemployment is higher for young workers. Their higher unemployment incidence may reflect the rational choice to engage in unemployed job search in the pursuit of better job matches.

Bowlus (1998) and Ferrall (1997) also show the value of the search framework as a lens through which to view the unemployment experience of the young. Both authors use panel data from Canada and the United States from the late 1980s to follow young workers as they move into and out of jobs. By specifying an econometric model of the decisions that workers make in response to the jobs they find, both authors are able to identify key features of the "matching process" in Canada and the United States. Bowlus finds that the higher unemployment rate of young and low-skilled Canadian workers is consistent with greater search frictions in the Canadian labour market: the Canadian jobs are shorter, and harder to find. These greater frictions also map into a higher degree of monopsony power for Canadian employers, which helps sustain the frictions. Ferrall's study focuses on similar workers, but his emphasis is on the impact of UI on individuals as they leave school. In particular, he asks whether the Canadian unemployment insurance system affects the search behaviour of these young workers. While his conclusions concerning the frictions in Canada's labour market are similar to Bowlus', Ferrall finds that unemployment insurance actually speeds up young Canadian's acceptance of their "first" job, as workers need to obtain employment in order to subsequently qualify for unemployment insurance.

[2]See Mortensen and Pissarides (1999) for an up-to-date and comprehensive review of the theoretical and empirical search literature.

In summary, labour market search is an important activity among the unemployed, some of the employed, and many employers. Most fundamentally, the economic analysis of job search helps explain the coexistence of unemployed workers and unfilled vacancies and the process through which these are matched. More specifically, search theory offers insights into several phenomena, including the duration of unemployment, the cyclical behaviour of quits and labour force participation, the sluggish adjustment of wages to changes in economic conditions, and the consequences of public policies such as unemployment insurance and the provision of labour market information.

IMPLICIT CONTRACTS

While search theory is concerned with the process of matching job vacancies and unemployed workers, **implicit contract theory** deals with issues that may arise when firms and workers are already engaged in a continuing employment relationship. In particular, implicit contract theory seeks to explain phenomena such as rigid wages and the use of quantity adjustments (layoffs and rehires) rather than wage adjustments to respond to variations in product demand. Our emphasis in this section is on the way in which implicit contract theory can generate rigid wages and layoffs as the optimal arrangement between willing workers and firms.

Implicit contract theory is based on the view that wage and employment behaviour reflects **risk-sharing** between employers and employees. Risk-sharing arises because of differences in attitudes toward risk between workers and the owners of firms. Specifically, workers are believed to be more risk-averse than the shareholders of firms. These differences in attitudes toward risk create potential gains from trade; that is, both parties can benefit from a risk-sharing arrangement. Because workers dislike fluctuations in their incomes, they prefer an arrangement whereby they receive a somewhat lower average or expected income provided their income is sufficiently less variable (more certain). The owners of firms also prefer this arrangement because average or expected profits are higher (due to lower labour costs), albeit more variable because of the stabilization of workers' incomes. In effect, the employment relation involves two transactions: (1) provision of labour services by employees in exchange for payment by employers and (2) provision of insurance services by employers in exchange for payment of an insurance premium (acceptance of a lower wage) by employees. For reasons discussed below, workers are generally unable to purchase insurance against the risk of income fluctuations in regular insurance markets such as those that exist for accident, property, and life insurance. However, the continuing nature of the employment relationship makes feasible the implicit purchase of income insurance from the employer.

Seminal contributions to implicit contract theory were made by Azariadis (1975), Baily (1974), and Gordon (1974). A large literature, much of it highly technical in nature, has subsequently developed. Our purpose in this section is to present the basic elements of implicit contract theory in as nontechnical a fashion as possible. Further details are available in surveys by Azariadis (1979), Azariadis and Stiglitz (1983), Hart (1983), and Rosen (1985).

Differences in attitudes toward risk between employers and employees provide the basis for both parties to benefit from a risk-sharing arrangement. Two reasons why workers may be more risk-averse than the owners of firms have been advanced. Perhaps the most significant factor is that for many workers their wealth consists largely of the value of their human capital, which cannot be diversified. In contrast, individuals whose wealth consists largely of financial capital can reduce the risk of a reduction in their wealth by holding a diversified portfolio; that is, by acquiring shares in (or income claims on) a variety of companies. It is not possible to diversify wealth holdings in the form of human capital because markets analogous to the stock market do not exist for buying and selling claims on the incomes of different individuals or groups of individuals. Such markets would constitute a form of slavery and would therefore be illegal, even if there were sufficient demand to make markets for trading in such claims viable. Workers, therefore, are in the awkward position of having most of their wealth in one risky asset—their human capital. As a consequence, they seek alternative ways of reducing the risk of fluctuations in the return on that asset, their employment income.

A second reason for differences in risk attitudes involves sorting according to innate risk preferences. Those who are venturesome—risk-neutral or perhaps even risk lovers—may be more likely to become entrepreneurs and thus the owners of firms. Cautious or risk-averse individuals may be more likely to become employees and wage earners.

If workers dislike the risk of fluctuations in their employment income, why do they not purchase income insurance from private insurance companies? Private markets for income insurance do not exist because of two phenomena—moral hazard and adverse selection—that may result in the selling of such insurance being an unprofitable activity, despite the demand that exists for the product. **Moral hazard** exists when individuals can influence the risk against which they are insured. For example, suppose workers are insured against reductions in their income associated with becoming unemployed. The fact that they are insured could affect their behaviour such that they are then more likely to be unemployed and collecting insurance—perhaps because such workers who become unemployed search longer for a better job when they are insured or because they become more willing to accept a job with a high risk of layoff than they would if they were not insured. Thus the profitability of selling such insurance is reduced, perhaps to the point at which selling such insurance is unprofitable.

Adverse selection occurs when the insurer cannot observe the risk that a particular insuree represents. The insurer thus charges each customer the same rate. However, the high-risk individuals are more likely and the low-risk individuals less likely to purchase insurance. Thus the average risk among those who purchase insurance will be higher than the risk for the population as a whole. The insurer will therefore earn less—perhaps incurring a loss—than would be expected on the basis of population risk statistics. Furthermore, raising its insurance rates may not increase profitability because fewer individuals will purchase insurance at the higher rates *and* those who decide not to purchase insurance because of the higher rates will be the customers facing the lowest risk. Thus, with each increase in its rates, the insurance company ends up selling to a smaller number of customers with a higher average risk. In these circumstances, there may be no price that would enable insurance to be sold at a profit.

Moral hazard and adverse selection may exist in any insurance market. In some cases—such as automobile insurance for most individuals and life insurance for individuals under 65—the reduction in profitability due to moral hazard and adverse selection is small enough that private insurance markets continue to exist. In other cases—such as life insurance for individuals over 65 and income insurance in the labour market—the reduction in profitability is evidently large enough that insurance against these risks cannot be purchased in the usual fashion. The central hypothesis of implicit contract theory is that employees purchase income insurance indirectly from the employer. The continuing nature of the employment relationship enables the employer to deal with the moral hazard and adverse selection problems. The firm provides insurance only to its own employees, thus avoiding adverse selection. In addition, the firm controls the probability of income loss due to layoff or wage and/or hours reduction, thus avoiding the moral hazard problem.

Implicit contract theory applies to situations in which there is a long-term attachment between the firm and its workers. Many economists have suggested that in labour markets with these characteristics wages do not adjust each period to equate demand and supply. In contrast, many product and asset markets behave like "Walrasian auction markets" in which the price adjusts each period to clear the market. According to implicit contract theory this difference in behaviour reflects risk-sharing in the labour market. The continuing nature of the employment relationship enables the firm to stabilize its employees' incomes over several periods by paying a wage above that which would exist with continuous market-clearing when product demand conditions are weaker than normal, and paying a wage below that which would exist with continuous market-clearing when product demand conditions are stronger than normal.

The reasons for the importance of long-term attachments in the labour market have been discussed in previous chapters. Specific human capital is perhaps the most fundamental factor. As discussed in Chapter 9 on human capital theory, when employees acquire firm-specific human capital due to on-the-job training and experience, then both the employer and the employees subsequently earn rents. The worker receives a wage greater than the alternative wage and the firm earns a marginal revenue product greater than the worker's wage. The fact that both parties are earning rents provides the incentive for each to continue the employment relationship. A second reason for long-term attachments in the labour market is the cost of search and mobility discussed in the previous section. Because finding a new job is costly to employees and hiring new workers is costly to employers, both parties usually prefer to maintain the employment relationship.

Although employers and employees are assumed to be involved in a continuing employment relationship, the basic model of implicit contracts can be explained in a two-period setting. In the initial period, firms offer wage and employment contracts to workers and workers decide which firm's contract to accept. The wages and employment stipulated in these contracts may be contingent on the state of product demand realized in the second period. The contracts agreed to in the first period are then carried out in the second. Thus workers are mobile ex ante (in the initial period when they are choosing which firm's contract to accept) but immobile ex post (in the second period when the uncertainty about product demand conditions is resolved and the terms of the contract are carried out). The assumption of ex post immobility is intended to reflect the continuing nature of the employment relationship and the cost of severing that relationship.

These contractual arrangements are not formal written agreements—hence the term "implicit contract"—but rather represent understandings that govern the behaviour of firms and workers. As stated colourfully by Okun (1981, p. 89), "Employers ... Rely heavily on the 'invisible handshake' as a substitute for the invisible hand that cannot operate effectively in the career labour market." The explicit contracts observed in the union sector may also reflect risk-sharing to some degree, but the purpose of the analysis is to explain behaviour in the unorganized sector.

To keep the analysis simple, we will assume that the workers are homogeneous, each with utility function u(y) where $y = w \times h$ is income, w is the wage rate and h is hours worked. To focus on wages and employment, hours of work will be assumed to be constant at h. A worker is thus either employed, working h hours, or unemployed, working zero hours. With hours of work fixed, an employed worker's utility can be written in terms of the wage rate alone, u(w). An unemployed worker receives utility u(k), where k is the value of leisure time and any unemployment benefit received from the unemployment insurance program. (Workers on layoff receive no income from the employer.) Because workers are homogeneous, which workers are laid off (should layoffs be required) is randomly determined.

Let N_0 be the number of workers attached to the firm; this is the number of workers who agreed to join the firm's "labour pool" given the contract offered in the first period. The firm's labour supply curve in the second period is thus shown by S in Figure 18.3. At wage rates equal to or greater than the reservation wage k, the firm can employ up to N_0 workers. The firm cannot employ any workers at wage rates below k.

We will discuss the case in which perfect competition prevails in the output market so that the price of output is not affected by the output produced and hence labour utilized. The analysis for other product market structures is similar. The firm's labour demand schedule is the locus of points for which wages are just equal to the value of the marginal

Figure 18.3 **Implicit Contracts**

The base case without implicit contracts is shown in panel (a). N_0 workers are attached to the firm, and the value of leisure is k. The supply curve to the firm is perfectly elastic at k for employment levels below N_0, perfectly inelastic at N_0 for wages above k. The firm's labour demand can either be "high," D_a or "low," D_b. Neither workers nor firms know which state will prevail before workers sign on with a firm. In the good state, N_0 workers are employed at W_a; in the bad state, N_b employed workers earn W_b, and unemployed workers "earn" k (not paid by the firm). Earnings variability can be reduced with implicit contracts. Panel (b) shows the case where workers and firms agree that, in the good state, employment will be at N_0 at a wage W*. In the bad state, employment will be higher than before, at N_b^* and wages will be W*, higher than the market-clearing case. For workers, this represents a reduction in risk (fewer layoffs and constant wages). As long as W* is not too low, risk-averse workers will find this attractive. For firms, the wage W* is lower than the expected wage under market-clearing, $\overline{W}$, so expected profits are higher. Firms and workers are thus better off with the risk sharing.

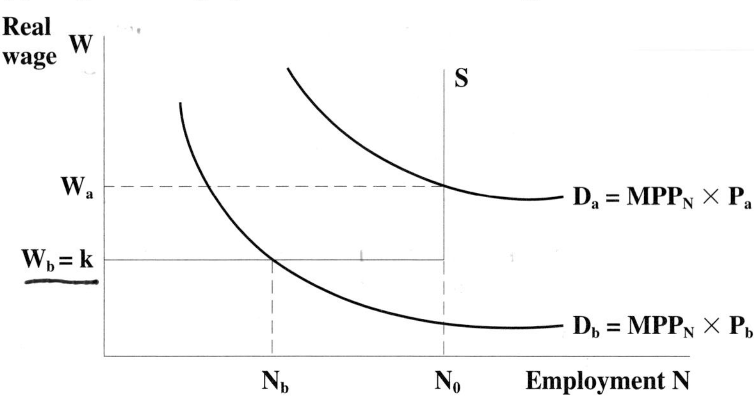

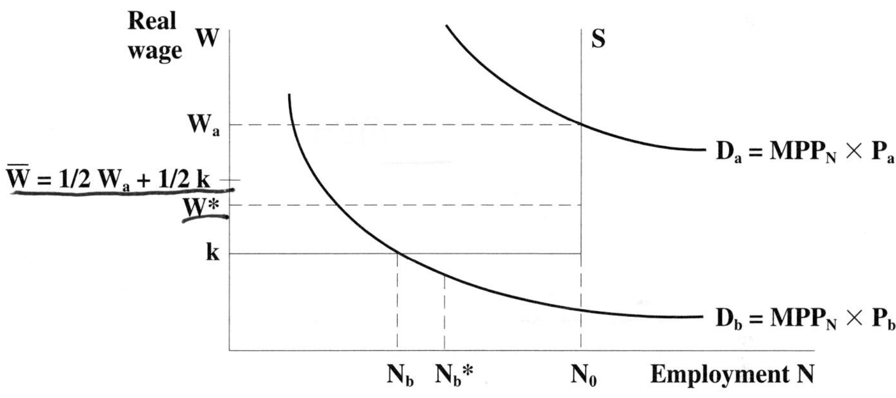

product of labour, which in turn equals the marginal product of labour times the price at which the extra output is sold. That is, $D = VMP_N = MPP_N P$ where MPP_N is the marginal product of labour, and P is the price of output.

There is uncertainty about the state of the product market. When product market conditions are strong, the product price and the demand for labour will be high. The opposite holds in weak product market conditions. For ease of exposition we will assume that there are only two possible states of the product market—the "good state" in which the product price is high at P_a and the "poor state" in which the product price is low at P_b—and that these are equally likely to occur. The assumption of two equi-probable outcomes does not affect the analysis in any way except to make the results easier to present. An important assumption, however, is that both the employer and employees observe the state which is realized. When this **symmetric information** assumption holds, the two parties can make the implicit wage-employment contract contingent on the observed state. When **asymmetric information** exists—for example, if the firm has better information about the state of the product market than the workers do—this type of contingent contract may not be optimal because the firm will usually have an incentive to cheat. For example, if the wage rate depends on the state, the firm may want to claim that the poor state has been realized—whatever the actual state—in order to pay a lower wage. The nature of contracts under asymmetric information is discussed further below.

The behaviour of a continuously clearing labour market, as shown in Figure 18.3(a), provides a useful benchmark for examining the influence of risk-sharing on wages and employment. In the good state the wage rises to W_a and all the workers in the firm's labour pool are employed ($N = N_0$). In the poor state the wage falls to W_b (equal to the reservation wage k) and employment declines to N_b.

It is important to note that there is no involuntary unemployment with market-clearing. In the poor state, the decline in demand produces excess labour supply and the wage rate declines. As the wage falls below k, some workers withdraw from employment. The result is an equilibrium at (W_b, N_b). Because the employed workers are paid the reservation wage k, unemployed workers do not envy the employed workers. Workers are indifferent between being employed and unemployed, given the equilibrium wage rate and their value of leisure time.

As is well known, in the absence of externalities and other sources of market failure, the competitive market-clearing outcome produces an efficient allocation of resources. In the case analyzed here, the allocation of labour among firms was determined ex ante. However, there remains the question of how to best utilize each firm's labour pool. The allocation of workers shown in Figure 18.3(a)—including the fact that N_bN_o workers are not employed in the poor state—is efficient in the sense that it maximizes the value of output produced and income generated in each state. However, with market-clearing, workers face an uncertain income stream. Income may fluctuate because both the wage rate and employment depend on the state which is realized. Because of this income uncertainty, the market-clearing outcome is not, in general, a Pareto-optimal arrangement—that is, it is possible through risk-sharing to make at least one of the parties better off without making the other party worse off—even though it does produce an efficient allocation of labour resources. An optimal arrangement takes into account both efficiency and risk-sharing considerations.

A Pareto-optimal contract between a risk-neutral firm and risk-averse workers has the following features: (1) the real wage rate is independent of the state which is realized, so that employed workers receive the same real wage whatever the level of product demand and (2) layoffs may occur in weak states of demand, though the number of workers laid off will be less than the number who would be voluntarily unemployed under market-clearing. Figure 18.3(b) shows an example of an optimal wage-employment contract. Employed workers receive the wage W* in each state. Employment equals N_0 in the good state and N_b^* in the poor state.

Several features of the optimal contract should be noted. First, the contract provides for a rigid real wage. Employed workers receive the same utility, whatever the state of product demand and the overall price level. The contract wage W* is lower than the market-clearing wage in the good state and higher than with market-clearing in the poor state. Second, there are layoffs in the poor state. However, the number of workers laid off ($N_b^*N_0$) is less than the number that would voluntarily withdraw from employment with market clearing (N_bN_o). Third, there is involuntary unemployment in the poor state, which is why layoffs are necessary. Employed workers receive utility u(W*) whereas unemployed workers receive utility u(k); laid-off workers would prefer to be employed, given that the wage does not decline in the poor state.

The way in which both parties may benefit from a risk-sharing arrangement can be seen in Figure 18.3. Even though the firm is paying a higher wage and employing more workers in the poor state than with market-clearing, the savings in labour costs in the good state are sufficiently large—given a contract wage W* less than the expected wage W—that expected profits are higher under the implicit contract. The risk-neutral firm will therefore be better off with risk-sharing. Although their expected income is somewhat lower, risk-averse workers are also better off because their income is more certain. The reduction in the variability of workers' real income comes from two sources: real wage fluctuations are eliminated and more workers are employed in the poor state than with market-clearing.

Workers' incomes are not fully stabilized, however. There remains some uncertainty due to the possibility of being laid off in weak demand conditions. In general, a contract that eliminates all income risk by stabilizing employment in addition to the wage is not optimal because in order for it to be in the firm's interest to employ all N_o workers in the poor state, the contract wage W* would have to be lower than the reservation wage k. In these circumstances the workers would prefer not to be employed. Thus the optimal contract reduces, but does not necessarily eliminate, the income uncertainty that workers face.

The optimal contract represents a tradeoff between risk-sharing and production efficiency. On the basis of risk-sharing alone, the risk-neutral firm should absorb all the risk and the risk-averse workers should receive a fixed real income. For production efficiency alone, the real wage and employment should fluctuate, as shown in Figure 18.3 (a). The optimal contract sacrifices some efficiency by employing more than N_b workers in the poor state. This inefficiency is reflected in the fact that the output produced by the additional N_b N_b^* workers is less than the value of their leisure time. However, there is a benefit in terms of risk-sharing because employing these additional N_b N_b^* workers in the poor state reduces the probability of a worker being laid off and not receiving the contract wage W*. However, completely eliminating income uncertainty would be too costly in terms of production efficiency. The optimal contract strikes a balance between these two competing considerations.

Several conclusions emerge from this discussion of risk-sharing between the firm and its workers. Implicit contract theory can account for real wage rigidity, the use of layoffs to respond to reductions in demand, and the existence of involuntary unemployment. The optimal contract provides for a constant real wage and reduction in employment in the poor state. Because workers would prefer to be employed and earning the contract wage, the reduction in employment takes the form of layoffs. Those workers laid off are involuntarily unemployed in an ex post sense: given that the weak demand state occurs, that they are selected for layoff, and that the contract wage exceeds their reservation wage, they would prefer to be employed. However, the unemployment may be considered voluntary in an ex ante sense because the workers chose a wage-employment contract with some risk of layoff, and would make the same choice again in identical circumstances, given the Pareto-optimal nature of the contractual arrangement. Thus the unemployment is involuntary in a rather limited sense.

Although implicit contract theory does provide a rigorous microeconomic explanation for wage rigidity, layoffs, and involuntary unemployment (in a restricted sense), the theory has been criticized for its inability to explain unemployment in excess of the amount that would be observed if wages adjusted each period to equate labour supply and demand (Akerlof and Miyazaki, 1980). Indeed, according to the basic implicit contract model discussed in this section, the number of workers involuntarily laid off in weak demand conditions is less than the number that would voluntarily withdraw from employment with market-clearing. However, this implication of the model is closely related to the assumption that both parties observe the state of demand. When this symmetric information assumption is relaxed, optimal contracts may imply unemployment in excess of the amount that would occur with market-clearing.

In many circumstances employers have more information than their employees on the true nature of the demand conditions they are facing. Thus it is not possible for the two parties to have wages and employment contingent on the state of demand, as was the case under symmetric information, because workers cannot verify the outcome. Contracts need to be contingent on some variable which both parties observe. In these circumstances, implicit contracts will generally involve layoffs rather than wage reductions in weak demand conditions. Contracts which provide for wage reductions in poor demand conditions will not work because the firm has an incentive to claim demand is weak, whatever the true state. This is so because paying a lower wage is not costly to the firm. However, layoffs do impose costs on the employer because output is lower with fewer employees, and the firm runs the risk of losing employees and has to incur rehiring costs. Rigid wage contracts that involve layoffs in poor states and rehires in good states discourage the firm from bluffing about the true nature of its product market, forcing the firm to reveal the true state of demand by its choice of employment. Thus, under asymmetric information there is an additional rationale for wage rigidity and layoff.

Because many of the key variables in implicit contract models are unobservable (that is one of the reasons they are called "implicit"), the empirical literature on this subject is not large. One approach adopted by researchers is to explore the features of "explicit" contracts, in order to gauge the degree to which it appears that firms are offering employment insurance to their unionized workers. Ragan (1995) examines a sample of Canadian union contracts. He posits that risk-averse unions should prefer shorter contracts, since this allows more flexible renegotiation in response to changed market conditions. On the other hand, risk-neutral firms would prefer longer contracts. He then investigates whether union members are compensated for bearing the risk of longer contracts, and finds that indeed, longer contracts are associated with higher wages. This provides favourable evidence for the underlying behavioural assumptions of implicit contract theory.

Beaudry and DiNardo (1991, 1995) use implicit contract theory to explain evidence of long-term attachment of workers to firms, which would otherwise be difficult to explain. For example, Beaudry and DiNardo (1991) show that the economic conditions that existed when a worker signed on with a firm have permanent effects on earnings. For example, if an employee started with a firm during a recession for a lower starting wage, this would have a significantly adverse effect on the entire profile of wages, as long as the employee remained at that firm. Allowing for the possibility of renegotiation, they also found that if economic conditions improved over the tenure of employment with the firm, the wage could be adjusted upward. The significant correlation of past economic conditions with current wages thus suggests that wages are not determined solely in a contemporaneously clearing spot market, and the attachment of workers to firms is thus consistent with a more general model where contracting is important. McDonald and Worswick (1999) replicate Beaudry and DiNardo's methodology with Canadian data (Surveys of Consumer Finance from 1981 to 1992), and reach similar conclusions. On the other hand, Kahn and Lang (1995) do not find that actual and desired hours line up with the predictions of implicit contract theory. Clearly, long-run firm-worker attachments are an important feature of the labour market, but the precise nature of this relationship, and its link to wages and unemployment, remain an important area for further research.

EFFICIENCY WAGES

Another explanation of wage rigidity and unemployment which has received considerable attention in recent years is the notion of **efficiency wages**. While implicit contract theory emphasized the role of wages and employment in risk-sharing, efficiency wage theory focuses on the effect of wages on incentives and worker productivity. The central hypothesis is that firms may choose to pay wages above the market-clearing level in order to enhance worker productivity.

Some of the basic features of efficiency wage theory were described in Chapter 10, where its implications for wage differentials were discussed. Here we focus on the theory's implications for unemployment.

The central assumption of efficiency wage theory is that firms may prefer to pay "above market" wages because doing so enhances worker productivity. There are several reasons why firms may benefit from paying a wage above the level necessary to attract labour. In less-developed countries, higher wages may result in better-fed and thus healthier and more productive workers. In developed economies wages may affect productivity in a variety of ways. Higher wages may improve worker morale, discourage shirking and absenteeism by raising the cost to workers of being fired, and reduce turnover. Firms may also prefer to pay high wages in order to reduce the threat of unionization or to obtain a larger and higher-quality pool of job applicants.

The incentive to pay high wages will generally differ across firms and industries. Efficiency wages are most likely to be observed when other methods of enhancing productivity—such as supervision and monitoring of employees or the use of piece-rate compensation systems—are costly or ineffective. The impact of employee work effort on the quality and quantity of output is also an important factor. Shirking by employees can have disastrous effects in some jobs (an example would be the operator in a nuclear power station or the driver of a bus), while in others the consequences are much less severe. Similarly, in some production processes the work is highly interdependent, so that poor work effort by one employee affects the output of the entire group; whereas in other situations only that employee's output is affected. Other determinants of efficiency wages may also differ from one firm or industry to another. For example, turnover is more costly to some employers than others because of differences in hiring and training costs. As discussed in Chapter 14 on union growth and incidence, some firms are more likely to become unionized than others because of factors such as size and capital intensity. Thus the incentive to pay high wages in order to discourage unionization will be stronger in some organizations than in others.

The primary objective of the model is to show why firms may be reluctant to hire an unemployed applicant, even if the applicant is willing to work for a lower wage than the current employees. If we can show why this is rational for firms, then we can explain the logical possibility of the coexistence of unemployment and rigid wages. For concreteness, we present a model motivated by the nutritional efficiency wage model used in development economics (see Exhibit 18.2). To sketch the model, assume that labour, L, is supplied inelastically to the firm (a rice farm). Output depends only on the labour input, which is measured in "efficiency units," eL. L measures the quantity of labour (in hours), while e is the quality, or efficiency of the work. Output of rice is given by the production function

$$Q = F(eL)$$

Clearly, the higher e is, the more efficiency units of labour are provided for each hour worked, and the higher is output. The key part of an efficiency wage model is that efficiency, e, depends on the wage paid:

$$e = e(W)$$

In the nutritional efficiency wage model, the efficiency of workers increases as they are paid more, and thus able to eat better, and work harder. The firm's profits are given by the difference between revenue and costs. If we normalize the price of output (e.g., rice) to one, profits are given by

$$\pi = F(e(W) \times L) - WL$$
$$= g(W;L) - WL$$

Exhibit 18.2 Nutritional Efficiency Wages

Some of the earliest papers on efficiency wages were motivated by their possible importance in the rural labour markets of low-income countries (Mirrlees, 1975; Stiglitz, 1976). There was significant concern that unemployment or underemployment was a defining feature of rural labour markets. In nutritional efficiency wage models, the labour market does not clear because wages cannot be cut without adversely affecting worker productivity and farm profits. If wages are the sole source of income for a worker, then if wages are set too low, the worker will not be able to afford to eat enough food to be productive, especially in physically demanding farm labour. Thus, no matter how persistent workers may be in offering their services below the prevailing wage, employers will not be willing to hire them at the lower wage, and unemployment will result.

Because the basic ingredients of the model are more or less observable—worker wages, nutritional intake, and farm productivity—this type of efficiency wage model has received more empirical attention, at least in terms of direct evaluation of its assumptions than those based on imperfect information. The first step in evaluating the model has been an estimation of the links between nutrition and labour productivity. Strauss (1986) estimates a relationship between individual caloric intake and farm productivity, and finds that better-fed farmers are also more productive. Of course, one obvious problem that Strauss must contend with is that the causality goes both ways: more productive farmers (i.e., richer farmers) also tend to be better fed. Strauss goes to considerable length to build a convincing case that at least some of the correlation between caloric intake and productivity is the productivity-enhancing effect of better nutrition, a key ingredient of the efficiency wage model.

Foster and Rosenzweig (1994) examine the productivity of workers under alternative payment schemes—straight-time wages, piece rates, sharecropping, and own-farm self-employment. Controlling for nutritional health status—Body Mass Index (BMI), an index that measures weight for height—they find that workers who eat more (i.e., consume more calories) are more productive in those pursuits for which there is the greatest payoff: piece-rate and own-farm work. Their research also addresses the moral hazard (shirking) explanation for efficiency wages. They find that workers who were paid by piece rates worked harder than those who were paid a flat-time wage. Work effort was measured by the decline in BMI after a day's work under different wage payment schemes. Evidently, those workers who's pay was not tied directly to their output did not "sweat" as much as those paid piece rates.

While these and other studies provide convincing evidence on the potential links between nutrition, health, and productivity, they still do not show that efficiency wages are an important feature of rural labour markets. As Subramanian and Deaton (1996) show, for example, in one part of rural India daily nutrients for a farmworker can be purchased with about 5 percent of the daily agricultural wage. At this level, it is unlikely that wage rigidities could be generated by nutritional concerns. For a more detailed discussion of these issues, see Strauss and Thomas (1995).

If there is full employment, the firm will have to pay the prevailing wage if it wants to hire any workers. In that case, the efficiency wage framework is less relevant—even if it would like to, the firm must at least pay the going wage rate. But consider the case where there are unemployed workers, and the firm has some discretion in setting the wage. It faces a tradeoff in making this decision. The firm reduces labour costs by paying a lower wage, but these labour savings may be offset by a drop in labour productivity, so that the lower wage actually reduces profits. The firm must balance the costs and benefits of higher wages. The solution is depicted in Figure 18.4.

The relationship between productivity and the wage is summarized by the function g(W;L).[3] In our depiction, the function is S-shaped. The corresponding "story" is that productivity increases only slowly at first, as the wage is increased. Only after workers are able to obtain a minimum threshold diet do we see an increase in efficiency. Eventually, diminishing returns take over—paying workers higher wages beyond some point will have only small impacts on productivity (only so much of the extra wage goes to food, and increased eating has only limited effects on productivity beyond some point, as these authors are all too aware!). The average cost of producing any given output (with one worker) is W/Q. It can be shown that maximizing profits implies minimizing this cost, or maximizing output per dollar spent, Q/W. The firm's objective is to choose the wage to maximize profits, subject to the efficiency relationship. Diagrammatically, any ray through the origin represents

Figure 18.4 **Determination of the Efficiency Wage**

The efficiency wage, W*, is the wage that maximizes profits when worker productivity depends on how much he/she is paid. The efficiency relationship linking productivity (output) and wages is given by g(W;L). Maximizing profits can be shown to imply minimizing the cost per unit of output, W/Q, or equivalently, maximizing Q/W. Any ray through the origin has a slope ("rise over run") equal to Q/W. Maximizing profits then requires choosing the wage on g(W;L) that lies on the steepest ray Q/W. The choice of a wage like W_1 yields output Q_1, and a slope of Q_1/W_1. The firm would do better by increasing the wage to W_2, but profits are maximized by raising the wage to W*, at the tangency between Q/W and g(W;L). This tangency implies that the slopes of the two functions are equal, that is $\frac{\Delta Q}{\Delta W} = \frac{Q}{W}$.

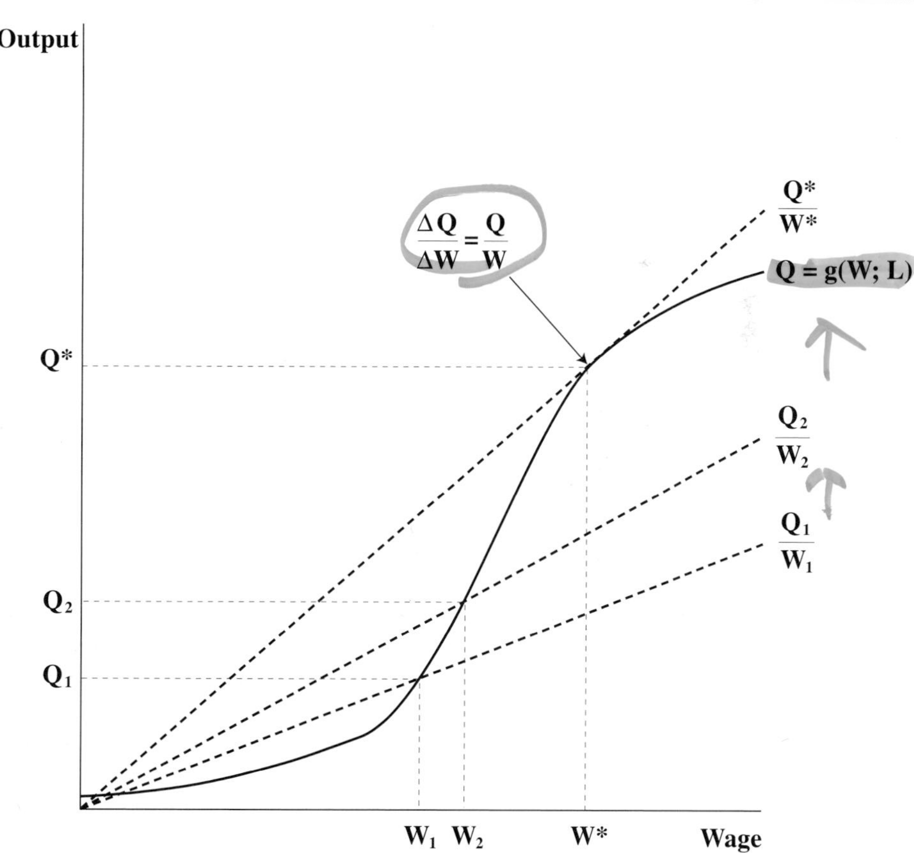

[3]Note we are conditioning on employment in this presentation. It is not difficult to derive the same conditions allowing the firm to choose both wages and employment.

a line with slope equal to Q/W. The firm's objective is to choose the wage on the g(W;L) function that has the steepest (highest) output per dollar spent (Q/W). Consider first the firm paying W_1. A worker with this wage produces Q_1, yielding output per dollar of Q_1/W_1. The firm would do better to increase the wage to W_2, yielding higher output per dollar, Q_2/W_2. This will continue to be true as long as the increase in the worker's productivity justifies the higher labour costs. The optimum occurs at W*, at the tangency between Q/W and g(W;L). This tangency is characterized by

$$\frac{\Delta Q}{\Delta W} = \frac{Q}{W} \quad \text{or} \quad \frac{\Delta Q}{\Delta W} \times \frac{W}{Q} = 1$$

Notice that this expression implies that profits are maximized when the elasticity of output with respect to the wage is equal to one. The intuition is straightforward. An increase in the wage by 1 percent will increase labour costs by 1 percent, no matter what happens to output. So the firm should increase the wage until the increase in benefits is also 1 percent (i.e., output increases by 1 percent). In summary, as long as the efficiency wage, W*, is higher than the going wage rate, the firm's optimal wage is independent of labour market conditions. No matter how much a worker offered to work for less, the firm would not want to hire him. Unemployment and rigid wages can coexist.

A theoretically tighter link between efficiency wages, productivity, and unemployment is provided by Shapiro and Stiglitz (1984). Their model is more applicable to rich industrial economies, and is the basis of most current efficiency wage models. In their model, unemployment serves as a "worker discipline device." Monitoring employee effort is difficult, but if employees are caught shirking, they are fired. The cost to the employee of being fired depends on how long it will take him to find another job that pays as well. Employees are thus assumed to work hard when they fear losing their jobs. Their work effort will be greatest when their wage is high relative to the next-best alternative, and/or when unemployment is high. The greater the unemployment rate, the longer the expected search period facing the fired worker, and therefore the greater the cost of shirking on the present job. The coexistence of unemployment and rigid wages is thus maintained by the unwillingness of firms to cut wages, because of the adverse work incentives on employees.

Testing whether efficiency wages are an important source of unemployment, let alone whether they exist, has been difficult. One problem is that the standard neoclassical theory also predicts a correlation between wages and productivity (W = VMP). It would be difficult to attribute such a correlation to a causal relationship between wages and productivity, at least as an alternative to the neoclassical model. One approach that researchers have taken is to look for evidence of cross-sector differences in wages that cannot be explained by productivity differentials, and that can reasonably be associated with efficiency wage considerations. Some of these results were outlined in Chapter 10, where it was noted that difficulties in controlling for unobserved productivity mean that a neoclassical explanation of the differentials cannot be precluded.

Another body of evidence that is consistent with efficiency wage theory is the negative relationship between unemployment and wage rates across markets, called the **wage curve**. Blanchflower and Oswald (1994) document this relationship in many settings, and in almost every country for which appropriate data are available. They offer a number of alternative theoretical interpretations; nevertheless, the preferred interpretation seems to be that this locus represents a "no-shirking" condition, as suggested by the Shapiro-Stiglitz model. With that model, in markets where there is a higher unemployment rate, workers face a higher penalty for being caught shirking. Therefore, with a higher penalty for being fired, firms need not pay as high wages. Across otherwise identical markets, then, there should be a negative relationship between wages and the unemployment rate. As noted by Card (1995) in his review of *The Wage Curve*, Blanchflower and Oswald have not yet pursued some of the other potentially testable implications of the efficiency wage explanation. At this point, the wage curve remains only suggestive of the possibility that efficiency wages and unemployment are related, as proposed by Shapiro and Stiglitz.

INSIDER-OUTSIDER THEORY

In the presence of excess supply, labour market equilibrium is restored by a decline in the real wage, and vice versa for excess labour demand. Persistent unemployment suggests that this natural equilibrating mechanism is not operating, or not operating sufficiently quickly. For this reason, explanations of persistent unemployment typically focus on the wage determination process, and in particular on reasons why wages may not adjust to eliminate excess supply or demand. Both the implicit contract and efficiency wage theories provided explanations for real-wage rigidity and unemployment that are consistent with rational behaviour on the part of employers and employees. **Insider-outsider theory** is another explanation of wage inflexibility and unemployment, one that has received considerable attention, especially in the context of the persistence of high unemployment in several European countries. (References include Lindbeck and Snower, 1986, 1987, 1988; Solow, 1985.)

The central theme of insider-outsider theory is that wage-setting is determined by bargaining between the employer and its existing work force (the "insiders"), with unemployed workers (the "outsiders") exerting little, if any, influence on the outcome. This view is based on the proposition that it is costly for the firm to replace all or some of its existing work force with new workers recruited from among the ranks of the unemployed. These costs give incumbent workers bargaining power which they can use to raise their wages, even in the presence of excess labour supply in the form of unemployed workers willing to work at lower wages.

Turnover costs are one potentially important source of insider power. As discussed in Chapter 6, there are often costs associated with recruiting and hiring new workers. There may also be significant costs associated with the dismissal of existing employees (severance pay, requirements for advance notice). Firm-specific training and work experience is another factor giving insiders power over outsiders. As discussed in Chapter 9, in the presence of firm-specific human capital, the employer is not indifferent between an experienced incumbent and an otherwise identical individual without the specific training.

In these circumstances, the fact that there exist unemployed job seekers willing to work at lower wages may not be enough of an incentive for employers to attempt to replace some or all of the existing work force with new employees.

Another potential source of insider power stressed by Lindbeck and Snower (1988) is the ability of incumbent employees to not cooperate with or even to harass new hires, especially if new hires are replacing otherwise incumbent workers.

Analytically, the insider-outsider theory is similar to wage determination under collective bargaining, as discussed in Chapter 15. Through bargaining between the employer and incumbent "insiders," the wage will be set above the market-clearing level, thus generating less employment than would occur in the absence of insider power. This reduced employment in sectors in which workers possess insider power will generate unemployment in the labour market as a whole unless wages fall enough in other sectors (sectors in which workers do not have insider power, perhaps because turnover costs and firm-specific training are unimportant) to absorb the excess supply.

Insider-outsider theory has been used to explain the persistence of high unemployment, combined with substantial real-wage growth among employed workers, observed in many European countries since the 1970s. The persistence of unemployment, including the phenomenon of "hysteresis"—according to which the level of unemployment may drift upward or downward rather than tending to return to its natural or equilibrium level—is discussed further in Chapter 19.

There have been very few attempts to directly test the implications of insider-outsider theory. One exception is provided by Doiron (1995a). In this paper, she examines a set of union contract provisions from the International Woodworkers of America in British Columbia to estimate the implicit weight that "insiders" (current union members) place on "outsiders" (potential union members). She rejects the insider-outsider specification, whereby existing union members would prefer increased rents to existing members as opposed to the expansion of membership.

Blanchflower, Oswald, and Sanfey (1996) provide indirect evidence supporting a more general prediction of insider-outsider theory, that workers earn rents at all. They examine cross-industry wage differentials in the United States. After controlling for worker demographic and education characteristics, they find that long-run profitability is correlated with wages. Thus, firm "ability to pay" is a significant determinant of wages. As long as individual productivity is fully accounted for, then this evidence is at odds with the purely competitive model, and consistent with models that emphasize that some workers earn rents, as in insider-outsider models. However, their paper draws no links between rents and queues of workers to work in the high-paying industries, and provides no evidence linking rents and unemployment.

SECTORAL SHIFTS AND UNEMPLOYMENT

The rapidity of structural adjustment (due to technological and economic change) in the economy may also affect the aggregate level of unemployment. Macroeconomists typically view aggregate fluctuations as arising from shocks to aggregate demand or supply. However, as emphasized by Lilien (1982), shifts in the sectoral composition of demand (by region, industry, or occupation) can raise the equilibrium level of unemployment, as time is required for labour and other resources to be reallocated to other sectors.

This **sectoral shift hypothesis** can be illustrated as follows. Consider two economies in which labour demand and labour supply are growing at equal average rates. If labour demand is growing at the same rate in each industry (or region or occupation) in economy A, but growing at above-average rates in some industries and below-average rates in other industries in economy B, the latter economy would have a higher natural unemployment rate due to the necessity for labour to be reallocated from those industries which are growing slowly (perhaps even declining) to those industries which are growing rapidly. For this reason, Lilien (1982) includes the variance of employment growth across U.S. industries as an additional variable explaining movements in the equilibrium level of unemployment in that country. Lilien's model was estimated for Canada by Sampson (1985) and Charette and Kaufman (1987). Both studies find a relationship between the variance of employment growth across industries and the unemployment rate.

Although periods of high dispersion of employment growth across industries are associated with periods of high unemployment, there is considerable disagreement as to whether this relationship confirms the structural shifts hypothesis. The problem arises because a standard macroeconomic model of the business cycle based on aggregate demand shocks is also likely to generate a positive relationship between the variance of employment growth across industries and unemployment (Abraham and Katz, 1986). In particular, some industries are more cyclically sensitive than others, so that shocks to aggregate demand will have a differential effect across industries, producing a rise in the dispersion of employment growth across industries at the same time as unemployment increases. Thus, it is difficult to separate cause and effect; in particular, it is difficult to determine whether sectoral shifts exert an independent influence on unemployment, or whether aggregate shocks cause both a rise in unemployment and a cyclically induced increase in the dispersion of employment growth across industries. In a Canadian study which attempts to separate out the cyclical from noncyclical components of changes in sectoral composition of demand, Neelin (1987) finds that noncyclical shifts in the variance in employment growth across industries do not have an independent effect on unemployment. Rather, the causation runs in the reverse direction; economy-wide shocks which influence the aggregate unemployment rate also cause shifts in the industrial composition of employment. However, Neelin does find evidence supporting the sectoral shifts hypothesis for changes in the regional composition of labour demand. Evidence reported in Gera (1991, Chap. 4) also suggests that increasing regional imbalances played an important role in the rise in unemployment in Canada during the 1970s and 1980s.

Adopting a different estimation framework to these studies, Altonji and Ham (1990) attempt to decompose the sources of employment fluctuations in Canada into those due to (1) U.S. aggregate shocks; (2) Canadian-specific aggregate shocks; (3) provincial shocks; (4) industry shocks; and (5) idiosyncratic shocks. They document the empirical difficulty of identifying the inherently "unobservable" shocks, and find that two-thirds of employment variation in Canada was due to U.S. shocks, and one-quarter due to aggregate Canadian shocks. Only one-tenth of employment variation could be explained by sectoral shocks, though they were more important in some individual industries and provinces.

Osberg (1991) analyzes microdata on the interindustry mobility of Canadian workers during the period 1980–1986. He finds that interindustry mobility falls sharply during economic downturns, in contrast to the implications of the sectoral shifts hypothesis. Murphy and Topel (1987) report similar findings for the United States. The tendency for recessions to "chill" the process of intersectoral labour mobility may contribute to the slow recovery from economic downturns.

Structural unemployment will increase if there is a mismatch between industries and regions experiencing growth in labour demand and those experiencing growth in labour supply. However, there are incentives for employers to adjust their hiring to the available labour supply, as well as for workers to acquire characteristics in demand by employers. Beach and Kaliski (1986) examine changes in the demographic and industry characteristics of employment in detailed Canadian industries during the period 1966–1983, when most of the growth in labour supply involved entry by youths and women. They find that changes in industry employment structure generally accommodated the changes on the supply side; most industries increased their proportions of women and young workers employed, and industries which employed women intensively grew more rapidly than average. Thus the interaction between changes in labour demand and those in the composition of labour supply facilitated employment growth and prevented the increase in structural unemployment that would occur in the absence of adjustments on both the demand and supply sides of the labour market.

Although the evidence supporting the sectoral shifts hypothesis is limited, the message that some economic shocks may have more severe consequences for unemployment than others (holding constant the overall magnitude of the shock) is an important one. The 1981–82 recession had a much larger impact in the western provinces (especially Alberta and British Columbia) than in central Canada, whereas the 1990–1992 downturn adversely affected Ontario more than it did the western provinces. Because of the additional need for interregional reallocation of labour resources, adjustment to these shocks is more difficult than adjustment to shocks that have an even impact across regions.

Storer (1996) pursues this in analyzing the differential effects that oil price shocks have played in Ontario and Alberta. In this paper, the oil price is treated as a sectoral shock, though Storer notes the "hazy" distinction between a sectoral shock, and an aggregate shock that has different effects across sectors. Nevertheless, he shows the important role played by this *observable* variable in explaining the differential unemployment experience in the two economies: oil price increases in the 1970s had detrimental effects on Ontario, but a positive effect on the labour market in Alberta, while the subsequent fall in oil prices in the 1980s reversed Alberta's advantage. While not looking at specifically sectoral issues, Carruth, Hooker, and Oswald (1995) also explore the remarkably high correlation between oil prices and Canada's aggregate unemployment rate, noting the similarity and robustness of the relationship in both Canada and the U.K. These papers have the merit of isolating what the "shocks" may be that are the driving variables in microeconomic models of unemployment.

Other features of economic shocks may also contribute to the ease or difficulty of adjustment. During the 1980s and 1990s, a considerable amount of economic dislocation involved losses in high-wage manufacturing jobs and growth in lower-wage service sector employment. In addition, there was substantial displacement among older workers with substantial job tenure. These features of displacement appear to contribute to a slow process of adjustment and high levels of unemployment. Osberg (1991) finds a very strong relationship between job tenure and interindustry labour mobility, consistent with the hypothesis that workers accumulate specific human capital on the job, as discussed in Chapter 9. Workers displaced from high-wage jobs are also generally found to have longer periods of nonemployment than comparable workers displaced from low-wage jobs (e.g., Kruse, 1988).

In fact, **displaced workers** have been the focus of considerable recent research. Much of this research stems from the particular challenge posed to policymakers by this subgroup of the unemployed. Fallick (1996) reviews much of this recent literature pertaining to the United States. He notes that the definition of "displaced worker" varies across researchers, and is often subject to the idiosyncracies of a particular sample survey design. Nevertheless, the common features one would ascribe to displaced workers are: (1) they were not fired for cause, but rather due to structural changes in the economy; (2) they have a limited ability to return to comparable employment; and (3) they had a strong attachment to their predisplacement job. Displaced workers are also likely to suffer either longer spells of unemployment, or lower postdisplacement earnings for a variety of reasons. The skills or human capital they had acquired in their previous jobs may no longer be valuable, especially if this was firm-specific. They will almost certainly lose their seniority, being forced to start at the bottom of the ladder again. They may have to switch industries, or out of union jobs, that had provided them rents. Finally, they may lose deferred wages (wages in excess of their productivity) that would have been paid on their previous job, but would not be paid in their new job (recall the discussion of deferred wages in Chapter 13). On the other hand, some of their earlier high wage in fact may have been a compensating wage premium for the risk of job loss— a risk that has now come to fruition.

Measuring the impact of displacement on these workers is not as easy as one might imagine. The problem, as we have seen before, is that we do not observe the path that their earnings would have followed if they had not been displaced. It is possible that their earnings would have declined anyway, for example as their industry declined, or monopoly rents were eroded. Most U.S. studies (see Neal, 1995; Jacobson, Lalonde, and Sullivan, 1993; Carrington, 1993; Carrington and Zaman, 1994; Fallick, 1993) estimate earnings losses on the order of 15 to 25 percent, even five years after being laid off. No matter how generous unemployment insurance may be in replacing temporary earnings loss, it appears that displaced workers suffer permanent damage to their earnings capacity.

The Canadian evidence tends to support most of the U.S. findings. Gray and Grenier (1995) summarize the characteristics associated with the unemployment duration of displaced workers, based on the 1986 Canadian Displaced Worker Survey. They find that the post-displacement unemployment spells are longer for older, less-educated workers, and women. They also find that local labour market conditions are important, as it takes longer for workers to obtain new jobs where the unemployment rate is higher. Crossley, Jones, and Kuhn (1994) contrast the earnings losses of men and women in a sample of displaced workers from Ontario. Unlike the Displaced Worker Survey, which may include individuals laid off for a variety of reasons, perhaps not corresponding to a more narrow definition of "displacement," the Ontario survey focused only on mass layoffs, most of which were plant closures. They find significant post-displacement earnings losses, larger for women than men. Men with three to five years of pre-displacement job tenure ended up in jobs paying 5 percent less than their previous jobs, while similar women suffered a 14 percent loss. For individuals with 15 to 25 years of job tenure, the earnings losses were a relatively devastating 25 percent for men, and 54 percent for women. Crossley, Kuhn, and Jones note that losses of this magnitude strongly suggest that firm-specific human capital is as important for women as men.

In their 1991 paper, Gibbons and Katz point out another problem that laid-off workers may face. If worker ability is only imperfectly observed when workers are hired, but is observed better after the worker has been employed for some time, then it is a generally bad signal to be seen as having been fired. Despite protestations that they were laid off for economic reasons, workers may have a difficult time distinguishing themselves from the "lemons" who were fired because they were inferior employees. The one advantage that truly displaced workers have is that they can make a more credible case that they are not "lemons," since the layoff was clearly beyond their control. Using the U.S. Displaced Worker Survey, they find evidence that workers who were the victims of mass layoffs indeed suffered lower post-layoff losses than comparable other laid-off workers. Doiron (1995b) has replicated this analysis in Canada, with the Canadian Displaced Worker Survey. She also finds that, at least for white-collar workers, those who had lost their jobs due to a plant closing suffered 5 percent lower losses than the average job loser, but there was no advantage for similar blue-collar workers.

The extent to which unemployment is associated with sectoral shifts and the process of labour, reallocation is important for policy purposes. Policies which facilitate adjustment to change (training, mobility assistance) are more likely to be useful in periods characterized by substantial sectoral adjustment, whereas macroeconomic stabilization policies are more likely to be useful in response to aggregate shocks.

Sectoral Shifts and Institutional Rigidities

Underlying the sectoral shifts explanation is the notion that labour market rigidities will matter most when the labour market is called upon to reallocate workers across sectors of the economy in response to demand shifts. This hypothesis has received recent attention as an explanation for higher unemployment levels in Europe than in the United States. As reviewed in Chapter 9, it is generally accepted that developed economies experienced a dramatic increase in the relative demand for skilled workers, due to technical change or increased world trade. This shift is believed to explain the sharp rise in wage inequality in the United States over the 1980s and early 1990s. At the same time, unemployment rates rose in Europe and Canada relative to the United States, while these countries had only modest (or no) increases in wage inequality. According to the "Krugman/OECD" hypothesis (see Krugman, 1994; Riddell, 1999), the explanation lies in differential degrees of labour market flexibility. The more flexible U.S. labour market transmitted the demand shocks through to prices, allowing quantities (employment) to fully adjust, while the more rigid European labour markets saw adjustments in quantities instead of prices. The main culprit in European inflexibility was government policy and inflexible labour market institutions, including employment protection laws, high minimum wages, and strong unions.

The story is certainly compelling, and it fits economists' preconceptions of the role of institutions in labour markets. However, like most good (and simple) stories in economics, while it contains a grain of truth it is largely incomplete—and wrong in some important dimensions. One study that directly tests the implications of the labour market rigidities hypothesis is Card, Kramarz, and Lemieux (2000). Using comparable microdata, the authors compare the labour market outcomes of high- and low-skilled workers in Canada, France, and the United States, evaluating the main premise of the skill-based sectoral shifts hypothesis. While they find that skill-based wage inequality indeed rose more in the United States than in France and Canada, they find only weak evidence that the employment of low-skilled workers underlies the overall increase in unemployment in France and Canada. So, while the skills-based part of the story concerning wages appears true, there is no evidence that the sectoral reallocation of low-skilled labour is behind the increase in aggregate unemployment.

A number of studies have also looked at the possible role played by labour market institutions. Kuhn (2000b) compares employment protection legislation in Canada and the United States, evaluating the theoretical possibility that these laws could generate higher unemployment in Canada. He argues that the cost to employers is simply too small to have any meaningful impact on labour demand in Canada relative to the United States. Nickell (1997) and Nickell and Layard (1999) investigate the role of a broad array of labour market policies on the unemployment and employment experiences of OECD countries. They make a number of important points. First, it is dangerous to oversimplify the institutional world, breaking it into two camps, "Europe" and "the United States": there is considerable variation within Europe concerning both institutions and unemployment experiences. Second, they find no evidence that, in aggregate, wages are less flexible in Europe than North America. Third, concerning unemployment directly, they find no evidence that employment protection laws, or labour standards more generally, can explain differences in unemployment levels across OECD countries. The effect of unions is more noticeable, though the potentially adverse impact on employment is ameliorated by centralized wage bargaining, which tends to take into balance consideration of the impact of wages on employment. Finally, their most striking finding, and the main "smoking gun" explanation of differences in unemployment rates, is the association of more generous unemployment insurance benefits with higher unemployment, especially if these benefits are not accompanied by strong incentives for recipients to get back to work. Their results suggest that unemployment insurance programs play a significant (but complicated) role in increasing unemployment rates. As this hypothesis has been prominent in Canadian public policy debates, we now turn our attention to the relationship between UI and unemployment in Canada.

Section Three: Unemployment Insurance and Unemployment

The relationship between unemployment insurance and unemployment has been the subject of considerable theoretical and empirical research. Unemployment insurance is intended to provide workers with protection against the risk of income loss due to unemployment. However, the unemployment insurance program may also affect the incidence and duration of unemployment by altering the incentives facing workers and firms. In this section we examine the influence of unemployment insurance on labour supply, job search, layoffs, seasonal unemployment, and interregional mobility. A brief description of the main features of Canada's unemployment insurance system is also provided.

ECONOMIC RATIONALE FOR UNEMPLOYMENT INSURANCE

Because economic circumstances continually change, risk and uncertainty are often present. As discussed previously in the context of implicit contract theory, labour market risks are especially significant because workers are generally unable to diversify their human capital wealth. In addition, comprehensive private insurance markets, which would enable most workers to purchase insurance against the risk of unemployment (and possibly other sources of loss of labour market income), have generally failed to emerge despite the demand that evidently exists for such insurance. According to the economic theory of risk and insurance, this absence of private insurance markets is probably due to moral hazard and adverse selection. In the context of unemployment insurance, moral hazard implies that individuals with insurance are more likely to become or remain unemployed. Adverse selecton in this context implies that the purchasers of insurance will be those who are most likely to become unemployed. Relative to a situation without moral hazard and adverse selection, these two effects reduce the profitability of selling insurance, and may result in a situation in which the sale of insurance is not profitable at any price.

The experience with Career Guard, an insurance plan to protect executives who might be fired, illustrates these effects. (See "Insurance against being fired: A plan that just didn't fly," *Financial Post*, May 29, 1983, p. 1.) Although this insurance policy didn't cover executives fired within six months of purchasing insurance, the entrepreneurs who started Career Guard nonetheless discovered that a very high proportion of those who purchased insurance were dismissed by their employers subsequent to the six-month qualifying period. It appears that Career Guard failed primarily because of adverse selection—those executives who knew they were likely to be dismissed were the main purchasers of insurance, and the insurer could not distinguish high-risk from low-risk customers. Moral hazard may also have played a role.

Moral hazard and adverse selection are generally present in any insurance situation. Whether they prevent the emergence of private insurance markets depends on their magnitudes. For example, in life insurance, moral hazard is not a serious problem because few individuals will take their own lives in order to collect insurance. Insurance companies often reduce the already small amount of moral hazard by not paying insurance in the event of suicides or murder by a beneficiary. Adverse selection is minimized by such means as not selling insurance to some high-risk groups (e.g., skydivers), charging differential fees to others (e.g., smokers), and requiring medical examinations for certain individuals seeking insurance.

For these reasons, the private sector may not provide the socially optimal amount of unemployment insurance. In the absence of private-sector provision, governments in many countries have introduced unemployment insurance as part of social policy. We briefly review the development of Canada's unemployment insurance system, called Employment Insurance.

CANADA'S UNEMPLOYMENT INSURANCE SYSTEM

Canada's unemployment insurance system was established in 1940, following the recommendations of the Royal Commission on Dominion-Provincial Relations and the resolution, through a constitutional amendment, of the difficulties which had resulted in an earlier attempt to introduce UI being declared outside the legislative authority of the federal government. The unemployment insurance fund is financed by premiums collected from employers and employees. Coverage is compulsory for those groups that come under the Act, a feature which significantly reduces the effects of adverse selection. However, as the empirical evidence reviewed below indicates, moral hazard effects do occur.

Canada's unemployment insurance system has evolved significantly over time. Between 1940 and 1971 there were gradual and modest changes in the eligibility, coverage, and benefit and financing provisions of the UI Act. Dramatic changes to these key features of the Act were made in 1971-72, including a substantial expansion in coverage, an increase in the benefit rate (benefits as a proportion of previous earnings), a reduction in the minimum period of employment required to qualify for benefits, an increase in the maximum benefit period, and the introduction of extended benefits in regions with high unemployment. With these changes, UI covered a much larger proportion of the labour force (about 90 percent) and became considerably more "generous." Making UI benefits taxable offset this increased generosity to some degree. The 1971-72 changes were also partially reversed by revisions made in 1978–79, and again in the 1990s. Nonetheless, the EI system of today contrasts sharply with that of pre-1971 in terms of coverage and the generosity of its provisions. These dramatic changes have provided a rather unusual "social experiment" for studying the impact of unemployment insurance on labour market behaviour. Accordingly, many of the Canadian empirical studies contrast pre- and post-1971–72 behaviour or pre- and post-1978–79 behaviour. Of course, the 1971–72 and 1978–79 changes did not constitute a controlled experiment. As is so frequently the case in empirical research, controlling for other factors which may have affected behaviour represents a major challenge.

The period from 1989 to 1994 saw continued modifications to UI, generally in the direction of reducing the generosity of the program changes that were made in 1971. The reforms of 1989 and 1994, for example, generally increased the qualification period, reduced the benefit rate, and reduced the maximum duration of benefits. One of the side effects of the 1989 change was the subsequent delay of passage of the enacting legislation by the Senate, which provided some limited "exogenous" variation in some of the UI program parameters. This variation was exploited in a number of papers (Green and Riddell, 1997; Baker and Rea, 1998) discussed in Chapter 4.

The mid-1990s witnessed dramatic changes, partly in response to concerns about the federal government's fiscal situation. In 1996 the Unemployment Insurance program was renamed Employment Insurance (EI), and several key parameters were changed. First, EI qualification became based on hours worked, not weeks. In the past, if an individual worked less than 15 hours per week, he or she would not be eligible to collect UI. Similarly, an individual working 15 or 50 hours per week accumulated the same credit toward UI eligibility. Under the new program, EI eligibility is obtained by working as few as 420 hours in the previous year (e.g., 12 weeks at 35 hours per week). The eligibility requirement rises in regions where the unemployment rate is lower, so that in any region where the unemployment rate is at 6 percent or less, the eligibility requirement is 700 hours. Second, the benefit level is based on an average of earnings over a longer period of time. Third, an "intensity rule" was introduced, whereby the replacement rate, while still 55 percent for most workers, was reduced slightly for repeat users. At the extreme, if someone collected UI for 100 weeks or more over the past five years, the replacement rate would be reduced to 50 percent. Finally, EI is more dependent on income (including family income) than UI. Low-income families receive an additional supplement, while higher-income individuals faced a higher tax-back rate for benefits.

The EI changes of 1996 were modified in the year 2000, primarily in the direction of relaxing some of the restrictions introduced in the 1996 reforms. Most importantly, the contentious intensity rule was dropped, so that the replacement rate is 55 percent for all beneficiaries, and not reduced for repeat users. The federal government also reduced the clawback of benefits for higher-income beneficiaries, especially those who made no previous use of unemployment insurance, or who were collecting maternity or parental benefits in the EI program. In fact, this change was part of a larger package of refinements to EI designed to improve the provisions for maternity and parental benefits.

On the basis of economic theory, changes in the provisions of the unemployment insurance system can be expected to affect labour force behaviour in several ways. Indeed, examining the impact of such changes provides a useful test of the theories of unemployment, discussed previously in this chapter, and of the analysis of the incentive effects of alternative income maintenance schemes discussed in Chapter 3. The following effects are discussed in turn: incidence and duration of search unemployment, temporary layoffs, employment instability and seasonal unemployment, labour force participation and labour supply, and interregional labour market mobility. More detailed surveys of the effects of unemployment insurance can be found in Phipps (1993), Corak (1994), Gunderson and Riddell (2001), and Riddell (1999).

THE ECONOMIC EFFECTS OF UNEMPLOYMENT INSURANCE

Incidence and Duration of Unemployment

Analysis of the relationship between unemployment and unemployment insurance is complicated by the fact that the unemployment insurance program has several key parameters, including the benefit rate, the minimum employment period to qualify for benefits, the maximum duration of benefits, the relation between weeks of previous employment and weeks of potential benefits, and the coverage of the labour force. Much of the empirical literature focuses on the consequences of changes in the benefit rate, and our discussion reflects this emphasis. However, other "program parameters" are also important, and we will discuss evidence regarding their impacts where this evidence is available.

Unemployment insurance can affect the incidence and duration of search unemployment by altering the costs and benefits of job search. Several cases need to be considered, depending on whether the individual is (1) employed, (2) unemployed and eligible for unemployment insurance benefits, and (3) not eligible for benefits. For the employed, an increase in the benefit rate makes unemployed search more attractive relative to employed search; as a consequence, the incidence of unemployment is predicted to rise. Evidence appears to support this prediction. Kaliski (1985) notes that the ratio of employed to unemployed search rose sharply following the introduction in 1978-79 of a reduced benefit rate and tighter qualification requirements.

For the unemployed who are eligible for benefits (because of a previous spell of employment), an increase in the benefit rate lowers the marginal cost of search. According to the theory of optimal search, the expected or average duration of job search will increase. This prediction has been extensively tested in the United States, the United Kingdom, and to a lesser extent Canada. Cousineau (1985) and Corak (1994) summarize various Canadian and U.S. studies, and Atkinson et al. (1984) and Atkinson and Micklewright (1991) critically evaluate U.S. and U.K. evidence. Early Canadian studies using aggregate data concluded that the 1971-72 changes to the UI Act—which increased the benefit rate from 43 to 67 percent, among other changes—raised the average duration of unemployment by $1\frac{1}{2}$ to 2 weeks (Cousineau and Green, 1978; Rea, 1977; Maki, 1977; Lazar, 1978). This increase of approximately 20 percent in duration corresponds to an increase in the unemployment rate of one to one-and-one-half percentage points.

More recent studies in Canada and the United States employ microdata which allow for more careful testing of UI effects. Using gross flow data, Beach and Kaliski (1983) find that the 1978-79 revisions—which lowered the benefit rate from 67 to 60 percent and tightened qualification requirements—resulted in an increase in the flow from unemployment to employment and a reduced duration of unemployment for all age-sex groups. Studies by Glenday and Alam (1982) and Ham and Rea (1987), using microdata on the employment and unemployment experience of individuals, find significant effects of UI entitlements on the duration of job search.

When UI benefits are exhausted, there is often a "spike" in the probability of leaving unemployment. This spike is present in both U.S. and Canadian data, and suggests that UI not only affects spell duration, but also may affect the outcome of search. Belzil (1995) documents the relationship between benefit exhaustion and unemployment duration in Canada. He also shows that for displaced workers, the subsidy to search provided by UI actually helped them find jobs that gave them a longer subsequent re-employment spell.

www.aeaweb.org/journal/contents/mar1995.html

Among the more convincing bodies of evidence that UI affects search behaviour, are the results of Unemployment Insurance Bonus Experiments in the U.S., surveyed in Meyer (1995, 1996). Woodbury and Spiegelman (1987) provide the earliest evidence on one specific experiment, conducted in Illinois. In that experiment, UI recipients were offered a $500 "prize" or bonus if they found a job within 11 weeks, and kept the job for at least

4 months. UI recipients were carefully assigned to treatment (bonus-eligible) and control (conventional-UI) groups, so that the effect of the bonus could be isolated. Woodbury and Spiegelman found that this bonus program significantly reduced the duration of unemployment, though not enough to offset the cost of paying the bonus. Their basic finding was confirmed in later versions of the experiment, and those conducted in other states. Thus, while bonuses may not represent a useful policy tool themselves, the results of the experiments point to the importance that incentives play in affecting (though not exclusively determining) unemployment duration.

Changes in the benefit rate may also affect the search behaviour of those who are not eligible for UI. Such individuals may be entering the labour force for the first time, they may be reentering after an extended absence from the labour force, or they may have exhausted their benefits. In these circumstances it may be rational to accept employment quickly, even temporary work, in order to subsequently qualify for UI benefits. In effect, a job has two components: the income received directly, and a "ticket" entitling the worker to benefits in the event of unemployment. Consequently, for individuals ineligible for benefits, an increase in the benefit rate does not affect the costs of search but lowers the marginal benefit of search, thus reducing optimal search duration (see Ferrall, 1997).

In summary, unemployment insurance affects job search behaviour in several ways. For workers who qualify for UI, a more generous benefit structure lowers the cost of job search, thus raising average search duration, and makes unemployed search more attractive relative to employed search, thus increasing the incidence of unemployment. Empirical evidence generally supports these predictions of the theory of optimal search behaviour. The impact on search duration has been most extensively investigated. Although most studies find that UI benefits do affect the duration of job search, the studies are not always robust to changes in specification (Atkinson et al., 1984; Atkinson and Micklewright, 1991). Possibly offsetting these effects to some extent, a more generous benefit structure may reduce search duration for those currently ineligible for UI. This latter effect is likely to be small, in which case the overall impact of a more generous benefit structure will be to increase search duration. Empirical studies of the 1971–72 UI liberalization conclude that the overall duration of unemployment did increase significantly.

Layoffs

The impact of UI on layoffs can be analyzed using implicit contract theory. As discussed previously in this chapter, optimal risk-sharing arrangements may provide for layoffs in adverse product market conditions when the value of the marginal product of labour falls below the workers' reservation wage. An increase in the benefit rate raises the reservation wage, thus increasing the number of states in which layoffs will occur and increasing the number of workers laid off in each adverse state. These predictions can be illustrated by shifting up the labour supply curve S in Figure 18.3(b).

The theory of compensating wage differentials discussed in Chapter 8 is also relevant to the analysis of layoffs. Although all firms and industries experience fluctuations in demand due to cyclical, seasonal, and other factors, these variations are much larger for some employers than others. Firms can adjust to these disturbances in various ways: through inventories, by altering the time lag between orders and shipments, by diversifying product lines, by saving work for slack periods, by adjusting wages and/or hours of work, and by layoffs and rehires. Firms will choose the least-cost method of adjustment. Unemployment insurance lowers the cost of adjusting through layoffs relative to other methods because, in the absence of UI, employers who rely extensively on layoffs will have to pay a compensating wage to attract employees. In this way a higher benefit rate may contribute to larger variations in employment in response to cyclical and seasonal fluctuations in demand.

The financing of the UI program is also relevant. Under **experience rating**, employers' UI premiums are related to the amount of benefit payments to their employees. Firms which rely heavily on layoffs will pay a penalty in the form of higher UI premiums, thus providing an incentive to utilize other forms of adjustment. Canada's unemployment insurance system is not experience-rated, a feature which has been the subject of considerable policy discussion (Kesselman, 1983; Riddell, 1985). As a consequence, industries with stable employment patterns cross-subsidize those with unstable employment. In the United States, various states have experience rating in their unemployment insurance programs. Anderson and Meyer (1993) document the high degree of cross-subsidization that still occurs with limited experience rating, as high-unemployment industries do not pay actuarially fair premiums. They find in particular that construction, manufacturing, and mining are net recipients of these subsidies.

Employment Instability

The relationship between UI and employment instability has been investigated in a number of empirical studies. Much of this research has been carried out in the United States, utilizing differences that exist across states in the degree to which UI is experience-rated. Studies by Feldstein (1978), Topel (1983), and Saffer (1982, 1983) indicate that incomplete experience rating has a significant impact on the incidence of layoffs; that is, the lower the degree of experience rating the greater the use of layoffs, ceteris paribus. In Canada, Kaliski (1976) found that for the majority of industries and provinces, the trend toward reduced seasonality in employment moderated, or even reversed, after 1971. The increase in seasonal fluctuations in employment was particularly large in construction, one of the industries most heavily subsidized by UI. Glenday and Alam (1982) conclude that the regional extended benefits (longer entitlement periods in regions with high unemployment) contribute to the amount of seasonal unemployment and short-term employment instability in high-unemployment regions.

The choice between hours reductions and layoffs has received special policy attention. As discussed in Reid (1985) and Riddell (1985), UI may bias employers and employees toward the use of layoffs as opposed to reductions in hours of work. This is so because workers on layoff qualify for UI benefits while those whose unemployment takes the form of reduced hours do not. This bias can be offset in one or two ways: (1) have UI premiums experience-rated so that firms pay a penalty for adjustments in the form of layoffs or (2) introduce a UI-assisted worksharing program. Canada has followed the latter route. As described in Chapter 3 and Reid (1985), the Canadian program basically provides UI benefits of two-thirds of each employee's lost wages for voluntarily giving up an average of one day of work per week so that other workers in the firm would not have to be laid off.

Labour Supply

Unemployment insurance also affects employment and unemployment through its impact on labour force participation. This aspect was analyzed in Chapter 3 using the income-leisure choice model, and the reader may wish to review that discussion at this time. The analysis applies to situations in which employees can adjust their weeks of employment and nonemployment in response to the incentives inherent in the UI system. The many individuals for whom a job entails being employed throughout the year do not fit in this category. The relevant group consists of those who work less than a full year either because the worker quits or is laid off after a certain period of employment or because the job itself is short-term in nature, as is the case in much seasonal work.

Our earlier analysis showed that more generous UI will decrease weeks worked by those who, prior to the change, worked more than the minimum number of weeks required to qualify for benefits, whereas more generous UI will increase weeks of employment for those who previously did not qualify. Most of the latter group would have been out of the labour force prior to the change; for these individuals, higher UI benefits make labour force participation sufficiently attractive to obtain at least enough employment to qualify for benefits. (In Chapter 3 we compared equilibriums with and without unemployment insurance. The analysis of equilibriums with different UI benefit levels is very similar.)

These two responses have offsetting effects on employment, reducing weeks worked by those with relatively strong labour force attachment and increasing weeks worked by those with little or no labour force attachment. Total employment may therefore increase or decrease. However, the impact on labour force participation and unemployment is unambiguous. Labour force participation is predicted to rise because of the entry by those who now wish to obtain enough work to qualify for UI. Those who previously qualified for benefits do not exit from the labour force, although they do work fewer weeks. Measured unemployment increases for both groups: those who previously qualified for UI because they now spend less time employed and more time unemployed, while those previously not eligible spend more time employed and unemployed and less "not in the labour force."

These predictions of the income-leisure choice model refer to desired combinations of employment and nonemployment given the individual's preferences and constraints. Of course, not all workers can achieve their desired allocation of time to work and nonmarket activity, especially in the short run. However, as discussed in Chapter 8, firms have an incentive to offer jobs with more desirable and fewer undesirable characteristics because doing so reduces the compensating wage that must be paid in equilibrium. Thus if short-term employment is desirable for some workers, jobs with these features can be expected to emerge. In this way, changes in the UI system may affect not only employee behaviour but also the structure of labour demand.

Glenday and Alam (1982) conclude that UI benefits contribute to the amount of employment instability; in particular, the regional differentiation of benefits reinforces the short-term and seasonal nature of much of the employment in high unemployment regions.

A variety of Canadian empirical evidence is available on these labour supply effects. Early studies by Cousineau and Green (1978), Rea (1977), and Sharir and Kuch (1978) found that the 1971–72 changes to the UI program increased aggregate labour force participation, especially among groups with lower average rates of labour force attachment. More recently, Phipps (1990, 1991a, 1991b) used the income-leisure choice framework discussed in Part 1 of this book (in particular, in Chapter 3) to analyze the impacts of UI parameters on labour force participation and employment. An important implication of Phipps' research is that changes in the UI program designed to increase work incentives (i.e., to increase labour supply) may have little effect if there are constraints on the demand side of the labour market (e.g., insufficient jobs in depressed regions or in economic downturns).

Green and Riddell (1993) examine the labour supply effects of UI coverage of older workers, a group generally considered to have a low degree of labour force attachment. In particular, they study the impact of a 1976 change in UI regulations which disenfranchised workers between 65 and 70 years of age, who were covered by the UI program prior to this change. They find that a large proportion of these individuals withdrew from the labour force on the removal of UI eligibility.

Corak (1993a, 1993b) uses UI administrative data covering the period 1971–90 to examine patterns of employment and nonemployment among participants in the UI program. He finds a high degree of repeat use of UI. For example, during the latter part of the 1980s, about 80 percent of the UI claimants in any year had previously received UI, with 40 to 50 percent having experienced five or more previous claims. The extent to which this degree of repeat use is due to the structure of labour demand (for example, the importance of seasonal work) or due to individuals adjusting their labour supply to the parameters of the UI program is an important question. Corak (1993b) shows that spell length of unemployment increases with repeat use of UI. Whether this reflects diminished human capital ("destroyed" by the experience of unemployment), repeated and compounding bad luck, or changed search behaviour remains unclear. Nevertheless, repeat use of UI appears detrimental to an individual's long-run labour market outcomes.

One possible explanation for repeat use is the lack of experience rating, discussed earlier. Repeat users—and their employers—do not pay actuarially fair EI premiums. The primary objective of the 1996 "intensity rule" (since abandoned) was to partially rectify this, by slightly reducing the benefits of repeat users. At the same time, the government planned a social experiment in order to evaluate the importance of incentives for repeat users to accept longer duration. It was called the "Earnings Supplement Project," and was rigorously designed along lines similar to the Self-Sufficiency Project described in Chapter 3. The basic idea was to offer an earnings supplement to repeat UI users, to top up their wages and encourage them to accept possibly lower-paying jobs. The experiment had to be scrapped, as it quickly became apparent that there would be no takers for the supplement. Instead, the budget was directed toward an intensive survey of repeat users, "Survey of Repeat Use of Employment Insurance." Preliminary results based on this survey are now available (Social Research and Demonstration Corporation, 2001a; 2001b). One conclusion—which is perhaps not surprising given the earlier work of Corak—is that there is considerable heterogeneity within the group of repeat EI users, and so it is unlikely any single explanation or policy response will fit. Second, the evidence from the survey, and the "failure" of the Earnings Supplement Project, is consistent with the view that employers and employees in high-turnover and seasonal industries adjust the terms of employment (job duration and pay) in response to EI system and its lack of experience rating (the implicit contracts interpretation discussed in the Layoffs and Employment Instability sections).

The regional extended benefit structure brought about by the changes made to the UI program in the late 1970s provides a relatively strong incentive for individuals in high unemployment regions to work at least 10 weeks, and thereby qualify for up to 42 weeks of benefits. In their study of Canada-U.S. unemployment, Card and Riddell (1993) find evidence that during the 1980s Canadians increasingly adjusted their labour supply to the parameters of the UI program. In particular, for both males and females the distributions of annual weeks of employment show "spikes" at 10 to 14 weeks (the minimum weeks required to qualify for UI), and the magnitudes of these spikes increased during the 1980s. As noted above, such behaviour could arise both because some individuals who would otherwise (i.e., in the absence of UI eligibility) not participate in the labour force work enough weeks to qualify for UI, and because some individuals who would otherwise work more weeks reduce their labour supply. By comparing the differences in these spikes over time and between Canada and the United States, Card and Riddell (1997) attribute as much as 80 percent of the increased unemployment differential to the increased likelihood that nonemployed individuals report being unemployed in Canada. In turn, the data suggest that the increased unemployment was associated with collection of UI benefits.

While they only look at aggregate measures of unemployment and UI generosity, Milbourne, Purvis, and Scoones (1991) show that by setting benefit levels as a function of the unemployment rate, UI benefits increase the persistence of unemployment. They show that the increased generosity of UI, and its link to benefits through the unemployment rate, can account for most of the divergence of the unemployment rates between Canada and the United States.

Green and Riddell (2000) explore the impact of the 1996 reforms on the UI system, in particular the movement to hours-based from weeks-based qualification. In principle, using hours instead of weeks could allow more people to become eligible for UI, especially those working less than 15 hours per week who were previously ineligible. In fact,

Green and Riddell find no evidence of a shift in UI eligibility patterns. However, they do find that the move to an hours-based system had two important effects. First, it distributed EI benefits toward those who could accumulate more hours per week—predominantly men and seasonal workers—and away from part-time workers—predominantly women. Second, because EI entitlement could be accumulated more quickly in high-weekly-hours seasonal jobs, the average weekly duration of these jobs declined, providing further evidence that firms and workers adjust their terms of employment in response to parameters of the EI system.

Interregional Mobility

Unemployment insurance may also affect the interregional mobility of the labour force. The regional extended benefits, in particular, appear to retard interregional mobility by providing benefits for longer periods in regions with high unemployment (Winer and Gauthier, 1982; Vanderkamp, 1986). The studies summarized in Chapter 3—Green and Riddell, (1997), Christofides and McKenna (1996), and Baker and Rea (1998)—also showed that the variable entrance requirements, a key feature of the regional differentiation of the UI program, were correlated with labour force attachment patterns. Jones and Corak (1995) estimate the impact of the regional extended benefits in increasing unemployment differentially across regions. They find that while the more generous extended benefits appeared related to unemployment duration, the effects were not large enough to explain the large increase in unemployment that occurred over the 1980s. There is also some evidence (Coulombe and Lee, 1995; Milne and Tucker, 1992) that transfers like UI have slowed the regional convergence of productivity and wages that otherwise is occurring slowly in Canada.

In summary, the unemployment insurance system has numerous effects on labour force behaviour, including the incidence and duration of search unemployment, layoffs, annual patterns of employment and unemployment, labour force participation, and interregional mobility. A substantial amount of empirical research has been devoted to estimating the size of these effects. Although there are some offsetting influences, the overall impact of a more generous UI benefit structure is to increase unemployment. This does not imply that improvements in UI generosity are undesirable or that changes which to some extent "tighten up" the UI program are desirable; it simply points up the fact that such changes affect our aggregate unemployment rate and that this should be considered in interpreting this statistic. More generally, the tradeoffs inherent in the unemployment insurance system need to be recognized in the design of UI financing and benefits. The more generous the benefit structure, the greater the insurance value of the program but also the larger the adverse incentive effects and the amount of induced unemployment. Optimal UI design must strike a balance between these social costs and benefits.

Summary

- The primary objective of this chapter is to provide an overview of the variety of theoretical explanations of unemployment, and furthermore to evaluate the extent to which unemployment insurance plays a role in the Canadian unemployment experience. The most important lesson to take away is that unemployment is complex, and no single explanation is sufficient. A corollary of this is that there is no single policy prescription that economists can provide that will yield "full employment."
- We begin with a "taxonomy" of the various types of unemployment discussed by economists. While the definitions are not mutually exclusive, economists often distinguish

between frictional, structural, demand-deficient, and seasonal unemployment, and between involuntary and voluntary unemployment.

- There are many microeconomic theories of unemployment, but all have a common theoretical thread. In the conventional neoclassical (supply and demand) model, unemployment only exists when some factor prevents the market wage from declining to clear the market. The various theories we review attempt provide microeconomic foundations for rigid wages.
- *Search unemployment.* Search theory provides a theory of frictional unemployment, and a model of individual behaviour in the presence of imperfect information. In this case, the imperfect information is incomplete knowledge of the wages being paid for a specific job.
- *Implicit contracts.* Implicit contract theory provided a rationale for rigid wages in the presence of unemployment. In this model, wages serve a dual function: they allocate labour as in the neoclassical model, but they are also the means by which firms offer layoff insurance to workers. Because of the risk-sharing of wages, these models show that unemployment and rigid wages can coexist.
- *Efficiency wages.* In efficiency wage models, firms will not lower their wages, even to "desperate" workers willing to work for less than the prevailing wage. Lowering the wage would actually lower firm profits, because lower wages reduce worker productivity in excess of the savings of labour costs.
- *Insider-outsider theory.* This class of models takes as its premise the existence of "rents" in the labour market. Because of various forms of imperfect competition, workers in high-wage firms are protected from competition in the outside labour market, and again, unemployment and rigid wages can coexist.
- *Sectoral shifts.* This class of models has a more traditional macroeconomic flavour, whereby the principal source of unemployment is an adverse demand shock, concentrated in specific sectors.
- *Sectoral shifts combined with institutional rigidities.* Increases in the demand for skilled labour are believed to have caused increases in wage inequality in the United States but almost no unemployment, whereas in Europe the adjustment to these shocks have been mostly reflected in high unemployment with little transmission to wage inequality. The difference in adjustment patterns is attributed to difference in labour market institutions, such as stronger employment protection laws and a greater degree of unionization in Europe.
- We review the motivation and development of unemployment insurance (UI, or EI) in Canada, and evaluate the evidence linking unemployment insurance to labour market behaviour. Whether one is looking at the impact of UI on the incidence and duration of unemployment, the layoff behaviour of firms, employment stability, labour supply behaviour, or interregional mobility, it is difficult to avoid the conclusion that UI "matters" in contributing to the observed patterns of unemployment. However, this does not mean the UI is a "bad program," merely that its impact must be taken into account in program design.

REVIEW QUESTIONS

1. Summarize the main types of unemployment, their causes, and the usual policies discussed to curb each type of unemployment. Can all unemployment be categorized into one of these types?

2. Indicate the basic differences between frictional and structural unemployment. If possible, provide examples of when it may be unclear as to whether to categorize a worker as frictionally or structurally unemployed.
3. Discuss the costs and benefits of job search for younger workers and women. Relate these factors to their expected unemployment duration.
4. Discuss the implications of job search theory for the following phenomena:
   - Unemployment duration
   - The cyclical behaviour of quits
   - Wage rigidity over the business cycle
5. Discuss the implications of implicit contract theory for the following phenomena:
   - Wage rigidity over the business cycle
   - Labour hoarding
   - Layoffs instead of wage reductions
6. Why don't we observe private insurance companies selling unemployment insurance? How could employers provide such insurance?
7. Discuss the various design features (policy parameters) of unemployment insurance that can affect the benefits from such insurance, and therefore the behaviour of recipients. What features of unemployment and other labour market behaviour might be explained, at least partially, by unemployment insurance?

PROBLEMS

1. "Frictional unemployment is optimal." True or false? Discuss.
2. The following figure illustrates the time series behaviour of the unemployment rate and hourly real wages in Canada (based on the same wage series as reported in Figure 7.10):

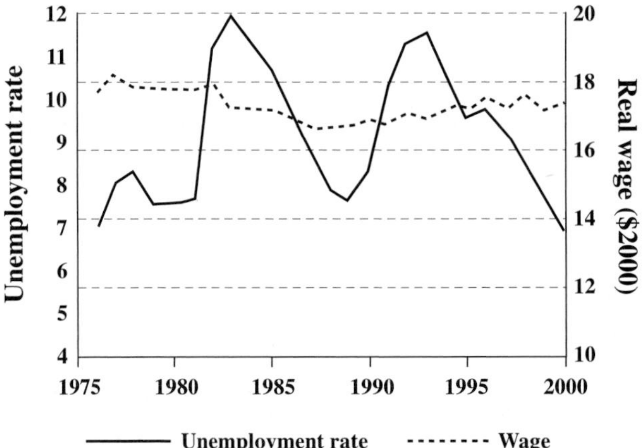

Explain why a decline in demand for new housing in the United States might generate shifts of the demand curve for labour in Canada. Using a supply-and-demand figure, evaluate the extent to which the above figure is consistent with such shifts of a labour demand schedule along a stable labour supply curve. Is it possible to account for this pattern by allowing a shifting supply curve? Interpret this possibility, and offer alternative explanations.

3. Assume that the productivity of farm labour depends on daily caloric intake, similarly to that depicted in Figure 18.4. Using this kind of diagram, compare the efficiency wages that would apply to the following two types of workers:

- A landless labourer
- A labourer with small plot of land on which he grows staple crops

Describe the likely equilibrium unemployment rates and wage rates for landless labourers and small landholders. Judging partially on the basis of this example, what sorts of data and what empirical strategies might you use to see whether nutritional efficiency wages were an important element in the rural labour markets of poor, rural economies?

4. Assume that the Shapiro-Stiglitz monitoring-based efficiency wage model is relevant for the Canadian economy. Using carefully labelled diagrams similar to Figure 18.4, evaluate the impact on the prevailing wage rate and unemployment rate of an increase in unemployment insurance benefits.

   Describe the type of data that you might be able to use, and empirical strategies you might pursue, to see whether the Shapiro-Stiglitz type of model could explain characteristics of the labour market like those depicted in the figure in Question 2.

5. Assume that the following relationship describes individual productivity as a function of the wage paid:

$$Q = \begin{cases} = 0 & \text{for} \quad W \leq \$8 \\ = -20 + 3W - 0.05W^2 & \text{for} \quad \$8 < W < \$30 \\ = 30 & \text{for} \quad W \geq \$30 \end{cases}$$

   (a) Plot this relationship, and interpret. *Hint:* You may use a spreadsheet if you wish.
   (b) Note that the slope of the efficiency function is given by $\frac{\Delta Q}{\Delta W} = 3 - 0.10W$ in the range $8 < W < $30. Evaluate whether the following wages are profit-maximizing: $10, $20, and $30. Interpret and explain.

6. When examining the frequency distribution for various durations of unemployment, a common feature is a sharply noticeable concentration (or "spike") of individuals who find jobs at the maximum benefit period for unemployment insurance. In other words, if the maximum number of weeks a person can collect unemployment insurance is 26 weeks, there is a significant fraction of unemployed workers who find jobs after exactly 26 weeks of unemployment.
   (a) Show how a labour supply explanation, similar to that developed in Chapter 3, could account for this pattern.
   (b) Show how a search-based explanation could account for this phenomenon.
   (c) What type of data and what empirical strategy would you employ to distinguish between the labour supply and search-based explanations?

7. (a) Assume that the marginal benefit of a week's job search is given by

$$MB = a - b \times \text{Weeks}; \quad a, b > 0$$

   where Weeks is the cumulative number of weeks of searching. What factors will affect the returns to search, that is, what factors will cause a or b to be higher or lower?

   (b) Assume as well that the marginal cost of a week's job search is given by

$$MC = c + d \times \text{Weeks}; \quad c, d > 0$$

   What factors will affect the marginal cost of search, that is, what factors will cause c or d to be higher or lower?

   (c) Solve for the optimal number of weeks of job search for the parameters a = 35, b = 1, c = 5, d = 1.

   (d) Find a general expression for the optimal number of weeks of search, that is, express the optimal number of weeks of search, W*, as a function of a, b, c, and d. Use this expression to discuss what happens to W* if there is an increase in b or an increase in d. Interpret.

8. Explain why search and monopsony often go together in a labour market. Use the monopsony model outlined in Chapter 7 to explore the impact on a labour market (wages and employment) of a change in search technology, like the advent of Internet job sites.
9. A firm produces donuts in a competitive industry. Demand conditions are such that either it's a hot day and demand is low, or a cold day and demand is high. The firm does not know in advance what the weather will be, but there is a 50-50 chance it could be either (i.e., the probability of each type of day is $\frac{1}{2}$). If the weather is hot, the zero-profit equilibrium wage to pay its "baker" is \$4 for a day; if the weather is cold, the zero-profit equilibrium wage to pay is \$16 for the day. The donut firm only cares about profits, and is risk-neutral.

   The baker has a utility function defined over his wage for the day, $u = \sqrt{W}$. Assume that the baker cares only about the expected utility of his wage income.

   Show that the baker and the donut shop owner would both be better off (on average) if the firm paid the baker \$9.50 irrespective of the weather. Interpret.

KEYWORDS

frictional unemployment 530
temporary layoffs 530
structural unemployment 531
demand-deficient unemployment 532
cyclical unemployment 532
seasonal unemployment 533
voluntary and involuntary unemployment 533
wage rigidity 534
job search 534
matching 534
stopping rule 536
reservation wage 536
dynamic monopsony 538
implicit contract theory 542
risk-sharing 542
moral hazard 543
adverse selection 543
symmetric information 545
asymmetric information 545
efficiency wages 548
wage curve 552
insider-outsider theory 553
sectoral shift hypothesis 554
displaced workers 556
experience rating 563

REFERENCES

Abraham, K., and L. F. Katz. 1986. Cyclical unemployment: Sectoral shifts or aggregate disturbances. *JPE* 94:507–22.

Akerlof, G., and H. Miyazaki. 1980. The implicit contract theory of unemployment meets the wage bill argument. *R.E. Studies* 47 (January):321–338.

Altonji, J. G., and J. C. Ham. 1990. Variation in employment growth in Canada: The role of external, national, regional, and industrial factors. *JOLE* 8 (Part):S198–236.

Anderson, P. M., and B. D. Meyer. 1993. Unemployment insurance in the United States: Layoff incentives and cross subsidies. *JOLE* 11 (Part):S70–95.

Atkinson, A., J. Gomulka, J. Micklewright, and N. Rau. 1984. Unemployment benefit, duration and incentives in Britain: How robust is the evidence? *JPubEc* 23 (February/March):3–26.

Atkinson, A. B., and J. Micklewright. 1991. Unemployment compensation and labor market transitions: A critical review. *JEL* 29 (December):1679–1727.

Azariadis, C. 1975. Implicit contracts and underemployment equilibria. *JPE* 83 (December):1183–1202.

______. 1979. Implicit contracts and related topics: A survey. In *The Economics of the Labour Market*, eds. Z. Hornstein et al. London: HMSO.

Azariadis, C., and J. E. Stiglitz. 1983. Implicit contracts and fixed price equilibria. *QJE* 98:1–22.

Baily, M. N. 1974. Wages and employment under uncertain demand. *R.E. Studies* 41 (January):37–50.

Baker, M., and S. Rea. 1998. Employment spells and unemployment insurance eligibility requirements. *R.E. Stats.* 80 (February):80–94.

Beach, C., and S. Kaliski. 1983. Measuring the duration of unemployment from gross flow data. *CJE* 16 (May):258–63.

______. 1986. Structural unemployment: Demographic change or industrial structure. *CPP* 12 (June):356–67.

Beaudry, P., and J. DiNardo. 1991. The effect of implicit contracts on the movement of wages over the business cycle: Evidence from micro data. *JPE* 99 (August):665–88.

______. 1995. Is the behavior of hours worked consistent with implicit contract theory? *QJE* 110 (August):743-68.

Belzil, C. 1993. An empirical model of job-to-job transition with self-selectivity. *CJE* 26:536-51.

______. 1995. Unemployment duration stigma and re-employment earnings. *CJE* 28 (August):568-87.

______. 1996. Relative efficiencies and comparative advantages in job search. *JOLE* 14 (January):126-53.

Blanchflower, D. G., and A. J. Oswald. 1994. *The Wage Curve*. Cambridge and London: MIT Press.

Blanchflower, D. G., A. J. Oswald, and P. Sanfey. 1996. Wages, profits, and rent-sharing. *QJE* 111 (February):227-51.

Bowlus, A. J. 1998. U.S.-Canadian unemployment rate and wage differences among young, low-skilled males in the 1980s. *CJE* 31 (May):437-64.

Card, D. 1995. The wage curve: A review. *JEL* 33 (June):285-99.

Card, D., F. Kramarz, and T. Lemieux. 1999. Changes in the relative structure of wages and employment: A comparison of Canada, France and the United States. *CJE* 32 (August):843-77.

Card, D., and W. C. Riddell. 1993. A comparative analysis of unemployment in Canada and the United States. In *Small Differences That Matter: Labor Markets and Income Maintenance in Canada and the United States*, eds. D. Card and R. B. Freeman. Chicago: University of Chicago Press.

______. 1997. Unemployment in Canada and the United States: A further analysis. In *Trade, Technology and Economics: Essays in Honour of Richard G. Lipsey*, eds. B. C. Eaton and R. G. Harris. Cheltenham, U.K. and Lyme, N.H: Elgar.

Carrington, W. J. 1993. Wage losses for displaced workers: Is it really the firm that matters? *JHR* 28 (Summer):435-62.

Carrington, W. J., and A. Zaman. 1994. Interindustry variation in the costs of job displacement. *JOLE* 12 (April):243-75.

Carruth, A., M. Hooker and A. Oswald. 1995. Unemployment, oil prices, and the real interest rate: Evidence from Canada and the United Kingdom. In *Aspects of Labour Market Behaviour: Essays in Honour of John Vanderkamp*, eds. L. Christofides, E. K. Grant, and R. Swidinsky. Toronto: University of Toronto Press.

Charette, M. F., and B. Kaufman. 1987. Short-run variation in the natural rate of unemployment. *Journal of Macroeconomics* 9:417-27.

Christofides, L. N., and C. J. McKenna. 1996. Unemployment insurance and job duration in Canada. *JOLE* 14 (April):286-312.

Corak, M. 1993a. Is unemployment insurance addictive? Evidence from the benefit durations of repeat users. *ILRR* 47 (October):62-72.

______. 1993b. Unemployment insurance once again: The incidence of repeat participation in the Canadian UI program. *CPP* 19:162-76.

______. 1994. Unemployment insurance, work disincentives and the Canadian labour market: An overview. In *Unemployment Insurance: How to Make It Work*, eds. C. Green, M. Corak, and D. Gross. Toronto: C. D. Howe Institute.

Coulombe, S., and F. C. Lee. 1995. Convergence across Canadian provinces, 1961 to 1991. *CJE* 28 (November):886-98.

Cousineau, J.-M. 1985. Unemployment insurance and labour market adjustments. In *Income Distribution and Economic Security in Canada*, ed. F. Vaillancourt. Toronto: University of Toronto Press.

Cousineau, J.-M., and C. Green. 1978. Structural unemployment in Canada: 1971-1974. Did it worsen? *RI/IR* 33 (2):175-92.

Crossley, T. F., S. R. G. Jones, and P. Kuhn. 1994. Gender differences in displacement cost: Evidence and implications. *JHR* 29:461-80.

Doiron, D. J. 1995. Lay-offs as signals: The Canadian evidence. *CJE* 28 (November):822-35.

______. 1995. A test of the insider-outsider hypothesis in union preferences. *Economica* 62 (August):281-90.

Fallick, B. C. 1993. The industrial mobility of displaced workers. *JOLE* 11 (April):302-23.

______. 1996. A review of the recent empirical literature on displaced workers. *ILRR* 50 (October):5-16.

Feldstein, M. 1978. The effect of unemployment insurance on temporary layoff unemployment. *AER* 68 (December):834-46.

Ferrall, C. 1997. Unemployment insurance eligibility and the school-to-work transition in Canada and the United States. *Journal of Business and Economic Statistics* 15 (April):115-29.

Foster, A. D., and M. R. Rosenzweig. 1994. A test for moral hazard in the labor market: Contractual arrangements, effort, and health. *R.E. Stats.* 76 (May):213-27.

Gera, S., Ed. 1991. *Canadian Unemployment*. Ottawa: Economic Council of Canada.

Gibbons, R., and L. F. Katz. 1991. Layoffs and lemons. *JOLE* (October):351-80.

Glenday, G., and J. Alam. 1982. The labour market experience of individuals: Unemployment insurance and regional effects. Processed, York University.

Gordon, D. 1974. A neoclassical theory of Keynesian unemployment. *EI* 12 (December):431-59.

Gray, D., and G. Grenier. 1995. The determinants of jobless durations of displaced workers in Canada. *Applied Economics* 27 (September):829-39.

Green, D. A., and W. C. Riddell. 1993. The economic effects of unemployment insurance in Canada: An empirical analysis of UI disentitlement. *JOLE* 11 (January).

______. 1997. Qualifying for unemployment insurance: An empirical analysis. *EJ* 107 (January):67–84.

______. 2000. The effects of the shift to an hours-based entrance requirement. Report prepared for strategic evaluation and monitoring evaluation and data development, strategic policy, Human Resources Development Canada.

Grenon, L. 1998. Looking for work. *Perspectives on Labour and Income* 10 (Autumn):22–26.

______. 1999. Obtaining a job. *Perspectives on Labour and Income* 11 (Spring):23–27.

Gunderson, M., and W. C. Riddell. 2001. Unemployment insurance: Lessons from Canada. In *Labor Market Policies in Canada and Latin America: Challenges of the New Millennium*, ed. A. Berry. Norwell, Massachusetts: Kluwer Academic Publisher.

Ham, J. C., and S. A. Rea. 1987. Unemployment insurance and male unemployment duration in Canada. *JOLE* 5 (July):325–53.

Hart, O. D. 1983. Optimal labour contracts under asymmetric information: an introduction. *R.E. Studies* 50 (January):3–35.

Jacobson, L. S., R. J. LaLonde, and D. G. Sullivan. 1993. Earnings losses of displaced workers. *AER* 83 (September):685–709.

Jones, S.R.G., and M. Corak. 1995. The persistence of unemployment: How important were regional extended benefits? *CJE* 28 (August):555–67.

Jones, S.R.G., and P. Kuhn. 1995. Mandatory notice and unemployment. *JOLE* 13 (October):599–622.

Kahn, S., and K. Lang. 1995. The causes of hours constraints: Evidence from Canada. *CJE* 28 (November):914–28.

Kaliski, S. F. 1976. Unemployment and unemployment insurance: Testing some corollaries. *CJE* 9 (November):705–12.

______.. 1985. Trends, changes and imbalances: A survey of the Canadian labour market. In *Work and Pay: The Canadian Labour Market*, ed. W. C. Riddell. Toronto: University of Toronto Press.

Kesselman, J. R. 1983. *Financing Canadian Unemployment Insurance*. Toronto: Canadian Tax Foundation.

Krugman, P. 1994. Past and prospective causes of high unemployment. In *Reducing Unemployment: Current Issues and Policy Options*. Symposium sponsored by the Federal Reserve Bank of Kansas City, Jackson Hole, Wyoming, August 25–27.

Kruse, D. 1988. International trade and the labor market experience of displaced workers. *ILRR* 41 (April):402–17.

Kuhn, P. J. 2000a. Policies for an Internet labour market. *Policy Options* (October):42–47.

______. 2000b. Canada and the OECD hypothesis: Does labour market inflexibility explain Canada's high level of unemployment? In *Adopting Public Policy to a Labour Market in Transition*, eds. W. C. Riddell and F. St-Hilaire. Montreal: Institute for Research on Public Policy.

Lazar, F. 1978. The impact of the 1971 unemployment insurance revisions on unemployment rates: Another look. *CJE* 11 (August):559–69.

Lilien, D. 1982. Sectoral shifts and cyclical unemployment. *JPE* 90 (August):777–93.

Lindbeck, A., and D. J. Snower. 1986. Cooperation, harassment, and involuntary unemployment. *AER* 78:167–88.

______. 1987. Efficiency wages versus insiders and outsiders. *European Economic Review* 31 (February March):407–16.

Lindbeck, A., and D. J. Snower. 1988. *The Insider-Outsider Theory of Employment and Unemployment*. Cambridge: The MIT Press.

Lippman, S., and J. McCall. 1976. The economics of job search: A survey. *EI* 14 (June):155–189 and (September):347–368; comment by G. Borjas and M. Goldberg 16 (January 1978):119–125.

Maki, D. 1971. *Search Behaviour in Canadian Job Markets*. Ottawa: Economic Council of Canada.

______. 1977. Unemployment benefits and the duration of claims in Canada. *Applied Economics* 9:227–36.

McDonald, J. T., and C. Worswick. 1999. Wages, implicit contracts, and the business cycle: Evidence from Canadian micro data. *JPE* 107 (August):884–92.

Meyer, B. D. 1995. Lessons from the U.S. unemployment insurance experiments. *JEL* 33 (March):91–131.

______. 1996. What have we learned from the Illinois reemployment bonus experiment? *JOLE* 14 (January):26–51.

Milbourne, R. D., D. D. Purvis, and W. D. Scoones. 1991. Unemployment insurance and unemployment dynamics. *CJE* 24 (November):804–26.

Milne, W., and M. Tucker. 1992. Income convergence across Canadian provinces: Does growth theory help explain the process? *Atlantic Canada Economics Association* 21:170–82.

Mirrlees, J. 1975. A pure theory of underdeveloped economies. In *Agriculture in Development Theory*, ed. L. Reynolds. New Haven: Yale University Press.

Mortensen, D. T., and C. A. Pissarides. 1999. New developments in models of search in the labor market. In *Handbook of Labor Economics*, eds. O. Ashenfelter and D. Card. New York and Oxford: Elsevier Science, North Holland.

Murphy, K., and R. Topel. 1987. Unemployment, risk and earnings. In *Unemployment and Its Structure of Labour Markets*, eds. K. Lang and J. Leonard. Oxford: Basil Blackwell.

Neal, D. 1995. Industry-specific human capital: Evidence from displaced workers. *JOLE* 13 (October):653-77.

Neelin, J. 1987. Sectoral shifts and Canadian unemployment. *R.E. Stats.* 69:718-32.

Nickell, S. 1997. Unemployment and labor market rigidities: Europe versus North America. *JEP* 11 (Summer):55-74.

Nickell, S., and R. Layard. 1999. Labor market institutions and economic performance. In *Handbook of Labor Economics*, eds. O. Ashenfelter and D. Card. New York and Oxford: Elsevier Science, North Holland.

Okun, A. M. 1981. *Prices and Quantities: A Macroeconomic Analysis*. Washington: The Brookings Institute.

Osberg, L. 1991. Unemployment and inter-industry labour mobility in Canada in the 1980s. *Applied Economics* 23: 1707-17.

Phelps, E. S. et al. 1970. *Microeconomic Foundations of Employment and Inflation Theory*. New York: Norton.

Phipps, S. A. 1990. Quantity-constrained household responses to unemployed insurance reform. *EJ* 100 (March):124-40.

______. 1991a. Behavioral response to UI reform in constrained and unconstrained models of labour supply. *CJE* 24 (February):34-54.

______. 1991b. Equity and efficiency consequences of unemployment insurance reform in Canada. *Economica* 58 (May):199-214.

______. 1993. Does unemployment insurance increase unemployment? *Canadian Business Economics* 1 (Spring):37-50.

Ragan, C. 1995. A risk-sharing view of real wages and contract length. *CJE* 28 (November):1161-79.

Rea, S. A. 1977. Unemployment insurance and labour supply: A simulation of the 1971 Unemployment Insurance Act. *CJE* 10 (May):263-78.

Reid, F. 1985. Reductions in worktime: An assessment of employment sharing to reduce unemployment. In *Work and Pay*, ed. W. C. Riddell. Toronto: University of Toronto Press.

Riddell, W. C. (Ed.). 1985. *Work and Pay: The Canadian Labour Market*. Toronto: University of Toronto Press.

Riddell, W. C. 1999. Canadian labour market performance in international perspective. *CJE* 32 (November):1097-134.

Rosen, S. 1985. Implicit contracts: A survey. *JEL* 23 (September):1144-75.

Ruhm, C. J. 1992. Advance notice and postdisplacement joblessness. *JOLE* 10 (January):1-32.

Saffer, H. 1982. Layoffs and unemployment insurance. *JPubEc* 19 (October):121-30.

______. 1983. The effects of unemployment insurance on temporary and permanent layoffs. *R.E. Stats.* 65 (October):647-52.

Sampson, L. 1985. A study of the impact of sectoral shifts on aggregate unemployment in Canada. *CJE* 18 (August):518-30.

Shapiro, C., and J. E. Stiglitz. 1984. Equilibrium unemployment as a worker discipline device. *AER* 74 (June):433-44.

Sharir, S., and P. Kuch. 1978. Contribution to unemployment of insurance-induced labour force participation: Canada 1972. *Economics Letters* 1:271-4.

Social Research and Demonstration Corporation. 2001a. Essays on the repeat use of unemployment insurance: The earnings supplement project.

______. 2001b. The frequent use of unemployment insurance in Canada: The earnings supplement project.

Solow, R. M. 1985. Insiders and outsiders in wage determination. *Scandinavian Journal of Economics* 87:411-28.

Stigler, G. J. 1962. Information in the labour market. *JPE* 70 (October):94-105.

Stiglitz, J. E. 1976. The efficiency wage hypothesis, surplus labour, and the distribution of income in L.D.C.s. *Oxford Economic Papers* 28 (July):185-207.

Storer, P. 1996. Separating the effects of aggregate and sectoral shocks with estimates from a Markov-switching search model. *Journal of Economic Dynamics and Control* 20 (January/March):93-121.

Strauss, J. 1986. Does better nutrition raise farm productivity? *JPE* 94 (April):297-320.

Strauss, J., and D. Thomas. 1995. Human resources: Empirical modeling of household and family decisions. In *Handbook of Development Economics, Volume 3*, eds. J. Behrman and T. N. Srinivasan. Amsterdam: North Holland.

Subramanian, S., and A. Deaton. 1996. The demand for food and calories. *JPE* 104 (February):133-62.

Swaim, P. L., and M. J. Podgursky. 1990. Advance notice and job search: The value of an early start. *JHR* 25 (Spring):147-78.

Topel, R. H. 1983. On layoffs and unemployment insurance. *AER* 73 (September):541-59.

Vanderkamp, J. 1986. The efficiency of the interregional adjustment process. In *Disparities and Interregional Adjustment*, ed. K. Norrie. Toronto: University of Toronto Press.

Winer, S. L., and D. Gauthier. 1982. *Internal Migration and Fiscal Structure*. Ottawa: Economic Council of Canada.

Woodbury, S., and R. Spiegelman. 1987. Bonuses to workers to reduce unemployment: Randomized trials in Illinois. *AER* 77 (September):513-30.

Chapter Nineteen

Wage Changes, Price Inflation, and Unemployment

Main Questions

- *What is the connection between aggregate wage changes and the unemployment rate?*
- *Is high inflation still associated with low unemployment; or, of more contemporary interest, can low inflation be associated with low unemployment?*
- *To what extent are anti-inflationary policies linked with high unemployment?*
- *Does unemployment have a tendency to persist, that is, can an economy become "trapped" in a high-unemployment state?*
- *What role does wage rigidity play at a macroeconomic level in generating unemployment?*

Previous chapters dealt with a variety of wage *structures*, such as the occupational, industrial, and regional wage structures and wage differences between males and females or union and nonunion workers. In this chapter, we deal with the aggregate wage *level* and its determinants, in particular how it is affected by other aggregate variables such as the price level and unemployment. Often this topic is analyzed at the macroeconomic level of aggregation of the economy as a whole; however, increased attention has been paid to its microeconomic foundations—that is, how aggregate wage changes and movements in aggregate employment and unemployment are the results of decisions made by many individual workers, unions, and firms. In addition, empirical analysis of the determinants of wage changes is often made at the more disaggregate level of the industry, or for individual wage contracts, as well as the economy as a whole.

The focus of our analysis is on the labour market dimensions of the issue. Since this is essentially a topic of macroeconomics, a more complete treatment is left to texts and courses in macroeconomics.

CANADIAN EXPERIENCE

Table 19.1 summarizes Canada's long-term experience with respect to inflation, unemployment, and related economic aggregates (see also Figure 17.1 and Table 17.1). In order to abstract from the effects of business cycles, the table shows average performance between the postwar cyclical peak years of 1956, 1966, 1973, 1981, 1989, and 2000. Average data for the period prior to 1947 are also included for historical perspective. However, because this period includes both the Great Depression and World War II, the averages mask considerable variability.

Overall economic performance was excellent during the first two decades of the postwar period. Two bursts of inflation occurred during this period, one immediately after the war and the second during the Korean War (1950–1953). Otherwise, inflation rates were low by the standards of both previous and subsequent experience and displayed no obvious trend until they began to creep upward in the mid-1960s. Unemployment rates were also low by the standards of other periods, although they did rise significantly during the 1957–58 recession and remained above normal levels until the early 1960s. Productivity and real income per capita grew at rapid rates from 1947 to 1973 compared to rates attained earlier and subsequently. Employment also grew rapidly.

Signs of emerging problems with inflation and unemployment, however, began to be apparent in the late 1960s and early 1970s. Inflation rates rose during the late 1960s, with the rate of price increase falling below 4 percent only during the brief recession of 1970–71. After that slowdown, Canada, together with most other Western countries, embarked on an expansionary path. Employment grew extremely rapidly during 1972–1974 but only a modest decline in unemployment took place. Wage and price inflation climbed substantially.

A marked deterioration in economic performance is evident in Table 19.1 during the period 1974–1981. The coexistence of high inflation and high unemployment—a phenomenon often referred to as **stagflation**—was the most significant departure from the

Table 19.1 Aggregate Economic Trends, Canada, 1927–2000

	Growth Rate[a] Of:			Annual Average	
Period	Real Income per Capita[b]	Productivity[c]	Employment[d]	Inflation Rate[e]	Unemployment Rate[f]
1927–1946	2.2	2.1	1.4	0.1	8.1
1947–1956	2.6	3.5	1.8	4.3	3.2
1957–1966	2.4	2.1	2.5	2.0	5.5
1967–1973	3.9	2.5	3.0	4.4	5.2
1974–1981	1.7	0.1	2.9	9.7	7.3
1982–1989	1.9	1.3	1.8	5.3	9.8
1990–2000	1.4	1.2	1.3	2.2	9.3

a. Growth rates are averages of compound increases from the level in the year before the period specified to the level in the final year of the period specified.
b. Real GDP divided by population.
c. Real GDP per person employed.
d. Civilian employment; minor noncomparabilities in series occur in 1946 and 1966.
e. As measured by the Consumer Price Index.
f. Minor noncomparabilities occur in 1946 and 1966.

Sources: M. C. Urquhart (ed.), *Historical Statistics of Canada,* Catalogue 11–516 (Toronto: Macmillan, 1965); Bank of Canada, *Bank of Canada Review,* various issues; Statistics Canada, *National Income and Expenditure Accounts,* Catalogue 13-533, various issues; CANSIM database <www.statcan.ca/english/CANSIM/>.

past. Prior to the 1970s, increases in unemployment were generally accompanied by decreases in the rate of inflation and vice versa. The 1973 OPEC oil price shock contributed to higher rates of inflation while at the same time causing a recession in many Western countries in 1974–75. The slowdown was milder here than in many countries for several reasons: Canada is a producer as well as consumer of oil, the federal government imposed price controls that prevented domestic oil prices from increasing as much as world oil prices, and the government pursued expansionary aggregate demand policies to offset declining demand for Canadian exports due to the world recession. Nonetheless, employment growth declined noticeably in 1974–75 and unemployment rose.

The other evident departure from earlier postwar experience was the sharp decline in productivity growth. Real income growth also slowed considerably. Only employment growth remained healthy during the period 1974–1981.

Faced with continuing escalation in wage and price increases and the deteriorating demand conditions associated with the world recession, the federal government introduced the Anti-Inflation Program (AIP) in October 1975. The key ingredients in the program were mandatory wage and price (or profit) controls and gradual reduction in the growth of aggregate demand through fiscal and monetary restraint.

During the 1975–1978 AIP, wage settlements declined substantially; price increases also fell, although by a smaller amount. As discussed later in this chapter, most empirical studies attribute some of this decline in inflation to the controls program. The reduction in demand due to fiscal and monetary restraint also played a role.

The combination of the 1974–1975 recession and the 1975–1978 AIP resulted in some moderation of inflationary pressures. Nonetheless, in the late 1970s inflation began to move upward again in Canada and elsewhere. In 1979 the second OPEC oil price increase occurred. By the end of the decade rates of price increase exceeded 10 percent in both the United States and Canada. A variety of aspects of economic behaviour suggested that expectations of continuing inflation were deeply entrenched.

The 1980s were dominated by the onset of and recovery from the severe recession of 1981–82. A consequence of the buildup of inflation during the 1960s and 1970s, together with the evidence that many individuals expected high inflation to continue, was the adoption of a much more determined anti-inflationary stance by the monetary authorities in the United States and subsequently in Canada. The sharp drop in money supply growth in 1981 and 1982 led to a major reduction in the growth of aggregate demand. Initially the impact of the reduction in aggregate demand fell primarily on output and employment: employment declined by over 3 percent in 1982 and unemployment soared to over 11 percent. As the impact of the downturn became more widely felt, inflation began to decline dramatically. The adoption in 1982 of the federal "6 and 5" wage restraint program and subsequent related provincial programs, which limited the increases of public-sector employees, may also have played a role in the decline in wage increases. By 1984 the rates of wage and price inflation were the lowest since the 1960s. The restrictive monetary policy, possibly with some additional contribution from the public-sector wage control programs, had clearly achieved its objectives of substantially reducing a deeply entrenched inflation. Equally clear was the enormous cost of such a policy—high unemployment, business failures, mortgage foreclosures, and reduced output.

www.bank-banque-canada.ca

During the long period of economic growth from 1983 to 1989, the Bank of Canada continued to follow a policy of reducing—or at least containing—inflation. Indeed, during this period the Bank of Canada increasingly adopted the view that its primary objective should be that of price stability. The principal concern was to prevent a return to the high-inflation era of the 1970s and early 1980s. Unemployment fell gradually during this period of economic expansion, and by 1989 the unemployment rate had returned to its pre-recession level of 7.5 percent. The policy of inflation reduction had met with considerable success. In the peak year of the business cycle (1989), the rate of inflation was 5.0

percent, a modest level by the standards of the previous 20 years. Nonetheless, even this reduced level of inflation was inconsistent with the Bank of Canada's stated goal of achieving "price stability."

During the 1980s, productivity growth recovered somewhat from the depressed levels experienced during 1974-1981, and real income growth increased. Employment growth remained healthy by historical standards, but lower than the very rapid pace set in the 1960s and 1970s.

http://economics.ca

The 1990s, like the previous decade, began with a major recession and ended with a period of strong growth. The 1990-92 recession—named "The Great Canadian Slump" by Fortin (1996) in his Presidential Address to the Canadian Economics Association—was Canada's worst since the Great Depression. The unemployment rate increased to a similar extent as in the 1981-82 recession—peaking at 11.3 percent in 1992—but the protracted nature of the early 1990s downturn and the slow and uneven recovery during 1993-1996 contributed to an unusually large cumulative loss in employment and output.

Beginning in the early 1990s, the Bank of Canada sought to bring about a reduction in inflation from the then-prevailing rate of about 5 percent. Formal "inflation reduction targets" were introduced in 1991. These provided for a gradual reduction in inflation, with mid-point ranges of 3 percent, 2.5 percent, and 2 percent during the period 1991-1994. Monetary policy was focused on achieving these targets even if doing so might bring about a period of slow growth and high unemployment.

The extent to which the Bank of Canada's new policy of **inflation targeting**—and the associated levels of money supply growth and interest rates—contributed to the severity of the 1990-1992 recession is a matter of debate. Fortin (1996) argues that monetary policy was the leading cause of the "Great Canadian Slump." Freedman and Macklem (1998) defend the Bank of Canada's actions, and suggest that the recession was much deeper and more prolonged than could be due to monetary policy alone. They claim that the Canadian economy was subject to an unusually large amount of structural adjustment during the early 1990s, and this structural change contributed to the weak economic conditions. As is often the case with aggregate time series data, it is difficult to convincingly evaluate the competing explanations.

Real incomes stagnated during the period 1990-1996, but the strong economic growth toward the end of the decade meant that living standards of Canadians saw at least some improvement during 1990-2000. Nonetheless, real income growth during this period was the poorest of any postwar business cycle, and was also worse than in most other advanced economies, so that Canadian living standards fell in relative terms (Fortin, 1999). Productivity and employment growth rates were also low by postwar standards. The only significant achievement was the low rate of inflation, the best in Canada since the early 1960s.

As this review of the Canadian experience indicates, inflation and unemployment have been dominant policy concerns for at least the past three decades. They remain major challenges facing policymakers today. We begin our discussion of the labour market dimensions of inflation and unemployment with an examination of the determinants of wage changes.

DETERMINANTS OF WAGE CHANGES

Wage changes play a significant role in the inflationary process. Labour costs are an important component of total cost and reductions in the rate of price increase are unlikely to occur, other than temporarily, without accompanying reductions in the rate of wage increase. For this reason, policies to control inflation are typically directed to achieving reductions in wage as well as price increases. The first step in the design of such policies is to understand the factors that influence wage determination.

Unemployment Rate

In his classic article based on data from the United Kingdom for the period 1861–1957, Phillips (1958) estimated a negative relationship between aggregate money wage changes and unemployment in the economy as a whole—a relationship now generally referred to as the **Phillips curve**, as depicted in Figure 19.1(e). Much subsequent research has been devoted to the theoretical underpinnings of this relationship as well as to empirical investigations of other determinants of aggregate wage changes.

Lipsey (1960) explained the negative relationship on the basis that (1) the unemployment rate is a measure of the overall excess demand or supply in the aggregate labour market, and (2) the rate of wage change is a function of the amount of excess labour demand or supply. Aggregation over individual labour markets, each with possibly different amounts of excess demand or supply, is a key aspect of this explanation.

Figure 19.1 illustrates the main elements of Lipsey's theory. At any point in time some labour markets are characterized by **excess demand** for labour and others by **excess supply**, as shown in panel (a) of Figure 19.1. Basic economic theory predicts that wages will be rising in those markets characterized by positive excess demand and falling in markets with negative excess demand (excess supply). The rate at which wages adjust is assumed to be related to the amount of excess demand. This relationship may take various forms; for purpose of illustration it is shown in Figure 19.1(b) as being linear throughout (heavy line). Alternatively, it could be linear with a kink at the origin (shown by the dashed line), if wages rise more quickly in response to positive excess demand than they fall in response to negative excess demand, or even nonlinear (not shown). Note that the amount of excess demand in market i, $D_i - S_i$ is expressed relative to the size of the market, $(D_i - S_i)/S_i$, because excess demand of 25 workers has a different impact in a market with 50 workers than in a market with 500 workers.

The aggregate rate of wage change $\dot{W}$ is simply the weighted sum of the wage changes[1] in each individual market, the weights α_i being employment in market i:

$$\dot{W} = \sum_i \alpha_i \dot{W}_i \tag{19.1}$$

Because the rate of wage change in market i is related to the amount of excess demand in that market, the aggregate rate of change of wages is a function of aggregate excess labour demand:

$$\dot{W} = f\left(\frac{D - S}{S}\right) \tag{19.2}$$

The next step is to relate aggregate excess labour demand to observable counterparts, the unemployment rate (U) and the **job vacancy rate** (V):

$$\frac{D - S}{S} = V - U \tag{19.3}$$

This implies a relationship between the rate of wage change and the excess of job vacancies over unemployment:

$$\dot{W} = f(V - U) \tag{19.4}$$

If there is a stable relationship between the unemployment rate and the job vacancy rate, as depicted in Figure 19.1(c), then U alone can be used to measure aggregate excess demand. Substituting the relationship

$$V = g(U) \tag{19.5}$$

[1]The notation $\dot{Y}$ for any variable Y refers to the rate of change of Y with respect to time, that is, $\frac{\Delta Y}{\Delta TIME}$.

into equations 19.3 and 19.4 gives

$$\frac{D - S}{S} = g(U) - U = h(U) \qquad 19.6$$

which is shown in Figure 19.1(d) and

$$\dot{W} = f(g(U) - U) = F(U) \qquad 19.7$$

which is the Phillips curve shown in panel (e) ($F'(U) < 0$).[2]

From equation 19.3 there will exist values of the job vacancy rate and unemployment rate which imply aggregate excess labour demand equals zero. These are shown as V^* and U^* in panels (c), (d), and (e) of Figure 19.1. At U^* the aggregate labour market is in equilibrium in the sense that aggregate demand for labour equals aggregate supply and the aggregate rate of wage change equals zero (i.e., $F(U^*) = 0$). For this reason, U^* is called the equilibrium or **natural unemployment rate**. Note, however, that individual labour markets need not be in equilibrium. As discussed in Chapter 18 on unemployment, because of imperfect information, the process of matching workers and jobs takes time. Thus unfilled job vacancies and unemployed workers will coexist at any point in time. This disequilibrium at the micro level is nonetheless consistent with aggregate labour market equilibrium in that the excess demand (unfilled job vacancies) in some markets is offset by an equal amount of excess supply (unemployed job seekers) in other markets. The aggregate rate of wage change equals zero because markets in which wages are rising due to excess demand are offset by markets in which wages are declining.

Under the assumptions illustrated in Figure 19.1, the aggregate labour market is in equilibrium when the unemployment rate equals the job vacancy rate, as depicted in panel (c). However, this outcome need not occur in general. In particular, if the relationship between wage changes and excess demand is kinked at the origin, as depicted by the dashed line in panel (b), aggregate labour market equilibrium will require an unemployment rate in excess of the job vacancy rate, such as is illustrated by U^{**} and V^{**} in Figure 19.1(c). In these circumstances, because wages fall less rapidly in response to excess supply than they rise in response to excess demand, the aggregate amount of excess supply must exceed the amount of excess demand in order for the aggregate rate of wage change to equal zero. Thus, downward wage rigidity—or, more generally, asymmetry in the response of wages to excess demand versus excess supply—results in a higher equilibrium unemployment rate.

The natural unemployment rate depends on numerous factors discussed in Chapters 17 and 18 such as the magnitude and frequency of seasonal, cyclical, and other economic disturbances, the job search behaviour of employers and workers and the efficiency of the matching process, the use of layoffs to respond to changes in demand, the amount of labour force turnover, the age-sex composition of the labour force, and labour market policies such as minimum wages and unemployment insurance. Although some of these factors remain approximately constant over time, others change and therefore alter the equilibrium level of unemployment. In these circumstances, the appropriate measure of aggregate excess demand for labour is the difference between the observed and natural unemployment rates, $U - U^*$, with $U > U^*$ implying excess supply of labour and $U < U^*$ implying excess demand. That is, when the equilibrium unemployment rate itself may be changing, the unemployment rate is not a reliable measure of aggregate excess demand and $U - U^*$ should be employed in the wage equation in lieu of U. This requires a modification of equation 19.7:

$$\dot{W} = F(U - U^*),\ F'(\cdot) < 0,\ F(0) = 0 \qquad (19.8)$$

[2]The notation $F'(U)$ refers to the slope of the function F, with respect to U, that is, $\frac{\Delta F}{\Delta U}$.

Figure 19.1 **Wage Changes, Excess Demand, and Unemployment**

The figure illustrates the derivation of an aggregate Phillips curve from the micro behaviour of two individual labour markets. Panel (a) shows two labour markets, one (market a) with excess labour supply of $(D_a - S_a)/S_a$ at the current wage rate W_a and the second (market b) with excess labour demand of $(D_b - S_b)/S_b$ at the current wage W_b. In market a the current wage exceeds the equilibrium wage rate W_a^* and vice versa in market b.

Panel (b) illustrates two possible relationships between the amount of excess demand or supply in an individual market and the rate of wage adjustment. The solid line shows a linear adjustment function in which the rate of wage change is $\dot{W}_a$ in market a and $\dot{W}_b$ in market b. The solid plus dashed lines shows a kinked adjustment function in which the rate of upward wage change in response to excess labour demand ($\dot{W}_a$) is greater than the rate of downward wage adjustment in response to excess supply ($\dot{W}_b'$).

Panel (c) shows an inverse relationship between the job vacancy rate (V) and the unemployment rate (U). U* and U** are two possible values of the equilibrium unemployment rate at which aggregate excess labour demand equals zero, as illustrated for U* in panel (d). This implies a negative nonlinear relationship between aggregate excess demand (D - S)/S and U and between W and U, as shown in panel (e).

(a) Disequilibrium in individual labour markets

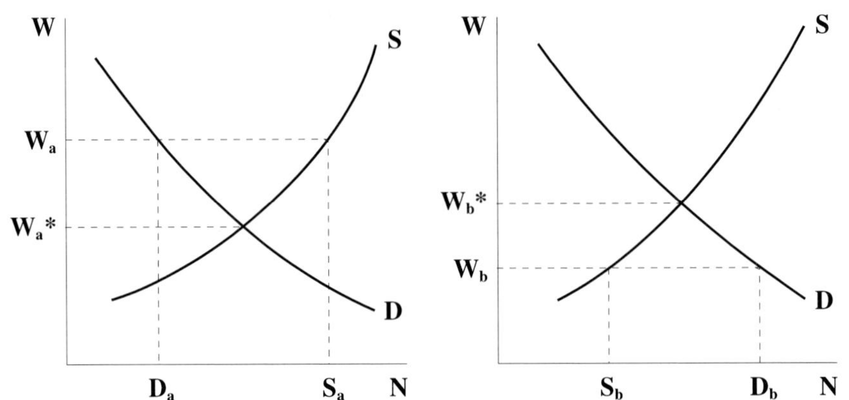

(b) The relationship between wage changes and excess demand

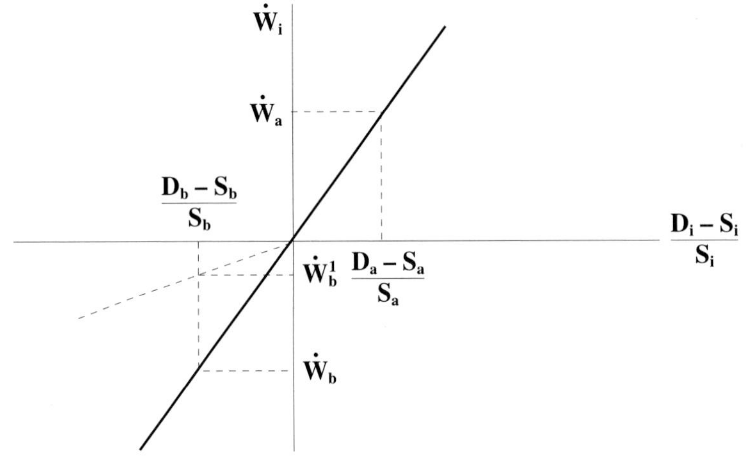

(c) The relationship between unemployment and job vacancies

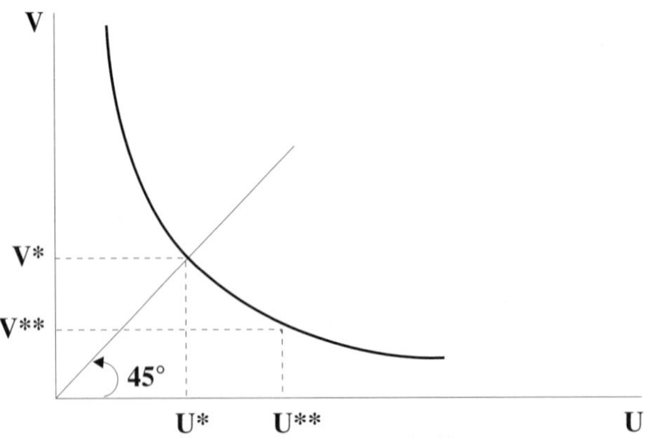

Figure 19.1 **Wage Changes, Excess Demand, and Unemployment *(continued)***

(d) The relationship between aggregate excess demand and unemployment

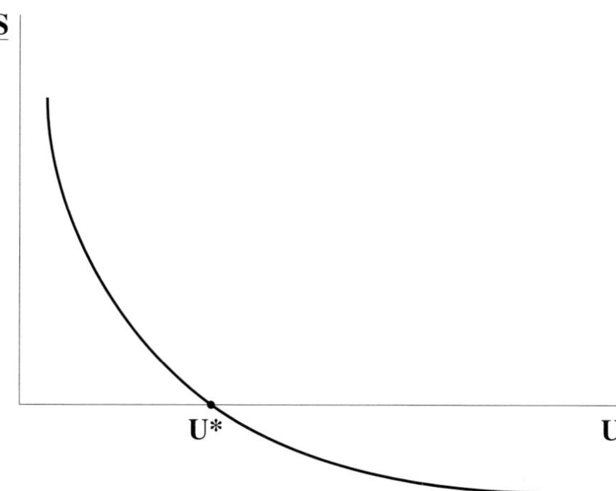

(e) The relationship between wage changes and unemployment

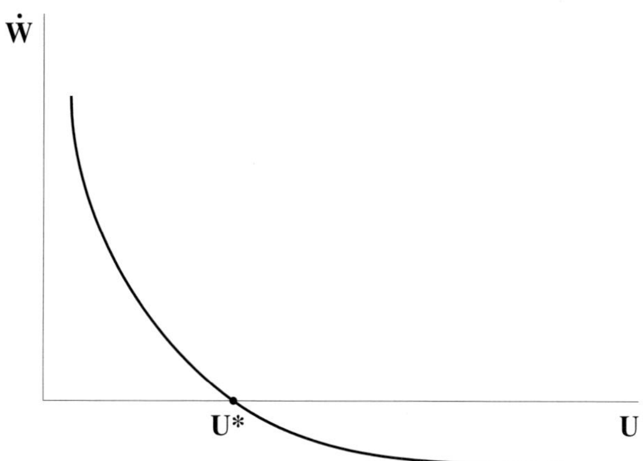

This clearly presents a challenge for empirical research on wage determination in that the natural unemployment rate is not directly observed. We discuss the way empirical studies have dealt with this issue in a subsequent section.

This discussion assumes that there is a unique equilibrium or natural unemployment rate U* and that U* is independent of the actual unemployment rate U. However, it is possible that there may be more than one unemployment rate at which the economy is in macroeconomic equilibrium. Similarly, it is also possible that economic shocks which lead to changes in the aggregate unemployment rate may also cause changes to occur in the natural unemployment rate. Both these possibilities have received attention from macro and labour economists, and are discussed later in this chapter under the heading "Unemployment Persistence."

An increase in the natural unemployment rate will shift the Phillips curve upward, resulting in larger wage increases at each unemployment rate, because there will be increased excess demand (or reduced excess supply) at each measured unemployment rate. The unemployment-vacancies relationship will also generally shift to the right because increased excess demand for labour at each unemployment rate is usually associated with more job vacancies at each level of measured unemployment. However, in some circumstances an increase in the natural rate is associated with a movement along, rather than a shift in, the U – V relationship. An example is the movement from U* to U** in Figure 19.1(c), which could have been caused by an increase in the degree of downward wage rigidity in the economy, as illustrated by the shift from the linear to the kinked relationship between wage changes and excess demand in Figure 19.1(b).

In summary, Lipsey's (1960) explanation of the Phillips curve is based on two stable relationships: a positive relation between wage changes and excess demand for labour and an inverse relation between excess demand for labour and the unemployment rate. The latter can be derived by expressing excess labour demand as the difference between the number of unfilled job vacancies and the number of unemployed workers, and assuming a stable (inverse) relation between unemployment and vacancies. The assumption of a stable relationship between the vacancy rate V and the unemployment rate U implies that there is a one-to-one relationship between excess demand and the unemployment rate.

Phillips' original paper indicated that the relationship between wage changes and unemployment in the United Kingdom had remained stable for almost a hundred years. However, in many countries, including Canada, the temporal stability of this relationship began to be questioned in the late 1960s and early 1970s; the upward drift in wage and price inflation beginning in the mid-1960s resulted in rates of wage increase well above those predicted by estimated Phillips curves. One explanation for this development was that the relationship between the unemployment rate and excess demand for labour had changed; as noted above, such a change could be due to an increase in the natural unemployment rate, perhaps associated with the changing composition of the labour force and revisions to the unemployment insurance system. Evidence relating to this explanation is discussed subsequently. Another leading explanation involved inflationary expectations.

Expected Inflation

Seminal contributions by Friedman (1968) and Phelps (1967, 1968) attacked the theoretical basis for a stable or permanent relationship between wage inflation and unemployment. Friedman and Phelps emphasized the role of inflationary expectations in the wage determination process. If both employers and employees expect prices to increase, they will adjust wage changes upward by the amount of **expected inflation** in order to achieve the desired change in real wages.

Expected wage or price inflation is a general term which includes several components: changes in the firm's product prices, in wages in similar firms and industries, and in the cost of living. These reflect the fact that what matters to employers and employees are *relative wages* and *real wages*. To workers, what is important are wages relative to those received by comparable workers in other firms and industries (relative wages) and relative to the cost of living (real wages). Thus, expectations about wage changes elsewhere and about changes in the cost of living will influence wage determination, especially when wages are not set or negotiated frequently. To firms, what is important are wages relative to wages elsewhere (which affects the firm's ability to attract and keep workers) and relative to the prices that the firm can charge for its products (which affects the firm's ability to pay). Thus expectations about product price increases should also be a factor in wage determination. In the analysis that follows we will focus on price expectations and thus on issues relating to real wages. The analysis of wage expectations and issues relating to relative wages results in similar conclusions (Phelps, 1968).

The role of expected inflation is illustrated in Figure 19.2. Two individual labour markets, market A with excess supply for labour at the current price level (p_0) and market B with excess demand at p_0, are used for purposes of illustration. During the period for which the wage rate is being determined, the price level is expected to rise from p_0 to p_1^e,

Figure 19.2 **Wage Changes and Expected Inflation**

The role of expected inflation is illustrated in two labour markets, market (a) with excess supply of labour at the current price level P_0 and market (b) with excess labour demand at P_0. In the initial situation the demand for labour is $D(P_0)$ and the supply is $S(P_0)$, giving equilibrium wages of W^*_a and W^*_b respectively. Initial period wages are $W_a > W^*_a$ and $W_b < W^*_b$. The price level is expected to rise from P_0 to P^e_1 resulting in upward shifts in labour demand from $D(P_0)$ to $D(P^*_1)$ and labour supply from $S(P_0)$ to $S(P^*_1)$. Because both demand and supply shift up vertically by the amount of expected inflation, an increase in expected inflation does not alter the equilibrium level of employment N^*_i in either market ($i = a,b$).

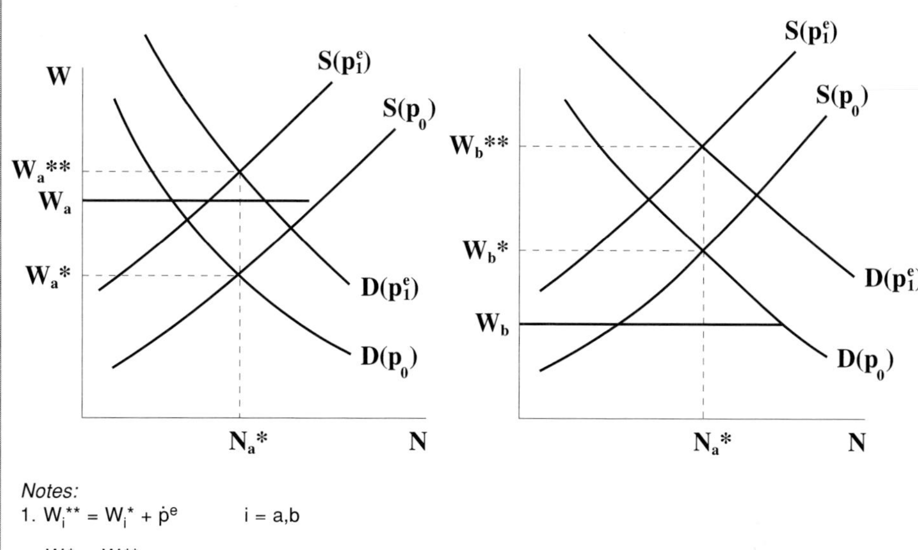

Notes:

1. $W_i^{**} = W_i^* + \dot{p}^e$ $\quad i = a,b$
2. $\frac{W_i^*}{p_0} = \frac{W_i^{**}}{p_1^e}$ $\quad i = a,b$

equivalent to an expected inflation rate of $\dot{p}^e$. Thus both the labour demand and labour supply curves shift up by the expected increase in the price level. Labour demand is a function of the price level because, as indicated in Chapter 5, the firm's labour demand schedule is the marginal revenue product of labour, defined as the marginal physical product times the price at which the product is sold. Hence, an increase in the price of output, other things being equal, will shift up the demand for labour by the amount of the price increase. The labour supply schedule is also a function of the price level, as discussed in Chapter 2 on labour supply, because the worker's desired supply of labour depends on the real wage—the money wage divided by the price level for consumption goods and services. An increase in these prices will thus increase the asking wage for any specific quantity of labour by exactly the increase in the price level. The labour supply curve thus shifts vertically upward by the amount of expected inflation.[3] Even though the current equilibrium wages in markets A and B are W_a^* and W_b^* respectively, the equilibrium wages for the period for which the wage rate is being determined are W_a^{**} and W_b^{**}. Thus the observed wage change will be from W_i to W_i^{**} in market A and B. This wage change can be expressed as the sum of two components: (1) from W_i to W_i^*, reflecting the current amount of excess demand or supply in market i, and (2) from W_i^* to W_i^{**}, reflecting the expected increase in the price level. Following the previous derivation of the relationship between wage changes and the current amount of aggregate excess demand for labour as measured by the unemployment rate, the Phillips curve becomes:

$$\dot{W} = F(U\text{-}U^*) + \dot{p}^e \qquad (19.9)$$

[3]The relevant price level in the labour supply function is the price level of consumption goods (e.g., the Consumer Price Index) while the relevant price in the labour demand function is the firm's product price. For expositional purposes, these are assumed to increase at the same rate. The analysis can easily be generalized to deal with differential rates of price increase.

This relationship—often referred to as the **expectations-augmented Phillips curve**, reflecting the addition of the expected inflation term $\dot{p}^e$—is illustrated in Figure 19.3. There are a family of Phillips curves, each based on a particular expected inflation rate. Increases in expected inflation shift the Phillips curve vertically upward by the amount of the increase in $\dot{p}^e$; decreases in inflationary expectations shift the relationship downward.

As before, the natural unemployment rate U* is defined as the level at which aggregate demand for labour equals aggregate supply. Because the aggregate labour market is in equilibrium, real wages are constant at U*.[4] However, changes in nominal wages may be taking place due to expected inflation, as illustrated by points a, c, and d in Figure 19.3. At each of these points money wages are increasing at the expected inflation rate, with the result that expected real wages are constant. At unemployment rates below U*, such as the point b in Figure 19.3, aggregate labour demand exceeds aggregate supply and expected real wages are increasing. At unemployment rates above U*, such as point e, expected real wages are declining, reflecting aggregate excess supply of labour.

An important aspect of the Friedman-Phelps theory of inflationary expectations is the prediction that both the labour demand and labour supply functions will shift upward by the anticipated increase in the price level. This prediction arises because firms' profits and workers' utility depend on the real wage; increases in the price level thus require an equal increase in the nominal wage at each level of employment to maintain the real wage. As a consequence, the equilibrium level of employment in each individual labour market is not altered by a change in the price level, once nominal wages have adjusted to the higher (expected) price level. This property can be seen in Figure 19.2. In both markets, the labour demand and labour supply functions shift up by the same amount, resulting in the same equilibrium level of employment N_i^* and equilibrium real wage as prevailed before the expected increase in the price level. Because the equilibrium in

Figure 19.3 **Wage Changes, Unemployment, and Expected Inflation**

The figure illustrates a family of short-run Phillips curves, each drawn for a given level of expected inflation. The Phillips curve shifts up vertically by the amount of expected inflation, thus leaving the equilibrium of natural unemployment rate U* unchanged.

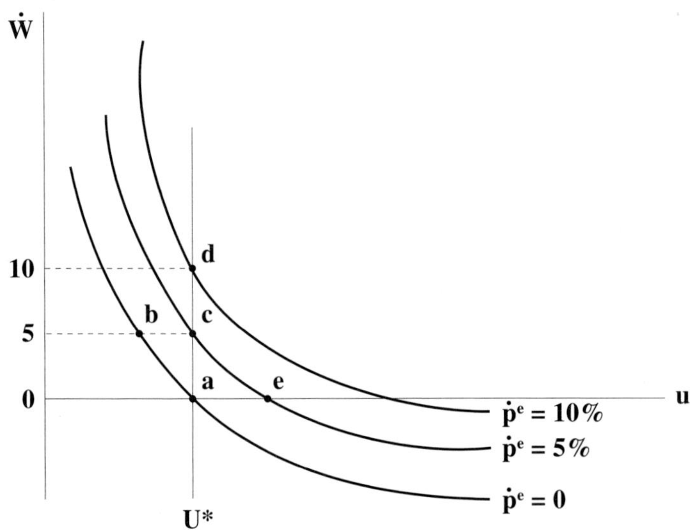

[4]The possibility of real wage growth due to productivity growth is discussed below. For the moment, aggregate productivity growth is assumed to be zero.

each market is unchanged, the unemployment rate at which aggregate demand for labour equals aggregate supply is also not altered by changes in the price level, once these changes are anticipated and taken into account by both employers and employees in wage determination. The Phillips curve thus shifts vertically upward by the anticipated increase in the price level, as depicted in Figure 19.3.

In contrast, if workers display **money illusion** by not raising their asking wage for a given quantity of labour by the same proportion as the anticipated increase in prices, then a change in the price level may alter the equilibrium level of employment in each market and the equilibrium unemployment rate for the economy as a whole. In these circumstances, wage changes do not adjust fully by the expected rate of inflation, so the expectations-augmented Phillips curve becomes

$$\dot{W} = F(U - U^{*}) + \lambda\, \dot{p}^{e} \qquad 19.10$$

where $\lambda < 1$ is a parameter reflecting the degree of money illusion, $\lambda = 1$ implying no money illusion. A number of empirical studies (discussed below) have tested the Friedman-Phelps prediction of a unit coefficient ($\lambda = 1$) in the wage equation.

In summary, Friedman (1968) and Phelps (1967, 1968) emphasized the role of inflationary expectations in the wage determination process. If wages are adjusted simply to eliminate the *current* amount of excess labour demand or supply, then the unemployment rate (or some other measure of excess demand) may be the sole determinant of wage changes. However, because wages are set or negotiated periodically, employers and employees look not only at current conditions but at the conditions *expected to prevail* during the remainder of the wage contract (or period for which the wage is set). This "forward-looking" aspect provides the rationale for including the expected inflation variable.

The role of inflationary expectations in wage determination is widely accepted. It is well grounded in the microeconomic theory of the behaviour of workers and firms; it is capable of explaining much of the upward drift in wage settlements since the 1960s; and it is evident to even the most casual observer of the wage determination process.

The relationship between wage changes, unemployment, and expected inflation summarized by equation 19.9 has profound implications for macroeconomic policy. In particular, it implies that there is no long-run tradeoff between inflation and unemployment even though these two variables may be inversely related in the short run. This important implication is discussed more fully subsequently in this chapter. At this point we continue to examine the main factors that influence wage changes.

Catch-up for Unanticipated Inflation

Wages are typically determined periodically, with the duration of the wage contract usually explicit in the union sector and implicit in the nonunion sector. No matter how much effort employers, employees, and their representatives devote to forecasting inflation and wage increases in other firms and industries, the actual changes in the price level and in wages elsewhere during the contract period may differ from the expected change. Consequently, the real or relative wage at the end of the contract will generally not equal the real or relative wage that was expected to prevail at the time the wage was originally determined. If inflation is greater than anticipated, workers will desire an additional "catch-up" wage increase because of the unanticipated decline in their purchasing power. Similarly, if the increase in wages in related industries and occupations is greater than expected, workers will desire an additional increase to restore wage relativities. In contrast, if prices or other firms' wages increase less rapidly than anticipated, there will be pressure from the firm to adjust wages downward, or to have them increase less quickly in the future.

The effect of unanticipated inflation is illustrated in Figure 19.4. For purposes of illustration, it is assumed that wages are set to yield labour market equilibrium at the end of the contract. At the beginning of the current contract period (end of previous contract), the wage is W_0. Given the anticipated rise in the price level to p_1^e, the appropriate wage increase is from W_0 to W_1^*. However, because the actual rise in the price level (to p_1^a) exceeds the expected rise, the actual equilibrium wage is W_1^a. An additional "catch-up" wage increase from W_1^* to W_1^a is therefore needed to restore equilibrium.

To account for the influence of this catch-up factor, a number of empirical studies have included, as an explanatory variable in the wage equation, a measure of the difference between the actual rate of inflation over the previous wage contract and the expected rate of inflation at the time the previous contract began (e.g., Turnovsky, 1972; Riddell, 1979; Christofides, Swidinsky, and Wilton, 1980). Note that this variable measures the amount of excess demand or supply due to unanticipated inflation, given by $D_1^a - S_1^a$ in Figure 19.4. Thus this catch-up variable would not be needed (and would not have any explanatory power) if the unemployment rate (or other measures of excess demand) were perfect measures of the excess demand or supply of labour. That is, unanticipated inflation should be reflected in the observed levels of job vacancies and unemployed job seekers. The catch-up variable should therefore be interpreted as a supplementary measure of excess demand or supply in the labour market; it is useful to the extent that movements in the unemployment rate do not fully capture all variations in excess demand for labour.

If inflation or other economic circumstances deviate substantially from the expectations upon which wages were determined, the parties may not wait until the end of the contract period to make an upward or downward adjustment. Such adjustments are more likely to occur in the nonunion sector where the wage rate and the length of the period for which it is in force are not part of a formal contract but rather are implicit understandings about normal behaviour. Nonetheless, even in the union sector, where wage agreements are legal contracts with a fixed duration, a significant change in economic conditions (relative to what was expected) may cause one side to request and the other to agree to renegotiate the terms of the contract. (Indeed, some contracts contain "reopener provisions" which stipulate the circumstances under which such renegotiation may be necessary.) Examples of such adjustments took place in Canada in the 1970s because of unanticipated increases in inflation and in the 1980s because of an unanticipated decline in inflation and in product market conditions due to the 1981–82 recession.

Figure 19.4 **Wage Changes and Unanticipated Inflation**

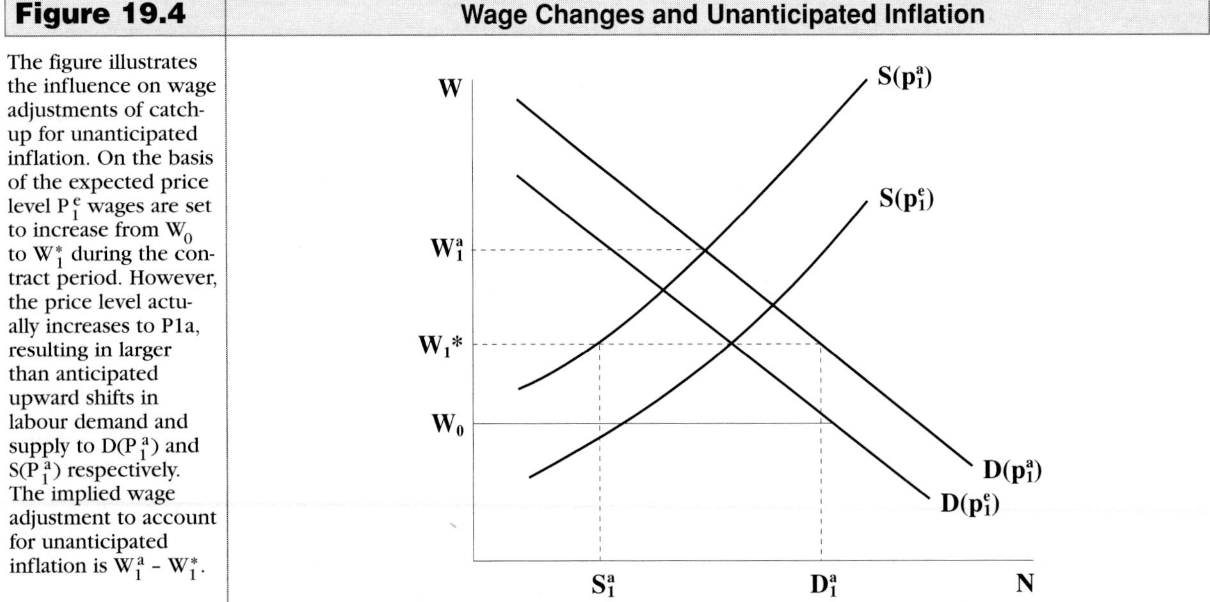

The figure illustrates the influence on wage adjustments of catch-up for unanticipated inflation. On the basis of the expected price level P_1^e wages are set to increase from W_0 to W_1^* during the contract period. However, the price level actually increases to P1a, resulting in larger than anticipated upward shifts in labour demand and supply to $D(P_1^a)$ and $S(P_1^a)$ respectively. The implied wage adjustment to account for unanticipated inflation is $W_1^a - W_1^*$.

Productivity Growth

In wage determination, the direct concern of employers and employees may be the nominal or money wage, but their ultimate concern is with the real wage. Thus any factors that influence real wage growth should also be included as explanatory variables in the wage equation. This can be seen by subtracting $\dot{p}^e$ from both sides of equation 19.9:

$$\dot{W} - \dot{p}^e = F(U - U^*) \qquad 19.11$$

The dependent variable is the (expected) growth in real wages; thus any additional determinants of real wage growth should be included on the right-hand side of equation 19.11.

The primary determinant of real wage growth is the trend rate of productivity growth. Over the long term, real wages have tended to increase at the rate of growth of productivity (Allen, 1986). This tendency is also evident in the postwar Canadian experience: the sharp decline in productivity growth after 1973 was accompanied by a decline in the rate of growth of real income per capita (Table 19.1) and in the rate of increase in real wages.

The relationship between productivity and real wage growth can be understood most easily at the level of the economy as a whole. Higher productivity implies that it is possible to produce more output with the same inputs. Thus, other factors being constant (including employment of inputs), an increase in productivity will increase the economy's total output or national income and therefore real income per capita. Wages and salaries make up over 75 percent of national income. Unless there is a shift toward profits in the functional distribution of income, an increase in real per capita income will be associated with higher real wages and salaries. The relationship between aggregate output, labour's share of total output or income, productivity, and real wages is discussed below.

Productivity growth influences wage negotiations by affecting workers' aspirations for real wage increases. If a steady rate of technical advance of, say, 3 percent per year has been experienced for some time, workers come to expect annual wage increases that exceed inflation by approximately 3 percent. However, there may be long lags between changes in the trend rate of productivity increase—such as the sharp decline in productivity growth that began in the early 1970s—and adjustments in workers' aspirations. If productivity growth declines—for example, from 3 to 1 percent—and workers' aspirations continue to reflect the historical experience of 3 percent annual real wage gains, there will be pressure for higher real wage increases than are warranted by the rate of productivity advance. As discussed subsequently in this chapter, these gains can occur if there is an increase in labour's share of national income (and a corresponding decrease in capital's share). Conversely, if the trend rate of technical advance increases, and workers' aspirations remain based on historical experience, there will be less pressure for real wage gains than can be sustained by the economy's higher productivity and an increase in capital's share of national income is likely to occur.

At the level of an individual labour market, the relationship between productivity and real wages is more complex (Allen, 1986). Higher productivity may either increase or decrease labour demand, depending on the magnitude of several offsetting factors. These include a displacement effect—less labour is required per unit of output—and a product demand effect—higher productivity lowers costs and therefore product prices, resulting in an increase in product demand and thus labour demand. As a consequence, productivity gains may result in lower real wages and/or employment in some labour markets.

Technical changes introduced in individual labour markets also have effects throughout the economy. These general equilibrium effects often provide the mechanism through which productivity gains result in real wage increases for the average worker. Increased efficiency in the production of one commodity lowers its price, resulting in higher real incomes for all consumers of that commodity. As a consequence, the demand for all normal goods increases, raising labour demand and therefore real wages throughout much of the economy. Average real wages rise, although there may be lower real wages in some individual labour markets. Productivity improvements tend to reduce costs of production, whereas wage increases raise costs. Thus productivity growth affects the relationship between wage changes and price changes. These aspects are discussed below.

Other Determinants of Money Wage Changes

In addition to productivity growth, expected inflation, catch-up for unanticipated inflation and unemployment, a number of other variables have been suggested as determinants of money wage changes. In many cases, these variables are included (a) to control for certain factors, given the particular nature of the data set employed in the empirical work or (b) to act as a proxy for other variables for which data was not available. In other cases, they are included in a more or less ad hoc fashion, often without a careful theoretical rationale, simply to reflect institutional features that are believed to affect money wage changes. While these factors may truly have an exogenous effect, they may also simply reflect a common set of underlying forces. Hence, it is important to have an appropriate theoretical foundation to sort out cause and effect—the crucial linkage for most policy purposes.

The rate of increase of wages in the United States, for example, may be regarded as a determinant of wage changes in Canada. This could occur through wage spillovers from key groups in the United States, through international unions, multinational corporations, or pressures for wage parity. Again, the extent to which U.S. wages would exert an independent influence, as opposed to Canadian and U.S. wages moving together in response to a common set of forces, might be a difficult issue to disentangle.

Profits have been regarded as a determinant of wage changes largely on the belief that high profits reflect a greater ability to pay or a higher opportunity cost of resisting wage demands and engaging in a strike. They could also reflect short-run demand changes over a business cycle, as well as reverse causation in that wage increases may affect profitability. Again, cause and effect becomes difficult to disentangle without a well-specified theoretical rationale.

Changes in unionization also have been regarded as an independent determinant of money wages. While unions can undoubtedly have an impact on the wages of their members, their impact on the rate of *change* of the *aggregate* wage level is a much more complicated matter. As discussed in Chapter 16, unions affect the wages and employment of both union and nonunion workers, the union-nonunion wage differential reflecting both higher wages for union members and a lower average wage in the nonunion sector (although some nonunion workers receive higher wages due to threat effects). The change in the aggregate wage level depends on the magnitude of these two offsetting effects. The empirical evidence indicates that, although unionization may lower the average wage in the nonunion sector, most of the differential is associated with higher wages in the union sector. Thus unionization may tend to raise the aggregate wage level. However, this constitutes a "one-time" increase associated with the creation of a union-nonunion wage differential. In order to have a continuing effect on the aggregate rate of wage change, either an increase in the union-nonunion wage differential or an increase in the extent of unionization must occur. Calculations indicate that these contribute relatively little to the aggregate rate of wage change. For example, the aggregate wage level increased by 44 percent in the United States between 1967 and 1973; Ashenfelter (1978) concluded that the combined effect of increases in union density and in the union-nonunion wage differential accounted for only one to two percentage points of this increase. Similar conclusions have been reached in other empirical studies.

Market imperfections also have been discussed, especially in the context of insulating wages from competitive pressures. In the context of dual labour market analysis, for example, aggregate money wage changes could emanate from institutional changes, and from changes in administrative practices, or segmentation of the labour market. This would be facilitated by the ability to pass wage cost increases on to consumers via administrative pricing in noncompetitive product markets. To a certain extent the belief in these market imperfections and noncompetitive forces—most notably monopoly power in the product market and union power in the labour market—were part of the rationale for wage-price controls and guidelines. The exact manner in which these imperfections would affect the wage and inflation process, however, was seldom spelled out clearly. In particular, while imperfections could explain why the price and wage *levels* are higher than they would be in the absence of the imperfections, they do not explain the *changes* in prices and wages, unless one believes that the imperfections themselves change rapidly.

Unusual events—in particular, large wage settlements in specific sectors of the economy—often have been discussed as important determinants of aggregate money wage changes in the economy as a whole. The belief is that unusually high settlements in specific sectors have set off a chain reaction, spilling over into other sectors. In Canada, such key settlements allegedly have included Seaway workers in the late 1960s, construction trades in the 1960s and early 1970s, and the public sector in the 1970s.

While it can be tempting to regard these settlements as setting off inflationary wage settlements elsewhere, there is a danger in such ad hoc theorizing about the impact of peculiar events. Certainly they can affect the magnitude of wages in a particular sector, and hence they can affect the wages of that sector relative to other sectors, at least in the short run. Nevertheless, the mechanism whereby this affects aggregate wages in the economy as a whole is not clear. What appears to be a spillover effect may simply be a variety of sectors responding to the same set of economic forces. And even if there are purely institutional spillover effects, it is not clear that they will persist in the long run. There will always be a group that stands out as receiving unusually large settlements in a given short period of time. Some of the gain may reflect a catch-up, some may reflect a short-run demand increase, and some may be a purely transitory gain that will be dissipated over time. Unusually high wage settlements in a particular sector may be a *symptom* of any of a variety of factors; it is another matter, however, to argue that they are the *cause* of general increases in aggregate money wages.

A variety of public policies may also affect aggregate wage changes. In some cases these effects are intended, while in others they are incidental consequences. Incomes policies are designed to restrain wage and price increases. In Canada these have generally taken the form of guidelines or direct controls on wage and price increases. The economic rationale for such policies and Canada's experience with them are discussed subsequently in this chapter. Changes in taxation may affect wage changes, although such effects are usually unintended consequences. Payroll taxes affect labour demand and income taxes affect labour supply. Thus if tax changes are large enough and apply throughout much of the economy, they may affect the aggregate wage level. As was the case with several other factors discussed in this section, such changes have a one-time impact on the aggregate wage level. However, if income tax rates are not indexed to changes in the price level then taxation may affect wage changes on a continuing basis in an inflationary period, as individuals are pushed into higher tax brackets due to increases in their nominal incomes associated with inflation.

In summary, in addition to the main determinants of wage changes, a number of other factors may affect labour demand or labour supply and therefore the wage level. In many cases these exert a one-time impact; however, some may exert a continuing influence on aggregate wage changes.

EMPIRICAL EVIDENCE

A large number of studies of the determinants of wage changes have been carried out in Canada. Early studies such as Kaliski (1964) and Turnovsky (1972) used as the dependent variable the annual or quarterly rate of change in an aggregate earnings index (such as average hourly earnings). Aggregate earnings indexes cover a substantial proportion of the labour force; however, there are several problems associated with their use in this context. Earnings depend not only on the hourly wage rate but also on factors such as overtime pay and bonuses. Average wage or earnings indexes may also be affected by changes in the composition of employment; for example, if firms lay off mainly junior, low-wage employees in a cyclical downturn and rehire these employees in the upturn, the average wage or earnings index will vary countercyclically even if wage rates and earnings for each type of employee do not. For this reason, it is preferable to use indexes based on fixed employment weights.

www.statcan.ca/english/econoind/cpia.htm

Another important measurement issue relates to the distinction between current and deferred wage changes. In the postwar period there has been a marked trend toward the use of multi-year contracts in the unionized sector. Multi-year contracts often contain deferred increases. The magnitude of these may be predetermined (i.e., fixed at the time the contract is signed) or indexed to changes in the Consumer Price Index via a **cost-of-living-allowance or COLA** clause. The observed change in average wages or earnings at any point in time is thus a mixture of current and deferred changes. Yet the determinants of these two types of wage change clearly differ.

Another implication of multi-year contracts is that the fraction of the labour force negotiating a new agreement varies from year to year. In some years as few as 30 percent of major collective agreements are renegotiated while in other years more than 60 percent are renegotiated. Thus, some of the variation in aggregate earnings (or wage) indexes is simply due to the timing of the "bargaining calendar."

In view of these difficulties associated with aggregate wage index data, researchers have increasingly turned to data on individual contracts. This approach treats each negotiated settlement as an observation and to a considerable extent circumvents the two problems discussed above. In particular, deferred increases are not so problematic in that all the increases to take effect during the contract are included in calculating the percentage change in wages, which is then explained in terms of economic conditions prevailing at the time the contract was signed. Similarly, variations in the proportion of the labour force bargaining in each period are evidently less of a problem in that one observes the underlying rate of change of wages. In addition to lessening the measurement difficulties associated with analyzing the determinants of wage changes, the use of contract data also provides considerably more micro detail and therefore permits the testing of some hypotheses which would simply not be feasible with more aggregative data. Canadian studies based on individual wage contracts include Riddell (1979), Christofides, Swidinsky, and Wilton (1980), and Card (1990).

Each of the empirical studies of Canadian wage changes employs the basic expectations-augmented Phillips curve specification discussed above. However, they differ in several ways, including the measurement of excess demand for labour, the measurement of inflationary expectations, and in the role of catch-up for unanticipated inflation.

Each of the studies includes a measure of excess demand for labour. Generally this variable is found to be a significant determinant of wage changes; however, in contrast to Phillips's original study, analyses incorporating data from the 1970s find that the aggregate unemployment rate is often insignificant or even perversely signed (e.g., Christofides, Swidinsky, and Wilton, 1980). This outcome is not unexpected. As discussed in Chapters 17 and 18 on unemployment, because of substantial changes in the age-sex composition of the labour force and in social programs such as unemployment insurance, the meaning of (say) a 6 percent unemployment rate in the 1970s differed considerably from that in the 1950s. In other words, the demographic trends and changes in social policies have raised the equilibrium unemployment rate, and consequently the aggregate unemployment rate has not remained a consistent measure of the "tightness" of the labour market.

There are several ways to deal with this situation. A number of authors have constructed adjusted unemployment-rate series which are intended to provide a consistent measure of excess demand and thus can be used in lieu of the measured unemployment rate to explain wage changes. These adjusted measures are typically weighted averages of the unemployment rates of different age-sex groups, with groups such as males aged 25 to 44 being assumed to contribute more to excess labour demand than females and youths. Alternatively, some authors use the job vacancy rate on the assumption that the developments that raised U^* did not significantly alter the equilibrium job vacancy rate V^* (Christofides, Swidinsky, and Wilton, 1980).

An alternative procedure, used for example by Riddell and Smith (1982), is to measure aggregate excess demand for labour as the difference between the actual and natural unemployment rates, $U - U^*$ as in equation 19.9. A second equation is added to account for changes in U^* in terms of the demographic, legislative, and other changes. When this is done, the coefficient on the excess demand variable has the predicted sign and is statistically significant.

The conclusion that excess demand for labour exerts a significant influence on wage changes implies that there is a relationship between wage inflation and unemployment in the short run, holding constant inflationary expectations and the natural unemployment rate. Changes in the natural rate have shifted this short-run Phillips curve upward, resulting in higher wage inflation at each measured unemployment rate. Another important conclusion is that the short-run Phillips curve is fairly flat. Because the relationship is generally found to be nonlinear, as depicted in Figure 19.3, the slope depends on the unemployment rate. Evaluated at the average unemployment rate during the sample period, a slope of 0.5 is a typical estimate, implying that a one percentage point increase in the unemployment rate reduces the rate of wage inflation by one-half of one percent. As discussed below, such estimates indicate that the costs of reducing inflation by monetary and fiscal restraint (thereby reducing excess demand in labour and product markets) may be extremely high.

Both expected inflation and catch-up for unanticipated inflation appear to play significant roles in wage determination. Empirical studies indicate that much of the upward shift in the Phillips curve during the 1960s and 1970s was associated with the rise in inflationary expectations. Catch-up forces also contributed to the upward shift in the late 1960s and early 1970s. This factor can work in either direction; more recently, with the decline in inflation in the 1980s and 1990s, lower-than-anticipated inflation has exerted additional downward pressure on wage increases.

A fundamental difficulty is that inflationary expectations are not generally observed. Empirical analysis thus requires constructing a proxy for expected inflation; as a consequence, the results represent a joint test of the theory of the determinants of aggregate wage changes and the theory of expectations formation. This joint hypothesis-testing problem is exacerbated by the fact that any errors in measuring expected inflation will also cause errors in the measurement of unanticipated inflation.

Early research was often based on the hypothesis of adaptive expectations, according to which the expected rate of inflation could be expressed as a distributed lag of previous inflation rates. This approach was criticized on the basis that these expectations need not be consistent with the actual process generating inflation. In other words, the adaptive expectations hypothesis implies that those involved in forming expectations may repeatedly over- or underpredict inflation without revising their forecasting behaviour. For this reason, economists have increasingly adopted the hypothesis of rational expectations, according to which individuals' expectations represent an optimal forecast, given the available information regarding the process that actually generates inflation. The most controversial aspect of rational expectations is the information set that market participants are assumed to possess and use in forming their expectations. In much theoretical work in macroeconomics, market participants are assumed to understand the structure of the economy, including knowing the parameters of the various relationships among variables. In empirical work on wage determination, much weaker versions of rational expectations are generally assumed. A common assumption is that in forecasting inflation individuals use only the previous inflationary experience as their information set. Rational expectations of inflation can generally be written as a distributed lag of previous inflation rates; however, the distributed lag weights must reflect the actual relationship between current and past inflation rather than being arbitrary, as is the case under adaptive expectations.

A central empirical issue is the prediction of Friedman (1968) and Phelps (1967, 1968) that wage changes will adjust fully to reflect changes in expected inflation. In these circumstances there is no long-run relationship between wage inflation and unemployment; the long-run Phillips curve is vertical at the natural unemployment rate as depicted in Figure 19.3. As noted previously, this prediction implies $\lambda = 1$ in equation 19.10. Tests of this "natural rate hypothesis" have generally confirmed the $\lambda = 1$ prediction. Some apparent exceptions are discussed below.

However expectations of future inflation are formed, they will often turn out to be incorrect. The catch-up variable is intended to capture the effects of over- or under-prediction of changes in the price level. When wage increases fully reflect expected inflation, the catch-up variable can be measured as the difference between the actual rate of inflation since the wage was last determined and the expected rate of inflation at that time, $\dot{p}_{t-1} - \dot{p}^e_{t-1}$. This catch-up specification was originally used by Turnovsky (1972) with aggregate data and subsequently employed by Riddell (1979) with individual contract data. Because the length of wage contracts varies considerably across bargaining units, it is difficult to incorporate the influence of unanticipated inflation adequately with aggregate data. With individual contract data, both expected inflation and catch-up can be precisely related to the actual timing of wage settlements.

The extent to which wages adjust to expected inflation on an ex ante versus ex post basis is clearly important for the short-run dynamics of unemployment and inflation. Even with full ex ante compensation for expected inflation, the existence of a catch-up adjustment for forecast errors implies that unanticipated disturbances will have effects that will persist for several years. The smaller the ex ante compensation and thus the larger the ex post compensation, the more significant are the delayed responses to economic shocks. Even if expectations are forward-looking, there is therefore an important backward-looking aspect to wage determination. Several Canadian studies suggest that this aspect is quantitatively significant.

The impact of the 1975-1978 Anti-Inflation Program on wage and price inflation has been extensively investigated. Studies include Auld, Christofides, Swidinsky, and Wilton (1979), Christofides and Wilton (1985), and Riddell and Smith (1982). Wage increases fell substantially during the period 1975–1978, with new non-COLA settlements declining from over 19 percent prior to the introduction of controls in October 1975 to under 11 percent in the first year of the program (1976) and under 8 percent in the last two years of the program (1977 and 1978). The main objective of the empirical research has been to determine how much of this decline (if any) can be attributed to the wage-price controls program and how much is associated with other factors such as the higher unemployment and slack economic conditions which prevailed during this period.

Empirical studies are unanimous in concluding that the controls program had a significant effect on the rate of wage increase. Most estimates of the impact on new wage settlements are in the range of 3 to 4 percent per year. This is a very large impact. Assuming the slope of the short-run Phillips curve to be approximately 0.5, the same direct effect on wage inflation would have required unemployment rates of 13 to 14 percent throughout the three-year period rather than the 7 to 8 percent unemployment rates actually experienced. Studies by Riddell and Smith (1982) and Christofides and Wilton (1985), which include data from the post-controls period, also conclude that the AIP was not followed by a wage explosion or "post-controls bubble," as has been the case in many other attempts at achieving wage restraint. The policy implications of these findings are discussed below.

PRICE INFLATION AND UNEMPLOYMENT

We have seen how actual and expected changes in the price level affect wages. However, because of their effect on labour costs, wage changes also influence prices. Thus any factor such as unemployment or expected inflation which affects the rate of change of wages will also affect the rate of change in prices as changes in labour costs associated with wage changes feed through into prices. This implies that there will exist a relationship between price inflation and unemployment, holding constant other factors, as well as between actual and expected price inflation. These relationships and their implications are briefly examined in this section. Further discussion is provided in textbooks on macroeconomics.

Because labour costs are a substantial proportion of total costs, a common assumption in empirical work on price determination is that the output price p can be written as a mark-up m times the labour cost per unit of output, or unit labour cost. The mark-up reflects both other costs such as raw materials and a normal rate of profit. Unit labour cost is simply the wage rate (dollars per employee-hour) divided by output Q per employee-hour N or average labour productivity. Thus

$$p = m \times \frac{W}{A} \qquad 19.12$$

where A is average labour productivity (Q/N). Totally differentiating (19.12), assuming the mark-up is approximately constant over time (dm = 0), and dividing the left-hand side by p and the right-hand by $m \cdot \frac{W}{A}$ gives

$$\dot{p} = \dot{W} - \dot{A} \qquad 19.13$$

where $\dot{p} = \frac{\Delta p}{p}$ and similarly for $\dot{W}$ and $\dot{A}$. Note that equation (19.13) can be rewritten as

$$\dot{W} - \dot{p} = \dot{A} \qquad 19.14$$

which states that, with a constant mark-up on unit labour costs, real wages will grow at the rate of productivity growth. The relationship between wage inflation, price inflation, and productivity growth can also be derived under competitive rather than mark-up pricing.[5] In that case, real wages will grow at the rate of productivity increase if the share of labour in national income is constant. Periods in which real wage gains exceed productivity growth will be associated with shifts in the distribution of income toward labour, and periods in which real wage gains fall below the rate of productivity increase will be accompanied by shifts in the distribution of income toward capital. The historical tendency for real wages to increase at the rate of productivity growth was discussed previously. This analysis provides an explanation for this phenomenon; namely, that mark-ups on unit labour cost are approximately constant in the long run, or, more generally, that the share of labour in national income is constant.

Combining equations 19.13 and 19.10 gives the relationship between price inflation and unemployment:

$$\dot{p} = F(U - U^*) - \dot{A} + \lambda \dot{p}^e \qquad 19.15$$

[5]See Problem 1 at the end of this chapter.

Holding constant productivity growth and expected inflation, price inflation and unemployment are inversely related in the same way as wage inflation and unemployment. Changes in productivity growth or expected inflation shift this relationship upward or downward. Figure 19.5 illustrates this "price Phillips curve" relationship for the case in which the Friedman-Phelps prediction that $\lambda = 1$ holds. As before, there is a family of price Phillips curves, each for a different expected inflation rate. These are referred to as short-run Phillips curves because they depict the relationship between inflation and unemployment during the period in which inflationary expectations do not adjust to changes in the actual rate of inflation. For example, by employing expansionary monetary and fiscal policy, it may be possible to move the economy from point a in Figure 19.5 to point b. However, the latter outcome is not sustainable in the long run because actual inflation exceeds expected inflation. The set of outcomes that can be maintained on a permanent basis are those points such as a, c, and d in Figure 19.5 at which actual and expected inflation are equal. At any other points, actual and expected inflation will diverge, causing employers and employees to adjust their expectations and consequently their behaviour.

This analysis implies that there is a temporary or short-run tradeoff between inflation and unemployment, other things being equal. However, there is no permanent or long-run tradeoff between these two variables.[6] The long-run relationship between inflation and unemployment is vertical at the natural or equilibrium unemployment rate U*, as depicted in Figure 19.5. Formally, macroeconomic equilibrium requires that

$$\dot{p}^e = \dot{p} \tag{19.16}$$

Substituting equation 19.16 into equation 19.15 gives the long-run or equilibrium relationship between inflation and unemployment:

$$F(U - U^*) - \dot{A} = 0 \tag{19.17}$$

Figure 19.5 **The Relationship Between Inflation and Unemployment**

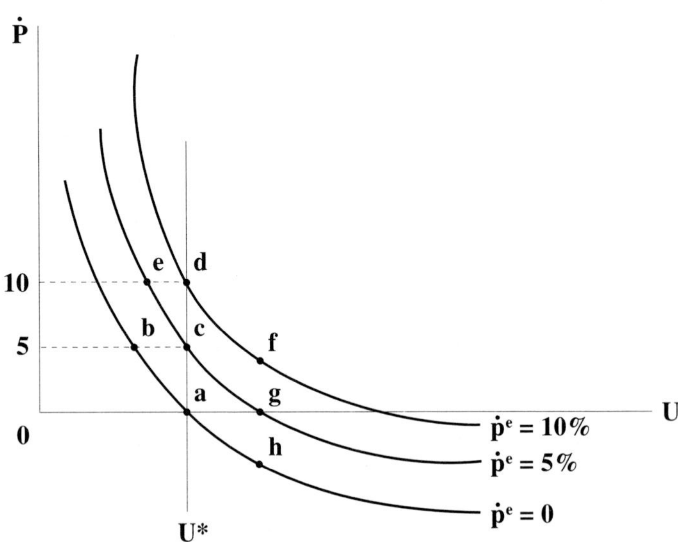

The figure illustrates the relationship between price inflation and unemployment. For each level of expected inflation there is a short-run relationship. The figure shows three short-run Phillips curves, for expected inflation of 0, 5, and 10 percent. The long-run relationship consists of points at which actual and expected inflation are equal. This relationship is the vertical line at U = U*, the natural unemployment rate or NAIRU.

[6] If workers display permanent money illusion ($\lambda < 1$ in Equation 19.15), there will be a tradeoff between inflation and unemployment even in the long run. This tradeoff will be steeper than the short-run counterpart. See problem 5 at the end of this chapter.

Because the rate of inflation does not appear in equation 19.17, equations 19.16 and 19.17 are consistent with any steady rate of inflation.

The absence of a permanent tradeoff can be illustrated by examining the implications of attempting to maintain unemployment below the natural unemployment rate U^* on a continuing basis. For example, beginning in long-run equilibrium at point a in Figure 19.5, the authorities may be able to move the economy to point b via expansionary monetary or fiscal policy. However, once workers and firms adjust to the higher rate of inflation, the short-run Phillips curve will shift up and the economy will return to U^* at c (given the higher level of inflationary expectations). Attempting to maintain the lower level of unemployment will require further stimulus to the economy, resulting in higher inflation such as at point e. Thus a policy of maintaining $U < U^*$ will be associated with increasing inflation. For this reason, U^* is often referred to as the **non-accelerating inflation rate of unemployment** or **NAIRU**. As the NAIRU designation emphasizes, at $U = U^*$ the rate of inflation will tend to remain constant, whereas inflation will tend to increase if $U < U^*$ is maintained over an extended period.

This discussion illustrates how overly expansionary aggregate demand policies may have contributed to the upward drift in inflation during the 1960s and early 1970s, as described previously in this chapter. Such policies may have been adopted for several reasons: (1) because of a belief that there existed a permanent tradeoff between inflation and unemployment (a view that was prevalent during that period) and that it was preferable to accept a bit more inflation in exchange for lower unemployment; (2) because of a belief that the unemployment rate consistent with steady inflation was in fact lower than the true value of U^*; or (3) possibly with full recognition that the consequences would be increased inflation in the longer term, albeit lower unemployment and a more buoyant economy in the short run.

The reduction of inflation by a policy of demand restraint can also be illustrated with reference to Figure 19.5. Beginning at a point like d with an ongoing inflationary spiral—in which wages are rising because workers and firms expect prices to rise and prices are rising due to higher wages—a sharp reduction in aggregate demand such as occurred in 1981–82 will cause unemployment to rise and inflation to fall, moving the economy to a point such as f in the short run. As expectations adjust to the lower rate of inflation, the Phillips curve shifts down, enabling the authorities to achieve a permanently lower rate of inflation, such as at point c. Alternatively, continued restraint such as Canada experienced in the early 1990s would move the economy from f to g to h, eventually resulting in a return to price stability at point a. This process of a gradual reduction in inflationary expectations characterizes the outcome of the anti-inflation policy followed in Canada during the 1980s and 1990s.

Supply Shocks

The price Phillips curve relationship illustrated in Figure 19.5 is traced out by variations in aggregate demand. An increase in aggregate demand affects many product markets, and this in turn increases demand in many labour markets. As a consequence, more labour markets have excess labour demand and fewer have excess supply. Job vacancies increase, the number of unemployed workers falls, and the economy moves along the U-V relationship depicted in Figure 19.1(c) . As unemployment falls the average rate of wage change rises, and the economy moves along the short-run wage and price Phillips curves shown in Figures 19.3 and 19.5.

Shifts in aggregate supply, or **supply shocks**, refer to developments that change the costs of producing goods and services and thus the prices that firms charge. Although many supply shocks have impacts that are limited to a few products—for example, poor growing conditions in coffee-producing regions will increase the relative price of coffee beans—others have impacts that are widely felt. Classic examples of adverse supply shocks are the oil price increases brought about by the Organization of Petroleum Exporting Countries

www.opec.org

(OPEC) during the 1970s. The 1973 oil price shock nearly doubled the world price of oil and the subsequent 1979 oil price increase raised the world price a further 40 percent. Such an adverse supply shock shifts the price Phillips curve up and to the right, resulting in higher inflation at each unemployment rate or higher unemployment at each inflation rate.

When significant supply shocks occur, the economy may deviate from its natural unemployment rate or NAIRU for an extended period. For example, in the United States, during the period 1973–1975 inflation rose from 6.2 percent in 1973 to 11 percent in 1974 (an increase of 4.8 percentage points) and the unemployment rate almost doubled, from 4.9 percent in 1973 to 8.5 percent in 1975, an increase of 3.6 percentage points. In Canada, for reasons discussed previously, the changes were less dramatic: inflation increased by 3.3 percentage points and unemployment rose by only 1.5 percentage points. An adverse supply shock is thus expected to result in an increase in both inflation and unemployment, with the mix between the two depending on the extent to which the monetary and fiscal authorities attempt to offset the tendency toward falling output and rising unemployment by expansionary aggregate demand policies.

Similarly, favourable supply shocks—such as the collapse of world oil prices in the 1980s or the steep decline in the price of computing that occurred in the 1990s—present countries with the opportunity to achieve, at least temporarily, both lower inflation and lower unemployment.

CHALLENGES TO THE NATURAL RATE HYPOTHESIS

During the 1960s the notion of a stable Phillips curve or tradeoff between inflation and unemployment became incorporated into macroeconomic thinking, and into the models used by policymakers and economic forecasters. This era began with the important early contributions by Phillips (1958) and Lipsey (1960). Canadian research along these lines included Kaliski (1964) and Bodkin et al. (1966). However, as discussed above, the notion of a stable tradeoff between inflation and unemployment was unable to account for observed behaviour during the late 1960s and 1970s, when both higher rates of inflation and unemployment were observed. In addition, this perspective came under increased attack on both theoretical and empirical grounds for its failure to take into account the role of expectations in the inflationary process. Following a flurry of theoretical and empirical research, together with a process of debate and controversy, the notion of a Phillips curve or tradeoff between inflation and unemployment was discarded and replaced by the model developed above, characterized by a unique natural unemployment rate or NAIRU and the absence of a tradeoff between inflation and unemployment in the long run. By the mid- to late-1970s, the Phelps-Friedman "natural rate" view had become economic orthodoxy.

However, macroeconomic experience during the 1980s and 1990s has resulted in considerable questioning of the natural rate paradigm. In this section we briefly discuss three features of recent experience that raise doubts about the theory that there is no long-run tradeoff between inflation and unemployment and about the usefulness of the concept of a natural unemployment rate or NAIRU. The first is the dramatic rise in unemployment in Europe and the persistence of high European unemployment without significant reductions in inflation. The second is the spectacular performance during the 1990s of the U.S. economy—in particular the combination of low inflation and unusually low unemployment experienced during the second half of the decade of the 1990s. The third issue discussed is whether downward wage rigidity will raise the costs of pursuing a low inflation strategy, such as Canada did during the 1990s.

The extent to which recent developments can be reconciled with the natural rate theory is the subject of much current research and debate. At this point it is uncertain whether this research will result in a significant modification of the natural rate hypothesis—or even rejection of the theory and its replacement by a better theoretical framework.

Unemployment Persistence

In many European countries, unemployment rates more than doubled between 1970 and 1980 and by the mid-1990s were three to five times their 1970 levels. Yet, in most countries, inflation during this period was approximately stable, or at best declined modestly. To be consistent with the natural rate view, this behaviour requires massive increases in the natural rate. Although some increases in the NAIRU may have occurred because of changes in social and labour market legislation and changes in the structure of the labour force, such changes appear unlikely to be able to explain a rise in the natural unemployment rate by a factor of three to five times. In Canada, many of the factors used to explain the rise in unemployment during the 1960s and early 1970s (increased labour force participation of women and youths, higher real minimum wages, more comprehensive and more generous unemployment insurance) either levelled off or were reversed during the latter half of the 1970s and during the 1980s and 1990s; on these grounds, the natural rate would have been expected to decline. However, average levels of unemployment in Canada were higher during the 1980s and 1990s rather than lower.

Economists have accordingly devoted increased attention to the possibility that changes in the actual unemployment rate may themselves result in changes in the natural rate, so that economic shocks which increase unemployment may also raise the NAIRU. This reassessment of the natural rate paradigm is an area of active research and debate. In this section we describe some of the central issues being examined; however, the conclusions at this stage must necessarily be very tentative.

Two related research issues are being addressed. First, are theoretical and empirical models capable of explaining the **persistence** of high levels of unemployment? As noted, this persistence is most evident in Europe, but has also characterized the Canadian experience, albeit to a lesser extent, during the 1980s and 1990s, as inspection of Figure 17.1 and Table 19.1 will confirm. (See Exhibit 17.1 for a summary of the European experience.) Explanations include insider-outsider models of wage-setting, the loss of physical and/or human capital during economic downturns, and persistence generated by the features of the unemployment insurance system. The second issue involves the possibility of multiple equilibriums, so that the economy could settle down at an equilibrium with a low natural unemployment rate or one with a high rate.

As discussed in Chapter 18, insider-outsider models emphasize the significant role played by currently employed (and perhaps also recently employed) workers in the wage-setting process (the "insiders") and the much less significant role of unemployed workers (the "outsiders") in that process. A shock to aggregate demand which reduces employment may thus reduce the number of insiders and increase the number of individuals who exert little influence on the wage determination process. The interests of workers laid off may be represented for a certain period of time, after which they drift away and become disenfranchised. Thus the increase in unemployment may not produce much downward pressure on wage changes, in contrast to the expectations-augmented Phillips curve model where increases in unemployment above the NAIRU produce downward pressure on wage settlements (relative to expected inflation).

Persistence in unemployment may also be associated with decay in physical or human capital during a recessionary period. Individuals who have been unemployed for a long period may suffer a deterioration in their labour market skills or in the intensity with which they search for work. Such effects would imply that their probability of re-employment falls with the duration of unemployment. It may also be the case that employers are less likely (other things being equal) to employ those who have been unemployed for a long period.

Decay in physical capital can arise due to bankruptcies and plant closures during a slump in economic activity. These events lower labour demand at each wage rate, thus lowering the equilibrium level of employment and raising the natural unemployment rate. If entry by new firms during the subsequent recovery occurs only slowly, one consequence of a recession may be a higher natural unemployment rate for an extended period of time.

These mechanisms imply that short-run shocks can have long-run (although not necessarily permanent) effects. An economic downturn can reduce the number of insiders, with the consequence that wages are subsequently set at the higher level required to employ the smaller number of insiders. This mechanism appears to be consistent with the combination of persistent high unemployment and substantial real wage growth among employed workers observed in many European countries during the 1970s and 1980s (Blanchard and Summers, 1986; Blanchard, 1991).

The deterioration of physical and/or human capital is also an example of a long-run consequence of a short-run cyclical phenomenon. During a recession, the number of unemployed job seekers rises and employment opportunities decline; consequently the probability of re-employment falls and the duration of unemployment rises. In a severe recession, many of the long-term unemployed may suffer a decline in their job-related skills, the intensity of their search effort, or they may become accustomed to public assistance in the form of unemployment insurance or social assistance. In these circumstances, the long-term unemployed may become "outsiders," a group with little labour market attachment and one which exerts little restraining influence on wage settlements. The reduced impact on wage bargaining (for a given level of the unemployment rate) implies an increase in the equilibrium level of unemployment.

The extreme case of **hysteresis** occurs when the unemployment rate may drift upward or downward, without any tendency to return to an equilibrium level. Hysteresis exists when short-run shocks have permanent effects, so that the concept of a natural unemployment rate becomes irrelevant.

Whether or not cyclical downturns have long-lasting "scarring" effects on the labour market—including whether or not the labour market is characterized by hysteresis—is an important policy issue. For example, according to the natural rate hypothesis, reducing inflation involves a tradeoff between temporary costs (higher unemployment and lower output during the period of monetary and fiscal restraint) and permanent gains (a permanently lower rate of inflation). The costs are temporary because once the rate of inflation has been brought down the economy can return to normal levels of output and employment. However, if economic downturns have long-run effects then the costs of reducing inflation by demand restraint are larger; in the extreme case of hysteresis the costs as well as the benefits are permanent. Because a substantial reduction in output and employment is required to achieve even small reductions in inflation, the wisdom of reducing inflation by demand restraint is very dependent on the degree to which recessions have long-run adverse effects.

The structure of Canada's unemployment insurance system may also contribute to persistence in unemployment, an aspect investigated by Milbourne, Purvis, and Scoones (1991). As discussed in Chapter 18, most research finds a relationship between the generosity and maximum duration of UI benefits and the duration of unemployment. This relationship, by itself, does not make unemployment more persistent, although a more generous UI program has the dual effects of making an economic downturn less painful (i.e., performing its primary role of providing insurance against the risk of unemployment) and making the increase in unemployment during a recession larger than it would otherwise be (because workers laid off take longer than they would in the absence of UI, or with less generous UI, to obtain work). However, since 1978–79, Canada's UI program has had a "regional extended benefit" provision which can contribute to persistence. Specifically, the maximum duration of UI benefits and the minimum number of weeks of benefits needed to qualify for UI depend on the regional unemployment rate. Thus as unemployment rises in an economic downturn, more and more regions have shorter qualifying periods and longer duration periods, thus making unemployment more likely to last longer. Milbourne,

Purvis, and Scoones (1991) find some evidence that the degree of persistence of Canadian unemployment did increase after 1978–79, a change which could be due to this institutional feature of Canada's UI program.

Related to the issue of hysteresis is the possibility of **multiple equilibrium**. The natural rate hypothesis is based on the assumption that the economy is characterized by a unique equilibrium level of employment and unemployment. Although a unique general equilibrium is predicted by an important class of economic models, many theoretical models which appear reasonable on a priori grounds are characterized by multiple equilibriums. In particular, equilibrium models of employer and employee search and matching in the labour market often have multiple rather than unique equilibriums, as discussed by Diamond (1982), Mortensen (1989), and Pissarides (1989).

For example, an economy may be characterized by two possible equilibriums, one in which employers and workers are optimistic, so that firms are searching for workers because they believe that expanding employment will be profitable in the future, and unemployed workers are actively seeking work because they believe employers will be hiring in the future. In contrast to this "high-level equilibrium" is an equilibrium at a low level of economic activity in which, because of pessimism about the future, most employers are not hiring and many workers are not actively searching. In these circumstances, the economy can become stuck in a low-level equilibrium—a situation (because it is an equilibrium) which the economy does not, on its own, have a tendency to move away from.

International evidence on hysteresis in unemployment is mixed. The evidence is strongest for Europe in the 1970s and especially the 1980s and 1990s (Blanchard and Summers, 1986; Dreze and Bean, 1990; Ball, 1999), but weaker when behaviour over longer periods and more countries is examined. The dramatic growth of long-term unemployment in Europe appears to have played an important role; many of the long-term unemployed seem to have become excluded from the labour market on a continuing basis. Whether this outcome is due to insider-outsider wage-setting, loss of job-related skills during unemployment, reduced search intensity and greater discouragement, or because employers are reluctant to hire those who have been unemployed the longest is an important area of research. Layard, Nickell, and Jackman (1991) report detailed findings on these questions for the U.K. labour market. There is also some evidence that persistence may work in reverse. Ball (1999) concludes that, during the period from the mid-1980s to the late 1990s, those European countries in which recessions were subsequently followed by sustained growth in aggregate demand were able to substantially reduce unemployment without significantly exacerbating inflationary pressures.

Canadian studies almost uniformly reject hysteresis (Cozier and Wilkinson, 1991; Fortin, 1991; Poloz and Wilkinson, 1992; see Jones, 1995 for a useful review and extension of Canadian evidence). However, there is some evidence of increased persistence in unemployment during the 1980s (Fortin, 1991). Whether this change is due to the changes made to Canada's UI system in the late 1970s, as is suggested by the work of Milbourne, Purvis, and Scoones (1991), or perhaps due to long-term effects of the severe 1981–82 recession, is an important unanswered question. Although Canada experienced two severe recessions in the early 1980s and early 1990s, in both cases these downturns were followed by a period of recovery and then very strong growth. This feature of the Canadian experience may have minimized the potentially detrimental long-term effects of periods of weak economic conditions.

U.S. Economic Performance in the 1990s

As noted by Stiglitz (1997), the behaviour of the United States economy appears to be broadly consistent with the predictions of the natural rate hypothesis. Since 1960, inflation rose in 26 of the 32 quarters when the demographically adjusted unemployment rate[7] was below 5 percent, and inflation fell in 24 of the 27 quarters in which unemployment was above 7 percent. Nonetheless, the remarkably good performance of the U.S. economy during the latter half of the 1990s—referred to by some observers as the "Goldilocks economy" (not too hot, not too cold, but just right)—has led many to question the usefulness of the natural rate or NAIRU concept. In particular, during this period the United States experienced unemployment rates below 5 percent—substantially below existing estimates of the NAIRU—for several consecutive years (see Exhibit 17.1) and low and stable rates of inflation. Is this an example of unemployment hysteresis—or at least persistence—in reverse?

However, as is frequently the case, there are a number of competing explanations for this very good performance on the inflation and unemployment front. These can be divided into two main groups: forces that may have reduced the natural unemployment rate and favourable supply shocks. In addition, there were improvements in the measurement of U.S. inflation, and these changes also resulted in lower measured rates of inflation (Gordon, 1998).

Gordon (1998) emphasizes the contribution of favourable supply developments during this period: declining energy prices, steep drops in the price of computing, and reductions in employer health care costs associated with the development of health maintenance organizations (HMOs). In addition, the U.S. dollar was strong during the period, which further contributed to keeping import prices and interest rates low.

Several factors also appear to have reduced the NAIRU during the 1990s. Several studies conclude that the aging of the labour force, largely associated with the "baby boom" generation, is contributing to a reduction in the natural unemployment rate because older workers experience less turnover and employment instability (Shimer, 1998; Katz and Kreuger, 1999). Dramatically rising rates of incarceration have also reduced measured unemployment because the "institutionalized population" is not included in the labour force, and many of those in U.S. jails are young men who, if they were not in prison, would have relatively high unemployment rates (see Katz and Kreuger, 1999 and Riddell, 1999). In addition, the rapid growth of temporary help agencies may have resulted in more efficient matching of labour demand and supply and reduced need for job search on the part of unemployed workers (Katz and Kreuger, 1999).

Whether these favourable supply shocks and forces tending to reduce the NAIRU are quantitatively important enough to fully account for the excellent U.S. economic performance during the 1990s remains an important subject for research.

Nominal Wage Rigidity and Low Inflation

As discussed in Chapter 18, unemployment and wage rigidity are often regarded as being closely linked. A central assumption of Keynesian economics is that the institutional features of the labour market result in downward nominal wage rigidity, even in the presence of substantial unemployment. In addition to the various potential sources of wage stickiness discussed in Chapter 18, workers may resist nominal wage cuts because of money illusion or notions of fairness in wage setting. One implication of nominal wage rigidity, emphasized for example by Tobin (1972), is that positive rates of price inflation may facilitate the adjustment of real and relative wages to economic shocks affecting individual labour markets. More recently, Akerlof, Dickens, and Perry (1996) point out that downward nominal wage rigidity may result in the long-run Phillips curve being downward-sloping at low rates of inflation, although vertical at moderate and high inflation rates.

[7] As discussed in Chapter 17, there are large differences in unemployment rates across demographic groups, especially between youths and adults. The demographically adjusted unemployment rate refers to the unemployment rate that would prevail if the age-sex structure of the labour force were held constant.

A simple example can be used to illustrate this point. Suppose that a particular set of shocks to individual product and labour markets result in real wage adjustments of −3 percent being required to restore equilibrium in one set of labour markets, 0 percent in another group of markets, and +3 percent in a third set of markets. If the rate of price inflation is 5 percent, these real wage adjustments can be achieved by having nominal wages grow at +2 percent, +5 percent, and +8 percent respectively in the three sets of labour markets. However, if the rate of price inflation is only 1 percent, the same real wage adjustments would require nominal wage changes of −2 percent, +1 percent and +4 percent respectively. In the low-inflation environment, downward nominal wage rigidity would impede the real wage adjustments needed to restore market equilibrium, and as a consequence the economy would experience higher unemployment and lower output. In the higher inflation environment, the necessary real wage adjustments could occur without any loss in output and employment. In this sense, inflation may "grease the wheels of the labour market."

This is an important challenge to the conventional view, because it implies that the pursuit of low inflation may have a permanent cost in the form of higher unemployment and reduced national output. According to the natural rate theory, reducing inflation from, say, 5 to 0 percent has a temporary cost in the form of higher unemployment (shown as the movement from c to g in Figure 19.5) but no permanent cost, as the economy will eventually be able to return to the NAIRU at the lower inflation rate (point a in Figure 19.5). However, if the long-run Phillips curve becomes downward-sloping at low rates of inflation, there is a permanent rather than temporary cost of pursuing low inflation. This permanent cost arises because downward nominal wage rigidity interferes with the relative wage adjustments needed for the efficient allocation of labour.

How important empirically is the resistance to nominal wage reductions? And does the amount of nominal wage rigidity in the Canadian economy imply that it is likely to be very costly for the monetary authorities to aim for price stability, or even low positive rates of inflation? These are important questions that research is attempting to address.[8]

A leading advocate of the view that nominal wage inflexibility is an empirically important phenomenon in Canada is Fortin (1996, 2001). He argues that Canada's very poor economic performance during the 1990s (especially the first half of that decade) can be principally attributed to the pursuit of low inflation (inflation targets in the 1 to 3 percent range) by the Bank of Canada. He further proposes that the Bank should increase rather than lower its inflation targets in the future.

Empirical studies with both Canadian and U.S. data do find a substantial "spike" at zero in the distribution of annual wage changes. That is, measured at annual intervals, many workers experience no wage increase or decrease. The challenge for empirical research is to estimate the extent to which this "spike" can be attributed to nominal wage rigidity versus other factors. For example, even if wages are fully flexible in both directions, zero wage changes will be appropriate in some cases. In other cases, wages may not change from one year to the next because they are fixed under long-term contracts. Thus studies must confront the counterfactual question of how much "zero wage change" would be observed in the absence of rigid nominal wages.

The careful study by Card and Hyslop (1997) addresses this counterfactual problem and concludes that there is a moderate amount of wage rigidity in the U.S. economy. They estimate that, in a typical year in the 1980s, downward nominal wage rigidities "held up" real wage changes of workers by up to 1 percent per year. Crawford and Harrison (1998) obtain similar results for Canada.

[8]See Crawford and Harrison (1998), Fares and Lemieux (2001), and Parkin (2001) for surveys of this literature with particular emphasis on the Canadian findings.

Although this and other research does suggest that nominal wage rigidity is an empirically important phenomenon in the Canadian labour market, researchers have been less successful in identifying the consequences of wage inflexibility for "real" variables such as employment and unemployment. For example, in their analysis of state-level data on wage changes and unemployment, Card and Hyslop (1997) found little evidence that the rate of wage adjustment across local labour markets is more rapid in a high-inflation environment. Fares and Lemieux (2001) estimate Phillips curves with Canadian data over the 1980s and 1990s. They exploit both the time series variation for Canada as a whole, and the variation in economic conditions across provinces and over time. The aggregate results for Canada as a whole provide some weak support for the hypothesis that there are adverse unemployment consequences of pursuing low inflation in that the negative Phillips curve relationship estimated for the 1980s "flattens out" (indeed, is no longer statistically significant) in the 1990s. However, their analysis of provincial data provides no support for the prediction of a flatter Phillips curve in the low-inflation environment of the 1990s. Overall, their results for Canada tend to reinforce the conclusions of Card and Hyslop (1997) for the United States—there is only weak evidence of negative employment consequences of downward wage rigidities in periods of low inflation.

ANTI-INFLATION POLICY

The problems of inflation and unemployment have been at the forefront of the policy agenda throughout the past several decades. They remain major challenges today. This section briefly examines the main policies that have been advocated and/or adopted in order to achieve price stability and low levels of unemployment. These policies are discussed in terms of the two major challenges that policymakers face in dealing with inflation and unemployment:

1. How to maintain desirable levels of employment without steadily increasing inflation
2. How to stop or reduce in severity an inflationary wage-price spiral should one develop

Full Employment and Price Stability

According to the natural unemployment rate paradigm described in this chapter, there is a tradeoff between inflation and unemployment in the short run but not in the long run. This conclusion, if correct, has significant implications for economic policy. In particular, it implies that attempting to achieve lower levels of unemployment in exchange for higher rates of inflation is not a feasible option on a continuing basis. Using monetary and fiscal policies to maintain the economy at an unemployment rate below the natural unemployment rate, or NAIRU, will lead to a continually increasing inflation rate. Thus, when the objectives of price stability and high levels of employment are considered together, the natural unemployment rate emerges as an appropriate definition of full employment: it is the unemployment rate that is feasible on a sustained basis and is compatible with price stability.

At the same time, the objectives of full employment and price stability are compatible with each other, providing that full employment is defined as the level of employment at which $U = U^*$. If an inflationary wage-price spiral develops, it may be necessary to accept higher unemployment and reduced output *temporarily* in order to restrain inflationary pressures, but it is not necessary to accept unemployment in excess of the natural rate on a *permanent* basis.

The natural unemployment rate, or NAIRU, is an appropriate definition of full employment in the sense that it is compatible with price stability (or any steady rate of inflation) whereas lower unemployment rates are not. However, U^* may be considered too high in terms of other social objectives such as minimizing the hardship, poverty, and lost output associated with unemployment and providing ample employment opportunities. In these circumstances, policymakers should attempt to lower U* directly, using structural and labour market policies, rather than attempting to lower U below U* using monetary and fiscal policies. Policies to reduce frictional, structural, and seasonal unemployment include mobility and adjustment assistance, provision of labour market information to improve the search and matching process, and training and retraining. Labour market policies that contribute to a higher NAIRU, such as minimum wages and unemployment insurance, could also be examined. In designing these programs, policymakers need to recognize the trade-off that exists between the immediate objectives of the program (such as providing insurance against the risk of unemployment in the case of UI) and the consequences of the program for the amount of frictional, structural, and seasonal unemployment in the economy.

Pursuing a full employment goal that is consistent with price stability (or a low stable rate of inflation) may succeed in preventing a wage-price spiral from developing, as occurred during the 1960s and 1970s. However, should wage and price inflation again climb to unacceptable levels several alternative policies are available for halting an inflationary spiral—ranging from pure reliance on demand restraint to various forms of incomes policies. The theoretical and empirical analysis discussed in this chapter sheds some light on the costs and benefits of these alternative anti-inflationary strategies.

DEMAND RESTRAINT

There is general agreement among economists that restraint in aggregate demand—in particular in the rate of increase of the money supply—must play a role in halting an inflationary wage-price spiral. There are, however, differences in opinion regarding how costly a policy of **demand restraint** will be in terms of high unemployment and reduced output. Those who believe that the costs of reducing inflation are extremely high often advocate additional policies such as wage and price controls.

In the context of the framework developed in this chapter, demand restraint reduces the amount of excess demand for labour (lowers U relative to U*), thus reducing the rates of wage and price increases. As actual inflation falls, expectations of future inflation decline and the short-run Phillips curve shifts down. Demand restraint may also impact directly on expectations. If those involved in wage and price determination form expectations rationally, they will realize that a policy of demand restraint will reduce wage and price inflation. Thus, if they believe the authorities are determined to follow this policy, they will lower their expectations, thus directly reducing wage and price increases.

The problem with this approach is that it may require a prolonged period of high unemployment and weak economic conditions in order to achieve a significant reduction in the rate of inflation. This will especially be the case if the restraint policy has little direct impact on expectations—either because those involved in wage and price determination do not form their expectations in a rational, forward-looking manner or because they do not believe that the announced policy will be followed. In these circumstances, the initial impact of the reduction in aggregate demand (or its rate of increase) will be on output and employment. The inflationary spiral can be broken, but only at a very high cost. Whether the costs are worth incurring depends on the benefits of achieving a (permanent) reduction in inflation. The approximate magnitude of these costs can be calculated from the empirical studies of the determinants of wage and price changes discussed previously in this chapter. If the slope of the short-run Phillips curve is approximately 0.5, each one percent reduction in the rate of wage and price inflation requires an increase in the unemployment rate of two percentage points. This estimate does not allow for any direct impact of demand restraint on expectations or for a variety of other factors which a complete analysis would want to take into account. Nonetheless, this rough estimate predicts the experience of the demand restraint policy implemented in the early 1980s reasonably well.

Between 1981 and 1985, price inflation declined from 12.5 to 4.0 percent, a drop of 8.5 percentage points. The decline in wage inflation was similar in magnitude. This reduction in wage and price inflation was accompanied by an increase in unemployment of 3.5 percentage points in 1982 (11.0 - 7.5), followed by increases of 4.4 in 1983 (11.9 - 7.5), 3.8 in 1984, and 3.0 in 1985. During this four-year period, the cumulative increase in unemployment above its previous level was 14.7 percentage points. The reduction in the rate of inflation was 8 percent, just slightly more than would be predicted by assuming a slope of 0.5 for the short-run Phillips curve and no direct impact on expectations.

The experience of the early 1990s was much less favourable. In this case, inflation declined from about 5 percent in 1990 to approximately 1.5 percent in 1994, a reduction of 3.5 percentage points. However, the cumulative increase in unemployment was much greater than in the 1980s (Fortin, 1996). In other words, the **sacrifice ratio**—defined as the loss of output relative to trend divided by the reduction in inflation—in the 1990s was much larger than in the 1980s, and larger than would have been predicted from a simple calculation based on a Phillips curve with slope equal to 0.5. Indeed, Debelle (1996) studies several periods of inflation reduction and estimates that the sacrifice ratio associated with the Canadian disinflation during the early 1990s was substantially higher than the earlier reductions in inflation in Canada during the 1970s and 1980s, as well as disinflations of a similar size in Australia and New Zealand. As discussed previously in this chapter, one explanation for the much greater employment loss experienced during the 1990s is that it is more costly to reduce inflation from 5 to 2 percent than from 8 to 5 percent. That is, inflation reduction runs into diminishing returns. Other explanations for Canada's weak performance during the period 1990–1996 are discussed in Freedman and Macklem (1998) and Riddell (1999).

The experience of the 1981–1982 and 1990–1992 recessions and their aftermaths provides a vivid illustration of both the effectiveness of a determined policy of demand restraint in bringing about a substantial reduction in inflation and the extraordinarily high costs associated with this approach. As a consequence of the latter, economists and policymakers have searched for—and in some cases implemented—alternative ways of making the transition to a lower inflation rate with less severe adverse consequences. The following are discussed in turn: enhancing credibility, incomes policies, and increased wage and price flexibility.

Enhancing Credibility

If those involved in wage and price determination form their expectations in a rational, forward-looking manner, they will take into account the policy stance of the monetary and fiscal authorities in predicting future inflation. In these circumstances, if the authorities can make believable their commitment to a policy of demand restraint, the transition to a lower rate of inflation can be made more easily due to the policy's direct impact on expectations. As a consequence, more of the reduction in aggregate demand falls on wages and prices and less on employment and output.

Establishing or enhancing credibility is not a simple matter. Simply announcing that a restraint policy will be followed is unlikely to be effective. The citizenry may be skeptical about the ability or willingness of the authorities to continue with such a potentially costly policy. Over time, credibility can be enhanced by adopting and maintaining a policy stance—such as nonaccommodation of inflation—which can be learned by firms, unions, and workers and taken into account in wage and price determination. For this reason, macroeconomists have increasingly focused on the question of the appropriate policy rules to be followed by the monetary and fiscal authorities (Taylor, 1999).

However, experience indicates that enhanced credibility is not easily achieved in the short run. A dramatic shift to a disinflationary stance was made by the monetary authorities in the United States and the United Kingdom in 1979. Canada followed in 1981. The determination to persist with this policy was clearly and repeatedly stated by the relevant authorities. This experience, particularly that of the United States and the United Kingdom, provides a test of the hypothesis that inflation can be reduced at low cost in terms of lost output and employment by committing to and carrying out a determined policy of demand restraint. A large number of studies of these policy experiments, reviewed in Riddell (1986, Chap. 3), have been carried out. The results do not support the hypothesis. The costs of reducing inflation by this determined policy of demand restraint were high and do not appear to have been significantly reduced by the attempt to make a clear commitment to a disinflationary stance.

In the 1990s, Canada and a number of other countries adopted a new approach to monetary policy—inflation targeting—which involved setting explicit targets for inflation rates and giving primary emphasis to inflation performance in central bank policy. This approach can be viewed as an attempt both to enhance the transparency and credibility of central bank policy and to directly influence inflation expectations. Bernanke and Mishkin (1997) and Bernanke et al. (1999) discuss this new approach to monetary policy and evaluate its effects to date. Johnson (1999) finds that inflation targeting reduced expected inflation in five countries that adopted this approach relative to a sample of countries that did not follow this policy.

Incomes Policies

The term **incomes policy** refers to a wide range of programs that intervene in wage and price setting in order to influence the rate of inflation. These include voluntary mechanisms, such as the setting of guidelines or attempting to reach agreement on norms for wage and price increases, mandatory controls on wages, prices or profits, and incentive-based incomes policies that employ taxes, subsidies, or other incentives to restrain wage and price increases.

In the postwar period governments have experimented with a variety of incomes policies. In Canada, these experiments included a number of attempts at voluntary restraint such as that involving the Prices and Incomes Commission during the late 1960s and early 1970s. In addition, mandatory wage and profit controls were a central part of the Anti-Inflation Program of 1975–1978. Wage controls were also applied to public sector employees in the federal "6-and-5" program and associated provincial programs introduced in 1982 to complement the demand restraint policy in effect at that time. Similarly, in the United States, incomes policies were employed during the Korean War period (the Wage Stabilization Board of 1950–1953), during the Kennedy and Johnson administrations (the guideposts of 1962–1966), during the Nixon administration (the wage-price controls of 1971–1974), and during the Carter administration (1977–1981). In many European countries, periods without incomes policies of some form were less common than periods with such policies. There is thus a rich history of experience with incomes policies from which we may be able to infer their advantages and disadvantages.

In principle, temporary wage and price controls can achieve a lasting reduction in inflation provided they are carefully coordinated with a program of demand restraint. In effect, the direct controls ensure that the reduction in aggregate demand (or in its rate of growth) falls primarily on wages and prices rather than on employment and output. Expectations of future inflation will also decline if the citizenry observes both lower actual inflation and monetary and fiscal policy that is appropriate for maintaining the lower rate of wage and price increase. This rationale for a temporary incomes policy combined with demand restraint is very similar to that for enhancing credibility. Both indicate the possibility of breaking an inflationary wage-price spiral without incurring severe adverse consequences in the form of high unemployment and reduced output.

Experience with wage and price control programs in the United Kingdom and the United States, reviewed in more detail in Riddell (1986, Chap. 4), has been mixed. In several cases the programs appear to have had little impact other than of a temporary nature. In other cases the policy appears to have achieved some moderation in inflation. A common characteristic of the unsuccessful programs is the failure of the authorities to combine the incomes policy with the appropriate demand restraint. In these circumstances the controls program and monetary and fiscal policy are working at cross purposes. Thus, even if controls are successful in restraining inflation in the short run, their long-run impact is minimal as wage and price increases move sharply upward in the post-controls period. In some cases the overly expansionary monetary and fiscal policy and the concomitant excess demand in product and labour markets led to the demise of the incomes policy.

The Canadian experience, in particular the Anti-Inflation Program of 1975–1978, has been more favourable. As discussed previously, econometric studies generally conclude that the wage and price controls reduced new wage settlements by 3–4 percent in each of the three years of the program, and price inflation by 1–3 percent per year, with the reduction in price inflation concentrated in the second half of the program and continuing well beyond the end of the AIP. The somewhat greater success of Canada's 1975–1978 controls program relative to the experience of the United States and the United Kingdom can probably be attributed to two key design features: the coordination of the wage and price controls with monetary and fiscal restraint, and the use of gradually declining norms for wage and price increases. The latter are important in Canada because wage contracts in the union sector are often two to three years in length. Attempting to achieve an extremely rapid reduction in the rate of wage change will cause larger inequities in the relative wage structure as groups whose contracts come up for renewal early in the controls program are treated substantially differently than those who renegotiated wages prior to the imposition of controls. Gradually declining norms for wage increases facilitate winding down the wage-price spiral without causing severe inequities that may undermine support for the program and impose high penalties on certain groups.

Although both economic theory and empirical evidence indicate that the combination of wage and price guidelines and appropriate restraint in aggregate demand represent an attractive alternative to reliance on demand restraint alone to reduce inflation, it would be a mistake to resort to controls on a regular basis. The interference with individual freedom and the inevitable inequities associated with mandatory limits on wage and price increases result in a loss of goodwill between different groups in society and alter the relationship between the citizens and the state. For this reason and others, controls should be limited to situations in which there is widespread agreement on the need to reduce inflation to more acceptable levels.

Because direct controls are a tool that should be used infrequently, and because the experience of some countries with their use has been disappointing, there has also been considerable interest in alternative policies for restraining inflation. Incentive-based incomes policies are schemes that create incentives for moderating wage and price increases without otherwise interfering with market forces. Tax-based incomes policies have received the most attention (Seidman, 1978; Layard, 1982). These utilize taxes or subsidies to provide incentives for wage and price restraint. There is little experience with these policies, but they continue to receive attention as an alternative to direct wage and price controls.

Some economists (Lerner, 1978; Lerner and Colander, 1980) have advocated elaborate schemes in which firms would require permits to increase prices (or wages) by a certain amount. The number of permits issued to firms would be restricted in order to achieve the desired overall rate of inflation. Permits would trade in an open market so that firms that wish to raise their prices more than average could purchase additional permits from firms wishing to raise prices less than average. In this way, relative prices can change despite the restraints on the overall rate of price increase.

Encouraging Wage and Price Flexibility

Disinflation via demand restraint is a costly policy to pursue because of the persistence or momentum in the inflationary process. Because of this inertia, most of the initial impact of the reduction in aggregate demand falls on output and employment. Only subsequently, as weak product and labour market conditions take their toll, do wage and price increases moderate. If wages and prices were more responsive to changes in economic conditions, inflation could be reduced without massive increases in unemployment. Enhanced credibility may be an effective means of increasing wage and price responsiveness if the main source of persistence is slowly adjusting expectations. However, if inertia is due to other factors, alternative approaches may be more successful. An approach that has received attention involves altering the institutional features of wage determination so that wages and prices adjust more quickly to changing economic conditions.

Countries differ considerably in their wage-setting arrangements (Gordon, 1982; Riddell, 1983). A distinguishing feature of the Japanese economy is the extensive use of bonus payments. These semiannual bonuses represent a substantial proportion of Japanese employees' total income (about 25 percent on average); their magnitude in any year depends in part on the economic performance of the firm and industry. Japan is also characterized by short-term wage contracts (one year) and synchronized bargaining (wage negotiations take place at approximately the same time) in the form of the "spring wage offensive." Canada and the United States are unique in the degree to which long-term (often two or three years) overlapping (rather than synchronized) wage contracts are common in the union sector. The extent of wage indexation in the form of cost-of-living-allowance clauses is low; thus real wages are not rigid, but nominal wages display considerable inertia. European countries vary. Some (e.g., Italy) employ long-term contracts but these do not overlap. Several (e.g., Sweden, Norway, Austria, Germany) have short duration contracts and synchronized, usually centralized, bargaining. The United Kingdom is characterized by one-year contracts (although these do not have a predetermined expiry date as in North America) and non-synchronized negotiations. Many European countries have wages either explicitly or implicitly indexed to changes in the price level; wages thus display "real wage rigidity."

These countries also differ substantially in their macroeconomic performance during the past three decades. Japan weathered the contractions of the postwar period, including the 1973 and 1979 OPEC oil price shocks, with relatively little increase in unemployment. Some of this is undoubtedly due to other factors, but their wage-setting institutions (synchronized bargaining, annual contracts, substantial bonus payments) probably contributed to this remarkable performance. Canada and the United States found it difficult to restrain inflation at low cost, and suffered significant increases in unemployment in response to the two oil price shocks. In both countries, however, unemployment subsequently began to decline. However, two severe recessions (in 1981–82 and 1990–92) were evidently needed to achieve a return to low levels of inflation. Although there are important differences among the European countries, as a group they suffered the largest increases in unemployment in response to the 1973 and 1979 OPEC oil price shocks. Furthermore, in many of these countries unemployment continued to rise during the 1980s and 1990s, often to levels that are three to five times those experienced in the 1960s.

Research by Taylor (1980, 1983) and others has indicated that the long-term overlapping contracts used in the union sector in the United States are an important source of persistence in wage and price inflation. Even with rational expectations and a fully credible disinflationary policy, wage and price changes respond only slowly to a reduction in aggregate demand. In Canada, the use of long-term overlapping contracts in the union sector is broadly similar to that in the United States (Riddell, 1983).

Although some economists have proposed imposing shorter wage contracts as a means of increasing wage and price responsiveness and thus reducing the costs of following a disinflationary policy, another proposed reform that has received attention is Weitzman's (1984) suggestion that profit-sharing be adopted on a widespread basis. The bonus payments used in Japan can be viewed as a form of profit-sharing (although bonuses are not explicitly tied to profits), and Weitzman has attributed Japan's remarkable economic performance during the 1970s and 1980s with respect to inflation and unemployment to the widespread use of these bonuses.

Weitzman (1984) argues that there is a fundamental difference between an economy in which workers are paid a fixed hourly wage and one in which workers are paid a share of revenue or profit. In the wage economy, the labour market is in equilibrium when the demand for labour equals the supply of labour. In the share economy, however, in equilibrium there is unsatisfied demand or unfilled job vacancies at the prevailing negotiated shares. This excess demand for labour will act as a cushion, protecting the economy from significant deviations from full employment. Any reduction in labour demand will be offset by the existence of unfilled vacancies.

The reason for this important difference is that with the share-compensation system the firm can increase profits by expanding employment and output because, with profit-sharing, the marginal cost of labour is a declining function of employment. Thus as the firm expands employment, the average cost of labour (and compensation per employee) declines. With the wage system, the firm will expand employment only to the point at which the additional revenue generated by the extra employment equals the additional cost which is the hourly wage.

Flexible compensation arrangements such as profit-sharing and gain-sharing, which relate employee remuneration to the economic performance of the firm or industry, are often recommended for their *micro* benefits at the level of the individual enterprise. By giving employees a greater financial stake in the enterprise and an opportunity for benefiting directly from its performance, the adversarial nature of labour-management relations may be replaced by a more cooperative, problem-solving approach. Additional potential benefits include increased levels of employee motivation, leading to higher productivity and organizational effectiveness and thus greater income to be shared by employers and employees. However, it may be the case that the most significant effects of these compensation arrangements are *macro* rather than micro benefits. Indeed, as Weitzman (1984) argues, there may be a rationale for public policy to encourage these compensation arrangements (e.g., by taxing income in the form of profit shares at a lower rate than income from a fixed wage) because of a "macroeconomic externality." In particular, benefits in the form of greater stability in employment and output accrue to society as a whole and not just to the parties choosing a compensation system.

In summary, inflation can be reduced by demand restraint, but experience shows that the costs of doing so are high. For this reason, a variety of additional or alternative approaches have been suggested and in some cases attempted. Determining the best way—or best combination of methods—of reducing inflation remains a major challenge for macro and labour economists.

Summary

- Canada's experience with respect to inflation, unemployment, and growth in productivity and real income has varied widely. Economic performance was excellent during the early postwar period (1950s and 1960s), although inflationary pressures had begun to emerge during the 1960s. The 1970s brought "stagflation"—increases in inflation and unemployment. During the 1960s and 1970s various policies—including demand restraint and wage and price controls—were introduced in an attempt to reduce or at least contain inflation. However, it was not until after the two major periods of monetary and fiscal restraint and the associated recessions of the early 1980s and early 1990s that a return to low rates of inflation was achieved.

- Wage changes play a significant role in the inflationary process. The aggregate relationship between the rate of wage change and the unemployment rate, called the "Phillips curve," can be derived from the micro behaviour of wage adjustment in individual labour markets. This derivation is based on two stable relationships: a positive relationship between wage changes and excess labour demand, and an inverse relationship between excess labour demand and the unemployment rate. The latter can be derived by expressing excess labour demand as the difference between the number of unfilled job vacancies and the number of unemployed workers, and assuming a stable inverse relationship between unemployment and job vacancies.
- Wage changes also depend on the expected rate of inflation. If both employers and employees expect prices to increase, they will adjust wages upward by the amount of expected inflation. Adding the expected inflation term to the relationship between wage changes and unemployment yields the "expectations-augmented Phillips curve." The absence of money illusion implies that the coefficient on expected inflation should be unity.
- Wages are typically set periodically, at annual or less frequent intervals, in implicit or explicit contracts. Even though at the time of contract negotiation the parties may take into account the inflation expected to prevail, the actual rate of price increase during the contract may differ from what was anticipated. The difference between actual and expected inflation over the previous contract will result in unanticipated excess demand or supply of labour, and an associated "catch-up" wage adjustment in the current contract. The catch-up wage adjustment will be positive if inflation was greater than anticipated and negative if inflation was lower than expected.
- The primary determinant of real wage growth is the economy's rate of productivity advance. Thus it is appropriate to include the trend rate of productivity growth as a right-hand-side variable in the wage change equation. Productivity growth influences wage negotiations by affecting workers' aspirations of real wage gains. There may thus be a lag between changes in the rate of productivity advance and the adjustment of workers' aspirations.
- A variety of additional factors may influence labour demand or supply and thus the wage level. In many cases—such as a change in the degree of unionization—these are expected to exert a one-time impact; however, some may exert a continuing influence on wage changes.
- Many empirical studies of the determinants of wage changes have been carried out in Canada. Some research uses as the dependent variable the annual or quarterly rate of change in an aggregate wage or earnings index, while other research uses individual contract data. The specification employed in most of this work is the basic expectations-augmented Phillips curve. When the unemployment rate is used as the measure of the state of excess demand or supply in the labour market, it is important to allow for changes over time in Canada's natural unemployment rate or NAIRU. When this is done, the unemployment rate is generally found to exert a significant influence on wage changes, with a slope of about 0.5, implying that a one percentage point increase in the unemployment rate reduces the annual rate of wage increase by about 0.5 percent. Most studies find that the coefficient on expected inflation is not significantly different from unity, implying that there is a short-run but no long-run relationship between inflation and unemployment. Catch-up for unanticipated inflation is also found in most studies to be an important part of the inflationary process.

- Empirical studies of the 1975-1978 Anti-Inflation Program, which imposed wage and price (or profit) controls, generally conclude that the program was successful in reducing wage settlements by 3 to 4 percent per year. If demand restraint alone had been employed, such a reduction would have required a large increase in unemployment.
- Wage changes influence prices, so the relationship between wage inflation and unemployment implies a relationship between price inflation and unemployment. The difference between the rate of wage change and the rate of price change—the rate of real wage growth—equals the rate of productivity growth when the shares of labour and capital in national income remain constant. The "price Phillips curve" relates the rate of price inflation to the unemployment rate, the rate of expected inflation, the rate of productivity growth, and other influences. The short-run Phillips curve refers to the relationship when expected inflation is held constant; this relationship is negatively sloped and implies that lower unemployment can be achieved in the short run at the expense of higher inflation. The long-run relationship refers to the situation in which actual and expected inflation are equal, so that there is no tendency for expected inflation to change. The absence of money illusion implies that the long-run relationship between inflation and unemployment is vertical at the natural unemployment rate U^*. This is often referred to as the "non-accelerating inflation rate of unemployment" or NAIRU because the theory implies that inflation will increase if $U < U^*$ and decrease if $U > U^*$.
- Adverse supply shocks—such as the dramatic increases in the world price of oil that occurred in the 1970s—shift the price Phillips curve up, resulting in higher inflation and unemployment. Favourable supply shocks shift the price Phillips curve down, allowing countries to enjoy, at least temporarily, both lower inflation and unemployment.
- According to the natural rate hypothesis, there is a short-run or temporary relationship between inflation and unemployment, but no long-run or permanent tradeoff between the two. Countries with unemployment below the NAIRU will experience increasing inflation, and vice versa for unemployment above the natural rate. Although this theory is now economic orthodoxy, several features of recent experience raise doubts about the theory and about the usefulness of the concept of a natural unemployment rate. The first is the dramatic rise of unemployment in Europe and the persistence of high unemployment without significant reductions in inflation. The second is the spectacular inflation-unemployment performance of the U.S. economy during the 1990s. The third is the issue of whether downward nominal wage rigidity implies that the long-run Phillips curve is downward-sloping rather than vertical at low inflation rates, thus raising the costs of pursuing a low-inflation strategy, as Canada did during the 1990s. These issues are controversial and the subject of ongoing research and debate.
- The experience of the 1980s and 1990s has confirmed that it is possible to significantly reduce inflation through a determined policy of demand restraint, but that the costs of doing so are very high. For this reason, a variety of additional or alternative approaches have been suggested, and in some cases implemented. These include enhancing credibility, inflation targeting, incomes policies, and encouraging wage and price flexibility. Determining the best way of reducing inflation—or the best combination of methods—remains a major challenge for macro and labour economists.

REVIEW QUESTIONS

1. Discuss the theoretical rationale, if any, for the use of the unemployment rate as a determinant of the rate of increase in aggregate money wages.
2. Distinguish between the wage inflation-unemployment tradeoff curve and the price inflation-unemployment tradeoff curve.

3. In the econometric estimation of aggregate money wage equations, the unemployment rate is often entered in reciprocal form (i.e., 1/U), with an expected positive sign, to capture the nonlinear relationship whereby the Phillips curve is convex to the origin. Illustrate why this is the case, and why a positive sign would reflect a negative relationship between $\dot{W}$ and U.
4. The original Phillips curve literature was often criticized for simply reflecting an unstable empirical relationship without any theoretical rationale for the relationship. Consequently, the policy implications were often wrong, and when the underlying causal determinants changed, the old empirical relationship no longer predicted well. This illustrates the importance of theory for accurate prediction and for policy prescriptions. Discuss.
5. Discuss the extent to which noncompetitive forces such as monopolies and powerful unions could lead to wage and price inflation.

PROBLEMS

1. Consider an economy with an aggregate Cobb-Douglas production function

$$Q = AL^{b}K^{1 - b}$$

(a) Derive the marginal product of labour in terms of the average product of labour Q/L.

(b) Show that under perfect competition in labour and product markets, b equals labour's share of the value of output (national income).

(c) Show that under perfect competition in labour and product markets, $\hat{W} - \hat{P} = \hat{A} + \hat{b}$, where the ^ above the variable denotes the rate of growth. Explain the implications of this equation for movements in price inflation, wage inflation, real wage growth, and productivity growth.

(d) In this economy what will happen to labour's share of the value of total output if real wages increase at the rate of productivity growth? What does this imply about how the benefits of productivity increases are shared by labour and capital?

2. Trace out the wage and price inflation–unemployment curves, in both the short run and the long run, from the adjustment process portrayed in Figure 19.2. What if the asking wage of labour increased by more than the inflation rate of a given year, perhaps because of a catch-up process or because of an anticipation of even higher inflation in the future? Illustrate this in Figure 19.2, and illustrate the new point in the inflation-unemployment tradeoffs. What if this were prevented by a wage-price control program that restricted wage increases to the price inflation of that year? (Illustrate on the diagram and on the tradeoff curves.) Could this provide a rationale for a controls program to move the economy toward its long-run equilibrium without experiencing a phase of high unemployment necessary to moderate wage demands? Does it matter if the original wage demands in excess of actual inflation were based on a catch-up for past inflation, or an expectation of future inflation? What if the controls were not accompanied by the appropriate monetary and fiscal policies to curb inflationary pressures? What if inflation continued in spite of the wage controls, perhaps because the price mark-up over labour costs were increased?
3. Illustrate how the adjustment process of Figure 19.2 could arise from a job search process whereby job seekers face a distribution of money wage offers and have an acceptance or reservation wage in money terms. That is, they will continue to remain unemployed and search (sample the distribution of money wage offers) until they receive their reservation wage. Indicate how an increase in aggregate demand and its accompanying increase in the aggregate price level may reduce search unemployment

in the short run, but may not reduce it in the long run when the reservation wage adjusts to the inflation.

4. "Any microeconomic theory of behaviour that requires wage rigidities due to such things as unanticipated inflation, wage lags, or money illusion in the collective bargaining or job search process, could only explain phenomena in the short run, not in the long run." Discuss.
5. Illustrate the long-run relationship between price inflation and unemployment for different values of λ in equations 19.10 and 19.15; for example, $\lambda = 0.5$, $\lambda = 0.8$, $\lambda = 0.95$. What happens as λ approaches unity?
6. "If price inflation is 6 percent and productivity growth 2 percent, and if money wages increase by 8 percent, then labour receives *all* of the productivity increase and nothing is left over for other factors of production." Discuss.
7. Assume that the following short-run *hypothetical* Phillips curve is estimated econometrically:

$$\dot{W} = 2.5 + 0.9\,\dot{p}^e - 0.25U$$

where $\dot{W}$ is the annual rate of change in money wages, $\dot{p}^e$ is the annual expected inflation rate, and U is the unemployment rate. All variables are expressed in percentage terms and their averages over the sample period are 10 for $\dot{W}$, 10 for $\dot{p}^e$, and 6 for U. The estimated coefficients are all significantly different from zero, and the coefficient of $\dot{p}^e$ is not significantly different from one, according to conventional significance tests.

(a) What is the rate of change of money wages that would result if expected inflation were 10 percent and the unemployment rate 6 percent?
(b) What would happen if the unemployment rate were raised to 10 percent?
(c) What would happen if expected inflation were moderated to 5 percent?
(d) What does the coefficient for the inflation-expectations variable imply about the formation of expectations?
(e) What does the coefficient of the unemployment rate variable imply about the shape of the Phillips curve?
(f) Plot a Phillips curve assuming expectations of inflation of 5 percent. Plot a Phillips curve assuming expectations of inflation of 10 percent. What happens to the Phillips curve if expectations of inflation increase from 5 to 10 percent?
(g) Assume that the short-run aggregate price equation was estimated as $\dot{p} = 2 - 0.25U + 1.1\,\dot{W}$. and that, in the long run, actual inflation equals expected inflation—that is, $\dot{p} = \dot{p}^e$. Utilize the short-run Phillips curve and aggregate price equations, and the long-run equilibrium condition to solve for the long-run Phillips curve. Compare the shape of the long-run and short-run Phillips curves. Solve for the long-run or natural rate of unemployment as a function of money wages.

KEYWORDS

stagflation 575
inflation targeting 577
Phillips curve 578
excess demand 578
excess supply 578
job vacancy rate 578
natural unemployment rate 579
expected inflation 582
expectations-augmented Phillips curve 584
money illusion 585
cost-of-living-allowance or COLA 590
non-accelerating inflation rate of unemployment (NAIRU) 595
supply shocks 595
persistence 597
hysteresis 598
multiple equilibriums 599
demand restraint 603
sacrifice ratio 604
incomes policy 605

REFERENCES

Akerlof, G., W. Dickens, and G. Perry. 1996. The macroeconomics of low inflation. *BPEA* 1(1996):1-76.

Allen, R. 1986. The impact of technical change on employment, wages and the distribution of skills: A historical perspective. In *Adapting to Change: Labour Market Adjustment in Canada*, ed. W. C. Riddell. Toronto: University of Toronto Press.

Ashenfelter, O. 1978. Union relative wage effects: New evidence and a survey of their implications for wage inflation. In *Econometric Contributions to Public Policy*, eds. R. Stone and W. Peterson. New York: St. Martin's Press.

Auld, D., L. Christofides, R. Swidinsky, and D. Wilton. 1979. The impact of the Anti-Inflation Board on negotiated wage settlements. *CJE* 12 (May):195-213.

Ball, L. 1999. Aggregate demand and long term unemployment. *BPEA* (2)(1999):189-236.

Bernanke, B., T. Laubach, F. Mishkin, and A. Posen. 1999. *Inflation Targeting: Lessons from the International Experience*. Princeton: Princeton University Press.

Bernanke, B., and F. Mishkin. 1997. Inflation targeting: A new framework for monetary policy? *JEP* 11 (Spring):97-116.

Blanchard, O. 1991. Wage bargaining and unemployment persistence. *Journal of Money, Credit, and Banking* 23 (August):277-92.

Blanchard, O., and L. H. Summers. 1986. Hysteresis and the European unemployment problem. *NBER Macroeconomic Annual*:15-78.

Bodkin, R., E. Bond, G. Reuber, and T. Robinson. 1966. *Price Stability and High Employment*. Ottawa: Economic Council of Canada.

Card, D. 1990. Unexpected inflation, real wages, and employment determination in union contracts. *AER* 80 (September):669-88.

Card, D., and D. Hyslop. 1997. Does inflation grease the wheels of the labor market? In *Reducing Inflation*, eds. C. Romer and D. Romer. Chicago: University of Chicago Press.

Christofides, L., R. Swidinsky, and D. Wilton. 1980. A microeconometric analysis of spill-overs within the Canadian wage determination process. *R.E. Stats.* 62 (May):213-21.

Christofides, L., and D. Wilton. 1985. Wage determination in the aftermath of controls. *Economica* 52 (February):51-64.

Cozier, B., and G. Wilkinson. 1991. Some evidence on hysteresis and the costs of disinflation in Canada. Bank of Canada, Technical Report No. 55.

Crawford, A., and A. Harrison. 1998. Testing for downward wage rigidity in nominal wage rates. In *Price Stability, Inflation Targets, and Monetary Policy*. Ottawa: Bank of Canada.

Debelle, G. 1996. The ends of three small inflations: Australia, New Zealand and Canada. *CPP* 22 (March):56-78.

Diamond, P. 1982. Aggregate demand management in search equilibrium. *JPE* 90 (August):881-94.

Dreze, J., and C. Bean. 1990. *Europe's Unemployment Problem*. Cambridge, Mass.: MIT Press.

Fares, J., and T. Lemieux. 2001. Downward nominal wage rigidity: A critical assessment and some new evidence for Canada. In *Price Stability and the Long Run Target for Monetary Policy*. Ottawa: Bank of Canada.

Fortin, P. 1991. The Phillips curve, macroeconomic policy, and the welfare of Canadians. *CJE* 24:774-803.

______. 1996. The Great Canadian Slump. *CJE* 29 (November):761-87.

______. 1999. *The Canadian Standard of Living: Is There a Way Up?* C. D. Howe Institute Benefactors Lecture. Toronto: C. D. Howe Institute.

______. 2001. Inflation targeting: The three percent solution. *Policy Matters*. Montreal: Institute for Research on Public Policy.

Freedman, C., and T. Macklem. 1998. A comment on "The great Canadian slump." *CJE* 31 (August) 646-65.

Friedman, M. 1968. The role of monetary policy. *AER* 58 (March):1-17.

Gordon, R. 1982. Why U.S. wage and employment behaviour differs from that in Britain and Japan. *EJ* 92 (March):13-44.

______. 1998. Foundations of the Goldilocks economy: Supply shocks and the time-varying NAIRU. *BPEA* (2)(1998):297-333.

Johnson, D. 1999. The effect of inflation targeting on the behaviour of expected inflation: Evidence from an 11 country panel. Working Paper, Wilfred Laurier University.

Jones, S. 1995. *The Persistence of Unemployment*. Montreal: McGill-Queen's University Press.

Kaliski, S. 1964. The relation between unemployment and the rate of change of money wages in Canada. *IER* 5 (January):1-33.

Katz, L., and A. Kreuger. 1999. The high pressure U.S. labor market of the 1990s. *BPEA* (1)(1999):1-65.

Layard, R. 1982. Is incomes policy the answer to unemployment? *Economica* 49 (August):219-39.

Layard, R., S. Nickell, and R. Jackman. 1991. *Unemployment: Macroeconomic Performance and the Labour Market*. Oxford: Oxford University Press.

Lerner, A. 1978. A wage increase permit plan to stop inflation. *BPEA* 2:491-505.

Lerner, A., and D. Colander. 1980. *MAP:A Market Anti-Inflation Plan*. New York: Harcourt Brace Jovanovich.

Lipsey, R. 1960. The relationship between unemployment and the rate of change of money wage rates in the United Kingdom, 1862-1957: A further analysis. *Economica* 27 (February):1-31.

Milbourne, R., D. Purvis, and W. D. Scoones. 1991. Unemployment insurance and unemployment dynamics. *CJE* 24 (November):804-26.

Mortensen, D. 1989. The persistence and indeterminacy of unemployment in search equilibrium. *Scandinavian Journal of Economics* 91:347-60.

Parkin, M. 2001. What have we learned about price stability? In *Price Stability and the Long Run Target for Monetary Policy*. Ottawa: Bank of Canada.

Phelps, E. 1967. Phillips curves, expectations of inflation and optimal unemployment over time. *Economica* 34 (August):254-81.

______. 1968. Money-wage dynamics and labor-market equilibrium. *JPE* 76 (July/August):678-711.

Phillips, A. 1958. The relation between unemployment and the rate of change of money wage rates in the United Kingdom, 1861-1957. *Economica* 25 (November, Comment by G. Routh 36. [1959] 299-315):283-99.

Pissarides, C. 1989. Unemployment and macroeconomics. *Economica* 56 (February):1-14.

Poloz, S., and G. Wilkinson. 1992. Is hysteresis a characteristic of the Canadian labour market? A tale of two studies. Bank of Canada.

Riddell, W. 1979. The empirical foundations of the Phillips curve: Evidence from Canadian wage contract data. *Ecta.* 47 (January):1-24.

______. 1983. The responsiveness of wage settlements in Canada and economic policy. *CPP* 9 (March):9-23.

______. 1986. *Dealing with Inflation and Unemployment in Canada*. Toronto: University of Toronto Press.

______. 1999. Canadian labour market performance in international perspective. *CJE* 32 (November): 1097-134.

Riddell, W., and P. Smith. 1982. Expected inflation and wage changes in Canada. *CJE* 15 (August):377-94.

Seidman, L. 1978. Tax-based incomes policies. *BPEA* 2:301-48.

Setterfield, M., D. Gordon, and L. Osberg. 1992. Searching for a will o' the wisp: An empirical study of the NAIRU in Canada. *EER* 36 (January):119-36.

Shimer, R. 1998. Why is the U.S. unemployment rate so much lower? *NBER Macroeconomics Annual 1998.*

Stiglitz, J. 1997. Reflections on the natural rate hypothesis. *JEP* 11 (Winter):3-10.

Taylor, J. 1980. Aggregate dynamics and staggered contracts. *JPE* 88 (February):1-23.

______. 1982. Establishing credibility: A rational expectations viewpoint. *AER* 72 (May):81-5.

______. 1983. Union wage settlements during a disinflation. *AER* 73 (December):981-93.

Taylor, J. (Ed.). 1999. *Monetary Policy Rules*. Chicago: University of Chicago Press.

Tobin, J. 1972. Inflation and unemployment. *AER* 62 (March):1-18.

Turnovsky, S. 1972. The expectations hypothesis and aggregate wage equation: Empirical evidence for Canada. *Economica* 39 (February):1-17.

Weitzman, M. L. 1984. *The Share Economy: Conquering Stagflation*. Cambridge, Mass.: Harvard University Press.

Glossary

ability bias: a pitfall that is involved in the empirical estimation of human capital earnings functions; the estimate of the rate of return on education might be systematically higher than the true value due to the role of the unobserved variable of innate ability

Aboriginal earnings differentials: the discrepancy in the average earnings between Aboriginal Canadians and non-Aboriginal Canadians, often after adjusting for human capital levels (see the definition for **human capital**)

added worker: a worker who normally does not participate in the labour force but searches for work in order to supplement the family income

administrative concept of value: a procedure for determining the value of a certain job that relies on explicit assessments of the average value of the job's characteristics; in contrast to the market or economic concept of value

adverse selection: a situation in which the insurer cannot observe the true risk involved in insuring the insuree, but the insuree knows it well; it imposes a difficulty on developing insurance contracts such as implicit contracts (see the definition for **implicit contracts**)

affirmative action: a particular form of equal employment opportunity legislation which seeks to implement a greater equality in results as opposed to focusing on more equal opportunities (see the definition for **equal employment opportunity legislation**)

age-earnings profile: the relationship between age and/or labour market experience and the wage level of an individual as he/she ages; the shape of an earnings stream

aggregate or time series data: data describing macroeconomic variables such as unemployment or inflation; there is a one-to-one correspondence between the time period and a data value, as the values vary over the dimension of time

alternative wage: the highest wage level that the worker could earn working for another firm; it may or may not be a unionized position

assessed and nonassessed classes: assessed classes are those immigrants whose applications are subjected to an evaluation of their likely contribution and success in the Canadian labour market; immigrants in nonassessed classes do not undergo an evaluation based on those criteria

asymmetric information: a situation in which both parties to a contract do not have the same information as far as work effort, production costs, or firm profit is concerned; there is often a disincentive to reveal full information to the other party

bargaining power: the power the union possesses in collective bargaining to raise wages without facing a major cost in the form of reduced employment; alternatively, the power to achieve a wage-employment outcome that approaches its ideal outcome

bargaining range: the range of wage outcomes that could feasibly emerge from collective bargaining; the lower bound is the alternative wage, and the higher bound generates zero profits for the firm (see the definition for **alternative wage**)

bargaining theory: a body of economic theory concerned with predicting the specific wage-employment outcome that might emerge from collective bargaining given the set of Pareto-efficient wage-employment contracts (see the definition for **Pareto-efficient wage-employment outcome**)

bargaining units: the group of workers whose wages and terms of employment are covered in the collective bargaining agreement (see the definition for **collective bargaining**)

brain drain: an economic choice in which highly skilled and highly educated individuals emigrate from Canada; Canada is thus the source country rather than the host country

budget constraint: the locus of all combinations of income and leisure that the worker can potentially reach given the wage and the level of non-market income

Canada/Quebec Pension Plan: these government programs, abbreviated CPP/QPP, are social insurance regimes providing payments to retired workers on the basis of their prior contributions to the regime; the payments are thus not in the form of demogrants, and the program is not universal

Canada-U.S. unemployment differential: the historical phenomenon of the unemployment rate in Canada exceeding the unemployment rate in the United States since the mid-1980s despite the many similarities between the two economies

certification: the legal process by which a group of unorganized workers attain representation by a labour union; the union then becomes the sole bargaining agent for that group

child-care subsidies: a government program that allocates payments to working parents to either pay the full cost of or defray the cost of child-care services

coefficient: a parameter of a regression model; a constant scalar value that, multiplied by the economic variable(s), gives the effect of the explanatory variable on the variable being explained (see the definitions for **regression analysis** and **parameter**)

cohort effect: a labour supply choice or effect that refers to a group of individuals who all entered the labour force at the same time (contexts of life-cycle labour supply and effects on wage levels)

collective agreement coverage: the percentage of paid workers whose wages and working conditions are covered by a collective agreement; in North America, nearly all of them are actual union members

collective bargaining: a process under which the union negotiates wages, nonwage benefits, working conditions, and the terms of employment with the firm; the union negotiates on behalf of all workers, and the terms of the contract apply to all workers (see the definition for **unions**)

comparable worth: a government policy designed to reduce the magnitude of the overall earnings gap between men and women; very similar to pay equity (see the definition for **pay equity**)

comparator jobs: a job class used to implement a pay equity scheme; the female-dominated job is paired with a male-dominated one thought to have very similar attributes and requirements

compensated elasticity (of labour supply)**:** the wage elasticity of labour supply adjusted for the income elasticity of labour supply, that is, the percentage change in the quantity supplied of labour divided by the percentage change in the wage after subtracting the income effect of the wage change

compensating risk premium: the rate at which the worker values a higher level of job safety in terms of the wage; the compensating differential that the worker offers to the labour market before the market wage differential is determined, and is determined by his/her preferences for job safety versus income (see the definition for **compensating wage differentials**)

compensating wage differentials: wage differentials designed to compensate a worker for amenities or disamenities associated with a job; positive for undesirable aspects and negative for desirable ones (see the definition for **wage differentials**)

competitive buyer of labour: a firm which obtains its labour in a competitive labour market; it faces a labour supply curve that is infinitely elastic at the going market wage, and is thus a wage "taker" (see definition for **competitive market**)

competitive market: an input market or an output market that meets the criteria of the model of perfect competition (a large number of buyers and/or sellers, a homogenous product/service, perfect information regarding prices and quality, and free entry of new buyers and sellers)

consumer's optimum: the worker's choice of market income received and number of hours worked within the labour supply model (context of the labour supply model)

consumption-leisure: the tradeoff facing any worker in the labour supply model, also called the income-leisure tradeoff

contract curve: the locus of all Pareto-efficient wage-employment combinations; drawn in wage-employment space (see the definition for **Pareto-efficient wage-employment contracts**)

control group: a group of workers involved in a research experiment that is not subjected to a certain process and is compared to the treatment group (see the definitions for **program evaluation** and **treatment group**)

conventional equal pay legislation: a government antidiscrimination policy that requires equal pay for equal work within the same job and within the same establishment

corner solution: a labour supply choice corresponding to either zero hours of leisure coupled with all hours allocated to work or zero hours of work coupled with all hours allocated to leisure

cost minimization: the assumption applied to the behavioural motive of firms as they determine the demand for labour; it applies in cases in which the level of output desired is fixed (see the definition for **profit maximization**)

cost-of-living allowance: the practice of tying the rate of wage increases stipulated in labour contracts to the rate of increase in the consumer price index

counterfactual: a case involved in the research of labour market issues; an estimate of an alternative, hypothetical labour market equilibrium that would have occurred in the absence of an economic event (such as in the absence of immigration activity)

craft unions: a labour union that represents workers within a particular trade or occupation (see the definition for **unions**)

cross-section microdata: data describing attributes of microeconomic units such as firms and workers; there is a one-to-one correspondence between the unit of observation and a data value; the values vary over the dimension of economic actors at the same time period

crowding hypothesis: a supply theory of discrimination according to which women, facing barriers to entry in many occupation, tend to be forced into certain female-dominated occupations, thereby expanding the supply of labour (see definition for **supply theories of discrimination**)

cyclical unemployment: see the definition for **demand-deficient unemployment**

deadweight loss: the loss in total output generated by an inefficient allocation of labour resources between two sectors (see the definitions of **inefficient allocation** and **two-sector model**)

decertification: the reverse of the certification process (see the definition for **certification**)

deferred compensation: a remuneration mechanism in which the worker's pay is typically below their marginal revenue product during the early phases of their career, but is above it during the later phases; non-wage benefits that can be redeemed by the worker only after he/she has worked for the firm for a specified time period; examples are pension benefits and vacation pay

defined benefit plans: a special type of employer-sponsored pension plan in which the benefits are set at a certain percentage of wages and the length of time worked, and the contributions are determined by the financial requirements of the pension obligations

defined contribution plans: a special type of employer-sponsored pension plan in which the contributions are set at a certain percentage of wages, and the benefits are determined by the amount of money in the fund at the time of retirement

delay costs: an element of Rubinstein's bargaining theory in which the parties can exercise leverage by threatening to delay a settlement, which imposes costs on the other party (see the definition for **Rubinstein's bargaining theory**)

demand-deficient unemployment: the type of aggregate unemployment associated with a level of aggregate demand that is insufficient to provide enough jobs for the entire labour force

demand for union representation: an economic variable reflecting the preferences of workers for union representation; it depends on its expected costs and benefits

demand restraint: a restrictive fiscal policy and/or restrictive monetary policy designed to reduce the actual and the expected rate of inflation

demand theories of discrimination: a source of labour market discrimination; demand for female labour is reduced relative to the demand for male labour, all other factors (especially productivity) held constant

demogrant: a lump-sum transfer allocated to the worker regardless of his/her work effort or how many or few hours that he/she works

derived demand: the demand for a productive resource or input that depends directly on the demand for the product or service it is employed to produce

diminishing marginal returns: a principle stating that, as successive increments of a variable factor such as labour are applied to a fixed factor, the marginal product of the variable factor declines; it applies only in the short run. (see definition for **marginal physical product**)

discouraged worker: a jobless worker who has ceased searching for work because he/she believes no work is available

disequilibrium: a state in which a market is not clearing such that quantity supplied is equal to quantity demanded; the transactions price is prevented from reaching the equilibrium price

displaced workers: workers who were formerly employed (and often attached to these jobs) but were permanently laid off lost their jobs; much research has been carried out on their subsequent job search

dualism: an analytical perspective that is an alternative to the neoclassical supply and demand approach; the labour market is segmented into two parts, the core and the periphery

duration of unemployment: the average length of time spent in the state of unemployment before leaving that state through finding employment or exiting from the labour force

dynamic factor demand: a framework for analyzing labour demand choices that incorporates quasi-fixed labour costs; given a change in the wage or the level of output, the adjustment to the new employment level is not instantaneous; the speed of adjustment and the path of adjustment are analyzed; in contrast with the static framework, both the number of hours and the number of employees adjust instantaneously, and the adjustment path is not examined

dynamic labour supply: choices

involving hours worked as a function of wages in the current period as well as wages in prior or subsequent periods; at the beginning of the time horizon, the worker plans his/her choices of how many hours to work in each subsequent time period over his/her career as a function of the wages and expected wages over his/her career

dynamic monopsony: a firm that is essentially a competitive buyer of labour, but may be facing an upward-sloping supply of labour in the short run; it thus has to raise the wage it pays in order to recruit workers at the margin (see the definitions for **competitive buyer of labour** and **monopsony**)

early retirement: the act of withdrawing from the labour force at an earlier age than normal; the worker often receives most of the pension benefit level he/she would otherwise have received

earnings function: a mathematical equation that models the wage earned by an individual; the wage is the dependent variable, and among the independent variables are the level of education and the level of experience

economic assimilation: the process by which a cohort of immigrants overcomes a negative entry effect and attains labour market outcomes (such as wage levels) that are on a par with those of their native counterparts (see the definition for **entry effect**)

economic rent: the difference between the going wage and the alternative wage (see the definition for **alternative wage**)

efficiency wages: a wage that exceeds that competitive, market-clearing level and is designed to enhance the productivity of the worker; thought to elicit greater effort from the worker

efficient contract: an agreed-upon arrangement between the employer (the principal) and the employee (the agent) which minimizes the potential disincentives, such as employee shirking or employer cheating

efficient wage and employment contracts: collective bargaining agreements for which both the level of the wage and the level of employment are subjected to negotiation

elasticity of demand for labour: the percentage change in quantity demanded of labour that results from a 1 percent change in the wage rate

employed: the state of holding a paying job

employer-sponsored/occupational pension plans: a private tier of pension funds that allocate pensions to retired workers; the beneficiaries are former employees of these firms, and typically both the employer and the employee have contributed

employment: the market quantity of labour that is hired and inputted into the production process

employment equity: (see the definition for **affirmative action**)

employment rate: the number of employed workers divided by the size of the working-age population

employment standards legislation: laws drafted by governments that apply to firms; they require the firm to provide certain nonwage benefits and job protections once the employee has served a certain length of time

endogenous preferences: antidiscrimination policies that are designed to alter tastes, perceptions, preferences, and attitudes regarding traditional male and female occupations; the objective is to encourage more females to enter male occupations

endogenous variables: variables within an economic model whose fluctuations are to be explained or determined by the fluctuations of exogenous variables; also called the dependent variables of a model; the analyst has no control over the fluctuations (see the definition for **exogenous variables**)

entry effect: the degree to which immigrants, upon arrival to Canada, earn lower wages than their native counterparts; also labelled the earnings penalty

equal employment opportunity legislation: a government policy designed to prevent discrimination in recruiting, hiring, promotion, and dismissals; influences personnel decisions rather than wage levels

equilibrium: the state of an economic model, such as the supply and demand framework, in which there are no forces acting to change the values of the economic variables

errors-in-variables problems: a difficulty involved in empirical analysis; an empirical proxy for an economic variable such as job safety does not measure the true variable very accurately

ethnic-white earnings differentials: differences between the average earnings levels of white Canadians and those of other ethnic groups, many of whom are visible minorities; these differences may stem from labour market discrimination

event study: a research methodology oriented around a particular occurrence; economic outcomes that occurred before this event are compared to those occurring after it in order to analyze the effect of the event

evolutionary wage change: a wage change reflected in a movement along an individual's age-earnings profile; these wage changes are associated with normal progress through one's career; there are typically increases during most of the career, but decreases are possible toward the end of the career

excess demand: a situation in the aggregate labour market characterized by demand that is greater than supply; associated with positive pressure on the wage

excess supply: a situation in the aggregate labour market characterized by supply that is greater than demand; associated with negative pressure on the wage

exit: a tactic for workers to exert pressure on their employers when and if they are dissatisfied with their terms of employment by quitting their job; an alternative strategy to voice (see the definition for **voice**)

exogenous variables: variables within an economic model whose fluctuations are controlled by the researcher; these variables serve to explain the fluctuations of endogenous variables (see the definition for **endogenous variables**)

expectations-augmented Phillips curve: a derived version of the simple Phillips curve that has a term for the expectation rate of inflation appended to it (see the definitions for **Phillips curve** and **expected inflation**)

expected inflation: the rate of inflation that workers and firms anticipate to occur in future periods

experience rating: an aspect of unemployment insurance programs in which premiums paid by the firm increase with the frequency with which its workers claim benefits

experimental evidence: a research technique that develops and carries out social experiments involving the parameters of the income maintenance scheme, and observes the labour market outcomes (context of supply and income maintenance schemes); an example is the negative income tax mechanism

explained and unexplained differentials: the two components of the Oaxaca decomposition of the observed wage gap; the first is attributable to differences in pre-market characteristics and the second is due to differences in the rate at which they are valued on the labour market (see the definitions for the **Oaxaca decomposition** and **pre-market characteristics**)

external production: a personnel practice whereby positions are filled from the pool of applicants outside the firm; the opposite of internal recruitment (see the definition for **internal promotion**)

facilitating policies: a particular form of equal employment opportunity policies that are designed to encourage greater employment opportunities and wages for the disfavoured group; there is less direct intervention in personnel decisions (see the definition for **equal employment opportunity legislation**)

factor of production: economic resources that function as inputs to the production process, such as land, labour, capital, and entrepreneurial ability

family class immigrants: one of the two nonassessed classes of immigrants; their applications are not evaluated according to the point system, but rather according to the immigrants' kinship with other immigrants who have been admitted

family investment hypothesis: an economic theory of immigrant behaviour according to which families facing borrowing constraints specialize their labour market participation patterns between the wife and the husband

feminist perspectives: a point of view on how the labour market works that has an underlying ideology that diverges greatly from the neoclassical perspective

fertility: issues having to do with bearing children and raising a family; they have profound effects on labour supply patterns of both men and women

fixed costs: a cost that does not vary with the length of time that the individual works (context of labour supply and child-care subsidies)

fixed costs: production costs expressed in levels which are invariant with respect to the level of output

fixed-effects model: a type of empirical wage-determination model in which the effect of many unobservable attributes on wage levels is removed from the estimation process; longitudinal data is required (see the definition for **longitudinal or panel data**)

frictional unemployment: the type of aggregate unemployment associated with normal turnover in the labour force; individual workers often take time to find suitable jobs while they are jobless

full income: the amount of income that corresponds to the maximum number of hours worked

general equilibrium effects: the impact of an income maintenance scheme on labour market choices within a dynamic framework

general training: human capital development, often occurring on the job, that can be applied at other firms in addition to the firm that provides it

glass ceilings: a discriminatory barrier to upward job mobility thought to apply to higher-skilled women, preventing them from reaching the highest echelons of the pay scale

gross flows: the total number of workers observed per month to be transiting from one labour force state (i.e., employment, unemployment, or out of the labour force) to another; movements in the two directions are counted separately

guaranteed income supplement: this program is very similar to the old age security regime (abbreviated GIS; see the definition for **old age security**)

hidden unemployment: the situation of jobless workers who are not officially classified as unemployed but nonetheless may desire work or otherwise exhibit some attachment to the labour force (see the section "Hidden Unemployment/Marginal Labour Force Attachment" in Chapter 17)

hold-up problem: a potential negative effect that unions can have on firm productivity; by threatening job action, they can appropriate some of the returns to investment in capital due to the immobility of capital

hours of work aspect: the element of the labour supply choice involving the number of hours that are worked per unit of time

human capital: characteristics individuals can acquire to improve the productivity of their labour; the most common examples are education and other forms of training, but more generally can include health, nutrition, and other investments in human productivity

human capital earnings function: an empirical equation that relates the wage level of a worker to the level of education; it includes as explanatory variables the level of education and an estimate of the level of labour market experience

human capital investment decision: the choice an individual makes regarding the level of education or training to which he/she is going to devote time and resources

human capital theory: a theory of the act of investment in human resources in the form of training and education with a view on raising the productivity of an individual

hysteresis: an extreme case of persistence in unemployment in which the actual rate of unemployment can drift upward or downward, without any tendency to return to an equilibrium level (see the definition for **persistence**)

immobility: a state in which a factor of production, such as labour, is constrained as to which sectors, occupations, or regions it can enter

impact of immigrants: an important economic issue related to immigration; the degree to which immigration activity has an impact on the equilibriums in labour markets of the host country, and hence on the welfare of native workers

imperfect information: a feature of labour markets in which the attributes of workers and the attributes of firms are unknown at the point of exchange, and are revealed only with the passage of time

implicit contracts: an agreement between the employer and the labour force that is not legally binding, but that tends to be self-enforcing because the firm's reputation and or the worker group's reputation could be at risk if it did not respect the contract

incidence of tax: the distribution between the demanders and the suppliers of the true burden of a tax, net of any adjustment of the market price in response to the imposition of the tax

incidence of unemployment: the proportion of the individuals in the labour force who become unemployed in any time interval

income effect: the portion of the change in quantity demanded resulting from a price change that is attributed to the change in income, holding relative prices constant

income elasticity (of labour supply): the percentage change in the quantity supplied of labour divided by the percentage change in the income

income-leisure: the tradeoff workers face as they determine their labour supply behaviour; both income and leisure are considered to be goods, and the worker has to choose how many units of each he/she wants given the wage and other income

income maintenance schemes: a government program that compensates individuals with payments for income losses and/or income deficiencies

incomes policy: a range of government policies designed to intervene in wage- and price-setting institutions in order to reduce the rate of inflation and the expected rate of inflation; suggested by some as an alternative to demand restraint policies (see the definition for **demand restraint**)

increased returns to education: the economic phenomenon of an apparent rise in the United States in the rate of return to education over the 1980s and 1990s (see the definition for **returns to schooling**)

independent immigrants: (see the definition for **assessed and nonassessed classes**)

indifference curves: the locus of all combinations of income and leisure that yield equal utility to the worker (context of the labour supply model)

industrial unions: a labour union that represents all workers within a particular firm or industry as opposed to a certain trade or occupation (see the definition for **unions**)

industry premiums: a difference in wages between two individuals attributable solely to the industries in which the workers are employed; factors such as human capital requirements and the occupation have been accounted for; it sometimes reflects non-pecuniary differences

inefficient allocation: an allocation of labour between two sectors of the labour market that fails to maximize total production and income; typically accompanied by disequilibrium wages (see the definition for **two-sector model**)

inferior good: a good whose quantity demanded decreases with the level of income

inflation targeting: a central bank policy of employing the standard tools of monetary policy with the aim of achieving a certain rate of inflation

insider-outsider theory: one theory that is designed to model aggregate unemployment is based on rigid and unduly high real wages; sometimes applied to explain the persistently high unemployment in continental Europe during the 1990s.

institutionalism: an analytical perspective that is an alternative to the neoclassical supply and demand approach; plays down the importance of the economic forces of supply and demand, and plays up the role of institutions, conventions, customs, social mores, and political forces

interindustry wage differentials: (see the definition for **industry premiums**)

interior solution: a labour supply choice corresponding to a positive number of hours of leisure and a positive number of hours of work

internal labour markets: labour markets in which the firm hires only its entry-level workers on the external market; always fill their open positions by promoting workers from within the ranks of their present labour force

internal promotion: a common feature of internal labour markets whereby positions above entry level are filled from the ranks of the existing labour force; there is no external recruitment for these positions (see the definition for **internal labour markets**)

internal rate of return: an implicit, calculated rate of return of investment in human capital (context of human capital)

interoccupational wage differentials: (see the definition for **occupational premiums**)

intertemporal substitution: a labour supply response to an anticipated, evolutionary wage change over the course of the life cycle. The worker adjusts his/her working patterns and savings patterns over the entire life cycle in response to changes in wages at other periods

isocost line: the locus of all combinations of inputs of labour and capital that generated the same level of total cost; represented graphically in capital-labour space

isoprofit curves: the locus of all combinations of the wage level and the employment level that yield equal profits to the employer; drawn in employment-wage space

isoprofit schedule: the locus of various combinations of the wage level and the job attribute (such as safety) that generate an equal level of profitability for the firm; drawn in wage–job attribute space

isoquant: the locus of all combinations of inputs of labour and capital that generate the same level of output; represented graphically in capital-labour space

job search: the process of workers seeking job offers and employment on the labour market; it takes place in an environment of imperfect information

job vacancy rate: the proportion of employment positions that are not currently held by an individual

labour demand curve model: a regime for collective bargaining in which the two parties agree upon a union wage, and the firm unilaterally sets the employment level; the wage-employment outcome always lies on the labour demand curve

labour demand: the relationship between the amount of labour that firms are willing to hire over a given time interval and the wage level offered by workers

labour force: the number of people who are either employed or unemployed

labour force participation decision: the decision to either work or seek work on the labour market

labour force participation rate: the ratio of the labour force to the size of the working-age population

labour force survey: a monthly data set containing information on the labour market status of individuals

labour hoarding: the employment practice of firms retaining workers during a cyclical downturn in labour and product demand even if the marginal revenue product is below the wage level in the current period

labour market discrimination: an instance in which seemingly equally productive workers, or workers having equal endowments of productivity-related attributes, of different races, genders, or ethnicities are paid different wages

labour market outcomes: the phenomena generated from the labour market as a result of the forces of labour supply and labour demand; primary examples are wages, employment levels, and unemployment levels

labour market turnover: the extent to which positions in the labour market are assumed by new workers; it includes quits, dismissals, layoffs, promotions, and rehires

labour supply: the relationship between the amount of work that workers are willing to provide over a given time interval and the wage level offered by firms

labour supply model: the analytical framework employed for determining the number of hours of work

labour supply schedule: the functional relationship between the wage offered and the quantity supplied of labour

leisure: time per day that is not allocated to working for a wage

life-cycle labour supply: the configuration (or time-path) of labour supply choices over an individual's adult life; analyzed as a function of wages, age, demographic factors such as fertility, and the income of spouses.

line-to-line: a procedure for implementing a pay equity scheme; the female line is raised vertically to the male line; the average pay of the female-dominated occupations is raised to the average level of the male-dominated ones for each set of comparator jobs (see the definitions for **payline, comparator jobs,** and **pay equity**)

logarithms: a mathematical function that is the inverse of the exponential function; frequently employed to transform economic data

long run: the time frame under which producers are able to adjust the quantities of all of the factors of production that they employ; a period in which all resources are variable and no resources are fixed

longitudinal or panel data: data consisting of the attributes of individuals (such as wages) that follows these individuals over time; time series observations exist for the same individual

mandatory retirement: a personnel management practice in which a worker is compelled to retire upon reaching either a certain age or a certain length of service; tied to the termination date for a compensation contract

mandatory retirement provisions: these provisions stipulate that the worker is compelled to withdraw from the labour force upon reaching a certain age

marginal cost: the increment to the firm's level of total cost that is obtained by producing one more unit of output

marginal labour force attachment: the state of being jobless but not necessarily actively searching for work; workers with marginal labour force attachment would not be considered to be officially unemployed, and they include discouraged workers (see the definition for **discouraged worker**)

marginal physical product: the increment to the total product, or the level of production, that stems from a change in the level of a variable factor (such as labour) that is employed

marginal rate of substitution: the rate at which the worker is willing to trade an increment of leisure for an increment of income, and vice versa (context of the labour supply model)

marginal rate of technical substitution: the rate at which the firm can increase its employment of labour (capital) and reduce its employment of capital (labour) and still generate the same level of output; graphically, the slope of the isoquant curve

marginal revenue: the increment to the firm's total revenue obtained by producing and selling one more unit of output

marginal revenue product: the increment to the firm's total revenue obtained by hiring one more unit of a variable factor such as labour on the input market

market-clearing model: the supply and demand model of equilibrium output and price determination; the market is said to clear when the equilibrium price is reached

market demand curve: the total demand for labour within a given labour market, representing the horizontal summation of the labour demand curves of the individual firms

market envelope curve: the outermost portions of the group of employers' isoprofit curves; sometimes called the outer shell or the employers' offer curve; represents the maximum compensating wage any employer is willing to pay given a certain level of job safety (see the definition for **isoprofit schedule**)

matching: the process by which workers searching for employment are paired with firms offering jobs; takes place in an environment of imperfect information

median voter model: a proposition that holds that when economic choices over a single variable (such as the union wage level) are made in a democratic fashion, the choice made by the group will be identical to the choices made by the median voter (i.e., one whose preferences are halfway through the range of the preferences of all of the voters)

migration: geographical mobility on the part of workers

minimum wage laws: laws that stipulate a floor on wages such that the employer is compelled to pay his/her employees a wage at least as high

money illusion: the macroeconomic phenomenon of workers failing to require wage increases (for a given quantity supplied of labour) that are in proportion to the rate of price inflation; as a consequence, the real wage declines

monitoring costs: the costs incurred in ensuring that employees are not shirking and that employers are meeting their commitments in terms of remunerating their workers

monopolist: a firm that operates in a market in which there are no other firms producing and selling its product/service; there is a single seller of the good/service

monopsony: a structure for an input market for which there is only one buyer (single employer in the context of a labour market); the labour supply curve facing the firm is upward-sloping

moonlighting: the choice of accepting additional work at a wage rate lower than that of the first job

moral hazard: a situation in which individuals can influence their risk of suffering a loss from which they have obtained insurance coverage; it imposes a difficulty on developing insurance contracts such as implicit contracts (see the definition for **implicit contracts**)

multiple equilibriums: a macroeconomic phenomenon related to hysteresis in the unemployment rate in which the aggregate labour market does not have a tendency to move toward an equilibrium at the unique, natural rate of unemployment; several different long-run equilibriums are possible (see the definition for **hysteresis**)

multiple regression: a regression model having more than one explanatory variable (see the definition for **regression model**)

Nash's solution: the specific wage-employment outcome generated by a particular type of bargaining theory; only the bargaining outcome is specified (see the definition for **bargaining theory**)

natural experiment: a research technique sometimes employed to isolate the impact of changes in one economic variable on the fluctuations of another economic variable; the possibility of unobserved and omitted economic variables affecting the estimation of that relationship is reduced

natural unemployment rate: the unemployment rate that corresponds to equilibrium in the aggregate labour market, where there is neither excess demand nor excess supply; essentially equivalent to the non-accelerating inflation rate of unemployment (NAIRU) (see the definition for **non-accelerating inflation rate of unemployment**)

negative income tax: a special type of social assistance program containing an incentive structure that does not penalize the act of working; a level of income is guaranteed, and the implicit tax rate on labour market earnings is not 100 percent, as is the case for conventional social assistance programs

neoclassical economics: the analytical approach used in mainstream economics: self-interested economic actors produce, consume, and exchange goods and services in markets

neoclassical supply and demand model: the analytical framework used for most of the field of labour markets; based on the self-interested choices of firms and workers who exchange services in labour market

net flows: the number of workers observed per month to be transiting from one labour force state (i.e., employment, unemployment, or out of the labour force) to another; movements in the opposite direction are subtracted

non-accelerating inflation rate of unemployment: the rate of unemployment associated with a stable rate of inflation (see the definition for **Phillips curve**)

non-competitive market: an input or output market that does not meet the criteria of the model of perfect competition; for output markets, monopoly, oligopoly, or monopolistic competition; for input markets, monopsony, oligopsony, or monopsonistic competition

non-competitive theories of discrimination: any theory regarding the nature of labour market discrimination such that the differentials are not eroded by the forces of competition in the labour market, but are permanent

nonexperimental evidence: a research technique that uses data and evidence relating measures of labour market supply to the parameters of the income maintenance scheme (context of labour supply and income maintenance schemes); it is the most commonly employed research technique, and it is based only on observed economic behaviour

nonmarket time: time per day not allocated to working for a wage; also called leisure time

non-pecuniary benefits: an amenity associated with a job that is not financial in nature; it thus has no bearing on wages or benefits

nonwage benefits: an element of the firm's labour costs and the compensation of workers that does not take the form of wages paid for time worked for the employer; examples are health care benefits, dental benefits, retirement pensions, and life insurance benefits

normal good: a good whose quantity demanded increases with the level of income (leisure in the context of the labour supply model)

Oaxaca decomposition: a mathematical equation that measures discrimination by decomposing the average wage differential between males and females into a portion attributable to differences in productive characteristics and a portion due to differences in the rates at which these productive characteristics determine wages; it is that latter element that is considered to be discriminatory

occupation: the function of a worker; the nature or content of the work performed

occupational premiums: a difference in wages between two individuals that is attributable solely to the functions of the workers (i.e., the trade) involved; factors such as human capital requirements and the industry of employment have been accounted for; it sometimes reflects non-pecuniary differences

offer-matching: the act of matching the salary offer that the raiding firm makes to one of the firms' top employees; a counteroffer from the current employer

old age security: a government program that provides payments to retired workers in the form of a demogrant; it is a universal program, but the benefits are clawed back for higher-income recipients; abbreviated OAS

omitted variable bias: a difficulty involved in empirical analysis: an economic variable thought to play an important role in determining the values of the endogenous variables (such as wages) is not included in the estimating equation at all

1/N problem: a pitfall involved in the remuneration practice of team-based compensation (all workers receive an equal share of the salary mass) whereby certain workers have an incentive to shirk

opportunity cost: the cost of the forgone alternative that has the highest value; the explicit costs of education and training plus the forgone earnings stemming from the training process (context of human capital investment)

optimal compensation system: a remuneration mechanism within a firm that generates a wage level such that the effort level and hence the workers' productivity is the highest possible given the level of labour costs

optimal degree of inequality: a characteristic of a remuneration system within an organization such that the degree of inequality of the salary scale achieves the proper tradeoff between generating proper incentives for individual effort versus achieving cooperative teamwork when necessary

ordinary least squares: a statistical or econometric technique employed to estimate the values of parameters of regression models having a linear form; applicable under certain conditions (see the definition for **parameter**)

overemployed: said of a worker who desires to work fewer hours at the going wage rate but is prevented from doing so due to labour market constraints

overtime premium: the wage premium that is awarded for hours worked beyond the standard work week, and that may be necessary to induce the overemployed worker to work longer hours (see the definition for **overemployed**)

parameter: an element of a regression model that links the economic variables; typically it takes the form of a slope coefficient or the intercept term (see the definition for **regression analysis**).

Pareto-efficient wage-employment outcome: a wage-employment outcome that makes the union as well off as possible given the level of profit for the firm, and makes the firm as well off as possible given the level of utility for the union; any other wage-employment outcome will necessarily make one party worse off

partial equilibrium effects: the impact of an income maintenance scheme on labour market choices within a static framework

pay equity: a government antidiscrimination policy that requires equal pay for work at different jobs that are assessed to have the same value; usually restricted to the public sector

payline: a mathematical tool in the form of a line that is used to implement pay equity schemes; the number of job evaluation points is related to the pay rates, and there is a line for both men and women

payroll taxes: a tax, typically levied on both the employer and the worker, that varies directly with earnings up to a ceiling; used to finance public pensions and the unemployment insurance regime

perfect capital markets: financial markets that allow an individual to borrow against his/her lifetime earnings and save for his/her lifetime earnings without constraint; in such markets an individual can base an investment decision on lifetime income rather than on current income

perfectly monopolistic wage differentiation: a particular type of monopsony equilibrium in which the employer is able to pay every single worker a different wage equal to the worker's reservation wage (see the definition for **monopsony**)

persistence: the tendency for shocks that cause increases or decreases in the actual rate of unemployment to have very-long-term effects that dissipate slowly; thus the natural rate of unemployment is affected by changes in the actual rate of unemployment

phantom jobs: the situation in which an appropriate (usually male) comparator job does not exist (see the definition for **comparator jobs**)

Phillips curve: a macroeconomic, negative mathematical relationship between the rate of unemployment and the rate of wage inflation

point system: the institutional procedure through which the applications of independent immigrants are evaluated; it consists of about a dozen criteria that can be evaluated in a relatively objective fashion

point-to-line: a procedure for implementing a pay equity scheme;

all of the points of female-dominated occupations are raised vertically to the male line; the pay of the female dominated occupations is raised to the average level of the male-dominated ones for each set of comparator jobs (see the definitions for **payline**, **comparator jobs**, and **pay equity**)

point-to-point: a procedure for implementing a pay equity scheme; all of the points for female occupations are raised vertically to the nearest point among the male-dominated occupations; the pay of the female-dominated occupations is raised to the lowest level of the male-dominated one given a set of comparator jobs (see the definitions for **payline** and **pay equity**)

polarization of wages: the economic phenomenon of an apparent rise in the earnings gap between the highly educated and the less-educated workers in the U.S. labour market; the distribution of wage levels among workers tends to diverge

policy capturing approach: a procedure for applying the administrative concept of value that simulates the market approach; the attributes of a job that have been estimated by the evaluators are then remunerated according to market rates prevailing for male-dominated jobs

positively selected: the degree to which immigrants, often having undergone an evaluation of their productive attributes according to the official point system, also possess unobservable characteristics (such as motivation) that strengthen economic assimilation (see the definitions for **economic assimilation** and **point system**)

postponed retirement: a provision that permits the worker to continue to work full-time past the normal retirement age; it almost always involves receiving less pension income than what would otherwise be the case

potential experience: the proxy variable for labour market experience that is frequently included in a human capital earnings function; typically estimated as Age *minus* Years of schooling *minus* 5 (see the definition for **human capital earnings function**)

potential income constraint: the highest level of income that can be reached corresponding to a given number of hours worked

preferences: the tastes the worker has for income versus leisure (context of labour supply model)

pre-market characteristics: the first component generated by the Oaxaca decomposition; also called the explained component of discrimination (see the definition for the **Oaxaca decomposition**)

present value: the value of the right to receive a payment or a series of payments in the future denominated in dollars of the current period

principal agent theory: a conceptual framework employed to analyze certain remuneration practices; the principal is the firm, which hires the employee (the agent) to work on its behalf

private costs and benefits: the costs and the benefits that are incurred by and accrue solely to the parties that make an economic choice (such as an investment in human capital)

proactive, system-wide: said of a procedure for applying comparable worth policies whereby employers would be required to have in place a bona fide job evaluative system to achieve pay equity; no complaint or grievance would have to be filed

production function: the technological relationship between the inputs to the production process and the level of output (see the definition for **factor of production**)

production possibility frontier: a curve that shows the locus of combinations of the levels of outputs of two goods or services that can be produced in a full-employment, full-production economy where the levels of inputs and the state of technology are fixed; also called a transformation curve

productivity: the relationship between the level of output and the level of input employed to produce it; stated as a ratio of either the level of output divided by the level of input, or the change in output divided by the change in input (see the definition for **marginal physical product**)

profitability: the level or the margin of profit, where profit is the total revenue of the firm minus the total costs

profit maximization: the assumption, applied to the behavioural motive of firms as they determine the demand for labour, that they will choose to employ that level of labour which yields the greatest possible level of profit

program evaluation: a research procedure that seeks to assess the efficacy of labour market programs such as job training in obtaining a desired result

protectionist labour standards: employment regulations designed to improve working conditions in certain male-dominated occupations so that females may find them more attractive

public-private sector wage differentials: a difference in wages between two workers that is attributable solely to the fact that one works in the private sector and one works for the public sector; factors such as human capital requirements and the occupation have been accounted for; sometimes reflects non-pecuniary differences (see the definition for **industry premiums**)

quasi-fixed labour costs: labour costs incurred by the firm that vary directly with the number of workers hired but are independent of the number of hours each person works

quasi-panel: a research methodology employing data series that follows a group of individuals over several time periods; growth in economic variables such as wages can be observed

queuing theories: theories regarding the nature of labour market discrimination according to which the wage differentials stem from the payment of efficiency wages; the efficiency wages cause workers to queue up for well-paying jobs that tend to be held by the favoured group (see the definition for **efficiency wages**)

radicalism: an analytical perspective based on a Marxian approach in which the primary forces are the economic classes rather than supply and demand; an alternative to the neoclassical supply and demand approach

raiding: a personnel management practice that involves very aggressive recruitment of workers of high skill level; lured from competing organizations

real costs: concrete costs stemming from an economic choice that involve the use of productive resources; may or may not have a monetary value

reduced form: a form for an economic model in which only exogenous variables and parameters appear on the right side of the model's equations

refugee class: one of the two non-assessed classes of immigrants; their applications are not evacuated according to the point system, but rather on their personal histories in foreign countries

regional wage differential: a difference in wages between two individuals attributable solely to geographical location; factors such as human capital requirements have been accounted for

regression analysis: a tool for empirical analysis in which the fluctuations in the dependent variable (or explained variable) are explained as a function of fluctuations in one or more independent variables (of explanatory variables); the regression model is a mathematical equation describing the relationship between a dependent variable and one or more independent variables; the primary elements are parameters and variables (see the definition for **parameter**)

reservation wage: the lowest wage required to prevent the worker from withdrawing from the labour force, or the wage threshold that suffices to induce a nonparticipating worker to join the labour force

retirement decision: a labour supply decision that typically involves labour supply and savings decisions that are made over the entire life cycle; the worker chooses to no longer participate in the labour force

retirement test: a provision of a retirement pension program that penalizes the beneficiary to the extent that he/she continues to work for a wage

returns to schooling: empirical evidence on the private benefits in the form of wage increases from an investment to schooling; a quantitative estimate of the differences between the earnings of groups of workers having various levels of education

risk sharing: a major element of the implicit contract approach to modelling wages and employment levels; workers accept lower wages in exchange for a greater degree of job security and a lower degree of wage variability

R-squared: the proportion of the fluctuations in the dependent variable of a regression model that can be explained by fluctuations in the independent variable (see the definition for **regression analysis**)

Rubinstein's bargaining theory: a specific bargaining theory specifying the bargaining process employed to reach the ultimate wage-employment outcome (see the definition for **bargaining theory**)

sacrifice ratio: the loss of aggregate output (GDP) relative to trend (potential GDP) divided by the reduction in the inflation rate; sometimes used as a measure of the efficacy of demand restraint policies (see the definition for **demand restraint**)

salaries as tournament prizes: a salary determination mechanism in which much of the compensation reflects a prize for being selected as the most productive worker rather than reflecting the marginal revenue product (see the definition for **superstar**)

sample selection bias: a difficulty involved in empirical analysis: the estimating sample is not representative of the underlying population whose economic behaviour the researcher wants to investigate; the sample is typically weighted toward workers with fairly extreme patterns of economic behaviour

sampling error: the error (inaccuracy) in the estimation process that stems from drawing data from a sample not totally representative of the population

scale effect: the change in quantity demanded of labour that results from a change in the wage rate, holding the relative prices of the inputs (usually labour versus capital) fixed; the portion of the change which is attributable solely to the level of output adjusting

seasonal unemployment: the type of aggregate unemployment associated with a level of aggregate demand insufficient to provide enough jobs for the entire labour force during a particular season; it has aspects of demand-deficient as well as frictional unemployment

sectoral shift hypothesis: a model for analyzing aggregate unemployment that stresses the role of adjustment of the allocation of labour in the face of frequent changes in technology and shocks to aggregate demand and supply; it stresses the dispersion in employment growth across sectors of the labour market

selection bias: a complication involved in the empirical elimination of the union-nonunion wage effect; the unobservable attributes of union workers are not the same as those of nonunion workers

self-sufficiency project: a pilot project involving social assistance recipients who were presented with strong financial incentives to accept paying jobs (see definition for **experimental evidence**)

shadow or implicit prices: the portion of the total market wage associated with a job amenity or disseminate; synonymous with a compensating wage differential

shock effect: a potential for the unionization of workers (with the accompanying increase in wages) to increase by the level of production at the firm by inducing the firm to adopt more efficient production techniques

short run: the time frame under which producers are able to adjust the quantities of some but not all of the factors of production they employ; a period in which some resources are fixed but some are variable

signalling: an event whereby a worker on the supply side of the labour market reveals information relevant to his/her true innate productivity or quality; only applies in a climate of imperfect information (see the definition for **imperfect information**)

simultaneity: a complication involved in the empirical elimination of the union-nonunion wage effect; the union status can affect the wage and vice versa, which can render a biased estimate

social assistance: (see the definition for **welfare program**)

social costs and benefits: the private costs and benefits faced by the parties that make an economic choice plus the third-party effects or externalities that accrue to parties not directly involved (such as an investment in human capital)

special retirement: the act of withdrawing from the labour force at an earlier age than is normal; unlike in the case of early retirement, the worker receives full pension

specific training: human capital development, often occurring on the job, that can be applied only at the firm that provides it

stagflation: a macroeconomic phenomenon of high inflation coupled with high unemployment, as opposed to the more normal relationship of a tradeoff

standard errors: a statistical measure of the dispersion of an economic variable or an estimator for a parameter

statistical and signalling theories of discrimination: a practice in which female workers (or some other group treated unfavourably on the labour market) are assessed according to the average performance of all females, and have their wages set accordingly

statistical significance: an indication that the true value of the parameter of the regression model is different from zero (see the definition for **regression analysis**)

steady-state condition: a situation in which the inflow to the state of unemployment is equal to the outflow from it, and the average duration of unemployment is constant

stock options: a method of compensation that frequently applies to business executives; they have the option of buying the firm's stock in the future at a guaranteed price

stopping rule: the condition under which the process of job search comes to an end; the wage of the offered job is equal to or greater than the reservation wage (see the definitions for **job search** and **reservation wage**)

structural unemployment: the type of aggregate unemployment associated with mismatches between the skills and/or the geographic location of the unemployed with the characteristics of job vacancies

substitution effect: the change in quantity demanded of labour that results from a change in the wage rate, holding the level of output fixed; the portion of the change attributable solely to the change in the relative factor prices

superstar: a worker whose compensation level far exceeds those of all of the other workers within the organization even though often his/her skill level is only slightly higher than the next most productive worker; the differential in salary is magnified relative to the differential in productivity

supply of union representation: an economic variable reflecting the costs of organizing and maintaining a union, and the costs of administering contract preferences of workers for union representation; depends on its expected costs and benefits; emanates from the staff of the union

supply shocks: shifts in the aggregate supply that alter the costs of producing goods and services, and thus have an impact on the aggregate price level

supply theories of discrimination: a source of labour market discrimination; supply of female labour is expanded relative to the supply of male labour, all other factors held constant

symmetric information: a situation in which the two parties in an employment relationship have the same amount of information regarding relevant variables such as the firm's profits, labour market conditions, the worker's productivity, etc.

systemic discrimination: labour market discrimination that may be the unintended by-product or side effect of conventional employment or pay practices that perpetuate the existing gender composition of the workplace

teamwork: work effort by an individual that is cooperative in nature and is harmonized with the efforts of the co-workers; the cross-marginal products are positive and high in this case

temporary layoffs: layoffs expected to be temporary; both the firm and the worker expect a recall

tenure: the length of service an employee has with the firm

threat effect: a positive effect on the wages of the nonunion sector that can stem from the possibility that those nonunion workers could organize; the employers in the nonunion sector grant a wage increase in order to discourage unionization (see the definition for **two-sector model**)

threat point: the point in union utility–firm utility space that corresponds to the outcome in which no collective bargaining agreement for the wage-employment outcome is reached; also called the disagreement point

total revenue product: the level of a firm's total revenue associated with an amount of a factor employed in the production process (such as labour)

transfer costs: costs stemming from an economic choice that do not involve the use of real, productive resources; they involve only a financial gain for one group and a financial loss for another

transfers in kind: a payment from the employer to the employee that does not take the form of cash, and can thus only be used for an explicitly stated purpose (see the definition for **nonwage benefits**)

transitory wage change: a wage change that is not evolutionary, but rather temporary (see the definition for **unanticipated wage increase**)

t-ratio: the ratio of the estimated parameter (i.e., the estimated slope coefficient or the estimated constant) to the estimated standard of error of the estimated parameter

treatment group: a group of workers that is involved in a research experiment that is subjected to a certain process; often they have participated in a program (see the definition for **program evaluation**)

two-sector model: an analytical framework based on supply and demand forces that can be used to analyze wage differentials between workers in unionized industries and those in nonunionized industries (also employed to analyze the male-female wage differential)

unanticipated wage increase: a one-time, unexpected wage increase that occurs at a particular point in time over the age-earnings profile; not thought to influence labour supply choices during other periods (see definition for **dynamic labour supply**)

uncompensated elasticity (of labour supply)**:** the total wage elasticity of labour supply, that is, the percentage change in the quantity supplied of labour divided by the percentage change in the wage

underemployed: said of a worker who is willing to work more hours at the going wage rate but is prevented from doing so due to labour market constraints

unemployed: the state of being jobless and actively searching for work or being jobless on temporary layoff

unemployment: human resources that are not employed on the job market; such workers are actively searching for work and are willing to work at the going market wage

unemployment insurance: an income maintenance program that allocates payments to workers who have suffered job loss; workers must have contributed while they were employed in order to be eligible for benefits

unemployment rate: the number of unemployed workers divided by the size of the labour force, which in turn is the sum of the number of unemployed workers plus the number of employed workers

union density: a quantitative measure of the extent of union organization; the number of organized union members divided by the number of potential union members

union membership: the state of belonging to a labour union; normally involves the payment of dues

union objectives: the goals of the labour union relating primarily to wages, employment levels, working conditions, and the terms of employment

union status: the individual worker's attribute of belonging or not belonging to a labour union

union-nonunion wage differential: the percentage difference in wages between union workers and otherwise comparable nonunion workers

unions: collective organizations of workers of a certain firm and/or occupations whose primary objective is to protect and improve the well-being of their members

unobserved heterogeneity: differences in attributes (often across individuals) of economic factors that are relevant for economic choices but are not observable to the researcher; examples are innate intelligence and entrepreneurial drive

up-or-out rules: a personnel management practice in which the firm's employees are evaluated at a certain stage of their career, and either promoted or terminated at that stage

utility: the level of well-being or satisfaction the worker receives from consuming given levels of income and leisure (context of the labour supply model)

utility function: a function relating the level of consumer satisfaction or well-being to the level of consumption of one or more goods

utility maximizing: the assumption thought to guide the behaviour of the worker (context of the labour supply model)

value of life: estimates of the value of a worker's life that only reflect the compensating differential generated by the labour market for a risky job or occupation; represents the price that the market assesses to reduce the risk of death to zero

value of marginal product: the increment to the firm's total revenue obtained by hiring one more unit of a variable factor such as labour on the input market; applies only when the output market is perfectly competitive (see the definition for **marginal revenue product**)

variable costs: production costs expressed in levels that vary directly with the level of output

voice: a tactic for workers to exert pressure on their employers when and if they are dissatisfied with their terms of employment by resorting to collective expression through the union; an alternative strategy to exit (see the definition for **exit**)

voluntary and involuntary unemployment: individuals are involuntarily unemployed if they are willing to work at the going wage rate for their skills or occupation but are unable to find employment; they are voluntarily unemployed if a suitable job is available but he/she is unwilling to accept it at the going wage

wage curve: a mathematical relationship between the wage level and the unemployment rate; the relationship is negative, and may be based on efficiency wages; graphed in wage-employment space (see the definition for **efficiency wages**)

wage differentials: a difference in the wage levels that arises when workers and jobs are heterogeneous with respect to attributes such as vocation, risk of injury, or working conditions

wage dispersion: the degree of variation or variance within the distribution of wages within the labour market

wage rate: (see the definition for **wages**)

wage rigidity: the failure of the transactions wage to adjust to a decline in aggregate demand, creating excess quantity supplied of labour, and hence involuntary unemployment (see the definition for **voluntary and involuntary unemployment**)

wage-safety locus: the locus of tendencies between the various isoprofit curves and the indifference curves; generates the equilibrium combinations of the wage and the job attribute (usually job safety) that prevail in the labour market

wage structures: the hierarchy or grid of wage levels relative to each other; a set of wage premiums associated with worker or job attributes such as education, training, and seniority

wage subsidy: a government program that allocates a wage supplement in addition to the wage paid by the employer; designed to encourage low-paid workers to increase their work hours

wages: the market price for a unit of labour

wait or queue unemployment: the phenomenon of unemployed workers who are unsuccessful in finding jobs in the union sector waiting for those scarce jobs to open up; there is thus less pressure on the supply of labour to the nonunion sector (see the definition for **two-sector model**)

welfare program: a social program (also called social assistance) that typically allocates demogrant payments to nonparticipants of the labour force; the amounts are based primarily on the survival needs of the family, and the implicit tax on labour market earnings is 100 percent

winner's curse: a possible result stemming from the personnel management practice of raiding other organizations (often competing organizations) for the most talented workers; there is a risk that the pay offer will not be justified by the recruit's marginal productivity (see the definition for **raiding**)

workers' compensation: an income maintenance program that allocates payments to workers who have suffered job-related illness or injury and are thus unable to work

work incentives: the reward and/or penalty effect associated with an income maintenance scheme that applies to the work effort of recipients

worksharing: a special type of unemployment insurance regime in which workers are compensated for partial rather than total job loss; they receive indemnities for the working hours which are reduced

years since migration: the number of years that have elapsed since the time in which the immigrant entered the host country; an important variable involved in assessing economic assimilation (see the definition for **economic assimilation**)

Index